OFFICIAL
BASEBALL
DOPE BOOK

1981 EDITION

PRESIDENT-CHIEF EXECUTIVE OFFICER
RICHARD WATERS

EDITORS
LARRY WIGGE
CRAIG CARTER
CARL CLARK

PUBLISHED BY

The Sporting News

1212 North Lindbergh Boulevard
P. O. Box 56, St. Louis, Mo. 63166

Copyright © 1981
The Sporting News Publishing Company
a Times Mirror company

ISBN 0-89204-073-4   51   ISSN 0162-5411

TABLE OF CONTENTS

ON THE COVER: All-Star and Gold Glove first baseman CECIL COOPER of the Milwaukee Brewers. Cooper had 219 hits and a brilliant .352 average while leading the American League in RBIs in 1980 with 122.
Photo by Nancy Hogue.

LELAND S. MacPHAIL, JR.
President
American League

BOWIE KUHN
Commissioner
of Baseball

CHARLES S. FEENEY
President
National League

Major League Directory

Commissioner of Baseball—Bowie Kuhn
Secretary-Treasurer—Alexander H. Hadden
Office of Baseball—75 Rockefeller Plaza, New York, N. Y. 10019
Executive Council—Bowie K. Kuhn, Commissioner; Leland S. MacPhail, Jr., President of American League; Charles S. Feeney, President of National League; John E. Fetzer, Edmund B. Fitzgerald, Ewing Kauffman and Haywood C. Sullivan, representatives of American League, and Daniel M. Galbreath, Robert L. Howsam, Robert A. Lurie and Peter F. O'Malley, representatives of National League.

Administrative Officer—William A. Murray
Special Assistants to the Commissioner—Joseph L. Reichler, Monte Irvin
Director of Information—Robert A. Wirz
Acting Co-Ordinator of Inter-American Baseball—Pedro Arias

AMERICAN LEAGUE

President—Leland S. MacPhail, Jr.
Chairman—Joseph E. Cronin
Secretary & Assistant to the President—Robert O. Fishel
League Office—280 Park Avenue, New York, N. Y. 10017

Umpires—Larry Barnett, Nick Bremigan, Joseph Brinkman, Alan Clark, Terry Cooney, Derryl Cousins, Don Denkinger, James Evans, Dale Ford, Rich Garcia, Russ Goetz, Bill Haller, Ted Hendry, Ken Kaiser, Greg Kosc, Bill Kunkel, George Maloney, Larry McCoy, James McKean, Durwood Merrill, Jerry Neudecker, Steve Palermo, Dallas Parks, David Phillips, Mike Reilly, John Shulock, Marty Springstead, Vic Voltaggio.

NATIONAL LEAGUE

President—Charles S. Feeney
Vice-President—John J. McHale
Administrator & Director of Public Relations—Blake Cullen
Business Manager—Louis H. Krems
League Office—1 Rockefeller Plaza, New York, N. Y. 10020

Umpires—Fred Brocklander, Nick Colosi, Jerry Crawford, Jerry Dale, Dave Davidson, Bob Engel, Steve Fields, Bruce Froemming, Eric Gregg, Lanny Harris, Doug Harvey, John Kibler, John McSherry, Ed Montague, Andy Olsen, Dave Pallone, Paul Pryor, Frank Pulli, Jim Quick, Dutch Rennert, Paul Runge, Dick Stello, Terry Tata, Ed Vargo, Harry Wendelstedt, Joe West, Lee Weyer, Bill Williams.

AMERICAN LEAGUE—Pennant Winners—1900-1980

1900—Chicago* .607	1927—New York .714	1954—Cleveland .721
1901—Chicago .610	1928—New York .656	1955—New York .623
1902—Philadelphia .610	1929—Philadelphia .693	1956—New York .630
1903—Boston .659	1930—Philadelphia .662	1957—New York .636
1904—Boston .617	1931—Philadelphia .704	1958—New York .597
1905—Philadelphia .622	1932—New York .695	1959—Chicago .610
1906—Chicago .616	1933—Washington .651	1960—New York .630
1907—Detroit .613	1934—Detroit .656	1961—New York .673
1908—Detroit .588	1935—Detroit .616	1962—New York .593
1909—Detroit .645	1936—New York .667	1963—New York .646
1910—Philadelphia .680	1937—New York .662	1964—New York .611
1911—Philadelphia .669	1938—New York .651	1965—Minnesota .630
1912—Boston .691	1939—New York .702	1966—Baltimore .606
1913—Philadelphia .627	1940—Detroit .584	1967—Boston .568
1914—Philadelphia .651	1941—New York .656	1968—Detroit .636
1915—Boston .669	1942—New York .669	1969—Baltimore .673
1916—Boston .591	1943—New York .636	1970—Baltimore .667
1917—Chicago .649	1944—St. Louis .578	1971—Baltimore .639
1918—Boston .595	1945—Detroit .575	1972—Oakland .600
1919—Chicago .629	1946—Boston .675	1973—Oakland .580
1920—Cleveland .636	1947—New York .630	1974—Oakland .556
1921—New York .641	1948—Cleveland† .626	1975—Boston .594
1922—New York .610	1949—New York .630	1976—New York .610
1923—New York .645	1950—New York .636	1977—New York .617
1924—Washington .597	1951—New York .636	1978—New York† .613
1925—Washington .636	1952—New York .617	1979—Baltimore .642
1926—New York .591	1953—New York .656	1980—Kansas City .599

*Not recognized as major league in 1900. †Defeated Boston in one-game playoff for pennant.

STANDING OF CLUBS AT CLOSE OF SEASON

EAST DIVISION

Club	N.Y.	Balt.	Mil.	Bos.	Det.	Clev.	Tor.	Cal.	Chi.	K.C.	Min.	Oak.	Sea.	Tex.	W.	L.	Pct.	G.B.
New York	..	6	8	10	8	8	10	10	7	4	8	8	9	7	103	59	.636	....
Baltimore....	7	..	7	8	10	6	11	10	6	6	10	7	6	6	100	62	.617	3
Milwaukee...	5	6	..	7	6	10	5	6	7	6	7	7	9	5	86	76	.531	17
Boston........	3	5	6	..	8	7	7	9	6	5	6	9	7	5	83	77	.519	19
Detroit........	5	3	7	5	..	10	9	7	10	2	6	6	10	4	84	78	.519	19
Cleveland....	5	7	3	6	3	..	8	6	7	5	9	6	8	6	79	81	.494	23
Toronto........	3	2	8	6	4	5	..	8	7	3	5	4	6	5	67	95	.414	36

WEST DIVISION

Club	K.C.	Oak.	Min.	Tex.	Chi.	Cal.	Sea.	Balt.	Bos.	Clev.	Det.	Mil.	N.Y.	Tor.	W.	L.	Pct.	G.B.
Kansas City..	..	6	5	10	8	8	7	6	7	7	10	6	8	9	97	65	.599	....
Oakland......	7	..	7	7	7	10	8	5	3	6	6	5	4	8	83	79	.512	14
Minnesota....	8	6	..	9	8	6	7	2	6	3	6	5	4	7	77	84	.478	19½
Texas	3	6	3	..	7	2	9	6	7	6	8	7	5	7	76	85	.472	20½
Chicago........	5	6	5	6	..	10	6	4	5	2	5	3	9		70	90	.438	26
California	5	3	7	11	3	..	11	2	3	4	5	2	3	6	65	95	.406	31
Seattle........	6	5	4	4	7	2	..	5	4	2	5	4	3	6	59	103	.364	38

Tie Games—Seattle at Detroit and Texas at Chicago (2).
Cancelled Games—Boston at Chicago (2), California at Cleveland (2) and Minnesota at Texas.
Championship Series—Kansas City defeated New York, three games to none.

AMERICAN LEAGUE 1980 DEPARTMENTAL LEADERS
INDIVIDUAL BATTING

Average
G. Brett, Kansas City .390
Cooper, Milwaukee .352
Dilone, Cleveland .341

Home Runs
Jackson, New York 41
Oglivie, Milwaukee 41
Thomas, Milwaukee 38

Earned-Run Average
May, New York 2.47
Norris, Oakland 2.54
Burns, Chicago 2.84

Shutouts
John, New York 6
Zahn, Minnesota 5
Gura, K.C.; McGregor, Balt.; Stieb, Tor. 4

Doubles
Yount, Milwaukee 49
Oliver, Texas 43
Morrison, Chicago 40

Runs Batted In
Cooper, Milwaukee 122
Oglivie, Milwaukee 118
G. Brett, Kansas City 117

INDIVIDUAL PITCHING

Complete Games
Langford, Oakland 28
Norris, Oakland 24
Keough, Oakland 20

Innings
Langford, Oakland 290
Norris, Oakland 284
Gura, Kansas City 283

Triples
Griffin, Toronto 15
Wilson, Kansas City 15
Landreaux, Minn.;
Washington, K.C. 11

Stolen Bases
Henderson, Oakland 100
Wilson, Kansas City 79
Dilone, Cleveland 61

Strikeouts
Barker, Cleveland 187
Norris, Oakland 180
Guidry, New York 166

Victories
Stone, Baltimore 25
Norris, Oakland 22
John, New York 22

Earl Weaver

BALTIMORE ORIOLES

Board Chairman—Edward Bennett Williams
President—Jerold C. Hoffberger
Exec. V. P.-General Manager—Henry J. Peters
Vice-Pres.-Stadium Operations—Jack Dunn, III
Vice-President-Finance—Joseph P. Hamper, Jr.
Traveling Secretary—Philip E. Itzoe
Public Relations Director—Robert W. Brown
Scouting, Player Development—Thomas A. Giordano
Special Assistant to General Manager—Jim Russo
Offices—Memorial Stadium
Memorial Stadium Capacity—52,696.

Farm System: AAA—Rochester. AA—Charlotte.
A—Miami. Rookie—Bluefield.

BALTIMORE ORIOLES' YEARLY STANDING

(Milwaukee Brewers, 1901; St. Louis Browns, 1902 to 1953, Inclusive)

Year—Position	W.	L.	Pct.	*G.B.	Manager	Attendance
1901—Eighth	48	89	.350	35½	Hugh Duffy	139,034
1902—Second.....	78	58	.574	5	James McAleer	272,283
1903—Sixth........	65	74	.468	26½	James McAleer	380,405
1904—Sixth........	65	87	.428	29	James McAleer	318,108
1905—Eighth	54	99	.354	40½	James McAleer	339,112
1906—Fifth........	76	73	.510	16	James McAleer	389,157
1907—Sixth........	69	83	.454	24	James McAleeu	419,025
1908—Fourth.....	83	69	.546	6½	James McAleer	618,947
1909—Seventh ...	61	89	.407	36	James McAleer	366,274
1910—Eighth	47	107	.305	57	John O'Connor	249,889
1911—Eighth	45	107	.296	56½	Roderick Wallace	207,984
1912—Seventh ...	53	101	.344	53	Roderick Wallace, George Stovall	214,070
1913—Eighth	57	96	.373	39	George Stovall, Branch Rickey	250,330
1914—Fifth........	71	82	.464	28½	Branch Rickey	244,714
1915—Sixth........	63	91	.409	39½	Branch Rickey	150,358
1916—Fifth........	79	75	.513	12	Fielder Jones	335,740
1917—Seventh ...	57	97	.370	43	Fielder Jones	210,486
1918—Fifth........	60	64	.484	14	Fldr. Jones, Jas. Austin, Jas. Burke..	122,076
1919—Fifth........	67	72	.482	20½	James Burke	349,350
1920—Fourth....	76	77	.497	21½	James Burke	419,311
1921—Third.......	81	73	.526	17½	Lee Fohl	355,978
1922—Second.....	93	61	.604	1	Lee Fohl	712,918
1923—Fifth........	74	78	.487	24	Lee Fohl, James Austin	430,296
1924—Fourth.....	74	78	.487	17	George Sisler	533,349
1925—Third.......	82	71	.536	15	George Sisler	462,898
1926—Seventh ...	62	92	.403	29	George Sisler	283,986
1927—Seventh ...	59	94	.336	50½	Dan Howley	247,879
1928—Third.......	82	72	.532	19	Dan Howley	339,497
1929—Fourth.....	79	73	.520	26	Dan Howley	280,697

BALTIMORE ORIOLES' YEARLY STANDING—Continued

Year–Position	W.	L.	Pct.	*G.B.	Manager	Attendance
1930–Sixth	64	90	.416	38	William Killefer	152,088
1931–Fifth	63	91	.409	45	William Killefer	179,126
1932–Sixth	63	91	.409	44	William Killefer	112,558
1933–Eighth	55	96	.364	43½	Killefer, Sothoron, Hornsby	88,113
1934–Sixth	67	85	.441	33	Rogers Hornsby	115,305
1935–Seventh	65	87	.428	28½	Rogers Hornsby	80,922
1936–Seventh	57	95	.375	44½	Rogers Hornsby	93,267
1937–Eighth	46	108	.299	56	Rogers Hornsby, James Bottomley	123,121
1938–Seventh	55	97	.362	44	Charles (Gabby) Street	130,417
1939–Eighth	43	111	.279	64½	Fred Haney	109,159
1940–Sixth	67	87	.435	23	Fred Haney	239,591
1941–Sixth†	70	84	.455	31	Fred Haney, J. Luther Sewell	176,240
1942–Third	82	69	.543	19½	J. Luther (Luke) Sewell	255,617
1943–Sixth	72	80	.474	25	J. Luther (Luke) Sewell	214,392
1944–First	89	65	.578	+ 1	J. Luther (Luke) Sewell	508,644
1945–Third	81	70	.536	6	J. Luther (Luke) Sewell	482,986
1946–Seventh	66	88	.429	38	J. Luther Sewell, Zack Taylor	526,435
1947–Eighth	59	95	.383	38	Herold (Muddy) Ruel	320,474
1948–Sixth	59	94	.386	37	James (Zack) Taylor	335,546
1949–Seventh	53	101	.344	44	James (Zack) Taylor	270,936
1950–Seventh	58	96	.377	40	James (Zack) Taylor	247,131
1951–Eighth	52	102	.338	46	James (Zack) Taylor	293,790
1952–Seventh	64	90	.416	31	Rogers Hornsby, Martin Marion	518,796
1953–Eighth	54	100	.351	46½	Martin Marion	297,238
1954–Seventh	54	100	.351	57	James Dykes	1,060,910
1955–Seventh	57	97	.370	39	Paul Richards	852,039
1956–Sixth	69	85	.448	28	Paul Richards	901,201
1957–Fifth	76	76	.500	21	Paul Richards	1,029,581
1958–Sixth	74	79	.484	17½	Paul Richards	829,991
1959–Sixth	74	80	.481	20	Paul Richards	891,926
1960–Second	89	65	.578	8	Paul Richards	1,187,849
1961–Third	95	67	.586	14	Paul Richards, C. Luman Harris	951,089
1962–Seventh	77	85	.475	19	William Hitchcock	790,254
1963–Fourth	86	76	.531	18½	William Hitchcock	774,343
1964–Third	97	65	.599	2	Henry Bauer	1,116,215
1965–Third	94	68	.580	8	Henry Bauer	781,649
1966–First	97	63	.606	+ 9	Henry Bauer	1,203,366
1967–Sixth†	76	85	.472	15½	Henry Bauer	955,053
1968–Second	91	71	.562	12	Henry Bauer, Earl Weaver	943,977

*Games behind pennant winner. †Tied for position.

EAST DIVISION

Year–Position	W.	L.	Pct.	*G.B.	Manager	Attendance
1969–First‡	109	53	.673	+19	Earl Weaver	1,058,168
1970–First‡	108	54	.667	+15	Earl Weaver	1,057,069
1971–First‡	101	57	.639	+12	Earl Weaver	1,023,037
1972–Third	80	74	.519	5	Earl Weaver	899,950
1973–First§	97	65	.599	+ 8	Earl Weaver	958,667
1974–First§	91	71	.562	+ 2	Earl Weaver	962,572
1975–Second	90	69	.566	4½	Earl Weaver	1,002,157
1976–Second	88	74	.543	10½	Earl Weaver	1,058,609
1977–Second†	97	64	.602	2½	Earl Weaver	1,195,769
1978–Fourth	90	71	.559	9	Earl Weaver	1,051,724
1979–First‡	102	57	.642	+ 8	Earl Weaver	1,681,009
1980–Second	100	62	.617	3	Earl Weaver	1,797,438

*Games behind winner. †Tied for position. ‡Won Championship Series. §Lost Championship Series.

BALTIMORE ORIOLES
(4) EARL WEAVER—Manager

No. PITCHERS—	Bts.	Thrs.	Hgt.	Wgt.	Birth-date	1980 Club	IP.	W.	L.	ERA.
52 Boddicker, Mike	R	R	5:11	172	8-23-57	Rochester	190	12	9	2.18
						Baltimore	7	0	1	6.43
46 Flanagan, Mike	L	L	6:00	195	12-16-51	Baltimore	251	16	13	4.12
21 Ford, Dave	R	R	6:04	200	12-29-56	Baltimore	70	1	3	4.24
30 Martinez, Dennis	R	R	6:01	183	5-14-55	Baltimore	100	6	4	3.96
						Miami	12	0	0	0.00
23 Martinez, Tippy	L	L	5:10	175	5-31-50	Baltimore	81	4	4	3.00
16 McGregor, Scott	B	L	6:01	190	1-18-54	Baltimore	252	20	8	3.32
22 Palmer, Jim	R	R	6:03	194	10-15-45	Baltimore	224	16	10	3.98
53 Stewart, Sammy	R	R	6:03	208	10-28-54	Baltimore	119	7	7	3.55
49 Stoddard, Tim	R	R	6:07	250	1-24-53	Baltimore	86	5	3	2.51
32 Stone, Steve	R	R	5:10	178	7-14-47	Baltimore	251	25	7	3.23

CATCHERS—	Bts.	Thrs.	Hgt.	Wgt.	Birth-date	1980 Club	G.	HR.	RBI.	Avg.
24 Dempsey, Rick	R	R	6:00	184	9-13-49	Baltimore	119	9	40	.262
41 Graham, Dan	L	R	6:01	212	7-19-54	Rochester	16	4	12	.346
						Baltimore	86	15	54	.278
34 Morales, Jose	R	R	6:00	195	12-30-44	Minnesota	97	8	36	.303

INFIELDERS—	Bts.	Thrs.	Hgt.	Wgt.	Birth-date	1980 Club	G.	HR.	RBI.	Avg.
7 Belanger, Mark	R	R	6:02	170	6- 8-44	Baltimore	113	0	22	.228
2 Bonner, Bob	R	R	6:00	185	8-12-56	Rochester	133	2	41	.241
						Baltimore	4	0	1	.000
10 Crowley, Terry	L	L	6:00	182	2-16-47	Baltimore	92	12	50	.288
25 Dauer, Rich	R	R	6:00	180	7-27-52	Baltimore	152	2	63	.284
11 DeCinces, Doug	R	R	6:02	195	8-29-50	Baltimore	145	16	64	.249
6 Krenchicki, Wayne	L	R	6:01	175	9-17-54	Rochester	87	2	39	.264
						Baltimore	9	0	0	.143
33 Murray, Eddie	B	R	6:02	200	2-24-56	Baltimore	158	32	116	.300
9 Rayford, Floyd	R	R	5:10	195	7-27-57	Baltimore	8	0	1	.222
						Rochester	107	9	46	.230
8 Ripken, Cal Jr.	R	R	6:04	200	8-24-60	Charlotte	144	25	78	.276
12 Sakata, Lenn	R	R	5:09	160	6- 8-53	Rochester	26	3	8	.344
						Baltimore	43	1	9	.193

OUTFIELDERS—	Bts.	Thrs.	Hgt.	Wgt.	Birth-date	1980 Club	G.	HR.	RBI.	Avg.
27 Ayala, Benny	R	R	6:01	195	2- 7-51	Baltimore	76	10	33	.265
1 Bumbry, Al	L	R	5:08	175	4-21-47	Baltimore	160	9	53	.318
15 Corey, Mark	R	R	6:02	205	11- 3-55	Rochester	82	3	25	.230
						Baltimore	36	1	2	.278
28 Dwyer, Jim	L	L	5:10	175	1- 3-50	Boston	93	9	38	.285
38 Lowenstein, John	L	R	6:01	180	1-27-47	Baltimore	104	4	27	.311
35 Roenicke, Gary	R	R	6:03	200	12- 5-54	Baltimore	118	10	28	.239
29 Singleton, Ken	B	R	6:04	212	6-10-47	Baltimore	156	24	104	.304

ELROD HENDRICKS (44)—Coach   CAL RIPKEN, SR. (47)—Coach
RAY MILLER (31)—Coach   RALPH ROWE (54)—Coach
JIMMY WILLIAMS (40)—Coach

MEMORIAL STADIUM

	Seats	Prices
Sky Boxes	12	....
Lower Box Seats	7,488	$7.75
Terrace Box Seats	3,519	6.75
Mezzanine Box Seats	1,947	6.75
Upper Boxes	3,610	5.50
Lower Reserved	5,098	4.75
Upper Reserved	9,278	4.75
General Admission		
Lower	13,555	3.75
Upper	8,189	3.75

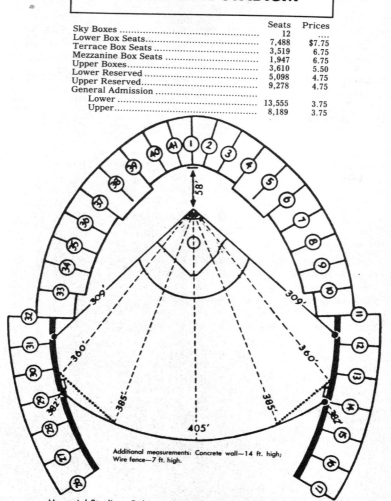

Additional measurements: Concrete wall—14 ft. high; Wire fence—7 ft. high.

Memorial Stadium, Baltimore—First A. L. Game Played April 15, 1954

BOSTON RED SOX

President—Jean R. Yawkey
Exec. Vice-Pres.-Gen. Mgr.—Haywood C. Sullivan
Exec. VP-Administration—Edward G. LeRoux
Treasurer—James M. Olivier
Secretary—Joseph H. LaCour
V. P., Director, Player Development—Edward F. Kenney
Director, Scouting—Edward M. Kasko
Traveling Secretary—John J. Rogers
V. P., Director of Public Relations—William C. Crowley
Director, Publicity—Richard L. Bresciani
Offices—24 Yawkey Way
Fenway Park Capacity—33,536

Farm System: AAA—Pawtucket. AA—Bristol, Conn.
A—Elmira, Winston-Salem, Winter Haven.

Ralph Houk

BOSTON RED SOX' YEARLY STANDING

Year—Position	W.	L.	Pct.	*G.B.	Manager	Attendance
1901—Second.....	79	57	.581	4	James Collins	289,448
1902—Third.....	77	60	.562	6½	James Collins	348,567
1903—First.......	91	47	.659	+14½	James Collins	379,338
1904—First.......	95	59	.617	+ 1½	James Collins	623,295
1905—Fourth.....	78	74	.513	16	James Collins	468,828
1906—Eighth.....	49	105	.318	45½	James Collins, Charles Stahl	410,209
1907—Seventh ...	59	90	.396	32½	G. Huff, R. Unglaub, J. McGuire	436,777
1908—Fifth.......	75	79	.487	15½	James McGuire, Fred Lake	473,048
1909—Third.......	88	63	.583	9½	Fred Lake	668,965
1910—Fourth.....	81	72	.529	22½	Patrick Donovan	584,619
1911—Fifth.......	78	75	.510	24	Patrick Donovan	503,961
1912—First.......	105	47	.691	+14	J. Garland Stahl	597,096
1913—Fourth.....	79	71	.527	15½	J. Garland Stahl, William Carrigan ...	437,194
1914—Second.....	91	62	.595	8½	William Carrigan	481,359
1915—First.......	101	50	.669	+ 2½	William Carrigan	539,885
1916—First.......	91	63	.591	+ 2	William Carrigan	496,397
1917—Second.....	90	62	.592	9	John Barry	387,856
1918—First.......	75	51	.595	+ 2½	Edward Barrow	249,513
1919—Sixth.......	66	71	.482	20½	Edward Barrow	417,291
1920—Fifth.......	72	81	.471	25½	Edward Barrow	402,445
1921—Fifth.......	75	79	.487	23½	Hugh Duffy	279,273
1922—Eighth	61	93	.396	33	Hugh Duffy	259,184
1923—Eighth	61	91	.401	37	Frank Chance	229,668
1924—Seventh ...	67	87	.435	25	Lee Fohl	448,556
1925—Eighth	47	105	.309	49½	Lee Fohl	267,782
1926—Eighth	46	107	.301	44½	Lee Fohl	285,155
1927—Eighth	51	103	.331	59	William Carrigan	305,275
1928—Eighth	57	96	.373	43½	William Carrigan	396,920
1929—Eighth	58	96	.377	48	William Carrigan	394,620

BOSTON RED SOX' YEARLY STANDING—Continued

Year—Position	W.	L.	Pct.	*G.B.	Manager	Attendance
1930—Eighth	52	102	.338	50	Charles (Heinie) Wagner	444,045
1931—Sixth........	62	90	.408	45	John Collins	350,975
1932—Eighth	43	111	.279	64	John Collins, Martin McManus	182,150
1933—Seventh ...	63	86	.423	34½	Martin McManus	268,715
1934—Fourth.....	76	76	.500	24	Stanley (Bucky) Harris	610,640
1935—Fourth.....	78	75	.510	16	Joseph Cronin	558,568
1936—Sixth.......	74	80	.481	28½	Joseph Cronin	626,895
1937—Fifth........	80	72	.526	21	Joseph Cronin	559,659
1938—Second.....	88	61	.591	9½	Joseph Cronin	646,459
1939—Second.....	89	62	.589	17	Joseph Cronin	573,070
1940—Fourth.....	82	72	.532	8	Joseph Cronin	716,234
1941—Second.....	84	70	.545	17	Joseph Cronin	718,497
1942—Second.....	93	59	.612	9	Joseph Cronin	730,340
1943—Seventh ...	68	84	.447	29	Joseph Cronin	358,275
1944—Fourth.....	77	77	.500	12	Joseph Cronin	506,975
1945—Seventh ...	71	83	.461	17½	Joseph Cronin	603,794
1946—First........	104	50	.675	+12	Joseph Cronin	1,416,944
1947—Third.......	83	71	.539	14	Joseph Cronin	1,427,315
1948—Second† ...	96	59	.619	1	Joseph McCarthy	1,558,798
1949—Second.....	96	58	.623	1	Joseph McCarthy	1,596,650
1950—Third.......	94	60	.610	4	Joseph McCarthy, Stephen O'Neill	1,344,080
1951—Third.......	87	67	.565	11	Stephen O'Neill	1,312,282
1952—Sixth.......	76	78	.494	19	Louis Boudreau	1,115,750
1953—Fourth.....	84	69	.549	16	Louis Boudreau	1,026,133
1954—Fourth.....	69	85	.448	42	Louis Boudreau	931,127
1955—Fourth.....	84	70	.545	12	Michael Higgins	1,203,200
1956—Fourth.....	84	70	.545	13	Michael Higgins	1,137,158
1957—Third.......	82	72	.532	16	Michael Higgins	1,181,087
1958—Third.......	79	75	.513	13	Michael Higgins	1,077,047
1959—Fifth........	75	79	.487	19	Michael Higgins, William Jurges	984,102
1960—Seventh ...	65	89	.422	32	William Jurges, Michael Higgins	1,129,866
1961—Sixth.......	76	86	.469	33	Michael Higgins	850,589
1962—Eighth	76	84	.475	19	Michael Higgins	733,080
1963—Seventh ...	76	85	.472	28	John Pesky	942,642
1964—Eighth	72	90	.444	27	John Pesky, William Herman	883,276
1965—Ninth	62	100	.383	40	William Herman	652,201
1966—Ninth	72	90	.444	26	Wm. Herman, Jas. (Pete) Runnels....	811,172
1967—First........	92	70	.568	+ 1	Richard Williams	1,727,832
1968—Fourth.....	86	76	.531	17	Richard Williams	1,940,788

*Games behind pennant winner. †Lost to Cleveland in pennant playoff.

EAST DIVISION

Year—Position	W.	L.	Pct.	*G.B.	Manager	Attendance
1969—Third.......	87	75	.537	22	R. Williams, Edward Popowski	1,833,246
1970—Third.......	87	75	.537	21	Edward Kasko	1,595,278
1971—Third.......	85	77	.525	18	Edward Kasko	1,678,732
1972—Second.....	85	70	.548	½	Edward Kasko	1,441,718
1973—Second.....	89	73	.549	8	Edward Kasko	1,481,002
1974—Third.......	84	78	.519	7	Darrell D. Johnson	1,556,411
1975—First‡	95	65	.594	+ 4½	Darrell D. Johnson	1,748,587
1976—Third.......	83	79	.512	15½	Darrell D. Johnson, Donald Zimmer..	1,895,846
1977—Second† ...	97	64	.602	2½	Donald Zimmer	2,074,549
1978—Second§ ...	99	64	.607	1	Donald Zimmer	2,320,643
1979—Third.......	91	69	.569	11½	Donald Zimmer	2,353,114
1980—Fourth.....	83	77	.519	19	Donald Zimmer, John Pesky	1,956,092

*Games behind winner. †Tied for position. ‡Won Championship Series.
§Lost to New York in pennant playoff.

BOSTON RED SOX

(35) RALPH HOUK—Manager

No. PITCHERS—	Bts.	Thrs.	Hgt.	Wgt.	Birth-date	1980 Club	IP.	W.	L.	ERA.
16 Burgmeier, Tom	L	L	5:11	180	8- 2-43	Boston	99	5	4	2.00
22 Campbell, Bill	R	R	6:03	190	8- 9-48	Boston	41	4	0	4.83
25 Clear, Mark	R	R	6:04	200	5-27-56	California	106	11	11	3.31
28 Crawford, Steve	R	R	6:05	225	4-29-58	Bristol	177	9	7	2.64
						Boston	32	2	0	3.66
43 Eckersley, Dennis	R	R	6:02	190	10- 3-54	Boston	198	12	14	4.27
42 Rainey, Chuck	R	R	5:11	195	7-14-54	Boston	87	8	3	4.86
49 Remmerswaal, Win	R	R	6:02	160	3- 8-54	Pawtucket	48	5	5	4.69
						Boston	35	2	1	4.63
46 Stanley, Bob	R	R	6:04	205	11-10-54	Boston	175	10	8	3.39
40 Tanana, Frank	L	L	6:03	195	7- 3-53	California	204	11	12	4.15
21 Torrez, Mike	R	R	6:05	210	8-28-46	Boston	207	9	16	5.09
30 Tudor, John	L	L	6:00	185	2- 2-54	Pawtucket	74	4	5	3.65
						Boston	92	8	5	3.03

CATCHERS—	Bts.	Thrs.	Hgt.	Wgt.	date	1980 Club	G.	HR.	RBI.	Avg.
39 Allenson, Gary	R	R	5:11	188	2- 4-55	Boston	36	0	10	.357
10 Gedman, Rich	L	R	6:00	210	9-26-59	Pawtucket	111	11	29	.236
						Boston	9	0	1	.208
50 Schmidt, Dave	R	R	6:01	190	12-22-56	Pawtucket	50	5	16	.229

INFIELDERS—	Bts.	Thrs.	Hgt.	Wgt.	date	1980 Club	G.	HR.	RBI.	Avg.
18 Hoffman, Glenn	R	R	6:02	170	7- 7-58	Boston	114	4	42	.285
4 Lansford, Carney	R	R	6:02	195	2- 7-57	California	151	15	80	.261
5 Perez, Tony	R	R	6:02	205	5-14-42	Boston	151	25	105	.275
2 Remy, Jerry	L	R	5:09	165	11- 8-52	Boston	63	0	9	.313
11 Stapleton, Dave	R	R	6:01	170	1-16-54	Pawtucket	37	3	19	.340
						Boston	106	7	45	.321
1 Walker, Chico	B	R	5:09	170	11-25-57	Pawtucket	139	8	52	.272
						Boston	19	1	5	.211

OUTFIELDERS—	Bts.	Thrs.	Hgt.	Wgt.	date	1980 Club	G.	HR.	RBI.	Avg.
24 Evans, Dwight	R	R	6:03	205	11- 3-51	Boston	148	18	60	.266
37 Hancock, Garry	L	L	6:00	175	1-23-54	Pawtucket	60	6	19	.241
						Boston	46	4	19	.287
3 Miller, Rick	L	L	6:00	185	4-19-48	California	129	2	38	.274
51 Nichols, Reid	R	R	5:11	165	8- 5-58	Pawtucket	134	4	42	.276
						Boston	12	0	3	.222
17 Poquette, Tom	L	R	5:11	175	10-30-51	(Did not play in 1980)				
14 Rice, Jim	R	R	6:02	205	3- 8-53	Boston	124	24	86	.294
26 Rudi, Joe	R	R	6:02	200	9- 7-46	California	104	16	53	.237
8 Yastrzemski, Carl	L	R	5:11	185	8-22-39	Boston	105	15	50	.275

JOHN PESKY(6)—Coach   LEE STANGE (34)—Coach
EDDIE YOST (36)—Coach   TOMMY HARPER (32)—Coach
WALT HRINIAK (33)—Coach

FENWAY PARK

	Seats	Prices
Roof Boxes	594	$8.50
Box Seats	13,250	....
Upper Boxes		6.50
Lower Boxes		7.50-6.50
Reserved Grandstand	12,274	5.75-5.25
General Admission		4.00
Bleachers	7,418	....
Reserved Bleachers	....	3.00
Upper Bleachers	....	2.00

Note—Proportion of reserved and general admission seats in grandstand dependent upon size of crowd anticipated.

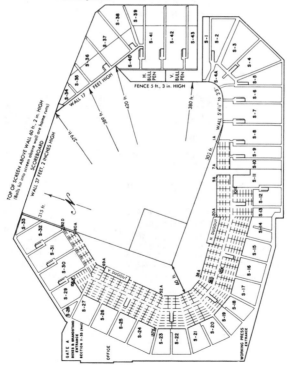

Fenway Park, Boston—First A. L. Game Played April 20, 1912

Jim Fregosi

CALIFORNIA ANGELS

Chairman of the Board—Gene Autry
Asst. to Chairman of the Board—Arthur E. Patterson
Exec. Vice-Pres.—E. J. (Buzzie) Bavasi
Vice-Pres.-Treasurer—Francis X. Leary
V.P.-Chief Administrative Officer—Mike Port
Director of Player Personnel—Gene Mauch
Director Public Relations—Tom Seeberg
Offices—Anaheim Stadium
Anaheim Stadium Capacity—65,158

Farm System: AAA—Salt Lake City. AA—Holyoke. A—Redwood, Salem. Rookie—Idaho Falls.

CALIFORNIA ANGELS' YEARLY STANDING

Year—Position	W.	L.	Pct.	*G.B.	Manager	Attendance
1961—Eighth	70	91	.435	38½	William Rigney	603,510
1962—Third	86	76	.531	10	William Rigney	1,144,063
1963—Ninth	70	91	.435	34	William Rigney	821,015
1964—Fifth........	82	80	.506	17	William Rigney	760,439
1965—Seventh ...	75	87	.463	27	William Rigney	566,727
1966—Sixth........	80	82	.494	18	William Rigney	1,400,321
1967—Fifth........	84	77	.522	7½	William Rigney	1,317,713
1968—Eighth†	67	95	.414	36	William Rigney	1,025,956

*Games behind pennant winner.   †Tied for position.

WEST DIVISION

Year—Position	W.	L.	Pct.	*G.B.	Manager	Attendance
1969—Third	71	91	.438	26	William Rigney, Harold (Lefty) Phillips	758,388
1970—Third	86	76	.531	12	Harold (Lefty) Phillips	1,077,741
1971—Fourth	76	86	.469	25½	Harold (Lefty) Phillips	926,373
1972—Fifth........	75	80	.484	18	Del Rice	744,190
1973—Fourth	79	83	.488	15	Bobby B. Winkles	1,058,206
1974—Sixth........	68	94	.420	22	Bobby B. Winkles, Richard Williams .	917,269
1975—Sixth........	72	89	.447	25½	Richard Williams	1,058,163
1976—Fourth† ...	76	86	.469	14	Richard Williams, Norman Sherry	1,006,774
1977—Fifth........	74	88	.457	28	Norman Sherry, David Garcia	1,432,633
1978—Second† ...	87	75	.537	5	David Garcia, James Fregosi	1,755,386
1979—First§	88	74	.543	† 3	James Fregosi	2,523,575
1980—Sixth........	65	95	.406	31	James Fregosi	2,297,327

*Games behind winner.   †Tied for position. §Lost Championship Series.

CALIFORNIA ANGELS

(11) JIM FREGOSI—Manager

No. PITCHERS—	Bts.	Thrs.	Hgt.	Wgt.	Birth-date	1980 Club	IP.	W.	L.	ERA.
46 Aase, Don	R	R	6:03	195	9- 8-54	California	175	8	13	4.06
28 D'Acquisto, John	R	R	6:03	205	12-24-51	S.D.-Mon.	88	2	5	3.38
43 Forsch, Ken	R	R	6:04	205	9- 8-46	Houston	222	12	13	3.20
37 Frost, Dave	R	R	6:06	235	11-17-52	California	78	4	8	5.31
41 Hassler, Andy	L	L	6:05	215	10-18-51	Pittsburgh	12	0	0	3.75
						California	83	5	1	2.49
34 Jefferson, Jesse	R	R	6:03	215	3- 3-50	Toronto	29	4	13	5.46
						Pittsburgh	1	1	0	1.29
24 Kison, Bruce	R	R	6:04	173	2-18-50	California	73	3	6	4.93
42 Knapp, Chris	R	R	6:05	200	9-16-53	California	117	2	11	6.15
27 Martinez, Fred	R	R	6:03	190	3-15-57	California	149	7	9	4.53
45 Renko, Steve	R	R	6:06	225	12-10-44	Boston	165	9	9	4.19
40 Sanchez, Luis	R	R	6:02	170	8-24-53	Aguila	177	14	9	2.03
						Albuquerque	22	2	1	5.32
26 Travers, Bill	L	L	6:06	200	10-27-52	Milwaukee	154	12	6	3.92
39 Witt, Mike	R	R	6:07	185	8-20-60	El Paso	70	5	5	5.79
						Salinas	90	7	3	2.10
38 Zahn, Geoff	L	L	6:01	185	12-19-46	Minnesota	233	14	18	4.40

No. CATCHERS—	Bts.	Thrs.	Hgt.	Wgt.	Birth-date	1980 Club	G.	HR.	RBI.	Avg.
5 Downing, Brian	R	R	5:10	200	10- 9-50	California	30	2	25	.290
14 Ott, Ed	L	R	5:10	190	7-11-51	Pittsburgh	120	8	41	.260

INFIELDERS—	Bts.	Thrs.	Hgt.	Wgt.	Birth-date	1980 Club	G.	HR.	RBI.	Avg.
7 Burleson, Rick	R	R	5:10	160	4-29-51	Boston	155	8	51	.278
19 Campaneris, Bert	R	R	5:10	160	3- 9-42	California	77	2	18	.252
29 Carew, Rod	L	R	6:00	182	10- 1-45	California	144	3	59	.331
4 Grich, Bobby	R	R	6:02	190	1-15-49	California	150	14	62	.271
13 Harris, John	L	L	6:03	215	9-13-54	Salt Lake C.	140	17	98	.333
						California	19	2	7	.293
10 Hobson, Butch	R	R	6:01	190	8-17-51	Boston	93	11	39	.228
2 Patek, Fred	R	R	5:06	150	10- 9-44	California	86	5	34	.264

OUTFIELDERS—	Bts.	Thrs.	Hgt.	Wgt.	Birth-date	1980 Club	G.	HR.	RBI.	Avg.
25 Baylor, Don	R	R	6:01	195	6-28-49	California	90	5	51	.250
12 Beniquez, Juan	R	R	5:11	165	5-13-50	Seattle	70	6	21	.228
3 Brunansky, Tom	R	R	6:04	205	8-20-60	Salt Lake C.	9	1	8	.344
						El Paso	128	24	97	.323
32 Clark, Bobby	R	R	6:00	190	6-13-55	Salt Lake C.	33	4	21	.345
						California	78	5	23	.230
15 Ford, Dan	R	R	6:01	185	5-19-52	California	65	7	26	.279
20 Harlow, Larry	L	L	6:02	176	11-13-51	California	109	4	27	.276
8 Lynn, Fred	L	L	6:01	190	2- 3-52	Boston	110	12	61	.301

BOB CLEAR (49)—Coach
PRESTON GOMEZ (18)—Coach
BOBBY KNOOP (1)—Coach

TOM MORGAN (47)—Coach
JIMMIE REESE (50)—Coach
MERV RETTENMUND (17)—Coach

ANAHEIM STADIUM

	Seats	Prices
Club Level Boxes	11,814	$5.50
Field Boxes	13,482	5.50
Terrace Level Boxes	12,827	4.50
View Level Reserved	7,863	3.50
View Level Unreserved	19,172	2.50

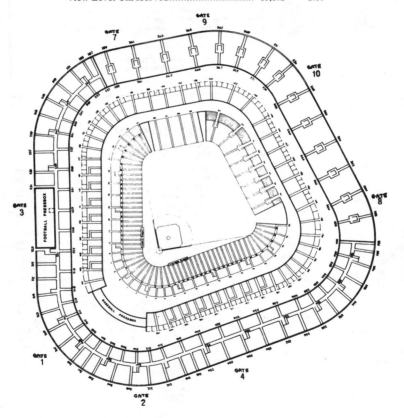

Anaheim Stadium, Anaheim—First A. L. Game Played April 19, 1966

CHICAGO WHITE SOX

Chairman of the Board—Jerry Reinsdorf
President—Edward M. Einhorn
Vice-President—Roland Hemond
Exec. Vice-Pres.—Howard Pizer
Treasurer—Leo Breen
Director, Public Relations—Chuck Shriver
Traveling Secretary—Glen Rosenbaum
Director, Player Development—Paul Richards
Offices—Comiskey Park
Comiskey Park Capacity—44,135

Farm System: AAA—Edmonton. AA—Glens Falls.
A—Appleton. Rookie—Sarasota.

Tony LaRussa

CHICAGO WHITE SOX' YEARLY STANDING

Year—Position	W.	L.	Pct.	*G.B.	Manager	Attendance
1901—First	83	53	.610	+ 4	Clark Griffith	354,350
1902—Fourth	74	60	.552	8	Clark Griffith	337,898
1903—Seventh	60	77	.438	30½	James Callahan	286,183
1904—Third	89	65	.578	6	James Callahan, Fielder Jones	557,123
1905—Second	92	60	.605	2	Fielder Jones	687,419
1906—First	93	58	.616	+ 3	Fielder Jones	585,202
1907—Third	87	64	.576	5½	Fielder Jones	666,307
1908—Third	88	64	.579	1½	Fielder Jones	636,096
1909—Fourth	78	74	.513	20	William Sullivan	478,400
1910—Sixth	68	85	.444	35½	Hugh Duffy	552,084
1911—Fourth	77	74	.510	24	Hugh Duffy	583,208
1912—Fourth	78	76	.506	28	James Callahan	602,241
1913—Fifth	78	74	.513	17½	James Callahan	644,501
1914—Sixth†	70	84	.455	30	James Callahan	469,290
1915—Third	93	61	.604	9½	Clarence Rowland	539,461
1916—Second	89	65	.578	2	Clarence Rowland	679,923
1917—First	100	54	.649	+ 9	Clarence Rowland	684,521
1918—Sixth	57	67	.460	17	Clarence Rowland	195,081
1919—First	88	52	.629	+ 3½	William Gleason	627,186
1920—Second	96	58	.623	2	William Gleason	833,492
1921—Seventh	62	92	.403	36½	William Gleason	543,650
1922—Fifth	77	77	.500	17	William Gleason	602,860
1923—Seventh	69	85	.448	30	William Gleason	573,778
1924—Eighth	66	87	.431	25½	Frank Chance, John Evers	606,658
1925—Fifth	79	75	.513	18½	Edward Collins	832,231
1926—Fifth	81	72	.529	9½	Edward Collins	710,339
1927—Fifth	70	83	.458	29½	Ray Schalk	614,423
1928—Fifth	72	82	.468	29	Ray Schalk, Russell Blackburne	494,152
1929—Seventh	59	93	.388	46	Russell Blackburne	426,795
1930—Seventh	62	92	.403	40	Owen (Donie) Bush	406,123

CHICAGO WHITE SOX' YEARLY STANDING—Continued

Year—Position	W.	L.	Pct.	*G.B.	Manager	Attendance
1931—Eighth	56	97	.366	51	Owen (Donie) Bush	403,550
1932—Seventh ...	49	102	.325	56½	Lewis Fonseca	233,198
1933—Sixth	67	83	.447	31	Lewis Fonseca	397,789
1934—Eighth	53	99	.349	47	Lewis Fonseca, James Dykes	236,559
1935—Fifth........	74	78	.487	19½	James Dykes	470,281
1936—Third.......	81	70	.536	20	James Dykes	440,810
1937—Third.......	86	68	.558	16	James Dykes	589,245
1938—Sixth.......	65	83	.439	32	James Dykes	338,278
1939—Fourth.....	85	69	.552	22½	James Dykes	594,104
1940—Fourth† ...	82	72	.532	8	James Dykes	660,336
1941—Third.......	77	77	.500	24	James Dykes	677,077
1942—Sixth.......	66	82	.446	34	James Dykes	425,734
1943—Fourth.....	82	72	.532	16	James Dykes	508,962
1944—Seventh ...	71	83	.461	18	James Dykes	563,539
1945—Sixth.......	71	78	.477	15	James Dykes	657,981
1946—Fourth.....	74	80	.481	30	James Dykes, Theodore Lyons	983,403
1947—Sixth.......	70	84	.455	27	Theodore Lyons	876,948
1948—Eighth	51	101	.336	44½	Theodore Lyons	777,844
1949—Sixth.......	63	91	.409	34	Jack Onslow	937,151
1950—Sixth.......	60	94	.390	38	Jack Onslow, John Corriden	781,330
1951—Fourth.....	81	73	.526	17	Paul Richards	1,328,234
1952—Third.......	81	73	.526	14	Paul Richards	1,231,675
1953—Third.......	89	65	.578	11½	Paul Richards	1,191,353
1954—Third.......	94	60	.610	17	Paul Richards, Martin Marion	1,231,629
1955—Third.......	91	63	.591	5	Martin Marion	1,175,684
1956—Third.......	85	69	.552	12	Martin Marion	1,000,090
1957—Second....	90	64	.584	8	Alfonso Lopez	1,135,668
1958—Second....	82	72	.532	10	Alfonso Lopez	797,451
1959—First........	94	60	.610	+ 5	Alfonso Lopez	1,423,144
1960—Third.......	87	67	.565	10	Alfonso Lopez	1,644,460
1961—Fourth.....	86	76	.531	23	Alfonso Lopez	1,146,019
1962—Fifth........	85	77	.525	11	Alfonso Lopez	1,131,562
1963—Second....	94	68	.580	10½	Alfonso Lopez	1,158,848
1964—Second....	98	64	.605	1	Alfonso Lopez	1,250,053
1965—Second....	95	67	.586	7	Alfonso Lopez	1,130,519
1966—Fourth.....	83	79	.512	15	Edward Stanky	990,016
1967—Fourth.....	89	73	.549	3	Edward Stanky	985,634
1968—Eighth†	67	95	.414	36	Edward Stanky, Alfonso Lopez	803,775

*Games behind pennant winner.   †Tied for position.

WEST DIVISION

Year—Position	W.	L.	Pct.	*G.B.	Manager	Attendance
1969—Fifth........	68	94	.420	29	Al Lopez, Donald Gutteridge	589,546
1970—Sixth........	56	106	.346	42	D. Gutteridge, Charles Tanner	495,355
1971—Third........	79	83	.488	22½	Charles Tanner	833,891
1972—Second.....	87	67	.565	5½	Charles Tanner	1,177,318
1973—Fifth........	77	85	.475	17	Charles Tanner	1,302,527
1974—Fourth......	80	80	.500	9	Charles Tanner	1,149,596
1975—Fifth........	75	86	.466	22½	Charles Tanner	750,802
1976—Sixth........	64	97	.398	25½	Paul Richards	914,945
1977—Third........	90	72	.556	12	Robert Lemon	1,657,135
1978—Fifth........	71	90	.441	20½	Robert Lemon, Lawrence Doby	1,491,100
1979—Fifth........	73	87	.456	14	Donald Kessinger, Anthony LaRussa	1,280,702
1980—Fifth........	70	90	.438	26	Anthony LaRussa	1,200,365

*Games behind winner.

CHICAGO WHITE SOX

(10) TONY LaRUSSA—Manager

No. PITCHERS—	Bts.	Thrs.	Hgt.	Wgt.	Birth-date	1980 Club	IP.	W.	L.	ERA.
46 Barrios, Francisco	R	R	6:03	195	6-10-53	Chicago	16	1	1	5.06
						Appleton	13	2	0	0.69
						Iowa	3	0	0	15.00
30 Baumgarten, Ross	L	L	6:01	180	5-27-55	Chicago	136	2	12	3.44
40 Burns, Britt	R	L	6:05	215	6- 8-59	Chicago	238	15	13	2.84
49 Dotson, Richard	R	R	6:00	185	1-10-59	Chicago	198	12	10	4.27
22 Farmer, Ed	R	R	6:05	205	10-18-49	Chicago	100	7	9	3.33
45 Hickey, Kevin	L	L	6:01	170	2-25-57	Glens Falls	169	9	7	4.31
36 Hoffman, Guy	L	L	5:09	175	7- 9-56	Iowa	75	6	3	3.60
						Chicago	38	1	0	2.61
31 Hoyt, Lamarr	R	R	6:03	190	1- 1-55	Iowa	62	5	2	2.90
						Chicago	112	9	3	4.58
43 Lamp, Dennis	R	R	6:03	190	9-23-52	Chicago NL	203	10	14	5.19
35 Robinson, Dewey	R	R	6:00	180	4-29-55	Iowa	73	5	5	2.84
						Chicago	35	1	1	3.09
33 Trout, Steve	L	L	6:04	195	7-20-57	Chicago	200	9	16	3.69

CATCHERS—	Bts.	Thrs.	Hgt.	Wgt.	Birth-date	1980 Club	G.	HR.	RBI.	Avg.
16 Essian, Jim	R	R	6:01	187	1- 2-51	Oakland	87	5	29	.232
72 Fisk, Carlton	R	R	6:02	220	12-26-47	Boston	131	18	62	.289
7 Hill, Marc	R	R	6:03	215	2-18-52	San Fran.	17	0	0	.171
						Seattle	29	2	9	.229

INFIELDERS—	Bts.	Thrs.	Hgt.	Wgt.	Birth-date	1980 Club	G.	HR.	RBI.	Avg.
34 Almon, Bill	R	R	6:03	170	11-21-52	Mtl.-N.Y.	66	0	7	.193
14 Bernazard, Tony	B	R	5:09	164	8-24-56	Montreal	82	5	18	.224
21 Cruz, Todd	R	R	6:00	175	11-23-55	Cal.-Chi.	108	3	23	.237
23 Johnson, Lamar	R	R	6:02	225	9- 2-50	Chicago	147	13	81	.277
12 Morrison, Jim	R	R	5:11	178	9-23-52	Chicago	162	15	57	.283
11 Pryor, Greg	R	R	6:00	175	10- 2-49	Chicago	122	1	29	.240
25 Squires, Mike	L	L	5:11	185	3- 5-52	Chicago	131	2	33	.283

OUTFIELDERS—	Bts.	Thrs.	Hgt.	Wgt.	Birth-date	1980 Club	G.	HR.	RBI.	Avg.
3 Baines, Harold	L	L	6:02	175	3-15-59	Chicago	141	13	49	.255
47 Kuntz, Rusty	R	R	6:03	190	2- 4-55	Iowa	91	11	54	.292
						Chicago	36	0	3	.226
8 LeFlore, Ron	R	R	6:00	200	6-16-48	Montreal	139	4	39	.257
44 Lemon, Chet	R	R	6:00	190	2-12-55	Chicago	147	11	51	.292
19 Luzinski, Greg	R	R	6:01	217	11-22-50	Philadelphia	106	19	56	.228
5 Molinaro, Bob	L	R	6:00	180	5-21-50	Chicago	119	5	36	.291
20 Nordhagen, Wayne	R	R	6:02	195	7- 4-48	Chicago	123	15	59	.277
48 Sutherland, Leo	L	L	5:10	165	4- 6-58	Iowa	96	2	23	.260
						Chicago	34	0	5	.258

LOREN BABE (42)—Coach
ART KUSNYER (15)—Coach
MINNIE MINOSO (9)—Coach

RON SCHUELER (37)—Coach
VADA PINSON (28)—Coach
BOBBY WINKLES (1)—Coach

COMISKEY PARK

	Seats	Prices
Box Seats	15,676	$7.00
Reserved Grandstand	4,780	5.00
Outfield Reserved	5,677	5.00
General Admission	18,002	3.00

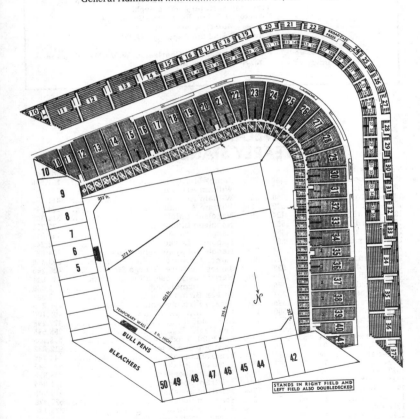

Comiskey Park, Chicago—First A. L. Game Played July 1, 1910

CLEVELAND INDIANS

President, Chief Exec. Officer—Gabe Paul
Chairman of the Board—F. J. Steve O'Neill
Secretary-Treasurer—Dudley S. Blossom III
Vice-Pres.-General Manager—Philip Seghi
V.P., Player Dev. & Scouting—Bob Quinn
Director of Stadium Operations—Daniel W. Zerbey
Traveling Secretary—Mike Seghi
Director of Public Relations—Bob DiBiasio
Offices—Municipal Stadium
Municipal Stadium Capacity—77,481

Farm System: AAA—Charleston, W. Va. AA—Chattanooga. A— Waterloo, Batavia.

Dave Garcia

CLEVELAND INDIANS' YEARLY STANDING

Year—Position	W.	L.	Pct.	*G.B.	Manager	Attendance
1901—Seventh ...	54	82	.397	29	James McAleer	131,380
1902—Fifth........	69	67	.507	14	William Armour	275,395
1903—Third.......	77	63	.550	15	William Armour	311,280
1904—Fourth.....	86	65	.570	7½	William Armour	264,749
1905—Fifth........	76	78	.494	19	Napoleon Lajoie	316,306
1906—Third.......	89	64	.582	5	Napoleon Lajoie	325,733
1907—Fourth.....	85	67	.559	8	Napoleon Lajoie	382,046
1908—Second.....	90	64	.584	½	Napoleon Lajoie	422,242
1909—Sixth........	71	82	.464	27½	Napoleon Lajoie, James McGuire.....	354,627
1910—Fifth........	71	81	.467	32	James McGuire	293,456
1911—Third.......	80	73	.523	22	James McGuire, George Stovall.......	406,296
1912—Fifth........	75	78	.490	30½	Harry Davis, Joseph Birmingham	336,844
1913—Third.......	86	66	.566	9½	Joseph Birmingham	541,000
1914—Eighth.....	51	102	.333	48½	Joseph Birmingham	185,997
1915—Seventh ...	57	95	.375	44½	Joseph Birmingham, Lee Fohl	159,285
1916—Sixth........	77	77	.500	14	Lee Fohl	492,106
1917—Third.......	88	66	.571	12	Lee Fohl	477,298
1918—Second.....	73	56	.566	3½	Lee Fohl	295,515
1919—Second.....	84	55	.604	3½	Lee Fohl, Tristram Speaker	538,135
1920—First........	98	56	.636	+ 2	Tristram Speaker	912,832
1921—Second.....	94	60	.610	4½	Tristram Speaker	748,705
1922—Fourth.....	78	76	.507	16	Tristram Speaker	528,145
1923—Third.......	82	71	.536	16½	Tristram Speaker	558,856
1924—Sixth........	67	86	.438	24½	Tristram Speaker	481,905
1925—Sixth........	70	84	.455	27½	Tristram Speaker	419,005
1926—Second.....	88	66	.571	3	Tristram Speaker	627,426
1927—Sixth........	66	87	.431	43½	Jack McCallister	373,138
1928—Seventh ...	62	92	.403	39	Roger Peckinpaugh	375,907
1929—Third.......	81	71	.533	24	Roger Peckinpaugh	536,210

CLEVELAND INDIANS' YEARLY STANDING—Continued

Year—Position	W.	L.	Pct.	*G.B.	Manager	Attendance
1930—Fourth.....	81	73	.536	21	Roger Peckinpaugh	528,657
1931—Fourth.....	78	76	.506	30	Roger Peckinpaugh	483,027
1932—Fourth.....	87	65	.572	19	Roger Peckinpaugh	468,953
1933—Fourth.....	75	76	.497	23½	Roger Peckinpaugh, Walter Johnson	387,936
1934—Third......	85	69	.552	16	Walter Johnson	391,338
1935—Third......	82	71	.536	12	Walter Johnson, Stephen O'Neill	397,615
1936—Fifth........	80	74	.519	22½	Stephen O'Neill	500,391
1937—Fourth.....	83	71	.539	19	Stephen O'Neill	564,849
1938—Third......	86	66	.566	13	Oscar Vitt	652,006
1939—Third......	87	67	.565	20½	Oscar Vitt	563,926
1940—Second.....	89	65	.578	1	Oscar Vitt	902,576
1941—Fourth† ...	75	79	.487	26	Roger Peckinpaugh	745,948
1942—Fourth.....	75	79	.487	28	Louis Boudreau	459,447
1943—Third......	82	71	.536	15½	Louis Boudreau	438,894
1944—Fifth†	72	82	.468	17	Louis Boudreau	475,272
1945—Fifth	73	72	.503	11	Louis Boudreau	558,182
1946—Sixth.......	68	86	.442	36	Louis Boudreau	1,057,289
1947—Fourth.....	80	74	.519	17	Louis Boudreau	1,521,978
1948—First‡	97	58	.626	+ 1	Louis Boudreau	2,620,627
1949—Third......	89	65	.578	8	Louis Boudreau	2,233,771
1950—Fourth.....	92	62	.597	6	Louis Boudreau	1,727,464
1951—Second.....	93	61	.604	5	Alfonso Lopez	1,704,984
1952—Second.....	93	61	.604	2	Alfonso Lopez	1,444,607
1953—Second.....	92	62	.597	8½	Alfonso Lopez	1,069,176
1954—First........	111	43	.721	+ 8	Alfonso Lopez	1,335,472
1955—Second.....	93	61	.604	3	Alfonso Lopez	1,221,780
1956—Second.....	88	66	.571	9	Alfonso Lopez	865,467
1957—Sixth.......	76	77	.497	21½	M. Kerby Farrell	722,256
1958—Fourth.....	77	76	.503	14½	Robert Bragan, Joseph Gordon	663,805
1959—Second.....	89	65	.578	5	Joseph Gordon	1,497,976
1960—Fourth.....	76	78	.494	21	Joseph Gordon, James Dykes	950,985
1961—Fifth........	78	83	.484	30½	James Dykes	725,547
1962—Sixth.......	80	82	.494	16	F. Melvin McGaha	716,076
1963—Fifth†	79	83	.488	25½	George (Birdie) Tebbetts	562,507
1964—Sixth†	79	83	.488	20	George (Birdie) Tebbetts	653,293
1965—Fifth........	87	75	.537	15	George (Birdie) Tebbetts	934,786
1966—Fifth........	81	81	.500	17	Geo. Tebbetts, Geo. Strickland	903,359
1967—Eighth	75	87	.463	17	Joseph Adcock	662,980
1968—Third......	86	75	.534	16½	Alvin Dark	857,994

*Games behind pennant winner. †Tied for position. ‡Defeated Boston in pennant playoff.

EAST DIVISION

Year—Position	W.	L.	Pct.	*G.B.	Manager	Attendance
1969—Sixth........	62	99	.385	46½	Alvin Dark	619,970
1970—Fifth........	76	86	.469	32	Alvin Dark	729,752
1971—Sixth........	60	102	.370	43	Alvin Dark, John Lipon	591,361
1972—Fifth........	72	84	.462	14	Ken Aspromonte	626,354
1973—Sixth........	71	91	.438	26	Ken Aspromonte	615,107
1974—Fourth.......	77	85	.475	14	Ken Aspromonte	1,114,262
1975—Fourth.....	79	80	.497	15½	Frank Robinson	977,039
1976—Fourth.....	81	78	.509	16	Frank Robinson	948,776
1977—Fifth........	71	90	.441	28½	Frank Robinson, Jeffrey Torborg	900,365
1978—Sixth........	69	90	.434	29	Jeffrey Torborg	800,584
1979—Sixth........	81	80	.503	22	Jeffrey Torborg, David Garcia	1,011,644
1980—Sixth........	79	81	.494	23	David Garcia	1,033,827

*Games behind winner.

CLEVELAND INDIANS
(1) DAVE GARCIA—Manager

No. PITCHERS—	Bts.	Thrs.	Hgt.	Wgt.	Birth-date	1980 Club	IP.	W.	L.	ERA.
39 Barker, Len	R	R	6:04	215	7- 7-55	Cleveland	246	19	12	4.17
28 Blyleven, Bert	R	R	6:03	207	4- 6-51	Pittsburgh	247	8	13	3.02
45 Brennan, Tom	R	R	6:01	180	10-30-52	Tacoma	152	9	3	2.49
38 Cuellar, Bobby	R	R	5:11	190	8-20-52	Tacoma	90	8	3	3.30
40 Denny, John	R	R	6:03	190	11- 8-52	Cleveland	109	8	6	4.38
17 Garland, Wayne	R	R	6:00	190	10-26-50	Cleveland	150	6	9	4.62
59 Glaser, Gordy	R	R	6:03	185	11-19-57	Chattanooga	100	6	4	2.61
						Tacoma	50	4	3	6.48
48 Grimsley, Ross	L	L	6:03	200	1- 7-50	Montreal	41	2	4	6.37
						Cleveland	75	4	5	6.72
35 Lacey, Bob	R	L	6:04	190	8-25-53	Oakland	80	3	2	2.94
43 Monge, Sid	B	L	6:02	195	4-11-51	Cleveland	94	3	5	3.54
37 Spillner, Dan	R	R	6:01	190	11-27-51	Cleveland	194	16	11	5.29
46 Stanton, Mike	R	R	6:02	200	9-25-52	Cleveland	86	1	3	5.44
36 Waits, Rick	L	L	6:03	195	5-15-52	Cleveland	224	13	14	4.46
22 Wihtol, Sandy	R	R	6:02	190	6- 1-55	Tacoma	58	4	9	3.57
						Cleveland	35	1	0	3.60
33 Wilkins, Eric	R	R	6:01	180	12- 9-56	Tacoma	101	7	4	3.92

CATCHERS—						1980 Club	G.	HR.	RBI.	Avg.
23 Bando, Chris	B	R	6:00	195	2- 4-56	Chattanooga	121	12	73	.349
16 Diaz, Bo	R	R	5:11	190	3-23-53	Cleveland	76	3	32	.227
9 Hassey, Ron	L	R	6:02	195	2-27-53	Cleveland	130	8	65	.318
13 Pruitt, Ron	R	R	6:00	185	10-21-51	Cleve.-Chi.	56	2	15	.302

INFIELDERS—										
7 Bannister, Alan	R	R	5:11	175	9- 3-51	Chi.-Clev.	126	1	41	.283
10 Dybzinski, Jerry	R	R	6:02	180	7- 7-55	Cleveland	114	1	23	.230
21 Hargrove, Mike	L	L	6:00	195	10-26-49	Cleveland	160	11	85	.304
11 Harrah, Toby	R	R	6:00	180	10-26-48	Cleveland	160	11	72	.267
8 Hayes, Von	L	R	6:05	185	8-31-58	Waterloo	134	15	90	.329
18 Kuiper, Duane	L	R	6:00	175	6-19-50	Cleveland	42	0	9	.282
12 Rosello, Dave	R	R	5:11	160	6-26-50	Cleveland	71	2	12	.248
29 Thornton, Andre	R	R	6:02	205	8-13-49	Cleveland	(Did not play in 1980)			
15 Veryzer, Tom	R	R	6:01	185	2-11-53	Cleveland	109	2	28	.271

OUTFIELDERS—										
34 Charboneau, Joe	R	R	6:02	200	6-17-55	Cleveland	131	23	87	.289
27 Dilone, Miguel	B	R	6:00	160	11- 1-54	Wichita	20	0	2	.238
						Cleveland	132	0	40	.341
25 Kelly, Pat	L	L	6:01	194	7-30-44	Baltimore	89	3	26	.260
32 Littleton, Larry	R	R	6:01	185	4- 3-54	Tacoma	148	17	80	.271
20 Manning, Rick	L	R	6:01	180	9- 2-54	Cleveland	140	3	52	.234
6 Orta, Jorge	L	R	5:10	175	11-26-50	Cleveland	129	10	64	.291

DAVE DUNCAN (4)—Coach
TOM McCRAW (14)—Coach

JOE NOSSEK (24)—Coach
DENNIS SOMMERS (2)—Coach

MUNICIPAL STADIUM

	Seats	Prices
Field Boxes	1,810	$7.00
Box Seats in Lower Deck	10,032	7.00
Box Seats in Upper Deck	7,535	7.00
Reserved Seats in Lower Deck	15,425	5.00
Reserved Seats in Upper Deck	14,941	5.00
General Admission	....	....
Lower Deck	11,469	3.50
Upper Deck	7,110	3.50
Bleachers	9,159	2.00

Note—Last five rows of Sections 1 to 43 used for general admission.

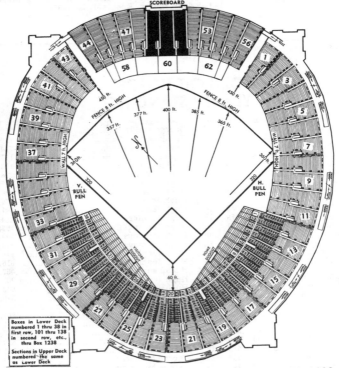

Municipal Stadium, Cleveland—First A. L. Game Played July 31, 1932
(Indians' Permanent Home Since 1947)

DETROIT TIGERS

Owner—John E. Fetzer
President-General Manager—James A. Campbell
Vice-President, Baseball—William R. Lajoie
V. P.-Secretary-Treasurer—Alex Callam
Dir. of Player Development—Walter "Hoot" Evers
Director of Public Relations—Dan Ewald
Traveling Secretary—Bill Brown
Offices—Tiger Stadium
Tiger Stadium Capacity—52,687

Farm System: AAA—Evansville. AA—Montgomery.
A—Lakeland, Macon. Rookie—Bristol, Va.

Sparky Anderson

DETROIT TIGERS' YEARLY STANDING

Year—Position	W.	L.	Pct.	*G.B.	Manager	Attendance
1901—Third	74	61	.548	8½	George Stallings	259,430
1902—Seventh	52	83	.385	30½	Frank Dwyer	189,469
1903—Fifth	65	71	.478	25	Edward Barrow	224,523
1904—Seventh	62	90	.408	32	Edward Barrow, Robert Lowe	177,796
1905—Third	79	74	.516	15½	William Armour	193,384
1906—Sixth	71	78	.477	21	William Armour	174,043
1907—First	92	58	.613	+ 1½	Hugh Jennings	297,079
1908—First	90	63	.588	+ ½	Hugh Jennings	436,199
1909—First	98	54	.645	+ 3½	Hugh Jennings	490,490
1910—Third	86	68	.558	18	Hugh Jennings	391,288
1911—Second	89	65	.578	13½	Hugh Jennings	484,988
1912—Sixth	69	84	.451	36½	Hugh Jennings	402,870
1913—Sixth	66	87	.431	30	Hugh Jennings	398,502
1914—Fourth	80	73	.523	19½	Hugh Jennings	416,225
1915—Second	100	54	.649	2½	Hugh Jennings	476,105
1916—Third	87	67	.565	5	Hugh Jennings	616,772
1917—Fourth	78	75	.510	21½	Hugh Jennings	457,289
1918—Seventh	55	71	.437	20	Hugh Jennings	203,719
1919—Fourth	80	60	.571	8	Hugh Jennings	643,805
1920—Seventh	61	93	.396	37	Hugh Jennings	579,650
1921—Sixth	71	82	.464	27	Tyrus Cobb	661,527
1922—Third	79	75	.513	15	Tyrus Cobb	861,206
1923—Second	83	71	.539	16	Tyrus Cobb	911,377
1924—Third	86	68	.558	6	Tyrus Cobb	1,015,136
1925—Fourth	81	73	.526	16½	Tyrus Cobb	820,766
1926—Sixth	79	75	.513	12	Tyrus Cobb	711,914
1927—Fourth	82	71	.536	27½	George Moriarty	773,716
1928—Sixth	68	86	.442	33	George Moriarty	474,323
1929—Sixth	70	84	.455	36	Stanley (Bucky) Harris	869,318
1930—Fifth	75	79	.487	27	Stanley (Bucky) Harris	649,450

DETROIT TIGERS' YEARLY STANDING—Continued

Year—Position	W.	L.	Pct.	*G.B.	Manager	Attendance
1931—Seventh ...	61	93	.396	47	Stanley (Bucky) Harris	434,056
1932—Fifth.......	76	75	.503	29½	Stanley (Bucky) Harris	397,157
1933—Fifth........	75	79	.487	25	Stanley Harris, Delmer Baker	320,972
1934—First........	101	53	.656	+ 7	Gordon (Mickey) Cochrane	919,161
1935—First........	93	58	.616	+ 3	Gordon (Mickey) Cochrane	1,034,929
1936—Second.....	83	71	.539	19½	Gordon (Mickey) Cochrane	875,948
1937—Second.....	89	65	.578	13	Gordon (Mickey) Cochrane	1,072,276
1938—Fourth.....	84	70	.545	16	Gordon Cochrane, Delmer Baker	799,557
1939—Fifth........	81	73	.526	26½	Delmer Baker	836,279
1940—First........	90	64	.584	+ 1	Delmer Baker	1,112,693
1941—Fourth† ...	75	79	.487	26	Delmer Baker	684,915
1942—Fifth........	73	81	.474	30	Delmer Baker	580,087
1943—Fifth........	78	76	.506	20	Stephen O'Neill	606,287
1944—Second.....	88	66	.571	1	Stephen O'Neill	923,176
1945—First........	88	65	.575	+ 1½	Stephen O'Neill	1,280,341
1946—Second.....	92	62	.597	12	Stephen O'Neill	1,722,590
1947—Second.....	85	69	.552	12	Stephen O'Neill	1,398,093
1948—Fifth........	78	76	.506	18½	Stephen O'Neill	1,743,035
1949—Fourth.....	87	67	.565	10	Robert (Red) Rolfe	1,821,204
1950—Second.....	95	59	.617	3	Robert (Red) Rolfe	1,951,474
1951—Fifth........	73	81	.474	25	Robert (Red) Rolfe	1,132,641
1952—Eighth......	50	104	.325	45	Robert Rolfe, Fred Hutchinson	1,026,846
1953—Sixth........	60	94	.390	40½	Fred Hutchinson	884,658
1954—Fifth........	68	86	.442	43	Fred Hutchinson	1,079,847
1955—Fifth........	79	75	.513	17	Stanley (Bucky) Harris	1,181,838
1956—Fifth........	82	72	.532	15	Stanley (Bucky) Harris	1,051,182
1957—Fourth.....	78	76	.506	20	John Tighe	1,272,346
1958—Fifth........	77	77	.500	15	John Tighe, Willis (Bill) Norman	1,098,924
1959—Fourth.....	76	78	.494	18	Willis Norman, James Dykes	1,221,221
1960—Sixth........	71	83	.461	26	James Dykes, Joseph Gordon	1,167,669
1961—Second.....	101	61	.623	8	Robert Scheffing	1,600,710
1962—Fourth.....	85	76	.528	10½	Robert Scheffing	1,207,881
1963—Fifth†	79	83	.488	25½	Robert Scheffing, Charles Dressen	821,952
1964—Fourth.....	85	77	.525	14	Charles (Chuck) Dressen	816,139
1965—Fourth.....	89	73	.549	13	Charles (Chuck) Dressen	1,029,645
1966—Third.......	88	74	.543	10	C. Dressen, R. Swift, F. Skaff	1,124,293
1967—Second† ..	91	71	.562	1	Mayo Smith	1,447,143
1968—First........	103	59	.636	+12	Mayo Smith	2,031,847

*Games behind pennant winner   †Tied for position.

EAST DIVISION

Year—Position	W.	L.	Pct.	*G.B.	Manager	Attendance
1969—Second.....	90	72	.566	19	Mayo Smith	1,577,481
1970—Fourth.....	79	83	.488	29	Mayo Smith	1,501,293
1971—Second.....	91	71	.562	12	Alfred (Billy) Martin	1,591,073
1972—First†	86	70	.551	+ ½	Alfred (Billy) Martin	1,892,386
1973—Third.......	85	77	.525	12	Alfred Martin, Joseph Schultz	1,724,146
1974—Sixth........	72	90	.444	19	Ralph Houk	1,243,080
1975—Sixth........	57	102	.358	37½	Ralph Houk	1,058,836
1976—Fifth........	74	87	.460	24	Ralph Houk	1,467,020
1977—Fourth.....	74	88	.457	26	Ralph Houk	1,359,863
1978—Fifth........	86	76	.531	13½	Ralph Houk	1,714,893
1979—Fifth........	85	76	.528	18	J. Lester Moss, George Anderson	1,630,929
1980—Fifth........	84	78	.519	19	George Anderson	1,785,293

*Games behind winner.   †Lost Championship Series.

BASEBALL DOPE BOOK

DETROIT TIGERS
(11) SPARKY ANDERSON—Manager

No.	PITCHERS—	Bts.	Thrs.	Hgt.	Wgt.	Birth-date	1980 Club	IP.	W.	L.	ERA.
60	Bailey, Howard	R	L	6:03	190	7-31-58	Montgomery	186	12	12	3.44
21	Kinney, Dennis	L	L	6:01	170	2-26-52	San Diego	83	4	6	4.23
29	Lopez, Aurelio	R	R	6:00	230	10- 5-48	Detroit	124	13	6	3.77
47	Morris, Jack	R	R	6:03	190	5-16-55	Detroit	250	16	15	4.18
46	Petry, Dan	R	R	6:04	200	11-13-58	Evansville	30	2	0	2.70
							Detroit	165	10	9	3.93
19	Rozema, Dave	R	R	6:04	200	8- 5-56	Detroit	145	6	9	3.91
49	Rucker, Dave	L	L	6:01	185	9- 1-58	Evansville	92	7	8	3.42
31	Saucier, Kevin	R	L	6:01	195	8- 9-56	Philadelphia	50	7	3	3.42
36	Schatzeder, Dan	L	L	6:00	195	12- 1-54	Detroit	193	11	13	4.01
45	Tobik, Dave	R	R	6:01	195	3- 2-53	Evansville	48	3	3	3.94
							Detroit	61	1	0	3.98
40	Underwood, Pat	L	L	6:00	175	2- 9-57	Detroit	113	3	6	3.58
44	Weaver, Roger	R	R	6:03	200	10- 6-54	Evansville	37	3	3	3.16
							Detroit	64	3	4	4.08
39	Wilcox, Milt	R	R	6:02	215	4-20-50	Detroit	199	13	11	4.48

No.	CATCHERS—	Bts.	Thrs.	Hgt.	Wgt.	Birth-date	1980 Club	G.	HR.	RBI.	Avg.
15	Dyer, Duffy	R	R	6:00	200	8-15-45	Detroit	48	4	11	.185
17	Fahey, Bill	L	R	6:00	200	6-14-50	San Diego	93	1	22	.257
13	Parrish, Lance	R	R	6:03	210	6-15-56	Detroit	144	24	82	.286
14	Wockenfuss, John	R	R	6:00	180	2-27-49	Detroit	126	16	65	.274

No.	INFIELDERS—	Bts.	Thrs.	Hgt.	Wgt.	Birth-date	1980 Club	G.	HR.	RBI.	Avg.
16	Brookens, Tom	R	R	5:10	170	8-10-53	Detroit	151	10	66	.275
2	Hebner, Richie	L	R	6:01	195	11-26-47	Detroit	104	12	82	.290
18	Kelleher, Mick	R	R	5:09	170	7-25-47	Chicago NL	105	0	4	.146
9	Papi, Stan	R	R	6:00	180	5-14-51	Okla. City	8	0	3	.333
							Bos.-Det.	47	3	17	.237
3	Trammell, Alan	R	R	6:00	170	2-21-58	Detroit	146	9	65	.300
1	Whitaker, Lou	L	R	5:11	160	5-12-57	Detroit	145	1	45	.233

No.	OUTFIELDERS—	Bts.	Thrs.	Hgt.	Wgt.	Birth-date	1980 Club	G.	HR.	RBI.	Avg.
34	Brown, Darrell	R	R	6:00	180	10-29-55	Evansville	123	3	43	.277
25	Corcoran, Tim	L	L	5:11	175	3-19-53	Detroit	84	3	18	.288
10	Cowens, Al	R	R	6:02	200	10-25-51	Cal.-Det.	142	6	59	.268
37	Filkins, Les	L	L	5:11	185	9-14-56	Montgomery	49	6	31	.287
							Evansville	83	7	38	.297
23	Gibson, Kirk	L	L	6:03	210	5-28-57	Detroit	51	9	16	.263
35	Jones, Lynn	R	R	5:09	175	1- 1-53	Evansville	34	0	11	.273
							Detroit	30	0	6	.255
33	Kemp, Steve	L	L	•6:00	190	8- 7-54	Detroit	135	21	101	.293
32	Peters, Rick	B	R	5:10	160	11-21-55	Detroit	133	2	42	.291
24	Summers, Champ	L	R	6:02	205	6-15-48	Detroit	120	17	60	.297

GATES BROWN (26)—Coach   DICK TRACEWSKI (53)—Coach
BILLY CONSOLO (50)—Coach   ALEX GRAMMAS (51)—Coach
ROGER CRAIG (38)—Coach

TIGER STADIUM

	Seats	Prices
Box Seats	11,718	$7.50
Reserved Grandstand	23,508	6.50
General Admission	6,269	4.25
Bleachers	11,192	2.75

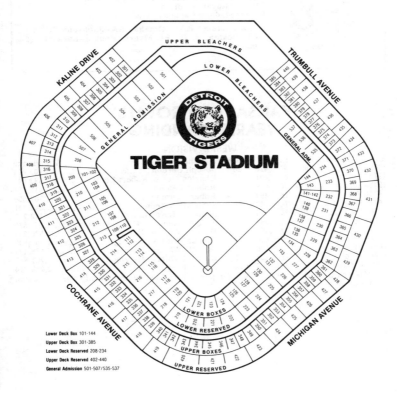

Lower Deck Box 101-144
Upper Deck Box 301-385
Lower Deck Reserved 208-234
Upper Deck Reserved 402-440
General Admission 501-507/535-537

Tiger Stadium, Detroit—First A. L. Game Played April 20, 1912

Jim Frey

KANSAS CITY ROYALS

President—Ewing Kauffman
Exec. Vice-Pres. & Gen. Manager—Joe Burke
V. P. Player Personnel—John Schuerholz
Vice-President-Administration—Spencer Robinson
Vice-President-Controller—Dale Rohr
Director of Public Relations—Dean Vogelaar
Traveling Secretary—Bill Beck
Director of Publications—Bruce Carnahan
Offices—Royals Stadium
Royals Stadium Capacity—40,628

Farm System: AAA—Omaha. AA—Jacksonville. A—Charleston, S. C., Ft. Myers. Rookie—Sarasota (2 clubs).

KANSAS CITY ROYALS' YEARLY STANDING

WEST DIVISION

Year—Position	W.	L.	Pct.	*G.B.	Manager	Attendance
1969—Fourth.....	69	93	.426	28	Joseph Gordon	902,414
1970—Fourth† ...	65	97	.401	33	Charles Metro, Robert Lemon	693,047
1971—Second.....	85	76	.528	16	Robert Lemon	910,784
1972—Fourth.....	76	78	.494	16½	Robert Lemon	707,656
1973—Second.....	88	74	.543	6	John A. McKeon	1,345,341
1974—Fifth........	77	85	.475	13	John A. McKeon	1,173,292
1975—Second.....	91	71	.562	7	J. A. McKeon, D. (Whitey) Herzog	1,151,836
1976—First‡	90	72	.556	+ 2½	Dorrel (Whitey) Herzog	1,680,265
1977—First‡	102	60	.630	+ 8	Dorrel (Whitey) Herzog	1,852,603
1978—First‡	92	70	.568	+ 5	Dorrel (Whitey) Herzog	2,255,493
1979—Second.....	85	77	.525	3	Dorrel (Whitey) Herzog	2,261,845
1980—First§	97	65	.599	+14	James Frey	2,288,714

*Games behind winner. †Tied for position. ‡Lost Championship Series. §Won Championship Series.

KANSAS CITY ROYALS
(41) JIM FREY—Manager

No. PITCHERS—	Bts.	Thrs.	Hgt.	Wgt.	Birth-date	1980 Club	IP.	W.	L.	ERA.
37 Berenguer, Juan	R	R	5:11	186	11-30-54	Tidewater	157	9	15	3.84
						New York NL	9	0	1	6.00
25 Brett, Ken	L	L	5:11	190	9-18-48	Omaha	9	0	0	4.00
						Kansas City	13	0	0	0.00
28 Chamberlain, Craig	R	R	6:01	190	2- 2-57	Omaha	170	11	10	4.76
						Kansas City	9	0	1	7.00
31 Christenson, Gary	L	L	6:05	212	5- 5-53	Omaha	41	2	4	2.41
						Kansas City	31	3	0	5.23
38 Gale, Rich	R	R	6:07	225	1-19-54	Kansas City	191	13	9	3.91
32 Gura, Larry	L	L	6:00	185	11-26-47	Kansas City	283	18	10	2.96
22 Leonard, Dennis	R	R	6:01	190	5- 8-51	Kansas City	280	20	11	3.79
27 Martin, Renie	R	R	6:04	185	8-30-55	Kansas City	137	10	10	4.40
29 Quisenberry, Dan	R	R	6:02	180	2- 7-54	Kansas City	128	12	7	3.09
34 Splittorff, Paul	L	L	6:03	210	10- 8-46	Kansas City	204	14	11	4.15
21 Twitty, Jeff	L	L	6:02	185	11-10-57	Omaha	48	6	3	1.88
						Kansas City	22	2	1	6.14
50 Wright, Jim	R	R	6:05	205	3- 3-55	Okla. City	106	9	9	5.35

CATCHERS—						1980 Club	G.	HR.	RBI.	Avg.
15 Grote, Jerry	R	R	5:10	190	10- 6-42	(Did not play in 1980)				
9 Quirk, Jamie	L	R	6:04	200	10-22-54	Kansas City	62	5	21	.276
12 Wathan, John	R	R	6:02	205	10- 4-49	Kansas City	126	6	58	.305

INFIELDERS—										
24 Aikens, Willie	L	R	6:02	220	10-14-54	Kansas City	151	20	98	.278
5 Brett, George	L	R	6:00	200	5-15-53	Kansas City	117	24	118	.390
17 Castillo, Manny	B	R	5:09	160	4- 1-57	Omaha	137	6	70	.289
						Kansas City	7	0	0	.200
7 Chalk, Dave	R	R	5:10	170	8-30-50	Kansas City	69	1	20	.251
						Jacksonville	74	12	44	.322
2 Concepcion, Onix	R	R	5:06	160	10- 5-57	Omaha	58	4	34	.281
						Kansas City	12	0	2	.133
33 Ireland, Tim	R	R	6:00	180	3-14-53	Omaha	126	12	63	.296
14 May, Lee	R	R	6:03	205	3-23-43	Baltimore	78	7	31	.243
18 Mulliniks, Rance	L	R	6:00	170	1-15-56	Kansas City	36	0	6	.259
16 Phelps, Ken	L	L	6:01	209	8- 6-54	Omaha	133	23,	72	.294
						Kansas City	3	0	0	.000
30 Washington, U. L.	B	R	5:11	175	10-27-53	Kansas City	153	6	53	.273
20 White, Frank	R	R	5:11	170	9- 4-50	Kansas City	154	7	60	.264

OUTFIELDERS—										
45 Garcia, Daniel	L	L	6:01	182	4-29-54	Omaha	120	1	49	.320
23 Geronimo, Cesar	L	L	6:02	175	3-11-48	Cincinnati	103	2	9	.255
10 Hurdle, Clint	L	L	6:03	195	7-30-57	Kansas City	130	10	60	.294
11 McRae, Hal	R	R	5:11	180	7-10-46	Kansas City	124	14	83	.297
26 Otis, Amos	R	R	5:11	166	4-26-47	Kansas City	107	10	53	.251
6 Wilson, Willie	B	R	6:03	187	7- 9-55	Kansas City	161	3	49	.326

BILL CONNORS (36)—Coach   JOSE MARTINEZ (42)—Coach
GORDY MacKENZIE (43)—Coach   JIMMY SCHAFFER (44)—Coach
RICK RENICK (46)—Coach

ROYALS STADIUM

	Seats	Prices
Club Boxes	2,492	$8.00
Field Box Seats	7,605	7.00
View Box Seats	4,543	5.00
Plaza Reserved Seats	7,639	5.00
View Reserved Seats	13,279	4.00
General Admission	5,070	1.50

NOTE: There are no seating sections as such. Seating is controlled by aisle numbers. Even numbers start behind home plate and go in ascending order toward right field, odd numbers toward left field.

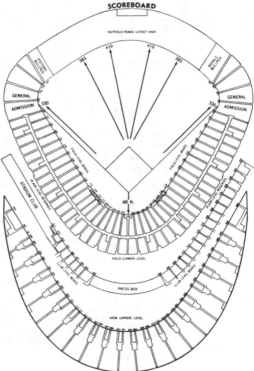

Royals Stadium, Harry S. Truman Sports Complex, Kansas City—
First A. L. Game Played April 10, 1973

Bob Rodgers

MILWAUKEE BREWERS

President—Allan (Bud) Selig
Exec. Vice-Pres.-General Manager—Harry Dalton
Vice Pres., Administration—Tom Ferguson
V. P. Marketing—Richard Hackett
Dir. Scouting, Player Development—Ray Poitevint
Director of Publicity—Tom Skibosh
Asst. Director; Publicity—Mario Ziino
Offices—County Stadium
County Stadium Seating Capacity—53,192

Farm System: AAA—Vancouver. AA—El Paso. A—Burlington, Ia., Stockton. Rookie—Butte.

MILWAUKEE BREWERS' YEARLY STANDING

(Seattle Pilots Prior To 1970)
WEST DIVISION

Year—Position	W.	L.	Pct.	*G.B.	Manager	Attendance
1969—Sixth	64	98	.395	33	Joseph Schultz	677,944
1970—Fourth†	65	97	.401	33	J. David Bristol	933,690
1971—Sixth	69	92	.429	32	J. David Bristol	731,531

*Games behind winner. †Tied for position.

EAST DIVISION

Year—Position	W.	L.	Pct.	*G.B.	Manager	Attendance
1972—Sixth	65	91	.417	21	J. David Bristol, Del Crandall	600,440
1973—Fifth	74	88	.457	23	Del Crandall	1,092,158
1974—Fifth	76	86	.469	15	Del Crandall	955,741
1975—Fifth	68	94	.420	28	Del Crandall	1,213,357
1976—Sixth	66	95	.410	32	Alexander Grammas	1,012,164
1977—Sixth	67	95	.414	33	Alexander Grammas	1,114,938
1978—Third	93	69	.574	6½	George Bamberger	1,601,406
1979—Second	95	66	.590	8	George Bamberger	1,918,343
1980—Third	86	76	.531	17	George Bamberger, Robert Rodgers	1,857,408

*Games behind winner.

MILWAUKEE BREWERS

(37) BOB RODGERS—Manager

No. PITCHERS—	Bts.	Thrs.	Hgt.	Wgt.	Birth-date	1980 Club	IP.	W.	L.	ERA.
46 Augustine, Jerry	L	L	6:00	185	7-24-52	Milwaukee	70	4	3	4.50
48 Caldwell, Mike	R	L	6:00	185	1-22-49	Milwaukee	225	13	11	4.04
25 Cleveland Reggie	R	R	6:01	200	5-23-48	Milwaukee	154	11	9	3.74
49 DiPino, Frank	L	L	5:10	175	10-22-56	Holyoke	76	7	0	1.30
						Vancouver	28	3	1	2.25
28 Easterly, Jamie	L	L	5:10	180	2-17-53	Denver	134	9	8	3.63
34 Fingers, Rollie	R	R	6:04	190	8-25-46	San Diego	103	11	9	2.80
30 Haas, Moose	R	R	6:00	170	4-22-56	Milwaukee	252	16	15	3.11
45 Keeton, Rickey	R	R	6:02	190	3-18-57	Milwaukee	28	2	2	4.82
						Vancouver	136	10	4	3.31
47 Lerch, Randy	L	L	6:03	195	10- 9-45	Philadelphia	150	4	14	5.16
10 McClure, Bob	B	L	5:11	170	4-29-53	Milwaukee	91	5	8	3.07
27 Moore, Balor	L	L	6:03	185	1-25-51	Syracuse	9	0	3	9.00
						Toronto	65	1	1	5.26
41 Slaton, Jim	R	R	6:00	185	6-19-50	Milwaukee	16	1	1	4.50
50 Vuckovich, Pete	R	R	6:04	220	10-27-52	St. Louis	222	12	9	3.41

CATCHERS—	Bts.	Thrs.	Hgt.	Wgt.	Birth-date	1980 Club	G.	HR.	RBI.	Avg.
21 Martinez, Buck	R	R	5:11	190	11- 7-48	Milwaukee	76	3	17	.224
22 Moore, Charlie	R	R	5:11	180	6-21-53	Milwaukee	111	2	30	.291
23 Simmons, Ted	B	R	6:00	200	8- 9-49	St. Louis	145	21	98	.303
5 Yost, Ned	R	R	6:01	185	8-19-55	Milwaukee	15	0	0	.161
						Vancouver	80	2	41	.309

INFIELDERS—	Bts.	Thrs.	Hgt.	Wgt.	Birth-date	1980 Club	G.	HR.	RBI.	Avg.
6 Bando, Sal	R	R	6:00	200	2-13-44	Milwaukee	78	5	31	.197
15 Cooper, Cecil	L	L	6:02	190	12-30-49	Milwaukee	153	25	122	.352
17 Gantner, Jim	L	R	5:11	175	1- 5-53	Milwaukee	132	4	40	.282
13 Howell, Roy	L	R	6:01	195	12-18-53	Toronto	142	10	57	.269
7 Money, Don	R	R	6:01	190	6- 7-47	Milwaukee	86	17	46	.256
11 Romero, Ed	R	R	5:11	150	12-19-57	Milwaukee	42	1	10	.260
						Vancouver	50	0	16	.273
19 Yount, Robin	R	R	6:00	170	9-16-55	Milwaukee	143	23	87	.293

OUTFIELDERS—	Bts.	Thrs.	Hgt.	Wgt.	Birth-date	1980 Club	G.	HR.	RBI.	Avg.
29 Brouhard, Mark	R	R	6:01	210	5-22-56	Milwaukee	45	5	16	.232
16 Edwards, Marshall	L	L	5:09	157	8-27-52	Vancouver	134	2	68	.291
9 Hisle, Larry	R	R	6:02	195	5- 5-47	Milwaukee	17	6	16	.283
4 Molitor, Paul	R	R	6:00	175	8-22-56	Milwaukee	111	9	37	.304
24 Oglivie, Ben	L	L	6:02	170	2-11-49	Milwaukee	156	41	118	.304
20 Thomas, Gorman	R	R	6:03	200	12-12-50	Milwaukee	162	38	105	.239

LARRY HANEY (12)—Coach   CAL McLISH (38)—Coach
HARVEY KUENN (32)—Coach   RON HANSEN (18)—Coach
HARRY WARNER (36)—Coach

COUNTY STADIUM

	Seats	Prices
Deluxe Mezzanine	76	$8.00
Mezzanine	933	7.50
Box Seats	11,572	....
Lower	6,885	7.00
Upper	4,687	7.00
Lower Grandstand	21,231	6.00
Upper Grandstand	13,380	4.50
General Admission	*	4.50
Bleachers	6,000	2.50

*Variable

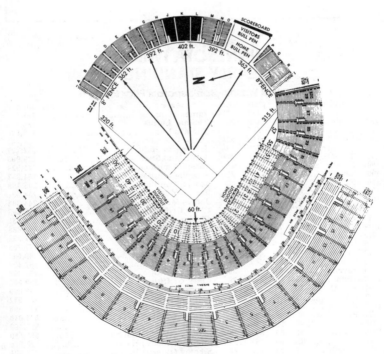

County Stadium, Milwaukee—First A. L. Game Played May 15, 1968

Johnny Goryl

MINNESOTA TWINS

President—Calvin R. Griffith
Vice-President—Mrs. Thelma Griffith Haynes
Exec. Vice-Pres.—Clark Griffith, Bruce G. Haynes,
   Howard T. Fox Jr.
Vice-Pres.-Farm Director—George Brophy
Asst. Farm Director—Jim Rantz
Director of Public Relations—Tom Mee
Offices—Metropolitan Stadium, Bloomington
Metropolitan Stadium Capacity—45,919

Farm System: AAA—Toledo. AA—Orlando. A—Visalia,
Wisconsin Rapids. Rookie—Elizabethton.

MINNESOTA TWINS' YEARLY STANDING

(Original Washington Senators Prior to 1961)

Year—Position	W.	L.	Pct.	*G.B.	Manager	Attendance
1901—Sixth	61	72	.459	20½	James Manning	161,661
1902—Sixth	61	75	.449	22	Thomas Loftus	188,158
1903—Eighth	43	94	.314	47½	Thomas Loftus	128,878
1904—Eighth	38	113	.251	55½	Patrick Donovan	131,744
1905—Seventh	64	87	.421	29½	J. Garland Stahl	252,027
1906—Seventh	55	95	.367	37½	J. Garland Stahl	129,903
1907—Eighth	49	102	.325	43½	Joseph Cantillon	221,929
1908—Seventh	67	85	.441	22½	Joseph Cantillon	264,252
1909—Eighth	42	110	.276	56	Joseph Cantillon	205,199
1910—Seventh	66	85	.437	36½	James McAleer	254,591
1911—Seventh	64	90	.416	38½	James McAleer	244,884
1912—Second	91	61	.599	14	Clark Griffith	350,663
1913—Second	90	64	.584	6½	Clark Griffith	325,831
1914—Third	81	73	.526	19	Clark Griffith	243,888
1915—Fourth	85	68	.556	17	Clark Griffith	167,332
1916—Seventh	76	77	.497	14½	Clark Griffith	177,265
1917—Fifth	74	79	.484	25½	Clark Griffith	89,682
1918—Third	72	56	.563	4	Clark Griffith	182,122
1919—Seventh	56	84	.400	32	Clark Griffith	234,096
1920—Sixth	68	84	.447	29	Clark Griffith	359,260
1921—Fourth	80	73	.523	18	George McBride	456,069
1922—Sixth	69	85	.448	25	Clyde Milan	458,552
1923—Fourth	75	78	.490	23½	Owen (Donie) Bush	357,406
1924—First	92	62	.597	+ 2	Stanley (Bucky) Harris	534,310
1925—First	96	55	.636	+ 8½	Stanley (Bucky) Harris	817,199
1926—Fourth	81	69	.540	8	Stanley (Bucky) Harris	551,580
1927—Third	85	69	.552	25	Stanley (Bucky) Harris	528,976
1928—Fourth	75	79	.487	26	Stanley (Bucky) Harris	378,501
1929—Fifth	71	81	.467	34	Walter Johnson	355,506

MINNESOTA TWINS' YEARLY STANDING—Continued

Year–Position	W.	L.	Pct.	*G.B.	Manager	Attendance
1930—Second....	94	60	.610	8	Walter Johnson	614,474
1931—Third......	92	62	.597	16	Walter Johnson	492,657
1932—Third......	93	61	.604	14	Walter Johnson	371,396
1933—First.......	99	53	.651	+ 7	Joseph Cronin	437,533
1934—Seventh...	66	86	.434	34	Joseph Cronin	330,074
1935—Sixth.......	67	86	.438	27	Stanley (Bucky) Harris	255,011
1936—Fourth.....	82	71	.536	20	Stanley (Bucky) Harris	379,525
1937—Sixth.......	73	80	.477	28½	Stanley (Bucky) Harris	397,799
1938—Fifth.......	75	76	.497	23½	Stanley (Bucky) Harris	522,694
1939—Sixth.......	65	87	.428	41½	Stanley (Bucky) Harris	339,257
1940—Seventh ...	64	90	.416	26	Stanley (Bucky) Harris	381,241
1941—Sixth†	70	84	.455	31	Stanley (Bucky) Harris	415,663
1942—Seventh ...	62	89	.411	39½	Stanley (Bucky) Harris	403,493
1943—Second....	84	69	.549	13½	Oswald Bluege	574,694
1944—Eighth.....	64	90	.416	25	Oswald Bluege	525,235
1945—Second.....	87	67	.565	1½	Oswald Bluege	652,660
1946—Fourth.....	76	78	.494	28	Oswald Bluege	1,027,216
1947—Seventh ...	64	90	.416	33	Oswald Bluege	850,758
1948—Seventh ...	56	97	.366	40	Joseph Kuhel	795,254
1949—Eighth.....	50	104	.325	47	Joseph Kuhel	770,745
1950—Fifth.......	67	87	.435	31	Stanley (Bucky) Harris	699,697
1951—Seventh ...	62	92	.403	36	Stanley (Bucky) Harris	695,167
1952—Fifth.......	78	76	.506	17	Stanley (Bucky) Harris	699,457
1953—Fifth.......	76	76	.500	23½	Stanley (Bucky) Harris	595,594
1954—Sixth.......	66	88	.429	45	Stanley (Bucky) Harris	503,542
1955—Eighth.....	53	101	.344	43	Charles (Chuck) Dressen	425,238
1956—Seventh ...	59	95	.383	38	Charles (Chuck) Dressen	431,647
1957—Eighth.....	55	99	.357	43	Chas. Dressen, Harry Lavagetto	457,079
1958—Eighth.....	61	93	.396	31	Harry (Cookie) Lavagetto	475,288
1959—Eighth.....	63	91	.409	31	Harry (Cookie) Lavagetto	615,372
1960—Fifth.......	73	81	.474	24	Harry (Cookie) Lavagetto	743,404
1961—Seventh ...	70	90	.438	38	Harry Lavagetto, Sam Mele	1,256,723
1962—Second....	91	71	.562	5	Sabath (Sam) Mele	1,433,116
1963—Third......	91	70	.565	13	Sabath (Sam) Mele	1,406,652
1964—Sixth†	79	83	.488	20	Sabath (Sam) Mele	1,207,514
1965—First.......	102	60	.630	+ 7	Sabath (Sam) Mele	1,463,258
1966—Second....	89	73	.549	9	Sabath (Sam) Mele	1,259,374
1967—Second† ...	91	71	.562	1	Sabath (Sam) Mele, Calvin Ermer	1,483,547
1968—Seventh ...	79	83	.488	24	Calvin Ermer	1,143,257

*Games behind pennant winner.   †Tied for position.

WEST DIVISION

Year–Position	W.	L.	Pct.	*G.B.	Manager	Attendance
1969—First‡	97	65	.599	+ 9	Alfred (Billy) Martin	1,349,328
1970—First‡	98	64	.605	+ 9	William Rigney	1,261,887
1971—Fifth.......	74	86	.463	26½	William Rigney	940,858
1972—Third......	77	77	.500	15½	William Rigney, Frank Quilici	797,901
1973—Third......	81	81	.500	13	Frank Quilici	907,499
1974—Third......	82	80	.506	8	Frank Quilici	662,401
1975—Fourth.....	76	83	.478	20½	Frank Quilici	737,156
1976—Third......	85	77	.525	5	Gene Mauch	715,394
1977—Fourth.....	84	77	.522	17½	Gene Mauch	1,162,727
1978—Fourth.....	73	89	.451	19	Gene Mauch	787,878
1979—Fourth.....	82	80	.506	6	Gene Mauch	1,070,521
1980—Third.......	77	84	.478	19½	Gene Mauch, John Goryl	769,206

*Games behind winner.   ‡Lost Championship Series.

MINNESOTA TWINS

(45) JOHNNY GORYL–Manager

No.	PITCHERS–	Bts.	Thrs.	Hgt.	Wgt.	Birth-date	1980 Club	IP.	W.	L.	ERA.
30	Arroyo, Fernando	R	R	6:02	190	3-21-52	Toledo	72	6	1	1.63
							Minnesota	92	6	6	4.70
34	Cooper, Don	R	R	6:00	175	2-15-57	Nashville	60	9	5	1.80
							Columbus	38	3	2	2.13
23	Corbett, Doug	R	R	6:01	192	11- 4-52	Minnesota	136	8	6	1.99
19	Erickson, Roger	R	R	6:03	199	8-30-56	Minnesota	191	7	13	3.25
37	Felton, Terry	R	R	6:02	185	10-29-57	Minnesota	18	0	3	7.00
							Toledo	146	7	8	4.01
31	Jackson, Darrell	L	L	5:10	143	4- 3-56	Minnesota	172	9	9	3.87
36	Koosman, Jerry	R	L	6:02	225	12-23-43	Minnesota	243	16	13	4.04
33	O'Connor, Jack	L	L	6:03	200	6- 2-58	W. Palm Bch.	139	9	6	2.40
							Memphis	29	1	2	7.76
17	Redfern, Pete	R	R	6:02	190	8-25-54	Minnesota	105	7	7	4.54
26	Sarmiento, Wally	R	R	6:00	160	11-25-58	Toledo	85	6	6	2.65
22	Verhoeven, John	R	R	6:05	207	7- 3-53	Minnesota	100	3	4	3.96
28	Williams, Al	R	R	6:04	190	5- 7-54	Toledo	107	9	3	2.10
							Minnesota	77	6	2	3.51

No.	CATCHERS–	Bts.	Thrs.	Hgt.	Wgt.	Birth-date	1980 Club	G.	HR.	RBI.	Avg.
11	Butera, Sal	R	R	6:00	189	9-25-52	Minnesota	34	0	2	.271
18	Smith, Ray	R	R	6:01	185	9-18-55	Toledo	115	0	46	.274
16	Wynegar, Butch	B	R	6:00	194	3-14-56	Minnesota	146	5	57	.255

No.	INFIELDERS–	Bts.	Thrs.	Hgt.	Wgt.	Birth-date	1980 Club	G.	HR.	RBI.	Avg.
24	Baker, Chuck	R	R	5:11	180	12- 6-52	Hawaii	114	9	45	.273
							San Diego	9	0	0	.136
2	Castino, John	R	R	5:11	169	10-23-54	Minnesota	150	13	64	.302
25	Goodwin, Danny	L	R	6:01	203	9- 2-53	Minnesota	55	1	11	.200
9	Hatcher, Mickey	R	R	6:02	195	3-15-55	Albuquerque	43	7	40	.326
							Los Angeles	57	1	5	.226
15	Jackson, Ron	R	R	6:00	217	5- 9-53	Minnesota	131	5	42	.265
14	Mackanin, Pete	R	R	6:02	196	8- 1-51	Minnesota	108	4	35	.266
5	Smalley, Roy	B	R	6:01	182	10-25-52	Minnesota	133	12	63	.278
50	Washington, Ron	R	R	5:11	160	4-29-52	Toledo	114	3	36	.287
7	Wilfong, Rob	L	R	6:01	185	9- 1-53	Minnesota	131	8	45	.248

No.	OUTFIELDERS–	Bts.	Thrs.	Hgt.	Wgt.	Birth-date	1980 Club	G.	HR.	RBI.	Avg.
8	Adams, Glenn	L	R	6:00	188	10- 4-47	Minnesota	99	6	38	.286
20	Engle, Dave	R	R	6:03	210	11-30-56	Toledo	133	7	73	.307
21	Johnston, Greg	L	L	6:00	175	2-12-55	Toledo	132	14	66	.296
							Minnesota	14	0	1	.185
10	Powell, Hosken	L	L	6:01	185	5-14-55	Minnesota	137	6	35	.262
12	Sofield, Rick	L	R	6:01	193	12-16-56	Minnesota	131	9	49	.247
32	Ward, Gary	R	R	6:02	207	12- 6-53	Toledo	128	13	66	.282
							Minnesota	13	1	10	.463

KARL KUEHL (41)–Coach   JOHNNY PODRES (46)–Coach
BILLY GARDNER (42)–Coach   RICK STELMASZEK (43)–Coach

METROPOLITAN STADIUM

	Seats	Prices
Deluxe Boxes	42	$7.50
Private Boxes	94	7.00
Box Seats	14,030	7.00
Reserved Grandstand	12,779	6.00
Unreserved Grandstand	4,547	6.00
General Admission	14,427	3.00

Note—Deluxe Boxes sold on season basis only.

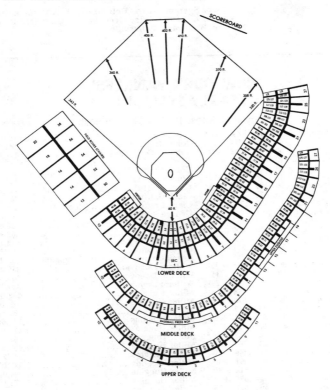

Metropolitan Stadium, Bloomington—First A. L. Game Played April 21, 1961

Gene Michael

NEW YORK YANKEES

Principal Owner—George M. Steinbrenner III
President—Lou Saban
Exec. Vice-President—Cedric Tallis
Vice-Pres., Gen. Manager—Gene Michael
Director of Media Relations—Larry Wahl
Asst. Director of Media Relations—David Szen
Traveling Secretary—Bill Kane

Offices—Yankee Stadium
Yankee Stadium Capacity—57,545

**Farm System: AAA—Columbus, O. AA—Nashville.
A—Ft. Lauderdale, Greensboro, Oneonta. Rookie—Bradenton, Paintsville.**

NEW YORK YANKEES' YEARLY STANDING

(Baltimore Orioles, 1901 to 1902, Inclusive)

Year—Position	W.	L.	Pct.	*G.B.	Manager	Attendance
1901—Fifth	68	65	.511	13½	John McGraw	141,952
1902—Eighth	50	88	.362	34	John McGraw, Wilbert Robinson	174,606
1903—Fourth	72	62	.537	17	Clark Griffith	211,808
1904—Second	92	59	.609	1½	Clark Griffith	438,919
1905—Sixth	71	78	.477	21½	Clark Griffith	309,100
1906—Second	90	61	.596	3	Clark Griffith	434,709
1907—Fifth	70	78	.473	21	Clark Griffith	350,020
1908—Eighth	51	103	.331	39½	Clark Griffith, Norman Elberfeld	305,500
1909—Fifth	74	77	.490	23½	George Stallings	501,000
1910—Second	88	63	.583	14½	George Stallings, Hal Chase	355,857
1911—Sixth	76	76	.500	25½	Hal Chase	302,444
1912—Eighth	50	102	.329	55	Harry Wolverton	242,194
1913—Seventh	57	94	.377	38	Frank Chance	357,551
1914—Sixth†	70	84	.455	30	Frank Chance, Roger Peckinpaugh	359,477
1915—Fifth	69	83	.454	32½	William Donovan	256,035
1916—Fourth	80	74	.519	11	William Donovan	469,211
1917—Sixth	71	82	.464	28½	William Donovan	330,294
1918—Fourth	60	63	.488	13½	Miller Huggins	282,047
1919—Third	80	59	.576	7½	Miller Huggins	619,164
1920—Third	95	59	.617	3	Miller Huggins	1,289,422
1921—First	98	55	.641	+ 4½	Miller Huggins	1,230,696
1922—First	94	60	.610	+ 1	Miller Huggins	1,026,134
1923—First	98	54	.645	+16	Miller Huggins	1,007,066
1924—Second	89	63	.586	2	Miller Huggins	1,053,533
1925—Seventh	69	85	.448	30	Miller Huggins	697,267
1926—First	91	63	.591	+ 3	Miller Huggins	1,027,095
1927—First	110	44	.714	+19	Miller Huggins	1,164,015
1928—First	101	53	.656	+ 2½	Miller Huggins	1,072,132
1929—Second	88	66	.571	18	Miller Huggins	960,148
1930—Third	86	68	.558	16	J. Robert Shawkey	1,169,230

NEW YORK YANKEES' YEARLY STANDING—Continued

Year—Position	W.	L.	Pct.	*G.B.	Manager	Attendance
1931—Second.....	94	59	.614	13½	Joseph McCarthy	912,437
1932—First.......	107	47	.695	+13	Joseph McCarthy	962,320
1933—Second.....	91	59	.607	7	Joseph McCarthy	728,014
1934—Second.....	94	60	.610	7	Joseph McCarthy	854,682
1935—Second.....	89	60	.597	3	Joseph McCarthy	657,508
1936—First.......	102	51	.667	+19½	Joseph McCarthy	976,913
1937—First.......	102	52	.662	+13	Joseph McCarthy	998,148
1938—First.......	99	53	.651	+ 9½	Joseph McCarthy	970,916
1939—First.......	106	45	.702	+17	Joseph McCarthy	859,785
1940—Third.......	88	66	.571	2	Joseph McCarthy	988,975
1941—First.......	101	53	.656	+17	Joseph McCarthy	964,722
1942—First.......	103	51	.669	+ 9	Joseph McCarthy	988,251
1943—First.......	98	56	.636	+13½	Joseph McCarthy	645,006
1944—Third.......	83	71	.539	6	Joseph McCarthy	822,864
1945—Fourth......	81	71	.533	6½	Joseph McCarthy	881,846
1946—Third.......	87	67	.565	17	J. McCarthy, W. Dickey, J. Neun	2,265,512
1947—First.......	97	57	.630	+12	Stanley (Bucky) Harris	2,178,937
1948—Third.......	94	60	.610	2½	Stanley (Bucky) Harris	2,373,901
1949—First.......	97	57	.630	+ 1	Chas. (Casey) Stengel	2,281,676
1950—First.......	98	56	.636	+ 3	Chas. (Casey) Stengel	2,081,380
1951—First.......	98	56	.636	+ 5	Chas. (Casey) Stengel	1,950,107
1952—First.......	95	59	.617	+ 2	Chas. (Casey) Stengel	1,629,665
1953—First.......	99	52	.656	+ 8½	Chas. (Casey) Stengel	1,537,811
1954—Second.....	103	51	.669	8	Chas. (Casey) Stengel	1,475,171
1955—First.......	96	58	.623	+ 3	Chas. (Casey) Stengel	1,490,138
1956—First.......	97	57	.630	+ 9	Chas. (Casey) Stengel	1,491,784
1957—First.......	98	56	.636	+ 8	Chas. (Casey) Stengel	1,497,134
1958—First.......	92	62	.597	+10	Chas. (Casey) Stengel	1,428,438
1959—Third.......	79	75	.513	15	Chas. (Casey) Stengel	1,552,030
1960—First.......	97	57	.630	+ 8	Chas. (Casey) Stengel	1,627,349
1961—First.......	109	53	.673	+ 8	Ralph Houk	1,747,725
1962—First.......	96	66	.593	+ 5	Ralph Houk	1,493,574
1963—First.......	104	57	.646	+10½	Ralph Houk	1,308,920
1964—First.......	99	63	.611	+ 1	Lawrence (Yogi) Berra	1,305,638
1965—Sixth.......	77	85	.475	25	John Keane	1,213,552
1966—Tenth......	70	89	.440	26½	John Keane, Ralph Houk	1,124,648
1967—Ninth......	72	90	.444	20	Ralph Houk	1,259,514
1968—Fifth.......	83	79	.512	20	Ralph Houk	1,185,666

*Games behind pennant winner.   †Tied for position.

EAST DIVISION

Year—Position	W.	L.	Pct.	*G.B.	Manager	Attendance
1969—Fifth........	80	81	.497	28½	Ralph Houk	1,067,996
1970—Second....	93	69	.574	15	Ralph Houk	1,136,879
1971—Fourth.....	82	80	.506	21	Ralph Houk	1,070,771
1972—Fourth.....	79	76	.510	6½	Ralph Houk	966,328
1973—Fourth.....	80	82	.494	17	Ralph Houk	1,262,103
1974—Second.....	89	73	.549	2	William Virdon	1,273,075
1975—Third.......	83	77	.519	12	William Virdon, Billy Martin	1,288,048
1976—First‡......	97	62	.610	+10½	Alfred (Billy) Martin	2,012,434
1977—First‡......	100	62	.617	+ 2½	Alfred (Billy) Martin	2,103,092
1978—First§‡.....	100	63	.613	+ 1	Alfred (Billy) Martin, Robert Lemon	2,335,871
1979—Fourth.....	89	71	.556	13½	Robert Lemon, Alfred (Billy) Martin	2,537,765
1980—First a	103	59	.636	+3	Richard Howser	2,627,417

*Games behind winner. ‡Won Championship Series. §Defeated Boston in pennant playoff. aLost Championship Series.

NEW YORK YANKEES
(11) GENE MICHAEL—Manager

No. PITCHERS—	Bts.	Thrs.	Hgt.	Wgt.	Birth-date	1980 Club	IP.	W.	L.	ERA.
43 Bird, Doug	R	R	6:04	180	3- 5-50	Columbus	48	6	0	2.25
						New York	51	3	0	2.65
35 Castro, Bill	R	R	5:11	170	12-13-53	Milwaukee	56	2	4	2.79
57 Cochran, Greg	R	R	6:02	195	11-15-53	Columbus	165	12	7	2.56
39 Davis, Ron	R	R	6:04	198	8- 6-55	New York	131	9	3	2.95
54 Gossage, Rich	R	R	6:03	217	7- 5-51	New York	99	6	2	2.27
49 Guidry, Ron	L	L	5:11	160	8-28-50	New York	220	17	10	3.56
25 John, Tommy	R	L	6:03	203	5-22-43	New York	265	22	9	3.43
34 LaRoche, Dave	L	L	6:02	195	5-14-48	California	128	3	5	4.08
45 May, Rudy	L	L	6:02	195	7-18-44	New York	175	15	5	2.47
46 Nelson, Gene	R	R	6:00	172	12- 3-60	Ft. Laud.	196	20	3	1.97
19 Righetti, Dave	L	L	6:03	195	11-29-58	Columbus	142	6	10	4.63
66 Ryder, Brian	R	R	6:06	175	2-13-60	Nashville	201	15	9	3.04
38 Underwood, Tom	L	L	5:11	185	12-22-53	New York	187	13	9	3.66

CATCHERS—						1980 Club	G.	HR.	RBI.	Avg.
10 Cerone, Rick	R	R	5:11	185	5-19-54	New York	147	14	85	.277
26 Oates, Johnny	L	R	5:11	185	1-21-46	New York	39	1	3	.188
47 Robinson, Bruce	L	R	6:02	194	4-16-54	Columbus	104	12	48	.240
						New York	4	0	0	.000
24 Werth, Dennis	R	R	6:01	201	12-29-52	Columbus	32	3	15	.220
						New York	39	3	12	.308

INFIELDERS—										
20 Dent, Bucky	R	R	5:11	184	11-25-51	New York	141	5	52	.262
18 Milbourne, Larry	B	R	6:00	165	2-14-51	Seattle	106	0	26	.264
9 Nettles, Graig	L	R	6:00	187	8-20-44	New York	89	16	45	.244
30 Randolph, Willie	R	R	5:11	163	7- 6-54	New York	138	7	46	.294
27 Rodriguez, Aurelio	R	R	5:11	180	12-28-47	San Diego	89	2	13	.200
						New York	52	3	14	.220
21 Soderholm, Eric	R	R	5:11	202	9-24-48	New York	95	11	35	.287
12 Spencer, Jim	L	L	6:02	205	7-30-47	New York	97	13	43	.236
28 Watson, Bob	R	R	6:02	212	4-10-46	New York	130	13.	68	.307

OUTFIELDERS—										
13 Brown, Bobby	B	R	6:01	198	5-24-54	New York	137	14	47	.260
17 Gamble, Oscar	L	R	5:11	187	12-20-49	New York	78	14	50	.278
44 Jackson, Reggie	L	L	6:00	206	5-18-46	New York	143	41	111	.300
22 Mumphrey, Jerry	B	R	6:02	185	9- 9-52	San Diego	160	4	59	.298
2 Murcer, Bobby	L	R	5:11	185	5-20-46	New York	100	13	57	.269
14 Piniella, Lou	R	R	6:02	199	8-28-43	New York	116	2	27	.287
31 Winfield, Dave	R	R	6:06	220	10- 3-51	San Diego	162	20	87	.276

JOE ALTOBELLI (48)—Coach
YOGI BERRA (8)—Coach
MIKE FERRARO (33)—Coach

STAN WILLIAMS (42)—Coach
JEFF TORBORG (41)—Coach
CHARLEY LAU (40)—Coach

YANKEE STADIUM

*Sold only on season basis.	Seats	Prices
Luxury Boxes	298	*
Field Boxes	7,521	$7.50
Main Level Boxes	8,098	7.50
Loge	6,302	7.50
Upper Boxes	7,955	7.50
Main Level Reserved	5,780	5.50
Upper Reserved	15,652	5.50
General Admission		2.50
Bleachers	5,939	1.50

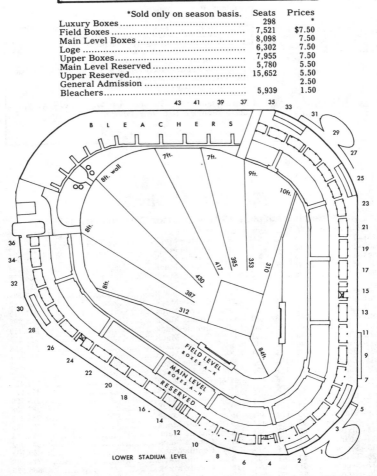

Yankee Stadium, New York—First A. L. Game Played April 18, 1923

OAKLAND A's

Billy Martin

President—Roy Eisenhardt
Executive Vice-President—Walter J. Haas
Field Manager-Dir. Player Development—Billy Martin
V.P. Baseball Administration—Carl A. Finley
V.P. Business Operations—Andy Dolich
Director of Scouting—Dick Wiencek
Director, Minor League Operations—Walt Jocketty
Dir. of Pub. Relations-Traveling Sec.—Mickey Morabito
Offices—Oakland-Alameda County Coliseum
Coliseum Capacity—49,217.

Farm System: AAA—Tacoma. AA—West Haven. A— Modesto, Medford, San Jose (Co-op).

OAKLAND A'S
YEARLY STANDING

(Philadelphia Athletics, 1901-54; Kansas City Athletics, 1955-67)

Year—Position	W.	L.	Pct.	*G.B.	Manager	Attendance
1901—Fourth	74	62	.544	9	Connie Mack	206,329
1902—First	83	53	.610	+ 5	Connie Mack	442,473
1903—Second	75	60	.556	14½	Connie Mack	420,078
1904—Fifth	81	70	.536	12½	Connie Mack	512,294
1905—First	92	56	.622	+ 2	Connie Mack	554,576
1906—Fourth	78	67	.538	12	Connie Mack	489,129
1907—Second	88	57	.607	1½	Connie Mack	625,581
1908—First	68	85	.444	22	Connie Mack	455,062
1909—Second	95	58	.621	3½	Connie Mack	674,915
1910—First	102	48	.680	+14½	Connie Mack	588,905
1911—First	101	50	.669	+13½	Connie Mack	605,749
1912—Third	90	62	.592	15	Connie Mack	517,653
1913—First	96	57	.627	+ 6½	Connie Mack	571,896
1914—First	99	53	.651	+ 8½	Connie Mack	346,641
1915—Eighth	43	109	.283	58½	Connie Mack	146,223
1916—Eighth	36	117	.235	54½	Connie Mack	184,471
1917—Eighth	55	98	.359	44½	Connie Mack	221,432
1918—Eighth	52	76	.402	24	Connie Mack	177,926
1919—Eighth	36	104	.257	52	Connie Mack	225,209
1920—Eighth	48	106	.312	50	Connie Mack	287,888
1921—Eighth	53	100	.346	45	Connie Mack	344,430
1922—Seventh	65	89	.422	29	Connie Mack	425,356
1923—Sixth	69	83	.454	29	Connie Mack	534,122
1924—Fifth	71	81	.467	20	Connie Mack	531,992
1925—Second	88	64	.579	8½	Connie Mack	869,703
1926—Third	83	67	.533	6	Connie Mack	714,308
1927—Second	91	63	.591	19	Connie Mack	605,529
1928—Second	98	55	.641	2½	Connie Mack	689,756
1929—First	104	46	.693	+18	Connie Mack	839,176

OAKLAND A's YEARLY STANDING—Continued

Year—Position	W.	L.	Pct.	*G.B.	Manager	Attendance
1930—First	102	52	.662	+ 8	Connie Mack	721,663
1931—First	107	45	.704	+13½	Connie Mack	627,464
1932—Second	94	60	.610	13	Connie Mack	405,500
1933—Third	79	72	.523	19½	Connie Mack	297,138
1934—Fifth	68	82	.453	31	Connie Mack	305,847
1935—Eighth	58	91	.389	34	Connie Mack	233,173
1936—Eighth	53	100	.346	49	Connie Mack	285,173
1937—Seventh	54	97	.358	46½	Connie Mack	430,733
1938—Eighth	53	99	.349	46	Connie Mack	385,357
1939—Seventh	55	97	.362	51½	Connie Mack	395,022
1940—Eighth	54	100	.351	36	Connie Mack	432,145
1941—Eighth	64	90	.416	37	Connie Mack	528,894
1942—Eighth	55	99	.357	48	Connie Mack	423,487
1943—Eighth	49	105	.318	49	Connie Mack	376,735
1944—Fifth†	72	82	.468	17	Connie Mack	505,322
1945—Eighth	52	98	.347	34½	Connie Mack	462,631
1946—Eighth	49	105	.318	55	Connie Mack	621,793
1947—Fifth	78	76	.506	19	Connie Mack	911,566
1948—Fourth	84	70	.545	12½	Connie Mack	945,076
1949—Fifth	81	73	.526	16	Connie Mack	816,514
1950—Eighth	52	102	.338	46	Connie Mack	309,805
1951—Sixth	70	84	.455	28	James Dykes	465,469
1952—Fourth	79	75	.513	16	James Dykes	627,100
1953—Seventh	59	95	.383	41½	James Dykes	362,113
1954—Eighth	51	103	.331	60	Edwin Joost	304,666
1955—Sixth	63	91	.409	33	Louis Boudreau	1,393,054
1956—Eighth	52	102	.338	45	Louis Boudreau	1,015,154
1957—Seventh	59	94	.386	38½	Louis Boudreau, Harry Craft	901,067
1958—Seventh	73	81	.474	19	Harry Craft	925,090
1959—Seventh	66	88	.429	28	Harry Craft	963,683
1960—Eighth	58	96	.377	39	Robert Elliott	774,944
1961—Ninth†	61	100	.379	47½	Joseph Gordon, Henry Bauer	683,817
1962—Ninth	72	90	.444	24	Henry Bauer	635,675
1963—Eighth	73	89	.451	31½	Edmund Lopat	762,364
1964—Tenth	57	105	.352	42	Edmund Lopat, F. Melvin McGaha	642,478
1965—Tenth	59	103	.364	43	Mel McGaha, Haywood Sullivan	528,344
1966—Seventh	74	86	.463	23	Alvin Dark	773,929
1967—Tenth	62	99	.385	29½	Alvin Dark, Luke Appling	726,639
1968—Sixth	82	80	.506	21	Robert Kennedy	837,466

*Games behind pennant winner. †Tied for position.

WEST DIVISION

Year—Position	W.	L.	Pct.	*G.B.	Manager	Attendance
1969—Second	88	74	.543	9	Henry Bauer, John McNamara	778,232
1970—Second	89	73	.549	9	John McNamara	778,355
1971—First‡‡	101	60	.627	+16	Richard Williams	914,993
1972—First‡‡	93	62	.600	+ 5½	Richard Williams	921,323
1973—First‡‡	94	68	.580	+ 6	Richard Williams	1,000,763
1974—First‡‡	90	72	.556	+ 5	Alvin Dark	845,693
1975—First‡	98	64	.605	+ 7	Alvin Dark	1,075,518
1976—Second	87	74	.540	2½	Charles Tanner	780,593
1977—Seventh	63	98	.391	38½	Jack McKeon, Bobby Winkles	495,599
1978—Sixth	69	93	.426	23	Bobby Winkles, Jack McKeon	526,999
1979—Seventh	54	108	.333	34	R. James Marshall	306,763
1980—Second	83	79	.512	14	Alfred (Billy) Martin	842,259

*Games behind winner. ‡Lost Championship Series. ‡‡Won Championship Series.

OAKLAND A's
(1) BILLY MARTIN—Manager

No. PITCHERS—	Bts.	Thrs.	Hgt.	Wgt.	Birth-date	1980 Club	IP.	W.	L.	ERA.
59 Beard, Dave	L	R	6:05	190	10- 2-59	Ogden	97	7	8	6.40
						Oakland	16	0	1	3.38
28 Bordi, Rich	R	R	6:07	210	4-18-59	West Haven	76	4	6	4.14
						Oakland	2	0	0	4.50
38 Jones, Jeff	R	R	6:03	210	7-29-56	Oakland	44	1	3	2.86
27 Keough, Matt	R	R	6:02	175	7- 3-55	Oakland	250	16	13	2.92
50 Kingman, Brian	R	R	6:01	190	7-27-54	Oakland	211	8	20	3.84
22 Langford, Rick	R	R	6:00	180	3-20-52	Oakland	290	19	12	3.26
54 McCatty, Steve	R	R	6:03	205	3-20-54	Oakland	222	14	14	3.85
34 McLaughlin, Bo	R	R	6:05	210	10-23-53	Richmond	28	1	1	4.50
32 Minetto, Craig	L	L	6:00	185	4-25-54	Ogden	41	3	2	4.61
						Oakland	8	0	2	7.88
17 Norris, Mike	R	R	6:02	172	3-19-55	Oakland	284	22	9	2.54
53 Owchinko, Bob	L	L	6:02	195	1- 1-55	Cleveland	114	2	9	5.29
36 Thomas, Roy	R	R	6:05	215	6-22-53	Springfield	37	5	1	3.41
						St. Louis	55	2	3	4.75

CATCHERS—						1980 Club	G.	HR.	RBI.	Avg.
2 Heath, Mike	R	R	5:11	176	2- 5-55	Oakland	92	1	33	.243
25 Hosley, Tim	R	R	5:11	190	5-10-47	Ogden	139	26	102	.301
44 Johnson, Cliff	R	R	6:04	225	7-22-47	Chicago NL	68	10	34	.235
						Cleveland	54	6	28	.230
5 Newman, Jeff	R	R	6:02	215	9-11-48	Oakland	127	15	56	.233

INFIELDERS—										
3 Babitt, Shooty	R	R	5:07	170	3- 9-59	West Haven	29	1	15	.290
						Ogden	93	1	25	.234
18 Doyle, Brian	L	R	5:10	170	1-26-54	Columbus	47	0	5	.225
						New York	34	1	5	.173
10 Gross, Wayne	L	R	6:02	205	1-14-52	Oakland	113	14	61	.281
12 Klutts, Mickey	R	R	5:11	189	9-30-54	Oakland	75	4	21	.269
39 McKay, Dave	B	R	6:00	195	3-14-50	Oakland	123	1	29	.244
8 Picciolo, Rob	R	R	6:02	185	2- 4-53	Oakland	95	5	18	.240
13 Revering, Dave	L	R	6:04	205	2-12-53	Oakland	106	15	62	.290
11 Stanley, Fred	R	R	5:11	167	8-13-47	New York AL	49	0	5	.209

OUTFIELDERS—										
20 Armas, Tony	R	R	6:01	182	7-12-53	Oakland	158	35	109	.279
16 Davis, Mike	L	L	6:02	165	6-11-59	Ogden	19	1	14	.304
						Oakland	51	1	8	.211
35 Henderson, Rickey	R	L	5:10	180	12-25-58	Oakland	158	9	53	.303
21 Murphy, Dwayne	L	R	6:01	180	3-18-55	Oakland	159	13	68	.274
6 Page, Mitchell	L	R	6:02	205	3- 1-53	Oakland	110	17	51	.244
14 Patterson, Mike	R	R	5:10	170	1-26-58	West Haven	114	15	50	.263
						Ogden	17	1	5	.304

CLETE BOYER (41)—Coach   LEE WALLS (43)—Coach
ART FOWLER (42)—Coach   GEORGE MITTERWALD (40)—Coach
JACKIE MOORE (45)—Coach

THE COLISEUM

	Seats	Prices
Loge Boxes	1,605	$6.00
Lower Deck Boxes (Second Level)	16,856	6.00
Mezzanine Boxes (Second Level)	11,219	5.00
Reserved Seats (Third Level)	13,537	4.00
Bleachers	6,000	2.00

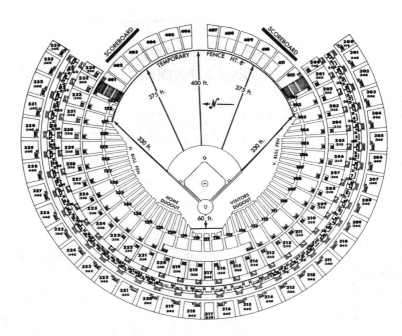

Oakland-Alameda County Coliseum Complex, Oakland—First A. L.
Game Played April 17, 1968

Maury Wills

SEATTLE MARINERS

Principal Owner—George L. Argyros
President & Chief Executive Officer—Daniel F. O'Brien
Executive Director—Kip Horsburgh
Director of Business Affairs—Jeff Odenwald
Director of Player Development—Hal Keller
Traveling Secretary—Lee Pelekoudas
Public Relations Director—Randy Adamack
Offices—P.O. Box 4100
Kingdome, King County Stadium, Capacity—59,438
Farm System: AAA—Spokane. AA—Lynn. A—Belling-
ham, Wausau.

SEATTLE MARINERS' YEARLY STANDING

Year—Position	W.	L.	Pct.	*G.B.	Manager	Attendance
1977—Sixth	64	98	.395	38	Darrell Johnson	1,338,511
1978—Seventh	56	104	.350	35	Darrell Johnson	877,440
1979—Sixth	67	95	.414	21	Darrell Johnson	844,447
1980—Seventh	59	103	.364	38	Darrell Johnson, Maurice Wills	836,204

*Games behind winner.

Game-Winning RBI Introduced to Majors

The RBI that gives a club the lead it never relinquishes: (GAME-WIN-NING RBI—Rule 10.04 (e) adopted prior to 1980 season).

For trivia buffs, the first game-winning RBI belonged to Cincinnati's George Foster. The Reds' left fielder drilled a first-inning double down the left-field line to start his club off and running toward a 9-0 rout over the Braves April 9.

Later in the day, Ted Cox of the Mariners hit a ground-rule double to score two runs and give Seattle a 4-2 lead—a lead the Mariners never relinquished en route to an 8-6 decision over the Blue Jays.

One of the most unusual game-winning RBIs was achieved by Mets pitcher Pete Falcone, who provided the key blow in New York's eight-run, second-inning outburst. Unfortunately, Falcone couldn't stand prosperity and only lasted 4⅓ innings and did not qualify for the victory, even though the Mets defeated the Pirates, 9-4, June 6.

SEATTLE MARINERS
(30) MAURY WILLS—Manager

No. PITCHERS—	Bts.	Thrs.	Hgt.	Wgt.	Birth-date	1980 Club	IP.	W.	L.	ERA.
17 Abbott, Glenn	R	R	6:06	200	2-16-51	Seattle	215	12	12	4.10
39 Anderson, Larry	R	R	6:03	180	5-16-53	Portland	93	5	7	1.74
25 Anderson, Rick	R	R	6:02	210	12-25-53	Spokane	80	6	0	3.26
						Seattle	10	0	0	3.60
19 Bannister, Floyd	L	L	6:01	190	6-10-55	Seattle	218	9	13	3.47
45 Beattie, Jim	R	R	6:06	205	7- 4-54	Seattle	187	5	15	4.86
46 Biercevicz, Greg	R	R	6:01	185	10-21-55	Spokane	126	10	9	4.93
48 Clark, Bryan	L	L	6:02	185	7-12-56	Spokane	41	5	5	5.27
						Lynn	116	9	5	3.10
21 Clay, Ken	R	R	6:02	195	4- 6-54	Columbus	138	9	4	1.96
						Texas	43	2	3	4.60
40 Drago, Dick	R	R	6:01	200	6-25-45	Boston	133	7	7	4.13
28 Gleaton, Jerry Don	L	L	6:03	210	9-14-57	Tulsa	178	13	7	3.64
						Texas	7	0	0	2.57
20 Parrott, Mike	R	R	6:04	205	12- 6-54	Seattle	94	1	16	7.28
						Spokane	22	1	2	0.82
41 Rawley, Shane	L	L	6:00	155	7-27-55	Seattle	114	7	7	3.32

CATCHERS—						1980 Club	G.	HR.	RBI.	Avg.
9 Bulling, Terry	R	R	6:01	200	12-15-52	Spokane	109	4	40	.279
27 Gulden, Brad	L	R	5:11	182	6-10-56	Columbus	14	2	10	.157
						Nashville	85	6	46	.237
						New York	2	1	2	.333
3 Narron, Jerry	L	R	6:03	205	1-15-56	Spokane	67	9	39	.283
						Seattle	48	4	18	.196

INFIELDERS—										
4 Anderson, Jim	R	R	6:00	170	2-23-57	Seattle	116	8	30	.227
16 Auerbach, Rick	R	R	6:00	175	2-15-50	Cincinnati	24	1	4	.333
23 Bochte, Bruce	L	L	6:03	200	11-12-50	Seattle	148	13	78	.300
6 Cruz, Julio	B	R	5:09	160	12- 2-54	Seattle	119	2	16	.209
24 Edler, Dave	R	R	6:00	185	8- 5-56	Spokane	140	10	72	.288
						Seattle	28	3	9	.225
1 Randle, Lenny	B	R	5:10	175	2-12-49	Chicago NL	130	5	39	.276

OUTFIELDERS—										
2 Allen, Kim	R	R	5:11	175	4- 5-53	Spokane	118	1	41	.294
						Seattle	23	0	3	.235
5 Burroughs, Jeff	R	R	6:00	200	3- 7-51	Atlanta	99	13	51	.263
29 Gray, Gary	R	R	6:00	187	9-21-52	Tacoma	96	20	73	.335
						Cleveland	28	2	4	.148
42 Henderson, Dave	R	R	6:02	210	7-21-58	Spokane	109	7	50	.279
7 Meyer, Dan	L	R	5:11	180	8- 3-52	Seattle	146	11	71	.275
14 Paciorek, Tom	R	R	6:04	210	11- 2-46	Seattle	126	15	59	.273
18 Simpson, Joe	L	L	6:03	175	12-31-51	Seattle	129	3	34	.249
22 Zisk, Richie	R	R	6:01	205	2- 6-49	Texas	135	19	77	.290

TOMMY DAVIS (12)—Coach   BENJAMIN "CANANEA" REYES (10)—Coach
FRANK FUNK (35)—Coach   WES STOCK (32)—Coach

THE KINGDOME

	Seats	Prices
Box Seats	10,377	$7.50
Bench Box Seats	2,087	6.50
Loge Seats	28,665	5.50
Reserved General Admission	7,352	2.50
General Admission	10,957	1.50

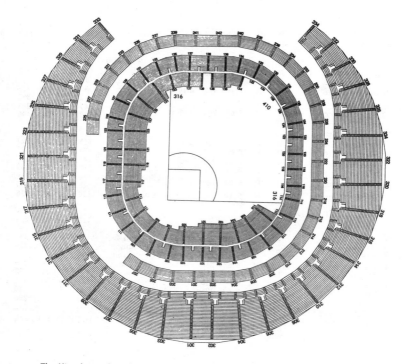

The Kingdome, Seattle, Wash. First A. L. Game Played April 6, 1977.

TEXAS RANGERS

Chairman of the Board—Eddie Chiles
Exec. Vice-Pres.-Baseball Operations—Eddie Robinson
Exec. V.P.-Business Operations—Samuel G. Meason
Dir. Player Develop.-Procurement—Joseph Klein
Public Relations Director—Burton Hawkins
Traveling Secretary—Dan Schimek
Offices—Arlington Stadium, Arlington, Tex.

Seating Capacity—41,284

Farm System: AAA—Wichita. AA—Tulsa. A—Asheville.
    Rookie—Sarasota.

Don Zimmer

TEXAS RANGERS' YEARLY STANDING

(Second Washington Senators Club prior to 1972)

Year—Position	W.	L.	Pct.	*G.B.	Manager	Attendance
1961—Ninth†	61	100	.379	47½	James (Mickey) Vernon	597,287
1962—Tenth......	60	101	.373	35½	James (Mickey) Vernon	729,775
1963—Tenth......	56	106	.346	48½	Mickey Vernon, Gilbert Hodges	535,604
1964—Ninth	62	100	.383	37	Gilbert Hodges	600,106
1965—Eighth	70	92	.432	32	Gilbert Hodges	560,083
1966—Eighth	71	88	.447	25½	Gilbert Hodges	576,260
1967—Sixth†	76	85	.472	15½	Gilbert Hodges	770,863
1968—Tenth......	65	96	.404	37½	James Lemon	546,661

*Games behind pennant winner. †Tied for position. (First Washington club's record is shown under Minnesota.)

EAST DIVISION

Year—Position	W.	L.	Pct.	*G.B.	Manager	Attendance
1969—Fourth.....	86	76	.531	23	Theodore Williams	918,106
1970—Sixth........	70	92	.432	38	Theodore Williams	824,789
1971—Fifth........	63	96	.396	38½	Theodore Williams	655,156

*Games behind winner.

WEST DIVISION

Year—Position	W.	L.	Pct.	*G.B.	Manager	Attendance
1972—Sixth........	54	100	.351	38½	Theodore Williams	662,974
1973—Sixth........	57	105	.352	37	D. (Whitey) Herzog, Billy Martin	686,085
1974—Second.....	84	76	.525	5	Alfred (Billy) Martin........................	1,193,902
1975—Third......	79	83	.488	19	A. (Billy) Martin, Frank Lucchesi	1,127,924
1976—Fourth† ...	76	86	.469	14	Frank Lucchesi.................................	1,164,982
1977—Second.....	94	68	.580	8	Frank Lucchesi, Ed Stanky, Connie Ryan, G. William Hunter	1,250,722
1978—Second† ..	87	75	.537	5	G. William Hunter, Patrick Corrales .	1,447,963
1979—Third......	83	79	.512	5	Patrick Corrales	1,519,671
1980—Fourth	76	85	.472	20½	Patrick Corrales	1,198,175

*Games behind winner. †Tied for position.

TEXAS RANGERS
(23) DON ZIMMER—Manager

No.	PITCHERS—	Bts.	Thrs.	Hgt.	Wgt.	Birth-date	1980 Club	IP.	W.	L.	ERA.
46	Babcock, Bob	R	R	6:05	190	8-25-49	Charleston	65	6	3	1.52
							Texas	23	1	2	4.70
11	Comer, Steve	B	R	6:03	207	1-13-54	Texas	42	2	4	7.93
							Tulsa	14	1	2	6.43
44	Darwin, Danny	R	R	6:03	195	10-25-55	Texas	110	13	4	2.62
35	Devine, Adrian	R	R	6:04	205	12- 2-51	Texas	28	1	1	4.42
40	Honeycutt, Rick	L	L	6:02	190	6-29-54	Seattle	203	10	17	3.95
49	Hough, Charlie	R	R	6:02	190	1- 5-48	Los Angeles	32	1	3	5.63
							Texas	61	2	2	3.98
31	Jenkins, Fergie	R	R	6:05	210	12-13-43	Texas	198	12	12	3.77
38	Johnson, John Henry	L	L	6:02	185	8-21-56	Charleston	77	3	9	3.86
							Texas	39	2	2	2.31
34	Kern, Jim	R	R	6:05	205	3-15-49	Texas	63	3	11	4.86
28	Lewallyn, Dennis	R	R	6:04	195	8-11-53	Albuquerque	127	15	2	2.13
							Texas	6	0	0	7.50
32	Matlack, Jon	L	L	6:03	200	1-19-50	Texas	235	10	10	3.68
33	Medich, Doc	R	R	6:05	227	12- 9-48	Texas	204	14	11	3.93
26	Rajsich, Dave	L	L	6:05	180	9-28-51	Texas	48	2	1	6.00
							Charleston	4	0	0	9.00
15	Whitehouse, Len	L	L	5:11	175	9-10-57	Tulsa	48	3	2	5.44
							Charleston	99	8	9	4.27

No.	CATCHERS—	Bts.	Thrs.	Hgt.	Wgt.	Birth-date	1980 Club	G.	HR.	RBI.	Avg.
20	Cox, Larry	R	R	5:11	190	9-11-47	Seattle	105	4	20	.202
9	Ellis, John	R	R	6:02	210	8-21-48	Texas	73	1	23	.236
10	Sundberg, Jim	R	R	6:00	196	5-18-51	Texas	151	10	63	.273

No.	INFIELDERS—	Bts.	Thrs.	Hgt.	Wgt.	Birth-date	1980 Club	G.	HR.	RBI.	Avg.
25	Bell, Buddy	R	R	6:02	185	8-27-51	Texas	129	17	83	.329
12	Davis, Odie	R	R	6:01	178	8-13-55	Charleston	110	2	29	.243
							Texas	17	0	0	.125
21	Duran, Dan	L	L	5:11	190	3-16-54	Charleston	116	13	71	.276
14	Mendoza, Mario	R	R	5:11	187	12-26-50	Seattle	114	2	14	.245
4	Norman, Nelson	B	R	6:02	160	5-23-58	Texas	17	0	1	.219
							Charleston	28	0	5	.242
18	Putnam, Pat	L	R	6:01	214	12- 3-53	Texas	147	13	55	.263
13	Stein, Bill	R	R	5:10	175	1-21-47	Seattle	67	5	27	.268
30	Wagner, Mark	R	R	6:01	175	3- 4-54	Detroit	45	0	3	.236
1	Wills, Bump	B	R	5:09	177	7-27-52	Texas	146	5	58	.263

No.	OUTFIELDERS—	Bts.	Thrs.	Hgt.	Wgt.	Birth-date	1980 Club	G.	HR.	RBI.	Avg.
6	Grubb, John	L	R	6:03	188	8- 4-48	Texas	110	9	32	.277
19	Norris, Jim	L	L	5:10	175	12-20-48	Texas	119	0	16	.247
0	Oliver, Al	L	L	6:01	203	10-14-46	Texas	163	19	117	.319
17	Rivers, Mickey	L	L	5:10	162	10-30-48	Texas	147	7	60	.333
7	Roberts, Leon	R	R	6:03	200	1-22-51	Seattle	119	10	33	.251
5	Sample, Billy	R	R	5:09	175	4- 2-55	Texas	99	4	19	.260

JACKIE BROWN (41)—Coach   WAYNE TERWILLIGER (42)—Coach
TOMMY HELMS (19)—Coach   FRED KOENIG (47)—Coach
DARRELL JOHNSON (22)—Coach

ARLINGTON STADIUM

	Seats	Prices
Field and Mezzanine Boxes	11,938	$7.50
Reserved Seats	5,487	6.00
Plaza Boxes	5,021	5.50
General Admission	18,838	3.00

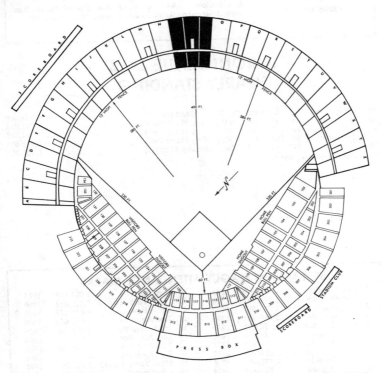

Arlington Stadium, Arlington, Tex.—First A. L. Game Played April 21, 1972

Bobby Mattick

TORONTO BLUE JAYS

Chairman of the Board—R. Howard Webster
Pres. & Chief Operating Officer—Peter Bavasi
Vice-Pres., Business Operations—Paul Beeston
Vice-Pres., Baseball Operations—Pat Gillick
Director of Operations—Ken Erskine
Administrator of Player Personnel—Elliott Wahle
Director of Team Travel—Ken Carson
Director of Public Relations—Howard Starkman
Offices—Exhibition Stadium

Exhibition Stadium Capacity—43,737

Farm System: AAA—Syracuse. AA—Knoxville. A—Kinston, Florence. Rookie—Bradenton, Medicine Hat.

TORONTO BLUE JAYS' YEARLY STANDING

Year—Position	W.	L.	Pct.	*G.B.	Manager	Attendance
1977—Seventh ...	54	107	.335	45½	Roy Hartsfield	1,701,052
1978—Seventh ...	59	102	.366	40	Roy Hartsfield	1,562,585
1979—Seventh ...	53	109	.327	50½	Roy Hartsfield	1,431,651
1980—Seventh ...	67	95	.414	36	Bobby Mattick	1,400,327

*Games behind winner.

BEST MAJOR LEAGUE ATTENDANCE MARKS

1. Los Angeles	3,347,845	1978	11. Cincinnati	2,629,708	1976
2. Los Angeles	3,249,287	1980	12. New York Yanks	2,627,417	1980
3. Los Angeles	2,955,087	1977	13. Cleveland	2,620,627	1948
4. Los Angeles	2,860,954	1979	14. Los Angeles	2,617,029	1966
5. Philadelphia	2,775,011	1979	15. Philadelphia	2,583,389	1978
6. Los Angeles	2,755,184	1962	16. Los Angeles	2,553,577	1965
7. Philadelphia	2,700,070	1977	17. Los Angeles	2,539,349	1975
8. New York Mets	2,697,479	1970	18. Los Angeles	2,538,602	1963
9. Philadelphia	2,651,650	1980	19. New York Yanks	2,537,765	1979
10. Los Angeles	2,632,474	1974	20. Cincinnati	2,532,497	1978

TORONTO BLUE JAYS
(3) BOBBY MATTICK—Manager

No.	PITCHERS—	Bts.	Thrs.	Hgt.	Wgt.	Birth-date	1980 Club	IP.	W.	L.	ERA.
46	Barlow, Mike	L	R	6:05	215	4-30-48	Syracuse	51	3	2	4.59
							Toronto	55	3	1	4.09
18	Clancy, Jim	R	R	6:04	202	12-18-55	Toronto	251	13	16	3.30
36	Garvin, Jerry	L	L	6:03	195	10-21-55	Toronto	83	4	7	2.28
25	Jackson, Roy Lee	R	R	6:02	195	5- 1-54	Tidewater	78	3	5	2.31
							New York NL	71	1	7	4.18
48	Leal, Luis	R	R	6:03	205	3-21-57	Syracuse	110	6	5	3.27
							Toronto	60	3	4	4.50
50	McLaughlin, Joey	R	R	6:02	205	7-11-56	Toronto	136	6	9	4.50
42	Mirabella, Paul	L	L	6:02	196	3-20-54	Syracuse	31	1	2	2.61
							Toronto	131	5	12	4.33
37	Stieb, Dave	R	R	6:01	185	7-22-57	Toronto	243	12	15	3.70
40	Todd, Jackson	R	R	6:02	190	11-20-51	Syracuse	153	7	9	3.41
							Toronto	85	5	2	4.02
23	Willis, Mike	L	L	6:02	200	12-26-50	Syracuse	69	7	4	2.48
							Toronto	26	2	1	1.73

No.	CATCHERS—	Bts.	Thrs.	Hgt.	Wgt.	Birth-date	1980 Club	G.	HR.	RBI.	Avg.
6	Whitmer, Dan	R	R	6:03	200	11-23-55	Salt Lake C.	59	3	27	.224
							California	48	0	7	.241
12	Whitt, Ernie	L	R	6:02	200	6-13-52	Toronto	106	6	34	.237

No.	INFIELDERS—	Bts.	Thrs.	Hgt.	Wgt.	Birth-date	1980 Club	G.	HR.	RBI.	Avg.
2	Ainge, Dan	R	R	6:04	175	3-17-59	Syracuse	80	2	17	.244
							Toronto	38	0	4	.243
7	Garcia, Damaso	R	R	6:00	170	2- 7-57	Toronto	140	4	46	.278
4	Griffin, Alfredo	B	R	5:11	165	3-10-57	Toronto	155	2	41	.254
16	Iorg, Garth	R	R	5:11	165	10-12-54	Syracuse	32	1	14	.299
							Toronto	80	2	14	.248
8	Macha, Ken	R	R	6:02	215	9-29-50	Montreal	49	1	8	.290
10	Mayberry, John	L	L	6:03	225	2-18-50	Toronto	149	30	82	.248
17	Ramos, Domingo	R	R	5:10	154	3-29-58	Syracuse	84	4	27	.251
							Toronto	5	0	0	.125
26	Upshaw, Willie	L	L	6:00	185	4-27-57	Syracuse	100	9	52	.254
							Toronto	34	1	5	.213

No.	OUTFIELDERS—	Bts.	Thrs.	Hgt.	Wgt.	Birth-date	1980 Club	G.	HR.	RBI.	Avg.
11	Bell, Jorge	R	R	6:01	190	10-21-59	Reading	22	0	11	.309
9	Bonnell, Barry	R	R	6:03	200	10-27-53	Toronto	130	13	56	.268
22	Bosetti, Rick	R	R	5:11	185	8- 5-53	Toronto	53	4	18	.213
49	Hodgson, Paul	R	R	6:02	190	4-14-60	Knoxville	59	5	26	.235
							Kinston	60	7	39	.352
							Toronto	20	1	5	.220
15	Moseby, Lloyd	L	R	6:03	200	11- 5-59	Syracuse	37	3	19	.322
							Toronto	114	9	46	.229
19	Velez, Otto	R	R	6:00	195	11-20-50	Toronto	104	20	62	.269
20	Woods, Al	L	L	6:03	200	8- 8-53	Toronto	109	15	47	.300

AL WIDMAR (41)—Coach
DENIS MENKE (14)—Coach
JIMY WILLIAMS (24)—Coach

JOHN FELSKE (28)—Coach
BOBBY DOERR (31)—Coach

EXHIBITION STADIUM

	Seats	Prices
Field Level, Chair	11,300	$8.00
Upper Level, Chair	6,600	6.50
First Base Reserved, Bench	5,100	5.00
Right Field Reserved, Bench	6,700	3.00
General Admission	14,037	2.00

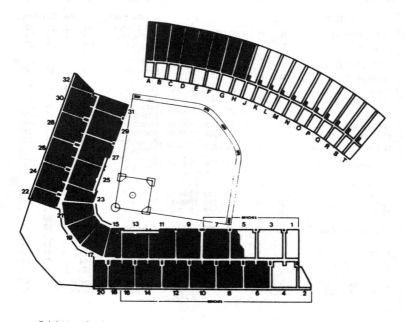

Exhibition Stadium, Toronto, Ont.—First A. L. Game Played April 7, 1977

NATIONAL LEAGUE—Pennant Winners—1876-1980

1876—Chicago	.788	1903—Pittsburgh	.650	1930—St. Louis	.597	1957—Milwaukee	.617
1877—Boston	.646	1904—New York	.693	1931—St. Louis	.656	1958—Milwaukee	.597
1878—Boston	.683	1905—New York	.686	1932—Chicago	.584	1959—Los Ang.‡	.564
1879—Providence	.705	1906—Chicago	.763	1933—New York	.599	1960—Pittsburgh	.617
1880—Chicago	.798	1907—Chicago	.704	1934—St. Louis	.621	1961—Cincinnati	.604
1881—Chicago	.667	1908—Chicago	.643	1935—Chicago	.649	1962—San Fran.§	.624
1882—Chicago	.655	1909—Pittsburgh	.724	1936—New York	.597	1963—Los Angeles	.611
1883—Boston	.643	1910—Chicago	.675	1937—New York	.625	1964—St. Louis	.574
1884—Providence	.750	1911—New York	.647	1938—Chicago	.586	1965—Los Angeles	.599
1885—Chicago	.777	1912—New York	.682	1939—Cincinnati	.630	1966—Los Angeles	.586
1886—Chicago	.726	1913—New York	.664	1940—Cincinnati	.654	1967—St. Louis	.627
1887—Detroit	.637	1914—Boston	.614	1941—Brooklyn	.649	1968—St. Louis	.599
1888—New York	.641	1915—Philadelphia	.592	1942—St. Louis	.688	1969—New York	.617
1889—New York	.659	1916—Brooklyn	.610	1943—St. Louis	.682	1970—Cincinnati	.630
1890—Brooklyn	.667	1917—New York	.636	1944—St. Louis	.682	1971—Pittsburgh	.599
1891—Boston	.630	1918—Chicago	.651	1945—Chicago	.636	1972—Cincinnati	.617
1892—Boston	.680	1919—Cincinnati	.686	1946—St. Louis*	.628	1973—New York	.509
1893—Boston	.662	1920—Brooklyn	.604	1947—Brooklyn	.610	1974—Los Angeles	.630
1894—Baltimore	.695	1921—New York	.614	1948—Boston	.595	1975—Cincinnati	.667
1895—Baltimore	.669	1922—New York	.604	1949—Brooklyn	.630	1976—Cincinnati	.630
1896—Baltimore	.698	1923—New York	.621	1950—Philadelphia	.591	1977—Los Angeles	.605
1897—Boston	.705	1924—New York	.608	1951—New York†	.624	1978—Los Angeles	.586
1898—Boston	.685	1925—Pittsburgh	.621	1952—Brooklyn	.627	1979—Pittsburgh	.605
1899—Brooklyn	.677	1926—St. Louis	.578	1953—Brooklyn	.682	1980—Philadelphia	.562
1900—Brooklyn	.603	1927—Pittsburgh	.610	1954—New York	.630		
1901—Pittsburgh	.647	1928—St. Louis	.617	1955—Brooklyn	.641		
1902—Pittsburgh	.741	1929—Chicago	.645	1956—Brooklyn	.604		

*Defeated Brooklyn, two games to none, in playoff for pennant. †Defeated Brooklyn, two games to one, in playoff for pennant. ‡Defeated Milwaukee, two games to none, in playoff for pennant. §Defeated Los Angeles, two games to one, in playoff for pennant.

STANDING OF CLUBS AT CLOSE OF SEASON

EAST DIVISION

Club	Phil.	Mon.	Pitt.	St.L.	N.Y.	Chi.	Atl.	Cin.	Hou.	L.A.	S.D.	S.F.	W.	L.	Pct.	G.B.
Philadelphia	..	9	7	9	12	13	7	5	9	6	8	6	91	71	.562	....
Montreal	9	..	6	12	10	12	7	9	7	1	10	7	90	72	.556	1
Pittsburgh	11	12	..	10	8	9	9	6	7	5	5	5	83	79	.512	8
St. Louis	9	6	8	..	9	9	6	7	5	5	5	1	74	88	.457	17
New York	6	8	10	9	..	9	4	4	5	1	3	6	67	95	.414	24
Chicago	5	6	8	9	10	..	4	7	1	5	4	5	64	98	.395	27

WEST DIVISION

Club	Hou.	L.A.	Cin.	Atl.	S.F.	S.D.	Chi.	Mon.	N.Y.	Phil.	Pitt.	St.L.	W.	L.	Pct.	G.B.
Houston	..	9	10	11	11	11	11	5	8	3	7	7	93	70	.571	....
Los Angeles	10	..	9	7	13	9	7	11	7	6	6	7	92	71	.564	1
Cincinnati	8	9	..	16	7	15	5	3	8	7	6	5	89	73	.549	3½
Atlanta	7	11	2	..	11	12	8	5	3	5	11	6	81	80	.503	11
San Francisco	7	5	11	6	..	8	7	5	9	6	4	7	75	86	.466	17
San Diego	7	9	3	6	10	..	8	2	11	4	6	7	73	89	.451	19½

NOTE: Standing includes one-game playoff between Houston and Los Angeles.
Tie Game—San Diego at Cincinnati.
Cancelled Game—San Francisco at Atlanta.
Championship Series—Philadelphia defeated Houston, three games to two.

NATIONAL LEAGUE 1980 DEPARTMENTAL LEADERS

INDIVIDUAL BATTING

Average
Buckner, Chicago	.324
Hernandez, St. Louis	.321
Templeton, St. Louis	.319

Doubles
Rose, Philadelphia	42
Buckner, Chicago	41
Dawson, Montreal	41

Triples
Moreno, Pittsburgh	13
Scott, Montreal	13
Herndon, S.F.; LeFlore, Mon	11

Home Runs
Schmidt, Philadelphia	48
Horner, Atlanta	35
Murphy, Atlanta	33

Runs Batted In
Schmidt, Philadelphia	121
Hendrick, St. Louis	109
Garvey, Los Angeles	106

Stolen Bases
LeFlore, Montreal	97
Moreno, Pittsburgh	96
Collins, Cincinnati	79

INDIVIDUAL PITCHING

Earned-Run Average
Sutton, Los Angeles	2.21
Carlton, Philadelphia	2.34
Reuss, Los Angeles	2.52

Complete Games
Rogers, Montreal	14
Carlton, Philadelphia	13
Niekro, Atl.; Niekro, Hou	11

Strikeouts
Carlton, Philadelphia	286
Ryan, Houston	200
Soto, Cincinnati	182

Shutouts
Reuss, Los Angeles	6
Richard, Houston	4
Rogers, Montreal	4

Innings
Carlton, Philadelphia	304
Rogers, Montreal	281
Niekro, Atlanta	275

Victories
Carlton, Philadelphia	24
Niekro, Houston	20
Bibby, Pittsburgh	19

Bobby Cox

ATLANTA BRAVES

Chairman of the Board—William C. Bartholomay
President—R. E. (Ted) Turner III
Exec. Vice-President—Al Thornwell
Vice-Pres.-Gen. Manager—John Mullen
Vice-President, Player Development—Hank Aaron
Dir. Public Relations-Promotions—Wayne Minshew
Offices—Atlanta Stadium
Atlanta Stadium Capacity—52,610

Farm System: AAA—Richmond. AA—Savannah. A—Anderson, Durham. Rookie—Bradenton.

ATLANTA BRAVES' YEARLY STANDING

(Boston Braves Prior to 1953; Milwaukee Braves 1953-65)

Year—Position	W.	L.	Pct.	*G.B.	Manager	Attendance
1901—Fifth	69	69	.500	20½	Frank Selee	146,502
1902—Third	73	64	.533	29	Albert Buckenberger	116,960
1903—Sixth	58	80	.420	32	Albert Buckenberger	143,155
1904—Seventh	55	98	.359	51	Albert Buckenberger	140,694
1905—Seventh	51	103	.331	54½	Fred Tenney	150,003
1906—Eighth	49	102	.325	66½	Fred Tenney	143,280
1907—Seventh	58	90	.392	47	Fred Tenney	203,221
1908—Sixth	63	91	.409	36	Joseph Kelley	253,750
1909—Eighth	45	108	.294	65½	Frank Bowerman, Harry Smith	195,188
1910—Eighth	53	100	.346	50½	Fred Lake	149,027
1911—Eighth	44	107	.291	54	Fred Tenney	116,000
1912—Eighth	52	101	.340	52	John Kling	121,000
1913—Fifth	69	82	.457	31½	George Stallings	208,000
1914—First	94	59	.614	+10½	George Stallings	382,913
1915—Second	83	69	.546	7	George Stallings	376,283
1916—Third	89	63	.586	4	George Stallings	313,495
1917—Sixth	72	81	.471	25½	George Stallings	174,253
1918—Seventh	53	71	.427	28½	George Stallings	84,938
1919—Sixth	57	82	.410	38½	George Stallings	167,401
1920—Seventh	62	90	.408	30	George Stallings	162,483
1921—Fourth	79	74	.516	15	Fred Mitchell	318,627
1922—Eighth	53	100	.346	39½	Fred Mitchell	167,965
1923—Seventh	54	100	.351	41½	Fred Mitchell	227,802
1924—Eighth	53	100	.346	40	David Bancroft	117,478
1925—Fifth	70	83	.458	25	David Bancroft	313,528
1926—Seventh	66	86	.434	22	David Bancroft	303,598
1927—Seventh	60	94	.390	34	David Bancroft	288,685
1928—Seventh	50	103	.327	44½	John Slattery, Rogers Hornsby	227,001
1929—Eighth	56	98	.364	43	Emil Fuchs, Walter Maranville	372,351

ATLANTA BRAVES' YEARLY STANDING—Continued

Year—Position	W.	L.	Pct.	*G.B.	Manager	Attendance
1930—Sixth........	70	84	.455	22	William McKechnie	464,835
1931—Seventh ...	64	90	.416	37	William McKechnie	515,005
1932—Fifth........	77	77	.500	13	William McKechnie	507,606
1933—Fourth....	83	71	.539	9	William McKechnie	517,803
1934—Fourth....	78	73	.517	16	William McKechnie	303,205
1935—Eighth....	38	115	.248	61½	William McKechnie	232,754
1936—Sixth........	71	83	.461	21	William McKechnie	340,585
1937—Fifth........	79	73	.520	16	William McKechnie	385,339
1938—Fifth........	77	75	.507	12	Charles (Casey) Stengel	341,149
1939—Seventh ...	63	88	.417	32½	Charles (Casey) Stengel	285,994
1940—Seventh ...	65	87	.428	34½	Charles (Casey) Stengel	241,616
1941—Seventh ...	62	92	.403	38	Charles (Casey) Stengel	263,680
1942—Seventh ...	59	89	.399	44	Charles (Casey) Stengel	285,332
1943—Sixth........	68	85	.444	36½	Charles (Casey) Stengel	271,289
1944—Sixth........	65	89	.422	40	Robert Coleman	208,691
1945—Sixth........	67	85	.441	30	R. Coleman, Adelphia Bissonette	374,178
1946—Fourth....	81	72	.529	15½	William Southworth	969,673
1947—Third......	86	68	.558	8	William Southworth	1,277,361
1948—First........	91	62	.595	+ 6½	William Southworth	1,455,439
1949—Fourth....	75	79	.487	22	William Southworth	1,081,795
1950—Fourth....	83	71	.539	8	William Southworth	944,391
1951—Fourth....	76	78	.494	20½	W. Southworth, T. Holmes	487,475
1952—Seventh ...	64	89	.418	32	Thomas Holmes, Charles Grimm	281,278
1953—Second....	92	62	.597	13	Charles Grimm	1,826,397
1954—Third......	89	65	.578	8	Charles Grimm	2,131,388
1955—Second....	85	69	.552	13½	Charles Grimm	2,005,836
1956—Second....	92	62	.597	1	Charles Grimm, Fred Haney	2,046,331
1957—First........	95	59	.617	+ 8	Fred Haney	2,215,404
1958—First........	92	62	.597	+ 8	Fred Haney	1,971,101
1959—Second†...	86	70	.551	2	Fred Haney	1,749,112
1960—Second....	88	66	.571	7	Charles Dressen	1,497,799
1961—Fourth....	83	71	.539	10	Chas. Dressen, Birdie Tebbetts	1,101,441
1962—Fifth........	86	76	.531	15½	George (Birdie) Tebbetts	766,921
1963—Sixth........	84	78	.519	15	Robert Bragan	773,018
1964—Fifth........	88	74	.543	5	Robert Bragan	910,911
1965—Fifth........	86	76	.531	11	Robert Bragan	555,584
1966—Fifth........	85	77	.525	10	Robert Bragan, Wm. Hitchcock	1,539,801
1967—Seventh ...	77	85	.475	24½	Wm. Hitchcock, Ken Silvestri	1,389,222
1968—Fifth........	81	81	.500	16	Luman Harris	1,126,540

*Games behind pennant winner.   †Lost to Los Angeles in pennant playoff.

WEST DIVISION

Year—Position	W.	L.	Pct.	*G.B.	Manager	Attendance
1969—First‡.....	93	69	.574	+ 3	Luman Harris	1,458,320
1970—Fifth.......	76	86	.469	26	Luman Harris	1,078,848
1971—Third......	82	80	.506	8	Luman Harris	1,006,320
1972—Fourth....	70	84	.455	25	Luman Harris, Edwin Mathews	752,973
1973—Fifth.......	76	85	.472	22½	Edwin Mathews	800,655
1974—Third......	88	74	.543	14	Edwin Mathews, Clyde King	981,085
1975—Fifth.......	67	94	.416	40½	Clyde King, Connie Ryan	534,672
1976—Sixth.......	70	92	.432	32	J. David Bristol	818,179
1977—Sixth.......	61	101	.377	37	J. David Bristol, Ted Turner	872,464
1978—Sixth.......	69	93	.426	26	Robert Cox	904,494
1979—Sixth.......	66	94	.413	23½	Robert Cox	769,465
1980—Fourth.....	81	80	.503	11	Robert Cox	1,048,411

*Games behind winner.   ‡Lost Championship Series.

ATLANTA BRAVES

(6) BOB COX—Manager

No. PITCHERS—	Bts.	Thrs.	Hgt.	Wgt.	Birth-date	1980 Club	IP.	W.	L.	ERA.
32 Bedrosian, Steve	R	R	6:03	200	12- 6-57	Savannah	203	14	10	3.19
40 Boggs, Tom	R	R	6:02	200	10-25-53	Atlanta	192	12	9	3.42
34 Bradford, Larry	R	L	6:01	205	12-21-51	Atlanta	55	3	4	2.45
43 Brizzolara, Tony	R	R	6:05	210	1-14-57	Richmond	206	10	15	3.71
37 Camp, Rick	R	R	6:01	198	6-10-53	Atlanta	108	6	4	1.92
26 Garber, Gene	R	R	5:10	175	11-13-47	Atlanta	82	5	5	3.84
49 Hanna, Preston	R	R	6:01	185	9-10-54	Atlanta	79	2	0	3.19
39 Hrabosky, Al	R	L	5:10	180	7-21-49	Atlanta	60	4	2	3.60
42 Mahler, Rick	R	R	6:01	190	8- 5-53	Richmond	188	12	6	2.59
						Atlanta	4	0	0	2.25
29 Matula, Rick	R	R	6:00	195	11-22-53	Atlanta	177	11	13	4.58
27 McWilliams, Larry	L	L	6:05	175	2-10-54	Atlanta	164	9	14	4.94
24 Montefusco, John	R	R	6:01	192	5-25-50	San Fran.	113	4	8	4.38
38 Morogiello, Dan	L	L	6:01	200	3-26-55	Richmond	196	11	12	4.04
35 Niekro, Phil	R	R	6:02	195	4- 1-39	Atlanta	275	15	18	3.63
36 Perry, Gaylord	R	R	6:04	215	9-15-38	Tex.-N.Y. AL	206	10	13	3.67
43 Walk, Bob	R	R	6:03	200	11-26-56	Okla. City	49	5	1	2.94
						Philadelphia	152	11	7	4.56

CATCHERS—	Bts.	Thrs.	Hgt.	Wgt.	Birth-date	1980 Club	G.	HR.	RBI.	Avg.
20 Benedict, Bruce	R	R	6:01	185	8-18-55	Richmond	3	0	0	.300
						Atlanta	120	2	34	.253
15 Nahorodny, Bill	R	R	6:02	195	8-31-53	Atlanta	59	5	18	.242
4 Pocoroba, Biff	B	R	5:10	170	7-25-53	Atlanta	70	2	8	.265
14 Sinatro, Matt	R	R	5:09	174	3-22-60	Savannah	122	11	50	.278

INFIELDERS—	Bts.	Thrs.	Hgt.	Wgt.	Birth-date	1980 Club	G.	HR.	RBI.	Avg.
10 Chambliss, Chris	L	R	6:01	215	12-26-48	Atlanta	158	18	72	.282
9 Gomez, Luis	R	R	5:09	150	8-19-51	Atlanta	121	0	24	.191
5 Horner, Bob	R	R	6:01	210	8- 6-57	Atlanta	124	35	89	.268
17 Hubbard, Glenn	R	R	5:08	165	9-25-57	Richmond	38	2	25	.315
						Atlanta	117	9	43	.248
28 Lum Mike	L	L	6:00	185	10-27-45	Atlanta	93	0	5	.205
16 Ramirez, Rafael	R	R	6:00	170	2-18-59	Richmond	80	5	38	.281
						Atlanta	50	2	11	.267

OUTFIELDERS—	Bts.	Thrs.	Hgt.	Wgt.	Birth-date	1980 Club	G.	HR.	RBI.	Avg.
30 Asselstine, Brian	L	R	6:01	190	9-23-53	Atlanta	87	3	25	.284
19 Harper, Terry	R	R	6:01	195	8-19-55	Richmond	140	13	72	.279
						Atlanta	21	0	3	.185
22 Landis, Craig	R	R	6:02	195	12-29-58	Phoenix	142	7	49	.282
25 Linares, Rufino	R	R	6:00	170	2-28-55	Savannah	51	2	38	.425
						Richmond	63	3	41	.329
45 Miller, Ed	B	R	5:09	165	6-29-57	Richmond	110	0	22	.209
						Atlanta	11	0	0	.158
3 Murphy, Dale	R	R	6:05	215	3-12-56	Atlanta	156	33	89	.281
1 Royster, Jerry	R	R	6:00	165	10-18-52	Atlanta	123	1	20	.242
18 Washington, Cld.	L	L	6:00	190	8-31-54	Chicago AL	32	1	12	.289
						New York NL	79	10	42	.275

TOMMIE AARON (23)—Coach   BOBBY DEWS (2)—Coach
CLOYD BOYER (48)—Coach   JOHN SULLIVAN (8)—Coach

ATLANTA STADIUM

	Seats	Prices
Club Level Box Seats	2,790	$7.50
Dugout Level Box Seats	2,278	7.50
Field Level Seats	16,757	6.00
Upper Level Seats	22,481	4.00
General Admission	7,884	2.50
Picnic Area	420	*1.00

*Children under 12

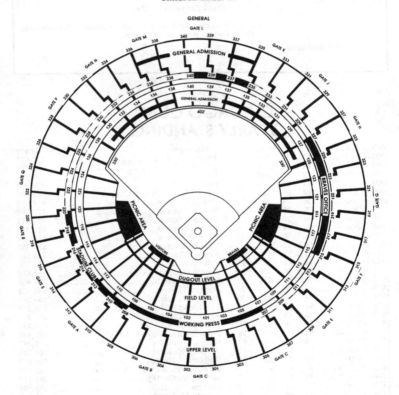

Atlanta Stadium, Atlanta—First N. L. Game Played April 12, 1966

Joe Amalfitano

CHICAGO CUBS

Chairman of Executive Committee—William Wrigley
Pres., Chief Exec. Officer, Treas.—Wm. J. Hagenah, Jr.
Executive Vice-President—Robert D. Kennedy
Secretary, Director of Park Operations—E. R. Saltwell
Director of Player Development—C. V. Davis
Director, Information & Marketing—Buck Peden
Traveling Secretary—Jim Davidovich
Offices—Wrigley Field
Wrigley Field Capacity—37,241

Farm System: AAA—Iowa. AA—Midland. A—Geneva,
Quad Cities. Rookie—Sarasota.

CHICAGO CUBS' YEARLY STANDING

Year—Position	W.	L.	Pct.	*G.B.	Manager	Attendance
1901—Sixth	53	86	.381	37	Thomas Loftus	205,071
1902—Fifth	68	69	.496	34	Frank Selee	263,700
1903—Third	82	56	.594	8	Frank Selee	386,205
1904—Second	93	60	.608	13	Frank Selee	439,100
1905—Third	92	61	.601	13	Frank Selee, Frank Chance	509,900
1906—First	116	36	.763	+20	Frank Chance	654,300
1907—First	107	45	.704	+17	Frank Chance	422,550
1908—First	99	55	.643	+ 1	Frank Chance	665,325
1909—Second	104	49	.680	6½	Frank Chance	633,480
1910—First	104	50	.675	+13	Frank Chance	526,152
1911—Second	92	62	.597	7½	Frank Chance	576,000
1912—Third	91	59	.607	11½	Frank Chance	514,000
1913—Third	88	65	.575	13½	John Evers	419,000
1914—Fourth	78	76	.506	16½	Henry (Hank) O'Day	202,516
1915—Fourth	73	80	.477	17½	Roger Bresnahan	217,058
1916—Fifth	67	86	.438	26½	Joseph Tinker	453,685
1917—Fifth	74	80	.481	24	Fred Mitchell	360,218
1918—First	84	45	.651	+10½	Fred Mitchell	337,256
1919—Third	75	65	.536	21	Fred Mitchell	424,430
1920—Fifth†	75	79	.487	18	Fred Mitchell	480,783
1921—Seventh	64	89	.418	30	John Evers, William Killefer	410,107
1922—Fifth	80	74	.519	13	William Killefer	542,283
1923—Fourth	83	71	.539	12½	William Killefer	703,705
1924—Fifth	81	72	.529	12	William Killefer	716,922
1925—Eighth	68	86	.442	27½	Killefer, W. Maranville, G. Gibson	622,610
1926—Fourth	82	72	.532	7	Joseph McCarthy	885,063
1927—Fourth	85	68	.556	8½	Joseph McCarthy	1,159,168
1928—Third	91	63	.591	4	Joseph McCarthy	1,143,740
1929—First	98	54	.645	+10½	Joseph McCarthy	1,485,166
1930—Second	90	64	.584	2	Joseph McCarthy, Rogers Hornsby	1,463,624

CHICAGO CUBS' YEARLY STANDING—Continued

Year—Position	W.	L.	Pct.	*G.B.	Manager	Attendance
1931—Third	84	70	.545	17	Rogers Hornsby	1,086,422
1932—First	90	64	.584	+ 4	Rogers Hornsby, Charles Grimm	974,688
1933—Third	86	68	.558	6	Charles Grimm	594,112
1934—Third	86	65	.570	8	Charles Grimm	707,525
1935—First	100	54	.649	+ 4	Charles Grimm	692,604
1936—Second†	87	67	.565	5	Charles Grimm	699,370
1937—Second	93	61	.604	3	Charles Grimm	895,020
1938—First	89	63	.586	+ 2	Chas. Grimm, Gabby Hartnett	951,640
1939—Fourth	84	70	.545	13	Charles (Gabby) Hartnett	726,663
1940—Fifth	75	79	.487	25½	Charles (Gabby) Hartnett	534,878
1941—Sixth	70	84	.455	30	James Wilson	545,159
1942—Sixth	68	86	.442	38	James Wilson	590,872
1943—Fifth	74	79	.484	30½	James Wilson	508,247
1944—Fourth	75	79	.487	30	James Wilson, Charles Grimm	640,110
1945—First	98	56	.636	+ 3	Charles Grimm	1,036,386
1946—Third	82	71	.536	14½	Charles Grimm	1,342,970
1947—Sixth	69	85	.448	25	Charles Grimm	1,364,039
1948—Eighth	64	90	.416	27½	Charles Grimm	1,237,792
1949—Eighth	61	93	.396	36	Charles Grimm, Frank Frisch	1,143,139
1950—Seventh	64	89	.418	26½	Frank Frisch	1,165,944
1951—Eighth	62	92	.403	34½	Frank Frisch, Philip Cavarretta	894,415
1952—Fifth	77	77	.500	19½	Philip Cavarretta	1,024,826
1953—Seventh	65	89	.422	40	Philip Cavarretta	763,658
1954—Seventh	64	90	.416	33	Stanley Hack	748,183
1955—Sixth	72	81	.471	26	Stanley Hack	875,800
1956—Eighth	60	94	.390	33	Stanley Hack	720,118
1957—Seventh†	62	92	.403	33	Robert Scheffing	670,629
1958—Fifth†	72	82	.468	20	Robert Scheffing	979,904
1959—Fifth†	74	80	.481	13	Robert Scheffing	858,255
1960—Seventh	60	94	.390	35	Charles Grimm, Louis Boudreau	809,770
1961—Seventh	64	90	.416	29	H. Craft, A. Himsl, L. Klein	673,057
1962—Ninth	59	103	.364	42½	E. Tappe, L. Klein, Chas. Metro	609,802
1963—Seventh	82	80	.506	17	Robert Kennedy	979,551
1964—Eighth	76	86	.469	17	Robert Kennedy	751,647
1965—Eighth	72	90	.444	25	Robert Kennedy, Louis Klein	641,361
1966—Tenth	59	103	.364	36	Leo Durocher	635,891
1967—Third	87	74	.540	14	Leo Durocher	977,226
1968—Third	84	78	.519	9	Leo Durocher	1,043,409

*Games behind pennant winner.   †Tied for position.

EAST DIVISION

Year—Position	W.	L.	Pct.	*G.B.	Manager	Attendance
1969—Second	92	70	.568	8	Leo Durocher	1,674,993
1970—Second	84	78	.519	5	Leo Durocher	1,642,705
1971—Third†	83	79	.512	14	Leo Durocher	1,653,007
1972—Second	85	70	.548	11	Leo Durocher, Whitey Lockman	1,299,163
1973—Fifth	77	84	.478	5	Carroll (Whitey) Lockman	1,351,705
1974—Sixth	66	96	.407	22	Whitey Lockman, James Marshall	1,015,378
1975—Fifth†	75	87	.463	17½	James Marshall	1,034,819
1976—Fourth	75	87	.463	26	James Marshall	1,026,217
1977—Fourth	81	81	.500	20	Herman Franks	1,439,834
1978—Third	79	83	.488	11	Herman Franks	1,525,311
1979—Fifth	80	82	.494	18	Herman Franks, J. Joseph Amalfitano	1,648,587
1980—Sixth	64	98	.395	27	Pedro (Preston) Gomez, J. Joseph Amalfitano	1,206,776

*Games behind winner.   †Tied for position.

CHICAGO CUBS
(5) JOE AMALFITANO–Manager

No. PITCHERS–	Bts.	Thrs.	Hgt.	Wgt.	Birth-date	1980 Club	IP.	W.	L.	ERA.
35 Capilla, Doug	L	L	5:08	175	1- 7-52	Chicago	90	2	8	4.10
36 Caudill, Bill	R	R	6:01	175	7-13-56	Chicago	128	4	6	2.18
49 Eastwick, Rawly	R	R	6:03	175	10-24-50	Omaha	28	2	2	2.10
						Kansas City	22	0	1	5.32
37 Kravec, Ken	L	L	6:00	180	7-29-51	Chicago AL	82	3	6	6.91
39 Krukow, Mike	R	R	6:04	195	1-21-52	Chicago	205	10	15	4.39
34 Martz, Randy	L	R	6:04	210	5-28-56	Wichita	107	8	6	3.11
						Chicago	30	1	2	2.10
40 McGlothen, Lynn	L	R	6:02	195	3-27-50	Chicago	182	12	14	4.80
42 Nastu, Phil	L	L	6:02	185	3- 8-55	Phoenix	93	4	8	5.42
						San Fran.	6	0	0	6.00
48 Reuschel, Rick	R	R	6:03	230	5-16-49	Chicago	257	11	13	3.40
46 Smith, Lee	R	R	6:05	220	12- 4-57	Wichita	90	4	7	3.70
						Chicago	22	2	0	2.86
41 Tidrow, Dick	R	R	6:04	213	5-14-57	Chicago	116	6	5	2.79

CATCHERS–						1980 Club	G.	HR.	RBI.	Avg.
9 Blackwell, Tim	B	R	5:11	185	8-19-52	Chicago	103	5	30	.272
7 Davis, Jody	R	R	6:04	192	11-12-56	Springfield	13	0	2	.167
						St. Pete.	45	6	27	.277
8 Foote, Barry	R	R	6:03	215	2-16-52	Chicago	63	6	28	.238

INFIELDERS–										
22 Buckner, Bill	L	L	6:01	185	12-14-49	Chicago	145	10	68	.324
11 DeJesus, Ivan	R	R	5:11	175	1- 9-53	Chicago	157	3	33	.259
15 Dillard, Steve	R	R	6:01	180	2- 8-51	Chicago	100	4	27	.225
12 Macko, Steve	L	R	5:10	160	9- 6-54	Wichita	89	9	42	.252
						Chicago	6	0	2	.300
44 Reitz, Ken	R	R	6:00	185	6-24-51	St. Louis	151	8	58	.270
20 Strain, Joe	R	R	5:10	169	4-30-54	San Fran.	77	0	16	.286
18 Tyson, Mike	R	R	5:09	170	1-13-50	Chicago	123	3	23	.238
21 Waller, Ty	R	R	6:00	180	3-14-57	Springfield	123	6	53	.262
						St. Louis	5	0	0	.083

OUTFIELDERS–										
27 Cruz, Hector	R	R	5:11	180	4- 2-53	Cincinnati	52	1	5	.213
10 Durham, Leon	L	L	6:01	185	7-31-57	Springfield	32	5	23	.258
						St. Louis	96	8	42	.271
28 Henderson, Steve	R	R	6:01	185	11-18-52	New York NL	143	8	58	.290
30 Lezcano, Carlos	R	R	6:02	185	9-30-55	Wichita	77	19	56	.232
						Chicago	42	3	12	.205
24 Morales, Jerry	R	R	5:10	165	2-18-49	New York NL	94	3	30	.254
25 Thompson, Scot	L	L	6:03	175	12- 7-55	Chicago	102	2	13	.212
23 Tracy, Jim	L	L	6:03	193	12-31-55	Wichita	112	16	63	.320
						Chicago	42	3	9	.254

GENE CLINES (3)–Coach   COOKIE ROJAS (1)–Coach
JACK HIATT (4)–Coach   LES MOSS (6)–Coach
                    PEANUTS LOWREY (2)–Coach

WRIGLEY FIELD

	Seats	Prices
Box Seats—First Ten Rows Lower Deck.....	3,254	$6.50
Box Seats—Balance of Lower Deck .... also Upper Deck	10,981	6.50
Reserved Grandstand	5,707	5.00
General Admission	13,999	3.50
Bleachers..	3,300	2.00

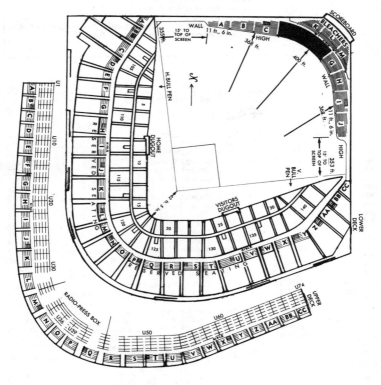

Wrigley Field, Chicago—First N. L. Game Played April 20, 1916

CINCINNATI REDS

Chairmen—James R. Williams, William J. Williams
Vice-Chairman—Robert L. Howsam
President, Chief Executive Officer—Richard Wagner
Vice-President, Marketing—Roger Ruhl
Vice-President, Player Personnel—Sheldon Bender
Vice-President, Scouting—Joe Bowen
Secretary—Henry W. Hobson, Jr.
Publicity Director—Jim Ferguson
Traveling Secretary—Doug Bureman
Offices—Riverfront Stadium
Riverfront Stadium Capacity—52,392

Farm System: AAA—Indianapolis. AA—Waterbury. A—Cedar Rapids, Tampa, Eugene. Rookie—Billings.

John McNamara

CINCINNATI REDS' YEARLY STANDING

Year—Position	W.	L.	Pct.	*G.B.	Manager	Attendance
1901—Eighth	52	87	.374	38	John McPhee	205,728
1902—Fourth	70	70	.500	33½	J. McPhee, F. Bancroft, J. Kelley	217,300
1903—Fourth	74	65	.532	16½	Joseph Kelley	351,680
1904—Third	88	65	.575	18	Joseph Kelley	391,915
1905—Fifth	79	74	.516	26	Joseph Kelley	313,927
1906—Sixth	64	87	.424	51½	Edward (Ned) Hanlon	330,056
1907—Sixth	66	87	.431	41½	Edward (Ned) Hanlon	317,500
1908—Fifth	73	81	.474	26	John Ganzel	399,200
1909—Fourth	77	76	.503	33½	Clark Griffith	424,643
1910—Fifth	75	79	.487	29	Clark Griffith	380,622
1911—Sixth	70	83	.458	29	Clark Griffith	300,000
1912—Fourth	75	78	.490	29	Henry (Hank) O'Day	344,000
1913—Seventh	64	89	.418	37½	Joseph Tinker	258,000
1914—Eighth	60	94	.390	34½	Charles (Buck) Herzog	100,791
1915—Seventh	71	83	.461	20	Charles (Buck) Herzog	218,878
1916—Seventh†	60	93	.392	33½	Buck Herzog, Christy Mathewson	255,846
1917—Fourth	78	76	.506	20	Christy Mathewson	269,056
1918—Third	68	60	.531	15½	Christy Mathewson, Henry Groh	163,009
1919—First	96	44	.686	+ 9	Patrick Moran	532,501
1920—Third	82	71	.536	10½	Patrick Moran	568,107
1921—Sixth	70	83	.458	24	Patrick Moran	311,227
1922—Second	86	68	.558	7	Patrick Moran	493,754
1923—Second	91	63	.591	4½	Patrick Moran	575,063
1924—Fourth	83	70	.542	10	John (Jack) Hendricks	437,707
1925—Third	80	73	.523	15	John (Jack) Hendricks	464,920
1926—Second	87	67	.565	2	John (Jack) Hendricks	672,987
1927—Fifth	75	78	.490	18½	John (Jack) Hendricks	442,164
1928—Fifth	78	74	.513	16	John (Jack) Hendricks	490,490
1929—Seventh	66	88	.429	33	John (Jack) Hendricks	295,040
1930—Seventh	59	95	.383	33	Daniel Howley	386,727

CINCINNATI REDS' YEARLY STANDING—Continued

Year—Position	W.	L.	Pct.	*G.B.	Manager	Attendance
1931—Eighth	58	96	.377	43	Daniel Howley	263,316
1932—Eighth	60	94	.390	30	Daniel Howley	356,950
1933—Eighth	58	94	.382	33	Owen (Donie) Bush	218,281
1934—Eighth	52	99	.344	42	Robert O'Farrell, Charles Dressen....	206,773
1935—Sixth........	68	85	.444	31½	Charles Dressen..............................	448,247
1936—Fifth........	74	80	.481	18	Charles Dressen..............................	466,245
1937—Eighth	56	98	.364	40	Charles Dressen, Roderick Wallace...	411,221
1938—Fourth.....	82	68	.547	6	William McKechnie	706,756
1939—First.......	97	57	.630	+ 4½	William McKechnie	981,443
1940—First.......	100	53	.654	+12	William McKechnie	850,180
1941—Third.......	88	66	.571	12	William McKechnie	643,513
1942—Fourth.....	76	76	.500	29	William McKechnie	427,031
1943—Second.....	87	67	.565	18	William McKechnie	379,122
1944—Third.......	89	65	.578	16	William McKechnie	409,567
1945—Seventh....	61	93	.396	37	William McKechnie	290,070
1946—Sixth........	67	87	.435	30	William McKechnie	715,751
1947—Fifth........	73	81	.474	21	John Neun	899,975
1948—Seventh....	64	89	.418	27	John Neun, William Walters	823,386
1949—Seventh....	62	92	.403	35	William (Bucky) Walters...................	707,782
1950—Sixth........	66	87	.431	24½	J. Luther Sewell..............................	538,794
1951—Sixth........	68	86	.442	28½	J. Luther Sewell..............................	588,268
1952—Sixth........	69	85	.448	27½	J. Luther Sewell, Rogers Hornsby ...	604,197
1953—Sixth........	68	86	.442	37	Rogers Hornsby, C. Buster Mills	548,086
1954—Fifth........	74	80	.481	23	George (Birdie) Tebbetts.................	704,167
1955—Fifth........	75	79	.487	23½	George (Birdie) Tebbetts.................	693,662
1956—Third.......	91	63	.591	2	George (Birdie) Tebbetts.................	1,125,928
1957—Fourth.....	80	74	.519	15	George (Birdie) Tebbetts.................	1,070,850
1958—Fourth.....	76	78	.494	16	Birdie Tebbetts, James Dykes..........	788,582
1959—Fifth†......	74	80	.481	13	E. Mayo Smith, Fred Hutchinson	801,289
1960—Sixth........	67	87	.435	28	Fred Hutchinson	663,486
1961—First.......	93	61	.604	+ 4	Fred Hutchinson	1,117,603
1962—Third.......	98	64	.605	3½	Fred Hutchinson	982,085
1963—Fifth........	86	76	.531	13	Fred Hutchinson	858,805
1964—Second†...	92	70	.568	1	Fred Hutchinson	862,466
1965—Fourth.....	89	73	.459	8	Richard Sisler	1,047,824
1966—Seventh ...	76	84	.475	18	Donald Heffner, J. David Bristol	742,958
1967—Fourth.....	87	75	.537	14½	J. David Bristol...............................	958,300
1968—Fourth.....	83	79	.512	14	J. David Bristol...............................	733,354

*Games behind pennant winner. †Tied for position.

WEST DIVISION

Year—Position	W.	L.	Pct.	*G.B.	Manager	Attendance
1969—Third.......	89	73	.549	4	J. David Bristol...............................	987,991
1970—First‡	102	60	.630	+14½	George (Sparky) Anderson	1,803,568
1971—Fourth† ...	79	83	.488	11	George (Sparky) Anderson	1,501,122
1972—First‡	95	59	.617	+10½	George (Sparky) Anderson	1,611,459
1973—First§	99	63	.611	+ 3½	George (Sparky) Anderson	2,017,601
1974—Second....	98	64	.605	4	George (Sparky) Anderson	2,164,307
1975—First‡	108	54	.667	+20	George (Sparky) Anderson	2,315,603
1976—First‡	102	60	.630	+10	George (Sparky) Anderson	2,629,708
1977—Second....	88	74	.543	10	George (Sparky) Anderson	2,519,670
1978—Second....	92	69	.571	2½	George (Sparky) Anderson	2,532,497
1979—First§	90	71	.559	+ 1½	John McNamara	2,356,933
1980—Third.......	89	73	.549	3½	John McNamara	2,022,450

*Games behind winner. †Tied for position.
‡Won Championship Series. §Lost Championship Series.

CINCINNATI REDS

(3) JOHN McNAMARA—Manager

No. PITCHERS—	Bts.	Thrs.	Hgt.	Wgt.	Birth-date	1980 Club	IP.	W.	L.	ERA.
40 Bair, Doug	R	R	6:00	185	8-22-49	Cincinnati	85	3	6	4.24
38 Berenyi, Bruce	R	R	6:03	215	8-21-54	Indianapolis	123	5	8	4.32
						Cincinnati	28	2	2	7.71
42 Bonham, Bill	R	R	6:03	195	10- 1-48	Tampa	16	1	0	0.56
						Cincinnati	19	2	1	4.74
37 Combe, Geoff	R	R	6:01	185	2- 1-56	Indianapolis	77	2	2	2.22
						Cincinnati	7	0	0	10.29
47 Hume, Tom	R	R	6:01	185	3-29-53	Cincinnati	137	9	10	2.56
51 LaCoss, Mike	R	R	6:04	190	5-30-56	Cincinnati	169	10	12	4.63
48 Lahti, Jeff	R	R	6:00	180	10- 8-56	Waterbury	91	7	8	2.77
44 Leibrandt, Charlie	R	L	6:04	200	10- 4-56	Cincinnati	174	10	9	4.24
31 Moskau, Paul	R	R	6:02	205	12-20-53	Cincinnati	153	9	7	4.00
35 Pastore, Frank	R	R	6:03	210	8-21-57	Cincinnati	185	13	7	3.26
49 Price, Joe	R	L	6:04	220	11-29-56	Indianapolis	79	4	4	3.87
						Cincinnati	111	7	3	3.57
41 Seaver, Tom	R	R	6:01	210	11-17-44	Cincinnati	168	10	8	3.64
36 Soto, Mario	R	R	6:00	185	7-12-56	Cincinnati	190	10	8	3.08

CATCHERS—						1980 Club	G.	HR.	RBI.	Avg.
5 Bench, Johnny	R	R	6:01	215	12- 7-47	Cincinnati	114	24	68	.250
9 O'Berry, Mike	R	R	6:02	190	4-20-54	Midland	57	1	23	.243
						Wichita	9	0	6	.261
						Chicago	19	0	5	.208
17 Nolan, Joe	L	R	6:00	190	5-12-51	Atl.-Cin.	70	3	26	.307

INFIELDERS—										
13 Concepcion, Dave	R	R	6:01	180	6-17-48	Cincinnati	156	5	77	.260
22 Driessen, Dan	L	R	5:11	190	7-29-51	Cincinnati	154	14	74	.265
26 Kennedy, Junior	R	R	6:00	185	8- 9-50	Cincinnati	104	1	34	.261
25 Knight, Ray	R	R	6:02	190	12-28-52	Cincinnati	162	14	78	.264
16 Oester, Ron	B	R	6:02	185	5- 5-56	Cincinnati	100	2	20	.277
12 Spilman, Harry	L	R	6:01	190	7-18-54	Cincinnati	65	4	19	267

OUTFIELDERS—										
33 Biittner, Larry	L	L	6:02	200	7-24-47	Chicago NL	127	1	34	.249
29 Collins, Dave	B	L	5:10	175	10-20-52	Cincinnati	144	3	35	.303
15 Foster, George	R	R	6:01	195	12- 1-48	Cincinnati	144	25	93	.273
30 Griffey, Ken	L	L	6:00	200	4-10-50	Cincinnati	146	13	85	.294
21 Householder, Paul	B	R	6:00	180	9- 4-58	Indianapolis	125	9	50	.295
						Cincinnati	20	0	7	.244
28 Mejias, Sam	R	R	6:00	170	5- 9-52	Cincinnati	71	1	10	.278
23 Vail, Mike	R	R	6:00	185	11-10-51	Chicago NL	114	6	47	.298

HARRY DUNLOP (4)—Coach
BILL FISCHER (6)—Coach

RUSS NIXON (2)—Coach
RON PLAZA (11)—Coach

RIVERFRONT STADIUM

	Seats	Prices
Club Boxes	2,180	$8.00
Box Seats	17,997	6.00
Reserved Grandstand	24,303	5.00
Loge Reserved	7,912	3.00

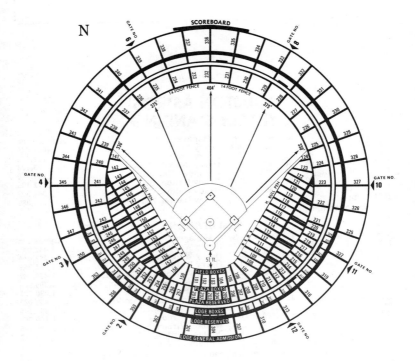

Riverfront Stadium, Cincinnati—First N. L. Game Played June 30, 1970

Bill Virdon

HOUSTON ASTROS

Chief Executive Officer—John J. McMullen
President and General Manager—Al Rosen
Asst. to Pres.—Traveling Sec.—Donald Davidson
Asst. General Manager—Tony Siegle
Director of Scouting—Lynwood Stallings
Publicity Director—Ed Wade
Offices—Astrodome
Astrodome Capacity—45,000

Farm System: AAA—Tucson. AA—Columbus, Ga. A—Daytona Beach. Rookie—Sarasota Orange and Blue.

HOUSTON ASTROS' YEARLY STANDING

Year—Position	W.	L.	Pct.	*G.B.	Manager	Attendance
1962—Eighth	64	96	.400	36½	Harry Craft	924,456
1963—Ninth	66	96	.407	33	Harry Craft	719,502
1964—Ninth	66	96	.407	27	Harry Craft, C. Luman Harris	725,773
1965—Ninth	65	97	.401	32	C. Luman Harris.............................	2,151,470
1966—Eighth	72	90	.444	23	Grady Hatton.................................	1,872,108
1967—Ninth	69	93	.426	32½	Grady Hatton.................................	1,348,303
1968—Tenth.......	72	90	.444	25	Grady Hatton, Harry Walker.............	1,312,887

*Games behind pennant winner.

WEST DIVISION

Year—Position	W.	L.	Pct.	*G.B.	Manager	Attendance
1969—Fifth........	81	81	.500	12	Harry Walker..................................	1,442,995
1970—Fourth.....	79	83	.488	23	Harry Walker..................................	1,253,444
1971—Fourth† ...	79	83	.488	11	Harry Walker..................................	1,261,589
1972—Second.....	84	69	.549	10½	Harry Walker, Leo Durocher	1,469,247
1973—Fourth.....	82	80	.506	17	Durocher, Pedro (Preston) Gomez....	1,394,004
1974—Fourth.....	81	81	.500	21	Pedro (Preston) Gomez..................	1,090,728
1975—Sixth........	64	97	.398	43½	Pedro Gomez, William Virdon..........	858,002
1976—Third.......	80	82	.494	22	William Virdon	886,146
1977—Third.......	81	81	.500	17	William Virdon	1,109,560
1978—Fifth........	74	88	.457	21	William Virdon	1,126,145
1979—Second.....	89	73	.549	1½	William Virdon	1,900,312
1980—First‡	93	70	.571	+1	William Virdon	2,278,217

*Games behind winner. †Tied for position. ‡Lost Championship Series. §Defeated Los Angeles in division playoff.

HOUSTON ASTROS
(7) BILL VIRDON—Manager

No. PITCHERS—	Bts.	Thrs.	Hgt.	Wgt.	Birth-date	1980 Club	IP.	W.	L.	ERA.
47 Andujar, Joaquin	B	R	5:11	180	12-21-52	Houston	122	3	8	3.91
39 Knepper, Bob	L	L	6:02	200	5-25-54	San Fran.	215	9	16	4.10
31 LaCorte, Frank	R	R	6:01	180	10-13-51	Houston	83	8	5	2.82
36 Niekro, Joe	R	R	6:01	190	11- 7-44	Houston	256	20	12	3.55
46 Niemann, Randy	L	L	6:04	200	11-15-55	Tucson	52	4	1	4.85
						Houston	33	0	1	5.45
26 Pladson, Gordie	R	R	6:04	210	7-31-56	Tucson	128	10	5	3.59
						Houston	41	0	4	4.39
50 Richard, J.R.	R	R	6:08	237	3- 7-50	Houston	114	10	4	1.89
42 Roberge, Bert	R	R	6:04	190	10- 3-54	Tucson	49	5	3	4.78
						Houston	24	2	0	6.00
48 Ruhle, Vern	R	R	6:01	187	1-25-51	Houston	159	12	4	2.38
34 Ryan, Nolan	R	R	6:02	195	1-31-47	Houston	234	11	10	3.35
35 Sambito, Joe	L	L	6:01	190	6-28-52	Houston	90	8	4	2.20
45 Smith, Dave	R	R	6:01	195	1-21-55	Houston	103	7	5	1.92
41 Sprowl, Bobby	L	L	6:02	190	4-14-56	Tucson	180	10	11	4.35
						Houston	1	0	0	0.00
20 Sutton, Don	R	R	6:01	190	4- 2-45	Los Angeles	212	13	5	2.21

CATCHERS—	Bts.	Thrs.	Hgt.	Wgt.	Birth-date	1980 Club	G.	HR.	RBI.	Avg.
14 Ashby, Alan	B	R	6:02	190	7- 8-51	Houston	116	3	48	.256
11 Knicely, Alan	R	R	6:00	194	5-19-55	Tucson	133	22	105	.318
						Houston	1	0	0	.000
6 Pujols, Luis	R	R	6:01	195	11-18-55	Houston	78	0	20	.199

INFIELDERS—	Bts.	Thrs.	Hgt.	Wgt.	Birth-date	1980 Club	G.	HR.	RBI.	Avg.
16 Bergman, Dave	L	L	6:02	185	6- 6-53	Houston	90	0	3	.256
23 Garcia, Kiko	R	R	5:11	178	10-14-53	Baltimore	111	1	27	.199
24 Heep, Danny	L	L	5:11	185	7- 3-57	Tucson	96	17	69	.343
						Houston	33	0	6	.276
18 Howe, Art	R	R	6:01	185	12-15-46	Houston	110	10	46	.283
17 Landestoy, Rafael	B	R	5:09	163	5-28-53	Houston	149	1	27	.247
12 Reynolds, Craig	L	R	6:01	175	12-27-52	Houston	137	3	28	.226
8 Roberts, Dave	R	R	6:03	205	2-17-51	Texas	101	10	30	.238
10 Thon, Dickie	R	R	5:11	150	6-20-58	Salt Lake C.	40	2	28	.394
						California	80	0	15	.255

OUTFIELDERS—	Bts.	Thrs.	Hgt.	Wgt.	Birth-date	1980 Club	G.	HR.	RBI.	Avg.
28 Cedeno, Cesar	R	R	6:02	195	2-25-51	Houston	137	10	73	.309
25 Cruz, Jose	L	L	6:00	175	8- 8-47	Houston	160	11	91	.302
30 Leonard, Jeff	R	R	6:04	200	9-22-55	Houston	87	3	20	.213
22 Loucks, Scott	R	R	6:00	178	11-11-56	Columbus	137	10	45	.243
						Houston	8	0	0	.333
21 Puhl, Terry	L	R	6:02	197	7- 8-56	Houston	141	13	55	.282
29 Walling, Denny	L	R	6:01	185	4-17-54	Houston	100	3	29	.299
15 Woods, Gary	R	R	6:02	190	7-20-54	Tucson	140	8	86	.313
						Houston	19	2	15	.377

DON LEPPERT (3)—Coach
DEACON JONES (4)—Coach

BOB LILLIS (5)—Coach
MEL WRIGHT (2)—Coach

THE ASTRODOME

	Seats	Prices
Sky Boxes	2,058	*
Club Level	789	$7.50
Field Level	10,532	6.50
Mezzanine Level	10,658	5.50
Loge Level	4,912	4.50
Gold Box	2,536	3.50
Gold Reserved	9,205	3.00
Pavilion	3,910	1.50

*Sky Boxes sold on season basis only.

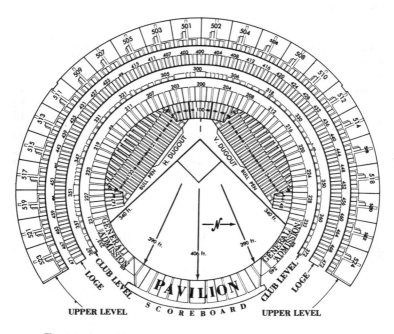

The Astrodome, Houston—First N. L. Game Played April 12, 1965

Tom Lasorda

LOS ANGELES DODGERS

President—Peter O'Malley
V.-P., Player Personnel—Al Campanis
V.-P., Public Relations, Promotions—Fred Claire
V.-P., Minor League Operat.—William P. Schweppe
V.-P., Marketing—Merritt Willey
Publicity Director—Steve Brener
Traveling Secretary—Bill DeLury
Offices—Dodger Stadium
Dodger Stadium Capacity—56,000

Farm System: AAA—Albuquerque. AA—San Antonio. A—Lodi, Vero Beach. Rookie—Lethbridge.

LOS ANGELES DODGERS' YEARLY STANDING

(Brooklyn Dodgers Prior to 1958)

Year—Position	W.	L.	Pct.	*G.B.	Manager	Attendance
1901—Third	79	57	.581	9½	Edward (Ned) Hanlon	189,200
1902—Second	75	63	.543	27½	Edward (Ned) Hanlon	199,868
1903—Fifth	70	66	.515	19	Edward (Ned) Hanlon	224,670
1904—Sixth	56	97	.366	50	Edward (Ned) Hanlon	214,600
1905—Eighth	48	104	.316	56½	Edward (Ned) Hanlon	227,924
1906—Fifth	66	86	.434	50	Patrick (Patsy) Donovan	227,400
1907—Fifth	65	83	.439	40	Patrick (Patsy) Donovan	312,500
1908—Seventh	53	101	.344	46	Patrick (Patsy) Donovan	275,600
1909—Sixth	55	98	.359	55½	Harry Lumley	321,300
1910—Sixth	64	90	.416	40	William Dahlen	279,321
1911—Seventh	64	86	.427	33½	William Dahlen	269,000
1912—Seventh	58	95	.379	46	William Dahlen	243,000
1913—Sixth	65	84	.436	34½	William Dahlen	347,000
1914—Fifth	75	79	.487	19½	Wilbert Robinson	122,671
1915—Third	80	72	.526	10	Wilbert Robinson	297,766
1916—First	94	60	.610	+ 2½	Wilbert Robinson	447,747
1917—Seventh	70	81	.464	26½	Wilbert Robinson	221,619
1918—Fifth	57	69	.452	25½	Wilbert Robinson	83,831
1919—Fifth	69	71	.493	27	Wilbert Robinson	360,721
1920—First	93	61	.604	+ 7	Wilbert Robinson	808,722
1921—Fifth	77	75	.507	16½	Wilbert Robinson	613,245
1922—Sixth	76	78	.494	17	Wilbert Robinson	498,856
1923—Sixth	76	78	.494	19½	Wilbert Robinson	564,666
1924—Second	92	62	.597	1½	Wilbert Robinson	818,883
1925—Sixth†	68	85	.444	27	Wilbert Robinson	659,435
1926—Sixth	71	82	.464	17½	Wilbert Robinson	650,819
1927—Sixth	65	88	.425	28½	Wilbert Robinson	637,230
1928—Sixth	77	76	.503	17½	Wilbert Robinson	664,863
1929—Sixth	70	83	.458	28½	Wilbert Robinson	731,886

LOS ANGELES DODGERS' YEARLY STANDING—Continued

Year—Position	W.	L.	Pct.	*G.B.	Manager	Attendance
1930—Fourth	86	68	.558	6	Wilbert Robinson	1,097,339
1931—Fourth	79	73	.520	21	Wilbert Robinson	753,133
1932—Third	81	73	.526	9	Max Carey	681,827
1933—Sixth	65	88	.425	26½	Max Carey	526,815
1934—Sixth	71	81	.467	23½	Charles (Casey) Stengel	434,188
1935—Fifth	70	83	.458	29½	Charles (Casey) Stengel	470,517
1936—Seventh	67	87	.435	25	Charles (Casey) Stengel	489,618
1937—Sixth	62	91	.405	33½	Burleigh Grimes	482,481
1938—Seventh	69	80	.463	18½	Burleigh Grimes	663,087
1939—Third	84	69	.549	12½	Leo Durocher	955,668
1940—Second	88	65	.575	12	Leo Durocher	975,978
1941—First	100	54	.649	+ 2½	Leo Durocher	1,214,910
1942—Second	104	50	.675	2	Leo Durocher	1,037,765
1943—Third	81	72	.529	23½	Leo Durocher	661,739
1944—Seventh	63	91	.409	42	Leo Durocher	605,905
1945—Third	87	67	.565	11	Leo Durocher	1,059,220
1946—Second‡	96	60	.615	2	Leo Durocher	1,796,824
1947—First	94	60	.610	+ 5	Burton Shotton	1,807,526
1948—Third	84	70	.545	7½	Leo Durocher, Burton Shotton	1,398,967
1949—First	97	57	.630	+ 1	Burton Shotton	1,633,747
1950—Second	89	65	.578	2	Burton Shotton	1,185,896
1951—Second‡	97	60	.618	1	Charles (Chuck) Dressen	1,282,628
1952—First	96	57	.627	+ 4½	Charles (Chuck) Dressen	1,088,704
1953—First	105	49	.682	+13	Charles (Chuck) Dressen	1,163,419
1954—Second	92	62	.597	2	Walter (Smokey) Alston	1,020,531
1955—First	98	55	.641	+13½	Walter (Smokey) Alston	1,033,589
1956—First	93	61	.604	+ 1	Walter (Smokey) Alston	1,213,562
1957—Third	84	70	.545	11	Walter (Smokey) Alston	1,028,258
1958—Seventh	71	83	.461	21	Walter (Smokey) Alston	1,845,556
1959—First§	88	68	.564	+ 2	Walter (Smokey) Alston	2,071,045
1960—Fourth	82	72	.532	13	Walter (Smokey) Alston	2,253,887
1961—Second	89	65	.578	4	Walter (Smokey) Alston	1,804,250
1962—Second‡	102	63	.618	1	Walter (Smokey) Alston	2,755,184
1963—First	99	63	.611	+ 6	Walter (Smokey) Alston	2,538,602
1964—Sixth†	80	82	.494	13	Walter (Smokey) Alston	2,228,751
1965—First	97	65	.599	+ 2	Walter (Smokey) Alston	2,553,577
1966—First	95	67	.586	+ 1½	Walter (Smokey) Alston	2,617,029
1967—Eighth	73	89	.451	28½	Walter (Smokey) Alston	1,664,362
1968—Seventh	76	86	.469	21	Walter (Smokey) Alston	1,581,093

*Games behind pennant winner. †Tied for position. ‡Lost pennant playoff. §Won pennant playoff.

WEST DIVISION

Year—Position	W.	L.	Pct.	*G.B.	Manager	Attendance
1969—Fourth	85	77	.525	8	Walter (Smokey) Alston	1,784,527
1970—Second	87	74	.540	14½	Walter (Smokey) Alston	1,697,142
1971—Second	89	73	.549	1	Walter (Smokey) Alston	2,064,594
1972—Third	85	70	.548	10½	Walter (Smokey) Alston	1,860,858
1973—Second	95	66	.590	3½	Walter (Smokey) Alston	2,136,192
1974—First‡	102	60	.630	+ 4	Walter (Smokey) Alston	2,632,474
1975—Second	88	74	.543	20	Walter (Smokey) Alston	2,539,349
1976—Second	92	70	.568	10	Walter (Smokey) Alston	2,386,301
1977—First‡	98	64	.605	+10	Thomas Lasorda	2,955,087
1978—First†‡	95	67	.586	+ 2½	Thomas Lasorda	3,347,845
1979—Third	79	83	.488	11½	Thomas Lasorda	2,860,954
1980—Second§	92	71	.564	1	Thomas Lasorda	3,249,287

*Games behind winner. ‡Won Championship Series. §Lost to Houston in division playoff.

LOS ANGELES DODGERS

(2) TOM LASORDA—Manager

No. PITCHERS—	Bts.	Thrs.	Hgt.	Wgt.	Birth-date	1980 Club	IP.	W.	L.	ERA.
27 Beckwith, Joe	L	R	6:03	185	1-28-55	Albuquerque	14	2	1	2.57
						Los Angeles	60	3	3	1.95
37 Castillo, Bobby	R	R	5:10	170	4-18-55	Los Angeles	98	8	6	2.76
51 Forster, Terry	L	L	6:03	210	1-14-52	Los Angeles	12	0	0	3.00
38 Goltz, Dave	R	R	6:04	215	6-23-49	Los Angeles	171	7	11	4.32
46 Hooton, Burt	R	R	6:01	200	2- 7-50	Los Angeles	207	14	8	3.65
57 Howe, Steve	L	L	6:01	180	3-10-58	Los Angeles	85	7	9	2.65
41 Reuss, Jerry	L	L	6:05	217	6-19-49	Los Angeles	229	18	6	2.52
26 Stanhouse, Don	R	R	6:02	198	2-12-51	Los Angeles	25	2	2	5.04
48 Stewart, Dave	R	R	6:02	200	2-19-57	Albuquerque	202	15	10	3.70
43 Sutcliffe, Rick	L	R	6:06	200	6-21-56	Los Angeles	110	3	9	5.56
34 Valenzuela, Fer'do	L	L	5:11	180	11- 1-60	San Antonio	174	13	9	3.10
						Los Angeles	18	2	0	0.00
35 Welch, Bob	R	R	6:03	190	11- 3-56	Los Angeles	214	14	9	3.28

CATCHERS—	Bts.	Thrs.	Hgt.	Wgt.	Birth-date	1980 Club	G.	HR.	RBI.	Avg.
13 Ferguson, Joe	R	R	6:02	215	9-19-46	Los Angeles	77	9	29	.238
14 Scioscia, Mike	L	R	6:02	200	11-27-58	Albuquerque	52	3	33	.331
						Los Angeles	54	1	8	.254
7 Yeager, Steve	R	R	6:00	200	11-24-48	Los Angeles	96	2	20	.211

INFIELDERS—	Bts.	Thrs.	Hgt.	Wgt.	Birth-date	1980 Club	G.	HR.	RBI.	Avg.
10 Cey, Ron	R	R	5:09	180	2-15-48	Los Angeles	157	28	77	.254
36 Frias, Pepe	R	R	5:10	165	7-14-48	Texas	116	0	10	.242
						Los Angeles	14	0	0	.222
6 Garvey, Steve	R	R	5:10	190	12-22-48	Los Angeles	163	26	106	.304
15 Lopes, Davey	R	R	5:09	170	5- 3-46	Los Angeles	141	10	49	.251
45 Perconte, Jack	L	R	5:10	160	8-31-54	Albuquerque	120	2	46	.326
						Los Angeles	14	0	2	.235
18 Russell, Bill	R	R	6:00	175	10-21-48	Los Angeles	130	3	34	.264

OUTFIELDERS—	Bts.	Thrs.	Hgt.	Wgt.	Birth-date	1980 Club	G.	HR.	RBI.	Avg.
12 Baker, Dusty	R	R	6:02	187	6-15-49	Los Angeles	153	.29	97	.294
28 Guerrero, Pedro	R	R	5:11	176	6-29-56	Los Angeles	75	7	31	.322
21 Johnstone, Jay	L	R	6:01	190	11-20-46	Los Angeles	109	2	20	.307
44 Landreaux, Ken	L	R	5:11	164	12-22-54	Minnesota	129	7	62	.281
3 Law, Rudy	L	L	6:01	165	10- 7-56	Los Angeles	128	1	23	.260
16 Monday, Rick	L	L	6:03	200	11-20-45	Los Angeles	96	10	25	.268
8 Smith, Reggie	B	R	6:00	195	4- 2-45	Los Angeles	92	15	55	.322
30 Thomas, Derrel	B	R	6:00	160	1-14-51	Los Angeles	117	1	22	.266

MONTY BASGALL (54)—Coach   MANNY MOTA (11)—Coach
MARK CRESSE (58)—Coach   DANNY OZARK (33)—Coach
RON PERRANOSKI (29)—Coach

DODGER STADIUM

	Seats	Prices
Dugout, Club Level Boxes	1,732	*
Field, Loge Box Seats	25,217	$5.50
Reserved Grandstand	18,785	4.00
General Admission	4,266	2.50
Pavilion	6,000	2.50

*Sold only on season basis.

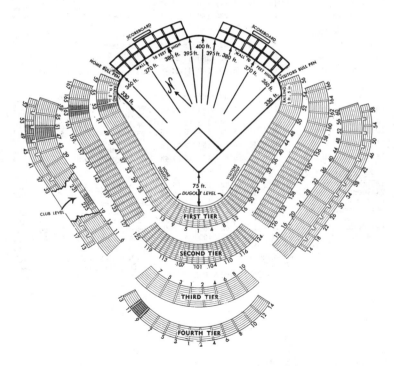

Dodger Stadium, Los Angeles—First N. L. Game Played April 10, 1962

Dick Williams

MONTREAL EXPOS

Chairman of the Board—Charles R. Bronfman
President & Chief Executive Officer—John J. McHale
Vice-President, Player Development—Jim Fanning
Vice-President, Secretary-Treasurer—Harry Renaud
Director of Scouting—Danny Menendez
Publicists—Monique Giroux, Richard Griffin
Traveling Secretary—Peter Durso
Offices—P. O. Box 500, Station M
Olympic Stadium Capacity—59,984

Farm System: AAA—Denver. AA—Memphis. A—Jamestown, West Palm Beach. Rookie—Calgary.

MONTREAL EXPOS' YEARLY STANDING

EAST DIVISION

Year—Position	W.	L.	Pct.	*G.B.	Manager	Attendance
1969—Sixth	52	110	.321	48	Gene Mauch	1,212,608
1970—Sixth	73	89	.451	16	Gene Mauch	1,424,683
1971—Fifth	71	90	.441	25½	Gene Mauch	1,290,963
1972—Fifth	70	86	.449	26½	Gene Mauch	1,142,145
1973—Fourth	79	83	.488	3½	Gene Mauch	1,246,863
1974—Fourth	79	82	.491	8½	Gene Mauch	1,019,134
1975—Fifth†	75	87	.463	17½	Gene Mauch	908,292
1976—Sixth	55	107	.340	46	Karl Kuehl, Charlie Fox	646,704
1977—Fifth	75	87	.463	26	Richard Williams	1,433,757
1978—Fourth	76	86	.469	14	Richard Williams	1,427,007
1979—Second	95	65	.594	2	Richard Williams	2,102,173
1980—Second	90	72	.556	1	Richard Williams	2,208,175

*Games behind winner. †Tied for position.

MONTREAL EXPOS

(23) DICK WILLIAMS—Manager

No. PITCHERS—	Bts.	Thrs.	Hgt.	Wgt.	Birth-date	1980 Club	IP.	W.	L.	ERA.
22 Bahnsen, Stan	R	R	6:02	198	12-15-44	Montreal	91	7	6	3.07
48 Burris, Ray	R	R	6:05	200	8-22-50	New York NL	170	7	13	4.02
28 Dues, Hal	R	R	6:03	185	9-22-54	Montreal	12	0	1	6.75
						Denver	98	7	4	3.40
35 Fryman, Woodie	R	L	6:02	215	4-12-40	Montreal	80	7	4	2.25
34 Gullickson, Bill	R	R	6:03	210	2-20-59	Montreal	141	10	5	3.00
						Denver	66	6	2	1.91
20 James, Bob	R	R	6:04	215	8-15-58	Denver	87	9	2	3.83
						Montreal	104	7	5	3.72
53 Lea, Charlie	R	R	6:04	194	12-25-56	Denver	12	0	0	1.50
						Memphis	75	9	0	0.84
37 Lee, Bill	L	L	6:03	190	12-28-46	Montreal	118	4	6	4.96
46 Palmer, David	R	R	6:01	205	10-19-57	Montreal	130	8	6	2.98
47 Ratzer, Steve	R	R	6:01	192	9- 9-53	Montreal	4	0	0	11.25
						Denver	163	15	4	3.59
45 Rogers, Steve	R	R	6:01	175	10-26-49	Montreal	281	16	11	2.98
21 Sanderson, Scott	R	R	6:05	198	7-22-56	Montreal	211	16	11	3.11
27 Sosa, Elias	R	R	6:02	205	6-10-50	Montreal	94	9	6	3.06
26 Wortham, Richard	R	L	6:00	185	10-22-53	Chicago AL	92	4	7	5.97

CATCHERS—	Bts.	Thrs.	Hgt.	Wgt.		1980 Club	G.	HR.	RBI.	Avg.
8 Carter, Gary	R	R	6:02	215	4- 8-54	Montreal	154	29	101	.264
44 Ramos, Bobby	R	R	5:11	208	11- 5-55	Montreal	13	0	2	.156
						Denver	74	4	30	.295
50 Wieghaus, Tom	R	R	6:00	195	2- 1-57	Memphis	120	4	44	.272

INFIELDERS—	Bts.	Thrs.	Hgt.	Wgt.			G.	HR.	RBI.	Avg.
49 Cromartie, Warren	L	L	6:00	200	9-23-53	Montreal	162	14	70	.288
14 Hutton, Tommy	L	L	5:11	172	4-20-46	Montreal	62	0	5	.218
43 Manuel, Jerry	R	R	6:00	155	12-23-53	Montreal	7	0	0	.000
						Denver	128	3	61	.277
2 Mills, Brad	L	R	6:00	195	1-19-57	Montreal	21	0	8	.300
						Denver	52	2	27	.289
						Memphis	55	6	44	.295
5 Montanez, Willie	L	L	6:01	185	4- 1-48	SD-Mont.	142	6	64	.272
15 Parrish, Larry	R	R	6:03	215	11-10-53	Montreal	126	15	72	.254
3 Scott, Rodney	B	R	6:00	155	10-16-53	Montreal	154	0	46	.224
4 Speier, Chris	R	R	6:01	175	6-28-50	Montreal	128	1	32	.265

OUTFIELDERS—	Bts.	Thrs.	Hgt.	Wgt.			G.	HR.	RBI.	Avg.
10 Dawson, Andre	R	R	6:03	192	7-10-54	Montreal	151	17	87	.308
25 Office, Rowland	L	L	6:00	170	10-25-52	Montreal	116	6	30	.267
24 Pate, Bob	R	R	6:03	196	12- 3-53	Montreal	23	0	5	.256
						Denver	67	8	65	.323
30 Raines, Tim	B	R	5:08	170	8-16-59	Montreal	15	0	0	.050
						Denver	108	6	64	.354
17 Valentine, Ellis	R	R	6:04	218	7-30-54	Montreal	86	13	67	.315
29 Wallach, Tim	R	R	6:03	220	9-14-58	Montreal	5	1	2	.182
						Denver	134	36	124	.281
18 White, Jerry	B	R	5:11	172	8-23-52	Montreal	110	7	23	.262

OZZIE VIRGIL (1)—Coach   NORM SHERRY (40)—Coach
VERN RAPP (9)—Coach   GALEN CISCO (36)—Coach
PAT MULLIN (39)—Coach   STEVE BOROS (41)—Coach

OLYMPIC STADIUM

	Seats	Prices
Level 200 (Mobile Field Dugout Seats)	5,498	$8.25
Level 300	12,889	7.00
Level 400	10,715	6.00
Level 500 (Mezzanine)	3,408	8.25
Level 600	8,173	4.00
Level 700	19,301	4.00
General Admission	*	1.00

*Variable

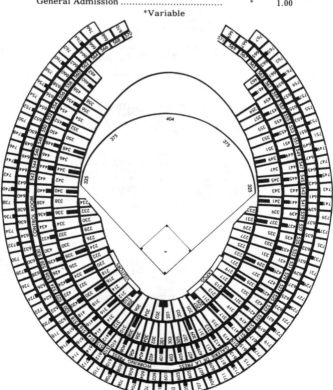

Olympic Stadium, Montreal—First N. L. Game Played April 15, 1977

Joe Torre

NEW YORK METS

Chairman of the Board—Nelson Doubleday
President—Fred Wilpon
Exec. V. P.-General Manager—Frank Cashen
Vice-Pres.-Baseball Operations—Lou Gorman
Vice-Pres.-Administration—James Nagourney
Vice-President—Alan Harazin
Director of Scouting—Joseph McIlvaine
Director of Minor Leagues—Christopher Kager
Asst. to G.M.-Traveling Secretary—Arthur Richman
Director of Public Relations—Jay Horwitz
Offices—Shea Stadium
Shea Stadium Capacity—55,300

Farm System: AAA—Tidewater. AA—Jackson. A— Little
Falls, Lynchburg, Shelby. Rookie—Kingsport.

NEW YORK METS' YEARLY STANDING

Year—Position	W.	L.	Pct.	*G.B.	Manager	Attendance
1962—Tenth	40	120	.250	60½	Charles (Casey) Stengel	922,530
1963—Tenth	51	111	.315	48	Charles (Casey) Stengel	1,080,108
1964—Tenth	53	109	.327	40	Charles (Casey) Stengel	1,732,597
1965—Tenth	50	112	.309	47	C. Stengel, Wesley Westrum	1,768,389
1966—Ninth	66	95	.410	28½	Wesley Westrum	1,932,693
1967—Tenth	61	101	.377	40½	W. Westrum, F. (Salty) Parker	1,565,492
1968—Ninth	73	89	.451	24	Gilbert Hodges	1,781,657

*Games behind pennant winner.

EAST DIVISION

Year—Position	W.	L.	Pct.	*G.B.	Manager	Attendance
1969—First†	100	62	.617	+ 8	Gilbert Hodges	2,175,373
1970—Third	83	79	.512	6	Gilbert Hodges	2,697,479
1971—Third‡	83	79	.512	14	Gilbert Hodges	2,266,680
1972—Third	83	73	.532	13½	Lawrence P. Berra	2,134,185
1973—First†	82	79	.509	+ 1½	Lawrence P. Berra	1,912,390
1974—Fifth	71	91	.438	17	Lawrence P. Berra	1,722,209
1975—Third‡	82	80	.506	10½	L. P. Berra, Roy McMillan	1,730,566
1976—Third	86	76	.531	15	Joe Frazier	1,468,754
1977—Sixth	64	98	.395	37	Joe Frazier, Joseph Torre	1,066,825
1978—Sixth	66	96	.407	24	Joseph Torre	1,007,328
1979—Sixth	63	99	.389	35	Joseph Torre	788,905
1980—Fifth	67	95	.414	24	Joseph Torre	1,192,073

*Games behind winner.   †Won Championship Series.   ‡Tied for position.

NEW YORK METS

(9) JOE TORRE—Manager

No. PITCHERS—	Bts.	Thrs.	Hgt.	Wgt.	Birth-date	1980 Club	IP.	W.	L.	ERA.
13 Allen, Neil	R	R	6:02	185	1-24-58	New York	97	7	10	3.71
33 Falcone, Pete	L	L	6:02	185	10- 1-53	New York	157	7	10	4.53
32 Hausman, Tom	R	R	6:05	200	3-31-53	New York	122	6	5	3.98
26 Holman, Scott	R	R	6:00	190	9-18-58	Tidewater	48	3	3	4.88
						New York	7	0	0	1.29
25 Jones, Randy	R	L	6:00	180	1-12-50	San Diego	154	5	13	3.92
38 Leary, Tim	R	R	6:03	195	12-23-58	Jackson	173	15	8	2.76
49 Miller, Dyar	R	R	6:01	202	5-29-46	Tidewater	52	4	2	4.67
						New York	42	1	2	1.93
47 Orosco, Jesse	R	L	6:02	174	4-21-57	Jackson	71	4	4	3.68
44 Reardon, Jeff	R	R	6:01	190	10- 1-55	New York	110	8	7	2.62
34 Roberts, Dave	L	L	6:03	192	9-11-44	Pittsburgh	2	0	1	4.50
						Seattle	80	2	3	4.39
30 Scott, Mike	R	R	6:03	215	4-26-55	Tidewater	170	13	7	2.96
						New York	29	1	1	4.34
27 Swan, Craig	R	R	6:03	215	11-30-50	New York	128	5	9	3.59
46 Von Ohlen, Dave	L	L	6:02	200	10-25-58	Tidewater	86	5	4	3.21
40 Zachry, Pat	R	R	6:05	175	4-24-52	New York	165	6	10	3.00

CATCHERS—	Bts.	Thrs.	Hgt.	Wgt.	Birth-date	1980 Club	G.	HR.	RBI.	Avg.
42 Hodges, Ron	L	R	6:01	185	6-22-49	New York	36	0	5	.238
12 Stearns, John	R	R	6:00	185	8-21-51	New York	91	0	45	.285
29 Trevino, Alex	R	R	5:10	165	8-26-57	New York	106	0	37	.256

INFIELDERS—	Bts.	Thrs.	Hgt.	Wgt.	Birth-date	1980 Club	G.	HR.	RBI.	Avg.
6 Backman, Wally	B	R	5:09	160	9-29-59	Tidewater	125	1	51	.293
						New York	27	0	9	.323
7 Brooks, Hubie	R	R	6:00	178	9-24-56	Tidewater	113	3	50	.297
						New York	24	1	10	.309
3 Cubbage, Mike	L	R	6:00	180	7-21-50	Minnesota	103	8	42	.246
23 Flynn, Doug	R	R	5:11	160	4-18-51	New York	128	0	24	.255
17 Giles, Brian	R	R	6:01	165	4-27-60	Jackson	132	10	57	.286
22 Jorgensen, Mike	L	L	6:00	192	8-16-48	New York	119	7	43	.255
10 Staub, Rusty	L	R	6:02	215	4- 1-44	Texas	109	9	55	.300
11 Taveras, Frank	R	R	6:00	170	12-24-50	New York	141	0	25	.279

OUTFIELDERS—	Bts.	Thrs.	Hgt.	Wgt.	Birth-date	1980 Club	G.	HR.	RBI.	Avg.
4 Bailor, Bob	R	R	5:10	160	7-10-51	Toronto	117	1	16	.236
5 Kingman, Dave	R	R	6:06	210	12-21-48	Chicago NL	81	18	57	.278
16 Mazzilli, Lee	B	R	6:01	180	3-25-55	New York	152	16	76	.280
1 Wilson, Mookie	B	R	5:10	170	2- 9-56	Tidewater	132	4	44	.295
						New York	27	0	4	.248
18 Youngblood, Joel	R	R	5:11	175	8-28-51	New York	146	8	69	.276

BOB GIBSON (45)—Coach   RUBE WALKER (54)—Coach
DERON JOHNSON (51)—Coach   CHUCK COTTIER (53)—Coach
JOE PIGNATANO (52)—Coach

SHEA STADIUM

	Seats	Prices
Field, Loge Level Boxes............................	12,792	$7.00
Mezzanine, Upper Level Boxes.................	7,680	5.50
Loge Level Reserved	6,582	5.50
Mezzanine Level Reserved........................	10,542	5.50
Upper Reserved..		4.00
General Admission	17,704	2.00

Note—Proportion of reserved and general admission seats in loge, mezzanine and upper deck dependent upon anticipated size of crowd.

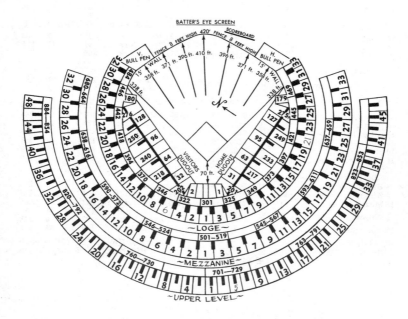

William A. Shea Stadium, New York—First N. L. Game Played April 17, 1964

Dallas Green

PHILADELPHIA PHILLIES

Chairman of the Board—R. R. M. Carpenter, Jr.
President—R. R. M. Carpenter, III
Executive Vice-President—William Y. Giles
Vice-President and Director of Player
                              Personnel—Paul Owens
Vice-President and Director of Finance—
                              George F. H. Harrison
Dir. of Minor Leagues & Scouting—Jim Baumer
Asst. Dir. of Minor Leagues & Scouting—Jack Pastore
Publicity and Public Relations Director—Larry Shenk
Traveling Secretary—Eddie Ferenz
Offices—Veterans Stadium
Veterans Stadium Capacity—65,454
Farm System: AAA—Oklahoma City. AA—Reading.
  A—Bend, Spartanburg, Peninsula. Rookie—Helena.

PHILADELPHIA PHILLIES' YEARLY STANDING

Year—Position	W.	L.	Pct.	*G.B.	Manager	Attendance
1901—Second.....	83	57	.593	7½	William Shettsline	234,937
1902—Seventh ...	56	81	.409	46	William Shettsline	112,066
1903—Seventh ...	49	86	.363	39½	Charles (Chief) Zimmer	151,729
1904—Eighth	52	100	.342	53½	Hugh Duffy	140,771
1905—Fourth	83	69	.546	21½	Hugh Duffy	317,932
1906—Fourth.....	71	82	.464	45½	Hugh Duffy	294,680
1907—Third......	83	64	.565	21½	William J. Murray	341,216
1908—Fourth.....	83	71	.539	16	William J. Murray	420,660
1909—Fifth.......	74	79	.484	36½	William J. Murray	303,177
1910—Fourth.....	78	75	.510	25½	Charles (Red) Dooin	296,597
1911—Fourth.....	79	73	.520	19½	Charles (Red) Dooin	416,000
1912—Fifth......	73	79	.480	30½	Charles (Red) Dooin	250,000
1913—Second.....	88	63	.583	12½	Charles (Red) Dooin	470,000
1914—Sixth.......	74	80	.481	20½	Charles (Red) Dooin	138,474
1915—First.......	90	62	.592	+ 7	Patrick Moran	449,898
1916—Second.....	91	62	.595	2½	Patrick Moran	515,365
1917—Second.....	87	65	.572	10	Patrick Moran	354,428
1918—Sixth.......	55	68	.447	26	Patrick Moran	122,266
1919—Eighth	47	90	.343	47½	John Coombs, Clifford Cravath	240,424
1920—Eighth	62	91	.405	30½	Clifford (Gavvy) Cravath	330,998
1921—Eighth	51	103	.331	43½	William Donovan, Irvin Wilhelm	273,961
1922—Seventh ...	57	96	.373	35½	Irvin Wilhelm	232,471
1923—Eighth	50	104	.325	45½	Arthur Fletcher	228,168
1924—Seventh ...	55	96	.364	37	Arthur Fletcher	299,818
1925—Sixth†	68	85	.444	27	Arthur Fletcher	304,905
1926—Eighth	58	93	.384	29½	Arthur Fletcher	240,600
1927—Eighth	51	103	.331	43	John (Stuffy) McInnis	305,420
1928—Eighth	43	109	.283	51	Burton Shotton	182,168
1929—Fifth........	71	82	.464	27½	Burton Shotton	281,200
1930—Eighth	52	102	.338	40	Burton Shotton	299,007

PHILADELPHIA PHILLIES' YEARLY STANDING—
Continued

Year—Position	W.	L.	Pct.	*G.B.	Manager	Attendance
1931—Sixth.......	66	88	.429	35	Burton Shotton	284,849
1932—Fourth	78	76	.506	12	Burton Shotton	268,914
1933—Seventh ...	60	92	.395	31	Burton Shotton	156,421
1934—Seventh ...	56	93	.376	37	James Wilson	169,885
1935—Seventh ...	64	89	.418	35½	James Wilson	205,470
1936—Eighth	54	100	.351	38	James Wilson	249,219
1937—Seventh ...	61	92	.399	34½	James Wilson	212,790
1938—Eighth	45	105	.300	43	James Wilson, John Lobert	166,111
1939—Eighth	45	106	.298	50½	James (Doc) Prothro	277,973
1940—Eighth	50	103	.327	50	James (Doc) Prothro	207,177
1941—Eighth	43	111	.279	57	James (Doc) Prothro	231,401
1942—Eighth	42	109	.278	62½	John (Hans) Lobert	230,183
1943—Seventh ...	64	90	.416	41	Stanley Harris, Fred Fitzsimmons	466,975
1944—Eighth	61	92	.399	43½	Fred Fitzsimmons	369,586
1945—Eighth	46	108	.299	52	Fred Fitzsimmons, Ben Chapman	285,057
1946—Fifth.......	69	85	.448	28	W. Benjamin Chapman	1,045,247
1947—Seventh†..	62	92	.403	32	W. Benjamin Chapman	907,332
1948—Sixth.......	66	88	.429	25½	B. Chapman, Al Cooke, Ed Sawyer....	767,429
1949—Third.......	81	73	.526	16	Edwin Sawyer	819,698
1950—First.......	91	63	.591	+ 2	Edwin Sawyer	1,217,035
1951—Fifth.......	73	81	.474	23½	Edwin Sawyer	937,658
1952—Fourth	87	67	.565	9½	Edwin Sawyer, Stephen O'Neill........	775,417
1953—Third†	83	71	.539	22	Stephen O'Neill	853,644
1954—Fourth	75	79	.487	22	Stephen O'Neill, Terry Moore	738,991
1955—Fourth	77	77	.500	21½	E. Mayo Smith	922,886
1956—Fifth.......	71	83	.461	22	E. Mayo Smith	934,798
1957—Fifth.......	77	77	.500	19	E. Mayo Smith	1,146,230
1958—Eighth	69	85	.448	23	E. Mayo Smith, Edwin Sawyer........	931,110
1959—Eighth	64	90	.416	23	Edwin Sawyer	802,815
1960—Eighth	59	95	.383	36	Edwin Sawyer, Gene Mauch	862,205
1961—Eighth	47	107	.305	46	Gene Mauch	590,039
1962—Seventh ...	81	80	.503	20	Gene Mauch	762,034
1963—Fourth	87	75	.537	12	Gene Mauch	907,141
1964—Second† ...	92	70	.568	1	Gene Mauch	1,425,891
1965—Sixth.......	85	76	.528	11½	Gene Mauch	1,166,376
1966—Fourth	87	75	.537	8	Gene Mauch	1,108,201
1967—Fifth.......	82	80	.506	19½	Gene Mauch	828,888
1968—Seventh†..	76	86	.469	21	Gene Mauch, Robert Skinner	664,546

*Games behind pennant winner. †Tied for position.

EAST DIVISION

Year—Position	W.	L.	Pct.	*G.B.	Manager	Attendance
1969—Fifth.......	63	99	.389	37	Robert Skinner, George Myatt	519,414
1970—Fifth.......	73	88	.453	15½	Frank Lucchesi	708,247
1971—Sixth.......	67	95	.414	30	Frank Lucchesi	1,511,223
1972—Sixth.......	59	97	.378	37½	Frank Lucchesi, Paul Owens	1,343,329
1973—Sixth.......	71	91	.438	11½	Daniel L. Ozark	1,475,934
1974—Third......	80	82	.494	8	Daniel L. Ozark	1,808,648
1975—Second....	86	76	.531	6½	Daniel L. Ozark	1,909,233
1976—First‡	101	61	.623	+ 9	Daniel L. Ozark	2,480,150
1977—First‡	101	61	.623	+ 5	Daniel L. Ozark	2,700,070
1978—First‡	90	72	.556	+ 1½	Daniel L. Ozark	2,583,389
1979—Fourth	84	78	.519	14	Daniel L. Ozark, G. Dallas Green.....	2,775,011
1980—First§	91	71	.562	+ 1	G. Dallas Green	2,651,650

*Games behind winner. ‡Lost Championship Series. §Won Championship Series.

PHILADELPHIA PHILLIES

(46) DALLAS GREEN—Manager

No.	PITCHERS—	Bts.	Thrs.	Hgt.	Wgt.	Birth-date	1980 Club	IP.	W.	L.	ERA.
40	Brusstar, Warren	R	R	6:03	200	2- 2-52	Peninsula	14	1	1	4.61
							Philadelphia	39	2	2	3.69
50	Bystrom, Marty	R	R	6:05	200	7-26-58	Okla. City	91	6	5	3.66
							Philadelphia	36	5	0	1.50
32	Carlton, Steve	L	L	6:05	219	12-22-44	Philadelphia	304	24	9	2.34
38	Christenson, Larry	R	R	6:04	213	11-10-53	Philadelphia	74	5	1	4.01
35	Espinosa, Nino	R	R	6:01	186	8-15-53	Spartanburg	17	1	1	2.65
							Philadelphia	76	3	5	3.79
39	Lyle, Sparky	L	L	6:01	195	7-22-44	Texas	81	3	2	4.67
							Philadelphia	14	0	0	1.93
45	McGraw, Tug	B	L	6:00	180	8-30-44	Philadelphia	92	5	4	1.47
48	Noles, Dickie	R	R	6:02	178	11-19-56	Philadelphia	81	1	4	3.89
30	Proly, Mike	R	R	5:10	184	12-15-50	Chicago AL	147	5	10	3.06
42	Reed, Ron	R	R	6:06	225	11- 2-42	Philadelphia	91	7	5	4.05
44	Ruthven, Dick	R	R	6:03	190	3-27-51	Philadelphia	223	17	10	3.55

No.	CATCHERS—	Bts.	Thrs.	Hgt.	Wgt.	Birth-date	1980 Club	G.	HR.	RBI.	Avg.
8	Boone, Bob	R	R	6:02	202	11-19-47	Philadelphia	141	9	55	.229
6	Moreland, Keith	R	R	6:00	200	5- 2-54	Philadelphia	62	4	29	.314

No.	INFIELDERS—	Bts.	Thrs.	Hgt.	Wgt.	Birth-date	1980 Club	G.	HR.	RBI.	Avg.
16	Aguayo, Luis	R	R	5:09	173	3-13-59	Okla. City	84	9	40	.244
							Philadelphia	20	1	8	.277
15	Aviles, Ramon	R	R	5:09	155	1-22-52	Okla. City	11	1	2	.279
							Philadelphia	51	2	9	.277
10	Bowa, Larry	B	R	5:10	155	12- 6-45	Philadelphia	147	2	39	.267
14	Rose, Pete	B	R	5:11	203	4-14-41	Philadelphia	162	1	64	.282
20	Schmidt, Mike	R	R	6:02	203	9-27-49	Philadelphia	150	48	121	.286
9	Trillo, Manny	R	R	6:01	164	12-25-50	Philadelphia	141	7	43	.292
18	Vukovich, John	R	R	6:01	190	7-31-47	Philadelphia	49	0	5	.161

No.	OUTFIELDERS—	Bts.	Thrs.	Hgt.	Wgt.	Birth-date	1980 Club	G.	HR.	RBI.	Avg.
26	Davis, Dick	R	R	6:00	195	9-25-53	Milwaukee	106	4	30	.271
23	Gross, Greg	L	L	5:11	175	8- 1-52	Philadelphia	127	0	12	.240
31	Maddox, Garry	R	R	6:03	185	9- 1-49	Philadelphia	143	11	73	.259
34	Matthews, Gary	R	R	6:03	190	7- 5-50	Atlanta	155	19	75	.278
21	McBride, Bake	L	R	6:02	184	2- 3-49	Philadelphia	137	9	87	.309
27	Smith, Lonnie	R	R	5:09	170	12-22-55	Philadelphia	100	3	20	.339
25	Unser, Del	L	L	5:11	180	12- 9-44	Philadelphia	96	0	10	.264

BILLY DeMARS (2)—Coach
BOBBY WINE (7)—Coach
HERM STARRETTE (4)—Coach

RUBEN AMARO (12)—Coach
MIKE RYAN (5)—Coach
LEE ELIA (3)—Coach

VETERANS STADIUM

	Seats	Prices
Super Boxes—Fourth Level	890	*
Deluxe Boxes	1,276	*
Field Boxes	10,361	$7.00
Terrace Boxes	10,870	6.00
Loge Boxes	5,711	6.00
Upper Reserved, 600 Level	11,367	5.00
Upper Reserved, 700 Level	9,360	4.00
General Admission	15,619	2.50

*Sold only on season basis.

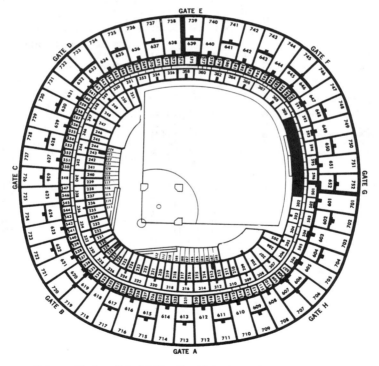

Veterans Stadium, Philadelphia—First N. L. Game Played April 10, 1971

Chuck Tanner

PITTSBURGH PIRATES

Chairman of the Board—John W. Galbreath
President—Daniel M. Galbreath
Executive Vice-President—Harding Peterson
Vice-President-Bus. Admin.—Joseph M. O'Toole
Vice-Pres.-P.R.-Marketing—Jack Shrom
Director of Publicity—Joseph Safety
Traveling Secretary—Charles Muse
Offices—Three Rivers Stadium
Three Rivers Stadium Capacity—54,356

Farm System: AAA—Portland. AA—Buffalo. A—Alexandria, Greenwood. Rookie—Bradenton.

PITTSBURGH PIRATES' YEARLY STANDING

Year—Position	W.	L.	Pct.	*G.B.	Manager	Attendance
1901—First	90	49	.647	+ 7½	Fred Clarke	251,955
1902—First	103	36	.741	+27½	Fred Clarke	243,826
1903—First	91	49	.650	+ 6½	Fred Clarke	326,855
1904—Fourth	87	66	.569	19	Fred Clarke	340,615
1905—Second	96	57	.627	9	Fred Clarke	369,124
1906—Third	93	60	.608	23½	Fred Clarke	394,877
1907—Second	91	63	.591	17	Fred Clarke	319,506
1908—Second†	98	56	.636	1	Fred Clarke	382,444
1909—First	110	42	.724	+ 6½	Fred Clarke	534,950
1910—Third	86	67	.562	17½	Fred Clarke	436,586
1911—Third	85	69	.552	14½	Fred Clarke	432,000
1912—Second	93	58	.616	10	Fred Clarke	384,000
1913—Fourth	78	71	.523	21½	Fred Clarke	296,000
1914—Seventh	69	85	.448	25½	Fred Clarke	139,620
1915—Fifth	73	81	.474	18	Fred Clarke	225,743
1916—Sixth	65	89	.422	29	James Callahan	289,132
1917—Eighth	51	103	.331	47	J. Callahan, J. Wagner, H. Bezdek	192,807
1918—Fourth	65	60	.520	17	Hugo Bezdek	213,610
1919—Fourth	71	68	.511	24½	Hugo Bezdek	276,810
1920—Fourth	79	75	.513	14	George Gibson	429,037
1921—Second	90	63	.588	4	George Gibson	701,567
1922—Third†	85	69	.552	8	Geo. Gibson, William McKechnie	523,675
1923—Third	87	67	.565	8½	William McKechnie	611,082
1924—Third	90	63	.588	3	William McKechnie	736,883
1925—First	95	58	.621	+ 8½	William McKechnie	804,354
1926—Third	84	69	.549	4½	William McKechnie	798,542
1927—First	94	60	.610	+ 1½	Owen (Donie) Bush	869,720
1928—Fourth	85	67	.559	9	Owen (Donie) Bush	495,070
1929—Second	88	65	.575	10½	Owen (Donie) Bush, Jewel Ens	491,377
1930—Fifth	80	74	.519	12	Jewel Ens	357,795

PITTSBURGH PIRATES' YEARLY STANDING—Continued

Year—Position	W.	L.	Pct.	*G.B.	Manager	Attendance
1931—Fifth	75	79	.487	26	Jewel Ens	260,392
1932—Second	86	68	.558	4	George Gibson	287,262
1933—Second	87	67	.565	5	George Gibson	288,747
1934—Fifth	74	76	.493	19½	Geo. Gibson, Harold Traynor	322,622
1935—Fourth	86	67	.562	13½	Harold (Pie) Traynor	352,885
1936—Fourth	84	70	.545	8	Harold (Pie) Traynor	372,524
1937—Third	86	68	.558	10	Harold (Pie) Traynor	459,679
1938—Second	86	64	.573	2	Harold (Pie) Traynor	641,033
1939—Sixth	68	85	.444	28½	Harold (Pie) Traynor	376,734
1940—Fourth	78	76	.506	22½	Frank Frisch	507,934
1941—Fourth	81	73	.526	19	Frank Frisch	482,241
1942—Fifth	66	81	.449	36½	Frank Frisch	448,897
1943—Fourth	80	74	.519	25	Frank Frisch	604,278
1944—Second	90	63	.588	14½	Frank Frisch	498,740
1945—Fourth	82	72	.532	16	Frank Frisch	604,694
1946—Seventh†	63	91	.409	34	Frank Frisch	749,962
1947—Seventh†	62	92	.403	32	William Herman, William Burwell	1,283,531
1948—Fourth	83	71	.539	8½	William Meyer	1,517,021
1949—Sixth	71	83	.461	26	William Meyer	1,499,435
1950—Eighth	57	96	.373	33½	William Meyer	1,166,267
1951—Seventh	64	90	.416	32½	William Meyer	980,590
1952—Eighth	42	112	.273	54½	William Meyer	686,673
1953—Eighth	50	104	.325	55	Fred Haney	572,757
1954—Eighth	53	101	.344	44	Fred Haney	475,494
1955—Eighth	60	94	.390	38½	Fred Haney	469,397
1956—Seventh	66	88	.429	27	Robert Bragan	949,878
1957—Seventh†	62	92	.403	33	Robert Bragan, Daniel Murtaugh	850,732
1958—Second	84	70	.545	8	Daniel Murtaugh	1,311,988
1959—Fourth	78	76	.506	9	Daniel Murtaugh	1,359,917
1960—First	95	59	.617	+ 7	Daniel Murtaugh	1,705,828
1961—Sixth	75	79	.487	18	Daniel Murtaugh	1,199,128
1962—Fourth	93	68	.578	8	Daniel Murtaugh	1,090,648
1963—Eighth	74	88	.457	25	Daniel Murtaugh	783,648
1964—Sixth†	80	82	.494	13	Daniel Murtaugh	759,496
1965—Third	90	72	.556	7	Harry Walker	909,279
1966—Third	92	70	.568	3	Harry Walker	1,196,618
1967—Sixth	81	81	.500	20½	Harry Walker, Daniel Murtaugh	907,012
1968—Sixth	80	82	.494	17	Lawrence Shepard	693,485

*Games behind pennant winner. †Tied for position.

EAST DIVISION

Year—Position	W.	L.	Pct.	*G.B.	Manager	Attendance
1969—Third	88	74	.543	12	Law. Shepard, Alex Grammas	769,369
1970—First‡	89	73	.549	+ 5	Daniel Murtaugh	1,341,947
1971—First§	97	65	.599	+ 7	Daniel Murtaugh	1,501,132
1972—First‡	96	59	.619	+11	William Virdon	1,427,460
1973—Third	80	82	.494	2½	William Virdon, Daniel Murtaugh	1,319,913
1974—First‡	88	74	.543	+ 1½	Daniel Murtaugh	1,110,552
1975—First‡	92	69	.571	+ 6½	Daniel Murtaugh	1,270,018
1976—Second	92	70	.568	9	Daniel Murtaugh	1,025,945
1977—Second	96	66	.593	5	Charles Tanner	1,237,349
1978—Second	88	73	.547	1½	Charles Tanner	964,106
1979—First§	98	64	.605	+ 2	Charles Tanner	1,435,454
1980—Third	83	79	.512	8	Charles Tanner	1,646,757

*Games behind winner. ‡Lost Championship Series. §Won Championship Series.

PITTSBURGH PIRATES

(7) CHUCK TANNER—Manager

No. PITCHERS—	Bts.	Thrs.	Hgt.	Wgt.	Birth-date	1980 Club	IP.	W.	L.	ERA.
26 Bibby, Jim	R	R	6:05	250	10-29-44	Pittsburgh	238	19	6	3.33
45 Candelaria, John	L	L	6:07	232	11- 6-53	Pittsburgh	233	11	14	4.02
49 Cruz, Victor	R	R	5:09	215	12-24-57	Cleveland	86	6	7	3.45
23 Jackson, Grant	B	L	6:00	204	9-28-42	Pittsburgh	71	8	4	2.92
46 Lee, Mark	R	R	6:04	225	6-14-53	Hawaii-Port.	66	6	6	4.09
						Pittsburgh	6	0	1	4.50
25 Perez, Pascual	R	R	6:02	162	5-17-57	Portland	160	12	10	4.05
						Pittsburgh	12	0	1	3.75
29 Rhoden, Rick	R	R	6:03	195	5-16-53	Portland	52	6	3	2.94
						Pittsburgh	127	7	5	3.83
43 Robinson, Don	R	R	6:04	231	6- 8-57	Pittsburgh	160	7	10	3.99
15 Romo, Enrique	R	R	5:11	185	7-15-47	Pittsburgh	124	5	5	3.27
19 Scurry, Rod	L	L	6:02	180	3-17-56	Pittsburgh	38	0	2	2.13
44 Solomon, Eddie	R	R	6:03	190	2- 9-51	Pittsburgh	100	7	3	2.70
27 Tekulve, Kent	R	R	6:04	175	3- 5-47	Pittsburgh	93	8	12	3.39

CATCHERS—						1980 Club	G.	HR.	RBI.	Avg.
35 Alexander, Gary	R	R	6:02	200	3-27-53	Cleveland	76	5	31	.225
16 Nicosia, Steve	R	R	5:10	185	8- 6-55	Pittsburgh	60	1	22	.216
6 Pena, Tony	R	R	6:00	175	11-20-57	Portland	124	9	77	.327
						Pittsburgh	8	0	1	.429

INFIELDERS—										
4 Berra, Dale	R	R	6:00	190	12-13-56	Pittsburgh	93	6	31	.220
11 Bevacqua, Kurt	R	R	6:02	195	1-23-48	S.D.-Pitt.	84	0	16	.228
10 Foli, Tim	R	R	6:00	175	12- 8-50	Pittsburgh	127	3	38	.265
3 Garner, Phil	R	R	5:10	177	4-30-49	Pittsburgh	151	5	58	.259
2 Law, Vance	R	R	6:02	185	10- 1-56	Portland	96	5	54	.295
						Pittsburgh	25	0	3	.230
5 Madlock, Bill	R	R	5:11	185	1-12-51	Pittsburgh	137	10	53	.277
34 Milner, John	L	L	6:00	183	12-28-49	Pittsburgh	114	8	34	.244
8 Stargell, Willie	L	L	6:03	225	3- 6-41	Pittsburgh	67	11	38	.262
30 Thompson, Jason	L	L	6:03	210	7- 6-54	Det.-Cal.	138	21	90	.288

OUTFIELDERS—										
12 Boyland, Dorian	L	L	6:04	204	1- 6-55	Portland	120	14	67	.281
24 Easler, Mike	L	R	6:01	196	11-29-50	Pittsburgh	132	21	74	.338
17 Lacy, Lee	R	R	6:01	175	4-10-48	Pittsburgh	109	7	33	.335
18 Moreno, Omar	L	L	6:03	170	10-24-52	Pittsburgh	162	2	36	.249
39 Parker, Dave	L	R	6:05	230	6- 9-51	Pittsburgh	139	17	79	.295
28 Robinson, Bill	R	R	6:03	197	6-26-43	Pittsburgh	100	12	36	.287

HARVEY HADDIX (31)—Coach   AL MONCHAK (42)—Coach
JOE LONNETT (32)—Coach   BOB SKINNER (48)—Coach

THREE RIVERS STADIUM

	Seats	Prices
Field Boxes	8,089	$7.00
Loge Boxes	7,621	7.00
Lounge Boxes	700	....
Special Boxes	265	....
Club Boxes	3,503	7.00
Terrace Boxes	2,839	6.00
Terrace Reserved	13,794	5.00
Loge Reserved	6,059	3.50
General Admission	11,486	2.50

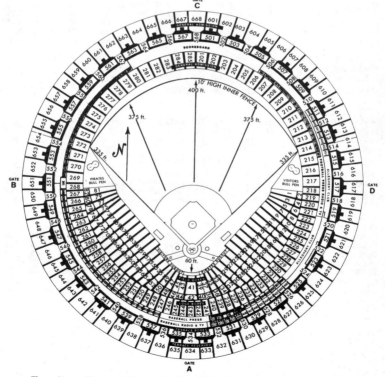

Three Rivers Stadium, Pittsburgh—First N. L. Game Played July 16, 1970

ST. LOUIS CARDINALS

Chairman of the Board and President—
August A. Busch, Jr.
Vice-President—August A. Busch III
General Manager-Manager—Whitey Herzog
Exec. Assisant-Baseball—Joe McDonald
Exec. Assisant-Business—Gary Blase
Exec. V.-P., Bus. Affairs—Joe McShane
Vice-Pres., Public Relations—James L. Toomey
Director of Player Development—Lee Thomas
Director of Scouting—Fred McAlister
Traveling Secretary—C. J. Cherre
Offices—Busch Memorial Stadium
Busch Memorial Stadium Capacity—50,222

Farm System: AAA—Springfield. AA—Arkansas. A—Erie, Gastonia, St. Petersburg. Rookie—Johnson City.

Whitey Herzog

ST. LOUIS CARDINALS' YEARLY STANDING

Year—Position	W.	L.	Pct.	*G.B.	Manager	Attendance
1901—Fourth	76	64	.543	14½	Patrick Donovan	379,988
1902—Sixth........	56	78	.418	44½	Patrick Donovan	226,417
1903—Eighth	43	94	.314	46½	Patrick Donovan	226,538
1904—Fifth........	75	79	.487	31½	Charles (Kid) Nichols	386,750
1905—Sixth........	58	96	.377	47½	C. Nichols, J. Burke, Stan Robison	292,800
1906—Seventh ...	52	98	.347	63	John McCloskey	283,770
1907—Eighth	52	101	.340	55½	John McCloskey	185,377
1908—Eighth	49	105	.318	50	John McCloskey	205,129
1909—Seventh ...	54	98	.355	56	Roger Bresnahan	299,982
1910—Seventh ...	63	90	.412	40½	Roger Bresnahan	355,668
1911—Fifth........	75	74	.503	22	Roger Bresnahan	447,768
1912—Sixth........	63	90	.412	41	Roger Bresnahan	241,759
1913—Eighth	51	99	.340	49	Miller Huggins	203,531
1914—Third	81	72	.529	13	Miller Huggins	256,099
1915—Sixth.......	72	81	.471	18½	Miller Huggins	252,666
1916—Seventh†..	60	93	.392	33½	Miller Huggins	224,308
1917—Third	82	70	.539	15	Miller Huggins	288,491
1918—Eighth	51	78	.395	33	John (Jack) Hendricks	110,599
1919—Seventh ...	54	83	.394	40½	Branch Rickey	167,059
1920—Fifth†	75	79	.487	18	Branch Rickey	326,836
1921—Third	87	66	.569	7	Branch Rickey	384,773
1922—Third†	85	69	.552	8	Branch Rickey	536,998
1923—Fifth........	79	74	.516	16	Branch Rickey	338,551
1924—Sixth.......	65	89	.422	28½	Branch Rickey	272,885
1925—Fourth	77	76	.503	18	B. Rickey, Rogers Hornsby	404,959
1926—First........	89	65	.578	+ 2	Rogers Hornsby	668,428
1927—Second.....	92	61	.601	1½	Robert O'Farrell	749,340
1928—First........	95	59	.617	+ 2	William McKechnie	761,574
1929—Fourth	78	74	.513	20	Wm. McKechnie, Wm. Southworth	399,887
1930—First........	92	62	.597	+ 2	Charles (Gabby) Street	508,501

*Games behind pennant winner. †Tied for position.

ST. LOUIS CARDINALS' YEARLY STANDING—Continued

Year—Position	W.	L.	Pct.	*G.B.	Manager	Attendance
1931—First	101	53	.656	+13	Charles (Gabby) Street	608,535
1932—Sixth†	72	82	.468	18	Charles (Gabby) Street	279,219
1933—Fifth	82	71	.536	9½	Gabby Street, Frank Frisch	256,171
1934—First	95	58	.621	+ 2	Frank Frisch	325,056
1935—Second	96	58	.623	4	Frank Frisch	506,084
1936—Second†	87	67	.565	5	Frank Frisch	448,078
1937—Fourth	81	73	.526	15	Frank Frisch	430,811
1938—Sixth	71	80	.470	17½	Frank Frisch, Mike Gonzalez	291,418
1939—Second	92	61	.601	4½	Raymond Blades	400,245
1940—Third	84	69	.549	16	R. Blades, M. Gonzalez, Southworth	324,078
1941—Second	97	56	.634	2½	William Southworth	633,645
1942—First	106	48	.688	+ 2	William Southworth	553,552
1943—First	105	49	.682	+18	William Southworth	517,135
1944—First	105	49	.682	+14½	William Southworth	461,968
1945—Second	95	59	.617	3	William Southworth	594,630
1946—First‡	98	58	.628	+ 2	Edwin Dyer	1,061,807
1947—Second	89	65	.578	5	Edwin Dyer	1,247,913
1948—Second	85	69	.552	6½	Edwin Dyer	1,111,440
1949—Second	96	58	.623	1	Edwin Dyer	1,430,676
1950—Fifth	78	75	.510	12½	Edwin Dyer	1,093,411
1951—Third	81	73	.526	15½	Martin Marion	1,013,429
1952—Third	88	66	.571	8½	Edward Stanky	913,113
1953—Third†	83	71	.539	22	Edward Stanky	880,242
1954—Sixth	72	82	.468	25	Edward Stanky	1,039,698
1955—Seventh	68	86	.442	30½	Edward Stanky, Harry Walker	849,130
1956—Fourth	76	78	.494	17	Fred Hutchinson	1,029,773
1957—Second	87	67	.565	8	Fred Hutchinson	1,183,575
1958—Fifth†	72	82	.468	20	Fred Hutchinson, Stanley Hack	1,063,730
1959—Seventh	71	83	.461	16	Solly Hemus	929,953
1960—Third	86	68	.558	9	Solly Hemus	1,096,632
1961—Fifth	80	74	.519	13	Solly Hemus, John Keane	855,305
1962—Sixth	84	78	.519	17½	John Keane	953,895
1963—Second	93	69	.574	6	John Keane	1,170,546
1964—First	93	69	.574	+ 1	John Keane	1,143,294
1965—Seventh	80	81	.497	16½	Albert (Red) Schoendienst	1,241,201
1966—Sixth	83	79	.512	12	Albert (Red) Schoendienst	1,712,980
1967—First	101	60	.627	+10½	Albert (Red) Schoendienst	2,090,145
1968—First	97	65	.599	+ 9	Albert (Red) Schoendienst	2,011,167

EAST DIVISION

Year—Position	W.	L.	Pct.	*G.B.	Manager	Attendance
1969—Fourth	87	75	.537	13	Albert (Red) Schoendienst	1,682,783
1970—Fourth	76	86	.469	13	Albert (Red) Schoendienst	1,629,736
1971—Second	90	72	.556	7	Albert (Red) Schoendienst	1,604,671
1972—Fourth	75	81	.481	21½	Albert (Red) Schoendienst	1,196,894
1973—Second	81	81	.500	1½	Albert (Red) Schoendienst	1,574,046
1974—Second	86	75	.534	1½	Albert (Red) Schoendienst	1,838,413
1975—Third†	82	80	.506	10½	Albert (Red) Schoendienst	1,695,270
1976—Fifth	72	90	.444	29	Albert (Red) Schoendienst	1,207,079
1977—Third	83	79	.512	18	Vernon Rapp	1,659,287
1978—Fifth	69	93	.426	21	Vernon Rapp, Kenton Boyer	1,278,215
1979—Third	86	76	.531	12	Kenton Boyer	1,627,256
1980—Fourth	74	88	.457	17	K. Boyer, W. Herzog, Schoendienst	1,385,147

*Games behind winner. †Tied for position. ‡Defeated Brooklyn in pennant playoff.

ST. LOUIS CARDINALS

(24) WHITEY HERZOG—Manager

No. PITCHERS—	Bts.	Thrs.	Hgt.	Wgt.	Birth-date	1980 Club	IP.	W.	L.	ERA.
44 Edelen, Joe	R	R	6:00	165	9-16-55	Arkansas	161	13	5	2.63
31 Forsch, Bob	R	R	6:04	200	1-13-50	St. Louis	215	11	10	3.77
40 Frazier, George	R	R	6:05	205	10-13-54	Springfield	60	1	3	3.00
						St. Louis	23	1	4	2.74
41 Fulgham, John	R	R	6:02	205	6- 9-56	Arkansas	5	0	0	0.00
						St. Louis	85	4	6	3.39
36 Kaat, Jim	L	L	6:06	195	11- 7-38	New York	5	0	1	7.20
						St. Louis	130	8	7	3.81
34 Littell, Mark	L	R	6:03	210	1-17-53	St. Louis	11	0	2	9.00
33 Martin, John	B	L	6:00	190	4-11-56	Ev.-Sprng.	38	2	2	5.92
						Arkansas	27	1	1	1.67
						St. Louis	42	2	3	4.29
35 Martinez, Silvio	R	R	5:11	160	8-31-55	St. Louis	120	5	10	4.80
						St. Pete.	6	0	0	1.50
40 Otten, Jim	R	R	6:02	195	7- 1-51	Springfield	48	6	0	1.69
						St. Louis	55	0	5	5.56
46 Rincon, Andy	R	R	6:03	195	3- 5-59	Arkansas	172	10	7	3.40
						St. Louis	31	3	1	2.61
32 Shirley, Bob	R	L	5:11	180	6-25-54	San Diego	137	11	12	3.55
39 Sorensen, Lary	R	R	6:02	200	10- 4-55	Milwaukee	196	12	10	3.67
42 Sutter, Bruce	R	R	6:02	190	1- 8-53	Chicago NL	102	5	8	2.65
38 Sykes, Bob	B	L	6:02	200	12-11-54	St. Louis	126	6	10	4.64

CATCHERS—	Bts.	Thrs.	Hgt.	Wgt.	Birth-date	1980 Club	G.	HR.	RBI.	Avg.
15 Porter, Darrell	L	R	6:01	195	1-17-52	Kansas City	118	7	51	.249
23 Sanchez, Orlando	L	R	6:00	185	9- 7-56	Okla. City	68	1	21	.307
18 Tenace, Gene	R	R	6:00	195	10-10-46	San Diego	133	17	50	.222

INFIELDERS—	Bts.	Thrs.	Hgt.	Wgt.	Birth-date	1980 Club	G.	HR.	RBI.	Avg.
14 Gonzalez, Julio	R	R	5:11	165	12-25-53	Tucson	38	2	25	.295
						Houston	40	0	1	.115
37 Hernandez, Keith	L	L	6:00	185	10-20-53	St. Louis	159	16	99	.321
28 Herr, Tom	B	R	6:00	175	4- 4-56	Springfield	37	1	16	.312
						St. Louis	76	0	15	.248
10 Oberkfell, Ken	L	R	6:01	185	5- 4-56	St. Louis	116	3	46	.303
5 Ramsey, Mike	B	R	6:01	170	3-29-54	Springfield	21	0	6	.261
						St. Louis	59	0	8	.262
1 Templeton, Garry	B	R	5:11	170	3-24-56	St. Louis	118	4	43	.319

OUTFIELDERS—	Bts.	Thrs.	Hgt.	Wgt.	Birth-date	1980 Club	G.	HR.	RBI.	Avg.
26 Braun, Steve	L	R	5:10	180	5- 8-48	Syracuse	19	2	11	.328
						K.C.-Tor.	51	1	10	.205
25 Hendrick, George	R	R	6:03	195	10-18-49	St. Louis	150	25	109	.302
19 Iorg, Dane	L	R	6:00	180	5-11-50	St. Louis	105	3	36	.303
21 Landrum, Tito	R	R	5:11	175	10-25-54	Springfield	93	12	46	.303
						St. Louis	35	0	7	.247
16 Lezcano, Sixto	R	R	5:10	175	11-28-53	Milwaukee	112	18	55	.229
30 Scott, Tony	B	R	6:00	175	9-18-51	St. Louis	143	0	28	.251

CHUCK HILLER (4)—Coach   HAL LANIER (8)—Coach
HUB KITTLE (9)—Coach   DAVE RICKETTS (3)—Coach
RED SCHOENDIENST (2)—Coach

BUSCH MEMORIAL STADIUM

	Seats	Prices
Deluxe Boxes	390	*
Box Seats	14,643	$7.00
Reserved Seats	23,025	5.50
General Admission	8,082	3.50
Bleachers	4,082	2.50

*Sold only on season basis

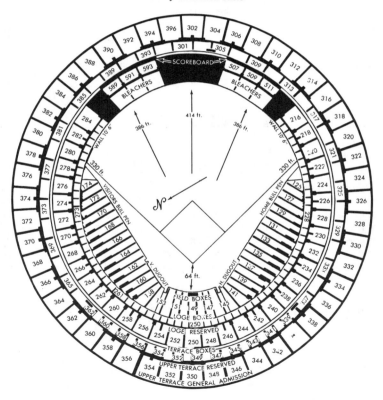

Busch Memorial Stadium, St. Louis—First N. L. Game Played May 12, 1966

Frank Howard

SAN DIEGO PADRES

Owner and Chairman of Board—Ray A. Kroc
Director—Joan Kroc
President and Director—Ballard Smith
Director, Baseball Operations—Jack McKeon
Director, Business Operations—Elten Schiller
Director, Minor Leagues—Jim Weigel
Director of Public Relations—Bob Chandler
Traveling Secretary—John Mattei
Offices—San Diego Stadium
San Diego Stadium Capacity—51,309

Farm System: AAA—Hawaii. AA—Amarillo. A—Reno,
Salem, Walla Walla. Rookie—Bradenton.

SAN DIEGO PADRES' YEARLY STANDING

WEST DIVISION

Year—Position	W.	L.	Pct.	*G.B.	Manager	Attendance
1969—Sixth	52	110	.321	41	Pedro (Preston) Gomez	512,970
1970—Sixth	63	99	.389	39	Pedro (Preston) Gomez	643,679
1971—Sixth	61	100	.379	28½	Pedro (Preston) Gomez	557,513
1972—Sixth	58	95	.379	36½	Preston Gomez, Donald Zimmer	644,273
1973—Sixth	60	102	.370	39	Donald Zimmer	611,826
1974—Sixth	60	102	.370	42	John McNamara	1,075,399
1975—Fourth	71	91	.438	37	John McNamara	1,281,747
1976—Fifth	73	89	.451	29	John McNamara	1,458,478
1977—Fifth	69	93	.426	29	John McNamara, Alvin Dark	1,376,269
1978—Fourth	84	78	.519	11	Roger Craig	1,670,107
1979—Fifth	68	93	.422	22	Roger Craig	1,456,967
1980—Sixth	73	89	.451	19½	Gerald Coleman	1,139,026

*Games behind winner.

SAN DIEGO PADRES

(33) FRANK HOWARD–Manager

No. PITCHERS–	Bts.	Thrs.	Hgt.	Wgt.	Birth-date	1980 Club	IP.	W.	L.	ERA.
30 Boone, Dan	L	L	5:08	135	1-14-54	Amarillo	73	5	4	2.96
						Hawaii	14	2	0	1.29
51 Curtis, John	L	L	6:02	185	3- 9-48	San Diego	187	10	8	3.51
13 Eichelberger, Juan	R	R	6:02	195	10-21-53	Hawaii	77	7	3	3.51
						San Diego	89	4	2	3.64
50 Littlefield, John	R	R	6:02	200	1- 5-54	Springfield	32	3	0	2.25
						St. Louis	66	5	5	3.14
48 Lollar, Tim	L	L	6:03	200	3-17-56	Columbus	49	2	1	2.57
						New York AL	32	1	0	3.38
25 Lucas, Gary	L	L	6:05	200	11- 8-54	San Diego	150	5	8	3.24
27 Mura, Steve	R	R	6:02	188	2-12-55	San Diego	169	8	7	3.67
46 Olmsted, Al	R	L	6:02	195	3-18-57	Arkansas	55	3	4	3.27
						Springfield	117	10	5	2.77
						St. Louis	35	1	1	2.83
45 Seaman, Kim	L	L	6:03	205	5- 6-57	Springfield	37	2	3	4.62
						St. Louis	24	3	2	2.38
42 Stablein, George	R	R	6:04	185	10-29-57	Hawaii	153	12	7	3.88
						San Diego	12	0	1	3.00
49 Tellmann, Tom	R	R	6:04	185	3-29-54	Hawaii	170	13	5	3.23
						San Diego	22	3	0	1.64
38 Urrea, John	R	R	6:03	205	2- 9-55	Springfield	92	5	4	3.52
						St. Louis	65	4	1	3.46
26 Welsh, Chris	L	L	6:02	185	4- 4-55	Columbus, O.	158	9	12	2.73
40 Wise, Rick	R	R	6:02	195	9-13-45	San Diego	154	6	8	3.68

CATCHERS–	Bts.	Thrs.	Hgt.	Wgt.	Birth-date	1980 Club	G.	HR.	RBI.	Avg.
16 Kennedy, Terry	L	R	6:04	220	6- 4-56	St. Louis	84	4	34	.254
7 Stimac, Craig	R	R	6:02	185	11-18-54	Hawaii	110	11	47	.298
						San Diego	20	0	7	.220
9 Swisher, Steve	R	R	6:02	205	8- 9-51	St. Louis	18	0	2	.250

INFIELDERS–	Bts.	Thrs.	Hgt.	Wgt.	Birth-date	1980 Club	G.	HR.	RBI.	Avg.
5 Bass, Randy	L	R	6:01	210	3-13-54	Denver	123	37	143	.333
						San Diego	19	3	8	.286
3 Bonilla, Juan	R	R	5:09	170	2-12-56	Tacoma	139	4	55	.303
8 Evans, Barry	R	R	6:01	180	11-30-56	San Diego	73	1	14	.232
						Hawaii	28	2	15	.250
6 Flannery, Tim	L	R	5:11	170	9-29-57	Hawaii	47	1	16	.346
						San Diego	95	0	25	.240
15 Perkins, Broderick	L	L	5:10	180	11-23-54	Hawaii	118	6	65	.312
						San Diego	43	2	14	.370
10 Phillips, Mike	L	R	6:01	185	8-19-50	St. Louis	63	0	7	.234
4 Salazar, Luis	R	R	6:00	185	5-19-56	Port.-Hawaii	127	9	64	.316
						San Diego	44	1	25	.337
1 Smith, Ozzie	B	R	5:10	150	12-26-54	San Diego	158	0	35	.230

OUTFIELDERS–	Bts.	Thrs.	Hgt.	Wgt.	Birth-date	1980 Club	G.	HR.	RBI.	Avg.
24 Edwards, Dave	R	R	6:00	170	2-24-54	Minnesota	81	2	20	.250
22 Jones, Ruppert	L	L	5:10	171	3-12-55	New York AL	83	9	42	.223
18 Lefebvre, Joe	L	R	5:10	170	2-22-56	New York AL	74	8	21	.227
						Columbus	56	10	26	.278
17 Richards, Gene	L	L	6:00	175	9-29-53	San Diego	158	4	41	.301
20 Turner, Jerry	L	L	5:09	180	1-17-54	San Diego	85	3	18	.288
53 Wiggins, Al	B	R	6:02	160	2-17-58	Lodi	135	0	35	.288

CHUCK ESTRADA (23)–Coach   BOBBY TOLAN (28)–Coach
JACK KROL (34)–Coach   ED BRINKMAN (37)–Coach

SAN DIEGO STADIUM

	Seats	Prices
Club-Press Box Seats	2,183	$6.50
Field Box Seats	6,394	6.50
Plaza Reserved Seats	11,945	5.50
Loge Reserved Seats	8,741	5.00
Upper Reserved Seats	2,228	4.50
General Admission	16,445	3.00
Right Field Pavilion	3,373	3.00

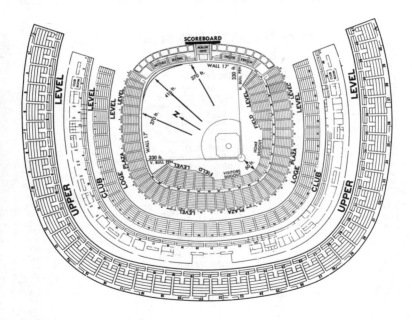

San Diego Stadium, San Diego—First N. L. Game Played April 8, 1969

Frank Robinson

SAN FRANCISCO GIANTS

President—Robert Lurie
Vice-Pres.-Administration—Corey Busch
Vice-Pres.-Baseball—Spec Richardson
Vice-Pres.-Business—Pat Gallagher
Baseball Consultant—Jerry Donovan
Director of Scouting and Minor League Operations—
                                    Jack Schwarz
Publicity Director—Duffy Jennings
Traveling Secretary-Statistician—Ralph Nelson
Offices—Candlestick Park
Candlestick Park Capacity—58,945

Farm System: AAA—Phoenix. AA—Shreveport. A—Clinton, Fresno. Rookie—Great Falls.

SAN FRANCISCO GIANTS' YEARLY STANDING

(New York Giants Prior to 1958)

Year—Position	W.	L.	Pct.	*G.B.	Manager	Attendance
1901—Seventh ...	52	85	.380	37	George S. Davis	297,650
1902—Eighth	48	88	.353	53½	H. Fogel, G. Smith, J. McGraw	302,875
1903—Second....	84	55	.604	6½	John McGraw	579,530
1904—First........	106	47	.693	+13	John McGraw	609,826
1905—First........	105	48	.686	+ 9	John McGraw	552,700
1906—Second....	96	56	.632	20	John McGraw	402,850
1907—Fourth.....	82	71	.536	25½	John McGraw	538,350
1908—Second† ...	98	56	.636	1	John McGraw	910,000
1909—Third......	92	61	.601	18½	John McGraw	783,700
1910—Second....	91	63	.591	13	John McGraw	511,785
1911—First........	99	54	.647	+ 7½	John McGraw	675,000
1912—First........	103	48	.682	+10	John McGraw	638,000
1913—First........	101	51	.664	+12½	John McGraw	630,000
1914—Second....	84	70	.545	10½	John McGraw	364,313
1915—Eighth	69	83	.454	21	John McGraw	391,850
1916—Fourth.....	86	66	.566	7	John McGraw	552,056
1917—First........	98	56	.636	+10	John McGraw	500,264
1918—Second.....	71	53	.573	10½	John McGraw	256,618
1919—Second.....	87	53	.621	9	John McGraw	708,857
1920—Second.....	86	68	.558	7	John McGraw	929,609
1921—First........	94	59	.614	+ 4	John McGraw	773,477
1922—First........	93	61	.604	+ 7	John McGraw	945,809
1923—First........	95	58	.621	+ 4½	John McGraw	820,780
1924—First........	93	60	.608	+ 1½	John McGraw	844,068
1925—Second.....	86	66	.566	8½	John McGraw	778,993
1926—Fifth........	74	77	.490	13½	John McGraw	700,362
1927—Third.......	92	62	.597	2	John McGraw	858,190
1928—Second.....	93	61	.604	2	John McGraw	916,191
1929—Third.......	84	67	.556	13½	John McGraw	868,806

SAN FRANCISCO GIANTS' YEARLY STANDING— Continued

Year—Position	W.	L.	Pct.	*G.B.	Manager	Attendance
1930—Third	87	67	.565	5	John McGraw	868,714
1931—Second	87	65	.572	13	John McGraw	812,163
1932—Sixth†	72	82	.468	18	John McGraw, William Terry	484,868
1933—First	91	61	.599	+ 5	William Terry	604,471
1934—Second	93	60	.608	2	William Terry	730,851
1935—Third	91	62	.595	8½	William Terry	748,748
1936—First	92	62	.597	+ 5	William Terry	837,952
1937—First	95	57	.625	+ 3	William Terry	926,887
1938—Third	83	67	.553	5	William Terry	799,633
1939—Fifth	77	74	.510	18½	William Terry	702,457
1940—Sixth	72	80	.474	27½	William Terry	747,852
1941—Fifth	74	79	.484	25½	William Terry	763,098
1942—Third	85	67	.559	20	Melvin Ott	779,621
1943—Eighth	55	98	.359	49½	Melvin Ott	466,095
1944—Fifth	67	87	.435	38	Melvin Ott	674,083
1945—Fifth	78	74	.513	19	Melvin Ott	1,016,468
1946—Eighth	61	93	.396	36	Melvin Ott	1,219,873
1947—Fourth	81	73	.526	13	Melvin Ott	1,600,793
1948—Fifth	78	76	.506	13½	Melvin Ott, Leo Durocher	1,459,269
1949—Fifth	73	81	.474	24	Leo Durocher	1,218,446
1950—Third	86	68	.558	5	Leo Durocher	1,008,876
1951—First‡	98	59	.624	+ 1	Leo Durocher	1,059,539
1952—Second	92	62	.597	4½	Leo Durocher	984,940
1953—Fifth	70	84	.455	35	Leo Durocher	811,518
1954—First	97	57	.630	+ 5	Leo Durocher	1,155,067
1955—Third	80	74	.519	18½	Leo Durocher	824,112
1956—Sixth	67	87	.435	26	William Rigney	629,179
1957—Sixth	69	85	.448	26	William Rigney	653,923
1958—Third	80	74	.519	12	William Rigney	1,272,625
1959—Third	83	71	.539	4	William Rigney	1,422,130
1960—Fifth	79	75	.513	16	William Rigney, Thomas Sheehan	1,795,356
1961—Third	85	69	.552	8	Alvin Dark	1,390,679
1962—First§	103	62	.624	+ 1	Alvin Dark	1,592,594
1963—Third	88	74	.543	11	Alvin Dark	1,571,306
1964—Fourth	90	72	.556	3	Alvin Dark	1,504,364
1965—Second	95	67	.586	2	Herman Franks	1,546,075
1966—Second	93	68	.578	1½	Herman Franks	1,657,192
1967—Second	91	71	.562	10½	Herman Franks	1,242,480
1968—Second	88	74	.543	9	Herman Franks	837,220

*Games behind pennant winner. †Tied for position. ‡Defeated Brooklyn in pennant playoff. §Defeated Los Angeles in pennant playoff.

WEST DIVISION

Year—Position	W.	L.	Pct.	*G.B.	Manager	Attendance
1969—Second	90	72	.556	3	Clyde King	873,603
1970—Third	86	76	.531	16	Clyde King, Charles Fox	740,720
1971—First†	90	72	.556	+ 1	Charles Fox	1,106,043
1972—Fifth	69	86	.445	26½	Charles Fox	647,744
1973—Third	88	74	.543	11	Charles Fox	834,193
1974—Fifth	72	90	.444	30	Charles Fox, Wesley Westrum	519,987
1975—Third	80	81	.497	27½	Wesley Westrum	522,919
1976—Fourth	74	88	.457	28	William Rigney	626,868
1977—Fourth	75	87	.463	23	Joseph Altobelli	700,056
1978—Third	89	73	.549	6	Joseph Altobelli	1,740,477
1979—Fourth	71	91	.438	19½	Joseph Altobelli, J. David Bristol	1,456,402
1980—Fifth	75	86	.466	17	J. David Bristol	1,096,115

*Games behind winner. †Lost Championship Series.

SAN FRANCISCO GIANTS

(20) FRANK ROBINSON—Manager

No. PITCHERS—	Bts.	Thrs.	Hgt.	Wgt.	Birth-date	1980 Club	IP.	W.	L.	ERA.
33 Alexander, Doyle	R	R	6:03	200	9- 4-50	Atlanta	232	14	11	4.19
14 Blue, Vida	B	L	6:00	200	7-28-49	San Fran.	224	14	10	2.97
34 Bordley, Bill	L	L	6:02	200	1- 9-58	Phoenix	111	4	8	5.35
						San Fran.	31	2	3	4.65
48 Breining, Fred	R	R	6:04	185	11-15-55	Phoenix	100	6	13	4.14
						San Fran.	7	0	0	5.14
43 Griffin, Tom	R	R	6:03	210	2-22-48	San Fran.	108	5	1	2.75
						Shreveport	81	2	6	1.78
40 Hargesheimer, Al	R	R	6:03	200	11-21-56	Phoenix	17	1	1	4.24
						San Fran.	75	4	6	4.32
19 Holland, Al	R	L	5:11	210	8-16-52	San Fran.	82	5	3	1.76
46 Lavelle, Gary	B	L	6:02	205	1- 3-49	San Fran.	100	6	8	3.42
38 Minton, Greg	B	R	6:02	191	7-29-51	San Fran.	91	4	6	2.47
17 Moffitt, Randy	R	R	6:03	195	10-13-48	San Fran.	17	1	1	4.76
45 Ripley, Allen	R	R	6:03	200	10-18-52	Phoenix	44	5	0	2.45
						San Fran.	113	9	10	4.14
28 Rowland, Mike	R	R	6:03	205	1-31-53	Phoenix	140	5	11	4.56
						San Fran.	27	1	1	2.33
32 Whitson, Ed	R	R	6:03	200	5-19-55	San Fran.	212	11	13	3.10

CATCHERS—						1980 Club	G.	HR.	RBI.	Avg.
7 May, Milt	L	R	6:00	192	8- 1-50	San Fran.	111	6	50	.260
3 Sadek, Mike	R	R	5:10	170	5-30-46	San Fran.	1	64	16	.252

INFIELDERS—										
23 Cabell, Enos	R	R	6:05	185	10- 8-49	Houston	152	2	55	.276
41 Evans, Darrell	L	R	6:02	205	5-26-47	San Fran.	154	20	78	.264
15 Ivie, Mike	R	R	6:04	215	8- 8-52	San Fran.	79	4	25	.241
10 LeMaster, Johnnie	R	R	6:02	165	6-19-54	San Fran.	135	3	31	.215
8 Morgan, Joe	L	R	5:07	160	9-19-43	Houston	141	11	49	.243
2 Pettini, Joe	R	R	5:09	165	1-26-55	Phoenix	85	2	32	.282
						San Fran.	63	1	9	.232
21 Smith, Billy	B	R	6:01	165	7-14-53	Okla. City	72	5	37	.278
6 Stennett, Rennie	R	R	5:11	185	4- 5-51	San Fran.	120	2	37	.244

OUTFIELDERS—										
22 Clark, Jack	R	R	6:03	205	11-10-55	San Fran.	127	22	82	.284
30 Davis, Charles	B	R	6:03	195	1-17-60	Shreveport	129	12	67	.294
18 Figueroa, Jesus	L	L	5:10	160	2-20-57	Wichita	11	1	3	.103
						Chicago	115	1	11	.253
31 Herndon, Larry	R	R	6:03	195	11- 3-53	San Fran.	139	8	49	.258
25 Martin, Jerry	R	R	6:01	195	5-11-49	Chicago NL	141	23	73	.227
36 North, Bill	B	R	5:11	185	5-15-48	San Fran.	128	1	19	.251
49 Venable, Max	L	R	5:10	185	6- 6-57	Phoenix	78	5	40	.285
						San Fran.	64	0	10	.268
1 Wohlford, Jim	R	R	5:11	175	2-28-51	San Fran.	91	1	24	.280

DON BUFORD (9)—Coach   JOHN VAN ORNUM (42)—Coach
JIM DAVENPORT (12)—Coach   DON McMAHON (47)—Coach
JIM LEFEBVRE (5)—Coach

CANDLESTICK PARK

	Seats	Prices
Mezzanine Boxes	556	$8.00
Box Seats	15,672	6.00
Reserved Seats	35,917	5.00
General Admission	6,800	1.00

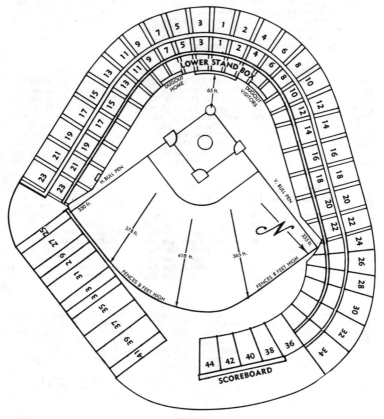

Candlestick Park, San Francisco—First N. L. Game Played April 12, 1960

The Sporting News
Major League All-Star Teams

1925
Bottomley, St. L. NL 1B
Hornsby, St. Louis NL .. 2B
Wright, Pittsburgh NL .. SS
Traynor, Pittsb'gh NL .. 3B
Cuyler, Pittsb'gh NL...... OF
Carey, Pittsb'gh NL ...,.. OF
Goslin, Wash'ton AL...... OF
Cochrane, Phila. AL...... C
Johnson, Wash'ton AL .. P
Rommel, Phila. AL........ P
Vance, Brooklyn NL ...... P

1926
G. Burns, Cleve. AL
Hornsby, St. Louis NL
J. Sewell, Cleve. AL
Traynor, Pittsb'gh NL
Goslin, Wash'ton AL
Mostil, Chicago AL
Ruth, New York AL
O'Farrell, St. Louis NL
Pennock, N. York AL
Uhle, Cleveland AL
Alexander, St. L. NL

1927
1B—Gehrig, N. York AL
2B—Hornsby, N. York NL
SS—Jackson, N. York AL
3B—Traynor, Pitts. NL
OF—Ruth, New York AL
OF—Simmons, Phila. AL
OF—P. Waner, Pitts. NL
C—Hartnett, Chicago NL
P—Root, Chicago, NL
P—Lyons, Chicago AL

1928
Gehrig, New York AL.... 1B
Hornsby, Boston NL 2B
Jackson, N. York NL .... SS
Lindstrom, N. Y. NL 3B
Ruth, New York AL ...... OF
Manush, St. Louis AL.... OF
P. Waner, Pitts. NL ...... OF
Cochrane, Phila. AL...... C
Grove, Phila'phia AL .... P
Hoyt, New York AL ...... P

1929
Foxx, Phila'phia AL
Hornsby, Chicago NL
Jackson, N. York NL
Traynor, Pittsb'gh NL
Simmons, Phila. AL
L. Wilson, Chi. NL
Ruth, New York AL
Cochrane, Phila. AL
Grove, Phila'phia AL
Grimes, Pittsburgh NL

1930
1B—Terry, New York NL
2B—Frisch, St. Louis NL
SS—Cronin, Wash'ton, AL
3B—Lindstrom, N. Y. NL
OF—Simmons, Phila. AL
OF—L. Wilson, Chi. NL
OF—Ruth, New York AL
C—Cochrane, Phila. AL
P—Grove, Phila'phia AL
P—W. Ferrell, Cleve. AL

1931
Gehrig, New York AL.... 1B
Frisch, St. Louis NL...... 2B
Cronin, Wash'ton AL .... SS
Traynor, Pittsb'gh NL .. 3B
Simmons, Phila. AL ...... OF
Averill, Cleve'd AL........ OF
Ruth, New York AL ...... OF
Cochrane, Phila. AL...... C
Grove, Phila'phia AL .... P
Earnshaw, Phila. AL .... P

1932
Foxx, Phila'phia AL
Lazzeri, N. York AL
Cronin, Wash'ton AL
Traynor, Pittsb'gh NL
O'Doul, Brooklyn NL
Averill, Cleveland AL
Klein, Phila'phia NL
Dickey, New York AL
Grove, Phila'phia AL
Warneke, Chicago NL

1933
1B—Foxx, Phila'phia AL
2B—Gehringer, Det. AL
SS—Cronin, Wash'ton AL
3B—Traynor, Pitts. NL
OF—Simmons, Chi. AL
OF—Berger, Boston NL
OF—Klein, Phila'phia NL
C—Dickey, N. York AL
P—Crowder, Wash'ton AL
P—Hubbell, N. York NL

1934
Gehrig, New York AL.... 1B
Gehringer, Det. AL........ 2B
Cronin, Wash'ton AL .... SS
Higgins, Phil'phia AL 3B
Simmons, Chicago AL .. OF
Averill, Cleveland AL .... OF
Ott, New York NL .... OF
Cochrane, Detroit AL C
Gomez, New York AL.... P
Rowe, Detroit AL .... P
J. Dean, St. Louis NL .... P

1935
Greenberg, Det. AL
Gehringer, Det. AL
Vaughan, Pitts. NL
J. Martin, St. L. NL
Medwick, St. L. NL
Cramer, Phila. AL
Ott, New York NL
Cochrane, Detroit AL
Hubbell, N. York NL
J. Dean, St. Louis NL

1936
1B—Gehrig, New York AL
2B—Gehringer, Det. AL
SS—Appling, Chicago AL
3B—Higgins, Phila. AL
OF—Medwick, St. L. NL
OF—Averill, Cleve. AL
OF—Ott, New York NL
C—Dickey, New York AL
P—Hubbell, N. York NL
P—J. Dean, St. Louis NL

1937

Gehrig, New York AL.... 1B
Gehringer, Det. AL...... 2B
Bartell, New York NL .. SS
Rolfe, New York AL...... 3B
Medwick, St. L. NL ...... OF
J. DiMaggio, N.Y. AL.... OF
P. Waner, Pitts. NL ...... OF
Hartnett, Chicago, NL .. C
Hubbell, New York NL .. P
Ruffing, New York AL .. P

1938

Foxx, Boston AL
Gehringer, Detroit AL
Cronin, Boston AL
Rolfe, New York AL
Medwick, St. Louis NL
J. DiMaggio, N. Y. AL
Ott, New York NL
Dickey, New York AL
Ruffing, New York AL
Gomez, New York AL
Vander Meer, Cin. NL

1939

1B—Foxx, Boston, AL
2B—Gordon, N. York AL
SS—Cronin, Boston AL
3B—Rolfe, New York AL
OF—Medwick, St. L. NL
OF—J. DiMaggio, N.Y. AL
OF—Williams, Boston AL
C—Dickey, N. York AL
P—Ruffing, N. York AL
P—Feller, Cleveland AL
P—Walters, Cinn. NL

1940

F. McCor'ick, Cin. NL .. 1B
Gordon, N. York AL 2B
Appling, Chicago AL...... SS
Hack, Chicago NL 3B
Greenberg, Det. AL ...... OF
J. DiMaggio, N.Y. AL.... OF
Williams, Boston AL .... OF
Danning, N. York NL C
Feller, Cleveland AL .... P
Walters, Cinn. NL.......... P
Derringer, Cinn. NL ...... P

1941

Camilli, Brooklyn NL
Gordon, N. York AL
Travis, Wash'ton AL
Hack, Chicago NL
Williams, Boston AL
J. DiMaggio, N. Y. AL
Reiser, Brooklyn NL
Dickey, New York AL
Feller, Cleveland AL
Wyatt, Brooklyn NL
Lee, Chicago NL

1942

1B—Mize, New York NL
2B—Gordon, N. York AL
SS—Pesky, Boston AL
3B—Hack, Chicago NL
OF—Williams, Boston AL
OF—J. DiMaggio, N. Y. AL
OF—Slaughter, St. L. NL
C—Owen, Brooklyn NL
P—M. Cooper, St. L. NL
P—Bonham, N. York AL
P—Hughson, Boston AL

1943

York, Detroit AL 1B
Herman, Brooklyn NL .. 2B
Appling, Chicago AL...... SS
Johnson, N. York AL 3B
Wakefield, Detroit AL.... OF
Musial, St. Louis NL...... OF
Nicholson, Chi. NL .... OF
W. Cooper, St. L. NL C
Chandler, N. Y. AL ...... P
M. Cooper, St. L. NL .... P
Sewell, Pittsburgh NL .. P

1944

Sanders, St. Louis NL
Doerr, Boston AL
Marion, St. Louis NL
Elliott, Pittsburgh NL
Musial, St. Louis NL
Wakefield, Detroit AL
F. Walker, Brkn. NL
W. Cooper, St. L. NL
Newhouser, Det. AL
M. Cooper, St. L. NL
Trout, Detroit AL

1945

1B—Cavarretta, Chi. NL
2B—Stirnweiss, N. Y. AL
SS—Marion, St. Louis NL
3B—Kurowski, St. L. NL
OF—Holmes, Boston NL
OF—Pafko, Chicago NL
OF—Rosen, Brooklyn, NL
C—Richards, Detroit AL
P—Newhouser, Detroit AL
P—Ferriss, Boston AL
P—Borowy, Chicago NL

1946

Musial, St. Louis NL...... 1B
Doerr, Boston AL 2B
Pesky, Boston AL.......... SS
Kell, Detroit AL 3B
Williams, Boston AL...... OF
D. DiMaggio, Bos. AL..... OF
Slaughter, St. Louis NL.. OF
Robinson, N. York AL .. C
Newhouser, Detroit AL.. P
Feller, Cleveland AL .... P
Ferriss, Boston AL........ P

1947

Mize, New York NL
Gordon, Cleveland AL
Boudreau, Cleve. AL
Kell, Detroit AL
Williams, Boston AL
J. DiMaggio, N.Y. AL
Kiner, Pittsburgh NL
W. Cooper, N. Y. NL
Blackwell, Cinn. NL
Feller, Cleveland AL
Branca, Brooklyn NL

1948

1B—Mize, New York NL
2B—Gordon, Clevel'd AL
SS—Boudreau, Cleve. AL
3B—Elliott, Boston NL
OF—Williams, Boston AL
OF—J. DiMaggio, N.Y. AL
OF—Musial, St. Louis NL
C—Tebbetts, Boston AL
P—Sain, Boston NL
P—Lemon, Cleveland AL
P—Brecheen, St. L. NL

1949

Henrich, N. York AL	1B
Robinson, Brkn. NL	2B
Rizzuto, N. York AL	SS
Kell, Detroit AL	3B
Williams, Boston AL	OF
Musial, St. Louis NL	OF
Kiner, Pittsburgh NL	OF
Campanella, Brkn. NL	C
Parnell, Boston AL	P
Kinder, Boston AL	P
Page, New York AL	P

1950

Dropo, Boston AL
Robinson, Brkn. NL
Rizzuto, New York AL
Kell, Detroit AL
Musial, St. Louis NL
Kiner, Pittsburgh NL
Doby, Cleveland AL
Berra, New York AL
Raschi, New York AL
Lemon, Cleveland AL
Konstanty, Phila. NL

1951

1B—Fain, Philadelphia AL
2B—Robinson, Brkn. NL
SS—Rizzuto, N. York AL
3B—Kell, Detroit AL
OF—Musial, St. Louis NL
OF—Williams, Boston AL
OF—Kiner, Pittsburgh NL
C—Campanella, Brkn. NL
P—Maglie, New York NL
P—Roe, Brooklyn NL
P—Reynolds, N. York AL

1952

Fain, Phila'phia AL	1B
Robinson, Brkn. NL	2B
Rizzuto, New York AL	SS
Kell, Boston AL	3B
Musial, St. Louis NL	OF
Sauer, Chicago NL	OF
Mantle, N. York AL	OF
Berra, New York AL	C
Roberts, Phila'phia NL	P
Shantz, Phila'phia AL	P
Reynolds, N. York AL	P

1953

Vernon, Wash'ton AL
Schoendi'st, St. L. NL
Reese, Brooklyn NL
Rosen, Cleveland AL
Musial, St. Louis NL
Snider, Brooklyn NL
Furillo, Brooklyn NL
Campanella, Brkn. NL
Roberts, Phila'phia NL
Spahn, Milwaukee NL
Porterfield, Wash. AL

1954

1B—Kluszewski, Cinn. NL
2B—Avila, Cleveland AL
SS—Dark, New York NL
3B—Rosen, Cleveland AL
OF—Mays, New York NL
OF—Musial, St. Louis NL
OF—Snider, Brooklyn NL
C—Berra, New York AL
P—Lemon, Cleveland AL
P—Antonelli, N. York NL
P—Roberts, Phila'phia NL

1955

Kluszewski, Cinn. NL	1B
Fox, Chicago AL	2B
Banks, Chicago NL	SS
Mathews, Milw. NL	3B
Snider, Brooklyn NL	OF
Williams, Boston AL	OF
Kaline, Detroit AL	OF
Campanella, Brkn. NL	C
Roberts, Phila. NL	P
Newcombe, Brkn. NL	P
Ford, New York AL	P

1956

Kluszewski, Cinn. NL
Fox, Chicago AL
Kuenn, Detroit AL
Boyer, St. Louis NL
Mantle, New York AL
Aaron, Milwaukee NL
Williams, Boston AL
Berra, New York AL
Newcombe, Brkn. NL
Ford, New York AL
Pierce, Chicago AL

1957

1B—Musial, St. Louis NL
2B—Scho'st, N.Y-Mil. NL
SS—McDougald, N.Y. AL
3B—Mathews, Milw. NL
OF—Mantle, N. Y. AL
OF—Williams, Boston AL
OF—Mays, New York NL
C—Berra, New York AL
P—Spahn, Milwaukee NL
P—Pierce, Chicago AL
P—Bunning, Detroit AL

1958

Musial, St. Louis NL	1B
Fox, Chicago AL	2B
Banks, Chicago NL	SS
Thomas, Pitts. NL	3B
Williams, Boston AL	OF
Mays, San Fran. NL	OF
Aaron, Milwaukee NL	OF
Crandall, Milw. NL	C
Turley, New York AL	P
Spahn, Milwaukee NL	P
Friend, Pittsburgh NL	P

1959

Cepeda, San Fran. NL
Fox, Chicago AL
Banks, Chicago NL
Mathews, Milw. NL
Minoso, Cleveland AL
Mays, San Fran. NL
Aaron, Milwaukee NL
Lollar, Chicago AL
Wynn, Chicago AL
S. Jones, S. Fran. NL
Antonelli, S. Fran. NL

1960

1B—Skowron, N. Y. AL
2B—Mazeroski, Pitts. NL
SS—Banks, Chicago NL
3B—Mathews, Milw. NL
OF—Minoso, Chicago AL
OF—Mays, San Fran. NL
OF—Maris, New York AL
C—Crandall, Milw. NL
P—Law, Pittsburgh NL
P—Spahn, Milw. NL
P—Broglio, St. Louis NL

1961–National

1B–Orlando Cepeda, San Francisco
2B–Frank Bolling, Milwaukee
SS–Maury Wills, Los Angeles
3B–Ken Boyer, St. Louis
OF–Willie Mays, San Francisco
OF–Frank Robinson, Cincinnati
OF–Roberto Clemente, Pittsburgh
C–Smoky Burgess, Pittsburgh
P–Joey Jay, Cincinnati
P–Warren Spahn, Milwaukee

1961–American

1B–Norm Cash, Detroit
2B–Bobby Richardson, New York
SS–Tony Kubek, New York
3B–Brooks Robinson, Baltimore
OF–Mickey Mantle, New York
OF–Roger Maris, New York
OF–Rocky Colavito, Detroit
C–Elston Howard, New York
P–Whitey Ford, New York
P–Frank Lary, Detroit

1962–National

1B–Orlando Cepeda, San Francisco
2B–Bill Mazeroski, Pittsburgh
SS–Maury Wills, Los Angeles
3B–Ken Boyer, St. Louis
OF–Tommy Davis, Los Angeles
OF–Willie Mays, San Francisco
OF–Frank Robinson, Cincinnati
C–Del Crandall, Milwaukee
P–Don Drysdale, Los Angeles
P–Bob Purkey, Cincinnati

1962–American

1B–Norm Siebern, Kansas City
2B–Bobby Richardson, New York
SS–Tom Tresh, New York
3B–Brooks Robinson, Baltimore
OF–Leon Wagner, Los Angeles
OF–Mickey Mantle, New York
OF–Al Kaline, Detroit
C–Earl Battey, Minnesota
P–Ralph Terry, New York
P–Dick Donovan, Cleveland

1963–National

1B–Bill White, St. Louis
2B–Jim Gilliam, Los Angeles
SS–Dick Groat, St. Louis
3B–Ken Boyer, St. Louis
OF–Tommy Davis, Los Angeles
OF–Willie Mays, San Francisco
OF–Hank Aaron, Milwaukee
C–John Edwards, Cincinnati
P–Sandy Koufax, Los Angeles
P–Juan Marichal, San Francisco

1963–American

1B–Joe Pepitone, New York
2B–Bobby Richardson, New York
SS–Luis Aparicio, Baltimore
3B–Frank Malzone, Boston
OF–Carl Yastrzemski, Boston
OF–Albie Pearson, Los Angeles
OF–Al Kaline, Detroit
C–Elston Howard, New York
P–Whitey Ford, New York
P–Gary Peters, Chicago

1964–American

1B–Dick Stuart, Boston
2B–Bobby Richardson, New York
SS–Jim Fregosi, Los Angeles
3B–Brooks Robinson, Baltimore
OF–Harmon Killebrew, Minnesota
OF–Mickey Mantle, New York
OF–Tony Oliva, Minnesota
C–Elston Howard, New York
P–Dean Chance, Los Angeles
P–Gary Peters, Chicago

1964–National

1B–Bill White, St. Louis
2B–Ron Hunt, New York
SS–Dick Groat, St. Louis
3B–Ken Boyer, St. Louis
OF–Billy Williams, Chicago
OF–Willie Mays, San Francisco
OF–Roberto Clemente, Pittsburgh
C–Joe Torre, Milwaukee
P–Sandy Koufax, Los Angeles
P–Jim Bunning, Philadelphia

1965–American

1B–Fred Whitfield, Cleveland
2B–Bobby Richardson, New York
SS–Zoilo Versalles, Minnesota
3B–Brooks Robinson, Baltimore
LF–Carl Yastrzemski, Boston
CF–Jimmie Hall, Minnesota
RF–Tony Oliva, Minnesota
C–Earl Battey, Minnesota
P–Jim Grant, Minnesota
P–Mel Stottlemyre, New York

1965–National

1B–Willie McCovey, San Francisco
2B–Pete Rose, Cincinnati
SS–Maury Wills, Los Angeles
3B–Deron Johnson, Cincinnati
LF–Willie Stargell, Pittsburgh
CF–Willie Mays, San Francisco
RF–Hank Aaron, Milwaukee
C–Joe Torre, Milwaukee
P–Sandy Koufax, Los Angeles
P–Juan Marichal, San Francisco

1966—American

1B—Boog Powell, Baltimore
2B—Bobby Richardson, New York
SS—Luis Aparicio, Baltimore
3B—Brooks Robinson, Baltimore
LF—Frank Robinson, Baltimore
CF—Al Kaline, Detroit
RF—Tony Oliva, Minnesota
C—Paul Casanova, Minnesota
P—Jim Kaat, Minnesota
P—Earl Wilson, Detroit

1966—National

1B—Felipe Alou, Atlanta
2B—Pete Rose, Cincinnati
SS—Gene Alley, Pittsburgh
3B—Ron Santo, Chicago
LF—Willie Stargell, Pittsburgh
CF—Willie Mays, San Francisco
RF—Roberto Clemente, Pittsburgh
C—Joe Torre, Atlanta
P—Sandy Koufax, Los Angeles
P—Juan Marichal, San Francisco

1967—American

1B—Harmon Killebrew, Minnesota
2B—Rod Carew, Minnesota
SS—Jim Fregosi, California
3B—Brooks Robinson, Baltimore
LF—Carl Yastrzemski, Boston
CF—Al Kaline, Detroit
RF—Frank Robinson, Baltimore
C—Bill Freehan, Detroit
P—Jim Lonborg, Boston
P—Earl Wilson, Detroit

1967—National

1B—Orlando Cepeda, St. Louis
2B—Bill Mazeroski, Pittsburgh
SS—Gene Alley, Pittsburgh
3B—Ron Santo, Chicago
LF—Hank Aaron, Atlanta
CF—Jim Wynn, Houston
RF—Roberto Clemente, Pittsburgh
C—Tim McCarver, St. Louis
P—Mike McCormick, San Francisco
P—Ferguson Jenkins, Chicago

1968—American

1B—Boog Powell, Baltimore
2B—Rod Carew, Minnesota
SS—Luis Aparicio, Chicago
3B—Brooks Robinson, Baltimore
OF—Ken Harrelson, Boston
OF—Willie Horton, Detroit
OF—Frank Howard, Washington
C—Bill Freehan, Detroit
P—Dave McNally, Baltimore
P—Denny McLain, Detroit

1968—National

1B—Willie McCovey, San Francisco
2B—Tommy Helms, Cincinnati
SS—Don Kessinger, Chicago
3B—Ron Santo, Chicago
OF—Billy Williams, Chicago
OF—Curt Flood, St. Louis
OF—Pete Rose, Cincinnati
C—Johnny Bench, Cincinnati
P—Bob Gibson, St. Louis
P—Juan Marichal, San Francisco

1969—American

1B—Boog Powell, Baltimore
2B—Rod Carew, Minnesota
SS—Rico Petrocelli, Boston
3B—Harmon Killebrew, Minnesota
OF—Frank Howard, Washington
OF—Paul Blair, Baltimore
OF—Reggie Jackson, Oakland
C—Bill Freehan, Detroit
RHP—Denny McLain, Detroit
LHP—Mike Cuellar, Baltimore

1969—National

1B—Willie McCovey, San Francisco
2B—Glenn Beckert, Chicago
SS—Don Kessinger, Chicago
3B—Ron Santo, Chicago
OF—Cleon Jones, New York
OF—Matty Alou, Pittsburgh
OF—Hank Aaron, Atlanta
C—Johnny Bench, Cincinnati
RHP—Tom Seaver, New York
LHP—Steve Carlton, St. Louis

1970—American

1B—Boog Powell, Baltimore
2B—Dave Johnson, Baltimore
SS—Luis Aparicio, Chicago
3B—Harmon Killebrew, Minnesota
OF—Frank Howard, Washington
OF—Reggie Smith, Boston
OF—Tony Oliva, Minnesota
C—Ray Fosse, Cleveland
RHP—Jim Perry, Minnesota
LHP—Sam McDowell, Cleveland

1970—National

1B—Willie McCovey, San Francisco
2B—Glenn Beckert, Chicago
SS—Don Kessinger, Chicago
3B—Tony Perez, Cincinnati
OF—Billy Williams, Chicago
OF—Bobby Tolan, Cincinnati
OF—Hank Aaron, Atlanta
C—Johnny Bench, Cincinnati
RHP—Bob Gibson, St. Louis
LHP—Jim Merritt, Cincinnati

1971—American

1B—Norm Cash, Detroit
2B—Cookie Rojas, Kansas City
SS—Leo Cardenas, Minnesota
3B—Brooks Robinson, Baltimore
LF—Merv Rettenmund, Baltimore
CF—Bobby Murcer, New York
RF—Tony Oliva, Minnesota
C—Bill Freehan, Detroit
RHP—Jim Palmer, Baltimore
LHP—Vida Blue, Oakland

1971—National

1B—Lee May, Cincinnati
2B—Glenn Beckert, Chicago
SS—Bud Harrelson, New York
3B—Joe Torre, St. Louis
LF—Willie Stargell, Pittsburgh
CF—Willie Davis, Los Angeles
RF—Hank Aaron, Atlanta
C—Manny Sanguillen, Pittsburgh
RHP—Ferguson Jenkins, Chicago
LHP—Steve Carlton, St. Louis

1972—American

1B—Dick Allen, Chicago
2B—Rod Carew, Minnesota
SS—Luis Aparicio, Boston
3B—Brooks Robinson, Baltimore
LF—Joe Rudi, Oakland
CF—Bobby Murcer, New York
RF—Richie Scheinblum, Kan. City
C—Carlton Fisk, Boston
RHP—Gaylord Perry, Cleveland
LHP—Wilbur Wood, Chicago

1972—National

1B—Willie Stargell, Pittsburgh
2B—Joe Morgan, Cincinnati
SS—Chris Speier, San Francisco
3B—Ron Santo, Chicago
LF—Billy Williams, Chicago
CF—Cesar Cedeno, Houston
RF—Roberto Clemente, Pittsburgh
C—Johnny Bench, Cincinnati
RHP—Ferguson Jenkins, Chicago
LHP—Steve Carlton, Philadelphia

1973—American

1B—John Mayberry, Kansas City
2B—Rod Carew, Minnesota
SS—Bert Campaneris, Oakland
3B—Sal Bando, Oakland
LF—Reggie Jackson, Oakland
CF—Amos Otis, Kansas City
RF—Bobby Murcer, New York
C—Thurman Munson, New York
RHP—Jim Palmer, Baltimore
LHP—Ken Holtzman, Oakland

1973—National

1B—Tony Perez, Cincinnati
2B—Dave Johnson, Atlanta
SS—Bill Russell, Los Angeles
3B—Darrell Evans, Atlanta
LF—Bobby Bonds, San Francisco
CF—Cesar Cedeno, Houston
RF—Pete Rose, Cincinnati
C—Johnny Bench, Cincinnati
RHP—Tom Seaver, New York
LHP—Ron Bryant, San Francisco

1974—American

1B—Dick Allen, Chicago
2B—Rod Carew, Minnesota
SS—Bert Campaneris, Oakland
3B—Sal Bando, Oakland
LF—Joe Rudi, Oakland
CF—Paul Blair, Baltimore
RF—Jeff Burroughs, Texas
C—Thurman Munson, New York
DH—Tommy Davis, Baltimore
RHP—Jim Hunter, Oakland
LHP—Mike Cuellar, Baltimore

1974—National

1B—Steve Garvey, Los Angeles
2B—Joe Morgan, Cincinnati
SS—Dave Concepcion, Cincinnati
3B—Mike Schmidt, Philadelphia
LF—Lou Brock, St. Louis
CF—Jim Wynn, Los Angeles
RF—Richie Zisk, Pittsburgh
C—Johnny Bench, Cincinnati
RHP—Andy Messersmith, Los Angeles
LHP—Don Gullett, Cincinnati

1975—American

1B—John Mayberry, Kansas City
2B—Rod Carew, Minnesota
SS—Toby Harrah, Texas
3B—Graig Nettles, New York
LF—Jim Rice, Boston
CF—Fred Lynn, Boston
RF—Reggie Jackson, Oakland
C—Thurman Munson, New York
DH—Willie Horton, Detroit
RHP—Jim Palmer, Baltimore
LHP—Jim Kaat, Chicago

1975—National

1B—Steve Garvey, Los Angeles
2B—Joe Morgan, Cincinnati
SS—Larry Bowa, Philadelphia
3B—Bill Madlock, Chicago
LF—Greg Luzinski, Philadelphia
CF—Al Oliver, Pittsburgh
RF—Dave Parker, Pittsburgh
C—Johnny Bench, Cincinnati
RHP—Tom Seaver, New York
LHP—Randy Jones, San Diego

1976—American

1B—Chris Chambliss, New York
2B—Bobby Grich, Baltimore
3B—George Brett, Kansas City
SS—Mark Belanger, Baltimore
LF—Joe Rudi, Oakland
CF—Mickey Rivers, New York
RF—Reggie Jackson, Baltimore
C—Thurman Munson, New York
DH—Hal McRae, Kansas City
RHP—Jim Palmer, Baltimore
LHP—Frank Tanana, California

1976—National

1B—Willie Montanez, San Fran.-Atlanta
2B—Joe Morgan, Cincinnati
3B—Mike Schmidt, Philadelphia
SS—Dave Concepcion, Cincinnati
LF—George Foster, Cincinnati
CF—Cesar Cedeno, Houston
RF—Ken Griffey, Cincinnati
C—Bob Boone, Philadelphia
RHP—Don Sutton, Los Angeles
LHP—Randy Jones, San Diego

1977—American

1B—Rod Carew, Minnesota
2B—Willie Randolph, New York
3B—Graig Nettles, New York
SS—Rick Burleson, Boston
OF—Jim Rice, Boston
OF—Larry Hisle, Minnesota
OF—Bobby Bonds, California
C—Carlton Fisk, Boston
DH—Hal McRae, Kansas City
RHP—Nolan Ryan, California
LHP—Frank Tanana, California

1977—National

1B—Steve Garvey, Los Angeles
2B—Joe Morgan, Cincinnati
3B—Mike Schmidt, Philadelphia
SS—Garry Templeton, St. Louis
OF—George Foster, Cincinnati
OF—Dave Parker, Pittsburgh
OF—Greg Luzinski, Philadelphia
C—Ted Simmons, St. Louis
RHP—Rick Reuschel, Chicago
LHP—Steve Carlton, Philadelphia

1978—American

1B—Rod Carew, Minnesota
2B—Frank White, Kansas City
3B—Graig Nettles, New York
SS—Robin Yount, Milwaukee
OF—Jim Rice, Boston
OF—Larry Hisle, Milwaukee
OF—Fred Lynn, Boston
C—Jim Sundberg, Texas
DH—Rusty Staub, Detroit
RHP—Jim Palmer, Baltimore
LHP—Ron Guidry, New York

1978—National

1B—Steve Garvey, Los Angeles
2B—Dave Lopes, Los Angeles
3B—Pete Rose, Cincinnati
SS—Larry Bowa, Philadelphia
OF—George Foster, Cincinnati
OF—Dave Parker, Pittsburgh
OF—Jack Clark, San Francisco
C—Ted Simmons, St. Louis
RHP—Gaylord Perry, San Diego
LHP—Vida Blue, San Francisco

1979—American

1B—Cecil Cooper, Milwaukee
2B—Bobby Grich, California
3B—George Brett, Kansas City
SS—Roy Smalley, Minnesota
LF—Jim Rice, Boston
CF—Fred Lynn, Boston
RF—Ken Singleton, Baltimore
C—Darrell Porter, Kansas City
DH—Don Baylor, California
RHP—Jim Kern, Texas
LHP—Mike Flanagan, Baltimore

1979—National

1B—Keith Hernandez, St. Louis
2B—Dave Lopes, Los Angeles
3B—Mike Schmidt, Philadelphia
SS—Garry Templeton, St. Louis
LF—Dave Kingman, Chicago
CF—Omar Moreno, Pittsburgh
RF—Dave Winfield, San Diego
C—Ted Simmons, St. Louis
RHP—Joe Niekro, Houston
LHP—Steve Carlton, Philadelphia

1980 American

1B—Cecil Cooper, Milwaukee
2B—Willie Randolph, New York
3B—George Brett, Kansas City
SS—Robin Yount, Milwaukee
LF—Ben Oglivie, Milwaukee
CF—Al Bumbry, Baltimore
RF-DH—Reggie Jackson, New York
C—Rick Cerone, New York
RHP—Steve Stone, Baltimore
LHP—Tommy John, New York

1980 National

1B—Keith Hernandez, St. Louis
2B—Manny Trillo, Philadelphia
3B—Mike Schmidt, Philadelphia
SS—Garry Templeton, St. Louis
LF—Dusty Baker, Los Angeles
CF—Cesar Cedeno, Houston
RF—George Hendrick, St. Louis
C—Gary Carter, Montreal
RHP—Jim Bibby, Pittsburgh
LHP—Steve Carlton, Philadelphia

The Sporting News
All-Star Fielding Teams

1957 Majors
P–Shantz, N. Y. AL
C–Lollar, Chicago AL
1B–Hodges, Brooklyn
2B–Fox, Chicago AL
3B–Malzone, Boston
SS–McMillan, Cin.
LF–Minoso, Chicago AL
CF–Mays, N. Y. NL
RF–Kaline, Detroit

1958 American
P–Shantz, New York
C–Lollar, Chicago
1B–Power, Cleveland
2B–Bolling, Detroit
3B–Malzone, Boston
SS–Aparicio, Chicago
LF–Siebern, New York
CF–Piersall, Boston
RF–Kaline, Detroit

1958 National
P–Haddix, Cincinnati
C–Crandall, Milwaukee
1B–Hodges, Los Angeles
2B–Mazeroski, Pitt.
3B–Boyer, St. Louis
SS–McMillan, Cin.
LF–Robinson, Cin.
CF–Mays, S. Francisco
RF–Aaron, Milwaukee

1959 American
P–Shantz, New York
C–Lollar, Chicago
1B–Power, Cleveland
2B–Fox, Chicago
3B–Malzone, Boston
SS–Aparicio, Chicago
LF–Minoso, Cleveland
CF–Kaline, Detroit
RF–Jensen, Boston

1959 National
P–Haddix, Pittsburgh
C–Crandall, Milwaukee
1B–Hodges, Los Angeles
2B–Neal, Los Angeles
3B–Boyer, St. Louis
SS–McMillan, Cincinnati
LF–Brandt, St. Louis
CF–Mays, San Francisco
RF–Aaron, Milwaukee

1960 American
P–Shantz, New York
C–Battey, Washington
1B–Power, Cleveland
2B–Fox, Chicago
3B–Robinson, Baltimore
SS–Aparicio, Chicago
LF–Minoso, Chicago
CF–Landis, Chicago
RF–Maris, New York

1960 National
P–Haddix, Pittsburgh
C–Crandall, Milwaukee
1B–White, St. Louis
2B–Mazeroski, Pittsburgh
3B–Boyer, St. Louis
SS–Banks, Chicago
LF–Moon, Los Angeles
CF–Mays, San Francisco
RF–Aaron, Milwaukee

1961 American
P–Lary, Detroit
C–Battey, Chicago
1B–Power, Cleveland
2B–Richardson, New York
3B–Robinson, Baltimore
SS–Aparicio, Chicago
OF–Kaline, Detroit
OF–Piersall, Cleveland
OF–Landis, Chicago

1961 National
P–Shantz, Pittsburgh
C–Roseboro, Los Angeles
1B–White, St. Louis
2B–Mazeroski, Pittsburgh
3B–Boyer, St. Louis
SS–Wills, Los Angeles
OF–Mays, San Francisco
OF–Clemente, Pittsburgh
OF–Pinson, Cincinnati

1962 American
P–Kaat, Minnesota
C–Battey, Minnesota
1B–Power, Minnesota
2B–Richardson, New York
3B–Robinson, Baltimore
SS–Aparicio, Chicago
OF–Landis, Chicago
OF–Mantle, New York
OF–Kaline, Detroit

1962 National
P–Shantz, St. Louis
C–Crandall, Milwaukee
1B–White, St. Louis
2B–Hubbs, Chicago
3B–Davenport, San Francisco
SS–Wills, Los Angeles
OF–Mays, San Francisco
OF–Clemente, Pittsburgh
OF–Virdon, Pittsburgh

1963 American

P—Kaat, Minnesota
C—Howard, New York
1B—Power, Minnesota
2B—Richardson, New York
3B—Robinson, Baltimore
SS—Versalles, Minnesota
OF—Kaline, Detroit
OF—Yastrzemski, Boston
OF—Landis, Chicago

1963 National

P—Shantz, St. Louis
C—Edwards, Cincinnati
1B—White, St. Louis
2B—Mazeroski, Pittsburgh
3B—Boyer, St. Louis
SS—Wine, Philadelphia
OF—Mays, San Francisco
OF—Clemente, Pittsburgh
OF—Flood, St. Louis

1964 American

P—Kaat, Minnesota
C—Howard, New York
1B—Power, Los Angeles
2B—Richardson, New York
3B—Robinson, Baltimore
SS—Aparicio, Baltimore
OF—Kaline, Detroit
OF—Landis, Chicago
OF—Davalillo, Cleveland

1964 National

P—Shantz, Philadelphia
C—Edwards, Cincinnati
1B—White, St. Louis
2B—Mazeroski, Pittsburgh
3B—Santo, Chicago
SS—Amaro, Philadelphia
OF—Mays, San Francisco
OF—Clemente, Pittsburgh
OF—Flood, St. Louis

1965 American

P—Kaat, Minnesota
C—Freehan, Detroit
1B—Pepitone, New York
2B—Richardson, New York
3B—Robinson, Baltimore
SS—Versalles, Minnesota
OF—Kaline, Detroit
OF—Tresh, New York
OF—Yastrzemski, Boston

1965 National

P—Gibson, St. Louis
C—Torre, Atlanta
1B—White, St. Louis
2B—Mazeroski, Pittsburgh
3B—Santo, Chicago
SS—Cardenas, Cincinnati
OF—Mays, San Francisco
OF—Clemente, Pittsburgh
OF—Flood, St. Louis

1966 American

P—Kaat, Minnesota
C—Freehan, Detroit
1B—Pepitone, New York
2B—Knoop, California
3B—B. Robinson, Baltimore
SS—Aparicio, Baltimore
OF—Kaline, Detroit
OF—Agee, Chicago
OF—Oliva, Minnesota

1966 National

P—Gibson, St. Louis
C—Roseboro, Los Angeles
1B—White, Philadelphia
2B—Mazeroski, Pittsburgh
3B—Santo, Chicago
SS—Alley, Pittsburgh
OF—Mays, San Francisco
OF—Flood, St. Louis
OF—Clemente, Pittsburgh

1967 American

P—Kaat, Minnesota
C—Freehan, Detroit
1B—Scott, Boston
2B—Knoop, California
3B—B. Robinson, Baltimore
SS—Fregosi, California
OF—Yastrzemski, Boston
OF—Blair, Baltimore
OF—Kaline, Detroit

1967 National

P—Gibson, St. Louis
C—Hundley, Chicago
1B—Parker, Los Angeles
2B—Mazeroski, Pittsburgh
3B—Santo, Chicago
SS—Alley, Pittsburgh
OF—Clemente, Pittsburgh
OF—Flood, St. Louis
OF—Mays, San Francisco

1968 American

P–Kaat, Minnesota
C–Freehan, Detroit
1B–Scott, Boston
2B–Knoop, California
3B–B. Robinson, Baltimore
SS–Aparicio, Chicago
OF–Stanley, Detroit
OF–Yastrzemski, Boston
OF–Smith, Boston

1969 American

P–Kaat, Minnesota
C–Freehan, Detroit
1B–Pepitone, New York
2B–Johnson, Baltimore
3B–B. Robinson, Baltimore
SS–Belanger, Baltimore
OF–Blair, Baltimore
OF–Stanley, Detroit
OF–Yastrzemski, Boston

1970 American

P–Kaat, Minnesota
C–Fosse, Cleveland
1B–Spencer, California
2B–Johnson, Baltimore
3B–B. Robinson, Baltimore
SS–Aparicio, Chicago
OF–Stanley, Detroit
OF–Blair, Baltimore
OF–Berry, Chicago

1971 American

P–Kaat, Minnesota
C–Fosse, Cleveland
1B–Scott, Boston
2B–Johnson, Baltimore
3B–B. Robinson, Baltimore
SS–Belanger, Baltimore
OF–Blair, Baltimore
OF–Otis, Kansas City
OF–Yastrzemski, Boston

1972 American

P–Kaat, Minnesota
C–Fisk, Boston
1B–Scott, Milwaukee
2B–Griffin, Boston
3B–Robinson, Baltimore
SS–Brinkman, Detroit
OF–Blair, Baltimore
OF–Murcer, New York
OF–Berry, California

1968 National

P–Gibson, St. Louis
C–Bench, Cincinnati
1B–Parker, Los Angeles
2B–Beckert, Chicago
3B–Santo, Chicago
SS–Maxvill, St. Louis
OF–Mays, San Francisco
OF–Clemente, Pittsburgh
OF–Flood, St. Louis

1969 National

P–Gibson, St. Louis
C–Bench, Cincinnati
1B–Parker, Los Angeles
2B–Millan, Atlanta
3B–Boyer, Atlanta
SS–Kessinger, Chicago
OF–Clemente, Pittsburgh
OF–Flood, St. Louis
OF–Rose, Cincinnati

1970 National

P–Gibson, St. Louis
C–Bench, Cincinnati
1B–Parker, Los Angeles
2B–Helms, Cincinnati
3B–Rader, Houston
SS–Kessinger, Chicago
OF–Clemente, Pittsburgh
OF–Agee, New York
OF–Rose, Cincinnati

1971 National

P–Gibson, St. Louis
C–Bench, Cincinnati
1B–Parker, Los Angeles
2B–Helms, Cincinnati
3B–Rader, Houston
SS–Harrelson, New York
OF–Clemente, Pittsburgh
OF–Bonds, San Francisco
OF–Davis, Los Angeles

1972 National

P–Gibson, St. Louis
C–Bench, Cincinnati
1B–Parker, Los Angeles
2B–Millan, Atlanta
3B–Rader, Houston
SS–Bowa, Philadelphia
OF–Clemente, Pittsburgh
OF–Cedeno, Houston
OF–Davis, Los Angeles

1973 American

P—Kaat, Chicago
C—Munson, New York
1B—Scott, Milwaukee
2B—Grich, Baltimore
3B—Robinson, Baltimore
SS—Belanger, Baltimore
OF—Blair, Baltimore
OF—Otis, Kansas City
OF—Stanley, Detroit

1973 National

P—Gibson, St. Louis
C—Bench, Cincinnati
1B—Jorgensen, Montreal
2B—Morgan, Cincinnati
3B—Rader, Houston
SS—Metzger, Houston
OF—Bonds, San Francisco
OF—Cedeno, Houston
OF—Davis, Los Angeles

1974 American

P—Kaat, Chicago
C—Munson, New York
1B—Scott, Milwaukee
2B—Grich, Baltimore
3B—Robinson, Baltimore
SS—Belanger, Baltimore
OF—Blair, Baltimore
OF—Otis, Kansas City
OF—Rudi, Oakland

1974 National

P—Messersmith, Los Angeles
C—Bench, Cincinnati
1B—Garvey, Los Angeles
2B—Morgan, Cincinnati
3B—Rader, Houston
SS—Concepcion, Cincinnati
OF—Cedeno, Houston
OF—Geronimo, Cincinnati
OF—Bonds, San Francisco

1975 American

P—Kaat, Chicago
C—Munson, New York
1B—Scott, Milwaukee
2B—Grich, Baltimore
3B—Robinson, Baltimore
SS—Belanger, Baltimore
OF—Blair, Baltimore
OF—Rudi, Oakland
OF—Lynn, Boston

1975 National

P—Messersmith, Los Angeles
C—Bench, Cincinnati
1B—Garvey, Los Angeles
2B—Morgan, Cincinnati
3B—Reitz, St. Louis
SS—Concepcion, Cincinnati
OF—Cedeno, Houston
OF—Geronimo, Cincinnati
OF—Maddox, Philadelphia

1976 American

P—Palmer, Baltimore
C—Sundberg, Texas
1B—Scott, Milwaukee
2B—Grich, Baltimore
3B—Rodriguez, Detroit
SS—Belanger, Baltimore
OF—Rudi, Oakland
OF—Evans, Boston
OF—Manning, Cleveland

1976 National

P—Kaat, Philadelphia
C—Bench, Cincinnati
1B—Garvey, Los Angeles
2B—Morgan, Cincinnati
3B—Schmidt, Philadelphia
SS—Concepcion, Cincinnati
OF—Cedeno, Houston
OF—Geronimo, Cincinnati
OF—Maddox, Philadelphia

1977 American

P—Palmer, Baltimore
C—Sundberg, Texas
1B—Spencer, Chicago
2B—White, Kansas City
3B—Nettles, New York
SS—Belanger, Baltimore
OF—Beniquez, Texas
OF—Yastrzemski, Boston
OF—Cowens, Kansas City

1977 National

P—Kaat, Philadelphia
C—Bench, Cincinnati
1B—Garvey, Los Angeles
2B—Morgan, Cincinnati
3B—Schmidt, Philadelphia
SS—Concepcion, Cincinnati
OF—Geronimo, Cincinnati
OF—Maddox, Philadelphia
OF—Parker, Pittsburgh

1978 American

P–Palmer, Baltimore
C–Sundberg, Texas
1B–Chambliss, New York
2B–White, Kansas City
3B–Nettles, New York
SS–Belanger, Baltimore
OF–Lynn, Boston
OF–Evans, Boston
OF–Miller, California

1978 National

P–Niekro, Atlanta
C–Boone, Philadelphia
1B–Hernandez, St. Louis
2B–Lopes, Los Angeles
3B–Schmidt, Philadelphia
SS–Bowa, Philadelphia
OF–Maddox, Philadelphia
OF–Parker, Pittsburgh
OF–Valentine, Montreal

1979 American

P–Palmer, Baltimore
C–Sundberg, Texas
1B–Cooper, Milwaukee
2B–White, Kansas City
3B–Bell, Texas
SS–Burleson, Boston
OF–Evans, Boston
OF–Lezcano, Milwaukee
OF–Lynn, Boston

1979 National

P–Niekro, Atlanta
C–Boone, Philadelphia
1B–Hernandez, St. Louis
2B–Trillo, Philadelphia
3B–Schmidt, Philadelphia
SS–Concepcion, Cincinnati
OF–Maddox, Philadelphia
OF–Parker, Pittsburgh
OF–Winfield, San Diego

1980 American

P–Norris, Oakland
C–Sundberg, Texas
1B–Cooper, Milwaukee
2B–White, Kansas City
3B–Bell, Texas
SS–Trammell, Detroit
OF–Lynn, Boston
OF–Murphy, Oakland
OF–Wilson, Kansas City

1980 National

P–Niekro, Atlanta
C–Carter, Montreal
1B–Hernandez, St. Louis
2B–Flynn, New York
3B–Schmidt, Philadelphia
SS–Smith, San Diego
OF–Dawson, Montreal
OF–Maddox, Philadelphia
OF–Winfield, San Diego

The Sporting News

Silver Slugger Teams

1980 American

1B–Cecil Cooper, Milwaukee
2B–Willie Randolph, New York
3B–George Brett, Kansas City
SS–Robin Yount, Milwaukee
OF–Ben Oglivie, Milwaukee
OF–Al Oliver, Texas
OF–Willie Wilson, Kansas City
C–Lance Parrish, Detroit
DH–Reggie Jackson, New York

1980 National

1B–Keith Hernandez, St. Louis
2B–Manny Trillo, Philadelphia
3B–Mike Schmidt, Philadelphia
SS–Garry Templeton, St. Louis
OF–Dusty Baker, Los Angeles
OF–Andre Dawson, Montreal
OF–George Hendrick, St. Louis
C–Ted Simmons, St. Louis
P–Bob Forsch, St. Louis

Cardinals Hurlers Made Impressive Debuts

Well-pitched games by three St. Louis Cardinals highlighted the comings out of 145 players—73 in the National League and 72 in the American—in 1980. Lefthander Al Olmsted pitched 9⅓ scoreless innings in the second game of a September 12 doubleheader at Philadelphia, but received no decision in the Cardinals' 5-0, 11-inning win. Andy Rincon allowed only five hits in defeating Chicago by a 5-1 score September 15. John Martin gained a victory over Houston August 27, surrendering only one run in seven innings of relief in the Cardinals' 10-2 triumph.

Three other pitchers made impressive debuts. Montreal's Charlie Lea worked the first eight innings of the Expos' 9-1 thrashing of San Diego June 12; Doug Corbett struck out six and gave up just one hit in the last five innings of Minnesota's 9-7, 12-inning victory over Oakland April 10; and John Butcher of Texas throttled the A's, 6-2, on six hits September 8.

Montreal's Tim Wallach, THE SPORTING NEWS College Player of the Year for California State-Fullerton in 1979 and the Expos' first pick in the June draft that year, became the 47th player to hit a home run in his first major league at-bat, connecting against Phil Nastu of San Francisco September 6.

Other batters experienced more success in their second game. Dave Stapleton cracked two homers for the Red Sox against Milwaukee May 31 to join the Yankees' Joe Lefebvre (who homered in each of his first two games) in tying an A.L. record for most home runs, first two major league games. Tito Landrum of St. Louis had four hits in his initial start, July 25 against San Diego.

Surprisingly, the world champion Phillies used 11 newcomers, only one fewer than the other division champions combined. Only Boston took in as many greenhorns.

An alphabetical list of players who made their big league debuts in 1980 follows:

Player	Pos.	Club	Date and Place of Birth	Debut
Aguayo, Luis	2B-SS	Philadelphia	3-13-59—Vega Baja, P.R.	4-19
Allen, Kim Bryant	2B-OF	Seattle	4- 5-53—Fontana, Calif.	9- 2
Aponte, Luis Eduardo	P	Boston	6-14-54—Lel Tigre, Venezuela	9- 4
Armstrong, Michael Dennis	P	San Diego	3- 7-54—Glen Cove, N.Y.	8-12
Backman, Walter Wayne	2B-SS	New York NL	9-22-59—Hillsboro, Ore.	9- 2
Baines, Harold Douglass	OF	Chicago AL	3-15-59—St. Michaels, Md.	4-10
Beard, David Charles	P	Oakland	10- 2-59—Chamblee, Ga.	7-16
Berenyi, Bruce Michael	P	Cincinnati	8-21-54—Bryan, O.	7- 5
Boddicker, Michael James	P	Baltimore	8-23-57—Cedar Rapids, Ia.	10- 4
Bonner, Robert Averill	SS	Baltimore	8-12-56—Uvalde, Tex.	9-12
Bordi, Richard Albert	P	Oakland	4-18-59—S. San Francisco, Calif.	7-16
Bordley, William Charles	P	San Francisco	1- 9-58—Rolling Hills Estates, Calif.	6-30
Bourjos, Christopher	OF	San Francisco	10-16-55—Chicago, Ill.	8-31
Brant, Marshall Lee	1B	New York AL	9-17-55—Garberville, Calif.	10- 1
Breining, Fred Lawrence	P	San Francisco	11-15-55—San Francisco, Calif.	9- 4
Brooks, Hubert Jr.	3B	New York NL	9-24-56—Los Angeles, Calif.	9- 4
Brouhard, Mark Steven	OF	Milwaukee	5-22-56—Burbank, Calif.	4-12
Butcher, John Daniel	P	Texas	3- 8-57—Glendale, Calif.	9- 8
Butera, Salvatore Philip	C	Minnesota	9-25-52—Richmond Hill, N.Y.	4-10
Bystrom, Martin Eugene	P	Philadelphia	7-26-58—Miami, Fla.	9- 7
Camacho, Ernie Carlos	P	Oakland	2- 1-56—Salinas, Calif.	5-22
Castillo, Esteban Manuel Antonio	3B	Kansas City	4- 1-57—Santo Domingo, D.R.	9- 1
Charboneau, Joseph	OF-DH	Cleveland	6-17-56—Belvedere, Ill.	4-11
Cliburn, Stanley Gene	C	California	12-19-56—Jackson, Miss.	5- 6
Combe, Geoffrey Wade	P	Cincinnati	2- 1-56—Melrose, Mass.	9- 2
Concepcion, Onix	SS	Kansas City	10- 5-57—Dorado, P.R.	8-30

Player	Pos.	Club	Date and Place of Birth	Debut
Contreras, Arnaldo Juan	P	Chicago AL	9-19-51 — Tampa, Fla.	5-23
Cooper, Gary Nathaniel	OF	Atlanta	12-22-56 — Savannah, Ga.	8-25
Corbett, Douglas Mitchell	P	Minnesota	11-14-52 — Sarasota, Fla.	4-10
Cosey, Donald Ray	OF	Oakland	2-15-56 — San Rafael, Calif.	4-14
Cox, Jeffrey Lindon	2B	Oakland	11- 9-55 — Los Angeles, Calif.	7- 1
Crawford, Steven Ray	P	Boston	4-29-58 — Pryor, Okla.	9- 2
Davis, Mark William	P	Philadelphia	10-19-60 — Livermore, Calif.	9-12
Davis, Michael Dwayne	OF	Oakland	6-11-59 — San Diego, Calif.	4-10
Davis, Odie Ernest	SS	Texas	8-13-55 — San Antonio, Tex.	9- 3
Dernier, Robert Eugene	OF	Philadelphia	1- 5-57 — Kansas City, Mo.	9- 7
De Sa, Joseph	1B-OF	St. Louis	7-27-59 — Honolulu, Hawaii	9- 6
Detherage, Robert Wayne	OF	Kansas City	9-20-54 — Springfield, Mo.	4-11
Dorsey, James Edward	P	California	8- 2-55 — Chicago, Ill.	9- 2
Durham, Leon	OF-1B	St. Louis	7-31-57 — Cincinnati, O.	5-27
Dybzinski, Jerome	SS	Cleveland	7- 7-55 — Cleveland, O.	4-11
Edler, David Delmar	3B	Seattle	8- 5-56 — Sioux City, Ia.	9- 4
Faedo, Leonardo L.	SS	Minnesota	5-13-60 — Tampa, Fla.	9- 6
Figueroa, Jesus Maria	OF	Chicago NL	2-20-57 — Santo Domingo, D.R.	4-22
Gedman, Richard Leo	C	Boston	9-26-59 — Worcester, Mass.	9- 7
Hargesheimer, Alan Robert	P	San Francisco	11-21-56 — Chicago, Ill.	7-14
Harper, Terry Joe	OF	Atlanta	8-19-55 — Douglasville, Ga.	9-12
Hart, James Michael	OF	Texas	12-20-51 — Portage, Mich.	6-12
Hayes, William Ernest	C	Chicago NL	10-24-57 — Cheverly, Md.	9-30
Hazewood, Drungo Larue	OF	Baltimore	9- 2-59 — Mobile, Ala.	9-19
Hodgson, Paul Joseph Dennis	OF	Toronto	4-14-60 — Montreal, Canada	8-31
Hoffman, Glenn Edward	3B-SS	Boston	7- 7-58 — Orange, Calif.	4-12
Holman, Randy Scott	P	New York NL	9-18-58 — Santa Paula, Calif.	9-20
Holt, Roger Boyd	2B	New York AL	4- 8-56 — Daytona Beach, Fla.	10- 4
Householder, Paul Wesley	OF	Cincinnati	9- 4-58 — Columbus, O.	8-26
Howe, Steven Roy	P	Los Angeles	3-10-58 — Pontiac, Mich.	4-11
Howell, Jay Canfield	P	Cincinnati	11-26-55 — Miami, Fla.	8-10
Hurst, Bruce Vee	P	Boston	3-24-58 — St. George, Utah	4-12
Isales, Orlando	OF	Philadelphia	12-22-59 — Santurce, P.R.	9-11
Johnson, Randall Stuart	1B-OF	Chicago AL	8-15-58 — Miami, Fla.	7- 5
Jones, Jeffrey Allen	P	Oakland	7-29-56 — Detroit, Mich.	4-10
Jones, Michael Carl	P	Kansas City	7-30-59 — Rochester, N.Y.	9- 6
Kainer, Donald Wayne	P	Texas	9- 3-55 — Houston, Tex.	9- 6
Keeton, Rickey	P	Milwaukee	3-18-57 — Cincinnati, O.	5-27
Kelly, Dale Patrick	C	Toronto	8-27-55 — Santa Barbara, Calif.	5-28
Kinnunen, Michael John	P	Minnesota	4- 1-58 — Seattle, Wash.	6-12
Kubski, Gilbert Thomas	OF	California	10-12-54 — Longview, Tex.	9- 2
Landrum, Terry Lee	OF	St. Louis	10-25-54 — Joplin, Mo.	7-23
LaPoint, David Jeffrey	P	Milwaukee	7-29-59 — Glens Falls, N.Y.	9-10
Law, Vance Aaron	SS	Pittsburgh	10- 1-56 — Boise, Ida.	6-12
Lea, Charles William	P	Montreal	12-25-56 — Orleans, France	5-25
Leal, Luis Enrique	P	Toronto	3-21-57 — Barquisimeto, Venezuela	5-22
Lefebvre, Joseph Henry	OF	New York AL	2-22-56 — Concord, N.H.	4-10
Lezcano, Carlos Manuel	OF	Chicago NL	9-30-55 — Arecibo, P.R.	9- 6
Little, Donald Jeffrey	P	St. Louis	12-25-54 — Fremont, O.	6- 8
Littlefield, John Andrew	P	St. Louis	1- 5-54 — Covina, Calif.	6-28
Lollar, William Timothy	P	New York AL	3-17-56 — Poplar Bluff, Mo.	9- 1
Loucks, Scott Gregory	OF	Houston	11-11-56 — Anchorage, Alaska	9- 2
Loviglio, John Paul	2B	Philadelphia	5-30-56 — Freeport, N.Y.	4-16
Lucas, Gary Paul	P	San Diego	11- 8-54 — Riverside, Calif.	8-31
Lynch, Edward Francis	P	New York NL	2-25-56 — Brooklyn, N.Y.	4-12
Lysander, Richard Eugene	P	Oakland	2-21-53 — Huntington Park, Calif.	5-10
MacWhorter, Keith	P	Boston	12-30-55 — Worcester, Mass.	8-27
Martin, John Robert	P	St. Louis	4-11-56 — Wyandotte, Mich.	9- 6
Martinez, Alfredo	P	California	3-15-57 — Los Angeles, Calif.	4-20
Martz, Randy Carl	P	Chicago NL	5-28-56 — Harrisburg, Pa.	9- 6
McCormack, Donald Ross	C	Philadelphia	9-18-55 — Omak, Wash.	9-30
Mills, James Bradley	3B	Montreal	1-19-57 — Lemoncove, Calif.	6- 8
Milner, Eddie James	OF	Cincinnati	5-21-55 — Columbus, O.	9- 2
Mitchell, Robert Van	OF	Los Angeles	4- 7-55 — Salt Lake City, Utah	9- 1
Moreno, Jose	2B-3B	New York NL	11- 2-57 — Santo Domingo, D.R.	5-24
Moseby, Lloyd Anthony	OF	Toronto	11- 5-59 — Portland, Ark.	5-24
Mullins, Francis Joseph	3B	Chicago AL	5-14-57 — Oakland, Calif.	9- 1
Munninghoff, Scott Andrew	P	Philadelphia	12- 5-58 — Cincinnati, O.	4-13
Murray, Richard Dale	1B	San Francisco	7- 6-57 — Los Angeles, Calif.	6- 7

Player	Pos.	Club	Date and Place of Birth	Debut
Nichols, Thomas Reid	OF	Boston	8- 5-58—Ocala, Fla.	9-16
Ojeda, Robert Michael	P	Boston	12-17-57—Los Angeles, Calif.	7-13
Olmsted, Alan Ray	P	St. Louis	3-18-57—St. Louis, Mo.	9-12
Pate, Robert Wayne	OF	Montreal	12- 3-53—Los Angeles, Calif.	6- 2
Pena, Antonio Francisco	C	Pittsburgh	6- 4-57—Monte Cristy, D.R.	9- 1
Perconte, John Patrick	2B	Los Angeles	8-31-54—Joliet, Ill.	9-13
Perez, Pascual	P	Pittsburgh	5-17-57—Haina, D.R.	5- 7
Pettini, Joseph Paul	SS-3B-2B	San Francisco	1-26-55—Windsor Heights, W. Va.	7-10
Phelps, Kenneth Allen	1B	Kansas City	8- 6-54—Seattle, Wash.	9-20
Price, Joseph Walter	P	Cincinnati	11-29-56—Inglewood, Calif.	6-14
Ramirez, Mario	SS-2B-3B	New York NL	9-12-57—Yauco, P.R.	4-25
Ramirez, Rafael	SS	Atlanta	2-18-59—San Pedro de Macoris, D.R.	8- 4
Ratzer, Stephen	P	Montreal	9- 9-53—Paterson, N.J.	10- 5
Rayford, Floyd Kinnard	3B	Baltimore	7-27-57—Memphis, Tenn.	4-17
Richardt, Michael Anthony	2B	Texas	5-24-58—N. Hollywood, Calif.	8-30
Rincon, Andrew John	P	St. Louis	3- 5-59—Pico Rivera, Calif.	9-15
Rowland, Michael Evan	P	San Francisco	1-31-53—Chicago, Ill.	7-25
Salazar, Luis Ernesto	3B-OF	San Diego	5-19-56—Barcelona, Venezuela	8-15
Schrom, Kenneth Marvin	P	Toronto	11-23-54—Grangeville, Ida.	8- 8
Scioscia, Michael Lorri	C	Los Angeles	11-27-58—Darby, Pa.	4-20
Scurry, Rodney Grant	P	Pittsburgh	3-17-56—Sacramento, Calif.	4-17
Seilheimer, Ricky Allen	C	Chicago AL	8-30-60—Brenham, Tex.	7- 5
Smith, David S. Jr.	P	Houston	1-21-55—San Francisco, Calif.	4-11
Smith, Lee Arthur	P	Chicago NL	12- 4-57—Jamestown, La.	9- 1
Souza, Kenneth Mark	P	Oakland	2- 1-54—Redwood City, Calif.	4-22
Stablein, George Charles	P	San Diego	10-29-57—Inglewood, Calif.	9-20
Stapleton, David Leslie	2B-1B	Boston	1-16-54—Fairhope, Ala.	5-30
Stember, Jeffrey Alan	P	San Francisco	3- 2-58—Elizabeth, N.J.	8- 5
Stimac, Craig Steven	C-3B	San Diego	11-18-54—Oak Park, Ill.	8-12
Sularz, Guy Patrick	2B-3B	San Francisco	11- 7-55—Minneapolis, Minn.	9- 2
Sutherland, Leonardo	OF	Chicago AL	4- 6-58—Santiago, Cuba	8-11
Tracy, James Edwin	OF-1B	Chicago NL	12-31-55—Hamilton, Ohio	7-20
Twitty, Jeffrey Dean	P	Kansas City	11-10-57—Lancaster, S.C.	7- 5
Ujdur, Gerald Raymond	P	Detroit	3- 5-57—Duluth, Minn.	8-17
Valdez, Julio	SS	Boston	7- 3-56—Nizao de Peravia, D.R.	9- 2
Valenzuela, Fernando	P	Los Angeles	11- 1-60—Navajoa, Mexico	9-15
Veselic, Robert Michael	P	Minnesota	9-27-55—Pittsburgh, Pa.	9-18
Virgil, Osvaldo Jose Jr.	C	Philadelphia	12- 7-56—Mayaguez, P.R.	10- 5
Vukovich, George Stephen	OF	Philadelphia	6-24-56—Chicago, Ill.	4-13
Walk, Robert Vernon	P	Philadelphia	11-26-56—Van Nuys, Calif.	5-26
Walker, Cleotha	2B	Boston	11-25-57—Jackson, Miss.	9- 2
Wallach, Timothy Charles	OF-1B	Montreal	9-14-57—Tustin, Calif.	9- 6
Waller, Elliott Tyrone	3B	St. Louis	3-14-57—Fresno, Calif.	9- 6
Walton, Reginald Sherard	OF	Seattle	10-24-52—Kansas City, Mo.	6-13
Weaver, Roger Edward	P	Detroit	10- 6-54—Amsterdam, N.Y.	6- 6
Weiss, Gary Lee	SS	Los Angeles	12-27-55—Brenham, Tex.	9-13
Whitmer, Daniel C.	C	California	11-23-55—Redlands, Calif.	7-20
Williams, Alberto	P	Minnesota	5- 7-54—Pearl Lagoon, Nicaragua	5- 7
Wilson, William Hayward	OF	New York NL	2- 9-56—Bamberg, S.C.	9- 2
Yost, Edgar Frederick	C	Milwaukee	8-19-55—Eureka, Calif.	4-12

No-Hit Games Listed by Clubs

AMERICAN LEAGUE

BALTIMORE ORIOLES

Pitcher–Opponent	Score	Date
Hoyt Wilhelm, New York	1-0	9-20-58
Steve Barber (8⅔)-Stu		
Miller (⅓), Detroit	1-2	4-30-67
Tom Phoebus, Boston	6-0	4-27-68
Jim Palmer, Oakland	8-0	8-13-69

BOSTON RED SOX

Pitcher–Opponent	Score	Date
Cy Young, Philadelphia	*3-0	5- 5-04
Jesse Tannehill, Chicago	6-0	8-17-04
Bill Dinneen, Chicago	2-0	9-27-05
Cy Young, New York	8-0	6-30-08
Joe Wood, St. Louis	5-0	7-29-11
George Foster, N. York	2-0	6-21-16
Hub Leonard, St. Louis	4-0	8-30-16
Ernie Shore, Washington	*4-0	6-23-17
Hub Leonard, Detroit	5-0	6- 3-18
Howard Ehmke, Phila.	4-0	9- 7-23
Mel Parnell, Chicago	4-0	7-14-56
Earl Wilson, Los Ang.	2-0	6-26-62
Bill Monbouquette, Chi.	1-0	8- 1-62
Dave Morehead, Cleve.	2-0	9-16-65
*Perfect game.		

CALIFORNIA ANGELS

Pitcher–Opponent	Score	Date
Bo Belinsky, Baltimore	2-0	5- 5-62
Clyde Wright, Oakland	4-0	7- 3-70
Nolan Ryan, Kansas City	3-0	5-15-73
Nolan Ryan, Detroit	6-0	7-15-73
Nolan Ryan, Minnesota	4-0	9-28-74
Nolan Ryan, Baltimore	1-0	6- 1-75

CHICAGO WHITE SOX

Pitcher–Opponent	Score	Date
Jim Callahan, Detroit	3-0	9-20-02
Frank Smith, Detroit	15-0	9- 6-05
Frank Smith, Phila.	1-0	9-20-08
Ed Walsh, Boston	5-0	8-27-11
Jim Scott, Washington	0-1	5-14-14
Lost on two hits in ten innings.		
Joe Benz, Cleveland	6-1	5-31-14
Ed Cicotte, St. Louis	11-0	4-14-17
Charles Robertson, Det.	*2-0	4-30-22
Ted Lyons, Boston	6-0	8-21-26
Vern Kennedy, Cleveland	5-0	8-31-35
Bill Dietrich, St. Louis	8-0	6- 1-37
Bob Keegan, Washington	6-0	8-20-57
Joe Horlen, Detroit	6-0	9-10-67
Johnny Odom (5) and Francisco		
Barrios (4), Oakland	2-1	7-28-76
*Perfect game.		

CLEVELAND INDIANS

Pitcher–Opponent	Score	Date
Earl Moore, Chicago	2-4	5- 9-01
Lost on two hits in ten innings.		
Bob Rhoades, Boston	2-1	9-18-08
Addie Joss, Chicago	*1-0	10- 2-08
Addie Joss, Chicago	1-0	4-20-10
Ray Caldwell, New York	3-0	9-10-19
Wes Ferrell, St. Louis	9-0	4-29-31
Bob Feller, Chicago	1-0	4-16-40
Bob Feller, New York	1-0	4-30-46
Don Black, Philadelphia	3-0	7-10-47
Bob Lemon, Detroit	2-0	6-30-48
Bob Feller, Detroit	2-1	7- 1-51

Pitcher–Opponent	Score	Date
Sonny Siebert, Wash.	2-0	6-10-66
Dick Bosman, Oakland	4-0	7-19-74
Dennis Eckersley, California	1-0	5-30-77
*Perfect game.		

DETROIT TIGERS

Pitcher–Opponent	Score	Date
George Mullin, St. Louis	7-0	7- 4-12
Virgil Trucks, Wash.	1-0	5-15-52
Virgil Trucks, New York	1-0	8-25-52
Jim Bunning, Boston	3-0	7-20-58

KANSAS CITY ROYALS

Pitcher–Opponent	Score	Date
Steve Busby, Detroit	3-0	4-27-73
Steve Busby, Milwaukee	2-0	6-19-74
Jim Colborn, Texas	6-0	5-14-77

MINNESOTA TWINS

Pitcher–Opponent	Score	Date
Jack Kralick, Kan. City	1-0	8-26-62
Dean Chance, Cleveland	2-1	8-25-67

NEW YORK YANKEES

Pitcher–Opponent	Score	Date
Tom Hughes, Cleveland	0-5	8-30-10
Yielded one hit in tenth; lost on seven hits in 11 innings.		
George Mogridge, Boston	2-1	4-24-17
Sam Jones, Philadelphia	2-0	9- 4-23
Monte Pearson, Cleve.	13-0	8-27-38
Allie Reynolds, Cleve.	1-0	7-12-51
Allie Reynolds, Boston	8-0	9-28-51
Don Larsen, Brooklyn	‡2-0	10- 8-56
‡World Series perfect game.		

OAKLAND ATHLETICS

Pitcher–Opponent	Score	Date
Jim Hunter, Minnesota	*4-0	5- 8-68
Vida Blue, Minnesota	6-0	9-21-70
Vida Blue (5), Glenn Abbott (1),		
Paul Lindblad (1),		
Rollie Fingers (2), California	5-0	9-28-75
*Perfect game.		

PHILADELPHIA ATHLETICS

Pitcher–Opponent	Score	Date
Weldon Henley, St. Louis	6-0	7-22-05
Chief Bender, Cleveland	4-0	5-12-10
Joe Bush, Cleveland	5-0	8-26-16
Dick Fowler, St. Louis	1-0	9- 9-45
Bill McCahan, Wash.	3-0	9- 3-47

ST. LOUIS BROWNS

Pitcher–Opponent	Score	Date
Earl Hamilton, Detroit	5-1	8-30-12
Ernie Koob, Chicago	1-0	5- 5-17
Bob Groom, Chicago	3-0	5- 6-17
Buck Newsom, Boston	1-2	9-18-34
Lost on one hit in tenth inning.		
Bobo Holloman, Phila.	6-0	5- 6-53

TEXAS RANGERS

Pitcher–Opponent	Score	Date
Jim Bibby, Oakland	6-0	7-30-73
Bert Blyleven, California	6-0	9-22-77

WASHINGTON SENATORS

Pitcher–Opponent	Score	Date
Walter Johnson, Boston	1-0	7- 1-20
Bob Burke, Boston	5-0	8- 31

NATIONAL LEAGUE
(PRESENT CLUBS)

ATLANTA BRAVES

Pitcher–Opponent	Score	Date
Phil Niekro, San Diego	9-0	8- 5-73

CHICAGO CUBS

Pitcher–Opponent	Score	Date
Larry Corcoran, Boston	6-0	8-19-80
Larry Corcoran, Worcester	5-0	9-20-82
Larry Corcoran, Providence	6-0	6-27-84
John Clarkson, Providence	4-0	7-27-85
Walter Thornton, Brkn.	2-0	8-21-98
Bob Wicker, New York	1-0	6-11-04

Yielded only hit in tenth; won in 12 innings.

Jimmy Lavender, N.Y.	2-0	8-31-15
Hippo Vaughn, Cincinnati	0-1	5- 2-17

Lost on two hits in tenth inning; Fred Toney, Cincinnati, pitched ten hitless innings in same game.

Sam Jones, Pittsburgh	4-0	5-12-55
Don Cardwell, St. Louis	4-0	5-16-60
Ken Holtzman, Atlanta	3-0	8-19-69
Ken Holtzman, Cin.	1-0	6- 3-71
Burt Hooton, Phila.	4-0	4-16-72
Milt Pappas, S. Diego	8-0	9- 2-72

CINCINNATI REDS

Pitcher–Opponent	Score	Date
Bumpus Jones, Pitts.	7-1	10-15-92
Theo. Breitenstein, Pitts.	11-0	4-22-98
Noodles Hahn, Phila.	4-0	7-12-00
Fred Toney, Chicago	†1-0	5- 2-17

Toney's opponent, Hippo Vaughn, pitched nine hitless innings.

Hod Eller, St. Louis	6-0	5-11-19
John Vander Meer, Bos.	3-0	6-11-38
John Vander Meer, Bkn.	6-0	6-15-38
Clyde Shoun, Boston	1-0	5-15-44
Ewell Blackwell, Boston	6-0	6-18-47
John Klippstein (7), Hersh Freeman (1), Joe Black (2½), Milwaukee	1-2	5-26-56

Trio yielded no hits until tenth; lost on three hits in 11th inning.

Jim Maloney, New York	0-1	6-14-65

Lost on two hits in eleventh inning.

Jim Maloney, Chicago	†1-0	8-19-65
George Culver, Phila.	6-1	7-29-68
Jim Maloney, Houston	10-0	4-30-69
Tom Seaver, St. Louis	4-0	6-16-78

†Ten innings.

HOUSTON ASTROS

Pitcher–Opponent	Score	Date
Don Nottebart, Phila.	4-1	5-17-63
Ken Johnson, Cincinnati	0-1	4-23-64

(FORMER CLUBS)

BALTIMORE ORIOLES

Pitcher–Opponent	Score	Date
Bill Hawke, Washington	5-0	8-16-93
Jim Hughes, Boston	8-0	4-22-98

BOSTON BRAVES

Pitcher–Opponent	Score	Date
John Stivetts, Brooklyn	11-0	8- 6-92
Vic Willis, Washington	7-1	8- 7-99
Frank Pfeffer, Cinn.	6-0	5- 8-07
George Davis, Phila.	7-0	9- 9-14

Pitcher–Opponent	Score	Date
Don Wilson, Atlanta	2-0	6-18-67
Don Wilson, Cincinnati	4-0	5- 1-69
Larry Dierker, Montreal	6-0	7- 9-76
Ken Forsch, Atlanta	6-0	4-17-79

LOS ANGELES DODGERS

Pitcher–Opponent	Score	Date
Sandy Koufax, New York	5-0	6-30-62
Sandy Koufax, San Fran.	8-0	5-11-63
Sandy Koufax, Phila.	3-0	6- 4-64
Sandy Koufax, Chicago	*1-0	9- 9-65
Bill Singer, Philadelphia	5-0	7-20-70
Jerry Reuss, San Francisco	8-0	6-27-80

*Perfect game.

MONTREAL EXPOS

Pitcher–Opponent	Score	Date
Bill Stoneman, Philadelphia	7-0	4-17-69
Bill Stoneman, New York	7-0	10- 2-72

PHILADELPHIA PHILLIES

Pitcher–Opponent	Score	Date
Charles Ferguson, Providence	1-0	8-29-85
Frank Donohue, Boston	5-0	7- 8-98
Chic Fraser, Chicago	10-0	9-18-03
John Lush, Brooklyn	6-0	5- 1-06
Jim Bunning, New York	*6-0	6-21-64
Rick Wise, Cincinnati	4-0	6-23-71

*Perfect game.

PITTSBURGH PIRATES

Pitcher–Opponent	Score	Date
Nick Maddox, Brooklyn	2-1	9-20-07
Cliff Chambers, Boston	3-0	5- 6-51
*Harvey Haddix, Milw.	0-1	5-26-59
Bob Moose, New York	4-0	9-20-69
Dock Ellis, San Diego	2-0	6-12-70
John Candelaria, Los Angeles	2-0	8- 9-76

*Pitched 12 perfect innings; lost on one hit in 13 innings.

ST. LOUIS CARDINALS

Pitcher–Opponent	Score	Date
George Bradley, Hartford	2-0	7-15-76
Jess Haines, Boston	5-0	7-17-24
Paul Dean, Brooklyn	3-0	9-21-34
Lon Warneke, Cincinnati	2-0	8-30-41
Ray Washburn, San Fran.	2-0	9-18-68
Bob Gibson, Pittsburgh	11-0	8-14-71
Bob Forsch, Philadelphia	5-0	4-16-78

SAN FRANCISCO GIANTS

Pitcher–Opponent	Score	Date
Juan Marichal, Houston	1-0	6-15-63
Gaylord Perry, St. Louis	1-0	9-17-68
Ed Halicki, New York	6-0	8-24-74
John Montefusco, Atlanta	9-0	9-29-76

Pitcher–Opponent	Score	Date
Tom Hughes, Pittsburgh	2-0	6-16-16
Jim Tobin, Brooklyn	2-0	4-27-44
Vern Bickford, Brooklyn	7-0	8-11-50

BROOKLYN DODGERS

Pitcher–Opponent	Score	Date
Tom Lovett, New York	4-0	6-22-91

Pitcher—Opponent	Score	Date
Mal Eason, St. Louis	2-0	7-20-06
Harry McIntire, Pitts.	0-1	8- 1-06

Yielded first hit in 11th inning; lost on four hits in 13th.

Nap Rucker, Boston	6-0	9- 5-08
Dazzy Vance, Phila.	10-1	9-13-25
Tex Carleton, Cinn.	3-0	4-30-40
Ed Head, Boston	5-0	4-23-46
Rex Barney, New York	2-0	9- 9-48
Carl Erskine, Chicago	5-0	6-19-52
Carl Erskine, New York	3-0	5-12-56
Sal Maglie, Philadelphia	5-0	9-25-56

BUFFALO

Pitcher—Opponent	Score	Date
Jim Galvin, Worcester	1-0	8-20-80
Jim Galvin, Detroit	18-0	8- 4-84

CLEVELAND

Hugh Dalley, Philadelphia	1-0	9-13-83
Cy Young, Cincinnati	6-0	9-18-97

LOUISVILLE

Alex Sanders, Baltimore	6-2	8-22-92
Deacon Phillippe, New York	7-0	5-25-99

MILWAUKEE BRAVES

Jim Wilson, Phila.	2-0	6-12-54
Lou Burdette, Phila.	1-0	8-18-60
Warren Spahn, Phila.	4-0	9-16-60
Warren Spahn, San Fran.	1-0	4-28-61

NEW YORK GIANTS

Amos Rusie, Brooklyn	6-0	7-31-91
Christy Mathewson, St. Louis	5-0	7-15-01

Pitcher—Opponent	Score	Date
Christy Mathewson, Chi.	1-0	6-13-05
George Wiltse, Phila.	†1-0	7- 4-08
Leon Ames, Brooklyn	0-3	4-15-09

Yielded one hit in tenth; lost on seven hits in 13 innings.

Jeff Tesreau, Philadelphia	3-0	9- 6-12
Rube Marquard, Brooklyn	2-0	4-15-15
Jesse Barnes, Philadelphia	6-0	5- 7-22
Carl Hubbell, Pittsburgh	11-0	5- 8-29

†Ten innings.

PROVIDENCE

John Ward, Buffalo	*5-0	6-17-80
Chas. Radbourn, Cleve.	8-0	7-25-83

*Perfect game.

WORCESTER

John Richmond, Cleve.	*1-0	6-12-80

*Perfect game.

NOTE—Present pitching distance of 60 feet, six inches was adopted effective with 1893 season.

JERRY REUSS joined no-hit elite in 1980.

Baseball's Hall of Fame

St. Louis Cardinals pitching great Bob Gibson was the only player to be elected to the Hall of Fame in the 1981 voting of the Baseball Writers' Association. Johnny Mize, a slugger for three major league teams from 1936 through 1953, and Andrew (Rube) Foster, founder of the Negro National League, were named by the Committee on Veterans. The selections increased the total number enshrined at Cooperstown to 176.

The lifetime major league totals of the Hall of Famers follow:

Player—Position	Years	G.	AB.	R.	H.	2B.	3B.	HR.	RBI.	B.A.	F.A.
Adrian (Cap) Anson, 1b.	22	2253	9084	1712	3081	530	129	92	....	.339	.971
Lucius Appling, ss	20	2422	8856	1319	2749	440	102	45	1116	.310	.948
H. Earl Averill, of.	14	1669	6352	1224	2019	401	128	238	1164	.318	.970
Frank (Home Run) Baker, 3b	13	1575	5983	887	1838	313	103	93	1012	.307	.943
David Bancroft, ss	16	1913	7182	1048	2004	320	77	32	579	.279	.944
Ernest Banks, ss-1b	19	2528	9421	1305	2583	407	90	512	1636	.274	.986
Jacob Beckley, 1b.	20	2373	9476	1601	2930	455	246	87	....	.309	.982
Lawrence (Yogi) Berra, c-of	19	2120	7555	1175	2150	321	49	358	1430	.285	.988
Louis Boudreau, ss	15	1646	6030	861	1779	385	66	68	789	.295	.973
Roger (Duke) Bresnahan, c	17	1410	4480	684	1251	222	72	26	....	.279	.969
Dennis (Dan) Brouthers, 1b	19	1658	6725	1507	2349	446	212	103	....	.349	.970
Jesse (Crab) Burkett, of	16	2063	8389	1708	2872	314	185	70	....	.342	.922
Roy Campanella, c	10	1215	4205	627	1161	178	18	242	856	.276	.988
Max Carey, of	20	2469	9363	1545	2665	419	159	69	797	.285	.966
Frank (Husk) Chance, 1b	17	1232	4279	796	1273	195	80	20	....	.297	.985
Fred Clarke, of	21	2204	8584	1620	2703	358	219	65	....	.315	.955
Roberto Clemente, of	18	2433	9454	1416	3000	440	166	240	1305	.317	.972
Tyrus Cobb, of.	24	3033	11436	2245	4190	723	298	117	1960	.367	.962
Gordon (Mickey) Cochrane, c	13	1482	5169	1041	1652	333	64	119	832	.320	.985
Edward Collins, 2b	25	2826	9946	1816	3309	437	186	47	1307	.333	.970
James Collins, 3b	14	1718	6792	1057	1999	333	117	62	....	.294	.929
Earle Combs, of.	12	1455	5746	1186	1866	309	154	58	629	.325	.973
*Charles Comiskey, 1b	13	1374	5780	981	1559	199	69	29	....	.270	.974
*John (Jocko) Conlan, of	2	128	365	55	96	18	4	0	31	.263	.957
Roger Connor, 1b	18	1987	7807	1607	2535	429	227	131	....	.325	.970
Samuel Crawford, of	19	2505	9579	1392	2964	455	312	95	....	.309	.968
Joseph Cronin, ss	20	2124	7579	1233	2285	516	118	170	1423	.301	.953
Hazen (Kiki) Cuyler, of.	18	1879	7161	1305	2299	394	157	127	1065	.321	.972
Edward Delahanty, of.	16	1825	7493	1596	2593	508	182	98	....	.346	.944
William Dickey, c	17	1789	6300	930	1969	343	72	202	1209	.313	.988
Joseph DiMaggio, of.	13	1736	6821	1390	2214	389	131	361	1537	.325	.978
Hugh Duffy, of.	17	1722	6999	1545	2307	310	117	103	....	.330	.941
John Evers, 2b	18	1776	6136	919	1659	216	70	12	....	.270	.955
William (Buck) Ewing, c	18	1281	5348	1118	1663	237	179	66	....	.311	.941
Elmer Flick, of.	13	1480	5601	951	1767	268	170	46	....	.315	.945
James Foxx, 1b	20	2317	8134	1751	2646	458	125	534	1921	.325	.952
Frank Frisch, 2b-3b	19	2311	9112	1532	2880	466	138	105	1242	.316	.971
H. Louis Gehrig, 1b	17	2164	8001	1888	2721	535	162	493	1990	.340	.991
Charles Gehringer, 2b	19	2323	8860	1774	2839	574	146	184	1427	.320	.976
Leon (Goose) Goslin, of.	18	2287	8656	1483	2735	500	173	248	1609	.316	.960
Henry Greenberg, 1b-of	13	1394	5193	1051	1628	379	71	331	1276	.313	.990
Charles (Chick) Hafey, of.	13	1283	4625	777	1466	341	67	164	833	.317	.971
William Hamilton, of.	14	1578	6262	1690	2157	225	94	37	....	.344	.929
Stanley (Bucky) Harris, 2b	12	1264	4736	722	1297	223	64	9	506	.274	.965
Charles (Gabby) Hartnett, c	20	1990	6432	867	1912	396	64	236	1179	.297	.984
Harry Heilmann, of.	17	2146	7787	1291	2660	542	151	183	1549	.342	.974
William Herman, 2b	15	1922	7707	1163	2345	486	82	47	839	.304	.968
Harry Hooper, of.	17	2308	8784	1429	2466	389	160	75	813	.281	.966
Rogers Hornsby, 2b	23	2259	8173	1579	2930	541	169	301	1579	.358	.957
*Miller Huggins, 2b	13	1573	5558	948	1474	146	50	9	....	.265	.956
†Monford Irvin, of.	8	764	2499	366	731	97	31	99	443	.293	.981
Hugh Jennings, ss	18	1264	4840	989	1520	227	88	19	....	.314	.946
Albert Kaline, of.	22	2834	10116	1622	3007	498	75	399	1583	.297	.987
William Keeler, of.	19	2124	8564	1720	2955	234	155	32	....	.345	.957
Joseph Kelley, of.	17	1829	6989	1425	2245	353	189	66	....	.321	.967
George Kelly, 1b	16	1622	5993	819	1778	337	76	148	1019	.297	.991
Michael (King) Kelly, c-of	16	1434	5922	1359	1853	351	109	65	....	.313	.865
Ralph Kiner, of.	10	1472	5205	971	1451	216	39	369	1015	.279	.975
Charles (Chuck) Klein, of.	17	1753	6486	1168	2076	398	74	300	1201	.320	.962
Napoleon (Larry) Lajoie, 2b	21	2475	9590	1506	3252	652	164	82	....	.339	.966
Frederick Lindstrom, 3b-of	13	1438	5611	895	1747	301	81	103	779	.311	.966
Alfonso Lopez, c	19	1950	5916	613	1547	206	42	52	652	.261	.984
*Connie Mack, c	11	695	2671	387	672	78	28	5	....	.252	.930
Mickey Mantle, of.	18	2401	8102	1677	2415	344	72	536	1509	.298	.985
Henry Manush, of.	17	2008	7654	1287	2524	491	160	110	1183	.330	.979
Walter (Rabbit) Maranville, ss	23	2670	10078	1255	2605	380	177	28	874	.258	.956

Player—Position	Years	G.	AB.	R.	H.	2B.	3B.	HR.	RBI.	B.A.	F.A.
Edwin Mathews, 3b	17	2391	8537	1509	2315	354	72	512	1453	.271	.959
Willie Mays, of	22	2992	10881	2062	3283	523	140	660	1903	.302	.981
Thomas McCarthy, of	13	1258	5055	1050	1485	194	58	43	....	.294	.899
*John McGraw, 3b	16	1082	3919	1019	1307	124	71	12	....	.334	.899
*William McKechnie, 3b	9	546	1822	163	471	40	22	5	160	.234	.963
Joseph Medwick, of	17	1984	7635	1198	2471	540	113	205	1383	.324	.980
John Mize, 1b	15	1884	6443	1118	2011	367	83	359	1337	.312	.992
Stanley Musial, of-1b	22	3026	10972	1949	3630	725	177	475	1951	.331	.989
James O'Rourke, of-1b	19	1750	7365	1425	2314	385	139	49	....	.314	.911
Melvin Ott, of-3b	22	2730	9456	1859	2876	488	72	511	1860	.304	.974
Edgar (Sam) Rice, of	20	2404	9269	1515	2987	498	184	34	1077	.322	.965
*Branch, Rickey, c	4	119	343	38	82	9	6	3	....	.239	.940
Jackie Robinson, 2b	10	1382	4877	947	1518	273	54	137	734	.311	.983
Wilbert Robinson, c	16	1316	4942	632	1388	210	54	17	....	.280	.949
Edd Roush, of	16	1748	6646	1000	2158	311	168	63	882	.325	.972
George (Babe) Ruth, of-p	22	2503	8397	2174	2873	506	136	714	2204	.342	.968
Raymond Schalk, c	14	1760	5306	579	1345	199	48	12	596	.253	.981
Joseph Sewell, ss-3b	14	1903	7132	1141	2226	436	68	49	1051	.312	.954
Aloysius Simmons, of	20	2215	8761	1507	2927	539	149	307	1827	.334	.982
George Sisler, 1b	15	2055	8267	1284	2812	425	165	100	1180	.340	.987
Edwin (Duke) Snider, of	18	2143	7161	1259	2116	358	85	407	1333	.295	.985
Tristram Speaker, of	22	2789	10196	1881	3515	793	222	116	1559	.345	.970
*Charles (Casey) Stengel, of	14	1277	4288	575	1219	182	89	60	518	.284	.964
William Terry, 1b	14	1721	6428	1120	2193	373	112	154	1078	.341	.992
Samuel Thompson, of	15	1405	6004	1259	2016	326	146	126	....	.336	.936
Joseph Tinker, ss	13	1642	5936	716	1565	238	106	29	....	.264	.937
Harold (Pie) Traynor, 3b	17	1941	7559	1183	2416	371	164	58	1273	.320	.945
John (Honus) Wagner, ss	21	2785	10427	1740	3430	651	252	101	....	.329	.946
Roderick (Bobby) Wallace, ss	25	2369	8629	1056	2308	395	149	36	....	.267	.940
Lloyd Waner, of	18	1993	7772	1201	2459	281	118	28	598	.316	.983
Paul Waner, of	20	2549	9459	1627	3152	605	191	113	1309	.333	.976
John Montgomery Ward, inf-of	17	1810	7597	1403	2151	232	95	26	....	.283	.905
Zachariah (Zach) Wheat, of	19	2406	9106	1289	2884	476	172	132	1265	.317	.966
Theodore Williams, of	19	2292	7706	1798	2654	525	71	521	1839	.344	.974
Lewis R. (Hack) Wilson, of	12	1348	4760	884	1461	266	67	244	1063	.307	.965
*George Wright, ss	7	315	1448	250	364	52	20	1	....	.251	.907
Royce (Ross) Youngs, of	10	1211	4627	812	1491	236	93	42	596	.322	.953

PITCHERS

Pitcher	Years	G.	IP.	W.	L.	Pct.	H.	R.	ER.	SO.	BB.	ERA.
Grover Cleveland Alexander	20	696	5189	373	208	.642	4868	1851	....	2198	951	....
Chas. Albert (Chief) Bender	15	433	2847	208	112	.650	2455	987	....	1630	667	....
Mordecai (Miner) Brown	12	411	2697	208	111	.652	2284	863	....	1166	548	....
John (Jack) Chesbro	11	392	2886	198	127	.609	2602	1202	....	1276	674	....
John Clarkson	12	517	4514	327	176	.650	4384	....	....	2013	1192	....
Stanley Coveleski	14	450	3092	214	141	.603	3055	1237	982	981	802	2.88
*William (Candy) Cummings	2	43	....	21	22	.488	....	....	....	....	....	....
Jay Hanna (Dizzy) Dean	12	317	1966	150	83	.644	1921	776	663	1155	458	3.04
Urban (Red) Faber	20	669	4087	254	212	.545	4104	1813	1430	1471	1213	3.15
Robert W. A. Feller	18	570	3828	266	162	.621	3271	1557	1384	2581	1764	3.25
Edward (Whitey) Ford	16	498	3171	236	106	.690	2766	1107	967	1956	1086	2.74
James (Pud) Galvin	14	685	5959	361	309	.539	6334	....	....	1786	744	....
Robert Gibson	14	528	3885	251	174	.591	3279	1420	1258	3117	1336	2.91
Vernon (Lefty) Gomez	14	368	2503	189	102	.649	2290	1091	929	1468	1095	3.34
Clark C. Griffith	21	416	3370	240	140	.632	3372	....	....	962	800	....
Burleigh Grimes	19	615	4178	270	212	.560	4406	2048	1636	1512	1295	3.52
Robert (Lefty) Grove	17	616	3940	300	141	.680	3849	1594	1339	2266	1187	3.06
Jesse Haines	19	555	3207	210	158	.571	3460	1556	1298	981	871	3.64
Waite Hoyt	21	675	3762	237	182	.566	4037	1780	1500	1206	1003	3.59
Carl Hubbell	16	535	3591	253	154	.622	3461	1380	1188	1677	725	2.98
Walter Johnson	21	802	5924	416	279	.599	4920	1902	1103	3508	1353	....
Adrian C. Joss	9	288	2340	160	96	.625	1885	....	....	933	382	....
Timothy Keefe	14	599	5050	344	225	.605	....	....	....	2542	1225	....
Sanford Koufax	12	397	2325	165	87	.655	1754	806	713	2396	817	2.76
Robert Lemon	13	460	2849	207	128	.618	2559	1185	1024	1277	1251	3.23
Theodore Lyons	21	594	4162	260	230	.531	4489	2056	1696	1073	1121	3.67
Richard (Rube) Marquard	18	536	3307	201	177	.532	3233	1443	....	1593	858	....
Christopher Mathewson	17	635	4781	373	188	.665	4203	1613	....	2505	837	....
Joseph McGinnity	10	467	3455	247	145	.630	3236	1442	....	1064	803	....
Charles (Kid) Nichols	15	582	5067	360	202	.641	4854	....	....	1866	1245	....
†Leroy (Satchel) Paige	6	179	463	28	31	.475	429	191	174	290	183	3.38
Herbert Pennock	22	617	3558	240	162	.597	3900	1699	1403	1227	916	3.60
Edward Plank	17	581	4234	305	181	.628	3688	1470	....	2112	984	....
Charles Radbourn	12	517	4543	308	191	.617	4500	2300	....	1746	856	....
Eppa Rixey	21	692	4494	266	251	.515	4633	1986	1572	1350	1082	3.15
Robin Roberts	19	676	4689	286	245	.539	4582	1962	1774	2357	902	3.40
Charles (Red) Ruffing	22	624	4342	273	225	.548	4294	2117	1833	1987	1541	3.80
Amos Rusie	11	412	....	241	158	.604	3177	1908	....	1953	1637	....
Warren Spahn	21	750	5246	363	245	.597	4830	2016	1798	2583	1434	3.08
*Albert Spalding	2	126	....	47	13	.783	....	....	....	....	....	....
Arthur (Dazzy) Vance	16	442	2967	197	140	.585	2809	1246	1068	2045	840	3.24

Pitcher	Years	G.	IP.	W.	L.	Pct.	H.	R.	ER.	SO.	BB.	ERA.
George (Rube) Waddell	13	407	2958	191	142	.574	2480	1079	....	2310	771	....
Edward Walsh	14	431	2968	195	126	.607	2335	882	....	1731	620	....
Michael (Mickey) Welch	13	564	4775	311	207	.600	4637	2548	....	1837	1305	....
Early Wynn	23	691	4566	300	244	.551	4291	2037	1796	2334	1775	3.54
Denton (Cy) Young	22	906	7377	511	313	.620	7078	3168	....	2819	1209	....

*Named to Hall of Fame chiefly for services to game apart from playing career.

†Named to Hall of Fame for contributions in Negro leagues.

Of the 176 in the Hall of Fame, 26 never played in the major leagues: Ed Barrow, Yankees' general manager; Morgan Bulkeley, first National League president; Alexander Cartwright, organizer of the first baseball team; Henry Chadwick, compiler of the first rule book; Tom Connolly, American League umpire; Ford Frick, commissioner; Ban Johnson, organizer of the American League; Bill Klem, National League umpire; Judge Kenesaw Landis, first commissioner; Joe McCarthy, manager of the Yankees; William (Harry) Wright, "Father of Professional Baseball,"; Billy Evans, umpire and club official; George Weiss, Yankees' executive; Will Harridge, American League president; Cal Hubbard, American League umpire; Leland S. MacPhail, Sr., pioneer of night baseball and executive; Warren Giles, National League president, Tom Yawkey, Red Sox owner, and Negro league stars Josh Gibson, Buck Leonard, Jim (Cool Papa) Bell, William Julius (Judy) Johnson, Oscar Charleston, John Henry Lloyd, Martin Dihigo and Andrew (Rube) Foster.

Hall of Fame form of **BOB GIBSON**

American League Lifetime Batting Records

Players with 100 or More Games Played Who Were Active in Majors in 1980

NOTE—Figures include complete major league totals of players who also played in National League.

Player	Yrs.	G.	AB.	R.	H.	TB.	2B.	3B.	HR.	RBI.	SB.	Pct.
Adams, Glenn	6	559	1331	137	389	557	65	5	31	189	6	.292
Aikens, Willie	3	309	1013	134	275	444	46	0	41	185	3	.271
Ainge, Danny	2	125	419	37	100	123	13	2	2	23	4	.239
Allenson, Gary	2	144	311	36	74	103	16	2	3	32	3	.238
Alston, Dell	3	189	332	48	79	103	7	4	3	35	20	.238
Anderson, Jim	3	260	659	85	151	213	27	1	11	60	5	.229
Armas, Tony	5	451	1514	159	384	636	41	14	61	210	8	.254
Ashford, Tucker	4	175	441	38	99	147	30	0	6	53	5	.224
Ault, Doug	4	256	713	66	168	258	29	5	17	86	4	.236
Ayala, Benny	5	164	353	54	87	160	14	1	19	56	0	.246
Baines, Harold	1	141	491	55	125	199	23	6	13	49	2	.255
Bando, Sal	15	1987	6995	972	1777	2858	285	38	240	1030	74	.254
Bannister, Alan	7	573	1796	264	488	629	83	20	6	170	57	.272
Baylor, Don	11	1232	4472	680	1192	1947	199	20	172	661	246	.267
Belanger, Mark	16	1898	5595	661	1281	1571	171	31	19	375	164	.229
Bell, Buddy	9	1278	4872	627	1377	1963	221	34	99	570	32	.283
Bell, Kevin	5	293	717	73	158	236	21	9	13	64	5	.220
Beniquez, Juan	9	760	2553	332	668	929	100	22	39	233	89	.262
Bernazard, Tony	2	104	223	37	53	82	9	1	6	26	10	.238
Blair, Paul	17	1946	6042	776	1513	2307	282	55	134	620	171	.250
Bochte, Bruce	7	885	3089	383	887	1256	160	19	57	403	26	.287
Bonnell, Barry	4	474	1502	179	402	567	64	10	27	162	30	.268
Borgmann, Glenn	9	474	1294	137	296	394	42	4	16	151	4	.229
Bosetti, Rick	5	405	1462	162	369	504	68	8	17	128	30	.252
Bosley, Thad	4	230	655	69	179	220	18	4	5	54	24	.273
Braun, Steve	10	1095	3285	430	895	1211	140	16	48	353	44	.272
Brett, George	8	1002	3944	619	1257	1959	244	82	98	578	111	.319
Brohamer, Jack	9	805	2500	262	613	818	91	12	30	227	23	.245
Brookens, Tom	2	211	699	87	190	284	30	11	14	87	23	.272
Brown, Bobby	7	171	490	73	124	193	15	6	14	50	29	.253
Bumbry, Al	9	934	3282	524	952	1310	153	41	41	270	199	.290
Burleson, Rick	7	1031	4064	571	1114	1473	203	21	38	360	67	.274
Burroughs, Jeff	11	1222	4269	579	1111	1904	179	13	196	701	15	.260
Campaneris, Bert	17	2213	8459	1151	2182	2892	306	85	78	625	638	.258
Cannon, J. J.	4	148	227	34	40	48	3	1	1	11	15	.176
Cardenal, Jose	18	2017	6964	936	1913	2752	333	46	138	775	329	.275
Carew, Rod	14	1889	7184	1102	2394	3188	354	100	80	836	312	.333
Castino, John	2	298	939	116	277	391	30	15	18	116	12	.295
Cerone, Rick	6	416	1398	151	344	509	70	10	25	177	2	.246
Chalk, Dave	8	876	2861	290	722	889	104	9	15	238	36	.252
Charboneau, Joe	1	131	453	76	131	221	17	2	23	87	2	.289
Cooper, Cecil	10	976	3592	516	1098	1721	201	28	122	541	60	.306
Corcoran, Tim	4	273	602	74	164	213	24	2	7	66	4	.272
Cowens, Al	7	954	3307	442	924	1308	137	47	51	433	86	.279
Cox, Larry	7	341	808	71	179	255	30	5	12	85	5	.222
Cox, Ted	4	256	721	59	174	225	25	1	8	70	3	.241
Crowley, Terry	12	682	1247	152	316	477	54	1	35	184	3	.253
Cruz, Julio	4	433	1585	238	380	451	42	7	5	77	168	.240
Cruz, Todd	3	166	455	37	105	143	21	1	5	40	2	.231
Cubbage, Mike	7	636	1871	209	486	693	72	18	33	247	6	.260
Dauer, Rich	5	534	1838	229	480	638	90	1	22	198	4	.261
Davis, Bob	7	289	663	50	131	174	19	3	6	51	0	.198
Davis, Dick	4	288	969	136	256	378	51	4	21	103	10	.264
DeCinces, Doug	8	758	2570	324	647	1091	138	12	94	342	39	.252
Dempsey, Rick	12	711	1988	213	481	673	97	7	27	182	14	.242
Dent, Bucky	8	1072	3553	366	899	1162	133	20	30	338	14	.253
Diaz, Bo	4	137	367	27	82	118	17	2	5	44	1	.223
Dilone, Miguel	7	415	982	168	277	344	39	11	2	61	153	.282
Donohue, Tom	2	122	325	31	65	91	7	2	5	28	7	.200
Downing, Brian	8	764	2286	304	607	853	91	7	47	285	27	.266
Dwyer, Jim	8	533	1096	148	273	396	44	6	22	117	17	.250
Dybzinski, Jerry	1	114	248	32	57	73	11	1	1	23	4	.230
Dyer, Duffy	13	720	1993	151	441	627	74	11	30	173	10	.221
Edwards, Mike	4	317	879	94	220	262	28	4	2	49	38	.250
Elliott, Randy	4	114	288	31	62	102	12	2	8	35	0	.215
Ellis, John	12	860	2614	257	691	1034	113	13	68	384	6	.264
Essian, Jim	8	524	1421	146	344	489	61	3	26	161	6	.242
Evans, Dwight	9	1064	3394	485	888	1521	187	31	128	443	39	.262
Fisk, Carlton	11	1078	3860	627	1097	1856	207	33	162	568	61	.284
Foley, Marvis	3	113	268	23	65	91	8	0	6	31	0	.243
Ford, Dan	6	777	2794	425	771	1229	143	30	85	414	44	.276
Gamble, Oscar	12	1198	3544	520	964	1613	142	27	151	509	40	.272
Gantner, Jim	5	295	836	100	228	298	34	6	8	79	19	.273
Garcia, Damaso	3	169	622	58	169	226	31	7	4	51	16	.272
Garcia, Kiko	5	392	1077	120	250	341	36	14	9	78	30	.232
Garr, Ralph	13	1317	5108	717	1562	2127	212	64	75	408	172	.306

Player	Yrs.	G.	AB.	R.	H.	TB.	2B.	3B.	HR.	RBI.	SB.	Pct.
Goodwin, Danny	5	176	433	48	105	168	24	6	9	56	0	.242
Grich, Bobby	11	1285	4490	662	1188	1852	211	36	127	535	91	.265
Griffin, Alfredo	5	339	1326	150	354	466	50	25	4	75	41	.267
Gross, Wayne	5	525	1596	183	376	631	70	7	57	198	14	.236
Grubb, John	9	893	2858	387	809	1183	149	21	61	295	26	.283
Guerrero, Mario	8	697	2251	166	578	702	79	12	7	170	8	.257
Hargrove, Mike	7	1038	3546	541	1043	1457	170	20	68	444	16	.294
Harlow, Larry	5	406	1012	146	254	353	47	8	12	68	25	.251
Harrah, Toby	11	1443	4975	729	1301	1964	198	24	139	632	177	.262
Harrelson, Bud	16	1533	4834	539	1120	1367	136	45	7	267	127	.232
Harris, Vic	8	579	1610	168	349	475	57	15	13	121	36	.217
Hassey, Ron	3	230	687	68	203	285	32	4	14	106	3	.295
Heath, Mike	3	199	655	52	161	200	21	3	4	68	4	.246
Hebner, Richie	13	1532	5306	770	1477	2367	248	54	178	776	23	.278
Henderson, Rickey	2	247	942	160	275	354	35	7	10	79	133	.292
Hill, Marc	8	471	1295	104	293	414	42	2	25	150	1	.226
Hisle, Larry	12	1161	4087	634	1122	1855	189	32	160	658	128	.275
Hobson, Butch	6	623	2230	285	561	979	98	19	94	358	10	.252
Hoffman, Glenn	1	114	312	37	89	124	15	4	4	42	2	.285
Horton, Willie	18	2028	7298	873	1993	3332	284	40	325	1163	20	.273
Howell, Roy	7	801	2889	319	763	1136	145	21	62	341	8	.264
Hurdle, Clint	4	331	1009	119	275	427	66	10	22	153	1	.273
Jackson, Reggie	14	1924	6863	1145	1874	3531	345	41	410	1231	212	.273
Jackson, Ron	6	641	2107	266	551	834	122	19	41	237	15	.262
Johnson, Cliff	9	730	1987	287	497	922	95	6	106	351	3	.250
Johnson, Lamar	7	646	2173	247	634	930	104	12	56	328	19	.292
Jones, Lynn	2	125	268	42	77	103	10	2	4	32	10	.287
Jones, Ruppert	5	562	2070	289	518	840	91	24	61	249	86	.250
Kelly, Pat	14	1337	4263	612	1131	1611	185	35	75	402	248	.265
Kemp, Steve	4	579	2132	326	608	972	96	14	80	373	15	.285
Kimm, Bruce	4	186	439	35	104	128	19	1	1	26	5	.237
Klutts, Mickey	5	107	290	27	73	111	18	1	6	29	1	.252
Kuiper, Duane	7	714	2659	266	733	861	73	26	1	207	49	.276
LaCock, Pete	9	715	1729	214	444	633	86	11	27	224	8	.257
Landreaux, Ken	4	396	1384	180	385	572	62	22	27	173	26	.278
Lansford, Carney	3	429	1709	264	478	704	80	10	42	211	54	.280
LeFlore, Ron	7	926	3787	627	1104	1514	147	49	55	304	391	.292
Lemon, Chet	6	690	2466	353	705	1098	155	23	64	298	40	.286
Lowenstein, John	11	923	2359	336	578	884	89	14	63	265	111	.245
Lynn, Fred	7	828	3062	523	944	1591	217	29	124	521	43	.308
Mackanin, Pete	8	471	1345	140	303	459	56	11	26	123	26	.225
Manning, Rick	6	758	2881	362	759	979	103	24	23	249	98	.263
Martinez, Buck	11	595	1643	131	374	524	65	8	23	167	3	.228
May, Lee	16	2003	7463	944	1987	3429	331	29	351	1224	39	.266
Mayberry, John	13	1440	4909	672	1253	2171	198	18	228	806	19	.255
McKay, Dave	6	488	1492	141	340	460	55	13	13	132	10	.228
McRae, Hal	12	1319	4680	629	1354	2131	325	46	120	688	100	.289
Mendoza, Mario	7	586	1091	87	232	287	27	8	4	79	79	.213
Meyer, Danny	7	812	2896	339	747	1135	114	26	74	361	56	.258
Milbourne, Larry	7	652	1522	196	379	472	42	15	7	118	33	.249
Miller, Rick	10	1010	2732	401	728	958	114	28	20	256	65	.266
Minoso, Minnie	17	1835	6579	1136	1963	3023	336	83	186	1023	205	.298
Molinaro, Bob	5	243	661	89	182	257	22	10	11	64	42	.275
Molitor, Paul	3	376	1555	242	467	665	82	22	24	144	97	.300
Money, Don	13	1521	5641	736	1488	2301	276	33	157	652	80	.264
Moore, Junior	5	289	774	83	204	259	20	7	7	73	5	.264
Moore, Charlie	8	696	2013	235	530	723	88	21	21	211	28	.263
Mora, Andres	4	235	700	71	156	268	27	2	27	83	1	.223
Morales, Jose	8	588	1114	115	327	460	61	6	20	177	0	.294
Morrison, Jim	4	287	959	119	257	410	55	1	32	103	21	.268
Moseby, Lloyd	1	114	389	44	89	142	24	1	9	46	4	.229
Mulliniks, Rance	4	186	512	57	119	159	19	3	5	41	3	.232
Murcer, Bobby	14	1784	6450	944	1795	2870	271	45	238	988	125	.278
Murphy, Dwayne	3	340	1013	158	266	380	30	6	24	113	41	.263
Murray, Eddie	4	638	2448	356	712	1190	127	9	111	398	23	.291
Narron, Jerry	2	109	230	24	42	74	6	1	8	36	0	.183
Nettles, Graig	14	1767	6111	865	1588	2704	238	19	280	910	30	.252
Newman, Jeff	5	512	1461	137	336	550	56	4	50	178	7	.230
Nordhagen, Wayne	5	343	991	115	280	449	62	7	31	146	1	.283
Norman, Nelson	3	187	409	41	92	109	11	3	0	23	4	.225
Norris, Jim	4	489	1282	173	338	450	57	17	7	110	59	.264
Norwood, Willie	4	294	854	109	207	313	40	6	18	93	41	.242
Oates, Johnny	10	583	1611	142	405	506	55	2	14	126	11	.251
Oglivie, Ben	10	1028	3352	470	938	1591	168	22	147	487	77	.280
Oliver, Al	13	1734	6699	919	2028	3086	382	68	180	999	71	.303
Orta, Jorge	9	1119	4042	520	1142	1683	180	47	89	520	72	.283
Otis, Amos	13	1636	5999	929	1675	2603	307	57	169	811	311	.279
Paciorek, Tom	11	751	2040	244	548	813	109	18	40	236	23	.269
Page, Mitchell	4	535	1843	256	504	812	74	21	64	238	96	.273
Papi, Stan	5	185	430	41	95	141	24	5	4	39	1	.221
Parrish, Lance	4	384	1380	191	366	643	73	12	60	195	12	.265
Patek, Fred	13	1623	5483	733	1329	1775	215	54	41	485	384	.242
Perez, Tony	17	2313	8503	1153	2399	4026	443	70	348	1462	48	.282

Player	Yrs.	G.	AB.	R.	H.	TB.	2B.	3B.	HR.	RBI.	SB.	Pct.
Peters, Rick	2	145	496	82	144	183	19	7	2	44	13	.290
Picciolo, Rob	4	436	1131	120	258	343	38	7	11	74	5	.228
Piniella, Lou	14	1503	5213	575	1512	2118	266	38	88	689	31	.290
Poquette, Tom	5	395	1098	121	310	436	60	18	10	126	12	.282
Powell, Hosken	3	362	1204	162	320	427	54	10	11	102	30	.266
Pruitt, Ron	6	330	781	87	212	283	27	4	12	90	8	.271
Pryor, Greg	4	352	1044	121	273	357	52	7	6	79	8	.261
Putnam, Pat	4	317	908	106	241	385	40	4	32	124	1	.265
Quirk, Jamie	6	301	645	53	161	231	33	2	11	67	3	.250
Rader, Dave	10	846	2405	254	619	840	107	12	30	235	8	.257
Randall, Bob	5	460	1325	154	341	412	50	9	1	91	11	.257
Randolph, Willie	6	727	2628	443	721	963	100	41	20	232	150	.274
Remy, Jerry	6	735	2765	380	749	918	92	28	7	200	168	.271
Rettenmund, Merv	13	1023	2555	393	693	1037	114	16	66	329	68	.271
Revering, Dave	3	383	1369	160	386	629	67	13	50	185	2	.282
Rice, Jim	7	926	3656	596	1124	1993	171	55	196	669	47	.307
Rivera, Bombo	5	330	821	108	219	310	39	11	10	83	11	.267
Rivers, Mickey	11	1151	4540	640	1348	1813	195	57	52	416	244	.297
Roberts, Leon	7	645	2068	275	560	896	94	25	4	259	21	.271
Rodriguez, Aurelio	14	1805	6215	583	1478	2191	269	45	118	606	35	.238
Roenicke, Gary	4	307	821	114	204	363	35	2	40	112	3	.248
Rosello, Dave	8	379	789	103	186	246	27	3	9	69	5	.236
Rudi, Joe	14	1427	5241	649	1405	2263	278	38	168	768	25	.268
Sakata, Lenn	4	130	329	34	63	87	11	2	3	25	4	.191
Sample, Bill	3	235	544	91	155	219	33	2	9	57	16	.285
Sanguillen, Manny	13	1448	5062	566	1500	2014	205	57	65	585	35	.296
Simmons, Ted	13	1564	5725	736	1704	2626	332	37	172	929	11	.298
Simpson, Joe	6	320	694	79	178	226	27	3	5	63	24	.256
Singleton, Ken	11	1561	5395	786	1569	2436	246	18	195	819	21	.291
Sizemore, Ted	12	1411	5011	577	1311	1610	188	21	23	430	59	.262
Skaggs, Dave	4	205	510	44	123	154	18	2	3	49	0	.241
Smalley, Roy	6	825	3040	414	788	1149	130	15	67	368	18	.259
Soderholm, Eric	9	894	2894	402	764	1218	120	14	102	383	18	.264
Sofield, Rick	2	166	510	60	131	189	23	4	9	61	6	.257
Spencer, Jim	13	1441	4573	515	1166	1806	168	26	140	581	10	.255
Squires, Mike	5	322	856	112	232	286	30	6	4	78	30	.271
Stanley, Fred	12	649	1277	149	284	345	27	5	8	96	9	.222
Stapleton, Dave	1	106	449	61	144	208	33	5	7	45	3	.321
Stein, Bill	9	672	2158	204	565	800	89	16	38	225	13	.262
Stinson, Bob	12	652	1634	166	408	582	61	7	33	180	8	.250
Summers, Champ	7	488	1005	160	264	457	47	4	46	163	14	.263
Sundberg, Jim	7	1026	3259	347	837	1128	136	19	39	356	14	.257
Terrell, Jerry	8	657	1626	218	412	494	48	11	4	125	50	.253
Thomas, Gorman	8	751	2305	332	526	1066	111	9	137	400	27	.228
Thompson, Jason	5	717	2516	338	664	1125	96	10	115	424	6	.264
Thon, Dickie	2	115	323	38	87	106	15	2	0	27	21	.269
Thornton, Andre	7	759	2434	405	614	1156	124	20	126	414	21	.252
Torres, Rusty	7	654	1314	159	279	439	45	5	35	126	13	.212
Trammell, Alan	4	446	1511	230	423	550	46	15	17	149	32	.280
Upshaw, Willie	2	129	285	36	66	84	11	3	2	22	5	.232
Velez, Otto	8	159	1485	207	389	682	77	9	66	238	5	.262
Veryzer, Tom	8	778	2411	221	583	720	74	12	13	206	7	.242
Wagner, Mark	5	220	490	44	120	145	7	6	2	37	4	.245
Walton, Danny	9	297	779	69	174	293	27	4	28	107	4	.223
Washington, U.L.	4	333	966	121	256	347	31	18	8	88	43	.265
Wathan, John	5	365	1003	125	287	388	37	14	12	140	25	.286
Watson, Bob	15	1595	5664	750	1697	2551	285	37	165	903	26	.300
Whitaker, Lou	4	442	1416	219	378	477	46	16	7	147	37	.267
White, Frank	8	989	3055	389	769	1081	133	31	39	313	120	.252
Whitt, Ernie	4	139	358	31	81	123	17	2	7	43	1	.226
Wilfong, Rob	4	436	1205	171	329	457	47	12	19	128	39	.273
Wills, Bump	4	601	2201	357	590	807	97	18	28	223	149	.268
Wilson, Willie	5	467	1531	299	470	613	56	30	9	115	216	.307
Winfield, Dave	8	1117	3997	599	1134	1853	179	39	154	626	133	.284
Wockenfuss, John	7	445	1245	166	324	553	49	9	54	183	3	.260
Wolfe, Larry	4	161	361	43	83	122	16	1	7	50	0	.230
Woods, Al	4	425	1469	188	411	595	71	13	29	143	19	.280
Wynegar, Butch	5	723	2510	305	642	871	103	9	36	307	8	.256
Yastrzemski, Carl	20	2967	10811	1689	3109	5066	586	57	419	1663	168	.288
Yount, Robin	7	988	3835	499	1050	1490	193	38	57	390	98	.274
Zisk, Richie	10	1138	3999	548	1150	1865	193	24	158	651	6	.288

National League Lifetime Batting Records

Players With 100 or More Games Played Who Were Active in Majors in 1980

NOTE—Figures include complete major league totals of players who also played in American League.

Player	Yrs.	G.	AB.	R.	H.	TB.	2B.	3B.	HR.	RBI.	SB.	Pct.
Alexander, Gary	6	411	1229	163	283	506	41	0	54	196	6	.230
Alexander, Matt	8	359	157	106	32	40	4	2	0	4	100	.204
Almon, Bill	7	495	1471	159	366	458	48	16	4	88	49	.249

Player	Yrs.	G	AB	R	H	TB	2B	3B	HR	RBI	SB	Pct.
Ashby, Alan	8	629	1885	170	432	609	81	9	26	208	4	.229
Asselstine, Brian	5	228	488	44	124	184	22	4	10	58	4	.254
Bailor, Bob	6	437	1891	232	498	637	75	20	8	138	46	.263
Baker, Dusty	13	1346	4788	661	1323	2104	229	15	174	700	97	.276
Bench, Johnny	14	1877	6771	1001	1811	3265	342	22	356	1259	67	.267
Benedict, Bruce	3	218	615	35	150	185	27	1	2	50	4	.244
Bergman, Dave	5	219	300	32	70	88	11	2	1	18	3	.233
Berra, Dale	4	210	543	48	115	180	16	2	15	63	5	.212
Bevacqua, Kurt	10	673	1593	156	374	520	64	11	20	189	10	.235
Biittner, Larry	11	1012	2790	286	759	1000	126	17	27	304	9	.272
Blackwell, Tim	7	339	829	68	190	248	27	8	5	64	1	.229
Bochy, Bruce	3	132	305	19	73	98	13	0	4	21	0	.239
Bonds, Bobby	13	1804	6880	1232	1851	3254	295	65	326	1005	456	.269
Boone, Bob	9	1049	3463	330	909	1299	165	21	61	432	21	.262
Bowa, Larry	11	1636	6455	782	1696	2083	192	78	13	390	272	.263
Buckner, Bill	12	1306	4936	575	1457	1990	249	25	78	545	117	.295
Cabell, Enos	9	995	3652	486	1006	1365	156	43	39	368	186	.275
Carter, Gary	7	850	2950	406	787	1332	135	16	126	444	28	.267
Cash, Dave	12	1422	5554	732	1571	1989	243	56	21	426	120	.283
Cedeno, Cesar	11	1430	5426	848	1576	2484	324	55	158	744	475	.290
Cey, Ron	10	1246	4348	611	1147	1935	185	15	191	713	17	.264
Chambliss, Chris	10	1446	5504	676	1552	2280	289	35	123	678	26	.282
Clark, Jack	6	596	2088	332	580	1006	114	24	88	329	47	.278
Collins, Dave	6	680	2135	298	582	749	71	16	18	162	183	.277
Concepcion, Dave	11	1505	5324	644	1430	1965	232	39	75	606	232	.269
Cromartie, Warren	6	675	2581	309	728	1038	153	23	37	224	36	.282
Cruz, Hector	7	554	1479	170	332	511	65	9	32	185	5	.224
Cruz, Jose	11	1325	4276	567	1209	1792	217	54	86	571	216	.283
Cubbage, Mike	7	636	1871	209	486	693	72	18	33	247	6	.260
Dawson, Andre	5	626	2435	343	676	1127	119	37	86	323	119	.278
DeJesus, Ivan	7	720	2628	380	702	913	111	29	14	164	134	.267
Dillard, Steve	6	369	853	129	213	294	40	4	11	86	15	.250
Driessen, Dave	8	1046	3364	478	915	1398	171	21	90	495	131	.272
Easler, Mike	7	244	546	84	170	283	31	5	24	94	6	.311
Evans, Barry	3	153	377	27	88	109	9	3	2	32	1	.233
Evans, Darrell	12	1468	5003	747	1251	2098	189	23	204	719	73	.250
Fahey, Bill	8	309	778	59	192	235	21	2	6	68	8	.247
Ferguson, Joe	11	936	2846	387	689	1182	117	11	118	429	22	.242
Figueroa, Jesus	1	115	198	20	50	58	5	0	1	11	2	.253
Flannery, Tim	2	117	357	17	80	94	12	1	0	29	2	.224
Flynn, Doug	6	749	2190	169	532	659	59	25	6	180	11	.243
Foli, Tim	11	1292	4721	460	1185	1471	194	16	20	378	70	.251
Foote, Barry	8	621	1932	175	456	723	94	10	51	217	10	.236
Foster, George	12	1199	4169	630	1190	2130	190	36	226	784	42	.285
Frias, Pepe	8	698	1310	126	314	381	48	8	1	105	12	.240
Garner, Phil	8	966	3286	407	863	1304	170	50	57	389	148	.263
Garvey, Steve	12	1455	5487	723	1670	2566	275	33	185	842	69	.304
Gomez, Luis	7	574	1216	104	256	292	26	5	0	89	6	.211
Gonzalez, Julio	4	296	839	79	197	242	27	6	2	54	12	.235
Griffey, Ken	8	946	3461	607	1063	1525	180	54	58	390	138	.307
Gross, Greg	8	907	2451	319	722	900	84	38	6	203	27	.295
Guerrero, Pedro	3	105	253	37	79	121	11	2	9	41	4	.312
Henderson, Steve	4	497	1800	267	516	762	79	31	35	227	55	.287
Hendrick, George	10	1226	4381	580	1222	1984	203	14	177	658	47	.279
Hernandez, Keith	7	847	2903	484	867	1318	190	36	63	427	49	.299
Herndon, Larry	6	598	1765	199	464	644	61	31	19	145	45	.263
Hodges, Ron	8	377	799	63	186	251	27	1	12	82	4	.233
Horner, Bob	3	334	1273	197	363	688	46	3	91	250	3	.285
Howe, Art	7	585	1758	179	458	690	97	18	33	207	7	.261
Hubbard, Glenn	3	258	919	104	224	309	37	3	14	85	9	.244
Hutton, Tommy	11	921	1626	195	407	550	63	7	22	184	15	.250
Iorg, Dane	4	261	577	56	166	224	40	3	4	67	2	.288
Ivie, Mike	8	732	2328	267	638	983	112	16	67	357	22	.274
Johnstone, Jay	15	1413	4110	506	1110	1617	188	35	83	453	49	.270
Jorgensen, Mike	12	1170	2877	372	708	1093	106	9	87	358	50	.246
Kennedy, Junior	3	298	733	84	191	232	25	5	2	62	11	.261
Kennedy, Terry	3	127	386	39	99	142	19	3	6	53	0	.256
Kingman, Dave	10	1143	3839	552	933	1938	155	20	270	720	65	.243
Knight, Ray	5	489	1337	151	377	564	85	12	26	176	6	.282
Lacy, Lee	9	740	1974	266	547	803	89	22	41	211	52	.277
Landestoy, Rafael	4	352	911	99	236	296	27	15	1	66	45	.259
Law, Rudy	2	139	400	57	104	120	5	4	1	24	43	.260
LeMaster, Johnnie	6	467	1328	124	293	405	57	14	9	100	21	.221
Leonard, Jeff	4	241	663	79	178	233	24	11	3	73	27	.268
Lezcano, Sixto	7	785	2722	360	749	1229	130	22	102	374	34	.275
Lopes, Dave	9	1149	4376	724	1160	1683	163	39	94	367	398	.265
Lum, Mike	14	1466	3485	398	862	1293	127	20	88	424	13	.247
Luzinski, Greg	11	1289	4630	618	1299	2263	253	21	223	811	29	.281
Maddox, Elliott	11	1029	2843	360	742	949	121	16	18	234	60	.261
Maddox, Garry	9	1251	4806	622	1388	2043	270	56	91	578	218	.289
Madlock, Bill	8	974	3592	519	1128	1628	193	29	83	435	115	.314
Martin, Jerry	7	735	1757	252	442	751	100	13	61	237	30	.252
Matthews, Gary	9	1182	4406	658	1267	1982	196	42	145	587	112*	.288

Player	Yrs.	G	AB	R	H	TB	2B	3B	HR	RBI	SB	Pct.
May, Milt	11	858	2688	242	703	1004	102	11	59	343	1	.262
Mazzilli, Lee	5	641	2331	313	640	956	119	16	55	269	122	.275
McBride, Bake	8	916	3317	493	95	1414	139	50	60	378	168	.300
Mejias, Sam	5	268	299	45	72	99	11	2	4	24	7	.241
Milner, John	10	1091	3248	437	814	1350	132	16	124	470	30	.251
Monday, Rick	15	1686	5571	864	1471	2453	232	57	212	681	95	.264
Montanez, Willie	12	1523	5695	633	1573	2313	278	24	138	794	32	.276
Moreno, Omar	6	683	2506	386	637	863	79	42	21	184	313	.254
Morgan, Joe	18	2186	7737	1413	2127	3352	373	90	224	939	625	.275
Mumphrey, Jerry	7	682	2135	283	602	772	84	25	12	193	118	.282
Murphy, Dale	5	448	1624	225	427	742	62	8	79	248	26	.263
Nahoodny, Bill	5	241	711	66	173	272	35	2	20	86	1	.243
Nicosia, Steve	3	133	372	38	93	132	24	0	5	35	0	.250
Nolan, Joe	6	324	715	79	184	265	27	6	14	78	5	.257
North, Bill	10	1123	3769	618	987	1219	113	31	19	218	369	.262
Oberkfell, Ken	4	284	850	118	246	327	47	11	4	82	6	.289
Oester, Ron	3	112	314	41	87	113	16	2	2	21	6	.277
Office, Rowland	8	868	2368	255	618	836	100	11	32	241	27	.261
Ott, Ed	7	492	1534	176	409	588	68	9	31	173	12	.267
Parker, Dave	8	1017	3812	590	1197	1952	234	52	139	612	98	.314
Parrish, Larry	7	870	3062	380	811	1318	189	21	92	400	17	.265
Perkins, Broderick	3	162	404	40	112	149	23	1	4	55	6	.277
Phillips, Mike	8	645	1625	160	393	516	44	23	11	140	11	.242
Pocoroba, Biff	6	424	1093	111	287	396	54	2	17	126	6	.263
Porter, Darrell	10	1092	3602	514	905	1464	148	33	115	527	24	.251
Puhl, Terry	4	507	1949	289	561	757	84	20	24	149	99	.288
Pujols, Luis	4	166	464	33	82	107	16	3	1	39	0	.177
Randle, Lenny	10	1026	3631	456	945	1226	134	39	23	296	143	.260
Reitz, Ken	9	1255	4507	356	1187	1641	234	11	66	520	10	.263
Reynolds, Craig	6	604	1984	204	515	664	60	25	13	144	29	.260
Richards, Gene	4	608	2267	337	668	884	85	40	17	159	178	.295
Roberts, David W.	8	654	1930	188	464	695	73	7	48	201	26	.240
Robinson, Bill	13	1357	4129	514	1072	1818	217	29	157	600	69	.260
Rose, Pete	18	2830	11479	1842	3557	4910	654	117	155	1077	167	.310
Royster, Jerry	8	735	2555	346	637	818	84	23	17	182	138	.249
Russell, Bill	12	1545	5461	600	1450	1898	222	50	42	479	127	.266
Sadek, Mike	7	364	777	83	178	228	27	4	5	71	6	.229
Schmidt, Mike	9	1234	4261	778	1104	2239	208	39	283	787	129	.259
Scott, Rodney	6	571	1745	266	425	514	34	23	3	123	168	.244
Scott, Tony	7	609	1664	209	419	555	66	20	10	163	83	.252
Smith, Lonnie	3	134	332	79	106	139	16	4	3	23	39	.319
Smith, Ozzie	3	473	1786	213	416	506	53	17	1	108	125	.233
Smith, Reggie	15	1840	6649	1067	1914	3264	351	57	295	1028	130	.288
Speier, Chris	10	1423	4969	544	1231	1735	202	40	74	497	28	.248
Spilman, Harry	3	112	161	22	40	59	7	0	4	24	0	.248
Stargell, Willie	19	2248	7794	1187	2198	4139	415	55	472	1514	17	.282
Staub, Rusty	18	2533	9108	1160	2547	3946	468	47	279	1364	46	.280
Stearns, John	7	620	2039	255	516	765	114	6	41	259	61	.253
Stennett, Rennie	10	1199	4434	492	1219	1598	177	41	40	425	73	.275
Strain, Joe	2	144	446	53	116	135	14	1	1	28	9	.260
Swisher, Steve	7	467	1328	104	291	407	48	7	18	121	4	.219
Tamargo, John	4	135	244	19	59	85	12	1	4	33	1	.242
Taveras, Frank	9	1018	3673	464	950	1164	128	40	2	199	280	.259
Templeton, Garry	5	633	2657	396	815	1118	109	61	24	248	130	.307
Tenace, Gene	12	1378	4075	602	987	1752	158	20	189	628	35	.242
Thomas, Derrel	10	1148	3805	464	950	1265	128	44	33	302	120	.250
Thomasson, Gary	9	901	2373	315	591	927	103	25	61	294	50	.249
Thompson, Scot	3	249	608	69	163	213	26	6	4	44	10	.268
Trevino, Alex	3	191	574	53	150	178	22	3	0	57	2	.261
Trillo, Manny	8	913	3190	312	834	1109	120	25	35	331	33	.261
Turner, Jerry	7	580	1466	194	384	577	70	9	35	203	44	.262
Tyson, Mike	9	967	2867	275	697	944	116	28	25	261	22	.243
Unser, Del	13	1718	5142	612	1335	1856	176	42	87	475	64	.260
Vail, Mike	6	488	1289	129	374	536	58	10	28	178	9	.290
Valentine, Ellis	6	616	2275	289	660	1091	133	11	92	343	56	.290
Venable, Max	2	119	223	25	51	59	6	1	0	13	11	.229
Walling, Dennis	6	317	718	83	205	284	26	13	9	104	16	.286
Washington, Claudell	7	824	3023	393	845	1242	154	36	57	370	149	.280
White, Jerry	7	453	904	126	241	338	38	7	15	82	45	.267
Whitfield, Terry	7	545	1615	210	465	645	78	12	26	145	17	.288
Wohlford, Jim	9	755	2158	264	566	730	80	27	10	204	78	.262
Yeager, Steve	9	855	2519	278	585	926	93	10	76	294	12	.232
Youngblood, Joel	5	567	1636	213	433	649	89	17	31	172	38	.265

American League Lifetime Pitching Records

Pitchers With 10 or More Decisions Who Were Active in Majors in 1980

Pitcher—N.L. Totals in Parentheses	Balt. W-L	Bos. W-L	Calif. W-L	Chi. W-L	Clev. W-L	Det. W-L	†K.C. W-L	‡Mil. W-L	Minn. W-L	N.Y. W-L	*Oak. W-L	Sea. W-L	§Tex. W-L	Tor. W-L	Totals W-L
Aase, Don	0-5	1-3	3-5	2-1	2-3	2-6	5-0	2-2	4-9	2-1	4-3	1-0	4-3	5-2	34-33
Abbott, Glenn	4-3	1-3	3-1	1-2	2-4	3-7	6-9	6-2	6-9	2-6	5-5		2-6	4-3	48-66
Arroyo, Fernando	0-4	3-3	3-1	2-6	1-4		6-9	1-1	2-5	0-3	5-3	0-1	2-6	1-3	17-26
Augustine, Jerry	4-9	2-5	4-4	5-3	3-1	6-6	5-3		2-5	7-6	2-1	4-0	2-2	3-2	49-51
Bacsik, Mike	0-0	1-1	3-0	0-1		0-0	1-0		2-0	0-1	2-1	1-0	0-3		8-6
Bannister, Floyd (11-18)	2-2	2-2	0-1	3-2	1-0	2-3	1-1	0-4	2-3	1-1	2-1		2-5	1-3	19-28
Barker, Len	2-5	2-1	0-0	3-2		3-1	3-1	0-5	4-0	1-1	2-1	2-1	5-0	1-3	31-24
Barlow, Mike (2-2)	1-1		1-0	2-0	0-1	0-2	1-0	1-0	1-1	0-1	0-0	0-0	0-0	0-0	8-4
Barr, Jim (81-90)	1-3		2-7	2-1				4-2	1-4	2-2	2-1	1-3	1-2	0-0	11-16
Barrios, Francisco	1-1	2-1	3-4		3-3	3-0	5-3	4-2	1-4	2-2	5-1	5-3	4-3	3-0	37-35
Baumgarten, Ross	1-3	2-1	1-2		2-3	2-3	1-3	1-1	1-0	1-2	0-2	1-2	3-0	2-0	17-22
Beattie, Jim	2-3	1-0	3-0	2-4	2-3	1-3	1-0	2-1	0-3		0-1	5-3	3-3	2-3	14-30
Billingham, Jack (119-95)	3-6	4-5	6-4	5-6	2-1	3-6	1-0	5-1	2-3	5-4	6-2	1-0	3-3	2-3	26-18
Bird, Doug (2-0)	9-9	7-8	18-10	12-13	7-11	9-6		5-1	5-3	8-10	6-2	0-2	9-7	0-0	52-36
Blyleven, Bert (34-28)	9-9	7-8	18-10	12-13	7-11	9-6	19-12	5-1		8-10	12-13	4-0	4-6	1-1	122-113
Brett, Ken (39-26)	3-8	4-2	1-7	3-3	5-4	2-5	2-7	2-1	5-2	3-5	5-3	0-2	4-2	1-1	43-58
Burgmeier, Tom	2-3	4-1	3-2	5-4	4-2	4-3		9-4	5-2	4-7	5-3	2-1	6-2	1-0	59-43
Burns, Britt	0-2	3-0	3-0		0-5	0-4	1-0	2-0	2-0	1-2	2-1	2-0	1-1	1-0	15-15
Busby, Steve	3-8	5-5	10-2	7-8	4-5	7-4		8-1	6-7	1-2	8-7	2-1	7-4	1-0	70-54
Buskey, Tom	1-5	3-4	0-2	2-1	2-2	3-4	1-0	2-2	6-7	0-2	0-0	2-1	2-1	1-0	21-27
Caldwell, Mike (35-50)	3-4	3-4	2-3	4-6	2-2	4-5	3-4		5-1	8-1	6-2	3-1	4-1	3-2	56-34
Campbell, Bill	3-1	2-2	8-2	4-0	4-6	7-3	7-4	6-2	1-1	1-4	6-3	3-3	6-1	2-3	59-39
Castro, Bill	1-3	1-4	1-4	0-0	4-2	1-3	1-6		0-1	3-0	3-3	1-2	3-5	2-1	25-23
Clancy, Jim	3-5	2-5	3-1	3-3	3-3	2-1	4-0	6-7	1-2	2-1	4-1	2-0	3-2		29-44
Clay, Ken	0-0	1-2	0-0	1-1	0-4	2-1	0-1	1-1	1-2	3-0	0-0	2-1	3-5	3-3	8-17
Clear, Mark	1-5	1-2		0-1	3-1	1-1	1-3	8-1	1-1	2-1	3-2	3-1	1-2	2-3	22-16
Cleveland, Reggie (40-41)	8-8	4-4	3-5	6-6	6-1	7-4	3-4	4-0	0-1	8-3	5-6	4-2	2-5	0-3	63-62
Comer, Steve	3-1	1-1	1-0	3-1	3-0	4-5	4-0	6-7	4-1	2-1	3-2	4-2		2-1	30-21
Corbett, Doug	0-2	3-0	2-3	0-0	3-1	2-1	0-1	1-1		1-0	1-0	4-2	0-0	3-1	8-6
Darwin, Danny	2-0	1-1	1-0	0-0	3-1	1-1	0-1	1-1	4-2	2-1	3-1	2-1		1-0	18-8
Davis, Ron	1-1	4-0	2-1	2-0	3-0	2-0	0-1	1-1	1-0		1-0	1-0	2-1	0-0	23-5
Denny, John (51-46)	1-0	1-1	0-2	0-0	0-1	1-0	0-1	1-0	1-0	1-0	0-1	1-0	1-2	0-0	8-6
Devine, Adrian (14-15)	1-0	0-2	2-1	1-1	0-1	0-1	0-1	3-0	0-0	2-1	1-0	1-0		0-0	12-7
Dotson, Richard	9-13	5-6	8-6		12-7	9-7	6-7	14-5	7-15	4-10	7-11	5-1		1-1	104-111
Drago, Dick	0-1	3-1	0-3	0-2		0-2	2-6	0-5	0-0	1-0	1-0		10-11	1-1	7-12
Dressler, Rob (4-11)	6-7	3-3	7-4	6-4	11-3	9-7	3-9	9-4	8-3	6-10	6-5	7-2	4-9	1-1	89-64
Eckersley, Dennis	3-2	2-3	3-6	6-3		2-3	3-9	4-4	1-3	1-2	6-5	1-1	6-1	7-0	24-36
Erickson, Roger	3-2	2-3	3-1	2-1	0-3	0-3	1-1	3-3		1-2	1-1	4-2	3-1	1-0	23-27
Farmer, Ed (2-1)	1-3	2-3	2-1	5-1	2-5	0-3	1-1	3-3	2-2	2-3	1-1	3-1	4-2	1-0	29-19
Fidrych, Mark	3-8	8-3	5-5	8-3	7-4		2-9	7-7	9-2	2-3	7-5	5-2	3-4	3-3	80-67
Figueroa, Ed	6-5	9-4	8-5	7-1	6-6	6-5	5-8	6-1	8-2	2-2	1-0	5-2	5-2	1-1	67-61
Fingers, Rollie (34-40)	5-6	5-3	8-3	5-4	4-4	6-5	7-4	6-4	8-2	6-7	10-3	6-2	4-2	1-0	76-53
Flanagan, Mike	3-3	4-3	2-4	2-2	2-3	1-3	5-8	6-1	8-2	2-2	2-2	3-1	2-2	1-0	24-36
Frost, Dave	2-3	2-3	1-0	3-4	2-3	1-3	2-0	2-2	9-2	2-3	2-2	0-3	6-3	3-1	36-27
Gale, Rich	4-2	5-6	3-4	4-3	3-1	8-3		6-1	8-2	6-7	10-4	6-2	2-2	10-4	36-27
Garland, Wayne	2-2	4-6	4-6	4-5		8-3	3-6	7-6	2-6	2-2	6-4	0-3	4-5	4-3	52-59

Pitcher—N.L. Totals in Parentheses	Balt. W-L	Bos. W-L	Calif. W-L	Chi. W-L	Cleve. W-L	Det. W-L	†K.C. W-L	‡Mil. W-L	Minn. W-L	N.Y. W-L	*Oak. W-L	Sea. W-L	§Tex. W-L	Tor. W-L	Totals W-L
Garvin, Jerry	1-3	1-2	3-0	2-2	0-7	4-2	1-3	0-7	5-1	1-5	1-5	2-2	2-3	2-1	18-38
Gossage, Rich (11-9)	1-3	2-3	8-4	1-0	8-5	4-3	5-7	0-7	5-3	2-3	1-2	0-2	3-5	3-1	50-52
Grimsley, Ross (69-49)	0-0	2-3	3-5	3-4	7-1	6-3	2-5	3-5	8-2	8-4	6-4	3-3	2-4	1-1	54-48
Guidry, Ron	5-0	7-2	3-3	3-2	7-1	10-4	6-2	9-6	8-2	7-1	8-1	3-3	2-4	9-0	76-29
Gura, Larry (3-7)	5-3	0-4	10-3	3-3	7-1	3-4		3-2	4-6	7-1	3-4	5-3	2-4	5-3	71-40
Haas, Moose	8-4	0-4	2-5	7-2	4-2	3-4	2-4		1-3	4-3	3-4	3-2	2-7	5-3	39-42
Hamilton, Dave (0-2)	4-4	4-3	2-7	4-0	4-2	2-3	5-5	2-3	5-4	4-3	0-0	1-0	5-6	4-0	39-39
Hartzell, Paul	3-1	0-2	2-0	2-2	1-2	1-3	0-3	3-4	0-2	1-8	4-3	2-3	5-8	1-1	27-38
Hassler, Andy (4-5)	2-3	2-4	0-0	3-6	1-2	4-2	0-3	2-4	0-9	2-0	3-5	1-3	3-1	1-2	33-56
Heaverlo, Dave (12-6)	0-0	1-3	1-3	0-2	2-1	1-3	5-3	0-3	1-4	0-1	0-0	0-2	2-8	0-2	13-20
Hiller, John	7-14	7-5	10-6	7-2	8-8		5-1	9-6	4-7	13-7	6-6	0-2	8-9	3-2	87-76
Holdsworth, Fred (3-3)	0-4	0-2	2-4	4-3	0-1	1-0	1-2	1-1		0-0	0-2	0-0	1-2	0-1	4-7
Honeycutt, Rick	0-1	0-1	1-0	0-0	0-2	2-5	1-5	2-0	6-2	0-5	2-5	1-1	1-0	1-0	26-41
Hoyt, LaMarr					2-0		0-3			1-5	3-0	1-1	1-0		9-3
Jackson, Darrell	9-5	8-3	8-9	8-12	8-6	5-5	8-10	11-8		8-12	12-7	6-5	10-8	4-3	17-19
Jenkins, Ferguson (149-109)	14-10	10-10	14-14	4-1	15-10	6-13	9-3	8-8	11-8	0-3	6-12	3-1	0-1	1-3	127-105
John, Tommy (87-42)	1-1	2-4	1-1	3-4	2-1	2-4	2-3	1-0	1-0	2-1	1-0	3-2	1-8	2-2	17-26
Johnson, John	3-6	2-4	3-6	0-6	1-3	2-4	4-3	2-4	2-3	0-1	5-3	3-2	0-4	1-1	27-48
Keough, Matt	0-1	4-4	2-5	7-2	2-1	2-0	4-3	5-1	2-3	2-1	4-4	3-2	0-3	3-3	45-46
Kern, Jim	1-4	0-2	2-1	4-2	1-3	2-0	4-3	0-3	4-1	4-4	5-4	1-2	1-3	1-2	32-36
Kingman, Brian	2-5	2-2	4-2	4-2	2-2	2-5	5-3	0-2	2-4	0-1		6-0	1-3	3-3	36-32
Knapp, Chris	2-5	1-3	2-1	3-2	1-3	2-0	4-3	4-1	2-6	2-6	5-2	4-3	1-2	6-2	36-26
Koosman, Jerry (140-137)	0-1	0-0	0-3	1-1	3-5	2-5	5-4	1-1	4-1	0-1	5-4	6-1	0-3	2-1	41-49
Kravec, Ken	2-5	1-2	4-2		1-1	0-2	1-1	1-1	0-5	1-7	2-1	2-2	1-2	2-1	18-24
Kucek, Jack (1-0)	0-1	1-3	0-3	2-0	0-5	0-1	1-0	1-0	0-0	0-1		4-6	0-3	5-2	6-16
Lacey, Bob	0-3	3-4	2-0	3-5	3-3	3-2	1-5	4-3	3-6	1-7		3-6	4-5	2-4	16-27
Langford, Rick (0-1)	5-6	3-4	8-4	5-4	4-0	3-2	3-5	4-4	8-3	5-5	3-4	3-6	2-7	4-3	48-60
LaRoche, Dave (9-7)	2-4	1-1	1-1	5-4	6-6	3-6	3-5	8-5	2-3	5-5	2-4	6-4	12-10	0-0	37-63
Lemanczyk, Dave	5-4	1-5	1-3	2-6	0-5	10-5	0-6	7-4	7-4	5-5	9-10	1-0	2-6	1-0	107-73
Leonard, Dennis	6-5	8-6	12-2	10-7	10-7	2-7		8-2	7-2	2-1	3-6	4-0	2-6	2-0	33-61
Lockwood, Skip (24-36)	2-8	0-7	3-0	2-7	2-4	3-1	6-4	0-1	0-1	2-1	4-4	1-3	2-0	0-2	23-11
Lopez, Aurelio (4-2)	3-0	3-2	0-5	3-4	4-5		3-5	0-2	0-2	4-1	4-4	1-1	2-7	5-2	27-45
Marshall, Mike (67-65)	1-5	2-3	2-1	0-2	0-1	3-1	1-0	0-2	1-2	0-5	0-0	0-0	4-0	5-2	10-13
Martin, Renie	0-2	1-1	4-3	1-0	0-1	0-1	1-0	1-4	1-1	1-5	4-0	0-3		5-2	52-40
Martin, Alfredo	7-10	2-3		0-2	5-2	4-2	4-3	6-4	1-1	1-5	3-3	8-1	4-0	2-1	28-14
Martinez, Dennis	2-2	1-1	4-1	2-2	0-1	0-1	1-0	1-2	1-4	8-3	3-3	3-1	2-1	2-1	30-27
Martinez, Tippy	0-0	0-1	0-1	0-1	4-1	0-1	4-3	8-9	1-1	0-1	3-3	3-1	2-2	2-1	121-121
Matlack, Jon (92-81)	2-0	2-2	2-2	2-2	1-6	15-12	1-3	11-10	13-11	8-14	13-14	1-0	8-4	1-2	15-26
May, Rudy (18-13)	3-13	2-1	6-6	13-11	10-2	2-2	4-8	1-2	2-3		0-1	3-1	2-1	1-1	51-33
McCatty, Steve	2-1	2-2	1-1	5-2	2-3	2-3	2-2	0-5	2-1	0-3		2-3	4-1	4-2	14-21
McClure, Bob	1-2	2-5	5-2	1-1	5-2	9-1	2-4	0-1	7-1	3-5	2-3	2-2	4-1	0-1	6-9
McGregor, Scott	1-2	2-3	2-0	1-0	0-0	0-1	3-1	0-4	2-0	0-1	0-2		3-1	5-2	94-72
McLaughlin, Byron	1-0	0-1	2-0	9-7	11-7	0-1	1-2	1-2	6-5	0-1	3-8	0-0	6-1	2-1	8-18
McLaughlin, Joey (5-3)	4-4	10-4	7-7	9-7	1-1	8-5	9-7	8-9	1-3	4-3	1-1	0-3	2-2	2-2	32-39
Medich, Doc (8-12)	0-3	2-2	1-0	0-3	2-3	2-0	1-2	1-2	6-3	0-4	1-0	3-5	3-7	4-1	26-30
Mirabella, Paul	1-5	1-0	3-1	5-3	3-2	0-1	0-4	0-1	1-3	0-3	0-8	0-3	4-1	2-3	21-21
Mitchell, Paul	3-1	1-4	3-1	3-3	2-1	2-1	3-1	0-4	0-9	3-3	1-2	3-5	2-1	2-0	21-21
Monge, Sid (3-5)	0-1	3-2	1-2	4-2		1-1	3-1	0-2	1-3	3-3	4-1	2-0	2-1	3-1	12-19
Montague, John (3-5)		1-1	1-2	2-1		2-1			1-2	1-2	0-1		1-1	2-0	
Moore, Balor (18-29)	0-1	1-1	1-2	1-2	2-1	2-1	1-2	0-2	1-2	1-2	0-1	1-1	1-1	0-0	

Pitcher—N.L. Totals in Parentheses	Balt. W-L	Bos. W-L	Calif. W-L	Chi. W-L	Cleve. W-L	Det. W-L	†K.C. W-L	‡Mil. W-L	Minn. W-L	N.Y. W-L	*Oak. W-L	Sea. W-L	§Tex. W-L	Tor. W-L	Totals W-L
Morris, Jack	3-2	2-4	4-3	3-1	4-3	—	2-3	5-1	2-2	3-2	3-3	3-3	1-2	3-1	37-28
Norris, Mike	2-1	3-4	4-2	4-4	2-2	2-1	2-4	5-1	2-2	3-2	—	3-1	3-4	4-2	34-34
Palmer, Jim	—	20-16	24-8	24-9	26-11	19-10	20-10	19-8	18-10	25-15	18-12	7-4	19-16	7-4	241-132
Parrott, Mike	1-2	1-3	4-2	2-3	2-2	1-2	0-3	2-3	0-3	1-1	0-2	—	1-5	1-0	16-33
Pattin, Marty	6-13	5-4	14-12	9-12	10-11	9-9	8-3	13-3	13-10	4-10	9-14	1-1	10-7	3-0	114-109
Paxton, Mike	3-3	1-2	3-1	2-0	5-2	2-6	2-3	4-9	4-2	1-4	0-3	3-4	1-3	3-0	30-24
Perry, Gaylord (167-126)	13-14	18-5	7-5	10-7	—	12-6	9-13	4-9	12-12	4-10	10-16	3-4	6-4	1-1	122-104
Petry, Dan	1-1	1-1	2-1	3-0	1-2	—	0-1	0-3	1-2	0-1	1-3	2-1	1-3	1-1	16-14
Proly, Mike (1-0)	1-0	1-1	2-1	0-0	2-0	3-0	2-0	0-3	1-1	1-0	1-3	2-1	3-2	0-2	13-20
Quisenberry, Dan	1-1	2-1	0-3	1-1	1-1	1-2	—	0-3	2-1	1-0	1-5	1-0	3-0	5-0	15-9
Rainey, Chuck	1-0	—	0-4	1-1	1-4	1-2	2-0	2-2	2-1	1-0	1-4	4-2	3-2	1-1	16-8
Rawley, Shane	3-1	0-1	0-3	2-2	2-5	3-2	1-1	2-3	0-1	3-0	2-1	4-2	4-2	2-1	16-25
Redfern, Pete	2-3	1-4	4-2	1-3	1-2	3-2	3-5	2-3	—	0-3	2-1	4-2	3-3	1-1	31-30
Renko, Steve (78-95)	1-1	1-5	2-1	0-1	0-0	1-2	1-7	4-2	3-3	4-1	2-1	0-0	1-0	1-0	22-30
Roberts, Dave (81-92)	1-2	3-5	2-1	3-1	5-0	0-2	0-2	4-3	2-4	0-3	1-6	0-1	4-3	3-2	34-32
Robbins, Bruce	0-0	1-2	2-0	0-2	3-0	—	1-0	1-1	1-0	1-1	0-0	2-2	1-0	3-1	7-5
Rozema, Dave	0-1	3-5	2-1	3-1	5-0	—	4-10	4-1	2-4	0-3	1-6	6-1	4-3	3-2	34-32
Scarbery, Randy	0-0	0-2	1-1	0-0	0-0	0-2	0-0	0-1	2-4	0-3	0-0	0-1	0-1	—	3-10
Schatzeder, Dan (19-13)	0-1	1-2	1-1	0-0	1-0	—	1-1	1-1	2-0	1-1	0-0	2-2	0-0	—	11-13
Slaton, Jim	9-11	9-8	12-6	8-12	10-8	10-12	4-10	—	13-7	7-13	8-12	6-1	6-7	6-4	105-113
Spillner, Dan (24-41)	1-1	2-4	5-1	3-4	9-8	11-6	3-1	3-1	1-2	1-1	1-2	3-0	0-7	1-5	28-17
Splittorff, Paul	9-7	5-4	7-14	19-17	4-6	7-8	—	4-7	5-0	11-11	15-12	11-7	11-7	7-5	137-117
Stanley, Bob	4-3	—	5-1	3-4	4-1	3-2	5-3	12-7	4-2	4-1	4-1	5-5	1-1	5-4	49-29
Stewart, Sammy	2-2	2-2	2-0	1-3	1-1	3-1	1-1	2-3	0-1	0-1	1-2	2-2	1-1	1-0	16-13
Stieb, Dave	0-4	2-2	2-0	1-0	1-2	1-2	0-1	3-1	1-0	0-3	1-2	2-1	2-1	2-0	20-23
Stoddard, Tim	1-4	1-0	8-3	1-1	1-0	0-1	0-1	1-1	0-0	1-1	1-2	2-2	0-3	1-1	8-5
Stone, Steve (34-37)	1-4	7-3	8-3	13-7	6-7	8-8	5-12	6-5	13-7	3-8	6-4	8-3	6-7	4-0	69-49
Tanana, Frank	10-4	6-3	—	20-12	14-5	28-17	6-15	9-5	18-16	5-8	23-10	6-1	19-17	9-0	102-78
Tiant, Luis	21-22	12-11	20-13	20-12	10-3	8-8	7-5	12-12	18-16	22-15	12-10	1-1	8-7	6-2	225-165
Torrez, Mike (61-50)	5-9	4-6	9-5	5-5	10-5	7-8	2-4	11-8	8-6	1-10	23-10	1-1	8-6	9-0	94-76
Travers, Bill	2-5	1-2	3-1	5-5	2-1	1-2	3-2	—	8-6	7-12	11-3	8-7	7-2	5-1	65-67
Trout, Steve	1-4	1-2	1-0	—	2-1	2-1	3-2	1-1	5-10	7-12	5-6	2-3	8-7	6-1	23-24
Tudor, John	1-1	—	0-0	0-0	1-1	—	3-2	1-1	2-2	1-2	3-3	2-0	1-2	1-0	9-7
Underwood, Pat	0-0	0-0	2-0	0-5	1-1	—	0-3	0-0	0-1	0-2	2-0	0-1	0-2	3-0	9-10
Underwood, Tom (34-29)	4-6	2-2	2-3	1-0	2-2	1-3	0-3	0-5	2-0	2-3	3-5	0-1	0-3	2-0	28-39
Verhoeven, John	1-0	0-1	0-1	0-5	0-0	0-0	0-1	1-1	0-1	1-1	0-1	0-1	0-2	1-1	3-8
Vuckovich, Pete (39-31)	2-1	6-2	3-4	7-3	2-2	2-11	4-6	2-3	2-4	2-3	0-4	3-1	3-1	2-1	14-12
Waits, Rick	6-6	2-9	3-4	5-4	4-2	2-11	3-6	8-4	2-1	8-8	4-4	6-1	4-8	8-2	64-60
Wilcox, Milt (5-4)	0-8	0-1	2-2	5-4	4-2	—	3-6	0-1	5-5	8-8	5-2	5-1	6-6	5-2	61-61
Willis, Mike	0-1	0-0	2-2	0-1	0-0	1-3	2-0	0-1	0-4	1-1	0-1	1-1	0-2	—	7-17
Wirth, Dennis	0-0	0-0	2-1	0-0	0-0	0-0	—	0-1	—	—	—	—	—	—	6-6
Zahn, Geoff	0-7	1-3	3-4	7-6	3-2	4-7	6-6	0-1	0-1	6-7	6-3	2-5	6-0	6-2	53-53

†Present club only. *Includes records vs. Kansas City Athletics. ‡Includes records vs. Seattle Pilots. §Includes records vs. Washington Senators.

National League Lifetime Pitching Records

Pitchers with 10 or More Decisions Who Were Active In Majors in 1980

Pitcher—A.L. Totals in Parentheses	†Atl. W-L	Chi. W-L	Cinn. W-L	Hous. W-L	L.A. W-L	Mont. W-L	N.Y. W-L	Phila. W-L	Pitts. W-L	St.L. W-L	S.D. W-L	S.F. W-L	Totals W-L
Alexander, Doyle (76-70)	0-1	3-1	0-6	3-1	3-0	1-1	1-2	3-1	1-0	1-2	2-2	2-0	20-17
Allen, Neil	0-1		0-2		1-2	0-2		1-3	3-1	1-1	2-2	1-0	10-17
Andujar, Joaquin	2-5	4-3	6-8	1-4	4-5	0-2	3-3	2-4	2-5	1-1	5-5	2-3	40-45
Bahnsen, Stan (125-126)	1-3	4-3	0-0	3-3	1-3	8-2	3-4	1-2	3-1	0-1	2-7	2-3	19-21
Bair, Doug (4-6)	5-2	0-3	0-0	3-3	1-3	0-1	2-1	4-3	0-0	2-0	7-0	4-0	21-19
Bibby, Jim (60-64)	6-3	6-1	2-1	5-6	2-2	1-1	3-2	4-3	3-1	6-14	7-0		40-22
Blue, Vida (124-86)	3-1	5-3	3-3	2-2	3-6	8-2	5-3	0-6	0-0	4-2	7-0		46-34
Blyleven, Bert (122-113)	1-0	6-1	1-2	1-6	3-3	3-4	5-3	0-0	0-1	4-3	7-0	2-2	34-28
Boggs, Tom (1-10)	1-0	1-1	0-1	0-0	1-0	1-1	0-2	2-2	0-1	3-0	0-1	0-1	14-19
Bomback, Mark	8-4	2-3	0-1	4-9	5-7	0-9	4-6	0-0	6-5	6-14	7-7	7-4	10-8
Bonham, Bill	12-2	8-1	6-5	3-0	3-7	4-4	4-6	10-10	5-2	6-5	7-5	7-5	75-83
Borbon, Pedro (2-3)	1-0	3-1	1-0	5-0	0-7	0-1	3-0	6-4	3-1	1-1	7-7	7-4	67-36
Brusstar, Warren	1-0	0-1	2-6	2-0	3-7	1-5	0-5	9-6	3-9	0-5	6-8	0-7	16-7
Burris, Ray (1-3)	1-6	11-2	0-0	0-3	3-7	12-9	9-4	2-3	2-1	6-5	3-4	9-7	62-73
Camp, Rick	9-2	0-1	8-3	6-3	3-5	6-6	3-0	8-3	2-1	6-7	4-8	9-7	14-12
Candelaria, John			9-17	1-3	13-11	6-6	3-0	8-3		2-3	18-12	21-16	81-52
Carlton, Steve	19-12	30-16		28-9		19-17	25-27		30-21	29-8			249-169
Castillo, Bob	0-0	0-0	2-1	0-2		0-3	1-0	2-1	0-1	1-1	3-2	0-1	11-10
Caudill, Bill	0-0	0-0	0-1	0-2	0-3	0-3		0-2	2-0			0-1	
Christenson, Larry	6-9	7-3	2-6	3-6	4-4	11-5	10-4		6-7	3-4	4-1	5-2	68-50
Curtis, John (26-23)	4-5	4-5	4-5	0-6	1-2	3-7	6-4	5-7	6-7	0-3	7-2	5-13	43-66
D'Acquisto, John	6-6	3-4	2-9	2-7	1-2	1-6	4-2	2-2	3-4	4-3	4-2		34-50
Dues, Hal	6-6	1-0	0-0	0-0	0-1		0-1	1-1	2-1	0-1	0-1	1-0	
Espinosa, Nino	4-5	5-5	3-1	3-1	2-5	4-7	5-1	3-7	5-6	2-6	3-5	1-5	42-50
Falcone, Pete	4-5	5-8	3-7	6-3	1-7	4-3	0-9	3-8	6-7	2-6	4-1	2-4	43-66
Fingers, Rollie (67-61)	2-5	8-2	3-4	5-7	7-4	7-5	7-5	3-4	4-6	3-11		4-5	34-40
Forsch, Bob	12-8	8-7	9-10		12-8	7-5	6-2	2-4	6-8		9-4	5-13	83-69
Forsch, Ken	7-6	12-5	4-7		5-7	10-6	9-6	12-10	6-8		6-3	7-5	78-81
Forster, Terry (26-42)		1-1	1-1	5-6	0-0	0-2	2-2	1-1	0-1	1-1	0-0	3-2	11-10
Frazier, George	6-6	1-0	1-1	1-6	0-12	0-7	1-4	0-1	1-0		0-0	12-10	3-11
Fryman, Woodie (22-25)	10-9	12-11	4-12	11-6	10-12	5-2	2-4	3-8	11-10	10-14	6-8	11-11	105-120
Fulgham, John	1-3	1-3	0-1	2-1	0-0	3-7	0-1	1-0	2-1		2-0	1-0	14-12
Garber, Gene (10-11)	3-3	5-7	2-3	3-6	7-2	3-4	9-4	1-0	4-5	2-7	3-2	6-4	48-50
Glynn, Ed (3-6)	0-1	1-0	1-0	0-2	0-1					0-1	1-0	0-1	4-7
Goltz, Dave (96-79)	0-3	1-1	1-1	0-3			2-1	3-6	0-2	0-1	14-7	2-1	7-11
Griffin, Tom (3-4)	6-6	2-8	6-10	9-6	5-11	7-3	5-9	3-6	6-5	12-4	4-7	3-8	65-79
Grimsley, Ross (54-48)	5-6	0-2	0-2	1-7	1-5	5-1	7-5	4-5	6-5	8-4	4-1	7-3	69-49
Gullickson, Bill	2-0	2-5	3-9	1-7	0-3		1-0	0-1	2-0	1-3	1-0	1-0	10-5
Halicki, Ed (3-1)	2-7	8-2	3-9	11-7	8-9	5-7	7-3	3-7	3-1	3-5	1-3		52-65
Hanna, Preston		0-0	1-2		0-2	0-2	1-0	1-3	2-1	1-3	0-0	2-2	12-20
Hargesheimer, Alan	1-2	0-0	1-1	0-1	2-2	0-2		0-2	0-1	0-1	0-2		4-6
Hausman, Tom (3-6)	0-2	1-3	1-1	0-1	0-0	2-1	2-1	1-3	2-1	1-1	2-2	2-1	11-14
Hernandez, Willie	0-2		3-1	3-2	2-1	0-3	2-1	0-1	3-3	5-5	2-2	2-1	21-22
Hooton, Burt	8-10	8-4	4-8	11-12	5-3	10-7	18-13	12-11	10-7	10-11	8-9	15-6	119-101

Pitcher—A.L. Totals in Parentheses	†Atl. W-L	Chi. W-L	Clnn. W-L	Hous. W-L	L.A. W-L	Mont. W-L	N.Y. W-L	Phila. W-L	Pitts. W-L	St.L. W-L	S.D. W-L	S.F. W-L	Totals W-L
Hough, Charlie (2-2)	8-9	4-2	4-7	7-5		3-3	5-3	1-3	3-3	2-4	3-3	7-4	47-46
Howe, Steve	0-1	2-1	0-2	3-1		3-1	1-0	0-1	0-1	0-0	0-1	0-1	7-9
Hrabosky, Al (17-11)	2-2	1-5	3-2	3-0	6-2	4-2	5-0	5-1	5-3		5-3	2-2	44-22
Hume, Tom	7-1	1-7		5-4	2-5	1-4	5-0	4-3	5-3	7-10	5-3	2-4	30-33
Jackson, Grant (30-12)	4-4	3-7	7-6	4-4	5-5	2-4	9-10	3-3	4-2	7-10	4-1	2-2	51-60
Jackson, Roy Lee	0-0	0-0	1-1	0-0	0-0	0-2	8-7	0-1	0-1	0-0	0-1	2-4	2-9
Jones, Randy	9-12	7-8	11-14	8-11	9-9	8-6	8-7	9-8	6-9	6-11	7-5	11-10	92-105
Kaat, Jim (237-191)	3-3	5-3	5-2	0-0	1-1	3-3	2-2	2-2	3-6	2-3		3-0	35-37
Kinney, Dennis (0-2)	0-0	3-0	0-2	0-0	1-1	0-1	0-1	1-1	0-1	2-1		0-0	4-7
Knepper, Bob	6-2	3-5	5-7	6-3	0-4	1-2	4-5	1-1	5-6	5-4	9-4	3-3	47-50
Knowles, Darold (44-44)	1-1	3-1	2-3	3-1	0-1	2-1	4-5	0-1	3-5	2-4	0-2	3-3	22-30
Kobel, Kevin (6-16)	1-1	4-1	0-2	1-3	2-5	1-1	0-0	2-8	1-5	5-6	2-3	1-3	12-18
Krukow, Mike	3-3		4-1	3-5	3-3	5-3	6-3	2-1	4-3	2-4	2-3	3-3	36-41
LaCorte, Frank	4-1	2-2	1-5	0-5	4-1	2-6	2-3	2-1	0-1	1-2	2-7	2-5	13-31
LaCoss, Mike	3-4	2-2		3-5	3-4	2-3	5-5	2-4	0-4	3-4	3-0	3-1	28-28
Lamp, Dennis	1-5	3-5	2-1	3-5	1-9	1-3	0-0	1-0	4-3	2-4	3-1	1-2	28-41
Larson, Dan	4-6	0-1		0-2	0-0	1-0	2-0	2-1	0-0	0-1	1-1		7-21
Lavelle, Gary	1-1	2-1	1-1	1-2	3-1	0-1	2-3	2-4	6-3	10-1	2-1	0-1	49-46
Lea, Charlie	3-0	1-1	1-1	1-2	1-1	0-1	1-1	1-0	0-0	0-1	0-0	1-0	7-5
Lee, Mark	2-1	5-4	1-2	2-0	2-1	2-2	5-2	2-3	5-6	3-2	2-1	2-5	7-6
Lee, Bill (94-68)	1-2	4-8	1-2	2-2	4-3	6-3	2-1	2-3	2-6	5-9	1-4	1-4	20-16
Leibrandt, Charlie	2-1	3-1	2-1	0-0	1-1	0-1	1-1	4-0	2-0				35-41
Lerch, Randy	1-0	1-1	2-1	1-2	1-1	0-2	1-1	1-0	2-0	1-2	0-1	1-0	13-14
Littell, Mark (18-13)	0-1	0-0		2-2	0-0	0-2	1-0	0-1	0-1	1-2	0-0	0-0	5-5
Littlefield, John	2-4	0-2	0-0	1-2	0-1	0-2	0-4	0-1	0-6	1-5	2-2	1-0	10-24
Lucas, Gary	2-2	4-3	2-1	2-2	2-3	3-2	5-2	1-3	0-1	1-2	2-2	3-0	29-26
Mahler, Mickey	4-3	2-2	9-6	2-2	3-2	3-2	2-2	1-2	3-1	1-0	4-0	2-2	19-23
Martinez, Silvio (0-1)	2-2	2-0	0-1	4-2	5-2	4-1	1-1	0-1	2-1	0-1	3-1	2-5	76-80
Matula, Rick	6-6	0-0	1-1	2-2	3-2	1-2	0-4	1-2	2-1	0-1	2-1	5-7	87-84
McGlothen, Lynn (9-9)	9-8	0-0	11-11	3-4	6-7	0-6	5-2	4-0	2-0	3-5	8-6	3-3	15-14
McGraw, Tug	4-6	3-4	3-6	4-5	10-5	5-1	5-5	7-5	3-3	3-4	6-3	2-2	35-46
McWilliams, Larry	2-3	7-5	3-4	3-5	1-1	5-5	5-5	5-5	2-0	1-1	5-3	5-7	59-62
Minton, Greg	4-6	25-15	3-7	1-5	2-1	0-2	0-3	1-0	1-0	3-1	1-2	3-3	15-14
Moffitt, Randy	6-7	9-8	3-4	5-5	8-8	0-2	3-3	7-5	2-6	3-5	8-6	1-3	26-21
Montefusco, John	4-2	0-1	1-5	6-7	1-1	6-3	5-6	3-2	3-3	3-4	4-0	1-2	12-13
Moore, Donnie	1-0	4-8	0-0	2-2	3-5	3-3	2-1	1-2	2-0	0-0	3-1	4-2	41-37
Moskau, Paul	3-1	3-1		2-2	3-2	4-1	6-1	0-2	3-3	0-0	1-1	1-3	115-98
Mura, Steve	7-10	4-6	0-4	3-11	7-2	4-1	6-1	3-5	5-6	10-5	3-1	4-2	233-209
Murray, Dale	17-12	7-5	13-17	3-5	8-9	8-7	9-6	3-7	12-19	14-17	15-5	11-8	4-8
Niekro, Joe (21-22)	0-0	25-15	25-32	22-23	23-28	14-14	21-13	23-15	22-19	14-17	20-18	24-15	115-98
Niekro, Phil	9-11	9-8	0-0	9-9	11-17	9-5	8-6		6-2	6-2	10-9	11-5	233-209
Noles, Dickie	2-0	0-1	6-0	10-9	0-0	0-0	1-0	1-1	10-14	6-4	0-9		4-8
Norman, Fredie (0-1)	5-1	5-12	1-2	12-10	11-17	9-5	8-6	7-7	10-14	6-1	10-9	11-5	104-102
Palmer, Dave	2-0	1-0		2-4	0-0	0-0	1-0	1-1	1-4	3-0	0-1	3-2	18-9
Pastore, Frank	5-1	1-0		1-0	0-0	2-6	1-0	2-0	4-6	2-0	3-0	0-3	19-14
Price, Joe	0-0	3-2		3-7	5-9	6-8	4-5	2-6	2-0	1-3	9-6	3-8	7-3
Rasmussen, Eric	11-4	2-2	8-11	11-6	6-8	9-2	4-5	5-0	2-6	7-3	9-6	12-8	46-69
Rau, Doug	7-3	3-2	2-3	3-7		9-2	5-0	5-5	4-6	7-3	9-4	12-1	80-58
Reardon, Jeff	0-0	0-0	1-1	2-1	1-0	3-5	0-0	2-6	0-2	0-2	0-2	0-0	9-9
Reed, Ron	5-2	7-16	16-13	13-13	12-13	16-13	11-8	7-8	12-12	6-15	13-8	12-15	127-125
Reuschel, Rick	10-6		11-11	8-10	9-11	16-13	8-17	13-8	13-17	12-8	12-4	13-9	125-114

Pitcher—A.L. Totals in Parentheses	†Atl. W-L	Chi. W-L	Cinn. W-L	Hous. W-L	L.A. W-L	Mont. W-L	N.Y. W-L	Phila. W-L	Pitts. W-L	St.L. W-L	S.D. W-L	S.F. W-L	Totals W-L
Reuss, Jerry	14-6	9-14	15-14	11-7	10-11	13-5	13-13	11-12	2-1	9-13	12-4	9-9	133-114
Rhoden, Rick	5-3	5-2	7-6	5-1	2-0	4-2	4-4	2-0	7-6	5-4	7-5	1-2	49-30
Richard, J. R.	14-6	10-4	9-12		15-4	10-5	9-3	6-7	2-9	5-4	14-8	13-9	107-71
Ripley, Alan (5-6)	1-1	1-1	2-0	1-0	2-0	1-2	0-1	3-1	0-0	13-8	0-3	3-14	9-10
Roberts, Dave (22-30)	9-11	4-5	4-9	4-5	10-13	5-6	7-6	5-3	4-8	3-8	8-3	2-0	81-92
Robinson, Don	3-2	5-5	2-2	2-2	9-10	4-0	1-2	10-4		3-0	2-1	8-8	29-24
Rogers, Steve	6-8	13-9	7-8	4-9	9-10		11-10	14-13	13-14	9-12	4-2	8-6	102-105
Romo, Enrique (19-17)	0-1	11-9	0-1	6-2	4-6	8-7	1-7	6-4		3-0	1-2	8-6	15-10
Rooker, Jim (21-44)	4-5	3-2	3-7		1-2	8-8	7-7	6-4		18-9	7-3	2-2	82-65
Ruhle, Vern (25-27)	5-2	11-7	1-2	7-11	2-12	8-8	0-3	0-0	2-1	7-10	11-2	12-4	17-13
Ruthven, Dick	4-4	7-1	3-5	3-7	1-8	3-4	3-4	5-4	5-6	5-4	3-5	3-1	77-80
Ryan, Nolan (138-121)	4-4	1-1	2-3		0-0	1-0	0-0	3-1	2-2	5-2	3-4	3-1	40-48
Sambito, Joe	2-3	3-3	2-0		0-0	0-0	3-2	5-2	3-6	3-1	1-1	1-0	28-27
Sanderson, Scott	1-1	0-1	0-1	2-1	1-2		2-5	5-2	1-1	1-1	1-1	1-1	29-21
Saucier, Kevin	2-0			1-0	0-0	1-2	2-5		1-1			1-0	8-8
Seaver, Tom	30-8	20-16	11-18	19-19	22-17	18-11	14-11	26-11	23-11	24-11	26-7	24-10	230-175
Shirley, Bob	3-7	1-0	0-0	6-5	6-5	1-5	0-5	0-5	1-0	5-9		1-6	7-5
Smith, Dave	0-0	4-0	0-2		2-2	0-1	3-2	0-0	1-0	4-0	2-0	1-1	25-30
Solomon, Eddie	0-0	2-3	3-5	3-1	2-2	4-4	2-5	3-2	2-3	0-3	2-2	1-3	46-40
Sosa, Elias (8-2)	5-1	6-1		3-4	3-5	1-2	6-2	5-3	3-1	5-2	6-7	1-3	16-16
Soto, Mario	3-1	1-4		2-3	1-3	0-2	2-1	2-1	1-1	0-1	4-2	0-3	21-24
Stanhouse, Don (17-29)	0-2	1-3	2-0	2-2	1-0	2-3	1-2	2-3	1-2	3-3	1-1	2-1	20-19
Sutcliffe, Rick	2-2	1-4	4-1	0-3		3-6	1-1	5-4	1-1	3-3	4-2	5-2	32-30
Sutter, Bruce	33-14	15-19	20-24	21-15	3-2	17-9	14-11	18-10	23-17	16-18	25-15	28-23	45-54
Sutton, Don	4-2	9-4	0-2	3-5	2-4	5-5	1-2	2-9	3-0	5-9	5-4	5-5	10-13
Swan, Craig	4-2	0-2	0-2	1-3	2-4	5-5		6-5	2-5	5-4	5-3	5-3	43-34
Sykes, Bob (11-13)	3-6	3-3	1-0	1-3	3-1	0-3	8-5	2-9	3-0	5-3	2-0	1-0	10-13
Tekulve, Kent	0-0	0-1	1-0	0-1	1-0	0-1	0-0	6-5		2-0	2-2	2-2	43-34
Thomas, Roy	2-1		5-1	1-0	1-1	3-0	4-3	3-1	2-3	0-0	1-1	2-2	6-8
Tidrow, Dick (70-67)	2-1	1-1	0-1	5-0	0-1	0-1	1-0	1-1	2-3	2-1	2-0	2-3	17-10
Tomlin, Dave	2-0	1-0	0-1	3-3	5-3	0-1	4-3	0-2	1-2		5-3	5-3	25-12
Urrea, John	5-2	4-3	4-2	3-3	5-2	2-4	2-1	2-3	1-1		1-2	1-1	15-16
Vuckovich, Pete (14-12)	1-1	3-0	1-0	4-2	1-1	2-1	2-0	5-4	1-4	1-3	2-6	5-0	39-31
Walk, Bob	2-3	2-0	2-2	4-2	2-2	2-1	2-1	2-2	0-2	1-2	1-1	0-0	11-7
Welch, Bob	4-1	2-1	3-5	4-2		2-3	2-2	2-2	0-4	3-2	4-5	5-0	26-19
Whitson, Ed (71-61)	0-2	3-1	8-10	12-8	3-4	3-3	1-2	3-2	0-2	5-11	8-4	12-11	24-30
Wise, Rick (71-61)	9-15	13-14	8-10	12-8	10-7	7-10	16-9		10-11	5-11	8-4	12-11	113-112
Zachry, Pat	7-2	6-4	2-2	1-6	6-5	4-2	0-2	2-5	3-3	6-2	6-1	2-3	45-37

History of the All-Star Game

The majors' annual All-Star Game was the brainchild of Arch Ward, late sports editor of the Chicago Tribune. Although the owners approved the first game in 1933 somewhat reluctantly, it has become as much a fixture of the baseball season as the World Series. Even those who at first were cool or indifferent to the idea have since agreed that the game gives baseball a decided midseason pickup.

While there had been talk of an All-Star Game for some years prior to 1933, it took Ward to sell the idea to Commissioner Kenesaw M. Landis and the major leagues as part of the sports program of Chicago's Century of Progress Exposition of that year. The first game was played at Comiskey Park, Chicago, July 6, 1933, and the mid-summer classic has been staged every year since except in 1945, when there was a one-year break because of the wartime curtailment on travel.

They have termed it the "Dream Game," and it has been all of that. The contests have produced some of the most dramatic moments in the history of the sport. The All-Star attractions have been featured by everything from Carl Hubbell striking out Babe Ruth, Lou Gehrig, Jimmie Foxx, Al Simmons and Joe Cronin in succession in the 1934 game to Ted Williams' two-out, two-on homer in the ninth inning to win the 1941 game.

Fortunately, the All-Star competition was started when such great players as Ruth, Gehrig, Hubbell, Simmons, Foxx, Frankie Frisch, Pie Traynor, Jimmie Dykes and others still were headliners. Playing in the first and second games at the age of 38 and 39, Ruth hit a homer and single in six times at bat.

The World Series pilots of the preceding fall usually draw the All-Star managerial nominations. However, in a touch of sentiment, League Presidents Will Harridge and John Heydler selected those grand leaders of the game, Connie Mack and John McGraw, as managers of the first game in 1933. McGraw had retired in midseason of 1932 and made the All-Star Game just in time, for he died the following February.

Of the 11 cities represented in the majors when the All-Star Game was originated, Brooklyn was the last to stage the game. The 1942 contest was awarded to Brooklyn, but because the proceeds were to go to war organizations, Lt.-Col. Larry MacPhail, then president of the Dodgers, permitted the game to be transferred to the Polo Grounds in New York so a larger crowd could be accommodated.

Unfortunately, afternoon showers and a hard downpour at game time held attendance to a disappointing 34,178. Ebbets Field finally was the scene of the midsummer classic in 1949.

The best and poorest crowds came in successive years. In 1935, a crowd of 69,831 packed Cleveland's Municipal Stadium to see the third game. The following year, only 25,556 turned out at Braves' Field in Boston. Confusion over unreserved seats was largely responsible. It had been announced that the reserved seats were all sold and Boston fans took that to mean the game was a sellout, with the result that thousands of unreserved seats remained unoccupied.

When Ward first advanced the plan of the Dream Game, it was his idea that the fans should pick the players for the rival teams. This plan was followed more or less in 1933 and 1934, with the managers reserving the right to use other players as they deemed necessary.

Starting in 1935, the magnates turned selection of the teams over to the managers. In 1947, the system of naming the performers was changed again, with the eight starters for each team—all but the pitchers—being picked in a nationwide fan poll and the rival managers selecting the remainder of their squads.

Late in 1957 it was decided to abandon this plan in favor of having the leagues' managers, coaches and players vote to choose the eight starters on each team with the rival managers picking the remainder of their squads. This plan was followed through 1969.

In 1970 Commissioner Bowie Kuhn returned the selection of the starting teams to the fans. Under the present system, ballots (computerized cards) are distributed in major and minor league ball parks throughout the month of June and voting is done by punching out a box next to the player preferred for each position.

There was considerable criticism in 1970 when Rico Carty, of the Atlanta Braves, was not listed among the nominees for outfielder on the National League team. He was leading the league in batting at the time and, indeed, he went on to win the National League batting championship for the season. However, the fans elected him through write-ins and he was in the starting lineup.

A radical change went into effect in 1959. At the request of the players, the owners agreed to an arrangement of two games each year to speed payment of pension fund indebtedness. Sixty percent of the All-Star gate receipts and radio-television money went into the pension fund. However, after playing two games each season for four years, the players approved a return to one game in December, 1962. The fans' interest was centered on one game and diminished with two.

The 1981 All-Star Game is scheduled to be played at night at Municipal Stadium in Cleveland, July 14.

Game of 1933—Comiskey Park, Chicago, July 6

Babe Ruth, with his genius for stealing the thunder, was the hero of the first All-Star Game as the American leaguers defeated the Nationals, 4-2. The Bambino's two-run homer in the third inning represented the margin of victory. In addition, Ruth made the game's best defensive play. He moved his 38-year-old legs fast over the turf to grab a steaming line drive by Chick Hafey in the eighth inning.

The American League players wore their regular home uniforms, but John Heydler, then National League president, dressed up the N.L. players in special uniforms for the occasion. They were steel gray with "National League" spelled out in blue letters across the blouses. The game yielded $52,000, of which $45,000 went to the Association of Professional Ball Players, the game's benevolent society.

Connie Mack stated that the American League was out to win rather than to see how many stars it could inject into the box score. He made only one change in his lineup apart from pitchers. By contrast, N.L. Manager John McGraw used 17 players.

McGraw started Bill Hallahan, Cardinal southpaw, in hopes of curbing Ruth and Lou Gehrig, but the selection was unfortunate for the National League. Hallahan was terribly wild, giving up five walks and three runs before he was derricked with none out in the third inning. All of the N.L. runs came off Alvin Crowder, Mack's middle pitcher.

Lefty Gomez was credited with the victory, but he still is prouder of the fact that he drove in the first run in All-Star competition. After Al Simmons flied out in the second inning, Jimmie Dykes coaxed a pass. Joe Cronin also worked Hallahan for a walk, but Rick Ferrell lined out. Gomez then surprised the N.L. contingent by lining a single over shortstop to plate Dykes. The box score:

NATIONALS	AB.	R.	H.	PO.	A.	E.	AMERICANS	AB.	R.	H.	PO.	A.	E.
Martin (Cardinals), 3b	4	0	0	3	0		Chapman (Yankees), lf-rf	5	0	1	1	0	0
Frisch (Cardinals), 2b	4	1	2	5	3	0	Gehringer (Tigers), 2b	3	1	0	1	3	0
Klein (Phillies), rf	4	0	1	3	0	0	Ruth (Yankees), rf	4	1	2	1	0	0
P. Waner (Pirates), rf	0	0	0	0	0	0	West (Browns), cf	0	0	0	0	0	0
Hafey (Reds), lf	4	0	1	0	0	0	Gehrig (Yankees), 1b	2	0	0	12	0	1
Terry (Giants), 1b	4	0	2	7	2	0	Simmons (Wh. Sox), cf-lf	4	0	1	4	0	0
Berger (Braves), cf	4	0	0	4	0	0	Dykes (White Sox), 3b	3	1	2	2	4	0
Bartell (Phillies), ss	2	0	0	0	3	0	Cronin (Senators), ss	3	1	1	2	4	0
cTraynor (Pirates)	1	0	1	0	0	0	R. Ferrell (Red Sox), c	3	0	0	4	0	0
Hubbell (Giants), p	0	0	0	0	0	0	Gomez (Yankees), p	1	0	1	0	0	0
eCuccinello (Dodgers)	1	0	0	0	0	0	Crowder (Senators), p	1	0	0	0	0	0
Wilson (Cardinals), c	1	0	0	2	0	0	bAverill (Indians)	1	0	1	0	0	0
aO'Doul (Giants)	1	0	0	0	0	0	Grove (Athletics), p	1	0	0	0	0	0
Hartnett (Cubs), c	1	0	0	2	0	0	Totals	31	4	9	27	11	1
Hallahan (Cardinals), p	1	0	0	1	0	0							
Warneke (Cubs), p	1	1	1	0	0	0							
dEnglish (Cubs), ss	1	0	0	0	0	0							
Totals	34	2	8	24	11	0							

```
National League ............................  0   0   0   0   2     0   0   0 — 2
American League ...........................  0   1   2   0   0   1     0   0   x — 4
```

Nationals	IP.	H.	R.	ER.	BB.	SO.	Americans	IP.	H.	R.	ER.	BB.	SO.
Hallahan (Cardinals)	2*	2	3	3	5	1	Gomez (Yankees)	3	2	0	0	0	1
Warneke (Cubs)	4	6	1	1	0	2	Crowder (Senators)	3	3	2	2	0	0
Hubbell (Giants)	2	1	0	0	1	1	Grove (Athletics)	3	3	0	0	0	3

*Pitched to three batters in third.

Winning pitcher—Gomez.   Losing pitcher—Hallahan.

aGrounded out for Wilson in sixth. bSingled for Crowder in sixth. cDoubled for Bartell in seventh. dFlied out for Warneke in seventh. eFanned for Hubbell in ninth. Runs batted in—Martin, Frisch, Ruth 2, Gomez, Averill. Two-base hit—Traynor. Three-base hit—Warneke. Home runs—Ruth, Frisch. Sacrifice hit—Ferrell. Stolen base—Gehringer. Double plays—Bartell, Frisch and Terry; Dykes and Gehrig. Left on bases—Americans 10, Nationals 5. Umpires—Dinneen and McGowan (A.L.), Klem and Rigler (N.L.). Time of game—2:05. Attendance—47,595.

Game of 1934—Polo Grounds, New York, July 10

For drama, excitement and a quick change in fortunes, the second All-Star Game was a real thriller-diller. Victory again went to the American League, 9-7, but only after a titanic struggle. Despite the big score, the game saw some of the greatest All-Star pitching by Carl Hubbell and Mel Harder.

The N. L. had all the better of it in the early going, grabbing a 4-0 lead as Hubbell performed his mound magic. After the first two A. L. stars reached base in the opening inning, the Giants' southpaw struck out Babe Ruth, Lou Gehrig and Jimmie Foxx in succession. In the second inning, he fanned Al Simmons and Joe Cronin to make it five strikeouts in succession. After Bill Dickey singled, Lefty Gomez became Hubbell's sixth whiff victim in two innings.

The Americans bounced back with a vengeance to score eight runs off Lon Warneke and Van Mungo in the fourth and fifth innings. The Nationals then kayoed Red Ruffing before he could retire a batter in their fifth turn, but Harder came on to perform his magic, holding the N. L. to one hit over the last five rounds.

Homers by Frank Frisch in the first inning and Joe Medwick with two aboard in the third staked the Nationals to their early 4-0 lead.

Earl Averill was the Americans' batting hero. He hammered a run-scoring triple as a pinch-hitter in the fourth inning and then doubled across two more runs in the fifth. The box score:

AMERICAN	AB.	R.	H.	PO.	A.	E.
Gehringer (Tigers), 2b	3	0	2	2	1	0
Manush (Senators), lf	2	0	0	0	0	0
Ruffing (Yankees), p	1	0	1	0	0	0
Harder (Indians), p	2	0	0	1	0	0
Ruth (Yankees), rf	2	1	0	0	0	0
Chapman (Yankees), rf	2	0	1	0	1	0
Gehrig (Yankees), 1b	4	1	0	11	1	1
Foxx (Athletics), 3b	5	1	2	1	2	0
Simmons (Wh. Sox), cf-lf	5	3	3	3	0	0
Cronin (Senators), ss	5	1	2	2	8	0
Dickey (Yankees), c	2	1	1	4	0	0
hCochrane (Tigers), c	1	0	0	1	1	0
Gomez (Yankees), p	1	0	0	0	0	0
bAverill (Indians), cf	4	1	2	1	0	0
West (Browns), cf	0	0	0	1	0	0
Totals	39	9	14	27	14	1

NATIONALS	AB.	R.	H.	PO.	A.	E.
Frisch (Cardinals), 2b	3	3	2	0	1	0
aHerman (Cubs), 2b	2	0	1	0	1	0
Traynor (Pirates), 3b	5	2	2	1	0	0
Medwick (Cardinals), lf	2	1	1	0	0	0
dKlein (Cubs), lf	3	0	1	1	0	0
Cuyler (Cubs), rf	2	0	0	2	0	0
eOtt (Giants), rf	2	0	0	0	1	0
Berger (Braves), cf	2	0	0	0	0	1
fP. Waner (Pirates), cf	2	0	0	1	0	0
Terry (Giants), 1b	3	0	1	4	0	0
Jackson (Giants), ss	2	0	0	1	0	0
gVaughan (Pirates), ss	2	0	0	4	0	0
Hartnett (Cubs), c	2	0	0	9	0	0
Lopez (Dodgers), c	2	0	0	5	1	0
Hubbell (Giants), p	0	0	0	0	0	0
Warneke (Cubs), p	0	0	0	0	0	0
Mungo (Dodgers), p	0	1	0	0	0	0
cMartin (Cardinals)	1	0	0	0	0	0
Dean (Cardinals), p	1	0	0	0	0	0
Frankhouse (Braves), p	1	0	0	0	1	0
Totals	36	7	8	27	5	1

American League	0	0	0	2	6	1	0	0	0	— 9
National League	1	3	0	3	0	0	0	0	0	— 7

Americans	IP.	H.	R.	ER.	BB.	SO.
Gomez (Yankees)	3	3	4	4	1	3
Ruffing (Yankees)	1†	4	3	3	1	0
Harder (Indians)	5	1	0	0	1	2

Nationals	IP.	H.	R.	ER.	BB.	SO.
Hubbell (Giants)	3	2	0	0	2	6
Warneke (Cubs)	1*	3	4	4	3	1
Mungo (Dodgers)	1	4	4	4	2	1
Dean (Cardinals)	3	5	1	1	4	0
Frankhouse (Braves)	1	0	0	0	1	0

*Pitched to two batters in fifth. †Pitched to four batters in fifth.

Winning pitcher—Harder. Losing pitcher—Mungo.

aPopped out for Hubbell in third but was permitted to replace Frisch in seventh. bTripled for Gomez in fourth. cWalked for Mungo in fifth. dSingled for Medwick in fifth. eFlied out for Cuyler in fifth. fFanned for Berger in fifth. gForced runner for Jackson in fifth. hRan for Dickey in sixth. Runs batted in—Frisch, Medwick 3, Cronin 2, Averill 3, Foxx, Simmons, Ruffing 2, Traynor, Klein. Two-base hits—Foxx, Simmons 2, Cronin, Averill, Herman. Three-base hits—Chapman, Averill. Home runs—Frisch, Medwick. Stolen bases—Gehringer, Manush, Traynor, Ott. Double play—Lopez and Vaughan. Left on bases—American 12, National 5. Umpires—Pfirman and Stark (n. L.) Owens and Moriarty (A. L.). Time of game—2:44. Attendance—48,363.

Game of 1935—Municipal Stadium, Cleveland, July 8

A crowd of 69,831—the largest throng to see an All-Star Game—packed Cleveland's big lakefront stadium for the third contest and, being largely American League rooters, thrilled to the junior circuit's third successive victory, 4-1.

Cardinals' Manager Frank Frisch, who piloted the National League team, started his own southpaw, Bill Walker. After retiring the A. L.'s first batter of the game, Walker passed Charley Gehringer, but Lou Gehrig forced him. Jimmie Foxx then applied his broad shoulders to a pitch and rode it into the left field stands for a homer and a 2-0 lead.

The Americans jumped on Walker for another run in the second inning on a triple by Rollie Hemsley and Joe Cronin's fly to Wally Berger. Hal Schumacher struck out five in his four-inning tour of duty for the Nationals, but yielded the Americans' final run in the fifth inning. With two out, Joe Vosmik singled and went to third on Gehringer's single. After Gehrig walked, filling the bases, Foxx singled Vosmik across.

Mickey Cochrane, American League manager, used just two pitchers, Lefty Gomez and Mel Harder. Gomez worked the first six innings, yielding three hits and the lone National League run. It came in the fourth inning when Arky Vaughan led off with a double to right and scored on Bill Terry's single.

Because Harder worked five innings in the 1934 game and Gomez went six in this contest, the National League had the All-Star rules changed so that no pitcher could hurl more than three innings unless a game went into overtime. Harder allowed only one hit in three innings this time, giving him a record of permitting only two hits in eight successive innings against the N. L.'s hardest hitters. The box score:

NATIONALS	AB.	R.	H.	PO.	A.	E.
Martin (Cardinals), 3b	4	0	1	0	0	1
Vaughan (Pirates), ss	3	1	1	2	2	0
Ott (Giants), rf	4	0	0	1	0	0
Medwick (Cardinals), lf	3	0	0	0	0	0
Terry (Giants), 1b	3	0	1	5	1	0
Collins (Cardinals), 1b	1	0	0	2	0	0
Berger (Braves), cf	2	0	0	1	0	0
bMoore (Giants), cf	2	0	0	1	0	0
Herman (Cubs), 2b	3	0	0	1	4	0
Wilson (Phillies), c	3	0	1	8	0	0
cWhitehead (Cardinals)	0	0	0	0	0	0
Hartnett (Cubs), c	0	0	0	3	0	0
Walker (Cardinals), p	0	0	0	0	0	0
aMancuso (Giants)	1	0	0	0	0	0
Schmacher (Giants), p	1	0	0	0	1	0
dP. Waner (Pirates)	1	0	0	0	0	0
Derringer (Reds), p	0	0	0	0	0	0
Dean (Cardinals), p	0	0	0	0	0	0
Totals	31	1	4	24	8	1

AMERICANS	AB.	R.	H.	PO.	A.	E.
Vosmik (Indians), rf	4	1	1	1	0	0
Gehringer (Tigers), 2b	3	0	2	1	3	0
Gehrig (Yankees), 1b	3	1	0	12	0	0
Foxx (Athletics), 3b	3	1	2	0	0	0
Bluege (Senators), 3b	0	0	0	0	0	0
Johnson (Athletics), ss	4	0	0	4	0	0
Chapman (Yankees), lf	0	0	0	0	0	0
Simmons (Wh. Sox), cf	4	0	2	2	0	0
Cramer (Athletics), cf	0	0	0	0	0	0
Hemsley (Browns), c	4	1	1	6	0	0
Cronin (Red Sox), ss	4	0	0	1	4	0
Gomez (Yankees), p	2	0	0	0	2	0
Harder (Indians), p	1	0	0	0	1	0
Totals	32	4	8	27	10	0

National League	0	0	0	1	0	0	0	0	0 – 1
American League	2	1	0	0	1	0	0	0	x – 4

Nationals	IP.	H.	R.	ER.	BB.	SO.
Walker (Cardinals)	2	2	3	3	1	2
Schumacher (Giants)	4	4	1	1	1	5
Derringer (Reds)	1	1	0	0	0	1
Dean (Cardinals)	1	0	0	0	1	1

Americans	IP.	H.	R.	ER.	BB.	SO.
Gomez (Yankees)	6	3	1	1	2	4
Harder (Indians)	3	1	0	0	0	1

Winning pitcher—Gomez. Losing pitcher—Walker.

aFlied out for Walker in third. bFlied out for Berger in seventh. cRan for Wilson in seventh. dGrounded out for Schumacher in seventh. Runs batted in—Foxx 3, Cronin, Terry. Two-base hits—Vaughan, Wilson, Gehringer, Simmons. Three-base hit—Hemsley. Home run—Foxx. Left on bases—Americans 7, Nationals 5. Umpires—Ormsby and Geisel (A. L.), Magerkurth and Sears (N. L.). Time of game—2:06. Attendance—69,831.

Game of 1936—Braves Field, Boston, July 7

After losing three straight, the National League gained its first All-Star victory, 4-3. An unfortunate mixup in the sale of unreserved seats resulted in only 25,556 fans attending, leaving some 10,000 empty seats.

Joe McCarthy, who went on to manage seven All-Star teams, got into his first game—as a pinch-manager for Mickey Cochrane. Cochrane, Detroit's fighting catcher-manager, was slated to be the American League manager, but he had a nervous breakdown in June and was sent to a Wyoming ranch to recuperate.

Joe DiMaggio, the Yankees' brilliant rookie center fielder, was the goat of the first A. L. defeat. Coming up repeatedly in the pinch, he failed to get a hit in five attempts, although one of his line drives almost spun Leo Durocher around.

DiMaggio, who played right field, also missed on an attempted shoestring catch on Gabby Hartnett in the second inning and the ball went for a triple. The hit helped the N. L. to a 2-0 lead. In the fifth frame, DiMag's fumble on a single by Billy Herman also proved costly, setting up the Nationals' final run. The error came just moments after Augie Galan smashed a drive which hit the right field flagpole for a home run.

Dizzy Dean, Carl Hubbell, Curt Davis and Lon Warneke pitched the N. L. to its first victory, although Davis almost wrecked his team's chances in his brief turn on the mound in the seventh inning. Lou Gehrig greeted Davis with a homer. After he retired the next two batters, a pair of singles and a walk filled the bases and Luke Appling's ace plated two more A. L. runs. Warneke then came on and, after passing Charley Gehringer to fill the bases, he faced DiMaggio. With a chance to redeem himself, DiMag hit a terrific liner just a bit to Durocher's right, but Leo gloved the ball just as it was about to sail to the outfield. The box score:

AMERICANS	AB.	R.	H.	PO.	A.	E.
Appling (Wh. Sox), ss	4	0	1	2	2	0
Gehringer (Tigers), 2b	3	0	2	2	1	0
DiMaggio (Yankees), rf	5	0	0	1	0	1
Gehrig (Yankees), 1b	2	1	1	7	0	0
Averill (Indians), cf	3	0	0	3	1	0
Chapman (Senators), cf	1	0	0	0	0	0
Ferrell (Red Sox), c	2	0	0	4	0	0
aDickey (Yankees), c	2	0	0	2	0	0
Radcliff (Wh. Sox), lf	2	0	1	2	0	0
Goslin (Tigers), lf	1	1	1	1	0	0
Higgins (Athletics), 3b	2	0	0	0	1	0
bFoxx (Red Sox), 3b	2	1	1	0	1	0
Grove (Red Sox), p	1	0	0	0	0	0
Rowe (Tigers), p	1	0	0	0	0	0
cSelkirk (Yankees)	0	0	0	0	0	0
Harder (Indians), p	0	0	0	0	1	0
fCrosetti (Yankees)	1	0	0	0	0	0
Totals	32	3	7	24	7	1

NATIONALS	AB.	R.	H.	PO.	A.	E.
Galan (Cubs), cf	4	1	1	1	0	0
Herman (Cubs), 2b	3	1	2	3	4	0
Collins (Cardinals), 1b	2	0	0	9	1	0
Medwick (Cardinals), lf	4	0	1	0	0	0
Demaree (Cubs), rf	3	1	1	1	0	0
dOtt (Giants), rf	1	0	1	0	0	0
Hartnett (Cubs), c	4	1	1	7	0	0
Whitney (Phillies), 3b	3	0	1	0	2	0
eRiggs (Reds), 3b	1	0	0	0	0	0
Durocher (Cardinals), ss	3	0	1	4	0	0
J. Dean (Cardinals), p	1	0	0	0	2	0
Hubbell (Giants), p	1	0	0	2	1	0
Davis (Cubs), p	0	0	0	0	1	0
Warneke (Cubs), p	1	0	0	0	0	0
Totals	31	4	9	27	11	0

American League	0	0	0	0	0	0	3	0	0	0—3
National League	0	2	0	0	2	0	0	0	x—4

Americans	IP.	H.	R.	ER.	BB.	SO.
Grove (Red Sox)	3	3	2	2	2	2
Rowe (Tigers)	3	4	2	1	1	2
Harder (Indians)	2	2	0	0	0	2

Nationals	IP.	H.	R.	ER.	BB.	SO.
J. Dean (Cardinals)	3	0	0	0	2	3
Hubbell (Giants)	3	2	0	0	1	2
Davis (Cubs)	⅔	4	3	3	1	0
Warneke (Cubs)	2⅓	1	0	0	3	2

Winning pitcher—J. Dean. Losing pitcher—Grove.

aGrounded out for Ferrell in seventh. bSingled for Higgins in seventh. cWalked for Rowe in seventh. dSingled for Demaree in eighth. eFanned for Whitney in eighth. fFanned for Harder in ninth. Runs batted in—Hartnett, Whitney, Medwick, Galan, Appling 2, Gehrig. Two-base hit—Gehringer. Three-base hit—Hartnett. Home runs—Galan, Gehrig. Double plays—Whitney, Herman and Collins; Appling, Gehringer and Gehrig. Left on bases—Americans 9, Nationals 6. Wild pitch—Hubbell. Umpires—Reardon and Stewart (N. L.), Summers and Kolls (A. L.). Time of game —2:00. Attendance—25,556.

Game of 1937—Griffith Stadium, Washington, July 7

The American League All-Stars, made up largely of Yankees, really dazzled, pounding out an easy 8-3 victory before a crowd of 31,391. The turnout included President Franklin D. Roosevelt, who drove on the field in an open car, plus cabinet officers and members of Congress.

Joe McCarthy, A. L. manager, had five of his Yankees in the starting line-up—Lou Gehrig, Red Rolfe, Joe DiMaggio, Bill Dickey and Lefty Gomez. All but Gomez played the entire game. Gehrig, enjoying his last big season, was the winners' batting star, driving in four runs with a homer and double.

Dizzy Dean, the Nationals' starting pitcher, remembered this game to the day he died. He began the day as baseball's outstanding pitcher, but a toe fracture suffered in the third inning started him on the downgrade and he never was the same thereafter.

It all began when Diz shook off Gabby Hartnett on a 3-and-2 pitch to Gehrig. Throwing a smoking fast ball instead of a curve, Dean saw Gehrig send it high over the distant right field wall for a two-run homer and a 2-0 lead. Earl Averill, next up, then hit a line drive back at Dean's foot with the force of a machine gun bullet. Dizzy managed to recover the ball and retire Averill, but when he reached the clubhouse, he discovered he had a broken toe on his left foot.

The Americans pretty well sewed up the game against Carl Hubbell in the fourth inning, tagging him for three runs on a walk, single, Rolfe's triple and a single by Charley Gehringer. The box score:

NATIONALS	AB.	R.	H.	PO.	A.	E.
P. Waner (Pirates), rf	5	0	0	0	0	0
Herman (Cubs), 2b	5	1	2	1	4	0
Vaughan (Pirates), 3b	5	0	2	3	0	0
Medwick (Cardinals), lf	5	1	4	1	0	0
Demaree (Cubs), cf	5	0	1	3	1	0
Mize (Cardinals), 1b	4	0	0	7	0	0
Hartnett (Cubs), c	3	1	1	6	0	0
bWhitehead (Giants)	0	0	0	0	0	0
Mancuso (Giants), c	1	0	0	1	0	0
Bartell (Giants), ss	4	0	1	2	3	0
J. Dean (Cardinals), p	1	0	0	0	1	0
Hubbell (Giants), p	0	0	0	0	0	0
Blanton (Pirates), p	0	0	0	0	0	0
aOtt (Giants)	1	0	1	0	0	0
Grissom (Reds), p	0	0	0	0	0	0
cCollins (Cubs)	1	0	1	0	0	0
Mungo (Dodgers), p	0	0	0	0	1	0
eMoore (Giants)	1	0	0	0	0	0
Walters (Phillies), p	0	0	0	0	1	0
Totals	41	3	13	24	11	0

AMERICANS	AB.	R.	H.	PO.	A.	E.
Rolfe, (Yankees), 3b	4	2	2	0	1	2
Gehringer (Tigers), 2b	5	1	3	2	5	0
DiMaggio (Yankees), rf	4	1	1	1	1	0
Gehrig (Yankees), 1b	4	1	2	10	1	0
Averill (Indians), cf	3	0	1	2	0	0
Cronin (Red Sox), ss	4	1	1	4	3	0
Dickey (Yankees), c	3	1	2	2	0	0
West (Browns), lf	4	1	1	5	0	0
Gomez (Yankees), p	1	0	0	0	0	0
Bridges (Tigers), p	1	0	0	0	1	0
dFoxx (Red Sox)	1	0	0	0	0	0
Harder (Indians), p	1	0	0	1	1	0
Totals	35	8	13	27	13	2

National League	0	0	1	1	1	0	0	0 – 3
American League	0	0	2	3	1	2	0	0	x – 8

Nationals	IP.	H.	R.	ER.	BB.	SO.
J. Dean (Cardinals)	3	4	2	2	1	2
Hubbell (Giants)	⅔	3	3	3	1	1
Blanton (Pirates)	1⅓	1	0	0	0	1
Grissom (Reds)	1	2	1	1	0	2
Mungo (Dodgers)	2	2	2	2	2	1
Walters (Phillies)	1	2	0	0	0	0

Americans	IP.	H.	R.	ER.	BB.	SO.
Gomez (Yankees)	3	1	0	0	0	0
Bridges (Tigers)	3	7	3	3	0	0
Harder (Indians)	3	5	0	0	0	0

Winning pitcher—Gomez. Losing pitcher—J. Dean.

aDoubled for Blanton in fifth. bRan for Hartnett in sixth. cSingled for Grissom in sixth. dGrounded out for Bridges in sixth. eForced runner for Mungo in eighth. Runs batted in—Gehrig 4, Rolfe 2, Gehringer, Dickey, P. Waner, Medwick, Mize. Two-base hits—Gehrig, Dickey, Cronin, Ott, Medwick 2. Three-base hit—Rolfe. Home run—Gehrig. Double play—Bartell and Mize. Left on bases—Nationals 11, Americans 7. Umpires—McGowan and Quinn (A. L.), Barr and Pinelli (N. L.) Time of game—2:30. Attendance—31,391.

Game of 1938—Crosley Field, Cincinnati, July 6

The strong-armed pitching of Johnny Vander Meer, Bill Lee and Mace Brown led the National League to a 4-1 victory. The trio limited the A.L. All-Stars to seven hits.

This was the year of Vander Meer's successive no-hitters, and the white-haired boy of the Cincinnati team didn't disappoint his 27,067 hometown fans in the midsummer classic. Manager Bill Terry gave him the distinction of starting the game. Vandy turned back the A.L. stars with one hit in his three innings.

Unlike his course in the 1934 and 1937 games, Terry made no effort to turn the game into a parade of National League stars. Except for pitchers, he didn't make a single change in his lineup, using only 12 players.

Lefty Gomez opened on the mound for the A.L. and suffered his first defeat, but it wasn't his fault. An error by Joe Cronin—the first of four A.L. boots—set up a run in the opening inning. Johnny Allen yielded a second run in the fourth on Mel Ott's triple and a single by Ernie Lombardi.

The N.L. scored two more off Lefty Grove in the seventh on the most ludicrous of All-Star plays. Frank McCormick greeted Grove with a single and Leo Durocher laid down a sacrifice bunt. It did as much damage as a home run because Jimmie Foxx, playing third base, threw the ball into right field. When Joe DiMaggio, after retrieving the ball, overthrew the plate trying for McCormick, Durocher continued running until he scored for a "bunt-home run."

The Americans pasted Mace Brown hard in the ninth inning, but he escaped with one run. A single by DiMaggio and Joe Cronin's long double produced the marker. Two great catches by Joe Medwick and Ival Goodman spared Brown from further trouble. The box score:

AMERICANS	AB.	R.	H.	PO.	A.	E.
Kreevich (Wh. Sox), lf	2	0	0	1	0	0
cCramer (Red Sox), lf	2	0	0	0	0	0
Gehringer (Tigers), 2b	3	0	1	2	2	0
Averill (Indians), cf	4	0	5	0	0	0
Foxx (Red Sox), 1b-3b	4	0	1	5	1	1
DiMaggio (Yankees), rf	4	1	1	2	0	1
Dickey (Yankees), c	4	0	1	8	0	1
Cronin (Red Sox), ss	3	0	2	0	2	1
Lewis (Senators), 3b	1	0	0	0	1	0
bGehrig (Yankees), 1b	3	0	1	1	0	0
Gomez (Yankees), p	1	0	0	0	0	0
Allen (Indians), p	1	0	0	0	0	0
dYork (Tigers)	1	0	0	0	0	0
Grove (Red Sox), p	0	0	0	0	0	0
eJohnson (Athletics)	1	0	0	0	0	0
Totals	34	1	7	24	6	4

NATIONALS	AB.	R.	H.	PO.	A.	E.
Hack (Cubs), 3b	4	1	1	1	2	0
Herman (Cubs), 2b	4	0	1	3	4	0
Goodman (Reds), rf	3	0	0	2	0	0
Medwick (Cardinals), lf	4	0	1	2	0	0
Ott (Giants), cf	4	1	1	3	0	0
Lombardi (Reds), c	4	0	2	5	0	0
McCormick (Reds), 1b	4	1	1	11	0	0
Durocher (Dodgers), ss	3	1	1	0	3	0
Vander Meer (Reds), p	0	0	0	0	3	0
aLeiber (Giants)	1	0	0	0	0	0
Lee (Cubs), p	1	0	0	0	0	0
Brown (Pirates), p	1	0	0	0	1	0
Totals	33	4	8	27	13	0

```
American League .......................... 0  0  0    0  0  0    0  0  1 — 1
National League .......................... 1  0  0    1  0  0    2  0  x — 4
```

Americans	IP.	H.	R.	ER.	BB.	SO.
Gomez (Yankees)	3	2	1	0	0	1
Allen (Indians)	3	2	1	1	0	3
Grove (Red Sox)	2	4	2	0	0	3

Nationals	IP.	H.	R.	ER.	BB.	SO.
Vander Meer (Reds)	3	1	0	0	0	1
Lee (Cubs)	3	1	0	0	1	2
Brown (Pirates)	3	5	1	1	1	2

Winning pitcher—Vander Meer. Losing pitcher—Gomez.

aLined out for Vander Meer in third. bGrounded out for Lewis in fifth. cGrounded out for Kreevich in sixth. dFanned for Allen in seventh. eStruck out for Grove in ninth. Runs batted in—Medwick, Lombardi, Cronin. Two-base hits—Dickey, Cronin. Three-base hit—Ott. Stolen bases—Goodman, DiMaggio. Left on bases—Americans 8, Nationals 6. Hit by pitcher—By Allen—(Goodman). Umpires—Ballanfant and Klem (N. L.), Basil and Geisel (A. L.). Time of game—1:58. Attendance—27,067.

Game of 1939—Yankee Stadium, New York, July 11

With six Yankees in the starting lineup, the American League stars emerged victorious, 3-1. The game was the second to be played in New York and was awarded to the Big Town because it was World's Fair year there. A crowd of 62,892 attended.

The announcer's introduction of six Yankees in the starting lineup prompted an inebriated fan with N.L. sympathies to pull a famous quip. "That isn't fair," he remarked. "They ought to make Joe McCarthy play an All-Star American League team. We can beat them, but we can't beat the Yankees."

McCarthy opened with a New York battery of Red Ruffing and Bill Dickey. Other Yankees in the lineup were Joe DiMaggio, George Selkirk, Joe Gordon and Red Rolfe. And the only time Marse Joe called on a pinch-hitter he used Myril Hoag, a former Yankee.

The N.L. was the first to score, picking up its lone run off Ruffing in the third inning on singles by Arky Vaughan and Stan Hack plus Lonnie Frey's double.

The Americans gained the lead with two tallies in the fourth at the expense of Bill Lee. With one out, Dickey walked and Hank Greenberg singled. Another ace by Selkirk plated one run and Greenberg subsequently scored when Vaughan bobbled Gordon's roller. DiMaggio closed the run-making with a homer in the fifth.

The A.L.'s big hero was Bob Feller. He took over in a ticklish situation in the sixth inning. The bases were full with one out and Vaughan at bat when Bob relieved Tommy Bridges. Feller didn't waste any time, retiring the side on one pitch, which Vaughan hit into a double play. The Cleveland fireballer then checked the N.L. on one hit over the last three frames. The box score:

NATIONALS	AB.	R.	H.	PO.	A.	E.
Hack (Cubs), 3b	4	0	1	1	1	0
Frey (Reds), 2b	4	0	1	0	4	0
Goodman (Reds), rf	1	0	0	0	0	0
cHerman (Cubs)	1	0	0	0	0	0
Moore (Cardinals), cf	1	0	0	0	0	0
McCormick (Reds), 1b	4	0	0	7	1	0
Lombardi (Reds), c	4	0	2	6	0	0
Medwick (Cardinals), lf	4	0	0	1	0	0
Ott (Giants), cf-rf	4	0	2	4	0	0
Vaughan (Pirates), ss	3	1	1	4	1	1
Derringer (Reds), p	1	0	0	0	0	0
bCamilli (Dodgers)	1	0	0	0	0	0
Lee (Cubs), p	0	0	0	0	0	0
dPhelps (Dodgers)	1	0	0	0	0	0
Fette (Braves), p	0	0	0	1	0	0
eMize (Cardinals)	1	0	0	0	0	0
Totals	34	1	7	24	7	1

AMERICANS	AB.	R.	H.	PO.	A.	E.
Cramer (Red Sox), rf	4	0	1	3	0	0
Rolfe (Yankees), 3b	4	0	1	1	0	0
DiMaggio (Yankees), cf	4	1	1	1	0	0
Dickey (Yankees), c	3	1	0	10	0	0
Greenberg (Tigers), 1b	3	1	1	7	1	0
Cronin (Red Sox), ss	4	0	1	2	3	1
Selkirk (Yankees), lf	2	0	1	0	0	0
Gordon (Yankees), 2b	4	0	0	2	5	0
Ruffing (Yankees), p	0	0	0	0	0	0
aHoag (Browns)	1	0	0	0	0	0
Bridges (Tigers), p	1	0	0	1	0	0
Feller (Indians), p	1	0	0	0	0	0
Totals	31	3	6	27	9	1

```
National League ....................................... 0   0   1     0   0   0     0   0   0 – 1
American League ..................................... 0   0   0     2   1   0     0   0   x – 3
```

Nationals	IP.	H.	R.	ER.	BB.	SO.
Derringer (Reds)	3	2	0	0	0	1
Lee (Cubs)	3	3	3	2	3	4
Fette (Braves)	2	1	0	0	1	0

Americans	IP.	H.	R.	ER.	BB.	SO.
Ruffing (Yankees)	3	4	1	1	1	4
Bridges (Tigers)	2⅓	2	0	0	1	3
Feller (Indians)	3⅔	1	0	0	1	2

Winning pitcher—Bridges. Losing pitcher—Lee.

aFanned for Ruffing in third. bStruck out for Derringer in fourth. cStruck out for Goodman in fifth. dGrounded out for Lee in seventh. eStruck out for Fette in ninth. Runs batted in—DiMaggio, Selkirk, Frey. Two-base hit—Frey. Home run—DiMaggio. Double play—Gordon, Cronin and Greenberg. Left on bases—Nationals 9, Americans 8. Umpires—Hubbard and Rommel (A. L.), Goetz and Magerkurth (N. L.). Time of game—1:55. Attendance—62,892.

Game of 1940—Sportsman's Park, St. Louis, July 9

The National League scored the first shutout of the All-Star series when five hurlers combined to blank the A. L. on three hits, 4-0. Bill McKechnie, senior circuit skipper, worked Paul Derringer, Bucky Walters, Whit Wyatt and Larry French in two-inning shifts and then used Carl Hubbell to wrap it up in the ninth inning.

Reverting to an earlier N. L. practice, McKechnie tried to show all of his stars, using no fewer than 22 players. Joe Cronin, who handled the Americans because the loop's magnates figured Joe McCarthy had had the honor often enough, took a cue from his senior circuit rival and employed 18 players himself.

The game was decided before many of the 32,373 fans had settled in their seats. Oddly enough, it was one of the lesser lights of the N. L. squad who was the hero. After Arky Vaughan and Billy Herman opened with singles off Red Ruffing in the first inning, Max West drove a home run into the stands in right-center, giving the Nationals a 3-0 lead before Ruffing retired a man.

In the very next inning, West crumpled in front of the right field wall while trying to make a leaping catch of Luke Appling's liner. Max had to be assisted from the field, but the injury was not serious.

Following their first-inning burst, the Nationals went out as regularly against Ruffing, Buck Newsom and Bob Feller as the Americans until they scored a parting run off Feller in the eighth. Mel Ott worked Feller for a walk, moved to second on a sacrifice and came home when Harry Danning singled. The box score:

AMERICANS	AB.	R.	H.	PO.	A.	E.
Travis (Senators), 3b	3	0	0	0	0	0
Keltner (Indians), 3b	1	0	0	2	1	0
Williams (Red Sox), lf	2	0	0	3	0	0
Finney (Red Sox), rf	0	0	0	0	0	0
Keller (Yankees), rf	2	0	0	4	0	0
Greenberg (Tigers), lf	2	0	0	0	0	0
DiMaggio (Yankees), cf	4	0	0	1	0	0
Foxx (Red Sox), 1b	3	0	0	4	2	0
Appling (White Sox), ss	3	0	2	0	0	0
Boudreau (Indians), ss	0	0	0	0	0	0
Dickey (Yankees), c	1	0	0	2	0	0
Hayes (Athletics), c	1	0	0	1	0	0
Hemsley (Indians), c	1	0	0	3	0	1
Gordon (Yankees), 2b	2	0	0	3	1	0
aMack (Indians), 2b	1	0	0	0	0	0
Ruffing (Yankees), p	1	0	0	0	0	0
Newsom (Tigers), p	1	0	1	0	0	0
Feller (Indians), p	1	0	0	1	0	0
Totals	29	0	3	24	4	1

NATIONALS	AB.	R.	H.	PO.	A.	E.
Vaughan (Pirates), ss	3	1	1	0	1	0
Miller (Braves), ss	1	0	0	2	1	0
Herman (Cubs), 2b	3	1	3	0	3	0
Coscarart (Dodgers), 2b	1	0	0	0	2	0
West (Braves), rf	1	1	1	0	0	0
Nicholson (Cubs), rf	2	0	0	1	0	0
Ott (Giants), rf	0	1	0	0	0	0
Mize (Cardinals), 1b	2	0	0	8	0	0
F. McCormick (Reds), 1b	1	0	0	2	0	0
Lombardi (Reds), c	2	0	1	3	0	0
Phelps (Dodgers), c	0	0	0	1	0	0
Danning (Giants), c	1	0	1	6	0	0
Medwick (Dodgers), lf	2	0	0	1	0	0
J. Moore (Dodgers), lf	2	0	0	1	0	0
Lavagetto (Dodgers), 3b	2	0	0	0	1	0
May (Phillies), 3b	1	0	0	0	0	0
T. Moore (Cardinals), cf	3	0	0	2	0	0
Derringer (Reds), p	1	0	0	1	0	0
Walters (Reds), p	0	0	0	0	1	0
Wyatt (Dodgers), p	1	0	0	0	0	0
French (Cubs), p	0	0	0	0	0	0
Hubbell (Giants), p	0	0	0	0	0	0
Totals	29	4	7	27	10	0

American League	0	0	0	0	0	0	0	0	0	—	0
National League	3	0	0	0	0	0	0	1	x	—	4

Americans	IP.	H.	R.	ER.	BB.	SO.
Ruffing (Yankees)	3	5	3	3	0	2
Newsom (Tigers)	3	1	0	0	1	1
Feller (Indians)	2	1	1	1	2	3

Nationals	IP.	H.	R.	ER.	BB.	SO.
Derringer (Reds)	2	1	0	0	1	3
Walters (Reds)	2	0	0	0	1	0
Wyatt (Dodgers)	2	1	0	0	0	1
French (Cubs)	2	1	0	0	0	2
Hubbell (Giants)	1	0	0	0	1	1

Winning pitcher—Derringer. Losing pitcher—Ruffing.

aStruck out for Gordon in eighth. Runs batted in—West 3, Danning. Two-base hit—Appling. Home run—West. Sacrifice hits—F. McCormick, French. Double play—Coscarart, Miller and F. McCormick. Left on bases—Nationals 7, Americans 4. Hit by pitcher—By Feller (May). Umpires—Reardon and Stewart (N. L.), Pipgras and Basil (A. L.). Time of game—1:53. Attendance—32,373.

Game of 1941—Briggs Stadium, Detroit, July 8

Few important games between the two leagues have left as many heartaches for the senior major as this contest. Leading by 5-4 with two out in the ninth inning, the Nationals seemed to have victory in the bag. But then Ted Williams, the Red Sox' great young hitter, sent a three-run homer into the upper right field stands and the Americans won, 7-5.

Never before or since has the finish of an All-Star Game produced such an explosion of uninhibited joy as the emotional outpouring staged in the A. L. dressing room. Manager Del Baker, not an overly demonstrative man, hugged and kissed the tall, grinning Williams.

The tough luck player of the day was Arky Vaughan. The Pirate shortstop hit successive two-run homers for the National League in the seventh and eighth innings, one off righthander Sid Hudson and the second off lefty Edgar Smith. Vaughan looked like the big hero of the game until Williams' tremendous drive made Arky's two round-trippers just incidents in another N. L. defeat.

Vaughan's second smash made the score 5-2, but the A. L. came back with one run in its half of the eighth against Claude Passeau. Joe DiMaggio doubled and scored when brother Dom DiMaggio singled.

That set the stage for the dramatic ninth. With one out, pinch-hitter Ken Keltner singled. Joe Gordon also singled and when Passeau walked Cecil Travis, the bags were full. Joe DiMaggio hit into a force play, scoring Keltner, and then came Williams' payoff blow. The box score:

NATIONALS	AB.	R.	H.	PO.	A.	E.		AMERICANS	AB.	R.	H.	PO.	A.	E.
Hack (Cubs), 3b	2	0	1	3	0	0		Doerr (Red Sox), 2b	3	0	0	0	0	0
fLavagetto (Dodgers, 3b	1	0	0	0	0	0		Gordon (Yankees), 2b	2	1	1	2	0	0
T. Moore (Cardinals), lf	5	0	0	-0	0	0		Travis (Senators), 3b	4	1	1	2	0	0
Reiser (Dodgers), cf	4	0	0	6	0	2		J. DiMaggio (Yanks), cf	4	3	1	1	0	0
Mize (Cardinals), 1b	4	1	1	5	0	0		Williams (Red Sox), lf	4	1	2	3	0	1
F. McCormick (Reds), 1b	0	0	0	0	0	0		Heath (Indians), rf	2	0	0	1	0	1
Nicholson (Cubs), rf	1	0	0	1	0	0		D. DiMaggio (R. Sox), rf	1	0	1	1	0	0
Elliott (Pirates), rf	1	0	0	0	0	0		Cronin (Yanks), ss	2	0	0	3	0	0
Slaughter (Cardinals), rf	2	1	1	0	0	0		York (Tigers), 1b	3	0	1	6	2	0
Vaughan (Pirates), ss	4	2	3	1	2	0		Foxx (Red Sox), 1b	1	0	0	2	2	0
Miller (Braves), ss	0	0	0	0	1	0		Dickey (Yankees), c	3	0	1	4	2	0
Frey (Reds), 2b	1	0	1	1	3	0		Hayes (Athletics), c	1	0	0	2	0	0
cHerman (Dodgers), 2b	3	0	2	3	0	0		Feller (Indians), p	0	0	0	0	1	0
Owen (Dodgers), c	1	0	0	0	0	0		bCullenbine (Browns)	1	0	0	0	0	0
Lopez (Pirates), c	1	0	0	3	0	0		Lee (White Sox), p	1	0	0	0	1	0
Danning (Giants), c	1	0	0	3	0	0		Hudson (Senators), p	0	0	0	0	0	0
Wyatt (Dodgers), p	0	0	0	0	0	0		eKeller (Yankees)	1	0	0	0	0	0
aOtt (Giants)	1	0	0	0	0	0		Smith (White Sox), p	0	0	0	1	0	1
Derringer (Reds), p	0	0	0	0	1	0		gKeltner, (Indians)	1	1	1	0	0	0
Walters (Reds), p	1	1	1	0	0	0		Totals	36	7	11	27	11	3
dMedwick (Dodgers)	1	0	0	0	0	0								
Passeau (Cubs), p	1	0	0	0	0	0								
Totals	35	5	10	26	7	2								

```
National League .................. 0   0   0     0   0   1     2   2   0 – 5
American League .................. 0   0   0     1   0   1     0   1   4 – 7
```

Two out when winning run scored.

Nationals	IP.	H.	R.	ER.	BB.	SO.		Americans	IP.	H.	R.	ER.	BB.	SO.
Wyatt (Dodgers)	2	0	0	0	1	0		Feller (Indians)	3	1	0	0	0	4
Derringer (Reds)	2	2	1	0	0	0		Lee (White Sox)	3	4	1	1	0	0
Walters (Reds)	2	3	1	1	2	2		Hudson (Senators)	1	3	2	2	1	1
Passeau (Cubs)	2⅔	6	5	4	1	3		Smith (White Sox)	2	2	2	2	0	2

Winning pitcher—Smith. Losing pitcher—Passeau.

aStruck out for Wyatt in third. bGrounded out for Feller in third. cSingled for Frey in fifth. dGrounded out for Walters in seventh. eStruck out for Hudson in eighth. fGrounded out for Hack in ninth. gSingled for Smith in ninth. Runs batted in—Williams 4, Moore, Boudreau, Vaughan 4, D. DiMaggio, J. DiMaggio. Two-base hits—Travis, Williams, Walters, Herman, J. DiMaggio. Home runs—Vaughan 2, Williams. Sacrifice hits—Hack, Lopez. Double plays—Frey, Vaughan and Mize; York and Cronin. Left on bases—Americans 7, Nationals 6. Umpires—Summers and Grieve (A. L.), Jorda and Pinelli (N. L.). Time of game—2:23. Attendance—54,674.

Game of 1942—Polo Grounds, New York, July 6

A first-inning home-run barrage against Mort Cooper, Cardinal ace, enabled the Americans to win, 3-1. The game, a twilight affair, was originally scheduled for Brooklyn, but since the proceeds were to go to war charities, Larry MacPhail permitted the contest to be transferred to the Polo Grounds because of its larger capacity.

Even so, the crowd of 34,178 fell far below expectations. There were, however, extenuating circumstances. Afternoon showers fell in New York, and shortly before the scheduled 6 p.m. game time, a cloudburst struck the Polo Grounds. The downpour ruined the sale of unreserved seats.

Because the winning team was scheduled to play the Service All-Stars, recruited from top-notch big leaguers in the Army and Navy, in Cleveland the next night, the three-inning rule for pitchers was suspended. Instead, the managers were permitted to work their pitchers as many as five innings. Joe McCarthy took advantage of the rule, using Spud Chandler the first four innings and Alton Benton the last five.

Lou Boudreau hit Mort Cooper's second pitch of the game into the upper left field stands for a home run. Tommy Henrich followed with a double. Cooper retired the next two batters, but then Rudy York sliced a drive into the lower right field stands about five feet inside the foul line, giving the A.L. a 3-0 lead.

The only N.L. run came in the eighth when Mickey Owen hit a pinch-homer into the left field stands. Ironically, he didn't sock a single home run in 133 league games that year. The box score:

AMERICANS	AB.	R.	H.	PO.	A.	E.
Boudreau (Indians), ss	4	1	1	4	5	0
Henrich (Yankees), rf	4	1	1	2	0	0
Williams (Red Sox), lf	4	0	1	0	0	0
J. DiMaggio (Yankees), cf	4	0	2	2	0	0
York (Tigers), 1b	4	1	1	11	3	0
Gordon (Yankees), 2b	4	0	0	1	4	0
Keltner (Indians), 3b	4	0	0	0	1	0
Tebbetts (Tigers), c	4	0	0	4	1	0
Chandler (Yankees), p	1	0	0	3	1	0
bJohnson (Athletics)	1	0	1	0	0	0
Benton (Tigers), p	1	0	0	0	1	0
Totals	35	3	7	27	16	0

NATIONALS	AB.	R.	H.	PO.	A.	E.
Brown (Cardinals), 2b	2	0	0	1	0	1
Herman (Dodgers), 2b	1	0	0	0	0	0
Vaughan (Dodgers), 3b	2	0	0	1	2	0
Elliott (Pirates), 3b	1	0	1	1	2	0
Reiser (Dodgers), cf	3	0	1	3	0	0
Moore (Cardinals), cf	1	0	0	1	0	0
Mize (Giants), 1b	2	0	0	3	0	0
F. McCormick (Reds), 1b	2	0	0	3	0	0
Ott (Giants), rf	4	0	0	1	0	0
Medwick (Dodgers), lf	2	0	0	1	0	0
Slaughter (Cardinals), lf	2	0	1	1	0	0
W. Cooper (Cardinals), c	2	0	1	7	0	0
Lombardi (Braves), c	1	0	0	2	0	0
Miller (Braves), ss	2	0	0	2	1	0
Reese (Dodgers), ss	1	0	0	0	1	0
M. Cooper (Cardinals), p	0	0	0	0	0	0
aMarshall (Giants)	1	0	0	0	0	0
Vander Meer (Reds), p	0	0	0	0	1	0
cLitwhiler (Phillies)	1	0	1	0	0	0
Passeau (Cubs), p	0	0	0	0	0	0
dOwen (Dodgers)	1	1	1	0	0	0
Walters (Reds), p	0	0	0	0	0	0
Totals	31	1	6	27	7	1

```
American League ....................................... 3 0   0   0    0 0   0   0   0 – 3
National League ...................................... 0 0   0   0    0 0   1   0 – 1
```

Americans	IP.	H.	R.	ER.	BB.	SO.
Chandler (Yankees)	4	2	0	0	0	2
Benton (Tigers)	5	4	1	1	2	1

Nationals	IP.	H.	R.	ER.	BB.	SO.
M. Cooper (Cardinals)	3	4	3	3	0	2
Vander Meer (Reds)	3	2	0	0	0	4
Passeau (Cubs)	2	1	0	0	0	1
Walters (Reds)	1	0	0	0	0	1

Winning pitcher—Chandler. Losing pitcher—M. Cooper.

aForced runner for M. Cooper in third. bSingled for Chandler in fifth. cSingled for Vander Meer in sixth. dHomered for Passeau in eighth. Runs batted in—Boudreau, York 2, Owen. Two-base hit—Henrich. Home runs—Boudreau, York, Owen. Double plays—Gordon, Boudreau and York; Boudreau and York. Hit by pitcher—By Chandler (Brown). Passed ball—Tebbetts. Left on bases—Nationals 6, Americans 5. Umpires—Ballanfant and Barlick (N. L.), Stewart and McGowan (A. L.). Time of game—2:07. Attendance—34,178.

Game of 1943—Shibe Park, Philadelphia, July 13

In the first night game in All-Star history, the American leaguers edged the Nationals, 5-3, for their eighth victory in 11 games. Mort Cooper, Cardinal ace, again was the victim, just as he had been the year before.

Although the Yankees qualified six players, more than any other team, Manager Joe McCarthy didn't use a single member of his club. The brazen move apparently stemmed from his resentment of accusations that he had favored his players in earlier games and a decision to prove that he could win without a single Yankee.

The fair-haired boy for the Americans was Bobby Doerr. The Red Sox second baseman tagged Mort Cooper for a three-run homer in the second inning. The blow, which erased a 1-0 lead the N.L. had taken against Dutch Leonard in the opening frame, followed a pair of walks.

Cooper still was wobbly in the third and the A.L. stars scored again on doubles by Ken Keltner and Dick Wakefield. After Vern Stephens sacrificed Wakefield to third, Manager Billy Southworth lifted Cooper in favor of Johnny Vander Meer, who struck out both Rudy York and Chet Laabs to end the inning.

Vander Meer fanned six in his two and two-thirds innings, but was on the mound when the Americans scored their fifth run in the fifth.

Vince DiMaggio, who entered the game in the fourth inning as a pinch-hitter, was the Nationals' batting hero. He was a one-man blitz with a single, triple and homer in three attempts. The box score:

NATIONALS	AB.	R.	H.	PO.	A.	E.
Hack (Cubs), 3b	5	1	3	0	2	1
Herman (Dodgers), 2b	5	0	2	3	3	2
Musial (Cardinals), lf-rf	4	0	1	0	0	0
Nicholson (Cubs), rf	2	0	0	0	0	0
cGalan (Dodgers), lf	1	0	0	1	0	0
Fletcher (Pirates), 1b	2	0	0	3	0	0
dDahlgren (Phillies), 1b	2	0	0	3	0	0
W. Cooper (Cardinals), c	2	0	1	7	1	0
eLombardi (Giants), c	2	0	0	3	0	0
H. Walker (Cards), cf	1	0	0	1	0	0
bDiMaggio (Pirates), cf	3	2	3	1	0	0
Marion (Cardinals), ss	2	0	0	2	2	0
gOtt (Giants)	1	0	0	0	0	0
Miller (Reds), ss	1	0	0	0	1	0
M. Cooper (Cardinals), p	1	0	0	0	1	0
Vander Meer (Reds), p	1	0	0	0	1	0
Sewell (Pirates), p	0	0	0	0	1	0
hF. Walker (Dodgers)	1	0	0	0	0	0
Javery (Braves), p	0	0	0	0	0	0
iFrey (Reds)	1	0	0	0	0	0
Totals	37	3	10	24	12	3

AMERICANS	AB.	R.	H.	PO.	A.	E.
Case (Senators), rf	2	1	0	0	0	0
Keltner (Indians), 3b	4	1	1	2	2	0
Wakefield (Tigers), lf	4	0	2	3	0	0
R. Johnson (Senators), lf	0	0	0	1	0	0
Stephens (Browns), ss	3	0	1	1	3	1
Siebert (Athletics), 1b	1	0	0	3	1	0
aYork (Tigers), 1b	3	0	1	4	0	0
Laabs (Browns), cf	3	1	0	7	0	0
Early (Senators), c	2	1	0	3	0	0
Doerr (Red Sox), 2b	4	1	2	3	3	0
Leonard (Senators), p	1	0	1	0	1	0
Newhouser (Tigers), p	1	0	0	0	0	0
fHeath (Indians)	1	0	0	0	0	0
Hughson (Red Sox), p	0	0	0	0	0	0
Totals	29	5	8	27	10	1

National League	1	0	0	0	0	0	1	0	1 – 3
American League	0	3	1	0	1	0	0	0	x – 5

Nationals	IP.	H.	R.	ER.	BB.	SO.
M. Cooper (Cardinals)	2⅓	4	4	4	2	1
Vander Meer (Reds)	2⅔	2	1	0	1	6
Sewell (Pirates)	1	0	0	0	0	0
Javery (Braves)	2	2	0	0	0	3

Americans	IP.	H.	R.	ER.	BB.	SO.
Leonard (Senators)	3	2	1	1	0	0
Newhouser (Tigers)	3	3	0	0	1	1
Hughson (Red Sox)	3	5	2	2	0	2

Winning pitcher—Leonard. Losing pitcher—M. Cooper.

aStruck out for Siebert in third. bSingled for H. Walker in fourth. cWalked for Nicholson in sixth. dHit into double play for Fletcher in sixth. eFlied out for W. Cooper in sixth. fFlied out for Newhouser in sixth. gStruck out for Marion in seventh. hFlied out for Sewell in seventh. iFlied out for Javery in ninth. Runs batted in—Musial, F. Walker, DiMaggio, Doerr 3, Wakefield. Two-base hits—Musial, Keltner, Wakefield. Three-base hit—DiMaggio. Home runs—Doerr, DiMaggio. Sacrifice hits—Stephens, Early. Double plays—Hack, Herman and Fletcher; Vander Meer, Marion and Herman; Miller, Herman and Dahlgren; Stephens, Doerr and York. Hit by pitcher—By M. Cooper (Case). Left on bases—Nationals 8, Americans 6. Umpires—Rommel and Rue (A. L.), Conlan and Dunn (N. L.). Time of game—2:07. Attendance—31,938.

Game of 1944—Forbes Field, Pittsburgh, July 11

Erupting for 12 hits, the Nationals romped to an easy 7-1 victory before an arc-light turnout of 29,589. It was only the fourth win for the senior circuit in 12 All-Star clashes.

Joe McCarthy started Hank Borowy, and the Yankee righthander not only blanked the N.L. on three hits in his three-inning stint, but also drove in the A.L.'s only run. The tally came off Bucky Walters.

Tex Hughson, Borowy's successor, breezed through the fourth inning, but blew up in the fifth. Connie Ryan opened the inning with a single and stole second. A pinch-double by Bill Nicholson drove in the tying run. Augie Galan followed with a single, scoring Nicholson. A pass and an error by George McQuinn filled the bases. Singles by Walker Cooper and Dixie Walker added two more runs.

In the seventh inning, with Hal Newhouser on duty, Whitey Kurowski doubled across a pair of N.L. runs to make the score 6-1. The final tally in the eighth came without the benefit of a hit. Marty Marion, leading off, struck out but reached base safely when Frank Hayes missed the third strike. Two walks subsequently filled the bases, and Marion counted on Musial's fly ball.

Phil Cavarretta set an All-Star Game record by reaching base safely five straight times on a triple, single and three walks. Each of the passes came from a different pitcher.

With $81,275 from gate receipts, $25,000 from Gillette Safety Razor Co. for broadcasting rights and a contribution by Sportservice from the concessions, the game produced net receipts of $100,999.39 to buy equipment for men in the armed forces. The box score:

AMERICANS	AB.	R.	H.	PO.	A.	E.
Tucker (White Sox), cf	4	0	0	4	0	0
Spence (Senators), rf	4	0	2	2	1	0
McQuinn (Browns), 1b	4	0	1	5	1	1
Stephens (Browns), ss	3	0	0	2	1	0
Johnson (Red Sox), lf	4	1	1	0	4	0
Keltner (Indians), 3b	3	0	0	4	1	1
Doerr (Red Sox), 2b	3	0	0	2	0	0
Hemsley (Yankees), c	2	0	0	3	0	1
Hayes (Athletics), c	1	0	1	0	0	0
Borowy (Yankees), p	1	0	1	0	0	0
Hughson (Red Sox), p	0	0	0	0	0	0
Muncrief (Browns), p	0	0	0	1	0	0
cHiggins (Tigers)	1	0	0	0	0	0
Newhouser (Tigers), p	0	0	0	0	1	0
Newsom (Athletics), p	0	0	0	0	0	0
Totals	32	1	6	24	9	3

NATIONALS	AB.	R.	H.	PO.	A.	E.
Galan (Dodgers), lf	4	1	1	2	0	0
Cavarretta, (Cubs), 1b	2	1	2	12	0	0
Musial (Cardinals), cf-rf	4	1	1	2	1	0
W. Cooper (Cardinals), c	5	1	2	5	2	0
Mueller (Reds), c	0	0	0	0	0	0
Walker (Dodgers), rf	4	0	2	0	0	0
DiMaggio (Pirates), cf	0	0	0	0	0	0
Elliott (Pirates), 3b	3	0	1	0	3	0
Kurowski (Cardinals), 3b	1	0	1	0	1	0
Ryan (Braves), 2b	4	1	2	4	4	1
Marion (Cardinals), ss	3	1	0	2	3	0
Walters (Reds), p	0	0	0	0	1	0
aOtt (Giants)	1	0	0	0	0	0
Raffensberger (Phils), p	0	0	0	0	0	0
bNicholson (Cubs)	1	1	1	0	0	0
Sewell (Pirates), p	1	0	0	0	0	0
dMedwick (Giants)	0	0	0	0	0	0
Tobin (Braves), p	0	0	0	0	0	0
Totals	33	7	12	27	15	1

American League	0	1	0	0	0	0	0	0 — 1
National League	0	0	0	0	4	0	2	1	x — 7

Americans	IP.	H.	R.	ER.	BB.	SO.
Borowy (Yankees)	3	3	0	0	1	0
Hughson (Red Sox)	1⅓	5	4	3	1	2
Muncrief (Browns)	1⅓	1	0	0	0	1
Newhouser (Tigers)	1⅓	3	3	2	2	1
Newsom (Athletics)	⅓	0	0	0	0	0

Nationals	IP.	H.	R.	ER.	BB.	SO.
Walters (Reds)	3	5	1	1	0	1
Raffensberger (Phillies)	2	1	0	0	0	2
Sewell (Pirates)	3	0	0	0	1	2
Tobin (Braves)	1	0	0	0	0	0

Winning pitcher—Raffensberger. Losing pitcher—Hughson.

aFlied out for Walters in third. bDoubled for Raffensberger in fifth. cGrounded out for Muncrief in seventh. dSacrificed for Sewell in eighth. Runs batted in—Kurowski 2, Nicholson, Galan, W. Cooper, Walker, Musial, Borowy. Two-base hits—Nicholson. Kurowski. Three-base hit—Cavarretta. Sacrifice hits—Marion, Musial, Medwick. Stolen base—Ryan. Double plays—Spence and Hemsley; Marion, Ryan and Cavarretta. Wild pitch—Muncrief. Left on bases—Nationals 9, Americans 5. Umpires—Barr and Sears (N. L.), Berry and Hubbard (A. L.). Time of game—2:11. Attendance—29,589.

Game of 1946—Fenway Park, Boston, July 9

After a one-year interruption because of war travel restrictions, the All-Star Game was resumed and the American League scored the most overwhelming triumph of the series, crushing the Nationals, 12-0.

Ted Williams, playing before his home fans, staged one of the most magnificent shows in the history of the midsummer classic. He hit two homers and two singles and drew a walk in five times at bat. In addition, he scored four runs and drove in five.

The Splendid Splinter's first homer was a terrific smash into the center field bleachers off Kirby Higbe in the fourth inning. In the eighth, swinging against a blooper pitch by Rip Sewell, Williams supplied the power to drive the ball into the right field bullpen for his second round-tripper.

The A.L. collected a total of 14 hits and gave an early intimation of the rout that followed when Charlie Keller bashed a homer off Claude Passeau following a walk to Williams in the first inning. Williams' first homer made it 3-0 in the fourth.

The Americans added three more runs in the fifth while kayoing Higbe. A double by Vern Stephens with the bags full and a single by Williams were the big blows. Ewell Blackwell was nicked for two runs in the seventh and then Williams capped the scoring with a three-run blast off Sewell in the eighth after Sam Chapman plated a run earlier in the inning with a fly ball. The box score:

NATIONALS	AB.	R.	H.	PO.	A.	E.
Schoendienst (Cards), 2b....	2	0	0	0	2	0
cGustine (Pirates), 2b	1	0	0	1	1	0
Musial (Cardinals), lf........	2	0	0	0	0	0
dEnnis (Phillies), lf	2	0	0	0	0	0
Hopp (Braves), lf	2	0	1	0	0	0
eLowrey (Cubs), cf.............	2	0	1	3	0	0
Walker (Dodgers), rf	3	0	0	1	0	0
Slaughter (Cardinals), rf....	1	0	0	0	0	0
Kurowski (Cardinals), 3b ..	3	0	0	2	1	0
iVerban (Phillies)	1	0	0	0	0	0
Mize (Giants), 1b	1	0	0	7	0	0
bMcCormick (Phils), 1b......	1	0	0	1	1	0
gCavarretta (Cardinals), 1b	1	0	1	0	0	0
Cooper (Giants), c	1	0	1	0	0	0
Masi (Braves), c	2	0	0	4	1	0
Marion (Cardinals), ss	3	0	0	4	6	0
Passeau (Cubs), p..............	1	0	0	0	1	0
Higbe (Dodgers), p.............	1	0	0	0	0	0
Blackwell (Reds), p	0	0	0	0	0	0
hLamanno (Reds)...............	1	0	0	0	0	0
Sewell (Pirates), p	0	0	0	0	0	0
Totals	31	0	3	24	13	0

AMERICANS	AB.	R.	H.	PO.	A.	E.
DiMaggio (R. Sox), cf	2	0	1	1	0	0
Spence (Senators), cf	0	1	0	1	0	0
Chapman (Athletics), cf	2	0	0	1	0	0
Pesky (Red Sox), ss	2	0	0	1	0	1
Stephens (Browns), ss	3	1	2	0	4	0
Williams (Red Sox), lf	4	4	4	1	0	0
Keller (Yankees), rf	4	2	1	1	0	0
Doerr (Red Sox), 2b	2	0	0	1	1	0
Gordon (Yankees), 2b	2	0	1	0	1	0
Vernon (Senators), 1b	2	0	0	2	1	0
York (Red Sox), 1b.............	2	0	1	5	0	0
Keltner (Indians), 3b	0	0	0	0	0	0
Stirnweiss (Yankees), 3b....	3	1	1	0	0	0
Hayes (Indians), c	1	0	0	3	0	0
Rosar (Athletics), c	2	1	1	5	0	0
Wagner (Red Sox), c	1	0	0	4	0	0
Feller (Indians), p	0	0	0	0	0	0
aAppling (White Sox)	1	0	0	0	0	0
Newhouser (Tigers), p	1	1	1	1	0	0
fDickey (Yankees)	1	0	0	0	0	0
Kramer (Browns), p...........	1	1	1	0	0	0
Totals	36	12	14	27	7	1

National League	0	0	0	0	0	0	0	0	0 – 0		
American League	2	0	0	1	3	0	2	4	x – 12		

Nationals	IP.	H.	R.	ER.	BB.	SO.
Passeau (Cubs)	3	2	2	2	2	0
Higbe (Dodgers)	1⅓	5	4	4	1	2
Blackwell (Reds)	2⅔	3	2	2	1	1
Sewell (Pirates)	1	4	4	4	0	0

Americans	IP.	H.	R.	ER.	BB.	SO.
Feller (Indians)	3	2	0	0	0	3
Newhouser (Tigers)	3	1	0	0	0	4
Kramer (Browns)	3	0	0	0	1	3

Winning pitcher—Feller. Losing pitcher—Passeau.

aGrounded out for Feller in third. bFlied out for Mize in fourth. cStruck out for Schoendienst in sixth. dStruck out for Musial in sixth. eSingled for Hopp in sixth. fStruck out for Newhouser in sixth. gStruck out for McCormick in seventh. hGrounded out for Blackwell in eighth. iFouled out for Kurowski in ninth. Runs batted in—Keller 2, Williams 5, Stephens 2, Gordon 2, Chapman. Two-base hits—Stephens, Gordon. Home runs—Williams 2, Keller. Double plays—Marion and Mize; Schoendienst, Marion and Mize. Wild pitch—Blackwell. Left on bases—Nationals 5, Americans 4. Umpires—Summers and Rommel (A. L.), Boggess and Goetz (N. L.). Time of game—2:19. Attendance—34,906.

Game of 1947—Wrigley Field, Chicago, July 8

The ability of two pinch-hitters to deliver in the clutch provided the American League with a 2-1 victory in a dramatic contest. The triumph was credited to Frank Shea of the Yankees, the first rookie to earn this distinction in All-Star competition.

Luke Appling and Stan Spence supplied the pinch-blows that enabled the A. L. to come from behind. The junior loop collected eight hits to the five permitted by four pitchers employed by Manager Joe Cronin.

Johnny Mize broke a scoreless battle when he stroked a Shea pitch for a home run in the fourth inning. The Americans knotted the game in the sixth against Harry Brecheen. Appling launched the rally with his pinch-single. Ted Williams followed with a single, sending Appling to third, and Luke then crossed the plate while the N. L. executed a double play on Joe DiMaggio's grounder to short.

Johnny Sain was on the mound in the seventh when the Americans tabbed their decisive run. Bobby Doerr singled and stole second. The A. L. got a break when Sain, attempting to pick Doerr off second, hit him with the ball, which bounced into center field, enabling the runner to go to third. He scored easily when Spence, batting for Shea, singled to right-center.

The Nationals threatened in the eighth, but reliever Joe Page came on to quell the threat, retiring Enos Slaughter with two runners on base. The box score:

AMERICANS	AB.	R.	H.	PO.	A.	E.
Kell (Tigers), 3b	4	0	0	0	0	0
Johnson (Yanks), 3b	0	0	0	0	0	0
Lewis (Senators), rf	2	0	0	1	0	0
bAppling (White Sox)	1	1	1	0	0	0
Henrich (Yankees), rf	1	0	0	3	0	0
Williams (Red Sox), lf	4	0	2	3	0	0
DiMaggio (Yanks), cf	3	0	1	1	0	0
Boudreau (Indians), ss	4	0	1	4	4	0
McQuinn (Yankees), 1b	4	0	0	9	1	0
Gordon (Yankees), 2b	2	0	1	0	4	0
Doerr (Red Sox), 2b	2	1	1	0	2	0
Rosar (Athletics), c	4	0	0	6	0	0
Newhouser (Tigers), p	1	0	0	0	0	0
Shea (Yankees), p	1	0	0	0	0	0
cSpence (Senators)	1	0	1	0	0	0
Masterson (Senators), p	0	0	0	0	0	0
Page (Yankees), p	0	0	0	0	0	0
Totals	34	2	8	27	11	0

NATIONALS	AB.	R.	H.	PO.	A.	E.
H. Walker (Phillies), cf	2	0	0	1	0	0
Pafko (Cubs), cf	2	0	1	2	0	0
F. Walker (Dodgers), rf	2	0	0	1	0	0
Marshall (Giants), rf	1	0	0	3	0	0
W. Cooper (Giants), c	3	0	0	6	0	0
Edwards (Dodgers), c	0	0	0	2	0	0
eCavarretta (Cubs), 1b	1	0	0	1	0	0
Mize (Giants), 1b	3	1	2	8	0	0
fMusi (Braves)	0	0	0	0	0	0
Slaughter (Cardinals), lf	3	0	0	1	0	0
Gustine (Pirates), 3b	2	0	0	2	0	0
Kurowski (Cards), 3b	2	0	0	0	1	0
Marion (Cardinals), ss	2	0	1	0	1	0
Reese (Dodgers), ss	1	0	0	2	0	0
Verban (Phillies), 2b	2	0	0	0	0	0
Stanky (Dodgers), 2b	2	0	0	2	2	0
Blackwell (Reds), p	0	0	0	0	0	0
aHaas (Reds)	1	0	1	0	0	0
Brecheen (Cardinals), p	1	0	0	0	0	0
Sain (Braves), p	0	0	0	0	0	1
dMusial (Cardinals)	1	0	0	0	0	0
Spahn (Braves), p	0	0	0	0	0	0
gRowe (Phillies)	1	0	0	0	0	0
Totals	32	1	5	27	9	1

American League	0	0	0		0	0	1		1	0	0 – 2
National League	0	0	1		0	0	0		0	0	0 – 1

Americans	IP.	H.	R.	ER.	BB.	SO.
Newhouser (Tigers)	3	1	0	0	0	2
Shea (Yankees)	3	3	1	1	2	2
Masterson (Senators)	1⅔	0	0	0	1	2
Page (Yankees)	1⅓	1	0	0	1	0

Nationals	IP.	H.	R.	ER.	BB.	SO.
Blackwell (Reds)	3	1	0	0	0	4
Brecheen (Cardinals)	3	5	1	1	0	2
Sain (Braves)	1	2	1	1	0	1
Spahn (Braves)	2	0	0	0	1	1

Winning pitcher—Shea. Losing pitcher—Sain.

aSingled for Blackwell in third. bSingled for Lewis in sixth. cSingled for Shea in seventh. dGrounded out for Sain in seventh. eStruck out for Edwards in eighth. fRan for Mize in eighth. gFlied out for Spahn in ninth. Runs batted in —Mize, Spence. Two-base hits—Williams, Gordon. Home run—Mize. Stolen base—Doerr. Double play—Reese, Stanky and Mize. Wild pitch—Blackwell. Passed ball—W. Cooper. Left on bases—Nationals 8, Americans 6. Umpires—Boyer and Passarella (A. L.), Conlan and Henline (N. L.). Time of game—2:19. Attendance—41,123.

Game of 1948—Sportsman's Park, St. Louis, July 13

Injuries prevented four of the American League's top performers—Ted Williams, Joe DiMaggio, George Kell and Hal Newhouser—from taking their regular places in the lineup, but the junior circuit still managed to win, 5-2, for its eleventh victory in 15 games.

Three of the A. L. cripples made brief appearances. DiMaggio, hobbled by a swollen left knee, and Williams, handicapped by a torn rib cartilage, served as pinch-hitters, while Newhouser, suffering from bursitis in his left shoulder, was used as a pinch-runner. Kell, who had a sprained ankle, did not see action.

Walter Masterson was the Americans' starting pitcher and the N. L. cuffed the Senator hurler for two quick runs in the opening frame on an infield hit by Richie Ashburn and a homer by Stan Musial. A single by Johnny Mize and a walk to Enos Slaughter kept Masterson in hot water, but he bore down to end the inning without further damage.

Masterson followed with two shutout innings, after which Vic Raschi and Joe Coleman completed the job of holding the N. L. in check.

Hoot Evers opened the junior loop's scoring with a homer off Ralph Branca in the second inning. Two walks, a double steal and Lou Boudreau's fly ball produced the tying run against Branca in the third.

With Johnny Schmitz on the hill, the A. L. filled the bases with one out in the fourth inning. Raschi then came through with a single, scoring two runs. Joe DiMaggio's long fly ball drove in another run. The box score:

NATIONALS	AB.	R.	H.	PO.	A.	E.
Ashburn (Phillies), cf	4	1	2	1	0	0
Kiner (Pirates), lf	1	0	0	1	0	0
Schoendienst (Cards), 2b	4	0	0	0	1	0
Rigney (Giants), 2b	0	0	0	2	0	0
Musial (Cardinals), lf-cf	4	1	2	3	0	0
Mize (Giants), 1b	4	0	1	4	1	0
Slaughter (Cardinals), rf	2	0	1	2	0	0
Holmes (Braves), rf	1	0	0	1	0	0
Pafko (Cubs), 3b	2	0	0	0	0	0
Elliott (Braves), 3b	2	0	1	0	0	0
Cooper (Giants), c	2	0	0	3	0	0
Masi (Braves), c	2	0	1	4	0	0
Reese (Dodgers), ss	2	0	0	2	2	0
Kerr (Giants), ss	2	0	0	1	0	0
Branca (Dodgers), p	1	0	0	0	0	0
bGustine (Pirates)	1	0	0	0	0	0
Schmitz (Cubs), p	0	0	0	0	0	0
Sain (Braves), p	0	0	0	0	0	0
dWaitkus (Cubs)	0	0	0	0	0	0
Blackwell (Reds), p	0	0	0	0	0	0
gThomson (Giants)	1	0	0	0	0	0
Totals	35	2	8	24	4	0

AMERICANS	AB.	R.	H.	PO.	A.	E.
Mullin (Tigers), rf	1	0	0	0	0	0
cDiMaggio (Yankees)	1	0	0	0	0	0
Zarilla (Browns), rf	2	0	0	2	0	0
Henrich (Yankees), lf	3	0	0	1	0	0
Boudreau (Indians), ss	2	0	0	2	0	0
Stephens (Red Sox), ss	2	0	1	0	0	0
Gordon (Indians), 2b	2	0	0	1	2	0
Doerr (Red Sox), 2b	2	0	0	0	3	0
Evers (Tigers), cf	4	1	1	0	0	0
Keltner (Indians), 3b	3	1	1	1	6	0
McQuinn (Yankees), 1b	4	1	2	14	0	0
Rosar (Athletics), c	1	0	0	1	0	0
Tebbetts (Red Sox), c	1	1	0	5	1	0
Masterson (Senators), p	0	0	0	0	0	0
aVernon (Senators)	0	1	0	0	0	0
Raschi (Yankees), p	1	0	1	0	1	0
eWilliams (Red Sox)	0	0	0	0	0	0
fNewhouser (Tigers)	0	0	0	0	0	0
Coleman (Athletics), p	0	0	0	0	1	0
Totals	29	5	6	27	14	0

National League				2	0	0	0 0 0	0 0	0 – 2
American League				0	1	1	3 0 0	0 0	x – 5

Nationals	IP.	H.	R.	ER.	BB.	SO.
Branca (Dodgers)	3	1	2	2	3	3
Schmitz (Cubs)	⅓	3	3	3	1	0
Sain (Braves)	1⅔	0	0	0	0	3
Blackwell (Reds)	3	2	0	0	3	1

Americans	IP.	H.	R.	ER.	BB.	SO.
Masterson (Senators)	3	5	2	2	1	1
Raschi (Yankees)	3	3	0	0	1	3
Coleman (Athletics)	3	0	0	0	2	3

Winning pitcher—Raschi. Losing pitcher—Schmitz.

aWalked for Masterson in third. bStruck out for Branca in fourth. cFlied out for Mullin in fourth, scoring Tebbetts from third. dWalked for Sain in sixth. eWalked for Raschi in sixth. fRan for Williams in sixth. gStruck out for Blackwell in ninth. Runs batted in—Musial 2, Evers, Boudreau, Raschi 2, DiMaggio. Home runs—Musial, Evers. Stolen bases—Ashburn, Vernon, Mullin, McQuinn. Sacrifice hit—Coleman. Wild pitch—Masterson. Left on bases— Nationals 10, American 8. Umpires—Berry and Paparella (A. L.), Reardon and Stewart (N. L.). Time of game—2:27. Attendance—34,009.

Game of 1949—Ebbets Field, Brooklyn, July 12

In a loosely-played game marred by six errors, five of them by the National League, the Americans continued their mastery by pounding out an 11-7 triumph.

The contest marked the first appearance of Negro players in All-Star competition. Jackie Robinson, Roy Campanella and Don Newcombe of the host Dodgers were named for the N.L. squad and Larry Doby of the Indians for the A.L. Newcombe, although charged with the defeat, came close to being the senior circuit's hero. With the bags full in the second inning, he smashed a long drive to the corner in left field. At first it looked like a home run, but the wind caught the ball and Ted Williams, racing over, speared it with one hand.

Manager Billy Southworth used seven of the eight pitchers on the N.L. team. Starter Warren Spahn was rapped for four runs, all unearned. Mel Parnell, the A.L.'s starter, also got his early bumps, being tagged for a two-run homer by Stan Musial in the opening frame.

Ralph Kiner's homer with a mate aboard in the sixth cut the Nationals' deficit to 8-7, but the A.L. jumped on Howie Pollet for three runs in the seventh to sew up the game. The box score:

AMERICANS	AB.	R.	H.	PO.	A.	E.
D. DiM'gio (R. Sox), rf-cf ..	5	2	2	2	0	0
Raschi (Yankees), p	1	0	0	0	1	0
Kell (Tigers), 3b	3	2	2	0	1	0
dDillinger (Browns), 3b......	1	2	1	0	2	0
Williams (Red Sox), lf	2	1	0	1	0	1
Mitchell (Indians), lf	1	0	1	1	0	0
J. DiMaggio (Yankees), cf..	4	1	2	0	0	0
eDoby (Indians), rf-cf	1	0	0	2	0	0
Joost (Athletics), ss	2	1	1	2	2	0
Stephens (Red Sox), ss	2	0	0	2	0	0
E. Robinson (Senators), 1b	5	1	1	8	0	0
Goodman (Red Sox), 1b......	0	0	0	1	1	0
Michaels (White Sox), 2b ..	2	0	0	1	3	0
J. Gordon (Indians), 2b	2	1	1	3	3	0
Tebbetts (Red Sox), c........	2	0	2	2	0	0
Berra (Yankees), c	3	0	0	0	1	0
Parnell (Red Sox), p	1	0	0	0	1	0
Trucks (Tigers), p	1	0	0	0	0	0
Brissie (Athletics), p	1	0	0	0	0	0
gWertz (Tigers), rf	2	0	0	0	0	0
Totals	41	11	13	27	15	1

NATIONALS	AB.	R.	H.	PO.	A.	E.
Reese (Dodgers), ss	5	0	0	3	3	1
J. Robinson (Dodgers), 2b..	4	3	1	1	1	0
Musial (Cardinals), cf-rf ..	4	1	3	2	0	0
Kiner (Pirates), lf	5	1	1	3	0	0
Mize (Giants), 1b	2	0	1	1	0	1
aHodges (Dodgers), 1b......	3	1	1	8	2	0
Marshall (Giants), rf	1	1	0	1	0	1
Bickford (Braves), p..........	0	0	0	0	0	0
fThomson (Giants)	1	0	0	0	0	0
Pollet (Cardinals), p	0	0	0	1	0	0
Blackwell (Reds), p	0	0	0	0	0	0
hSlaughter (Cardinals)	1	0	0	0	0	0
Roe (Dodgers), p...............	0	0	0	0	0	0
Kazak (Cardinals), 3b	2	0	2	0	1	0
S. Gordon (Giants), 3b......	2	0	1	0	4	0
Seminick (Phillies), c........	1	0	0	3	0	1
Campanella (Dodgers), c ...	2	0	0	2	0	1
Spahn (Braves), p	0	0	0	0	0	0
Newcombe (Dodgers), p......	1	0	0	0	0	0
bSchoendienst (Cardinals)	1	0	1	0	0	0
Munger (Cardinals), p........	0	0	0	0	0	0
cPafko (Cubs), cf	2	0	1	2	0	0
Totals	37	7	12	27	11	5

American League				4	0	0	2	0	2	3	0	0 — 11
National League				2	1	2	0	0	2	0	0	0 — 7

Americans	IP.	H.	R.	ER.	BB.	SO.
Parnell (Red Sox).............	1*	3	3	3	1	1
Trucks (Tigers)..............	2	3	2	2	2	0
Brissie (Athletics)............	3	5	2	2	2	1
Raschi (Yankees).............	3	1	0	0	3	1

Nationals	IP.	H.	R.	ER.	BB.	SO.
Spahn (Braves)	1⅓	4	4	0	2	3
Newcombe (Dodgers)	2⅔	3	2	2	1	0
Munger (Cardinals)	1	0	0	0	1	0
Bickford (Braves)	1	2	2	2	1	0
Pollet (Cardinals)	1	4	3	3	0	0
Blackwell (Reds)	1	0	0	0	0	2
Roe (Dodgers)	1	0	0	0	0	0

*Pitched to three batters in second inning.

Winning pitcher—Trucks. Losing pitcher—Newcombe.

aRan for Mize in third. bSingled for Newcombe in fourth. cStruck out for Munger in fifth. dRan for Kell in sixth. eRan for J. DiMaggio in sixth. fFlied out for Bickford in sixth. gFlied out for Brissie in seventh. hFlied out for Blackwell in eighth. Runs batted in—J. DiMaggio 3, E. Robinson, Tebbetts, Musial 2, Newcombe, Kazak, Joost 2, Kiner 2, D. DiMaggio, Dillinger, Mitchell. (Joost scored on Reese's error in first.) (J. Robinson scored when Kiner hit into double play in third.) Two-base hits—J. Robinson, Tebbetts, S. Gordon, D. DiMaggio, J. Gordon, Mitchell. Home runs—Musial, Kiner. Stolen base—Kell. Double plays—Michaels, Joost and E. Robinson; Joost, Michaels and E. Robinson; J. Robinson, Reese and Hodges. Hit by pitcher—By Parnell (Seminick). Left on bases—Nationals 12, Americans 8. Umpires—Barlick, Gore and Ballanfant (N.L.), Hubbard, Summers and Grieve (A.L.). Time of game—3:04. Attendance—32,577.

Game of 1950—Comiskey Park, Chicago, July 11

Red Schoendienst's fourteenth-inning home run gave the National League a dramatic 4-3 victory, snapping a long-time jinx. The triumph marked the senior circuit's first in nine All-Star games played in American League parks and was the old loop's first win since 1944.

The game, one of the most thrilling in the series, was the first to go extra innings. The Nationals gained the decision by employing the American leaguers' old home-run weapon. Besides Schoendienst's winning wallop, Ralph Kiner smashed a ninth-inning homer off Art Houtteman to tie the score.

An injury to Ted Williams marred the contest, although the extent of the mishap wasn't known until the next day. In the first inning the Red Sox slugger bumped against the wall while pulling down a long drive by Kiner. Williams hurt his left elbow in the crash, but despite considerable pain he remained in the game until the ninth inning. X-rays the next day showed a fracture, which sidelined Ted until late in the season.

Enos Slaughter helped the N.L. to a 2-0 lead in the second inning with a triple. The Americans picked up one run off Robin Roberts in the third and then tore into Don Newcombe two innings later for two runs and a 3-2 lead. Williams singled across the tie-breaking marker. The box score:

NATIONALS	AB.	R.	H.	PO.	A.	E.
Jones (Phillies), 3b	7	0	1	2	3	0
Kiner (Pirates), lf	6	1	2	1	0	0
Musial (Cardinals), 1b	5	0	0	11	1	0
Robinson (Dodgers), 2b	4	1	1	3	2	0
fWyrostek (Reds), rf	2	0	0	0	0	0
Slaughter (Cards), cf-rf	4	1	2	3	0	0
Schoendienst (Cards), 2b	1	1	1	1	1	0
Sauer (Cubs), rf	2	0	0	1	0	0
Pafko (Cubs), cf	4	0	2	4	0	0
Campanella (Dodgers), c	6	0	0	13	2	0
Marion (Cardinals), ss	2	0	0	0	2	0
Konstanty (Phillies), p	0	0	0	0	0	0
Jansen (Giants), p	2	0	0	1	0	0
gSnider (Dodgers)	1	0	0	0	0	0
Blackwell (Reds), p	1	0	0	0	1	0
Roberts (Phillies), p	1	0	0	0	0	0
Newcombe (Dodgers), p	0	0	0	0	1	0
cSisler (Phillies)	1	0	1	0	0	0
dReese (Dodgers), ss	3	0	0	2	4	0
Totals	52	4	10	42	17	0

AMERICANS	AB.	R.	H.	PO.	A.	E.
Rizzuto (Yankees), ss	6	0	2	2	2	0
Doby (Indians), cf	6	1	2	9	0	0
Kell (Tigers), 3b	6	0	0	2	4	0
Williams (Red Sox), lf	4	0	1	2	0	0
D. DiMaggio (R. Sox), lf	2	0	1	0	0	0
Dropo (Red Sox), 1b	3	0	1	8	1	0
eFain (Athletics), 1b	3	0	1	2	1	0
Evers (Tigers), rf	2	0	0	1	0	0
J. DiMaggio (Yanks), rf	3	0	0	3	0	0
Berra (Yankees), c	2	0	0	2	0	0
bHegan (Indians), c	3	0	0	7	1	0
Doerr (Red Sox), 2b	3	0	0	1	4	0
Coleman (Yankees), 2b	2	0	0	0	0	1
Raschi (Yankees), p	0	0	0	0	0	0
aMichaels (Senators)	1	1	1	0	0	0
Lemon (Indians), p	0	1	0	1	0	0
Houtteman (Tigers), p	1	0	1	0	0	0
Reynolds (Yankees), p	1	0	0	0	0	0
hHenrich (Yankees)	1	0	0	0	0	0
Gray (Tigers), p	0	0	0	0	0	0
Feller (Indians), p	0	0	0	0	0	0
Totals	49	3	8	42	13	1

```
National League.............. 0 2 0   0 0 0   0 0 1   0 0 0   0 1 — 4
American League............. 0 0 1   0 2 0   0 0 0   0 0 0   0 0 — 3
```

Nationals	IP.	H.	R.	ER.	BB.	SO.
Roberts (Phillies)	3	3	1	1	1	1
Newcombe (Dodgers)	2	3	2	2	1	1
Konstanty (Phillies)	1	0	0	0	0	0
Jansen (Giants)	5	0	0	0	0	6
Blackwell (Reds)	3	1	0	0	0	2

Americans	IP.	H.	R.	ER.	BB.	SO.
Raschi (Yankees)	3	2	2	2	0	1
Lemon (Indians)	3	0	0	0	0	2
Houtteman (Tigers)	3	3	1	1	0	0
Reynolds (Yankees)	3	1	0	0	1	2
Gray (Tigers)	1⅓	3	1	1	0	1
Feller (Indians)	⅔	0	0	0	1	1

Winning pitcher—Blackwell.   Losing pitcher—Gray.

aDoubled for Raschi in third. bRan for Berra in fourth. cSingled for Newcombe in sixth. dRan for Sisler in sixth. ePopped out for Dropo in eighth. fFlied out for Robinson in eleventh. gFlied out for Jansen in twelfth. hFlied out for Reynolds in twelfth. Runs batted in—Slaughter, Sauer, Kell 2, Williams, Kiner, Schoendienst. Three-base hits—Slaughter. Two-base hits—Michaels, Doby, Kiner. Home runs—Kiner, Schoendienst. Double plays—Rizzuto, Doerr and Dropo; Jones, Schoendienst and Musial. Wild pitch—Roberts. Passed ball—Hegan. Left on bases—Nationals 9, Americans 6. Umpires—McGowan, Rommel and Stevens (A.L.); Pinelli, Conlan and Robb (N.L.). Time of game—3:19. Attendance—46,127.

Game of 1951—Briggs Stadium, Detroit, July 10

Exploding a record total of four home runs, the National League trounced the A. L., 8-3, in the eighteenth annual classic. The victory was the old loop's second in succession, marking the first time the N. L. had won in consecutive years.

The practice of having the two leagues alternate as host was broken when the game was played in the Motor City. Originally, it was slated for Philadelphia under the auspices of the Phillies, but the magnates agreed to switch it to Detroit as part of that city's 250th anniversary.

The four N. L. homers accounted for six runs. The senior circuit's siege guns went to work in the fourth inning. Stan Musial hit Ed Lopat's first pitch for a home run and Bob Elliott also connected later in the inning with a mate aboard for a 4-1 lead.

Gil Hodges unloaded a two-run homer off Fred Hutchinson in the sixth inning and Ralph Kiner connected against Mel Parnell in the eighth to climax the day's scoring.

American League hitters unloaded two homers, making a record total of six for the game. Both were by members of the host club—Vic Wertz and George Kell.

Joe DiMaggio, who announced his retirement at the close of the season, was a member of the A. L. squad, but a leg injury prevented The Yankee Clipper from seeing action. The box score:

NATIONALS	AB.	R.	H.	PO.	A.	E.
Ashburn (Phillies), cf	4	2	2	4	1	0
Snider (Dodgers), cf	0	0	0	0	0	0
Dark (Giants), ss	5	0	1	0	3	0
Reese (Dodgers), ss	0	0	0	0	1	0
Musial (Cards), lf-rf-lf	4	1	2	0	0	0
Westlake (Cardinals), lf	0	0	0	0	0	0
J. Robinson (Dodgers), 2b	4	1	2	3	1	1
Schoendienst (Cards), 2b	0	0	0	0	0	0
Hodges (Dodgers), 1b	5	2	2	6	0	0
Elliott (Braves), 3b	2	1	1	1	1	0
Jones (Phillies), 3b	2	0	0	3	0	0
Ennis (Phillies), rf	2	0	0	0	0	0
Kiner (Pirates), lf	2	1	1	1	0	0
Wyrostek (Reds), rf	1	0	0	0	0	0
Campanella (Dodgers), c	4	0	0	9	1	0
Roberts (Phillies), p	0	0	0	0	0	0
aSlaughter (Cardinals)	1	0	0	0	0	0
Maglie (Giants), p	1	0	0	0	1	0
Newcombe (Dodgers), p	2	0	1	0	1	0
Blackwell (Reds), p	0	0	0	0	0	0
Totals	39	8	12	27	9	1

AMERICANS	AB.	R.	H.	PO.	A.	E.
D. DiMaggio (R. Sox), cf	5	0	1	1	0	0
Fox (White Sox), 2b	3	0	1	3	1	1
eDoerr (Red Sox), 2b	1	0	1	1	4	0
Kell (Tigers), 3b	3	1	1	4	2	0
Williams (Red Sox), lf	3	0	1	3	0	0
Busby (White Sox), lf	0	0	0	0	0	0
Berra (Yankees), c	4	1	1	4	2	1
Wertz (Tigers), rf	3	1	1	2	0	0
Rizzuto (Yankees), ss	1	0	0	1	2	0
Fain (Athletics), 1b	3	0	1	5	0	0
fE. Robin'n (W. Sox), 1b	1	0	0	0	1	0
Carrasquel (Wh. Sox), ss	2	0	1	0	3	0
cMinoso (White Sox), rf	2	0	0	2	0	0
Garver (Browns), p	1	0	0	0	0	0
Lopat (Yankees), p	0	0	0	0	0	0
bDoby (Indians)	1	0	0	0	0	0
Hutchinson (Tigers), p	0	0	0	1	0	0
dStephens (Red Sox)	1	0	0	0	0	0
Parnell (Red Sox), p	0	0	0	0	0	0
Lemon (Indians), p	0	0	0	1	0	0
gHegan (Indians)	1	0	1	0	0	0
Totals	35	3	10	27	11	2

National League					1	0	0	3	0	2		1	1	0 — 8
American League					0	1	0	1	1	0		0	0	0 — 3

Nationals	IP.	H.	R.	ER.	BB.	SO.
Roberts (Phillies)	2	4	1	1	1	1
Maglie (Giants)	3	3	2	2	1	1
Newcombe (Dodgers)	3	2	0	0	0	3
Blackwell (Reds)	1	1	0	0	1	2

Americans	IP.	H.	R.	ER.	BB.	SO.
Garver (Browns)	3	1	1	0	1	1
Lopat (Yankees)	1	3	3	3	0	0
Hutchinson (Tigers)	3	3	3	3	2	0
Parnell (Red Sox)	1	3	1	1	0	1
Lemon (Indians)	1	2	0	0	1	1

Winning pitcher—Maglie. Losing pitcher—Lopat.

aLined out for Roberts in third. bPopped out for Lopat in fourth. cGrounded out for Carrasquel in sixth. dStruck out for Hutchinson in seventh. eSingled for Fox in eighth. fGrounded out for Fain in eighth. gDoubled for Lemon in ninth. Runs batted in—Fain, Musial, Elliott 2, Wertz, Kell, Hodges 2, J. Robinson, Kiner. Two-base hits—Ashburn, Hegan. Three-base hits—Fain, Williams. Home runs—Musial, Elliott, Wertz, Kell, Hodges, Kiner. Sacrifice hit—Kell. Double play—Berra and Kell. Left on bases—Nationals 8, Americans 9. Passed ball—Campanella. Umpires—Passarella, Hurley and Honochick (A. L.), Robb, Jorda and Dascoli (N. L.). Time of game—2:41. Attendance—52,075.

Game of 1952—Shibe Park, Philadelphia, July 8

For the first time in All-Star history, rain cut short a game, halting play after five innings with the Nationals emerging victorious, 3-2. The defeat was the third straight for the American League.

The N. L. again employed the home-run punch. Jackie Robinson accounted for the game's initial run when he clouted a Vic Raschi pitch into the stands in the opening inning, and then Hank Sauer unloaded a two-run homer off Bob Lemon in the fourth for what proved to be the margin of victory.

Rain, which fell intermittently during the morning and almost steadily during the game, made footing insecure, but the crowd saw an exceptionally well-played game. Because of the weather, both teams dispensed with pre-game drills, and the start of the contest was delayed nearly 20 minutes in the hope there might be a letup in the showers.

From a pitching standpoint, two southpaws from the home-town clubs—Curt Simmons of the host Phillies and Bobby Shantz of the Athletics—stole the show. Simmons blanked the Americans on one hit over the first three innings. Shantz was the last of three hurlers used by Casey Stengel, and rain limited him to one inning. In that brief appearance, the A's diminutive portsider performed one of the top mound feats in All-Star history, fanning Whitey Lockman, Jackie Robinson and Stan Musial in succession.

Rain deprived Shantz of a chance to go after Carl Hubbell's record of whiffing five in succession in the 1934 game.

The Americans scored their two runs off Bob Rush in the fourth inning. Minnie Minoso led off with a pinch-double. Following a walk and an out, Eddie Robinson singled for one run and another scored when Bobby Avila beat out an infield hit. The box score:

AMERICANS	AB.	R.	H.	PO.	A.	E.
DiMaggio (Red Sox), cf	2	0	1	1	0	0
Doby (Indians), cf	0	0	0	0	0	0
Bauer (Yankees), rf	3	0	1	2	0	0
Jensen (Senators), rf	0	0	0	0	0	0
Mitchell (Indians), lf	1	0	0	1	0	0
cMinoso (White Sox), lf	1	1	1	0	0	0
Rosen (Indians), 3b	1	1	0	3	1	0
Berra (Yankees), c	2	0	0	6	0	0
E. Robin'n (W. Sox), 1b	2	0	1	1	0	0
Avila (Indians), 2b	2	0	1	0	0	0
Rizzuto (Yankees), ss	2	0	0	1	0	0
Raschi (Yankees), p	0	0	0	0	0	0
aMcDougald (Yankees)	1	0	0	0	0	0
Lemon (Indians), p	1	0	0	0	0	0
Shantz (Athletics), p	0	0	0	0	0	0
Totals	18	2	5	15	1	0

NATIONALS	AB.	R.	H.	PO.	A.	E.
Lockman (Giants), 1b	3	0	0	5	0	0
J. Robinson (Dodgers), 2b	3	1	1	2	2	0
Musial (Cardinals), cf	2	1	0	1	0	0
Sauer (Cubs), lf	2	1	1	0	0	0
Campanella (Dodgers), c	1	0	0	5	1	0
Slaughter (Cardinals), rf	2	0	1	0	0	0
Thomson (Giants), 3b	2	0	0	1	1	0
Hamner (Phillies), ss	1	0	0	1	3	0
Simmons (Phillies), p	0	0	0	0	0	0
bReese (Dodgers)	1	0	0	0	0	0
Rush (Cubs), p	1	0	0	0	0	0
Totals	18	3	3	15	7	0

American League	0	0	0	2	0 – 2
National League	1	0	0	2	0 – 3

Stopped by rain.

Americans	IP.	H.	R.	ER.	BB.	SO.
Raschi (Yankees)	2	1	1	1	0	3
Lemon (Indians)	2	2	2	2	0	0
Shantz (Athletics)	1	0	0	0	0	3

Nationals	IP.	H.	R.	ER.	BB.	SO.
Simmons (Phillies)	3	1	0	0	1	3
Rush (Cubs)	2	4	2	2	1	1

Winning pitcher—Rush. Losing pitcher—Lemon.

aGrounded out for Raschi in third. bFlied out for Simmons in third. cDoubled for Mitchell in fourth. Runs batted in—J. Robinson, E. Robinson, Avila, Sauer 2. Two-base hits—DiMaggio, Minoso, Slaughter. Home runs—J. Robinson, Sauer. Double play—Hamner, J. Robinson and Lockman. Left on bases—Americans 3, Nationals 3. Hit by pitcher—By Lemon (Musial). Umpires—Barlick, Boggess and Warneke (N. L.), Berry, Summers and Soar (A. L.). Time of game—1:29. Attendance—32,785.

Game of 1953—Crosley Field, Cincinnati, July 14

Combining a ten-hit attack with effective pitching, the National League gained its fourth straight victory, 5-1. By winning four years in a row, the N.L. matched the Americans' best run of victories. Curiously, the manager of the four-time A.L. losers was Casey Stengel, who went on to lead the Yankees to a fifth successive flag in 1953.

The game was more one-sided than the score would indicate. For eight innings the Americans were held to two hits. Only one runner reached second base in that time. In the ninth inning, Murry Dickson yielded three singles for the lone A.L. run.

Aside from the pitchers, the Nationals' top star was Enos Slaughter. The 37-year-old Cardinal outfielder collected two hits and a walk, drove in one, scored two and made a catch which compared with the best fielding plays ever seen in the midsummer classic. It came in the sixth inning when Harvey Kuenn smashed a drive down the right field line for what seemed a sure hit until Slaughter skidded on his left shoulder to grab the ball.

For the first time since 1944, there were no home runs. The N.L. scored twice off Allie Reynolds in the fifth inning and once off Mike Garcia in the seventh. Satchel Paige, ageless Negro pitcher, yielded the last two runs in the eighth, with Slaughter driving in one and Dickson the other. The box score:

AMERICANS	AB.	R.	H.	PO.	A.	E.
Goodman (Red Sox), 2b	2	0	0	1	1	0
Fox (White Sox), 2b	1	0	0	1	0	0
Vernon (Senators), 1b	3	0	0	6	0	0
Fain (White Sox), 1b	1	1	1	1	1	0
Bauer (Yankees), rf	2	0	0	3	0	0
jMize (Yankees)	1	0	1	0	0	0
Mantle (Yankees), cf	2	0	0	0	0	0
eHunter (Browns)	0	0	0	0	0	0
Doby (Indians), cf	1	0	0	1	1	0
Rosen (Indians), 3b	4	0	0	2	4	0
Zernial (Athletics), lf	2	0	1	1	0	0
Minoso (White Sox), lf	2	0	2	0	0	0
Berra (Yankees), c	4	0	0	4	0	0
Carrasquel (Wh. Sox), ss	2	0	0	2	1	0
gKell (Red Sox)	1	0	0	0	0	0
Rizzuto (Yankees), ss	0	0	0	1	0	0
Pierce (White Sox), p	1	0	0	0	0	0
Reynolds (Yankees), p	0	0	0	0	0	0
cKuenn (Tigers)	1	0	0	0	0	0
Garcia (Indians), p	0	0	0	1	0	0
hE. Robinson (Athletics)	1	0	0	0	0	0
Paige (Browns), p	0	0	0	0	0	0
Totals	31	1	5	24	8	0

NATIONALS	AB.	R.	H.	PO.	A.	E.
Reese (Dodgers), ss	4	0	2	1	1	0
Hamner (Phillies), ss	0	0	0	0	0	0
Schoendienst (Cards), 2b	3	0	0	0	3	0
Williams (Giants), 2b	0	0	0	2	0	0
Musial (Cardinals), lf	4	0	2	3	0	0
Kluszewski (Reds), 1b	3	0	1	5	0	0
dHodges (Dodgers), 1b	1	0	0	1	0	0
Campanella (Dodgers), c	4	1	1	6	2	0
Mathews (Braves), 3b	3	1	0	0	0	0
Bell (Reds), cf	3	0	0	4	0	0
iSnider (Dodgers), cf	0	1	0	1	0	0
Slaughter (Cardinals), rf	3	2	2	4	0	0
Roberts (Phillies), p	0	0	0	0	1	0
aKiner (Cubs)	1	0	0	0	0	0
Spahn (Braves), p	0	0	0	0	0	0
bAshburn (Phillies)	1	0	1	0	0	0
Simmons (Phillies), p	0	0	0	0	0	0
fJ. Robinson (Dodgers)	1	0	0	0	0	0
Dickson (Pirates), p	1	0	1	0	0	0
Totals	32	5	10	27	7	0

American League	0	0	0	0	0	0	0	0	1 – 1		
National League	0	0	0	0	2	0	1	2	x – 5		

Americans	IP.	H.	R.	ER.	BB.	SO.
Pierce (White Sox)	3	1	0	0	0	1
Reynolds (Yankees)	2	2	2	2	2	1
Garcia (Indians)	2	4	1	1	1	2
Paige (Browns)	1	3	2	2	1	0

Nationals	IP.	H.	R.	ER.	BB.	SO.
Roberts (Phillies)	3	1	0	0	1	2
Spahn (Braves)	2	0	0	0	1	2
Simmons (Phillies)	2	1	0	0	1	1
Dickson (Pirates)	2	3	1	1	0	0

Winning pitcher—Spahn. Losing pitcher—Reynolds.

aStruck out for Roberts in third. bSingled for Spahn in fifth. cLined out for Reynolds in sixth. dRan for Kluszewski in sixth. eRan for Mantle in seventh. fPopped out for Simmons in seventh. gFlied out for Carrasquel in eighth. hLined out for Garcia in eighth. iWalked for Bell in ninth. jSingled for Bauer in ninth. Runs batted in—Ashburn, Reese 2, Slaughter, Dickson, Minoso. Two-base hit—Reese. Stolen base—Slaughter. Double play—Carrasquel and Vernon. Left on bases—Nationals 7, Americans 6. Hit by pitcher—By Reynolds (Mathews). Umpires—Conlan, Donatelli and Engeln (N. L.). Stevens, McKinley and Napp (A. L.). Time of game—2:19. Attendance—30,846.

Game of 1954—Municipal Stadium, Cleveland, July 13

In a spectacular slugfest that set All-Star marks for runs and hits by the two clubs, the American League edged the National, 11-9, before 68,751 fans—only 1,080 under the record set in the same park in 1935. With increased ticket prices, gross gate receipts were $292,678, topping the former high by more than $100,000.

The slugfest produced six home runs, including four by the A. L. Both were record-equalling totals. Ironically, the decisive hit was a blooper over second base by Nellie Fox with the bags loaded and the score 9-all in the eighth inning. The bleeder, which barely eluded shortstop Alvin Dark, scored the winning runs.

Three Indians—Al Rosen, Larry Doby and Bobby Avila—starred before their hometown crowd. They drove in eight of the A. L. runs, with Rosen walloping two successive home runs and a single to bat in five runs. His two homers and five RBIs tied All-Star records.

A two-run pinch-homer by Gus Bell in the eighth put the Nationals ahead, 9-8. Later in the inning, immediately after Dean Stone took the mound, Red Schoendienst made a surprise attempt to steal home, but the A. L. hurler hurried his motion and nailed him. The National leaguers argued that Stone had balked, but Plate Umpire Bill Stewart disagreed. Though Stone faced no other batter, he was the winner. The box score:

NATIONALS	AB.	R.	H.	PO.	A.	E.
Hammer (Phillies), 2b	3	0	0	0	0	0
Schoendienst (Cards), 2b	2	0	0	1	0	0
Dark (Giants), ss	5	0	1	1	2	0
Snider (Dodgers), cf-rf	4	2	3	2	0	0
Musial (Cards), rf-lf	5	1	2	2	1	0
Kluszewski (Reds), 1b	4	2	2	5	0	0
Hodges, (Dodgers), 1b	1	0	0	1	0	0
Jablonski (Cards), 3b	3	1	1	0	1	0
Jackson (Cubs), 3b	2	0	0	1	1	0
Robinson (Dodgers), lf	2	1	1	0	0	0
Mays (Giants), cf	2	1	1	1	0	0
Campanella (Dodgers), c	3	0	1	9	0	0
Burgess (Phillies), c	0	0	0	1	0	0
Roberts (Phillies), p	1	0	0	0	0	0
aMueller (Giants)	1	0	1	0	0	0
Antonelli (Giants), p	0	0	0	0	0	0
cThomas (Pirates)	1	0	0	0	0	0
Spahn (Braves), p	0	0	0	0	0	0
Grissom (Giants), p	0	0	0	0	0	0
eBell (Reds)	1	1	1	0	0	0
Conley (Braves), p	0	0	0	0	0	0
Erskine (Dodgers), p	0	0	0	0	0	0
Totals	40	9	14	24	5	0

AMERICANS	AB.	R.	H.	PO.	A.	E.
Minoso (White Sox), lf-rf	4	1	2	1	0	1
Piersall (Red Sox), rf	1	0	0	0	0	0
Avila (Indians), 2b	3	1	3	1	1	0
Keegan (White Sox), p	0	0	0	0	0	0
Stone (Senators), p	0	0	0	0	0	0
fDoby (Indians), cf	1	1	1	0	0	0
Mantle (Yankees), cf	5	1	2	2	0	0
Trucks (White Sox), p	0	0	0	0	0	0
Berra (Yankees), c	4	2	2	5	0	0
Rosen (Indians), 1b-3b	4	2	3	7	0	0
Boone (Tigers), 3b	4	1	1	1	3	0
gVernon (Senators), 1b	1	0	0	1	0	0
Bauer (Yankees), rf	2	0	1	1	0	0
Porterfield (Senators), p	1	0	0	0	0	0
dFox (White Sox), 2b	2	0	1	1	0	0
Carrasquel (Wh. Sox), ss	5	1	1	5	4	0
Ford (Yankees), p	1	0	0	0	0	0
Consuegra (White Sox), p	0	0	0	0	0	0
Lemon (Indians), p	0	0	0	0	0	0
bWilliams (Red Sox), lf	2	1	0	2	0	0
Noren (Yankees), lf	0	0	0	0	0	0
Totals	39	11	17	27	8	1

National League	0	0	0	5	2	0	0	2	0	—	9
American League	0	0	4	1	2	1	0	3	x	—	11

Nationals	IP.	H.	R.	ER.	BB.	SO.
Roberts (Phillies)	3	5	4	4	2	5
Antonelli (Giants)	2	4	3	3	0	2
Spahn (Braves)	⅔	4	1	1	1	0
Grissom (Giants)	1⅓	0	0	0	0	2
Conley (Braves)	⅓	3	3	3	1	0
Erskine (Dodgers)	⅔	1	0	0	0	1

Americans	IP.	H.	R.	ER.	BB.	SO.
Ford (Yankees)	3	1	0	0	1	0
Consuegra (White Sox)	⅓	5	5	5	0	0
Lemon (Indians)	⅔	1	0	0	0	0
Porterfield (Senators)	3	4	2	2	0	1
Keegan (White Sox)	⅔	3	2	2	0	1
Stone (Senators)	⅓	2	0	0	1	0
Trucks (White Sox)	1	0	0	0	1	0

Winning pitcher—Stone. Losing pitcher—Conley.

aDoubled for Roberts in fourth. bStruck out for Lemon in fourth. cStruck out for Antonelli in sixth. dStruck out for Porterfield in seventh. eHomered for Grissom in eighth. fHomered for Stone in eighth. gStruck out for Boone in eighth. Runs batted in—Rosen 5, Boone, Kluszewski 3, Jablonski, Robinson 2, Mueller, Avila 2, Bell 2, Doby, Fox 2. Two-base hits—Robinson, Mueller, Snider. Home runs—Rosen 2, Boone, Kluszewski, Bell, Doby. Sacrifice fly—Avila. Double play—Avila, Carrasquel and Rosen. Left on bases—Nationals 6, Americans 9. Umpires—Rommel, Honochick and Paparella (A. L.), Ballanfant, Stewart and Gorman (N. L.). Time of game—3:10. Attendance—68,751.

Game of 1955—County Stadium, Milwaukee, July 12

Stan Musial's home run on the first pitch in the twelfth inning climaxed a stirring uphill battle that enabled the Nationals to nose out a 6-5 victory. Victim of the blast was Frank Sullivan.

Moments before Musial broke up the game, the crowd of 45,643 gave Gene Conley, Braves' hurler, a standing ovation. He earned the plaudits by fanning three of the Americans' greatest hitters—Al Kaline, Mickey Vernon and Al Rosen—in succession in the top half of the frame.

Robin Roberts had another sad experience as the starting N. L. pitcher. Famed as a control pitcher, he uncorked a wild pitch that let in the first A. L. run in the opening inning and moments later saw Mickey Mantle smash a 430-foot homer over the center field fence for three more runs.

Trailing by 5-0, the Nationals rallied for two runs off Whitey Ford in the seventh inning on a single by Willie Mays, a walk, another ace by Johnny Logan and Chico Carrasquel's error. After the Yankee lefty retired the first two batters in the eighth, the N. L. combined singles by Mays, Ted Kluszewski, Randy Jackson and Hank Aaron with Al Rosen's error for three runs to knot the score, paving the way for extra innings and the thrilling finish. The box score:

AMERICANS	AB.	R.	H.	PO.	A.	E.
Kuenn (Tigers), ss	3	1	1	1	0	0
Carrasquel (Wh. Sox), ss	3	0	2	1	3	1
Fox (White Sox), 2b	3	1	1	2	0	0
Avila (Indians), 2b	1	0	0	1	2	0
Williams (Red Sox), lf	3	1	1	1	0	0
Smith (Indians), lf	1	0	0	0	0	0
Mantle (Yankees), cf	6	1	2	3	0	0
Berra (Yankees), c	6	1	1	8	2	0
Kaline (Tigers), rf	4	0	1	6	0	0
Vernon (Senators), 1b	5	0	1	8	0	0
Finigan (Athletics), 3b	3	0	0	2	0	0
Rosen (Indians), 3b	2	0	0	0	0	1
Pierce (White Sox), p	0	0	0	0	0	0
bJensen (Red Sox)	1	0	0	0	0	0
Wynn (Indians), p	0	0	0	0	1	0
gPower (Athletics)	1	0	0	0	0	0
Ford (Yankees), p	1	0	0	0	1	0
Sullivan (Red Sox), p	1	0	0	0	0	0
Totals	44	5	10	33	9	2

NATIONALS	AB.	R.	H.	PO.	A.	E.
Schoendienst (Cards), 2b	6	0	2	3	2	0
Ennis (Phillies), lf	1	0	0	1	0	0
cMusial (Cardinals), lf	4	1	1	0	0	0
Snider (Dodgers), cf	2	0	0	3	0	0
Mays (Giants), cf	3	2	2	3	0	0
Kluszewski (Reds), 1b	5	1	2	9	1	0
Mathews (Braves), 3b	2	0	0	0	3	1
Jackson (Cubs), 3b	3	1	1	0	0	0
Mueller (Giants), rf	2	0	1	0	0	0
dAaron (Braves), rf	2	1	2	0	0	0
Banks (Cubs), ss	2	0	0	2	1	0
Logan (Braves), ss	3	0	1	1	1	0
Crandall (Braves), c	1	0	0	1	0	0
eBurgess (Phillies), c	1	0	0	2	0	0
hLopata (Phillies), c	3	0	0	10	0	0
Roberts (Phillies), p	0	0	0	1	1	0
aThomas (Pirates)	1	0	0	0	0	0
Haddix (Cardinals), p	0	0	0	0	2	0
fHodges (Dodgers)	1	0	1	0	0	0
Newcombe (Dodgers), p	0	0	0	0	0	0
iBaker (Cubs)	1	0	0	0	0	0
Jones (Cubs), p	0	0	0	0	0	0
Nuxhall (Reds), p	2	0	0	0	1	0
Conley (Braves), p	0	0	0	0	0	0
Totals	45	6	13	36	12	1

```
American League ....................4  0  0    0  0  1    0  0  0    0  0  0—5
National League ....................0  0  0    0  0  0    2  3  0    0  0  1—6
                None out when winning run scored.
```

Americans	IP.	H.	R.	ER.	BB.	SO.
Pierce (White Sox)	3	1	0	0	0	3
Wynn (Indians)	3	3	0	0	0	1
Ford (Yankees)	1⅔	5	5	3	1	0
Sullivan (Red Sox)	3⅓*	4	1	1	1	4

*Pitched to one batter in twelfth.

Nationals	IP.	H.	R.	ER.	BB.	SO.
Roberts (Phillies)	3	4	4	4	1	0
Haddix (Cardinals)	3	3	1	1	0	2
Newcombe (Dodgers)	1	1	0	0	0	1
Jones (Cubs)	⅔	0	0	0	2	1
Nuxhall (Reds)	3⅓	2	0	0	3	5
Conley (Braves)	1	0	0	0	0	3

Winning pitcher—Conley. Losing pitcher—Sullivan.

aPopped out for Roberts in third. bPopped out for Pierce in fourth. cStruck out for Ennis in fourth. dRan for Mueller in fifth. eHit into force play for Crandall in fifth. fSingled for Haddix in sixth. gPopped out for Wynn in seventh. hSafe on error for Burgess in seventh. iFlied out for Newcombe in seventh. Runs batted in—Mantle 3, Vernon, Logan, Jackson, Aaron, Musial. Two-base hits—Kluszewski, Kaline. Home runs—Mantle, Musial. Sacrifice hits—Pierce, Avila. Double plays—Kluszewski, Banks and Roberts; Wynn, Carrasquel and Vernon. Left on bases—Americans 12, Nationals 8. Hit by pitcher—By Jones (Kaline). Wild pitch—Roberts. Passed ball—Crandall. Umpires—Barlick, Boggess and Secory (N. L.), Soar, Summers and Runge (A. L.). Time of game—3:17. Attendance—45,643.

Game of 1956—Griffith Stadium, Washington, July 10

Capitalizing on a power-packed lineup, the Nationals breezed to a 7-3 victory. The triumph was the senior circuit's sixth in the last seven contests and whittled the A. L.'s once-overwhelming edge to 13-10.

In a sense, the outcome vindicated the judgment of the fans, who again selected the starting lineups. Although Cincinnati was battling for first place, there was considerable criticism when, as the result of a campaign by a Cincinnati radio station, five Reds were named to the N. L. lineup and three other regulars were runnersup at their positions.

The Nationals had numerous standouts, but the real star was Ken Boyer. The Cardinal third baseman went 3-for-5 at bat and in the field broke the hearts of the American leaguers with three sizzling plays.

The N. L. cracked the scoring ice with a run in the third and then made it 3-0 when Willie Mays tagged Whitey Ford for a two-run homer as a pinch-hitter in the fourth.

Down by 5-0, the Americans came to life in the sixth inning, routing Warren Spahn. Nellie Fox opened with a single and then Ted Williams and Mickey Mantle smashed successive homers. Johnny Antonelli replaced Spahn and blanked the A. L. the remainder of the way.

The Nationals added their final two runs in the seventh inning. Stan Musial homered into the left-center field bleachers. Later, Willie Mays walked and scored on Ted Kluszewski's two-bagger. The box score:

NATIONALS	AB.	R.	H.	PO.	A.	E.
Temple (Reds), 2b	4	1	2	2	3	0
Robinson (Reds), lf	2	0	0	1	0	0
dSnider (Dodgers), cf	3	0	0	1	0	0
Musial (Cardinals), rf-lf	4	1	1	2	0	0
Aaron (Braves), lf	1	0	0	0	0	0
Boyer (Cardinals), 3b	5	1	3	3	1	0
Bell (Reds), cf	1	0	0	2	0	0
bMays (Giants), cf-rf	3	2	1	2	0	0
Long (Pirates), 1b	2	0	0	6	0	0
fKluszewski (Reds), 1b	2	1	2	2	0	0
Bailey (Reds), c	3	0	0	3	1	0
Campanella (Dodgers), c	0	0	0	1	0	0
McMillan (Reds), ss	3	1	2	1	5	0
Friend (Pirates), p	0	0	0	0	0	0
cRepulski (Cardinals)	1	0	0	0	0	0
Spahn (Braves), p	1	0	0	0	0	0
Antonelli (Giants), p	1	0	0	1	0	0
Totals	36	7	11	27	10	0

AMERICANS	AB.	R.	H.	PO.	A.	E.
Kuenn (Tigers), ss	5	0	1	2	3	0
Fox (White Sox), 2b	4	1	2	1	0	0
Williams (Red Sox), lf	4	1	1	2	0	0
Mantle (Yankees), cf	4	1	1	0	0	0
Berra (Yankees), c	2	0	2	10	1	0
gLollar (White Sox), c	2	0	1	4	0	0
Kaline (Tigers), rf	3	0	1	0	0	0
Piersall (Red Sox), rf	1	0	0	1	0	0
Vernon (Red Sox), 1b	2	0	0	4	0	0
hPower (Athletics), 1b	2	0	1	3	0	0
Kell (Orioles), 3b	4	0	1	0	1	0
Pierce (White Sox), p	0	0	0	0	1	0
aSimpson (Athletics)	1	0	0	0	0	0
Ford (Yankees), p	0	0	0	0	0	0
Wilson (White Sox), p	0	0	0	0	1	0
eMartin (Yankees)	1	0	0	0	0	0
Brewer (Red Sox), p	0	0	0	0	0	0
iBoone (Tigers)	1	0	0	0	0	0
Score (Indians), p	0	0	0	0	0	0
Wynn (Indians), p	0	0	0	0	0	0
jSievers (Senators)	1	0	0	0	0	0
Totals	37	3	11	27	7	0

National League	0	0	1	2	1	1	2	0	0 —	7
American League	0	0	0	0	0	3	0	0	0 —	3

Nationals	IP.	H.	R.	ER.	BB.	SO.
Friend (Pirates)	3	3	0	0	0	3
Spahn (Braves)	2*	4	3	3	0	1
Antonelli (Giants)	4	4	0	0	0	1

*Pitched to three batters in sixth.

Americans	IP.	H.	R.	ER.	BB.	SO.
Pierce (White Sox)	3	1	1	1	1	5
Ford (Yankees)	1	3	2	2	1	2
Wilson (White Sox)	1	2	1	1	0	1
Brewer (Red Sox)	2	4	3	3	1	2
Score (Indians)	1	0	0	0	1	1
Wynn (Indians)	1	0	0	0	0	0

Winning pitcher—Friend. Losing pitcher—Pierce.

aStruck out for Pierce in third. bHomered for Bell in fourth. cFouled out for Friend in fourth. dFlied out for Robinson in fifth. eGrounded out for Wilson in fifth. fDoubled for Long in sixth. gSingled for Berra in sixth. hFlied out for Vernon in sixth. iLined out for Brewer in seventh. jPopped out for Wynn in ninth. Runs batted in—Temple, Mays 2, Boyer, Williams 2, Mantle, Musial, Kluszewski. Two-base hits—Kluszewski 2. Home runs—Mays, Williams, Mantle, Musial. Stolen base—Temple. Sacrifice hit—Friend. Double play—McMillan, Temple and Kluszewski. Left on bases—Nationals 7, Americans 7. Wild pitches—Brewer 2. Umpires—Berry, Hurley and Flaherty (A. L.), Pinelli, Gore and Jackowski (N. L.). Time of game—2:45. Attendance—28,843.

Game of 1957—Busch Stadium, St. Louis, July 9

In a contest which saw most of the action packed into the ninth inning, the Americans emerged victorious, 6-5. The game produced almost everything except a home run.

A deluge of 500,000 late votes from Cincinnati resulted in all of the Reds' regulars except first baseman George Crowe being the leaders at their respective positions. However, because of the over-balance of Cincinnati votes, Commissioner Ford Frick ordered outfielder Gus Bell and Wally Post dropped from consideration. Manager Walter Alston later added Bell to his squad.

The Americans jumped off to a 2-0 lead in the second inning against Curt Simmons and Lou Burdette on three walks and a pair of singles and added another run in the sixth.

The N.L. got back in the game in the seventh when a pinch-double by Bell plated two runs, but in the ninth the A.L. expanded its lead to 6-2. However, the Nationals gave the crowd a thrill in their final turn. A walk to Stan Musial, Willie Mays' triple and a wild pitch produced two quick runs. When Hank Foiles followed with a single and Bell walked, Manager Casey Stengel rushed in Don Mossi. A single by Ernie Banks added the final run, but Bell was nailed trying to go from first to third. Gil Hodges then lined sharply to left field to end the game. The box score:

AMERICANS	AB.	R.	H.	PO.	A.	E.
Kuenn (Tigers), ss	2	0	0	0	1	0
McDougald (Yankees), ss ..	2	1	0	1	0	0
Fox (White Sox), 2b	4	0	0	2	4	0
Kaline (Tigers), rf	5	1	2	1	1	0
Mantle (Yankees), cf	4	1	1	4	0	0
Minoso (White Sox), lf	3	1	0	2	0	0
Williams (Red Sox), lf	1	0	1	1	1	0
Skowron (Yankees), 1b	3	1	2	5	1	0
Berra (Yankees), c	3	0	1	6	0	0
Kell (Orioles), 3b	2	0	0	0	1	0
Malzone (Red Sox), 3b	2	0	0	1	1	0
Bunning (Tigers), p	1	0	0	0	0	0
aMaxwell (Tigers)	1	0	1	0	0	0
Loes (Orioles), p	1	0	0	0	1	0
Wynn (Indians), p	0	0	0	0	0	0
Pierce (White Sox), p	1	1	1	1	0	0
Mossi (Indians), p	0	0	0	0	0	0
Grim (Yankees), p	0	0	0	0	0	0
Totals	37	6	10	27	11	0

NATIONALS	AB.	R.	H.	PO	A.	E.
Temple (Reds), 2b	2	0	0	3	0	0
eSchoend'nst (Braves), 2b ..	2	0	0	0	0	1
Aaron (Braves), rf	4	0	1	2	0	0
Musial (Cardinals), 1b	3	1	1	9	0	0
Mays (Giants), cf	4	2	2	2	0	0
Bailey (Reds), c	3	1	1	2	0	0
hFoiles (Pirates)	1	1	1	0	0	0
Robinson (Reds), lf	2	0	1	5	0	0
fBell (Reds), lf	1	0	1	0	0	0
Hoak (Reds), 3b	1	0	0	1	0	0
bMathews (Braves), 3b	3	0	0	1	0	0
McMillan (Reds), ss	1	0	0	2	0	0
cBanks (Cubs), ss	3	0	1	0	3	0
Simmons (Phillies), p	0	0	0	0	0	0
Burdette (Braves), p	1	0	0	0	0	0
Sanford (Phillies), p	0	0	0	0	0	0
dMoon (Cardinals)	1	0	0	0	0	0
Jackson (Cardinals), p	0	0	0	0	1	0
gCimoli (Dodgers)	1	0	0	0	0	0
Labine (Dodgers), p	0	0	0	0	1	0
iHodges (Dodgers)	1	0	0	0	0	0
Totals	34	5	9	27	5	1

American League	0	2	0	0	0	1	0	0	3 — 6
National League	0	0	0	0	0	0	2	0	3 — 5

Americans	IP.	H.	R.	ER.	BB.	SO.
Bunning (Tigers)	3	0	0	0	0	1
Loes (Orioles)	3	0	0	0	1	0
Wynn (Indians)	⅓	3	2	2	0	0
Pierce (White Sox)	1⅔†	3	3	3	2	3
Mossi (Indians)	⅔	1	0	0	0	0
Grim (Yankees)	⅓	0	0	0	0	1

Nationals	IP.	H.	R.	ER.	BB.	SO.
Simmons (Phillies)	1*	2	2	2	0	0
Burdette (Braves)	4	2	0	0	1	0
Sanford (Phillies)	1	2	1	0	0	0
Jackson (Cardinals)	2	1	0	0	1	0
Labine (Dodgers)	1	3	3	1	0	1

*Pitched to four batters in second. †Pitched to four batters in ninth.

Winning pitcher—Bunning. Losing pitcher—Simmons.

aSingled for Bunning in fourth. bHit into force play for Hoak in fifth. cHit into double play for McMillan in fifth. dGrounded out for Sanford in sixth. eFlied out for Temple in sixth. fDoubled for Robinson in seventh. gCalled out on strikes for Jackson in eighth. hSingled for Bailey in ninth. iFlied out for Labine in ninth. Runs batted in—Wertz, Kuenn, Berra, Bell 2, Kaline 2, Minoso, Mays, Banks. Two-base hits—Musial, Skowron, Bell, Minoso. Three-base hit —Mays. Sacrifice hit—Fox. Double play—Malzone, Fox and Skowron. Left on bases—Americans 9, Nationals 4. Wild pitches—Sanford, Pierce. Umpires—Dascoli, Dixon and Landes (N.L.); Napp, Stevens and Chylak (A.L.). Time of game—2:43. Attendance—30,693.

Game of 1958—Memorial Stadium, Baltimore, July 8

Pitchers stole the show as the American League stars edged their N.L. rivals, 4-3. The game produced only 13 hits, all of them singles. It was the first time in the history of the midsummer classic that there was no extra-base blow.

Vice-President Richard Nixon was among the capacity crowd of 48,829. He came over from Washington to throw out the first ball.

Except for Bob Turley, who went on to win the Cy Young Award as the year's outstanding pitcher, American League hurlers enjoyed a banner afternoon. The Yankee ace gave up all three runs and three of the four hits collected by the Nationals.

Turley was in trouble right at the start. Willie Mays led off with a single; another ace by Stan Musial and Hank Aaron's sacrifice fly produced a quick run. After a hit batsman and walk filled the bases, Turley uncorked a wild pitch, enrolling another run.

The Americans got one of these runs back in their turn, but the N.L. scored once in the second when Mays, after forcing Warren Spahn, stole second, continued to third on catcher Gus Triandos' throwing error and tallied when Bob Skinner singled.

The Americans counted once again in their half and then tied the score at 3-all in the fifth. They tabbed the winning run in the sixth on singles by Frank Malzone and Gil McDougald sandwiched around an error.

While Early Wynn received credit for the victory, Billy O'Dell was the real mound hero for the A.L. The Baltimore southpaw blotted out nine successive batters over the last three innings to protect the one-run lead. The box score:

NATIONALS	AB.	R.	H.	PO.	A.	E.
Mays (Giants), cf	4	2	1	1	0	0
Skinner (Pirates), lf	3	0	1	2	0	0
gWalls (Cubs), lf	1	0	0	0	0	0
Musial (Cardinals), 1b	4	1	1	7	0	0
Aaron (Braves), rf	2	0	0	2	0	0
Banks, (Cubs), ss	3	0	0	2	3	1
Thomas (Pirates), 3b	3	0	1	1	3	1
Mazeroski (Pirates), 2b	4	0	0	4	5	0
Crandall (Braves), c	4	0	0	5	0	0
Spahn (Braves), p	0	0	0	0	1	0
aBlasingame (Cardinals)	1	0	0	0	0	0
Friend (Pirates), p	0	0	0	0	0	0
Jackson (Cardinals), p	0	0	0	0	0	0
fLogan (Braves)	1	0	0	0	0	0
Farrell (Phillies), p	0	0	0	0	0	0
Totals	30	3	4	24	12	2

AMERICANS	AB.	R.	H.	PO.	A.	E.
Fox (White Sox), 2b	4	1	2	5	3	1
Mantle (Yankees), cf	2	0	1	3	0	0
Jensen (Red Sox), rf	4	0	0	1	0	0
Cerv (Athletics), lf	2	0	1	4	0	0
O'Dell (Orioles), p	0	0	0	0	0	0
Skowron (Yankees), 1b	4	0	0	8	0	0
Malzone (Red Sox), 3b	4	1	1	0	2	0
Triandos (Orioles), c	2	0	1	1	0	1
cBerra (Yankees), c	2	0	0	3	0	0
Aparicio (White Sox), ss	2	1	0	1	1	0
dWilliams (Red Sox), lf	2	0	1	0	0	0
Kaline (Tigers), lf	0	0	0	0	0	0
Turley (Yankees), p	0	0	0	0	0	0
Narleski (Indians), p	1	0	1	0	0	0
bVernon (Indians)	1	1	1	0	0	0
Wynn (White Sox), p	0	0	0	0	0	0
eMcDougald (Yanks), ss	1	0	1	0	3	0
Totals	31	4	9	27	9	2

```
National League .............................. 2  1  0   0  0  0   0  0  0 – 3
American League .............................. 1  1  0   0  1  1   0  0  x – 4
```

Nationals	IP.	H.	R.	ER.	BB.	SO.
Spahn (Braves)	3	5	2	1	0	0
Friend (Pirates)	2⅓	4	2	1	2	0
Jackson (Cardinals)	⅔	0	0	0	0	0
Farrell (Phillies)	2	0	0	0	1	4

Americans	IP.	H.	R.	ER.	BB.	SO.
Turley (Yankees)	1⅔	3	3	3	2	0
Narleski (Indians)	3⅓	1	0	0	1	0
Wynn (White Sox)	1	0	0	0	0	0
O'Dell (Orioles)	3	0	0	0	0	2

Winning pitcher—Wynn. Losing pitcher—Friend.

aFlied out for Spahn in fourth. bSingled for Narieski in fifth. cPopped out for Triandos in sixth. dSafe on error for Aparicio in sixth. eSingled for Wynn in sixth. fFlied out for Jackson in seventh. gGrounded out for Skinner in seventh. Runs batted in—Skinner, Aaron, Fox, Jensen, McDougald. Sacrifice hit—O'Dell. Sacrifice fly—Aaron. Stolen base—Mays. Left on bases—Nationals 5, Americans 7. Double plays—Thomas, Mazeroski and Musial; Malzone, Fox and Skowron; Banks, Mazeroski and Musial 2. Hit by pitcher—By Turley (Banks). Wild pitch—Turley. Umpires—Rommel, McKinley and Umont (A.L.); Gorman, Conlan and Secory (N.L.). Time of game—2:13. Attendance—48,829.

First Game of 1959—Forbes Field, Pittsburgh, July 7

Breaking with tradition, the owners and players agreed to expand the All-Star Game into a double feature in 1959. The regularly-scheduled contest was played in Pittsburgh as part of that city's bicentennial celebration and saw the Nationals returned the victors, 5-4.

For six and one-half innings, the crowd of 35,277, which included Vice-President Richard Nixon, saw a tremendous pitching duel, but then the sluggers took charge.

Homers by Eddie Mathews in the first inning and Al Kaline in the fourth accounted for the only tallies as Don Drysdale and Lou Burdette, pitching for the Nationals, and Early Wynn and Ryne Duren, for the Americans, battled on even terms through the first six innings.

In the seventh, the N. L. rocked Jim Bunning for two runs on a double by Ernie Banks and singles by Del Crandall and Bill Mazeroski.

Roy Face, Pittsburgh relief ace who was 12-0 at the time, retired the first two A. L. batters in the eighth, but two singles, a walk and Gus Triandos' double scored three runs for a 4-3 lead. Johnny Antonelli relieved at that point and halted the threat.

The Nationals won the game in their turn. Whitey Ford was the victim. Singles by Ken Boyer and Hank Aaron sandwiched around a sacrifice accounted for the tying run and then Willie Mays tripled to score Aaron with the decisive marker. The box score:

AMERICANS	AB.	R.	H.	PO.	A.	E.
Minoso (Indians), lf	5	0	0	0	1	0
Fox (White Sox), 2b	5	1	2	2	0	0
Kaline (Tigers), cf	3	1	1	1	0	0
Kuenn (Tigers), cf	1	1	0	0	0	0
Skowron (Yankees), 1b	3	0	2	3	0	0
Power (Indians), 1b	1	1	1	3	0	0
Colavito (Indians), rf	3	0	1	1	0	0
bWilliams (Red Sox)	0	0	0	0	0	0
cMcDougald (Yanks)	0	0	0	0	0	0
Triandos (Orioles), c	4	0	1	8	0	0
fMantle (Yankees), rf	0	0	0	0	0	0
Killebrew (Senators), 3b	3	0	0	0	1	0
Bunning (Tigers), p	0	0	0	0	0	0
dRunnels (Red Sox)	0	0	0	0	0	0
eSievers (Senators)	0	0	0	0	1	0
Ford (Yankees), p	0	0	0	0	0	0
Daley (Athletics), p	0	0	0	0	0	0
Aparicio (White Sox), ss	3	0	0	4	2	0
gLollar (White Sox), c	1	0	0	1	0	0
Wynn (White Sox), p	1	0	0	1	0	0
Duren (Yankees), p	1	0	0	0	0	0
Malzone (Red Sox), 3b	2	0	0	0	0	0
Totals	36	4	8	24	5	0

NATIONALS	AB.	R.	H.	PO.	A.	E.
Temple (Reds), 2b	2	0	0	1	3	0
aMusial (Cardinals)	1	0	0	0	0	0
Face (Pirates), p	0	0	0	0	0	0
Antonelli (Giants), p	0	0	0	0	0	0
hBoyer, (Cardinals), 3b	1	1	1	1	0	0
Mathews (Braves), 3b	3	1	1	2	1	1
iGroat (Pirates)	0	0	0	0	0	0
Elston (Cubs), p	0	0	0	0	0	0
Aaron (Braves), rf	4	1	2	2	0	0
Mays (Giants), cf	4	0	1	2	0	0
Banks (Cubs), ss	3	1	2	1	2	0
Cepeda (Giants), 1b	4	0	0	6	0	0
Moon (Dodgers), lf	2	0	0	1	0	0
Crandall (Braves), c	3	1	1	10	0	0
Drysdale (Dodgers), p	1	0	0	0	0	0
Burdette (Braves), p	1	0	0	0	0	0
Mazeroski (Pirates), 2b	1	0	1	1	0	0
Totals	30	5	9	27	6	1

American League	0	0	0	1	0	0	0	3	0 – 4
National League	1	0	0	0	0	0	2	2	x – 5

Americans	IP.	H.	R.	ER.	BB.	SO.
Wynn (White Sox)	3	2	1	1	1	3
Duren (Yankees)	3	1	0	0	1	4
Bunning (Tigers)	1	3	2	2	0	1
Ford (Yankees)	⅓	3	2	2	0	0
Daley (Athletics)	⅔	0	0	0	0	1

Nationals	IP.	H.	R.	ER.	BB.	SO.
Drysdale (Dodgers)	3	0	0	0	0	4
Burdette (Braves)	3	4	1	1	0	2
Face (Pirates)	1⅔	3	3	3	2	2
Antonelli (Giants)	⅓	0	0	0	1	0
Elston (Cubs)	1	1	0	0	1	0

Winning pitcher—Antonelli. Losing pitcher—Ford.

aPopped out for Temple in sixth. bWalked for Colavito in eighth. cRan for Williams in eighth. dAnnounced as batter for Bunning in eighth. eWalked for Runnels in eighth. fRan for Triandos in eighth. gHit into force play for Aparicio in eighth. hSingled for Antonelli in eighth. iSacrificed for Mathews in eighth. Runs batted in—Kaline, Power, Triandos 2, Mathews, Aaron, Mays, Crandall, Mazeroski. Two-base hits—Banks 2, Triandos. Three-base hit—Mays. Home runs—Mathews, Kaline. Sacrifice hit—Groat. Double play—Aparicio and Skowron. Left on bases—Americans 8, Nationals 4. Wild pitch—Elston. Umpires—Barlick, Donatelli and Crawford (N. L.), Runge, Paparella and Rice (A. L.). Time of game—2:33. Attendance—35,277.

2nd Game of 1959—Memorial Col., Los Angeles, Aug. 3

In the Dream Game encore, the Americans gained sweet revenge by winning, 5-3. To avoid the early-afternoon heat and also to permit more fans in the East and Midwest to view the telecast, the game began at 4 o'clock.

With 60 per cent of the gate and radio-TV revenue going into the players' pension fund, the contest produced an extra $307,401 to meet back service obligations.

Unhampered by any restrictions on the use of players, Casey Stengel placed six lefthanded swingers at the head of the A. L. lineup to face Don Drysdale, Dodger righthander, and the move paid off.

Home runs accounted for six of the game's eight runs. After the Nationals jumped on Jerry Walker for a tally in the opening frame, Frank Malzone lofted a Drysdale pitch just barely over the chummy left field screen in the second to tie the score.

Yogi Berra's long smash over the right field fence with one aboard in the third made it 3-1, but Frank Robinson narrowed the N. L. deficit when he homered deep into the left field seats in the fifth.

After going hitless for three innings, the Americans reached Sam Jones for a run in the seventh on a walk, two errors and Nellie Fox's single. The Nationals got the run back in their turn on Jim Gilliam's homer over the left field screen, but Rocky Colavito duplicated in the eighth for the game's final tally. The box score:

AMERICANS	AB.	R.	H.	PO.	A.	E.
Runnels (Red Sox), 1b	3	0	0	9	0	0
Power (Indians), 1b	1	0	0	4	0	0
Fox (White Sox), 2b	4	1	2	3	1	0
Williams (Red Sox), lf	3	0	0	0	0	0
Kaline (Tigers), lf-cf	2	0	0	0	0	0
Berra (Yankees), c	3	1	1	2	0	0
Lollar (White Sox), c	0	0	0	2	0	0
Mantle (Yankees), cf	3	0	1	3	0	0
O'Dell (Orioles), p	0	0	0	0	0	0
McLish (Indians), p	0	0	0	0	0	0
Maris (Athletics), rf	2	0	0	1	0	0
Colavito (Indians), rf	2	1	1	0	0	0
Malzone (Red Sox), 3b	4	1	1	1	6	0
Aparicio (White Sox), ss	3	0	0	1	2	0
Walker (Orioles), p	1	0	0	0	0	0
bWoodling (Orioles)	1	0	0	0	0	0
Wynn (White Sox), p	0	0	0	1	0	0
Wilhelm (Orioles), p	0	0	0	0	0	0
fKubek (Yankees), lf	1	1	0	0	0	0
Totals	33	5	6	27	9	0

NATIONALS	AB.	R.	H.	PO.	A.	E.
Temple (Reds), 2b	2	1	1	1	1	0
dGilliam (Dodgers), 3b	2	1	1	0	0	0
Boyer (Cardinals), 3b	2	0	0	0	1	0
Neal (Dodgers), 2b	1	0	0	0	2	0
Aaron (Braves), rf	3	0	0	2	0	0
Mays (Giants), cf	4	0	3	3	0	0
Banks (Cubs), ss	4	0	0	2	0	1
Musial (Cardinals), 1b	0	0	0	3	1	0
Robinson (Reds), lf	3	1	3	3	0	1
Moon (Dodgers), lf	2	0	0	1	0	0
Crandall (Braves), c	2	0	1	7	1	0
Smith (Cardinals), c	2	0	0	5	0	0
Drysdale (Dodgers), p	0	0	0	0	0	0
aMathews (Braves)	1	0	0	0	0	0
Conley (Phillies), p	0	0	0	0	1	0
cCunningham (Cardinals)	1	0	0	0	0	0
ePinson (Reds)	1	0	0	0	0	0
Jones (Giants), p	0	0	0	0	0	1
gGroat (Pirates)	1	0	0	0	0	0
Face (Pirates), p	0	0	0	0	0	0
hBurgess (Pirates)	1	0	0	0	0	0
Totals	31	3	6	27	7	3

American League	0	1	2	0	0	0	1	1	0 – 5
National League	1	0	0	0	1	0	1	0	0 – 3

Americans	IP.	H.	R.	ER.	BB.	SO.
Walker (Orioles)	3	2	1	1	1	0
Wynn (White Sox)	2	1	1	1	3	1
Wilhelm (Orioles)	1	1	0	0	0	0
O'Dell (Orioles)	1	1	1	1	0	0
McLish (Indians)	2	1	0	0	1	2

Nationals	IP.	H.	R.	ER.	BB.	SO.
Drysdale (Dodgers)	3	4	3	3	3	5
Conley (Phillies)	2	0	0	0	1	2
Jones (Giants)	2	1	1	0	2	3
Face (Pirates)	2	1	1	1	0	2

Winning pitcher—Walker. Losing pitcher—Drysdale.

aStruck out for Drysdale in third. bGrounded out for Walker in fourth. cHit into force play for Conley in fifth. dWalked for Temple in fifth. eRan for Cunningham in fifth. fWalked for Wilhelm in seventh. gGrounded out for Jones in seventh. hGrounded out for Face in ninth. Runs batted in—Fox, Berra 2, Colavito, Malzone, Gilliam, Aaron, Robinson. Two-base hit—Temple. Home runs—Malzone, Berra, Robinson, Gilliam, Colavito. Sacrifice fly—Aaron. Stolen base—Aparicio. Double play—Runnels (unassisted). Left on bases—Americans 7, Nationals 7. Umpires—Jackowski, Venzon and Burkhart (N. L.), Berry, Summers and Soar (A. L.). Time of game—2:42. Attendance—55,105.

1st Game of 1960—Municipal Stadium, Kansas City, July 11

Despite a heat wave that sent the temperature soaring to 101, a capacity crowd of 30,619 turned out for the first All-Star Game ever played in Kansas City and saw the Nationals nose out a 5-3 victory.

The N. L. wasted little time in spoiling the occasion for the American League partisans, jumping on Bill Monbouquette and Chuck Estrada for all of their runs in the first three innings.

Willie Mays opened the game with a triple and Bob Skinner followed with a single. Monbouquette retired the next two batters, but then Ernie Banks homered and it was 3-0.

Del Crandall also hit for the circuit in the second inning and Estrada yielded the final N. L. run in the third on a double by Banks and singles by Joe Adcock and Bill Mazeroski.

Blanked for five innings by Bob Friend and Mike McCormick, the Americans jumped on the Giant lefty for a run in the sixth, but with the bags full and one out, Roy Face snuffed out the threat.

Bob Buhl yielded the Americans' other runs in the eighth when he served up a home run to Al Kaline following Charlie Neal's error on a grounder by Kuenn. The box score:

NATIONALS	AB.	R.	H.	PO.	A.	E.
Mays (Giants), cf	4	1	3	4	0	0
Pinson (Reds), cf	1	0	0	1	0	0
Skinner (Pirates), lf	4	1	1	1	0	0
Cepeda (Giants), lf	1	0	0	0	0	0
Mathews (Braves), 3b	4	0	0	1	0	2
Boyer (Cardinals), 3b	0	0	0	0	2	0
Aaron (Braves), rf	4	0	0	0	1	0
Clemente (Pirates), rf	1	0	0	2	0	0
Banks (Cubs), ss	4	2	2	2	2	0
Groat (Pirates), ss	0	0	0	0	1	0
Adcock (Braves), 1b	3	0	2	3	0	0
bWhite (Cardinals), 1b	1	0	0	4	0	0
Mazeroski (Pirates), 2b	2	0	1	2	2	0
eMusial (Cardinals)	1	0	1	0	0	0
Neal (Dodgers), 2b	0	0	0	0	0	1
Crandall (Braves), c	3	1	2	4	0	0
Burgess (Pirates), c	1	0	0	3	0	1
Friend (Pirates), p	2	0	0	0	0	0
McCormick (Giants), p	1	0	0	0	0	0
Face (Pirates), p	0	0	0	0	0	0
gLarker (Dodgers)	1	0	0	0	0	0
Buhl (Braves), p	0	0	0	0	0	0
Law (Pirates), p	0	0	0	0	0	0
Totals	38	5	12	27	8	4

AMERICANS	AB.	R.	H.	PO.	A.	E.
Minoso (White Sox), lf	3	0	0	0	0	0
Lemon (Senators), lf	1	0	0	1	0	0
Malzone (Red Sox), 3b	3	0	0	1	1	0
Robinson (Orioles), 3b	2	0	0	0	0	0
Maris (Yankees), rf	2	0	0	1	0	0
Kuenn (Indians), rf	3	1	1	1	0	0
Mantle (Yankees), cf	0	0	0	2	0	0
Kaline (Tigers), cf	2	2	1	1	0	0
Skowron (Yankees), 1b	3	0	1	9	0	0
Lary (Tigers), p	0	0	0	0	0	0
hLollar (White Sox)	1	0	0	0	0	0
B. Daley (Athletics), p	0	0	0	0	0	1
Berra (Yankees), c	2	0	0	5	0	0
Howard (Yankees), c	1	0	0	4	0	0
Runnels (Red Sox), 2b	1	0	0	0	1	0
Fox (White Sox), 2b	2	0	1	1	3	0
Hansen (Orioles), ss	2	0	1	0	0	0
Aparicio (White Sox), ss	2	0	0	1	1	0
Monbouquette (R. Sox), p	0	0	0	0	0	0
aWilliams (Red Sox)	1	0	0	0	0	0
Estrada (Orioles), p	0	0	0	0	0	0
Coates (Yankees), p	0	0	0	0	1	0
cSmith (White Sox)	1	0	0	0	0	0
Bell (Indians), p	0	0	0	0	1	0
dGentile (Orioles), 1b	2	0	1	0	0	0
Totals	34	3	6	27	8	1

National League	3	1	1	0	0	0	0	0	0 – 5
American League	0	0	0	0	0	1	0	2	0 – 3

Nationals	IP.	H.	R.	ER.	BB.	SO.
Friend (Pirates)	3	1	0	0	1	2
McCormick (Giants)	2⅓	3	1	0	3	2
Face (Pirates)	1⅔	2	0	0	0	2
Buhl (Braves)	1⅓	2	2	1	1	1
Law (Pirates)	⅔	0	0	0	0	0

Americans	IP.	H.	R.	ER.	BB.	SO.
Monbouquette (Red Sox)	2	5	4	4	0	2
Estrada (Orioles)	1	4	1	1	0	1
Coates (Yankees)	2	2	0	0	0	0
Bell (Indians)	2	0	0	0	0	0
Lary (Tigers)	1	1	0	0	0	1
B. Daley (Athletics)	1	0	0	0	1	2

Winning pitcher—Friend. Losing pitcher—Monbouquette.

aGrounded out for Monbouquette in second. bRan for Adcock in fifth. cFiled out for Coates in fifth. dStruck out for Bell in seventh. eSingled for Mazeroski in eighth. fRan for Musial in eighth. gGrounded into force play for Face in eighth. hGrounded out for Lary in eighth. Runs batted in—Skinner, Banks 2, Mazeroski, Crandall, Kaline 2, Fox. Two-base hits—Banks, Mays, Adcock. Three-base hit—Mays. Home runs—Banks, Crandall, Kaline. Stolen base—Skinner. Double plays—Malzone and Skowron; Banks, Mazeroski and White. Left on bases—Nationals 8, Americans 9. Hit by pitcher—By Coates (Mazeroski). Wild pitch—Friend. Balk—Friend. Umpires—Honochick, Chylak and Stevens (A. L.), Gorman, Boggess and Smith (N. L.). Time of game—2:39. Attendance—30,619.

Second Game of 1960—Yankee Stadium, New York, July 13

Displaying a blase approach to a second All-Star game, only 38,362 New York fans turned out for the 1960 encore. They saw the National League make a sweep of the two-game set by winning, 6-0.

Both squads were exactly the same as for the earlier game at Kansas City, even down to the coaches.

Led by Willie Mays, who made a triumphant return to New York, the N. L. stars banged four home runs. Meantime, Walter Alston's six-man pitching relay blanked the Americans on eight hits.

Mays repeated his heroics of the first clash at Kansas City, rapping three hits, including a homer. Eddie Mathews, Stan Musial and Ken Boyer delivered the other round-trippers.

Whitey Ford took another defeat when Mathews solved him for a two-run homer in the second inning and Mays connected in the third.

Musial walloped his four-bagger as a pinch-hitter against Gerry Staley in the seventh and then Boyer capped the N. L.'s explosive afternoon by homering against Gary Bell with a mate aboard in the ninth. The box score:

NATIONALS	AB.	R.	H.	PO.	A.	E.
Mays (Giants), cf	4	1	3	5	0	0
Pinson (Reds), cf	0	0	0	0	0	0
Skinner (Pirates), lf	3	0	1	2	0	0
Cepeda (Giants), lf	2	0	0	0	0	0
Aaron (Braves), rf	3	0	0	1	0	0
hClemente (Pirates), rf	0	0	0	0	0	0
Banks (Cubs), ss	3	0	1	2	3	0
iGroat (Pirates), ss	1	0	0	0	1	0
Adcock (Braves), 1b	2	1	1	3	0	0
White (Cardinals), 1b	1	0	0	2	0	0
kLarker (Cardinals), 1b	0	1	0	3	0	0
Mathews (Braves), 3b	3	1	1	0	1	0
Boyer (Cardinals), 3b	1	1	1	1	0	0
Mazeroski (Pirates), 2b	2	0	0	0	0	0
Neal (Dodgers), 2b	1	0	1	1	2	0
Taylor (Phillies), 2b	1	0	1	2	1	0
Crandall (Braves), c	2	0	0	3	0	0
S. Williams (Dodgers), p	0	0	0	0	0	0
dMusial (Cardinals)	1	1	1	0	0	0
Jackson (Cardinals), p	0	0	0	0	0	0
Bailey (Reds), c	1	0	0	0	0	0
Law (Pirates), p	1	0	0	0	1	0
Podres (Dodgers), p	0	0	0	0	1	0
bBurgess (Pirates), c	2	0	0	2	0	0
Henry (Reds), p	0	0	0	0	0	0
McDaniel (Cardinals), p	0	0	0	0	0	0
Totals	34	6	10	27	10	0

AMERICANS	AB.	R.	H.	PO.	A.	E.
Minoso (White Sox), lf	2	0	0	1	0	0
eT. Williams (Red Sox)	1	0	1	0	0	0
fRobinson (Orioles), 3b	1	0	0	0	0	0
Runnels (Red Sox), 2b	2	0	0	0	1	0
Staley (White Sox), p	0	0	0	1	1	0
gKaline (Tigers), lf	1	0	1	3	0	0
Maris (Yankees), rf	4	0	0	0	0	0
Mantle (Yankees), cf	4	0	1	3	0	0
Skowron (Yankees), 1b	1	0	1	6	0	0
Power (Indians), 1b	2	0	0	5	1	0
Berra (Yankees), c	2	0	0	4	1	0
Lollar (White Sox), c	2	0	1	0	0	0
Malzone (Red Sox), 3b	2	0	0	2	2	0
Lary (Tigers), p	0	0	0	0	0	0
jSmith (White Sox)	1	0	0	0	0	0
Bell (Indians), p	0	0	0	0	1	0
Hansen (Orioles), ss	4	0	2	2	4	0
Ford (Yankees), p	0	0	0	0	0	0
aKuenn (Tigers)	1	0	0	0	0	0
Wynn (White Sox), p	0	0	0	0	0	0
cFox (White Sox), 2b	3	0	1	0	1	0
Totals	33	0	8	27	12	0

National League	0	2	1	0	0	0	1	0	2 —	6
American League	0	0	0	0	0	0	0	0	0 —	0

Nationals	IP.	H.	R.	ER.	BB.	SO.
Law (Pirates)	2	1	0	0	0	1
Podres (Dodgers)	2	1	0	0	3	1
S. Williams (Dodgers)	2	2	0	0	1	2
Jackson (Cardinals)	1	1	0	0	2	0
Henry (Reds)	1	2	0	0	0	0
McDaniel (Cardinals)	1	1	0	0	0	1

Americans	IP.	H.	R.	ER.	BB.	SO.
Ford (Yankees)	3	5	3	3	0	1
Wynn (White Sox)	2	0	0	0	0	2
Staley (White Sox)	2	2	1	1	0	0
Lary (Tigers)	1	1	0	0	1	0
Bell (Indians)	1	2	2	2	0	0

Winning pitcher—Law. Losing pitcher—Ford.

aFiled out for Ford in third. bStruck out for Podres in fifth. cSingled for Wynn in fifth. dHomered for S. Williams in seventh. eSingled for Minoso in seventh. fRan for T. Williams in seventh. gWalked for Staley in seventh. hWalked for Aaron in eighth. iHit into double play for Banks in eighth. jPopped out for Lary in eighth. kWalked for White in ninth. Runs batted in—Mays, Mathews 2, Boyer 2, Musial. Two-base hit—Lollar. Home runs—Mathews, Mays, Musial, Boyer. Stolen base—Mays. Caught stealing—Mays. Sacrifice hit—Henry. Double plays—Law, Banks and Adcock; Banks, Neal and White; Fox, Hansen and Power. Left on bases—Nationals 5, Americans 12. Umpires—Chylak, Honochick and Stevens (A. L.), Boggess, Gorman and Smith (N. L.). Time of game—2:42. Attendance—38,362.

1st Game of 1961—Candlestick Park, San Francisco, July 11

A near gale contributed to a wild climax as the Nationals came from behind in the tenth inning to win, 5-4, in a game marked by a record seven errors, five of them by the winning team.

The victory marked the first time either loop had pulled a game from the fire in overtime. It also gave the N.L. a 3-0 record in extra-inning All-Star encounters.

The gale-like winds which struck in the late innings were responsible for many of the errors. Ken Boyer, Cardinal third baseman, was guilty of two of the worst miscues. The game produced two homers, both by pinch-hitters—Harmon Killebrew and George Altman.

As the A.L. came to bat in the ninth, trailing 3-1, the wind began blowing and turned the game into a weird nightmare. With one run in and two runners on base, Stu Miller relieved and the near gale caused him to commit a costly balk, after which Boyer bobbled a grounder, permitting the tying run to score.

In the tenth, Boyer made a wild throw that allowed Nellie Fox to score all the way from first base. However, the Nationals came back with two runs in their turn when Hank Aaron singled, Willie Mays doubled and Roberto Clemente came through with a single. The box score:

AMERICANS	AB.	R.	H.	PO.	A.	E.
Temple (Indians), 2b	3	0	0	1	2	0
fGentile (Orioles), 1b	2	0	0	2	0	1
Cash (Tigers), 1b	4	0	1	6	1	0
gFox (White Sox), 2b	0	2	0	1	0	0
Mantle (Yankees), cf	3	0	0	3	0	0
Kaline (Tigers), cf	2	1	1	1	0	0
Maris (Yankees), rf	4	0	1	3	0	0
Colavito (Tigers), lf	4	0	0	1	0	0
Kubek (Yankees), ss	4	0	0	1	2	1
Romano (Indians), c	3	0	0	7	0	0
hBerra (Yankees), c	1	0	0	0	0	0
Howard (Yankees), c	0	0	0	0	0	0
B. Robinson (Ori.), 3b	2	0	0	2	0	0
dBrandt (Orioles)	1	0	0	0	0	0
Fornieles (Red Sox), p	0	0	0	0	0	0
Wilhelm (Orioles), p	1	0	0	0	0	0
Ford (Yankees), p	1	0	0	1	0	0
Lary (Tigers), p	0	0	0	0	0	0
Donovan (Senators), p	0	0	0	0	0	0
cKillebrew (Twins), 3b	2	1	1	0	0	0
Howser (Athletics), 3b	1	0	0	0	1	0
Totals	38	4	4	27	8	2

NATIONALS	AB.	R.	H.	PO.	A.	E.
Wills (Dodgers), ss	5	0	1	0	2	0
Mathews (Braves), 3b	2	0	0	0	0	0
Purkey (Reds), p	0	0	0	1	0	0
bMusial (Cardinals)	1	0	0	0	0	0
McCormick (Giants), p	0	0	0	0	0	0
eAltman (Cubs)	1	1	1	0	0	0
Face (Pirates), p	0	0	0	0	0	0
Koufax (Dodgers), p	0	0	0	0	0	0
Miller (Giants), p	0	0	0	0	0	0
iAaron (Braves)	1	1	1	0	0	0
Mays (Giants), cf	5	2	2	3	0	1
Cepeda (Giants), lf	3	0	0	1	0	1
F. Robinson (Reds), lf	1	0	1	2	0	0
Clemente (Pirates), rf	4	1	2	2	0	0
White (Cardinals), 1b	3	0	1	7	1	0
Bolling (Braves), 2b	3	0	0	1	3	0
Zimmer (Cubs), 2b	1	0	0	0	0	0
Burgess (Pirates), c	4	0	1	13	0	1
Spahn (Braves), p	0	0	0	0	0	0
aStuart (Pirates)	1	0	1	0	0	0
Boyer (Cardinals), 3b	2	0	0	0	1	2
Totals	37	5	11	30	8	5

```
American League .......................... 0 0 0    0 0 1    0 0 2    1 – 4
National League .......................... 0 1 0    1 0 0    0 1 0    2 – 5
```

None out when winning run scored.

Americans	IP.	H.	R.	ER.	BB.	SO.
Ford (Yankees)	3	2	1	1	0	2
Lary (Tigers)	0*	1	0	0	0	0
Donovan (Senators)	2	4	0	0	0	1
Bunning (Tigers)	2	0	0	0	0	2
Fornieles (Red Sox)	⅓	2	1	1	0	0
Wilhelm (Orioles)	1⅔‡	3	2	2	1	0

Nationals	IP.	H.	R.	ER.	BB.	SO.
Spahn (Braves)	3	0	0	0	0	3
Purkey (Reds)	2	0	0	0	0	0
McCormick (Giants)	3	1	1	1	1	3
Face (Pirates)	⅓	2	2	2	0	1
Koufax (Dodgers)	0†	1	0	0	0	0
Miller (Giants)	1⅔	0	1	0	1	4

*Pitched to one batter in fourth. †Pitched to one batter in ninth. ‡Pitched to four batters in tenth.

Winning pitcher—Miller. Losing pitcher—Wilhelm.

aDoubled for Spahn in third. bFlied out for Purkey in fifth. cHomered for Donovan in sixth. dStruck out for Bunning in eighth. eHomered for McCormick in eighth. fStruck out for Temple in ninth. gRan for Cash in ninth. hSafe on error for Romano in ninth. iSingled for Miller in tenth. Runs batted in—Kaline, Colavito, Killebrew, Altman, Mays, Clemente 2, White. Two-base hits—Stuart, Cash, Mays. Three-base hit—Clemente. Home runs—Killebrew, Altman. Stolen base—F. Robinson. Sacrifice flies—Clemente, White. Left on bases—Americans 6, Nationals 9. Hit by pitcher—By Wilhelm (F. Robinson). Balk—Miller. Passed ball—Howard. Umpires—Landes, Crawford and Vargo (N. L.), Umont, Runge and Drummond (A. L.). Time of game—2:53. Attendance— 44,115.

Second Game of 1961—Fenway Park, Boston, July 31

Just as in the year's first contest, the elements played a prominent role in the encore. A heavy downpour that fell just as the ninth inning ended forced the two clubs to settle for a 1-1 stalemate.

Except for a misplayed grounder, the game might have resulted in the first 1-0 decision in All-Star history. As it was, the crowd of 31,851 witnessed the best-pitched game in the long series.

A first-inning homer by Rocky Colavito off Bob Purkey accounted for the American League's lone score. The blow was the A. L.'s only hit off Purkey and Art Mahaffey in the first four innings.

Jim Bunning started for the junior loop and worked three hitless innings. Don Schwall was on the mound when the Nationals tied the score in the sixth. With one away, he walked Eddie Mathews; one out later, he nicked Orlando Cepeda with a pitch.

Luis Aparicio then was guilty of a mental lapse which helped the N.L. to its run. On Eddie Kasko's dribbler toward shortstop, Aparicio waited for the ball instead of moving in for it. The last bounce was a tricky one, and by the time the White Sox shortstop got the ball, it was too late for a play. The infield hit filled the bases.

A moment later Aparicio made a great play which proved a game-saver for the Americans. Bill White slapped a sharp grounder toward the box, which Schwall barely deflected. Dashing behind second, Aparicio made a tremendous stop. One run scored on the hit, but Aparicio's play forced Cepeda to stop at third. Schwall then retired the next batter.

A heavy downpour began falling as the ninth inning ended, and after a 30-minute wait the umpires called the game. The box score:

NATIONALS	AB.	R.	H.	PO.	A.	E.
Wills (Dodgers), ss	2	0	1	1	1	0
Aaron (Braves), rf	2	0	0	1	0	0
Miller (Giants), p	0	0	0	0	0	0
Mathews (Braves), 3b	3	1	0	0	2	0
Mays (Giants), cf	3	0	1	1	0	0
Cepeda (Giants), lf	3	0	0	0	0	0
Clemente (Pirates), rf	2	0	0	0	0	0
Kasko (Reds), ss	1	0	1	2	4	0
eBanks (Cubs), ss	1	0	0	0	0	0
White (Cardinals), 1b	4	0	2	11	1	0
Bolling (Braves), 2b	4	0	0	3	2	1
Burgess (Pirates), c	1	0	0	2	0	0
Roseboro (Dodgers), c	3	0	0	6	0	0
Purkey (Reds), p	0	0	0	0	1	0
aStuart (Pirates)	1	0	0	0	0	0
Mahaffey (Phillies), p	0	0	0	0	0	0
cMusial (Cardinals)	1	0	0	0	0	0
Koufax (Dodgers), p	0	0	0	0	0	0
dAltman (Cubs), rf	1	0	0	0	0	0
Totals	32	1	5	27	11	1

AMERICANS	AB.	R.	H.	PO.	A.	E.
Cash (Tigers), 1b	4	0	0	11	0	0
Colavito (Tigers), lf	4	1	1	3	0	0
Kaline (Tigers), rf	4	0	2	1	0	0
Mantle (Yankees), cf	3	0	0	2	0	0
Romano (Indians), c	1	0	0	1	0	0
bMaris (Yankees)	1	0	0	0	0	0
Howard (Yankees), c	2	0	0	6	0	0
Aparicio (Wh. Sox), ss	2	0	0	1	3	0
fSievers (White Sox)	1	0	0	0	0	0
Temple (Indians), 2b	2	0	0	2	3	0
B. Robinson (Orioles), 3b	3	0	1	0	3	0
Bunning (Tigers), p	1	0	0	0	0	0
Schwall (Red Sox), p	1	0	0	0	0	0
Pascual (Twins), p	1	0	0	0	0	0
Totals	30	1	4	27	9	0

National League	0	0	0	0	0	1	0	0	0 — 1
American League	1	0	0	0	0	0	0	0	0 — 1

Called because of rain.

Nationals	IP.	H.	R.	ER.	BB.	SO.
Purkey (Reds)	2	1	1	1	2	2
Mahaffey (Phillies)	2	0	0	0	1	0
Koufax (Dodgers)	2	2	0	0	0	1
Miller (Giants)	3	1	0	0	0	5

Americans	IP.	H.	R.	ER.	BB.	SO.
Bunning (Tigers)	3	0	0	0	0	1
Schwall (Red Sox)	3	5	1	1	1	2
Pascual (Twins)	3	0	0	0	1	4

aGrounded out for Purkey in third. bPopped out for Romano in fourth. cFanned for Mahaffey in fifth. dFlied out for Koufax in seventh. eFanned for Kasko in ninth. fFanned for Aparicio in ninth. Runs batted in—White, Colavito. Two-base hit—White. Home run—Colavito. Stolen base—Kaline. Double plays—Bolling, Kasko and White; White, Kasko and Bolling. Left on bases—Nationals 7, Americans 5. Hit by pitcher—By Schwall (Cepeda). Passed ball—Burgess. Umpires—Napp, Flaherty and Smith (A. L.), Secory, Sudol and Pelekoudas (N. L.). Time of game—2:27. Attendance—31,851.

First Game of 1962—D. C. Stadium, Washington, July 10

The Nationals scored their 11th victory in the last 15 decisions by nipping the Americans, 3-1, in a sharply-pitched game. A capacity crowd of 45,480, including President John F. Kennedy and Vice-President Lyndon Johnson, jammed Washington's new stadium for the game. President Kennedy threw out the first ball.

Maury Wills shared the spotlight with the four-hit chucking of four N. L. pitchers. Although he didn't enter the game until the sixth inning—when it was still scoreless—Wills literally stole the show.

Veteran Stan Musial launched the first scoring drive when he singled as a pinch-hitter in the sixth. Wills ran for him and promptly stole second and scored on Dick Groat's single. Roberto Clemente followed with his third successive hit, and Groat subsquently scored on an infield out.

The Americans tallied their lone run in the bottom of the sixth on singles by Rich Rollins and Billy Moran plus a long fly ball by Roger Maris which Willie Mays caught against the wall in right-center.

Wills gave the crowd another thrill in the eighth. Leading off with a single, he daringly raced to third on Jim Davenport's single to left. When Felipe Alou followed with a foul fly to Leon Wagner in short right field, Wills tagged up and slid across the plate with the Nationals' third run.

The Americans made an abortive bid to tie the score in the ninth inning. With Bob Shaw on the hill, Rocky Colavito led off with a single. After Shaw retired the next two batters, John Romano singled and Luis Aparicio smashed a drive to deep right-center. For a moment, it looked like a triple, but Mays caught it to end the game. The box score:

NATIONALS	AB.	R.	H.	PO.	A.	E.
Groat (Pirates), ss	3	1	1	3	3	0
Davenport (Giants), 3b	1	0	1	0	1	0
Clemente (Pirates), rf	3	0	3	2	0	0
F. Alou (Giants), rf	0	0	0	0	0	0
Mays (Giants), cf	3	0	0	3	0	0
Cepeda (Giants), 1b	3	0	0	2	2	0
Purkey (Reds), p	0	0	0	0	1	0
eCallison (Phillies)	1	0	1	0	0	0
Shaw (Braves), p	0	0	0	1	0	0
T. Davis (Dodgers), lf	4	0	0	2	0	0
Boyer (Cardinals), 3b	2	0	0	1	0	0
Banks (Cubs), 1b	2	0	0	4	1	0
Crandall (Braves), c	4	0	0	5	0	0
Mazeroski (Pirates), 2b	2	0	0	1	0	0
Bolling (Braves), 2b	2	0	0	1	3	0
Drysdale (Dodgers), p	1	0	0	1	0	0
Marichal (Giants), p	0	0	0	0	0	0
cMusial (Cardinals)	1	0	1	0	0	0
dWills (Dodgers), ss	1	2	1	1	1	0
Totals	32	3	8	27	12	0

AMERICANS	AB.	R.	H.	PO.	A.	E.
Rollins (Twins), 3b	2	1	1	1	3	0
Robinson (Orioles), 3b	0	0	0	0	1	0
Moran (Angels), 2b	3	0	1	0	0	0
Richardson (Yankees), 2b	1	0	0	1	0	0
Maris (Yankees), cf	2	0	0	2	0	0
Landis (White Sox), cf	1	0	0	2	0	0
Mantle (Yankees), rf	1	0	0	0	0	0
bColavito (Tigers), lf	1	0	1	0	0	0
Gentile (Orioles), 1b	3	0	0	8	0	0
Wagner (Angels), lf-rf	4	0	0	4	0	0
Battey (Twins), c	2	0	0	4	1	0
Romano (Indians), c	2	0	1	1	0	0
Aparicio (White Sox), ss	4	0	1	3	2	0
Bunning (Tigers), p	0	0	0	0	0	0
aL. Thomas (Angels)	1	0	0	0	0	0
Pascual (Twins), p	1	0	0	0	1	0
Donovan (Indians), p	0	0	0	0	0	0
fSiebern (Athletics)	1	0	0	0	0	0
Pappas (Orioles), p	0	0	0	0	0	0
Totals	29	1	4	27	8	0

National League	0	0	0	0	2	0	1	0 – 3
American League	0	0	0	0	1	0	0	0 – 1

Nationals	IP.	H.	R.	ER.	BB.	SO.
Drysdale (Dodgers)	3	1	0	0	1	3
Marichal (Giants)	2	0	0	0	1	0
Purkey (Reds)	2	2	1	1	0	1
Shaw (Braves)	2	1	0	0	1	1

Americans	IP.	H.	R.	ER.	BB.	SO.
Bunning (Tigers)	3	1	0	0	0	2
Pascual (Twins)	3	4	2	2	1	1
Donovan (Indians)	2	3	1	1	0	0
Pappas (Orioles)	1	0	0	0	0	0

Winning pitcher—Marichal. Losing pitcher—Pascual.

aPopped out for Bunning in third. bRan for Mantle in fourth. cSingled for Marichal in sixth. dRan for Musial in sixth. eSingled for Purkey in eighth. fGrounded out for Donovan in eighth. Runs batted in—Groat, Cepeda, Maris, F. Alou. Two-base hit—Clemente. Three-base hit—Aparicio. Stolen bases—Mays, Wills. Caught stealing—Clemente. Sacrifice flies—Maris. F. Alou. Double plays—Cepeda, Groat and Drysdale; Battey and Rollins. Left on bases—Nationals 5, Americans 7. Hit by pitcher—By Drysdale (Rollins), by Shaw (Robinson). Umpires—Hurley, Stewart and Schwarts (A. L.), Donatelli, Venzon and Steiner (N. L.). Time of game—2:33. Attendance—45,480.

Second Game of 1962—Wrigley Field, Chicago, July 30

The National League muffed an opportunity to deadlock the All-Star series when the Americans hauled out the lethal home-run weapon to hammer out an easy 9-4 victory.

Both teams collected ten hits, but three A. L. homers spelled the difference. The first came from a surprise source, Pete Runnels. The Boston infielder, who had previously hit only 45 round-trippers in 12 years in the majors, connected against Art Mahaffey in the third inning.

Leon Wagner belted Mahaffey for a two-run homer in the fourth to make it 3-1. After the Americans picked up another run off Bob Gibson in the sixth, Rocky Colavito virtually iced the game by smashing a three-run homer off Dick Farrell in the seventh.

The Nationals got to Hank Aguirre for single tallies in the seventh and eighth, but the Americans added two insurance runs in the ninth off Juan Marichal on a double error by Eddie Mathews, Roger Maris' double, a wild pitch and a sacrifice fly by Rocky Colavito. For Colavito it was his fourth RBI of the day.

John Roseboro wound up the afternoon's run making by socking the Nationals' lone homer—off Milt Pappas—in the ninth. The box score:

AMERICANS	AB.	R.	H.	PO.	A.	E.	NATIONALS	AB.	R.	H.	PO.	A.	E.
Rollins (Twins), 3b	3	0	1	0	1	0	Groat (Pirates), ss	3	0	2	3	3	1
B. Robinson (Orioles), 3b	1	1	0	1	0	0	Wills (Dodgers), ss	1	0	0	0	1	0
Moran (Angels), 2b	4	0	1	1	4	0	Clemente (Pirates), rf	2	0	0	2	0	0
fBerra (Yankees)	1	0	0	0	0	0	F. Robinson (Reds), rf	3	0	0	1	0	0
gRich'dson (Yankees), 2b	0	1	0	2	0	0	Mays (Giants), cf	2	0	2	2	0	0
Maris (Yankees), cf	4	2	1	4	0	0	H. Aaron (Braves), cf	2	0	0	1	0	0
Colavito (Tigers), rf	4	1	1	2	0	0	Cepeda (Giants), 1b	1	0	0	2	0	0
Gentile (Orioles), 1b	4	0	1	10	0	0	Banks (Cubs), 1b	2	1	1	1	1	0
Battey (Twins), c	2	1	0	2	0	0	T. Davis (Dodgers), lf	1	0	0	0	1	1
dKaline (Tigers)	0	1	0	0	0	0	bMusial (Cardinals), lf	2	0	0	0	1	0
Howard (Yankees), c	2	0	0	2	0	0	Williams (Cubs), lf	1	0	0	2	0	0
Wagner (Angels), lf	4	1	3	1	0	0	Boyer (Cardinals), 3b	3	0	1	1	2	0
L. Thomas (Angels), lf	0	0	0	1	0	0	Mathews (Braves), 3b	1	0	0	0	0	2
Aparicio (White Sox), ss	2	0	0	2	3	0	Crandall (Braves), c	1	0	0	3	0	0
Tresh (Yankees), ss	2	0	1	0	4	0	Roseboro (Dodgers), c	3	1	1	6	0	0
Stenhouse (Senators), p	0	0	0	0	0	0	Mazeroski (Pirates), 2b	1	0	0	0	0	0
aRunnels (Red Sox)	1	1	1	0	0	0	cAltman (Cubs)	1	0	0	0	0	0
Herbert (White Sox), p	1	0	0	0	0	0	Gibson (Cardinals), p	0	0	0	0	0	0
Aguirre (Tigers), p	2	0	0	0	0	0	Farrell (Colts), p	0	0	0	0	0	0
Pappas (Orioles), p	0	0	0	0	0	0	eAshburn (Mets)	1	1	1	0	0	0
Totals	37	9	10	27	13	0	Marichal (Giants), p	0	0	0	0	0	0
							hCallison (Phillies)	0	0	0	0	0	0
							Podres (Dodgers), p	1	1	1	0	0	0
							Mahaffey (Phillies), p	0	0	0	0	0	0
							Bolling (Braves), 2b	3	0	1	3	1	0
							Totals	35	4	10	27	10	4

American League								
American League	0	0	1	2	0	1	3 0	2 — 9
National League	1	0	0	0	0	1	1	1 — 4

Americans	IP.	H.	R.	ER.	BB.	SO.
Stenhouse (Senators)	2	3	1	1	1	1
Herbert (White Sox)	3	3	0	0	0	0
Aguirre (Tigers)	3	3	2	2	0	2
Pappas (Orioles)	1	1	1	1	1	0

Nationals	IP.	H.	R.	ER.	BB.	SO.
Podres (Dodgers)	2	2	0	0	0	2
Mahaffey (Phillies)	2	2	3	3	1	1
Gibson (Cardinals)	2	1	1	1	2	1
Farrell (Colts)	1	3	3	3	1	2
Marichal (Giants)	2	2	2	1	0	2

Winning pitcher—Herbert. Losing pitcher—Mahaffey.

aHomered for Stenhouse in third. bGrounded out for T. Davis in third. cFiled out for Mazeroski in fourth. dRan for Battey in sixth. eSingled for Farrell in seventh. fSafe on error for Moran in ninth. gRan for Berra in ninth. hWalked for Marichal in ninth. Runs batted in—Groat 2, Runnels, Wagner 2, Tresh, Colavito 4, Williams, Maris, Roseboro. Two-base hits—Podres, Tresh, Bolling, Maris. Three-base hit—Banks. Home runs—Runnels, Wagner, Colavito, Roseboro. Sacrifice fly—Colavito. Double plays—Aparicio, Moran and Gentile; Moran, Aparicio and Gentile. Left on bases—Americans 6, Nationals 7. Hit by pitcher—By Stenhouse (Groat). Wild pitches—Marichal 2, Stenhouse. Umpires—Conlan, Burkhart and Forman (N. L.), McKinley, Rice and Kinnamon (A. L.). Time of game—2:28. Attendance—38,359.

Game of 1963—Municipal Stadium, Cleveland, July 9

After four years as a double feature, the All-Star Game went back to a single performance and it found the National League utilizing its speed to run past the American League stars, 5-3. Only 44,160 fans—nearly 30,000 under capacity—attended.

Willie Mays was easily the standout performer. He collected only one hit, but drove in two runs, walked once, stole two bases, scored twice and contributed the game's most scintillating catch.

Oddly, the Americans outhit the Nationals, 11 to six, and had the only extra-base blow. However, Mays' two stolen bases and another by Bill White each set up a run for the senior circuit.

Mays started the N. L. on the road to victory when he walked in the second inning, swiped second and scored on Dick Groat's single. After the Americans knotted the score in their turn, the senior loop came up with two more runs in the third on a single by Tommy Davis, an infield out, a run-scoring ace by Mays, his theft and a hit by Ed Bailey.

The Americans got the two runs back in their turn against Larry Jackson. Albie Pearson doubled and tallied on Frank Malzone's single. An infield out and Earl Battey's single fetched in the tying marker.

The N. L. broke the deadlock against Jim Bunning in the fifth on a walk, an error by Bobby Richardson and Willie Mays' infield out. The Nationals added their final run in the eighth when White singled off Dick Radatz, stole second and scored on Ron Santo's ace. The box score:

NATIONALS	AB.	R.	H.	PO.	A.	E.
T. Davis (Dodgers), lf	3	1	1	2	1	0
eSnider (Mets), lf	1	0	0	0	0	0
H. Aaron (Braves), rf	4	1	0	3	0	0
White (Cardinals), 1b	4	1	1	5	3	0
Mays (Giants), cf	3	2	1	1	0	0
Clemente (Pirates), cf	0	0	0	0	0	0
Bailey (Giants), c	3	0	1	4	1	0
aMusial (Cardinals)	1	0	0	0	0	0
Culp (Phillies), p	0	0	0	0	1	0
Santo (Cubs), 3b	1	0	1	0	0	0
Boyer (Cardinals), 3b	3	0	0	0	0	0
Woodeshick (Colts), p	0	0	0	0	1	0
dMcCovey (Giants)	1	0	0	0	0	0
Drysdale (Dodgers), p	0	0	0	0	0	0
Groat (Cardinals), ss	4	0	1	2	2	0
Javier (Cardinals), 2b	4	0	0	4	1	0
O'Toole (Reds), p	1	0	0	0	0	0
Jackson (Cubs), p	1	0	0	1	0	0
Edwards (Reds), c	2	0	0	5	0	0
Totals	34	5	6	27	10	0

AMERICANS	AB.	R.	H.	PO.	A.	E.
Fox (White Sox), 2b	3	0	1	3	1	0
Richardson (Yankees), 2b	2	0	0	0	1	1
Pearson (Angels), cf	4	1	2	4	0	0
Tresh (Yankees), cf	0	0	0	0	0	0
Kaline (Tigers), rf	3	0	0	2	0	0
Allison (Twins), rf	1	0	0	0	0	0
Malzone (Red Sox), 3b	3	1	1	1	3	0
Bouton (Yankees), p	0	0	0	0	0	0
Pizarro (White Sox), p	0	0	0	0	0	0
cKillebrew (Twins)	1	0	0	0	0	0
Radatz (Red Sox), p	0	0	0	0	0	0
Wagner (Angels), lf	3	1	2	1	0	0
Howard (Yankees), c	1	0	0	5	0	0
Battey (Twins), c	2	0	1	1	0	0
bYastrzemski (R. Sox), lf	2	0	0	1	0	0
Pepitone (Yankees), 1b	4	0	0	8	0	0
Versalles (Twins), ss	1	0	1	0	2	0
Aparicio (Orioles), ss	1	0	0	0	0	0
McBride (Angels), p	1	0	1	0	0	0
Bunning (Tigers), p	0	0	0	0	0	0
Robinson (Orioles), 3b	2	0	2	1	1	0
Totals	34	3	11	27	8	1

```
National League ...................................... 0   1   2     0   1   0     0   1   0 – 5
American League ..................................... 0   1   2     0   0   0     0   0   0 – 3
```

Nationals	IP.	H.	R.	ER.	BB.	SO.
O'Toole (Reds)	2	4	1	1	0	1
Jackson (Cubs)	2	4	2	2	0	3
Culp (Phillies)	1	1	0	0	0	0
Woodeshick (Colts)	2	1	0	0	1	3
Drysdale (Dodgers)	2	1	0	0	0	2

Americans	IP.	H.	R.	ER.	BB.	SO.
McBride (Angels)	3	4	3	3	2	1
Bunning (Tigers)	2	0	1	0	1	0
Bouton (Yankees)	1	0	0	0	0	0
Pizarro (White Sox)	1	0	0	0	0	0
Radatz (Red Sox)	2	2	1	1	0	5

Winning pitcher—Jackson. Losing pitcher—Bunning.

aLined out for Bailey in fifth. bFouled out for Battey in fifth. cCalled out on strikes for Pizarro in seventh. dStruck out for Woodeshick in eighth. eCalled out on strikes for T. Davis in ninth. Runs batted in—Mays 2, Bailey, Santo, Groat, Malzone, Battey, McBride. Two-base hit—Pearson. Stolen bases—Mays 2, White. Sacrifice hit—Bunning. Double plays—T. Davis and Bailey; Groat, Javier and White; White, Groat and White. Left on bases—Nationals 5, Americans 7. Hit by pitcher—By O'Toole (Versalles). Umpires—Soar, Smith and Haller (A. L.), Jackowski, Pryor and Harvey (N. L.). Time of game—2:20. Attendance—44,160.

Game of 1964—Shea Stadium, New York, July 7

Staging a dramatic ninth-inning rally, the Nationals came from behind to win, 7-4, and knot the All-Star series at 17 victories each. It also was the N. L.'s sixth win in the last seven decisions.

The Americans led, 4-3, going into the bottom of the ninth. Dick Radatz, Red Sox relief ace, was on the mound and had already hurled two hitless innings. However, Willie Mays wheedled a walk out of him to start the ninth. Then, in an unorthodox move, he stole second.

Orlando Cepeda followed with a bloop hit to short right field and Mays raced home with the tying run when first baseman Joe Pepitone, who retrieved the ball, made a bad throw to the plate. Following two outs sandwiched around a walk, Johnny Callison smashed the ball into the right field seats to break up the game.

The Nationals' first two runs came in the fourth inning when Billy Williams and Ken Boyer tagged Johnny Wyatt for homers. The N. L. made it 3-1 with a run off Camilo Pascual with two out in the fifth on a single by Roberto Clemente and Dick Groat's double. However, Brooks Robinson tripled across two A. L. mates in the sixth to tie the score.

Dick Farrell was pitching when the Americans went ahead, 4-3, in the seventh inning. He hit Elston Howard with a pitch and Rocky Colavito then singled Howard to third. Jim Fregosi followed with a sacrifice fly that scored Howard. That set the stage for the N. L.'s thrilling rally in the ninth inning. The box score:

AMERICANS	AB.	R.	H.	PO.	A.	E.
Fregosi (Angels), ss	4	1	1	4	1	0
Oliva (Twins), rf	4	0	0	0	0	0
Radatz (Red Sox), p	1	0	0	0	0	0
Mantle (Yankees), cf	4	1	1	2	0	0
Hall (Twins), cf	0	0	0	0	0	0
Killebrew (Twins), lf	4	1	3	0	0	0
Hinton (Senators), lf	0	0	0	0	0	0
Allison (Twins), 1b	3	0	0	9	0	0
fPepitone (Yankees), 1b	0	0	0	1	0	1
Robinson (Orioles), 3b	4	0	2	1	2	0
Richardson (Yankees), 2b	4	0	1	0	4	0
Howard (Yankees), c	3	1	0	9	0	0
Chance (Angels), p	1	0	0	0	1	0
Wyatt (Athletics), p	0	0	0	0	1	0
bSiebern (Orioles)	1	0	0	0	0	0
Pascual (Twins), p	0	0	0	0	1	0
eColavito (Athletics), rf	2	0	1	0	0	0
Totals	35	4	9	26	10	1

NATIONALS	AB.	R.	H.	PO.	A.	E.
Clemente (Pirates), rf	3	1	1	1	0	0
Short (Phillies), p	0	0	0	0	1	0
Farrell (Colts), p	0	0	0	0	0	0
gWhite (Cardinals)	1	0	0	0	0	0
Marichal (Giants), p	0	0	0	0	0	0
Groat (Cardinals), ss	3	0	1	0	0	0
dCardenas (Reds)	1	0	0	1	0	0
Williams (Cubs), lf	4	1	1	1	0	0
Mays (Giants), cf	3	1	0	7	0	0
Cepeda (Giants), 1b	4	0	1	6	0	0
hFlood (Cardinals)	1	0	0	0	0	0
Boyer (Cardinals), 3b	4	1	2	0	2	0
Torre (Braves), c	2	0	0	5	0	0
Edwards (Reds), c	1	0	0	5	0	0
Hunt (Mets), 2b	3	0	1	1	0	0
iAaron (Braves)	1	0	0	0	0	0
Drysdale (Dodgers), p	0	0	0	0	3	0
aStargell (Pirates)	1	0	0	0	0	0
Bunning (Phillies), p	0	0	0	0	0	0
cCallison (Phillies), rf	3	1	1	0	0	0
Totals	34	7	8	27	6	0

American League	1	0	0	0	0	2	1	0	0	— 4
National League	0	0	0	2	1	0	0	0	4	— 7

Two out when winning run scored.

Americans	IP.	H.	R.	ER.	BB.	SO.
Chance (Angels)	3	2	0	0	0	2
Wyatt (Athletics)	1	2	2	2	0	0
Pascual (Twins)	2	2	1	1	0	1
Radatz (Red Sox)	2⅔	2	4	4	2	5

Nationals	IP.	H.	R.	ER.	BB.	SO.
Drysdale (Dodgers)	3	2	1	0	0	3
Bunning (Phillies)	2	2	0	0	0	4
Short (Phillies)	1	3	2	2	0	1
Farrell (Colts)	2	2	1	1	1	1
Marichal (Giants)	1	0	0	0	0	1

Winning pitcher—Marichal. Losing pitcher—Radatz.

aGrounded out for Drysdale in third. bFlied out for Wyatt in fifth. cPopped out for Bunning in fifth. dRan for Groat in fifth. eDoubled for Pascual in seventh. fRan for Allison in eighth. gStruck out for Farrell in eighth. hRan for Cepeda in ninth. iStruck out for Hunt in ninth. Runs batted in—Killebrew, Williams, Boyer, Groat, Robinson 2, Fregosi, Callison 3. Two-base hits—Groat, Colavito. Three-base hit—Robinson. Home runs—Williams, Boyer, Callison. Stolen base—Mays. Sacrifice fly—Fregosi. Left on bases—Americans 7, Nationals 3. Hit by pitcher—By Farrell (Howard). Wild pitch—Drysdale. Passed ball—Torre. Umpires—Sudol, Secory and Harvey (N. L.), Paparella, Chylak and Salerno (A. L.). Time of game—2:37. Attendance—50,844.

Game of 1965—Metropolitan Stadium, Minnesota, July 13

For the first time since the All-Star Game was launched in 1933, the National League gained the lead in the series when it defeated the American League, 6-5. In posting its seventh victory in the last eight decisions, the senior circuit took an 18-17 edge.

Willie Mays and Juan Marichal were the N. L. standouts. Mays hit a homer, drew two walks and scored the winning run. Marichal breezed through the first three innings, permitting only one hit and facing the minimum of nine batters.

The Nationals jumped on Milt Pappas for three quick runs in the opening inning. Mays led off with a 415-foot homer and Joe Torre duplicated later with a mate aboard. The old loop then made it 5-0 at the expense of Mudcat Grant in the second inning when Willie Stargell homered with Marichal aboard via a single.

After picking up one run in the fourth, the Americans exploded for four runs against Jim Maloney with two away in the fifth to knot the score. Both Dick McAuliffe and Harmon Killebrew homered with one on.

The N. L. broke the tie in the seventh inning against Sam McDowell. Mays worked him for a walk, raced to third on Hank Aaron's single and scored on Ron Santo's nubber to shortstop Zoilo Versalles, who was unable to make a play. The box score:

NATIONALS	AB.	R.	H.	PO.	A.	E.
Mays (Giants), cf	3	2	1	4	0	0
Aaron (Braves), rf	5	0	1	0	0	0
Stargell (Pirates), lf	3	2	2	1	0	0
fClemente (Pirates), lf	2	0	0	0	0	0
Allen (Phillies), 3b	3	0	1	0	1	0
Santo (Cubs), 3b	2	0	1	2	0	0
Torre (Braves), c	4	1	1	5	1	0
Banks (Cubs), 1b	4	0	2	11	0	0
Rose (Reds), 2b	2	0	0	1	5	0
Wills (Dodgers), ss	4	0	1	2	3	0
Cardenas (Reds), ss	0	0	0	0	0	0
Marichal (Giants), p	1	1	1	0	0	0
bRojas (Phillies)	1	0	0	0	0	0
Maloney (Reds), p	0	0	0	0	0	0
Drysdale (Dodgers), p	0	0	0	0	0	0
dF. Robinson (Reds)	1	0	0	0	0	0
Koufax (Dodgers), p	0	0	0	0	0	0
Farrell (Astros), p	0	0	0	0	0	0
gWilliams (Cut s)	1	0	0	0	0	0
Gibson (Cardinals), p	0	0	0	1	0	0
Totals	36	6	11	27	10	0

AMERICANS	AB.	R.	H.	PO.	A.	E.
McAuliffe (Tigers), ss	3	2	2	3	0	0
McDowell (Indians), p	0	0	0	0	1	0
eOliva (Twins), rf	2	0	1	0	0	0
B. Robinson (Orioles), 3b	4	1	1	1	2	0
Alvis (Indians), 3b	1	0	0	0	0	0
Killebrew (Twins), 1b	3	1	1	7	1	0
Colavito (Indians), rf	4	0	1	1	0	0
Fisher (White Sox), p	0	0	0	1	1	0
hPepitone (Yankees)	1	0	0	0	0	0
Horton (Tigers), lf	3	0	0	2	0	0
Mantilla (Red Sox), 2b	2	0	0	1	1	0
Richardson (Yankees), 2b	2	0	0	2	1	0
Davalillo (Indians), cf	2	0	1	1	0	0
Versalles (Twins), ss	1	0	0	0	2	0
Battey (Twins), c	2	0	0	4	1	0
Freehan (Twins), c	1	0	1	4	0	0
Pappas (Orioles), p	0	0	0	0	1	0
Grant (Twins), p	0	0	0	0	0	0
aKaline (Tigers)	1	0	0	0	0	0
Richert (Senators), p	0	0	0	0	0	0
cHall (Twins), cf	2	1	0	0	0	0
Totals	34	5	8	27	11	0

National League	3	2	0	0	0	0	1	0	0 – 6
American League	0	0	0	1	4	0	0	0	0 – 5

Nationals	IP.	H.	R.	ER.	BB.	SO.
Marichal (Giants)	3	1	0	0	0	0
Maloney (Reds)	1⅔	5	5	5	2	1
Drysdale (Dodgers)	⅓	0	0	0	0	0
Koufax (Dodgers)	1	0	0	0	2	1
Farrell (Astros)	1	0	0	0	1	0
Gibson (Cardinals)	2	2	0	0	1	3

Americans	IP.	H.	R.	ER.	BB.	SO.
Pappas (Orioles)	1	4	3	3	1	0
Grant (Twins)	2	2	2	1	3
Richert (Senators)	2	1	0	0	0	2
McDowell (Indians)	2	3	1	1	1	2
Fisher (White Sox)	2	1	0	0	0	0

Winning pitcher—Koufax. Losing pitcher—McDowell.

aGrounded out for Grant in third. bFlied out for Marichal in fourth. cWalked for Richert in fifth. dStruck out for Drysdale in sixth. eGrounded out for McDowell in seventh. fHit into force play for Stargell in seventh. gGrounded out for Farrell in eighth. hStruck out for Fisher in ninth. Runs batted in—Mays, Stargell 2. Santo, Torre 2. McAuliffe 2, Killebrew 2, Colavito. Two-base hit—Oliva. Home runs—Mays, Torre, Stargell, McAuliffe, Killebrew. Sacrifice hit—Rose. Double plays—B. Robinson, Mantilla and Killebrew; Wills, Rose and Banks; McDowell, Richardson and Killebrew. Left on bases—Nationals 7, Americans 8. Wild pitch—Maloney. Umpires—Stevens, DiMuro and Valentine (A. L.), Weyer, Williams and Kibler (N. L.). Time of game—2:45. Attendance—46,706.

Game of 1966—Busch Memorial Stadium, St. Louis, July 12

Most of the 49,936 fans who attended the 1966 contest will best remember the occasion for the searing 105-degree temperature, but they also have memories of a sparkling 2-1 National League victory in ten innings. The game was played out of turn in St. Louis to help commemorate the city's bicentennial and to celebrate the opening of the new riverfront stadium.

The contest marked only the fourth in the midsummer series to go extra innings, and as on two previous occasions, a member of the Cardinals played a decisive role. Tim McCarver, a St. Louis catcher, scored the winning run on a single by Maury Wills after opening the tenth inning with a hit and advancing to second on a sacrifice. Pete Richert, who took the mound in the tenth, was the victim.

Although allowing just one hit in three innings, Sandy Koufax permitted the lone A. L. run. With one out in the second, Brooks Robinson smashed a liner to left field and wound up with a triple when Hank Aaron lost sight of the ball momentarily in the background of white shirts and it skipped past him to the wall. Robinson scored when Koufax uncorked a wild pitch.

The Nationals tied the game against Jim Kaat in the fourth frame. Willie Mays and Roberto Clemente led off with singles, and after Willie McCovey forced Clemente, Ron Santo beat out a slow roller as Mays raced across the plate. The box score:

AMERICANS	AB.	R.	H.	PO.	A.	E.
McAuliffe (Tigers), ss	3	0	0	1	1	0
Stottlemyre (Yankees), p	0	0	0	0	0	0
hColavito (Indians)	1	0	0	0	0	0
Siebert (Indians), p	0	0	0	0	1	0
Richert (Senators), p	0	0	0	0	1	0
Kaline (Tigers), cf	4	0	1	3	0	0
Agee (White Sox), cf	0	0	0	1	0	0
F. Robinson (Orioles), lf	4	0	0	2	0	0
Oliva (Twins), rf	4	0	0	0	0	0
B. Robinson (Orioles), 3b	4	1	3	4	4	0
Scott (Red Sox), 1b	2	0	0	4	1	0
eCash (Tigers), 1b	2	0	0	4	0	0
Freehan (Tigers), c	2	0	1	4	0	0
Battey (Twins), c	1	0	0	1	0	0
Knoop (Angels), 2b	2	0	0	3	1	0
gRichardson (Yanks), 2b	2	0	0	1	1	0
McLain (Tigers), p	1	0	0	0	1	0
Kaat (Twins), p	0	0	0	0	0	0
cKillebrew (Twins)	1	0	1	0	0	0
dFregosi (Angels), ss	2	0	0	1	0	0
Totals	35	1	6	28	11	0

NATIONALS	AB.	R.	H.	PO.	A.	E.
Mays (Giants), cf	4	1	1	3	0	0
Clemente (Pirates), rf	4	0	2	2	0	0
Aaron (Braves), lf	4	0	0	2	0	0
McCovey (Giants), 1b	3	0	0	10	1	0
Santo (Cubs), 3b	4	0	1	2	2	0
Torre (Braves), c	3	0	0	5	0	0
McCarver (Cardinals), c	1	1	1	1	0	0
Lefebvre (Dodgers), 2b	2	0	0	2	0	0
Hunt (Mets), 2b	1	0	0	0	1	0
Cardenas (Reds), ss	2	0	0	2	2	0
fStargell (Pirates)	1	0	0	0	0	0
Wills (Dodgers), ss	1	0	1	1	1	0
Koufax (Dodgers), p	0	0	0	0	0	0
aFlood (Cardinals)	1	0	0	0	0	0
Bunning (Phillies), p	0	0	0	0	0	0
bAllen (Phillies)	1	0	0	0	0	0
Marichal (Giants), p	0	0	0	0	0	0
iHart (Giants)	1	0	0	0	0	0
Perry (Giants), p	0	0	0	0	0	0
Totals	33	2	6	30	7	0

American League	0	1	0	0	0	0	0	0	0	0 – 1
National League	0	0	0	1	0	0	0	0	0	1 – 2

One out when winning run scored.

Americans	IP.	H.	R.	ER.	BB.	SO.
McLain (Tigers)	3	0	0	0	0	3
Kaat (Twins)	2	3	1	1	0	1
Stottlemyre (Yankees)	2	0	0	0	1	0
Siebert (Indians)	2	0	0	0	0	1
Richert (Senators)	⅓	2	1	1	0	0

Nationals	IP.	H.	R.	ER.	BB.	SO.
Koufax (Dodgers)	3	1	1	1	0	1
Bunning (Phillies)	2	1	0	0	0	2
Marichal (Giants)	3	3	0	0	0	2
Perry (Giants)	2	1	0	0	1	1

Winning pitcher—Perry. Losing pitcher—Richert.

aGrounded out for Koufax in third. bStruck out for Bunning in fifth. cSingled for Kaat in sixth. dRan for Killebrew in sixth. eGrounded into double play for Scott in seventh. fFouled out for Cardenas in seventh. gGrounded out for Knoop in eighth. hFlied out for Stottlemyre in eighth. iStruck out for Marichal in eighth. Runs batted in—Santo, Wills. Two-base hit—Clemente. Three-base hit—B. Robinson. Sacrifice hit—Hunt. Double play—McCovey, Cardenas and McCovey. Left on bases—Americans 5, Nationals 5. Wild pitches—Koufax, Perry. Umpires—Barlick, Vargo and Engel (N. L.). Umont, Honochick and Neudecker (A. L.). Time of game—2:19. Attendance—49,936.

Game of 1967—Anaheim Stadium, California, July 11

The longest and, some said, the dullest of the mid-season classics took place in the California Angels' one-year-old park, Anaheim Stadium, before 46,309 fans, many of whom weren't around at the finish, 3:41 after the beginning. The National League finally won, 2-1, in the 15th inning.

The contest was noteworthy because of the 30 strikeouts registered by the 12 pitchers who appeared in the game. And because home runs accounted for all the scoring.

Philadelphia's Richie Allen put the N.L. one up in the second inning when he homered off A.L. starter Dean Chance of Minnesota. Baltimore's Brooks Robinson evened the score in the sixth when he banged a four-bagger off Chicago Cubs' righthander Ferguson Jenkins.

Finally, in the top of the 15th, Cincinnati's Tony Perez separated Kansas City hurler Jim (Catfish) Hunter's one-strike fast ball from the gathering gloom and hit it out of the park.

NATIONALS	AB.	R.	H.	PO.	A.	E.
Brock (Cardinals), lf	2	0	0	1	0	0
cMays (Giants), cf	4	0	0	3	0	0
Clemente (Pirates), rf	6	0	1	6	0	0
Aaron (Braves), cf-lf	6	0	1	2	0	0
Cepeda (Cardinals), 1b	6	0	0	6	0	0
Allen (Phillies), 3b	4	1	1	0	2	0
Perez (Reds), 3b	2	1	1	0	3	0
Torre (Braves), c	2	0	0	4	1	0
Haller (Giants), c	1	0	0	7	0	0
gBanks (Cubs)	1	0	1	0	0	0
McCarver (Cardinals), c	2	0	2	7	1	0
Mazeroski (Pirates), 2b	4	0	0	7	1	0
Drysdale (Dodgers), p	0	0	0	0	0	0
kHelms (Reds)	1	0	0	0	0	0
Seaver (Mets), p	0	0	0	0	0	0
Alley (Pirates), ss	5	0	0	1	3	0
Marichal (Giants), p	1	0	0	0	0	0
Jenkins (Cubs), p	1	0	0	0	0	0
Gibson (Cardinals), p	0	0	0	0	1	0
fWynn (Astros)	1	0	1	0	0	0
Short (Phillies), p	0	0	0	0	1	0
iStaub (Astros)	1	0	1	0	0	0
Cuellar (Astros), p	0	0	0	0	0	0
jRose (Reds), 2b	1	0	0	1	0	0
Totals	51	2	9	45	13	0

AMERICANS	AB.	R.	H.	PO.	A.	E.
B. Robinson (Orioles), 3b	6	1	1	0	6	0
Carew (Twins), 2b	3	0	0	2	3	0
McAuliffe (Tigers), 2b	3	0	0	3	2	0
Oliva (Twins), cf	6	0	2	4	0	0
Killebrew (Twins), 1b	6	0	0	15	1	0
Conigliaro (Red Sox), rf	6	0	0	4	0	0
Yastrzemski (Red Sox), lf	4	0	3	2	0	0
Freehan (Tigers), c	5	0	1	13	0	0
Petrocelli (Red Sox), ss	1	0	0	0	1	0
McGlothlin (Angels), p	0	0	0	0	0	0
bMantle (Yankees)	1	0	0	0	0	0
Peters (White Sox), p	0	0	0	0	1	0
dMincher (Angels)	1	0	1	0	0	0
eAgee (White Sox)	0	0	0	0	0	0
Downing (Yankees), p	0	0	0	0	0	0
hAlvis (Indians)	1	0	0	0	0	0
Hunter (Athletics), p	1	0	0	0	0	0
lBerry (White Sox)	1	0	0	0	0	0
Chance (Twins), p	0	0	0	0	0	0
aFregosi (Angels), ss	4	0	1	2	3	0
Totals	49	1	8	45	17	0

Nationals	0	1	0	0	0	0	0	0	0	0	0	0	0	1 – 2
Americans	0	0	0	0	1	0	0	0	0	0	0	0	0	0 – 1

Nationals	IP.	H.	R.	ER.	BB.	SO.
Marichal (Giants)	3	1	0	0	0	3
Jenkins (Cubs)	3	3	1	1	0	6
Gibson (Cardinals)	2	2	0	0	0	2
Short (Phillies)	2	0	0	0	1	1
Cuellar (Astros)	2	1	0	0	0	2
Drysdale (Dodgers)	2	1	0	0	0	2
Seaver (Mets)	1	0	0	0	1	1

Americans	IP.	H.	R.	ER.	BB.	SO.
Chance (Twins)	3	2	1	1	0	1
McGlothlin (Angels)	2	1	0	0	0	2
Peters (White Sox)	3	0	0	0	0	4
Downing (Yankees)	2	2	0	0	0	2
Hunter (Athletics)	5	4	1	1	0	4

Winning pitcher—Drysdale.   Losing pitcher—Hunter.

aSingled for Chance in third inning. bStruck out for McGlothlin in fifth inning. cStruck out for Brock in sixth inning. dSingled for Peters in eighth inning. eRan for Mincher in eighth inning. fSingled for Gibson in ninth inning. gSingled for Haller in tenth inning. hGrounded into fielder's choice for Downing in tenth inning. iSingled for Short in eleventh inning. jFlied out for Cuellar in thirteenth inning. kLined into double play for Drysdale in 15th inning. lStruck out for Hunter in 15th inning. Runs batted in—Allen, Perez, B. Robinson. Two-base hits—Yastrzemski, McCarver. Home runs—Allen, Perez, B. Robinson. Double plays—B. Robinson, Carew and Killebrew; McAuliffe and Killebrew. Stolen base—Aaron. Sacrifice hits—Fregosi, Freehan, Mazeroski. Left on bases—Nationals 5, Americans 7. Bases on balls—Off Short (Yastrzemski), off Seaver (Yastrzemski). Strikeouts—By Marichal 3 (Oliva, Yastrzemski, Freehan), by Jenkins 6 (Killebrew, Conigliaro, Mantle, Fregosi, Carew, Oliva), by Gibson 2 (Conigliaro, Freehan), by Short (Fregosi), by Cuellar 2 (B. Robinson, Oliva), by Drysdale 2 (Hunter, Killebrew), by Seaver (Berry), by Chance (Clemente), by McGlothlin 2 (Allen, Alley), by Peters 4 (Mays, Clemente, Cepeda, Allen), by Downing 2 (Clemente, Allen), by Hunter 4 (Alley 2, Clemente, Perez). Umpires—Runge (A.L.), at plate; Secory (N.L.), first base; DiMuro (A.L.), second base; Burkhart (N.L.), third base; Ashford (A.L.), left field line; Pelekoudas (N.L.), right field line. Time of game—3:41. Attendance—46,309. Gross receipts—$324,428. Official scorers—Bob Addie, Washington Post; Ross Newhan, Long Beach Independent Press-Telegram, and Bob Hunter, Los Angeles Herald-Examiner.

Game of 1968—Astrodome, Houston, July 9

In the first 1-0 game in the 36-year history of All-Star competition, the National League scored an unearned run in the first inning and defeated the American League for the sixth straight time. The game, first in the classic series to be played indoors, packed the Astrodome with a crowd of 48,321 fans, who paid a record total of $383,733 at the gate.

Willie Mays, San Francisco's veteran star, was not scheduled to be in the N.L.'s starting lineup, but drew the assignment because of an injury to Pete Rose of Cincinnati. Batting in the leadoff spot, Mays grounded a single to left field. Cleveland's Luis Tiant, the A.L.'s starting pitcher, attempted to pick Mays off first, but his throw got by Killebrew, allowing Willie to reach second. Curt Flood of St. Louis walked, the fourth ball being a wild pitch that sent Mays to third. From this point, Mays was able to score the game's only run when his San Francisco teammate, Willie McCovey, grounded into a double play.

The N.L. collected only five hits and the A.L. just three. The total of eight tied the previous low set in the five-inning, rain-curtailed game at Philadelphia in 1952.

AMERICANS	AB.	R.	H.	RBI.	PO.	A.
Fregosi (Angels), ss	3	0	1	0	1	6
Campaneris (Athletics), ss	1	0	0	0	1	0
Carew (Twins), 2b	3	0	0	0	2	2
Johnson (Orioles), 2b	1	0	0	0	1	1
Yastr'ski (Red Sox), cf-lf	4	0	0	0	0	0
Howard (Senators), rf	2	0	0	0	0	0
Oliva (Twins), rf	1	0	1	0	2	0
Horton (Tigers), lf	2	0	0	0	1	0
Azcue (Indians), c	1	0	0	0	5	0
Josephson (White Sox), c	0	0	0	0	0	0
Killebrew (Twins), 1b	1	0	0	0	4	0
Powell (Orioles), 1b	2	0	0	0	2	0
Freehan (Tigers), c	2	0	0	0	4	0
McLain (Tigers), p	0	0	0	0	0	0
McDowell (Indians), p	0	0	0	0	0	0
eMantle (Yankees)	1	0	0	0	0	0
Stottlemyre (Yankees), p	0	0	0	0	0	0
John (White Sox), p	0	0	0	0	0	0
Robinson (Orioles), 3b	2	0	0	0	0	1
Wert (Tigers), 3b	1	0	1	0	1	0
Tiant (Indians), p	0	0	0	0	0	0
aHarrelson (Red Sox)	1	0	0	0	0	0
Odom (Athletics), p	0	0	0	0	0	0
Monday (Athletics), cf	2	0	0	0	0	0
Totals	30	0	3	0	24	10

NATIONALS	AB.	R.	H.	RBI.	PO.	A.
Mays (Giants), cf	4	1	1	0	0	0
Flood (Cardinals), lf	1	0	0	0	1	0
M. Alou (Pirates), lf	1	0	1	0	1	0
Javier (Cardinals), 2b	0	0	0	0	0	0
McCovey (Giants), 1b	4	0	0	0	10	0
Aaron (Braves), rf	3	0	1	0	1	0
Santo (Cubs), 3b	2	0	1	0	1	1
Perez (Reds), 3b	0	0	0	0	0	1
Helms (Reds), 2b	3	0	1	0	1	2
Reed (Braves), p	0	0	0	0	0	0
Koosman (Mets), p	0	0	0	0	0	0
Grote (Mets), c	2	0	0	0	3	0
Carlton (Cardinals), p	0	0	0	0	0	1
cStaub (Astros)	1	0	0	0	0	0
Seaver (Mets), p	0	0	0	0	0	0
F. Alou (Braves), lf	0	0	0	0	0	0
Kessinger (Giants), ss	2	0	0	0	1	2
dWilliams (Cubs)	1	0	0	0	0	0
Cardenas (Reds), ss	0	0	0	0	0	0
Drysdale (Dodgers), p	1	0	0	0	0	1
Marichal (Giants), p	0	0	0	0	0	0
bHaller (Dodgers), c	2	0	0	0	6	0
Bench (Reds), c	0	0	0	0	2	0
Totals	27	1	5	0	27	9

Americans	0	0	0	0	0	0	0	0	0	0—0		
Nationals	1	0	0	0	0	0	0	0	0	x—1		

Americans	IP.	H.	R.	ER.	BB.	SO.
Tiant (Indians)	2	2	1	0	2	2
Odom (Athletics)	2	0	0	0	2	2
McLain (Tigers)	2	1	0	0	2	1
McDowell (Indians)	1	1	0	0	0	3
Stottlemyre (Yankees)	⅓	0	0	0	0	1
John (White Sox)	⅔	1	0	0	0	0

Nationals	IP.	H.	R.	ER.	BB.	SO.
Drysdale (Dodgers)	3	1	0	0	0	0
Marichal (Giants)	2	0	0	0	0	3
Carlton (Cardinals)	1	0	0	0	0	1
Seaver (Mets)	2	2	0	0	0	5
Reed (Braves)	⅔	0	0	0	0	1
Koosman (Mets)	⅓	0	0	0	0	1

Winning pitcher—Drysdale.   Losing pitcher—Tiant.

aFlied out for Tiant in third. bFlied out for Marichal in fifth. cPopped out for Carlton in sixth. dFlied out for Kessinger in sixth. eStruck out for McDowell in eighth. Error—Killebrew. Double plays—Carew, Fregosi and Killebrew; Johnson and Powell. Left on bases—Americans 3, Nationals 8. Two-base hits—Fregosi, Helms, Oliva, Wert. Stolen base—Aaron. Bases on balls—Off Tiant 2 (Flood, Aaron), off Odom 2 (Santo, Helms), off McLain 2 (Flood, Santo). Struck out—By Tiant 2 (Grote, Kessinger), by Odom 2 (McCovey, Aaron), by McLain 1 (McCovey), by McDowell 3 (Haller, Mays, McCovey), by Stottlemyre 1 (Aaron), by Marichal 3 (Howard, Powell, Freehan), by Carlton 1 (Fregosi), by Seaver 5 (Yastrzemski, Azcue, Powell, Mantle, Monday), by Reed 1 (Johnson), by Koosman 1 (Yastrzemski). Wild pitch—Tiant. Umpires—Crawford (N.L.), at plate; Napp (A.L.), first base; Steiner (N.L.), second base; Kinnamon (A.L.), third base; Wendelstedt (N.L.), right field line; Odom (A.L.), left field line. Time of game—2:10. Attendance—48,321.

Game of 1969—Robert F. Kennedy Memorial Stadium, Washington, July 23

The National League battered the American League, 9-3, for their seventh consecutive All-Star victory as 45,259 paid $417,832, a new record gate. The win gave the N. L. a margin of 22 victories to the A. L.'s 17, with one game ending in a tie.

The game had been scheduled for Tuesday evening, July 22, but a torrential rain forced postponement until the following day. Willie McCovey of the Giants was the hitting star with two homers, only the fourth player in All-Star history to accomplish the feat. The issue was decided early as the N. L. scored an unearned run in the first, added two in the second on the Reds' Johnny Bench's homer with one on and sent nine men to the plate in the third as they tallied five times, two runs scoring on McCovey's first homer. Willie hit for the circuit again in the fourth to complete his club's scoring. Frank Howard of the host Senators homered in the second and Bill Freehan of the Tigers duplicated in the third. Freehan singled in another run in the fourth for the A. L.'s last tally.

NATIONALS	AB.	R.	H.	RBI.	PO.	A.
Alou (Pirates), cf	4	1	2	0	5	0
Kessinger (Cubs), ss	3	0	0	0	0	0
eMays (Giants)	1	0	0	0	0	0
Menke (Astros), ss	1	0	0	0	1	0
Aaron (Braves), rf	4	1	1	0	0	0
Singer (Dodgers), p	0	0	0	0	0	0
Beckert (Cubs), 2b	1	0	0	0	0	0
McCovey (Giants), 1b	4	2	2	3	2	0
L. May (Reds), 1b	1	0	0	0	3	0
Santo (Cubs), 3b	3	0	0	0	2	1
Perez (Reds), 3b	1	0	0	0	1	1
Jones (Mets), lf	4	2	2	0	3	0
Rose (Reds), lf	1	0	0	0	2	0
Bench (Reds), c	3	2	2	4	4	0
Hundley (Cubs), c	1	0	0	0	3	0
Millan (Braves), 2b	4	1	1	2	1	1
Koosman (Mets), p	0	0	0	0	0	0
Dierker (Astros), p	0	0	0	0	0	0
Niekro (Braves), p	0	0	0	0	0	1
Carlton (Cardinals), p	2	0	1	1	0	1
Gibson (Cardinals), p	0	0	0	0	0	0
dBanks (Cubs)	1	0	0	0	0	0
Clemente (Pirates), rf	1	0	0	0	0	0
Totals	40	9	11	8	27	5

AMERICANS	AB.	R.	H.	RBI.	PO.	A.
Carew (Twins), 2b	3	0	0	0	0	2
Andrews (Red Sox), 2b	1	0	0	0	0	0
Jackson (Athletics), cf-rf	2	0	0	0	2	0
Yastrzemski (Red Sox), lf	1	0	0	0	1	0
F. Robinson (Orioles), rf	2	0	0	0	0	0
Blair (Orioles), cf	2	0	0	0	2	0
Powell (Orioles), 1b	4	0	1	0	9	1
Howard (Senators), lf	1	1	1	1	0	0
bSmith (Red Sox), lf-rf	2	1	0	0	0	0
Bando (Athletics), 3b	3	0	1	0	0	1
McDowell (Indians), p	0	0	0	0	0	0
Culp (Red Sox), p	0	0	0	0	0	0
fWhite (Yankees)	1	0	0	0	0	0
Petrocelli (Red Sox), ss	3	0	1	0	1	3
Fregosi (Angels), ss	1	0	0	0	0	0
Freehan (Tigers), c	2	1	2	4	4	0
Roseboro (Twins), c	1	0	0	0	6	0
gC. May (White Sox)	1	0	0	0	0	0
Stottlemyre (Yankees), p	0	0	0	0	1	0
Odom (Athletics), p	0	0	0	0	0	0
Knowles (Senators), p	0	0	0	0	0	0
aKillebrew (Twins)	1	0	0	0	0	0
McLain (Tigers), p	0	0	0	0	0	0
cMincher (Pilots)	1	0	0	0	0	0
McNally (Orioles), p	0	0	0	0	0	0
B. Robinson (Orioles), 3b ..	1	0	0	1	1	1
Totals	33	3	6	3	27	8

National		1	2	5	1	0	0	0	0	0 – 9
American		0	1	1	1	0	0	0	0	0 – 3

Nationals	IP.	H.	R.	ER.	BB.	SO.
Carlton (Cardinals)	3	2	2	2	1	2
Gibson (Cardinals)	1	2	1	1	1	2
Singer (Dodgers)	2	0	0	0	0	0
Koosman (Mets)	1⅔	1	0	0	0	1
Dierker (Astros)	⅓	1	0	0	0	0
Niekro (Braves)	1	0	0	0	0	2

American	IP.	H.	R.	ER.	BB.	SO.
Stottlemyre (Yankees)	2	4	3	2	0	1
Odom (Athletics)	⅓	5	5	4	0	0
Knowles (Senators)	⅔	0	0	0	0	0
McLain (Tigers)	1	1	1	1	2	2
McNally (Orioles)	2	1	0	0	1	1
McDowell (Indians)	2	0	0	0	0	4
Culp (Red Sox)	1	0	0	0	0	2

Winning pitcher—Carlton. Losing pitcher—Stottlemyre.

aFlied out for Knowles in third. bRan for Howard in fourth. cStruck out for McLain in fourth. dLined out for Gibson in fifth. eFlied out for Kessinger in fifth. fStruck out for Culp in ninth. gStruck out for Roseboro in ninth. Errors—Howard, Petrocelli. Left on bases—Nationals 7, Americans 5. Two-base hits—Millan, Carlton, Petrocelli. Home runs—Bench, Howard, McCovey 2, Freehan. Bases on balls—Off Carlton 1 (Jackson), off Gibson 1 (Howard), off McLain 2 (Santo, Bench), off McNally 1 (Alou). Struck out—By Carlton 2 (F. Robinson, Petrocelli), by Gibson 2 (Powell, Mincher), by Koosman 1 (B. Robinson), by Niekro 2 (White, C. May), by Stottlemyre 1 (Carlton), by McLain 2 (Aaron, Millan), by McNally 1 (McCovey), by McDowell 4 (Clemente, Alou, Menke, L. May), by Culp 2 (Perez, Hundley). Wild pitch—Stottlemyre. Umpires—Flaherty (AL) plate, Donatelli (NL) first base, Stewart (AL) second base, Gorman (NL) third base, Springstead (AL) left field line, Venzon (NL) right field line. Time of game—2:38. Attendance—45,259.

Game of 1970—Riverfront Stadium, Cincinnati, July 14

The 1970 All-Star game was one inning too long as far as the American League was concerned and the Nationals scored their eighth straight win of the series, 5-4, in 12 innings.

The Americans held a 4-1 lead going into the last half of the ninth inning, but a home run by San Francisco's Dick Dietz, singles by New York's Bud Harrelson, Houston's Joe Morgan and San Francisco's Willie McCovey and a sacrifice fly by Pittsburgh's Roberto Clemente tied the score.

The decisive run came across in the 12th on successive two-out singles by Cincinnati's Pete Rose, Los Angeles' Bill Grabarkewitz and Chicago's Jim Hickman.

Carl Yastrzemski, of the Boston Red Sox, with four hits, was selected as the outstanding player of the game.

AMERICANS	AB.	R.	H.	RBI.	PO.	A.
Aparicio (White Sox), ss	6	0	0	0	1	4
Yastrzemski (Red Sox), cf-1b	6	1	4	1	8	0
F. Robinson (Orioles), rf-lf	3	0	0	0	1	0
Horton (Tigers), lf	2	1	2	0	1	0
Powell (Orioles), 1b	3	0	0	0	5	0
Otis (Royals), cf	3	0	0	0	2	0
Killebrew (Twins), 3b	2	0	1	0	0	0
bHarper (Brewers)	0	0	0	0	0	0
B. Robinson (Orioles), 3b	3	1	2	2	1	1
Howard (Senators), lf	2	0	0	0	0	0
Oliva (Twins), rf	2	0	1	0	0	0
D. Johnson (Orioles), 2b	5	0	1	0	5	1
Wright (Angels), p	0	0	0	0	0	0
Freehan (Tigers), c	1	0	0	0	4	0
Fosse (Indians), c	2	1	1	1	7	0
Palmer (Orioles), p	1	0	0	0	0	0
McDowell (Indians), p	0	0	0	0	0	3
dA. Johnson (Angels)	1	0	0	0	0	0
J. Perry (Twins), p	0	0	0	0	0	0
fFregosi (Angels)	1	0	0	0	0	0
Hunter (Athletics), p	0	0	0	0	0	0
Peterson (Yankees), p	0	0	0	0	0	0
Stottlemyre (Yankees), p	0	0	0	0	0	0
Alomar (Angels), 2b	1	0	0	0	0	2
Totals	44	4	12	4	35	11

NATIONALS	AB.	R.	H.	RBI.	PO.	A.
Mays (Giants), cf	3	0	0	0	3	0
G. Perry (Giants), p	0	0	0	0	0	2
eMcCovey (Giants), 1b	2	0	1	1	1	0
gOsteen (Dodgers), p	0	0	0	0	1	0
iTorre (Cardinals)	1	0	0	0	0	0
Allen (Cardinals), 1b	3	0	0	0	4	0
Gibson (Cardinals), p	0	0	0	0	0	0
hClemente (Pirates), rf	1	0	0	1	2	0
Aaron (Braves), rf	2	0	0	0	1	0
Rose (Reds), rf-lf	3	1	1	0	3	0
Perez (Reds), 3b	3	0	0	0	1	1
Grabarkewitz (Dodgers), 3b	3	0	1	0	0	1
Carty (Braves), lf	1	0	0	0	0	0
Hickman (Cubs), lf-1b	4	0	1	1	6	1
Bench (Reds), c	3	0	0	0	5	1
Dietz (Giants), c	2	1	1	1	2	0
Kessinger (Cubs), ss	2	0	2	0	0	0
Harrelson (Mets), ss	3	2	2	0	0	4
Beckert (Cubs), 2b	2	0	0	0	2	1
Gaston (Padres), cf	2	0	0	0	2	0
Seaver (Mets), p	0	0	0	0	0	0
aStaub (Expos)	1	0	0	0	0	0
Merritt (Reds), p	0	0	0	0	0	0
cMenke (Astros), 2b	0	0	0	0	2	1
Morgan (Astros), 2b	2	1	1	0	1	2
Totals	43	5	10	4	36	14

Americans	0	0	0	0	1	1	2	0	0	0	0'-	4
Nationals	0	0	0	0	0	1	0	3	0	0	1-	5

†Two out when winning run scored.

Americans	IP.	H.	R.	ER.	BB.	SO.
Palmer (Orioles)	3	1	0	0	1	3
McDowell (Indians)	3	1	0	0	3	3
J. Perry (Twins)	2	1	1	1	1	3
Hunter (Athletics)	1/3	3	3	3	0	0
Peterson (Yankees)	0*	1	0	0	0	0
Stottlemyre (Yankees)	1 2/3	0	0	0	0	2
Wright (Angels)	1 2/3	3	1	1	0	0

Nationals	IP.	H.	R.	ER.	BB.	SO.
Seaver (Mets)	3	1	0	0	0	4
Merritt (Reds)	2	1	0	0	0	1
G. Perry (Giants)	2	4	2	2	1	0
Gibson (Cardinals)	2	3	2	2	1	2
Osteen (Dodgers)	3	3	0	0	1	0

*Pitched to one batter in ninth.

Winning pitcher—Osteen. Losing pitcher—Wright.

aFlied out for Seaver in third. bRan for Killebrew in fifth. cWalked for Merritt in fifth. dHit into force play for McDowell in seventh. eGrounded into double play for G. Perry in seventh. fFlied out for J. Perry in ninth. gRan for McCovey in ninth. hHit sacrifice fly for Gibson in ninth. iGrounded out for Osteen in twelfth. Errors—None. Double plays—Aparicio and Yastrzemski; Harrelson, Morgan and Hickman. Left on bases—Americans 9, Nationals 10. Two-base hits—Oliva, Yastrzemski. Three-base hit—B. Robinson. Home run—Dietz. Sacrifice hit—McDowell. Sacrifice flies—Fosse, Clemente. Caught stealing—Harper. Struck out—By Palmer 3 (Mays, Bench, Perez), by McDowell 3 (Perez, Bench 2), by J. Perry 3 (Allen, Rose, Fregosi), by Stottlemyre 2 (Rose, Hickman), by Seaver 4 (Aparicio, F. Robinson, Killebrew, Howard), by Merritt 1 (F. Robinson), by Gibson 2 (D. Johnson, Aparicio). Bases on balls—Off Palmer 1 (Carty), off McDowell 3 (Menke, Allen, Rose), off J. Perry 1 (Gaston), off G. Perry 1 (Oliva), off Gibson 1 (Fosse), off Osteen 1 (Horton). Hit by pitcher—J. Perry (Menke). Umpires—Barlick (NL) plate, Rice (AL) first base, Secory (NL) second base, Haller (AL) third base, Dezelan (NL) left field, Goetz (AL) right field. Official scorers—Bob Hunter, Los Angeles Herald Examiner; Earl Lawson, Cincinnati Post and Times-Star; Si Burick, Dayton News. Time of game—3:19. Attendance—51,838.

Game of 1971—Tiger Stadium, Detroit, July 13

In a contest featured by six home runs, three for each side, the American League finally snapped the National League's All-Star Game winning streak at eight with a 6-4 triumph that pleased the majority of the crowd of 53,559 that paid a record All-Star Game gate of $435,134.

For a while, though, it seemed that the senior circuit would add another notch to its string as homers by Cincinnati's Johnny Bench and Atlanta's Hank Aaron off of Oakland's young lefty, Vida Blue, gave the Nationals an early 3-0 lead. But the Americans fell on Pittsburgh's voluble Dock Ellis in the third inning when Baltimore's Frank Robinson and Oakland's Reggie Jackson connected for four-ply swats, each coming with a man on base. This gave the Americans a one-run lead and they were never headed thereafter.

The lead was increased later when the Minnesota bomber, Harmon Killebrew, hit a circuit clout with a mate aboard in the sixth inning. Roberto Clemente, the Pittsburgh Pirates' great star, closed out the scoring with a home run in the eighth.

As a result of the victory, the American League, which once led the series, 12 games to four, closed the gap to 23-18, with one tie.

Frank Robinson won the Arch Ward Trophy as the game's most valuable player.

NATIONALS	AB.	R.	H.	RBI.	PO.	A.
Mays (Giants), cf	2	0	0	0	0	0
Clemente (Pirates), rf	2	1	1	1	1	0
Millan (Braves), 2b	0	0	0	0	1	1
Aaron (Braves), rf	2	1	1	1	0	0
May (Reds), 1b	1	0	0	0	6	0
Torre (Cardinals), 3b	3	0	0	0	1	0
fSanto (Cubs), 3b	1	0	0	0	0	1
Stargell (Pirates), lf	2	1	0	0	2	0
gBrock (Cardinals)	1	0	0	0	0	0
McCovey (Giants), 1b	2	0	0	0	4	0
Marichal (Giants), p	0	0	0	0	0	1
Kessinger (Cubs), ss	2	0	0	0	1	1
Bench (Reds), c	4	1	2	2	5	0
Beckert (Cubs), 2b	3	0	0	0	0	5
Rose (Reds), rf	0	0	0	0	0	0
Harrelson (Mets), ss	2	0	0	0	1	2
Jenkins (Cubs), p	0	0	0	0	0	0
cColbert (Padres)	1	0	0	0	0	0
Wilson (Astros), p	0	0	0	0	0	0
Ellis (Pirates), p	1	0	0	0	0	0
Davis (Dodgers), cf	1	0	1	0	2	0
eBonds (Giants), cf	1	0	0	0	0	0
Totals	31	4	5	4	24	11

AMERICANS	AB.	R.	H.	RBI.	PO.	A.
Carew (Twins), 2b	1	1	0	0	1	2
Rojas (Royals), 2b	1	0	0	0	1	1
Murcer (Yankees), cf	3	0	1	0	1	0
Cuellar (Orioles), p	0	0	0	0	0	0
dBuford (Orioles)	1	0	0	0	0	0
Lolich (Tigers), p	0	0	0	0	0	3
Yastrzemski (Red Sox), lf	3	0	0	0	0	0
F. Robinson (Orioles), rf	2	1	1	2	2	0
Kaline (Tigers), rf	2	1	0	2	0	0
Cash (Tigers), 1b	2	0	0	0	7	0
Killebrew (Twins), 1b	2	1	1	2	4	0
B. Robinson (Orioles), 3b	3	0	1	0	1	3
Freehan (Tigers), c	3	0	0	0	6	1
Munson (Yankees), c	0	0	0	0	1	0
Aparicio (Red Sox), ss	3	1	1	0	1	2
Blue (Athletics), p	0	0	0	0	0	0
aJackson (Athletics)	1	1	1	2	0	0
Palmer (Orioles), p	0	0	0	0	0	0
bHoward (Senators)	1	0	0	0	0	0
Otis (Royals), cf	1	0	0	0	0	0
Totals	29	6	7	6	27	12

Nationals	0	2	1	0	0	0	0	1	0 – 4
Americans	0	0	4	0	0	2	0	0	x – 6

Nationals	IP.	H.	R.	ER.	BB.	SO.
Ellis (Pirates)	3	4	4	4	1	2
Marichal (Giants)	2	0	0	0	1	1
Jenkins (Cubs)	1	3	2	2	0	0
Wilson (Astros)	2	0	0	0	1	2

Americans	IP.	H.	R.	ER.	BB.	SO.
Blue (Athletics)	3	2	3	3	0	3
Palmer (Orioles)	2	1	0	0	0	2
Cuellar (Orioles)	2	1	0	0	1	2
Lolich (Tigers)	2	1	1	1	0	1

Winning pitcher—Blue. Losing pitcher—Ellis.

aHomered for Blue in third. bGrounded out for Palmer in fifth. cStruck out for Jenkins in seventh. dStruck out for Cuellar in seventh. eStruck out for Davis in eighth. fGrounded out for Torre in eighth. gBunted and was thrown out for Stargell in ninth. Errors—None. Double plays—B. Robinson, Rojas and Killebrew; Beckert, Kessinger and May; Santo, Millan and May. Left on bases—Nationals 2, Americans 2. Home runs—Bench, Aaron, Jackson, F. Robinson, Killebrew, Clemente. Bases on balls—Off Ellis 1 (Carew), off Marichal 1 (Carew), off Wilson 1 (Yastrzemski), off Cuellar 1 (May). Strikeouts—By Ellis 2 (Cash 2), by Marichal 1 (Carew), by Wilson 2 (Buford, Kaline), by Blue 3 (McCovey, Ellis, Torre), by Palmer 2 (Stargell, Clemente), by Cuellar 2 (Stargell, Colbert), by Lolich 1 (Bonds). Hit by pitcher—By Blue (Stargell). Umpires—Umont (AL) plate, Pryor (NL) first base, O'Donnell (AL) second base, Harvey (NL) third base, Denkinger (AL) right field, Colosi (NL) left field. Time—2:05. Attendance—53,559.

Game of 1972—Atlanta Stadium, Atlanta, July 25

Late-inning tallies by the National League gave it a 4-3 ten-inning victory over the American League and enabled the senior circuit to resume its winning ways in the annual All-Star Game.

The triumph gave the Nationals a 24-18 margin in the series (there was one tie) and their ninth win in the last ten games.

A home run with a man on by Kansas City's Cookie Rojas in the eighth inning had given the Americans a 3-2 lead going into the last of the ninth. Rojas' blast, which added to an American run scored earlier in the contest, had offset Atlanta's Henry Aaron's home run with a mate aboard in the sixth frame.

But in the bottom of the ninth, singles by the Cubs' Billy Williams and the Pirates' Manny Sanguillen opened the door for the run that tied the game. It came while a forceout was being made at second base on a grounder by the Astros' Lee May.

San Diego's Nate Colbert drew a walk to start the lower half of the tenth inning and was sacrificed to second by San Francisco's Chris Speier. Cincinnati's Joe Morgan, who was voted the Arch Ward Trophy as the game's most valuable player, then shot a line single to right-center field and Colbert scored easily with the winning run.

NATIONALS	AB.	R.	H.	RBI.	PO.	A.
Morgan (Reds), 2b	4	0	1	1	3	5
Mays (Mets), cf	2	0	0	0	2	0
Cedeno (Astros), cf	2	1	1	0	0	0
Aaron (Braves), rf	3	1	1	2	0	0
Oliver (Pirates), rf	1	0	0	0	0	0
Stargell (Pirates), lf	1	0	0	0	0	0
Williams (Cubs), lf	2	1	1	0	0	0
Bench (Reds), c	2	0	1	0	3	0
Sanguillen (Pirates), c	2	0	1	0	6	0
May (Astros), 1b	4	0	1	1	13	0
Torre (Cardinals), 3b	3	0	1	0	1	2
Santo (Cubs), 3b	1	0	0	0	0	0
Kessinger (Cubs), ss	2	0	0	0	0	0
Carlton (Phillies), p	0	0	0	0	0	0
Stoneman (Expos), p	1	0	0	0	0	0
McGraw (Mets), p	0	0	0	0	0	0
eColbert (Padres)	0	1	0	0	0	0
Gibson (Cardinals), p	0	0	0	0	1	0
Blass (Pirates), p	0	0	0	0	0	0
aBeckert (Cubs)	1	0	0	0	0	0
Sutton (Dodgers), p	0	0	0	0	0	0
Speier (Giants), ss	2	0	0	0	1	5
Totals	33	4	8	4	30	14

AMERICANS	AB.	R.	H.	RBI.	PO.	A.
Carew (Twins), 2b	2	0	1	1	2	3
cRojas (Royals), 2b	1	1	1	2	3	1
Murcer (Yankees), cf	3	0	0	0	1	0
Scheinblum (Royals), rf	1	0	0	0	1	0
Jackson (Athletics), rf-cf	4	0	2	0	5	0
Allen (White Sox), 1b	3	0	0	0	4	0
Cash (Tigers), 1b	1	0	0	0	3	0
Yastrzemski (Red Sox), lf ..	3	0	0	0	3	0
Grich (Orioles), ss	4	0	0	0	0	3
Robinson (Orioles), 3b	2	0	0	0	0	1
Bando (Athletics), 3b	2	0	0	0	1	1
Freehan (Tigers), c	1	0	0	0	3	0
Fisk (Red Sox), c	2	1	1	0	2	0
Palmer (Orioles), p	0	0	0	0	0	0
Lolich (Tigers), p	1	0	0	0	0	0
Perry (Indians), p	0	0	0	0	0	0
bSmith (Red Sox)	1	0	0	0	0	0
Wood (White Sox), p	0	0	0	0	0	0
dPiniella (Royals)	1	0	0	0	0	0
McNally (Orioles), p	0	0	0	0	0	1
Totals	33	3	6	3	28	10

Americans	0	0	0	0	2	0	0 – 3
Nationals	0	0	2	0	0	1	1 – 4

One out when winning run scored.

Americans	IP.	H.	R.	ER.	BB.	SO.
Palmer (Orioles)	3	1	0	0	1	2
Lolich (Tigers)	2	2	0	0	1	1
Perry (Indians)	2	3	2	2	0	1
Wood (White Sox)	2	2	1	1	1	1
McNally (Orioles)	1/3	1	1	1	1	0

Nationals	IP.	H.	R.	ER.	BB.	SO.
Gibson (Cardinals)	2	1	0	0	0	0
Blass (Pittsburgh)	1	1	1	1	1	0
Sutton (Dodgers)	2	1	0	0	0	2
Carlton (Phillies)	1	0	0	0	1	0
Stoneman (Expos)	2	2	2	2	0	2
McGraw (Mets)	2	1	0	0	0	4

Winning pitcher—McGraw. Losing pitcher—McNally.

aFlied out for Blass in third. bStruck out for Perry in eighth. cHomered for Carew in eighth. dGrounded out for Wood in tenth. eWalked for McGraw in tenth. Errors—None. Double plays—Carew and Allen; May unassisted; May, Speier and May; Bando, Rojas and Cash. Left on bases—Americans 3, Nationals 5. Two-base hits—Jackson, Rudi. Home runs—Aaron, Rojas. Sacrifice hits—Palmer, Speier. Stolen base—Morgan. Bases on balls—Off Palmer 1 (Stargell), off Wood 1 (Morgan), off McNally 1 (Colbert), off Blass 1 (Freehan), off Carlton 1 (Carew). Strikeouts—By Palmer 2 (Aaron, Torre), by Lolich 1 (Mays), by Perry 1 (Stoneman), by Wood 1 (Cedeno), by Sutton 2 (Grich, Lolich), by Stoneman 2 (Yastrzemski, Smith), by McGraw 4 (Jackson, Cash, Grich, Fisk). Umpires—Landes (NL) plate, Di-Muro (AL) first base, Weyer (NL) second base, Neudecker (AL) third base, Dale (NL) left field, Kunkel (AL) right field. Time—2:26. Attendance—53,107.

Game of 1973—Royals Stadium, Kansas City, July 24

The 1973 All-Star Game was generally agreed to be one of the least exciting as the National League, paced by San Francisco's Bobby Bonds, posted a lopsided 7-1 win, its 10th in the last 11 games.

Bonds entered the game in the fourth inning and, on his first at bat in the fifth, belted a home run off California's Bill Singer. Then, in the seventh frame, the Giants' super star cracked a line drive to center and stretched what should have been a single into a double.

Cincinnati's Johnny Bench and Los Angeles' Willie Davis also hit homers. A record 54 players appeared in the contest.

The N. L. now leads the series 25-18, with one tie.

NATIONALS	AB.	R.	H.	RBI.	PO.	A.	AMERICANS	AB.	R.	H.	RBI.	PO.	A.
Rose (Reds), lf	3	1	0	0	1	0	Campaneris (Athletics), ss	3	0	0	0	1	2
Twitchell (Phillies), p	0	0	0	0	0	0	Brinkman (Tigers), ss	1	0	0	0	1	1
Giusti (Pirates), p	0	0	0	0	0	0	Carew (Twins), 2b	3	0	0	0	5	1
jMota (Dodgers), lf	1	0	0	0	0	0	Rojas (Royals), 2b	0	0	0	1	1	1
Brewer (Dodgers), p	0	0	0	0	0	0	Mayberry (Royals), 1b	3	0	1	0	8	0
Morgan (Reds), 2b	3	2	1	0	2	2	Jackson (Athletics), rf	4	1	1	0	0	0
Johnson (Braves), 2b	1	0	0	0	1	1	Blair (Orioles), cf	0	0	0	0	1	0
Cedeno (Astros), cf	3	0	1	3	0	0	Otis (Royals), cf	2	0	2	1	0	0
Russell (Dodgers), ss	2	0	0	0	0	2	May (Brewers), cf-rf	2	0	0	0	0	0
Aaron (Braves), 1b	2	0	1	1	3	1	Murcer (Yankees), lf	3	0	0	0	0	1
Torre (Cards), 1b-3b	3	0	0	0	5	0	Fisk (Red Sox), c	2	0	0	0	3	0
Williams (Cubs), rf	2	0	1	0	0	0	Munson (Yankees), c	2	0	0	0	5	1
Bonds (Giants), rf	2	1	2	2	0	0	Robinson (Orioles), 3b	2	0	0	1	1	3
Bench (Reds), c	3	1	1	1	3	0	Bando (Athletics), 3b	1	0	0	0	0	1
fSimmons (Cards), c	1	0	0	0	1	1	Nelson (Rangers), 3b	0	0	0	0	1	0
Santo (Cubs), 3b	1	1	1	0	0	1	kHorton (Tigers)	1	0	0	0	0	0
hColbert (Padres)	1	0	0	0	0	0	Hunter (Athletics), p	0	0	0	0	0	0
Fairly (Expos), 1b	0	0	0	0	4	0	Holtzman (Athletics), p	0	0	0	0	0	0
Speier (Giants), ss	2	0	0	0	1	1	Blyleven (Twins), p	0	0	0	0	0	0
dStargell (Pirates), lf	1	0	0	0	1	0	bBell (Indians)	1	0	1	0	0	0
iMays (Mets)	1	0	0	0	0	0	Singer (Angels), p	0	0	0	0	0	1
Seaver (Mets), p	0	0	0	0	0	1	cKelly (White Sox)	1	0	0	0	0	0
Watson (Astros), lf	0	0	0	0	0	0	Ryan (Angels), p	0	0	0	0	0	0
Wise (Cardinals), p	0	0	0	0	1	0	gSpencer (Rangers)	1	0	0	0	0	0
aEvans (Braves)	0	0	0	0	0	0	Lyle (Yankees), p	0	0	0	0	0	0
Osteen (Dodgers), p	0	0	0	0	0	1	Fingers (Athletics), p	0	0	0	0	0	0
Sutton (Dodgers), p	0	0	0	0	0	1	Totals	32	1	5	1	27	12
eDavis (Dodgers), cf	2	1	2	2	1	0							
Totals	34	7	10	7	27	12							

Nationals	0	2		1	2	2		0	0	0 − 7
Americans	1	0		0	0	0		0	0	0 − 1

Nationals	IP.	H.	R.	ER.	BB.	SO.	Americans	IP.	H.	R.	ER.	BB.	SO.
Wise (Cardinals)	2	2	1	1	0	1	Hunter (Athletics)	1⅓	1	0	0	0	1
Osteen (Dodgers)	2	2	0	0	1	1	Holtzman (Athletics)	⅔	1	0	0	0	0
Sutton (Dodgers)	1	0	0	0	0	0	Blyleven (Twins)	1	2	2	2	2	0
Twitchell (Phillies)	1	1	0	0	0	1	Singer (Angels)	2	3	3	3	1	2
Giusti (Pirates)	1	0	0	0	0	0	Ryan (Angels)	2	2	2	2	2	2
Seaver (Mets)	1	0	0	0	1	0	Lyle (Yankees)	1	1	0	0	0	1
Brewer (Dodgers)	1	0	0	0	1	2	Fingers (Athletics)	1	0	0	0	0	0

Winning pitcher—Wise. Losing pitcher—Blyleven.

aWalked for Wise in third. bTripled for Blyleven in third. cPopped out for Singer in fifth. dStruck out for Speier in sixth. eHomered for Sutton in sixth. fCalled out on strikes for Bench in seventh. gFlied out for Ryan in seventh. hFouled out for Santo in eighth. iStruck out for Stargell in eighth. jHit into force play for Giusti in eighth. kStruck out for Nelson in ninth. Errors—None. Double play—Rojas, Brinkman and Mayberry. Left on bases—Nationals 6, Americans 7. Two-base hits—Jackson, Morgan, Mayberry, Bonds. Three-base hit—Bell. Home runs—Bench, Bonds, Davis. Sacrifice hit—Osteen. Stolen base—Otis. Passed ball—Fisk. Bases on balls—Off Blyleven 2 (Evans, Morgan), off Singer 1 (Santo), off Ryan 2 (Santo, Rose), off Osteen 1 (Mayberry), off Seaver 1 (Rojas), off Brewer 1 (Murcer). Strikeouts—By Hunter 1 (Cedeno), by Singer 2 (Speier, Cedeno), by Ryan 2 (Stargell, Simmons), by Lyle 1 (Mays), by Wise 1 (Campaneris), by Osteen 1 (Campaneris), by Twitchell 1 (Jackson), by Brewer 2 (Munson, Horton). Umpires—Chylak (AL) plate, Burkhart (NL) first base, Barnett (AL) second base, W. Williams (NL) third base, Luciano (AL) left field, Engel (NL) right field. Time—2:45. Attendance—40,849.

Official scorers—Sid Bordman, Kansas City Star; Russell Schneider, Cleveland Plain Dealer; Dick Young, New York Daily News.

Game of 1974—Three Rivers Stadium, Pittsburgh, July 23

The National League captured its 11th victory out of the last 12 All-Star engagements by posting an easy 7-2 win. The triumph gave the Nationals a 26-18 margin in the series, with one tie.

Los Angeles first baseman Steve Garvey, who wasn't even listed on the official All-Star ballot but had been voted in as a write-in candidate, justified the fans' confidence in him by emerging as the star of the game. Garvey had a single and a double, drove in a run, scored once and sparkled in the field.

St. Louis' Reggie Smith homered for the Nationals. Four hurlers appeared for the American League and none escaped unscathed.

The Americans scored two runs in the third inning for a 2-1 lead and threatened a big inning. However, with two runners on base and two out, Garvey took Bobby Murcer's smash and threw to pitcher Andy Messersmith for the out.

Garvey's double keyed a two-run fourth inning, giving the Nationals the lead for keeps.

AMERICANS	AB.	R.	H.	RBI.	PO.	A.
Carew (Twins), 2b	1	1	0	0	0	1
Grich (Orioles), 2b	3	0	1	0	0	2
Campaneris (Athletics), ss	4	0	0	0	2	3
Jackson (Athletics), rf	3	0	0	0	3	0
Allen (White Sox), 1b	2	0	1	1	2	0
Yastrz'ski (Red Sox), 1b	1	0	0	0	5	0
Murcer (Yankees), cf	2	0	0	0	0	0
Hendrick (Indians), cf	2	0	1	0	3	0
Burroughs (Rangers), lf	0	0	0	0	1	0
Rudi (Athletics), lf	2	0	0	0	1	0
B. Robinson (Orioles), 3b	3	0	0	0	0	0
hMayberry (Royals)	1	0	0	0	0	0
Fingers (Athletics), p	0	0	0	0	0	0
Munson (Yankees), c	3	1	1	0	7	0
Perry (Indians), p	0	0	0	0	0	0
bKaline (Tigers)	1	0	0	0	0	0
Tiant (Red Sox), p	0	0	0	0	0	0
dF. Robinson (Angels)	1	0	0	0	0	0
Hunter (Athletics), p	0	0	0	0	0	0
Chalk (Angels), 3b	1	0	0	0	0	0
Totals	30	2	4	1	24	6

NATIONALS	AB.	R.	H.	RBI.	PO.	A.
Rose (Reds), lf	2	0	0	0	1	0
Brett (Pirates), p	0	0	0	0	0	0
cBrock (Cardinals)	1	1	1	0	0	0
Smith (Cardinals), rf	2	1	1	1	2	0
Morgan (Reds), 2b	2	0	1	1	3	4
gCash (Phillies), 2b	1	0	0	0	0	1
Aaron (Braves), rf	2	0	0	0	0	0
Cedeno (Astros), cf	2	0	0	0	2	0
Bench (Reds), c	3	1	2	0	7	0
Grote (Mets), c	0	0	0	0	1	0
Wynn (Dodgers), cf-rf	3	1	1	0	0	0
Matlack (Mets), p	0	0	0	0	0	0
Grubb (Padres), lf	1	0	0	0	0	0
Garvey (Dodgers), 1b	4	1	2	1	6	2
Cey (Dodgers), 3b	2	0	1	2	0	0
eSchmidt (Phillies), 3b	0	1	0	0	0	1
Bowa (Phillies), ss	2	0	0	0	2	0
fPerez (Reds)	1	0	0	0	0	0
Kessinger (Cubs), ss	1	1	1	1	1	0
Messersmith (Dodgers), p	0	0	0	0	2	1
aGarr (Braves), lf	3	0	0	0	0	0
McGlothen (Cardinals), p	0	0	0	0	0	0
Marshall (Dodgers), p	1	0	0	0	0	1
Totals	33	7	10	6	27	10

Americans	0	0	2	0	0	0	0	0	0 – 2
Nationals	0	1	0	2	1	0	1	2	x – 7

Americans	IP.	H.	R.	ER.	BB.	SO.
Perry (Indians)	3	3	1	1	0	4
Tiant (Red Sox)	2	4	3	2	1	0
Hunter (Athletics)	2	2	1	1	1	3
Fingers (Athletics)	1	1	2	2	1	0

Nationals	IP.	H.	R.	ER.	BB.	SO.
Messersmith (Dodgers)	3	2	2	2	3	4
Brett (Pirates)	2	1	0	0	1	0
Matlack (Mets)	1	1	0	0	1	0
McGlothen (Cardinals)	1	0	0	0	0	1
Marshall (Dodgers)	2	0	0	0	1	2

Winning pitcher—Brett. Losing pitcher—Tiant.

aStruck out for Messersmith in third. bFouled out for Perry in fourth. cSingled for Brett in fifth. dHit into force play for Tiant in sixth. eWalked for Cey in sixth. fStruck out for Bowa in sixth. gFlied out for Morgan in seventh. hGrounded out for B. Robinson in eighth. Errors—Bench, Munson. Double plays—None. Left on bases—Americans 8, Nationals 6. Two-base hits—Cey, Munson, Morgan, Garvey. Three-base hit—Kessinger. Home run—Smith. Stolen bases—Carew, Brock. Sacrifice hit—Perry. Sacrifice fly—Morgan. Wild pitch—Fingers. Bases on balls—Off Tiant 1 (Bench), off Hunter 1 (Schmidt), off Fingers 1 (Schmidt), off Messersmith 3 (Burroughs, Carew, Jackson), off Brett 1 (Burroughs), off Matlack 1 (Munson), off Marshall 1 (Yastrzemski). Strikeouts—By Perry 4 (Rose, Morgan, Bench, Garr), by Hunter 3 (Garvey, Perez, Cedeno), by Messersmith 4 (Campaneris 2, Jackson, Allen), by McGlothen 1 (Jackson), by Marshall 2 (Rudi, Chalk). Umpires—Sudol (NL) plate, Frantz (AL) first base, Vargo (NL) second base, Anthony (AL) third base, Kibler (NL) left field, Maloney (AL) right field. Time—2:37. Attendance—50,706.

Official scorers—Joe Heiling, Houston Post; Charley Feeney, Pittsburgh Post-Gazette; Luke Quay, McKeesport Daily News.

Game of 1975—County Stadium, Milwaukee, July 15

Chicago Cub third baseman Bill Madlock's bases-loaded single in the ninth snapped a 3-3 tie and sent the National League on to a 6-3 victory over the American League in the 46th All-Star Game.

Carl Yastrzemski's three-run homer in the sixth inning had enabled the Americans to overcome an early 3-0 National lead. The Red Sox veteran's blast came off the New York Mets' Tom Seaver.

Madlock and Mets' pitcher Jon Matlack were voted the outstanding players of the game.

The result gave the Nationals a 27-18 margin in the series, with one game ending in a tie.

Reggie Smith opened the N. L. ninth with a bloop single. After Al Oliver had doubled, Larry Bowa was hit by a pitch from reliever Rich Gossage. Madlock grounded a single past third for two runs and Pete Rose hit a sacrifice fly, scoring Bowa to complete the uprising.

NATIONALS	AB.	R.	H.	RBI.	PO.	A.
Rose (Reds), rf-lf	4	0	2	1	4	0
Carter (Expos), lf	0	0	0	0	1	0
Brock (Cardinals), lf	3	1	1	0	2	0
Murcer (Giants), rf	2	0	0	0	1	0
Jones (Padres), p	0	0	0	0	0	1
Morgan (Reds), 2b	4	0	1	0	0	1
Cash (Phillies), 2b	1	0	0	0	0	1
Bench (Reds), c	4	0	1	1	10	1
Garvey (Dodgers), 1b	3	1	2	1	4	1
iPerez (Reds), 1b	1	0	0	0	1	1
Wynn (Dodgers), cf	2	1	1	1	1	0
Smith (Cardinals), cf-rf	2	1	1	0	0	0
Cey (Dodgers), 3b	3	0	1	0	0	1
Seaver (Mets), p	0	0	0	0	0	0
Matlack (Mets), p	0	0	0	0	0	0
jOliver (Pirates), cf	1	1	1	0	0	0
Concepcion (Reds), ss	2	0	1	0	1	1
hLuzinski (Phillies)	1	0	0	0	0	0
Bowa (Phillies), ss	0	1	0	0	2	0
Reuss (Pirates), p	1	0	0	0	0	0
bWatson (Astros)	1	0	0	0	0	0
Sutton (Dodgers), p	0	0	0	0	0	0
Madlock (Cubs), 3b	2	0	1	2	0	0
Totals	37	6	13	6	27	8

AMERICANS	AB.	R.	H.	RBI.	PO.	A.
Bonds (Yankees), cf	3	0	0	0	0	1
Scott (Brewers), 1b	2	0	0	0	5	0
Carew (Twins), 2b	5	0	1	0	3	1
Munson (Yankees), c	2	0	1	0	1	1
dWashington (Ath.), cf-lf	1	1	0	1	0	0
Jackson (Athletics), rf	3	0	1	0	2	0
Dent (White Sox), ss	1	0	0	0	0	1
Rudi (Athletics), lf	3	0	1	0	5	0
eHendrick (Indians), rf	1	1	1	0	0	0
Nettles (Yankees), 3b	4	0	1	0	2	2
Tenace (Athletics), 1b-c	3	1	0	0	4	0
Campaneris (Ath.), ss	2	0	2	0	3	2
fLynn (Red Sox), cf	2	0	0	0	1	0
Blue (Athletics), p	0	0	0	0	0	1
aAaron (Brewers)	1	0	0	0	0	0
Busby (Royals), p	0	0	0	0	0	0
cHargrove (Rangers)	1	0	0	0	0	0
Kaat (White Sox), p	0	0	0	0	0	0
gYastrzemski (Red Sox)	1	1	1	3	0	0
Hunter (Yankees), p	0	0	0	0	0	0
Gossage (White Sox), p	0	0	0	0	0	0
kMcRae (Royals)	1	0	0	0	0	0
Totals	36	3	10	3	27	9

```
National ........... 0  2  1    0  0  0    0  0  3 — 6
Americans ......... 0  0  0    0  0  3    0  0  0 — 3
```

Nationals	IP.	H.	R.	ER.	BB.	SO.
Reuss (Pirates)	3	3	0	0	0	2
Sutton (Dodgers)	2	3	0	0	0	1
Seaver (Mets)	1	2	3	3	1	2
Matlack (Mets)	2	2	0	0	0	4
Jones (Padres)	1	0	0	0	0	0

Americans	IP.	H.	R.	ER.	BB.	SO.
Blue (Athletics)	2	5	2	2	0	1
Busby (Royals)	2	4	1	1	0	0
Kaat (White Sox)	2	0	0	0	0	0
Hunter (Yankees)	2*	3	2	2	0	2
Gossage (White Sox)	1	1	1	0	1	0

*Pitched to two batters in ninth.

Winning pitcher—Matlack. Losing pitcher—Hunter.

aLined out for Blue in second. bFlied out for Reuss in fourth. cFlied out for Busby in fourth. dRan for Munson in fifth. eRan for Rudi in sixth. fFlied out for Campaneris in sixth. gHomered for Kaat in sixth. hStruck out for Concepcion in seventh. iCalled out on strikes for Garvey in eighth. jDoubled for Matlack in ninth. kGrounded out for Gossage in ninth. Errors—Concepcion, Tenace. Double plays—None. Left on bases—Nationals 6, Americans 8. Two-base hit—Oliver. Home runs—Garvey, Wynn, Yastrzemski. Stolen bases—Brock, Washington, Hendrick, Nettles. Caught stealing—Concepcion, Washington. Sacrifice fly—Rose. Hit by pitcher—By Reuss (Munson), by Gossage (Bowa). Balk—Busby. Passed ball—Bench. Bases on balls—Off Seaver 1 (Tenace). Strikeouts—By Blue 1 (Concepcion), by Hunter 2 (Luzinski, Perez), by Reuss 2 (Jackson, Bonds), by Sutton 1 (Jackson), by Seaver 2 (Nettles, Scott), by Matlack 4 (Carew, Dent, Tenace, Lynn), by Jones 1 (Scott). Umpires—Haller (AL) plate, Pelekoudas (NL) first base, Springstead (AL) second base, Froemming (NL) third base, Goetz (AL) left field, McSherry (NL) right field. Time—2:35. Attendance—51,480. Official scorers—Charley Feeney, Pittsburgh Post-Gazette; Jerome Holtzman, Chicago Sun-Times; Tom Briere, Minneapolis Tribune.

Game of 1976—Veterans Stadium, Philadelphia, July 13

The National League continued its mastery over the American League, thumping the junior circuit's All-Stars, 7-1, in a game witnessed by 63,974 fans —third largest crowd in All-Star Game history—and which produced gate receipts of $772,346, a record for the mid-summer classic.

The game was held in Philadelphia to help celebrate the American Bicentennial, but the only celebrating was done by the National Leaguers.

Five N. L. pitchers throttled the Americans on five hits. The lone A. L. tally came on a homer by Boston's Fred Lynn.

George Foster of Cincinnati and Cesar Cedeno of Houston hit homers for the Nationals and Foster, who drove in three runs, was voted the game's Most Valuable Player.

The victory was the Nationals' 13th out of the last 14 games played and stretched their current winning streak in All-Star competition to five. The N. L. leads the overall standings, 28-18, with one tie.

The N. L. stars greeted Detroit rookie Mark Fidrych for two runs in the first inning and Foster put the game on ice with his two-run clout in the third.

AMERICANS	AB.	R.	H.	RBI.	PO.	A.	NATIONALS	AB.	R.	H.	RBI.	PO.	A.
LeFlore (Tigers), lf	2	0	1	0	2	0	Rose (Reds), 3b	3	1	2	0	0	1
Yastrzemski (Red Sox), lf	2	0	0	0	0	0	Oliver (Pirates), rf-lf	1	0	0	0	1	0
Carew (Twins), 1b	3	0	0	0	9	2	Garvey (Dodgers), 1b	3	1	1	1	6	0
Brett (Royals), 3b	2	0	0	0	0	1	Cash (Phillies), 2b	1	1	1	0	1	1
Money (Brewers), 3b	1	0	0	0	0	1	Morgan (Reds), 2b	3	1	1	0	2	3
Munson (Yankees), c	2	0	0	0	4	0	Perez (Reds), 1b	0	0	0	0	2	0
Fisk (Red Sox), c	1	0	0	0	1	0	Foster (Reds), cf-rf	3	1	1	3	0	0
dChambliss (Yankees)	1	0	0	0	0	0	Montefusco (Giants), p	0	0	0	0	0	0
Lynn (Red Sox), cf	3	1	1	1	0	0	Russell (Dodgers), ss	1	0	0	0	1	2
eOtis (Royals)	1	0	0	0	0	0	Luzinski (Phillies), lf	3	0	0	0	0	0
Harrah (Rangers), ss	2	0	0	0	0	0	Griffey (Reds), rf	1	1	1	1	1	0
Belanger (Orioles), ss	1	0	0	0	1	1	Bench (Reds), c	2	0	1	0	1	0
Patek (Royals), ss	0	0	0	0	0	1	Cedeno (Astros), cf	2	1	1	2	1	0
Staub (Tigers), rf	2	0	2	0	1	0	Kingman (Mets), rf	2	0	0	0	1	0
Tiant (Red Sox), p	0	0	0	0	0	0	Boone (Phillies), c	2	0	0	0	5	0
cWynegar (Twins)	1	0	0	0	0	0	Concepcion (Reds), ss	2	0	1	0	2	3
Tanana (Angels), p	0	0	0	0	1	0	Bowa (Phillies), ss	1	0	0	0	2	1
Grich (Orioles), 2b	2	0	0	0	1	1	Rhoden (Dodgers), p	0	0	0	0	0	0
Garner (Athletics), 2b	1	0	0	0	1	1	Cey (Dodgers), 3b	0	0	0	0	0	0
Fidrych (Tigers), p	0	0	0	0	1	0	Jones (Padres), p	1	0	0	0	1	1
aMcRae (Royals)	1	0	0	0	0	0	Seaver (Mets), p	1	0	0	0	0	0
Hunter (Yankees), p	0	0	0	0	0	0	Schmidt (Phillies), 3b	1	0	0	0	0	0
bRivers (Yankees), rf	2	0	1	0	2	0	Forsch (Astros), p	0	0	0	0	0	0
Totals	29	1	5	1	24	8	Totals	33	7	10	7	27	12

Americans	0	0	0	1	0	0	0	0	0 — 1
Nationals	2	0	2	0	0	0	0	3	x — 7

Americans	IP.	H.	R.	ER.	BB.	SO.	Nationals	IP.	H.	R.	ER.	BB.	SO.
Fidrych (Tigers)	2	4	2	2	0	1	Jones (Padres)	3	2	0	0	1	1
Hunter (Yankees)	2	2	2	2	0	3	Seaver (Mets)	2	1	1	0	1	2
Tiant (Red Sox)	2	1	0	0	0	1	Montefusco (Giants)	2	0	0	0	2	2
Tanana (Angels)	2	3	3	3	1	0	Rhoden (Dodgers)	1	1	0	0	0	0
							Forsch (Astros)	1	0	0	0	0	1

Winning pitcher—Jones. Losing pitcher—Fidrych.

aGrounded out for Fidrych in third. bStruck out for Hunter in fifth. cWalked for Tiant in seventh. dGrounded out for Fisk in ninth. eStruck out for Lynn in ninth. Errors—None. Double plays—Morgan, Concepcion and Garvey; Morgan, Bowa and Garvey; Cash, Russell and Perez; Money, Garner and Carew. Left on bases—Americans 4, Nationals 3. Three-base hits—Garvey, Rose. Home runs—Foster, Lynn, Cedeno. Stolen base—Carew. Passed ball—Munson. Bases on balls—Off Jones 1 (Brett), off Montefusco 2 (Carew, Wynegar), off Tanana 1 (Perez). Strikeouts—By Jones 1 (LeFlore), by Seaver 1 (Rivers), by Montefusco 2 (Lynn, Garner), by Forsch 1 (Otis), by Fidrych 1 (Jones), by Hunter 3 (Bench, Kingman, Seaver), by Tiant 1 (Cedeno). Umpires—Wendelstedt (NL) plate, Neudecker (AL) first base, Olsen (NL) second base, Denkinger (AL) third base, Davidson (NL) left field, Evans (AL) right field. Time—2:12. Attendance—63,974. Official scorers—Richard Dozer, Chicago Tribune; Ray Kelly, Philadelphia Bulletin, and Bill Liston, Boston Herald-American.

Game of 1977—Yankee Stadium, New York, July 19

Embroiled in a tiff with California righthander Nolan Ryan, Yankee Manager Billy Martin was hit with a further migraine when Cincinnati's Joe Morgan and Greg Luzinski of Philadelphia belted home runs in the first inning as the National League struck for four runs in their 7-5 verdict over the Americans.

It was the sixth N.L. victory in a row and their 14th in the last 15 games. The Nationals lead the overall standings, 29-18, with one tie.

Los Angeles righthander Don Sutton and San Francisco reliever Gary Lavelle each one-hit the A.L. over the first five innings. Sutton, the winning pitcher, was selected to receive the Arch Ward Trophy as MVP of the game.

Morgan became the fourth player in All-Star history to lead off with a homer. Cincinnati's George Foster doubled home Dave Parker of Pittsburgh, before Luzinski connected off Jim Palmer, capping the opening-inning outburst against the Baltimore hurler.

NATIONALS	AB.	R.	H.	RBI.	PO.	A.
Morgan (Reds), 2b	4	1	1	1	1	0
Trillo (Cubs), 2b	1	0	0	0	0	1
Garvey (Dodgers), 1b	3	1	1	1	1	0
Montanez (Braves), 1b	2	0	0	0	6	1
Parker (Pirates), rf	3	1	1	0	2	0
Templeton (Cardinals), ss	1	1	1	0	1	2
Foster (Reds), cf	3	1	1	1	2	0
Morales (Cubs), cf	0	0	0	0	1	0
Luzinski (Phillies), lf	2	1	1	2	0	0
Winfield (Padres), lf	2	0	2	2	1	0
Cey (Dodgers), 3b	2	0	0	0	0	0
Seaver (Reds), p	0	0	0	0	0	1
eSmith (Dodgers)	1	0	1	0	0	0
fSchmidt (Phillies)	0	0	0	0	0	0
R. Reuschel (Cubs), p	0	0	0	0	0	0
Stearns (Mets), c	0	0	0	0	2	0
Bench (Reds), c	2	0	0	0	4	0
cRose (Dodgers), 3b	0	0	0	0	0	0
Lavelle (Giants), p	2	0	0	0	0	1
Valentine (Expos), rf	1	0	0	0	1	1
Sutton (Dodgers), p	1	0	0	0	0	1
Simmons (Cardinals), c	3	0	0	0	5	0
Gossage (Pirates), p	0	0	0	0	0	0
Totals	33	7	9	7	27	8

AMERICANS	AB.	R.	H.	RBI.	PO.	A.
Carew (Twins), 1b	3	1	1	0	7	0
Scott (Red Sox), 1b	2	1	1	2	4	0
Randolph (Yankees), 2b	5	0	1	1	2	6
Brett (Royals), 3b	2	0	0	0	2	1
Campbell (Red Sox), p	0	0	0	0	0	0
dFairly (Blue Jays)	1	0	0	0	0	0
Lyle (Yankees), p	0	0	0	0	0	0
gMunson (Yankees)	1	0	0	0	0	0
Yastrzemski (Red Sox), cf	2	0	0	0	0	0
Lynn (Red Sox), cf	1	1	0	0	2	0
Zisk (White Sox), lf	3	0	2	2	0	0
Singleton (Orioles), rf	0	0	0	0	0	0
Jackson (Yankees), rf	2	0	1	0	0	0
Rice (Red Sox), rf-lf	2	0	1	0	1	0
Fisk (Red Sox), c	2	0	0	0	6	1
Wynegar (Twins), c	2	1	1	0	3	0
Burleson (Red Sox), ss	2	0	0	0	0	0
Campaneris (Rangers), ss	1	1	0	0	0	1
Palmer (Orioles), p	0	0	0	0	0	0
Kern (Indians), p	0	0	0	0	0	0
aJones (Mariners)	1	0	0	0	0	0
Eckersley (Indians), p	0	0	0	0	0	1
bHisle (Twins)	1	0	0	0	0	0
LaRoche (Angels), p	0	0	0	0	0	0
Nettles (Yankees), 3b	2	0	0	0	0	1
Totals	35	5	8	5	27	11

Nationals										
Nationals	4	0	1	0	0	0	2	0	0	— 7
Americans	0	0	0	0	0	2	1	0	2	— 5

Nationals	IP.	H.	R.	ER.	BB.	SO.
Sutton (Dodgers)	3	1	0	0	1	4
Lavelle (Giants)	2	1	0	0	0	2
Seaver (Reds)	2	4	3	2	1	2
R. Reuschel (Cubs)	1	1	0	0	0	0
Gossage (Pirates)	1	1	2	2	1	2

Americans	IP.	H.	R.	ER.	BB.	SO.
Palmer (Orioles)	2*	5	5	5	1	3
Kern (Indians)	1	0	0	0	0	2
Eckersley (Indians)	2	0	0	0	0	1
LaRoche (Angels)	1	1	0	0	1	0
Campbell (Red Sox)	1	0	0	0	1	2
Lyle (Yankees)	2	3	2	2	0	1

*Pitched to one batter in third.
Winning pitcher—Sutton. Losing pitcher—Palmer.

aFlied out for Kern in third. bFlied out for Eckersley in fifth. cFlied out for Lavelle in sixth. dStruck out for Campbell in seventh. eSingled for Seaver in eighth. fRan for Smith in eighth. gStruck out for Lyle in ninth. Error—Templeton. Double plays—Randolph and Scott; Montanez, Templeton and Montanez. Left on bases—Nationals 4, Americans 7. Two-base hits—Foster, Winfield, Zisk, Templeton. Home runs—Morgan, Luzinski, Garvey, Scott. Caught stealing—Concepcion. Sacrifice hit—Sutton. Wild pitches—Palmer, Lyle. Hit by pitch—By Lyle (Morales), by R. Reuschel (Singleton). Bases on balls—Off Palmer 1 (Concepcion), off LaRoche 1 (Cey), off Campbell 1 (Valentine), off Sutton 1 (Brett), off Seaver 1 (Lynn), off Gossage 1 (Campaneris). Strikeouts—By Palmer 3 (Garvey, Cey, Bench), by Kern 2 (Parker, Foster), by Eckersley 1 (Garvey), by Campbell 2 (Morgan, Montanez), by Lyle 1 (Trillo), by Sutton 4 (Randolph 2, Zisk, Fisk), by Lavelle 2 (Yastrzemski, Jackson), by Seaver 2 (Campaneris, Fairly), by Gossage 2 (Nettles, Munson). Umpires—Kunkel (A.L.) plate, Harvey (N.L.) first base, Phillips (A.L.) second base, Stello (N.L.) third base, Pulli (N.L.) left field, Brinkman (A.L.) right field. Time—2:34. Attendance—56,683. Official scorers—Earl Lawson, Cincinnati Post Times & Star; Red Foley, New York Daily News and Ken Nigro, Baltimore Morning Sun.

Game of 1978—San Diego Stadium, San Diego, July 11

For the first time in history, the Most Valuable Player of the All-Star Game was a repeat winner, as the Dodgers' Steve Garvey, who won the honor in 1974, singled home two runs to tie the game and then tripled in the eighth inning to trigger a four-run outburst which carried the National League to a 7-3 triumph over the Americans.

It was the seventh N.L. victory in a row and their 15th in the last 16 games. The Nationals lead the overall standings, 30-18, with one tie.

The A.L. bolted to a 3-0 lead thanks in large part to a record-setting pair of triples by Rod Carew of the Twins. However, a bases-loaded walk to the Phillies' Greg Luzinski and Garvey's two-run single tied the contest in the third. Garvey's opposite-field triple was followed by a wild pitch by losing hurler Rich Gossage. Bob Boone later stroked a two-run single and Dave Lopes plated Boone. Bruce Sutter of the Cubs retired five straight batters to gain the victory.

AMERICANS	AB.	R.	H.	RBI.	PO.	A.
Carew (Twins), 1b	4	2	2	0	6	1
Brett (Royals), 3b	3	1	2	2	0	2
Gossage (Yankees), p	0	0	0	0	0	0
Rice (Red Sox), lf	4	0	0	0	2	0
Lemon (White Sox), lf	0	0	0	0	0	0
Zisk (Rangers), rf	2	0	1	0	0	0
Evans (Red Sox), rf	1	0	0	0	3	0
Fisk (Red Sox), c	2	0	0	1	4	0
Sundberg (Rangers), c	0	0	0	0	2	1
fThompson (Tigers)	1	0	0	0	0	0
Lynn (Red Sox), cf	4	0	1	0	3	0
Money (Brewers), 2b	2	0	0	0	1	1
White (Royals), 2b	1	0	0	0	1	2
gPorter (Royals)	1	0	0	0	0	0
Patek (Royals), ss	3	0	1	0	1	1
Palmer (Orioles), p	1	0	0	0	1	0
Keough (A's), p	0	0	0	0	0	0
bHowell (Blue Jays)	1	0	0	0	0	0
Sorensen (Brewers), p	0	0	0	0	0	1
cHisle (Brewers)	1	0	1	0	0	0
Kern (Indians), p	0	0	0	0	0	0
Guidry (Yankees), p	0	0	0	0	0	0
Nettles (Yankees), 3b	0	0	0	0	0	1
Totals	31	3	8	3	24	10

NATIONALS	AB.	R.	H.	RBI.	PO.	A.
Rose (Reds), 3b	4	0	1	0	1	0
dLopes (Dodgers), 2b	1	0	1	1	0	1
Morgan (Reds), 2b	3	1	0	0	2	1
Clark (Giants), rf	1	0	0	0	0	0
Foster (Reds), cf	2	1	0	0	2	0
Luzinski (Phillies), lf	2	0	1	1	0	0
Fingers (Padres), p	0	0	0	0	0	1
eStargell (Pirates)	1	0	0	0	0	0
Sutter (Cubs), p	0	0	0	0	0	0
Niekro (Braves), p	0	0	0	0	0	0
Garvey (Dodgers), 1b	3	1	2	2	7	1
Simmons (Cardinals), c	3	0	1	0	4	1
Concepcion (Reds), ss	0	1	0	0	2	0
Monday (Dodgers), rf	2	0	0	0	1	0
Rogers (Expos), p	0	0	0	0	0	0
Winfield (Padres), lf	2	1	1	0	1	0
Bowa (Phillies), ss	3	1	2	0	2	4
Boone (Phillies), c	1	1	1	2	3	1
Pocoroba (Braves), c	0	0	0	0	0	0
Blue (Giants), p	0	0	0	0	0	1
aSmith (Padres), rf	3	0	0	0	1	0
Cey (Dodgers), 3b	1	0	0	0	1	0
Totals	32	7	10	6	27	11

Americans	2	0	1	0	0	0	0	0	0 – 3
Nationals	0	0	3	0	0	0	0	4	x – 7

Americans	IP.	H.	R.	ER.	BB.	SO.
Palmer (Orioles)	2⅔	3	3	3	4	4
Keough (A's)	⅓	1	0	0	0	0
Sorensen (Brewers)	3	1	0	0	0	0
Kern (Indians)	⅔	1	0	0	1	1
Guidry (Yankees)	⅓	0	0	0	0	0
Gossage (Yankees)	1	4	4	4	1	1

Nationals	IP.	H.	R.	ER.	BB.	SO.
Blue (Giants)	3	5	3	3	1	2
Rogers (Expos)	2	2	0	0	2	0
Fingers (Padres)	2	1	0	0	1	1
Sutter (Cubs)	1⅔	0	0	0	0	2
Niekro (Braves)	⅓	0	0	0	0	0

Winning pitcher—Sutter. Losing pitcher—Gossage.

aStruck out for Blue in third. bGrounded out for Keough in fourth. cSingled for Sorensen in seventh. dRan for Rose in seventh. eFlied out for Fingers in seventh. fFlied out for Sundberg in ninth. gFouled out for White in ninth. Error—Lemon. Double play—Brett, Money and Carew. Left on bases—Americans 4, Nationals 7. Two-base hits—Brett, Rose. Three-base hits—Carew 2, Garvey. Stolen bases—Bowa, Brett. Caught stealing—Zisk, Carew, Lopes. Sacrifice flies—Fisk, Brett. Wild pitches—Rogers, Gossage. Passed ball—Sundberg. Bases on balls—Off Palmer 4 (Garvey, Morgan, Foster, Luzinski), off Kern 1 (Foster), off Gossage 1 (Concepcion), off Blue 1 (Zisk). Strikeouts—By Palmer 4 (Morgan, Foster, Simmons, Smith), by Kern 1 (Smith), by Gossage 1 (Clark), by Blue 2 (Lynn, Money), by Rogers 2 (Rice, Zisk), by Fingers 1 (Patek), by Sutter 2 (Rice, Evans). Umpires—Pryor (N.L.) plate, Chylak (A.L.) first base, Tata (N.L.) second base, Deegan (A.L.) third base, Runge (N.L.) left field, McCoy (A.L.) right field. Time—2:37. Attendance—51,549. Official scorers—Bill Liston, Boston Herald American; Phil Collier, San Diego Union; Dick Miller, Los Angeles Herald-Examiner.

Game of 1979—Kingdome, Seattle, July 17

Lee Mazzilli of the Mets produced an eighth-inning pinch-homer to tie the game and an inning later he coaxed a walk with the bases loaded to give the Nationals a 7-6 victory in the majors' All-Star Game.

In addition to going 1-for-3 with an RBI, Pittsburgh's Dave Parker took MVP honors by throwing out two runners, including Brian Downing at the plate in the eighth with the score tied, 6-6.

It was the eighth NL victory in a row and their 16th in the last 17 games. The Nationals lead the overall series, 31-18, with one tie.

NATIONALS	AB.	R.	H.	RBI.	PO.	A.
Lopes (Dodgers), 2b	3	0	1	0	4	1
iMorgan (Reds), 2b	1	1	0	0	1	1
Parker (Pirates), rf	3	0	1	1	0	2
Garvey (Dodgers), 1b	2	1	0	0	5	0
Perry (Padres), p	0	0	0	0	0	0
Sambito (Astros), p	0	0	0	0	0	1
Reynolds (Astros), ss	2	0	0	0	0	0
Schmidt (Phillies), 3b	3	2	2	1	1	1
Cey (Dodgers), 3b	1	0	0	0	0	0
Parrish (Expos), 3b	0	0	0	0	0	1
Foster (Reds), lf	1	0	1	1	0	0
Matthews (Braves), lf	2	0	0	0	2	0
jMazzilli (Mets), cf	1	1	1	2	0	0
Winfield (Padres), cf-lf	5	0	1	1	3	0
Boone (Phillies), c	2	1	1	0	0	0
Carter (Expos), c	2	0	0	1	6	1
Bowa (Phillies), ss	2	0	0	0	1	3
LaCoss (Reds), p	1	0	0	0	0	0
kHernandez (Cardinals)	0	0	0	0	0	1
Sutter (Cubs), p	0	0	0	0	0	0
Carlton (Phillies), p	0	0	0	0	0	0
aBrock (Cardinals)	1	0	1	0	0	0
Andujar (Astros), p	1	0	0	0	0	0
cClark (Giants)	0	0	0	0	0	0
Rogers (Expos), p	0	0	0	0	0	0
eRose (Phillies), 1b	2	0	0	0	2	0
Totals	35	7	10	7	27	12

AMERICANS	AB.	R.	H.	RBI.	PO.	A.
Smalley (Twins), ss	3	0	0	0	2	2
Grich (Angels), 2b	1	0	0	0	2	0
Brett (Royals), 3b	3	1	0	0	1	2
Nettles (Yankees), 3b	1	0	1	0	1	2
Baylor (Angels), lf	4	2	2	1	1	0
Kern (Rangers), p	0	0	0	0	0	0
Guidry (Yankees), p	0	0	0	0	0	0
lSingleton (Orioles)	1	0	0	0	0	0
Rice (Red Sox), rf-lf	5	0	1	0	3	0
Lynn (Red Sox), cf	1	1	1	2	0	0
Lemon (White Sox), cf	2	1	0	0	2	0
Yastrzemski (Red Sox), 1b	3	0	2	1	5	1
fBurleson (Red Sox), ss	2	1	0	0	0	1
Porter (Royals), c	3	0	1	0	2	0
Downing (Angels), c	1	0	1	0	3	0
White (Royals), 2b	2	0	0	0	2	2
gBochte (Mariners), 1b	1	0	1	1	2	0
Ryan (Angels), p	0	0	0	0	0	0
bCooper (Brewers)	1	0	0	0	0	0
Stanley (Red Sox), p	0	0	0	0	1	0
dKemp (Tigers)	1	0	0	0	0	0
Clear (Angels), p	0	0	0	0	0	0
hJackson (Yankees), rf	1	0	0	0	0	0
Totals	35	6	10	5	27	10

Nationals	2	1	1	0	0	1	0	1	1 – 7
Americans	3	0	2	0	0	1	0	0	0 – 6

Nationals	IP.	H.	R.	ER.	BB.	SO.
Carlton (Phillies)	1	2	3	3	1	0
Andujar (Astros)	2	2	2	1	1	0
Rogers (Expos)	2	0	0	0	0	2
Perry (Padres)	0*	3	1	1	0	0
Sambito (Astros)	⅔	0	0	0	1	0
LaCoss (Reds)	1⅓	1	0	0	0	0
Sutter (Cubs)	2	2	0	0	2	3

Americans	IP.	H.	R.	ER.	BB.	SO.
Ryan (Angels)	2	5	3	3	1	2
Stanley (Red Sox)	2	1	1	0	0	0
Clear (Angels)	2	2	1	1	1	0
Kern (Rangers)	2⅔	2	2	2	3	3
Guidry (Yankees)	⅓	0	0	0	1	0

*Pitched to three batters in sixth.

Winning pitcher—Sutter. Losing pitcher—Kern.

aSingled for Carlton in second. bWalked for Ryan in second. cGrounded out for Andujar in fourth. dLined out for Stanley in fourth. eGrounded into double play for Rogers in sixth. fRan for Yastrzemski in sixth. gSingled for White in sixth. hGrounded into force play for Clear in ninth. iStruck out for Lopes in seventh. jHomered for Matthews in eighth. kStruck out for LaCoss in eighth. lGrounded out for Guidry in ninth. Error—Schmidt. Double plays—Brett, White and Yastrzemski; White, Smalley and Yastrzemski. Left on bases—Nationals 8, Americans 9. Two-base hits—Foster, Baylor, Schmidt, Winfield, Porter, Rice. Three-base hit—Schmidt. Home runs—Lynn, Mazzilli. Sacrifice hit—Bochte. Sacrifice fly—Parker. Wild pitch—Andujar. Balk—By pitcher—By Andujar (Lemon). Balk—Kern. Bases on balls—Off Carlton 1 (Brett), off Andujar 1 (Cooper), off Sambito 1 (Smalley), off Sutter 2 (Jackson, Lemon), off Ryan 1 (Garvey), off Clear 1 (Bowa), off Kern 3 (Morgan, Parker, Cey), off Guidry 1 (Mazzilli). Strikeouts—By Rogers 2 (Rice, Lemon), by Sutter 3 (Grich, Rice, Burleson), by Ryan 2 (Lopes, Parker), by Kern 3 (Morgan, Winfield, Hernandez). Umpires—Maloney (A.L.) plate, Weyer (N.L.) first base, Bremigan (A.L.) second base, W. Williams (N.L.) third base, Cooney (A.L.) left field, Rennert (N.L.) right field. Time—3:11. Attendance—58,905. Official scorers—Jean-Paul Sarault, Montreal Metro-Matin; Dick Dozer, Chicago Tribune; Mike Kenyon, Seattle Post-Intelligencer.

Game of 1980—Dodger Stadium, Los Angeles, July 8

American League Cy Young winner Steve Stone had become the first pitcher since Denny McLain in 1966 to toss three perfect innings, Fred Lynn had hit a two-run homer for his third career All-Star Game home run and Tommy John had continued the A. L.'s perfect game until two were out in the fifth inning when Cincinnati's Ken Griffey belted a home run. Round-tripper sparked the National League to a 4-2 victory—their ninth consecutive victory —for a 32-18-1 series advantage.

Consecutive singles by Ray Knight, Phil Garner and George Hendrick produced the first of two N. L. tallies in the sixth. Garner then scored the go-ahead run when Dave Winfield's one-hopper hancuffed second baseman Willie Randolph for an error. Dave Concepcion scored an insurance run on a wild pitch in the seventh. Griffey, the game's MVP, started the inning with a single.

Jerry Reuss of the Dodgers struck out the side in the sixth and was credited with the victory. His strikeouts, along with three by J.R. Richard, four by Bob Welch and one by Bruce Sutter were one short of the record (12).

AMERICANS	AB.	R.	H.	RBI.	PO.	A.
Randolph (Yankees), 2b.....	4	0	2	0	0	3
Stieb (Blue Jays), p	0	0	0	0	0	0
Trammell (Tigers), ss........	0	0	0	0	0	0
Carew (Angels), 1b...........	2	1	2	0	4	0
Cooper (Brewers), 1b.........	1	0	0	0	6	0
Lynn (Red Sox), cf...........	3	1	1	2	2	0
Bumbry (Orioles), cf	1	0	0	0	2	0
Jackson (Yankees), rf.........	2	0	1	0	0	0
aLandreaux (Twins), rf.......	1	0	0	0	1	0
Oglivie (Brewers), lf	2	0	0	0	1	0
Oliver (Rangers), lf...........	1	0	0	0	0	0
Gossage (Yankees), p	0	0	0	0	0	0
Fisk (Red Sox), c	2	0	0	0	5	0
Porter (Royals), c............	1	0	0	0	0	1
Henderson (A's), lf...........	1	0	0	0	0	0
Nettles (Yankees), 3b.........	2	0	0	0	0	1
Bell (Rangers), 3b...........	2	0	0	0	0	0
Dent (Yankees), ss...........	2	0	1	0	0	1
John (Yankees), p	1	0	0	0	0	1
Farmer (White Sox), p.......	0	0	0	0	0	0
Grich (Angels), 2b...........	0	0	0	0	0	1
Stone (Orioles), p	1	0	0	0	0	1
Yount (Brewers), ss	2	0	0	0	3	2
Parrish (Tigers), c	1	0	0	0	0	0
Totals...................	32	2	7	2	24	12

NATIONALS	AB.	R.	H.	RBI.	PO.	A.
Lopes (Dodgers), 2b...........	1	0	0	0	0	2
Garner (Pirates), 2b..........	2	1	1	0	1	3
Smith (Dodgers), cf	2	0	0	0	0	0
Hendrick (Cardinals), cf	2	0	1	1	0	0
Sutter (Cubs), p	0	0	0	0	0	0
Parker (Pirates), rf...........	2	0	0	0	0	0
Winfield (Padres), rf.........	2	0	0	1	2	0
Garvey (Dodgers), 1b.........	2	0	0	0	7	0
bHernandez (Cards), 1b.......	2	0	2	0	5	0
Bench (Reds), c..............	1	0	0	0	5	0
Stearns (Mets), c	1	0	0	0	5	0
cRose (Phillies)	1	0	0	0	0	0
Bibby (Pirates), p	0	0	0	0	0	0
Murphy (Braves), cf..........	1	0	0	0	0	0
Kingman (Cubs), lf...........	1	0	0	0	0	0
Griffey (Reds), lf............	3	1	2	1	0	0
Reitz (Cardinals), 3b	2	0	0	0	1	0
Reuss (Dodgers), p...........	0	0	0	0	0	0
Concepcion (Reds), ss........	1	1	0	0	0	2
Russell (Dodgers), ss.........	2	0	0	0	2	2
Carter (Expos), c	1	0	0	0	1	0
Richard (Astros), p..........	0	0	0	0	0	0
Welch (Dodgers), p	1	0	0	0	0	1
Knight (Reds), 3b	1	1	1	0	0	1
Totals...................	31	4	7	3	27	11

```
Americans........................ 0   0   0     0   2   0     0   0   0 — 2
Nationals........................ 0   0   0     0   1   2     1   0   x — 4
```

Americans	IP.	H.	R.	ER.	BB.	SO.
Stone (Orioles)	3	0	0	0	0	3
John (Yankees)	2⅓	4	3	3	0	1
Farmer (White Sox)	⅔	1	0	0	0	0
Stieb (Blue Jays).............	1	1	1	1	0	2
Gossage (Yankees)	1	1	0	0	0	0

Nationals	IP.	H.	R.	ER.	BB.	SO.
Richard (Astros)	2	1	0	0	2	3
Welch (Dodgers)	3	5	2	2	1	4
Reuss (Dodgers)	1	0	0	0	0	3
Bibby (Pirates)	1	1	0	0	0	0
Sutter (Cubs)	2	0	0	0	1	1

Winning pitcher—Reuss. Losing pitcher—John. Save—Sutter.

aRan for Jackson in fifth. bSingled for Garvey in sixth. cGrounded into double play for Stearns in sixth. Errors—Randolph 2. Double plays—Randolph, Yount and Cooper; Concepcion, Garner and Hernandez. Left on bases—Americans 7, Nationals 5. Two-base hit—Carew. Home runs—Lynn, Griffey. Stolen bases—Carew, Knight, Garner. Caught stealing—None. Wild pitches—Welch, Stieb 2. Passed ball—Porter. Bases on balls—Off Stieb 2 (Knight, Garner), off Richard 2 (Carew, Oglivie), off Welch 1 (Jackson), off Sutter 1 (Grich). Strikeouts—By Stone 3 (Parker, Kingman, Welch), by John 1 (Garner), by Richard 3 (Jackson, Fisk, Stone), by Welch 4 (Lynn, Oglivie, Fisk, Dent), by Reuss 3 (Porter, Bell, John), by Sutter 1 (Parrish). Umpires—Kibler (NL) plate, Barnett (AL) first base, Colosi (NL) second base, McKean (AL) third base, Dale (NL) left field, Garcia (AL) right field. Time—2:33. Attendance—56,088. Official scorers—Phil Collier, San Diego Union; Ed Browalski, Polish News; Bob Hunter, Valley News.

All-Star Game Squads

When the All-Star Game first was introduced in 1933, each squad included 18 players. The size of the teams was increased to 20 the following year and then to 21 in 1936, to 23 in 1937 and to 25 in 1939. With the expansion to 24 clubs in 1969 the squad size was hiked to 28.

Each club now must be represented by at least one player. This wasn't true in the early years of the game. As a result, several teams did not have a single player on the All-Star team.

The procedure of selecting the eight starting players for each team—all but the pitchers—in a poll was begun in 1947. At first, this was done in a fan poll. However, beginning in 1958 the league's managers, coaches and players voted to choose the eight starters for each team. This continued until 1970 when the fan voting was resumed.

Following are the yearly All-Star squads, with those players who were voted to the starting team each year since 1947 being designated by a black dot before their names:

1933

AMERICAN LEAGUE—Connie Mack, Philadelphia, manager; Edward Collins, Boston, and Arthur Fletcher, New York, coaches. **Boston (1)**—Richard Ferrell, c. **Chicago (2)**—James Dykes, 3b; Aloysius Simmons, of. **Cleveland (3)**—H. Earl Averill, of; Wesley Ferrell, p; Oral Hildebrand, p. **Detroit (1)**—Charles Gehringer, 2b. **New York (6)**—W. Benjamin Chapman, of; William Dickey, c; H. Louis Gehrig, 1b; Vernon Gomez, p; Anthony Lazzeri, 2b; George Ruth, of. **Philadelphia (2)**—James Foxx, 1b; Robert Grove, p. **St. Louis (1)**—Samuel West, of. **Washington (2)**—Joseph Cronin, ss; Alvin Crowder, p.

NATIONAL LEAGUE—John McGraw, New York, manager; William McKechnie, Boston, and Max Carey, Brooklyn, coaches. **Boston (1)**—Walter Berger, of. **Brooklyn (1)**—Anthony Cuccinello, 2b. **Chicago (3)**—Elwood English, ss; Charles Hartnett, c; Lonnie Warneke, p. **Cincinnati (1)**—Charles Hafey, of. **New York (4)**—Carl Hubbell, p; Frank O'Doul, of; Harold Schumacher, p; William Terry, 1b. **Philadelphia (2)**—Richard Bartell, ss; Charles Klein, of. **Pittsburgh (2)**—Harold Traynor, 3b; Paul Waner, of. **St. Louis (4)**—Frank Frisch, 2b; William Hallahan, p; John Martin, 3b; James Wilson, c.

1934

AMERICAN LEAGUE—Joseph Cronin, Washington, manager; Walter Johnson, Cleveland, and Albertus Schacht, Washington, coaches. **Boston (1)**—Richard Ferrell, c. **Chicago (2)**—James Dykes, 3b; Aloysius Simmons, of. **Cleveland (2)**—H. Earl Averill, of; Melvin Harder, p. **Detroit (3)**—Thomas Bridges, p; Gordon Cochrane, c; Charles Gehringer, 2b. **New York (6)**—W. Benjamin Chapman, of; William Dickey, c; H. Louis Gehrig, 1b; Vernon Gomez, p; Charles Ruffing, p; George Ruth, of. **Philadelphia (2)**—James Foxx, 1b; Michael Higgins, 3b. **St. Louis (1)**—Samuel West, of. **Washington (3)**—Joseph Cronin, ss; Henry Manush, of; Jack Russell, p.

NATIONAL LEAGUE—William Terry, manager; Charles Stengel, Brooklyn and William McKechnie, Boston, coaches. **Boston (2)**—Walter Berger, of; Frederick Frankhouse, p. **Brooklyn (2)**—Alfonso Lopez, c; Van Mungo, p. **Chicago (4)**—Charles Hartnett, c; William Herman, 2b; Charles Klein, of; Lonnie Warneke, p. **Cincinnati**—None. **New York (5)**—Carl Hubbell, p; Travis Jackson, ss; Joseph Moore, of; Melvin Ott, of; William Terry, 1b. (Moore replaced by Hazen Cuyler, of, Chicago). **Philadelphia**—None. **Pittsburgh (3)**—Harold Traynor, 3b; J. Floyd Vaughan, ss; Paul Waner, of. **St. Louis (4)**—Jerome Dean, p; Frank Frisch, 2b; John Martin, 3b; Joseph Medwick, of.

1935

AMERICAN LEAGUE—Gordon Cochrane, Detroit, manager; Delmer Baker, Detroit, and Rogers Hornsby, St. Louis, coaches. **Boston (3)**—Joseph Cronin, ss; Richard Ferrell, c; Robert Grove, p. **Chicago (1)**—Aloysius Simmons, of. **Cleveland (3)**—H. Earl Averill, of; Melvin Harder, p; Joseph Vosmik, of (Averill replaced by Roger Cramer, of,

Philadelphia). **Detroit (4)**—Thomas Bridges, p; Gordon Cochrane, c; Charles Gehringer, 2b; Lynwood Rowe, p. **New York (3)**—W. Benjamin Chapman, of; H. Louis Gehrig, 1b; Vernon Gomez, p. **Philadelphia (2)**—James Foxx, 1b; Robert Johnson, of. **St. Louis (2)**—Ralston Hemsley, c; Samuel West, of. **Washington (2)**—Oswald Bluege, 3b; Charles Myer, 2b.

NATIONAL LEAGUE—Frank Frisch, St. Louis, manager; Charles Grimm, Chicago, and Charles Dressen, Cincinnati, coaches. **Boston (1)**—Walter Berger, of. **Brooklyn**—None. **Chicago (2)**—Charles Hartnett, c; William Herman, 2b. **Cincinnati (1)**—Paul Derringer, p. **New York (6)**—Carl Hubbell, p; August Mancuso, c; Joseph Moore, of; Melvin Ott, of; Harold Schumacher, p; William Terry, 1b. **Philadelphia (1)**—James Wilson, c. **Pittsburgh (2)**—J. Floyd Vaughan, ss; Paul Waner, of. **St. Louis (7)**—James Collins, 1b; Jerome Dean, p; Frank Frisch, 2b; John Martin, 3b; Joseph Medwick, of; William Walker, p; Burgess Whitehead, 2b.

1936

NATIONAL LEAGUE—Charles Grimm, Chicago, manager; Harold Traynor, Pittsburgh, and William McKechnie, Boston, coaches. **Boston (1)**—Walter Berger, of. **Brooklyn (1)**—Van Mungo, p. **Chicago (6)**—Curtis Davis, p; J. Frank Demaree, of; August Galan, of; Charles Hartnett, c; William Herman, 2b; Lonnie Warneke, p. **Cincinnati (2)**—Ernest Lombardi, c; Lewis Riggs, 3b. **New York (3)**—Carl Hubbell, p; Joseph Moore, of; Melvin Ott, of. **Philadelphia (1)**—Arthur Whitney, 3b. **Pittsburgh (2)**—August Suhr, 1b; J. Floyd Vaughan, ss. **St. Louis (5)**—James Collins, 1b; Jerome Dean, p; Leo Durocher, ss; Stuart Martin, 2b; Joseph Medwick, of.

AMERICAN LEAGUE—Joseph McCarthy, New York, manager; Joseph Cronin, Boston, and Arthur Fletcher, New York, coaches. **Boston (3)**—Richard Ferrell, c; James Foxx, 3b; Robert Grove, p. **Chicago (2)**—Lucius Appling, ss; Raymond Radcliff, of. **Cleveland (2)**—H. Earl Averill, of; Melvin Harder, p. **Detroit (4)**—Thomas Bridges, p; Charles Gehringer, 2b; Leon Goslin, of; Lynwood Rowe, p (Bridges replaced by L. Vernon Kennedy, p, Chicago). **New York (7)**—Frank Crosetti, ss; William Dickey, c; Joseph DiMaggio, of; H. Louis Gehrig, 1b; Vernon Gomez, p; M. Monte Pearson, p; George Selkirk, of. **Philadelphia (1)**—Michael Higgins, 3b. **St. Louis (1)**—Ralston Hemsley, c. **Washington (1)**—W. Benjamin Chapman, of.

1937

AMERICAN LEAGUE—Joseph McCarthy, New York, manager; Delmar Baker, Detroit, and Arthur Fletcher, New York, coaches. **Boston (4)**—Roger Cramer, of; Joseph Cronin, ss; James Foxx, 1b; Robert Grove, p. **Chicago (2)**—J. Luther Sewell, c; Monty Stratton, p (Stratton replaced by John Murphy, p, New York). **Cleveland (2)**—H. Earl Averill, of; Melvin Harder, p. **Detroit (4)**—Thomas Bridges, p; Charles Gehringer, 2b; Henry Greenberg, 1b; Gerald Walker, of (Walker replaced by Samuel West, of, St. Louis). **New York (5)**—William Dickey, c; Joseph DiMaggio, of; H. Louis Gehrig, 1b; Vernon Gomez, p; Robert Rolfe, 3b. **Philadelphia (1)**—Wallace Moses, of. **St. Louis (2)**—Roy Bell, of; Harlond Clift, 3b. **Washington (3)**—Richard Ferrell, c; Wesley Ferrell, p; Charles Myer, 2b.

NATIONAL LEAGUE—William Terry, New York, manager; Charles Dressen, Cincinnati; Frank Frisch, St. Louis, and Jesse Haines, St. Louis, coaches. **Boston (1)**—Eugene Moore, of. **Brooklyn (1)**—Van Mungo, p. **Chicago (5)**—James Collins, 1b; J. Frank Demaree, of; Charles Hartnett, c; William Herman, 2b; William Jurges, ss. **Cincinnati (2)**—Lee Grissom, p; Ernesto Lombardi, c. **New York (6)**—Richard Bartell, ss; Carl Hubbell, p; August Mancuso, c; Joseph Moore, of; Melvin Ott, of; Burgess Whitehead, 2b. **Philadelphia (1)**—William Walters, p. **Pittsburgh (3)**—Darrell Blanton, p; J. Floyd Vaughan, 3b; Paul Waner, of. **St. Louis (4)**—Jerome Dean, p; John Martin, of; Joseph Medwick, of; John Mize, 1b

1938

NATIONAL LEAGUE—William Terry, New York, manager; William McKechnie, Cincinnati, and Frank Frisch, St. Louis, coaches. **Boston (2)**—Anthony Cuccinello, 2b; James Turner, p. **Brooklyn (3)**—Leo Durocher, ss; Harry Lavagetto, 3b; E. Gordon Phelps, c (Phelps replaced by Harry Danning, c, New York). Chicago (4)—Stanley Hack, 3b; Charles Hartnett, c; William Herman, 2b; William Lee, p. **Cincinnati (5)**—Paul Derringer, p; Ival Goodman, of; Ernesto Lombardi, c; Frank McCormick, 1b; John Vander

Meer, p. **New York (4)**—Carl Hubbell, p; Henry Leiber, of; Joseph Moore, of; Melvin Ott, of. **Philadelphia (1)**—Hershel Martin, of. **Pittsburgh (3)**—Mace Brown, p; J. Floyd Vaughan, ss; Lloyd Waner, of. **St. Louis (1)**—Joseph Medwick, of.

AMERICAN LEAGUE—Joseph McCarthy, New York, manager; Delmer Baker, Detroit, and Arthur Fletcher, New York, coaches. **Boston (4)**—Roger Cramer, of; Joseph Cronin, ss; James Foxx, 1b-3b; Robert Grove, p. **Chicago (1)**—Michael Kreevich, of. **Cleveland (3)**—John Allen, p; Robert Feller, p; H. Earl Averill, of. **Detroit (4)**—Charles Gehringer, 2b; Henry Greenberg, 1b; L. Vernon Kennedy, p; Rudolph York, c (Greenberg replaced by John Murphy, p, New York). **New York (6)**—William Dickey, c; Joseph DiMaggio, of; H. Louis Gehrig, 1b; Vernon Gomez, p; Robert Rolfe, 3b; Charles Ruffing, p. **Philadelphia (1)**—Robert Johnson, of. **St. Louis (1)**—Louis Newsom, p. **Washington (3)**—Richard Ferrell, c; John Lewis, of; Cecil Travis, ss.

1939

AMERICAN LEAGUE—Joseph McCarthy, New York, manager; Arthur Fletcher, New York, and Russell Blackburne, Philadelphia, coaches. **Boston (4)**—Roger Cramer, of; Joseph Cronin, ss; James Foxx, 1b; Robert Grove, p. **Chicago (2)**—Lucius Appling, ss; Theodore Lyons, p. **Cleveland (2)**—Robert Feller, p; Ralston Hemsley, c. **Detroit (3)**—Thomas Bridges, p; Henry Greenberg, 1b; Louis Newsom, p. **New York (9)**—Frank Crosetti, ss; William Dickey, c; Joseph DiMaggio, of; Vernon Gomez, p; Joseph Gordon, 2b; John Murphy, p; Robert Rolfe, 3b; Charles Ruffing, p; George Selkirk, of. **Philadelphia (2)**—Frank Hayes, c; Robert Johnson, of. **St. Louis (2)**—Myril Hoag, of; George McQuinn, 1b. **Washington (1)**—George Case, of. (NOTE—H. Louis Gehrig, 1b, New York, who retired as an active player in May because of illness, was named an honorary member of squad.)

NATIONAL LEAGUE—Charles Hartnett, Chicago, manager; John Corriden, Chicago, and William Terry, New York, coaches. **Boston (1)**—Louis Fette, p. **Brooklyn (4)**—Adolph Camilli, 1b; Harry Lavagetto, 3b; Ernest Phelps, c; Whitlow Wyatt, p. **Chicago (3)**—Stanley Hack, 3b; William Herman, 2b; William Lee, p. **Cincinnati (7)**—Paul Derringer, p; Linus Frey, 2b; Ival Goodman, of; Ernesto Lombardi, c; Frank McCormick, 1b; John Vander Meer, p; William Walters, p. **New York (3)**—Harry Danning, c; William Jurges, ss; Melvin Ott, of. **Philadelphia (1)**—Morris Arnovich, of. **Pittsburgh (1)**—J. Floyd Vaughan, ss. **St. Louis (5)**—Curtis Davis, p; Joseph Medwick, of; John Mize, 1b; Terry Moore, of; Lonnie Warneke, p.

1940

NATIONAL LEAGUE—William McKechnie, Cincinnati, manager; Charles Stengel, Boston, and James Prothro, Philadelphia, coaches. **Boston (1)**—Max West, of. **Brooklyn (6)**—Peter Coscarart, 2b; Leo Durocher, ss; Harry Lavagetto, 3b; Joseph Medwick, of; Ernest Phelps, c; Whitlow Wyatt, p. **Chicago (3)**—Lawrence French, p; William Herman, 2b; Henry Leiber, of (Leiber replaced by William Nicholson, of, Chicago). **Cincinnati (4)**—Paul Derringer, p; Ernesto Lombardi, c; Frank McCormick, 1b; William Walters, p. **New York (7)**—Harry Danning, c; Carl Hubbell, p; William Jurges, ss; Joseph Moore, of; Melvin Ott, of (Jurges replaced by Edward Miller, ss, Boston). **Philadelphia (3)**—W. Kirby Higbe, p; Merrill May. 3b; Hugh Mulcahy, p. **Pittsburgh (1)**—J. Floyd Vaughan, ss. **St. Louis (2)**—John Mize, 1b; Terry Moore, of.

AMERICAN LEAGUE—Joseph Cronin, Boston, manager; Thomas Daly, Boston, and Delmer Baker, Detroit, coaches. **Boston (4)**—Roger Cramer, of; Louis Finney, of; James Foxx, 1b; Theodore Williams, of. **Chicago (1)**—Lucius Appling, ss. **Cleveland (6)**—Louis Boudreau, ss; Robert Feller, p; Ralston Hemsley, c; Kenneth Keltner, 3b; Raymond Mack, 2b; Albert Milnar, p. **Detroit (3)**—Thomas Bridges, p; Henry Greenberg, of; Louis Newsom, p. **New York (7)**—William Dickey, c; Joseph DiMaggio, of; Joseph Gordon, 2b; Charles Keller, of; M. Monte Pearson, p; Robert Rolfe, 3b; Charles Ruffing, p (Rolfe replaced by Cecil Travis, 3b, Washington). **Philadelphia (2)**—Frank Hayes, c; Robert Johnson, of. **St. Louis (1)**—George McQuinn, 1b. **Washington (1)**—Emil Leonard, p.

1941

AMERICAN LEAGUE—Delmer Baker, Detroit, manager; Mervyn Shea, Detroit, and Arthur Fletcher, New York, coaches. **Boston (5)**—Joseph Cronin, ss; Dominic DiMaggio, of; Robert Doerr, 2b; James Foxx, 1b; Theodore Williams, of. **Chicago (3)**—Lucius Appling, ss; Thornton Lee, p; Edgar Smith, p. **Cleveland (4)**—Louis Boudreau, ss;

Robert Feller, p; J. Geoffrey Heath, of; Kenneth Keltner, 3b. **Detroit (3)**—J. Alton Benton, p; George Tebbetts, c; Rudolph York, 1b. **New York (6)**—William Dickey, c; Joseph DiMaggio, of; Joseph Gordon, 2b; Charles Keller, of; Charles Ruffing, p; Marius Russo, p. **Philadelphia (1)**—Frank Hayes, c. **St. Louis (1)**—Roy Cullenbine, of. **Washington (2)**—Sidney Hudson, p; Cecil Travis, 3b.

NATIONAL LEAGUE—William McKechnie, Cincinnati, manager; Leo Durocher, Brooklyn, and James Wilson, Chicago, coaches. **Boston (1)**—Edward Miller, ss. **Brooklyn (6)**—Adolph Camilli, 1b; William Herman, 2b; Harry Lavagetto, 3b; Arnold Owen, c; Harold Reiser, of; Whitlow Wyatt, p. (Camilli replaced by Frank McCormick, 1b, Cincinnati). **Chicago (4)**—Stanley Hack, 3b; Henry Leiber, of; William Nicholson, of; Claude Passeau, p. (Leiber replaced by Joseph Medwick, of, Brooklyn). **Cincinnati (3)**—Paul Derringer, p; Linus Frey, 2b; William Walters, p. **New York (3)**—Harry Danning, c; Carl Hubbell, p; Melvin Ott, of. **Philadelphia (1)**—Darrell Blanton, p. **Pittsburgh (3)**—Robert Elliott, of; Alfonso Lopez, c; J. Floyd Vaughan, ss. **St. Louis (4)**—John Mize, 1b; Terry Moore, of; Enos Slaughter, of; Lonnie Warneke, p.

1942

AMERICAN LEAGUE—Joseph McCarthy, New York, manager; Arthur Fletcher, New York, and Stanley Harris, Washington, coaches. **Boston (4)**—Dominic DiMaggio, of; Robert Doerr, 2b; Cecil Hughson, p; Theodore Williams, of. **Chicago (1)**—Edgar Smith, p. **Cleveland (3)**—James Bagby, p; Louis Boudreau, ss; Kenneth Keltner, 3b. **Detroit (4)**—J. Alton Benton, p; Harold Newhouser, p; George Tebbetts, c; Rudolph York, 1b. **New York (9)**—Ernest Bonham, p; Spurgeon Chandler, p; William Dickey, c; Joseph DiMaggio, of; Joseph Gordon, 2b; Thomas Henrich, of; Philip Rizzuto, ss; Warren Rosar, c; Charles Ruffing, p. (Dickey replaced by Harold Wagner, c, Philadelphia). **Philadelphia (1)**—Robert Johnson, of. **St. Louis (1)**—George McQuinn, 1b. **Washington (2)**—Sidney Hudson, p; Stanley Spence, of.

NATIONAL LEAGUE—Leo Durocher, Brooklyn, manager; William McKechnie, Cincinnati, and Frank Frisch, Pittsburgh, coaches. **Boston (2)**—Ernesto Lombardi, c; Edward Miller, ss. **Brooklyn (7)**—William Herman, 2b; Joseph Medwick, of; Arnold Owen, c; Harold Reese, ss; Harold Reiser, of; J. Floyd Vaughan, 3b; Whitlow Wyatt, p. **Chicago (1)**—Claude Passeau, p. **Cincinnati (4)**—Paul Derringer, p; Frank McCormick, 1b; John Vander Meer, p; William Walters, p. (Derringer replaced by Raymond Starr, p, Cincinnati). **New York (5)**—Carl Hubbell, p; Willard Marshall, of; Clifford Melton, p; John Mize, 1b; Melvin Ott, of. **Philadelphia (1)**—Daniel Litwhiler, of. **Pittsburgh (1)**—Robert Elliott, 3b. **St. Louis (5)**—James Brown, 2b; Morton Cooper, p; W. Walker Cooper, c; Terry Moore, of; Enos Slaughter, of.

1943

AMERICAN LEAGUE—Joseph McCarthy, New York, manager; Arthur Fletcher, New York, and Russell Blackburne, Philadelphia, coaches. **Boston (3)**—Robert Doerr, 2b; Cecil Hughson, p; Oscar Judd, p. **Chicago (1)**—Lucius Appling, ss. **Cleveland (6)**—James Bagby, p; Louis Boudreau, ss; J. Geoffrey Heath, of; Kenneth Keltner, 3b; Warren Rosar, c; Alfred Smith, p. **Detroit (2)**—Harold Newhouser, p; Rudolph York, 1b. **New York (6)**—Ernest Bonham, p; Spurgeon Chandler, p; William Dickey, c; Joseph Gordon, 2b; Charles Keller, of; John Lindell, of. (Keller replaced by Richard Wakefield, of, Detroit.) **Philadelphia (1)**—Richard Siebert, 1b. **St. Louis (1)**—Chester Laabs, of; Vernon Stephens, ss. **Washington (4)**—George Case, of; Jacob Early, c; Robert Johnson, of; Emil Leonard, p.

NATIONAL LEAGUE—William Southworth, St. Louis, manager; Frank Frisch, Pittsburgh, and Miguel Gonzalez, St. Louis, coaches. **Boston (1)**—Alva Javery, p. **Brooklyn (4)**—August Galan, of; William Herman, 2b; Arnold Owen, c; Fred Walker, of. **Chicago (3)**—Stanley Hack, 3b; William Nicholson, of; Claude Passeau, p. **Cincinnati (3)**—Linus Frey, 2b; Frank McCormick, 1b; Edward Miller, ss; John Vander Meer, p. (McCormick replaced by Elburt Fletcher, 1b, Pittsburgh.) **New York (2)**—Ernesto Lombardi, c; Melvin Ott, of. **Philadelphia (1)**—Ellsworth Dahlgren, 1b. **Pittsburgh (2)**—Vincent DiMaggio, of; Truett Sewell, p. **St. Louis (8)**—Morton Cooper, p; W. Walker Cooper, c; George Kurowski, 3b; H. Max Lanier, p; Martin Marion, ss; Stanley Musial, of; Howard Pollet, p; Harry Walker, of. (Pollet replaced by Ace Adams, p, New York.)

1944

NATIONAL LEAGUE—William Southworth, St. Louis, manager; Fred Fitzsimmons, Philadelphia; John Wagner, Pittsburgh, and Miguel Gonzalez, St. Louis, coaches. **Boston (3)**—Nathan Andrews, p; Alva Javery, p; Cornelius Ryan, 2b. **Brooklyn (3)**—August Galan, of; Arnold Owen, c; Fred Walker, of. **Chicago (3)**—Philip Cavarretta, 1b; Donald Johnson, 2b; William Nicholson, of. **Cincinnati (4)**—Frank McCormick, 1b; Edward Miller, ss; Raymond Mueller, c; William Walters, p. (Miller replaced by Frank Zak, ss, Pittsburgh). **New York (2)**—Joseph Medwick, of; Melvin Ott, of. **Philadelphia (1)**—Kenneth Raffensberger, p. **Pittsburgh (3)**—Vincent DiMaggio, of; Robert Elliott, 3b; Truett Sewell, p. **St. Louis (6)**—W. Walker Cooper, c; George Kurowski, 3b; H. Max Lanier, p; Martin Marion, ss; George Munger, p; Stanley Musial, of, (Lanier and Munger replaced by James Tobin, p, Boston, and William Voiselle, p, New York).

AMERICAN LEAGUE—Joseph McCarthy, New York, manager; Joseph Cronin, Boston, and Arthur Fletcher, New York, coaches. **Boston (3)**—Robert Doerr, 2b; Cecil Hughson, p; Robert Johnson, of. **Chicago (2)**—L. Orval Grove, p; Thurman Tucker, of. **Cleveland (4)**—Louis Boudreau, ss; Roy Cullenbine, of; Oris Hockett, of; Kenneth Keltner, 3b. **Detroit (4)**—Michael Higgins, 3b; Harold Newhouser, p; Paul Trout, p; Rudolph York, 1b. **New York (3)**—Henry Borowy, p; Ralston Hemsley, c; Joseph Page, p. **Philadelphia (2)**—Frank Hayes, c; Louis Newsom, p. **St. Louis (3)**—George McQuinn, 1b; Robert Muncrief, p; Vernon Stephens, ss. **Washington (4)**—George Case, of; Richard Ferrell, c; Emil Leonard, p; Stanley Spence, of. (Case replaced by Ervin Fox, of, Boston).

1945—No Game

1946

AMERICAN LEAGUE—Stephen O'Neill, Detroit manager; Arthur Mills, Detroit, and J. Luther Sewell, St. Louis, coaches. **Boston (8)**—Dominic DiMaggio, of; Robert Doerr, 2b; David Ferriss, p; Maurice Harris, p; John Pesky, ss; Harold Wagner, c; Theodore Williams, of; Rudolph York, 1b. **Chicago (1)**—Lucius Appling, ss. **Cleveland (3)**—Robert Feller, p; Frank Hayes, c; Kenneth Keltner, 3b. **Detroit (1)**—Harold Newhouser, p. **New York (6)**—Spurgeon Chandler, p; William Dickey, c; Joseph DiMaggio, of; Joseph Gordon, 2b; Charles Keller, of; George Stirnweiss, 3b. **Philadelphia (2)**—Samuel Chapman, of; Warren Rosar, c. **St. Louis (2)**—John Kramer, p; Vernon Stephens, ss. **Washington (2)**—Stanley Spence, of; James Vernon, 1b.

NATIONAL LEAGUE—Charles Grimm, Chicago, manager; William Southworth, Boston, and William McKechnie, Cincinnati, coaches. **Boston (3)**—Morton Cooper, p; John Hopp, of; Philip Masi, c. **Brooklyn (4)**—W. Kirby Higbe, p; Harold Reese, ss; Harold Reiser, of; Fred Walker, of. (Reese replaced by Frank McCormick, 1b, Philadelphia). **Chicago (4)**—Philip Cavarretta, 1b; Harry Lowrey, of; Claude Passeau, p; John Schmitz, p. **Cincinnati (3)**—Ewell Blackwell, p; Raymond Lamanno, c; Edward Miller, ss. (Miller replaced by Emil Verban, 2b, Philadelphia). **New York (2)**—W. Walker Cooper, c; John Mize, 1b. **Philadelphia (1)**—Delmer Ennis, of. **Pittsburgh (2)**—Frank Gustine, 2b; Truett Sewell, p. **St. Louis (6)**—George Kurowski, 3b; Martin Marion, ss; Stanley Musial, of; Howard Pollet, p; Albert Schoendienst, 2b; Enos Slaughter, of

1947

AMERICAN LEAGUE—Joseph Cronin, Boston, manager; Delmer Baker, Boston, and Stephen O'Neill, Detroit, coaches. **Boston (2)**—Robert Doerr, 2b; ●Theodore Williams, of. **Chicago (2)**—Lucius Appling, ss; Rudolph York, 1b. **Cleveland (4)**—●Louis Boudreau, ss; ●Joseph Gordon, 2b; Robert Feller, p; James Hegan, c. (Feller replaced by Early Wynn, p, Washington). **Detroit (4)**—●George Kell, 3b; Patrick Mullin, of; Harold Newhouser, p; Paul Trout, p. **New York (8)**—Spurgeon Chandler, p; ●Joseph DiMaggio, of; Charles Keller, of; William Johnson, 3b; ●George McQuinn, 1b; Joseph Page, p; Aaron Robinson, c; Francis Shea, p. (Keller replaced by Thomas Henrich, of, New York). **Philadelphia (1)**—Warren Rosar, c. **St. Louis (1)**—John Kramer, p. **Washington (3)**—●John Lewis, of; Walter Masterson, p; Stanley Spence, of.

NATIONAL LEAGUE—Edwin Dyer, St. Louis, manager; Melvin Ott, New York, and W. Benjamin Chapman, Philadelphia, coaches. **Boston (4)**—●Robert Elliott, 3b; Philip Masi, c; John Sain, p; Warren Spahn, p. (Elliott replaced by George Kurowski, 3b, St. Louis). **Brooklyn (4)**—Ralph Branca, p; C. Bruce Edwards, c; Edward Stanky, 2b; ●Fred Walker of. **Chicago (2)**—Philip Cavarretta, of; Andrew Pafko, of. **Cincinnati (3)**—Ewell

Blackwell, p; Berthold Haas, of; •Edward Miller, ss (Miller replaced by Harold Reese, ss, Brooklyn). **New York (3)**−•W. Walker Cooper, c; Willard Marshall, of; •John Mize, 1b. **Philadelphia (3)**−Lynwood Rowe, p; •Emil Verban, 2b; •Harry Walker, of. **Pittsburgh (1)**−Frank Gustine, 3b. **St. Louis (5)**−Harry Brecheen, p; Martin Marion, ss; George Munger, p; Stanley Musial, 1b; •Enos Slaughter, of.

1948

AMERICAN LEAGUE−Stanley Harris, New York manager; John Corriden, New York, and Charles Dressen, New York, coaches. **Boston (4)**−Robert Doerr, 2b; Vernon Stephens, ss; George Tebbetts, c; •Theodore Williams, of. **Chicago (1)**−Joseph Haynes, p. **Cleveland (5)**−•Louis Boudreau, ss; Robert Feller, p; •Joseph Gordon, 2b; Kenneth Keltner, 3b; Robert Lemon, p. (Feller replaced by Joseph Dobson, p, Boston). **Detroit (4)**−Walter Evers, of; •George Kell, 3b; •Patrick Mullin, of; Harold Newhouser, p. **New York (6)**−Lawrence Berra, c; •Joseph DiMaggio, of; Thomas Henrich, of; •George McQuinn, 1b; Joseph Page, p; Victor Raschi, p. **Philadelphia (2)**−Joseph Coleman, p; •Warren Rosar, c. **St. Louis (1)**−Allen Zarilla, of. **Washington (2)**−Walter Masterson, p; James Vernon, 1b.

NATIONAL LEAGUE−Leo Durocher, Brooklyn, manager; Melvin Ott, New York, and Edwin Dyer, St. Louis, coaches. **Boston (5)**−Robert Elliott, 3b; Thomas Holmes, of; Philip Masi, c; John Sain, p; •Edward Stanky, 2b. (Stanky replaced by William Rigney, 2b, New York). **Brooklyn (2)**−Ralph Branca, p; •Harold Reese, ss. **Chicago (4)**−Clyde McCullough, c; •Andrew Pafko, 3b; John Schmitz, p; Edward Waitkus, 1b. **Cincinnati (1)**−Ewell Blackwell, p. **New York (4)**−•W. Walker Cooper, c; Sidney Gordon, 3b; •John Mize, 1b; Robert Thomson, of. **Philadelphia (1)**−•Richie Ashburn, of. **Pittsburgh (3)**−Frank Gustine, 3b; Ralph Kiner, of; Elmer Riddle, p. **St. Louis (5)**−Harry Brecheen, p; Martin Marion, ss; •Stanley Musial, of; Albert Schoendienst, 2b; •Enos Slaughter, of. (Marion replaced by John Kerr, ss, New York).

1949

AMERICAN LEAGUE−Louis Boudreau, Cleveland, manager; William McKechnie, Cleveland, and Herold Ruel, Cleveland, coaches. **Boston (6)**−•Dominic DiMaggio, of; William Goodman, 1b; Melvin Parnell, p; Vernon Stephens, ss; •George Tebbetts, c; •Theodore Williams, of. **Chicago (1)**−•Casimer Michaels, 2b. **Cleveland (5)**−Lawrence Doby, of; Joseph Gordon, 2b; James Hegan, c; Robert Lemon, p; L. Dale Mitchell, of. **Detroit (3)**−•George Kell, 3b; Virgil Trucks, p; Victor Wertz, of. **New York (5)**−Lawrence Berra, c; Joseph DiMaggio, of; •Thomas Henrich, of; Victor Raschi, p; Allie Reynolds, p. **Philadelphia (3)**−Leland Brissie, p. •Alexander Kellner, p. **St. Louis (1)**−Robert Dillinger, 3b. **Washington (1)**−•W. Edward Robinson, 1b.

NATIONAL LEAGUE−William Southworth, Boston, manager; Burton Shotton, Brooklyn, and William Walters, Cincinnati, coaches. **Boston (2)**−Vernon Bickford, p; Warren Spahn, p. **Brooklyn (7)**−Ralph Branca, p; Roy Campanella, c; Gilbert Hodges, 1b; Donald Newcombe, p; •Harold Reese, ss; •Jack Robinson, 2b; Elwin Roe, p. **Chicago (1)**−Andrew Pafko, of. **Cincinnati (2)**−Ewell Blackwell, p; W. Walker Cooper, c. **New York (4)**−Sidney Gordon, 3b; •Willard Marshall, of; •John Mize, 1b; Robert Thomson, of. **Philadelphia (1)**−Andrew Seminick, c. **Pittsburgh (1)**−•Ralph Kiner, of. **St. Louis (7)**−•Edward Kazak, 3b; Martin Marion, ss; George Munger, p; •Stanley Musial, of; Howard Pollet, p; Albert Schoendienst, 2b; Enos Slaughter, of. (NOTE−Edward Waitkus, 1b, Philadelphia, sidelined by gunshot wound, was named honorary member of squad).

1950

AMERICAN LEAGUE−Charles Stengel, New York, manager; Frank Crosetti, New York, and William Dickey, New York, coaches. **Boston (5)**−Dominic DiMaggio, of; •Robert Doerr, 2b; •Walter Dropo, 1b; Vernon Stephens, ss; •Theodore Williams, of. **Chicago (1)**−Ray Scarborough, p. **Cleveland (4)**−•Lawrence Doby, of; Robert Feller, p; James Hegan, c; Robert Lemon, p. **Detroit (4)**−•Walter Evers, of; Theodore Gray, p; Arthur Houtteman, p; •George Kell, 3b. **New York (8)**−•Lawrence Berra, c; Thomas Byrne, p; Gerald Coleman, 2b; Joseph DiMaggio, of; Thomas Henrich, 1b; Victor Raschi, p; Allie Reynolds, p; •Philip Rizzuto, ss. **Philadelphia (1)**−Ferris Fain, 1b. **St. Louis (1)**−J. Sherman Lollar, c. **Washington (1)**−Casimer Michaels, 2b.

NATIONAL LEAGUE–Burton Shotton, Brooklyn, manager; Jacob Pitler, Brooklyn, and Milton Stock, Brooklyn, coaches. **Boston (2)**–W. Walker Cooper, c; Warren Spahn, p. **Brooklyn (7)**–●Roy Campanella, c; Gilbert Hodges, 1b; Donald Newcombe, p; Harold Reese, ss; ●Jack Robinson, 2b; Elwin Roe, p; Edwin Snider, of. **Chicago (3)**–Andrew Pafko, of; Robert Rush, p; ●Henry Sauer, of. **Cincinnati (2)**–Ewell Blackwell, p; John Wyrostek, of. **New York (2)**–Lawrence Jansen, p; Edward Stanky, 2b. **Philadelphia (4)**–●Willie Jones, 3b; James Konstanty, p; Robin Roberts, p; Richard Sisler, of. **Pittsburgh (1)**–●Ralph Kiner, of. **St. Louis (4)**–Martin Marion, ss; ●Stanley Musial, 1b; Albert Schoendienst, 2b; ●Enos Slaughter, of.

1951

AMERICAN LEAGUE–Charles Stengel, New York, manager; William Dickey, New York, and Thomas Henrich, New York, coaches. **Boston (5)**–●Dominic DiMaggio, of; Robert Doerr, 2b; Melvin Parnell, p; Vernon Stephens, 3b; ●Theodore Williams, of. **Chicago (6)**–James Busby, of; ●Alfonso Carrasquel, ss; ●J. Nelson Fox, 2b; Randall Gumpert, p; Orestes Minoso, of; W. Edward Robinson, 1b. **Cleveland (3)**–Lawrence Doby, of; James Hegan, c; Robert Lemon, p. **Detroit (3)**–Frederick Hutchinson, p; ●George Kell, 3b; ●Victor Wertz, of. **New York (4)**–●Lawrence Berra, c; Joseph DiMaggio, of; Edmund Lopat, p; Philip Rizzuto, ss. **Philadelphia (2)**–●Ferris Fain, 1b; Robert Shantz, p. **St. Louis (1)**–Ned Garver, p. **Washington (1)**–Conrado Marrero, p.

NATIONAL LEAGUE–Edwin Sawyer, Philadelphia, manager; Bernard Bengough, Allen Cooke and Ralph Perkins, all of Philadelphia, coaches. **Boston (2)**–●Robert Elliott, 3b; Warren Spahn, p. **Brooklyn (7)**–●Roy Campanella, c; ●Gilbert Hodges, 1b; Donald Newcombe, p; Harold Reese, ss; ●Jack Robinson, 2b; Elwin Roe, p; Edwin Snider, of. **Chicago (2)**–C. Bruce Edwards, c; Emil Leonard, p. **Cincinnati (2)**–Ewell Blackwell, p; John Wyrostek, of. **New York (3)**–●Alvin Dark, ss; Lawrence Jansen, p; Salvatore Maglie, p. **Philadelphia (4)**–●Richie Ashburn, of; ●Delmer Ennis, p; Willie Jones, 3b; Robin Roberts, p. **Pittsburgh (1)**–Ralph Kiner, of. **St. Louis (4)**–●Stanley Musial, of; Albert Schoendienst, 2b; Enos Slaughter, of; Waldon Westlake, of.

1952

AMERICAN LEAGUE–Charles Stengel, New York, manager; Anthony Cuccinello, Cleveland, and Alfonso Lopez, Cleveland, coaches. **Boston (2)**–●Dominic DiMaggio, of; George Kell, 3b (Kell replaced by Gil McDougald, 2b, New York). **Chicago (3)**–J. Nelson Fox, 2b; Orestes Minoso, of; ●W. Edward Robinson, 1b. **Cleveland (7)**–●Roberto Avila, 2b; Lawrence Doby, of; E. Mike Garcia, p; James Hegan, c; Robert Lemon, p; ●L. Dale Mitchell, of; ●Albert Rosen, 3b. **Detroit (1)**–Victor Wertz, of. **New York (6)**–●Henry Bauer, of; ●Lawrence Berra, c; Mickey Mantle, of; Victor Raschi, p; Allie Reynolds, p; ●Philip Rizzuto, ss. **Philadelphia (3)**–Ferris Fain, 1b; Edwin Joost, ss; Robert Shantz, p. **St. Louis (1)**–Leroy Paige, p. **Washington (2)**–Jack Jensen, of; Edward Yost, 3b.

NATIONAL LEAGUE–Leo Durocher, New York, manager; Frank Shellenback, New York, and Edward Stanky, St. Louis, coaches. **Boston (1)**–Warren Spahn,p. **Brooklyn (7)**–●Roy Campanella, c; Carl Furillo, of; Gilbert Hodges, 1b; Harold Reese, ss; Jack Robinson, 2b; Elwin Roe, p; Edwin Snider, of (Roe replaced by James Hearn, p, New York). **Chicago (3)**–Maurice Atwell, c; Robert Rush, p; ●Henry Sauer, of. **Cincinnati (1)**–Grady Hatton, 3b. **New York (6)**–Alvin Dark, ss; Monford Irvin, of (injured); ●Carroll Lockman, 1b; Salvatore Maglie, p; ●Robert Thomson, 3b; Wesley Westrum, c. **Philadelphia (3)**–●Granville Hamner, ss; Robin Roberts, p; Curtis Simmons, p. **Pittsburgh (1)**–Ralph Kiner, of. **St. Louis (4)**–●Stanley Musial, of; Albert Schoendienst, 2b; ●Enos Slaughter, of; Gerald Staley, p.

1953

AMERICAN LEAGUE–Charles Stengel, New York, manager; Louis Boudreau, Boston, and James Turner, New York, coaches. **Boston (3)**–●William Goodman, 2b; George Kell, 3b; Samuel White, c. **Chicago (5)**–●Alfonso Carrasquel, ss; Ferris Fain, 1b; J. Nelson Fox, 2b; Orestes Minoso, of; W. William Pierce, p. **Cleveland (4)**–Lawrence Doby, of; E. Mike Garcia, p; Robert Lemon, p; ●Albert Rosen, 3b. **Detroit (1)**–Harvey Kuenn, ss. **New York (7)**–●Henry Bauer, of; ●Lawrence Berra, c; ●Mickey Mantle, of; John Mize, 1b; Allie Reynolds, p; Philip Rizzuto, ss; John Sain, p. **Philadelphia (2)**–W. Edward Robinson. 1b; ●Gus Zernial, of. **St. Louis (2)**–G. William Hunter, ss;

Leroy Paige, p. **Washington (1)**–•James Vernon, 1b. (NOTE–Theodore Williams, of, Boston, just released from military service, was named honorary member of squad.)

NATIONAL LEAGUE–Charles Dressen, Brooklyn, manager; William Herman, Harry Lavagetto and Jacob Pitler, all of Brooklyn, coaches. **Brooklyn (6)**–•Roy Campanella, c; Carl Furillo, of; Gilbert Hodges, 1b; •Harold Reese, ss; Jack Robinson, 3b; Edwin Snider, of. **Chicago (1)**–Ralph Kiner, of. **Cincinnati (2)**–•David Bell, of; •Theodore Kluszewski, 1b. **Milwaukee (3)**–Delmar Crandall, c; •Edwin Mathews, 3b; Warren Spahn, p (Crandall replaced by Clyde McCullough, c, Chicago). **New York (2)**–J. Hoyt Wilhelm, p; David Williams, 2b. **Philadelphia (4)**–Richie Ashburn, of; Granville Hamner, ss; Robin Roberts, p; Curtis Simmons, p. **Pittsburgh (1)**–Murry Dickson, p. **St. Louis (6)**–Harvey Haddix, p; •Stanley Musial, of; Delbert Rice, c; •Albert Schoendienst, 2b; •Enos Slaughter, of; Gerald Staley, p (Rice replaced by Wesley Westrum, c, New York.)

1954

AMERICAN LEAGUE–Charles Stengel, New York, manager; Martin Marion, Chicago, and Frederick Hutchinson, Detroit, coaches. **Baltimore (1)**–Robert Turley, p. **Boston (2)**–James Piersall, of; Theodore Williams, of. **Chicago (8)**–•Alfonso Carrasquel, ss; Ferris Fain, 1b; J. Nelson Fox, 2b; Robert Keegan, p; George Kell, 3b; J. Sherman Lollar, c; •Orestes Minoso, of; Virgil Trucks, p (Fain replaced by D. Dean Stone, p, Washington, and Kell by James Vernon, 1b, Washington). **Cleveland (5)**–•Roberto Avila, 2b; Lawrence Doby, of; E. Mike Garcia, p; Robert Lemon, p; •Albert Rosen, 1b (Garcia replaced by Sandalio Consuegra, p, Chicago). **Detroit (2)**–•Raymond Boone, 3b; Harvey Kuenn, ss. **New York (5)**–•Henry Bauer, of; •Lawrence Berra, c; Edward Ford, p; •Mickey Mantle, of; Allie Reynolds, p (Reynolds replaced by Irving Noren, of, New York). **Philadelphia (1)**–James Finigan, 3b. **Washington (1)**–Erwin Porterfield, p.

NATIONAL LEAGUE–Walter Alston, Brooklyn, manager; Charles Grimm, Milwaukee, and Leo Durocher, New York, coaches. **Brooklyn (6)**–•Roy Campanella, c; Carl Erskine, p; Gilbert Hodges, 1b; Harold Reese, ss; •Jack Robinson, of; •Edwin Snider, of. **Chicago (1)**–Ransom Jackson, 3b. **Cincinnati (2)**–David Bell, of; •Theodore Kluszewski, 1b. **Milwaukee (3)**–Delmar Crandall, c; D. Eugene Conley, p; Warren Spahn, p. **New York (5)**–John Antonelli, p; •Alvin Dark, ss; Marvin Grissom, p; Willie Mays, of; Donald Mueller, of. **Philadelphia (3)**–Forrest Burgess, c; •Granville Hamner, 2b; Robin Roberts, p. **Pittsburgh (1)**–Frank Thomas, of. **St. Louis (4)**–Harvey Haddix, p; •Raymond Jablonski, 3b; •Stanley Musial, of; Albert Schoendienst, 2b (Haddix replaced by James Wilson, p, Milwaukee).

1955

AMERICAN LEAGUE–Alfonso Lopez, Cleveland, manager; Donald Gutteridge, Chicago, and Anthony Cuccinello, Cleveland, coaches. **Baltimore (1)**–James Wilson, p. **Boston (3)**–Jack Jensen, of; Franklin Sullivan, p; •Theodore Williams, of. **Chicago (5)**–Alfonso Carrasquel, ss; •J. Nelson Fox, 2b; Richard Donovan, p; J. Sherman Lollar, c; W. William Pierce, p. **Cleveland (6)**–Roberto Avila, 2b; Lawrence Doby, of; Albert Rosen, 3b; Alphonse Smith, of; Herbert Score, p; Early Wynn, p. **Detroit (3)**–William Hoeft, p; •Albert Kaline, of; •Harvey Kuenn, ss. **Kansas City (2)**–•James Finigan, 3b; Victor Power, 1b. **New York (4)**–•Lawrence Berra, c; Edward Ford, p; •Mickey Mantle, of; Robert Turley, p. **Washington (1)**–•James Vernon, 1b.

NATIONAL LEAGUE–Leo Durocher, New York, manager; E. Mayo Smith, Philadelphia, and Fred Haney, Pittsburgh, coaches. **Brooklyn (4)**–•Roy Campanella, c; Gilbert Hodges, 1b; Donald Newcombe, p; •Edwin Snider, of (Campanella replaced by Stanley Lopata, c, Philadelphia). **Chicago (4)**–Eugene Baker, 2b; •Ernest Banks, ss; Ransom Jackson, 3b; Samuel Jones, p. **Cincinnati (3)**–Forrest Burgess, c; •Theodore Kluszewski, 1b; Joseph Nuxhall, p. **Milwaukee (5)**–D. Eugene Conley, p; Delmar Crandall, c; John Logan, ss; •Edwin Mathews, 3b; Henry Aaron, of. **New York (2)**–Willie Mays, of; •Donald Mueller, of. **Philadelphia (2)**–•Delmer Ennis, of; Robin Roberts, p. **Pittsburgh (1)**–Frank Thomas, of. **St. Louis (4)**–•Luis Arroyo, p; Harvey Haddix, p; Stanley Musial, 1b; •Albert Schoendienst, 2b.

1956

AMERICAN LEAGUE–Charles Stengel, New York, manager; James Turner, New York, and Charles Dressen, Washington, coaches. **Baltimore (1)**–•George Kell, 3b. **Boston (5)–Thomas Brewer, p; James Piersall, of; •James Vernon, 1b; Franklin Sullivan, p; •Theodore Williams, of. **Chicago (4)**–•J. Nelson Fox, 2b; J. Sherman Lollar, c; W. William Pierce, p; James Wilson, p. **Cleveland (2)**–Raymond Narleski, p; Early Wynn, p (Narleski replaced by Herbert Score, p, Cleveland). **Detroit (4)**–Raymond Boone, 3b; •Albert Kaline, of; •Harvey Kuenn, ss; Charles Maxwell, of. **Kansas City (2)**–Victor Power, 1b; Harry Simpson, of. **New York (6)**–•Lawrence Berra, c; Edward Ford, p; John Kucks, p; •Mickey Mantle, of; Alfred Martin, 2b; Gilbert McDougald, ss. **Washington (1)**–Roy Sievers.

NATIONAL LEAGUE–Walter Alston, Brooklyn, manager; George Tebbetts, Cincinnati, and Frederick Hutchinson, St. Louis, coaches. **Brooklyn (4)**–Roy Campanella, c; James Gilliam, 2b; Clement Labine, p; Edwin Snider, of. **Chicago (1)**–Ernest Banks, ss. **Cincinnati (8)**–•L. Edgar Bailey, c; •David Bell, of; Theodore Kluszewski, 1b; Brooks Lawrence, p; •Roy McMillan, ss; Joseph Nuxhall, p; •Frank Robinson, of; •John Temple, 2b. **Milwaukee (4)**–Henry Aaron, of; Delmar Crandall, c; Edwin Mathews, 3b; Warren Spahn, p (Crandall replaced by Stanley Lopata, c, Philadelphia). **New York (2)**–John Antonelli, p; Willie Mays, of. **Philadelphia (1)**–Robin Roberts, p. **Pittsburgh (2)**–Robert Friend, p; •R. Dale Long, 1b. **St. Louis (3)**–•Kenton Boyer, 3b; •Stanley Musial, of; Eldon Repulski, of.

1957

AMERICAN LEAGUE–Charles Stengel, New York, manager; Frank Crosetti, New York, and James Turner, New York, coaches. **Baltimore (3)**–•George Kell, 3b; William Loes, p; Augustus Triandos, c. **Boston (2)**–Frank Malzone, 3b; •Theodore Williams, of. **Chicago (3)**–•J. Nelson Fox, 2b; Orestes Minoso, of; W. William Pierce, p. **Cleveland (3)**–Donald Mossi, p; •Victor Wertz, 1b; Early Wynn, p. **Detroit (4)**–James Bunning, p; •Albert Kaline, of; •Harvey Kuenn, ss; Charles Maxwell, of. **Kansas City (1)**–Joseph DeMaestri, ss. **New York (8)**–•Lawrence Berra, c; Robert Grim, p; Elston Howard, c; •Mickey Mantle, of; Gilbert McDougald, ss; Robert Richardson, 2b; Robert Shantz, p; William Skowron, 1b. **Washington (1)**–Roy Sievers, of.

NATIONAL LEAGUE–Walter Alston, Brooklyn, manager; Robert Scheffing, Chicago, and Robert Bragan, Pittsburgh, coaches. **Brooklyn (3)**–Gino Cimoli, of; Gilbert Hodges, 1b; Clement Labine, p. **Chicago (1)**–Ernest Banks, ss. **Cincinnati (6)**–•L. Edgar Bailey, c; David Bell, of; •Donald Hoak, 3b; •Roy McMillan, ss; •Frank Robinson, of; •John Temple, 2b. **Milwaukee (6)**–•Henry Aaron, of; S. Lewis Burdette, p; John Logan, ss; Edwin Mathews, 3b; Albert Schoendienst, 2b; Warren Spahn, p. **New York (2)**–John Antonelli, p; •Willie Mays, of. **Philadelphia (2)**–John Sanford, p; Curtis Simmons, p. **Pittsburgh (1)**–Henry Foiles, c. **St. Louis (4)**–Lawrence Jackson, p; Wallace Moon, of; •Stanley Musial, 1b; Harold Smith, c. (NOTE–David Bell and Wally Post of Cincinnati led voting for center and right field positions, respectively, but because of avalanche of Cincinnati votes, Commissioner Ford Frick arbitrarily named Mays and Aaron to starting lineup at those positions.)

1958

AMERICAN LEAGUE–Charles Stengel, manager; C. Luman Harris, Baltimore, and James Turner, New York, coaches. **Baltimore (2)**–William O'Dell, p; •Augustus Triandos, c. **Boston (3)**–•Jack Jensen, of, •Frank Malzone, 3b; Theodore Williams, of. **Chicago (5)**–•Luis Aparicio, ss; •J. Nelson Fox, 2b; J. Sherman Lollar, c; W. William Pierce, p; Early Wynn, p. **Cleveland (2)**–Raymond Narleski, p; James Vernon, 1b. **Detroit (2)**–Albert Kaline, of; Harvey Kuenn, of. **Kansas City (1)**–•Robert Cerv, of. **New York (9)**–Lawrence Berra, c; Rinold Duren, p; Edward Ford, p; Elston Howard, of; Anthony Kubek, ss; •Mickey Mantle, of; Gilbert McDougald, 2b; •William Skowron, 1b; Robert Turley p. **Washington (1)**–Everett Bridges, ss.

NATIONAL LEAGUE–Fred Haney, Milwaukee, manager; William Rigney, New York and E. Mayo Smith, Philadelphia, coaches. **Chicago (3)**–•Ernest Banks, ss; Walter Moryn, of; R. Lee Walls, of. **Cincinnati (2)**–George Crowe, 1b; Robert Purkey, p. **Los Angeles (2)**–John Podres, p; John Roseboro, c. **Milwaukee (6)**–•Henry Aaron, of; •Delmar Crandall, c; John Logan, ss; Edwin Mathews, 3b; Donald McMahon, p; Warren Spahn, p. **Philadelphia (2)**–Richie Ashburn, of; Richard Farrell, p. **Pittsburgh (4)**–Robert Friend, p; •William Mazeroski, 2b; •Robert Skinner, of; •Frank Thomas, 3b. **St. Louis (3)**–Donald Blasingame, 2b; Lawrence Jackson, p; •Stanley Musial, 1b. **San Francisco (3)**–John Antonelli, p; •Willie Mays, of; Robert Schmidt, c.

1959

AMERICAN LEAGUE–Charles Stengel, New York, manager; Anthony Cuccinello, White Sox, and Harry Craft, Kansas City, coaches. **Baltimore (2)**–●Augustus Triandos, c; J. Hoyt Wilhelm, p. **Boston (3)**–Frank Malzone, 3b; James Runnels, 2b; Theodore Williams, of. **Chicago (5)**–●Luis Aparicio, ss; ●J. Nelson Fox, 2b; J. Sherman Lollar, c; W. William Pierce, p; Early Wynn, p. **Cleveland (3)**–●Rocco Colavito, of; ●Orestes Minoso, of; Victor Power, 1b. **Detroit (3)**–James Bunning, p; ●Albert Kaline, of; Harvey Kuenn, of. **Kansas City (1)**–Roy Sievers, 1b. **New York (6)**–Lawrence Berra, c; Rinold Duren, p; Edward Ford, p; Mickey Mantle, of; Gilbert McDougald, ss; ●William Skowron, 1b. **Washington (2)**–●Harmon Killebrew, 3b; Roy Sievers, 1b. **SECOND GAME CHANGES: Players Replaced**–Bunning, Ford, Kuenn, McDougald, Pierce, Skowron, Triandos. **Additions**–Frank Crosetti, New York, and Harry Lavagetto, Washington, coaches; William O'Dell, p; Jerry Walker, p, and Eugene Woodling, of, Baltimore; Calvin McLish, p, Cleveland; Roger Maris, of, Kansas City; Elston Howard, c-of, Anthony Kubek, ss, and Robert Richardson, 2b, New York; Camilo Pascual, p, and W. Robert Allison, of, Washington (Pascual replaced by Pedro Ramos, p, Washington).

NATIONAL LEAGUE–Fred Haney, Milwaukee, manager; Edwin Sawyer, Philadelphia, and Daniel Murtaugh, Pittsburgh, coaches. **Chicago (1)**–●Ernest Banks, ss. **Cincinnati (3)**–Vada Pinson, of; Frank Robinson, 1b; ●John Temple, 2b. **Los Angeles (2)**–Donald Drysdale, p; ●Wallace Moon, of. **Milwaukee (5)**–●Henry Aaron, of; S. Lewis Burdette, p; ●Delmar Crandall, c; ●Edwin Mathews, 3b; Warren Spahn, p. **Philadelphia (1)**–D. Eugene Conley, p. **Pittsburgh (4)**–Forrest Burgess, c; El Roy Face, p; Richard Groat, ss; William Mazeroski, 2b. **St. Louis (6)**–Kenton Boyer, 3b; Joseph Cunningham, of; Wilmer Mizell, p; Stanley Musial, 1b; Harold Smith, c; William White, of (Mizell replaced by Donald Elston, p, Chicago.) **San Francisco (3)**–John Antonelli, p; ●Orlando Cepeda, 1b; ●Willie Mays, of. **SECOND GAME CHANGES: Players Replaced**–White. **Additions**–William Herman, Milwaukee, and John Fitzpatrick, Milwaukee, coaches; James Gilliam, inf-of and Charles Neal, ss, Los Angeles; John Logan, ss, Milwaukee; Samuel Jones, p, San Francisco.

1960

AMERICAN LEAGUE–Alfonso Lopez, Chicago, manager; Anthony Cuccinello, Chicago, and Donald Gutteridge, Chicago, coaches. **Baltimore (4)**–Charles Estrada, p; James Gentile, 1b; ●Ronald Hansen, ss; Brooks Robinson, 3b. **Boston (4)**–●Frank Malzone, 3b; William Monbouquette, p; ●James Runnels, 2b; Theodore Williams, of. **Chicago (7)**–Luis Aparicio, ss; J. Nelson Fox, 2b; J. Sherman Lollar, c; ●Orestes Minoso, of; Alphonse Smith, of; Gerald Staley, p; ●Early Wynn, p. **Cleveland (4)**–Gary Bell, p; Harvey Kuenn, of; Victor Power, 1b; Richard Stigman, p. **Detroit (2)**–Albert Kaline, of; Frank Lary, p; **Kansas City (1)**–Buddy Daley, p. **New York (7)**–●Lawrence Berra, c; James Coates, p; Edward Ford, p; Elston Howard, c; ●Mickey Mantle, of; ●Roger Maris, of; ●William Skowron, 1b. **Washington (1)**–Camilo Pascual, p (replaced by James Lemon, of, Washington). **SECOND GAME CHANGES:** None.

NATIONAL LEAGUE–Walter Alston, Los Angeles, manager; Frederick Hutchinson, Cincinnati, and Solly Hemus, St. Louis, coaches. **Chicago (1)**–●Ernest Banks, ss. **Cincinnati (3)**–L. Edgar Bailey, c; William Henry, p; ●Vada Pinson, of. **Los Angeles (4)**–Norman Larker, 1b; Charles Neal, 2b; John Podres, p; Stanley Williams, p. **Milwaukee (5)**–●Henry Aaron, of; ●Joseph Adcock, 1b; Robert Buhl, p; ●Delmar Crandall, c; ●Edwin Mathews, 3b. **Philadelphia (1)**–Antonio Taylor, 2b. **Pittsburgh (8)**–Forrest Burgess, c; Roberto Clemente, of; El Roy Face, p; Robert Friend, p; Richard Groat, ss; Vernon Law, p; ●William Mazeroski, 2b; Robert Skinner, of. **St. Louis (5)**–Kenton Boyer, 3b; Lawrence Jackson, p; Lyndall McDaniel, p; Stanley Musial, of; William White, 1b. **San Francisco (3)**–Orlando Cepeda, of; ●Willie Mays, of; Michael McCormick, p. **SECOND GAME CHANGES:** None.

1961

AMERICAN LEAGUE–Paul Richards, Baltimore, manager; Frank Crosetti, New York, and James Vernon, Washington, coaches. **Baltimore (4)**–John Brandt, of; James Gentile, 1b; ●Brooks Robinson, 3b; J. Hoyt Wilhelm, p. **Boston (1)**–J. Miguel Fornieles, p. **Chicago (2)**–J. Nelson Fox, 2b; W. William Pierce, p. **Cleveland (3)**–James Perry, p;

●John Romano, c; ●John Temple, 2b. **Detroit (5)**–●Norman Cash, 1b; ●Rocco Colavito, of; Albert Kaline, of; Frank Lary, p; James Bunning, p. **Kansas City (1)**–Richard Howser, ss. **Los Angeles (1)**–Rinold Duren, p. **Minnesota (1)**–Harmon Killebrew, 3b. **New York (6)**–Lawrence, Berra, of-c; Edward Ford, p; Elston Howard, c; ●Anthony Kubek, ss; ●Mickey Mantle, of; ●Roger Maris, of. **Washington (1)**–Richard Donovan, p. **SECOND GAME CHANGES: Players Replaced**–Duren, Fornieles, Lary, Perry, Pierce. **Additions**–James Adair, Baltimore, and Michael Higgins, Boston, coaches; Donald Schwall, p, Boston; Roy Sievers, 1b, and Luis Aparicio, ss, Chicago; John Francona, of-1b, and A. Barry Latman, p, Cleveland; Kenneth McBride, p, Los Angeles; Camilo Pascual, p, Minnesota; Luis Arroyo, p, and William Skowron, 1b, New York.

    NATIONAL LEAGUE–Daniel Murtaugh, Pittsburgh, manager; Gene Mauch, Philadelphia, and Alvin Dark, San Francisco, coaches. **Chicago (2)**–George Altman, of; Donald Zimmer, 2b. **Cincinnati (4)**–Joseph Jay, p; Edward Kasko, ss; Robert Purkey, p; Frank Robinson, of. **Los Angeles (3)**–Sanford Koufax, p; John Roseboro, c; ●Maurice Wills, ss. **Milwaukee (4)**–Henry Aaron, of; ●Frank Bolling, 2b; ●Edwin Mathews, 3b; Warren Spahn, p. **Philadelphia (1)**–Art Mahaffey, p. **Pittsburgh (4)**–●Forrest Burgess, c; ●Roberto Clemente, of; El Roy Face, p; Richard Stuart, 1b. **St. Louis (3)**–Kenton Boyer, 3b; Stanley Musial, of; ●William White, 1b. **San Francisco (4)**–●Orlando Cepeda, of; ●Willie Mays, of; Michael McCormick, p; Stuart Miller, p. **SECOND GAME CHANGES: Players Replaced**–None. **Additions**–Elvin Tappe, Chicago, and Charles Dressen, Milwaukee, coaches; Ernest Banks, ss, Chicago; Donald Drysdale, p, Los Angeles; L. Edgar Bailey, c, San Francisco.

1962

    AMERICAN LEAGUE–Ralph Houk, New York, manager; William Hitchcock, Baltimore, and James Vernon, Washington, coaches. **Baltimore (3)**–●James Gentile, 1b; Brooks Robinson, 3b; J. Hoyt Wilhelm, p (Wilhelm replaced by Milton Pappas, p, Baltimore). **Boston (1)**–William Monbouquette, p. **Chicago (2)**–●Luis Aparicio, ss; James Landis, of. **Cleveland (2)**–Richard Donovan, p; John Romano, c. **Detroit (3)**–Henry Aguirre, p; James Bunning, p; Rocco Colavito, of. **Kansas City (1)**–Norman Siebern, 1b. **Los Angeles (3)**–●William Moran, 2b; J. LeRoy Thomas, of; ●Leon Wagner, of. **Minnesota (3)**–●Earl Battey, c; Camilo Pascual, p; ●Richard Rollins, 3b. **New York (6)**–Elston Howard, c; ●Mickey Mantle, of; ●Roger Maris, of; Robert Richardson, 2b; Ralph Terry, p; Thomas Tresh, ss. **Washington (1)**–David Stenhouse, p. **SECOND GAME CHANGES: Players Replaced**–Monbouquette, Landis. **Additions**–Henry Bauer, Kansas City, and William Rigney, Los Angeles, coaches; James Runnels, 1b, Boston; Al Kaline, of, Detroit; Kenneth McBride, p, Los Angeles; James Kaat, p, Minnesota; Lawrence Berra, c, New York (McBride replaced by Ray Herbert, p, Chicago).

    NATIONAL LEAGUE–Frederick Hutchinson, Cincinnati, manager; Charles Stengel, New York, and John Keane, St. Louis, coaches. **Chicago (1)**–Ernest Banks, 1b. **Cincinnati (1)**–Robert Purkey, p. **Houston (1)**–Richard Farrell, p. **Los Angeles (5)**–●H. Thomas Davis, of; Donald Drysdale, p; Sanford Koufax, p; John Roseboro, c; ●Maurice Wills, ss. **Milwaukee (4)**–Henry Aaron, of; Frank Bolling, 2b; ●Delmar Crandall, c; Robert Shaw, p (Aaron replaced by Warren Spahn, p, Milwaukee). **New York (1)**–Richie Ashburn, of. **Philadelphia (1)**–John Callison, of. **Pittsburgh (3)**–●Roberto Clemente, of; ●Richard Groat, ss; ●William Mazeroski, 2b. **St. Louis (3)**–●Kenton Boyer, 3b; Robert Gibson, p; Stanley Musial, of. **San Francisco (5)**–Felipe Alou, of; ●Orlando Cepeda, 1b; James Davenport, 3b; Juan Marichal, p; ●Willie Mays, of. **SECOND GAME CHANGES: Players Replaced**–Koufax, Shaw, Drysdale, Alou. **Additions**–Harry Craft, Houston, and George Tebbetts, Milwaukee, coaches; Billy Williams, of, and George Altman, of, Chicago; Frank Robinson, of, Cincinnati; John Podres, p, Los Angeles; Henry Aaron, of, and Edwin Mathews, 3b, Milwaukee; Arthur Mahaffey, p, Philadelphia.

1963

    AMERICAN LEAGUE–Ralph Houk, New York, manager; John Pesky, Boston, and Sabath Mele, Minnesota, coaches. **Baltimore (3)**–Luis Aparicio, ss; Stephen Barber, p; Brooks Robinson, 3b (Barber replaced by William Monbouquette, p, Boston). **Boston (3)**–●Frank Malzone, 3b; Richard Radatz, p; Carl Yastrzemski, of. **Chicago (2)**–●J. Nelson Fox, 2b; Juan Pizarro, p. **Cleveland (1)**–James Grant, p. **Detroit (2)**–James Bunning, p; ●Albert Kaline, of. **Kansas City (1)**–Norman Siebern, 1b-of. **Los Angeles (3)**–

Kenneth McBride, p; ●Albert Pearson, of; ●Leon Wagner, of. **Minnesota (4)**—W. Robert Allison, of; ●Earl Battey, c; Harmon Killebrew, of; ●Zoilo Versalles, ss. **New York (6)**—James Bouton, p; Elston Howard, c; ●Mickey Mantle, of; ●Joseph Pepitone, 1b; Robert Richardson, 2b; Thomas Tresh, of. **Washington (1)**—Donald Leppert, c. **NOTE**—Mantle was sidelined with fracture of left foot when he was voted on team and was not included in squad.

NATIONAL LEAGUE—Alvin Dark, San Francisco, manager; Robert Kennedy, Chicago, and Gene Mauch, Philadelphia, coaches. **Chicago (2)**—Lawrence Jackson, p; Ronald Santo, 3b. **Cincinnati (2)**—John Edwards, c; James O'Toole, p. **Houston (1)**—Harold Woodeshick, p. **Los Angeles (4)**—●H. Thomas Davis, of; Donald Drysdale, p; Sanford Koufax, p; Maurice Wills, ss. **Milwaukee (3)**—●Henry Aaron, of; Warren Spahn, p; Joseph Torre, c. **New York (1)**—Edwin Snider, of. **Philadelphia (1)**—Raymond Culp, p. **Pittsburgh (2)**—Roberto Clemente, of; ●William Mazeroski, 2b (Mazeroski replaced by Julian Javier, 2b, St. Louis). **St. Louis (4)**—●Kenton Boyer, 3b; ●Richard Groat, ss; Stanley Musial, of; ●William White, 1b. **San Francisco (5)**—●L. Edgar Bailey, c; Orlando Cepeda, 1b; Juan Marichal, p; ●Willie Mays, of; Willie McCovey, of.

1964

AMERICAN LEAGUE—Alfonso Lopez, Chicago, manager; Anthony Cuccinello, Chicago, and Gilbert Hodges, Washington, coaches. **Baltimore (3)**—Luis Aparicio, ss; ●Brooks Robinson, 3b; Norman Siebern, 1b (Aparicio replaced by Edward Bressoud, ss, Boston). **Boston (2)**—Frank Malzone, 3b; Richard Radatz, p. **Chicago (2)**—Gary Peters, p; Juan Pizarro, p. **Cleveland (1)**—John Kralick, p. **Detroit (3)**—William Freehan, c; Albert Kaline, of; Jerry Lumpe, 2b (Kaline replaced by Rocco Colavito, of, Kansas City). **Kansas City (1)**—Jonathan Wyatt, p. **Los Angeles (2)**—W. Dean Chance, p; ●James Fregosi, ss. **Minnesota (5)**—●W. Robert Allison, 1b; Jimmie Hall, of; ●Harmon Killebrew, of; ●Pedro Oliva, of; Camilo Pascual, p. **New York (5)**—Edward Ford, p; ●Elston Howard, c; ●Mickey Mantle, of; Joseph Pepitone, 1b; ●Robert Richardson, 2b. **Washington (1)**—Charles Hinton, of.

NATIONAL LEAGUE—Walter Alston, Los Angeles, manager; Frederick Hutchinson, Cincinnati, and Charles Stengel, New York, coaches. **Chicago (3)**—Richard Ellsworth, p; Ronald Santo, 3b; ●Billy Williams, of. **Cincinnati (2)**—Leonardo Cardenas, ss; John Edwards, c. **Houston (1)**—Richard Farrell, p. **Los Angeles (2)**—Donald Drysdale, p; Sanford Koufax, p. **Milwaukee (2)**—●Henry Aaron, of; ●Joseph Torre, c. **New York (1)**—●Ronald Hunt, 2b. **Philadelphia (3)**—James Bunning, p; John Callison, of; Christopher Short, p. **Pittsburgh (4)**—Forrest Burgess, c; ●Roberto Clemente, of; William Mazeroski, 2b; Wilver Stargell, of. **St. Louis (4)**—●Kenton Boyer, 3b; Curtis Flood, of; ●Richard Groat, ss; William White, 1b. **San Francisco (3)**—●Orlando Cepeda, 1b; Juan Marichal, p; ●Willie Mays, of.

1965

AMERICAN LEAGUE—Alfonso Lopez, Chicago, manager; Donald Gutteridge, Chicago, and Sabath Mele, Minnesota, coaches. **Baltimore (2)**—Milton Pappas, p; ●Brooks Robinson, 3b. **Boston (2)**—●Felix Mantilla, 2b; Carl Yastrzemski, of (Yastrzemski replaced by William Freehan, c, Detroit). **Chicago (2)**—Eddie Fisher, p; ●William Skowron, 1b (Skowron replaced by Joe Pepitone, 1b, New York). **Cleveland (4)**—R. Maxwell Alvis, 3b; ●Rocco Colavito, of; ●Victor Davalillo, of; Samuel McDowell, p. **Detroit (3)**—●Willie Horton, of; Albert Kaline, of; ●Richard McAuliffe, ss. **Kansas City (1)**—John O'Donoghue, p. **Los Angeles (1)**—Robert Lee, p. **Minnesota (5)**—●Earl Battey, c; James Grant, p; Jimmie Hall, of; Harmon Killebrew, 3b; Zoilo Versalles, ss. **New York (4)**—Elston Howard, c; Mickey Mantle, of; Robert Richardson, 2b; Melvin Stottlemyre, p (Mantle replaced by Pedro Oliva, of, Minnesota). **Washington (1)**—Pete Richert, p.

NATIONAL LEAGUE—Gene Mauch, Philadelphia, manager; Richard Sisler, Cincinnati, and Robert Bragan, Milwaukee, coaches. **Chicago (3)**—●Ernest Banks, 1b; Ronald Santo, 3b; Billy Williams, of. **Cincinnati (6)**—Leonardo Cardenas, ss; John Edwards, c; Samuel Ellis, p; James Maloney, p; Frank Robinson, of; ●Peter Rose, 2b. **Houston (1)**—Richard Farrell, p. **Los Angeles (3)**—Donald Drysdale, p; Sanford Koufax, p; ●Maurice Wills, ss. **Milwaukee (2)**—●Henry Aaron, of; ●Joseph Torre, c. **New York (1)**—Edward Kranepool, 1b. **Philadelphia (3)**—●Richard Allen, 3b; John Callison, of; Octavio Rojas, 2b. **Pittsburgh (3)**—Roberto Clemente, of; ●Wilver Stargell, of; Robert Veale, p. **St. Louis (1)**—Robert Gibson, p. **San Francisco (2)**—Juan Marichal, p; ●Willie Mays, of.

1966

AMERICAN LEAGUE—Sabath Mele, Minnesota, manager; Henry Bauer, Baltimore, and George Tebbetts, Cleveland, coaches. **Baltimore (4)**—Stephen Barber, p; Andrew Etchebarren, c; ●Brooks Robinson, 3b; ●Frank Robinson, of. **Boston (2)**—●George Scott, 1b; Carl Yastrzemski, of. **California (2)**—James Fregosi, ss; ●Robert Knoop, 2b. **Chicago (1)**—Tommie Agee, of. **Cleveland (3)**—Gary Bell, p; Rocco Colavito, of; Samuel McDowell, p (McDowell replaced by Wilfred Siebert, p, Cleveland). **Detroit (5)**—Norman Cash, 1b; ●William Freehan, c; ●Albert Kaline, of; ●Richard McAuliffe, ss; Dennis McLain, p. **Kansas City (1)**—James Hunter, p. **Minnesota (4)**—Earl Battey, c; James Kaat, p; Harmon Killebrew, 3b; ●Pedro Oliva, of. **New York (2)**—Robert Richardson, 2b; Melvin Stottlemyre, p. **Washington (1)**—Peter Richert, p.

NATIONAL LEAGUE—Walter Alston, Los Angeles, manager; Herman Franks, San Francisco, and Harry Walker, Pittsburgh, coaches. **Atlanta (3)**—●Henry Aaron, of; Felipe Alou, 1b; ●Joseph Torre, c. **Chicago (1)**—Ronald Santo, 3b. **Cincinnati (2)**—●Leonardo Cardenas, ss; William McCool, p. **Houston (2)**—●Joe Morgan, 2b; J. Claude Raymond, p. **Los Angeles (3)**—Sanford Koufax, p; James Lefebvre, 2b; Maurice Wills, ss. **New York (1)**—Ronald Hunt, 2b. **Philadelphia (2)**—Richard Allen, of; James Bunning, p. **Pittsburgh (3)**—●Roberto Clemente, of; Wilver Stargell, of; Robert Veale, p. **St. Louis (3)**—Curtis Flood, of; Robert Gibson, p; J. Timothy McCarver, c (Gibson replaced by Philip Regan, p, Los Angeles). **San Francisco (6)**—Thomas Haller, c; James Hart, 3b; Juan Marichal, p; ●Willie Mays, of; ●Willie McCovey, 1b; Gaylord Perry, p. (NOTE—Morgan was sidelined with fractured kneecap after being named to starting lineup and was not included on squad).

1967

AMERICAN LEAGUE—Henry Bauer, Baltimore, manager; William Rigney, California, and Edward Stanky, Chicago, coaches. **Baltimore (3)**—●Brooks Robinson, 3b; Andrew Etchebarren, c; ●Frank Robinson, of (Frank Robinson replaced by A. Kenneth Berry, of, Chicago). **Boston (4)**—Anthony Conigliaro, of; James Lonborg, p; ●Americo Petrocelli, ss; ●Carl Yastrzemski, of. **California (3)**—James Fregosi, ss; James McGlothlin, p; Donald Mincher, 1b. **Chicago (3)**—Tommie Agee, of; Joel Horlen, p; Gary Peters, p. **Cleveland (2)**—R. Maxwell Alvis, 3b; Steve Hargan, p. **Detroit (3)**—●William Freehan, c; ●Albert Kaline, of; Richard McAuliffe, ss (Kaline replaced by Pedro Oliva, of, Minnesota). **Kansas City (1)**—James Hunter, p. **Minnesota (3)**—●Rodney Carew, 2b; W. Dean Chance, p; ●Harmon Killebrew, 1b. **New York (2)**—Alphonso Downing, p; Mickey Mantle, 1b. **Washington (1)**—Paulino Casanova, c.

NATIONAL LEAGUE—Walter Alston, Los Angeles, manager; Herman Franks, San Francisco, and Harry Walker, Pittsburgh, coaches. **Atlanta (3)**—●Henry Aaron, of; ●Joseph Torre, c; Denver Lemaster, p (Lemaster replaced by Chris Short, p, Philadelphia). **Chicago (2)**—Ernest Banks, 1b; Ferguson Jenkins, p. **Cincinnati (3)**—Tommy Helms, 2b; Atanasio Perez, 3b; Peter Rose, of. **Houston (3)**—Miguel Cuellar, p; Daniel Staub, of; James Wynn, of. **Los Angeles (2)**—Donald Drysdale, p; Claude Osteen, p. **New York (1)**—G. Thomas Seaver, p. **Philadelphia (3)**—●Richard Allen, 3b. **Pittsburgh (3)**—●L. Eugene Alley, ss; ●Roberto Clemente, of; ●William Mazeroski, 2b. **St. Louis (4)**—●Louis Brock, of; ●Orlando Cepeda, 1b; Robert Gibson, p; J. Timothy McCarver, c. **San Francisco (3)**—Thomas Haller, c; Juan Marichal, p; Willie Mays, of.

1968

AMERICAN LEAGUE—Richard Williams, Boston, manager; Calvin Ermer, Minnesota, and E. Mayo Smith, Detroit, coaches. **Baltimore (3)**—David Johnson, 2b; John Powell, 1b; ●Brooks Robinson, 3b. **Boston (3)**—Kenneth Harrelson, of; Jose Santiago, p; ●Carl Yastrzemski, of (Santiago replaced by Gary Bell, p, Boston). **California (1)**—●James Fregosi, ss. **Chicago (2)**—Thomas John, p; Duane Josephson, c. **Cleveland (3)**—Jose Azcue, c; Samuel McDowell, p; Luis Tiant, p. **Detroit (4)**—●William Freehan, c; ●Willie Horton, of; Dennis McLain, p; Donald Wert, 3b. **Minnesota (3)**—●Rodney Carew, 2b; ●Harmon Killebrew, 1b; Pedro Oliva, of. **New York (2)**—Mickey Mantle, of; Melvin Stottlemyre, p. **Oakland (3)**—Dagoberto Campaneris, ss; Robert Monday, of; Johnny Odom, p. **Washington (1)**—●Frank Howard, of.

NATIONAL LEAGUE—Albert Schoendienst, St. Louis, manager; J. David Bristol, Cincinnati, and Herman Franks, San Francisco, coaches. **Atlanta (3)**—●Henry Aaron, of; Felipe Alou, of; Ronald Reed, p. **Chicago (2)**−•Donald Kessinger, ss; •Ronald Santo, 3b. **Cincinnati (4)**−Johnny Bench, c; •Tommy Helms, 2b; Atanasio Perez, 3b; •Peter Rose, of (Rose replaced by Billy Williams, of, Chicago). **Houston (1)**−Daniel Staub, 1b. **Los Angeles (2)**−Donald Drysdale, p; Thomas Haller, c. **New York (3)**−•Gerald Grote, c; Jerry Koosman, p; G. Thomas Seaver, p. **Philadelphia (1)**−Woodrow Fryman, p. **Pittsburgh (2)**−L. Eugene Alley, ss; Mateo Alou, of (Alley replaced by Leonardo Cardenas, ss, Cincinnati). **St. Louis (4)**−Steven Carlton, p; •Curtis Flood, of; Robert Gibson, p; M. Julian Javier, 2b. **San Francisco (3)**−Juan Marichal, p; Willie Mays, of; •Willie McCovey, 1b.

1969

AMERICAN LEAGUE−E. Mayo Smith, Detroit, manager; Alvin Dark, Cleveland, Earl Weaver, Baltimore, and Theodore Williams, Washington, coaches. **Baltimore (6)**−Paul Blair, of; David Johnson, 2b; David McNally, p; •John Powell, 1b; Brooks Robinson, 3b; •Frank Robinson, of (Johnson replaced by Michael Andrews, 2b, Boston). **Boston (4)**−Raymond Culp, p; •Americo Petrocelli, ss; C. Reginald Smith, of; Carl Yastrzemski, of. **California (1)**−James Fregosi, ss. **Chicago (1)**−Carlos May, of. **Cleveland (1)**−Samuel McDowell, p. **Detroit (3)**−•William Freehan, c; Michael Lolich, p; Dennis McLain, p. **Kansas City (1)**−Eliseo Rodriguez, c. **Minnesota (4)**−•Rodney Carew, 2b; Harmon Killebrew, 1b; Pedro Oliva, of; John Roseboro, c (Oliva replaced by Roy White, of, New York). **New York (1)**−Melvin Stottlemyre, p. **Oakland (3)**−•Salvatore Bando, 3b; •Reginald Jackson, of; Johnny Odom, p. **Seattle (1)**−J. Michael Hegan, of-1b (Hegan replaced by Donald Mincher, 1b, Seattle). **Washington (2)**−•Frank Howard, of; Darold Knowles, p.

NATIONAL LEAGUE−Albert Schoendienst, St. Louis, manager; Léo Durocher, Chicago, and J. David Bristol, Cincinnati, coaches. **Atlanta (3)**−•Henry Aaron, of; •Felix Millan, 2b; Philip Niekro, p. **Chicago (5)**−Ernest Banks, 1b; Glenn Beckert, 2b; C. Randolph Hundley, c; •Donald Kessinger, ss; •Ronald Santo, 3b. **Cincinnati (4)**−•Johnny Bench, c; Lee May, 1b; Atanasio Perez, 3b; Peter Rose, of. **Houston (2)**−Lawrence Dierker, p; Denis Menke, ss. **Los Angeles (1)**−William Singer, p. **Montreal (1)**−Daniel Staub, of. **New York (3)**−•Cleon Jones, of; Jerry Koosman, p; G. Thomas Seaver, p. **Philadelphia (1)**−Grant Jackson, p. **Pittsburgh (2)**−•Mateo Alou, of; Roberto Clemente, of. **St. Louis (2)**−Steven Carlton, p; Robert Gibson, p. **San Diego (1)**−Christopher Cannizzaro, c. **San Francisco (3)**−Juan Marichal, p; Willie Mays, of; •Willie McCovey, 1b.

1970

AMERICAN LEAGUE−Earl Weaver, Baltimore, manager; Ralph Houk, New York, Harold (Lefty) Phillips, California, coaches. **Baltimore (6)**−Miguel Cuellar, p; David McNally, p; James Palmer, p; •John Powell, 1b; Brooks Robinson, 3b; •Frank Robinson, of. **Boston (2)**−Gerald Moses, c; •Carl Yastrzemski, of. **California (4)**−Santos Alomar, 2b; James Fregosi, ss; Alexander Johnson, of; Clyde Wright, p. **Chicago (1)**−•Luis Aparicio, ss. **Cleveland (2)**−Raymond Fosse, c; Samuel McDowell, p. **Detroit (2)**−•William Freehan, c; Willie Horton, of. **Kansas City (1)**−Amos Otis, of. **Milwaukee (1)**−Tommy Harper, 3b. **Minnesota (4)**−•Rodney Carew, 2b; •Harmon Killebrew, 3b; Pedro Oliva, of; James Perry, p (Carew replaced by David Johnson, 2b, Baltimore). **New York (3)**−Fred Peterson, p; Melvin Stottlemyre, p; Roy White, of. **Oakland (1)**−James Hunter, p. **Washington (1)**−•Frank Howard, of.

NATIONAL LEAGUE−Gilbert Hodges, New York, manager; Leo Durocher, Chicago, Luman Harris, Atlanta, coaches. **Atlanta (4)**−•Henry Aaron, of; •Ricardo Carty, of; Felix Millan, 2b; J. Hoyt Wilhelm, p (Millan replaced by Joe Morgan, 2b, Houston). **Chicago (3)**−•Glenn Beckert, 2b; James Hickman, of; •Donald Kessinger, ss. **Cincinnati (5)**−•Johnny Bench, c; James Merritt, p; •Atanasio Perez, 3b; Peter Rose, of; Wayne Simpson, p. **Houston (1)**−Denis Menke, ss. **Los Angeles (2)**−Billy Grabarkewitz, 3b; Claude Osteen, p. **Montreal (1)**−Daniel Staub, of. **New York (2)**−Derrel Harrelson, ss; G. Thomas Seaver, p. **Philadelphia (1)**−Joseph Hoerner, p. **Pittsburgh (1)**−Roberto Clemente, of. **St. Louis (3)**−•Richard Allen, 1b; Robert Gibson, p; Joseph Torre, c. **San Diego (1)**−Clarence Gaston, of. **San Francisco (4)**−Richard Dietz, c; •Willie Mays, of; Willie McCovey, 1b; Gaylord Perry, p.

1971

AMERICAN LEAGUE—Earl Weaver, Baltimore, manager; G. William Hunter, Baltimore, Alfred (Billy) Martin, Detroit, coaches. **Baltimore (6)**—Donald Buford, of; Miguel Cuellar, p; James Palmer, p; ●John Powell, 1b; ●Brooks Robinson, 3b; ●Frank Robinson, of (Powell replaced by Norman Cash, 1b, Detroit). **Boston (3)**—Luis Aparicio, ss; Wilfred Siebert, p; ●Carl Yastrzemski, of. **California (1)**—John Messersmith, p. **Chicago (1)**—William Melton, 3b. **Cleveland (2)**—●Raymond Fosse, c; Samuel McDowell, p (Fosse replaced by David Duncan, c, Oakland and McDowell replaced by Wilbur Wood, p, Chicago). **Detroit (3)**—William Freehan, c; Albert Kaline, of; Michael Lolich, p. **Kansas City (2)**—Amos Otis, of; Octavio Rojas, 2b. **Milwaukee (1)**—Martin Pattin, p. **Minnesota (5)**—Leo Cardenas, ss; ●Rodney Carew, 2b; Harmon Killebrew, 3b; ●Pedro Oliva, of; James Perry, p (Oliva replaced by Reginald Jackson, of, Oakland). **New York (2)**—Thurman Munson, c; Bobby Murcer, of. **Oakland (1)**—Vida Blue, p. **Washington (1)**—Frank Howard, of.

NATIONAL LEAGUE—George (Sparky) Anderson, Cincinnati, manager; Walter Alston, Los Angeles, Pedro (Preston) Gomez, San Diego, Daniel Murtaugh, Pittsburgh, coaches. **Atlanta (2)**—●Henry Aaron, of; Felix Millan, 2b. **Chicago (4)**—●Glenn Beckert, 2b; Ferguson Jenkins, p; Donald Kessinger, ss; Ronald Santo, 3b. **Cincinnati (4)**—●Johnny Bench, c; Clay Carroll, p; Lee May, 1b; Peter Rose, of. **Houston (1)**—Lawrence Dierker, p (Dierker replaced by Donald Wilson, p, Houston). **Los Angeles (1)**—William Davis, of. **Montreal (1)**—Daniel Staub, of. **New York (2)**—Derrel Harrelson, ss; G. Thomas Seaver, p. **Philadelphia (1)**—Richard Wise, p. **Pittsburgh (4)**—Roberto Clemente, of; Dock Ellis, p; Manuel Sanguillen, c; ●Wilver Stargell, of. **St. Louis (3)**—Louis Brock, of; Steven Carlton, p; ●Joseph Torre, 3b. **San Diego (1)**—Nathan Colbert, 1b. **San Francisco (4)**—Bobby Bonds, of; Juan Marichal, p; ●Willie Mays, of; ●Willie McCovey, 1b.

1972

AMERICAN LEAGUE—Earl Weaver, Baltimore, manager; Robert Lemon, Kansas City, Richard Williams, Oakland, coaches. **Baltimore (4)**—Patrick Dobson, p; David McNally, p; James Palmer, p; ●Brooks Robinson, 3b. **Boston (3)**—●Luis Aparicio, ss; Carlton Fisk, c; ●Carl Yastrzemski, of (Aparicio replaced by Toby Harrah, ss, Texas, who was replaced by Robert Grich, ss, Baltimore). **California (1)**—L. Nolan Ryan, p. **Chicago (3)**—●Richard Allen, 1b; Carlos May, of; Wilbur Wood, p. **Cleveland (1)**—Gaylord Perry, p. **Detroit (2)**—Norman Cash, 1b; Joseph Coleman, p; ●William Freehan, c; Michael Lolich, p (Coleman replaced by Kenneth Holtzman, p, Oakland). **Kansas City (5)**—Amos Otis, of; Freddie Patek, ss; Louis Piniella, of; Octavio Rojas, 2b; Richard Scheinblum, of (Patek replaced by Dagoberto Campaneris, ss, Oakland and Otis replaced by C. Reginald Smith, of, Boston). **Milwaukee (1)**—Eliseo Rodriguez, c. **Minnesota (1)**—●Rodney Carew, 2b. **New York (1)**—●Bobby Murcer, of. **Oakland (1)**—Salvatore Bando, 3b; James Hunter, p; ●Reginald Jackson, of; Joseph Rudi, of. **Texas (0)**.

NATIONAL LEAGUE Daniel Murtaugh, Pittsburgh, manager; Charles Fox, San Francisco, Albert Schoendienst, St. Louis, coaches. **Atlanta (1)**—●Henry Aaron, of. **Chicago (4)**—Glenn Beckert, 2b; ●Donald Kessinger, ss; Ronald Santo, 3b; Billy Williams, of. **Cincinnati (4)**—●Johnny Bench, c; Clay Carroll, p; ●Joe Morgan, 2b; Gary Nolan, p (Nolan replaced by Ferguson Jenkins, p, Chicago). **Houston (2)**—Cesar Cedeno, of; ●Lee May, 1b. **Los Angeles (1)**—Donald Sutton, p. **Montreal (1)**—William Stoneman, p. **New York (3)**—Willie Mays, of; Frank McGraw, p; G. Thomas Seaver, p. **Philadelphia (1)**—Steven Carlton, p. **Pittsburgh (5)**—Stephen Blass, p; ●Roberto Clemente, of; Albert Oliver, of; Manuel Sanguillen, c; ●Wilver Stargell, of. **St. Louis (4)**—Louis Brock, of; Robert Gibson, p; Ted Simmons, c; ●Joseph Torre, 3b. **San Diego (1)**—Nathan Colbert, 1b. **San Francisco (1)**—Chris Speier, ss.

1973

AMERICAN LEAGUE—Richard Williams, Oakland, manager; Charles Tanner, Chicago, Dorrel Herzog, Texas, coaches. **Baltimore (2)**—Paul Blair, of; ●Brooks Robinson, 3b; **Boston (3)**—●Carlton Fisk, c; William Lee, p; Carl Yastrzemski, 1b (Yastrzemski replaced by James Spencer, 1b, Texas). **California (2)**—L. Nolan Ryan, p; William Singer, p. **Chicago (1)**—●Richard Allen, 1b (Allen replaced by H. Patrick Kelly, of, Chicago). **Cleveland (1)**—David Bell, 3b. **Detroit (3)**—Edwin Brinkman, ss; William Freehan, c;

Willie Horton, of. **Kansas City (3)**—John Mayberry, 1b; •Amos Otis, of; Octavio Rojas, 2b. **Milwaukee (2)**—James Colborn, p; David May, of. **Minnesota (2)**—Rikalbert Blyleven, p; •Rodney Carew, 2b. **New York (3)**—Albert Lyle, p; Thurman Munson, c; •Bobby Murcer, of. **Oakland (6)**—Salvatore Bando, 3b; •Dagoberto Campaneris, ss; Roland Fingers, p; Kenneth Holtzman, p; James Hunter, p; •Reginald Jackson, of. **Texas (1)**—David Nelson, 2b.

NATIONAL LEAGUE—George (Sparky) Anderson, Cincinnati, manager; Gene Mauch, Montreal, William Virdon, Pittsburgh, coaches. **Atlanta (3)**—•Henry Aaron, 1b; Darrell Evans, 3b; David Johnson, 2b. **Chicago (2)**—•Ronald Santo, 3b; •Billy Williams, of. **Cincinnati (5)**—•Johnny Bench, c; John Billingham, p; David Concepcion, ss; •Joe Morgan, 2b; •Pete Rose, of (Concepcion replaced by William Russell, ss, Los Angeles). **Houston (2)**—•Cesar Cedeno, of; Robert Watson, of. **Los Angeles (5)**—James Brewer, p; William Davis, of; Manuel Mota, of; Claude Osteen, p; Donald Sutton, p. **Montreal (1)**—Ronald Fairly, 1b. **New York (2)**—Willie Mays, of; G. Thomas Seaver, p. **Philadelphia (1)**—Wayne Twitchell, p. **Pittsburgh (2)**—J. David Giusti, p; Wilver Stargell, of. **St. Louis (3)**—Ted Simmons, c; Joseph Torre, 3b; Richard Wise, p. **San Diego (1)**—Nathan Colbert, 1b. **San Francisco (2)**—Bobby Bonds, of; •Chris Speier, ss.

1974

AMERICAN LEAGUE—Richard Williams, manager; Earl Weaver, Baltimore, honorary manager; Dorrel Herzog, California, John McKeon, Kansas City, coaches. **Baltimore (3)**—Miguel Cuellar, p; Robert Grich, 2b; •Brooks Robinson, 3b. **Boston (3)**—•Carlton Fisk, c; Luis Tiant, p; Carl Yastrzemski, of (Fisk replaced by Edward Herrmann, c, Chicago, who was later replaced by James Sundberg, c, Texas). **California (2)**—David Chalk, 3b; Frank Robinson, of. **Chicago (2)**—•Richard Allen, 1b; Wilbur Wood, p. **Cleveland (2)**—George Hendrick, of; Gaylord Perry, p. **Detroit (2)**—John Hiller, p; Albert Kaline, of. **Kansas City (3)**—Steven Busby, p; John Mayberry, 1b; Octavio Rojas, 2b. **Milwaukee (1)**—Darrell Porter, c. **Minnesota (1)**—•Rodney Carew, 2b. **New York (2)**—Thurman Munson, c; •Bobby Murcer, of. **Oakland (6)**—Salvatore Bando, 3b; •Dagoberto Campaneris, ss; Roland Fingers, p; James Hunter, p; •Reginald Jackson, of; Joseph Rudi, of (Bando replaced by Donald Money, 3b, Milwaukee). **Texas (1)**—•Jeffrey Burroughs, of.

Earl Weaver stepped down as manager of the A.L. in favor of Richard Williams, manager of the 1973 A.L. champion Oakland Athletics, who was inactive at the time of the All-Star Game.

NATIONAL LEAGUE—Lawrence (Yogi) Berra, New York, manager; George (Sparky) Anderson, Cincinnati, Albert (Red) Schoendienst, St. Louis, coaches. **Atlanta (3)**—•Henry Aaron, of; Lee Capra, p; Ralph Garr, of. **Chicago (1)**—Donald Kessinger, ss. **Cincinnati (4)**—•Johnny Bench, c; •Joseph Morgan, 2b; Atanasio Perez, 1b; •Pete Rose, of. **Houston (1)**—Cesar Cedeno, of. **Los Angeles (5)**—Ronald Cey, 3b; •Steven Garvey, 1b; Michael Marshall, p; John Messersmith, p; •James Wynn, of. **Montreal (1)**—Stephen Rogers, p. **New York (2)**—Gerald Grote, c; Jonathan Matlack, p. **Philadelphia (4)**—•Lawrence Bowa, ss; Steven Carlton, p; David Cash, 2b; Michael Schmidt, 3b. **Pittsburgh (1)**—Kenneth Brett, p. **St. Louis (4)**—Louis Brock, of; Lynn McGlothen, p; Ted Simmons, c; Reginald Smith, of. **San Diego (1)**—John Grubb, of. **San Francisco (1)**—Chris Speier, ss.

1975

AMERICAN LEAGUE—Alvin Dark, Oakland, manager; Delmar Crandall, Milwaukee, Alfred Martin, Texas, coaches. **Baltimore (1)**—James Palmer, p. **Boston (2)**—Fredric Lynn, of; Carl Yastrzemski, of. **California (2)**—David Chalk, 3b; L. Nolan Ryan, p. **Chicago (4)**—Russell Dent, ss; Richard Gossage, p; James Kaat, p; Jorge Orta, 2b (Orta replaced by Colbert Harrah, ss, Texas). **Cleveland (1)**—George Hendrick, of. **Detroit (1)**—William Freehan, c. **Kansas City (2)**—Steven Busby, p; Harold McRae, of. **Milwaukee (2)**—Henry Aaron, of; George Scott, 1b. **Minnesota (1)**—•Rodney Carew, 2b. **New York (4)**—•Bobby Bonds, of; James Hunter, p; •Thurman Munson, c; •Graig Nettles, 3b. **Oakland (7)**—Vida Blue, p; •Dagoberto Campaneris, ss; Roland Fingers, p; •Reginald Jackson, of; •Joseph Rudi, of; •F. Gene Tenace, 1b; Claudell Washington, of. **Texas (1)**—D. Michael Hargrove, 1b.

NATIONAL LEAGUE—Walter Alston, Los Angeles, manager; Daniel Murtaugh,

Pittsburgh, Albert Schoendienst, St. Louis, coaches. **Atlanta (1)**—Philip Niekro, p. **Chicago (1)**—Bill Madlock, 3b. **Cincinnati (5)**—•Johnny Bench, c; •David Concepcion, ss; •Joe Morgan, 2b; Atanasio Perez, 1b; •Peter Rose, of. **Houston (1)**—Robert Watson, 1b. **Los Angeles (6)**—•Ronald Cey, 3b; •Steven Garvey, 1b; Michael Marshall, p; John Messersmith, p; Donald Sutton, p; •James Wynn, of. **Montreal (1)**—Gary Carter, of. **New York (2)**—Jonathan Matlack, p; G. Thomas Seaver, p. **Philadelphia (4)**—Lawrence Bowa, ss; David Cash, 2b; Gregory Luzinski, of; Frank McGraw, p. **Pittsburgh (3)**—Albert Oliver, of; Jerry Reuss, p; Manuel Sanguillen, c. **St. Louis (2)**—•Louis Brock, of; C. Reginald Smith, of. **San Diego (1)**—Randall Jones, p. **San Francisco (1)**—Bobby Murcer, of.

1976

AMERICAN LEAGUE—Darrell Johnson, Boston, manager; Gene Mauch, Minnesota, Frank Robinson, Cleveland, coaches. **Baltimore (2)**—Mark Belanger, ss; •Robert Grich, 2b. **Boston (4)**—Carlton Fisk, c; •Fredric Lynn, of; Luis Tiant, p; Carl Yastrzemski, 1b. **California (1)**—Frank Tanana, p. **Chicago (1)**—Richard Gossage, p. **Cleveland (1)**—David LaRoche, p. **Detroit (3)**—Mark Fidrych, p; •Ronald LeFlore, of; •Daniel Staub, of. **Kansas City (4)**—•George Brett, 3b; Harold McRae, of; Amos Otis, of; Freddie Patek, ss. **Milwaukee (2)**—Donald Money, 3b; William Travers, p. **Minnesota (2)**—•Rodney Carew, 1b; Harold Wynegar, c. **New York (6)**—C. Christopher Chambliss, 1b; James Hunter, p; Albert Lyle, p; •Thurman Munson, c; William Randolph, 2b (replaced by Philip Garner, 2b, Oakland); John Rivers, of. **Oakland (1)**—Roland Fingers, p. **Texas (1)**—•Colbert Harrah, ss.

NATIONAL LEAGUE—George (Sparky) Anderson, Cincinnati, manager; John McNamara, San Diego, Daniel Ozark, Philadelphia, coaches. **Atlanta (1)**—John Messersmith, p (replaced by Richard Ruthven, p, Atlanta). **Chicago (1)**—Steven Swisher, c. **Cincinnati (7)**—•Johnny Bench, c; •David Concepcion, ss; •George Foster, of; G. Kenneth Griffey, of; •Joe Morgan, 2b; Atanasio Perez, 1b; •Peter Rose, 3b. **Houston (2)**—Cesar Cedeno, of; Kenneth Forsch, p. **Los Angeles (4)**—Ronald Cey, 3b; •Steven Garvey, 1b; Richard Rhoden, p; William Russell, ss. **Montreal (1)**—Woodrow Fryman, p. **New York (3)**—•David Kingman, of; Jonathan Matlack, p; G. Thomas Seaver, p. **Philadelphia (5)**—Robert Boone, c; Lawrence Bowa, ss; David Cash, 2b; •Gregory Luzinski, of; Michael Schmidt, 3b. **Pittsburgh (1)**—Albert Oliver, of. **St. Louis (1)**—Arnold McBride, of. **San Diego (1)**—Randall Jones, p. **San Francisco (1)**—John Montefusco, p.

1977

AMERICAN LEAGUE—Alfred (Billy) Martin, New York, manager; Alexander Grammas, Milwaukee, Robert Lemon, Chicago, coaches. **Baltimore (2)**—James Palmer, p; Kenneth Singleton, of. **Boston (7)**—•Richard Burleson, ss; William Campbell, p; •Carlton Fisk, c; Fredric Lynn, of; James Rice, of; George Scott, 1b; •Carl Yastrzemski, of. **California (1)**—Frank Tanana, p (replaced by David LaRoche, p, California, who replaced L. Nolan Ryan, p, California). **Chicago (1)**—•Richard Zisk, of. **Cleveland (1)**—Dennis Eckersley, p. **Detroit (2)**—Mark Fidrych, p (replaced by James Kern, p, Cleveland); Jason Thompson, 1b. **Kansas City (1)**—•George Brett, 3b. **Milwaukee (1)**—Donald Money, 2b (replaced by James Slaton, p, Milwaukee). **Minnesota (3)**—•Rodney Carew, 1b; Larry Hisle, of; Harold Wynegar, c. **New York (5)**—•Reginald Jackson, of; Albert Lyle, p; Thurman Munson, c; Graig Nettles, 3b; •William Randolph, 2b. **Oakland (1)**—Vida Blue, p (replaced by Wayne Gross, 3b, Oakland). **Seattle (1)**—Ruppert Jones, of. **Texas (1)**—Dagoberto Campaneris, ss. **Toronto (1)**—Ron Fairly, 1b.

NATIONAL LEAGUE—George (Sparky) Anderson, Cincinnati, manager; Thomas Lasorda, Los Angeles, Daniel Ozark, Philadelphia, coaches. **Atlanta (1)**—Guillermo Montanez, 1b. **Chicago (4)**—Julio Morales, of; Ricky Reuschel, p; H. Bruce Sutter, p (replaced by Richard Gossage, p, Pittsburgh); J. Manuel Trillo, 2b. **Cincinnati (7)**—•Johnny Bench, c; •David Concepcion, ss; •George Foster, of; G. Kenneth Griffey, of; •Joe Morgan, 2b; Peter Rose, 3b; G. Thomas Seaver, p. **Houston (1)**—Joaquin Andujar, p. **Los Angeles (4)**—•Ronald Cey, 3b; •Steve Garvey, 1b; C. Reginald Smith, of; Donald Sutton, p. **Montreal (1)**—Ellis Valentine, of. **New York (1)**—John Stearns, c. **Philadelphia (3)**—Steven Carlton, p; •Gregory Luzinski, of; Michael Schmidt, 3b. **Pittsburgh (2)**—John Candelaria, p; •David Parker, of. **St. Louis (2)**—Ted Simmons, c; Garry Templeton, ss. **San Diego (1)**—David Winfield, of. **San Francisco (1)**—Gary Lavelle, p.

1978

AMERICAN LEAGUE—Alfred (Billy) Martin, New York, manager; Dorrel Herzog, Kansas City, Donald Zimmer, Boston, coaches. **Baltimore (3)**—Michael Flanagan, p; Eddie Murray, 1b; James Palmer, p. **Boston (5)**—Richard Burleson, ss (replaced by Gerald Remy, 2b, Boston); •Carlton Fisk, c; Fredric Lynn, of; •James Rice, of; Carl Yastrzemski, of (replaced by Dwight Evans, of, Boston). **California (1)**—Frank Tanana, p. **Chicago (1)**—Chester Lemon, of. **Cleveland (1)**—James Kern, p. **Detroit (1)**—Jason Thompson, 1b. **Kansas City (3)**—•George Brett, 3b; •Freddie Patek, ss; Frank White, 2b. **Milwaukee (2)**—•Donald Money, 2b; Lary Sorensen, p. **Minnesota (1)**—•Rodney Carew, 1b. **New York (5)**—Richard Gossage, p; Ronald Guidry, p; •Reginald Jackson, of (replaced by Graig Nettles, 3b, New York, who in turn was replaced by Larry Hisle, of, Milwaukee); Thurman Munson, c (replaced by Darrell Porter, c, Kansas City). **Oakland (1)**—Matthew Keough, p. **Seattle (1)**—G. Craig Reynolds, ss. **Texas (2)**—James Sundberg, c; •Richard Zisk, of. **Toronto (1)**—Roy Howell, 3b.

NATIONAL LEAGUE—Thomas Lasorda, Los Angeles, manager; Charles Tanner, Pittsburgh, Daniel Ozark, Philadelphia, coaches. **Atlanta (2)**—Jeffrey Burroughs, of; Philip Niekro, p. **Chicago (1)**—H. Bruce Sutter, p. **Cincinnati (6)**—•Johnny Bench, c (replaced by Biff Pocoroba, c, Atlanta); David Concepcion, ss; •George Foster, of; •Joe Morgan, 2b; •Peter Rose, 3b; G. Thomas Seaver, p. **Houston (1)**—Terry Puhl, of. **Los Angeles (6)**—Ronald Cey, 3b; •Steven Garvey, 1b; Thomas John, p; David Lopes, 2b; •Robert Monday, of; C. Reginald Smith, of. **Montreal (2)**—Ross Grimsley, p; Stephen Rogers, p. **New York (1)**—Patrick Zachry, p. **Philadelphia (3)**—Robert Boone, c; •Lawrence Bowa, ss; •Gregory Luzinski, of. **Pittsburgh (1)**—Wilver Stargell, 1b. **St. Louis (1)**—Ted Simmons, c. **San Diego (2)**—Roland Fingers, p; David Winfield, of. **San Francisco (2)**—Vida Blue, p; Jack Clark, of.

1979

AMERICAN LEAGUE—Robert Lemon, New York, manager; Patrick Corrales, Texas, Roy Hartsfield, Toronto, Darrell Johnson, Seattle, coaches. **Baltimore (2)**—Kenneth Singleton, of; Donald Stanhouse, p. **Boston (5)**—Richard Burleson, ss; •Fredric Lynn, of; •James Rice, of; Robert Stanley, p; •Carl Yastrzemski, of. **California (6)**—Donald Baylor, of; •Rodney Carew, 1b (replaced by Cecil Cooper, 1b, Milwaukee); Mark Clear, p; Brian Downing, c; Robert Grich, 2b; L. Nolan Ryan, p. **Chicago (1)**—Chester Lemon, of. **Cleveland (1)**—Isidro Monge, p. **Detroit (1)**—Steven Kemp, of. **Kansas City (3)**—•George Brett, 3b; •Darrell Porter, c; •Frank White, 2b. **Minnesota (1)**—•Roy Smalley, ss. **New York (4)**—Ronald Guidry, p; Reginald Jackson, of; Thomas John, p; Graig Nettles, 3b. **Oakland (1)**—Jeffrey Newman, c. **Seattle (1)**—Bruce Bochte, 1b. **Texas (1)**—James Kern, p. **Toronto (1)**—David Lemanczyk, p.

NATIONAL LEAGUE—Thomas Lasorda, Los Angeles, manager; Daniel Ozark, Philadelphia, Charles Tanner, Pittsburgh, coaches. **Atlanta (1)**—Gary Matthews, of. **Chicago (2)**—David Kingman, of (replaced by Keith Hernandez, 1b, St. Louis); H. Bruce Sutter, p. **Cincinnati (4)**—David Concepcion, ss (replaced by Larry Parrish, 3b, Montreal); •George Foster, of; Michael LaCoss, p; Joe Morgan, 2b. **Houston (3)**—Joaquin Andujar, p; Joseph Niekro, p; Joseph Sambito, p. **Los Angeles (3)**—Ronald Cey, 3b; •Steven Garvey, 1b; •David Lopes, 2b. **Montreal (2)**—Gary Carter, c; Stephen Rogers, p. **New York (1)**—Lee Mazzilli, of. **Philadelphia (5)**—Robert Boone, c; •Lawrence Bowa, ss; Steven Carlton, p; Peter Rose, 1b; •Michael Schmidt, 3b. **Pittsburgh (1)**—•David Parker, of. **St. Louis (3)**—Louis Brock, of; •Ted Simmons, c (replaced by Johnny Bench, c, Cincinnati, who in turn was replaced by John Stearns, c, New York); Garry Templeton, ss (replaced by G. Craig Reynolds, ss, Houston). **San Diego (2)**—Gaylord Perry, p; •David Winfield, of. **San Francisco (1)**—Jack Clark, of.

1980

AMERICAN LEAGUE—Earl Weaver, Baltimore, manager; Frank Robinson, Baltimore, James Frey, Kansas City, coaches. **Baltimore (2)**—Alonza Bumbry, of; Steven Stone, p. **Boston (4)**—Thomas Burgmeier, p; •Carlton Fisk, c; •Fredric Lynn, of; •James Rice, of (replaced due to injury). **California (2)**—•Rodney Carew, 1b; Robert Grich, 2b. **Chicago (1)**—Edward Farmer, p. **Cleveland (1)**—Jorge Orta, of. **Detroit (2)**—

Lance Parrish, c; Alan Trammell, ss. **Kansas City (3)**–•George Brett, 3b (replaced due to injury); Lawrence Gura, p; Darrell Porter, c. **Milwaukee (4)**–Cecil Cooper, 1b; •Paul Molitor, 2b (replaced due to injury); Benjamin Oglivie, of; Robin Yount, ss. **Minnesota (1)**–Kenneth Landreaux, of. **New York (6)**–•Russell Dent, ss; Richard Gossage, p; •Reginald Jackson, of; Thomas John, p; Graig Nettles, 3b; William Randolph, 2b. **Oakland (1)**–Rickey Henderson, of. **Seattle (1)**–Frederick Honeycutt, p. **Texas (2)**–David Bell, 3b; Albert Oliver, of. **Toronto (1)**–David Stieb, p.

NATIONAL LEAGUE–Charles Tanner, Pittsburgh, manager; John McNamara, Cincinnati, William Virdon, Houston, coaches. **Atlanta (1)**–Dale Murphy, of. **Chicago (2)**–•David Kingman, of; H. Bruce Sutter, p. **Cincinnati (3)**–•Johnny Bench, c; David Concepcion, ss; G. Kenneth Griffey, of. **Houston (2)**–Jose Cruz, of; J. Rodney Richard, p. **Los Angeles (6)**–•Steven Garvey, 1b; •David Lopes, 2b; Jerry Reuss, p; •William Russell, ss; •C. Reginald Smith, of; Robert Welch, p. **Montreal (1)**–Gary Carter, c. **New York (1)**–John Stearns, c. **Philadelphia (3)**–Steven Carlton, p; Peter Rose, 1b; •Michael Schmidt, 3b (replaced by C. Ray Knight, 3b, Cincinnati). **Pittsburgh (4)**–James Bibby, p; Philip Garner, 2b; •David Parker, of; Kenton Tekulve, p. **St. Louis (3)**–George Hendrick, of; Keith Hernandez, 1b; Kenneth Reitz, 3b. **San Diego (1)**–David Winfield, of. **San Francisco (1)**–Vida Blue, p (replaced by Eddie Whitson, p, San Francisco).

National Leaguers exchange glad hands after their ninth straight All-Star Game victory, 4-2, at Los Angeles.

ALL-STAR HOME RUNS (112)

Player	Date	Inning	On	Pitcher
George Ruth, A. L.	July 6, 1933	3	1	William Hallahan
Frank Frisch, N. L.	July 6, 1933	6	0	Alvin Crowder
Frank Frisch, N. L.	July 10, 1934	1	0	Vernon Gomez
Joseph Medwick, N. L.	July 10, 1934	3	2	Vernon Gomez
James Foxx, A. L.	July 8, 1935	1	1	William Walker
August Galan, N. L.	July 7, 1936	5	0	Lynwood Rowe
H. Louis Gehrig, A. L.	July 7, 1936	7	0	Curtis Davis
H. Louis Gehrig, A. L.	July 7, 1937	3	1	Jerome Dean
Joseph DiMaggio, A. L.	July 11, 1939	5	0	William Lee
Max West, N. L.	July 9, 1940	1	2	Charles Ruffing
J. Floyd Vaughan, N. L.	July 8, 1941	7	1	Sidney Hudson
J. Floyd Vaughan, N. L.	July 8, 1941	8	1	Edgar Smith
Theodore Williams, A. L.	July 8, 1941	9	2	Claude Passeau
Louis Boudreau, A. L.	July 6, 1942	1	0	Morton Cooper
Rudolph York, A. L.	July 6, 1942	1	1	Morton Cooper
Arnold Owen, N. L.	July 6, 1942	8	0	J. Alton Benton
Robert Doerr, A. L.	July 13, 1943	2	2	Morton Cooper
Vincent DiMaggio, N. L.	July 13, 1943	9	0	Cecil Hughson
Charles Keller, A. L.	July 9, 1946	1	1	Claude Passeau
Theodore Williams, A. L.	July 9, 1946	4	0	W. Kirby Higbe
Theodore Williams, A. L.	July 9, 1946	8	2	Truett Sewell
John Mize, N. L.	July 8, 1947	4	0	Francis Shea
Stanley Musial, N. L.	July 13, 1948	1	1	Walter Masterson
Walter Evers, A. L.	July 13, 1948	2	0	Ralph Branca
Stanley Musial, N. L.	July 12, 1949	1	1	Melvin Parnell
Ralph Kiner, N. L.	July 12, 1949	6	1	Louis Brissie
Ralph Kiner, N. L.	July 11, 1950	9	0	Arthur Houtteman
Albert Schoendienst, N. L.	July 11, 1950	14	0	Theodore Gray
Stanley Musial, N. L.	July 10, 1951	4	0	Edmund Lopat
Robert Elliott, N. L.	July 10, 1951	4	1	Edmund Lopat
Victor Wertz, A. L.	July 10, 1951	4	0	Salvatore Maglie
George Kell, A. L.	July 10, 1951	5	0	Salvatore Maglie
Gilbert Hodges, N. L.	July 10, 1951	6	1	Frederick Hutchinson
Ralph Kiner, N. L.	July 10, 1951	8	0	Melvin Parnell
Jack Robinson, N. L.	July 8, 1952	1	0	Victor Raschi
Henry Sauer, N. L.	July 8, 1952	4	1	Robert Lemon
Albert Rosen, A. L.	July 13, 1954	3	2	Robin Roberts
Raymond Boone, A. L.	July 13, 1954	3	0	Robin Roberts
Theodore Kluszewski, N. L.	July 13, 1954	5	1	Ervin Porterfield
Albert Rosen, A. L.	July 13, 1954	5	1	John Antonelli
David (Gus) Bell, N. L.	July 13, 1954	8	1	Robert Keegan
Lawrence Doby, A. L.	July 13, 1954	8	0	D. Eugene Conley
Mickey Mantle, A. L.	July 12, 1955	1	2	Robin Roberts
Stanley Musial, N. L.	July 12, 1955	12	0	Franklin Sullivan
Willie Mays, N. L.	July 10, 1956	4	1	Edward Ford
Theodore Williams, A. L.	July 10, 1956	6	1	Warren Spahn
Mickey Mantle, A. L.	July 10, 1956	6	0	Warren Spahn
Stanley Musial, N. L.	July 10, 1956	7	0	Thomas Brewer
Edwin Mathews, N. L.	July 7, 1959	1	0	Early Wynn
Albert Kaline, A. L.	July 7, 1959	4	0	Lewis Burdette
Frank Malzone, A. L.	Aug. 3, 1959	2	0	Donald Drysdale
Lawrence Berra, A. L.	Aug. 3, 1959	3	1	Donald Drysdale
Frank Robinson, N. L.	Aug. 3, 1959	5	0	Early Wynn
James Gilliam, N. L.	Aug. 3, 1959	7	0	William O'Dell
Rocco Colavito, A. L.	Aug. 3, 1959	8	0	ElRoy Face
Ernest Banks, N. L.	July 11, 1960	1	1	William Monbouquette
Delmar Crandall, N. L.	July 11, 1960	2	0	William Monbouquette
Albert Kaline, A. L.	July 11, 1960	8	0	Robert Buhl
Edwin Mathews, N. L.	July 13, 1960	2	1	Edward Ford
Willie Mays, N. L.	July 13, 1960	3	0	Edward Ford
Stanley Musial, N. L.	July 13, 1960	7	0	Gerald Staley
Kenton Boyer, N. L.	July 13, 1960	9	1	Gary Bell
Harmon Killebrew, A. L.	July 11, 1961	6	0	Michael McCormick
George Altman, N. L.	July 11, 1961	8	0	J. Miguel Fornieles
Rocco Colavito, A. L.	July 31, 1961	1	0	Robert Purkey
James Runnels, A. L.	July 30, 1962	3	0	Arthur Mahaffey
Leon Wagner, A. L.	July 30, 1962	4	1	Arthur Mahaffey
Rocco Colavito, A. L.	July 30, 1962	7	2	Richard Farrell
John Roseboro, N. L.	July 30, 1962	9	0	Milton Pappas
Billy Williams, N. L.	July 7, 1964	4	0	Johnathan Wyatt
Kenton Boyer, N. L.	July 7, 1964	4	0	Johnathan Wyatt
John Callison, N. L.	July 7, 1964	9	2	Richard Radatz
Willie Mays, N. L.	July 13, 1965	1	0	Milton Pappas
Joseph Torre, N. L.	July 13, 1965	1	1	Milton Pappas
Wilver Stargell, N. L.	July 13, 1965	2	1	James Grant
Richard McAuliffe, A. L.	July 13, 1965	5	1	James Maloney
Harmon Killebrew, A. L.	July 13, 1965	5	⁄1	James Maloney
Richard Allen, N. L.	July 11, 1967	2	0	Dean Chance
Brooks Robinson, A. L.	July 11, 1967	6	0	Ferguson Jenkins

ALL-STAR HOME RUNS (112)—Continued

Player	Date	Inning	On	Pitcher
Atanasio (Tony) Perez, N. L.	July 11, 1967	15	0	James Hunter
Johnny Bench, N. L.	July 23, 1969	2	1	Melvin Stottlemyre
Frank Howard, A. L.	July 23, 1969	2	0	Steven Carlton
Willie McCovey, N. L.	July 23, 1969	3	1	Johnny Odom
William Freehan, A. L.	July 23, 1969	3	0	Steven Carlton
Willie McCovey, N. L.	July 23, 1969	4	0	Dennis McLain
Richard Dietz, N. L.	July 14, 1970	9	0	James Hunter
Johnny Bench, N. L.	July 13, 1971	2	1	Vida Blue
Henry Aaron, N. L.	July 13, 1971	3	0	Vida Blue
Reginald Jackson, A. L.	July 13, 1971	3	1	Dock Ellis
Frank Robinson, A. L.	July 13, 1971	3	1	Dock Ellis
Harmon Killebrew, A. L.	July 13, 1971	6	1	Ferguson Jenkins
Roberto Clemente, N. L.	July 13, 1971	8	0	Michael Lolich
Henry Aaron, N. L.	July 25, 1972	6	1	Gaylord Perry
Octavio Rojas, A. L.	July 25, 1972	8	1	William Stoneman
Johnny Bench, N. L.	July 24, 1973	4	0	William Singer
Bobby Bonds, N. L.	July 24, 1973	5	1	William Singer
William Davis, N. L.	July 24, 1973	6	1	L. Nolan Ryan
C. Reginald Smith, N. L.	July 23, 1974	7	0	James Hunter
Steven Garvey, N. L.	July 15, 1975	2	0	Vida Blue
James Wynn, N. L.	July 15, 1975	2	0	Vida Blue
Carl Yastrzemski, A. L.	July 15, 1975	6	2	G. Thomas Seaver
George Foster, N. L.	July 13, 1976	3	1	James Hunter
Fredric Lynn, A. L.	July 13, 1976	4	0	G. Thomas Seaver
Cesar Cedeno, N. L.	July 13, 1976	8	1	Frank Tanana
Joe Morgan, N. L.	July 19, 1977	1	0	James Palmer
Gregory Luzinski, N. L.	July 19, 1977	1	1	James Palmer
Steven Garvey, N. L.	July 19, 1977	3	0	James Palmer
George Scott, A. L.	July 19, 1977	9	1	Richard Gossage
Fredric Lynn, A. L.	July 17 1979	1	1	Steven Carlton
Lee Mazzilli, N. L.	July 17 1979	8	0	James Kern
Fredric Lynn, A. L.	July 8, 1980	5	1	Robert Welch
G. Kenneth Griffey, N. L.	July 8, 1980	5	0	Thomas John

KEN GRIFFEY'S fifth-inning homer sparked N.L. to 1980 All-Star triumph.

All-Star Game Records

INDIVIDUAL BATTING, BASE-RUNNING—GAME, INNING

Most At-Bats, Nine-Inning Game
5—28 times—Held by 27 players.
Last Players—David M. Winfield, N. L., July 17, 1979.
James E. Rice, A. L., July 17, 1979.

Most At-Bats, Extra-Inning Game
7—Willie E. Jones, N. L., July 11, 1950, 14 innings.

Most Times Faced Pitcher, Inning
2—George H. Ruth, A. L., July 10, 1934, fifth inning.
H. Louis Gehrig, A. L., July 10, 1934, fifth inning.

Most Runs, Game
4—Theodore S. Williams, A. L., July 9, 1946.

Most Runs, Inning
1—Held by many players.

Most Runs Batted In, Game
5—Theodore S. Williams, A. L., July 9, 1946.
Albert L. Rosen, A. L., July 13, 1954.

Most Runs Batted In, Inning
3—Held by many players.

Most Hits, Game
4—Joseph M. Medwick, N. L., July 7, 1937 (5 at bats, 2 singles, 2 doubles), consecutive on last four plate appearances.
Theodore S. Williams, A. L., July 9, 1946 (4 at bats, 2 singles, 2 homers, also one base on balls), consecutive on last four plate appearances.
Carl M. Yastrzemski, A. L., July 14, 1970, night game, 12 innings, (6 at bats, 3 singles, 1 double).

Most Times Reached First Base Safely, Game
5—Philip J. Cavarretta, N. L., July 11, 1944 (3 bases on balls, one single, one triple).
Theodore S. Williams, A. L., July 9, 1946 (2 singles, 2 homers, one base on balls).

Most Hits, Inning
1—Held by many players.

Most One-Base Hits, Game (7 times)
3—Charles L. Gehringer, A. L., July 7, 1937.
William J. Herman, N. L., July 9, 1940.
Stanley C. Hack, N. L., July 13, 1943.
Roberto F. Avila, A. L., July 13, 1954.
Kenton L. Boyer, N. L., July 10, 1956.
Harmon Killebrew, A. L., July 7, 1964.
Carl M. Yastrzemski, A. L., July 14, 1970, night game, 12 innings.

Most One-Base Hits, Inning
1—Held by many players.

Most Two-Base Hits, Game
2—Joseph M. Medwick, N. L., July 7, 1937.
   Aloysius H. Simmons, A. L., July 10, 1934.
   Theodore B. Kluszewski, N. L., July 10, 1956.
   Ernest Banks, N. L., July 7, 1959.

Most Two-Base Hits, Inning
1—Held by many players.

Two-Base Hit, Inning, Batting in Three Runs
Never accomplished.

Most Three-Base Hits, Game
2—Rodney C. Carew, A. L., July 11, 1978.

Most Three-Base Hits, Inning
1—30 times, held by 24 players.

Three-Base Hit, Inning, Batting in Three runs
Never accomplished.

Most Home Runs, Game
2—J. Floyd Vaughan, N. L., July 8, 1941 (consecutive).
   Theodore S. Williams, A. L., July 9, 1946.
   Albert L. Rosen, A. L., July 13, 1954 (consecutive).
   Willie L. McCovey, N. L., July 23, 1969 (consecutive).

Most Home Runs, Inning
1—Held by many players. Accomplished 112 times. 66 by N. L., 46 by A. L.

Hitting Home Run in First At-Bat (7)
Max West, N. L., July 9, 1940, first inning, two on base.
Walter Evers, A. L., July 13, 1948, second inning, none on base.
James Gilliam, N. L., Aug. 3, 1959, seventh inning, none on base.
George Altman, N. L., July 11, 1961, eighth inning, none on base.
Johnny Bench, N. L., July 23, 1969, second inning, one on base.
Richard Dietz, N. L., July 14, 1970, ninth inning, none on base.
Lee Mazzilli, N. L., July 17, 1979, eighth inning, none on base.

Most Home Runs, Inning or Game, Pinch-Hitter (13)
1—Arnold M. Owen, N. L., July 6, 1942, eighth inning, none on base.
   David R. Bell, N. L., July 13, 1954, eighth inning, one on base.
   Lawrence E. Doby, A. L., July 13, 1954, eighth inning, none on base.
   Willie H. Mays, N. L., July 10, 1956, fourth inning, one on base.
   Stanley F. Musial, N. L., July 13, 1960, seventh inning, none on base.
   Harmon C. Killebrew, A. L., July 11, 1961, sixth inning, none on base.
   George L. Altman, N. L., July 11, 1961, eighth inning, none on base.
   James E. Runnels, A. L., July 30, 1962, third inning, none on base.
   Reginald M. Jackson, A. L., July 13, 1971, third inning, one on base.
   Octavio V. Rojas, A. L., July 25, 1972, eighth inning, one on base.
   William H. Davis, N. L., July 24, 1973, sixth inning, one on base.
   Carl M. Yastrzemski, A. L., July 15, 1975, sixth inning, two on base.
   Lee L. Mazzilli, N. L., July 17, 1979, eighth inning, none on base.

Most Times Home Run as Leadoff Batter, Start of Game
1—Frank F. Frisch, N. L., July 10, 1934.
   Louis Boudreau, A. L., July 6, 1942.
   Willie H. Mays, N. L., July 13, 1965.
   Joe L. Morgan, N. L., July 19, 1977.

Most Long Hits, Game
    2—Held by many players.

Most Long Hits, Inning
    1—Held by many players.

Most Total Bases, Game
    10—Theodore S. Williams, A. L., July 9, 1946.

Most Total Bases, Inning
    4—Held by many players.

Most Sacrifice Hits, Game or Inning
    1—Held by many players.

Most Sacrifice Flies, Game or Inning
    1—Held by many players.

Most Bases on Balls, Game
    3—Charles L. Gehringer, A. L., July 10, 1934.
       Philip J. Cavarretta, N. L., July 11, 1944 (also one single, one triple; 5 plate appearances).

Most Bases on Balls, Inning
    1—Held by many players.

Most Strikeouts, Nine-Inning Game
    3—H. Louis Gehrig, A. L., July 10, 1934.
       Robert L. Johnson, A. L., July 8, 1935.
       Stanley C. Hack, N. L., July 11, 1939.
       Joseph L. Gordon, A. L., July 6, 1942.
       Kenneth F. Keltner, A. L., July 13, 1943.
       James E. Hegan, A. L., July 11, 1950.
       Mickey C. Mantle, A. L., July 10, 1956.
       John Roseboro, N. L., July 31, 1961.
       Willie L. McCovey, N. L., July 9, 1968.
       Johnny L. Bench, N. L., July 14, 1970, night game; caught first six innings.

Most Strikeouts, Extra-Inning Game
    4—Roberto W. Clemente, N. L., July 11, 1967 (consecutive).

Most Strikeouts, Inning
    1—Held by many players.

Most Stolen Bases, Inning or Game
    2—Willie H. Mays, N. L., July 9, 1963.

Stealing Home, Game
    1—Harold J. Traynor, N. L., July 10, 1934, fifth inning (front end of a double steal with Mel Ott).

Most Times Caught Stealing, Nine-Inning Game
    1—Held by many players

Most Times Caught Stealing, Extra-Inning Game
    2—Pedro (Tony) Oliva, A. L., July 11, 1967, 15 innings.

Most Hit by Pitch, Inning or Game
    1—Accomplished 24 times. (Held by 24 players.)

Most Grounded Into Double Plays, Game
    2—Robert C. Richardson, A. L., July 9, 1963

INDIVIDUAL BATTING, BASE-RUNNING—TOTAL GAMES

Most Games

24—Stanley F. Musial, N. L., 1943, 1944, 1946, 1947, 1948, 1949, 1950, 1951, 1952, 1953, 1954, 1955, 1956, 1957, 1958, 1959, 1959, 1960, 1960, 1961, 1961, 1962, 1962, 1963 (consecutive).

Willie H. Mays, N. L., 1954, 1955, 1956, 1957, 1958, 1959, 1959, 1960, 1960, 1961, 1961, 1962, 1962, 1963, 1964, 1965, 1966, 1967, 1968, 1969, 1970, 1971, 1972, 1973 (consecutive).

Henry L. Aaron, N. L., 1955, 1956, 1957, 1958, 1959, 1959, 1960, 1960, 1961, 1961, 1962, 1963, 1964, 1965, 1966, 1967, 1968, 1969, 1970, 1971, 1972, 1973, 1974 (23 games), A. L., 1975, (1 game).

Most Games, Pinch-Hitter

10—Stanley F. Musial, 1947, 1955, 1959, first game, 1960, 1960, 1961, 1961, 1962, 1962, 1963 10 pinch-hit at-bats.

Highest Batting Average, Five or More Games

.500—Charles L. Gehringer, A. L., 1933, 1934, 1935, 1936, 1937, 1938 (6 games, 20 at-bats).

Most At-Bats, Total Games

75—Willie H. Mays, N. L., 1954, 1955, 1956, 1957, 1958, 1959, 1959, 1960, 1960, 1961, 1961, 1962, 1962, 1963, 1964, 1965, 1966, 1967, 1968, 1969, 1970, 1971, 1972, 1973 (24 games).

Most At-Bats, Total Games, Without a Hit

10—Terry B. Moore, N. L., 1939, 1940, 1941, 1942 (4 games).

Most Runs, Total Games

20—Willie H. Mays, N. L., 1954, 1955, 1956, 1957, 1958, 1959, 1959, 1960, 1960, 1961, 1961, 1962, 1962, 1963, 1964, 1965, 1966, 1967, 1968, 1969, 1970, 1971, 1972, 1973 (24 games).

Most Runs Batted In, Total Games

12—Theodore S. Williams, A. L., 1940, 1941, 1942, 1946, 1947, 1948, 1949, 1950, 1951, 1954, 1955, 1956, 1957, 1958, 1959, 1959, 1960, 1960 (18 games).

Most Hits, Total Games

23—Willie H. Mays, N. L., 1954, 1955, 1956, 1957, 1958, 1959, 1959, 1960, 1960, 1961, 1961, 1962, 1962, 1963, 1964, 1965, 1966, 1967, 1968, 1969, 1970, 1971, 1972, 1973 (24 games).

Most Consecutive Games Batted Safely, Total Games

7—Mickey C. Mantle, A. L., 1954, 1955, 1956, 1957, 1958, 1959 (second game), 1960 (second game). 1959, first game, pinch runner; 1960, first game, two bases on balls.

Joe L. Morgan, N. L., 1970, 1972, 1973, 1974, 1975, 1976, 1977 (was not on team in 1971).

6—Stanley F. Musial, N. L., 1953, 1954, 1955, 1956, 1957, 1958.

Willie H. Mays, N. L., 1954, 1955, 1956, 1957, 1958, 1959, first game.

Johnny Bench, N. L., 1971, 1972, 1973, 1974, 1975, 1976.

Most Hits, Total Games, as Pinch-Hitter

3—Stanley F. Musial, N. L., 1943, 1944, 1946, 1947, 1948, 1949, 1950, 1951, 1952, 1953, 1954, 1955, 1956, 1957, 1958, 1959, 1959, 1960, 1960, 1961, 1961, 1962, 1962, 1963 (24 games).

Most Two-Base Hits, Total Games

3—Aloysius H. Simmons, A. L., 1933, 1934, 1935 (3 games).

Joseph F. Cronin, A. L., 1933, 1934, 1935, 1937, 1938, 1939, 1941 (7 games).

Most Two-Base Hits, Total Games—Continued

Joseph L. Gordon, A. L., 1939, 1940, 1941, 1942, 1946, 1947, 1948, 1949 (8 games).

Theodore B. Kluszewski, N. L., 1953, 1954, 1955, 1956 (4 games).

Ernest Banks, N. L., 1955, 1957, 1958, 1959, 1959, 1960, 1960, 1961, 1962, 1962, 1965, 1967, 1969, 1970 (14 games).

Pedro (Tony) Oliva, A. L., 1964, 1965, 1966, 1967, 1968, 1970 (6 games).

Most Three-Base Hits, Total Games

3—Willie H. Mays, N. L., 1954, 1955, 1956, 1957, 1958, 1959, 1959, 1960, 1960, 1961, 1961, 1962, 1962, 1963, 1964, 1965, 1966, 1967, 1968, 1969, 1970, 1971, 1972, 1973 (24 games).

Brooks C. Robinson, A. L., 1960, 1960, 1961, 1961, 1962, 1962, 1963, 1964, 1965, 1966, 1967, 1968, 1969, 1970, 1971, 1972, 1973, 1974 (18 games).

Most Home Runs, Total Games

6—Stanley F. Musial, N. L., 1943, 1944, 1946, 1947, 1948, 1949, 1950, 1951, 1952, 1953, 1954, 1955, 1956, 1957, 1958, 1959, 1959, 1960, 1960, 1961, 1961, 1962, 1962, 1963 (24 games).

Most Total Bases, Total Games

40—Stanley F. Musial, N. L., 1943, 1944, 1946, 1947, 1948, 1949, 1950, 1951, 1952, 1953, 1954, 1955, 1956, 1957, 1958, 1959, 1959, 1960, 1960, 1961, 1961, 1962, 1962, 1963 (24 games).

Willie H. Mays, N. L., 1954, 1955, 1956, 1957, 1958, 1959, 1959, 1960, 1960, 1961, 1961, 1962, 1962, 1963, 1964, 1965, 1966, 1967, 1968, 1969, 1970, 1971, 1972, 1973 (24 games).

Most Long Hits, Total Games

8—Stanley F. Musial, N. L., 1943, 1944, 1946, 1947, 1948, 1949, 1950, 1951, 1952, 1953, 1954, 1955, 1956, 1957, 1958, 1959, 1959, 1960, 1960, 1961, 1961, 1962, 1962, 1963 (24 games, two doubles, six home runs).

Willie H. Mays, N. L., 1954, 1955, 1956, 1957, 1958, 1959, 1959, 1960, 1960, 1961, 1961, 1962, 1962, 1963, 1964, 1965, 1966, 1967, 1968, 1969, 1970, 1971, 1972, 1973 (24 games, two doubles, three triples, three home runs.)

Most Extra Bases on Long Hits, Total Games

20—Stanley F. Musial, N. L., 1943, 1944, 1946, 1947, 1948, 1949, 1950, 1951, 1952, 1953, 1954, 1955, 1956, 1957, 1958, 1959, 1959, 1960, 1960, 1961, 1961, 1962, 1962, 1963 (24 games).

Most Sacrifice Hits, Total Games

1—Held by many players.

Most Sacrifice Flies, Total Games

2—Henry L. Aaron, N. L., 1955, 1956, 1957, 1958, 1959 (2), 1960 (2), 1961 (2), 1962, 1963, 1964, 1965, 1966, 1967, 1968, 1969, 1970, 1971, 1972, 1973, 1974(23 games). A. L., 1975, (one game).

Roberto W. Clemente, N. L., 1960, 1960, 1961, 1961, 1962, 1962, 1963, 1964, 1965, 1966, 1967, 1969, 1970, 1971 (14 games).

Most Bases on Balls, Total Games

11—Theodore S. Williams, A. L., 1940, 1941, 1942, 1946, 1947, 1948, 1949, 1950, 1951, 1955, 1956, 1957, 1958, 1959, 1959, 1960, 1960 (18 games).

Most Strikeouts, Total Games

17—Mickey C. Mantle, A. L., 1953, 1954, 1955, 1956, 1957, 1958, 1959, 1959, 1960, 1960, 1961, 1961, 1962, 1964, 1967, 1968 (16 games).

Most Stolen Bases, Total Games

6—Willie H. Mays, N. L., 1954, 1955, 1956, 1957, 1958, 1959, 1959, 1960, 1960,

1961, 1961, 1962, 1962, 1963, 1964, 1965, 1966, 1967, 1968, 1969, 1970, 1971, 1972, 1973 (24 games).

Most Hit by Pitch, Total Games

1—Accomplished 24 times. (Held by 24 players).

Most Times Grounded Into Double Plays, Total Games

3—Joseph P. DiMaggio, A. L., 1936, 1937, 1938, 1939, 1940, 1941, 1942, 1947, 1948, 1949, 1950 (11 games).
  Peter E. Rose, N. L., 1965, 1967, 1969, 1970, 1971, 1973, 1974, 1975, 1976, 1977, 1978, 1979, 1980 (13 games).

Most Times Playing on Winning Club

17—Willie H. Mays, N. L., 1955, 1956, 1959 first game, 1960, 1960, 1961 first game, 1962 first game, 1963, 1964, 1965, 1966, 1967, 1968, 1969, 1970, 1972, 1973 (1 tie—1961 second game). (8 consecutive).
  Henry L. Aaron, N. L., 1955, 1956, 1959 first game, 1960, 1960, 1961 first game, 1963, 1964, 1965, 1966, 1967, 1968, 1969, 1970, 1972, 1973, 1974 (1 tie— 1961 second game). (8 consecutive).

Most Times Playing on Losing Club

15—Brooks C. Robinson, A. L., 1960, 1960, 1961 first game, 1962 first game, 1963, 1964, 1965, 1966, 1967, 1968, 1969, 1970, 1972, 1973, 1974 (1 tie—1961 second game). (8 consecutive).
  11—Mickey C. Mantle, A. L., 1953, 1955, 1956, 1959 first game, 1960, 1960, 1961 first game, 1962 first game, 1964, 1967, 1968. (1 tie—1961 second game).
  Carl M. Yastrzemski, A. L., 1963, 1967, 1968, 1969, 1970, 1972, 1974, 1975, 1976, 1977, 1979.
  Rodney C. Carew, A. L., 1967, 1968, 1969, 1972, 1973, 1974, 1975, 1976, 1977, 1978, 1980.
  10—Stanley F. Musial, N. L., 1943, 1946, 1947, 1948, 1949, 1954, 1957, 1958, 1959 second game, 1962 second game (1 tie—1961 second game).

Most Fielding Positions Played, Game

2—Held by many players.

Most Fielding Positions Played, Total Games

5—Peter E. Rose, N. L., Second base, left field, right field, third base, first base, 13 games.
  4—Stanley F. Musial, N. L., Left field, right field, center field, first base, 24 games.
  Henry L. Aaron, N. L., A. L., Right field, center field, left field, first base, 24 games.

CLUB BATTING, BASE-RUNNING—GAME, INNING

Most Official At-Bats, Nine-Inning Game, One Club

41—N. L., July 7, 1937.
  A. L., July 12, 1949.

Most Official At-Bats, Nine-Inning Game, Both Clubs

79—N. L., (40), A. L. (39), July 13, 1954.

Fewest Official At-Bats, Nine-Inning Game, One Club

27—N. L., July 9, 1968 (8 innings).
  29—N. L., July 9, 1940 (8 innings).
  A. L., July 9, 1940 (9 innings).
  A. L., July 13, 1943 (8 innings).
  A. L., July 13, 1948 (8 innings).
  A. L., July 10, 1962 (9 innings).
  A. L., July 13, 1976 (9 innings).

Fewest Official At-Bats, Nine-Inning Game, Both Clubs
57—A. L. (30), N. L. (27), July 9, 1968.

Most Runs, Game, One Club
12—A. L., July 9, 1946.

Most Runs, Game, Both Clubs
20—A. L. (11), N. L. (9), July 13, 1954.

Most Batters Facing Pitcher, Inning, One Club
11—A. L., July 10, 1934, fifth inning.

Most Batters Facing Pitcher, Inning, Both Clubs
19—A. L. (11), N. L. (8), July 10, 1934, fifth inning.

Most Consecutive Batters Facing Pitcher, Game, One Club, None Reaching Base
20—A. L., July 9, 1968. (James L. Fregosi, doubled, start of game, then 20 consecutive batters were retired until Pedro (Tony) Oliva doubled in seventh inning).

Most Runs, Inning, One Club
6—A. L., July 10, 1934, fifth inning.

Most Runs, Inning, Both Clubs
9—A. L. (6), N. L. (3), July 10, 1934, fifth inning.

Most Innings Scored, Game, One Club
5—A. L., July 9, 1946.
N. L., July 10, 1951.
A. L., July 13, 1954.
N. L., July 10, 1956.
A. L., July 30, 1962.
N. L., July 23, 1974.

Most Innings Scored, Game, Both Clubs
9—A. L. (5), N. L. (4), July 30, 1962.

Most Consecutive Scoreless Innings, Total Games, One League
19—American League; Last 9 innings 1967; all 9 innings, 1968, first inning, 1969.

Most Hits, Game, One Club
17—A. L., July 13, 1954.

Most Hits, Game, Both Clubs
31—A. L. (17), N. L. (14), July 13, 1954.

Fewest Hits, Game, One Club
3—A. L., July 9, 1940.
N. L., July 9, 1946.
A. L., July 9, 1968.

Fewest Hits, Game, Both Clubs
8—N. L. (5), A. L. (3), July 9, 1968.

Highest Batting Average, Game, One Club
.436—A. L., July 13, 1954, 39 at-bats, 17 hits.

Lowest Batting Average, Game, One Club
.097—N. L., July 9, 1946, 31 at-bats, 3 hits.

Most One-Base Hits, Game, One Club
13—A. L., July 13, 1954.

Most One-Base Hits, Game, Both Clubs
22—A. L. (13), N. L. (9), July 13, 1954.

Fewest One-Base Hits, Game, One Club
0—A. L., July 9, 1968.

Fewest One-Base Hits, Game, Both Clubs
4—N. L. (4), A. L. (0), July 9, 1968.

Most Two-Base Hits, Game, One Club
5—A. L., July 10, 1934.
A. L., July 12, 1949.

Most Two-Base Hits, Game, Both Clubs
7—A. L. (5), N. L. (2), July 12, 1949.

Fewest Two-Base Hits, Game, One Club
0—Made in many games.

Fewest Two-Base Hits, Game, Both Clubs
0—July 6, 1942; July 9, 1946; July 13, 1948; July 8, 1958; July 13, 1976.

Most Three-Base Hits, Game, One Club
2—A. L., July 10, 1934.
A. L., July 10, 1951.
N. L., July 13, 1976.
A. L., July 11, 1978.

Most Three-Base Hits, Game, Both Clubs
3—A. L. (2), N. L. (1), July 11, 1978.

Fewest Three-Base Hits, Game, One Club
0—Made in many games.

Fewest Three-Base Hits, Game, Both Clubs
0—Made in many games.

Most Home Runs, Game, One Club
4—N. L., July 10, 1951.
A. L., July 13, 1954.
N. L., July 13, 1960.

Most Home Runs, Game, Both Clubs
6—N. L. (4), A. L. (2), July 10, 1951.
A. L. (4), N. L. (2), July 13, 1954.
A. L. (3), N. L. (3), July 13, 1971.

Most Home Runs, Extra-Inning Game, Both Clubs, No Other Runs
3—N. L. (2), A. L. (1), July 11, 1967.

Fewest Home Runs, Game, One Club
0—Made in many games.

Fewest Home Runs, Game, Both Clubs
0—July 6, 1938; July 11, 1944; July 14, 1953; July 9, 1957; July 8, 1958; July 10, 1962; July 9, 1963; July 12, 1966; July 9, 1968, July 11, 1978.

Most Home Runs, Inning, One Club (10 times)
2—A. L., July 6, 1942, first inning (Boudreau, York).

Most Home Runs, Inning, One Club (10 times)—Continued

    N. L., July 10, 1951, fourth inning (Musial, Elliott).
    A. L., July 13, 1954, third inning (Rosen, Boone) (consecutive).
    A. L., July 10, 1956, sixth inning (Williams, Mantle) (consecutive).
    N. L., July 7, 1964, fourth inning (Williams, Boyer).
    N. L., July 13, 1965, first inning (Mays, Torre).
    A. L., July 13, 1965, fifth inning (McAuliffe, Killebrew).
    A. L., July 13, 1971, third inning (Jackson, F. Robinson).
    N. L., July 15, 1975, second inning (Garvey, Wynn) (consecutive).
    N. L., July 19, 1977, first inning (Morgan, Luzinski).

Most Home Runs, Inning, Both Clubs

    3—N. L., 2 (Musial, Elliott), A. L., 1 (Wertz), July 10, 1951, fourth inning.
    A. L., 2 (Jackson, F. Robinson), N. L., 1 (Aaron), July 13, 1971, third inning.

Most Consecutive Games, One or More Home Runs

    9—N. L.—1969, 1970, 1971, 1972, 1973, 1974, 1975, 1976, 1977.

Most Total Bases, Game, One Club

    29—A. L., July 13, 1954.

Most Total Bases, Game, Both Clubs

    52—A. L. (29), N. L. (23), July 13, 1954.

Fewest Total Bases, Game, One Club

    3—N. L., July 9, 1946.

Fewest Total Bases, Game, Both Clubs

    12—A. L. (6), N. L. (6), 1968.

Most Long Hits, Game, One Club

    7—A. L., July 10, 1934, five doubles, two triples.

Most Long Hits, Game, Both Clubs

    10—N. L. (5), one double, four home runs; A. L. (5), one double, two triples, two
        home runs, July 10, 1951.

Fewest Long Hits, Game, One Club

    0—A. L., July 11, 1944.
    N. L., July 9, 1946.
    A. L., July 14, 1953.
    N. L., July 8, 1958.
    A. L., July 8, 1958.
    N. L., July 9, 1963.

Fewest Long Hits, Game, Both Clubs

    0—July 8, 1958.

Most Extra Bases on Long Hits, Game, One Club

    13—N. L., July 10, 1951.

Most Extra Bases on Long Hits, Game, Both Clubs

    24—N. L. (13), A. L. (11), July 10, 1951.

Fewest Extra Bases on Long Hits, Game, One Club

    0—A. L., July 11, 1944.
    N. L., July 9, 1946.
    A. L., July 14, 1953.
    N. L., July 8, 1958.
    A. L., July 8, 1958.
    N. L., July 9, 1963.

Fewest Extra Bases on Long Hits, Game, Both Clubs
    0—July 8, 1958.

Most Sacrifice Hits, Nine-Inning Game, One Club
    3—N. L., July 11, 1944.

Most Sacrifice Hits, Nine-Inning Game, Both Clubs
    3—N. L. (3), A. L. (0), July 11, 1944.

Fewest Sacrifice Hits, Game, One Club
    0—Made in many games.

Fewest Sacrifice Hits, Game, Both Clubs
    0—Made in many games.

Most Stolen Bases, Game, One Club
    3—A. L., July 13, 1948.
        N. L., July 9, 1963.
        A. L., July 15, 1975.

Most Stolen Bases, Game, Both Clubs
    4—N. L. (2), A. L. (2), July 10, 1934.
        A. L. (3), N. L. (1), July 15, 1975.

Fewest Stolen Bases, Game, One Club
    0—Made in many games.

Fewest Stolen Bases, Game, Both Clubs
    0—Made in 22 games.

Most Bases on Balls, Game, One Club
    9—A. L., July 10, 1934.

Most Bases on Balls, Game, Both Clubs
    13—N. L. (8), A. L. (5), July 12, 1949.

Fewest Bases on Balls, Nine-Inning Game, One Club (7 times)
    0—N. L., July 6, 1933.
        N. L., July 7, 1937.
        N. L., July 6, 1938.
        A. L., July 6, 1942.
        A. L., July 10, 1956.
        A. L., July 9, 1968.
        N. L., July 15, 1975.

Fewest Bases on Balls, Extra-Inning Game, One Club
    0—N. L., July 11, 1967 (15 innings).

Fewest Bases on Balls, Nine-Inning Game, Both Clubs
    1—A. L. (1), N. L. (0), July 15, 1975.

Fewest Bases on Balls Extra-Inning Game, Both Clubs
    2—A. L. (2), N. L. (0), July 11, 1967 (15 innings).

Most Strikeouts, Game, One Club
    17—A. L., July 11, 1967 (15 innings).
    13—N. L., July 11, 1967 (15 innings).
    12—A. L., July 10, 1934.
        A. L., July 11, 1950 (14 innings).
        A. L., July 12, 1955 (12 innings).
        N. L., July 10, 1956.
        A. L., August 3, 1959.
        A. L., July 11, 1961 (10 innings).

Most Strikeouts, Nine-Inning Game, Both Clubs
20—A. L. (11), N. L. (9), July 9, 1968.

Most Strikeouts, Extra-Inning Game, Both Clubs
30—A. L. (17), N. L. (13), July 11, 1967 (15 innings).
20—A. L. (12), N. L. (8), July 12, 1955 (12 innings).

Fewest Strikeouts, Game, One Club
0—N. L., July 7, 1937.

Fewest Strikeouts, Game, Both Clubs
6—A. L. (4), N. L. (2), July 8, 1958.

Most Runs Batted In, Game, One Club
12—A. L., July 9, 1946.

Most Runs Batted In, Game, Both Clubs
20—A. L. (11), N. L. (9), July 13, 1954.

Fewest Runs Batted in, Game, One Club
0—A. L., July 9, 1940.
N. L., July 9, 1946.
A. L., July 13, 1960.
A. L., July 12, 1966.
A. L., July 9, 1968.
N. L., July 9, 1968.

Fewest Runs Batted In, Game, Both Clubs
0—A. L. (0), N. L. (0), July 9, 1968.

Most Left on Bases, Game, One Club
12—A. L., July 10, 1934.
N. L., July 12, 1949.
A. L., July 13, 1960.

Most Left on Bases, Game, Both Clubs
20—N. L. (12), A. L. (8), July 12, 1949.

Fewest Left on Bases, Game, One Club
2—N. L., July 13, 1971 (Batted 9 innings).
A. L., July 13, 1971 (Batted 8 innings).

Fewest Left on Bases, Game, Both Clubs
4—N. L. (2), A. L. (2), July 13, 1971.

Most Hit by Pitch, Game, One Club
2—A. L., July 10, 1962.

Most Hit by Pitch, Game, Both Clubs
2—A. L. (2), N. L. (0), July 10, 1962.
A. L. (1), N. L. (1), July 15, 1975.
A. L. (1), N. L. (1), July 19, 1977.

Fewest Hit by Pitch, Game, One Club
0—Made in many games.

Fewest Hit by Pitch, Game, Both Clubs
0—Made in 27 games.

Most Earned Runs, Game, One Club
12—A. L., July 9, 1946.

Most Earned Runs, Game, Both Clubs
>   20—A. L. (11), N. L. (9), July 13, 1954.

Fewest Earned Runs, Game, One Club
>   0—N. L., July 11, 1939.
>   A. L., July 9, 1940.
>   N. L., July 9, 1946.
>   A. L., July 13, 1960.
>   A. L., July 9, 1968.
>   N. L., July 9, 1968.

Fewest Earned Runs, Game, Both Clubs
>   0—A. L. (0), N. L. (0), July 9, 1968.

INDIVIDUAL FIELDING

FIRST BASEMEN'S FIELDING RECORDS

Most Games Played
>   8—John R. Mize, N. L., 1937, 1940, 1941, 1942, 1946, 1947, 1948, 1949.

Most Putouts, Total Games
>   53—H. Louis Gehrig, A. L., 1933, 1934, 1935, 1936, 1937, 1938.

Most Assists, Total Games
>   5—P. Rudolph York, A. L., 1941, 1942, 1943, 1946.
>   William D. White, N. L., 1960 (2), 1961 (2), 1963.

Most Chances Accepted, Total Games
>   55—H. Louis Gehrig, A. L., 1933, 1934, 1935, 1936, 1937, 1938.

Most Errors, Total Games
>   2—H. Louis Gehrig, A. L., 1933, 1934, 1935, 1936, 1937, 1938.

Most Double Plays, Total Games
>   6—William D. White, N. L., 1960 (2), 1961 (2), 1963.
>   Harmon C. Killebrew, A. L., 1965, 1967, 1968, 1971.

Most Putouts, Nine-Inning Game
>   14—George H. McQuinn, A. L., July 13, 1948.

Most Putouts, Extra-Inning Game
>   15—Harmon C. Killebrew, A. L., July 11, 1967.

Most Assists, Nine-Inning Game
>   3—P. Rudolph York, A. L., July 6, 1942.
>   William D. White, N. L., July 9, 1963.

Most Chances Accepted, Nine-Inning Game
>   14—P. Rudolph York, A. L., July 6, 1942, 11 putouts, 3 assists.
>   George H. McQuinn, A. L., July 13, 1948, 14 putouts.

Most Chances Accepted, Extra-Inning Game
>   16—Harmon C. Killebrew, A. L., July 11, 1967, 15 putouts, 1 assist.

Most Errors, Game
>   1—Held by eight first basemen.

Most Double Plays, Game
>   3—Stanley F. Musial, N. L., July 8, 1958.

Most Unassisted Double Plays, Game
1—James E. Runnels, A. L., August 3, 1959, second inning.
Lee A. May, N. L., July 25, 1972, third inning.

SECOND BASEMEN'S FIELDING RECORDS

Most Games Played
13—J. Nelson Fox, A. L., 1951, 1953, 1954, 1955, 1956, 1957, 1958, 1959 (2), 1960 (2), 1961, 1963.

Most Putouts, Total Games
25—J. Nelson Fox, A. L., 1951, 1953, 1954, 1955, 1956, 1957, 1958, 1959 (2), 1960 (2), 1961, 1963.

Most Assists, Total Games
23—William J. Herman, N. L., 1934, 1935, 1936, 1937, 1938, 1940, 1941, 1942, 1943.

Most Chances Accepted, Total Games
39—J. Nelson Fox, A. L., 1951, 1953, 1954, 1955, 1956, 1957, 1958, 1959 (2), 1960 (2), 1961, 1963 (25 putouts, 14 assists).

Most Errors, Total Games
2—William J. Herman, N. L., 1934, 1935, 1936, 1937, 1938, 1940, 1941, 1942, 1943.
J. Nelson Fox, A. L., 1951, 1953, 1954, 1955, 1956, 1957, 1958, 1959 (2), 1960 (2), 1961, 1963.
William L. Randolph, A. L., 1977, 1980.

Most Double Plays, Total Games
4—William J. Herman, N. L., 1934, 1935, 1936, 1937, 1938, 1940, 1941, 1942, 1943.
William S. Mazeroski, N. L., 1958, 1959, 1960 (2).

Most Putouts, Nine-Inning Game
5—Frank F. Frisch, N. L., July 6, 1933.

Most Assists, Nine-Inning Game
6—William L. Randolph, A. L., July 19, 1977.

Most Chances Accepted, Nine-Inning Game
9—William S. Mazeroski, N. L., July 8, 1958.

Most Errors, Game
2—William J. Herman, N. L., July 13, 1943.
William L. Randolph, A. L., July 8, 1980.

Most Double Plays, Game
3—William J. Herman, N. L., July 13, 1943.
William S. Mazeroski, N. L., July 8, 1958.

Most Unassisted Double Plays, Game
Never accomplished.

THIRD BASEMEN'S FIELDING RECORDS

Most Games Played
18—Brooks C. Robinson, A. L., 1960, 1960, 1961, 1961, 1962, 1962, 1963, 1964, 1965, 1966, 1967, 1968, 1969, 1970, 1971, 1972, 1973, 1974 (consecutive).

Most Putouts, Total Games

11—Brooks C. Robinson, A. L., 1960, 1960, 1961, 1961, 1962, 1962, 1963, 1964, 1965, 1966, 1967, 1968, 1969, 1970, 1971, 1972, 1973, 1974 (18 games).

Most Assists, Total Games

32—Brooks C. Robinson, A. L., 1960, 1960, 1961, 1961, 1962, 1962, 1963, 1964, 1965, 1966, 1967, 1968, 1969, 1970, 1971, 1972, 1973, 1974 (18 games).

Most Chances Accepted, Total Games

43—Brooks C. Robinson, A. L., 1960, 1960, 1961, 1961, 1962, 1962, 1963, 1964, 1965, 1966, 1967, 1968, 1969, 1970, 1971, 1972, 1973, 1974 (18 games), 11 putouts (32 assists).

Most Errors, Total Games

6—Edwin L. Mathews, N. L., 1953, 1955, 1957, 1959, 1960, 1960, 1961, 1961, 1962 second game.

Most Double Plays, Total Games

3—Frank J. Malzone, A. L., 1957, 1958, 1959, 1959, 1960, 1960, 1963.
Brooks C. Robinson, A. L., 1960, 1960, 1961, 1961, 1962, 1962, 1963, 1964, 1965, 1966, 1967, 1968, 1969, 1970, 1971, 1972, 1973, 1974 (18 games).

Most Putouts, Nine-Inning Game

4—George C. Kell, A. L., July 10, 1951.

Most Putouts, Extra-Inning Game

4—Brooks C. Robinson, A. L., July 12, 1966, 9⅓ innings.

Most Assists, Nine-Inning Game

6—Kenneth F. Keltner, A. L., July 13, 1948.
Frank J. Malzone, A. L., August 3, 1959.

Most Chances Accepted, Nine-Inning Game

7—Kenneth F. Keltner, A. L., July 13, 1948, 1 putout, 6 assists.
Frank J. Malzone, A. L., August 3, 1959, 1 putout, 6 assists.

Most Chances Accepted, Extra-Inning Game

8—Brooks C. Robinson, A. L., July 12, 1966, 9⅓ innings, 4 putouts, 4 assists.

Most Errors, Game

2—Robert A. Rolfe, A. L., July 7, 1937.
Edwin L. Mathews, N. L., July 11, 1960; July 30, 1962.
Kenton L. Boyer, N. L., July 11, 1961 (ten innings).

Most Errors, Inning

2—Edwin L. Mathews, N. L., July 30, 1962, ninth inning.

Most Double Plays, Game

1—Accomplished 18 times.

Most Unassisted Double Plays, Game

Never accomplished.

SHORTSTOPS' FIELDING RECORDS

Most Games Played

10—Luis E. Aparicio, A. L., 1958, 1959, 1959, 1960 first game, 1961 second game, 1962, 1962, 1963, 1970, 1971.

Most Putouts, Total Games

15—Luis E. Aparicio, A. L., 1958, 1959, 1959, 1960 first game, 1961 second game, 1962, 1962, 1963, 1970, 1971.

Most Assists, Total Games

    24—Joseph E. Cronin, A. L., 1933, 1934, 1935, 1937, 1938, 1939, 1941.

Most Chances Accepted, Total Games

    38—Joseph E. Cronin, A. L., 1933, 1934, 1935, 1937, 1938, 1939, 1941.

Most Errors, Total Games

    2—Joseph E. Cronin, A. L., 1933, 1934, 1935, 1937, 1938, 1939, 1941.
       Ernest Banks, N. L., 1955, 1957, 1958, 1959, 1959, 1960, 1960, 1961.

Most Double Plays, Total Games

    6—Ernest Banks, N. L., 1955, 1957, 1958, 1959, 1959, 1960, 1960, 1961.

Most Putouts, Nine-Inning Game

    5—Alfonso Carrasquel, A. L., July 13, 1954.

Most Assists, Nine-Inning Game

    8—Joseph E. Cronin, A. L., July 10, 1934.

Most Chances Accepted, Nine-Inning Game

    10—Joseph E. Cronin, A. L., July 10, 1934, 2 putouts, 8 assists.
       Martin W. Marion, N. L., July 9, 1946, 4 putouts, 6 assists.

Most Errors, Game

    1—13 times, held by 11 shortstops.

Most Double Plays, Game

    2—Louis Boudreau, A. L., July 6, 1942.
       Martin W. Marion, N. L., July 9, 1946.
       Edwin J. Joost, A. L., July 12, 1949.
       Ernest Banks, N. L., July 8, 1958.
       Ernest Banks, N. L., July 13, 1960.
       Edward Kasko, N. L., July 31, 1961.
       Luis E. Aparicio, A. L., July 30, 1962.
       Richard M. Groat, N. L., July 9, 1963.

Most Unassisted Double Plays, Game

    Never accomplished.

OUTFIELDERS' FIELDING RECORDS

Most Games Played

    22—Willie H. Mays, N. L., 1954, 1955, 1956, 1957, 1958, 1959, 1959, 1960, 1960,
       1961, 1961, 1962, 1962, 1963, 1964, 1965, 1966, 1967, 1968, 1970, 1971, 1972
       (19 consecutive).

Most Putouts, Total Games

    55—Willie H. Mays, N. L., 1954, 1955, 1956, 1957, 1958, 1959, 1959, 1960, 1960,
       1961, 1961, 1962, 1962, 1963, 1964, 1965, 1966, 1967, 1968, 1970, 1971, 1972
       (22 games).

Most Assists, Total Games

    3—Stanley F. Musial, N. L., 1943, 1944, 1946, 1948, 1949, 1951, 1952, 1953, 1954,
       1955, 1956, 1962 second game (1947, 1959 first game, 1960 and 1961 both
       games, 1962 first game and 1963, pinch-hitter; 1950, 1957, 1958, 1959
       second game, first base).

Most Chances Accepted, Total Games

    55—Willie H. Mays, N. L., 1954, 1955, 1956, 1957, 1958, 1959, 1959, 1960, 1960,
       1961, 1961, 1962, 1962, 1963, 1964, 1965, 1966, 1967, 1968, 1970, 1971, 1972
       (22 games).

Most Errors, Total Games
> 2—Harold H. Reiser, N. L., 1941, 1942.
> Joseph P. DiMaggio, A. L., 1936, 1937, 1938, 1939, 1940, 1941, 1942, 1947, 1949, 1950.

Most Double Plays, Total Games
> 1—Stanley O. Spence, A. L., 1944, 1946, 1947.
> H. Thomas Davis, N. L., 1962 (2), 1963.

Most Putouts, Center Field, Nine-Inning Game
> 7—Chester P. Laabs, A. L., July 13, 1943.
> Willie H. Mays, N. L., July 7, 1964.

Most Putouts, Center Field, Fourteen-Inning Game
> 9—Lawrence E. Doby, A. L., July 11, 1950.

Most Putouts, Left Field, Nine-Inning Game
> 5—Samuel F. West, A. L., July 7, 1937.
> Frank Robinson, N. L., July 9, 1957.
> Joseph O. Rudi, A. L., July 15, 1975.

Most Putouts, Right Field, Nine-Inning Game
> 4—Charles E. Keller, A. L., July 9, 1940.

Most Putouts, Right Field, Extra-Inning Game
> 6—Roberto W. Clemente, N. L., July 11, 1967 (15 innings).

Most Assists, Game, Center Field
> 1—6 times; held by six outfielders.

Most Assists, Game, Left Field
> 1—7 times; held by six outfielders.

Most Assists, Game, Right Field
> 2—David G. Parker, N. L., July 17, 1979.

Most Chances Accepted, Center Field, Nine-Inning Game
> 7—Chester P. Laabs, A. L., July 13, 1943, 7 putouts.
> Willie H. Mays, N. L., July 7, 1964, 7 putouts.

Most Chances Accepted, Center Field, Fourteen-Inning Game
> 9—Lawrence E. Doby, A. L., July 11, 1950, 9 putouts.

Most Chances Accepted, Left Field, Nine-Inning Game
> 5—Samuel F. West, A. L., July 7, 1937, 5 putouts.
> Joseph O. Rudi, A. L., July 15, 1975.

Most Chances Accepted, Right Field, Nine-Inning Game
> 4—Charles E. Keller, A. L., July 9, 1940, 4 putouts.

Most Errors, Game, Center Field
> 2—Harold P. Reiser, N. L., July 8, 1941.

Most Errors, Game, Left Field
> 1—6 times; held by six outfielders.

Most Errors, Game, Right Field
> 1—3 times; held by three outfielders.

Most Double Plays, Game, Center Field
> None.

Most Double Plays, Game, Left Field
　　　1—H. Thomas Davis, N. L., July 9, 1963.

Most Double Plays, Game, Right Field
　　　1—Stanley O. Spence, A. L., July 11, 1944.

Most Unassisted Double Plays, Game, Center field, Left field, Right field
　　　Never accomplished.

CATCHER'S FIELDING RECORDS

Most Games Played
　　　14—Lawrence P. Berra, A. L., 1949, 1950, 1951, 1952, 1953, 1954, 1955, 1956, 1957, 1958, 1959, 1960, 1960, 1961.

Most Putouts, Total Games
　　　61—Lawrence P. Berra, A. L., 1949, 1950, 1951, 1952, 1953, 1954, 1955, 1956, 1957, 1958, 1959, 1960, 1960, 1961.

Most Assists, Total Games
　　　7—Lawrence P. Berra, A. L., 1949, 1950, 1951, 1952, 1953, 1954, 1955, 1956, 1957, 1958, 1959, 1960, 1960, 1961.

Most Chances Accepted, Total Games
　　　68—Lawrence P. Berra, A. L., 1949, 1950, 1951, 1952, 1953, 1954, 1955, 1956, 1957, 1958, 1959, 1960, 1960, 1961.

Most Errors, Total Games
　　　2—Forrest H. Burgess, N. L., 1954, 1955, 1960, 1960, 1961, 1961, (pinch-hitter only in 1959, second game).

Most Double Plays, Total Games
　　　1—Held by many catchers.

Most Passed Balls, Total Games
　　　1—Held by 12 catchers.

Most Putouts, Nine-Inning Game
　　　10—William M. Dickey, A. L., July 11, 1939 (9 strikeouts).
　　　　　Lawrence P. Berra, A. L., July 10, 1956 (9 strikeouts).
　　　　　Delmar W. Crandall, N. L., July 7, 1959 (9 strikeouts).
　　　　　Johnny L. Bench, N. L., July 15, 1975 (10 strikeouts).

Most Putouts, Extra-Inning Game
　　　13—Roy Campanella, N. L., July 11, 1950 (14 innings—12 strikeouts).
　　　　　Forrest H. Burgess, N. L., July 11, 1961 (10 innings—12 strikeouts).
　　　　　William A. Freehan, A. L., July 11, 1967 (15 innings—13 strikeouts).

Most Assists, Game
　　　2—W. Walker Cooper, N. L., July 11, 1944.
　　　　Roy Campanella, N. L., July 11, 1950 (14 innings).
　　　　Lawrence P. Berra, A. L., July 10, 1951.
　　　　Roy Campanella, N. L., July 14, 1953.
　　　　Lawrence P. Berra, A. L., July 12, 1955 (11 innings).

Most Chances Accepted, Nine-Inning Game
　　　11—Lawrence P. Berra, A. L., July 10, 1956 (10 putouts, 1 assist).
　　　　　Johnny L. Bench, N. L., July 15, 1975 (10 putouts, 1 assist).

Most Chances Accepted, Extra-Inning Game
　　　15—Roy Campanella, N. L., July 11, 1950 (14 innings—13 putouts, 2 assists).

Most Errors, Game
>   1—Held by ten catchers.

Most Double Plays, Game
>   1—Held by four catchers.

Most Unassisted Double Plays, Game
>   Never accomplished.

Most Passed Balls, Game
>   1—13 times (held by 13 catchers).

Most Innings Caught, Game
>   15—William A. Freehan, A. L. July 11, 1967 (complete game).

PITCHERS' FIELDING RECORDS

Most Games Played
>   8—James P. Bunning, A. L., 1957, 1959 (first game), 1961 (2), 1962 (first game), 1963; N. L., 1964, 1966.
>   Donald S. Drysdale, N. L., 1959 (2), 1962 (first game), 1963, 1964, 1965, 1967, 1968.
>   Juan A. Marichal, N. L., 1962 (2), 1964, 1965, 1966, 1967, 1968, 1971.

Most Putouts, Total Games
>   3—Spurgeon F. Chandler, A. L., 1942.

Most Assists, Total Games
>   5—John S. Vander Meer, N. L., 1938, 1942, 1943.

Most Chances Accepted, Total Games
>   5—Melvin L. Harder, A. L., 1934, 1935, 1936, 1937 (2 putouts, 3 assists).
>   John S. Vander Meer, N. L., 1938, 1942, 1943 (5 assists).
>   Donald S. Drysdale, N. L., 1959 (2), 1962, (first game), 1963, 1964, 1965, 1967, 1968 (1 putout, 4 assists).

Most Errors, Total Games
>   1—Edgar Smith, A. L., 1941.
>   John F. Sain, N. L., 1947, 1948.
>   Samuel Jones, N. L., 1955, 1959.
>   Buddy L. Daley, A. L., 1960.

Most Double Plays, Total Games
>   1—Held by many pitchers.

Most Putouts, Game
>   3—Spurgeon F. Chandler, A. L., July 6, 1942.

Most Assists, Game
>   3—John S. Vander Meer, N. L., July 6, 1938.
>   Donald S. Drysdale, N. L., July 7, 1964.
>   Michael S. Lolich, A. L., July 13, 1971.

Most Chances Accepted, Game
>   4—Spurgeon F. Chandler, A. L., July 6, 1942 (3 putouts, 1 assist).

Most Errors, Game
>   1—Edgar Smith, A. L., July 8, 1941.
>   John F. Sain, N. L., July 8, 1947.
>   Samuel Jones, N. L., August 3, 1959.
>   Buddy L. Daley, A. L., July 11, 1960.

Most Double Plays, Game
    1—Held by many pitchers.

Most Unassisted Double Plays, Game
    Never accomplished.

CLUB FIELDING

Most Assists, Nine-Inning Game, One Club
    16—A. L., July 6, 1942.

Most Assists, Nine-Inning Game, Both Clubs
    26—A. L. (15), N. L. (11), July 12, 1949.

Fewest Assists, Eight-Inning Game, One Club
    4—A. L., July 9, 1940.
        N. L., July 13, 1948.

Fewest Assists, Nine-Inning Game, One Club
    5—N. L., July 10, 1934.
        N. L., July 9, 1957.
        N. L., July 23, 1969.

Fewest Assists, Nine-Inning Game, Both Clubs
    11—N. L. (6), A. L. (5), July 7, 1959.

Most Errors, Game, One Club
    5—N. L., July 12, 1949.
        N. L., July 11, 1961.

Most Errors, Nine-Inning Game, Both Clubs
    6—N. L. (5), A. L. (1), July 12, 1949.

Most Errors, Extra-Inning Game, Both Clubs
    7—N. L. (5), A. L. (2), July 11, 1961 (ten innings).

Fewest Errors, Game, One Club
    0—Made in many games.

Fewest Errors, Nine-Inning Game, Both Clubs
    0—July 13, 1948; July 14, 1953; July 10, 1956; July 13, 1960; July 10, 1962; July
        13, 1971; July 24, 1973, July 13, 1976.

Fewest Errors, Extra-Inning Game, Both Clubs
    0—July 11, 1967, 15 innings.
        July 14, 1970, 12 innings.
        July 12, 1966, 10 innings.
        July 25, 1972, 10 innings.

Most Consecutive Errorless Games, One Club
    11—N. L., July 9, 1963; July 7, 1964; July 13, 1965; July 12, 1966; July 11, 1967;
        July 9, 1968; July 23, 1969; July 14, 1970; July 13, 1971; July 25, 1972;
        July 24, 1973.

Most Double Plays, Game, One Club
    3—N. L., July 13, 1943.
        N. L., July 8, 1958.
        N. L., July 9, 1963.
        N. L., July 13, 1976.

Most Double Plays, Game, Both Clubs

    4—N. L. (3), A. L. (1), July 13, 1943.
        N. L. (3), A. L. (1), July 8, 1958.
        N. L. (2), A. L. (2), July 25, 1972, 10 innings.
        N. L. (3), A. L. (1), July 13, 1976.

Fewest Double Plays, Game, One Club

    0—Made in many games.

Fewest Double Plays, Game, Both Clubs

    0—July 8, 1935; July 6, 1938; July 13, 1948; July 11, 1961 (10 innings); July 7, Leroy Paige, 1953; 48 years, 7 days.

Most Players One or More Putouts, Game, Nine Innings, One Club

    14—N. L., July 13, 1976.

Most Players One or More Putouts, Game, Nine Innings, Both Clubs

    25—N. L. (14), A. L. (11), July 13, 1976.

Most Players One or More Assists, Game, Nine Innings, One Club

    10—N. L., July 24, 1973.

Most Players One or More Assists, Game, Nine Innings, Both Clubs

    19—N. L. (10), A. L. (9), July 24, 1973.

INDIVIDUAL PITCHING RECORDS

Most Games Pitched

    8—James P. Bunning, A. L., 1957, 1959 (first game), 1961 (2), 1962 (first game), 1963; N. L., 1964, 1966.
        Donald S. Drysdale, N. L., 1959 (2), 1962 (first game), 1963, 1964, 1965, 1967, 1968.
        Juan A. Marichal, N. L., 1962 (2), 1964, 1965, 1966, 1967, 1968, 1971.

Most Consecutive Games Pitched

    6—Ewell Blackwell, N. L., 1946, 1947, 1948, 1949, 1950, 1951.
        Early Wynn, A. L., 1955, 1956, 1957, 1958, 1959 (2).

Most Games Started

    5—Vernon Gomez, A. L., 1933, 1934, 1935, 1937, 1938.
        Robin E. Roberts, N. L., 1950, 1951, 1953, 1954, 1955.
        Donald S. Drysdale, N. L., 1959 (2), 1962 (first game), 1964, 1968.

Most Games Finished

    4—Melvin L. Harder, A. L., 1934, 1935, 1936, 1937.

Most Games Won

    3—Vernon Gomez, A. L., 1933, 1935, 1937.

Most Games Lost

    2—Morton C. Cooper, N. L., 1942, 1943.
        Claude W. Passeau, N. L., 1941, 1946.
        Edward C. Ford, A. L., 1959 (first game), 1960 (second game).
        Luis C. Tiant, A. L., 1968, 1974.
        James A. Hunter, A. L., 1967, 1975.

Most Innings Pitched, Total Games

    19⅓—Donald S. Drysdale, N. L., 1959 (2), 1962 (first game), 1963, 1964, 1965, 1967, 1968 (8 games).

Most Innings, Game
> 6—Vernon Gomez, A. L., July 8, 1935.

Most Runs Allowed, Total Games
> 13—Edward C. Ford, A. L., 1954, 1955, 1956, 1959, 1960, 1961.

Most Earned Runs Allowed, Total Games
> 11—Edward C. Ford, A. L., 1954, 1955, 1956, 1959, 1960, 1961.

Most Runs Allowed, Game
> 5—Claude W. Passeau, N. L., July 8, 1941.
> Sandalio S. Consuegra, A. L., July 13, 1954.
> Edward C. Ford, A. L., July 12, 1955.
> James W. Maloney, N. L., July 13, 1965.
> Johnny L. Odom, A. L., July 23, 1969.
> James A. Palmer, A. L., July 19, 1977.

Most Earned Runs Allowed, Game
> 5—Claude W. Passeau, N. L., July 8, 1941.
> Sandalio S. Consuegra, A. L., July 13, 1954.
> James W. Maloney, N. L., July 13, 1965.
> James A. Palmer, A. L., July 19, 1977.

Most Runs Allowed, Inning
> 5—Sandalio S. Consuegra, A. L., July 13, 1954, fourth inning.
> Johnny L. Odom, A. L., July 23, 1969, third inning.

Most Earned Runs, Inning
> 5—Sandalio S. Consuegra, A. L., July 13, 1954, fourth inning.

Most Hits Allowed, Total Games
> 19—Edward C. Ford, A. L., 1954, 1955, 1956, 1959, 1960, 1961.

Most Hits Allowed, Inning
> 5—Cecil G. Hughson, A. L., July 11, 1944, fifth inning.
> Sandalio S. Consuegra, A. L., July 13, 1954, fourth inning.
> Johnny L. Odom, A. L., July 23, 1969, third inning.

Most Hits Allowed, Game
> 7—Thomas D. Bridges, A. L., July 7, 1937.

Most Home Runs Allowed, Total Games
> 4—Vida Blue, A. L., 1971 (2), 1975 (2).
> James A. Hunter, A. L., 1967, 1970, 1974, 1976.

Most Home Runs Allowed, Game
> 3—James A. Palmer, A. L., July 19, 1977.

Most Home Runs Allowed, Inning (10)
> 2—Morton C. Cooper, N. L., July 6, 1942, first inning.
> Edmund W. Lopat, A. L., July 10, 1951, fourth inning.
> Robin E. Roberts, N. L., July 13, 1954, third inning (consecutive).
> Warren E. Spahn, N. L., July 10, 1956, sixth inning (consecutive).
> John T. Wyatt, A. L., July 7, 1964, fourth inning.
> Milton S. Pappas, A. L., July 13, 1965, first inning.
> James W. Maloney, N. L., July 13, 1965, fifth inning.
> Dock P. Ellis, N. L., July 13, 1971, third inning.
> Vida Blue, A. L., July 15, 1975, second inning (consecutive).
> James A. Palmer, A. L., July 19, 1977 (first inning).

Most Bases on Balls, Total Games
> 7—James A. Palmer, A. L., 1970 (1), 1972 (1), 1977 (1), 1978 (4).

Most Bases on Balls, Game

    5—William A. Hallahan, N. L., July 6, 1933, 2 innings.

Most Strikeouts, Total Games

    19—Donald S. Drysdale, N. L., 1959, 1959, 1962, 1963, 1964, 1965, 1967, 1968 (8 games).

Most Strikeouts, Game

    6—Carl O. Hubbell, N. L., July 10, 1934, 3 innings.
       John S. Vander Meer, N. L., July 13, 1943, 2⅔ innings.
       Lawrence J. Jansen, N. L., July 11, 1950, 5 innings.
       Ferguson A. Jenkins, N. L., July 11, 1967, 3 innings.

Most Consecutive Strikeouts, Game

    5—Carl O. Hubbell, N. L., July 10, 1934; 3 in first inning, 2 in second inning (Ruth, Gehrig, Foxx, Simmons, Cronin). Then Dickey singled, Gomez struck out.

Most Wild Pitches, Total Games

    2—Ewell Blackwell, N. L., 1946, 1947, 1948, 1949, 1950, 1951.
       Robin E. Roberts, N. L., 1950, 1951, 1953, 1954, 1955,
       Thomas A. Brewer, A. L., 1956.
       Juan A. Marichal, N. L., 1962, 1962, 1964, 1965, 1966, 1967, 1968, 1971.
       David A. Stieb, A. L., 1980.

Most Wild Pitches, Game

    2—Thomas A. Brewer, A. L., July 10, 1956, sixth and seventh innings.
       Juan A. Marichal, N. L., July 30, 1962, ninth inning.
       David A. Stieb, A. L., July 8, 1980, seventh inning.

Most Wild Pitches, Inning

    2—Juan A. Marichal, N. L., July 30, 1962, ninth inning.
       David A. Stieb, A. L., July 8, 1980, seventh inning.

Most Hit Batsmen, Inning or Game

    1—Held by 24 pitchers.

Most Balks, Inning or Game

    1—Robert B. Friend, N. L., July 11, 1960.
       Stuart L. Miller, N. L., July 11, 1961.
       Steven L. Busby, A. L., July 15, 1975.
       James L. Kern, A. L., July 17, 1979.

GENERAL RECORDS

Earliest Date for All-Star Game

    July 6, 1933 at Comiskey Park, Chicago.
    July 6, 1938 at Crosley Field, Cincinnati.
    July 6, 1942 at Polo Grounds, New York.

Latest Date for All-Star Game

    August 3, 1959 at Memorial Coliseum, Los Angeles.

All-Star Night Games

    July 13, 1943 at Shibe Park, Philadelphia.
    July 11, 1944 at Forbes Field, Pittsburgh.
    July 9, 1968 at The Astrodome, Houston.
    July 14, 1970 at Riverfront Stadium, Cincinnati.
    July 13, 1971 at Tiger Stadium, Detroit.
    July 25, 1972 at Atlanta Stadium, Atlanta.

All-Star Night Games—Continued

July 24, 1973 at Royals Stadium, Kansas City.
July 23, 1974 at Three Rivers Stadium, Pittsburgh.
July 15, 1975 at County Stadium, Milwaukee.
July 13, 1976 at Veterans Stadium, Philadelphia.
July 19, 1977 at Yankee Stadium, New York.
July 11, 1978 at San Diego Stadium, San Diego.

Largest Attendance, Game

69,831 at Municipal Stadium, Cleveland, July 8, 1935.

Smallest Attendance, Game

25,556 at Braves Field, Boston, July 7, 1936.

Longest Game, by Innings

15 innings—at Anaheim Stadium, California, July 11, 1967. National League 2, American League 1.
14 innings—at Comiskey Park, Chicago, July 11, 1950. National League 4, American League 3.

Shortest Game, by Innings

5 innings—at Shibe Park, Philadelphia, July 8, 1952 (rain). National League 3, American League 2.

Longest Nine-Inning Game, by Time

3 hours, 10 minutes, at Municipal Stadium, Cleveland, July 13, 1954. American League 11, National League 9.

Shortest Nine-Inning Game, by Time

1 hour, 53 minutes, at Sportsman's Park, St. Louis, July 9, 1940. National League 4, American League 0.

Longest Extra-Inning Game, by Time

3 hours, 41 minutes, at Anaheim Stadium, California, July 11, 1967. National League 2, American League 1, 15 innings.
3 hours, 19 minutes, at Comiskey Park, Chicago, July 11, 1950. National League 4, American League 3, 14 innings.
3 hours, 19 minutes, at Riverfront Stadium, Cincinnati, July 14, 1970, night game, National League 5, American League 4, 12 innings.

Most Players, Nine-Inning Game, One Club

28—N. L., July 24, 1973.

Most Players, Extra-Inning Game, One Club

25—N. L., July 14, 1970.

Most Players, Nine-Inning Game, Both Clubs

54—N. L. (28), A. L. (26), July 24, 1973.

Most Players, Extra-Inning Game, Both Clubs

49—N. L. (25), A. L. (24), July 14, 1970, night game, 12 innings.

Fewest Players, Game, One Club

11—A. L., July 6, 1942.

Fewest Players, Game, Both Clubs

27—A. L. (15), N. L. (12), July 1, 1938.

Most Pitchers, Nine-Inning Game, One Club

7—N. L., July 12, 1949.
A. L., July 13, 1954.
A. L., July 23, 1969.

A. L., July 24, 1973.
N. L., July 24, 1973.
N. L., July 17, 1979.

Most Pitchers, Extra-Inning Game, One Club
7—N. L., July 11, 1967.
   A. L., July 14, 1970.

Most Pitchers, Nine-Inning Game, Both Clubs
14—A. L. (7), N. L. (7), July 24, 1973.

Fewest Pitchers, Game, One Club
2—A. L., July 8, 1935.
   A. L., July 6, 1942.

Fewest Pitchers, Game, Both Clubs
6—N. L. (3), A. L. (3), July 6, 1933.
   N. L. (4), A. L. (2), July 8, 1935.
   N. L. (3), A. L. (3), July 6, 1938.
   N. L. (3), A. L. (3), July 11, 1939.

Most Catchers, Nine-Inning Game, One Club
3—9 games—N. L.—1940, 1941, 1947, 1955, 1960, second game; 1968, 1977, 1978, 1980.
   5 games—A. L.—1940, 1946, 1961, first game; 1968, 1980.

Most Catchers, Nine-Inning Game, Both Clubs
6—N. L. (3), A. L. (3), July 9, 1940.
   N. L. (3), A. L. (3), July 9, 1968.
   N. L. (3), A. L. (3), July 8, 1980.

Most First Basemen, Nine-Inning Game, One Club
3—N. L., July 9, 1946.
   N. L., July 13, 1960, second game.
   N. L., July 24, 1973.

Most First Basemen, Nine-Inning Game, Both Clubs
5—N. L. (3), A. L. (2), July 9, 1946.
   N. L. (3), A. L. (2), July 13, 1960, second game.

Most Second Basemen, Nine-Inning Game, One Club
3—N. L., July 13, 1960, second game.

Most Second Basemen, Nine-Inning Game, Both Clubs
5—N. L. (3), A. L. (2), July 13, 1960, second game.

Most Third Basemen, Nine-Inning Game, One Club
3—A. L., July 11, 1961, first game.
   A. L., July 24, 1973.
   N. L., July 13, 1976.

Most Third Basemen, Nine-Inning Game, Both Clubs
5—A. L. (3), N. L. (2), July 11, 1961, first game.
   A. L. (3), N. L. (2), July 24, 1973.
   N. L. (3), A. L. (2), July 13, 1976.

Most Shortstops, Nine-Inning Game, One Club
3—A. L., July 13, 1976.
   N. L., July 13, 1976.
   A. L., July 8, 1980.

Most Shortstops, Nine-Inning Game, Both Clubs
6—A. L. (3), N. L. (3), July 13, 1976.

Most Infielders, Game, One Club
10—N. L., July 13, 1960, second game.
N. L., July 14, 1970, 12 innings.
N. L., July 13, 1976.

Most Infielders, Game, Both Clubs
18—N. L. (10), A. L. (8), July 13, 1976.

Most Outfielders, Nine-Inning Game, One Club
8—N. L., July 24, 1973.

Most Outfielders, Nine-Inning Game, Both Clubs
14—N. L. (7), A. L. (7), July 8, 1980.

Most Outfielders, Extra-Inning Game, Both Clubs
13—N. L. (7), A. L. (6), July 14, 1970, 12 innings.

Most Right Fielders, Nine-Inning Game, One Club
4—N. L., July 13, 1976.

Most Right Fielders, Nine-Inning Game, Both Clubs
6—N. L. (4), A. L. (2), July 13, 1976.

Most Center Fielders, Nine-Inning Game, One Club
3—A. L., July 10, 1934; A. L., July 9, 1946; A. L., July 12, 1949; N. L., July 15, 1975.

Most Center Fielders, Nine-Inning Game, Both Clubs
5—A. L. (3), N. L. (2), July 10, 1934; A. L. (3), N. L. (2), July 9, 1946; A. L. (3), N. L. (2), July 12, 1949; N. L. (3), A. L. (2), July 15, 1975.

Most Left Fielders, Nine-Inning Game, One Club
3—N. L., July 1, 1951; A. L., July 13, 1954; N. L., August 3, 1959, second game; N. L., July 9, 1968; A. L., July 23, 1969; N. L., July 15, 1975; A. L., July 8, 1980.

Most Left Fielders, Nine-Inning Game, Both Clubs
5—N. L. (3), A. L. (2), July 10, 1951; A. L. (3), N. L. (2), July 13, 1954; N. L. (3), A. L. (2), July 9, 1968; A. L. (3), N. L. (2), July 23, 1969; N. L. (3), A. L. (2), July 15, 1975; A. L. (3), N. L. (2), July 8, 1980.

Most Left Fielders, Extra-Inning Game, Both Clubs
6—N. L. (3), A. L., (3), July 14, 1970, 12 innings.

Most Pinch-Hitters, Nine-Inning Game, One Club
8—N. L., July 9, 1957.

Most Pinch-Hitters, Nine-Inning Game, Both Clubs
11—N. L. (7), A. L. (4), July 24, 1973.

Most Pinch-Hitters, Extra-Inning Game, Both Clubs
11—N. L. (6), A. L. (5), July 11, 1967, 15 innings.

Fewest Pinch-Hitters, Game, One Club
0—A. L., July 8, 1935.
N. L., July 9, 1940.
A. L., July 8, 1980.

Fewest Pinch-Hitters, Game, Both Clubs
1—A. L., (1), N. L. (0), July 9, 1940.

Youngest Player to Participate in All-Star Game

Harold D. Wynegar, 1976; 20 years, 3 months, 30 days.

Oldest Player to Participate in All-Star Game

Leroy Paige, 1953; 48 years, 7 days.

Players Participating in All-Star Game, Each League (26)

Henry L. Aaron, National League, 1955, 1956, 1957, 1958, 1959 (2), 1960 (2), 1961 (2), 1962, 1963, 1964, 1965, 1966, 1967, 1968, 1969, 1970, 1971, 1972, 1973, 1974. American League, 1975.

Richard A. Allen, National League, 1965, 1966, 1967, 1970. American League, 1972, 1974.

Vida R. Blue, American League, 1971, 1975. National League, 1978.

Bobby L. Bonds, National League, 1971, 1973. American League, 1975.

James P. Bunning, American League, 1957, 1959, 1961 (2), 1962, 1963. National League, 1964, 1966.

Miguel Cuellar, National League, 1967. American League, 1971.

Raymond L. Culp, National League, 1963. American League, 1969.

Ronald R. Fairly, National League, 1973. American League, 1977.

Roland G. Fingers, American League, 1973, 1974. National League, 1978.

Philip M. Garner, American League, 1976. National League, 1980.

Richard M. Gossage, American League, 1975, 1978, 1980. National League, 1977.

George A. Hendrick, American League, 1974, 1975. National League, 1980.

David A. Johnson, American League, 1968, 1970. National League, 1973.

John R. Mize, National League, 1937, 1939, 1940, 1941, 1942, 1946, 1947, 1948, 1949. American League, 1953.

Robert J. Monday, American League, 1968. National League, 1978.

Bobby R. Murcer, American League, 1971, 1972, 1973, 1974; National League, 1975.

Albert Oliver, National League, 1972, 1975, 1976. American League, 1980.

Gaylord J. Perry, National League, 1966, 1970, 1979; American League, 1972, 1974.

Frank Robinson, National League, 1956, 1957, 1959, 1961, 1962, 1965. American League, 1966, 1969, 1970, 1971, 1974.

Octavio V. Rojas, National League, 1965. American League, 1971, 1972, 1973.

John Roseboro, National League, 1961, 1962. American League, 1969.

C. Reginald Smith, American League, 1969, 1972. National League, 1974, 1975, 1977, 1978, 1980.

William R. Singer, National League, 1969. American League, 1973.

Lynwood T. Rowe, American League, 1936. National League, 1947.

Daniel J. Staub, National League, 1967, 1968, 1970. American League, 1976.

John E. Temple, National League, 1956, 1957, 1959 (2). American League, 1961 (2).

Pitchers Starting in All-Star Game, Each League (1)

Vida R. Blue, American League, 1971. National League, 1978.

All-Star Games Won

32—National League (one tie). (Lost 18).

18—American League (one tie). (Lost 32).

Most Consecutive All-Star Games Won

9—National League, 1972, 1973, 1974, 1975, 1976, 1977, 1978, 1979, 1980.

Most Consecutive All-Star Games Lost

9—American League, 1972, 1973, 1974, 1975, 1976, 1977, 1978, 1979, 1980.

Most All-Star Games Managed

10—Charles D. Stengel, A. L., 1950, 1951, 1952, 1953, 1954, 1956, 1957, 1958, 1959 (2) (won 4, lost 6).

Most Consecutive All-Star Games Managed

5—Charles D. Stengel, A. L., 1950, 1951, 1952, 1953, 1954; also 1956, 1957, 1958, 1959 (2).

Most All-Star Games Won as Manager

7—Walter E. Alston, N. L., 1956, 1960 (2), 1964, 1966, 1967, 1975, (lost 1).

Most All-Star Games Lost as Manager

6—Charles D. Stengel, A. L., 1950, 1951, 1952, 1953, 1956, 1959 first game (won 4).

Most Consecutive Defeats as All-Star Manager

5—Alfonso R. Lopez, A. L., 1955, 1960 (2), 1964, 1965.

Most Consecutive Years Managing All-Star Losers

4—Charles D. Stengel, A. L., 1950, 1951, 1952, 1953.

All-Star Game's most distinguished managers, Casey Stengel and Walter Alston.

All-Star Game Composite Averages
BATTING AVERAGES
American League

Player, Club and Years Played	Pos.	G.	AB.	R.	H.	2B.	3B.	HR.	RBI.	B.A.
Aaron, Henry, 1975 Milwaukee	PH	1	1	0	0	0	0	0	0	.000
Agee, Tommie, 1966-67 Chicago	OF-PR	2	0	0	0	0	0	0	0	.000
Aguirre, Henry, 1962 Detroit	P	1	2	0	0	0	0	0	0	.000
Allen, John, 1938 Cleveland	P	1	1	0	0	0	0	0	0	.000
Allen, Richard, 1972-74 Chicago	1B	2	5	0	1	0	0	0	1	.200
Allison, W. Robert, 1963-64 Minnesota	OF-1B	2	4	0	0	0	0	0	0	.000
Alomar, Santos, 1970 California		1	1	0	0	0	0	0	0	.000
Alvis, R. Maxwell, 1965-67 Cleveland	3B-PH	2	2	0	0	0	0	0	0	.000
Andrews, Michael, 1969 Boston	2B	1	1	0	0	0	0	0	0	.000
Aparicio, Luis, 1958-59 (2)-60-61-62 (2) Chicago; 1963 Baltimore; 1970 Chicago; 1971 Boston	SS	10	28	2	2	0	1	0	0	.071
Appling, Lucius, 1936-40-46-47 Chicago	SS-PH	4	9	1	4	1	0	0	2	.444
Averill, Earl, 1933-34-36-37-38 Cleveland	OF-PH	5	15	1	4	1	1	0	4	.267
Avila, Roberto, 1952-54-55 Cleveland	2B	3	6	1	4	0	0	0	3	.667
Azcue, Jose, 1968 Cleveland	C	1	1	0	0	0	0	0	0	.000
Bando, Salvatore, 1969-72-73 Oakland	3B	3	6	0	1	0	0	0	0	.167
Battey, Earl, 1962 (2)-63-65-66 Minnesota	C	5	9	1	1	0	0	0	1	.111
Bauer, Henry, 1952-53-54 New York	OF	3	7	0	2	0	0	0	0	.286
Baylor, Donald, 1979 California	OF	1	4	2	2	1	0	0	1	.500
Belanger, Mark, 1976 Baltimore	SS	1	1	0	0	0	0	0	0	.000
Bell, David, 1973 Cleveland; 1980 Texas	PH-3B	2	3	0	1	0	1	0	0	.333
Bell, Gary, 1960 (2) Cleveland	P	2	0	0	0	0	0	0	0	.000
Benton, J. Alton, 1942 Detroit	P	1	1	0	0	0	0	0	0	.000
Berra, Lawrence, 1949-50-51-52-53-54-55-56-57-58-59-60 (2)-61-62 New York	C-PH	15	41	5	8	0	0	1	3	.195
Berry, A. Kenneth, 1967 Chicago	PH	1	1	0	0	0	0	0	0	.000
Blair, Paul, 1969-73 Baltimore	OF	2	2	0	0	0	0	0	0	.000
Blue, Vida, 1971-75 Oakland	P	2	0	0	0	0	0	0	0	.000
Bluege, Oswald, 1935 Washington	3B	1	0	0	0	0	0	0	0	.000
Blyleven, Rikalbert, 1973 Minnesota	P	1	0	0	0	0	0	0	0	.000
Bochte, Bruce, 1979 Seattle	PH-1B	1	1	0	1	0	0	0	1	1.000
Bonds, Bobby, 1975 New York	OF	1	3	0	0	0	0	0	0	.000
Boone, Raymond, 1954-56 Detroit	3B-PH	2	5	1	1	0	0	1	1	.200
Borowy, Henry, 1944 New York	P	1	1	0	1	0	0	0	1	1.000
Boudreau, Louis, 1940-41-42-47-48 Cleveland	SS	5	12	1	4	0	0	1	3	.333
Bouton, James, 1963 New York	P	1	0	0	0	0	0	0	0	.000
Brandt, Jack, 1961 Baltimore	PH	1	1	0	0	0	0	0	0	.000
Brett, George, 1976-77-78-79 Kansas City	3B	4	10	2	2	1	0	0	2	.200
Brewer, Thomas, 1956 Boston	P	1	0	0	0	0	0	0	0	.000
Bridges, Thomas, 1937-39 Detroit	P	2	2	0	0	0	0	0	0	.000
Brinkman, Edwin, 1973 Detroit	SS	1	1	0	0	0	0	0	0	.000
Brissie, Leland, 1949 Philadelphia	P	1	1	0	0	0	0	0	0	.000
Buford, Donald, 1971 Baltimore	PH	1	1	0	0	0	0	0	0	.000
Bumbry, Alonza, 1980 Baltimore	OF	1	1	0	0	0	0	0	0	.000
Bunning, James, 1957-59-61 (2)-62-63 Detroit	P	6	2	0	0	0	0	0	0	.000
Burleson, Rick, 1977-79 Boston	SS-PR	2	4	1	0	0	0	0	0	.000
Burroughs, Jeffrey, 1974 Texas	OF	1	0	0	0	0	0	0	0	.000
Busby, James, 1951 Chicago	OF	1	0	0	0	0	0	0	0	.000
Busby, Steven, 1975 Kansas City	P	1	0	0	0	0	0	0	0	.000
Campaneris, Dagoberto, 1968-73-74-75 Oak.; 1977 Tex.	SS	5	11	1	2	0	0	0	0	.182
Campbell, William, 1977 Boston	P	1	0	0	0	0	0	0	0	.000
Carew, Rodney, 1967-68-69-71-72-73-74-75-76-77-78 Minn.; 1980 California	2B-1B	12	33	6	7	1	2	0	1	.212
Cash, Norman, 1961 (2)-66-71-72 Detroit	1B	5	13	0	1	1	0	0	0	.077
Carrasquel, Alfonso, 1951-53-54-55 Chicago	SS	4	12	1	4	0	0	0	0	.333
Case, George, 1943 Washington	OF	1	2	1	0	0	0	0	0	.000
Cerv, Robert, 1958 Kansas City	OF	1	2	0	1	0	0	0	0	.500
Chalk, David, 1974 California	3B	1	1	0	0	0	0	0	0	.000
Chambliss, C. Christopher, 1976 New York	PH	1	1	0	0	0	0	0	0	.000
Chance, Dean, 1964 Los Angeles; 1967 Minnesota	P	2	1	0	0	0	0	0	0	.000
Chandler, Spurgeon, 1942 New York	P	1	1	0	0	0	0	0	0	.000
Chapman, Benjamin, 1933-34-35 N. Y.; 1936 Wash.	OF	4	8	0	2	0	1	0	0	.250
Chapman, Samuel, 1946 Philadelphia	OF	1	2	0	0	0	0	0	1	.000
Clear, Mark, 1979 California	P	1	0	0	0	0	0	0	0	.000
Coates, James, 1960 New York	P	1	0	0	0	0	0	0	0	.000
Cochrane, Gordon, 1934 Detroit	C	1	1	0	0	0	0	0	0	.000
Colavito, Rocco, 1959 (2) Clev.; 1961 (2)-62 (2) Det.; 1964 K. C.; 1965-66 Cleve.	OF-PH	9	25	3	6	1	0	3	8	.240
Coleman, Gerald, 1950 New York	2B	1	1	0	0	0	0	0	0	.000
Coleman, Joseph, 1948 Philadelphia	P	1	0	0	0	0	0	0	0	.000
Conigliaro, Anthony, 1967 Boston	OF	1	6	0	0	0	0	0	0	.000
Consuegra, Sandalio, 1954 Chicago	P	1	0	0	0	0	0	0	0	.000
Cooper, Cecil, 1979-80 Milwaukee	PH-1B	2	1	0	0	0	0	0	0	.000
Cramer, Roger, 1935 Philadelphia; 1938-39 Boston	OF	3	6	0	1	0	0	0	0	.167
Cronin, Joseph, 1933-34 Wash.; 1935-37-38-39-41 Boston	SS	7	25	3	7	3	0	0	4	.280
Crosetti, Frank, 1936 New York	PH	1	1	0	0	0	0	0	0	.000

Player, Club and Years Played	Pos.	G.	AB.	R.	H.	2B.	3B.	HR.	RBI.	B.A.
Crowder, Alvin, 1933 Washington	P	1	1	0	0	0	0	0	0	.000
Cuellar, Miguel, 1971 Baltimore	P	1	0	0	0	0	0	0	0	.000
Cullenbine, Roy, 1941 St. Louis	PH	1	1	0	0	0	0	0	0	.000
Culp, Raymond, 1969 Boston	P	1	0	0	0	0	0	0	0	.000
Daley, Buddy, 1959-60 Kansas City	P	2	0	0	0	0	0	0	0	.000
Davalillo, Victor, 1965 Cleveland	OF	1	2	0	1	0	0	0	0	.500
Dent, Russell, 1975 Chicago; 1980 New York	SS	2	3	0	1	0	0	0	0	.333
Dickey, William, 1934-36-37-38-39-40-41-46 New York.	C-PH	8	19	3	5	2	0	0	1	.263
Dillinger, Robert, 1949 St. Louis	3B	1	1	2	1	0	0	0	1	1.000
DiMaggio, Dominic, 1941-46-49-50-51-52 Boston	OF	6	17	2	6	2	0	0	2	.353
DiMaggio, Joseph, 1936-37-38-39-40-41-42- 47-48-49-50 New York	OF-PH	11	40	7	9	2	0	1	6	.225
Doby, Lawrence, 1949-50-51-52-53-54 Cleveland	OF-PH	6	10	2	3	1	0	1	1	.300
Doerr, Robert, 1941-43-44-46-47-48-50-51 Boston	2B	8	20	2	4	0	0	1	3	.200
Donovan, Richard, 1961 Washington; 1962 Cleveland	P	2	0	0	0	0	0	0	0	.000
Downing, Alphonso, 1967 New York	P	1	0	0	0	0	0	0	0	.000
Downing, Brian, 1979 California	C	1	1	0	1	0	0	0	0	1.000
Dropo, Walter, 1950 Boston	1B	1	3	0	1	0	1	0	0	.333
Duren, Ryne, 1959 New York	P	1	1	0	0	0	0	0	0	.000
Dykes, James, 1933 Chicago	3B	1	3	1	2	0	0	0	0	.667
Early, Jacob, 1948 Washington	C	1	2	1	0	0	0	0	0	.000
Eckersley, Dennis, 1977 Cleveland	P	1	0	0	0	0	0	0	0	.000
Estrada, Charles, 1960 Baltimore	P	1	0	0	0	0	0	0	0	.000
Evans, Dwight, 1978 Boston	OF	1	1	0	0	0	0	0	0	.000
Evers, Walter, 1948-50 Detroit	OF	2	6	1	1	0	0	1	1	.167
Fain, Ferris, 1950-51 Philadelphia; 1953 Chicago	1B	3	7	1	3	0	1	0	1	.429
Fairly, Ronald, 1977 Toronto	PH	1	1	0	0	0	0	0	0	.000
Farmer, Edward 1980 Chicago	P	1	0	0	0	0	0	0	0	.000
Feller, Robert, 1939-40-41-46-50 Cleveland	P	5	2	0	0	0	0	0	0	.000
Ferrell, Richard, 1933-36 Boston	C	2	5	0	0	0	0	0	0	.000
Fidrych, Mark, 1976 Detroit	P	1	0	0	0	0	0	0	0	.000
Fingers, Roland, 1973-74 Oakland	P	2	0	0	0	0	0	0	0	.000
Finigan, James, 1955 Kansas City	3B	1	3	0	0	0	0	0	0	.000
Finney, Louis, 1940 Boston	OF	1	0	0	0	0	0	0	0	.000
Fisher, Eddie, 1965 Chicago	P	1	0	0	0	0	0	0	0	.000
Fisk, Carlton, 1972-73-76-77-78-80 Boston	C	6	11	1	1	0	0	0	1	.091
Ford, Edward, 1954-55-56-59-60-61 New York	P	6	3	0	0	0	0	0	0	.000
Fornieles, J. Miguel, 1961 Boston	P	1	0	0	0	0	0	0	0	.000
Fosse, Raymond, 1970 Cleveland	C	1	2	1	1	0	0	0	1	.500
Fox, J. Nelson, 1951-53-54-55-56-57-58-59(2)- 60(2)-61-63 Chicago	2B-PH	13	38	7	14	0	0	0	5	.368
Foxx, James, 1934-35 Phila.; 1936-37-38-40-41 Boston	1B-3B	7	19	3	6	1	0	1	4	.316
Freehan, William, 1965-66-67-68-69-70-71-72 Detroit	C	8	17	2	4	0	0	1	2	.235
Fregosi, James, 1964 L.A.; 1966-67-68-69-70 Calif.	SS-PH	6	15	1	3	1	0	0	1	.200
Garcia, E. Mike, 1953 Cleveland	P	1	0	0	0	0	0	0	0	.000
Garner, Philip, 1976 Oakland	2B	1	1	0	0	0	0	0	0	.000
Garver, Ned, 1951 St. Louis	P	1	1	0	0	0	0	0	0	.000
Gehrig, H. Louis, 1933-34-35-36-37-38 New York	1B	6	18	4	4	1	0	2	5	.222
Gehringer, Charles, 1933-34-35-36-37-38 Detroit	2B	6	20	2	10	2	0	0	1	.500
Gentile, James, 1960-61-62 (2) Baltimore	PH-1B	4	11	0	2	0	0	0	0	.182
Gomez, Vernon, 1933-34-35-37-38 New York	P	5	6	0	1	0	0	0	1	.167
Goodman, William, 1949-53 Boston	1B-2B	2	2	0	0	0	0	0	0	.000
Gordon, Joseph, 1939-40-41-42-46 N. Y.; 1947-48-49 Cleve.	2B	8	20	2	4	3	0	0	2	.200
Goslin, Leon, 1936 Detroit	OF	1	1	1	1	0	0	0	0	1.000
Gossage, Richard, 1975 Chicago; 1978-80 New York	P	3	0	0	0	0	0	0	0	.000
Grant, James, 1965 Minnesota	P	1	0	0	0	0	0	0	0	.000
Gray, Theodore, 1950 Detroit	P	1	0	0	0	0	0	0	0	.000
Greenberg, Henry, 1939-40 Detroit	1B-OF	2	5	1	1	0	0	0	0	.200
Grich, Robert, 1972-74-76 Baltimore; 1979-80 California	SS-2B	5	10	0	1	0	0	0	0	.100
Grim, Robert, 1957 New York	P	1	0	0	0	0	0	0	0	.000
Grove, Robert, 1933 Philadelphia; 1936-38 Boston	P	3	2	0	0	0	0	0	0	.000
Guidry, Ronald, 1978-79 New York	P	2	0	0	0	0	0	0	0	.000
Hall, Jimmie, 1964-65 Minnesota	OF-PH	2	2	1	0	0	0	0	0	.000
Hansen, Ronald, 1960 (2) Baltimore	SS	2	6	0	3	0	0	0	0	.500
Harder, Melvin, 1934-35-36-37 Cleveland	P	4	4	0	0	0	0	0	0	.000
Hargrove, D. Michael, 1975 Texas	PH	1	1	0	0	0	0	0	0	.000
Harper, Tommy, 1970 Milwaukee	PR	1	0	0	0	0	0	0	0	.000
Harrah, Colbert, 1976 Texas	SS	1	2	0	0	0	0	0	0	.000
Harrelson, Kenneth, 1968 Boston	PH	1	1	0	0	0	0	0	0	.000
Hayes, Frank, 1940-41-44 Philadelphia; 1946 Cleveland	C	4	4	0	0	0	0	0	0	.000
Heath, J. Geoffrey, 1941-43 Cleveland	OF-PH	2	3	0	0	0	0	0	0	.000
Hegan, James, 1950-51 Cleveland	C-PH	2	4	0	1	1	0	0	0	.250
Hemsley, Ralston, 1935 St. Louis; 1940 Cleve.; 1944 N. Y.	C	3	7	1	1	0	1	0	0	.143
Henderson, Rickey, 1980 Oakland	OF	1	1	0	0	0	0	0	0	.000
Hendrick, George, 1974-75 Cleveland	OF-PR	2	3	1	2	0	0	0	0	.667
Henrich, Thomas, 1942-47-48-50 New York	OF-PH	4	9	1	1	1	0	0	0	.111
Herbert, Raymond, 1962 Chicago	P	1	1	0	0	0	0	0	0	.000
Higgins, Michael, 1936 Philadelphia; 1944 Detroit	3B-PH	2	3	0	0	0	0	0	0	.000
Hinton, Charles, 1964 Washington	OF	1	0	0	0	0	0	0	0	.000
Hisle, Larry, 1977 Minnesota; 1978 Milwaukee	PH	2	2	0	1	0	0	0	0	.500
Hoag, Myril, 1939 St. Louis	PH	1	1	0	0	0	0	0	0	.000
Holtzman, Kenneth, 1973 Oakland	P	1	0	0	0	0	0	0	0	.000
Horton, Willie, 1965-68-70-73 Detroit	OF-PH	4	8	1	2	0	0	0	0	.250

Player, Club and Years Played	Pos.	G.	AB.	R.	H.	2B.	3B.	HR.	RBI.	B.A.
Houtteman, Arthur, 1950 Detroit	P	1	1	0	0	0	0	0	0	.000
Howard, Elston, 1960-61 (2)-62-63-64 New York	C	6	9	1	0	0	0	0	0	.000
Howard, Frank, 1968-69-70-71 Washington	PH-OF	4	6	1	1	0	0	1	1	.167
Howell, Roy, 1978 Toronto	PH	1	1	0	0	0	0	0	0	.000
Howser, Richard, 1961 Kansas City	3B	1	1	0	0	0	0	0	0	.000
Hudson, Sidney, 1941 Washington	P	1	0	0	0	0	0	0	0	.000
Hughson, Cecil, 1943-44 Boston	P	2	1	0	0	0	0	0	0	.000
Hunter, G. William, 1953 St. Louis	PR	1	0	0	0	0	0	0	0	.000
Hunter, James, 1967 Kansas City; 1970-73-74-75 Oakland; 1976 New York	P	6	1	0	0	0	0	0	0	.000
Hutchinson, Fred, 1951 Detroit	P	1	0	0	0	0	0	0	0	.000
Jackson, Reginald, 1969-71-72-73-74-75 Oak.; 1977-79-80 N. Y.	PH-OF	9	22	2	7	2	0	1	2	.318
Jensen, Jack, 1952 Washington; 1955-58 Boston	OF-PH	3	5	0	0	0	0	0	1	.000
John, Thomas, 1968 Chicago; 1980 New York	P	2	1	0	0	0	0	0	0	.000
Johnson, Alexander, 1970 California	PH	1	1	0	0	0	0	0	0	.000
Johnson, David, 1968-70 Baltimore	2B	2	6	0	1	0	0	0	0	.167
Johnson, Robert, 1935-38-42 Philadelphia; 1943 Washington; 1944 Boston	OF-PH	5	9	0	1	0	0	0	0	.111
Johnson, William, 1947 New York	3B	1	0	0	0	0	0	0	0	.000
Jones, Ruppert, 1977 Seattle	PH	1	1	0	0	0	0	0	0	.000
Joost, Edwin, 1949 Philadelphia	SS	1	2	1	1	0	0	0	2	.500
Josephson, Duane, 1968 Chicago	C	1	0	0	0	0	0	0	0	.000
Kaat, James, 1966 Minnesota; 1975 Chicago	P	2	0	0	0	0	0	0	0	.000
Kaline, Albert, 1955-56-57-58-59 (2)-60 (2)-61 (2)-62-63-65-66-71-74 Detroit	OF-PH-PR	16	37	7	12	1	0	2	6	.324
Keegan, Robert, 1954 Chicago	P	1	0	0	0	0	0	0	0	.000
Kell, George, 1947-49-50-51 Det.; 1953 Bos.; 1956-57 Balt.	3B-PH	7	23	3	4	0	0	1	3	.174
Keller, Charles, 1940-41-46 New York	OF	3	7	2	1	0	0	1	2	.143
Kelly, H. Patrick, 1973 Chicago	PH	1	1	0	0	0	0	0	0	.000
Keltner, Kenneth, 1940-41-42-43-44-46-48 Cleveland	3B-PH	7	17	4	4	1	0	0	0	.235
Kemp, Steven, 1979 Detroit	PH	1	1	0	0	0	0	0	0	.000
Keough, Matthew, 1978 Oakland	P	1	0	0	0	0	0	0	0	.000
Kern, James, 1977-78 Cleveland; 1979 Texas	P	3	0	0	0	0	0	0	0	.000
Killebrew, Harmon, 1959 Wash.; 1961-63-64-65-66-67- 68-69-70-71 Minnesota	3B-PH-OF-1B	11	26	4	8	0	0	3	6	.308
Knoop, Robert, 1966 California	2B	1	2	0	0	0	0	0	0	.000
Knowles, Darold, 1969 Washington	P	1	0	0	0	0	0	0	0	.000
Kramer, John, 1946 St. Louis	P	1	1	1	1	0	0	0	0	1.000
Kreevich, Michael, 1938 Chicago	OF	1	2	0	0	0	0	0	0	.000
Kubek, Anthony, 1959-61 New York	PH-SS	2	5	1	0	0	0	0	0	.000
Kuenn, Harvey, 1953-55-56-57-59 Det.; 1960 (2) Clev.	PH-SS-OF	7	16	3	3	0	0	0	1	.188
Laabs, Chester, 1943 St. Louis	OF	1	3	1	0	0	0	0	0	.000
Landis, James, 1962 Chicago	OF	1	1	0	0	0	0	0	0	.000
Landreaux, Kenneth, 1980 Minnesota	OF	1	1	0	0	0	0	0	0	.000
LaRoche, David, 1977 California	P	1	0	0	0	0	0	0	0	.000
Lary, Frank, 1960 (2)-61 Detroit	P	3	0	0	0	0	0	0	0	.000
Lee, Thornton, 1941 Chicago	P	1	1	0	0	0	0	0	0	.000
LeFlore, Ronald, 1976 Detroit	OF	1	2	0	1	0	0	0	0	.500
Lemon, Chester, 1978-79 Chicago	OF	2	2	1	0	0	0	0	0	.000
Lemon, James, 1960 Washington	OF	1	1	0	0	0	0	0	0	.000
Lemon, Robert, 1950-51-52-54 Cleveland	P	4	1	1	0	0	0	0	0	.000
Leonard, Emil, 1943 Washington	P	1	1	0	1	0	0	0	0	1.000
Lewis, John, 1938-47 Washington	3B-OF	2	3	0	0	0	0	0	0	.000
Loes, William, 1957 Baltimore	P	1	1	0	0	0	0	0	0	.000
Lolich, Michael, 1971-72 Detroit	P	2	1	0	0	0	0	0	0	.000
Lollar, J. Sherman, 1956-59 (2)-60 (2) Chicago	C-PH	5	6	0	2	1	0	0	0	.333
Lopat, Edmund, 1951 New York	P	1	0	0	0	0	0	0	0	.000
Lyle, Albert, 1973-77 New York	P	2	0	0	0	0	0	0	0	.000
Lynn, Fredric, 1975-76-77-78-79-80 Boston	PH-OF	6	14	4	4	0	0	3	5	.286
Mack, Raymond, 1940 Cleveland	2B	1	1	0	0	0	0	0	0	.000
Malzone, Frank, 1957-58-59 (2)-60 (2)-63 Boston	3B	7	20	3	3	0	0	1	2	.150
Mantle, Mickey, 1953-54-55-56-57-58-59 (2)- 60 (2)-61 (2)-62-64-67-68 New York	OF-PH	16	43	5	10	0	0	2	4	.233
Mantilla, Felix, 1965 Boston	2B	1	2	0	0	0	0	0	0	.000
Manush, Henry, 1934 Washington	OF	1	2	0	0	0	0	0	0	.000
Maris, Roger, 1959 K. C.; 1960 (2)-61 (2)-62 (2) N. York	OF-PH	7	19	2	2	1	0	0	2	.105
Martin, Alfred, 1956 New York	PH	1	1	0	0	0	0	0	0	.000
Masterson, Walter, 1947-48 Washington	P	2	0	0	0	0	0	0	0	.000
Maxwell, Charles, 1957 Detroit	PH	1	1	0	1	0	0	0	0	1.000
May, Carlos, 1969 Chicago	PH	1	1	0	0	0	0	0	0	.000
May, David, 1973 Milwaukee	PH	1	2	0	0	0	0	0	0	.000
Mayberry, John, 1973-74 Kansas City	1B-PH	2	4	0	1	1	0	0	0	.250
McAuliffe, Richard, 1965-66-67 Detroit	SS-2B	3	9	2	2	0	0	1	2	.222
McBride, Kenneth, 1962 Los Angeles	P	1	1	0	1	0	0	0	1	1.000
McDougald, Gilbert, 1952-57-58-59 New York	PH-SS-PR	4	4	1	1	0	0	0	1	.250
McDowell, Samuel, 1965-68-69-70 Cleveland	P	4	0	0	0	0	0	0	0	.000
McGlothlin, James, 1967 California	P	1	0	0	0	0	0	0	0	.000
McLain, Dennis, 1966-68-69 Detroit	P	3	1	0	0	0	0	0	0	.000
McLish, Calvin, 1959 Cleveland	P	1	0	0	0	0	0	0	0	.000
McNally, David, 1969-70-72 Baltimore	P	2	0	0	0	0	0	0	0	.000
McQuinn, George, 1944 St. Louis; 1947-48 New York	1B	3	12	1	3	0	0	0	0	.250
McRae, Harold, 1975-76 Kansas City	PH	2	2	0	0	0	0	0	0	.000

Player, Club and Years Played	Pos.	G.	AB.	R.	H.	2B.	3B.	HR.	RBI.	B.A.
Michaels, Casimer, 1949 Chicago; 1950 Washington	2B-PH	2	3	1	1	1	0	0	0	.333
Mincher, Donald, 1967 California; 1969 Seattle	PH	2	2	0	1	0	0	0	0	.500
Minoso, Orestes, 1951-52-53-54-57-60 (2) Chi.; 1959 Clev.	OF	8	20	2	6	2	0	0	2	.300
Mitchell, L. Dale, 1949-52 Cleveland	OF	2	2	0	1	1	0	0	1	.500
Mize, John, 1953 New York	PH	1	1	0	1	0	0	0	1	1.000
Monbouquette, William, 1960 Boston	P	1	0	0	0	0	0	0	0	.000
Monday, Robert, 1968 Oakland	OF	1	2	0	0	0	0	0	0	.000
Money, Donald, 1976-78 Milwaukee	3B-2B	2	3	0	0	0	0	0	0	.000
Moran, William, 1962 (2) Los Angeles	2B	2	7	0	2	0	0	0	0	.286
Mossi, Donald, 1957 Cleveland	P	1	0	0	0	0	0	0	0	.000
Mullin, Patrick, 1948 Detroit	OF	1	1	0	0	0	0	0	0	.000
Muncrief, Robert, 1948 St. Louis	P	1	0	0	0	0	0	0	0	.000
Munson, Thurman, 1971-73-74-75-76-77 New York	PH-C	6	10	1	2	1	0	0	0	.200
Murcer, Bobby, 1971-72-73-74 New York	OF	4	11	0	1	0	0	0	0	.091
Narleski, Raymond, 1958 Cleveland	P	1	1	0	1	0	0	0	0	1.000
Nelson, David, 1973 Texas	3B	1	0	0	0	0	0	0	0	.000
Nettles, Graig, 1975-77-78-79-80 New York	3B	5	9	0	2	0	0	0	0	.222
Newhouser, Harold 1943-44-46-47-48 Detroit	P-PR	5	3	1	1	0	0	0	0	.333
Newsom, Louis, 1940 Detroit; 1944 Philadelphia	P	2	1	0	1	0	0	0	0	1.000
Noren, Irving, 1954 New York	OF	1	0	0	0	0	0	0	0	.000
O'Dell, William, 1958-59 Baltimore	P	2	0	0	0	0	0	0	0	.000
Odom, Johnny, 1968-69 Oakland	P	2	0	0	0	0	0	0	0	.000
Oglivie, Benjamin, 1980 Milwaukee	OF	1	2	0	0	0	0	0	0	.000
Oliva, Pedro (Tony) 1964-65-66-67-68-70 Minnesota	OF-PH	6	19	0	5	3	0	0	0	.263
Oliver, Albert, 1980 Texas	OF	1	1	0	0	0	0	0	0	.000
Otis, Amos, 1970-71-73-76 Kansas City	OF-PH	4	7	0	2	0	0	0	0	.286
Page, Joseph, 1947 New York	P	1	0	0	0	0	0	0	0	.000
Paige, Leroy, 1953 St. Louis	P	1	0	0	0	0	0	0	0	.000
Palmer, James, 1970-71-72-77-78 Baltimore	P	5	2	0	0	0	0	0	0	.000
Pappas, Milton, 1962 (2)-65 Baltimore	P	3	0	0	0	0	0	0	0	.000
Parnell, Melvin, 1949-51 Boston	P	2	1	0	0	0	0	0	0	.000
Parrish, Lance, 1980 Detroit	C	1	1	0	0	0	0	0	0	.000
Pascual, Camilo, 1961-62-64 Minnesota	P	3	2	0	0	0	0	0	0	.000
Patek, Freddie, 1976-78 Kansas City	SS	2	3	0	1	0	0	0	0	.333
Pearson, Albert, 1963 Los Angeles		1	4	1	2	1	0	0	0	.500
Pepitone, Joseph, 1963-64-65 New York	1B-PR-PH	3	5	0	0	0	0	0	0	.000
Perry, Gaylord, 1972-74 Cleveland	P	2	0	0	0	0	0	0	0	.000
Perry, James, 1970 Minnesota	P	1	0	0	0	0	0	0	0	.000
Pesky, John, 1946 Boston	SS	1	2	0	0	0	0	0	0	.000
Peters, Gary, 1967 Chicago	P	1	0	0	0	0	0	0	0	.000
Peterson, Fred, 1970 New York	P	1	0	0	0	0	0	0	0	.000
Petrocelli, Americo, 1967-69 Boston	SS	2	4	0	1	1	0	0	0	.250
Pierce, W. William, 1953-55-56-57 Chicago	P	4	1	1	1	0	0	0	0	1.000
Piersall, James, 1954-56 Boston	OF	2	1	0	0	0	0	0	0	.000
Piniella, Louis, 1972 Kansas City	PH	1	1	0	0	0	0	0	0	.000
Pizarro, Juan, 1963 Chicago	P	1	0	0	0	0	0	0	0	.000
Porter, Darrell, 1978-79-80 Kansas City	PH-C	3	5	0	1	1	0	0	0	.200
Porterfield, Ervin, 1954 Washington	P	1	1	0	0	0	0	0	0	.000
Powell, John, 1968-69-70 Baltimore	1B	3	9	0	1	0	0	0	0	.111
Power, Victor, 1955-56 K. C.; 1959 (2)-60 Clev.	PH-1B	5	7	1	2	0	0	0	1	.286
Radcliff, Raymond, 1936 Chicago	OF	1	2	0	1	0	0	0	0	.500
Radatz, Richard, 1963-64 Boston	P	2	1	0	0	0	0	0	0	.000
Randolph, William, 1977-80 New York	2B	2	9	0	3	0	0	0	1	.333
Raschi, Victor, 1948-49-50-52 New York	P	4	2	0	1	0	0	0	0	.500
Reynolds, Allie, 1950-53 New York	P	2	1	0	0	0	0	0	0	.000
Rice, James, 1977-78-79 Boston	OF	3	11	0	2	1	0	0	0	.182
Richardson, Robert, 1962 (2)-63-64-65-66 N. York	2B-PR-PH	6	11	1	1	0	0	0	0	.091
Richert, Peter, 1965-66 Washington	P	2	0	0	0	0	0	0	0	.000
Rivers, John, 1976 New York	PH-OF	1	2	0	1	0	0	0	0	.500
Rizzuto, Philip, 1950-51-52-53 New York	SS	4	9	0	2	0	0	0	0	.222
Robinson, Brooks, 1960 (2)-61 (2)-62 (2)-63-64-65-66-67-68-69-70-71-72-73-74 Baltimore	3B-PH	18	45	5	13	0	3	1	5	.289
Robinson, Frank, 1966-69-70-71 Balt.; 1974 Calif.	OF-PH	5	12	1	1	0	0	1	2	.083
Robinson, W. Edward, 1949 Wash.; 1951-52 Chi.; 1953 Philadelphia	1B-PH	4	9	1	2	0	0	0	2	.222
Rojas, Octavio, 1971-72-73 Kansas City	2B-PH	3	2	1	1	0	0	1	2	.500
Rollins, Richard, 1962 (2) Minnesota	3B	2	8	2	3	0	1	0	2	.375
Romano, John, 1961 (2)-62 Cleveland	C	2	5	1	2	0	0	0	0	.400
Rosar, Warren, 1946-47-48 Philadelphia	C	3	6	0	1	0	0	0	0	.167
Roseboro, John, 1969 Minnesota	C	3	7	1	1	0	0	0	0	.143
Rosen, Albert, 1952-53-54-55 Cleveland	3B-1B	4	11	3	3	0	0	2	5	.273
Rowe, Lynwood, 1936 Detroit	P	1	1	0	0	0	0	0	0	.000
Rudi, Joseph, 1972-74-75 Oakland	OF	3	6	0	2	1	0	0	0	.333
Ruffing, Charles, 1934-39-40 New York	P	3	2	0	1	0	0	0	0	.500
Runnels, James, 1959 (2)-60 (2)-62 Boston	PH-1B	5	7	1	1	0	0	1	1	.143
Ruth, George, 1933-34 New York	Of	2	6	2	2	0	0	1	2	.333
Ryan, J. Nolan, 1973-79 California	P	2	0	0	0	0	0	0	0	.000
Scheinblum, Richard, 1972 Kansas City	OF	1	1	0	0	0	0	0	0	.000
Schwall, Donald, 1961 Boston	P	1	1	0	0	0	0	0	0	.000
Score, Herbert, 1956 Cleveland	P	1	0	0	0	0	0	0	0	.000
Scott, George, 1966-77 Boston; 1975 Milwaukee	1B	3	6	1	1	0	0	1	2	.167
Selkirk, George, 1936-39 New York	OF-PH	2	2	0	1	0	0	0	1	.500

Player, Club and Years Played	Pos.	G.	AB.	R.	H.	2B.	3B.	HR.	RBI.	B.A.
Shantz, Robert, 1952 Philadelphia	P	1	0	0	0	0	0	0	0	.000
Shea, Francis, 1947 New York	P	1	1	0	0	0	0	0	0	.000
Siebern, Norman, 1962 K. C., 1964 Baltimore	PH	2	2	0	0	0	0	0	0	.000
Siebert, Richard, 1943 Philadelphia	1B	1	1	0	0	0	0	0	0	.000
Siebert, Wilfred, 1966 Cleveland	P	1	0	0	0	0	0	0	0	.000
Sievers, Roy, 1956-59 Wash.; 1961 Chicago	PH	3	2	0	0	0	0	0	0	.000
Simmons, Aloysius, 1933-34-35 Chicago	OF	3	13	3	6	3	0	0	1	.462
Simpson, Harry, 1956 Kansas City	PH	1	1	0	0	0	0	0	0	.000
Singer, William, 1973 California	P	1	0	0	0	0	0	0	0	.000
Singleton, Kenneth, 1977-79 Baltimore	OF-PH	2	1	0	0	0	0	0	0	.000
Skowron, William, 1957-58-59-60 (2) New York	1B	5	14	1	6	1	0	0	0	.429
Smalley, Roy F. III, 1979 Minnesota	SS	1	3	0	0	0	0	0	0	.000
Smith, Alphonse, 1955 Cleve.; 1960 (2) Chicago	OF-PH	3	3	0	0	0	0	0	0	.000
Smith, Edgar, 1941 Chicago	P	1	1	0	0	0	0	0	0	.000
Smith, C. Reginald, 1969-72 Boston	PH-PR-OF	2	3	1	0	0	0	0	0	.000
Sorensen, Lary, 1978 Milwaukee	P	1	0	0	0	0	0	0	0	.000
Spence, Stanley, 1944-46-47 Washington	OF	3	5	1	3	0	0	0	1	.600
Spencer, James, 1973 Texas	PH	1	1	0	0	0	0	0	0	.000
Staley, Gerald, 1960 Chicago	P	1	0	0	0	0	0	0	0	.000
Stanley, Robert, 1979 Boston	P	1	0	0	0	0	0	0	0	.000
Staub, Daniel, 1976 Detroit	OF	1	2	0	2	0	0	0	0	1.000
Stenhouse, David, 1962 Washington	P	1	0	0	0	0	0	0	0	.000
Stephens, Vernon, 1943-44 St. L.; 1946-48-49-51 Bos.	SS-PH	6	15	1	5	1	0	0	2	.333
Stieb, David, 1980 Toronto	P	1	0	0	0	0	0	0	0	.000
Stirnweiss, George, 1946 New York	2B	1	3	1	1	0	0	0	0	.333
Stone, D. Dean, 1954 Washington	P	1	0	0	0	0	0	0	0	.000
Stone, Steven, 1980 Baltimore	P	1	1	0	0	0	0	0	0	.000
Stottlemyre, Melvin, 1966-68-69-70 New York	P	4	0	0	0	0	0	0	0	.000
Sullivan, Franklin, 1955 Boston	P	1	1	0	0	0	0	0	0	.000
Sundberg, James, 1978 Texas	C	1	0	0	0	0	0	0	0	.000
Tanana, Frank, 1976 California	P	1	0	0	0	0	0	0	0	.000
Tebbetts, George, 1942 Detroit; 1948-49 Boston	C	3	7	1	2	1	0	0	1	.286
Temple, John, 1961 (2) Cleveland	2B	2	5	0	0	0	0	0	0	.000
Tenace, F. Gene, 1975 Oakland	1B-C	1	3	1	0	0	0	0	0	.000
Thomas, J. Leroy, 1962 (2) Los Angeles	PH-OF	2	1	0	0	0	0	0	0	.000
Thompson, Jason, 1978 Detroit	PH	1	1	0	0	0	0	0	0	.000
Tiant, Luis, 1968 Cleveland; 1974-76 Boston	P	3	1	0	0	0	0	0	0	.000
Trammell, Alan, 1980 Detroit	SS	1	0	0	0	0	0	0	0	.000
Travis, Cecil, 1940-41 Washington	SS	2	7	1	1	1	0	0	0	.143
Tresh, Thomas, 1962-63 New York	SS-OF	2	2	0	1	1	0	0	1	.500
Triandos, Augustus, 1958-59 Baltimore	C	2	6	0	2	1	0	0	2	.333
Trucks, Virgil, 1949 Detroit; 1954 Chicago	P	2	1	0	0	0	0	0	0	.000
Tucker, Thurman, 1944 Chicago	OF	1	4	0	0	0	0	0	0	.000
Turley, Robert, 1958 New York	P	1	0	0	0	0	0	0	0	.000
Vernon, James, 1946-48-53-54-55 Washington; 1956 Boston; 1958 Cleveland	1B-PH	7	14	2	2	0	0	0	1	.143
Versalles, Zoilo, 1963-65 Minnesota	SS	2	2	0	1	0	0	0	0	.500
Vosmik, Joseph, 1935 Cleveland	OF	1	4	1	1	0	0	0	0	.250
Wagner, Harold, 1946 Boston	C	1	1	0	0	0	0	0	0	.000
Wagner, Leon, 1962 (2)-63 Los Angeles	OF	3	11	2	5	0	0	1	2	.455
Wakefield, Richard, 1943 Detroit	OF	1	4	0	2	1	0	0	1	.500
Walker, Jerry, 1959 Baltimore	P	1	1	0	0	0	0	0	0	.000
Washington, Claudell, 1975 Oakland	PR-OF	1	1	0	1	0	0	0	0	1.000
Wert, Donald, 1968 Detroit	3B	1	1	0	1	1	0	0	0	1.000
Wertz, Victor, 1949-51 Detroit; 1957 Cleveland	OF-1B	3	7	1	2	0	0	1	2	.286
West, Samuel, 1933-34-37 St. Louis	OF	3	4	1	1	0	0	0	0	.250
White, Frank, 1978-79 Kansas City	2B	2	3	0	0	0	0	0	0	.000
White, Roy, 1969 New York	PH	1	1	0	0	0	0	0	0	.000
Wilhelm, J. Hoyt, 1959-61 Baltimore	P	2	1	0	0	0	0	0	0	.000
Williams, Theodore, 1940-41-42-46-47-48-49-50-51-54-55-56-57-58-59 (2)-60 (2) Boston	OF-PH	18	46	10	14	2	1	4	12	.304
Wilson, James, 1956 Chicago	P	1	0	0	0	0	0	0	0	.000
Wood, Wilbur, 1972 Chicago	P	1	0	0	0	0	0	0	0	.000
Woodling, Eugene, 1959 Baltimore	PH	1	1	0	0	0	0	0	0	.000
Wright, Clyde, 1970 California	P	1	0	0	0	0	0	0	0	.000
Wyatt, Johnathan, 1964 Kansas City	P	1	0	0	0	0	0	0	0	.000
Wynegar, Harold, 1976-77 Minnesota	PH-C	2	2	1	1	0	0	0	0	.500
Wynn, Early, 1955-56-57 Clev.; 1958-59 (2)-60 Chicago	P	7	1	0	0	0	0	0	0	.000
Yastrzemski, Carl, 1963-67-68-69-70-71-72-74-75-76-77-79 Boston	OF-1B-PH	12	32	2	10	2	0	1	5	.313
York, Rudolph, 1938-41-42-43 Detroit; 1946 Boston	1B-PH	5	13	1	4	0	0	1	2	.308
Yount, Robin, 1980 Minnesota	SS	1	2	0	0	0	0	0	0	.000
Zarilla, Allen, 1948 St. Louis	OF	1	2	0	0	0	0	0	0	.000
Zernial, Gus, 1953 Philadelphia	OF	1	2	0	1	0	0	0	0	.500
Zisk, Richard, 1977 Chicago; 1978 Texas	OF	2	5	0	3	1	0	0	2	.600

PITCHING RECORDS

American League

Player, Club and Years Pitched	G.	IP.	H.	R.	BB.	SO.	W.	L.	Pct.
Aguirre, Henry, 1962 Detroit	1	3	3	2	0	2	0	0	.000

Player, Club and Years Pitched	G.	IP.	H.	R.	BB.	SO.	W.	L.	Pct.
Allen, John, 1938 Cleveland	1	3	2	1	0	3	0	0	.000
Bell, Gary, 1960 (2) Cleveland	2	3	2	2	2	0	0	0	.000
Benton, J. Alton, 1942 Detroit	1	5	4	1	2	1	0	0	.000
Blue, Vida, 1971-75 Oakland	2	5	7	5	0	4	1	0	1.000
Blyleven, Rikalbert, 1973 Minnesota	1	1	2	2	2	0	0	1	.000
Borowy, Henry, 1944 New York	1	3	3	0	1	0	0	0	.000
Bouton, James, 1963 New York	1	1	0	0	0	0	0	0	.000
Brewer, Thomas, 1956 Boston	1	2	4	3	1	2	0	0	.000
Bridges, Thomas, 1937-39 Detroit	2	5⅓	9	3	1	3	1	0	1.000
Brissie, Leland, 1949 Philadelphia	1	3	5	2	2	1	0	0	.000
Busby, Steven, 1975 Kansas City	1	2	4	1	0	0	0	0	.000
Bunning, James, 1957-59-61 (2)-62-63 Detroit	6	14	4	3	1	7	1	1	.500
Campbell, William, 1977 Boston	1	1	0	0	1	2	0	0	.000
Chance, Dean, 1964 Los Angeles; 1967 Minnesota	2	6	4	1	0	3	0	0	.000
Chandler, Spurgeon, 1942 New York	1	4	2	0	0	2	1	0	1.000
Clear, Mark, 1979 California	1	2	2	1	1	0	0	0	.000
Coates, James, 1960 New York	1	2	2	0	0	0	0	0	.000
Coleman, Joseph, 1948 Philadelphia	1	3	0	0	2	3	0	0	.000
Consuegra, Sandalio, 1954 Chicago	1	⅓	5	5	0	0	0	0	.000
Crowder, Alvin, 1933 Washington	1	3	3	2	0	0	0	0	.000
Cuellar, Miguel, 1971 Baltimore	1	2	1	0	1	2	0	0	.000
Culp, Raymond, 1969 Boston	1	1	0	0	0	2	0	0	.000
Daley, Buddy, 1959-60 Kansas City	2	1⅔	0	0	1	3	0	0	.000
Donovan, Richard, 1961 Washington; 1962 Cleveland	2	4	7	1	0	1	0	0	.000
Downing, Alphonso, 1967 New York	1	2	2	0	0	2	0	0	.000
Duren, Ryne, 1959 New York	1	3	1	0	1	4	0	0	.000
Eckersley, Dennis, 1977 Cleveland	1	2	0	0	0	1	0	0	.000
Estrada, Charles, 1960 Baltimore	1	1	4	1	0	1	0	0	.000
Farmer, Edward, 1980 Chicago	1	⅔	1	0	0	0	0	0	.000
Feller, Robert, 1939-40-41-46-50 Cleveland	5	12⅓	5	1	4	13	1	0	1.000
Fidrych, Mark, 1976 Detroit	1	2	4	2	0	1	0	1	.000
Fingers, Roland, 1973-74 Oakland	2	2	1	2	1	0	0	0	.000
Fisher, Eddie, 1965 Chicago	1	2	1	0	0	0	0	0	.000
Ford, Edward, 1954-55-56-59-60-61 New York	6	12	19	13	3	5	0	2	.000
Fornieles, J. Miguel, 1961 Boston	1	⅓	2	1	0	0	0	0	.000
Garcia, E. Mike, 1953 Cleveland	1	2	4	1	1	2	0	0	.000
Garver, Ned, 1951 St. Louis	1	3	1	1	1	1	0	0	.000
Gomez, Vernon, 1933-34-35-37-38 New York	5	18	11	6	3	9	3	1	.750
Gossage, Richard, 1975 Chicago; 1978-80 New York	3	3	6	5	1	1	0	1	.000
Grant, James, 1965 Minnesota	1	2	2	2	1	3	0	0	.000
Gray, Theodore, 1950 Detroit	1	1⅓	3	1	0	1	0	1	.000
Grim, Robert, 1957 New York	1	⅓	0	0	0	0	0	0	.000
Grove, Robert, 1933 Philadelphia; 1936-38 Boston	3	8	10	4	2	8	0	1	.000
Guidry, Ronald, 1978-79 New York	2	⅔	0	0	1	0	0	0	.000
Harder, Melvin, 1934-35-36-37 Cleveland	4	13	9	0	1	5	1	0	1.000
Herbert, Raymond, 1962 Chicago	1	3	3	0	0	0	1	0	1.000
Holtzman, Kenneth, 1973 Oakland	1	⅔	1	0	0	0	0	0	.000
Houtteman, Arthur, 1960 Detroit	1	3	3	1	1	0	0	0	.000
Hudson, Sidney, 1941 Washington	1	1	3	2	1	1	0	0	.000
Hughson, Cecil, 1943-44 Boston	2	4⅔	10	6	1	4	0	1	.000
Hunter, James, 1967 Kansas City; 1970-73-74-75 Oakland; 1976 New York	6	12⅔	15	9	1	13	0	2	.000
Hutchinson, Frederick, 1951 Detroit	1	3	3	3	2	0	0	0	.000
John, Thomas, 1968 Chicago; 1980 New York	2	3	5	3	0	1	0	1	.000
Kaat, James, 1966 Minnesota; 1975 Chicago	2	4	3	1	0	1	0	0	.000
Keegan, Robert, 1954 Chicago	1	1⅔	3	2	0	1	0	0	.000
Keough, Matthew, 1978 Oakland	1	⅓	1	0	0	0	0	0	.000
Kern, James, 1977-78 Cleveland; 1979 Texas	3	4⅓	3	2	4	6	0	1	.000
Knowles, Darold, 1969 Washington	1	⅔	0	0	0	0	0	0	.000
Kramer, John, 1946 St. Louis	1	3	0	0	1	3	0	0	.000
LaRoche, David, 1977 California	1	1	1	0	1	0	0	0	.000
Lary, Frank, 1960 (2)-61 Detroit	3	2	2	1	1	1	0	0	.000
Lee, Thornton, 1941 Chicago	1	3	4	1	0	0	0	0	.000
Lemon, Robert, 1950-51-52-54 Cleveland	4	6⅔	6	2	3	3	0	1	.000
Leonard, Emil, 1943 Washington	1	3	2	1	0	0	1	0	1.000
Loes, William, 1957 Baltimore	1	3	3	0	0	1	0	0	.000
Lolich, Michael, 1971-72 Detroit	2	4	2	1	0	2	0	0	.000
Lopat, Edmund, 1951 New York	1	1	3	3	0	0	0	1	.000
Lyle, Albert, 1973-77 New York	2	3	4	2	0	2	0	0	.000
Masterson, Walter, 1947-48 Washington	2	4⅔	5	2	2	3	0	0	.000
McBride, Kenneth, 1963 Los Angeles	1	3	4	3	2	1	0	0	.000
McDowell, Samuel, 1965-68-69-70 Cleveland	4	8	5	1	4	12	0	1	.000
McGlothlin, James, 1967 California	1	2	1	0	0	2	0	0	.000
McLain, Dennis, 1966-68-69 Detroit	3	6	2	1	4	6	0	0	.000
McLish, Calvin, 1959 Cleveland	1	2	1	0	1	2	0	0	.000
McNally, David, 1969-72 Baltimore	2	2⅓	2	1	2	1	0	1	.000
Monbouquette, William, 1960 Boston	1	2	5	4	0	2	0	1	.000
Mossi, Donald, 1957 Cleveland	1	⅔	1	0	0	1	0	0	.000
Muncrief, Robert, 1944 St. Louis	1	1⅓	1	0	0	1	0	0	.000
Narleski, Raymond, 1958 Cleveland	1	3⅓	1	0	1	0	0	0	.000
Newhouser, Harold, 1943-44-46-47 Detroit	4	10⅔	8	3	3	8	0	0	.000
Newsom, Louis, 1940 Detroit; 1944 Philadelphia	2	3⅓	1	0	1	1	0	0	.000
O'Dell, William, 1958-59 Baltimore	2	4	1	1	0	2	0	0	.000

Player, Club and Years Pitched	G.	IP.	H.	R.	BB.	SO.	W.	L.	Pct.
Odom, Johnny, 1968-69 Oakland	2	2⅓	5	5	2	2	0	0	.000
Page, Joseph, 1947 New York	1	1⅓	1	0	1	0	0	0	.000
Paige, Leroy, 1953 St. Louis	1	3	2	1	0	0	0	0	.000
Palmer, James, 1970-71-72-77-78 Baltimore	5	12⅔	11	8	7	14	0	1	.000
Pappas, Milton, 1962 (2)-65 Baltimore	3	3	5	4	2	0	0	0	.000
Parnell, Melvin, 1949-51 Boston	2	2	6	4	1	2	0	0	.000
Pascual, Camilo, 1961-62-64 Minnesota	3	8	6	3	2	6	0	1	.000
Perry, Gaylord, 1972-74 Cleveland	2	5	6	3	0	5	0	0	.000
Perry, James, 1970 Minnesota	1	2	1	1	1	3	0	0	.000
Peters, Gary, 1967 Chicago	1	3	0	0	0	4	0	0	.000
Peterson, Fred, 1970 New York	1	0	1	0	0	0	0	0	.000
Pierce, W. William, 1953-55-56-57 Chicago	4	10⅔	6	4	3	12	0	1	.000
Pizarro, Juan, 1963 Chicago	1	1	0	0	0	0	0	0	.000
Porterfield, Erwin, 1954 Washington	1	3	4	2	0	1	0	0	.000
Radatz, Richard, 1963-64 Boston	2	4⅔	4	5	2	10	0	1	.000
Raschi, Victor, 1948-49-50-52 New York	4	11	7	3	4	8	1	0	1.000
Reynolds, Allie, 1950-53 New York	2	5	3	2	2	2	0	1	.000
Richert, Peter, 1965-66 Washington	1	2	3	1	0	2	0	0	.000
Rowe, Lynwood, 1936 Detroit	1	3	4	2	1	2	0	0	.000
Ruffing, Charles, 1934-39-40 New York	3	7	13	7	2	6	0	1	.000
Ryan, L. Nolan, 1973-79 California	2	4	7	5	3	4	0	0	.000
Schwall, Donald, 1961 Boston	1	3	5	1	1	2	0	0	.000
Score, Herbert, 1956 Cleveland	1	1	1	0	0	1	0	0	.000
Shantz, Robert, 1952 Philadelphia	1	1	0	0	0	3	0	0	.000
Shea, Francis, 1947 New York	1	3	3	1	2	2	1	0	1.000
Siebert, Wilfred, 1966 Cleveland	1	2	0	0	1	0	0	0	.000
Singer, William, 1973 California	1	2	3	3	1	2	0	0	.000
Smith, Edgar, 1941 Chicago	1	2	2	0	2	1	1	0	1.000
Sorensen, Lary, 1978 Milwaukee	1	3	1	0	0	0	0	0	.000
Stanley, Robert, 1979 Boston	1	2	1	1	0	0	0	0	.000
Stenhouse, David, 1962 Washington	1	2	3	1	1	1	0	0	.000
Stieb, D. Dean, 1980 Toronto	1	1	1	1	2	0	0	0	.000
Stone, D. Dean, 1954 Washington	1	⅓	0	0	0	0	1	0	1.000
Stone, Steven, 1980 Baltimore	1	3	0	0	0	3	0	0	.000
Stottlemyre, Melvin, 1966-68-69-70 New York	4	6	5	3	1	4	0	1	.000
Sullivan, Franklin, 1955 Boston	1	3⅓	4	1	1	4	0	1	.000
Staley, Gerald, 1960 Chicago	1	2	2	1	0	0	0	0	.000
Tanana, Frank, 1976 California	1	3	3	3	1	0	0	0	.000
Tiant, Luis, 1968 Cleveland; 1974-76 Boston	3	6	7	4	3	3	0	2	.000
Trucks, Virgil, 1949 Detroit; 1954 Chicago	2	3	3	2	3	0	1	0	1.000
Turley, Robert, 1958 New York	1	3	3	2	0	0	0	0	.000
Walker, Jerry, 1959 Baltimore	1	3	2	1	1	1	1	0	1.000
Wilhelm, J. Hoyt, 1959-61 Baltimore	2	2⅔	4	2	1	1	0	1	.000
Wyatt, Johnathan, 1964 Kansas City	1	1	2	2	0	0	0	0	.000
Wilson, James, 1956 Chicago	1	1	2	1	0	1	0	0	.000
Wood, Wilbur, 1972 Chicago	1	2	2	1	1	1	0	0	.000
Wright, Clyde, 1970 California	1	1⅔	3	1	0	0	0	1	.000
Wynn, Early, 1955-56-57 Clev.; 1958-59 (2)-60 Chicago	7	12⅓	9	4	4	8	1	0	1.000

BATTING AVERAGES

National League

Player, Club and Years Played	Pos.	G.	AB.	R.	H.	2B.	3B.	HR.	RBI.	B.A.
Aaron, Henry, 1955-56-57-58-59 (2)-60 (2)-61 (2)-62-63-64-65 Milw.; 1966-67-68-69-70-71-72-73-74 Atlanta	1B-OF-PH	23	66	7	13	0	0	2	8	.197
Adcock, Joseph, 1960 (2) Milwaukee	1B	2	5	1	3	1	0	0	0	.600
Allen, Richard, 1965-66-67 Phila.; 1970 St. Louis	3B-PH-1B	4	11	1	2	0	0	1	1	.182
Alley, L. Eugene, 1967 Pittsburgh	SS	1	5	0	0	0	0	0	0	.000
Alou, Felipe, 1962 San Francisco, 1968 Atlanta	OF	2	0	0	0	0	0	0	1	.000
Alou, Mateo, 1968-69 Pittsburgh	OF	2	5	1	3	0	0	0	0	.600
Altman, George A., 1961 (2)-62 Chicago	PH-OF	3	3	1	1	0	0	1	1	.333
Andujar, Joaquin, 1979 Houston	P	1	0	0	0	0	0	0	0	.000
Antonelli, John A., 1954-56, N. Y.; 1959 San Francisco	P	3	1	0	0	0	0	0	0	.000
Ashburn, Richie, 1948-51-53 Phil.; 1962 New York	OF-PH	4	10	4	6	1	0	0	1	.600
Bailey, L. Edgar, 1956-57-60 Cinn.; 63 San Francisco	C	4	8	1	2	0	0	0	1	.250
Baker, Eugene, 1955 Chicago	PH	1	1	0	0	0	0	0	0	.000
Banks, Ernest, 1955-57-58-59 (2)-60(2)-61-62 (2)-65-67-69 Chicago	PH-SS-1B	13	33	4	10	3	1	1	3	.303
Bartell, Richard, 1933 Philadelphia; 1937 New York	SS	2	6	0	1	0	0	0	0	.167
Beckert, Glenn, 1969-70-71-72 Chicago	2B-PH	4	7	0	0	0	0	0	0	.000
Bell, David (Gus), 1953-54-56-57 Cincinnati	OF-PH	4	6	1	2	1	0	1	4	.333
Bench, Johnny, 1969-70-71-72-73-74-75-76-77-80 Cincinnati	C	11	27	5	10	0	0	3	6	.370
Berger, Walter, 1933-34-35 Boston	OF	3	8	0	0	0	0	0	0	.000
Bibby, James, 1980 Pittsburgh	P	1	0	0	0	0	0	0	0	.000
Bickford, Vernon, 1949 Boston	P	1	0	0	0	0	0	0	0	.000
Blackwell, Ewell, 1946-47-48-49-50-51 Cincinnati	P	6	1	0	0	0	0	0	0	.000
Blanton, Darrell, 1937 Pittsburgh	P	1	0	0	0	0	0	0	0	.000
Blasingame, Donald, 1958 St. Louis	PH	1	1	0	0	0	0	0	0	.000
Blass, Stephen, 1972 Pittsburgh	P	1	0	0	0	0	0	0	0	.000

Player, Club and Years Played	Pos.	G.	AB.	R.	H.	2B.	3B.	HR.	RBI.	B.A.
Blue, Vida, 1978 San Francisco	P	1	0	0	0	0	0	0	0	.000
Bolling, Frank, 1961 (2)-62 (2) Milwaukee	2B	8	12	0	1	0	0	0	0	.083
Bonds, Bobby, 1971-73 San Francisco	PH-OF	4	23	1	1	1	0	0	0	.043
Boone, Robert, 1976-78-79 Philadelphia	C	3	3	1	2	1	0	1	2	.667
Bowa, Lawrence, 1974-75-76-78-79 Philadelphia	SS	3	5	2	2	0	0	0	2	.400
Boyer, Kenton, 1956-59(2)-60(2)-61-62(2)-63-64 St.L.	3B-PH	5	8	2	2	0	0	0	0	.250
Branca, Ralph, 1948 Brooklyn	P	10	23	4	8	0	0	2	4	.348
Brecheen, Harry, 1947 St. Louis	P	1	1	0	0	0	0	0	0	.000
Brett, Kenneth, 1974 Pittsburgh	P	1	1	0	0	0	0	0	0	.000
Brewer, James, 1973 Los Angeles	P	1	0	0	0	0	0	0	0	.000
Brock, Louis, 1967-71-74-75-79 St. Louis	OF-PH	5	8	2	3	0	0	0	0	.375
Brown, James, 1942 St. Louis	2B	1	0	0	0	0	0	0	0	.000
Brown, Mace, 1938 Pittsburgh	P	1	2	0	0	0	0	0	0	.000
Buhl, Robert, 1960 Milwaukee	P	1	1	0	0	0	0	0	0	.000
Burdette, S. Lewis, 1957-59 Milwaukee	P	1	0	0	0	0	0	0	0	.000
Bunning, James, 1964-66 Philadelphia	P	2	2	0	0	0	0	0	0	.000
Burgess, Forrest, 1954 Philadelphia; 1955 Cincinnati; 1959-60 (2)-61 (2) Pittsburgh	P	2	0	0	0	0	0	0	0	.000
	C-PH	7	10	0	1	0	0	0	0	.100
Callison, John, 1962 (2)-64 Philadelphia	PH-OF	3	4	1	2	0	0	1	3	.500
Camilli, Adolph, 1939 Brooklyn	PH	1	1	0	0	0	0	0	0	.000
Campanella, Roy, 1949-50-51-52-53-54-56 Brooklyn	C	7	20	1	2	0	0	0	0	.100
Cardenas, Leonardo, 1964-65-66-68 Cincinnati	PR-SS	4	3	0	0	0	0	0	0	.000
Carlton, Steven, 1968-69 St. Louis; 1972-79 Phialdelphia	P	4	2	0	1	1	0	0	1	.500
Carter, Gary, 1975-79-80 Montreal	OF-C	3	3	0	1	0	0	0	1	.333
Carty, Ricardo, 1970 Atlanta	OF	1	1	0	0	0	0	0	0	.000
Cash, David, 1974-75-76 Philadelphia	PH-2B	3	3	1	1	0	0	0	0	.333
Cavarretta, Philip, 1944-46-47 Chicago	2B-PH	3	4	1	2	0	1	0	0	.500
Cedeno, Cesar, 1972-73-74-76 Houston	OF	4	9	2	3	0	0	1	3	.333
Cepeda, Orlando, 1959-60 (2)-61 (2)-62 (2)-64 S. F.; 1967 St. Louis										
	1B-OF	9	27	0	1	0	0	0	1	.037
Cey, Ronald, 1974-75-76-77-78-79 Los Angeles	3B	6	9	0	2	1	0	0	2	.222
Cimoli, Gino, 1957 Brooklyn	PH	1	1	0	0	0	0	0	0	.000
Clark, Jack, 1978-79 San Francisco	PH	2	2	0	0	0	0	0	0	.000
Clemente, Roberto, 1960(2)-61(2)-62(2)-63-64-65-66-67-69-70-71 Pittsburgh										
	OF-PH	14	31	3	10	2	1	1	4	.323
Colbert, Nathan, 1971-72-73 San Diego	PH	3	2	1	0	0	0	0	0	.000
Collins, James, 1935-36 St. Louis; 1937 Chicago	SS	3	4	0	1	0	0	0	0	.250
Concepcion, David, 1975-76-77-78-80 Cincinnati	SS	5	6	2	2	0	0	0	0	.333
Conley, D. Eugene, 1954-55 Milw.; 1959 Phila	P	3	0	0	0	0	0	0	0	.000
Cooper, Morton, 1942-43 St. Louis	P	2	1	0	0	0	0	0	0	.000
Cooper, Walker, 1942-43-44 St. L.; 1946-47-48 New York	C	6	15	1	5	0	0	0	1	.333
Coscarart, Peter, 1940 Brooklyn	2B	1	0	0	0	0	0	0	0	.000
Crandall, Delmar, 1955-58-59(2)-60(2)-62(2) Milw	C	8	20	2	4	0	0	1	2	.200
Cuccinello, Anthony, 1933 Brooklyn	PH	1	1	0	0	0	0	0	0	.000
Cuellar, Miguel, 1967 Houston	P	1	0	0	0	0	0	0	0	.000
Culp, Raymond, 1963 Philadelphia	P	1	0	0	0	0	0	0	0	.000
Cunningham, Joseph, 1959 St. Louis	PH	1	1	0	0	0	0	0	0	.000
Cuyler, Hazen, 1934 Chicago	OF	1	2	0	0	0	0	0	0	.000
Dahlgren, Ellsworth, 1943 Philadelphia	1B	1	2	0	0	0	0	0	0	.000
Danning, Harry, 1940-41 New York	C	2	2	0	1	0	0	0	1	.500
Dark, Alvin, 1951-54 New York	SS	2	10	0	2	0	0	0	0	.200
Davenport, James, 1962 San Francisco	3B	1	1	0	1	0	0	0	0	1.000
Davis, Curtis, 1936 Chicago	P	1	0	0	0	0	0	0	0	.000
Davis, H. Thomas, 1962(2)-63 Los Angeles	OF	3	8	1	1	0	0	0	0	.125
Davis, William, 1971-73 Los Angeles	PH-OF	2	3	1	3	0	0	1	2	1.000
Dean, Jerome, 1934-35-36-37 St. Louis	P	4	3	0	0	0	0	0	0	.000
Demaree, Frank, 1936-37 Chicago	OF	2	8	1	2	0	0	0	0	.250
Derringer, Paul, 1935-39-40-41 Cincinnati	P	4	2	0	0	0	0	0	0	.000
Dickson, Murry, 1953 Pittsburgh	P	1	1	0	1	0	0	0	1	1.000
Dierker, Lawrence, 1969 Houston	P	1	0	0	0	0	0	0	0	.000
Dietz, Richard, 1970 San Francisco	C	1	2	1	1	0	0	1	1	.500
DiMaggio, Vincent, 1943-44 Pittsburgh	OF-PH	2	3	2	3	0	1	1	1	1.000
Drysdale, Donald, 1959(2)-62-63-64-65-67-68 Los Angeles	P	8	33	0	0	0	0	0	0	.000
Durocher, Leo, 1936 St. Louis; 1938 Brooklyn	SS	2	6	1	2	0	0	0	0	.333
Edwards, Bruce, 1947 Brooklyn	C	1	1	0	0	0	0	0	0	.000
Edwards, John, 1963-64 Cincinnati	C	2	3	1	0	0	0	0	0	.000
Elliott, Robert, 1941-42-44 Pitts.; 1948-51 Boston	3B-OF	5	9	1	3	0	0	1	2	.333
Ellis, Dock, 1971 Pittsburgh	P	1	1	0	0	0	0	0	0	.000
Elston, Donald, 1959 Chicago	P	1	0	0	0	0	0	0	0	.000
English, Elwood, 1933 Chicago	SS	1	1	0	0	0	0	0	0	.000
Ennis, Delmer, 1946-51-55 Philadelphia	OF	3	5	0	0	0	0	0	0	.000
Erskine, Carl, 1954 Brooklyn	P	1	0	0	0	0	0	0	0	.000
Evans, Darrell, 1973 Atlanta	PH	1	0	0	0	0	0	0	0	.000
Face, ElRoy, 1959(2)-60-61 Pittsburgh	P	4	0	0	0	0	0	0	0	.000
Fairly, Ronald, 1973 Montreal	1B	1	0	0	0	0	0	0	0	.000
Farrell, Richard, 1958 Phila.; 1962-64-65 Houston	P	4	0	0	0	0	0	0	0	.000
Fette, Louis, 1939 Boston	P	1	0	0	0	0	0	0	0	.000
Fingers, Roland, 1978 San Diego	P	1	0	0	0	0	0	0	0	.000
Fletcher, Elburt, 1943 Pittsburgh	1B	1	2	0	0	0	0	0	0	.000
Flood, Curtis, 1964-66-68 St. Louis	PR-PH	3	2	1	0	0	0	0	0	.000
Foiles, Henry, 1957 Pittsburgh	PH	1	1	1	1	0	0	0	0	1.000
Foster, George, 1976-77-78-79 Cincinnati	OF	4	9	3	3	2	0	1	5	.333
Forsch, Kenneth, 1976 Houston	P	1	0	0	0	0	0	0	0	.000

Player, Club and Years Played	Pos.	G.	AB.	R.	H.	2B.	3B.	HR.	RBI.	B.A.
Frankhouse, Fred, 1934 Boston	P	1	1	0	0	0	0	0	0	.000
French, Lawrence, 1940 Chicago	P	1	0	0	0	0	0	0	0	.000
Friend, Robert, 1956-58-60 Pittsburgh	P	3	2	0	0	0	0	0	0	.000
Frey, Linus, 1939-41-42 Cincinnati	2B-PH	3	6	0	2	1	0	0	1	.333
Frisch, Frank, 1933-34 St. Louis	2B	2	7	4	4	0	0	2	2	.571
Galan, August, 1936 Chicago; 1943-44 Brooklyn	OF	3	9	2	2	0	0	1	2	.222
Garner, Philip, 1980 Pittsburgh	2B	1	2	1	1	0	0	0	0	.500
Garr, Ralph, 1974 Atlanta	PH-OF	1	3	0	0	0	0	0	0	.000
Garvey, Steven, 1974-75-76-77-78-79-80 Los Angeles	1B	7	20	6	8	1	2	2	6	.400
Gaston, Clarence, 1970 San Diego	OF	1	2	0	0	0	0	0	0	.000
Gibson, Robert, 1962-65-67-69-70-72 St. Louis	P	6	0	0	0	0	0	0	0	.000
Gilliam, James, 1959 Los Angeles	3B	1	2	1	1	0	0	1	1	.500
Giusti, J. David, 1973 Pittsburgh	P	1	0	0	0	0	0	0	0	.000
Goodman, Ival, 1938-39 Cincinnati	OF	2	4	0	0	0	0	0	0	.000
Gordon, Sidney, 1949 New York	3B	1	2	0	1	1	0	0	0	.500
Gossage, Richard, 1977 Pittsburgh	P	1	0	0	0	0	0	0	0	.000
Grabarkewitz, Billy, 1970 Los Angeles	3B	1	3	0	1	0	0	0	0	.333
Griffey, G. Kenneth, 1976-80 Cincinnati	OF	2	4	2	3	0	0	1	2	.750
Grissom, Lee, 1937 Cincinnati	P	1	0	0	0	0	0	0	0	.000
Grissom, Marvin, 1954 New York	P	1	0	0	0	0	0	0	0	.000
Groat, Richard, 1959(2)-60(2)-62(2) Pitts.; 1963-64 St. L.	PH-SS	8	15	1	5	1	0	0	4	.333
Grote, Gerald, 1968-74 New York	C	2	2	0	0	0	0	0	0	.000
Grubb, John, 1974 San Diego	OF	1	1	0	0	0	0	0	0	.000
Gustine, Frank, 1946-47-48 Pittsburgh	2B-3B-PR	3	4	0	0	0	0	0	0	.000
Haas, Berthold, 1947 Cincinnati	PH	1	1	0	1	0	0	0	0	1.000
Hack, Stanley, 1938-39-41-43 Chicago	3B	4	15	2	6	0	0	0	0	.400
Haddix, Harvey, 1955 St. Louis	P	1	0	0	0	0	0	0	0	.000
Hafey, Charles, 1933 Cincinnati	OF	1	4	0	1	0	0	0	0	.250
Hallahan, William, 1933 St. Louis	P	1	1	0	0	0	0	0	0	.000
Haller, Thomas, 1967 San Fran.; 1968 Los Angeles	C-PH	2	3	0	0	0	0	0	0	.000
Hamner, Granville, 1952-53-54 Philadelphia	SS-3B	3	4	0	0	0	0	0	0	.000
Harrelson, Derrel, 1970-71 New York	SS	2	5	2	2	0	0	0	0	.400
Hart, James, 1966 San Francisco	PH	1	1	0	0	0	0	0	0	.000
Hartnett, Charles, 1933-34-35-36-37 Chicago	C	5	10	2	2	0	1	0	1	.200
Helms, Tommy, 1967-68 Cincinnati	PH-2B	2	3	0	1	1	0	0	0	.333
Hendrick, George, 1980 St. Louis	OF	1	2	0	1	0	0	0	1	.500
Henry, William, 1960 Cincinnati	P	1	0	0	0	0	0	0	0	.000
Herman, William, 1934-35-36-37-38-39-40 Chicago; 1941-42-43 Brooklyn	2B-PH	10	30	3	13	2	0	0	0	.433
Hernandez, Keith, 1979-80 St. Louis	PH-1B	2	3	0	2	0	0	0	0	.667
Hickman, James, 1970 Chicago	OF-1B	1	4	0	1	0	0	0	1	.250
Higbe, W. Kirby, 1946 Brooklyn	P	1	1	0	0	0	0	0	0	.000
Hoak, Donald, 1957 Cincinnati	3B	1	1	0	0	0	0	0	0	.000
Hodges, Gilbert, 1949-51-53-54-55-57 Brooklyn	1B-PR-PH	6	12	3	4	0	0	1	2	.333
Holmes, Thomas, 1948 Boston	OF	1	1	0	0	0	0	0	0	.000
Hopp, John, 1946 Boston	OF	1	2	0	1	0	0	0	0	.500
Hubbell, Carl, 1933-34-36-37-40 New York	P	5	1	0	0	0	0	0	0	.000
Hundley, C. Randolph, 1969 Chicago	C	1	1	0	0	0	0	0	0	.000
Hunt, Ronald, 1964-66 New York	2B	2	4	0	1	0	0	0	0	.250
Jablonski, Raymond, 1954 St. Louis	3B	1	3	1	1	0	0	0	1	.333
Jackson, Lawrence, 1957-58-60 St. L.; 1963 Chicago	P	4	1	0	0	0	0	0	0	.000
Jackson, Ransom, 1954-55 Chicago	3B	2	5	1	1	0	0	0	1	.200
Jackson, Travis, 1934 New York	SS	1	2	0	0	0	0	0	0	.000
Javery, Alva, 1943 Boston	P	1	0	0	0	0	0	0	0	.000
Javier, Julian, 1963-68 St. Louis	2B	2	4	0	0	0	0	0	0	.000
Jenkins, Ferguson, 1967-71 Chicago	P	2	1	0	0	0	0	0	0	.000
Johnson, David, 1973 Atlanta	2B	1	1	0	0	0	0	0	0	.000
Jones, Cleon, 1969 New York	OF	1	4	2	2	0	0	0	0	.500
Jones, Randall, 1975-76 San Diego	P	2	1	0	0	0	0	0	0	.000
Jones, Samuel, 1955 Chicago; 1959 San Francisco	P	2	0	0	0	0	0	0	0	.000
Jones, Willie, 1950-51 Philadelphia	3B	2	9	0	1	0	0	0	0	.111
Kasko, Edward, 1961 Cincinnati	SS	1	1	0	1	0	0	0	0	1.000
Kazak, Edward, 1949 St. Louis	3B	1	2	0	2	0	0	0	1	1.000
Kerr, John, 1948 New York	SS	1	2	0	0	0	0	0	0	.000
Kessinger, Donald, 1968-69-70-71-72-74 Chicago	SS	6	12	1	3	0	1	0	1	.250
Kiner, Ralph, 1948-49-50-51 Pitts.; 1953 Chicago	OF-PH	5	15	3	4	1	0	3	4	.267
Kingman, David, 1976 San Francisco; 1980 Chicago	OF	2	3	0	0	0	0	0	0	.000
Klein, Charles, 1933 Philadelphia; 1934 Chicago	OF	2	7	0	2	0	0	1	1	.286
Kluszewski, Theodore, 1953-54-55-56 Cincinnati	1B	4	14	4	7	3	0	1	4	.500
Knight, C. Ray, 1980 Cincinnati	3B	1	1	1	1	0	0	0	0	1.000
Konstanty, C. James, 1950 Philadelphia	P	1	0	0	0	0	0	0	0	.000
Koosman, Jerry, 1968-69 New York	P	2	0	0	0	0	0	0	0	.000
Koufax, Sanford, 1961(2)-65-66 Los Angeles	P	4	0	0	0	0	0	0	0	.000
Kurowski, George, 1944-46-47 St. Louis	3B	3	6	0	1	1	0	0	2	.167
Labine, Clement, 1957 Brooklyn	P	1	0	0	0	0	0	0	0	.000
LaCoss, Michael, 1979 Cincinnati	P	1	0	0	0	0	0	0	0	.000
Lamanno, Raymond, 1946 Cincinnati	PH	1	1	0	0	0	0	0	0	.000
Larker, Norman, 1960(2) Los Angeles	PH	2	1	1	0	0	0	0	0	.000
Lavagetto, Harry, 1940-41 Brooklyn	3B	2	3	0	0	0	0	0	0	.000
Lavelle, Gary, 1977 San Francisco	P	1	0	0	0	0	0	0	0	.000
Law, Vernon, 1960(2) Pittsburgh	P	2	1	0	0	0	0	0	0	.000
Lee, William, 1938-39 Chicago	P	2	1	0	0	0	0	0	0	.000
Lefebvre, James, 1966 Los Angeles	2B	1	2	0	0	0	0	0	0	.000

Player, Club and Years Played	Pos.	G.	AB.	R.	H.	2B.	3B.	HR.	RBI.	B.A.
Leiber, Henry, 1938 New York	PH	1	1	0	0	0	0	0	0	.000
Litwhiler, Daniel, 1942 Philadelphia	PH	1	1	0	1	0	0	0	0	1.000
Lockman, Carroll, 1952 New York	1B	1	3	0	0	0	0	0	0	.000
Logan, John, 1955-58 Milwaukee	SS-PH	2	4	0	1	0	0	0	1	.250
Lombardi, Ernest, 1938-39-40 Cin.; 1942 Bos.; 1943 N.Y.	C	5	13	0	5	0	0	0	1	.385
Long, R. Dale, 1956 Pittsburgh	1B	1	2	0	0	0	0	0	0	.000
Lopata, Stanley, 1955 Philadelphia	C	1	3	0	0	0	0	0	0	.000
Lopes, David, 1978-79-80 Los Angeles	PR-2B	3	5	0	2	0	0	0	1	.400
Lopez, Alfonso, 1934 Brooklyn; 1941 Pittsburgh	C	2	3	0	0	0	0	0	0	.000
Lowrey, Harry, 1946 Chicago	OF	1	2	0	1	0	0	0	0	.500
Luzinski, Gregory, 1975-76-77-78 Philadelphia	PH-OF	4	8	1	2	0	0	1	3	.250
Madlock, Bill, 1975 Chicago	3B	1	2	0	1	0	0	0	2	.500
Maglie, Salvatore, 1951 New York	P	1	1	0	0	0	0	0	0	.000
Mahaffey, Arthur, 1961-62 Philadelphia	P	2	0	0	0	0	0	0	0	.000
Maloney, James, 1965 Cincinnati	P	1	0	0	0	0	0	0	0	.000
Mancuso, August, 1935-37 New York	PH-C	2	2	0	0	0	0	0	0	.000
Marichal, Juan, 1962(2)-64-65-66-67-68-71 San Francisco	P	8	2	1	1	0	0	0	0	.500
Marion, Martin, 1943-44-46-47-50 St. Louis	SS	5	12	1	1	0	0	0	0	.083
Marshall, Michael, 1974 Los Angeles	P	1	1	0	0	0	0	0	0	.000
Marshall, Willard, 1942-47-49 New York	OF-PH	3	3	1	0	0	0	0	0	.000
Martin, John, 1933-34-35 St. Louis	3B	3	8	1	1	0	0	0	1	.125
Masi, Philip, 1946-47-48 Boston	C-PR	3	4	0	1	0	0	0	0	.250
Mathews, Edwin, 1953-55-57-59(2)-60(2)-61(2)-62 Milw.	PH-3B	10	25	4	2	0	0	2	3	.080
Matlack, Jonathan, 1974-75 New York	P	2	0	0	0	0	0	0	0	.000
Matthews, Gary, 1979 Atlanta	OF	1	2	0	0	0	0	0	0	.000
May, Lee, 1969-71 Cincinnati; 1972 Houston	1B	3	6	0	1	0	0	0	1	.167
May, Merrill, 1940 Philadelphia	3B	1	1	0	0	0	0	0	0	.000
Mays, Willie, 1954-55-56-57 N.Y.; 1958-59(2)-60(2)-61(2)-63-64-65-66-67-68-69-70-71 San Fran.; 1972-73 N.Y.	OF-PH	24	75	20	23	2	3	3	9	.307
Mazeroski, William, 1958-59-60(2)-62(2)-67 Pittsburgh	2B	7	16	0	2	0	0	0	0	.125
Mazzilli, Lee, 1979 New York	PH-OF	1	1	1	1	0	0	1	2	1.000
McCarver, J. Timothy, 1966-67 St. Louis	C	2	3	0	3	1	0	0	0	1.000
McCormick, Frank, 1938-39-40-41-42 Cinn.; 1946 Phila.	1B	6	12	1	1	0	0	0	0	.083
McCormick, Michael, 1960-61 San Francisco	P	2	1	0	0	0	0	0	0	.000
McCovey, Willie, 1963-66-68-69-70-71 San Fran.	1B-PH	6	16	2	3	0	0	2	4	.188
McDaniel, Lyndall, 1960 St. Louis	P	1	0	0	0	0	0	0	0	.000
McGlothen, Lynn, 1974 St. Louis	P	1	0	0	0	0	0	0	0	.000
McGraw, Frank, 1972 New York	P	1	0	0	0	0	0	0	0	.000
McMillan, Roy, 1956-57 Cincinnati	SS	2	4	1	2	0	0	0	0	.000
Medwick, Joseph, 1934-35-36-37-38-39 St. Louis; 1940-41-42 Brooklyn; 1944 New York	OF-PH	10	27	2	7	2	0	1	6	.259
Menke, Denis, 1969-70 Houston	SS-PH-2B	2	1	0	0	0	0	0	0	.000
Merritt, James, 1970 Cincinnati	P	1	0	0	0	0	0	0	0	.000
Messersmith, John, 1974 Los Angeles	P	1	0	0	0	0	0	0	0	.000
Millan, Felix, 1969-71 Atlanta	2B	2	4	1	1	1	0	0	2	.250
Miller, Edward, 1940-41-42 Boston; 1943 Cincinnati	SS	4	4	0	0	0	0	0	0	.000
Miller, Stuart, 1961(2) San Francisco	P	2	0	0	0	0	0	0	0	.000
Mize, John, 1937-39-40-41 St. L.; 1942-46-47-48-49 N.Y.	1B-PH	9	23	2	5	1	0	1	2	.217
Monday, Robert, 1978 Los Angeles	OF	1	2	0	0	0	0	0	0	.000
Montanez, Guillermo, 1977 Atlanta	1B	1	2	0	0	0	0	0	0	.000
Montefusco, John, 1976 San Francisco	P	1	0	0	0	0	0	0	0	.000
Moon, Wallace, 1957 St. Louis; 1959(2) Los Angeles	PH-OF	3	5	0	0	0	0	0	0	.000
Moore, Joseph, 1935-37-40 New York	OF	3	5	0	0	0	0	0	0	.000
Moore, Terry, 1939-40-41-42 St. Louis	OF	4	10	0	0	0	0	0	1	.000
Morales, Julio, 1977 Chicago	P	1	0	1	0	0	0	0	0	.000
Morgan, Joe, 1970 Hous.; 1972-73-74-75-76-77-78-79 Cincinnati	2B-PH	9	26	7	7	2	0	1	3	.269
Mota, Manuel, 1973 Los Angeles	PH-OF	1	1	0	0	0	0	0	0	.000
Mueller, Donald, 1954-55 New York	PH-OF	2	3	0	2	1	0	0	1	.667
Mueller, Raymond, 1944 Cincinnati	C	1	0	0	0	0	0	0	0	.000
Munger, George, 1949 St. Louis	P	1	0	0	0	0	0	0	0	.000
Mungo, Van, 1934-37 Brooklyn	P	2	0	0	0	0	0	0	0	.000
Murcer, Bobby, 1975 San Francisco	OF	1	2	0	0	0	0	0	0	.000
Murphy, Dale, 1980 Atlanta	OF	1	1	0	0	0	0	0	0	.000
Musial, Stanley, 1943-44-46-47-48-49-50-51-52-53-54-55-56-57-58-59(2)-60(2)-61(2)-62(2)-63 St. Louis	OF-PH-1B	24	63	11	20	2	0	6	10	.317
Neal, Charles, 1959-60(2) Los Angeles	2B	3	2	0	0	0	0	0	0	.000
Newcombe, Donald, 1949-50-51-55 Brooklyn	P	4	3	0	1	0	0	0	0	.333
Nicholson, William, 1940-41-43-44 Chicago	OF-PH	4	6	1	1	1	0	0	1	.167
Niekro, Philip, 1969-78 Atlanta	P	2	1	0	0	0	0	0	0	.000
Nuxhall, Joseph, 1955 Cincinnati	P	1	2	0	0	0	0	0	0	.000
O'Doul, Francis, 1933 New York	PH	1	1	0	0	0	0	0	0	.000
Oliver, Albert, 1972-75-76 Pittsburgh	OF-PH	3	3	1	1	1	0	0	0	.333
Osteen, Claude, 1970-73 Los Angeles	PR-P	2	0	0	0	0	0	0	0	.000
O'Toole, James, 1963 Cincinnati	P	1	1	0	0	0	0	0	0	.000
Ott, Melvin, 1934-35-36-37-38-39-40-41-42-43-44 New York	OF-PH	11	23	2	5	1	0	0	0	.217
Owen, Arnold, 1941-42 Brooklyn	C	2	2	1	1	0	0	1	1	.500
Pafko, Andrew, 1948-49-50 Chicago	OF-3B	4	10	0	4	0	0	0	0	.400
Parker, David, 1977-79-80 Pittsburgh	OF	3	8	1	2	0	0	0	1	.250
Parrish, Larry, 1979 Montreal	3B	1	1	0	0	0	0	0	0	.000
Passeau, Claude, 1941-42-46 Chicago	P	3	2	0	0	0	0	0	0	.000
Perez, Atanasio, 1967-68-69-70-74-75-76 Cincinnati	3B-PH-1B	7	8	1	1	0	0	1	1	.125

Player, Club and Years Played	Pos.	G.	AB.	R.	H.	2B.	3B.	HR.	RBI.	B.A.
Perry, Gaylord, 1966-70 San Francisco; 1979 San Diego	P	3	0	0	0	0	0	0	0	.000
Phelps, Ernest, 1939-40 Brooklyn	P	2	1	0	0	0	0	0	0	.000
Pinson, Vada, 1959-60(2) Cincinnati	PR-OF	4	3	0	0	0	0	0	0	.000
Pocoroba, Biff, 1978 Atlanta	C	1	0	0	0	0	0	0	0	.000
Podres, John, 1960-62 Los Angeles	P	2	1	1	1	0	0	0	0	1.000
Pollet, Howard, 1949 St. Louis	P	1	0	0	0	0	0	0	0	.000
Purkey, Robert, 1961(2)-62 Cincinnati	P	3	0	0	0	0	0	0	0	.000
Raffensberger, Kenneth, 1944 Philadelphia	P	1	0	0	0	0	0	0	0	.000
Reed, Ronald, 1968 Atlanta	P	1	0	0	0	0	0	0	0	.000
Reese, Harold, 1942-47-48-49-50-51-52-53 Brooklyn	SS-PH	8	17	0	2	1	0	0	2	.118
Reiser, Harold, 1941-42 Brooklyn	OF	2	7	0	1	0	0	0	0	.143
Reitz, Kenneth, 1980 St. Louis	3B	1	2	0	0	0	0	0	0	.000
Reuschel, Rick, 1977 Cincinnati	P	1	0	0	0	0	0	0	0	.000
Reuss, Jerry, 1975 Pittsburgh; 1980 Los Angeles	P	2	1	0	0	0	0	0	0	.000
Repulski, Eldon, 1956 St. Louis	PH	1	1	0	0	0	0	0	0	.000
Reynolds, G. Craig, 1979 Houston	SS	1	2	0	0	0	0	0	0	.000
Rhoden, Richard, 1976 Los Angeles	P	1	0	0	0	0	0	0	0	.000
Richard, J. R., 1980 Houston	P	1	0	0	0	0	0	0	0	.000
Riggs, Lewis, 1936 Cincinnati	PH-3B	1	1	0	0	0	0	0	0	.000
Rigney, William, 1948 New York	2B	1	0	0	0	0	0	0	0	.000
Roberts, Robin, 1950-51-53-54-55 Philadelphia	P	5	2	0	0	0	0	0	0	.000
Robinson, Frank, 1956-57-59-61-62-65 Cinn.	OF-1B-PH	6	12	1	5	0	0	1	1	.417
Robinson, Jack, 1949-50-51-52-53-54 Brooklyn	2B-PH-OF	6	18	7	6	2	0	1	4	.333
Roe, Elwin, 1949 Brooklyn	P	1	0	0	0	0	0	0	0	.000
Rogers, Stephen, 1978-79 Montreal	P	2	0	0	0	0	0	0	0	.000
Rojas, Octavio, 1965 Philadelphia	PH	1	1	0	0	0	0	0	0	.000
Rose, Peter, 1965-67-69-70-71-73-74-75-76-77-78 Cin.; 1979-80 Phila.	PH-2B-OF-3B-1B	13	28	3	6	1	1	0	1	.214
Roseboro, John, 1961-62 Los Angeles	C	2	6	1	1	0	0	1	1	.167
Rowe, Lynwood, 1947 Philadelphia	PH	1	1	0	0	0	0	0	0	.000
Rush, Robert, 1952 Chicago	P	1	1	0	0	0	0	0	0	.000
Russell, William, 1973-76-80 Los Angeles	SS	3	5	0	0	0	0	0	0	.000
Ryan, Cornelius, 1944 Boston	2B	1	4	1	2	0	0	0	0	.500
Sain, John, 1947-48 Boston	P	2	0	0	0	0	0	0	0	.000
Sambito, Joseph, 1979 Houston	P	1	0	0	0	0	0	0	0	.000
Sanford, John, 1957 Philadelphia	P	1	0	0	0	0	0	0	0	.000
Sanguillen, Manuel, 1972 Pittsburgh	C	1	2	0	1	0	0	0	0	.500
Santo, Ronald, 1963-65-66-68-69-71-72-73 Chicago	PH-3B	8	15	1	5	0	0	0	3	.333
Sauer, Henry, 1950-52 Chicago	OF	2	4	1	1	0	0	1	3	.250
Schmidt, Michael, 1974-76-77-79 Philadelphia	PR-PH-3B	4	4	3	2	1	1	0	1	.500
Schmitz, John, 1948 Chicago	P	1	0	0	0	0	0	0	0	.000
Schoendienst, Albert, 1946-48-49-50-51-53-54-55 St. Louis; 1957 Milwaukee	2B-PH	9	21	1	4	0	0	1	1	.190
Schumacher, Harold, 1935 New York	P	1	1	0	0	0	0	0	0	.000
Seaver, G. Thomas, 1967-68-70-73-75-76 N.Y.; 1977 Cin.	P	7	1	0	0	0	0	0	0	.000
Seminick, Andrew, 1949 Philadelphia	C	1	1	0	0	0	0	0	0	.000
Sewell, Truett, 1943-44-46 Pittsburgh	P	3	1	0	0	0	0	0	0	.000
Shaw, Robert, 1962 Milwaukee	P	1	0	0	0	0	0	0	0	.000
Short, Christopher, 1964-67 Philadelphia	P	2	0	0	0	0	0	0	0	.000
Simmons, Curtis, 1952-53-57 Philadelphia	P	3	0	0	0	0	0	0	0	.000
Simmons, Ted, 1973-77-78 St. Louis	C	3	7	0	1	0	0	0	0	.143
Singer, William, 1969 Los Angeles	P	1	0	0	0	0	0	0	0	.000
Sisler, Richard, 1950 Philadelphia	PH	1	1	0	1	0	0	0	0	1.000
Skinner, Robert, 1958-60(2) Pittsburgh	PH	3	1	0	0	0	0	0	0	.000
Slaughter, Enos, 1941-42-46-47-48-49-50-51-52-53 St. Louis..	OF	3	10	1	3	0	0	0	2	.300
Smith, C. Reginald, 1974-75 St. Louis; 1977-78-80 Los Angeles	OF-PH	10	21	4	8	1	1	0	2	.381
	PH-OF	5	10	2	3	0	0	1	1	.300
Smith, Harold, 1959 St. Louis	C	1	2	0	0	0	0	0	0	.000
Snider, Edwin, 1950-51-53-54-55-56 Brkn.; 1963 N. Y.	PH-OF	7	11	3	3	1	0	0	0	.273
Spahn, Warren, 1947-49 Bos.; 1953-54-56-58-61 Milw.	P	7	1	0	0	0	0	0	0	.000
Speier, Chris, 1972-73 San Francisco	SS	2	4	0	0	0	0	0	0	.000
Stanky, Edward, 1947 Brooklyn	2B	1	2	0	0	0	0	0	0	.000
Stargell, Wilver, 1964-65-66-71-72-73-78 Pittsburgh	PH-OF	7	10	3	2	0	0	1	2	.200
Staub, Daniel, 1967-68 Hous.; 1970 Montreal	PH	3	3	0	1	0	0	0	0	.333
Stearns, John, 1977-80 New York	C	2	1	0	0	0	0	0	0	.000
Stuart, Richard, 1961(2) Pittsburgh	PH	2	2	0	1	1	0	0	0	.500
Stoneman, William, 1972 Montreal	P	1	1	0	0	0	0	0	0	.000
Sutter, H. Bruce, 1978-79-80 Chicago	P	3	0	0	0	0	0	0	0	.000
Sutton, Donald, 1972-73-75-77 Los Angeles	P	4	0	0	0	0	0	0	0	.000
Taylor, Antonio, 1960(2) Philadelphia	PR-2B	2	1	0	1	0	0	0	0	1.000
Temple, John, 1956-57-59(2) Cincinnati	2B	4	10	2	3	1	0	0	1	.300
Templeton, Garry, 1977 St. Louis	SS	1	1	1	1	1	0	0	0	1.000
Terry, William, 1933-34-35 New York	P	3	10	0	4	0	0	0	1	.400
Thomas, Frank, 1954-55-58 Pittsburgh	PH-3B	3	5	0	1	0	0	0	0	.200
Thomson, Robert, 1948-49-52 New York	PH-3B	3	4	0	0	0	0	0	0	.000
Tobin, James, 1944 Boston	P	1	0	0	0	0	0	0	0	.000
Torre, Joseph, 1964-65 Milw.; 1966-67 Atlanta; 1970-71-72-73 St. Louis	PH-C-3B-1B	8	21	1	2	0	0	1	2	.095
Traynor, Harold, 1933-34 Pittsburgh	3B	2	6	2	3	1	0	0	1	.500
Trillo, Jesus, 1977 Chicago	2B	1	1	0	0	0	0	0	0	.000
Twitchell, Wayne, 1973 Pittsburgh	P	1	0	0	0	0	0	0	0	.000
Valentine, Ellis, 1977 Montreal	OF	1	1	0	0	0	0	0	0	.000
Vander Meer, John, 1938-42-43 Cincinnati	P	3	1	0	0	0	0	0	0	.000

Player, Club and Years Played	Pos.	G.	AB.	R.	H.	2B.	3B.	HR.	RBI.	B.A.
▽Vaughan, Floyd, 1934-35-37-39-40-41 Pitts.; 1942 Brkn	3B-SS	7	22	5	8	1	0	2	4	.364
Verban, Emil, 1946-47 Philadelphia	2B-PH	2	3	0	0	0	0	0	0	.000
Waitkus, Edward, 1948 Chicago	PH	1	0	0	0	0	0	0	0	.000
Walker, Fred, 1943-44-46-47 Brooklyn	OF-PH	4	10	0	2	0	0	0	2	.200
Walker, Harry, 1943 St. Louis; 1947 Philadelphia	OF	2	3	0	0	0	0	0	0	.000
Walker, William, 1935 St. Louis	P	1	0	0	0	0	0	0	0	.000
Walls, Lee, 1958 Chicago	P	1	1	0	0	0	0	0	0	.000
Walters, William, 1937 Phila.; 1940-41-42-44 Cinn.	PH-OF	1	1	0	0	0	0	0	0	.000
Waner, Paul, 1933-34-35-37 Pittsburgh	OF	5	1	1	1	1	0	0	0	1.000
Warneke, Lonnie, 1933-34-36 Chicago	P	4	8	0	0	0	0	0	0	.000
Watson, Robert, 1973-75 Houston	OF-PH	3	2	1	1	0	1	0	0	.500
Welch, Robert, 1980 Los Angeles	P	2	1	0	0	0	0	0	0	.000
West, Max, 1940 Boston	OF	1	1	0	0	0	0	0	0	.000
Westlake, Waldon, 1951 St. Louis	OF	1	1	1	1	0	0	1	3	1.000
White, William, 1960(2)-61(2)-63-64 St. Louis	PR-1B	6	14	1	4	1	0	0	2	.286
Whitehead, Burgess, 1935 St. Louis; 1938 New York	PR	2	0	0	0	0	0	0	0	.000
Whitney, Arthur, 1936 Philadelphia	3B	1	3	0	1	0	0	0	0	.333
Williams, Billy, 1962-64-65-68-72-73 Chicago	OF-PH	6	11	2	3	0	0	1	2	.273
Williams, David, 1954 New York	2B	1	0	0	0	0	0	0	0	.000
Williams, Stanley, 1960 Los Angeles	P	1	0	0	0	0	0	0	0	.000
Wills, Maurice, 1961(2)-62(2)-65-66 Los Angeles	SS-PR	6	14	2	5	0	0	0	1	.357
Wilson, Donald, 1971 Houston	P	1	0	0	0	0	0	0	0	.000
Wilson, James, 1933 St. Louis; 1935 Philadelphia	C	2	4	0	1	1	0	0	0	.250
Winfield, David, 1977-78-79-80 San Diego	OF	4	11	2	4	2	0	0	3	.364
Wise, Richard, 1973 St. Louis	P	1	0	0	0	0	0	0	0	.000
Woodeshick, Harold, 1963 Houston	P	1	0	0	0	0	0	0	0	.000
Wyatt, Whitlow, 1940-41 Brooklyn	P	2	1	0	0	0	0	0	0	.000
Wynn, James, 1967 Houston; 1974-75 Los Angeles	PH-OF	3	6	2	3	0	0	1	1	.500
Wyrostek, John, 1950-51 Cincinnati	OF	2	3	0	0	0	0	0	0	.000
Zimmer, Donald, 1961 Chicago	2B	1	1	0	0	0	0	0	0	.000

PITCHING RECORDS

National League

Player, Club and Years Pitched	G.	IP.	H.	R.	BB.	SO.	W.	L.	Pct.
Andujar, Joaquin, 1979 Houston	1	2	2	2	1	0	0	0	.000
Antonelli, John, 1954-56 New York; 1959 San Francisco	3	6⅓	8	3	1	3	1	0	1.000
Bibby, James, 1980 Pittsburgh	1	1	1	0	0	0	0	0	.000
Bickford, Vernon, 1949 Boston	1	1	0	0	0	0	0	0	.000
Blackwell, Ewell, 1946-47-48-49-50-51 Cincinnati	6	13⅔	8	2	5	12	1	0	1.000
Blanton, Darrell, 1937 Pittsburgh	1	⅓	0	0	0	1	0	0	.000
Blass, Stephen, 1972 Pittsburgh	1	1	1	1	1	0	0	0	.000
Blue, Vida, 1978 San Francisco	1	3	5	3	1	2	0	0	.000
Branca, Ralph, 1948 Brooklyn	1	3	1	2	3	3	0	0	.000
Brecheen, Harry, 1947 St. Louis	1	3	5	1	0	2	0	0	.000
Brett, Kenneth, 1974 Pittsburgh	1	2	1	0	1	0	1	0	1.000
Brewer, James, 1973 Los Angeles	1	1	0	0	0	0	0	0	.000
Brown, Mace, 1938 Pittsburgh	1	3	5	1	1	2	0	0	.000
Buhl, Robert, 1960 Milwaukee	1	1⅓	3	1	1	0	0	0	.000
Bunning, James, 1961-66 Philadelphia	2	4	3	1	0	6	0	0	.000
Burdette, S. Lewis, 1957-59 Milwaukee	2	7	6	1	1	2	0	0	.000
Carlton, Steven, 1968-69 St. Louis; 1972-79 Philadelphia	4	6	4	5	3	3	1	0	1.000
Conley, D. Eugene, 1954-55 Milwaukee; 1959 Philadelphia	3	3⅓	3	3	2	5	1	1	.500
Cooper, Morton, 1942-43 St. Louis	2	5⅓	8	7	2	3	0	2	.000
Cuellar, Miguel, 1967 Houston	1	2	1	0	0	2	0	0	.000
Culp, Raymond, 1963 Philadelphia	1	1	1	0	0	0	0	0	.000
Davis, Curtis, 1936 Chicago	1	⅔	4	3	1	0	0	0	.000
Dean, Jerome, 1934-35-36-37 St. Louis	4	10	4	3	1	0	0	0	.000
Derringer, Paul, 1935-39-40-41 Cincinnati	4	10	10	2	5	10	1	1	.500
Dickson, Murry, 1953 Pittsburgh	1	8	6	1	1	6	1	0	1.000
Dierker, Lawrence, 1969 Houston	1	⅓	1	0	0	0	0	0	.000
Drysdale, Donald, 1959(2)-62-63-64-65-67-68 Los Angeles	8	19⅓	10	4	4	19	2	1	.667
Ellis, Dock, 1971 Pittsburgh	1	3	4	4	1	2	0	1	.000
Elston, Donald, 1959 Chicago	1	1	1	0	1	0	0	0	.000
Erskine, Carl, 1954 Brooklyn	1	⅔	1	0	0	1	0	0	.000
Face, ElRoy, 1959(2)-60-61 Pittsburgh	4	5⅔	6	2	0	0	0	0	.000
Farrell, Richard, 1958 Phila.; 1962-64-65 Houston	4	5¾	6	2	7	0	0	0	.000
Fette, Louis, 1939 Boston	1	6	5	4	4	7	0	0	.000
Fingers, Roland, 1978 San Diego	1	2	1	0	1	1	0	0	.000
Forsch, Kenneth, 1976 Houston	1	2	1	0	0	1	0	0	.000
Frankhouse, Fred, 1934 Boston	1	1	0	0	0	1	0	0	.000
French, Lawrence, 1940 Chicago	1	2	1	0	0	2	0	0	.000
Friend, Robert, 1956-58-60 Pittsburgh	3	8⅓	8	2	3	5	2	1	.667
Gibson, Robert, 1962-65-67-69-70-72 St. Louis	6	11	11	4	5	10	0	0	.000
Giusti, J. David, 1973 Pittsburgh	1	1	0	0	0	0	0	0	.000
Gossage, Richard, 1977 Pittsburgh	1	1	1	2	1	2	0	0	.000
Grissom, Lee, 1937 Cincinnati	1	1	1	2	1	2	0	0	.000
Grissom, Marvin, 1954 New York	1	1⅓	0	0	0	2	0	0	.000

Player, Club and Years Pitched	G.	IP.	H.	R.	BB.	SO.	W.	L.	Pct.
Haddix, Harvey, 1955 St. Louis	1	3	3	1	0	2	0	0	.000
Hallahan, William, 1933 St. Louis	1	2	2	3	5	1	0	1	.000
Henry, William, 1960 Cincinnati	1	1	2	0	0	0	0	0	.000
Higbe, W. Kirby, 1946 Brooklyn	1	1⅓	5	4	1	2	0	0	.000
Hubbell, Carl, 1933-34-36-37-40 New York	5	9⅔	8	3	6	11	0	0	.000
Jackson, Lawrence, 1957-58-60 St. Louis; 1963 Chicago	4	5⅔	6	2	3	3	1	0	1.000
Jansen, Lawrence, 1950 New York	1	5	1	0	0	6	0	0	.000
Javery, Alva, 1943 Boston	1	2	2	0	0	3	0	0	.000
Jenkins, Ferguson, 1967-71 Chicago	2	4	6	3	0	6	0	0	.000
Jones, Randall, 1975-76 San Diego	2	4	0	0	1	2	1	0	1.000
Jones, Samuel, 1955 Chicago; 1959 San Francisco	2	2⅔	1	1	4	4	0	0	.000
Konstanty, C. James, 1950 Philadelphia	1	1	0	0	0	2	0	0	.000
Koosman, Jerry, 1968-69 New York	2	2	1	0	0	2	0	0	.000
Koufax, Sanford 1961(2)-65-66 Los Angeles	4	6	4	1	2	3	1	0	1.000
Labine, Clement, 1957 Brooklyn	1	3	3	0	1	0	0	0	.000
LaCoss, Michael, 1979 Cincinnati	1	1⅓	1	0	0	0	0	0	.000
Lavelle, Gary, 1977 San Francisco	1	2	1	0	0	2	0	0	.000
Law, Vernon, 1960(2) Pittsburgh	2	2⅔	1	0	0	1	1	0	1.000
Lee, William, 1938-39 Chicago	2	6	4	3	4	6	0	1	.000
Maglie, Salvatore, 1951 New York	1	3	3	2	1	1	1	0	1.000
Mahaffey, Arthur, 1961-62 Philadelphia	2	4	2	3	2	1	0	1	.000
Maloney, James, 1965 Cincinnati	1	1⅔	5	5	2	1	0	0	.000
Marichal, Juan, 1962(2)-64-65-66-67-68-71 San Fran.	8	18	7	2	6	9	2	0	1.000
Marshall, Michael, 1974 Los Angeles	1	2	0	0	1	2	0	0	.000
Matlack, Jonathan, 1974-75 New York	2	3	3	0	1	4	1	0	1.000
McCormick, Michael, 1960-61 San Francisco	2	5⅓	4	2	4	5	0	0	.000
McDaniel, Lyndall, 1960 St. Louis	1	1	0	0	0	0	0	0	.000
McGlothen, Lynn, 1974 St. Louis	1	1	0	0	1	0	0	0	.000
McGraw, Frank, 1972 New York	1	2	1	0	0	4	1	0	1.000
Merritt, James, 1970 Cincinnati	1	2	1	0	1	0	0	0	.000
Messersmith, John, 1974 Los Angeles	1	3	2	2	3	4	1	0	1.000
Miller, Stuart, 1961(2) San Francisco	2	4⅔	1	1	1	9	1	0	1.000
Montefusco, John, 1976 San Francisco	1	2	0	0	2	2	0	0	.000
Munger, George, 1949 St. Louis	1	1	0	0	1	0	0	0	.000
Mungo, Van, 1934-37 Brooklyn	2	3	6	6	4	2	0	1	.000
Newcombe, Donald, 1949-50-51-55 Brooklyn	4	8⅔	9	4	2	5	0	1	.000
Niekro, Philip, 1969-78 Atlanta	2	1½	0	0	0	2	0	0	.000
Nuxhall, Joseph, 1955 Cincinnati	1	3⅓	2	0	3	5	0	0	.000
Osteen, Claude, 1970-73 Los Angeles	2	5	5	0	2	1	1	0	1.000
O'Toole, James, 1963 Cincinnati	1	2	4	1	0	1	0	0	.000
Passeau, Claude, 1941-42-46 Chicago	3	7⅔	9	7	3	4	0	2	.000
Perry, Gaylord, 1966-70 San Francisco; 1979 San Diego	3	4	8	3	2	1	1	0	1.000
Podres, John, 1960-62 Los Angeles	2	4	3	0	3	3	0	0	.000
Pollet, Howard, 1949 St. Louis	1	1	4	3	0	0	0	0	.000
Purkey, Robert, 1961(2)-62 Cincinnati	3	6	3	2	2	4	0	0	.000
Raffensberger, Kenneth, 1944 Philadelphia	1	2	1	0	0	2	1	0	1.000
Reed, Ronald, 1968 Atlanta	1	⅔	0	0	0	1	0	0	.000
Reuschel, Rick, 1977 Chicago	1	1	0	0	0	0	0	0	.000
Reuss, Jerry, 1975 Pittsburgh; 1980 Los Angeles	2	4	3	0	0	5	1	0	1.000
Rhoden, Richard, 1976 Los Angeles	1	1	1	0	0	0	0	0	.000
Richard, J. R., 1980 Houston	1	2	1	0	2	3	0	0	.000
Roberts, Robin, 1950-51-53-54-55 Philadelphia	5	14	17	10	6	9	0	0	.000
Roe, Elwin, 1949 Brooklyn	1	1	0	0	0	0	0	0	.000
Rogers, Stephen, 1978-79 Montreal	2	4	2	0	0	4	0	0	.000
Rush, Robert, 1952 Chicago	1	2	4	2	1	1	1	0	1.000
Sain, John, 1947-48 Boston	2	2⅔	2	1	0	4	0	1	.000
Sambito, Joseph, 1979 Houston	1	⅔	0	0	1	0	0	0	.000
Sanford, John, 1957 Philadelphia	1	1	2	1	0	0	0	0	.000
Schmitz, John, 1948 Chicago	1	⅓	3	3	1	0	0	1	.000
Schumacher, Harold, 1935 New York	1	4	4	1	1	5	0	0	.000
Seaver, G. Thomas, 1967-68-70-73-75-76 N.Y.; 1977 Cin.	7	12	11	7	4	15	0	0	.000
Sewell, Truett, 1943-44-46 Pittsburgh	3	5	4	4	1	2	0	0	.000
Shaw, Robert, 1962 Milwaukee	1	2	1	0	1	1	0	0	.000
Short, Christopher, 1964-67 Philadelphia	2	3	3	2	1	2	0	0	.000
Simmons, Curtis, 1952-53-57 Philadelphia	3	6	4	2	4	4	0	1	.000
Singer, William, 1969 Los Angeles	1	2	0	0	0	0	0	0	.000
Spahn, Warren, 1947-49 Boston; 1953-54-56-58-61 Milwaukee	7	14	17	10	5	10	1	0	1.000
Stoneman, William, 1972 Montreal	1	2	2	2	0	2	0	0	.000
Sutter, H. Bruce, 1978-79-80 Chicago	3	5⅔	2	0	3	6	2	0	1.000
Sutton, Donald, 1972-73-75-77 Los Angeles	4	8	5	0	1	5	1	0	1.000
Tobin, James, 1944 Boston	1	1	0	0	0	0	0	0	.000
Twitchell, Wayne, 1973 Philadelphia	1	1	1	0	0	1	0	0	.000
Vander Meer, John, 1938-42-43 Cincinnati	3	8⅔	5	1	1	11	1	0	1.000
Walker, William, 1935 St. Louis	1	2	2	3	1	2	0	1	.000
Walters, William, 1937 Phila.; 1940-41-42-44 Cincinnati	5	9	10	2	2	4	0	0	.000
Warneke, Lonnie, 1933-34-36 Chicago	3	7⅓	10	5	6	5	0	0	.000
Welch, Robert, 1980 Los Angeles	1	3	5	2	1	4	0	0	.000
Williams, Stanley, 1960 Los Angeles	1	2	2	0	1	2	0	0	.000
Wilson, Donald, 1971 Houston	1	2	0	0	1	2	0	0	.000
Wise, Richard, 1973 St. Louis	1	2	2	1	0	1	1	0	1.000
Woodeshick, Harold, 1963 Houston	1	2	1	0	1	3	0	0	.000
Wyatt, J. Whitlow, 1940-41 Brooklyn	2	4	1	0	1	1	0	0	.000

OFFICIAL
CHAMPIONSHIP SERIES RECORDS

Complete Box Scores
Of All Games...

1969 - 1980

Compiled by

CRAIG CARTER

CHAMPIONSHIP SERIES RESULTS

AMERICAN LEAGUE

Year-Winner	Loser
1969—Baltimore (East), 3 games;	Minnesota (West), 0 games.
1970—Baltimore (East), 3 games;	Minnesota (West), 0 games.
1971—Baltimore (East), 3 games;	Oakland (West), 0 games.
1972—Oakland (West), 3 games;	Detroit (East), 2 games.
1973—Oakland (West), 3 games;	Baltimore (East), 2 games.
1974—Oakland (West), 3 games;	Baltimore (East), 1 game.
1975—Boston (East), 3 games;	Oakland (West), 0 games.
1976—New York (East), 3 games;	Kansas City (West), 2 games.
1977—New York (East), 3 games;	Kansas City (West), 2 games.
1978—New York (East), 3 games;	Kansas City (West), 1 game.
1979—Baltimore (East), 3 games;	California (West), 1 game.
1980—Kansas City (West), 3 games;	New York (East), 0 games.

NATIONAL LEAGUE

Year-Winner	Loser
1969—New York (East), 3 games;	Atlanta (West), 0 games.
1970—Cincinnati (West), 3 games;	Pittsburgh (East), 0 games.
1971—Pittsburgh (East), 3 games;	San Francisco (West), 1 game.
1972—Cincinnati (West), 3 games;	Pittsburgh (East), 2 games.
1973—New York (East), 3 games;	Cincinnati (West), 2 games.
1974—Los Angeles (West), 3 games;	Pittsburgh (East), 1 game.
1975—Cincinnati (West), 3 games;	Pittsburgh (East), 0 games.
1976—Cincinnati (West), 3 games;	Philadelphia (East), 0 games.
1977—Los Angeles (West), 3 games;	Philadelphia (East), 1 game.
1978—Los Angeles (West), 3 games;	Philadelphia (East), 1 game.
1979—Pittsburgh (East), 3 games;	Cincinnati (West), 0 games.
1980—Philadelphia (East), 3 games;	Houston (West), 2 games.

AMERICAN LEAGUE
Championship Series of 1969

	W.	L.	Pct.
Baltimore (East)	3	0	1.000
Minnesota (West)	0	3	.000

Baltimore was the belle of the American League ball in 1969. The Orioles overwhelmed the opposition in winning the East Division title by 19 games. They were equally devastating in their treatment of the West Division champion Minnesota Twins in the A. L. Championship Series.

The Orioles disposed of the Twins in three straight games, vindicating those who had crowed that Baltimore was the best team to represent the American League since the New York Yankees' halcyon days.

The Twins were stubborn foes in the first two matches, played in Baltimore. The Orioles had to go 12 innings in taking the opener, 4-3, on October 4. Next day, Baltimore prevailed in 11 innings, 1-0. That was the Twins' last gasp. When the series moved to the Twin Cities October 6, the Orioles lowered the boom in an 11-2 romp.

Mike Cuellar and Dave McNally were Baltimore's 20-game winners. Cuellar performed satisfactorily in the playoff opener, though failing to receive credit for a victory. McNally pitched brilliantly in blanking Minnesota in the second game. Jim Palmer, author of a no-hitter against Oakland during the regular season, coasted to victory behind Baltimore's 18-hit attack in the playoff finale.

Oriole bats were impressive, too. Frank Robinson, Mark Belanger and Boog Powell rapped homers in the opener. The winning hit, however, was a perfectly executed bunt by Paul Blair, who squeezed Belanger home from third in the 12th inning.

Blair, the swift center fielder who enjoyed a banner season, whacked five hits and drove in five runs in the third-game rout. Left fielder Don Buford contributed four hits after going 0-for-9 in the first two games.

Oriole Manager Earl Weaver employed simple strategy to deal with Minnesota's Harmon Killebrew, A. L. home run and RBI champ: Walk him in any dangerous situation. The Killer got nothing good to swing at until the third game was on ice. Baltimore pitchers walked him five times in the first two games and pitched to him only when he could not wreck them with one swing.

Rod Carew and Tony Oliva were the Twins' other top hitters during the season. Carew, A. L. batting champ, was a dud in the playoffs, going 1-for-14. Oliva hit safely in each of the three games, including a homer in the opener, but was guilty of some shoddy fielding in the third game.

In the opener, 20-game winner Jim Perry held a 3-2 lead over the Orioles entering the ninth inning. Powell tied the score with a smash over the right field fence. Reliever Ron Perranoski, who worked in all three games, shut off Baltimore's offense at that point.

Then, with two down in the 12th and Belanger on third, Blair stepped to the plate. Acting on his own, he bunted toward third. Neither third sacker Killebrew nor catcher John Roseboro could make a play as Belanger sped across the plate with the winning run. Dick Hall, who pitched two-thirds of an inning, was the winner. Perranoski didn't allow a ball to leave the infield in the 12th, but was the loser nevertheless.

Winner of 15 games in a row during the season, McNally was saddled with a "lucky" tag because Baltimore frequently rallied to win after Dave had left on the short end of the score. He won the second game of the playoffs on his own exceptional pitching and Curt Motton's 11th-inning pinch-single. It scored Powell from second base with the only run of the game. McNally's victim was Dave Boswell, who was a mighty tough opponent. McNally yielded only three hits, none after the fourth inning.

Twins' Manager Billy Martin, confronted with a pitching shortage, started Bob Miller, normally a reliever, in the third game. Miller lasted less than two innings, and his six successors fared no better. Every Oriole except pitcher Palmer hit safely in an assult which eliminated Minnesota and sent Baltimore into the World Series.

GAME OF SATURDAY, OCTOBER 4, AT BALTIMORE

Minnesota	AB.	R.	H.	RBI.	PO.	A.
Tovar, cf	4	0	0	0	3	0
Carew, 2b	5	0	1	0	3	1
Killebrew, 3b	2	1	0	0	3	2
Oliva, rf	5	2	2	2	3	0
Allison, lf	3	0	0	1	3	0
Uhlaender, lf	1	0	1	0	0	0
Reese, 1b	4	0	0	0	10	1
Cardenas, ss	5	0	0	0	5	3
Mitterwald, c	4	0	0	0	5	2
Roseboro, c	1	0	0	0	0	0
Perry, p	3	0	0	0	0	1
Perranoski, p	1	0	0	0	0	0
Totals	38	3	4	3	35	10

Baltimore	AB.	R.	H.	RBI.	PO.	A.
Buford, lf	6	0	0	0	3	0
Blair, cf	5	0	1	1	1	0
F. Robinson, rf	3	1	1	1	1	0
Powell, 1b	5	1	2	1	13	0
B. Robinson, 3b	5	0	4	0	2	4
Hendricks, c	3	0	0	0	9	0
Motton, ph	1	0	0	0	0	0
Watt, p	0	0	0	0	0	0
Salmon, ph	1	0	0	0	0	0
Lopez, p	0	0	0	0	0	0
Hall, p	0	0	0	0	0	0
Johnson, 2b	5	0	0	0	3	3
Belanger, ss	5	2	2	1	1	2
Cuellar, p	2	0	0	0	0	0
May, ph	1	0	0	0	0	0
Richert, p	0	0	0	0	0	0
Rettenmund, ph	0	0	0	0	0	0
Etchebarren, c	1	0	0	0	3	0
Totals	43	4	10	4	36	9

Minnesota	0	0	0		0	1	0		2	0	0		0 0 0 – 3
Baltimore	0	0	0		1	1	0		0	0	1		0 0 1 – 4

Two out when winning run scored.

Minnesota	IP.	H.	R.	ER.	BB.	SO.
Perry	8*	6	3	3	3	3
Perranoski (Loser)	3⅔	4	1	1	0	1

Baltimore	IP.	H.	R.	ER.	BB.	SO.
Cuellar	8	3	3	2	1	7
Richert	1	0	0	0	2	2
Watt	2	0	0	0	0	2
Lopez	⅓	1	0	0	2	0
Hall (Winner)	⅔	0	0	0	0	1

*Pitched to two batters in ninth.

Errors—F. Robinson. Uhlaender. Carew. Double play—Baltimore 1. Left on bases—Minnesota 5. Baltimore 8. Two-base hit—Oliva. Home runs—F. Robinson, Belanger, Oliva, Powell. Stolen base—Tovar. Sacrifice hit—Etchebarren. Sacrifice fly—Allison. Wild pitch—Lopez. Umpires—Chylak, Runge, Umont, Stewart. Rice and Flaherty. Time of game—3:29. Attendance—39,324.

GAME OF SUNDAY, OCTOBER 5, AT BALTIMORE

Minnesota	AB.	R.	H.	RBI.	PO.	A.
Tovar, cf	5	0	1	0	2	0
Carew, 2b	4	0	0	0	2	1
Killebrew, 3b	3	0	0	0	1	0
Oliva, rf	4	0	1	0	1	0
Allison, lf	5	0	0	0	3	0
Reese, 1b	4	0	0	0	11	3
Mitterwald, c	3	0	1	0	5	2
Cardenas, ss	4	0	0	0	6	5
Boswell, p	4	0	0	0	1	4
Perranoski, p	0	0	0	0	0	0
Totals	36	0	3	0	32	15

Baltimore	AB.	R.	H.	RBI.	PO.	A.
Buford, lf	3	0	0	0	1	0
Blair, rf	4	0	0	0	6	0
F. Robinson, rf	5	0	2	0	1	0
Powell, 1b	3	1	1	0	10	0
B. Robinson, 3b	4	0	2	0	3	3
Johnson, 2b	4	0	2	0	1	2
Belanger, ss	5	0	0	0	0	4
Etchebarren, c	3	0	0	0	8	0
Hendricks, ph-c	0	0	0	0	3	0
Motton, ph	1	0	1	1	0	0
McNally, p	4	0	0	0	0	0
Totals	36	1	8	1	33	9

Minnesota			0 0 0	0 0 0	0 0 0	0	0 – 0
Baltimore			0 0 0	0 0 0	0 0 0	0	1 – 1

Two out when winning run scored.

Minnesota	IP.	H.	R.	ER.	BB.	SO.
Boswell (Loser)	10⅔	7	1	1	7	4
Perranoski	0*	1	0	0	0	0
Baltimore	IP.	H.	R.	ER.	BB.	SO.
McNally (Winner)	11	3	0	0	5	11

*Pitched to one batter in eleventh.

Error—Cardenas. Double plays—Minnesota 2. Left on bases—Minnesota 8, Baltimore 11. Two base hits—F. Robinson 2. Stolen base—Oliva. Sacrifice hit—B. Robinson. Wild pitch—Boswell. Umpires—Runge, Umont, Stewart, Rice, Flaherty and Chylak. Time of game—3.17. Attendance—41,704.

GAME OF MONDAY, OCTOBER 6, AT MINNESOTA

Baltimore	AB.	R.	H.	RBI.	PO.	A.
Buford, lf	5	3	4	1	4	0
Blair, cf	6	1	5	5	1	0
F. Robinson, rf	4	0	1	1	0	0
Powell, 1b	5	0	2	0	11	0
B. Robinson, 3b	5	1	1	0	1	3
Johnson, 2b	4	2	1	0	1	6
Hendricks, c	5	2	2	3	6	0
Belanger, ss	5	2	2	0	3	3
Palmer, p	5	0	0	0	0	1
Totals	44	11	18	10	27	13

Minnesota	AB.	R.	H.	RBI.	PO.	A.
Uhlaender, lf	5	0	0	0	4	0
Carew, 2b	5	0	0	0	1	1
Oliva, rf	4	1	2	0	2	1
Killebrew, 3b	3	1	1	0	2	1
Reese, 1b	4	0	2	2	5	1
Tovar, cf	4	0	0	0	5	0
Roseboro, c	4	0	1	0	6	1
Cardenas, ss	4	0	2	0	2	4
Miller, p	0	0	0	0	0	0
Woodson, p	1	0	1	0	0	0
Hall, p	0	0	0	0	0	0
Manuel, ph	1	0	0	0	0	0
Worthington, p	0	0	0	0	0	0
Grzenda, p	0	0	0	0	0	0
Renick, ph	1	0	0	0	0	0
Chance, p	0	0	0	0	0	0
Perranoski, p	0	0	0	0	0	0
Nettles, ph	1	0	1	0	0	0
Totals	36	2	10	2	27	9

Baltimore		0	3 0	2 0 0	1	0 2	3 – 11
Minnesota		1	0 0	0 1 0	0	0 0	0 – 2

Baltimore	IP.	H.	R.	ER.	BB.	SO.
Palmer (Winner)	9	10	2	2	2	4
Minnesota	IP.	H.	R.	ER.	BB.	SO.
Miller (Loser)	1⅓	5	3	1	0	0
Woodson	1⅔	3	2	2	3	2
Hall	⅔	0	0	0	0	0
Worthington	1⅓	3	1	1	0	1
Grzenda	⅔	0	0	0	0	0
Chance	2*	4	3	3	0	2
Perranoski	1	3	2	2	0	0

*Pitched to one batter in ninth.

Errors—Oliva 2, B. Robinson 1, Minnesota 1. Left on base—Baltimore 9, Minnesota 9. Two-base hits—Oliva, B. Robinson, Hendricks 2, Blair 2, Killebrew, Buford. Three-base hits—Belanger, Cardenas. Home run—Blair. Wild pitch—Palmer. Umpires—Umont, Stewart, Rice, Flaherty, Chylak and Runge. Time of game—2:48. Attendance—32,735.

BALTIMORE ORIOLES' BATTING AND FIELDING AVERAGES

Player–Position	G.	AB.	R.	H.	TB.	2B.	3B.	HR.	RBI.	B.A.	PO.	A.	E.	F.A.
B. Robinson, 3b	3	14	1	7	8	1	0	0	0	.500	6	10	0	1.000
Motton, ph	2	2	0	1	1	0	0	0	1	.500	0	0	0	.000
Blair, cf	3	15	1	6	11	2	0	1	6	.400	8	0	0	1.000
Powell, 1b	3	13	2	5	8	0	0	1	1	.385	34	0	0	1.000
F. Robinson, rf	3	12	1	4	9	2	0	1	2	.333	2	0	1	.667
Buford, lf	3	14	3	4	5	1	0	0	1	.286	8	0	0	1.000
Belanger, ss	3	15	4	4	9	0	1	1	1	.267	4	9	0	1.000
Hendricks, ph-c	3	8	2	2	4	2	0	0	3	.250	18	0	0	1.000
Johnson, 2b	3	13	2	3	3	0	0	0	0	.231	5	11	0	1.000
Watt, p	1	0	0	0	0	0	0	0	0	.000	0	0	0	.000
Lopez, p	1	0	0	0	0	0	0	0	0	.000	0	0	0	.000
R. Hall, p	1	0	0	0	0	0	0	0	0	.000	0	0	0	.000
Richert, p	1	0	0	0	0	0	0	0	0	.000	0	0	0	.000
Rettenmund, ph	1	0	0	0	0	0	0	0	0	.000	0	0	0	.000
Salmon, ph	1	1	0	0	0	0	0	0	0	.000	0	0	0	.000
May, ph	1	1	0	0	0	0	0	0	0	.000	0	0	0	.000
Cuellar, p	1	2	0	0	0	0	0	0	0	.000	0	0	0	.000
Etchebarren, c	2	4	0	0	0	0	0	0	0	.000	11	0	0	1.000
McNally, p	1	4	0	0	0	0	0	0	0	.000	0	0	0	.000
Palmer, p	1	5	0	0	0	0	0	0	0	.000	0	1	0	1.000
Totals	3	123	16	36	58	8	1	4	15	.293	96	31	1	.992

MINNESOTA TWINS' BATTING AND FIELDING AVERAGES

Player–Position	G.	AB.	R.	H.	TB.	2B.	3B.	HR.	RBI.	B.A.	PO.	A.	E.	F.A.
Nettles, ph	1	1	0	1	1	0	0	0	0	1.000	0	0	0	.000
Woodson, p	1	1	0	1	1	0	0	0	0	1.000	0	0	0	.000
Oliva, rf	3	13	3	5	10	2	0	1	2	.385	6	1	2	.778
Roseboro, c	2	5	0	1	1	0	0	0	0	.200	6	1	0	1.000
Reese, 1b	3	12	0	2	2	0	0	0	2	.167	26	5	0	1.000
Uhlaender, lf	2	6	0	1	1	0	0	0	0	.167	4	0	1	.800
Cardenas, ss	3	13	0	2	4	0	1	0	0	.154	13	12	1	.962
Mitterwald, c	2	7	0	1	1	0	0	0	0	.143	10	4	0	1.000
Killebrew, 3b	3	8	2	1	2	1	0	0	0	.125	6	3	0	1.000
Tovar, cf	3	13	0	1	1	0	0	0	0	.077	10	0	0	1.000
Carew, 2b	3	14	0	1	1	0	0	0	0	.071	6	3	1	.900
Chance, p	1	0	0	0	0	0	0	0	0	.000	0	0	0	.000
Miller, p	1	0	0	0	0	0	0	0	0	.000	0	0	0	.000
T. Hall, p	1	0	0	0	0	0	0	0	0	.000	0	0	0	.000
Manuel, ph	1	0	0	0	0	0	0	0	0	.000	0	0	0	.000
Worthington, p	1	0	0	0	0	0	0	0	0	.000	0	0	0	.000
Grzenda, p	1	0	0	0	0	0	0	0	0	.000	0	0	0	.000
Renick, ph	1	1	0	0	0	0	0	0	0	.000	0	0	0	.000
Perranoski, p	3	1	0	0	0	0	0	0	0	.000	0	0	0	.000
Perry, p	1	3	0	0	0	0	0	0	0	.000	0	1	0	1.000
Boswell, p	1	4	0	0	0	0	0	0	0	.000	1	4	0	1.000
Allison, lf	2	8	0	0	0	0	0	0	1	.000	6	0	0	1.000
Totals	3	110	5	17	25	3	1	1	5	.155	94	34	5	.962

BALTIMORE ORIOLES' PITCHING RECORDS

Pitcher	G.	GS.	CG.	IP.	H.	R.	ER.	BB.	SO.	HB.	WP.	W.	L.	Pct.	ERA.
McNally	1	1	1	11	3	0	0	5	11	0	0	1	0	1.000	0.00
Watt	1	0	0	2	0	0	0	0	2	0	0	0	0	.000	0.00
Richert	1	0	0	1	0	0	0	2	2	0	0	0	0	.000	0.00
R. Hall	1	0	0	⅔	1	0	0	0	1	0	0	1	0	1.000	0.00
Lopez	1	0	0	⅓	1	0	0	2	0	0	1	0	0	.000	0.00
Palmer	1	1	1	9	10	2	2	2	4	0	1	1	0	1.000	2.00
Cuellar	1	1	0	8	3	3	2	1	7	0	0	0	0	.000	2.25
Totals	3	3	2	32	17	5	4	12	27	0	2	3	0	1.000	1.13

Shutout—McNally. No saves.

MINNESOTA TWINS' PITCHING RECORDS

Pitcher	G.	GS.	CG.	IP.	H.	R.	ER.	BB.	SO.	HB.	WP.	W.	L.	Pct.	ERA.
Grzenda	1	0	0	⅔	0	0	0	0	0	0	0	0	0	.000	0.00
T. Hall	1	0	0	⅔	0	0	0	0	0	0	0	0	0	.000	0.00
Boswell	1	1	0	10⅔	7	1	1	7	4	0	1	0	1	.000	0.84
Perry	1	1	0	8	6	3	3	3	3	0	0	0	0	.000	3.38
Miller	1	1	0	1⅔	5	3	1	0	0	0	0	0	1	.000	5.40
Perranoski	3	0	0	4⅔	8	3	3	0	2	0	0	0	1	.000	5.79
Worthington	1	0	0	1⅓	1	1	1	0	1	0	0	0	0	.000	6.75
Woodson	1	0	0	1⅔	3	2	2	3	2	0	0	0	0	.000	10.80
Chance	1	0	0	2	4	3	3	0	2	0	0	0	0	.000	13.50
Totals	3	3	0	31⅓	36	16	14	13	14	0	1	0	3	.000	4.02

No shutouts or saves.

COMPOSITE SCORE BY INNINGS

Baltimore	0	3	0	3	1	1	0	2	4	0	1	1—16
Minnesota	1	0	0	0	2	0	2	0	0	0	0	0— 5

Sacrifice hits—Etcheṭarren, B. Robinson.
Sacrifice fly—Allison.
Stolen bases—Oliva, Tovar.
Caught stealing—B. Robinson 2, Buford, Blair.
Double plays—Johnson and Powell; Belanger, Johnson and Powell; Cardenas and Reese; Boswell, Cardenas and Reese; Carew, Cardenas and Reese.
Hit by pitcher—None.
Passed balls—None.
Balks—None.
Left on bases—Baltimore 28—8, 11, 9; Minnesota 22—5, 8, 9.
Time of games—First game, 3:29; second game, 3:17; third game, 2:48.
Attendance—First game, 39,324; second game, 41,704; third game, 32,735.
Umpires—Chylak, Runge, Umont, Stewart, Rice and Flaherty.
Official scorers—Arno Goethel, St. Paul Pioneer Press; Neal Eskridge, Baltimore News-Post.

NATIONAL LEAGUE
Championship Series of 1969

	W.	L.	Pct.
New York (East)	3	0	1.000
Atlanta (West)	0	3	.000

Thirty-to-one shots do come through occasionally. And the National League's first experience with the two-division playoff system provided one of those rare instances. Note the East Division playoff.

Adding another lustrous chapter, the New York Mets swept the Atlanta Braves into oblivion in three Championship Series games to win their first league title after five tenth-place and two ninth-place finishes.

In the first game, played before 50,122 at Atlanta October 4, Tom Seaver, the Mets' 25-game winner, hooked up with Phil Niekro, winner of 23 decisions for the Braves.

Neither righthander finished. Niekro lasted eight innings, including the five-run eighth by which the Mets sewed up the verdict. Seaver departed for a pinch-hitter in the same decisive inning.

Wayne Garrett opened the tell-tale frame with a double and tied the score at 5-5 when Cleon Jones singled. Art Shamsky's third hit sent Jones to second. When Ken Boswell missed an attempted sacrifice, Jones was trapped off second. Catcher Bob Didier committed the cardinal sin of throwing behind the runner and Jones beat the relay throw to third base.

When Boswell bounced to the mound, the Braves retired only one runner, Al Weis, who ran for Shamsky at second base. On Ed Kranepool's grounder to first base, Orlando Cepeda fired wildly to the plate, Jones scoring the go-ahead run.

After Jerry Grote was retired, Bud Harrelson was walked intentionally, loading the bases. With Seaver due to bat, Hodges went to his bench and found just what he wanted. J. C. Martin pinch-singled two runs across the plate, providing the margin of victory, 9-5.

In the second game, witnessed by 50,270 October 5, Jerry Koosman, New

York's 17-game winner, was staked to leads of 8-0 and 9-1, yet failed to survive the fifth inning.

The Mets tagged Ron Reed for four runs in one and two-thirds innings, added two off Paul Doyle and three off Milt Pappas before the Atlanta guns went to work.

A homer by Hank Aaron, who hit for the circuit in each of the three games, provided three runs. A single by Felix Millan, double by Cepeda and single by Clete Boyer accounted for two more tallies and shelled Koosman, then leading by only 9-6.

Ron Taylor and Tug McGraw shut out the Braves on two hits the rest of the way. The Mets picked up their final runs in the seventh when Jones homered with Tommie Agee on base, making the score 11-6.

With the series switched to New York, the Mets applied the clincher before 53,195 delirious devotees on October 6.

This game belonged to Nolan Ryan, who replaced Gary Gentry with none out in the third inning, runners on second and third and the Braves leading, 2-0.

Ryan fanned Rico Carty as a starter, walked Cepeda intentionally, whiffed Boyer and got Didier on a fly to left to escape damage.

The hard-throwing righthander made his only mistake in the fifth, when he grooved a two-run homer pitch to Cepeda, that gave the Braves a 4-3 margin.

Ryan quickly made amends for that boner, leading off the home portion of the inning with a single. Agee was retired, but Garrett, who had hit his last homer on May 6, exactly five months earlier, clouted Jarvis' first pitch into the upper stands in right and the Mets were in front to stay.

Ryan, who had appeared in only 89 innings during the regular season, allowed three hits in his seven innings, walked two and fanned seven, in addition to collecting a second hit in the 7-4 victory.

GAME OF SATURDAY, OCTOBER 4, AT ATLANTA

New York	AB.	R.	H.	RBI.	PO.	A.	Atlanta	AB.	R.	H.	RBI.	PO.	A.
Agee, cf	5	0	0	0	2	0	Millan, 2b	5	1	2	0	3	2
Garrett, 3b	4	1	2	0	1	2	Gonzalez, cf	5	2	2	0	1	0
Jones, lf	5	1	1	1	5	0	H. Aaron, rf	5	1	2	2	1	0
Shamsky, rf	4	1	3	0	2	0	Carty, lf	3	1	1	0	0	0
Weis, pr-2b	0	0	0	0	1	1	Lum, lf	1	0	1	0	0	0
Boswell, 2b	3	2	0	0	0	1	Cepeda, 1b	4	0	1	0	14	0
Gaspar, rf	0	0	0	0	0	0	Boyer, 3b	1	0	0	1	2	5
Kranepool, 1b	4	2	1	0	7	2	Didier, c	4	0	0	0	5	0
Grote, c	3	1	1	1	5	1	Garrido, ss	4	0	1	0	2	7
Harrelson, ss	3	1	1	2	2	1	Niekro, p	3	0	0	0	0	3
Seaver, p	3	0	0	0	1	1	Aspromonte, ph	1	0	0	0	0	0
Martin, ph	1	0	1	2	0	0	Upshaw, p	0	0	0	0	0	1
Taylor, p	0	0	0	0	1	0	Totals	36	5	10	5	27	19
Totals	35	9	10	6	27	9							

New York		0	2	0	2	0	0	0	5	0 – 9
Atlanta		0	1	2	0	1	0	1	0	0 – 5

New York	IP.	H.	R.	ER.	BB.	SO.
Seaver (Winner)	7	8	5	5	3	2
Taylor (Save)	2	2	0	0	0	2

Atlanta	IP.	H.	R.	ER.	BB.	SO.
Niekro (Loser)	8	9	9	4	4	4
Upshaw	1	1	0	0	0	1

Errors—Boswell, Cepeda, Gonzalez. Double plays—Atlanta 2. Left on bases—New York 3, Atlanta 9. Two-base hits—Carty, Millan, Gonzalez, H. Aaron, Garrett, Lum. Three-base hit—Harrelson. Home runs—Gonzalez, H. Aaron. Stolen bases—Cepeda, Jones. Sacrifice fly—Boyer. Hit by pitcher—By Seaver (Cepeda). Passed balls—Didier, Grote. Umpires—Barlick, Donatelli, Sudol, Vargo, Pelekoudas and Steiner. Time of game—2:37. Attendance—50,122.

GAME OF SUNDAY, OCTOBER 5, AT ATLANTA

New York	AB.	R.	H.	RBI.	PO.	A.
Agee, cf	4	3	2	2	3	0
Garrett, 3b	5	1	2	1	0	1
Jones, lf	5	2	3	3	3	0
Shamsky, rf	5	1	3	1	0	0
Gaspar, pr-rf	0	0	0	0	2	0
Boswell, 2b	5	1	1	2	2	1
McGraw, p	0	0	0	0	0	0
Kranepool, 1b	4	0	1	1	9	0
Grote, c	5	1	0	0	9	0
Harrelson, ss	5	1	1	1	2	2
Koosman, p	2	1	0	0	0	1
Taylor, p	0	0	0	0	0	0
Martin, ph	1	0	0	0	0	0
Weis, 2b	1	0	0	0	0	2
Totals	42	11	13	11	27	7

Atlanta	AB.	R.	H.	RBI.	PO.	A.
Millan, 2b	2	1	2	0	0	5
Gonzalez, cf	4	1	1	0	2	0
H. Aaron, rf	5	1	1	3	3	0
Carty, lf	4	2	1	0	1	0
Cepeda, 1b	4	1	2	1	8	0
Boyer, 3b	4	0	1	2	1	2
Didier, c	4	0	0	0	12	1
Garrido, ss	4	0	1	0	0	0
Reed, p	0	0	0	0	0	1
Doyle, p	0	0	0	0	0	0
Pappas, p	1	0	0	0	0	0
T. Aaron, ph	1	0	0	0	0	0
Britton, p	0	0	0	0	0	0
Upshaw, p	1	0	0	0	0	0
Aspromonte, ph	1	0	0	0	0	0
Neibauer, p	0	0	0	0	0	0
Totals	35	6	9	6	27	9

```
New York .......................... 1   3   2     2   1   0     2   0   0 — 11
Atlanta ............................ 0   0   0     1   5   0     0   0   0 —  6
```

New York	IP.	H.	R.	ER.	BB.	SO.
Koosman	4⅔	7	6	6	4	5
Taylor (Winner)	1⅓	1	0	0	0	2
McGraw (Save)	3	1	0	0	1	1

Atlanta	IP.	H.	R.	ER.	BB.	SO.
Reed (Loser)	1⅔	5	4	4	3	3
Doyle	1	2	2	0	1	3
Pappas	2⅓	4	3	3	0	4
Britton	⅓	0	0	0	1	0
Upshaw	2⅔	2	2	2	1	1
Neibauer	1	0	0	0	0	0

Errors—H. Aaron, Cepeda, Harrelson, Boyer. Double plays—New York 2, Atlanta 1. Left on bases—New York 10, Atlanta 7. Two-base hits—Jones, Harrelson, Carty, Garrett, Cepeda. Home runs—Agee, Boswell, H. Aaron, Jones. Stolen bases—Agee 2, Garrett, Jones. Umpires—Donatelli, Sudol, Vargo, Pelekoudas, Steiner and Barlick. Time of game—3:10. Attendance—50,270.

GAME OF MONDAY, OCTOBER 6, AT NEW YORK

Atlanta	AB.	R.	H.	RBI.	PO.	A.
Millan, 2b	5	0	0	0	0	2
Gonzalez, cf	5	1	2	0	1	0
H. Aaron, rf	4	1	2	2	0	1
Carty, lf	3	1	1	0	2	0
Cepeda, 1b	3	1	2	2	7	1
Boyer, 3b	4	0	0	0	1	1
Didier, c	3	0	0	0	7	0
Lum, ph	1	0	1	0	0	0
Jackson, ss	0	0	0	0	0	0
Garrido, ss	2	0	0	0	2	1
Alou, ph	1	0	0	0	0	0
Tillman, c	0	0	0	0	2	0
Jarvis, p	2	0	0	0	1	2
Stone, p	1	0	0	0	1	1
Upshaw, p	0	0	0	0	0	0
Aspromonte, ph	1	0	0	0	0	0
Totals	35	4	8	4	24	9

New York	AB.	R.	H.	RBI.	PO.	A.
Agee, cf	5	1	3	2	4	0
Garrett, 3b	4	1	1	2	0	3
Jones, lf	4	1	2	0	3	0
Shamsky, rf	4	1	1	0	1	0
Gaspar, pr-rf	0	0	0	0	0	0
Boswell, 2b	4	1	3	3	1	0
Weis, 2b	0	0	0	0	0	0
Kranepool, 1b	4	0	1	0	7	1
Grote, c	4	1	1	0	8	0
Harrelson, ss	3	0	0	0	2	3
Gentry, p	0	0	0	0	0	0
Ryan, p	4	1	2	0	1	0
Totals	36	7	14	7	27	7

```
Atlanta ........................... 2   0   0     0   2   0     0   0   0 — 4
New York ......................... 0   0   1     2   3   1     0   0   x — 7
```

Atlanta	IP.	H.	R.	ER.	BB.	SO.
Jarvis (Loser)	4⅓	10	6	6	0	6
Stone	1	2	1	1	0	0
Upshaw	2⅔	2	0	0	0	2

New York	IP.	H.	R.	ER.	BB.	SO.
Gentry	2*	5	2	2	1	1
Ryan (Winner)	7	3	2	2	2	7

*Pitched to three batters in third.

Error—Millan. Double play—Atlanta 1. Left on bases—Atlanta 7, New York 6. Two-base hits—Cepeda, Agee, H. Aaron, Kranepool, Jones, Grote. Home runs—H. Aaron, Agee, Boswell, Cepeda, Garrett. Sacrifice hit—Harrelson. Umpires—Sudol, Vargo, Pelekoudas, Steiner, Barlick and Donatelli. Time of game—2:24. Attendance—53,195.

NEW YORK METS' BATTING AND FIELDING AVERAGES

Player–Position	G.	AB.	R.	H.	TB.	2B.	3B.	HR.	RBI.	B.A.	PO.	A.	E.	F.A.
Shamsky, rf	3	13	3	7	7	0	0	0	1	.538	3	0	0	1.000
Ryan, p	1	4	1	2	2	0	0	0	0	.500	1	0	0	1.000
Martin, ph	2	2	0	1	1	0	0	0	2	.500	0	0	0	.000
Jones, lf	3	14	4	6	11	2	0	1	4	.429	11	0	0	1.000
Garrett, 3b	3	13	3	5	10	2	0	1	3	.385	1	6	0	1.000
Agee, cf	3	14	4	5	12	1	0	2	4	.357	9	0	0	1.000
Boswell, 2b	3	12	4	4	10	0	0	2	5	.333	3	2	1	.833
Kranepool, 1b	3	12	2	3	4	1	0	0	1	.250	20	3	0	1.000
Harrelson, ss	3	11	2	2	5	1	1	0	3	.182	6	6	1	.923
Grote, c	3	12	3	2	3	1	0	0	1	.167	22	1	0	1.000
Gaspar, rf-pr	3	0	0	0	0	0	0	0	0	.000	2	0	0	1.000
McGraw, p	1	0	0	0	0	0	0	0	0	.000	0	0	0	.000
Gentry, p	1	0	0	0	0	0	0	0	0	.000	0	0	0	.000
Taylor, p	2	0	0	0	0	0	0	0	0	.000	1	0	0	1.000
Weis, pr-2b	3	1	0	0	0	0	0	0	0	.000	1	3	0	1.000
Koosman, p	1	2	1	0	0	0	0	0	0	.000	0	1	0	1.000
Seaver, p	1	3	0	0	0	0	0	0	0	.000	1	1	0	1.000
Totals	3	113	27	37	65	8	1	6	24	.327	81	23	2	.981

ATLANTA BRAVES' BATTING AND FIELDING AVERAGES

Player–Position	G.	AB.	R.	H.	TB.	2B.	3B.	HR.	RBI.	B.A.	PO.	A.	E.	F.A.
Lum, lf-ph	2	2	0	2	3	1	0	0	0	1.000	0	0	0	.000
Cepeda, 1b	3	11	2	5	10	2	0	1	3	.455	29	1	2	.938
H. Aaron, rf	3	14	3	5	16	2	0	3	7	.357	4	1	1	.833
Gonzalez, cf	3	14	4	5	9	1	0	1	2	.357	3	1	1	.800
Millan, 2b	3	12	2	4	5	1	0	0	0	.333	3	9	1	.923
Carty, lf	3	10	4	3	5	2	0	0	0	.300	3	0	0	1.000
Garrido, ss	3	10	0	2	2	0	0	0	0	.200	4	8	0	1.000
Boyer, 3b	3	9	0	1	1	0	0	0	3	.111	4	8	1	.923
Tillman, c	1	0	0	0	0	0	0	0	0	.000	2	0	0	1.000
Reed, p	1	0	0	0	0	0	0	0	0	.000	0	1	0	1.000
Jackson, ss	1	0	0	0	0	0	0	0	0	.000	0	0	0	.000
Doyle, p	1	0	0	0	0	0	0	0	0	.000	0	0	0	.000
Britton, p	1	0	0	0	0	0	0	0	0	.000	0	0	0	.000
Neibauer, p	1	0	0	0	0	0	0	0	0	.000	0	0	0	.000
Stone, p	1	1	0	0	0	0	0	0	0	.000	1	1	0	1.000
Upshaw, p	1	1	0	0	0	0	0	0	0	.000	0	1	0	1.000
T. Aaron, ph	1	1	0	0	0	0	0	0	0	.000	0	0	0	.000
Alou, ph	1	1	0	0	0	0	0	0	0	.000	0	0	0	.000
Pappas, p	1	1	0	0	0	0	0	0	0	.000	0	0	0	.000
Jarvis, p	1	2	0	0	0	0	0	0	0	.000	1	2	0	1.000
Aspromonte, ph	3	3	0	0	0	0	0	0	0	.000	0	0	0	.000
Niekro, p	1	3	0	0	0	0	0	0	0	.000	0	3	0	1.000
Didier, c	3	11	0	0	0	0	0	0	0	.000	24	1	0	1.000
Totals	3	106	15	27	51	9	0	5	15	.255	78	37	6	.950

NEW YORK METS' PITCHING RECORDS

Pitcher	G.	GS.	CG.	IP.	H.	R.	ER.	BB.	SO.	HB.	WP.	W.	L.	Pct.	ERA.
Taylor	2	0	0	3⅓	3	0	0	4	0	0	1	0	1.000	0.00
McGraw	1	0	0	3	1	0	0	1	1	0	0	0	0	.000	0.00
Ryan	1	0	0	7	3	2	2	2	7	0	0	1	0	1.000	2.57
Seaver	1	1	0	7	8	5	5	3	2	1	0	1	0	1.000	6.43
Gentry	1	1	0	2	5	2	2	1	1	0	0	0	0	.000	9.00
Koosman	1	1	0	4⅔	7	6	6	4	5	0	0	0	0	.000	11.57
Totals	3	3	0	27	27	15	15	11	20	1	0	3	0	1.000	5.00

Saves—Taylor, McGraw. No shutouts.

ATLANTA BRAVES' PITCHING RECORDS

Pitcher	G.	GS.	CG.	IP.	H.	R.	ER.	BB.	SO.	HB.	WP.	W.	L.	Pct.	ERA.
Neibauer	1	0	0	1	0	0	0	0	1	0	0	0	0	.000	0.00
Doyle	1	0	0	1	2	2	0	1	3	0	0	0	0	.000	0.00
Britton	1	0	0	⅓	0	0	0	1	0	0	0	0	0	.000	0.00
Upshaw	3	0	0	6⅓	5	2	2	1	4	0	0	0	0	.000	2.84
Niekro	1	1	0	8	9	9	4	4	4	0	0	0	1	.000	4.50
Stone	1	0	0	1	2	1	1	0	0	0	0	0	0	.000	9.00
Pappas	1	0	0	2⅓	4	3	3	0	4	0	0	0	0	.000	11.57
Jarvis	1	1	0	4⅓	6	6	6	0	6	0	0	0	1	.000	12.46
Reed	1	1	0	1⅔	5	4	4	3	3	0	0	0	1	.000	21.60
Totals	3	3	0	26	37	27	20	10	25	0	0	0	3	.000	6.92

No shutouts or saves.

COMPOSITE SCORE BY INNINGS

New York	1	5	3	6	4	1	2	5	0	–	27
Atlanta	2	1	2	1	8	0	1	0	0	–	15

Sacrifice hit—Harrelson.
Sacrifice fly—Boyer.
Stolen bases—Cepeda, Jones 2, Garrett, Agee 2.
Caught stealing—Kranepool.
Double plays—Garrido, Millan and Cepeda; Upshaw, Garrido and Cepeda; Didier and Boyer; Javis and Garrido; Harrelson, Boswell and Kranepool; Weis, Harrelson and Kranepool.
Hit by pitcher—By Seaver (Cepeda).
Passed balls—Didier, Grote.
Balks—None.
Left on bases—New York 19—3, 10, 6; Atlanta 23—9, 7, 7.
Time of games—First game, 2:37; second game, 3:10; third game, 2:24.
Attendance—First game, 50,122; second game, 50,270; third game, 53,195.
Umpires—Barlick, Donatelli, Sudol, Vargo, Pelekoudas, and Steiner.
Official scorers—Jack Lang, Long Island Press; Wayne Minshew, Atlanta Constitution.

AMERICAN LEAGUE
Championship Series of 1970

	W.	L.	Pct.
Baltimore (East)	3	0	1.000
Minnesota (West)	0	3	.000

Sweeping success was once more the name of the game for the Baltimore Orioles in the 1970 American League Championship Series.

And for the Minnesota Twins, it was again dismal defeat in three games.

For Manager Earl Weaver's Baltimore brigade, which won a total of 217 games in two seasons, the playoff sweep was a continuation of their winning ways in the regular A. L. campaign, which finished with 11 consecutive victories.

The Twins enjoyed the lead only once, a 1-0 edge in the first inning of the opening game. Their only tie was forged one inning later. At all other points, the Baltimore behemoths dominated action.

Mike Cuellar, half of Baltimore's 24-win duo, received the Oriole opening game assignment in the Twin Cities. Although staked to an early 9-3 lead, the Cuban lefthander was unable to attain maximum efficiency on the cool and windy afternoon and departed in the fifth inning. Dick Hall, 40-year-old relief specialist, allowed only one hit in the final 4⅔ innings to pick up the victory.

With the teams deadlocked, 2-2, the Orioles put the game beyond Minnesota reach in the fourth inning, aided considerably by Cuellar's bat and the lusty blasts of a strong wind blowing across Metropolitan Stadium from right field.

Two singles and Brooks Robinson's sacrifice fly produced one fourth-inning run off Jim Perry, the Twins' 24-game winner, and the Orioles then loaded the bases with one out.

The lefthanded-hitting Cuellar, with an .089 batting average and seven RBIs to show for his season's efforts, then pulled a Perry pitch toward foul territory in right field. As the ball passed first base it was patently foul, maybe as much as 15 feet. Cuellar, himself stood transfixed at the plate, watching the pellet transcribe a high parabola in the direction of the right field seats.

As the ball soared into the 29-mile-an-hour current, however, it started drifting toward fair territory. Cuellar started jogging from the plate. By the time he arrived at first base, the wind had worked its deviltry against the home forces, depositing the ball over the fence in fair territory, and giving Cuellar a grand slam homer.

Before the inning was completed, Don Buford cuffed Perry for a knock-out homer and Bill Zepp yielded a left-field round-tripper to southpaw-swinging Boog Powell to complete the seven-run outburst.

Dave McNally, who registered a ten-inning, 1-0 three-hitter in the second game of the 1969 playoffs, received the second-game assignment again and once more responded with victory, although with considerably more ease.

The Birds handed McNally a four-run cushion. Powell doubled home Mark Belanger in the first inning, Frank Robinson homered with Belanger aboard in the third and McNally himself singled home Andy Etchebarren in the fourth.

The Twins nearly erased that lead with two swings of the bat in their turn, Killebrew connecting for a homer after a pass to Leo Cardenas and Tony Oliva hitting a solo smash.

Stan Williams, following Tom Hall and Bill Zepp to the Twin mound, blanked Baltimore the next three frames and Ron Perranoski zeroed the visitors in the eighth before the East Division champs erupted for their second seven-run rally in the series.

McNally's bat ignited the conflagration with a wrong-field double and Dave Johnson concluded it with a three-run homer. All the Birds except Blair participated in the 13-hit feast, Belanger and Powell accounting for three apiece.

When the series shifted to Baltimore, October 5, Weaver called on his workhorse, Jim Palmer, to wrap it all up.

The big righthander, just ten days short of his twenty-fifth birthday and two years removed from an arm ailment that threatened his career, was razor-sharp, scattering seven hits.

In fairness, Palmer was entitled to a shutout. A brilliant sun blinded Frank Robinson while he was tracking down Cesar Tovar's fifth-inning fly that fell for a single. Cardenas' single produced a run, but that was all for the Twins.

A 20-game winner with a 2.71 ERA in regular play, Palmer set a personal career high of 12 strikeouts and issued only three walks.

He also laced a double and figured prominently in the second-inning Oriole run when his looper to short center field was misplayed for a two-base error. Palmer subsequently scored on Buford's double.

The Minnesota starting assignment went to Jim Kaat, a 14-game winner who had been handicapped by late-season arm miseries. The lefthander departed with none out in the third after yielding six hits. By that time the trend of the game had been established and three successors, while more effective, were helpless to change the outcome, the Birds cruising to an easy 6-1 victory.

Two singles, around a sacrifice, netted one Oriole run in the opening frame and Palmer made the score 2-0 in the second. A double by Brooks

Robinson and Johnson's single shelled Kaat in the third. With 19-year-old Bert Blyleven on duty, Etchebarren grounded to Cardenas. The shortstop's throw to the plate was in time, but Robbie's crunching slide dislodged the ball from Paul Ratliff's mitt. Palmer's double made the score, 4-0, and Buford's sacrifice fly plated a fifth run.

Johnson's second homer of the series concluded the scoring in the seventh inning.

GAME OF SATURDAY, OCTOBER 3, AT MINNESOTA

Baltimore	AB.	R.	H.	RBI.	PO.	A.
Buford, lf	3	1	1	1	0	0
Blair, cf	5	0	0	0	3	0
Powell, 1b	5	1	2	2	10	1
F. Robinson, rf	4	1	1	0	0	0
Hendricks, c	5	2	2	0	5	0
B. Robinson, 3b	3	1	3	1	2	1
Johnson, 2b	3	1	1	0	4	2
Belanger, ss	4	1	1	1	2	5
Cuellar, p	2	1	1	4	1	3
Hall, p	2	1	1	0	0	0
Totals	36	10	13	9	27	12

Minnesota	AB.	R.	H.	RBI.	PO.	A.
Tovar, cf-2b	5	1	2	1	1	0
Cardenas, ss	4	0	0	0	2	5
Killebrew, 3b	5	1	2	2	1	1
Oliva, rf	4	1	3	0	3	0
Alyea, lf	3	1	0	0	0	0
Reese, 1b	4	0	0	0	10	1
Mitterwald, c	4	2	3	2	7	1
Thompson, 2b	3	0	1	0	1	3
Williams, p	0	0	0	0	0	0
Holt, ph-cf	1	0	0	0	0	0
Perry, p	1	0	0	1	1	0
Zepp, p	0	0	0	0	0	0
Allison, ph	1	0	0	0	0	0
Woodson, p	0	0	0	0	1	1
Quilici, 2b	1	0	0	0	0	0
Carew, ph	1	0	0	0	0	0
Perranoski, p	0	0	0	0	0	0
Totals	37	6	11	6	27	12

Baltimore	0	2	0	7	0	1	0	0	0 – 10
Minnesota	1	1	0	1	3	0	0	0	0 – 6

Baltimore	IP.	H.	R.	ER.	BB.	SO.
Cuellar	4⅓	10	6	6	1	2
Hall (Winner)	4⅔	1	0	0	0	3

Minnesota	IP.	H.	R.	ER.	BB.	SO.
Perry (Loser)	3⅓	8	8	7	1	1
Zepp	⅔	1	1	1	0	2
Woodson	1*	2	1	1	1	0
Williams	3	2	0	0	1	1
Perranoski	1	0	0	0	0	2

*Pitched to two batters in sixth.

Errors—Thompson, Killebrew. Double plays—Baltimore 1, Minnesota 3. Left on bases—Baltimore 4, Minnesota 6. Two-base hits—Thompson, Oliva 2, B. Robinson. Home runs—Cuellar, Buford, Powell, Killebrew. Sacrifice hit—Cardenas. Sacrifice fly—B. Robinson. Hit by pitcher—By Perry (Johnson). Umpires—Stevens, Deegan, Satchell and Berry. Time—2:36. Attendance—26,847.

GAME OF SUNDAY, OCTOBER 4, AT MINNESOTA

Baltimore	AB.	R.	H.	RBI.	PO.	A.
Belanger, ss	4	3	3	0	1	5
Blair, cf	4	0	0	0	0	0
F. Robinson, rf	3	2	1	2	1	0
Powell, 1b	5	1	3	3	9	0
Rettenmund, lf	3	1	1	1	3	1
B. Robinson, 3b	5	1	1	0	1	4
Johnson, 2b	5	1	1	3	5	1
Etchebarren, c	5	1	1	0	7	0
McNally, p	5	1	2	1	0	0
Totals	39	11	13	10	27	11

Minnesota	AB.	R.	H.	RBI.	PO.	A.
Tovar, cf-lf	4	0	1	0	2	0
Cardenas, ss	3	1	1	0	4	3
Killebrew, 1b	3	1	1	2	7	0
Oliva, rf	4	1	1	1	4	2
Alyea, lf	3	0	0	0	0	0
Holt, pr-cf	0	0	0	0	0	0
Mitterwald, c	4	0	1	0	9	0
Renick, 3b	4	0	1	0	1	3
Thompson, 2b	4	0	0	0	0	0
Hall, p	1	0	0	0	0	0
Zepp, p	0	0	0	0	0	0
Williams, p	0	0	0	0	0	0
Allison, ph	0	0	0	0	0	0
Perranoski, p	0	0	0	0	0	1
Tiant, p	0	0	0	0	0	0
Quilici, ph	1	0	0	0	0	0
Totals	31	3	6	3	27	9

Baltimore	1	0	2	1	0	0	0	0	7 – 11
Minnesota	0	0	0	3	0	0	0	0	0 – 3

Baltimore	IP.	H.	R.	ER.	BB.	SO.
McNally (Winner)	9	6	3	3	5	5

Minnesota	IP.	H.	R.	ER.	BB.	SO.
Hall (Loser)	3⅓	6	4	4	3	4
Zepp	⅔*	1	0	0	2	0
Williams	3	0	0	0	0	1
Perranoski	1⅓	5	5	5	1	1
Tiant	⅔	1	2	1	0	0

*Pitched to three batters in fifth.

Errors—Cardenas 2. Double plays—Baltimore 1, Minnesota 2. Left on bases—Baltimore 7, Minnesota 6. Two-base hits—Powell 2, Mitterwald, McNally. Home runs—F. Robinson, Killebrew, Oliva, Johnson. Stolen base—Rettenmund. Umpires—Haller, Odom, Neudecker, Honochick, Goetz and Springstead. Time—2:59. Attendance—27,490.

GAME OF MONDAY, OCTOBER 5, AT BALTIMORE

Minnesota	AB.	R.	H.	RBI.	PO.	A.
Tovar, lf	4	1	2	0	3	0
Cardenas, ss	4	0	1	1	0	3
Oliva, rf	4	0	2	0	3	0
Killebrew, 3b	3	0	0	0	0	3
Holt, cf	4	0	0	0	3	0
Ratliff, c	4	0	1	0	7	0
Reese, 1b	3	0	1	0	6	1
Tiant, pr	0	0	0	0	0	0
Thompson, 2b	1	0	0	0	1	0
Allison, ph	1	0	0	0	0	0
Quilici, 2b	0	0	0	0	0	0
Alyea, ph	1	0	0	0	0	0
Kaat, p	1	0	0	0	0	0
Blyleven, p	0	0	0	0	1	0
Manuel, ph	1	0	0	0	0	0
Hall, p	0	0	0	0	0	0
Carew, ph	1	0	0	0	0	0
Perry, p	0	0	0	0	0	0
Renick, ph	1	0	0	0	0	0
Totals	33	1	7	1	24	7

Baltimore	AB.	R.	H.	RBI.	PO.	A.
Buford, lf	4	1	2	2	2	0
Blair, cf	4	0	1	0	1	0
F. Robinson, rf	3	0	0	0	1	0
Powell, 1b	4	0	1	1	5	0
B. Robinson, 3b	4	1	3	0	0	0
Johnson, 2b	3	2	2	1	2	1
Etchebarren, c	4	0	0	0	12	0
Belanger, ss	4	1	0	0	3	4
Palmer, p	4	1	1	1	1	1
Totals	34	6	10	5	27	6

Minnesota	0	0	0	0	1	0	0	0	0 – 1
Baltimore	1	3	0	0	0	1	0	x – 6

Minnesota	IP.	H.	R.	ER.	BB.	SO.
Kaat (Loser)	2*	6	4	2	2	1
Blyleven	2	2	1	0	0	2
Hall	2	0	0	0	1	2
Perry	2	2	1	1	0	2

Baltimore	IP.	H.	R.	ER.	BB.	SO.
Palmer (Winner)	9	7	1	1	3	12

*Pitched to two batters in third.

Errors—Holt, Ratliff. Double play—Baltimore 1. Left on bases—Minnesota 8, Baltimore 9. Two-base hits—Buford, B. Robinson, Palmer. Three-base hit—Tovar. Home run—Johnson. Sacrifice hit—Blair. Sacrifice fly—Buford. Umpires—Odom, Neudecker, Springstead, Honochick, Haller and Goetz. Time—2:20. Attendance—27,608.

BALTIMORE ORIOLES' BATTING AND FIELDING AVERAGES

Player—Position	G.	AB.	R.	H.	TB.	2B.	3B.	HR.	RBI.	B.A.	PO.	A.	E.	F.A.
B. Robinson, 3b	3	12	3	7	9	2	0	0	1	.583	3	5	0	1.000
Cuellar, p	1	2	1	1	4	0	0	1	4	.500	1	3	0	1.000
R. Hall, p	1	2	1	1	1	0	0	0	0	.500	0	0	0	.000
Powell, 1b	3	14	2	6	11	2	0	1	6	.429	24	1	0	1.000
Buford, lf	2	7	2	3	7	1	0	1	3	.429	2	0	0	1.000
Hendricks, c	1	5	2	2	2	0	0	0	0	.400	5	0	0	1.000
McNally, p	1	5	1	2	3	1	0	0	1	.400	0	0	0	.000
Johnson, 2b	3	11	4	4	10	0	0	2	4	.364	11	4	0	1.000
Belanger, ss	3	12	5	4	4	0	0	0	1	.333	6	14	0	1.000
Rettenmund, lf	1	3	1	1	1	0	0	0	1	.333	3	1	0	1.000
Palmer, p	1	4	1	1	2	1	0	0	1	.250	1	1	0	1.000
F. Robinson, rf	3	10	3	2	5	0	0	1	2	.200	2	0	0	1.000
Etchebarren, c	2	9	1	1	1	0	0	0	0	.111	19	0	0	1.000
Blair, cf	3	13	0	1	1	0	0	0	0	.077	4	0	0	1.000
Totals	3	109	27	36	61	7	0	6	24	.330	81	29	0	1.000

MINNESOTA TWINS' BATTING AND FIELDING AVERAGES

Player–Position	G.	AB.	R.	H.	TB.	2B.	3B.	HR.	RBI.	B.A.	PO.	A.	E.	F.A.
Oliva, rf	3	12	2	6	11	2	0	1	1	.500	10	2	0	1.000
Mitterwald, c	2	8	2	4	5	1	0	0	2	.500	16	1	0	1.000
Tovar, cf-2b-lf	3	13	2	5	7	0	1	0	1	.385	6	0	0	1.000
Killebrew, 3b-1b	3	11	2	3	9	0	0	2	4	.273	8	4	1	.923
Ratliff, c	1	4	0	1	1	0	0	0	0	.250	7	0	1	.875
Renick, 3b-ph	2	5	0	1	1	0	0	0	0	.200	1	3	0	1.000
Cardenas, ss	3	11	1	2	2	0	0	0	1	.182	6	11	2	.895
Reese, 1b	2	7	0	1	1	0	0	0	0	.143	16	2	0	1.000
Thompson, 2b	3	8	0	1	2	1	0	0	0	.125	2	3	1	.833
Blyleven, p	1	0	0	0	0	0	0	0	0	.000	1	0	0	1.000
Perranoski, p	2	0	0	0	0	0	0	0	0	.000	0	1	0	1.000
Tiant, p-pr	2	0	0	0	0	0	0	0	0	.000	0	0	0	.000
Williams, p	2	0	0	0	0	0	0	0	0	.000	0	0	0	.000
Woodson, p	1	0	0	0	0	0	0	0	0	.000	0	0	0	.000
Zepp, p	2	0	0	0	0	0	0	0	0	.000	0	0	0	.000
T. Hall, p	2	1	0	0	0	0	0	0	0	.000	0	0	0	.000
Kaat, p	1	1	0	0	0	0	0	0	0	.000	0	0	0	.000
Manuel, ph	1	1	0	0	0	0	0	0	0	.000	0	0	0	.000
Perry, p	2	1	0	0	0	0	0	0	1	.000	1	0	0	1.000
Allison, ph	3	2	0	0	0	0	0	0	0	.000	0	0	0	.000
Carew, ph	2	2	0	0	0	0	0	0	0	.000	0	0	0	.000
Quilici, 2b-ph	3	2	0	0	0	0	0	0	0	.000	1	1	0	1.000
Holt, ph-cf-pr	3	5	0	0	0	0	0	0	0	.000	3	0	1	.750
Alyea, lf-ph	3	7	1	0	0	0	0	0	0	.000	0	0	0	.000
Totals	3	101	10	24	39	4	1	3	10	.238	78	28	6	.946

BALTIMORE ORIOLES' PITCHING RECORDS

Pitcher	G.	GS.	CG.	IP.	H.	R.	ER.	BB.	SO.	HB.	WP.	W.	L.	Pct.	ERA.
R. Hall	1	0	0	4⅔	1	0	0	3	0	0	1	0		1.000	0.00
Palmer	1	1	1	9	7	1	1	3	12	0	0	1	0	1.000	1.00
McNally	1	1	1	9	6	3	3	5	5	0	0	1	0	1.000	3.00
Cuellar	1	1	0	4⅓	10	6	6	1	2	0	0	0	0	.000	12.46
Totals	3	3	2	27	24	10	10	9	22	0	0	3	0	1.000	3.33

No shutouts or saves.

MINNESOTA TWINS' PITCHING RECORDS

Pitcher	G.	GS.	CG.	IP.	H.	R.	ER.	BB.	SO.	HB.	WP.	W.	L.	Pct.	ERA.
Williams	2	0	0	6	2	0	0	1	2	0	0	0	0	.000	0.00
Blyleven	1	0	0	2	2	1	0	0	2	0	0	0	0	.000	0.00
T. Hall	2	1	0	5⅓	6	4	4	4	6	0	0	0	1	.000	6.75
Zepp	2	0	0	1⅓	2	1	1	2	2	0	0	0	0	.000	6.75
Kaat	1	1	0	2	6	4	2	2	1	0	0	0	1	.000	9.00
Woodson	1	0	0	1	2	1	1	1	0	0	0	0	0	.000	9.00
Perry	2	1	0	5⅓	10	9	8	1	3	1	0	0	1	.000	13.50
Tiant	1	0	0	⅔	1	2	1	0	0	0	0	0	0	.000	13.50
Perranoski	2	0	0	2⅓	5	5	5	1	3	0	0	0	0	.000	19.29
Totals	3	3	0	26	36	27	22	12	19	1	0	0	3	.000	7.62

No shutouts or saves.

COMPOSITE SCORE BY INNINGS

Baltimore	2	3	5	8	0	1	1	0	7 – 27
Minnesota	1	1	0	4	4	0	0	0	0 – 10

Sacrifice hits–Cardenas, Blair.
Sacrifice flies–B. Robinson, Buford.
Stolen base–Rettenmund.
Caught stealing–None.
Double plays–Johnson, Belanger and Powell 2; Belanger, Johnson and Powell; Thompson, Cardenas and Reese; Reese, Mitterwald and Reese; Cardenas, Quilici and Reese; Oliva and Mitterwald; Perranoski, Cardenas and Killebrew.
Hit by pitcher–By Perry (Johnson).
Passed balls–None.
Balks–None.
Left on bases–Baltimore 20–4, 7, 9; Minnesota 20–6, 6, 8.
Time of games–First game, 2:36; second game, 2:59; third game, 2:20.
Attendance–First game, 26,847; second game, 27,490; third game, 27,608.
Umpires–Stevens, Deegan, Satchell and Berry (first game); Haller, Odom, Neudecker, Honochick, Goetz and Springstead (second and third games).
Official scorers–Tom Briere, Minneapolis Tribune; Phil Jackman, Baltimore Evening Sun.

NATIONAL LEAGUE
Championship Series of 1970

	W.	L.	Pct.
Cincinnati (West)	3	0	1.000
Pittsburgh (East)	0	3	.000

A potent attack and a question-mark pitching staff. That was the consensus view of the Cincinnati Reds as the 1970 National League Championship Series began in Pittsburgh's Three Rivers Stadium October 3. Two days later, it was all over. The Reds reigned as National League champions, but not because of their menacing bats. It was that shaky pitching staff which carried the Reds to three successive victories over the Pirates.

Cincinnati sluggers had whacked 191 home runs in cruising to the West Division title by 14½ games. East Division champ Pittsburgh wasn't that easy for the Reds, despite their three-game sweep. The Reds had all they could handle in each conquest, particularly the finale, in which the Pirates repeatedly threatened but could not deliver.

Cincinnati boasted dual heroes in subduing the Pirates, 3-0, in 10 innings in the playoff opener. Gary Nolan, an 18-game winner during the regular season, pitched nine shutout innings to edge Dock Ellis. Nolan departed for pinch-hitter Ty Cline in the 10th, which turned out to be a stroke of genius by Red Manager Sparky Anderson. Cline socked a triple to lead off the inning. He scored the decisive run on Pete Rose's single, and Lee May doubled to provide two insurance tallies, sealing Ellis' fate. Reliever Clay Carroll protected Nolan's victory by holding Pittsburgh hitless in the 10th.

Another key contributor to the Reds' opening triumph was second baseman Tommy Helms. With Pirate runners on second and third and two out in the third inning, Dave Cash rifled a shot to Helms' right. Tommy's diving stop and quick throw to first prevented two Buc runs.

Four minor league umpires worked the opener while the regularly assigned arbiters (and several others) picketed the Pittsburgh park. The umps were striking for higher pay in the pennant playoffs and World Series. An hour before game two was scheduled to start, the striking umps reached an agreement with the major leagues and returned to work.

The Reds didn't cut it quite as close in game two. They led from the third inning on, but never by much, in posting a 3-1 victory. Pittsburgh's chief tormentors in this one were Bobby Tolan, the swift center fielder, and Don Gullett, 19-year-old fireballing reliever.

Tolan was a complete mystery to Buc starter Luke Walker. Bobby began his three-hit salvo with a single in the third inning. He stole second base and wound up at third on catcher Manny Sanguillen's wild peg into center field. Walker's wild pitch permitted Tolan to score. Bobby delivered his kayo punch in the fifth, belting a home run over the wall in right-center, and capped his big day with a single off reliever Dave Giusti in the eighth.

Lefty Jim Merritt, Cincinnati's lone 20-game winner, was the second-game starter. Arm trouble had kept Merritt on the shelf in the closing weeks of the regular season, but Manager Anderson had precedent going for him in this case. Merritt had beaten the Pirates six times in six starts over a two-year period. He made it seven for seven by lasting 5⅓ innings this time. Carroll relieved Merritt in the sixth, but gave up two hits and had retired only one batter when Anderson signaled for Gullett.

That did it. Gullett shut off the Pirate threat immediately, striking out the side in the seventh and finishing with 3⅓ hitless rounds.

When the scene shifted to Cincinnati for game three, the Reds wrapped it up, 3-2, but not without a struggle. The Pirates scored a run in the first inning off Tony Cloninger, who averted disaster three times before Anderson finally yanked him for a pinch-hitter in the fifth with the score 2-2.

The slugging Reds uncorked their only power show of the playoffs in the first inning, Tony Perez and Bench smacking successive homers off Bob Moose. Pirate starter Moose showed more courage than stuff in the early going. But he hung on and proceeded to halt the Reds until he had two out in the eighth. Then he walked pinch-hitter Cline and gave up a single to Rose.

With Tolan coming up, Pirate Manager Danny Murtaugh brought in lefty Joe Gibbon. Tolan whacked a single to left. Cline took off from second and sped for the plate. He arrived just a hair ahead of Willie Stargell's peg, and the Reds had a 3-2 lead.

The Reds had a pitching star in this one, too, young Milt Wilcox, who worked three shutout innings in relief of Cloninger and earned the victory. Wilcox vanished for pinch-hitter Cline in the eighth. Wayne Granger tried to protect the Reds' 3-2 lead in the ninth, but was removed with two down and a runner on first. Gullett was Anderson's choice to wrap it up. The teen-ager wasn't invincible this time, yielding a single to Stargell. But with runners on first and third, Al Oliver swung at Gullett's first pitch and grounded to Helms.

GAME OF SATURDAY, OCTOBER 3, AT PITTSBURGH

Cincinnati	AB.	R.	H.	RBI.	PO.	A.	Pittsburgh	AB.	R.	H.	RBI.	PO.	A.
Rose, rf	5	1	2	1	1	0	Alou, cf	3	0	2	0	4	0
Tolan, cf	5	0	1	0	2	0	Cash, 2b	5	0	0	0	3	3
Perez, 3b-1b	4	0	1	0	1	1	Clemente, rf	5	0	0	0	3	0
Bench, c	3	1	0	0	8	0	Stargell, lf	4	0	3	0	2	0
May, 1b	5	0	1	2	9	0	Jeter, pr-lf	1	0	0	0	2	0
Concepcion, pr-ss	0	0	0	0	0	0	Oliver, 1b	3	0	0	0	10	0
Carbo, lf	3	0	0	0	0	0	Sanguillen, c	4	0	1	0	2	0
McRae, ph	1	0	0	0	0	0	Hebner, 3b	4	0	2	0	0	2
Carroll, p	0	0	0	0	0	0	Alley, ss	3	0	0	0	4	3
Helms, 2b	4	0	2	0	5	5	Ellis, p	2	0	0	0	0	3
Woodward, ss-3b	4	0	0	0	4	4	Gibbon, p	0	0	0	0	0	0
Nolan, p	3	0	1	0	0	2	Totals	34	0	8	0	30	11
Cline, ph-lf	1	1	1	0	0	0							
Totals	38	3	9	3	30	15							

Cincinnati	0	0	0	0	0	0	0	0	0	3 – 3			
Pittsburgh	0	0	0	0	0	0	0	0	0	0 – 0			

Cincinnati	IP.	H.	R.	ER.	BB.	SO.
Nolan (Winner)	9	8	0	0	4	6
Carroll (Save)	1	0	0	0	0	2
Pittsburgh	IP.	H.	R.	ER.	BB.	SO.
Ellis (Loser)	9⅔	9	3	3	4	1
Gibbon	⅓	0	0	0	0	1

Errors—None. Double play—Pittsburgh 1. Left on bases—Cincinnati 9, Pittsburgh 10. Two-base hits—Alou, Perez, Stargell, May. Three-base hit—Cline. Sacrifice hits—Ellis 2. Umpires—Grimsley. Blandford, Morgenweck and Grygiel. Time—2:23. Attendance—33,088.

GAME OF SUNDAY, OCTOBER 4, AT PITTSBURGH

Cincinnati	AB.	R.	H.	RBI.	PO.	A.
Rose, rf	4	0	0	0	2	0
Tolan, cf	4	3	3	1	2	0
Perez, 3b	4	0	2	1	2	3
Concepcion, ss	0	0	0	0	1	1
Bench, c	3	0	0	0	5	0
May, 1b	4	0	1	0	10	0
McRae, lf	3	0	0	0	2	0
Carroll, p	0	0	0	0	0	0
Gullett, p	1	0	0	0	0	0
Helms, 2b	4	0	1	0	3	3
Woodward, ss-3b	3	0	1	0	0	2
Merritt, p	2	0	0	0	0	2
Stewart, lf	2	0	0	0	0	0
Totals	34	3	8	2	27	11

Pittsburgh	AB.	R.	H.	RBI.	PO.	A.
Alou, cf	4	0	0	0	1	0
Cash, 2b	3	1	1	0	3	5
Clemente, rf	4	0	1	1	2	0
Sanguillen, c	4	0	1	0	6	0
Robertson, 1b	4	0	1	0	11	1
Stargell, lf	4	0	0	0	1	0
Pagan, 3b	3	0	1	0	0	4
Alley, ss	4	0	0	0	2	4
Walker, p	2	0	0	0	0	0
Jeter, ph	1	0	0	0	0	0
Giusti, p	0	0	0	0	1	0
Totals	33	1	5	1	27	14

```
Cincinnati ............ 0   0  1   0  1  0   0  1  0 – 3
Pittsburgh ............ 0   0  0   0  0  1   0  0  0 – 1
```

Cincinnati	IP.	H.	R.	ER.	BB.	SO.
Merritt (Winner)	5⅓	3	1	1	0	2
Carroll	⅓	2	0	0	0	0
Gullett (Save)	3⅓	0	0	0	2	3

Pittsburgh	IP.	H.	R.	ER.	BB.	SO.
Walker (Loser)	7	5	2	1	1	5
Giusti	2	3	1	1	1	0

Errors—Walker, Perez, Sanguillen. Double plays—Pittsburgh 2. Left on bases—Cincinnati 6, Pittsburgh 7. Two-base hits—Robertson, Cash, Perez. Home run—Tolan. Stolen base—Tolan. Wild pitch—Walker. Umpires—Landes, Pryor, Harvey, Engel, Wendelstedt and Colosi. Time—2:10. Attendance—39,317.

GAME OF MONDAY, OCTOBER 5, AT CINCINNATI

Pittsburgh	AB.	R.	H.	RBI.	PO.	A.
Patek, ss	3	0	0	0	1	2
Robertson, ph	1	0	0	0	0	0
Alou, cf	5	1	1	0	1	0
Clemente, rf	5	1	2	0	2	0
Stargell, lf	4	0	3	1	1	0
Jeter, pr	0	0	0	0	0	0
Oliver, 1b	5	0	2	1	12	1
Sanguillen, c	4	0	0	0	5	1
Hebner, 3b	2	0	2	0	0	2
Mazeroski, 2b	2	0	0	0	1	4
Moose, p	4	0	0	0	1	2
Gibbon, p	0	0	0	0	0	0
Giusti, p	0	0	0	0	0	0
Totals	35	2	10	2	24	12

Cincinnati	AB.	R.	H.	RBI.	PO.	A.
Rose, rf	4	0	1	0	0	0
Tolan, cf	3	0	1	1	1	0
Perez, 3b	4	1	1	1	3	2
Granger, p	0	0	0	0	0	0
Gullett, p	0	0	0	0	0	0
Bench, c	3	1	2	1	7	0
May, 1b	3	0	0	0	12	1
Carbo, lf	3	0	0	0	0	0
Helms, 2b	3	0	0	0	3	4
Woodward, ss-3b	3	0	0	0	1	3
Cloninger, p	1	0	0	0	0	2
Bravo, ph	1	0	0	0	0	0
Wilcox, p	0	0	0	0	0	1
Cline, ph	0	1	0	0	0	0
Concepcion, ss	0	0	0	0	0	0
Totals	28	3	5	3	27	13

```
Pittsburgh ............ 1   0  0   0  1  0   0  0  0 – 2
Cincinnati ............ 2   0  0   0  0  0   0  1  x – 3
```

Pittsburgh	IP.	H.	R.	ER.	BB.	SO.
Moose (Loser)	7⅔	4	3	3	2	4
Gibbon	0*	1	0	0	0	0
Giusti	⅓	0	0	0	0	1

Cincinnati	IP.	H.	R.	ER.	BB.	SO.
Cloninger	5	7	2	2	4	1
Wilcox (Winner)	3	1	0	0	2	5
Granger	⅔	1	0	0	0	0
Gullett (Save)	⅓	1	0	0	0	0

*Pitched to one batter in eighth.

Errors—None. Double play—Cincinnati 1. Left on bases—Pittsburgh 12, Cincinnati 3. Two-base hits—Hebner 2. Home runs—Perez, Bench. Wild pitch—Cloninger. Umpires—Pryor, Harvey, Engel, Wendelstedt, Colosi and Landes. Time—2:38. Attendance—40,538.

CINCINNATI REDS' BATTING AND FIELDING AVERAGES

Player–Position	G.	AB.	R.	H.	TB.	2B.	3B.	HR.	RBI.	B.A.	PO.	A.	E.	F.A.
Cline, ph-lf	2	1	2	1	3	0	1	0	0	1.000	0	0	0	.000
Tolan, cf	3	12	3	5	8	0	0	1	2	.417	5	0	0	1.000
Perez, 3b-1b	3	12	1	4	9	2	0	1	2	.333	6	6	1	.923
Nolan, p	1	3	0	1	1	0	0	0	0	.333	0	2	0	1.000
Helms, 2b	3	11	0	3	3	0	0	0	0	.273	11	12	0	1.000
Rose, rf	3	13	1	3	3	0	0	0	1	.231	3	0	0	1.000
Bench, c	3	9	2	2	5	0	0	1	1	.222	20	3	0	1.000
May, 1b	3	12	0	2	3	1	0	0	2	.167	31	1	0	1.000
Woodward, ss-3b	3	10	0	1	1	0	0	0	0	.100	5	9	0	1.000
Carroll, p	2	0	0	0	0	0	0	0	0	.000	0	0	0	.000
Concepcion, pr-ss	3	0	0	0	0	0	0	0	0	.000	1	1	0	1.000
Granger, p	1	0	0	0	0	0	0	0	0	.000	0	0	0	.000
Wilcox, p	1	0	0	0	0	0	0	0	0	.000	0	1	0	1.000
Bravo, ph	1	0	0	0	0	0	0	0	0	.000	0	0	0	.000
Cloninger, p	1	1	0	0	0	0	0	0	0	.000	0	2	0	1.000
Gullett, p	2	1	0	0	0	0	0	0	0	.000	0	0	0	.000
Merritt, p	1	2	0	0	0	0	0	0	0	.000	0	2	0	1.000
Stewart, lf	1	2	0	0	0	0	0	0	0	.000	0	0	0	.000
McRae, ph-lf	2	4	0	0	0	0	0	0	0	.000	2	0	0	1.000
Carbo, lf	2	6	0	0	0	0	0	0	0	.000	0	0	0	.000
Totals	3	100	9	22	36	3	1	3	8	.220	84	39	1	.992

PITTSBURGH PIRATES' BATTING AND FIELDING AVERAGES

Player–Position	G.	AB.	R.	H.	TB.	2B.	3B.	HR.	RBI.	B.A.	PO.	A.	E.	F.A.
Hebner, 3b	2	6	0	4	6	2	0	0	0	.667	0	4	0	1.000
Stargell, lf	3	12	0	6	7	1	0	0	0	.500	4	0	0	1.000
Pagan, 3b	1	3	0	1	1	0	0	0	0	.333	0	4	0	1.000
Alou, cf	3	12	1	3	4	1	0	0	0	.250	6	0	0	1.000
Oliver, 1b	2	8	0	2	2	0	0	0	1	.250	22	1	0	1.000
Clemente, rf	3	14	1	3	3	0	0	0	1	.214	7	0	0	1.000
Robertson, 1b-ph	2	5	0	1	2	1	0	0	0	.200	11	1	0	1.000
Sanguillen, c	3	12	0	2	2	0	0	0	0	.167	13	1	1	.933
Cash, 2b	2	8	1	1	2	1	0	0	0	.125	6	8	0	1.000
Gibbon, p	2	0	0	0	0	0	0	0	0	.000	0	0	0	.000
Giusti, p	2	0	0	0	0	0	0	0	0	.000	1	0	0	1.000
Ellis, p	1	2	0	0	0	0	0	0	0	.000	0	3	0	1.000
Jeter, pr-lf-ph	3	2	0	0	0	0	0	0	0	.000	2	0	0	1.000
Mazeroski, 2b	1	2	0	0	0	0	0	0	0	.000	1	4	0	1.000
Walker, p	1	2	0	0	0	0	0	0	0	.000	0	0	1	.000
Patek, ss	1	3	0	0	0	0	0	0	0	.000	1	2	0	1.000
Moose, p	1	4	0	0	0	0	0	0	0	.000	1	2	0	1.000
Alley, ss	2	7	0	0	0	0	0	0	0	.000	6	7	0	1.000
Totals	3	102	3	23	29	6	0	0	3	.225	81	37	2	.983

CINCINNATI REDS' PITCHING RECORDS

Pitcher	G.	GS.	CG.	IP.	H.	R.	ER.	BB.	SO.	HB.	WP.	W.	L.	Pct.	ERA.
Nolan	1	1	0	9	8	0	0	4	6	0	0	1	0	1.000	0.00
Gullett	2	0	0	3⅔	1	0	0	2	3	0	0	0	0	.000	0.00
Wilcox	1	0	0	3	1	0	0	2	5	0	0	1	0	1.000	0.00
Carroll	2	0	0	1⅓	2	0	0	0	2	0	0	0	0	.000	0.00
Granger	1	0	0	⅔	1	0	0	0	0	0	0	0	0	.000	0.00
Merritt	1	1	0	5⅓	3	1	1	0	2	0	0	1	0	1.000	1.69
Cloninger	1	1	0	5	7	2	2	4	1	0	1	0	0	.000	3.60
Totals	3	3	0	28	23	3	3	12	19	0	1	3	0	1.00	0.96

Shutout–Nolan-Carroll (combined). Saves–Carroll, Gullett 2.

PITTSBURGH PIRATES' PITCHING RECORDS

Pitcher	G.	GS.	CG.	IP.	H.	R.	ER.	BB.	SO.	HB.	WP.	W.	L.	Pct.	ERA.
Gibbon	2	0	0	⅓	1	0	0	0	1	0	0	0	0	.000	0.00
Walker	1	1	0	7	5	2	1	1	5	0	0	0	1	.000	1.29
Ellis	1	1	0	9⅔	9	3	3	4	1	0	0	0	1	.000	2.79
Moose	1	1	0	7⅔	4	3	3	2	4	0	0	0	1	.000	3.52
Giusti	2	0	0	2⅓	3	1	1	1	1	0	1	0	0	.000	3.86
Totals	3	3	0	27	22	9	8	8	12	0	1	0	3	.000	2.67

No shutouts or saves.

COMPOSITE SCORE BY INNINGS

Cincinnati	2	0	1	0	1	0	0	2	0	3	– 9
Pittsburgh	1	0	0	0	1	1	0	0	0	0	– 3

Sacrifice hits—Ellis 2.
Stolen base—Tolan.
Caught stealing—Alou, Patek, Tolan.
Double plays—Alley, Cash and Oliver; Alley and Cash; Alley, Cash and Robertson; Perez, Helms and May.
Hit by pitchers—None.
Passed balls—None.
Balks—None.
Left on bases—Cincinnati 18—9, 6, 3; Pittsburgh 29—10, 7, 12.
Time of games—First game, 2:23; second game, 2:10; third game, 2:38.
Attendance—First game, 33,088; second game, 39,317; third game, 40,538.
Umpires—Grimsley, Blandford, Morgenweck and Grygiel (first game); Landes, Pryor, Harvey, Engel, Wendelstedt and Colosi (second and third games).
Official scorers—Charles Feeney, Pittsburgh Post-Gazette; Earl Lawson, Cincinnati Post and Times-Star.

AMERICAN LEAGUE
Championship Series of 1971

	W.	L.	Pct.
Baltimore (East)	3	0	1.000
Oakland (West)	0	3	.000

In 1971 the Orioles' victims were the Oakland A's, who had cruised to the West Division crown as impressively as the Orioles had shattered their Eastern rivals.

Oakland never was in it after seeing ace Vida Blue clubbed for four runs in the seventh inning of the opener October 3 in Baltimore. Blue went into that frame with a 3-1 lead. He emerged a 5-3 loser, and the A's might as well have capitulated then and there. They fell before Mike Cuellar, 5-1, the next day, and the day after that Jim Palmer killed them off, 5-3, in Oakland.

That made it nine victories in nine playoff games for the Orioles, starting in 1969, when they flattened the Minnesota Twins. The Twins came back for another dose of the same in 1970.

Baltimore entered the '71 playoffs with a pitching staff bristling with aces—four 20-game winners. The Orioles were the first to boast that kind of pitching firepower since the 1920 White Sox.

Dave McNally, Cuellar, Palmer and Pat Dobson were Manager Earl Weaver's 20-win artists. McNally defeated Blue in the playoff opener, Cuellar won the second game and Palmer the third. Dobson, despite his 20-8 record, delivered not a single pitch in the playoffs.

The Orioles fired a four-homer salvo, including two by Boog Powell, off Catfish Hunter in game two. Aside from that, Baltimore's noted sluggers were not devastating. Frank Robinson, longtime kingpin of the Oriole offense, made only one hit in 12 trips off Oakland pitching.

McNally, a 20-game winner for the fourth season in a row, survived a rocky start to win the opener. He trailed, 3-0, after 3½ innings, giving up three doubles and a triple. The A's had McNally tottering in the second. With two runs home, a runner on second and none out, second baseman Dick Green came to bat.

It was at this point that A's Manager Dick Williams made the first of several ultra-cautious moves which were to fuel criticism of his playoff strategy. He ordered Green to sacrifice, which put runner Dave Duncan on third with one out.

The next batter was Blue, whose bunting ability is well known. Vida tried to squeeze the run home, but the O's had guessed correctly on what was coming. McNally pitched out and Duncan was nailed in a rundown. Blue proceeded to strike out, and the A's splurge was over.

McNally gave up another run in the fourth, but that ended the A's scoring forays. Meanwhile, 24-game winner Blue yielded just one run and three hits the first six innings.

However, disaster overtook Vida in the very next frame. Frank Robinson led off with a walk and Powell struck out. Brooks Robinson's single sent F. Robby to second, after which Andy Etchebarren's fly to right advanced F. Robby to third.

Now there were runners on first and third with two down, and Blue appeared likely to quell the flurry without damage. After all, he'd beaten the O's twice in two tries during the season. And the next hitter was shortstop Mark Belanger, hardly a nemesis to any pitcher. But Belanger rifled a single to center to score F. Robby and ignite thunderous cheering from the crowd of 42,621.

Then Curt Motton, pinch-hitter hero of a '69 Oriole playoff victory over Minnesota, stepped up to bat for McNally. Curt slammed a double to the left field corner, plating B. Robby and tying the score. Center fielder Paul Blair followed with the blow that doomed Vida, a two-run double to left.

Reliever Eddie Watt blanked the A's the last two innings and Oakland was one game down. Skipper Williams was subjected to further sharpshooting for his failure to remove Blue, or even visit the mound, during the seventh-inning barrage.

Next day, the A's put it to 20-game winner Hunter to stop the crafty Cuellar, who had won 20 for the third consecutive year.

The Catfish held Baltimore to seven hits, but unfortunately for him, four of them were home runs. Powell walloped two, Brooks Robinson and Ellie Hendricks the others.

Cuellar displayed his usual pitching artistry, a baffling assortment of curves and change-ups which the A's solved for a mere six hits.

Typical of the A's super-cautious approach to their task was an incident in the sixth inning when they were trailing, 2-1. Reggie Jackson led off against Cuellar with a double. Cleanup hitter Tommy Davis was up next and to the surprise of everyone in the park, he bunted. The next two hitters were easy outs. Davis' sacrifice, it turned out, was not ordered by Williams.

Now one game from oblivion, the A's had to send Diego Segui against Palmer in Oakland October 5. Segui got the call in place of Chuck Dobson, Oakland's No. 3 starter, who had a sore elbow.

Palmer's performance was not among his most noteworthy—he permitted three home runs, two of them by the slugging Jackson and the other by Sal Bando. But all three shots were struck with the bases empty, and Palmer had more than enough to pitch Baltimore's pennant clincher for the third straight year.

Loser of his only two starts against Baltimore during the season, Segui reached the fifth inning October 5 with the score 1-1. Then he met his Waterloo. The crusher was Brooks Robinson's two-run single. It came after Williams ordered an intentional pass to Hendricks, loading the bases.

Bando's homer cut the A's deficit to 3-2 in the sixth; but, in the seventh, F. Robby's double and Darold Knowles' wild pitch scored two runs and put Baltimore out of danger. The Orioles collected 12 hits off Segui and his four successors, with Don Buford's triple and two singles leading the way.

GAME OF SUNDAY, OCTOBER 3, AT BALTIMORE

Oakland	AB.	R.	H.	RBI.	PO.	A.
Campaneris, ss	4	0	1	0	0	0
Rudi, lf	4	0	1	0	2	0
Jackson, rf	4	0	0	0	3	0
Davis, 1b	4	1	1	0	4	0
Bando, 3b	4	1	2	0	2	1
Mangual, cf	4	1	2	2	2	0
Duncan, c	3	0	2	1	9	0
Epstein, ph	1	0	0	0	0	0
Green, 2b	1	0	0	0	2	3
Blue, p	3	0	0	0	0	1
Fingers, p	0	0	0	0	0	0
Totals	32	3	9	3	24	5

Baltimore	AB.	R.	H.	RBI.	PO.	A.
Blair, cf	4	0	1	2	2	0
Johnson, 2b	4	1	1	0	1	3
Rettenmund, lf	4	0	1	1	3	0
F. Robinson, rf	3	1	0	0	2	0
Powell, 1b	4	0	1	0	9	1
B. Robinson, 3b	3	1	1	0	0	2
Etchebarren, c	3	0	0	0	7	0
Belanger, ss	2	1	1	1	3	4
McNally, p	2	0	0	0	0	2
Motton, ph	1	0	1	1	0	0
Palmer, pr	0	1	0	0	0	0
Watt, p	0	0	0	0	0	1
Totals	30	5	7	5	27	13

Oakland	0	2	0	0	0	0	0	0	0	0 – 3
Baltimore	0	0	0	1	0	0	4	0	x – 5

Oakland	IP.	H.	R.	ER.	BB.	SO.
Blue (Loser)	7	7	5	5	2	8
Fingers	1	0	0	0	0	1

Baltimore	IP.	H.	R.	ER.	BB.	SO.
McNally (Winner)	7	7	3	3	1	5
Watt (Save)	2	2	0	0	0	1

Error—Johnson. Double plays—Oakland 1, Baltimore 2. Left on base—Oakland 4, Baltimore 3. Two-base hits—Rudi, Bando, Duncan, Mangual, Johnson, Rettenmund, Motton, Blair, Campaneris. Three-base hit—Mangual. Sacrifice hit—Green. Umpires—Soar, Napp, DiMuro, O'Donnell, Luciano and Kunkel. Time—2:23. Attendance—42,621.

GAME OF MONDAY, OCTOBER 4, AT BALTIMORE

Oakland	AB.	R.	H.	RBI.	PO.	A.
Campaneris, ss	4	0	1	0	2	3
Rudi, lf	3	0	0	0	2	0
Jackson, rf	4	0	1	0	4	1
Davis, 1b	3	0	1	0	4	0
Bando, 3b	4	1	1	0	2	0
Mangual, cf	4	0	0	0	2	0
Duncan, c	3	0	1	1	6	0
Green, 2b	3	0	1	0	2	0
Hunter, p	3	0	0	0	0	0
Totals	31	1	6	1	24	4

Baltimore	AB.	R.	H.	RBI.	PO.	A.
Buford, lf	3	0	0	0	1	0
Blair, cf	0	0	0	0	0	0
Johnson, 2b	3	1	0	0	1	1
Powell, 1b	4	2	2	3	12	0
F. Robinson, rf	4	0	0	0	4	0
Rettenmund, cf-lf	4	0	1	0	4	0
B. Robinson, 3b	3	1	1	1	1	3
Hendricks, c	3	1	2	1	2	0
Belanger, ss	3	0	0	0	2	4
Cuellar, p	3	0	1	0	0	2
Totals	30	5	7	5	27	10

Oakland	0	0	0	1	0	0	0	0	0 – 1
Baltimore	0	1	1	0	0	0	1	2	x – 5

Oakland	IP.	H.	R.	ER.	BB.	SO.
Hunter (Loser)	8	7	5	5	2	6

Baltimore	IP.	H.	R.	ER.	BB.	SO.
Cuellar (Winner)	9	6	1	1	1	2

Errors—None. Left on base—Oakland 5, Baltimore 3. Two-base hits—Davis, Bando, Jackson. Home runs—B. Robinson, Powell 2, Hendricks. Sacrifice hit—Davis. Umpires—Napp, O'Donnell, Luciano, DiMuro, Kunkel and Soar. Time—2:04. Attendance—35,003.

GAME OF TUESDAY, OCTOBER 5, AT OAKLAND

Baltimore	AB.	R.	H.	RBI.PO.	A.
Buford, lf	4	1	3	0 0	0
Rettenmund, pr-lf	0	0	0	0 0	0
Blair, cf	5	1	2	0 3	0
Powell, 1b	2	2	0	0 7	1
F. Robinson, rf	5	1	1	1 1	0
Hendricks, c	1	0	0	1 4	0
Etchebarren, ph-c	2	0	0	0 4	0
B. Robinson, 3b	5	2	2	2 3	2
Johnson, 2b	3	0	2	0 3	2
Belanger, ss	3	0	1	0 1	3
Palmer, p	5	0	1	0 1	0
Totals	35	5	12	4 27	8

Oakland	AB.	R.	H.	RBI.PO.	A.
Campaneris, ss	4	0	0	0 1	3
Monday, cf	3	0	0	0 4	0
Jackson, rf	4	2	3	2 2	0
Epstein, 1b	4	0	1	0 4	0
Bando, 3b	3	1	1	1 2	1
Mangual, lf	4	0	0	0 2	0
Tenace, c	3	0	0	0 8	0
Green, 2b	3	0	1	0 4	1
Hegan, ph	1	0	0	0 0	0
Segui, p	2	0	0	0 0	0
Fingers, p	0	0	0	0 0	0
Knowles, p	0	0	0	0 0	0
Locker, p	0	0	0	0 0	0
Davis, ph	1	0	1	0 0	0
Grant, p	0	0	0	0 0	1
Blefary, ph	1	0	0	0 0	0
Totals	33	3	7	3 27	6

Baltimore	1	0	0	0	2	0		2	0	0 – 5
Oakland	0	0	1	0	0	1		0	1	0 – 3

Baltimore	IP.	H.	R.	ER.	BB.	SO.
Palmer (Winner)	9	7	3	3	3	8

Oakland	IP.	H.	R.	ER.	BB.	SO.
Segui (Loser)	4⅔	6	3	3	6	4
Fingers	1⅓*	2	2	2	1	1
Knowles	⅓	1	0	0	0	0
Locker	⅔	0	0	0	2	0
Grant	2	3	0	0	0	2

*Pitched on two batters in seventh.

Errors—None. Double plays—Baltimore 1, Oakland 3. Left on base—Baltimore 13, Oakland 6. Two-base hits—Johnson, F. Robinson, B. Robinson. Three-base hit—Buford. Home runs—Jackson 2, Bando. Sacrifice fly—Hendricks. Wild pitches—Palmer, Knowles. Umpires—DiMuro, Luciano, Soar, Kunkel, O'Donnell and Napp. Time—2:49. Attendance—33,176.

BALTIMORE ORIOLES' BATTING AND FIELDING AVERAGES

Player—Position	G.	AB.	R.	H.	TB.	2B.	3B.	HR.	RBI.	B.A.	PO.	A.	E.	F.A.
Motton, ph	1	1	0	1	2	1	0	0	1	1.000	0	0	0	.000
Hendricks, c	2	4	1	2	5	0	0	1	2	.500	6	0	0	1.000
Buford, lf	2	7	1	3	5	0	1	0	0	.429	4	0	0	1.000
B. Robinson, 3b	3	11	2	4	8	1	0	1	3	.364	4	7	0	1.000
Blair, cf	3	9	1	3	4	1	0	0	2	.333	5	0	0	1.000
Cuellar, p	1	3	0	1	1	0	0	0	0	.333	0	2	0	1.000
Johnson, 2b	3	10	2	3	5	2	0	0	0	.300	5	6	1	.917
Powell, 1b	3	10	4	3	9	0	0	2	3	.300	28	2	0	1.000
Belanger, ss	3	8	1	2	2	0	0	0	1	.250	6	11	0	1.000
Rettenmund, lf-cf-pr	3	8	0	2	3	1	0	0	1	.250	7	0	0	1.000
Palmer, pr-p	2	5	1	1	1	0	0	0	0	.200	1	0	0	1.000
F. Robinson, rf	3	12	2	1	2	1	0	0	1	.083	7	0	0	1.000
Watt, p	1	0	0	0	0	0	0	0	0	.000	0	1	0	1.000
McNally, p	1	2	0	0	0	0	0	0	0	.000	0	2	0	1.000
Etchebarren, c-ph	2	5	0	0	0	0	0	0	0	.000	11	0	0	1.000
Totals	3	95	15	26	47	7	1	4	14	.274	81	31	1	.991

OAKLAND ATHLETICS' BATTING AND FIELDING AVERAGES

Player—Position	G.	AB.	R.	H.	TB.	2B.	3B.	HR.	RBI.	B.A.	PO.	A.	E.	F.A.
Duncan, c	2	6	0	3	4	1	0	0	2	.500	15	0	0	1.000
Davis, 1b-ph	3	8	1	3	4	1	0	0	0	.375	8	0	0	1.000
Bando, 3b	3	11	3	4	9	2	0	1	1	.364	6	2	0	1.000
Jackson, rf	3	12	2	4	11	1	0	2	2	.333	9	1	0	1.000
Green, 2b	3	7	0	2	2	0	0	0	0	.286	8	4	0	1.000
Epstein, ph-1b	2	5	0	1	1	0	0	0	0	.200	4	0	0	1.000
Campaneris, ss	3	12	0	2	3	1	0	0	0	.167	3	6	0	1.000
Mangual, cf-lf	3	12	1	2	5	1	1	0	2	.167	6	0	0	1.000
Rudi, lf	2	7	0	1	2	1	0	0	0	.143	4	0	0	1.000
Fingers, p	2	0	0	0	0	0	0	0	0	.000	0	0	0	.000
Grant, p	1	0	0	0	0	0	0	0	0	.000	0	1	0	1.000
Knowles, p	1	0	0	0	0	0	0	0	0	.000	0	0	0	.000
Locker, p	1	0	0	0	0	0	0	0	0	.000	0	0	0	.000

Player—Position	G.	AB.	R.	H.	TB.	2B.	3B.	HR.	RBI.	B.A.	PO.	A.	E.	F.A.
Blefary, ph	1	1	0	0	0	0	0	0	0	.000	0	0	0	.000
Hegan, ph	1	1	0	0	0	0	0	0	0	.000	0	0	0	.000
Segui, p	1	2	0	0	0	0	0	0	0	.000	0	0	0	.000
Blue, p	1	3	0	0	0	0	0	0	0	.000	0	1	0	1.000
Hunter, p	1	3	0	0	0	0	0	0	0	.000	0	0	0	.000
Monday, cf	1	3	0	0	0	0	0	0	0	.000	4	0	0	1.000
Tenace, c	1	3	0	0	0	0	0	0	0	.000	8	0	0	1.000
Totals	3	96	7	22	41	8	1	3	7	.229	75	15	0	1.000

BALTIMORE ORIOLES' PITCHING RECORDS

Pitcher	G.	GS.	CG.	IP.	H.	R.	ER.	BB.	SO.	HB.	WP.	W.	L.	Pct.	ERA.
Watt	1	0	0	2	2	0	0	0	1	0	0	0	0	.000	0.00
Cuellar	1	1	1	9	6	1	1	1	2	0	0	1	0	1.000	1.00
Palmer	1	1	1	9	7	3	3	3	8	0	1	1	0	1.000	3.00
McNally	1	1	0	7	7	3	3	1	5	0	0	1	0	1.000	3.86
Totals	3	3	2	27	22	7	7	5	16	0	1	3	0	1.000	2.33

No shutouts. Save—Watt.

OAKLAND ATHLETICS' PITCHING RECORDS

Pitcher	G.	GS.	CG.	IP.	H.	R.	ER.	BB.	SO.	HB.	WP.	W.	L.	Pct.	ERA.
Grant	1	0	0	2	3	0	0	0	2	0	0	0	0	.000	0.00
Locker	1	0	0	⅔	0	0	0	2	0	0	0	0	0	.000	0.00
Knowles	1	0	0	⅓	1	0	0	0	0	1	0	0	0	.000	0.00
Hunter	1	1	1	8	7	5	5	2	6	0	0	0	1	.000	5.63
Segui	1	1	0	4⅔	6	3	3	6	4	0	0	0	1	.000	5.79
Blue	1	1	0	7	7	5	5	2	8	0	0	0	1	.000	6.43
Fingers	2	0	0	2⅓	2	2	2	1	2	0	0	0	0	.000	7.71
Totals	3	3	1	25	26	15	15	13	22	0	1	0	3	.000	5.40

No shutouts or saves.

COMPOSITE SCORE BY INNINGS

Baltimore	1	1	1	1	2	0	7	2	0 – 15
Oakland	0	2	1	2	0	1	0	1	0 – 7

Sacrifice hits—Green, Davis.
Sacrifice fly—Hendricks.
Stolen bases—None.
Caught stealing—Davis, Duncan.
Double plays—Bando, Green and Davis; Johnson, Belanger and Powell; Belanger, Johnson and Powell 2; Campaneris and Green; Green and Epstein; Bando and Epstein.
Hit by pitcher—None.
Passed balls—None.
Balks—None.
Left on bases—Baltimore 19–3, 3, 13; Oakland 15–4, 5, 6.
Time of games—First game, 2:23; second game, 2:04; third game, 2:49.
Attendance—First game, 42,621; second game, 35,003; third game, 33,176.
Umpires—Soar, Napp, DiMuro, O'Donnell, Luciano and Kunkel.
Official scorers—Dick O'Connor, Palo Alto Times; Lou Hatter, Baltimore Morning Sun.

NATIONAL LEAGUE
Championship Series of 1971

	W.	L.	Pct.
Pittsburgh (East)	3	1	.750
San Francisco (West)	1	3	.250

The big bat that led all major league home run hitters in 1971 was strangely silent during the National League Championship Series.

But another bat, swung by Bob Robertson, produced at a frenzied pace and the Pittsburgh Pirates defeated the San Francisco Giants, three games to one, to capture their first pennant since 1960.

While Willie Stargell drew a complete blank in the four games, going 0-for-14, Robertson collected seven hits in 16 trips to the plate, cracked four home runs and drove in six runs.

The big first baseman, who was inactivated by a kidney ailment for the entire 1968 season and by a knee condition for 31 games in 1971, enjoyed his most productive performance in the second contest, at Candlestick Park in San Francisco.

The Pirates, who lost the opening game, 5-4, although outhitting the Giants, 9 to 7, trailed, 2-1, after three innings of the second encounter. At this point, Robertson, who had doubled and scored in the second inning, hit a John Cumberland pitch into the right field seats for a home run.

In the seventh inning, Robertson poled a three-run shot to left field off Ron Bryant and, in the ninth, he connected off Steve Hamilton, driving the ball over the left-center field fence.

The 9-4 victory, credited to Dock Ellis, first of three Pittsburgh pitchers, was the Pirates' first at Candlestick Park after six consecutive defeats.

When the series shifted to Pittsburgh, Manager Danny Murtaugh nominated Nelson Briles (8-4 for the season) as the Pirates' starting pitcher.

In warming up however, the righthander suffered a recurrence of a hamstring pull and Bob Johnson, who compiled a 9-10 regular-season record, was tabbed as a replacement.

The 28-year-old righthander, who was allowed extra time to warm up, duelled Juan Marichal, the Giants' 18-game winner, on equal terms for seven innings and was returned a 2-1 winner when Richie Hebner poled a right field home run in the last of the eighth..

Marichal, with a 25-10 lifetime record against the Pirates, yielded only three hits in the first seven innings, including a no-harm single to Roberto Clemente in the first inning, Robertson's second-inning homer, his third in as many consecutive trips, and Hebner's non-productive single in the sixth.

In the eighth, Hebner drilled "a screwball out over the plate" to deep right field where Bonds missed a leaping catch by about five inches, the ball falling into home run territory for the deciding tally.

With the Pirates just one victory away from the pennant that eluded them in 1970 via three consecutive losses to the Cincinnati Reds, Murtaugh called on Steve Blass to face his first-game opponent, Perry.

Blass, who lasted five innings in the opener, was less a mystery in his second try. In two innings, the righthander yielded eight hits and five runs, two of the blows being homers by Chris Speier and Willie McCovey.

Trailing, 5-2, the Pirates tagged Perry for three second-inning runs. Sanguillen and Bill Mazeroski singled around a fielder's choice and Hebner again reached home run territory in right field, knotting the score at 5-5.

Perry, touched for 10 of the Pirates' 11 hits, blanked the N. L. East champions for the next three innings.

In the sixth stanza, however, the Bucs tagged him for one run on singles by Dave Cash and Clemente, around an infield out.

After Jerry Johnson relieved Perry, a passed ball permitted Cash to score and Clemente to go to second base. An intentional walk to Stargell was followed by Al Oliver's home run, giving the Pirates a 9-5 edge.

Bruce Kison, 20-year-old righthander who took over Pittsburgh mound duties in the third inning and allowed only two hits in $4\frac{2}{3}$ innings, ran into trouble in the seventh inning when the Giants placed two runners on base.

Dave Giusti, who saved 30 Pittsburgh wins in the regular season and appeared in the first three championship contests, responded again and turned back the Giants without a run.

GAME OF SATURDAY, OCTOBER 2, AT SAN FRANCISCO

Pittsburgh	AB.	R.	H.	RBI.	PO.	A.
Cash, 2b	5	2	2	1	3	2
Hebner, 3b	5	0	1	0	0	0
Clemente, rf	4	0	0	0	3	0
Stargell, lf	4	0	0	0	1	0
Oliver, cf	4	0	1	2	3	0
Robertson, 1b	4	0	2	0	1	1
Sanguillen, c	4	0	1	0	10	0
Hernandez, ss	2	1	1	0	1	0
Davalillo, ph	1	0	0	0	0	0
Moose, p	0	0	0	0	0	0
May, ph	1	0	0	0	0	0
Giusti, p	0	0	0	0	0	0
Blass, p	1	0	0	0	1	1
Alley, ss	2	1	1	0	1	1
Totals	37	4	9	3	24	5

San Francisco	AB.	R.	H.	RBI.	PO.	A.
Henderson, lf	4	0	2	1	2	0
Fuentes, 2b	4	1	1	2	2	3
Mays, cf	2	1	1	0	0	0
McCovey, 1b	3	1	1	2	12	0
Kingman, rf	3	0	0	0	3	0
Bonds, rf	1	0	0	0	1	0
Dietz, c	4	0	0	0	5	1
Gallagher, 3b	2	0	0	0	0	1
Lanier, 3b	1	0	0	0	1	0
Speier, ss	3	2	2	0	1	5
Perry, p	1	0	0	0	0	2
Totals	28	5	7	5	27	12

Pittsburgh	0	0	2	0	0	0	2	0	0 – 4
San Francisco	0	0	1	0	4	0	0	0	x – 5

Pittsburgh	IP.	H.	R.	ER.	BB.	SO.
Blass (Loser)	5	6	5	5	2	9
Moose	2	0	0	0	0	0
Giusti	1	1	0	0	1	1

San Francisco	IP.	H.	R.	ER.	BB.	SO.
Perry (Winner)	9	9	4	3	1	5

Errors—McCovey, Speier. Double play—Pittsburgh 1. Left on base—Pittsburgh 9, San Francisco 4. Two-base hits—Cash, Henderson, Mays. Home runs—Fuentes, McCovey. Sacrifice hits—Blass, Perry 2. Hit by pitcher—By Perry (Stargell). Umpires—Gorman, Crawford, Weyer, Olsen, Stello and Davidson. Time—2:44. Attendance—40,977.

GAME OF SUNDAY, OCTOBER 3, AT SAN FRANCISCO

Pittsburgh	AB.	R.	H.	RBI.	PO.	A.
Cash, 2b	5	1	3	0	3	3
Clines, cf	3	1	1	1	1	0
Oliver, ph-cf	1	1	1	0	0	0
Clemente, rf	5	1	3	1	3	0
Stargell, lf	5	0	0	0	1	0
Robertson, 1b	5	4	4	5	9	1
Sanguillen, c	5	1	2	1	5	0
Pagan, 3b	1	0	0	0	1	2
Hebner, ph-3b	3	0	0	0	1	0
Hernandez, ss	4	0	1	1	2	2
Ellis, p	3	0	0	0	0	0
Miller, p	1	0	0	0	1	0
Giusti, p	0	0	0	0	0	0
Totals	41	9	15	9	27	9

San Francisco	AB.	R.	H.	RBI.	PO.	A.
Henderson, lf	3	0	1	1	0	0
Fuentes, 2b	5	2	2	0	4	0
Mays, cf	5	1	2	3	2	0
McCovey, 1b	3	0	1	0	4	0
Rosario, 1b	0	0	0	0	0	0
Kingman, rf	4	0	1	0	2	0
Dietz, c	4	0	0	0	14	1
Gallagher, 3b	4	0	0	0	0	0
Speier, ss	3	1	2	0	1	5
Cumberland, p	0	0	0	0	0	0
Barr, p	1	0	0	0	0	0
McMahon, p	0	0	0	0	0	0
Duffy, ph	1	0	0	0	0	0
Carrithers, p	0	0	0	0	0	0
Bryant, p	0	0	0	0	0	0
Hart, ph	1	0	0	0	0	0
Hamilton, p	0	0	0	0	0	0
Totals	34	4	9	4	27	6

Pittsburgh	0	1	0	2	1	0	4	0	1 – 9
San Francisco	1	1	0	0	0	0	0	0	2 – 4

Pittsburgh	IP.	H.	R.	ER.	BB.	SO.
Ellis (Winner)	5‡	6	2	2	4	1
Miller	3x	3	2	2	3	3
Giusti (Save)	1	0	0	0	0	0

San Francisco	IP.	H.	R.	ER.	BB.	SO.
Cumberland (Loser)	3*	7	3	3	0	4
Barr	1†	3	1	1	0	2
McMahon	2	0	0	0	0	2
Carrithers	0§	3	3	3	0	0
Bryant	2	1	1	1	1	2
Hamilton	1	1	1	1	0	3

*Pitched to two batters in fourth.
†Pitched to two batters in fifth.
‡Pitched to two batters in sixth.
§Pitched to three batters in seventh.
xPitched to three batters in ninth.

Errors—None. Double plays—Pittsburgh 1, San Francisco 1. Left on base—Pittsburgh 7, San Francisco 12. Two-base hits—Mays, Robertson, Speier, Cash, Fuentes. Home runs—Robertson 3, Clines, Mays. Sacrifice hit—Cumberland. Stolen bases—Henderson, Sanguillen. Hit by pitcher—By Ellis (Gallagher), by Bryant (Hebner). Passed ball—Sanguillen. Umpires—Crawford, Weyer, Olsen, Stello, Davidson and Gorman. Time—3:23. Attendance—42,562.

GAME OF TUESDAY, OCTOBER 5, AT PITTSBURGH

San Francisco	AB.	R.	H.	RBI.	PO.	A.	Pittsburgh	AB.	R.	H.	RBI.	PO.	A.
Henderson, lf	4	1	1	0	2	0	Cash, 2b	4	0	0	0	2	4
Fuentes, 2b	3	0	0	0	1	2	Hebner, 3b	4	1	2	1	1	1
Mays, cf	4	0	1	0	0	0	Clemente, rf	4	0	1	0	5	0
McCovey, 1b	3	0	1	0	11	2	Stargell, lf	3	0	0	0	2	0
Bonds, rf	3	0	1	0	1	0	Oliver, cf	3	0	0	0	0	0
Dietz, c	3	0	0	0	7	0	Robertson, 1b	3	1	1	1	8	0
Gallagher, 3b	3	0	1	0	0	3	Sanguillen, c	3	0	0	0	7	1
Hart, ph	1	0	0	0	0	0	Hernandez, ss	3	0	0	0	2	5
Speier, ss	4	0	0	0	2	0	Johnson, p	2	0	0	0	0	0
Marichal, p	3	0	0	0	2	4	Davalillo, ph	1	0	0	0	0	0
Kingman, ph	1	0	0	0	0	0	Giusti, p	0	0	0	0	0	0
Totals	32	1	5	0	24	13	Totals	30	2	4	2	27	11

San Francisco	0	0	0	0	0	1	0	0	0 – 1
Pittsburgh	0	0	1	0	0	0	0	1	x – 2

San Francisco	IP.	H.	R.	ER.	BB.	SO.
Marichal (Loser)	8	4	2	2	0	6

Pittsburgh	IP.	H.	R.	ER.	BB.	SO.
Johnson (Winner)	8	5	1	0	3	7
Giusti (Save)	1	0	0	0	0	0

Errors—Bonds, Hebner. Fuentes. Left on base—San Francisco 8, Pittsburgh 4. Home runs—Robertson, Hebner. Sacrifice hit—Fuentes. Stolen base—Mays. Wild pitches—Marichal 2. Umpires—Weyer, Olsen, Stello, Davidson, Gorman and Crawford. Time—2:26. Attendance—38,322.

GAME OF WEDNESDAY, OCTOBER 6, AT PITTSBURGH

San Francisco	AB.	R.	H.	RBI.	PO.	A.	Pittsburgh	AB.	R.	H.	RBI.	PO.	A.
Henderson, lf	5	2	1	0	0	0	Cash, 2b	5	2	3	0	3	2
Fuentes, 2b	4	1	2	0	2	0	Hebner, 3b	5	2	2	3	2	1
Mays, cf	4	0	0	0	3	0	Clemente, rf	5	1	2	3	1	0
McCovey, 1b	5	1	3	4	7	1	Stargell, lf	2	1	0	0	2	0
Bonds, rf	4	0	1	0	1	0	Oliver, cf	4	1	1	3	2	0
Dietz, c	4	0	1	0	8	0	Robertson, 1b	4	0	0	0	7	0
Hart, 3b	3	0	0	0	0	2	Sanguillen, c	3	1	1	0	2	2
Gallagher, 3b	1	0	0	0	0	0	Hernandez, ss	4	1	1	0	0	1
Speier, ss	4	1	1	1	1	2	Blass, p	0	0	0	0	0	0
Perry, p	3	0	1	0	1	0	Mazeroski, ph	1	1	1	0	0	0
Johnson, p	0	0	0	0	0	0	Kison, p	2	0	0	0	0	1
Kingman, ph	1	0	0	0	0	0	Giusti, p	1	0	0	0	0	1
McMahon, p	0	0	0	0	1	1	Totals	36	9	11	9	27	7
Totals	38	5	10	5	24	6							

San Francisco	1	4	0	0	0	0	0	0	0 – 5
Pittsburgh	2	3	0	0	0	4	0	0	x – 9

San Francisco	IP.	H.	R.	ER.	BB.	SO.
Perry (Loser)	5⅔	10	7	7	2	6
Johnson	1⅓	1	2	2	1	2
McMahon	1	0	0	0	0	1

Pittsburgh	IP.	H.	R.	ER.	BB.	SO.
Blass	2	8	5	4	0	2
Kison (Winner)	4⅔	2	0	0	2	3
Giusti (Save)	2⅓	0	0	0	1	2

Errors—Cash, Hernandez. Double play—Pittsburgh 1. Left on base—San Francisco 9, Pittsburgh 6. Two-base hit—Hebner. Home runs—Speier, McCovey, Hebner, Oliver. Stolen base—Cash. Wild pitches—Perry, Kison. Passed ball—Dietz. Umpires—Olsen, Stello, Davidson, Gorman, Crawford and Weyer. Time—3:00. Attendance—35,487.

PITTSBURGH PIRATES' BATTING AND FIELDING AVERAGES

Player—Position	G.	AB.	R.	H.	TB.	2B.	3B.	HR.	RBI.	B.A.	PO.	A.	E.	F.A.
Mazeroski, ph	1	1	1	1	1	0	0	0	0	1.000	0	0	0	.000
Alley, ss	1	2	1	1	1	0	0	0	0	.500	1	1	0	1.000
Robertson, 1b	4	16	5	7	20	1	0	4	6	.438	25	2	0	1.000
Cash, 2b	4	19	5	8	10	2	0	0	1	.421	11	11	1	.957
Clemente, rf	4	18	2	6	6	0	0	0	4	.333	12	0	0	1.000
Clines, cf	1	3	1	1	4	0	0	1	1	.333	1	0	0	1.000
Hebner, 3b-ph	4	17	3	5	12	1	0	2	4	.294	4	3	1	.875
Sanguillen, c	4	15	1	4	4	0	0	0	1	.267	30	1	0	1.000
Oliver, cf-ph	4	12	2	3	6	0	0	1	5	.250	5	0	0	1.000
Hernandez, ss	4	13	2	3	3	0	0	0	1	.231	7	9	1	.941
Moose, p	1	0	0	0	0	0	0	0	0	.000	0	0	0	.000
Blass, p	2	1	0	0	0	0	0	0	0	.000	1	1	0	1.000
Giusti, p	4	1	0	0	0	0	0	0	0	.000	0	1	0	1.000
May, ph	1	1	0	0	0	0	0	0	0	.000	0	0	0	.000
Miller, p	1	1	0	0	0	0	0	0	0	.000	1	0	0	1.000
Pagan, 3b	1	1	0	0	0	0	0	0	0	.000	1	2	0	1.000
Davalillo, ph	2	2	0	0	0	0	0	0	0	.000	0	0	0	.000
R. Johnson, p	1	2	0	0	0	0	0	0	0	.000	0	0	0	.000
Kison, p	1	2	0	0	0	0	0	0	0	.000	0	1	0	1.000
Ellis, p	1	3	0	0	0	0	0	0	0	.000	0	0	0	.000
Stargell, lf	4	14	1	0	0	0	0	0	0	.000	6	0	0	1.000
Totals	4	144	24	39	67	4	0	8	23	.271	105	32	3	.979

SAN FRANCISCO GIANTS' BATTING AND FIELDING AVERAGES

Player—Position	G.	AB.	R.	H.	TB.	2B.	3B.	HR.	RBI.	B.A.	PO.	A.	E.	F.A.
McCovey, 1b	4	14	2	6	12	0	0	2	6	.429	34	3	1	.974
Speier, ss	4	14	4	5	9	1	0	1	1	.357	3	14	1	.944
Fuentes, 2b	4	16	4	5	9	1	0	1	2	.313	9	5	1	.933
Henderson, lf	4	16	3	5	6	1	0	0	0	.313	4	0	0	1.000
Mays, cf	4	15	2	4	9	2	0	1	3	.267	5	0	0	1.000
Bonds, rf	3	8	0	2	2	0	0	0	0	.250	3	0	1	.750
Perry, p	2	4	0	1	1	0	0	0	0	.250	1	2	0	1.000
Kingman, rf-ph	4	9	0	1	1	0	0	0	0	.111	5	0	0	1.000
Gallagher, 3b	4	10	0	1	1	0	0	0	0	.100	0	4	0	1.000
Dietz, c	4	15	0	1	1	0	0	0	0	.067	34	2	0	1.000
Bryant, p	1	0	0	0	0	0	0	0	0	.000	0	0	0	.000
Carrithers, p	1	0	0	0	0	0	0	0	0	.000	0	0	0	.000
Cumberland, p	1	0	0	0	0	0	0	0	0	.000	0	0	0	.000
Hamilton, p	1	0	0	0	0	0	0	0	0	.000	0	0	0	.000
J. Johnson, p	1	0	0	0	0	0	0	0	0	.000	0	0	0	.000
McMahon, p	2	0	0	0	0	0	0	0	0	.000	1	1	0	1.000
Rosario, pr	1	0	0	0	0	0	0	0	0	.000	0	0	0	.000
Barr, p	1	1	0	0	0	0	0	0	0	.000	0	0	0	.000
Duffy, ph	1	1	0	0	0	0	0	0	0	.000	0	0	0	.000
Lanier, 3b	1	1	0	0	0	0	0	0	0	.000	1	0	0	1.000
Marichal, p	1	3	0	0	0	0	0	0	0	.000	2	4	0	1.000
Hart, ph-3b	3	5	0	0	0	0	0	0	0	.000	0	2	0	1.000
Totals	4	132	15	31	51	5	0	5	14	.235	102	37	4	.972

PITTSBURGH PIRATES' PITCHING RECORDS

Pitcher	G.	GS.	CG.	IP.	H.	R.	ER.	BB.	SO.	HB.	WP.	W.	L.	Pct.	ERA.
R. Johnson	1	1	0	8	5	1	0	3	7	0	0	1	0	1.000	0.00
Giusti	4	0	0	5⅓	1	0	0	2	3	0	0	0	0	.000	0.00
Kison	1	0	0	4⅔	2	0	0	2	3	0	1	1	0	1.000	0.00
Moose	1	0	0	2	0	0	0	0	0	0	0	0	0	.000	0.00
Ellis	1	1	0	5	6	2	2	4	1	1	0	1	0	1.000	3.60
Miller	1	0	0	3	3	2	2	3	0	0	0	0	0	.000	6.00
Blass	2	2	0	7	14	10	9	2	11	0	0	0	1	.000	11.57
Totals	4	4	0	35	31	15	13	16	28	1	1	3	1	.750	3.34

No shutouts. Saves—Giusti 3.

SAN FRANCISCO GIANTS' PITCHING RECORDS

Pitcher	G.	GS.	CG.	IP.	H.	R.	ER.	BB.	SO.	HB.	WP.	W.	L.	Pct.	ERA.
McMahon	2	0	0	3	0	0	0	0	3	0	0	0	0	.000	0.00
Marichal	1	1	1	8	4	2	2	0	6	0	2	0	1	.000	2.25
Bryant	1	0	0	2	1	1	1	1	2	1	0	0	0	.000	4.50
Perry	2	2	1	14⅔	19	11	10	3	11	1	1	1	1	.500	6.14
Cumberland	1	1	0	3	7	3	3	0	4	0	0	0	1	.000	9.00
Barr	1	0	0	1	3	1	1	0	2	0	0	0	0	.000	9.00
Hamilton	1	0	0	1	1	1	1	0	3	0	0	0	0	.000	9.00
J. Johnson	1	0	0	1⅓	1	2	2	1	2	0	0	0	0	.000	13.50
Carrithers	1	0	0	0*	3	3	3	0	0	0	0	0	0	.000	......
Totals	4	4	2	34	39	24	23	5	33	2	3	1	3	.250	6.09

*Pitched to three batters in seventh inning of second game.
No shutouts or saves.

COMPOSITE SCORE BY INNINGS

Pittsburgh	2	5	2		2	1	4	6	1	1 — 24
San Francisco	2	5	1		0	4	1	0	0	2 — 15

Sacrifice hits—Blass, Perry 2, Cumberland, Fuentes.
Stolen bases—Henderson, Sanguillen, Mays, Cash.
Caught stealing—Cash.
Double plays—Alley, Cash and Robertson; Dietz and Fuentes; Hernandez, Cash and Robertson; Cash, Hernandez and Robertson.
Left on bases—Pittsburgh 26—9, 7, 4, 6; San Francisco 33—4, 12, 8, 9.
Hit by pitchers—By Perry (Stargell), by Ellis (Gallagher), by Bryant (Hebner).
Passed balls—Sanguillen, Dietz.
Balks—None.
Time of games—First game, 2:44; second game, 3:23; third game, 2:26; fourth game, 3:00.
Attendance—First game, 40,977; second game, 42,562; third game, 38,322; fourth game, 35,487.
Umpires—Gorman, Crawford, Weyer, Olsen, Stello and Davidson.
Official scorers—Bill Christine, Pittsburgh Press; Jack Hanley, San Jose Mercury-News and Charles Feeney, Pittsburgh Post-Gazette.

AMERICAN LEAGUE
Championship Series of 1972

	W.	L.	Pct.
Oakland (West)	3	2	.600
Detroit (East)	2	3	.400

Back in 1931, the Philadelphia A's won their third straight American League pennant. The A's were to wait 41 years for their next. When it finally came in 1972, the A's were long gone from Philadelphia, having traipsed across the country to Oakland after a stop in Kansas City.

Retaining their West Division crown in a breeze in '72, the A's outfought the East champion Detroit Tigers in a memorable pennant playoff, three games to two. It was the first A. L. Championship Series in the four-year history of the event that did not end in a three-game sweep.

The A's scored only 13 runs and logged just 38 hits, including one homer, in five playoff games, two of which were extra-inning struggles. Their eight-man pitching staff was equal to the task, granting the Tigers a mere 10 runs and 32 hits.

Blue Moon Odom, who pitched a shutout in winning game two, 5-0, was the only Oakland pitcher to go the route in the playoffs. That was no indictment of the A's starters. Rather, it was indicative of the superb relief pitching Manager Dick Williams could and did call upon at the first hint of trouble.

Vida Blue nursed a season-long grudge against Owner Charlie Finley, the aftermath of Blue's holdout well into May. Nevertheless, the griping Blue was a brilliant fireman in the playoffs, blanking the Tigers for 5⅓ innings in four appearances.

The playoffs dripped with drama and suspense from start to finish. Tiger ace Mickey Lolich carried a 2-1 lead into the last of the 11th in the opener. The A's thereupon scored twice to win it. The hero was Gonzalo Marquez, an obscure late addition to the A's roster. He lashed a pinch-single off Chuck Seelbach with one out and two aboard to score the tying run. On the same play, right fielder Al Kaline's throw shot past third sacker Aurelio Rodriguez, enabling Gene Tenace to cross the plate with the winning tally.

Kaline was charged with an error, which rubbed out his hero halo in a hurry. Kaline had belted a homer off Fingers in the top of the 11th to give Detroit a 2-1 edge.

Buoyed by their opening success, the A's came on strong the next day, handing the Tigers a 5-0 beating behind Odom's three-hitter. Shortstop Campy Campaneris, with three singles, two runs and two stolen bases, was the Tigers' No. 1 nemesis. He also precipitated a near riot in the seventh inning when he threw his bat at Lerrin LaGrow, who had plunked Campy on the ankle with a pitch.

Tiger Manager Billy Martin, noted for his fistic conquests, dashed from the dugout, along with his players. Three umpires managed to keep Martin from Campaneris, a feat which nipped a budding brawl. Plate umpire Nestor Chylak banished both Campy and LaGrow. Later, A. L. President Joe Cronin fined Campaneris $500 and suspended him from the remaining playoff games. He was allowed to play in the World Series, but sat out the first seven games of the 1973 season by order of the Commissioner.

Needing one more win to kill off the Tigers, the A's proceeded to swoon, 3-0, before Joe Coleman's 14-strikeout job October 10 as the scene shifted to Detroit. Coleman's whiff total surpassed the old playoff record of 12 set by Baltimore's Jim Palmer against Minnesota in 1970.

Nobody could brand the Tigers quitters. Still one game from oblivion, they tied the series the next day in a 10-inning thriller, 4-3.

Lolich pitched creditably for Detroit, as he had in the opener, but left for a pinch-hitter in the ninth with the score 1-1. The A's appeared to have the pennant wrapped up when they rocked Seelbach, Lolich's successor, for two runs in the 10th.

Then came Detroit's remarkable rally at the expense of Oakland relievers Bob Locker, Joe Horlen and Dave Hamilton. The carnage began with singles by Dick McAuliffe and Kaline, Horlen's wild pitch and a walk to Gates Brown. It continued with Tenace's muff of a throw on a force-play attempt while he was trying to play second base, Hamilton's bases-loaded walk to Norm Cash and Jim Northrup's winning hit to right field.

Next day, with a chill wind blowing and Detroit fans in one of their boisterous, destructive moods, the A's put it all together. Behind Odom and Blue, they turned back the Tigers and Woodie Fryman, 2-1, to hoist the pennant.

GAME OF SATURDAY, OCTOBER 7, AT OAKLAND

Detroit	AB.	R.	H.	RBI.	PO.	A.
McAuliffe, 2b	5	0	0	0	2	3
Kaline, rf	5	1	1	1	2	0
Sims, c	5	0	2	0	4	0
Cash, 1b	3	1	1	1	12	0
Horton, lf	3	0	0	0	3	0
G. Brown, ph	1	0	0	0	0	0
Stanley, cf	1	0	0	0	1	0
Northrup, cf-lf	3	0	1	0	5	0
Rodriguez, 3b	4	0	0	0	1	4
Brinkman, ss	4	0	1	0	1	2
Lolich, p	4	0	0	0	0	3
Seelbach, p	0	0	0	0	0	0
Totals	38	2	6	2	31	12

Oakland	AB.	R.	H.	RBI.	PO.	A.
Campaneris, ss	4	1	0	0	3	5
Alou, rf	5	0	1	0	0	0
Rudi, lf	4	0	0	1	4	0
Jackson, cf	5	0	2	0	2	4
Bando, 3b	4	0	2	0	0	0
Odom, pr	0	0	0	0	0	0
Epstein, 1b	3	0	2	0	14	0
Hegan, pr	0	1	0	0	0	0
Tenace, c	5	1	0	0	5	0
Green, 2b	0	0	0	0	1	0
Mangual, ph	1	0	0	0	0	0
Kubiak, 2b	2	0	1	0	0	5
Hendrick, ph	1	0	0	0	0	0
Maxvill, ss	0	0	0	0	0	1
Marquez, ph	1	0	1	1	0	0
Hunter, p	3	0	1	0	0	0
Blue, p	0	0	0	0	0	0
Fingers, p	1	0	0	0	0	0
Totals	39	3	10	2	33	15

```
Detroit ............... 0 1 0   0 0 0   0 0 0   0   1 - 2
Oakland ............... 0 0 1   0 0 0   0 0 0   0   2 - 3
```
One out when winning run scored.

Detroit	IP.	H.	R.	ER.	BB.	SO.
Lolich (Loser)	10‡	9	3	2	3	4
Seelbach	⅓	1	0	0	0	0

Oakland	IP.	H.	R.	ER.	BB.	SO.
Hunter	8*	4	1	1	2	4
Blue	0†	0	0	0	0	0
Fingers (Winner)	3	1	2	1	0	1

*Pitched to one batter in ninth.
†Pitched to one batter in ninth.
‡Pitched to two batters in eleventh.

Errors—McAuliffe, Kubiak, Kaline. Double plays—Detroit 1, Oakland 1. Left on base—Detroit 6, Oakland 10. Two-base hits—Brinkman, Sims. Three-base hit—Sims. Home runs—Cash, Kaline. Sacrifice hits—Bando, Cash. Sacrifice fly—Rudi. Umpires—Flaherty, Chylak, Rice, Denkinger, Barnett and Frantz. Time—3:09. Attendance—29,536.

GAME OF SUNDAY, OCTOBER 8, AT OAKLAND

Detroit	AB.	R.	H.	RBI.	PO.	A.
McAuliffe, ss	4	0	0	0	4	1
Kaline, rf	4	0	1	0	3	0
Sims, c	3	0	0	0	9	1
Cash, 1b	3	0	1	0	2	2
Horton, lf	3	0	0	0	3	0
Northrup, cf	3	0	1	0	1	0
Taylor, 2b	3	0	0	0	1	1
Rodriguez, 3b	3	0	1	0	1	0
Fryman, p	1	0	0	0	0	1
Zachary, p	0	0	0	0	0	0
Scherman, p	0	0	0	0	0	0
Haller, ph	1	0	0	0	0	0
LaGrow, p	0	0	0	0	0	0
Hiller, p	0	0	0	0	0	0
G. Brown, ph	1	0	0	0	0	0
Totals	29	0	3	0	24	6

Oakland	AB.	R.	H.	RBI.	PO.	A.
Campaneris, ss	3	2	3	0	0	2
Maxvill, pr-ss	0	0	0	0	0	0
Alou, rf	4	1	1	1	3	0
Rudi, lf	3	1	2	1	2	0
Jackson, cf	4	0	1	2	3	0
Bando, 3b	4	0	0	0	1	6
Epstein, 1b	3	0	0	0	13	2
Hegan, 1b	0	0	0	0	1	0
Tenace, c	3	0	0	0	2	2
Green, 2b	1	0	0	0	1	2
Hendrick, ph	1	1	1	0	0	0
Kubiak, 2b	1	0	0	0	1	1
Odom, p	2	0	0	0	0	2
Totals	29	5	8	4	27	15

```
Detroit ............... 0   0 0   0 0 0   0 0   0 - 0
Oakland ............... 1   0 0   0 4 0   0 0   x - 5
```

Detroit	IP.	H.	R.	ER.	BB.	SO.
Fryman (Loser)	4⅓	7	4	4	1	5
Zachary	0*	0	1	1	1	0
Scherman	⅔	1	0	0	0	1
LaGrow	1†	0	0	0	0	1
Hiller	2	0	0	0	0	1

Oakland	IP.	H.	R.	ER.	BB.	SO.
Odom (Winner)	9	3	0	0	0	2

*Pitched to one batter in fifth.
†Pitched to one batter in seventh.
Error—McAuliffe. Double play—Detroit 1. Left on base—Detroit 2, Oakland 4. Two-base hits—Rudi, Jackson. Stolen bases—Campaneris 2. Sacrifice hit—Odom. Hit by pitch—By LaGrow (Campaneris). Wild pitches—Zachary 2. Umpires—Chylak, Rice, Frantz, Barnett, Denkinger and Flaherty. Time—2:37. Attendance—31,088.

GAME OF TUESDAY, OCTOBER 10, AT DETROIT

Oakland	AB.	R.	H.	RBI.	PO.	A.
Alou, rf	5	0	3	0	1	0
Maxvill, ss	2	0	0	0	1	2
Duncan, ph-c	1	0	0	0	1	0
Rudi, lf	4	0	3	0	2	0
Jackson, cf	4	0	0	0	4	0
Epstein, 1b	4	0	0	0	9	0
Bando, 3b	4	0	1	0	0	3
Tenace, c-2b	2	0	0	0	3	3
Green, 2b	1	0	0	0	1	0
Mincher, ph	1	0	0	0	0	0
Kubiak, 2b	0	0	0	0	2	2
Marquez, ph	1	0	0	0	0	0
Cullen, ss	1	0	0	0	0	0
Holtzman, p	1	0	0	0	0	1
Mangual, ph	1	0	0	0	0	0
Fingers, p	0	0	0	0	0	0
Blue, p	0	0	0	0	0	0
Hegan, ph	1	0	0	0	0	0
Locker, p	0	0	0	0	0	0
Hendrick, ph	1	0	0	0	0	0
Totals	34	0	7	0	24	11

Detroit	AB.	R.	H.	RBI.	PO.	A.
Taylor, 2b	4	0	0	0	2	3
Rodriguez, 3b	4	0	0	0	0	0
Kaline, rf	3	1	2	0	0	0
Freehan, c	3	2	2	1	14	1
Horton, lf	2	0	0	0	0	0
Northrup, lf	1	0	0	0	1	0
Stanley, cf	3	0	1	0	3	0
I. Brown, 1b	2	0	1	2	2	0
Cash, ph-1b	1	0	0	0	0	1
McAuliffe, ss	3	0	1	0	5	2
Coleman, p	2	0	1	0	0	0
Totals	28	3	8	3	27	7

	1	2	3	4	5	6	7	8	9	R
Oakland	0	0	0	0	0	0	0	0	0	0
Detroit	0	0	0	2	0	0	0	1	x	3

Oakland	IP.	H.	R.	ER.	BB.	SO.
Holtzman (Loser)	4	4	2	2	2	2
Fingers	1⅔	2	0	0	1	1
Blue	⅓	0	0	0	0	0
Locker	2	1	1	1	0	1

Detroit	IP.	H.	R.	ER.	BB.	SO.
Coleman (Winner)	9	7	0	0	3	14

Error—McAuliffe. Double plays—Oakland 3, Detroit 1. Left on base—Oakland 10, Detroit 5. Two-base hits—Alou 2, Freehan. Home run—Freehan. Stolen bases—Alou, Maxvill. Sacrifice hit—Freehan. Umpires—Rice, Denkinger, Chylak, Frantz, Flaherty and Barnett. Time—2:27. Attendance—41,156.

GAME OF WEDNESDAY, OCTOBER 11, AT DETROIT

Oakland	AB.	R.	H.	RBI.	PO.	A.
Alou, rf	5	1	2	1	1	0
Maxvill, ss	2	0	1	0	0	1
Hendrick, ph	1	0	0	0	0	0
Cullen, ss	0	0	0	0	0	2
Mangual, ph	1	0	0	0	0	0
Kubiak, ss	1	0	1	1	0	0
Rudi, lf	5	0	0	0	3	0
Jackson, cf	5	0	2	0	3	0
Bando, 3b	5	0	0	0	1	2
Epstein, 1b	3	1	1	1	9	0
Tenace, c-2b	4	0	0	0	5	0
Green, 2b	2	0	1	0	1	3
Duncan, ph-c	1	0	0	0	4	1
Hunter, p	3	0	0	0	0	0
Fingers, p	0	0	0	0	0	0
Blue, p	0	0	0	0	0	0
Marquez, ph	1	1	1	0	0	0
Locker, p	0	0	0	0	0	0
Horlen, p	0	0	0	0	0	0
Hamilton, p	0	0	0	0	0	0
Totals	39	3	9	3	27	9

Detroit	AB.	R.	H.	RBI.	PO.	A.
McAuliffe, ss	4	2	2	1	1	1
Kaline, rf	3	1	1	0	1	0
Sims, lf	3	0	1	0	2	0
Stanley, cf	1	0	1	0	3	0
G. Brown, ph	0	1	0	0	0	0
Freehan, c	5	0	1	1	7	0
Cash, 1b	4	0	1	1	12	0
Northrup, cf-lf	5	0	1	1	2	0
Taylor, 2b	4	0	2	0	1	2
Rodriguez, 3b	2	0	0	0	0	7
Lolich, p	3	0	0	0	1	0
Horton, ph	1	0	0	0	0	0
Seelbach, p	0	0	0	0	0	0
Hiller, p	0	0	0	0	0	0
Totals	35	4	10	4	30	10

	1	2	3	4	5	6	7	8	9	10	R
Oakland	0	0	0	0	0	0	1	0	0	2	3
Detroit	0	0	1	0	0	0	0	0	0	3	4

None out when winning run scored.

Oakland	IP.	H.	R.	ER.	BB.	SO.
Hunter	7⅓	6	1	1	3	5
Fingers	⅔	0	0	0	0	1
Blue	1	1	0	0	1	2
Locker	0*	2	2	2	0	0
Horlen (Loser)	0†	0	1	1	1	0
Hamilton	0‡	1	0	0	1	0

Detroit	IP.	H.	R.	ER.	BB.	SO.
Lolich	9	5	1	1	2	6
Seelbach	⅔	3	2	2	0	0
Hiller (Winner)	⅓	1	0	0	0	0

*Pitched to two batters in tenth.
†Pitched to two batters in tenth.
‡Pitched to two batters in tenth.

Errors—Jackson, Rodriguez, Tenace. Double play—Oakland 1. Left on base—Oakland 8, Detroit 11. Two-base hits—Sims, Green, Taylor 2, Alou 2. Home runs—McAuliffe, Epstein. Sacrifice hit—Kaline. Wild pitch—Horlen. Umpires—Denkinger, Chylak, Rice, Flaherty, Barnett and Frantz. Time—3:04. Attendance—37,615.

GAME OF THURSDAY, OCTOBER 12, AT DETROIT

Oakland	AB.	R.	H.	RBI.	PO.	A.
Alou, rf	2	0	1	0	3	0
Maxvill, ss	4	0	0	0	2	4
Rudi, lf	4	0	0	0	2	0
Jackson, cf	0	1	0	0	0	0
Hendrick, cf	3	1	0	0	1	0
Bando, 3b	3	0	1	0	2	1
Epstein, 1b	3	0	0	0	10	0
Tenace, c	3	0	1	1	6	0
Green, 2b	4	0	0	0	1	2
Odom, p	2	0	1	0	0	1
Blue, p	1	0	0	0	0	1
Totals	29	2	4	1	27	9

Detroit	AB.	R.	H.	RBI.	PO.	A.
McAuliffe, ss	4	1	1	0	0	3
Kaline, rf	4	0	0	0	6	0
Sims, lf	3	0	0	0	1	0
Freehan, c	4	0	0	1	3	2
Cash, 1b	4	0	1	0	13	0
Niekro, pr	0	0	0	0	0	0
Northrup, cf	2	0	2	0	3	0
Stanley, ph	1	0	0	0	0	0
Taylor, 2b	4	0	0	0	1	3
Rodriguez, 3b	3	0	0	0	0	3
Fryman, p	2	0	0	0	0	2
Horton, ph	1	0	1	0	0	0
Knox, pr	0	0	0	0	0	0
Hiller, p	0	0	0	0	0	0
Totals	32	1	5	1	27	13

Oakland	0	1	0	1	0	0	0	0	0 – 2
Detroit	1	0	0	0	0	0	0	0	0 – 1

Oakland	IP.	H.	R.	ER.	BB.	SO.
Odom (Winner)	5	2	1	0	2	3
Blue (Save)	4	3	0	0	0	3

Detroit	IP.	H.	R.	ER.	BB.	SO.
Fryman (Loser)	8	4	2	1	1	3
Hiller	1	0	0	0	1	0

Errors—McAuliffe, Sims. Double play—Detroit 1. Left on base—Oakland 6, Detroit 6. Two-base hit—Odom. Stolen bases—Jackson 2, Epstein. Sacrifice hits—Bando, Alou. Hit by pitch—By Fryman (Epstein, Alou). Wild pitch—Odom. Balk—Fryman. Passed ball—Tenace. Umpires—Chylak, Rice, Barnett, Flaherty, Frantz and Denkinger. Time—2:48. Attendance—50,276.

OAKLAND ATHLETICS' BATTING AND FIELDING AVERAGES

Player—Position	G.	AB.	R.	H.	TB.	2B.	3B.	HR.	RBI.	B.A.	PO.	A.	E.	F.A.
Marquez, ph	3	3	1	2	2	0	0	0	0	.667	0	0	0	.000
Kubiak, 2b-ss	4	4	0	2	2	0	0	0	1	.500	3	8	1	.917
Campaneris, ss	2	7	3	3	3	0	0	0	0	.429	3	7	0	1.000
Alou, rf	5	21	2	8	12	4	0	0	2	.381	14	0	1	.933
Jackson, cf	5	18	1	5	6	1	0	0	2	.278	14	0	1	.933
Rudi, lf	5	20	1	5	6	1	0	0	2	.250	11	0	0	1.000
Odom, pr-p	3	4	0	1	2	1	0	0	0	.250	2	1	0	1.000
Bando, 3b	5	20	0	4	4	0	0	0	0	.200	6	16	0	1.000
Epstein, 1b	5	16	1	3	6	0	0	1	1	.188	55	2	0	1.000
Hunter, p	2	6	0	1	1	0	0	0	0	.167	0	0	0	.000
Hendrick, ph-cf	5	7	2	1	1	0	0	0	0	.143	1	0	0	1.000
Green, 2b	5	8	0	1	2	1	0	0	0	.125	5	7	0	1.000
Maxvill, 2b-pr-ss	5	8	0	1	1	0	0	0	0	.125	3	8	0	1.000
Tenace, c-2b	5	17	1	1	1	0	0	0	1	.059	21	5	1	.963
Hamilton, p	1	0	0	0	0	0	0	0	0	.000	0	0	0	.000
Horlen, p	1	0	0	0	0	0	0	0	0	.000	0	0	0	.000
Locker, p	2	0	0	0	0	0	0	0	0	.000	0	0	0	.000

Player—Position	G.	AB.	R.	H.	TB.	2B.	3B.	HR.	RBI.	B.A.	PO.	A.	E.	F.A.
Holtzman, p	1	1	0	0	0	0	0	0	0	.000	0	1	0	1.000
Mincher, ph	1	1	0	0	0	0	0	0	0	.000	0	0	0	.000
Cullen, ss	2	1	0	0	0	0	0	0	0	.000	0	2	0	1.000
Fingers, p	3	1	0	0	0	0	0	0	0	.000	0	0	0	.000
Hegan, pr-1b-ph	3	1	1	0	0	0	0	0	0	.000	1	0	0	1.000
Blue, p	4	1	0	0	0	0	0	0	0	.000	0	1	0	1.000
Duncan, ph-c	2	2	0	0	0	0	0	0	0	.000	5	1	0	1.000
Mangual, ph	3	3	0	0	0	0	0	0	0	.000	0	0	0	.000
Totals	5	170	13	38	49	8	0	1	10	.224	138	59	3	.985

DETROIT TIGERS' BATTING AND FIELDING AVERAGES

Player—Position	G.	AB.	R.	H.	TB.	2B.	3B.	HR.	RBI.	B.A.	PO.	A.	E.	F.A.
I. Brown, 1b	1	2	0	1	1	0	0	0	2	.500	2	0	0	1.000
Coleman, p	1	2	0	1	1	0	0	0	0	.500	0	0	0	.000
Northrup, cf-lf	5	14	0	5	5	0	0	0	1	.357	12	0	0	1.000
Stanley, cf-ph	4	6	0	2	2	0	0	0	0	.333	7	0	0	1.000
Cash, 1b-ph	5	15	1	4	7	0	0	1	2	.267	39	3	0	1.000
Kaline, rf	5	19	3	5	8	0	0	1	1	.263	12	0	1	.923
Freehan, c	3	12	2	3	7	1	0	1	3	.250	24	3	0	1.000
Brinkman, ss	1	4	0	1	2	1	0	0	0	.250	1	2	0	1.000
Sims, c-lf	4	14	0	3	7	2	1	0	0	.214	16	1	1	.944
McAuliffe, 2b-ss	5	20	3	4	7	0	0	1	1	.200	12	10	4	.846
Taylor, 2b	4	15	0	2	4	2	0	0	0	.133	5	9	0	1.000
Horton, lf-ph	5	10	0	1	1	0	0	0	0	.100	6	0	0	1.000
Knox, pr	1	0	0	0	0	0	0	0	0	.000	0	0	0	.000
LaGrow, p	1	0	0	0	0	0	0	0	0	.000	0	0	0	.000
Niekro, pr	1	0	0	0	0	0	0	0	0	.000	0	0	0	.000
Scherman, p	1	0	0	0	0	0	0	0	0	.000	0	0	0	.000
Zachary, p	1	0	0	0	0	0	0	0	0	.000	0	0	0	.000
Seelbach, p	2	0	0	0	0	0	0	0	0	.000	0	0	0	.000
Hiller, p	3	0	0	0	0	0	0	0	0	.000	0	0	0	.000
Haller, ph	1	1	0	0	0	0	0	0	0	.000	0	0	0	.000
G. Brown, ph	3	2	1	0	0	0	0	0	0	.000	0	0	0	.000
Fryman, p	2	3	0	0	0	0	0	0	0	.000	0	3	0	1.000
Lolich, p	2	7	0	0	0	0	0	0	0	.000	1	3	0	1.000
Rodriguez, 3b	5	16	0	0	0	0	0	0	0	.000	2	14	1	.941
Totals	5	162	10	32	52	6	1	4	10	.198	139	48	7	.964

OAKLAND ATHLETICS' PITCHING RECORDS

Pitcher	G.	GS.	CG.	IP.	H.	R.	ER.	BB.	SO.	HB.	WP.	W.	L.	Pct.	ERA.
Odom	2	2	1	14	5	1	0	2	5	0	1	2	0	1.000	0.00
Blue	4	0	0	5⅓	4	0	0	1	5	0	0	0	0	.000	0.00
Hamilton	1	0	0	0*	1	0	0	1	0	0	0	0	0	.000	0.00
Hunter	2	2	0	15⅓	10	2	2	5	9	0	0	0	0	.000	1.17
Fingers	3	0	0	5⅓	4	1	1	3	0	0	1	1	0	1.000	1.69
Holtzman	1	1	0	4	4	2	2	2	2	0	0	0	1	.000	4.50
Locker	2	0	0	2	4	3	3	0	1	0	0	0	0	.000	13.50
Horlen	1	0	0	0*	0	1	1	1	0	0	0	1	1	.000	....
Totals	5	5	1	46	32	10	9	13	25	0	2	3	2	.600	1.76

Shutout—Odom. Save—Blue.

DETROIT TIGERS' PITCHING RECORDS

Pitcher	G.	GS.	CG.	IP.	H.	R.	ER.	BB.	SO.	HB.	WP.	W.	L.	Pct.	ERA.
Coleman	1	1	1	9	7	0	0	3	14	0	0	1	0	1.000	0.00
Hiller	3	0	0	3⅓	1	0	0	1	1	0	0	1	0	1.000	0.00
LaGrow	1	0	0	1	0	0	0	1	1	0	0	0	0	.000	0.00
Scherman	1	0	0	⅔	1	0	0	1	0	0	0	0	0	.000	0.00
Lolich	2	2	0	19	14	4	3	5	10	0	0	0	1	.000	1.42
Fryman	2	2	0	12⅓	11	6	5	2	8	2	0	0	2	.000	3.65
Seelbach	2	0	0	1	4	2	2	0	0	0	0	0	0	.000	18.00
Zachary	1	0	0	0†	0	1	1	1	0	0	2	0	0	.000	....
Totals	5	5	1	46⅓	38	13	11	12	35	3	2	2	3	.400	2.11

*Pitched to two batters in tenth inning of fourth game. †Pitched to one batter in fifth inning of second game.
Shutout—Coleman. No saves.

COMPOSITE SCORE BY INNINGS

Oakland	1	1	1	1	4	0	1	0	0	2	2 – 13
Detroit	1	1	1	2	0	0	0	1	0	3	1 – 10

Sacrifice hits—Cash, Bando 2, Odom, Freehan, Kaline, Alou.
Sacrifice fly—Rudi.
Stolen bases—Campaneris 2, Alou, Maxvill, Jackson 2, Epstein.
Caught stealing—Northrup, Alou, Tenace, McAuliffe.
Double plays—Rodriguez and McAuliffe; Kubiak, Campaneris and Epstein; Taylor, McAuliffe and Cash; Maxvill and Epstein; Maxvill, Kubiak and Epstein; Bando, Tenace and Epstein; Freehan and McAuliffe; Cullen, Green and Epstein; Rodriguez, Taylor and Cash.
Left on bases—Oakland 38—10, 4, 10, 8, 6; Detroit 30—6, 2, 5, 11, 6.
Hit by pitchers—By LaGrow (Campaneris), by Fryman (Alou, Epstein).
Passed ball—Tenace.
Balk—Fryman.
Time of games—First game, 3:09; second game, 2:37; third game, 2:27; fourth game, 3:04; fifth game, 2:48.
Attendance—First game, 29,536; second game, 31,088; third game, 41,156; fourth game, 37,615; fifth game, 50,276.
Umpires—Flaherty, Chylak, Rice, Denkinger, Barnett and Frantz.
Official scorers—Watson Spoelstra, Detroit News; Dick O'Connor, Palo Alto Times.

NATIONAL LEAGUE
Championship Series of 1972

	W.	L.	Pct.
Cincinnati (West)	3	2	.600
Pittsburgh (East)	2	3	.400

So you're ahead by one run in the last of the ninth and the other team has its righthanded power hitters coming up? So whom do you want to pitch?

That was the situation facing Pittsburgh Pirate Manager Bill Virdon in the final game of the 1972 National League Championship Series.

And the Buc skipper brought in his best—righthander Dave Giusti, who had saved 22 games and won seven others during the regular season. But, unfortunately for the Pirates, Virdon went to the well and came up dry.

The first batter Giusti faced was Johnny Bench, home run king of the senior circuit during the regular season. Bench unloaded one of his specialties over the right field fence and the score was tied at 3-3.

When Tony Perez and Denis Menke followed with singles, Virdon came to the mound and led Giusti away, replacing him with another righthander, Bob Moose.

Cesar Geronimo flied out deep to right, sending George Foster, running for Perez, to third. Darrel Chaney popped out for the second out.

With Hal McRae, batting for relief pitcher Clay Carroll at the plate, Moose uncorked a pitch that bounced in front of the plate and skipped past catcher Manny Sanguillen. Foster raced home with the run that gave the Reds the National League pennant.

Up to the fifth game, the two teams had staged a series which had held the interest of fans throughout the country and put to rest speculation that the Championship Series had failed to catch on.

Joe Morgan, second man up in the opener, hit a home run off Steve Blass.

But that was just a prelude to the Pirate shooting. Rennie Stennett singled, Al Oliver tripled, Willie Stargell doubled and Hebner singled. It all added up to three runs, more than enough, as events proved, to win the game.

But Pittsburgh got two more in the fifth on another single by Stennett and a homer by Oliver. All of the Buc runs came off Don Gullett.

The Reds returned the favor the next day with their own big first inning as starter Moose failed to retire a batter. Pete Rose and Morgan singled and Bobby Tolan, Bench and Perez hit successive doubles to plate a total of four runs.

The Pirates picked up singletons in the fourth, fifth and sixth and actually were in good position to get much more in the fifth. They had two men on with two out and a two-ball, no-strike count on Stargell when Tom Hall replaced starter Jack Billingham on the hill for the Reds. He got Stargell on a called third strike.

The scene shifted to Cincinnati Riverfront Stadium for the third game and the Pirates won it, 3-2. But only after a tense struggle.

Cincinnati jumped off to a lead with two runs in the third on singles by Chaney, Morgan and Tolan. A stolen base by Morgan had set up the second run.

Sanguillen's homer off starter Gary Nolan gave the Bucs a counter in the fifth. Nolan left the game after hurling six innings when his arm tightened.

Pedro Borbon took the mound for the Reds in the seventh and hit Hebner with a pitch. Sanguillen singled and Gene Alley's sacrifice moved the runners along. Carroll relieved Borbon and issued an intentional pass to Vic Davalillo, pinch-hitting for Nelson Briles. A run came in on a hit by Stennett which bounced over the head of Perez at first. A double play got the Reds out of the inning with the score tied.

But Pittsburgh was not to be denied in the eighth. With one out, Stargell walked, Oliver doubled and Hebner was purposely passed to load the bases. Sanguillen forced Hebner at second, Chaney to Morgan, but the Pirates' catcher beat the relay to first and the winning run scored.

Pittsburgh was in a position at that stage to clinch its second successive flag but the Pirates never came close the next day. Lefty Ross Grimsley set them down with just two hits, both by Roberto Clemente, as his teammates battered four Pirate pitchers for 11 hits and seven runs.

That brought the teams to the climactic fifth game.

GAME OF SATURDAY, OCTOBER 7, AT PITTSBURGH

Cincinnati	AB.	R.	H.	RBI.	PO.	A.
Rose, lf	5	0	2	0	1	0
Morgan, 2b	4	1	1	1	0	6
Tolan, cf	5	0	1	0	4	0
Bench, c	3	0	0	0	3	0
Perez, 1b	4	0	1	0	14	0
Menke, 3b	3	0	1	0	0	1
Geronimo, rf	4	0	0	0	2	0
Chaney, ss	4	0	0	0	0	4
Gullett, p	2	0	1	0	0	0
Uhlaender, ph	1	0	1	0	0	0
Borbon, p	0	0	0	0	0	0
Hague, ph	0	0	0	0	0	0
Totals	35	1	8	1	24	11

Pittsburgh	AB.	R.	H.	RBI.	PO.	A.
Stennett, lf	4	2	2	0	7	0
Oliver, cf	4	2	2	3	8	0
Clemente, rf	4	0	0	0	3	0
Stargell, 1b	3	1	1	1	2	0
Robertson, 1b	0	0	0	0	1	0
Sanguillen, c	3	0	0	0	2	0
Hebner, 3b	3	0	1	1	0	0
Cash, 2b	3	0	0	0	0	2
Alley, ss	3	0	0	0	3	0
Blass, p	3	0	0	0	1	0
R. Hernandez, p	0	0	0	0	0	0
Totals	30	5	6	5	27	2

Cincinnati	1	0	0	0	0	0	0	0 — 1
Pittsburgh	3	0	0	0	2	0	0	0	x — 5

Cincinnati	IP.	H.	R.	ER.	BB.	SO.
Gullett (Loser)	6	6	5	5	0	3
Borbon	2	0	0	0	0	0

Pittsburgh	IP.	H.	R.	ER.	BB.	SO.
Blass (Winner)	8⅓	8	1	1	4	1
R. Hernandez (Save)	⅔	0	0	0	0	1

Errors—None. Left on base—Cincinnati 11, Pittsburgh 1. Two-base hits—Stargell, Rose. Three-base hit—Oliver. Home runs—Morgan, Oliver. Passed ball—Bench. Umpires—Donatelli, Burkhart, Harvey, Williams, Kibler and Wendelstedt. Time—1:57. Attendance—50,476.

GAME OF SUNDAY, OCTOBER 8, AT PITTSBURGH

Cincinnati	AB.	R.	H.	RBI.	PO.	A.		Pittsburgh	AB.	R.	H.	RBI.	PO.	A.
Rose, lf	4	1	1	0	2	0		Stennett, lf-2b	4	0	1	0	2	0
Morgan, 2b	4	2	2	1	3	4		Oliver, cf	5	1	2	0	3	0
Tolan, cf	4	1	2	2	1	0		Clemente, rf	3	0	0	1	1	0
Bench, c	4	1	1	0	8	0		Stargell, 1b-lf	3	0	0	0	6	0
Perez, 1b	4	0	1	2	7	2		Hebner, 3b	4	0	0	0	1	3
Menke, 3b	3	0	0	0	1	2		May, c	2	0	1	1	8	1
Geronimo, rf	4	0	1	0	1	0		Sanguillen, ph-c	2	1	1	0	2	0
Chaney, ss	2	0	0	0	2	2		Cash, 2b	4	0	1	1	2	1
Concepcion, ph-ss	2	0	0	0	0	0		Giusti, p	0	0	0	0	0	0
Billingham, p	2	0	0	0	0	1		Alley, ss	3	1	0	0	1	1
Hall, p	1	0	0	0	1	0		Moose, p	0	0	0	0	0	0
Totals	34	5	8	5	27	10		Johnson, p	1	0	0	0	0	0
								Mazeroski, ph	1	0	1	0	0	0
								Ellis, pr	0	0	0	0	0	0
								Kison, p	0	0	0	0	0	0
								Clines, ph	1	0	0	0	0	0
								R. Hernandez, p	0	0	0	0	0	2
								Robertson, 1b	0	0	0	0	1	0
								Totals	33	3	7	3	27	8

Cincinnati	4	0	0		0	0	0		0	1	0 – 5
Pittsburgh	0	0	0		1	1	1		0	0	0 – 3

Cincinnati	IP.	H.	R.	ER.	BB.	SO.
Billingham	4⅔	5	2	2	2	4
Hall (Winner)	4⅓	2	1	1	2	4

Pittsburgh	IP.	H.	R.	ER.	BB.	SO.
Moose (Loser)	0*	5	4	4	0	0
Johnson	5	1	0	0	1	6
Kison	2	0	0	0	0	2
R. Hernandez	1	1	1	1	0	1
Giusti	1	1	0	0	0	1

*Pitched to five batters in first.

Errors—Bench, Cash. Double plays—Cincinnati 1, Pittsburgh 2. Left on base—Cincinnati 3, Pittsburgh 8. Two-base hits—Tolan, Bench, Perez, Oliver, Sanguillen. Home run—Morgan. Hit by pitcher—By Billingham (Alley). Wild pitch—Johnson. Umpires—Burkhart, Harvey, Williams, Kibler, Wendelstedt and Donatelli. Time—2:43. Attendance—50,584.

GAME OF MONDAY, OCTOBER 9, AT CINCINNATI

Pittsburgh	AB.	R.	H.	RBI.	PO.	A.		Cincinnati	AB.	R.	H.	RBI.	PO.	A.
Stennett, lf	5	0	2	1	4	1		Rose, lf	4	0	3	0	3	0
Cash, 2b	5	0	1	0	1	0		Morgan, 2b	4	1	1	1	5	1
Clemente, rf	3	0	1	0	2	0		Tolan, cf	4	0	1	1	2	0
Stargell, 1b	3	0	0	0	4	2		Bench, c	4	0	1	0	5	2
Clines, pr	0	1	0	0	0	0		Perez, 1b	4	0	1	0	5	0
Robertson, 1b	0	0	0	0	0	1		Concepcion, pr	0	0	0	0	0	0
Oliver, cf	4	0	1	0	1	1		Menke, 3b	3	0	0	0	1	3
Hebner, 3b	2	1	1	0	1	0		Geronimo, rf	4	0	0	0	4	1
Sanguillen, c	4	1	2	2	8	0		Chaney, ss	3	1	1	0	2	3
Alley, ss	3	0	0	0	4	1		Nolan, p	2	0	0	0	0	0
Briles, p	2	0	0	0	1	1		Borbon, p	0	0	0	0	0	0
Davalillo, ph	0	0	0	0	0	0		Carroll, p	0	0	0	0	0	1
Kison, p	0	0	0	0	0	0		Hague, ph	1	0	0	0	0	0
Giusti, p	1	0	0	0	1	0		McGlothlin, p	0	0	0	0	0	0
Totals	32	3	7	3	27	8		Totals	33	2	8	2	27	11

Pittsburgh	0	0	0		0	1	0		1	1	0 – 3
Cincinnati	0	0	2		0	0	0		0	0	0 – 2

Pittsburgh	IP.	H.	R.	ER.	BB.	SO.
Briles	6	6	2	2	1	3
Kison (Winner)	1⅓	1	0	0	0	1
Giusti (Save)	1⅔	1	0	0	0	2

Cincinnati	IP.	H.	R.	ER.	BB.	SO.
Nolan	6	4	1	1	1	4
Borbon	⅓	1	1	1	0	0
Carroll (Loser)	1⅔	2	1	1	3	0
McGlothlin	1	0	0	0	0	0

Error—Chaney. Double plays—Pittsburgh 1, Cincinnati 1. Left on base—Pittsburgh 8, Cincinnati 5. Two-base hits—Rose 2, Clemente, Oliver. Three-base hit—Bench. Home run—Sanguillen. Stolen base—Morgan. Sacrifice hit—Alley. Hit by pitcher—By Borbon (Hebner). Wild pitch—Nolan. Umpires—Harvey, Williams, Kibler, Wendelstedt, Donatelli and Burkhart. Time—2:33. Attendance—52,420.

GAME OF TUESDAY, OCTOBER 10, AT CINCINNATI

Pittsburgh	AB.	R.	H.	RBI.	PO.	A.
Stennett, lf	4	0	0	0	3	0
Oliver, cf	4	0	0	0	4	0
Clemente, rf	4	1	2	1	1	0
Stargell, 1b	3	0	0	0	7	1
Sanguillen, c	3	0	0	0	5	0
Cash, 2b	3	0	0	0	0	2
Hebner, 3b	3	0	0	0	3	5
Alley, ss	3	0	0	0	1	1
Ellis, p	1	0	0	0	0	0
Mazeroski, ph	1	0	0	0	0	0
Johnson, p	0	0	0	0	0	0
Walker, p	0	0	0	0	0	0
Clines, ph	1	0	0	0	0	0
Miller, p	0	0	0	0	0	0
Totals	30	1	2	1	24	9

Cincinnati	AB.	R.	H.	RBI.	PO.	A.
Rose, lf	4	0	2	1	1	0
Morgan, 2b	3	1	1	0	1	4
Tolan, cf	4	2	1	1	4	0
Bench, c	3	1	2	1	5	0
Perez, 1b	4	0	0	0	11	0
Menke, 3b	4	1	2	0	0	1
Geronimo, rf	4	1	0	0	2	0
Chaney, ss	3	1	1	1	3	6
Grimsley, p	4	0	2	1	0	0
Totals	33	7	11	5	27	11

Pittsburgh 0   0   0   0   0   0   1   0   0 – 1
Cincinnati 1   0   0   2   0   2   2   0   x – 7

Pittsburgh	IP.	H.	R.	ER.	BB.	SO.
Ellis (Loser)	5	5	3	0	1	3
Johnson	1	3	2	2	1	1
Walker	1	3	2	2	0	0
Miller	1	0	0	0	0	1

Cincinnati	IP.	H.	R.	ER.	BB.	SO.
Grimsley (Winner)	9	2	1	1	0	5

Errors—Sanguillen, Chaney, Alley 2. Left on base—Pittsburgh 2, Cincinnati 6. Two-base hits—Grimsley, Menke. Three-base hit—Tolan. Home run—Clemente. Stolen bases—Bench 2, Chaney. Sacrifice hit—Morgan. Sacrifice fly—Bench. Umpires—Williams, Kibler, Wendelstedt, Donatelli, Burkhart and Harvey. Time—1:58. Attendance—39,447.

GAME OF WEDNESDAY, OCTOBER 11, AT CINCINNATI

Pittsburgh	AB.	R.	H.	RBI.	PO.	A.
Stennett, lf	4	0	1	0	1	0
Oliver, cf	3	0	0	0	1	0
Clemente, rf	3	0	1	0	3	0
Stargell, 1b	4	0	0	0	13	0
Robertson, 1b	0	0	0	0	0	0
Sanguillen, c	4	2	2	0	5	0
Hebner, 3b	4	1	2	0	0	2
Cash, 2b	4	0	2	2	2	5
Alley, ss	4	0	0	0	1	1
Blass, p	3	0	0	0	0	3
R. Hernandez, p	0	0	0	0	0	0
Giusti, p	0	0	0	0	0	0
Moose, p	0	0	0	0	0	0
Totals	33	3	8	2	26	11

Cincinnati	AB.	R.	H.	RBI.	PO.	A.
Rose, lf	3	0	1	1	3	0
Morgan, 2b	4	0	0	0	2	3
Tolan, cf	4	0	0	0	2	0
Bench, c	4	1	2	1	7	1
Perez, 1b	4	0	1	0	8	1
Foster, pr	0	1	0	0	0	0
Menke, 3b	3	0	1	0	1	4
Geronimo, rf	4	1	1	1	2	0
Chaney, ss	4	1	1	0	1	1
Gullett, p	0	0	0	0	0	0
Borbon, p	0	0	0	0	1	0
Uhlaender, ph	1	0	0	0	0	0
Hall, p	0	0	0	0	0	0
Hague, ph	0	0	0	0	0	0
Concepcion, pr	0	0	0	0	0	0
Carroll, p	0	0	0	0	0	0
McRae, ph	0	0	0	0	0	0
Totals	31	4	7	3	27	10

Pittsburgh	0	2	0	1	0	0	0	0	0 – 3
Cincinnati	0	0	1	0	1	0	0	0	2 – 4

Two out when winning run scored.

Pittsburgh	IP.	H.	R.	ER.	BB.	SO.
Blass	7⅓	4	2	2	2	4
R. Hernandez	⅔	0	0	0	0	1
Giusti (Loser)	0†	3	2	2	0	0
Moose	⅔	0	0	0	0	0

Cincinnati	IP.	H.	R.	ER.	BB.	SO.
Gullett	3*	6	3	3	0	2
Borbon	2	1	0	0	0	1
Hall	3	1	0	0	1	4
Carroll (Winner)	1	0	0	0	0	0

*Pitched to two batters in fourth.
†Pitched to three batters in ninth.

Error—Chaney. Double play—Cincinnati 1. Left on base—Pittsburgh 5, Cincinnati 5. Two-base hits—Hebner, Rose. Home runs—Geronimo, Bench. Sacrifice hits—Gullett, Oliver, Rose. Wild pitches—Gullett, Moose. Umpires—Donatelli, Kibler, Wendelstedt, Burkhart, Harvey and Williams. Time—2:19. Attendance—41,887.

CINCINNATI REDS' BATTING AND FIELDING AVERAGES

Player–Position	G.	AB.	R.	H.	TB.	2B.	3B.	HR.	RBI.	B.A.	PO.	A.	E.	F.A.
Grimsley, p	1	4	0	2	3	1	0	0	1	.500	0	0	0	.000
Gullett, p	2	2	0	1	1	0	0	0	0	.500	0	0	0	.000
Uhlaender, ph	2	2	0	1	1	0	0	0	0	.500	0	0	0	.000
Rose, lf	5	20	1	9	13	4	0	0	2	.450	10	0	0	1.000
Bench, c	5	18	3	6	12	1	1	1	2	.333	28	3	1	.969
Morgan, 2b	5	19	5	5	11	0	0	2	3	.263	11	18	0	1.000
Menke, 3b	5	16	1	4	5	1	0	0	0	.250	3	11	0	1.000
Tolan, cf	5	21	3	5	8	1	1	0	4	.238	13	0	0	1.000
Perez, 1b	5	20	0	4	5	1	0	0	2	.200	45	3	0	1.000
Chaney, ss	5	16	3	3	3	0	0	0	1	.188	8	16	3	.889
Geronimo, rf	5	20	2	2	5	0	0	1	3	.100	11	1	0	1.000
Foster, pr	1	0	1	0	0	0	0	0	0	.000	0	0	0	.000
McGlothlin, p	1	0	0	0	0	0	0	0	0	.000	0	0	0	.000
McRae, ph	1	0	0	0	0	0	0	0	0	.000	0	0	0	.000
Carroll, p	2	0	0	0	0	0	0	0	0	.000	0	1	0	1.000
Borbon, p	3	0	0	0	0	0	0	0	0	.000	1	0	0	1.000
Hague, ph	3	1	0	0	0	0	0	0	0	.000	0	0	0	.000
Hall, p	2	1	0	0	0	0	0	0	0	.000	1	0	0	1.000
Billingham, p	1	2	0	0	0	0	0	0	0	.000	1	0	0	1.000
Nolan, p	1	2	0	0	0	0	0	0	0	.000	0	0	0	.000
Concepcion, ph-ss-pr	3	2	0	0	0	0	0	0	0	.000	0	0	0	.000
Totals	5	166	19	42	67	9	2	4	16	.253	132	53	4	.979

PITTSBURGH PIRATES' BATTING AND FIELDING AVERAGES

Player–Position	G.	AB.	R.	H.	TB.	2B.	3B.	HR.	RBI.	B.A.	PO.	A.	E.	F.A.
May, c	1	2	0	1	1	0	0	0	1	.500	8	1	0	1.000
Mazeroski, ph	2	2	0	1	1	0	0	0	0	.500	0	0	0	.000
Sanguillen, c-ph	5	16	4	5	9	1	0	1	2	.313	22	0	1	.957
Stennett, lf-2b	5	21	2	6	6	0	0	0	1	.286	17	1	0	1.000
Oliver, cf	5	20	3	5	12	2	1	1	3	.250	17	1	0	1.000
Clemente, rf	5	17	1	4	8	1	0	1	2	.235	10	0	0	1.000
Cash, 2b	5	19	0	4	4	0	0	0	3	.211	5	10	1	.938
Hebner, 3b	5	16	2	3	4	1	0	0	1	.188	5	11	0	1.000
Stargell, 1b-lf	5	16	1	1	2	1	0	0	1	.063	32	3	0	1.000
Davalillo, ph	1	0	0	0	0	0	0	0	0	.000	0	0	0	.000
Miller, p	1	0	0	0	0	0	0	0	0	.000	0	0	0	.000
Walker, p	1	0	0	0	0	0	0	0	0	.000	0	0	0	.000
Kison, p	2	0	0	0	0	0	0	0	0	.000	0	0	0	.000
Moose, p	2	0	0	0	0	0	0	0	0	.000	0	0	0	.000
R. Hernandez, p	3	0	0	0	0	0	0	0	0	.000	0	2	0	1.000
Robertson, 1b	4	0	0	0	0	0	0	0	0	.000	2	1	0	1.000
Ellis, pr-p	2	1	0	0	0	0	0	0	0	.000	0	0	0	.000
Johnson, p	2	1	0	0	0	0	0	0	0	.000	0	1	0	1.000
Giusti, p	3	1	0	0	0	0	0	0	0	.000	1	0	0	1.000
Briles, p	1	2	0	0	0	0	0	0	0	.000	1	1	0	1.000
Clines, ph-pr	3	2	1	0	0	0	0	0	0	.000	0	0	0	.000
Blass, p	2	6	0	0	0	0	0	0	0	.000	1	3	0	1.000
Alley, ss	5	16	1	0	0	0	0	0	0	.000	10	4	2	.875
Totals	5	158	15	30	47	6	1	3	14	.190	131	38	4	.977

CINCINNATI REDS' PITCHING RECORDS

Pitcher	G.	GS.	CG.	IP.	H.	R.	ER.	BB.	SO.	HB.	WP.	W.	L.	Pct.	ERA.
McGlothlin	1	0	0	1	0	0	0	0	0	0	0	0	0	.000	0.00
Grimsley	1	1	1	9	2	1	1	0	5	0	0	1	0	1.000	1.00
Hall	2	0	0	7⅓	3	1	1	3	8	0	0	1	0	1.000	1.23
Nolan	1	1	0	6	4	1	1	1	4	0	1	0	0	.000	1.50
Borbon	3	0	0	4⅓	2	1	1	0	1	1	0	0	0	.000	2.08
Carroll	2	0	0	2⅔	2	1	1	3	0	0	0	1	1	.500	3.38
Billingham	1	1	0	4⅔	5	2	2	2	4	1	0	0	0	.000	3.86
Gullett	2	2	0	9	12	8	8	0	5	0	1	0	1	.000	8.00
Totals	5	5	1	44	30	15	15	9	27	2	2	3	2	.600	3.07

No shutouts or saves.

PITTSBURGH PIRATES' PITCHING RECORDS

Pitcher	G.	GS.	CG.	IP.	H.	R.	ER.	BB.	SO.	HB.	WP.	W.	L.	Pct.	ERA.
Ellis	1	1	0	5	5	3	0	1	3	0	0	0	1	.000	0.00
Kison	2	0	0	2⅓	1	0	0	0	3	0	0	1	0	1.000	0.00
Miller	1	0	0	1	0	0	0	0	1	0	0	0	0	.000	0.00
Blass	2	2	0	15⅔	12	3	3	6	5	0	0	1	0	1.000	1.72
R. Hernandez	3	0	0	3⅓	1	1	1	0	3	0	0	0	0	.000	2.70
Briles	1	1	0	6	6	2	2	1	3	0	0	0	0	.000	3.00
Johnson	2	0	0	6	4	2	2	2	7	0	1	0	0	.000	3.00
Giusti	3	0	0	2⅔	5	2	2	0	3	0	0	0	1	.000	6.75
Walker	1	0	0	1	3	2	2	0	0	0	0	0	0	.000	18.00
Moose	2	1	0	⅔	5	4	4	0	0	0	1	0	1	.000	54.00
Totals	5	5	0	43⅔	42	19	16	10	28	0	2	2	3	.400	3.30

No shutouts. Saves—R. Hernandez, Giusti.

COMPOSITE SCORE BY INNINGS

Cincinnati	6	0	3		2	1	2		2	1	2 – 19
Pittsburgh	3	2	0		2	4	1		2	1	0 – 15

Sacrifice hits—Alley, Morgan, Oliver, Rose, Gullett.
Sacrifice fly—Bench.
Stolen bases—Morgan, Bench 2, Chaney.
Caught stealing—Tolan, Stennett.
Double plays—Morgan, Chaney and Perez 2; Hebner and Stargell; May and Cash; Stennett and Sanguillen; Geronimo, Bench and Morgan.
Left on bases—Cincinnati 30—11, 3, 5, 6, 5; Pittsburgh 24—1, 8, 8, 2, 5.
Hit by pitcher—By Billingham (Alley); by Borbon (Hebner).
Passed ball—Bench.
Balks—None.
Time of games—First game, 1:57; second game, 2:43; third game, 2:33; fourth game, 1:58; fifth game, 2:19.
Attendance—First game, 50,476; second game, 50,584; third game, 52,420; fourth game, 39,447; fifth game, 41,887.
Umpires—Donatelli, Burkhart, Harvey, Williams, Kibler and Wendelstedt.
Official scorers—Jim Ferguson, Dayton Daily News; Luke Quay, McKeesport Daily News.

AMERICAN LEAGUE
Championship Series of 1973

	W.	L.	Pct.
Oakland (West)	3	2	.600
Baltimore (East)	2	3	.400

The Oakland A's won their second straight American League pennant when they downed the Baltimore Orioles in a five-game Championship Series.

They almost won it in four games, but a last-ditch Baltimore rally sent the series to a climactic fifth game.

The Orioles, who had been in three previous Championship Series (1969,

1970, 1971) and had never lost a game, continued their winning ways in the opening contest, played at Memorial Stadium, Baltimore.

Jim Palmer spent 16 minutes retiring the side in the top of the first inning. He walked the first two batters and struck out the next three.

The Orioles went to work against lefty Vida Blue and his successor, Horacio Pina, and during that time, Merv Rettenmund singled, Paul Blair walked, Tommie Davis doubled, Don Baylor walked, Earl Williams singled, Andy Etchebarren was hit by a pitch and Mark Belanger singled. When the carnage was over, the Orioles had four runs. It was much more than they needed as Palmer proceeded to hurl a five-hit shutout, striking out 12 A's along the way. The final score was 6-0.

The Orioles' playoff winning streak was snapped at 10 the next day when Sal Bando hit two home runs off Dave McNally, Campy Campaneris and Joe Rudi hit one apiece and Catfish Hunter, who served so many during the season that he threatened an A.L. record, didn't allow any, and the A's won the game, 6-3.

The third game, postponed a day by rain—the postponement triggered a rhubarb between A. L. President Joe Cronin and A's President Charlie Finley—was played at the Oakland-Alameda County Coliseum and produced a brilliant pitching battle between a pair of southpaws, Mike Cuellar of Baltimore and Ken Holtzman. It was decided in favor of the A's when Campaneris, first man up in the bottom of the eleventh, snapped a 1-1 tie by hitting Cuellar's second pitch over the left field fence for a home run.

Up to that point, Cuellar had allowed only three hits. He had a one-hit shutout for the first seven innings as he carefully nursed a 1-0 lead given him by Earl Williams' homer in the second inning. But in the eighth, pinch-hitter Jesus Alou singled and pinch-runner Allan Lewis was sacrificed to second by Mike Andrews. The play was controversial in that Cuellar appeared to have a force out at second base, but he ignored catcher Etchebarren's yells and took the safe out at first. This proved costly as, one out later, Joe Rudi singled home Lewis to tie the score.

The Oakland club appeared to have the flag safely tucked away in the fourth contest but it escaped them.

The A's knocked out Palmer with a three-run outburst in the second inning and, going into the top of the seventh, Blue was breezing along with a 4-0 bulge when he suddenly came apart at the seams. Williams drew a base on balls and Baylor followed with a single. Brooks Robinson came through with a run-producing single and Etchebarren hit the very next pitch for a home run, making the score 4-4.

The tie didn't last long. The next inning Bobby Grich hit a home run off Rollie Fingers and that, coupled with Grant Jackson's stout relief pitching, gave the game to the Orioles and set up the contest for all the money the next afternoon.

A surprisingly small crowd of 24,265 showed up for the final game and they saw Hunter pitch a five-hit shutout, winning 3-0. Righthander Doyle Alexander was the Baltimore starter but he lasted only until the fourth inning. In that frame he was the victim of singles by Gene Tenace and Alou wrapped around a triple by Vic Davalillo. He was relieved by Palmer who shut out Oakland the rest of the way but the Orioles were helpless against Hunter's powerful pitching.

GAME OF SATURDAY, OCTOBER 6, AT BALTIMORE

Oakland	AB.	R.	H.	RBI.	PO.	A.
Campaneris, ss	3	0	1	0	0	2
Rudi, lf	2	0	0	0	4	0
Bando, 3b	3	0	0	0	2	2
Jackson, rf	4	0	1	0	1	0
Johnson, dh	2	0	0	0	0	0
Bourque, dh	1	0	0	0	0	0
Tenace, 1b-c	4	0	1	0	5	0
Mangual, cf	4	0	0	1	0	0
Fosse, c	2	0	0	0	8	1
Davalillo, ph-1b	2	0	2	0	1	0
Green, 2b	2	0	0	0	2	0
Alou, ph	1	0	0	0	0	0
Kubiak, 2b	1	0	0	0	0	0
Blue, p	0	0	0	0	0	0
Pina, p	0	0	0	0	0	0
Odom, p	0	0	0	0	0	1
Fingers, p	0	0	0	0	0	0
Totals	31	0	5	0	24	6

Baltimore	AB.	R.	H.	RBI.	PO.	A.
Rettenmund, rf	4	1	1	0	0	0
Grich, 2b	5	0	0	0	3	0
Blair, cf	4	2	1	0	2	0
Davis, dh	5	1	3	1	0	0
Baylor, lf	3	2	2	1	4	0
Robinson, 3b	5	0	0	0	0	0
Williams, 1b	4	0	2	2	3	1
Etchebarren, c	3	0	2	1	12	0
Belanger, ss	3	0	1	1	2	2
Palmer, p	0	0	0	0	1	0
Totals	36	6	12	6	27	5

```
Oakland .......... 0   0  0     0  0  0     0  0  0 – 0
Baltimore ........ 4   0  0     0  0  0     1  1  x – 6
```

Oakland	IP.	H.	R.	ER.	BB.	SO.
Blue (Loser)	⅔	3	4	4	2	2
Pina	2	3	0	0	1	1
Odom	5	6	2	1	2	4
Fingers	⅓	0	0	0	0	0
Baltimore	IP.	H.	R.	ER.	BB.	SO.
Palmer (Winner)	9	5	0	0	5	12

Error—Campaneris. Double plays—Oakland 1, Baltimore 1. Left on base—Oakland 9, Baltimore 12. Two-base hits—Davis, Williams, Davalillo. Stolen base—Campaneris. Hit by pitch—By Pina (Etchebarren). Wild pitch—Blue. Umpires—Chylak, Haller, Maloney, Odom, Anthony and McCoy. Time—2:51. Attendance—41,279.

GAME OF SUNDAY, OCTOBER 7, AT BALTIMORE

Oakland	AB.	R.	H.	RBI.	PO.	A.
Campaneris, ss	5	2	3	2	5	3
Rudi, lf	4	1	2	1	2	0
Bando, 3b	4	2	2	3	1	1
R. Jackson, rf	5	0	0	0	3	0
Tenace, 1b	3	0	1	0	6	1
Johnson, dh	4	0	1	0	1	0
Mangual, cf	4	1	0	0	7	0
Fosse, c	3	0	0	0	1	4
Green, 2b	4	0	0	0	1	0
Hunter, p	0	0	0	0	1	0
Fingers, p	0	0	0	0	0	0
Totals	36	6	9	6	27	9

Baltimore	AB.	R.	H.	RBI.	PO.	A.
Bumbry, lf	4	1	0	0	2	0
Coggins, rf-cf	5	1	2	0	2	0
Davis, dh	5	0	2	1	0	0
Powell, 1b	4	1	0	0	7	0
Williams, c	4	0	2	1	8	0
Blair, cf	3	0	0	0	4	0
Crowley, ph-rf	1	0	0	0	1	0
Robinson, 3b	3	0	1	1	0	2
Hood, pr	0	0	0	0	0	0
Baker, ss	0	0	0	0	0	0
Grich, 2b	2	0	0	0	2	0
Belanger, ss	3	0	1	0	0	6
Baylor, ph	1	0	0	0	0	0
Brown, 3b	0	0	0	0	0	0
McNally, p	0	0	0	0	0	0
Reynolds, p	0	0	0	0	1	0
G. Jackson, p	0	0	0	0	0	0
Totals	35	3	8	3	27	8

```
Oakland .......... 1   0  0     0  0  2     0  2  1 – 6
Baltimore ........ 1   0  0     0  0  1     0  1  0 – 3
```

Oakland	IP.	H.	R.	ER.	BB.	SO.
Hunter (Winner)	7⅓	7	3	3	3	5
Fingers (Save)	1⅔	1	0	0	1	1
Baltimore	IP.	H.	R.	ER.	BB.	SO.
McNally (Loser)	7⅔	7	5	5	2	7
Reynolds	1	2	1	1	1	2
G. Jackson	⅓	0	0	0	0	0

Errors—None. Left on base—Oakland 7, Baltimore 9. Two-base hit—Williams. Home runs—Campaneris, Rudi, Bando 2. Stolen bases—Campaneris 2. Sacrifice hit—Fosse. Wild pitch—McNally. Passed ball—Williams. Umpires—Haller, Chylak, Maloney, Odom, Anthony and McCoy. Time—2:42. Attendance—48,425.

GAME OF TUESDAY, OCTOBER 9, AT OAKLAND

Baltimore	AB.	R.	H.	RBI.	PO.	A.
Rettenmund, rf	5	0	0	0	2	0
Grich, 2b	5	0	1	0	1	4
Blair, cf	4	0	1	0	1	0
Davis, dh	3	0	0	0	0	0
Baylor, lf	4	0	0	0	1	0
Robinson, 3b	4	0	0	0	0	4
Williams, 1b	4	1	1	1	13	0
Etchebarren, c	4	0	0	0	10	1
Belanger, ss	4	0	0	0	2	2
Cuellar, p	0	0	0	0	0	2
Totals	37	1	3	1	30	13

Oakland	AB.	R.	H.	RBI.	PO.	A.
Campaneris, ss	5	1	1	1	1	3
Rudi, lf	4	0	1	1	1	0
Bando, 3b	4	0	0	0	2	2
Jackson, rf	4	0	0	0	4	0
Tenace, 1b-c	4	0	1	0	9	1
Johnson, dh	2	0	0	0	0	0
Conigliaro, cf	4	0	0	0	5	0
Fosse, c	1	0	0	0	6	0
Alou, ph	1	0	1	0	0	0
Lewis, pr	0	1	0	0	0	0
Davalillo, 1b	1	0	0	0	2	0
Green, 2b	2	0	0	0	2	2
Andrews, ph	0	0	0	0	0	0
Kubiak, 2b	1	0	0	0	0	1
Holtzman, p	0	0	0	0	1	2
Totals	33	2	4	2	33	11

Baltimore	0	1	0	0	0	0	0	0	0	0	0 – 1
Oakland	0	0	0	0	0	0	0	1	0	0	1 – 2

None out when winning run scored.

Baltimore	IP.	H.	R.	ER.	BB.	SO.
Cuellar (Loser)	10*	4	2	2	3	11

Oakland	IP.	H.	R.	ER.	BB.	SO.
Holtzman (Winner)	11	3	1	1	1	7

*Pitched to one batter in eleventh.

Errors—Green 2, Davalillo. Double play—Oakland 1. Left on base—Baltimore 4, Oakland 5. Home runs—Williams, Campaneris. Sacrifice hit—Andrews. Umpires—Maloney, Haller, Anthony, Chylak, McCoy and Odom. Time—2:23. Attendance—34,367.

GAME OF WEDNESDAY, OCTOBER 10, AT OAKLAND

Baltimore	AB.	R.	H.	RBI.	PO.	A.
Rettenmund, rf	2	0	0	0	1	0
Grich, 2b	4	1	1	1	4	3
Blair, cf	4	0	1	0	0	0
Davis, dh	4	0	1	0	0	0
Williams, 1b	3	1	0	0	9	0
Baylor, lf	3	1	1	0	2	0
Robinson, 3b	4	1	2	1	1	3
Etchebarren, c	4	1	2	3	6	1
Belanger, ss	4	0	0	0	4	2
Palmer, p	0	0	0	0	0	0
Reynolds, p	0	0	0	0	0	0
Watt, p	0	0	0	0	0	1
G. Jackson, p	0	0	0	0	0	0
Totals	32	5	8	5	27	10

Oakland	AB.	R.	H.	RBI.	PO.	A.
Campaneris, ss	4	0	1	0	0	3
Rudi, lf	4	0	0	0	2	0
Bando, 3b	3	0	0	0	0	1
R. Jackson, rf	4	0	1	0	7	0
Tenace, 1b-c	3	2	1	0	7	1
Davalillo, cf	3	1	2	0	1	0
Mangual, ph-cf	1	0	0	0	0	0
Johnson, dh	2	0	0	0	0	0
Bourque, ph-dh	0	0	0	0	0	0
Andrews, ph-1b	1	0	0	0	1	0
Fosse, c	2	1	1	3	3	2
Lewis, pr	0	0	0	0	0	0
Kubiak, 2b	0	0	0	0	0	0
Green, 2b	3	0	1	1	5	3
Alou, ph	1	0	0	0	0	0
Fingers, p	0	0	0	0	0	0
Blue, p	0	0	0	0	1	0
Totals	31	4	7	4	27	10

Baltimore	0	0	0	0	0	0	4	1	0 – 5
Oakland	0	3	0	0	0	1	0	0	0 – 4

Baltimore	IP.	H.	R.	ER.	BB.	SO.
Palmer	1⅓	4	3	3	2	2
Reynolds	4⅔*	3	1	1	2	3
Watt	⅓	0	0	0	0	0
G. Jackson (Winner)	2⅔	0	0	1	1	0

Oakland	IP.	H.	R.	ER.	BB.	SO.
Blue	6⅓	5	4	4	3	1
Fingers (Loser)	2⅔	3	1	1	1	3

*Pitched to one batter in seventh.

Errors—None. Double plays—Oakland 2. Left on base—Baltimore 4, Oakland 8. Two-base hits—Tenace, Fosse, Green, Robinson. Home runs—Etchebarren, Grich. Sacrifice hit—Rudi. Sacrifice fly—Fosse. Hit by pitch—By Watt (Bando). Umpires—Chylak, Haller, Maloney, Odom, Anthony and McCoy. Time—2:31. Attendance—27,497.

GAME OF THURSDAY, OCTOBER 11, AT OAKLAND

Baltimore	AB.	R.	H.	RBI.	PO.	A.
Bumbry, lf	3	0	0	0	2	1
Coggins, rf	4	0	2	0	2	0
Davis, dh	4	0	0	0	0	0
Williams, 1b	3	0	0	0	10	1
Blair, cf	3	0	0	0	1	0
Robinson, 3b	4	0	2	0	1	3
Grich, 2b	4	0	0	0	6	2
Etchebarren, c	3	0	1	0	2	0
Belanger, ss	2	0	0	0	0	5
Crowley, ph	1	0	0	0	0	0
Baker, ss	0	0	0	0	0	0
Alexander, p	0	0	0	0	0	2
Palmer, p	0	0	0	0	0	1
Totals	31	0	5	0	24	15

Oakland	AB.	R.	H.	RBI.	PO.	A.
Campaneris, ss	4	0	1	0	0	4
Rudi, lf	4	0	1	1	2	0
Bando, 3b	4	0	1	0	2	4
Jackson, rf	4	0	1	0	4	0
Tenace, 1b	3	1	1	0	13	0
Davalillo, cf	2	1	1	1	3	0
Alou, dh	3	0	1	1	0	0
Fosse, c	3	1	0	0	1	1
Green, 2b	2	0	0	0	2	2
Hunter, p	0	0	0	0	0	0
Totals	29	3	7	3	27	11

Baltimore	0	0	0		0	0	0		0	0	0 – 0
Oakland	0	0	1		2	0	0		0	0	x – 3

Baltimore	IP.	H.	R.	ER.	BB.	SO.
Alexander (Loser)	3⅔	5	3	2	0	1
Palmer	4⅓	2	0	0	1	1

Oakland	IP.	H.	R.	ER.	BB.	SO.
Hunter (Winner)	9	5	0	0	2	1

Errors– Robinson, Bumbry. Double play– Baltimore 1. Left on base– Baltimore 7, Oakland 5. Two-base hits– Etchebarren, Coggins, Campaneris, Robinson. Three-base hit– Davalillo. Stolen base– Bumbry. Sacrifice hit– Green. Hit by pitch– By Hunter (Blair), by Alexander (Tenace). Umpires– Haller, Chylak, Maloney, Odom, Anthony and McCoy. Time– 2:11. Attendance– 24,265.

OAKLAND ATHLETICS' BATTING AND FIELDING AVERAGES

Player–Position	G.	AB.	R.	H.	TB.	2B.	3B.	HR.	RBI.	B.A.	PO.	A.	E.	F.A.
Davalillo, ph-1b-cf	4	8	2	5	8	1	1	0	1	.625	7	0	1	.875
Campaneris, ss	5	21	3	7	14	1	0	2	3	.333	6	15	1	.955
Alou, ph-dh	4	6	0	2	2	0	0	0	1	.333	0	0	0	.000
Tenace, 1b-c	5	17	3	4	5	1	0	0	0	.235	40	3	0	1.000
Rudi, lf	5	18	1	4	7	0	0	1	3	.222	11	0	0	1.000
Bando, 3b	5	18	2	3	9	0	0	2	3	.167	7	10	0	1.000
R. Jackson, rf	5	21	0	3	3	0	0	0	0	.143	19	0	0	1.000
Mangual, cf-ph	3	9	1	1	1	0	0	0	0	.111	2	0	0	1.000
Johnson, dh	4	10	0	1	1	0	0	0	0	.100	0	0	0	.000
Fosse, c	5	11	2	1	2	1	0	0	3	.091	25	4	0	1.000
Green, 2b	5	13	0	1	2	1	0	0	1	.077	12	11	2	.920
Lewis, pr	2	0	1	0	0	0	0	0	0	.000	0	0	0	.000
Blue, p	2	0	0	0	0	0	0	0	0	.000	1	0	0	1.000
Fingers, p	3	0	0	0	0	0	0	0	0	.000	0	0	0	.000
Holtzman, p	1	0	0	0	0	0	0	0	0	.000	1	2	0	1.000
Hunter, p	2	0	0	0	0	0	0	0	0	.000	1	0	0	1.000
Odom, p	1	0	0	0	0	0	0	0	0	.000	0	1	0	1.000
Pina, p	1	0	0	0	0	0	0	0	0	.000	0	0	0	.000
Andrews, ph-1b	2	1	0	0	0	0	0	0	0	.000	1	0	0	1.000
Bourque, ph-dh	2	1	0	0	0	0	0	0	0	.000	0	0	0	.000
Kubiak, 2b	3	2	0	0	0	0	0	0	0	.000	0	1	0	1.000
Conigliaro, cf	1	4	0	0	0	0	0	0	0	.000	5	0	0	1.000
Totals	5	160	15	32	54	5	1	5	15	.200	138	47	4	.979

BALTIMORE ORIOLES' BATTING AND FIELDING AVERAGES

Player–Position	G.	AB.	R.	H.	TB.	2B.	3B.	HR.	RBI.	B.A.	PO.	A.	E.	F.A.
Coggins, rf-cf	2	9	1	4	5	1	0	0	0	.444	4	0	0	1.000
Etchebarren, c	4	14	1	5	9	1	0	1	4	.357	30	2	0	1.000
Davis, dh	5	21	1	6	7	1	0	0	2	.286	0	0	0	.000
Williams, 1b-c	5	18	2	5	10	2	0	1	4	.278	43	2	0	1.000
Baylor, lf-ph	4	11	3	3	3	0	0	0	1	.273	7	0	0	1.000
Robinson, 3b	5	20	1	5	7	2	0	0	2	.250	2	14	1	.941
Blair, cf	5	18	2	3	3	0	0	0	0	.167	8	0	0	1.000
Belanger, ss	5	16	0	2	2	0	0	0	1	.125	8	17	0	1.000
Grich, 2b	5	20	1	2	5	0	0	1	1	.100	16	9	0	1.000
Rettenmund, rf	3	11	1	1	1	0	0	0	0	.091	3	0	0	1.000
Alexander, p	1	0	0	0	0	0	0	0	0	.000	0	2	0	1.000
Baker, ss	2	0	0	0	0	0	0	0	0	.000	0	0	0	.000
Brown, 3b	1	0	0	0	0	0	0	0	0	.000	0	0	0	.000

Player—Position	G.	AB.	R.	H.	TB.	2B.	3B.	HR.	RBI.	B.A.	PO.	A.	E.	F.A.
Cuellar, p	1	0	0	0	0	0	0	0	0	.000	0	2	0	1.000
Hood, pr	1	0	0	0	0	0	0	0	0	.000	0	0	0	.000
G. Jackson, p	2	0	0	0	0	0	0	0	0	.000	0	0	0	.000
McNally, p	1	0	0	0	0	0	0	0	0	.000	0	0	0	.000
Palmer, p	3	0	0	0	0	0	0	0	0	.000	1	1	0	1.000
Reynolds, p	2	0	0	0	0	0	0	0	0	.000	1	0	0	1.000
Watt, p	1	0	0	0	0	0	0	0	0	.000	0	1	0	1.000
Crowley, ph-rf	2	2	0	0	0	0	0	0	0	.000	1	0	0	1.000
Powell, 1b	1	4	1	0	0	0	0	0	0	.000	7	0	0	1.000
Bumbry, lf	2	7	1	0	0	0	0	0	0	.000	4	1	1	.833
Totals	5	171	15	36	52	7	0	3	15	.211	135	51	2	.989

OAKLAND ATHLETICS' PITCHING RECORDS

Pitcher	G.	GS.	CG.	IP.	H.	R.	ER.	BB.	SO.	HB.	WP.	W.	L.	Pct.	ERA.
Pina	1	0	0	2	3	0	0	1	1	1	0	0	0	.000	0.00
Holtzman	1	1	1	11	3	1	1	7	0	0	1	0	0	1.000	0.82
Hunter	2	2	1	16⅓	12	3	3	5	6	1	0	2	0	1.000	1.65
Odom	1	0	0	5	6	2	1	2	4	0	0	0	0	.000	1.80
Fingers	3	0	0	4⅔	4	1	1	2	4	0	0	1	0	1.000	1.93
Blue	2	2	0	7	8	8	8	5	3	0	1	0	1	.000	10.29
Totals	5	5	2	46	36	15	14	16	25	2	1	3	2	.600	2.74

Shutout—Hunter. Save—Fingers.

BALTIMORE ORIOLES' PITCHING RECORDS

Pitcher	G.	GS.	CG.	IP.	H.	R.	ER.	BB.	SO.	HB.	WP.	W.	L.	Pct.	ERA.
G. Jackson	2	0	0	3	0	0	0	1	0	0	0	1	0	1.000	0.00
Watt	1	0	0	⅓	0	0	0	0	1	0	0	0	0	.000	0.00
Cuellar	1	1	1	10	4	2	2	3	11	0	0	0	1	.000	1.80
Palmer	3	2	1	14⅔	11	3	3	8	15	0	0	1	0	1.000	1.84
Reynolds	2	0	0	5⅔	5	2	2	3	5	0	0	0	0	.000	3.18
Alexander	1	1	0	3⅔	5	3	2	0	1	1	0	0	1	.000	4.91
McNally	1	1	0	7⅔	7	5	5	2	7	0	1	0	1	.000	5.87
Totals	5	5	2	45	32	15	14	17	39	1	1	2	3	.400	2.80

Shutout—Palmer. No Saves.

COMPOSITE SCORE BY INNINGS

Oakland	1	3	1	2	0	3	0	3	1	0	1 – 15
Baltimore	5	1	0	0	0	1	5	3	0	0	0 – 15

Sacrifice hits—Fosse, Andrews, Rudi, Green.
Sacrifice fly—Fosse.
Stolen bases—Campaneris 3, Bumbry.
Caught stealing—Rettenmund 2, Davis, R. Jackson, Blair.
Double plays—Fosse and Green 2; Williams, Belanger and Palmer; Holtzman, Green and Tenace; Campaneris, Green and Tenace; Alexander, Grich and Williams.
Left on bases—Oakland 34—9, 7, 5, 8, 5; Baltimore 36—12, 9, 4, 4, 7.
Hit by pitcher—By Pina (Etchebarren); ;by Watt (Bando); by Alexander (Tenace); by Hunter (Blair).
Passed ball—Williams.
Balks—None.
Time of games—First game, 2:51; second game, 2:42; third game, 2:23; fourth game, 2:31; fifth game, 2:11.
Attendance—First game, 41,279; second game, 48,425; third game, 34,367; fourth game, 27,497; fifth game, 24,265.
Umpires—Chylak, Haller, Maloney, Odom, Anthony and McCoy.
Official scorers—Jim Elliott, Baltimore Morning Sun; Herb Michelson, Sacramento Bee.

NATIONAL LEAGUE
Championship Series of 1973

	W.	L.	Pct.
New York (East)	3	2	.600
Cincinnati (West)	2	3	.400

The New York Mets dethroned the Cincinnati Reds in a five-game Championship Series in 1973 marked by riotous scenes unparalleled in baseball history.

The New Yorkers pinned their hopes in the Championship Series on pitching and to that end they sent their big ace, Tom Seaver, to the mound in the opening game, played at Cincinnati's Riverfront Stadium.

Seaver almost staged a personal tour de force. His double drove in his team's lone run in the second inning and the lead held up until the eighth inning when Pete Rose, later to become a storm center in the series, hit a home run. Johnny Bench hit a home run in the ninth inning and so Seaver, who had walked none and struck out 13, came out on the losing end.

While Seaver had come close to a shutout in the opener, teammate Jon Matlack did post a shutout the next afternoon. He yielded but two singles while the Mets collected five runs and seven hits off four Cincinnati pitchers.

Paced by Rusty Staub's two home runs and the steady pitching of lefty Jerry Koosman, the Mets had an easy win in the third game, played at Shea Stadium. Easy, that is, if only the box score is considered. For it was in this game that the fireworks were ignited.

In the fifth inning, Rose slid hard into Bud Harrelson in an attempt to break up a double play.

Harrelson completed the play and then he and Rose began pushing and shoving and finally fell to the ground flailing away at each other. Players from both benches and bullpens raced onto the field.

It took several minutes to restore peace, but neither Rose nor Harrelson was ejected.

When Rose returned to left field, the fans began throwing bottles, garbage and other assorted debris at him. The barrage became so intense that Manager Sparky Anderson pulled the Reds off the field.

Finally, Yogi Berra, Willie Mays, Staub, Cleon Jones and Seaver walked out to left field and pleaded with the fans to cease and desist. The appeal was heeded and the game proceeded to its finish.

Game No. 4 could be aptly entitled "Rose's Revenge." The peppery Cincinnati outfielder hit a home run in the 12th inning to give his team a 2-1 victory and square the series at two games apiece. Earlier in the contest, while out in the field, Rose had been given a beer shower by a Met "fan."

The New York club salted the final game away in the fifth inning. With the score tied at 2-2, Wayne Garrett opened the frame with a double. Then Red rookie third baseman Dan Driessen made a grievous mental blunder. When Felix Millan laid down a sacrifice bunt, pitcher Jack Billingham fielded the ball and threw to third, apparently in plenty of time to get the runner. But Driessen, thinking (or not thinking) he had a force play, stepped on the bag but neglected to tag the runner. Jones then doubled, and Milner walked. Mays got a pinch-hit single to score another run and still another scored on a fielder's choice before Harrelson's single plated the fourth and final tally of the inning.

Seaver, pitching for the Mets, protected his lead with the help of Tug McGraw's relief and the Mets were National League Champions for 1973.

The final game will remain indelibly etched in the memories of those who saw it, either in person or on television. For not only was it the day the Mets clinched the pennant, it was the day that several thousand of their followers staged a reenactment of the storming of the Bastille. Unruly Mets' partisans tore up everything that wasn't nailed down.

GAME OF SATURDAY, OCTOBER 6, AT CINCINNATI

New York	AB.	R.	H.	RBI.	PO.	A.	Cincinnati	AB.	R.	H.	RBI.	PO.	A.
Garrett, 3b	4	0	1	0	2	1	Rose, lf	4	1	1	1	2	0
Millan, 2b	3	0	0	0	1	1	Morgan, 2b	4	0	0	0	2	6
Staub, rf	2	0	0	0	2	0	Driessen, 3b	4	0	1	0	0	0
Milner, 1b	3	0	1	0	3	1	Perez, 1b	4	0	0	0	11	1
Jones, lf	4	0	0	0	2	0	Bench, c	4	1	3	1	6	0
Grote, c	4	0	0	0	13	0	Griffey, rf	2	0	0	0	1	0
Hahn, cf	3	0	0	0	0	0	Geronimo, cf	3	0	1	0	5	0
Harrelson, ss	2	1	0	0	2	1	Chaney, ss	2	0	0	0	0	2
Seaver, p	3	0	1	1	0	0	Stahl, ph	1	0	0	0	0	0
							Crosby, ss	0	0	0	0	0	2
Totals	28	1	3	1	25	4	Billingham, p	1	0	0	0	0	1
							King, ph	1	0	0	0	0	0
							Hall, p	0	0	0	0	0	0
							Borbon, p	0	0	0	0	0	0
							Totals	30	2	6	2	27	12

New York .... 0 1 0   0 0 0   0 0 0 – 1
Cincinnati .... 0 0 0   0 0 0   0 1 1 – 2
One out when winning run scored.

New York	IP.	H.	R.	ER.	BB.	SO.
Seaver (Loser)	8⅓	6	2	2	0	13

Cincinnati	IP.	H.	R.	ER.	BB.	SO.
Billingham	8	3	1	1	3	6
Hall	0*	0	0	0	1	0
Borbon (Winner)	1	0	0	0	0	0

*Pitched to one batter in ninth.

Errors–None. Double play–Cincinnati 1. Left on base–New York 5, Cincinnati 5. Two-base hits–Seaver, Bench, Driessen. Home runs–Rose, Bench. Sacrifice hits–Millan, Billingham. Hit by pitch–By Seaver (Griffey). Umpires–Sudol, Vargo, Pelekoudas, Engel, Froemming and Dale. Time–2:00. Attendance–53,431.

GAME OF SUNDAY, OCTOBER 7, AT CINCINNATI

New York	AB.	R.	H.	RBI.	PO.	A.	Cincinnati	AB.	R.	H.	RBI.	PO.	A.
Garrett, 3b	5	0	0	0	0	3	Rose, lf	4	0	0	0	2	0
Millan, 2b	4	1	1	0	1	0	Morgan, 2b	4	0	0	0	3	3
Staub, rf	3	2	1	1	3	0	Perez, 1b	4	0	0	0	5	1
Jones, lf	3	1	1	1	2	0	Bench, c	4	0	0	0	7	0
Milner, 1b	3	1	0	0	6	2	Kosco, rf	2	0	2	0	4	0
Grote, c	4	0	1	2	9	0	Driessen, 3b	3	0	0	0	1	1
Hahn, cf	3	0	2	0	3	0	Geronimo, cf	3	0	0	0	3	0
Harrelson, ss	4	0	1	1	3	4	Chaney, ss	0	0	0	0	1	1
Matlack, p	2	0	0	0	0	1	Armbrister, ph	1	0	0	0	0	0
Totals	31	5	7	5	27	10	Hall, p	0	0	0	0	1	0
							Borbon, p	0	0	0	0	0	0
							Gullett, p	0	0	0	0	0	0
							Gagliano, ph	1	0	0	0	0	0
							Carroll, p	0	0	0	0	0	1
							Menke, ph-ss	1	0	0	0	0	0
							Totals	27	0	2	0	27	9

New York .... 0 0 0   1 0 0   0 0 4 – 5
Cincinnati .... 0 0 0   0 0 0   0 0 0 – 0

New York	IP.	H.	R.	ER.	BB.	SO.
Matlack (Winner)	9	2	0	0	3	9

Cincinnati	IP.	H.	R.	ER.	BB.	SO.
Gullett (Loser)	5	2	1	1	2	3
Carroll	3	0	0	0	1	2
Hall	⅓	2	4	4	2	0
Borbon	⅔	3	0	0	0	1

Errors–None. Double play–Cincinnati 1. Left on base–New York 5, Cincinnati 4. Home run–Staub. Sacrifice hits–Gullett, Matlack. Umpires–Vargo, Pelekoudas, Engel, Froemming, Dale and Sudol. Time–2:19. Attendance –54,041.

GAME OF MONDAY, OCTOBER 8, AT NEW YORK

Cincinnati	AB.	R.	H.	RBI.	PO.	A.
Rose, lf	4	0	2	0	3	0
Morgan, 2b	4	0	1	1	0	5
Perez, 1b	4	0	0	0	8	0
Bench, c	4	0	1	0	6	0
Kosco, rf	4	0	0	0	4	0
Armbrister, cf	4	0	1	0	3	0
Menke, 3b	4	1	1	1	0	1
Chaney, ss	3	0	0	0	0	1
Gagliano, ph	1	0	0	0	0	0
Grimsley, p	0	0	0	0	0	0
Hall, p	0	0	0	0	0	0
Stahl, ph	1	1	1	0	0	0
Tomlin, p	0	0	0	0	0	0
Nelson, p	1	0	0	0	0	0
King, ph	1	0	1	0	0	0
Borbon, p	0	0	0	0	0	1
Totals	35	2	8	2	24	8

New York	AB.	R.	H.	RBI.	PO.	A.
Garrett, 3b	4	0	0	1	1	0
Millan, 2b	3	2	1	1	2	0
Staub, rf	5	2	2	4	0	0
Jones, lf	3	1	2	0	1	0
Milner, 1b	4	0	1	1	4	1
Grote, c	3	2	1	0	9	0
Hahn, cf	4	1	2	0	8	0
Harrelson, ss	4	0	0	0	2	3
Koosman, p	4	1	2	1	0	0
Totals	34	9	11	8	27	4

```
Cincinnati ............. 0   2   0 0 0   0 0   0 - 2
New York ............... 1 5 1   2 0 0   0 0   x - 9
```

Cincinnati	IP.	H.	R.	ER.	BB.	SO.
Grimsley (Loser)	1⅔	5	5	5	1	2
Hall	⅔	1	1	1	1	1
Tomlin	1⅓	5	3	3	1	1
Nelson	2⅓	0	0	0	1	0
Borbon	2	0	0	0	0	2

New York	IP.	H.	R.	ER.	BB.	SO.
Koosman (Winner)	9	8	2	2	0	9

Errors—Kosco, Garrett. Double play—New York 1. Left on base—Cincinnati 6, New York 6. Two-base hits—Jones, Bench. Home runs—Staub 2, Menke. Sacrifice fly—Garrett. Umpires— Pelekoudas, Engel, Froemming, Dale, Sudol and Vargo. Time—2:48. Attendance—53,967.

GAME OF TUESDAY, OCTOBER 9, AT NEW YORK

Cincinnati	AB.	R.	H.	RBI.	PO.	A.
Rose, lf	5	1	3	1	3	0
Morgan, 2b	4	0	0	0	4	7
Perez, 1b	6	1	1	1	13	0
Bench, c	4	0	1	0	7	0
Kosco, rf	4	0	1	0	4	0
Menke, 3b-ss	4	0	1	0	0	3
Geronimo, cf	5	0	0	0	2	0
Chaney, ss	2	0	0	0	0	3
Armbrister, ph	1	0	0	0	0	0
Crosby, ss	1	0	1	0	1	0
Driessen, pr-3b	1	0	0	0	1	0
Norman, p	1	0	0	0	1	0
Stahl, ph	1	0	0	0	0	0
Gullett, p	1	0	0	0	1	0
Gagliano, ph	1	0	0	0	0	0
Carroll, p	0	0	0	0	0	0
Griffey, ph	1	0	0	0	0	0
Borbon, p	0	0	0	0	0	1
Totals	42	2	8	2	36	15

New York	AB.	R.	H.	RBI.	PO.	A.
Garrett, 3b	5	0	0	0	1	1
Millan, 2b	5	0	2	1	4	3
Staub, rf	5	0	0	0	5	0
Jones, lf	5	0	0	0	5	0
Milner, 1b	4	0	0	0	10	1
Grote, c	4	0	1	0	7	1
Hahn, cf	3	1	0	0	0	0
Harrelson, ss	4	0	0	0	2	5
Stone, p	1	0	0	0	1	2
McGraw, p	1	0	0	0	1	0
Boswell, ph	1	0	0	0	0	0
Parker, p	0	0	0	0	0	0
Totals	38	1	3	1	36	13

```
Cincinnati .......... 0 0 0   0 0 0   1 0 0   0 0   1 - 2
New York ............ 0 0 1   0 0 0   0 0 0   0 0   0 - 1
```

Cincinnati	IP.	H.	R.	ER.	BB.	SO.
Norman	5	1	1	1	3	3
Gullett	4	2	0	0	0	3
Carroll (Winner)	2	0	0	0	0	0
Borbon (Save)	1	0	0	0	0	0

New York	IP.	H.	R.	ER.	BB.	SO.
Stone	6⅔	3	1	1	2	4
McGraw	4⅓	4	0	0	3	3
Parker (Loser)	1	1	1	1	0	0

Errors—McGraw, Grote. Double plays—Cincinnati 1, New York 2. Left on base—Cincinnati 10, New York 4. Home runs—Perez, Rose. Sacrifice hit—Morgan. Wild pitch—McGraw. Umpires—Engel, Froemming, Dale, Sudol, Vargo and Pelekoudas. Time—3:07. Attendance—50,786.

GAME OF WEDNESDAY, OCTOBER 10, AT NEW YORK

Cincinnati	AB.	R.	H.	RBI.	PO.	A.
Rose, lf	4	1	2	0	0	1
Morgan, 2b	4	1	1	0	3	6
Driessen, 3b	4	0	1	1	2	1
Perez, 1b	4	0	1	1	10	1
Bench, c	3	0	0	0	5	0
Griffey, rf	4	0	1	0	1	0
Geronimo, cf	4	0	0	0	1	1
Chaney, ss	2	0	0	0	1	3
Stahl, ph	1	0	0	0	0	0
Billingham, p	2	0	0	0	0	1
Gullett, p	0	0	0	0	0	0
Carroll, p	0	0	0	0	0	1
Crosby, ph	1	0	0	0	0	0
Grimsley, p	0	0	0	0	1	0
King, ph	0	0	0	0	0	0
Totals	33	2	7	2	24	15

New York	AB.	R.	H.	RBI.	PO.	A.
Garrett, 3b	5	1	1	0	0	1
Millan, 2b	4	2	2	0	1	7
Jones, rf-lf	5	1	3	2	0	0
Milner, 1b	3	1	1	0	14	1
Kranepool, lf	2	0	1	2	2	0
Mays, ph-cf	3	1	1	1	1	0
Grote, c	4	0	1	0	4	0
Hahn, cf-rf	4	0	0	1	1	0
Harrelson, ss	4	0	2	1	3	1
Seaver, p	3	1	1	0	0	3
McGraw, p	0	0	0	0	1	0
Totals	37	7	13	7	27	13

Cincinnati	0	0	1		0	1	0		0	0	0 – 2
New York	2	0	0		0	4	1		0	0	x – 7

Cincinnati	IP.	H.	R.	ER.	BB.	SO.
Billingham (Loser)	4*	6	5	5	1	3
Gullett	0†	0	1	1	1	0
Carroll	2	5	1	1	0	0
Grimsley	2	2	0	0	1	1

New York	IP.	H.	R.	ER.	BB.	SO.
Seaver (Winner)	8⅓	7	2	1	5	4
McGraw (Save)	⅔	0	0	0	0	0

*Pitched to three batters in fifth.
†Pitched to one batter in fifth.

Errors—Jones, Driessen. Left on base—Cincinnati 10, New York 10. Two-base hits—Morgan, Griffey, Rose, Garrett, Jones, Seaver. Sacrifice hit—Millan. Sacrifice fly—Driessen. Wild pitch—Seaver. Umpires—Froemming, Dale, Sudol, Vargo, Pelekoudas and Engel. Time—2:40. Attendance—50,323.

CINCINNATI REDS' BATTING AND FIELDING AVERAGES

Player—Position	G.	AB.	R.	H.	TB.	2B.	3B.	HR.	RBI.	B.A.	PO.	A.	E.	F.A.
Stahl, ph	4	4	1	2	2	0	0	0	0	.500	0	0	0	.000
Crosby, ss-ph	3	2	0	1	1	0	0	0	0	.500	1	2	0	1.000
King, ph	3	2	0	1	1	0	0	0	0	.500	0	0	0	.000
Rose, lf	5	21	3	8	15	1	0	2	2	.381	10	1	0	1.000
Kosco, rf	3	10	0	3	3	0	0	0	0	.300	12	0	1	.923
Bench, c	5	19	1	5	10	2	0	1	1	.263	31	2	0	1.000
Menke, ph-ss-1b	3	9	1	2	5	0	0	1	1	.222	0	4	0	1.000
Driessen, 3b-pr	4	12	0	2	3	1	0	0	1	.167	3	2	1	.833
Armbrister, ph-cf	3	6	0	1	1	0	0	0	0	.167	3	0	0	1.000
Griffey, rf-ph	3	7	0	1	2	1	0	0	0	.143	2	0	0	1.000
Morgan, 2b	5	20	1	2	3	1	0	0	1	.100	12	27	0	1.000
Perez, 1b	5	22	1	2	5	0	0	1	2	.091	47	4	0	1.000
Geronimo, cf	4	15	0	1	1	0	0	0	0	.067	11	1	0	1.000
Borbon, p	4	0	0	0	0	0	0	0	0	.000	0	2	0	1.000
Carroll, p	3	0	0	0	0	0	0	0	0	.000	0	2	0	1.000
Grimsley, p	2	0	0	0	0	0	0	0	0	.000	1	0	0	1.000
Hall, p	3	0	0	0	0	0	0	0	0	.000	1	0	0	1.000
Tomlin, p	1	0	0	0	0	0	0	0	0	.000	0	0	0	.000
Gullett, p	3	1	0	0	0	0	0	0	0	.000	1	0	0	1.000
Nelson, p	1	1	0	0	0	0	0	0	0	.000	0	0	0	.000
Norman, p	1	1	0	0	0	0	0	0	0	.000	1	0	0	1.000
Billingham, p	2	3	0	0	0	0	0	0	0	.000	0	2	0	1.000
Gagliano, ph	3	3	0	0	0	0	0	0	0	.000	0	0	0	.000
Chaney, ss	5	9	0	0	0	0	0	0	0	.000	2	10	0	1.000
Totals	5	167	8	31	52	6	0	5	8	.186	138	59	2	.990

NEW YORK METS' BATTING AND FIELDING AVERAGES

Player—Position	G.	AB.	R.	H.	TB.	2B.	3B.	HR.	RBI.	B.A.	PO.	A.	E.	F.A.
Koosman, p	1	4	1	2	2	0	0	0	1	.500	0	0	0	.000
Kranepool, lf	1	2	0	1	1	0	0	0	2	.500	2	0	0	1.000
Seaver, p	2	6	1	2	4	2	0	0	1	.333	0	3	0	1.000
Mays, ph-cf	1	3	1	1	1	0	0	0	1	.333	1	0	0	1.000
Millan, 2b	5	19	5	6	6	0	0	0	2	.316	9	11	0	1.000
Jones, lf-rf	5	20	3	6	8	2	0	0	3	.300	10	0	1	.909
Hahn, cf-rf	5	17	2	4	4	0	0	0	1	.235	2	0	0	1.000
Grote, c	5	19	2	4	4	0	0	0	2	.211	42	1	1	.977
Staub, rf	4	15	4	3	12	0	0	3	5	.200	10	0	0	1.000
Milner, 1b	5	17	2	3	3	0	0	0	1	.176	37	6	0	1.000
Harrelson, ss	5	18	1	3	3	0	0	0	2	.167	12	14	0	1.000
Garrett, 3b	5	23	1	2	3	1	0	0	1	.087	4	6	1	.909
Parker, p	1	0	0	0	0	0	0	0	0	.000	0	0	0	.000
Boswell, ph	1	1	0	0	0	0	0	0	0	.000	0	0	0	.000
McGraw, p	2	1	0	0	0	0	0	0	0	.000	2	0	1	.667
Stone, p	1	1	0	0	0	0	0	0	0	.000	1	2	0	1.000
Matlack, p	1	2	0	0	0	0	0	0	0	.000	0	1	0	1.000
Totals	5	168	23	37	51	5	0	3	22	.220	142	44	4	.979

CINCINNATI REDS' PITCHING RECORDS

Pitcher	G.	GS.	CG.	IP.	H.	R.	ER.	BB.	SO.	HB.	WP.	W.	L.	Pct.	ERA.
Borbon	4	0	0	4⅔	3	0	0	0	3	0	0	1	0	1.000	0.00
Nelson	1	0	0	2⅓	0	0	0	1	0	0	0	0	0	.000	0.00
Carroll	3	0	0	7	5	1	1	1	2	0	0	1	0	1.000	1.29
Norman	1	1	0	5	1	1	1	3	3	0	0	0	0	.000	1.80
Gullett	3	1	0	9	4	2	2	3	6	0	0	0	1	.000	2.00
Billingham	2	2	0	12	9	6	6	4	9	0	0	0	1	.000	4.50
Grimsley	2	1	0	3⅔	7	5	5	2	3	0	0	0	1	.000	12.27
Tomlin	1	0	0	1⅔	5	3	3	1	1	0	0	0	0	.000	16.20
Hall	3	0	0	⅔	3	5	5	4	1	0	0	0	0	.000	67.50
Totals	5	5	0	46	37	23	23	19	28	0	0	2	3	.400	4.50

No shutouts. Save—Borbon.

NEW YORK METS' PITCHING RECORDS

Pitcher	G.	GS.	CG.	IP.	H.	R.	ER.	BB.	SO.	HB.	WP.	W.	L.	Pct.	ERA.
Matlack	1	1	1	9	2	0	0	3	9	0	0	1	0	1.000	0.00
McGraw	2	0	0	5	4	0	0	3	3	0	1	0	0	.000	0.00
Stone	1	1	0	6⅔	3	1	1	2	4	0	0	0	0	.000	1.35
Seaver	2	2	1	16⅔	13	4	3	5	17	1	1	1	1	.500	1.62
Koosman	1	1	1	9	8	2	2	0	9	0	0	1	0	1.000	2.00
Parker	1	0	0	1	1	1	1	0	0	0	0	0	1	.000	9.00
Totals	5	5	3	47⅓	31	8	7	13	42	1	2	3	2	.600	1.33

Shutout—Matlack. Save—McGraw.

COMPOSITE SCORE BY INNINGS

New York	3	6	2	3	4	1	0	0	4	0	0	0 — 23
Cincinnati	0	0	3	0	1	0	1	1	1	0	0	1 — 8

Sacrifice hits—Millan 2, Billingham, Matlack, Gullett, Morgan.
Sacrifice flies—Garrett, Driessen.
Stolen bases—None.
Caught stealing—Driessen.
Double plays—Chaney, Morgan and Perez 2; Morgan, Chaney and Perez; Milner, Harrelson and Milner; Millan, Harrelson and Milner; Harrelson, Millan and Milner.
Left on bases—New York 30—5, 5, 6, 4, 10; Cincinnati 35—5, 4, 6, 10, 10.
Hit by pitcher—By Seaver (Griffey).
Passed balls—None.
Balks—None.
Time of games—First game, 2:00; second game, 2:19; third game, 2:48; fourth game, 3:07; fifth game, 2:40.
Attendance—First game, 53,431; second game, 54,041; third game, 53,967; fourth game, 50,786; fifth game, 50,323.
Umpires—Sudol, Vargo, Pelekoudas, Engel, Froemming and Dale.
Official scorers—Jack Lang, Long Island Press; Bob Hertzel, Cincinnati Enquirer.

AMERICAN LEAGUE
Championship Series of 1974

	W.	L.	Pct.
Oakland (West)	3	1	.750
Baltimore (East)	1	3	.250

The Oakland A's won their third consecutive American League pennant when they downed the Baltimore Orioles, three games to one, in the Championship Series.

The Orioles, who came into their fifth playoff in the last six years on the impetus of nine straight victories and 28 wins in their last 34 games of the regular season, carried their momentum into the Championship Series opener, played at Oakland.

The Birds jumped all over the ace of the Oakland staff, Jim Hunter, pounding him for six runs and eight hits, including three homers, in less than five innings. Hunter had a skein of seven straight decisions over the Birds going into the game. Southpaw Mike Cuellar pitched steady ball for the winners and got the decision with relief help in the ninth inning from Ross Grimsley.

A portent of things to happen came in the first inning when Paul Blair, second man in the batting order, hit a Hunter pitch for a home run. Bert Campaneris' single that followed a fielder's choice and a stolen base by Bill North gave the A's a temporary tie in the third inning. But a double by Bobby Grich and Tommy Davis' single put the Orioles ahead to stay in the fourth. A four-run outburst in the fifth, featured by homers on the part of Brooks Robinson and Bobby Grich, locked up the game and sent Hunter to the showers.

When Cuellar yielded a single to Jesus Alou and a double to Claudell Washington, both pinch-hitters, to open the last of the ninth, he was derricked in favor of Grimsley who got the last three outs without trouble. The final score was 6-3.

The A's assumed command the next day when Ken Holtzman permitted the Orioles only five hits en route to a 5-0 triumph. The Oakland club got an unearned run in the fourth when Bobby Grich dropped a foul pop by Sal Bando for an error. Two pitches later, Bando drove a Dave McNally pitch over the left field fence for a homer. Joe Rudi tripled home North in the sixth for the second run. In the eighth inning, with two men on—the result of a walk and an error—Ray Fosse hit a home run off reliever Grant Jackson to put the game on ice.

The third game of the set, played in Baltimore, produced a brilliant pitching duel between A's lefty Vida Blue and Jim Palmer. Blue hurled a two-hitter and Palmer a four-hitter. But one of the four safe blows yielded by the Oriole righthander was a home run by Bando in the fourth inning. It was the only run of the game.

The fourth game saw the A's capture a 2-1 verdict, although their batting order was able to produce only one safe hit for the afternoon. Cuellar pitched a no-hitter for four and two-thirds innings but walked four consecutive batters to give Oakland a run. During his stint on the mound, the Oriole lefty walked no less than nine batters and was removed while yet to give up a hit.

The run which was to prove decisive came in the seventh off reliever Grimsley. Bando walked and Reggie Jackson stroked a double off the left field wall to plate Bando.

The Orioles almost pulled the game out of the bag in their last turn at bat. With one out and Rollie Fingers pitching in relief of Hunter, Blair walked and Grich singled. A force play provided the second out of the inning but Boog Powell's single drove in one run. Fingers, however, was equal to the occasion, striking out Baylor on a fast ball to clinch the league crown for Oakland.

The triumph of the A's was notable in a couple of ways. Besides marking Oakland's third straight pennant, it placed Manager Alvin Dark in the company of only two other managers who have won pennants in both major leagues. Joe McCarthy did it with the Cubs and the Yankees and Yogi Berra did it with the Yankees and the Mets.

GAME OF SATURDAY, OCTOBER 5, AT OAKLAND

Baltimore	AB.	R.	H.	RBI.	PO.	A.
Coggins, rf	4	0	0	0	3	0
Blair, cf	4	2	2	2	2	0
Grich, 2b	4	2	2	2	1	2
Davis, dh	4	0	2	1	0	0
Powell, 1b	4	0	0	0	8	1
Baylor, lf	4	0	2	0	2	0
Robinson, 3b	4	1	1	1	0	5
Hendricks, c	4	1	1	0	5	0
Belanger, ss	3	0	0	0	6	2
Cuellar, p	0	0	0	0	0	3
Grimsley, p	0	0	0	0	0	0
Totals	35	6	10	6	27	13

Oakland	AB.	R.	H.	RBI.	PO.	A.
North, cf	5	2	1	0	3	0
Campaneris, ss	4	0	3	3	0	5
Jackson, rf	4	0	0	0	0	0
Bando, 2b	4	0	1	0	1	2
Rudi, lf	4	0	0	0	2	0
Tenace, 1b	3	0	0	0	12	1
Mangual, dh	4	0	1	0	0	0
Fosse, c	2	0	1	0	6	0
Alou, ph	1	0	1	0	0	0
Trillo, pr	0	1	0	0	0	0
Green, 2b	2	0	0	0	2	3
C. Washington, ph	1	0	1	0	0	0
Hunter, p	0	0	0	0	1	1
Odom, p	0	0	0	0	0	0
Fingers, p	0	0	0	0	0	0
Totals	34	3	9	3	27	12

Baltimore	1	0	0		1	4	0		0	0	0 – 6
Oakland	0	0	1		0	1	0		0	0	1 – 3

Baltimore	IP.	H.	R.	ER.	BB.	SO.
Cuellar (Winner)	8*	9	3	3	4	4
Grimsley	1	0	0	0	0	0

Oakland	IP.	H.	R.	ER.	BB.	SO.
Hunter (Loser)	4⅔	8	6	6	0	3
Odom	3⅓	1	0	0	0	1
Fingers	1	1	0	0	0	1

*Pitched to two batters in ninth.

Errors—None. Double play—Oakland 1. Left on base—Baltimore 3, Oakland 9. Two-base hits—Grich, North, C. Washington. Home runs—Blair, Robinson, Grich. Stolen bases—North, Campaneris. Sacrifice hit—Belanger. Sacrifice fly—Campaneris. Passed ball—Fosse. Umpires—Napp, Neudecker, Goetz, Phillips, Springstead and Deegan. Time—2:29. Attendance—41,609.

GAME OF SUNDAY, OCTOBER 6, AT OAKLAND

Baltimore	AB.	R.	H.	RBI.	PO.	A.
Belanger, ss	3	0	0	0	0	1
Motton, ph	1	0	0	0	0	0
Baker, ss	0	0	0	0	1	0
Blair, cf	3	0	1	0	0	0
Grich, 2b	4	0	0	0	7	5
Davis, dh	4	0	1	0	0	0
Baylor, lf	4	0	0	0	2	0
Robinson, 3b	2	0	0	1	3	0
Williams, 1b	3	0	0	0	7	1
Cabell, rf	3	0	1	0	2	0
Etchebarren, c	3	0	2	0	3	0
Bumbry, pr	0	0	0	0	0	0
Hendricks, c	0	0	0	0	1	1
McNally, p	0	0	0	0	0	0
Garland, p	0	0	0	0	0	0
Reynolds, p	0	0	0	0	0	0
G. Jackson, p	0	0	0	0	0	0
Totals	30	0	5	0	24	11

Oakland	AB.	R.	H.	RBI.	PO.	A.
Campaneris, ss	4	0	0	0	0	6
North, cf	2	1	0	0	6	0
Bando, 3b	3	1	1	1	1	4
R. Jackson, dh	3	0	0	0	0	0
H. Washington, pr	0	0	0	0	0	0
Rudi, lf	4	0	2	1	1	0
Tenace, 1b	3	1	0	0	13	0
C. Washington, rf	4	1	1	0	0	0
Fosse, c	4	1	3	3	3	1
Green, 2b	1	0	1	0	1	2
Holt, ph	0	0	0	0	0	0
Odom, pr	0	0	0	0	0	0
Maxvill, 2b	1	0	0	0	2	1
Holtzman, p	0	0	0	0	0	1
Totals	29	5	8	5	27	15

Baltimore			0	0	0	0	0	0	0	0 – 0
Oakland	0	0	0	1	0	1	0	3	x – 5

Baltimore	IP.	H.	R.	ER.	BB.	SO.
McNally (Loser)	5⅔	6	2	1	2	2
Garland	⅔	1	0	0	1	0
Reynolds	1⅓	0	1	0	3	1
G. Jackson	⅓	1	2	0	0	1

Oakland	IP.	H.	R.	ER.	BB.	SO.
Holtzman (Winner)	9	5	0	0	2	3

Errors – Grich, Baker. Double plays – Baltimore 2, Oakland 2. Left on base – Baltimore 5, Oakland 7. Two-base hit – Fosse. Three-base hit – Rudi. Home runs – Bando, Fosse. Stolen base – Tenace. Sacrifice hit – Green. Wild pitch – McNally. Umpires – Neudecker, Goetz, Phillips, Springstead, Deegan and Napp. Time – 2:23. Attendance – 42,810.

GAME OF TUESDAY, OCTOBER 8, AT BALTIMORE

Oakland	AB.	R.	H.	RBI.	PO.	A.
Campaneris, ss	4	0	0	0	1	2
North, cf	4	0	0	0	2	0
Bando, 3b	4	1	1	1	0	1
Jackson, dh	4	0	1	0	0	0
Rudi, lf	4	0	0	0	2	0
Tenace, 1b	2	0	0	0	6	0
Holt, 1b	0	0	0	0	1	0
H. Washington, pr	0	0	0	0	0	0
C. Washington, rf	2	0	1	0	4	0
Fosse, c	2	0	0	0	7	1
Green, 2b	3	0	1	0	4	2
Blue, p	0	0	0	0	0	1
Totals	29	1	4	1	27	7

Baltimore	AB.	R.	H.	RBI.	PO.	A.
Coggins, rf	3	0	0	0	2	0
Cabell, ph	1	0	0	0	0	0
Blair, cf	4	0	0	0	2	0
Grich, 2b	4	0	1	0	3	2
Davis, dh	3	0	0	0	0	0
Baylor, lf	3	0	1	0	4	0
Robinson, 3b	3	0	0	0	2	3
Williams, 1b	3	0	0	0	9	0
Etchebarren, c	3	0	0	0	4	1
Belanger, ss	3	0	0	0	1	3
Palmer, p	0	0	0	0	0	2
Totals	30	0	2	0	27	11

Oakland	0	0	0	1	0	0	0	0	0 – 1
Baltimore	0	0	0	0	0	0	0	0	0 – 0

Oakland	IP.	H.	R.	ER.	BB.	SO.
Blue (Winner)	9	2	0	0	0	7

Baltimore	IP.	H.	R.	ER.	BB.	SO.
Palmer (Loser)	9	4	1	1	1	4

Errors – Williams, Green 2. Double play – Baltimore 1. Left on base – Oakland 4, Baltimore 3. Home run – Bando. Sacrifice hit – Fosse. Hit by Pitch – By Palmer (C. Washington). Umpires – Goetz, Phillips, Springstead, Deegan, Napp and Neudecker. Time – 1:57. Attendance – 32,060.

GAME OF WEDNESDAY, OCTOBER 9, AT BALTIMORE

Oakland	AB.	R.	H.	RBI.	PO.	A.
Campaneris, ss	5	0	0	0	2	4
North, cf	5	0	0	0	3	0
Bando, 3b	2	2	0	1	1	1
Jackson, dh	1	0	1	1	0	0
Odom, pr	0	0	0	0	0	0
Rudi, lf	1	0	0	0	0	0
Tenace, 1b	3	0	0	1	4	1
C. Washington, rf	4	0	0	0	7	0
Fosse, c	4	0	0	0	5	1
Green, 2b	3	0	0	0	3	1
Hunter, p	0	0	0	0	2	1
Fingers, p	0	0	0	0	0	0
Totals	28	2	1	2	27	9

Baltimore	AB.	R.	H.	RBI.	PO.	A.
Coggins, rf	4	0	0	0	1	0
Blair, cf	3	1	1	0	3	0
Grich, 2b	4	0	1	0	2	3
Davis, dh	4	0	1	0	0	0
Cabell, pr	0	0	0	0	0	0
Powell, 1b	4	0	1	1	14	0
Palmer, pr	0	0	0	0	0	0
Baylor, lf	4	0	1	0	1	0
Robinson, 3b	3	0	0	0	1	2
Hendricks, c	2	0	0	0	5	0
Belanger, ss	0	0	0	0	0	6
Bumbry, ph	1	0	0	0	0	0
Baker, ss	0	0	0	0	0	1
Cuellar, p	0	0	0	0	0	2
Grimsley, p	0	0	0	0	0	1
Totals	29	1	5	1	27	15

Oakland	0	0	0		0	1	0		1	0	0 – 2
Baltimore	0	0	0		0	0	0		0	1	1 – 1

Oakland	IP.	H.	R.	ER.	BB.	SO.
Hunter (Winner)	7*	3	0	0	2	3
Fingers (Save)	2	2	1	1	1	2

Baltimore	IP.	H.	R.	ER.	BB.	SO.
Cuellar (Loser)	4⅔	0	1	1	9	2
Grimsley	4⅓	1	1	1	2	2

*Pitched to one batter in eighth.

Error—Belanger. Double plays—Oakland 1, Baltimore 1. Left on base—Oakland 10, Baltimore 5. Two-base hit—Jackson. Sacrifice hit—Belanger. Wild pitch—Cuellar. Umpires—Phillips, Springstead, Deegan, Napp, Neudecker and Goetz. Time—2:46. Attendance—28,136.

OAKLAND ATHLETICS' BATTING AND FIELDING AVERAGES

Player—Position	G.	AB.	R.	H.	TB.	2B.	3B.	HR.	RBI.	B.A.	PO.	A.	E.	F.A.
Alou, ph	1	1	0	1	1	0	0	0	0	1.000	0	0	0	.000
Fosse, c	4	12	1	4	8	1	0	1	3	.333	7	3	0	1.000
C. Washington, ph-rf	4	11	1	3	4	1	0	0	0	.273	11	0	0	1.000
Mangual, dh	1	4	0	1	1	0	0	0	0	.250	0	0	0	.000
Bando, 3b	4	13	4	3	9	0	0	2	2	.231	3	8	0	1.000
Green, 2b	4	9	0	2	2	0	0	0	0	.222	10	8	2	.900
Campaneris, ss	4	17	0	3	3	0	0	0	3	.176	3	17	0	1.000
R. Jackson, rf-dh	4	12	0	2	3	1	0	0	1	.167	0	0	0	.000
Rudi, lf	4	13	0	2	4	0	1	0	1	.154	5	0	0	1.000
North, cf	4	16	3	1	2	1	0	0	0	.063	14	0	0	1.000
Blue, p	1	0	0	0	0	0	0	0	0	.000	0	1	0	1.000
Fingers, p	2	0	0	0	0	0	0	0	0	.000	0	0	0	.000
Holt, ph-1b	2	0	0	0	0	0	0	0	0	.000	1	0	0	1.000
Holtzman, p	1	0	0	0	0	0	0	0	0	.000	0	1	0	1.000
Hunter, p	2	0	0	0	0	0	0	0	0	.000	3	2	0	1.000
Odom, p-pr	3	0	0	0	0	0	0	0	0	.000	0	0	0	.000
Trillo, pr	1	0	1	0	0	0	0	0	0	.000	0	0	0	.000
H. Washington, pr	2	0	0	0	0	0	0	0	0	.000	0	0	0	.000
Maxvill, 2b	1	1	0	0	0	0	0	0	0	.000	2	1	0	1.000
Tenace, 1b	4	11	1	0	0	0	0	0	1	.000	35	2	0	1.000
Totals	4	120	11	22	37	4	1	3	11	.183	108	43	2	.987

BALTIMORE ORIOLES' BATTING AND FIELDING AVERAGES

Player—Position	G.	AB.	R.	H.	TB.	2B.	3B.	HR.	RBI.	B.A.	PO.	A.	E.	F.A.
Etchebarren, c	2	6	0	2	2	0	0	0	0	.333	7	1	0	1.000
Blair, cf	4	14	3	4	7	0	0	1	2	.268	7	0	0	1.000
Baylor, lf	4	15	0	4	4	0	0	0	0	.267	9	0	0	1.000
Davis, dh	4	15	0	4	4	0	0	0	1	.267	0	0	0	.000
Grich, 2b	4	16	2	4	8	1	0	1	2	.250	13	12	1	.962
Cabell, rf-ph-pr	3	4	0	1	1	0	0	0	0	.250	2	0	0	1.000
Hendricks, c	3	6	1	1	1	0	0	0	0	.167	11	1	0	1.000
Powell, 1b	2	8	0	1	1	0	0	0	1	.125	22	1	0	1.000
Robinson, 3b	4	12	1	1	4	0	0	1	1	.083	4	13	0	1.000
Baker, ss	2	0	0	0	0	0	0	0	0	.000	1	1	1	.667
Cuellar, p	2	0	0	0	0	0	0	0	0	.000	0	5	0	1.000

Player–Position	G.	AB.	R.	H.	TB.	2B.	3B.	HR.	RBI.	B.A.	PO.	A.	E.	F.A.
Garland, p	1	0	0	0	0	0	0	0	0	.000	0	0	0	.000
Grimsley, p	2	0	0	0	0	0	0	0	0	.000	0	1	0	1.000
G. Jackson, p	1	0	0	0	0	0	0	0	0	.000	0	0	0	.000
McNally, p	1	0	0	0	0	0	0	0	0	.000	0	0	0	.000
Palmer, p-pr	2	0	0	0	0	0	0	0	0	.000	0	2	0	1.000
Reynolds, p	1	0	0	0	0	0	0	0	0	.000	0	0	0	.000
Bumbry, pr-ph	2	1	0	0	0	0	0	0	0	.000	0	0	0	.000
Motton, ph	1	1	0	0	0	0	0	0	0	.000	0	0	0	.000
Williams, 1b	2	6	0	0	0	0	0	0	0	.000	16	1	1	.944
Belanger, ss	4	9	0	0	0	0	0	0	0	.000	7	12	1	.950
Coggins, rf	3	11	0	0	0	0	0	0	0	.000	6	0	0	1.000
Totals	4	124	7	22	32	1	0	3	7	.177	105	50	4	.975

OAKLAND ATHLETICS' PITCHING RECORDS

Pitcher	G.	GS.	CG.	IP.	H.	R.	ER.	BB.	SO.	HB.	WP.	W.	L.	Pct.	ERA.
Blue	1	1	1	9	2	0	0	0	7	0	0	1	0	1.000	0.00
Holtzman	1	1	1	9	5	0	0	2	3	0	0	1	0	1.000	0.00
Odom	1	0	0	3⅓	1	0	0	0	1	0	0	0	0	.000	0.00
Fingers	2	0	0	3	3	1	1	1	3	0	0	0	0	.000	3.00
Hunter	2	2	0	11⅔	11	6	6	2	6	0	0	1	1	.500	4.63
Totals	4	4	2	36	22	7	7	5	20	0	0	3	1	.750	1.75

Shutouts–Blue, Holtzman. Save–Fingers.

BALTIMORE ORIOLES' PITCHING RECORDS

Pitcher	G.	GS.	CG.	IP.	H.	R.	ER.	BB.	SO.	HB.	WP.	W.	L.	Pct.	ERA.
Reynolds	1	0	0	1⅓	0	1	0	3	1	0	0	0	0	.000	0.00
Garland	1	0	0	⅔	1	0	0	1	0	0	0	0	0	.000	0.00
G. Jackson	1	0	0	⅓	1	2	0	1	0	0	0	0	0	.000	0.00
Palmer	1	1	1	9	4	1	1	4	1	0	0	0	1	.000	1.00
McNally	1	1	0	5⅔	6	2	1	2	2	0	1	0	1	.000	1.59
Grimsley	2	0	0	5⅓	1	1	1	2	2	0	0	0	0	.000	1.69
Cuellar	2	2	0	12⅔	9	4	4	13	6	0	1	1	1	.500	2.84
Totals	4	4	1	35	22	11	7	22	16	1	2	1	3	.250	1.80

No shutouts or saves.

COMPOSITE SCORE BY INNINGS

Oakland	0	0	1	2	2	1	1	3	1	11
Baltimore	1	0	0	1	4	0	0	0	1	7

Sacrifice hits–Belanger 2, Green, Fosse.
Sacrifice fly–Campaneris.
Stolen bases–North, Campaneris, Tenace.
Caught stealing–Campaneris, Blair 2, H. Washington 2, Baylor.
Double plays–Bando, Green and Tenace; Fosse and Green; Bando, Maxvill and Tenace; Green, Campaneris and Tenace; Grich and Williams; Belanger, Grich and Williams; Robinson and Williams; Belanger, Grich and Powell.
Left on bases–Oakland 30–9, 7, 4, 10; Baltimore 16–3, 5, 3, 5.
Hit by pitcher–By Palmer (C. Washington).
Passed ball–Fosse.
Balks–None.
Time of games–First game, 2:29; second game, 2:23; third game, 1:57; fourth game, 2:46.
Attendance–First game, 41,609; second game, 42,810; third game, 32,060; fourth game, 28,136.
Umpires–Napp, Neudecker, Goetz, Phillips, Springstead and Deegan.
Official scorers–Jim Henneman, Baltimore News-American; Jim Street, San Jose Mercury-News.

NATIONAL LEAGUE
Championship Series of 1974

	W.	L.	Pct.
Los Angeles (West)	3	1	.750
Pittsburgh (East)	1	3	.250

With Don Sutton giving up only one run in 17 innings of pitching in two starting assignments, the Los Angeles Dodgers subdued the Pittsburgh Pirates in the National League Championship Series, three games to one in 1974.

The Dodgers had been winless in six games played at Pittsburgh's Three Rivers Stadium during the regular season but they remedied that situation in post-season play. In the opening game, Sutton was opposed by Jerry Reuss. The Pirate lefty yielded just one run in seven innings of work but left the game in favor of an ineffectual pinch-hitter. Dave Giusti came on in the eighth inning and gave up two insurance tallies. Meanwhile, Sutton let the Pittsburgh club down on four hits and no runs while striking out six and walking only one.

The Pittsburgh string of scoreless innings was extended to 15 before the Bucs finally got on the board in the seventh inning of the second game. But when they did score, there were no big base hits. One run came in on a groundout and the other on a high bouncer that escaped an infielder's glove and was scored as a single. But those two runs were enough to enable the Pirates to equalize the two runs that Los Angeles had scored earlier off starter Jim Rooker.

With the game tied going into the eighth stanza, it was a battle between ace relievers Mike Marshall, of Los Angeles, and Giusti. It was, however, strictly no contest. Marshall retired six straight batters in the last two innings but Giusti couldn't retire even one. He was clubbed for three runs and four hits before getting the hook. An error by his catcher, Manny Sanguillen, didn't help matters. The final score was 5-2 and on the plane trip to Los Angeles the Pirates had time to think about getting only a dozen singles in 18 innings and failing to score in 17 innings.

A record crowd for Dodger Stadium—55,953—showed up for the third game, confidently expecting the local nine to apply the coup de grace. But the home partisans were sorely disappointed. Dodger starter Doug Rau lingered on the premises for barely 10 minutes, during which time he was bombed for five runs. With Bruce Kison pitching effectively for Pittsburgh and the Dodgers contributing five errors, the game was, for all practical purposes, over early. Kison gave up only two hits in the six and two-thirds innings he worked and his reliever, Ramon Hernandez, slammed the door the rest of the way. The big blows for the Bucs were home runs by Willie Stargell and Richie Hebner. At game's end the Pirates had seven runs and the Dodgers had none.

Sutton and Reuss, as in the opener, were the opposing pitchers in the fourth game. Sutton was just as good as he ever was, permitting but one run and three hits and striking out seven in eight innings of work before allowing the ubiquitous Marshall to mop up. Reuss simply didn't have his best stuff and was kayoed in the third inning. His successors didn't fare much better. The unfortunate Giusti made his third appearance of the series and was just as ineffective as he had been in the first two, being charged with three runs in an inning and a third of toil. The biggest thunder came off the bat of Dodger first baseman Steve Garvey. He had four hits, including two homers and drove in four runs. The final score was 12-1, a decisive margin by any standard and the largest in any game played in a Championship Series.

GAME OF SATURDAY, OCTOBER 5, AT PITTSBURGH

Los Angeles	AB.	R.	H.	RBI.	PO.	A.
Lopes, 2b	4	1	0	1	2	4
Buckner, lf	5	0	1	0	3	0
Wynn, cf	3	1	1	1	2	0
Garvey, 1b	4	0	2	0	9	1
Ferguson, rf	4	1	2	1	1	0
Cey, 3b	3	0	0	0	0	3
Russell, ss	5	0	2	0	3	2
Yeager, c	4	0	0	0	6	1
Sutton, p	3	0	1	0	1	0
Totals	35	3	9	3	27	11

Pittsburgh	AB.	R.	H.	RBI.	PO.	A.
Stennett, 2b	4	0	0	0	5	1
Hebner, 3b	3	0	0	0	1	3
Oliver, cf	4	0	0	0	5	0
Stargell, lf	4	0	2	0	5	0
Zisk, rf	4	0	0	0	0	0
Sanguillen, c	4	0	1	0	3	0
Kirkpatrick, 1b	3	0	0	0	5	0
Taveras, ss	2	0	0	0	2	1
Popovich, ph-ss	1	0	1	0	1	0
Reuss, p	2	0	0	0	0	0
Parker, ph	1	0	0	0	0	0
Giusti, p	0	0	0	0	0	2
Totals	32	0	4	0	27	7

Los Angeles	0	1	0		0	0	0		0	0	2 – 3
Pittsburgh	0	0	0		0	0	0		0	0	0 – 0

Los Angeles	IP.	H.	R.	ER.	BB.	SO.
Sutton (Winner)	9	4	0	0	1	6

Pittsburgh	IP.	H.	R.	ER.	BB.	SO.
Reuss (Loser)	7	5	1	1	4	3
Giusti	2	4	2	2	3	0

Errors—Cey 2. Double play—Los Angeles 1. Left on base—Los Angeles 13, Pittsburgh 7. Two-base-hits—Garvey, Buckner, Wynn. Stolen base—Lopes. Sacrifice hit—Ferguson. Hit by pitch—By Sutton (Hebner). Umpires—Colosi, Pryor, Weyer, McSherry, Crawford and Davidson. Time—2:25. Attendance—40,638.

GAME OF SUNDAY, OCTOBER 6, AT PITTSBURGH

Los Angeles	AB.	R.	H.	RBI.	PO.	A.
Lopes, 2b	4	1	2	1	3	7
Buckner, lf	5	0	2	0	2	0
Wynn, cf	2	0	0	3	0	0
Garvey, 1b	5	0	1	1	13	1
Ferguson, rf-c	5	2	4	1	0	0
Cey, 3b	5	1	1	0	3	3
Russell, ss	3	0	0	0	0	0
Yeager, c	2	1	1	1	0	0
Crawford, ph-rf	3	0	0	0	1	2
Messersmith, p	1	0	1	1	0	0
Mota, ph	0	0	0	0	0	0
Lacy, pr	0	0	0	0	0	0
Marshall, p	0	0	0	0	0	0
Totals	38	5	12	5	27	13

Pittsburgh	AB.	R.	H.	RBI.	PO.	A.
Stennett, 2b	3	0	0	0	2	0
Hebner, 3b	3	0	1	1	2	1
Oliver, cf	4	0	1	1	3	0
Stargell, lf	3	1	0	0	0	0
Giusti, p	0	0	0	0	0	0
Demery, p	0	0	0	0	0	0
Hernandez, p	0	0	0	0	0	1
Parker, rf	4	0	0	0	3	0
Sanguillen, c	4	0	2	0	7	1
Kirkpatrick, 1b	4	0	0	0	9	0
Taveras, ss	0	0	0	0	0	0
Mendoza, ss	1	0	0	0	0	1
Popovich, ph-ss	2	1	1	0	1	0
Rooker, p	2	0	1	0	0	3
Zisk, ph	1	0	1	0	0	0
Clines, pr-lf	1	1	0	0	0	0
Totals	32	2	8	2	27	7

Los Angeles	1	0	0		1	0	0		0	3	0 – 5
Pittsburgh	0	0	0		0	0	0		2	0	0 – 2

Los Angeles	IP.	H.	R.	ER.	BB.	SO.
Messersmith (Winner)	7	8	2	2	3	0
Marshall	2	0	0	0	0	0

Pittsburgh	IP.	H.	R.	ER.	BB.	SO.
Rooker	7	6	2	2	5	4
Giusti (Loser)	0*	4	3	3	0	0
Demery	0†	1	0	0	0	0
Hernandez	2	1	0	0	1	1

*Pitched to four batters in eighth.
†Pitched to one batter in eighth.

Errors—Sanguillen 2, Rooker. Double plays—Los Angeles 2, Pittsburgh 1. Left on base—Los Angeles 12, Pittsburgh 8. Two-base hits—Cey 2. Home run—Cey. Stolen bases—Taveras, Wynn, Lopes. Sacrifice hit—Stennett. Hit by pitch—By Messersmith (Taveras). Wild pitch—Demery. Umpires—Pryor, Weyer, McSherry, Crawford, Davidson and Colosi. Time—2:44. Attendance 49,247.

GAME OF TUESDAY, OCTOBER 8, AT LOS ANGELES

Pittsburgh	AB.	R.	H.	RBI.	PO.	A.
Stennett, 2b	5	1	1	0	4	4
Sanguillen, c	5	0	1	0	6	1
Oliver, cf	3	1	1	0	1	0
Stargell, lf	5	2	2	3	3	0
Zisk, rf	5	1	2	0	2	0
Clines, rf	0	0	0	0	0	0
Robertson, 1b	5	1	0	0	11	0
xHebner, 3b	3	1	2	3	1	0
Mendoza, ss	3	0	1	1	1	5
Kison, p	3	0	0	0	1	1
Hernandez, p	1	0	0	0	0	0
Totals	38	7	10	7	27	11

Los Angeles	AB.	R.	H.	RBI.	PO.	A.
Lopes, 2b	3	0	0	0	3	5
Buckner, lf	3	0	0	0	0	0
Mota, ph-lf	1	0	0	0	1	0
Wynn, cf	3	0	0	0	4	0
Garvey, 1b	4	0	0	0	9	0
Crawford, rf	2	0	0	0	0	0
Paciorek, ph-rf	1	0	1	0	0	0
Cey, 3b	4	0	0	0	1	0
Ferguson, c	3	0	0	0	3	0
Russell, ss	4	0	2	0	6	7
Rau, p	0	0	0	0	0	0
Hough, p	0	0	0	0	0	0
Joshua, ph	0	0	0	0	0	0
Downing, p	1	0	0	0	0	0
McMullen, ph	1	0	0	0	0	0
Solomon, p	0	0	0	0	0	0
Auerbach, ph	1	0	1	0	0	0
Totals	31	0	4	0	27	12

Pittsburgh	5	0	2		0	0	0		0	0	0 – 7
Los Angeles	0	0	0		0	0	0		0	0	0 – 0

Pittsburgh	IP.	H.	R.	ER.	BB.	SO.
Kison (Winner)	6⅔	2	0	0	6	5
Hernandez	2⅓	2	0	0	0	1

Los Angeles	IP.	H.	R.	ER.	BB.	SO.
Rau (Loser)	⅔	3	5	3	1	0
Hough	2⅓	4	2	2	0	2
Downing	4	1	0	0	1	1
Solomon	2	2	0	0	1	1

xAwarded first base on catcher's interference. Errors—Garvey, Hough, Lopes, Ferguson, Downing. Double plays—Los Angeles 3. Left on bases—Pittsburgh 8, Los Angeles 10. Two-base hits—Sanguillen, Auerbach. Home runs—Stargell, Hebner. Passed balls—Ferguson, Sanguillen. Umpires—Weyer, McSherry, Crawford, Davidson, Colosi and Pryor. Time—2:41. Attendance—55,953.

GAME OF WEDNESDAY, OCTOBER 9, AT LOS ANGELES

Pittsburgh	AB.	R.	H.	RBI.	PO.	A.
Stennett, 2b	4	0	0	0	2	5
Hebner, 3b	4	0	0	0	1	3
Oliver, cf	3	0	0	0	0	0
Stargell, lf	3	1	1	1	5	0
Parker, rf	3	0	1	0	1	1
Sanguillen, c	3	0	0	0	3	0
Kirkpatrick, 1b	2	0	0	0	8	0
Mendoza, ss	1	0	0	0	3	1
Popovich, ph-ss	2	0	1	0	0	0
Reuss, p	0	0	0	0	0	0
Brett, p	1	0	0	0	0	1
Demery, p	0	0	0	0	0	1
Giusti, p	0	0	0	0	1	0
Pizarro, p	0	0	0	0	0	0
Howe, ph	1	0	0	0	0	0
Totals	27	1	3	1	24	12

Los Angeles	AB.	R.	H.	RBI.	PO.	A.
Lopes, 2b	4	2	2	1	1	2
Buckner, lf	5	0	0	0	1	0
Wynn, cf	2	3	1	1	2	0
Garvey, 1b	5	4	4	4	9	0
Ferguson, rf	2	2	1	3	0	0
Cey, 3b	4	0	1	0	1	1
Russell, ss	5	0	2	3	1	4
Yeager, c	2	1	0	0	8	0
Sutton, p	4	0	1	1	1	3
Mota, ph	1	0	0	0	0	0
Marshall, p	0	0	0	0	0	0
Totals	34	12	12	11	27	10

Pittsburgh	0	0	0		0	0	0		1	0	0 – 1
Los Angeles	1	0	2		0	2	2		2	3	x – 12

Pittsburgh	IP.	H.	R.	ER.	BB.	SO.
Reuss (Loser)	2⅔	2	3	3	4	0
Brett	2⅓	3	2	2	2	1
Demery	1*	2	4	4	2	0
Giusti	1⅓	5	3	3	2	1
Pizarro	⅔	0	0	0	1	0

Los Angeles	IP.	H.	R.	ER.	BB.	SO.
Sutton (Winner)	8	3	1	1	1	7
Marshall	1	0	0	0	0	1

*Pitched to two batters in seventh.

Error—Stennett. Double plays—Pittsburgh 1, Los Angeles 2. Left on bases—Pittsburgh 1, Los Angeles 9. Two-base hits—Wynn, Cey. Three-base hit—Lopes. Home runs—Garvey 2, Stargell. Stolen bases—Lopes, Yeager. Sacrifice hit—Reuss. Umpires—McSherry, Crawford, Davidson, Colosi, Pryor and Weyer. Time—2:36. Attendance—54,424.

LOS ANGELES DODGERS' BATTING AND FIELDING AVERAGES

Player–Position	G.	AB.	R.	H.	TB.	2B.	3B.	HR.	RBI.	B.A.	PO.	A.	E.	F.A.
Auerbach, ph	1	1	0	1	2	1	0	0	0	1.000	0	0	0	.000
Paciorek, ph-rf	1	1	0	1	1	0	0	0	0	1.000	0	0	0	.000
Garvey, 1b	4	18	4	7	14	1	0	2	5	.389	40	2	1	.977
Russell, ss	4	18	1	7	7	0	0	0	3	.389	13	16	0	1.000
Mota, ph-lf	3	3	0	1	1	0	0	0	1	.333	1	0	0	1.000
Cey, 3b	4	16	2	5	11	3	0	1	1	.313	2	4	2	.750
Sutton, p	2	7	0	2	2	0	0	0	1	.286	2	3	0	1.000
Lopes, 2b	4	15	4	4	6	0	1	0	3	.267	9	18	1	.964
Crawford, rf-c	2	4	1	1	1	0	0	0	1	.250	0	0	0	.000
Ferguson, rf-c	4	13	3	3	3	0	0	0	2	.231	9	0	1	.900
Wynn, cf	4	10	4	2	4	2	0	0	2	.200	11	0	0	1.000
Buckner, lf	4	18	0	3	4	1	0	0	0	.167	6	0	0	1.000
Hough, p	1	0	0	0	0	0	0	0	0	.000	0	0	1	.000
Josuha, ph	1	0	0	0	0	0	0	0	0	.000	0	0	0	.000
Lacy, pr	1	0	0	0	0	0	0	0	0	.000	0	0	0	.000
Marshall, p	2	0	0	0	0	0	0	0	0	.000	0	0	0	.000
Rau, p	1	0	0	0	0	0	0	0	0	.000	0	0	0	.000
Solomon, p	1	0	0	0	0	0	0	0	0	.000	0	0	0	.000
Downing, p	1	1	0	0	0	0	0	0	0	.000	0	0	1	.000
McMullen, ph	1	1	0	0	0	0	0	0	0	.000	0	0	0	.000
Messersmith, p	1	3	0	0	0	0	0	0	0	.000	1	2	0	1.000
Yeager, c	3	9	1	0	0	0	0	0	0	.000	14	1	0	1.000
Totals	4	138	20	37	56	8	1	3	19	.268	108	46	7	.957

PITTSBURGH PIRATES' BATTING AND FIELDING AVERAGES

Player–Position	G.	AB.	R.	H.	TB.	2B.	3B.	HR.	RBI.	B.A.	PO.	A.	E.	F.A.
Popovich, ph-ss	3	5	1	3	3	0	0	0	0	.600	2	0	0	1.000
Rooker, p	1	2	0	1	1	0	0	0	0	.500	0	3	1	.750
Stargell, lf	4	15	3	6	12	0	0	2	4	.400	13	0	0	1.000
Zisk, rf-ph	3	10	1	3	3	0	0	0	0	.300	2	0	0	1.000
Sanguillen, c	4	16	0	4	5	1	0	0	0	.250	19	2	2	.913
Hebner, 3b	4	13	1	3	6	0	0	1	4	.231	5	7	0	1.000
Mendoza, ss	3	5	0	1	1	0	0	0	1	.200	4	7	0	1.000
Oliver, cf	4	14	1	2	2	0	0	0	1	.143	9	0	0	1.000
Parker, ph-rf	3	8	0	1	1	0	0	0	0	.125	4	1	0	1.000
Stennett, 2b	4	16	1	1	1	0	0	0	0	.063	10	10	1	.952
Demery, p	2	0	0	0	0	0	0	0	0	.000	1	0	0	1.000
Giusti, p	3	0	0	0	0	0	0	0	0	.000	1	2	0	1.000
Pizarro, p	1	0	0	0	0	0	0	0	0	.000	0	0	0	.000
Brett, p	1	0	0	0	0	0	0	0	0	.000	0	1	0	1.000
Clines, pr-lf-rf	2	1	1	0	0	0	0	0	0	.000	0	0	0	.000
Hernandez, p	2	1	0	0	0	0	0	0	0	.000	0	1	0	1.000
Howe, ph	1	1	0	0	0	0	0	0	0	.000	0	0	0	.000
Reuss, p	2	2	0	0	0	0	0	0	0	.000	0	0	0	.000
Taveras, ss	2	2	0	0	0	0	0	0	0	.000	2	1	0	1.000
Kison, p	1	3	0	0	0	0	0	0	0	.000	1	1	0	1.000
Robertson, 1b	1	5	1	0	0	0	0	0	0	.000	11	0	0	1.000
Kirkpatrick, 1b	3	9	0	0	0	0	0	0	0	.000	22	0	0	1.000
Totals	4	129	10	25	35	1	0	3	10	.194	105	37	4	.973

LOS ANGELES DODGERS' PITCHING RECORDS

Pitcher	G.	GS.	CG.	IP.	H.	R.	ER.	BB.	SO.	HB.	WP.	W.	L.	Pct.	ERA.
Downing	1	0	0	4	1	0	0	1	0	0	0	0	0	.000	0.00
Marshall	2	0	0	3	0	0	0	1	0	0	0	0	0	.000	0.00
Solomon	1	0	0	2	0	0	0	1	1	0	0	0	0	.000	0.00
Sutton	2	2	1	17	7	1	1	2	13	1	0	2	0	1.000	0.53
Messersmith	1	1	0	7	8	2	2	3	0	1	0	1	0	1.000	2.57
Hough	1	0	0	2⅓	0	2	2	0	0	0	0	0	0	.000	7.71
Rau	1	1	0	⅔	3	5	3	1	0	0	0	0	1	.000	40.50
Totals	4	4	1	36	25	10	8	8	17	2	0	3	1	.750	2.00

PITTSBURGH PIRATES' PITCHING RECORDS

Pitcher	G.	GS.	CG.	IP.	H.	R.	ER.	BB.	SO.	HB.	WP.	W.	L.	Pct.	ERA.
Kison	1	1	0	6⅔	2	0	0	6	5	0	0	1	0	1.000	0.00
Hernandez	2	0	0	4⅓	3	0	0	1	2	0	0	0	0	.000	0.00
Pizarro	1	0	0	⅔	0	0	0	1	0	0	0	0	0	.000	0.00
Rooker	1	1	0	7	6	2	2	5	4	0	0	0	0	.000	2.57
Reuss	2	2	0	9⅔	7	4	4	8	3	0	0	0	2	.000	3.72
Brett	1	0	0	2⅓	3	2	2	2	1	0	0	0	0	.000	7.71
Giusti	3	0	0	3⅓	13	8	8	5	1	0	0	0	1	.000	21.60
Demery	2	0	0	1	3	4	4	2	0	0	1	0	0	.000	36.00
Totals	4	4	0	35	37	20	20	30	16	0	1	1	3	.250	5.14

COMPOSITE SCORE BY INNINGS

Los Angeles	2	1	2	1	2	2	2	6	2 – 20
Pittsburgh	5	0	2	0	0	0	3	0	0 – 10

Catcher's interference—Hebner awarded first base on interference by Ferguson.
Sacrifice hits—Ferguson, Stennett, Reuss.
Sacrifice flies—None.
Stolen bases—Lopes 3, Wynn, Taveras, Yeager.
Caught stealing—None.
Double plays—Cey, Lopes and Garvey; Messersmith, Russell and Garvey; Lopes, Russell and Garvey 2; Russell and Lopes; Russell (unassisted); Russell and Garvey; Sutton and Garvey; Hernandez, Sanguillen and Kirkpatrick; Hebner, Stennett and Kirkpatrick.
Left on bases—Los Angeles 44—13, 12, 10, 9; Pittsburgh 24—7, 8, 8, 1.
Hit by pitcher—By Sutton (Hebner); by Messersmith (Taveras).
Passed balls—Ferguson, Sanguillen.
Balks—None.
Time of games—First game, 2:25; second game, 2:44; third game, 2:41; fourth game, 2:36.
Attendance—First game, 40,638; second game, 49,247; third game, 55,953; fourth game, 54,424.
Umpires—Colosi, Pryor, Weyer, McSherry, Crawford and Davidson.
Official scorers—Bob Hunter, Los Angeles Herald-Examiner; Bob Smizik, Pittsburgh Press.

AMERICAN LEAGUE
Championship Series of 1975

	W.	L.	Pct.
Boston (East)	3	0	1.000
Oakland (West)	0	3	.000

The Boston Red Sox captured their first pennant since 1967 and stopped the Oakland A's bid for their fourth straight American League title by sweeping the Championship Series in three straight games.

Many observers had felt before the playoffs that the A's might be at a disadvantage because the first two games of the set were slated for Boston's Fenway Park, a nightmare arena for lefthanders. But the A's were still rated favorites on the strength of their championship experience, despite their heavy reliance on southpaw starters.

In the opener, Luis Tiant pitched a three-hitter as the Bosox batted out lefty Ken Holtzman in less than seven innings. Holtzman's cause wasn't helped at all by four errors behind him, three of the miscues coming on two consecutive first-inning plays.

The tone of the series was set in the opening inning when, with two out and Carl Yastrzemski on first, Bando let Carlton Fisk's grounder go through him. A's outfielder Claudell Washington threw over the cutoff man's head, off Bando's glove. As Yastrzemski scored, Fisk moved to second from where he immediately scored on an error by second baseman Phil Garner.

The Sox added five more tallies in the seventh frame as a dropped fly by Bill North and Washington's problems at the wall added to the A's troubles.

The A's jumped off to a three-run lead in the second game, Reggie Jackson's two-run homer in the first being the big blow. But the Sox chased lefty Vida Blue in the fourth inning on the strength of Yastrzemski's two-run homer, Fisk's double, Fred Lynn's single and a double play grounder.

Fisk's single plated Yastrzemski, who had doubled, with the go-ahead run in the sixth. Rico Petrocelli's homer in the seventh and an RBI single by Lynn in the eighth added to the margin.

The A's going down to the wire with resolute obstinacy, tried in the third game with another lefthander. It was again Holtzman, this time with just two days' rest.

The lefty left the game in the fifth inning with four runs charged against him, enough for the Boston victory.

GAME OF SATURDAY, OCTOBER 4, AT BOSTON

Oakland	AB.	R.	H.	RBI.	PO.	A.
North, cf	3	0	0	1	2	0
Washington, lf	4	0	0	0	1	4
Bando, 3b	4	0	0	1	0	0
Jackson, rf	4	0	1	0	2	0
Tenace, c	4	0	1	0	10	1
Rudi, 1b	3	0	0	0	0	0
Williams, dh	0	0	0	0	0	0
Hopkins, pr-dh	4	1	0	0	1	2
Campaneris, ss	2	0	0	0	2	1
Garner, 2b	1	0	1	0	0	0
Holt, ph	0	0	0	0	0	0
Martinez, pr-2b	0	0	0	0	1	1
Holtzman, p	0	0	0	0	0	0
Todd, p	0	0	0	0	0	0
Lindblad, p	0	0	0	0	0	0
Bosman, p	0	0	0	0	0	0
Abbott, p	0	0	0	0	0	0
Totals	32	1	3	1	24	10

Boston	AB.	R.	H.	RBI.	PO.	A.
Beniquez, dh	4	1	2	1	0	0
Doyle, 2b	3	1	0	1	0	1
Yastrzemski, lf	4	1	1	0	3	0
Fisk, c	4	2	1	0	9	0
Lynn, cf	4	0	1	2	7	0
Petrocelli, 3b	4	0	0	1	0	0
Evans, rf	4	1	1	0	4	0
Cooper, 1b	3	0	1	0	2	0
Burleson, ss	3	1	1	1	1	0
Tiant, p	0	0	0	0	0	1
Totals	33	7	8	5	27	2

```
Oakland ............... 0   0   0   0   0   0   0   1   0 – 1
Boston ................ 2   0   0   0   0   0   5   0   x – 7
```

Oakland	IP.	H.	R.	ER.	BB.	SO.
Holtzman (Loser)	6⅓	5	4	2	1	4
Todd	0*	1	1	1	0	0
Lindblad	⅓	2	2	0	0	0
Bosman	⅓	0	0	0	0	0
Abbott	1	0	0	0	0	0

Boston	IP.	H.	R.	ER.	BB.	SO.
Tiant (Winner)	9	3	1	0	3	8

*Pitched to one batter in seventh.

Errors—Bando, Washington, Garner, Lynn, North, Burleson, Cooper. Left on bases—Oakland 7, Boston 5. Two-base hits—Evans, Burleson, Lynn, Holt. Stolen bases—Beniquez 2. Sacrifice hit—Cooper. Sacrifice fly—Doyle. Umpires—Denkinger, DiMuro, Kunkel, Luciano, Evans and Morgenweck. Time—2:40. Attendance—35,578.

GAME OF SUNDAY, OCTOBER 5, AT BOSTON

Oakland	AB.	R.	H.	RBI.	PO.	A.
North, cf	4	0	0	0	0	0
Campaneris, ss	3	0	0	0	1	6
Bando, 3b	4	1	4	0	0	3
Jackson, rf	4	1	2	2	1	1
Tenace, 1b-c	4	0	0	0	11	1
Rudi, lf	4	1	2	0	1	0
Washington, dh	4	0	2	1	0	0
Garner, 2b	2	0	0	0	4	2
Harper, ph	0	0	0	0	0	0
Holt, 1b	1	0	0	0	1	2
Fosse, c	2	0	0	0	3	0
Williams, ph	1	0	0	0	0	0
Martinez, 2b	0	0	0	0	1	0
Tovar, ph	1	0	0	0	0	0
Blue, p	0	0	0	0	0	0
Todd, p	0	0	0	0	0	0
Fingers, p	0	0	0	0	1	0
Totals	34	3	10	3	24	15

Boston	AB.	R.	H.	RBI.	PO.	A.
Beniquez, dh	4	1	1	0	0	0
Doyle, 2b	3	1	1	0	2	1
Yastrzemski, lf	3	2	2	2	1	0
Fisk, c	4	1	2	1	4	0
Lynn, cf	4	0	2	1	4	1
Petrocelli, 3b	4	1	1	1	2	3
Evans, rf	3	0	0	0	1	0
Cooper, 1b	3	0	2	0	11	0
Burleson, ss	2	0	1	0	1	6
Cleveland, p	0	0	0	0	0	1
Moret, p	0	0	0	0	0	0
Drago, p	0	0	0	0	0	0
Totals	30	6	12	5	27	13

Oakland	2	0	0		1	0	0		0	0	0 – 3
Boston	0	0	0		3	0	1		1	1	x – 6

Oakland	IP.	H.	R.	ER.	BB.	SO.
Blue	3*	6	3	3	0	2
Todd	1†	1	0	0	0	0
Fingers (Loser)	4	5	3	3	1	. 3

Boston	IP.	H.	R.	ER.	BB.	SO.
Cleveland	5‡	7	3	3	1	2
Moret (Winner)	1§	1	0	0	1	0
Drago (Save)	3	2	0	0	0	2

*Pitched to four batters in fourth.
†Pitched to one batter in fifth.
‡Pitched to one batter in sixth.
§Pitched to one batter in seventh.

Errors—None. Double plays—Oakland 4, Boston 2. Left on bases—Oakland 6, Boston 3. Two-base hits—Bando 2, Rudi 2, Washington. Fisk, Cooper 2, Yastrzemski. Home runs—Jackson. Yastrzemski, Petrocelli. Sacrifice hits—Burleson, Doyle. Wild pitch—Drago. Umpires—DiMuro, Kunkel, Luciano, Evans, Morgenweck and Denkinger. Time—2:27. Attendance—35,578.

GAME OF TUESDAY, OCTOBER 7, AT OAKLAND

Boston	AB.	R.	H.	RBI.	PO.	A.	Oakland	AB.	R.	H.	RBI.	PO.	A.
Beniquez, dh	4	0	0	0	0	0	Campaneris, ss	4	0	0	0	0	2
Doyle, 2b	5	1	2	1	3	6	Washington, lf	4	1	1	0	0	0
Yastrzemski, lf	4	1	2	0	2	1	Bando, 3b	4	0	2	2	2	4
Fisk, c	4	1	2	1	2	0	Jackson, rf	4	0	2	1	2	0
Lynn, cf	3	1	1	0	1	0	Rudi, 1b	4	0	0	0	11	1
Petrocelli, 3b	4	0	1	1	1	0	Williams, dh	4	0	0	0	0	0
Evans, rf	3	0	0	0	2	0	Tenace, c	2	0	0	0	4	0
Cooper, 1b	4	0	1	1	11	1	North, cf	3	0	0	0	4	1
Burleson, ss	4	1	2	0	2	6	Garner, 2b	1	0	0	0	1	1
Wise, p	0	0	0	0	2	3	Tovar, ph-2b	1	2	1	0	2	2
Drago, p	0	0	0	0	1	1	Martinez, 2b	0	0	0	0	0	0
Totals	35	5	11	4	27	18	Holt, ph	1	0	0	0	0	0
							Holtzman, p	0	0	0	0	0	0
							Todd, p	0	0	0	0	0	0
							Lindblad, p	0	0	0	0	1	4
							Totals	32	3	6	3	27	15

Boston	0	0	0		1	3	0		0	1	0 – 5
Oakland	0	0	0		0	0	1		0	2	0 – 3

Boston	IP.	H.	R.	ER.	BB.	SO.
Wise (Winner)	7⅓	6	3	2	3	2
Drago (Save)	1⅔	0	0	0	1	0

Oakland	IP.	H.	R.	ER.	BB.	SO.
Holtzman (Loser)	4⅔	7	4	3	0	3
Todd	0*	1	0	0	0	0
Lindblad	4⅓	3	1	0	1	0

*Pitched to one batter in fifth.

Errors—Washington. Tovar, Doyle. Double play—Boston 1. Left on bases—Boston 6, Oakland 6. Two-base hit—Burleson. Stolen base—Fisk. Sacrifice hits—Beniquez, Lynn. Wild pitch—Lindblad. Umpires—Kunkel, Luciano, Evans, Morgenweck, Denkinger and DiMuro. Time—2:30. Attendance—49,358.

BOSTON RED SOX' BATTING AND FIELDING AVERAGES

Player—Position	G.	AB.	R.	H.	TB.	2B.	3B.	HR.	RBI.	B.A.	PO.	A.	E.	F.A.
Yastrzemski, lf	3	11	4	5	9	1	0	1	2	.455	7	2	0	1.000
Burleson, ss	3	9	2	4	6	2	0	0	1	.444	4	12	1	.941
Fisk, c	3	12	4	5	6	1	0	0	2	.417	15	0	0	1.000
Cooper, 1b	3	10	0	4	6	2	0	0	1	.400	24	1	1	.962
Lynn, cf	3	11	1	4	5	1	0	0	3	.364	12	1	1	.929
Doyle, 2b	3	11	3	3	3	0	0	0	2	.273	5	8	1	.929
Beniquez, dh	3	12	2	3	3	0	0	0	1	.250	0	0	0	.000
Petrocelli, 3b	3	12	1	2	5	0	0	1	2	.167	4	3	0	1.000
Evans, rf	3	10	1	1	2	1	0	0	0	.100	7	0	0	1.000
Cleveland, p	1	0	0	0	0	0	0	0	0	.000	0	1	0	1.000
Drago, p	2	0	0	0	0	0	0	0	0	.000	1	1	0	1.000
Moret, p	1	0	0	0	0	0	0	0	0	.000	0	0	0	.000
Tiant, p	1	0	0	0	0	0	0	0	0	.000	0	1	0	1.000
Wise, p	1	0	0	0	0	0	0	0	0	.000	2	3	0	1.000
Totals	3	98	18	31	45	8	0	2	14	.316	81	33	4	.966

OAKLAND ATHLETICS' BATTING AND FIELDING AVERAGES

Player—Position	G.	AB.	R.	H.	TB.	2B.	3B.	HR.	RBI.	B.A.	PO.	A.	E.	F.A.
Bando, 3b	3	12	1	6	8	2	0	0	2	.500	3	11	1	.933
Tovar, ph-2b	2	2	2	1	1	0	0	0	0	.500	2	2	1	.800
Jackson, rf	3	12	1	5	8	0	0	1	3	.417	5	1	0	1.000
Holt, ph-1b	3	3	0	1	2	1	0	0	0	.333	1	2	0	1.000
Rudi, 1b-lf	3	12	1	3	5	2	0	0	0	.250	22	2	0	1.000
Washington, lf-dh	3	12	1	3	4	1	0	0	1	.250	1	0	2	.333
Fosse, c	1	2	0	0	0	0	0	0	0	.000	3	0	0	1.000
Garner, 2b	3	5	0	0	0	0	0	0	0	.000	7	4	1	.917
Williams, dh-ph	3	8	0	0	0	0	0	0	0	.000	0	0	0	.000
Tenace, c-1b	3	9	0	0	0	0	0	0	0	.000	19	1	0	1.000
North, cf	3	10	0	0	0	0	0	0	1	.000	6	1	1	.875
Campaneris, ss	3	11	1	0	0	0	0	0	0	.000	2	10	0	1.000
Abbott, p	1	0	0	0	0	0	0	0	0	.000	0	0	0	.000
Blue, p	1	0	0	0	0	0	0	0	0	.000	0	0	0	.000
Bosman, p	1	0	0	0	0	0	0	0	0	.000	1	0	0	1.000
Fingers, p	1	0	0	0	0	0	0	0	0	.000	0	0	0	.000
Harper, ph	2	0	0	0	0	0	0	0	0	.000	1	1	0	1.000
Holtzman, p	1	0	0	0	0	0	0	0	0	.000	0	0	0	.000
Hopkins, pr-dh	2	0	0	0	0	0	0	0	0	.000	1	4	0	1.000
Lindblad, p	2	0	0	0	0	0	0	0	0	.000	1	1	0	1.000
Martinez, pr-2b	3	0	0	0	0	0	0	0	0	.000	0	0	0	.000
Todd, p	3	0	0	0	0	0	0	0	0	.000	0	0	0	.000
Totals	3	98	7	19	28	6	0	1	7	.194	75	40	6	.950

BOSTON RED SOX' PITCHING RECORDS

Pitcher	G.	GS.	CG.	IP.	H.	R.	ER.	BB.	SO.	HB.	WP.	W.	L.	Pct.	ERA.
Tiant	1	1	1	9	3	1	0	3	8	0	1	1	0	1.000	0.00
Drago	2	0	0	4⅔	2	0	0	1	2	0	1	0	0	.000	0.00
Moret	1	0	0	1	1	0	0	1	0	0	1	0	0	1.000	0.00
Wise	1	1	0	7⅓	6	3	2	3	2	0	0	1	0	1.000	2.45
Cleveland	1	1	0	5	7	3	3	1	2	0	0	0	0	.000	5.40
Totals	3	3	1	27	19	7	5	9	14	0	1	3	0	1.000	1.67

No shutouts. Saves—Drago 2.

OAKLAND ATHLETICS' PITCHING RECORDS

Pitcher	G.	GS.	CG.	IP.	H.	R.	ER.	BB.	SO.	HB.	WP.	W.	L.	Pct.	ERA.
Lindblad	2	0	0	4⅔	5	3	0	1	0	0	1	0	0	.000	0.00
Abbott	1	0	0	1	0	0	0	0	0	0	0	0	0	.000	0.00
Bosman	1	0	0	⅓	0	0	0	0	0	0	0	0	0	.000	0.00
Holtzman	2	2	0	11	12	8	5	1	7	0	0	0	2	.000	4.09
Fingers	1	0	0	4	5	3	3	1	3	0	0	0	1	.000	6.75
Blue	1	1	0	3	6	3	3	0	2	0	0	0	0	.000	9.00
Todd	3	0	0	1	3	1	1	0	0	0	0	0	0	.000	9.00
Totals	3	3	0	25	31	18	12	3	12	0	1	0	3	.000	4.32

No shutouts or saves.

COMPOSITE SCORE BY INNINGS

Boston	2	0	0	4	3	1	6	2	0	— 18
Oakland	2	0	0	1	0	1	0	3	0	— 7

Sacrifice hits—Cooper, Doyle, Burleson, Beniquez, Lynn.
Sacrifice fly—Doyle.
Stolen bases—Beniquez 2, Fisk.
Caught stealing—None.
Double plays—Campaneris, Garner and Tenace 2; Jackson and Fosse; Tenace, Campaneris and Tenace; Petrocelli, Doyle and Cooper; Lynn and Cooper; Burleson, Doyle and Cooper.
Left on bases—Boston 14—5, 3, 6; Oakland 19—7, 6, 6.
Hit by pitcher—None.
Passed balls—None.
Balks—None.
Time of games—First game, 2:40; second game, 2:27; third game, 2:30.
Attendance—First game, 35,578; second game, 35,578; third game, 49,358.
Umpires—Denkinger, DiMuro, Kunkel, Luciano, Evans and Morgenweck.
Official scorers—Glenn Schwarz, San Francisco Examiner; George Bankert, Quincy Patriot Ledger.

NATIONAL LEAGUE
Championship Series of 1975

	W.	L.	Pct.
Cincinnati (West)	3	0	1.000
Pittsburgh (East)	0	3	.000

The Cincinnati Reds, easy winners of the National League's West Division, were expected to have little trouble with their Championship Series rivals, the Pittsburgh Pirates. And that's just the way things turned out.

The Cincinnati club swept the three-game series and only the third game provided any of the dramatics that one might expect from two clubs contesting for baseball's oldest title, the National League pennant.

The Rhinelanders cuffed four Bucco hurlers for 11 hits in the opener, breezing to an 8-3 triumph. Even Reds' pitcher Don Gullett got into the act, getting two hits, one a home run, and driving in three runs.

The Cincinnati regulars took batting practice in the second game, banging out 12 hits as four more Pirate hurlers trudged to the mound. Tony Perez was the big cannon in the Reds' artillery, getting three hits, one a homer, as he drove in three runs. The final score was 6-1.

The high drama of the series came in the third game, played at Pittsburgh's Three Rivers Stadium.

The home team sent lefthander John Candelaria to the hill to try and stem the Red tide and the 21-year-old rookie responded magnificently. He yielded a solo homer to Concepcion in the second inning, but going into the eighth had a 2-1 lead, the result of Al Oliver's two-run homer in the Pirate sixth.

Candelaria struck out the first two batters in the eighth. That gave him a total of 14 for the game, a new playoff record. Concepcion's circuit clout had been the only Red hit to that point.

But, inexplicably, he lost his control and walked the weak-hitting Merv Rettenmund, a pinch-hitter. Pete Rose then blasted a home run to put the Reds ahead, 3-2. When Joe Morgan followed Rose's homer with a double, Candelaria left the game.

The Pirates tied the game in the ninth when Reds' relief pitcher Rawly Eastwick walked in the tying run with the bases loaded and two out.

But it all served to merely delay the inevitable.

The Reds got three hits and two runs off veteran Ramon Hernandez, the third Pittsburgh hurler, in the top of the 10th and so clinched the pennant.

The Reds' showed complete superiority and dazzled with their superior baserunning skills. The Reds stole 11 bases during the three games and the Pirates were simply unable to cope with this display of speed.

It was the third straight time in Championship Series competition that the Reds had defeated the Pirates.

The finale was the first night game ever played in Championship Series history.

GAME OF SATURDAY, OCTOBER 4, AT CINCINNATI

Pittsburgh	AB.	R.	H.	RBI.	PO.	A.
Stennett, 2b	5	0	1	0	1	5
Sanguillen, c	4	0	1	0	5	1
Oliver, cf	4	0	1	0	3	0
Stargell, 1b	4	0	0	0	8	0
Zisk, lf	4	0	1	0	2	0
Parker, rf	2	0	0	0	4	0
Hebner, 3b	4	1	2	1	0	1
Taveras, ss	3	0	1	1	1	2
Reuss, p	1	0	0	0	0	1
Brett, p	0	0	0	0	0	0
Robinson, ph	1	0	0	0	0	0
Demery, p	0	0	0	0	0	0
Randolph, ph	0	0	0	0	0	0
Ellis, p	1	0	0	0	0	0
Robertson, ph	1	0	1	0	0	0
Reynolds, pr	0	0	0	0	0	0
Totals	34	3	8	3	24	10

Cincinnati	AB.	R.	H.	RBI.	PO.	A.
Rose, 3b	5	0	2	0	0	0
Morgan, 2b	3	1	0	0	1	2
Bench, c	4	1	1	0	5	0
Perez, 1b	4	2	2	1	6	3
Foster, lf	4	2	2	0	2	0
Concepcion, ss	3	0	1	0	0	3
Griffey, rf	4	1	1	3	2	1
Geronimo, cf	3	0	0	1	7	0
Gullett, p	4	1	2	3	4	1
Totals	34	8	11	8	27	10

Pittsburgh	0	2	0	0	0	0	0	0	1 – 3
Cincinnati	0	1	3	0	4	0	0	0	x – 8

Pittsburgh	IP.	H.	R.	ER.	BB.	SO.
Reuss (Loser)	2⅔	4	4	4	4	1
Brett	1⅓	1	0	0	0	1
Demery	2	4	4	4	1	1
Ellis	2	2	0	0	0	2

Cincinnati	IP.	H.	R.	ER.	BB.	SO.
Gullett (Winner)	9	8	3	3	2	5

Errors—None. Left on bases—Pittsburgh 7, Cincinnati 8. Two-base hits—Hebner, Griffey. Home run—Gullett. Stolen bases—Morgan 3. Sacrifice fly—Geronimo. Hit by pitch—By Gullett (Parker). Wild pitch—Gullett. Passed balls—Sanguillen 2. Umpires—Kibler, Olsen, Pulli, W. Williams, Gorman and A. Williams. Time—3:00. Attendance —54,633.

GAME OF SUNDAY, OCTOBER 5, AT CINCINNATI

Pittsburgh	AB.	R.	H.	RBI.	PO.	A.
Stennett, 2b	4	0	2	0	0	3
Sanguillen, c	4	0	0	0	9	0
Oliver, cf	2	0	0	0	0	0
Stargell, 1b	3	1	1	0	6	0
Zisk, lf	3	0	2	0	2	0
Parker, rf	4	0	0	0	4	1
Hebner, 3b	3	0	0	1	0	1
Taveras, ss	3	0	0	0	3	3
Robertson, ph	1	0	0	0	0	0
Rooker, p	1	0	0	0	0	0
Robinson, ph	1	0	0	0	0	0
Tekulve, p	0	0	0	0	0	0
Brett, p	0	0	0	0	0	0
Kirkpatrick, ph	1	0	0	0	0	0
Kison, p	0	0	0	0	0	0
Totals	30	1	5	1	24	8

Cincinnati	AB.	R.	H.	RBI.	PO.	A.
Rose, 3b	4	1	1	0	0	1
Morgan, 2b	3	1	1	0	1	2
Bench, c	4	0	0	0	5	3
Perez, 1b	4	1	3	3	12	2
Foster, lf	4	1	2	0	2	0
Concepcion, ss	4	1	3	0	5	4
Griffey, rf	4	1	2	1	0	0
Geronimo, cf	3	0	0	0	1	0
Norman, p	1	0	0	1	0	1
Armbrister, ph	0	0	0	0	0	0
Crowley, ph	0	0	0	0	0	0
Rettenmund, ph	1	0	0	0	0	0
Eastwick, p	0	0	0	0	1	0
Totals	32	6	12	5	27	13

Pittsburgh	0	0	0	1	0	0	0	0	0 – 1
Cincinnati	0	0	0	2	0	1	1	0	x – 6

Pittsburgh	IP.	H.	R.	ER.	BB.	SO.
Rooker (Loser)	4	7	4	4	0	5
Tekulve	1*	3	1	1	1	2
Brett	1	0	0	0	0	0
Kison	2	2	1	1	1	1

Cincinnati	IP.	H.	R.	ER.	BB.	SO.
Norman (Winner)	6	4	1	1	5	4
Eastwick (Save)	3	1	0	0	0	1

*Pitched to two batters in sixth.

Error—Concepcion. Double plays—Pittsburgh 3, Cincinnati 2. Left on bases—Pittsburgh 7, Cincinnati 5. Two-base hits—Stargell, Zisk, Morgan. Home run—Perez. Stolen base—Foster, Concepcion 2, Griffey 3, Morgan. Sacrifice fly—Norman. Wild pitch—Norman. Balk—Brett. Umpires—Olsen, Pulli, W. Williams, Gorman, A. Williams and Kibler. Time—2:51. Attendance—54,752.

GAME OF TUESDAY, OCTOBER 7, AT PITTSBURGH (N)

Cincinnati	AB.	R.	H.	RBI.	PO.	A.
Rose, 3b	5	2	2	2	2	0
Morgan, 2b	5	0	2	1	2	5
Bench, c	5	0	0	0	8	1
Perez, 1b	4	0	0	0	9	0
Foster, lf	3	0	0	0	3	0
Concepcion, ss	4	1	1	1	1	1
Griffey, rf	4	1	1	0	2	0
Geronimo, cf	4	0	0	0	5	0
Nolan, p	2	0	0	0	0	0
C. Carroll, p	0	0	0	0	0	1
Rettenmund, ph	0	1	0	0	0	0
McEnaney, p	0	0	0	0	0	0
Eastwick, p	0	0	0	0	0	0
Armbrister, ph	0	0	0	1	0	0
Borbon, p	0	0	0	0	0	0
Totals	36	5	6	5	30	8

Pittsburgh	AB.	R.	H.	RBI.	PO.	A.
Stennett, 2b-ss	5	0	0	0	2	0
Hebner, 3b	5	1	2	0	0	0
Oliver, cf	5	1	1	2	2	0
Stargell, 1b	4	0	1	0	1	0
Randolph, pr-2b	1	1	0	0	0	1
Parker, rf	4	0	0	0	5	0
Zisk, lf	3	0	2	0	4	0
Sanguillen, c	4	0	1	0	15	0
Taveras, ss	1	0	0	0	0	1
Kirkpatrick, ph	1	0	0	0	0	0
Reynolds, ss	1	0	0	0	0	0
Robertson, ph-1b	0	0	0	0	1	0
Candelaria, p	3	0	0	0	0	0
Giusti, p	0	0	0	0	0	0
Dyer, p	0	0	0	1	0	0
Hernandez, p	0	0	0	0	0	0
Tekulve, p	0	0	0	0	0	0
Totals	37	3	7	3	30	2

Cincinnati	0	1	0	0 0 0	0	2	0	2 – 5
Pittsburgh	0	0	0	0 0 2	0	0	1	0 – 3

Cincinnati	IP.	H.	R.	ER.	BB.	SO.
Nolan	6	5	2	2	0	5
C. Carroll	1	0	0	0	1	1
McEnaney	1⅓	1	1	1	0	1
Eastwick (Winner)	⅔	1	0	0	2	0
Borbon (Save)	1	0	0	0	0	1

Pittsburgh	IP.	H.	R.	ER.	BB.	SO.
Candelaria	7⅔	3	3	3	2	14
Giusti	1⅓	0	0	0	0	1
Hernandez (Loser)	⅔	3	2	2	0	0
Tekulve	⅓	0	0	0	0	0

Errors—Reynolds, Sanguillen. Left on bases—Cincinnati 4, Pittsburgh 7. Two-base hits—Morgan 2. Home runs—Concepcion, Oliver, Rose. Stolen base—Bench. Sacrifice fly—Armbrister. Balk—Hernandez. Umpires—Pulli, W. Williams, Gorman, A. Williams, Kibler and Olsen. Time—2:47. Attendance—46,355.

CINCINNATI REDS' BATTING AND FIELDING AVERAGES

Player-Position	G.	AB.	R.	H.	TB.	2B.	3B.	HR.	RBI.	B.A.	PO.	A.	E.	F.A.
Gullett, p	1	4	1	2	5	0	0	1	3	.500	4	1	0	1.000
Concepcion, ss	3	11	2	5	8	0	0	1	1	.455	6	8	1	.933
Perez, 1b	3	12	3	5	8	0	0	1	4	.417	27	5	0	1.000
Foster, lf	3	11	3	4	4	0	0	0	0	.364	7	0	0	1.000
Rose, 3b	3	14	3	5	8	0	0	1	2	.357	2	1	0	1.000
Griffey, rf	3	12	3	4	5	1	0	0	4	.333	4	1	0	1.000
Morgan, 2b	3	11	2	3	6	3	0	0	1	.273	2	9	0	1.000
Bench, c	3	13	1	1	1	0	0	0	0	.077	18	4	0	1.000
Norman, p	1	1	0	0	0	0	0	0	1	.000	0	1	0	1.000
Rettenmund, ph	2	1	1	0	0	0	0	0	0	.000	0	0	0	.000
Nolan, p	1	2	0	0	0	0	0	0	0	.000	0	0	0	.000
Geronimo, cf	3	10	0	0	0	0	0	0	1	.000	13	0	0	1.000
Armbrister, ph	2	0	0	0	0	0	0	0	1	.000	0	0	0	.000
Borbon, p	1	0	0	0	0	0	0	0	0	.000	0	0	0	.000
Carroll, p	1	0	0	0	0	0	0	0	0	.000	0	1	0	1.000
Crowley, ph	1	0	0	0	0	0	0	0	0	.000	0	0	0	.000
Eastwick, p	2	0	0	0	0	0	0	0	0	.000	1	0	0	1.000
McEnaney, p	1	0	0	0	0	0	0	0	0	.000	0	0	0	.000
Totals	3	102	19	29	45	4	0	4	18	.284	84	31	1	.991

PITTSBURGH PIRATES' BATTING AND FIELDING AVERAGES

Player-Position	G.	AB.	R.	H.	TB.	2B.	3B.	HR.	RBI.	B.A.	PO.	A.	E.	F.A.
Zisk, lf	3	10	0	5	6	1	0	0	0	.500	8	0	0	1.000
Robertson, ph-1b	3	2	0	1	1	0	0	0	1	.500	1	0	0	1.000
Hebner, 3b	3	12	2	4	5	1	0	0	2	.333	0	2	0	1.000
Stennett, 2b-ss	3	14	0	3	3	0	0	0	0	.214	3	8	0	1.000
Oliver, cf	3	11	1	2	5	0	0	1	2	.182	5	0	0	1.000

Player–Position	G.	AB.	R.	H.	TB.	2B.	3B.	HR.	RBI.	B.A.	PO.	A.	E.	F.A.
Stargell, 1b	3	11	1	2	3	1	0	0	0	.182	15	0	0	1.000
Sanguillen, c	3	12	0	2	2	0	0	0	0	.167	29	1	1	.968
Taveras, ss	3	7	0	1	1	0	0	0	1	.143	4	6	0	1.000
Reuss, p	1	1	0	0	0	0	0	0	0	.000	0	1	0	1.000
Reynolds, pr-ss	2	1	0	0	0	0	0	0	0	.000	0	0	1	.000
Rooker, p	1	1	0	0	0	0	0	0	0	.000	0	0	0	.000
Kirkpatrick, ph	2	2	0	0	0	0	0	0	0	.000	0	0	0	.000
Randolph, ph-pr-2b	2	2	1	0	0	0	0	0	0	.000	0	1	0	1.000
Robinson, ph	2	2	0	0	0	0	0	0	0	.000	0	0	0	.000
Candelaria, p	1	3	0	0	0	0	0	0	0	.000	0	0	0	.000
Parker, rf	3	10	2	0	0	0	0	0	0	.000	13	1	0	1.000
Brett, p	2	0	0	0	0	0	0	0	0	.000	0	0	0	.000
Demery, p	1	0	0	0	0	0	0	0	0	.000	0	0	0	.000
Dyer, ph	1	0	0	0	0	0	0	0	1	.000	0	0	0	.000
Ellis, p	1	0	0	0	0	0	0	0	0	.000	0	0	0	.000
Giusti, p	1	0	0	0	0	0	0	0	0	.000	0	0	0	.000
Hernandez, p	1	0	0	0	0	0	0	0	0	.000	0	0	0	.000
Kison, p	1	0	0	0	0	0	0	0	0	.000	0	0	0	.000
Tekulve, p	2	0	0	0	0	0	0	0	0	.000	0	0	0	.000
Totals	3	101	7	20	26	3	0	1	7	.198	78	20	2	.980

CINCINNATI REDS' PITCHING RECORDS

Pitcher	G.	GS.	CG.	IP.	H.	R.	ER.	BB.	SO.	HB.	WP.	W.	L.	Pct.	ERA.
Eastwick	2	0	0	3⅔	2	0	0	2	1	0	0	1	0	1.000	0.00
Borbon	1	0	0	1	0	0	0	0	1	0	0	0	0	.000	0.00
Carroll	1	0	0	1	0	0	0	1	1	0	0	0	0	.000	0.00
Norman	1	1	0	6	4	1	1	5	4	0	1	1	0	1.000	1.50
Gullett	1	1	1	9	8	3	3	2	5	1	1	1	0	1.000	3.00
Nolan	1	1	0	6	5	2	2	0	5	0	0	0	0	.000	3.00
McEnaney	1	0	0	1⅓	1	1	1	0	1	0	0	0	0	.000	6.75
Totals	3	3	1	28	20	7	7	10	18	1	2	3	0	1.000	2.25

No shutouts. Saves–Eastwick, Borbon.

PITTSBURGH PIRATES' PITCHING RECORDS

Pitcher	G.	GS.	CG.	IP.	H.	R.	ER.	BB.	SO.	HB.	WP.	W.	L.	Pct.	ERA.
Brett	2	0	0	2⅓	1	0	0	0	3	0	0	0	0	.000	0.00
Ellis	1	0	0	2	2	0	0	2	0	0	0	0	0	.000	0.00
Giusti	1	0	0	1⅓	0	0	0	1	0	0	0	0	0	.000	0.00
Candelaria	1	1	0	7⅔	3	3	3	2	14	0	0	0	0	.000	3.52
Kison	2	0	0	2	2	1	1	1	0	0	0	0	0	.000	4.50
Tekulve	1	0	0	1⅓	1	1	1	2	0	0	0	0	0	.000	6.75
Rooker	1	1	0	4	7	4	4	0	5	0	0	0	1	.000	9.00
Reuss	1	1	0	2⅔	4	4	4	4	1	0	0	0	1	.000	13.50
Demery	1	0	0	2	4	4	4	1	0	0	0	0	0	.000	18.00
Hernandez	1	0	0	⅔	3	2	2	0	0	0	0	0	1	.000	27.00
Totals	3	3	0	26	29	19	19	9	28	0	0	0	3	.000	6.58

No shutouts or saves.

COMPOSITE SCORE BY INNINGS

Cincinnati	2	2	3	2	4	1		1	2	0		2 – 19
Pittsburgh	0	2	0	1	0	2		0	0	2		0 – 7

Sacrifice hits–None.
Sacrifice flies–Ambrister, Geronimo, Norman.
Stolen bases–Morgan 4, Griffey 3. Concepcion 2, Bench, Foster.
Caught stealing–None.
Double plays–Concepcion and Perez; Morgan, Concepcion and Perez; Parker and Sanguillen; Stennett, Taveras and Stargell 2.
Left on bases–Cincinnati 17–8, 5, 4; Pittsburgh 21–7, 7, 7.
Hit by pitcher–By Gullett (Parker).
Passed balls–Sanguillen 2.
Balks–Brett, Hernandez.
Time of games–First game, 3:00; second game, 2:51; third game, 2:47.
Attendance–First game 54,633; second game, 54,752; third game, 46,355.
Umpires–Kibler, Olsen, Pulli, W. Williams, Gorman and A. Williams.
Official scorers–Earl Lawson, Cincinnati Post; Luke Quay, McKeesport Daily News.

AMERICAN LEAGUE
Championship Series of 1976

	W.	L.	Pct.
New York (East)	3	2	.600
Kansas City (West)	2	3	.400

With one swing of the bat, New York Yankee first baseman Chris Chambliss propelled his team to its first American League pennant since 1964 and touched off one of the wildest mob scenes in the history of American sports.

With the score tied, 6-6, in the bottom of the ninth inning in the fifth game of the Championship Series, Chambliss sent the first pitch from the Kansas City Royals' fireballing righthander, Mark Littell, over the right field fence. Littell had yielded only one homer during the regular season.

As soon as it was clear that the 1976 American League season was over and the Yankees were winners, Yankee fans, who had been wandering in a desert of pennantless seasons—something to which they were not accustomed—rushed onto the field.

By the time Chambliss reached first base, he was surrounded by spectators. When he reached second, the bag had already been removed by a souvenir collector and Chambliss had to reach out to touch it. He never did reach third and came nowhere near home, although his teammates brought him out later to stamp his feet in the general vicinity of home plate.

The hero of the evening was fortunte to escape without serious injury, as were his teammates. The fans' victory "celebration" turned into an orgy of hoodlumism and looting and resulted in about $100,000 worth of damage being done to Yankee Stadium.

Chambliss' homer was the climax of an exciting game. After the lead seesawed back and forth in the early going, the Yankees finally managed to carry a 6-3 bulge into the eighth frame. But the Royals' third baseman, George Brett, tied the game with a three-run home run. That set the stage for the pulsating finish.

The Yankees had been substantial favorites to win the playoff but the Royals, even after losing ace center fielder Amos Otis because of a leg injury in the first game, battled right down to the wire.

The Series opened in Kansas City and the Royals showed their nervousness by handing the Yanks two runs in the first inning with Brett committing a pair of misplays. Catfish Hunter subdued the home team easily, giving up only five hits, and the New Yorkers captured the game, 4-1.

In the second contest, the Royals found Yankee 19-game winner Ed Figueroa no puzzle and pounded out a 7-3 triumph.

The Yankees won the third engagement, 5-3, as Chambliss got two hits, including a home run, and drove in three runs.

The Royals knocked Hunter out of the box in the fourth inning of the fourth game, and copped a 7-4 decision to deadlock the Series.

That set up the climactic game of the 1976 American League season wherein Chambliss' big blow was the hit of the year.

GAME OF SATURDAY, OCTOBER 9, AT KANSAS CITY

New York	AB.	R.	H.	RBI.	PO.	A.
Rivers, cf	5	2	2	0	0	0
R. White, lf	4	0	1	2	4	0
Munson, c	5	1	1	0	5	2
Piniella, dh	4	0	2	0	0	0
Chambliss, 1b	4	0	2	1	7	0
Nettles, 3b	4	0	0	0	3	3
Maddox, rf	4	0	1	0	4	0
Randolph, 2b	4	0	0	0	2	2
Stanley, ss	4	1	3	0	2	1
Hunter, p	0	0	0	0	0	2
Totals	38	4	12	3	27	10

Kansas City	AB.	R.	H.	RBI.	PO.	A.
Otis, cf	1	0	0	0	0	0
Wohlford, lf	3	0	0	0	2	0
Brett, 3b	4	0	3	0	1	3
McRae, dh	4	0	0	0	0	0
Mayberry, 1b	3	0	0	0	10	0
Cowens, rf-cf	3	1	1	0	3	0
Poquette, lf-rf	3	0	0	1	4	0
F. White, 2b	2	0	0	0	2	3
Rojas, ph-2b	1	0	0	0	0	0
Patek, ss	3	0	1	0	1	3
Martinez, c	2	0	0	0	4	0
Quirk, ph	0	0	0	0	0	0
Wathan, c	0	0	0	0	0	0
Stinson, ph	1	0	0	0	0	0
Gura, p	0	0	0	0	0	0
Littell, p	0	0	0	0	0	0
Totals	30	1	5	1	27	9

New York	2	0	0		0	0	0		0	0	2 – 4
Kansas City	0	0	0		0	0	0		0	1	0 – 1

New York	IP.	H.	R.	ER.	BB.	SO.
Hunter (Winner)	9	5	1	1	0	5

Kansas City	IP.	H.	R.	ER.	BB.	SO.
Gura (Loser)	8⅔	12	4	3	1	4
Littell	⅓	0	0	0	0	0

Errors—Brett 2. Double play—Kansas City 1. Left on base—New York 8, Kansas City 2. Two-base hits—Stanley, R. White. Three-base hits—Chambliss, Cowens. Umpires—Brinkman, Haller, Maloney, Barnett, Franz and McCoy. Time—2:06. Attendance—41,077.

GAME OF SUNDAY, OCTOBER 10, AT KANSAS CITY (N)

New York	AB.	R.	H.	RBI.	PO.	A.
Rivers, cf	4	0	0	0	3	0
R. White, lf	4	1	2	0	2	0
Munson, c	5	1	2	1	2	1
Chambliss, 1b	5	0	3	1	9	1
May, dh	5	1	2	0	0	0
Nettles, 3b	3	0	1	0	2	5
Gamble, rf	4	0	1	1	3	0
Randolph, 2b	3	0	0	0	1	3
Stanley, ss	3	0	1	0	0	4
Piniella, ph	1	0	0	0	0	0
Mason, ss	0	0	0	0	1	0
Figueroa, p	0	0	0	0	0	0
Tidrow, p	0	0	0	0	0	0
Totals	37	3	12	3	24	14

Kansas City	AB.	R.	H.	RBI.	PO.	A.
Wohlford, lf	4	1	1	0	2	0
Cowens, cf	5	1	1	0	5	0
Brett, 3b	3	1	1	1	0	1
Mayberry, 1b	4	1	1	1	12	0
McRae, dh	3	0	0	0	0	0
Poquette, rf	3	1	2	2	2	0
F. White, 2b	4	1	1	0	3	5
Patek, ss	4	1	1	1	1	6
Martinez, c	4	0	1	2	2	0
Leonard, p	0	0	0	0	0	0
Splittorff, p	0	0	0	0	0	1
Mingori, p	0	0	0	0	0	0
Totals	34	7	9	7	27	13

New York	0	1	2		0	0	0		0	0	0 – 3
Kansas City	2	0	0		0	0	2		0	3	x – 7

New York	IP.	H.	R.	ER.	BB.	SO.
Figueroa (Loser)	5⅓	6	4	4	2	2
Tidrow	2⅔	3	3	2	1	0

Kansas City	IP.	H.	R.	ER.	BB.	SO.
Leonard	2⅓	6	3	3	2	0
Splittorff (Winner)	5⅔	4	0	0	2	0
Mingori	1	2	0	0	0	1

Errors—Munson 2, Chambliss, Stanley, Gamble. Double plays—Kansas City 2. Left on base—New York 11, Kansas City 7. Two-base hits—May, R. White, Munson, Stanley, Nettles, Poquette. Three-base hit—Brett. Stolen bases—Cowens 2, Wohlford. Sacrifice fly—Brett. Umpires—Barnett, Maloney, Haller, Frantz, McCoy and Brinkman. Time—2:45. Attendance—41,091.

GAME OF TUESDAY, OCTOBER 12, AT NEW YORK (N)

Kansas City	AB.	R.	H.	RBI.	PO.	A.
Wohlford, lf	2	1	0	0	0	0
Cowens, cf	4	0	1	0	1	0
Brett, 3b	3	1	2	1	1	0
Mayberry, 1b	4	1	1	0	11	0
McRae, dh	2	0	0	1	0	0
Poquette, rf	3	0	1	1	2	0
Nelson, ph	1	0	0	0	0	0
F. White, 2b	2	0	0	0	1	3
Rojas, ph-2b	1	0	0	0	0	1
Patek, ss	3	0	1	0	3	5
Martinez, c	2	0	0	0	5	1
Quirk, ph	1	0	0	0	0	0
Stinson, c	0	0	0	0	0	0
Hassler, p	0	0	0	0	0	0
Pattin, p	0	0	0	0	0	0
Hall, p	0	0	0	0	0	0
Mingori, p	0	0	0	0	0	0
Littell, p	0	0	0	0	0	1
Totals	28	3	6	3	24	11

New York	AB.	R.	H.	RBI.	PO.	A.
Rivers, cf	5	0	1	0	1	0
R. White, lf	3	1	0	0	0	0
Munson, c	4	1	2	0	5	2
Piniella, dh	2	1	1	0	0	0
May, ph-dh	1	0	0	0	0	0
Chambliss, 1b	4	2	2	3	10	2
Nettles, 3b	3	0	1	1	0	3
Maddox, rf	4	0	1	1	4	0
Randolph, 2b	3	0	1	0	3	3
Stanley, ss	3	0	0	0	3	4
Ellis, p	0	0	0	0	1	0
Lyle, p	0	0	0	0	0	0
Totals	32	5	9	5	27	14

Kansas City	3	0	0		0	0	0		0	0	0 – 3
New York	0	0	0		2	0	3		0	0	x – 5

Kansas City	IP.	H.	R.	ER.	BB.	SO.
Hassler (Loser)	5*	4	4	4	3	3
Pattin	0†	0	1	1	1	0
Hall	⅓	1	0	0	0	0
Mingori	0‡	1	0	0	0	0
Littell	2⅔	3	0	0	1	2

New York	IP.	H.	R.	ER.	BB.	SO.
Ellis (Winner)	8	6	3	3	2	5
Lyle (Save)	1	0	0	0	1	0

*Pitched two batters in sixth.
†Pitched to one batter in sixth.
‡Pitched to one batter in sixth.

Errors—None. Double plays—Kansas City 1, New York 2. Left on base—Kansas City 3, New York 8. Two-base hits—Poquette, Piniella, Munson, Maddox. Home run—Chambliss. Stolen bases—Wohlford, Chambliss, Randolph. Sacrifice fly—McRae. Hit by Pitcher—By Ellis (McRae). Passed ball—Munson. Umpires—Maloney, Haller, Frantz, McCoy, Brinkman and Barnett. Time—3:00. Attendance—56,808.

GAME OF WEDNESDAY, OCTOBER 13, AT NEW YORK

Kansas City	AB.	R.	H.	RBI.	PO.	A.
Cowens, cf	5	0	0	0	4	0
Poquette, lf-rf	4	0	0	0	3	0
Brett, 3b	4	0	0	1	2	2
Mayberry, 1b	3	1	0	0	9	0
McRae, rf	4	2	2	0	2	0
Wohlford, lf	0	0	0	0	3	0
Quirk, dh	2	1	1	2	0	0
Nelson, ph-dh	1	0	0	0	0	0
Rojas, 2b	3	1	2	1	1	3
F. White, pr-2b	0	1	0	0	0	0
Patek, ss	4	1	3	3	3	3
Martinez, c	3	0	1	1	1	1
Gura, p	0	0	0	0	0	0
Bird, p	0	0	0	0	0	1
Mingori, p	0	0	0	0	0	0
Totals	33	7	9	7	27	10

New York	AB.	R.	H.	RBI.	PO.	A.
Rivers, cf	4	0	1	0	5	0
R. White, lf	4	0	1	0	7	0
Munson, c	4	0	2	0	2	1
Piniella, dh	4	0	0	0	0	0
Chambliss, 1b	4	1	1	0	9	0
Nettles, 3b	4	2	2	3	0	2
Maddox, rf	1	0	0	0	1	0
Gamble, ph-rf	2	1	1	0	1	0
Velez, ph	1	0	0	0	0	0
Randolph, 2b	4	0	1	1	1	1
Stanley, ss	2	0	1	0	1	1
Hendricks, ph	1	0	1	0	0	0
Guidry, pr	0	0	0	0	0	0
Mason, ss	0	0	0	0	0	2
Alomar, ph	1	0	0	0	0	0
Hunter, p	0	0	0	0	0	1
Tidrow, p	0	0	0	0	0	0
Jackson, p	0	0	0	0	0	1
Totals	36	4	11	4	27	9

Kansas City	0	3	0		2	0	1		0	1	0 – 7
New York	0	2	0		0	0	0		1	0	1 – 4

Kansas City	IP.	H.	R.	ER.	BB.	SO.
Gura	2*	6	2	2	0	0
Bird (Winner)	4⅔	4	1	1	0	1
Mingori (Save)	2⅓	1	1	1	0	0

New York	IP.	H.	R.	ER.	BB.	SO.
Hunter (Loser)	3†	5	5	5	1	0
Tidrow	3⅔	2	1	1	2	0
Jackson	2⅓	2	1	1	1	2

*Pitched to one batter in third.
†Pitched to two batters in fourth.

Error—Bird. Double play—Kansas City 1. Left on base—Kansas City 5, New York 5. Two-base hits—R. White, Patek 2, McRae, Gamble. Three-base hits—Quirk, McRae. Home runs—Nettles 2. Sacrifice flies—Rojas, Quirk. Umpires—Haller, Frantz, McCoy, Brinkman, Barnett and Maloney. Time—2:50. Attendance—56,355.

GAME OF THURSDAY, OCTOBER 14, AT NEW YORK (N)

Kansas City	AB.	R.	H.	RBI.	PO.	A.
Cowens, cf	4	1	1	0	2	0
Poquette, lf	3	0	0	0	2	0
Wohlford, ph-lf	2	1	1	0	0	0
Brett, 3b	4	2	2	3	0	1
Mayberry, 1b	4	1	2	2	6	1
McRae, rf	4	0	0	0	3	1
Quirk, dh	4	0	0	0	0	0
Rojas, 2b	4	1	1	0	3	2
Patek, ss	4	0	1	0	5	1
Martinez, c	4	0	3	1	3	2
Leonard, p	0	0	0	0	0	0
Splittorff, p	0	0	0	0	0	0
Pattin, p	0	0	0	0	0	0
Hassler, p	0	0	0	0	0	0
Littell, p	0	0	0	0	0	0
Totals	37	6	11	6	24	8

New York	AB.	R.	H.	RBI.	PO.	A.
Rivers, cf	5	3	4	0	2	0
R. White, lf	2	2	1	1	4	0
Munson, c	5	0	3	2	4	0
Chambliss, 1b	4	2	3	3	15	0
May, dh	4	0	0	0	0	0
Alomar, pr-dh	0	0	0	0	0	0
Nettles, 3b	3	0	0	0	0	1
Gamble, rf	2	0	0	0	0	0
Randolph, 2b	3	0	0	0	1	5
Stanley, ss	3	0	0	0	1	5
Figueroa, p	0	0	0	0	0	2
Jackson, p	0	0	0	0	0	0
Tidrow, p	0	0	0	0	0	0
Totals	31	7	11	6	27	13

Kansas City	2	1	0	0	0	0	0	3	0–6
New York	2	0	2	0	0	2	0	0	1–7

None out when winning run scored.

Kansas City	IP.	H.	R.	ER.	BB.	SO.
Leonard	0*	3	2	2	0	0
Splittorff	3⅔	3	2	2	3	1
Pattin	⅓	0	0	0	0	0
Hassler	2⅓	4	2	1	3	1
Littell (Loser)	1⅔‡	1	1	1	0	1

New York	IP.	H.	R.	ER.	BB.	SO.
Figueroa	7†	8	4	4	0	3
Jackson	1	2	2	2	0	1
Tidrow (Winner)	1	1	0	0	1	0

*Pitched to three batters in first.
†Pitched to one batter in eighth.
‡Pitched to one batter in ninth.

Errors—Gamble, Brett. Double play—New York 1. Left on bases—Kansas City 5, New York 9. Two-base hits—Brett, Chambliss. Three-base hit—Rivers. Home runs—Mayberry, Brett, Chambliss. Stolen bases—R. White, Rojas, Chambliss. Sacrifice hits—R. White, Gamble. Sacrifice fly—Chambliss. Umpires—Frantz, McCoy, Brinkman, Barnett, Maloney and Haller. Time—3:13. Attendance—56,821.

NEW YORK YANKEES' BATTING AND FIELDING AVERAGES

Player—Position	G.	AB.	R.	H.	TB.	2B.	3B.	HR.	RBI.	B.A.	PO.	A.	E.	F.A.
Hendricks, ph	1	1	0	1	1	0	0	0	0	1.000	0	0	0	.000
Chambliss, 1b	5	21	5	11	20	1	1	2	8	.524	50	3	1	.981
Munson, c	5	23	3	10	12	2	0	0	3	.435	18	6	2	.923
Rivers, cf	5	15	1	5	7	2	0	0	0	.333	7	15	1	.957
Stanley, ss	5	23	5	8	10	0	1	0	0	.348	11	0	0	1.000
R. White, lf	5	17	4	5	8	3	0	0	3	.294	17	0	0	1.000
Piniella, dh-ph	4	11	1	3	4	1	0	0	0	.273	0	0	0	.000
Gamble, rf-ph	3	8	1	2	3	1	0	0	1	.250	4	0	2	.667
Nettles, 3b	5	17	2	4	11	1	0	2	4	.235	5	14	0	1.000
Maddox, rf	3	9	0	2	3	1	0	0	1	.222	9	0	0	1.000
May, dh-ph	3	10	1	2	3	1	0	0	0	.200	0	0	0	.000
Randolph, 2b	5	17	0	2	2	0	0	0	1	.118	8	14	0	1.000
Ellis, p	1	0	0	0	0	0	0	0	0	.000	1	0	0	1.000
Guidry, pr	1	0	0	0	0	0	0	0	0	.000	0	0	0	.000
Lyle, p	1	0	0	0	0	0	0	0	0	.000	0	0	0	.000
Figueroa, p	2	0	0	0	0	0	0	0	0	.000	0	2	0	1.000
Hunter, p	2	0	0	0	0	0	0	0	0	.000	0	3	0	1.000

Player—Position	G.	AB.	R.	H.	TB.	2B.	3B.	HR.	RBI.	B.A.	PO.	A.	E.	F.A.
Jackson, p	2	0	0	0	0	0	0	0	0	.000	0	1	0	1.000
Mason, ss	2	0	0	0	0	0	0	0	0	.000	0	1	0	1.000
Tidrow, p	3	0	0	0	0	0	0	0	0	.000	1	2	0	1.000
Alomar, ph-pr-dh	2	1	0	0	0	0	0	0	0	.000	0	0	0	.000
Velez, ph	1	1	0	0	0	0	0	0	0	.000	0	0	0	.000
Totals	5	174	23	55	84	13	2	4	21	.316	132	60	6	.970

KANSAS CITY ROYALS' BATTING AND FIELDING AVERAGES

Player—Position	G.	AB.	R.	H.	TB.	2B.	3B.	HR.	RBI.	B.A.	PO.	A.	E.	F.A.
Brett, 3b	5	18	4	8	14	1	1	1	5	.444	3	7	3	.769
Patek, ss	5	18	2	7	9	2	0	0	4	.389	13	18	0	1.000
Martinez, c	5	15	0	5	5	0	0	0	4	.333	15	4	0	1.000
Rojas, ph-2b	4	9	2	3	3	0	0	0	1	.333	4	6	0	1.000
Mayberry, 1b	5	18	4	4	7	0	0	1	3	.222	48	1	0	1.000
Cowens, rf-cf	5	21	3	4	6	0	1	0	0	.190	15	0	0	1.000
Poquette, lf-cf	5	16	1	3	5	2	0	0	4	.188	13	0	0	1.000
Wohlford, lf-ph	5	11	3	2	2	0	0	0	0	.182	7	0	0	1.000
Quirk, ph-dh	4	7	1	1	3	0	1	0	2	.143	0	0	0	.000
F. White, 2b-pr	4	8	2	1	1	0	0	0	0	.125	6	11	0	1.000
McRae, dh-rf	5	17	2	2	5	1	1	0	1	.118	5	1	0	1.000
Bird, p	1	0	0	0	0	0	0	0	0	.000	0	1	1	.500
Hall, p	1	0	0	0	0	0	0	0	0	.000	0	0	0	.000
Wathan, c	1	0	0	0	0	0	0	0	0	.000	0	0	0	.000
Gura, p	2	0	0	0	0	0	0	0	0	.000	0	0	0	.000
Hassler, p	2	0	0	0	0	0	0	0	0	.000	0	0	0	.000
Leonard, p	2	0	0	0	0	0	0	0	0	.000	0	0	0	.000
Pattin, p	2	0	0	0	0	0	0	0	0	.000	0	0	0	.000
Splittorff, p	2	0	0	0	0	0	0	0	0	.000	0	1	0	1.000
Littell, p	3	0	0	0	0	0	0	0	0	.000	0	1	0	1.000
Mingori, p	3	0	0	0	0	0	0	0	0	.000	0	0	0	.000
Otis, cf	1	1	0	0	0	0	0	0	0	.000	0	0	0	.000
Stinson, ph-c	2	1	0	0	0	0	0	0	0	.000	0	0	0	.000
Nelson, ph-dh	2	2	0	0	0	0	0	0	0	.000	0	0	0	.000
Totals	5	162	24	40	60	6	4	2	24	.247	129	51	4	.978

NEW YORK YANKEES' PITCHING RECORDS

Pitcher	G.	GS.	CG.	IP.	H.	R.	ER.	BB.	SO.	HB.	WP.	W.	L.	Pct.	ERA.
Lyle	1	0	0	1	0	0	0	1	0	0	0	0	0	.000	0.00
Ellis	1	1	0	8	6	3	3	2	1	0	0	0	0	.000	3.38
Tidrow	3	0	0	7⅓	6	4	3	4	0	0	0	1	0	1.000	3.68
Hunter	2	2	1	12	10	6	6	1	5	0	0	1	0	1.000	4.50
Figueroa	2	2	0	12⅓	14	8	8	2	5	0	0	1	1	.500	5.84
Jackson	2	0	0	3⅓	4	3	3	1	3	0	0	0	1	.000	8.10
Totals	5	5	1	44	40	24	23	11	18	1	0	3	2	.600	4.70

No shutouts. Save—Lyle.

KANSAS CITY ROYALS' PITCHING RECORDS

Pitcher	G.	GS.	CG.	IP.	H.	R.	ER.	BB.	SO.	HB.	WP.	W.	L.	Pct.	ERA.
Hall	1	0	0	⅓	1	0	0	0	0	0	0	0	0	.000	0.00
Splittorff	2	0	0	9⅓	7	2	2	5	2	0	0	1	0	.000	1.93
Bird	1	0	0	4⅔	4	1	1	0	1	0	0	1	0	1.000	1.93
Littell	3	0	0	4⅔	4	1	1	1	3	0	0	0	1	1.000	1.93
Mingori	3	0	0	3⅓	4	1	1	0	1	0	0	0	0	.000	2.70
Gura	2	2	0	10⅔	18	6	5	1	4	0	0	0	1	.000	4.22
Hassler	2	1	0	7⅓	8	6	5	4	0	0	0	0	1	.000	6.14
Leonard	2	2	0	2⅓	9	5	5	2	0	0	0	0	0	.000	19.29
Pattin	2	0	0	⅓	0	1	1	1	0	0	0	0	0	.000	27.00
Totals	5	5	0	43	55	23	21	16	15	0	0	2	3	.400	4.40

No shutouts. Save—Mingori.

COMPOSITE SCORE BY INNINGS

New York	4	3	4	2	0	5		1	0	4 – 23
Kansas City	7	4	0	2	0	3		0	8	0 – 24

Sacrifice hits—Gamble, R. White.
Sacrifice flies—Brett, Chambliss, McRae, Quirk, Rojas.
Stolen bases—Chambliss 2, Cowens 2, Wohlford 2, Randolph, Rojas, R. White.
Caught stealing—Patek 3, Alomar, Brett, McRae, Munson, Rivers.
Double plays—Randolph and Chambliss; Chambliss, Stanley and Randolph; Stanley and Chambliss; Brett, F. White and Mayberry; Patek, F. White and Mayberry; Patek and Mayberry; Martinez and F. White; Rojas, Patek and Mayberry.
Left on bases—New York 41—8, 11, 8, 5, 9; Kansas City 22—2, 7, 3, 5, 5.

Hit by pitcher—By Ellis (McRae).
Passed ball—Munson.
Balks—None.
Time of games—First game, 2:06; second game, 2:45; third game, 3:00; fourth game, 2:50; fifth game, 3:13.
Attendance—First game, 41,077; second game, 41,091; third game, 56,808; fourth game, 56,355; fifth game, 56,821.
Umpires—Brinkman, Haller, Maloney, Barnett, Frantz and McCoy.
Official scorers—Sid Bordman, Kansas City Star; Phil Pepe, New York Daily News.

NATIONAL LEAGUE
Championship Series of 1976

	W.	L.	Pct.
Cincinnati (West).......................................	3	0	1.000
Philadelphia (East)...................................	0	3	.000

For most of the summer of 1976, baseball fans had been looking forward to what promised to be a great Championship Series between two fine teams, the Cincinnati Reds and the Philadelphia Phillies, each of whom had been impressive winners in their respective divisions.

The Series began in Philadelphia with each club sending its ace lefthander to the mound, Don Gullett for the Reds and Steve Carlton for the Phils. It was no contest. After a spate of first-inning wildness, Gullett was in command all the way, finishing an eight-inning stint with only one run and two hits against his record.

Carlton, meanwhile, was the victim of some shoddy support. A liner by Pete Rose was misplayed into a triple by right fielder Ollie Brown and that gave Cincinnati one of its runs. The Reds got another of their tallies when Phil third sacker Mike Schmidt passed up an easy throw to first base and attempted, unsuccessfully, to tag a runner off third. Carlton was finally kayoed in the eighth frame and his successor, Tug McGraw, was rapped for a couple of hits resulting in three runs that put the game out of reach for the home team.

After Gullett left the game with an injury to his left leg, the Phils managed to score a pair of runs off reliever Rawly Eastwick. But it was a meaningless gesture and served only to make the final score a respectable 6-3.

The largest crowd ever to see a Championship Series game—62,651—saw Phil righthander Jim Lonborg ride a 2-0 lead and a no-hitter into the sixth inning of the second contest.

But in the sixth he walked leadoff batter Dave Concepcion, who moved to second on a groundout. Rose then got the first hit off Lonborg, a single to right that plated Concepcion. Ken Griffey followed with a single sending Rose to third and took second on the futile throw trying to head off Pete. Lonborg was given the hook and replaced by Gene Garber. Joe Morgan drew an intentional walk to load the bases and Tony Perez then rammed a hot liner down the first base line. Dick Allen was unable to handle it, two runs scored and the sun had begun to set on the Phillies' season.

Cincinnati added another run before the inning was over and again pounded McGraw in the next inning to walk away with a 6-2 victory.

The third game, played at Cincinnati's Riverfront Stadium, was the most exciting. The Phils carried a 6-4 lead into the bottom of the ninth but were hit by lightning in the form of successive home runs by the first two batters of the inning, George Foster and Johnny Bench. Both blows came off reliever Ron Reed.

After Bench's homer, Garber relieved and stayed only long enough to give up a single to Concepcion. Lefty Tom Underwood came on and loaded the bases on a walk, a sacrifice and another walk. Griffey then ended the 1976 National League season by chopping a high bounding hit off the glove of first baseman Bobby Tolan. Concepcion raced home with the run that gave the Reds a 7-6 triumph and their second straight flag.

GAME OF SATURDAY, OCTOBER 9, AT PHILADELPHIA (N)

Cincinnati	AB.	R.	H.	RBI.	PO.	A.
Rose, 3b	5	1	3	1	1	2
Griffey, rf	4	0	1	0	5	0
Morgan, 2b	2	0	0	0	1	1
Eastwick, p	0	0	0	0	0	1
Perez, 1b	3	0	0	1	8	0
Foster, lf	5	1	1	1	4	0
Bench, c	5	1	2	0	4	2
Concepcion, ss	3	2	1	0	0	2
Geronimo, cf	4	0	0	4	0	0
Gullett, p	4	1	2	3	0	0
Flynn, 2b	0	0	0	0	0	0
Totals	35	6	10	6	27	8

Philadelphia	AB.	R.	H.	RBI.	PO.	A.
Cash, 2b	4	1	1	0	2	0
Maddox, cf	4	1	2	0	2	0
Schmidt, 3b	3	0	0	1	3	3
Luzinski, lf	3	1	1	1	2	0
Allen, 1b	3	0	1	0	5	0
Brown, rf	2	0	0	0	2	0
Johnstone, ph	1	0	1	1	0	0
McCarver, c	3	0	0	0	6	0
McGraw, p	0	0	0	0	0	0
Tolan, ph	1	0	0	0	0	0
Bowa, ss	3	0	0	0	1	4
Hutton, ph	1	0	0	0	0	0
Carlton, p	2	0	0	0	0	0
Boone, c	1	0	0	0	4	0
Totals	31	3	6	3	27	7

Cincinnati	0	0	1		0	0	2		0	3	0 – 6
Philadelphia	1	0	0		0	0	0		0	0	2 – 3

Cincinnati	IP.	H.	R.	ER.	BB.	SO.
Gullett (Winner)	8	2	1	1	3	4
Eastwick	1	4	2	2	0	0

Philadelphia	IP.	H.	R.	ER.	BB.	SO.
Carlton (Loser)	7*	8	5	4	5	6
McGraw	2	2	1	1	1	4

*Pitched to two batters in eighth.

Error—Schmidt. Double plays—Philadelphia 2. Left on bases—Cincinnati 9, Philadelphia 5. Two-base hits—Rose 2, Concepcion, Bench, Gullett, Cash, Luzinski. Three-base hits—Rose, Griffey. Home run—Foster. Stolen bases—Griffey, Bench, Morgan 2. Sacrifice flies—Schmidt, Perez. Wild pitches—McGraw, Eastwick. Umpires—Sudol, Dale, Stello, Vargo, Harvey and Tata. Time—2:39. Attendance—62,640.

GAME OF SUNDAY, OCTOBER 10, AT PHILADELPHIA

Cincinnati	AB.	R.	H.	RBI.	PO.	A.
Rose, 3b	5	2	2	1	1	2
Griffey, rf	4	1	2	1	4	0
Morgan, 2b	2	1	0	0	5	1
Perez, 1b	3	0	0	1	10	1
Foster, lf	4	0	0	1	0	0
Bench, c	4	0	1	0	4	1
Geronimo, cf	4	0	1	0	1	0
Concepcion, ss	3	1	0	0	1	5
Zachry, p	1	0	0	0	1	3
Driessen, ph	1	0	0	0	0	0
Borbon, p	2	1	0	0	0	0
Totals	33	6	6	4	27	13

Philadelphia	AB.	R.	H.	RBI.	PO.	A.
Cash, 2b	5	0	2	0	0	3
Maddox, cf	4	0	0	0	6	0
Schmidt, 3b	5	0	1	0	0	2
Luzinski, lf	4	1	1	1	4	0
Allen, 1b	3	1	1	0	12	0
Johnstone, rf	4	0	3	0	1	0
Boone, c	3	0	2	1	3	2
Bowa, ss	2	0	0	0	1	4
Lonborg, p	1	0	0	0	0	2
Garber, p	0	0	0	0	0	0
Tolan, ph	1	0	0	0	0	0
McGraw, p	0	0	0	0	0	1
Reed, p	0	0	0	0	0	0
McCarver, ph	1	0	0	0	0	0
Totals	33	2	10	2	27	14

| Cincinnati | 0 | 0 | 0 | 0 | 0 | 4 | 2 | 0 | 0 – 6 |
| Philadelphia | 0 | 1 | 0 | 0 | 1 | 0 | 0 | 0 | 0 – 2 |

Cincinnati	IP.	H.	R.	ER.	BB.	SO.
Zachry (Winner)	5	6	2	2	3	3
Borbon (Save)	4	4	0	0	1	0

Philadelphia	IP.	H.	R.	ER.	BB.	SO.
Lonborg (Loser)	5⅓	2	3	1	2	2
Garber	⅔	1	1	0	1	0
McGraw	⅓	2	2	2	0	1
Reed	2⅔	1	0	0	1	1

Error—Allen. Double plays—Cincinnati 2. Left on bases—Cincinnati 5, Philadelphia 10. Home run—Luzinski. Stolen base—Griffey. Sacrifice hits—Boone, Lonborg. Sacrifice fly—Perez. Wild pitch—McGraw. Umpires—Dale, Stello, Vargo, Harvey, Tata and Sudol. Time—2:24. Attendance—62,651.

GAME OF TUESDAY, OCTOBER 12, AT CINCINNATI

Philadelphia	AB.	R.	H.	RBI.	PO.	A.
Cash, 2b	4	0	1	1	6	5
Maddox, cf	5	1	1	1	1	0
Schmidt, 3b	5	1	3	1	1	4
Luzinski, lf	4	0	1	1	0	0
Reed, p	1	0	0	0	0	0
Garber, p	0	0	0	0	0	0
Underwood, p	0	0	0	0	0	0
Allen, 1b	3	0	0	0	11	0
Martin, lf	1	1	0	0	1	0
Johnstone, rf	4	1	3	1	2	0
Boone, c	3	0	0	0	1	0
Harmon, pr	0	1	0	0	0	0
Oates, c	1	0	0	0	1	0
Bowa, ss	3	1	1	1	0	3
Kaat, p	2	0	1	0	0	1
Tolan, lf-1b	0	0	0	0	1	0
Totals	36	6	11	6	25	13

Cincinnati	AB.	R.	H.	RBI.	PO.	A.
Rose, 3b	4	0	1	0	0	1
Griffey, rf	5	1	2	1	2	0
Morgan, 2b	3	1	0	0	3	3
Perez, 1b	4	1	2	1	9	1
Foster, lf	3	2	1	1	3	0
Bench, c	3	1	1	3	3	1
Concepcion, ss	4	1	1	0	1	5
Geronimo, cf	3	0	1	2	5	0
Nolan, p	0	0	0	0	1	0
Sarmiento, p	1	0	0	0	0	0
Borbon, p	0	0	0	0	0	0
Lum, ph	1	0	0	0	0	0
Eastwick, p	0	0	0	0	0	0
Armbrister, ph	0	0	0	0	0	0
Totals	31	7	9	7	27	11

| Philadelphia | 0 | 0 | 0 | 1 | 0 | 0 | 2 | 2 | 1 – 6 |
| Cincinnati | 0 | 0 | 0 | 0 | 0 | 0 | 4 | 0 | 3 – 7 |

One out when winning run scored.

Philadelphia	IP.	H.	R.	ER.	BB.	SO.
Kaat	6*	2	2	2	2	1
Reed	2†	5	4	4	1	1
Garber (Loser)	0‡	1	1	1	0	0
Underwood	⅓	1	0	0	2	0

Cincinnati	IP.	H.	R.	ER.	BB.	SO.
Nolan	5⅔	6	1	1	2	1
Sarmiento	1	2	2	2	1	0
Borbon	⅓	0	0	0	0	0
Eastwick (Winner)	2	3	3	2	2	1

*Pitched to two batters in seventh.
†Pitched to two batters in ninth.
‡Pitched to one batter in ninth.

Errors—Rose, Perez. Double plays—Philadelphia 1, Cincinnati 1. Left on bases—Philadelphia 10, Cincinnati 6. Two-base hits—Maddox, Schmidt 2, Luzinski, Johnstone, Bowa. Three-base hits—Johnstone, Geronimo. Home runs—Foster, Bench. Sacrifice hits—Kaat, Armbrister. Sacrifice flies—Cash, Foster. Wild pitch—Eastwick. Umpires—Stello, Vargo, Harvey, Tata, Sudol and Dale. Time—2:43. Attendance—55,047.

PHILADELPHIA PHILLIES' BATTING AND FIELDING AVERAGES

Player–Position	G.	AB.	R.	H.	TB.	2B.	3B.	HR.	RBI.	B.A.	PO.	A.	E.	F.A.
Johnstone, ph-rf	3	9	1	7	10	1	1	0	2	.778	3	0	0	1.000
Kaat, p	2	2	0	1	1	0	0	0	0	.500	0	1	0	1.000
Cash, 2b	3	13	1	4	5	1	0	0	1	.308	8	8	0	1.000
Schmidt, 3b	3	13	1	4	6	2	0	0	2	.308	4	9	1	.929
Boone, c	3	7	0	2	2	0	0	0	1	.286	8	2	0	1.000
Luzinski, lf	3	11	2	3	8	2	0	1	3	.273	6	0	0	1.000
Maddox, cf	3	13	2	3	4	1	0	0	1	.231	9	0	0	1.000
Allen, 1b	3	9	1	2	2	0	0	0	0	.222	28	0	1	.966
Bowa, ss	3	8	1	1	2	1	0	0	1	.125	2	11	0	1.000
Garber, p	2	0	0	0	0	0	0	0	0	.000	0	0	0	.000
Harmon, pr	1	0	1	0	0	0	0	0	0	.000	0	0	0	.000

Player—Position	G.	AB.	R.	H.	TB.	2B.	3B.	HR.	RBI.	B.A.	PO.	A.	E.	F.A.
McGraw, p	2	0	0	0	0	0	0	0	0	.000	0	1	0	1.000
Underwood, p	1	0	0	0	0	0	0	0	0	.000	0	0	0	.000
Hutton, ph	1	1	0	0	0	0	0	0	0	.000	0	0	0	.000
Lonborg, p	1	1	0	0	0	0	0	0	0	.000	0	2	0	1.000
Martin, lf	1	1	1	0	0	0	0	0	0	.000	1	0	0	1.000
Oates, c	1	1	0	0	0	0	0	0	0	.000	1	0	0	1.000
Reed, p	2	1	0	0	0	0	0	0	0	.000	0	0	0	.000
Brown, rf	1	2	0	0	0	0	0	0	0	.000	2	0	0	1.000
Carlton, p	1	2	0	0	0	0	0	0	0	.000	0	0	0	.000
Tolan, ph-lf-1b	3	2	0	0	0	0	0	0	0	.000	1	0	0	1.000
McCarver, c-ph	2	4	0	0	0	0	0	0	0	.000	6	0	0	1.000
Totals	3	100	11	27	40	8	1	1	11	.270	79	34	2	.983

CINCINNATI REDS' BATTING AND FIELDING AVERAGES

Player—Position	G.	AB.	R.	H.	TB.	2B.	3B.	HR.	RBI.	B.A.	PO.	A.	E.	F.A.
Gullett, p	1	4	1	2	3	1	0	0	3	.500	0	0	0	.000
Rose, 3b	3	14	3	6	10	2	1	0	2	.429	2	5	1	.875
Griffey, rf	3	13	2	5	7	0	1	0	2	.385	11	0	0	1.000
Bench, c	3	12	3	4	8	1	0	1	1	.333	11	4	0	1.000
Concepcion, ss	3	10	4	2	3	1	0	0	0	.200	2	12	0	1.000
Perez, 1b	3	10	1	2	2	0	0	0	3	.200	27	2	1	.967
Geronimo, cf	3	11	0	2	4	0	1	0	2	.182	10	0	0	1.000
Foster, lf	3	12	2	2	8	0	0	2	4	.167	7	0	0	1.000
Armbrister, ph	1	0	0	0	0	0	0	0	0	.000	0	0	0	.000
Eastwick, p	2	0	0	0	0	0	0	0	0	.000	0	1	0	1.000
Flynn, 2b	1	0	0	0	0	0	0	0	0	.000	0	0	0	.000
Nolan, p	1	0	0	0	0	0	0	0	0	.000	1	0	0	1.000
Driessen, ph	1	1	0	0	0	0	0	0	0	.000	0	0	0	.000
Lum, ph	1	1	0	0	0	0	0	0	0	.000	0	0	0	.000
Sarmiento, p	1	1	0	0	0	0	0	0	0	.000	0	0	0	.000
Zachry, p	1	1	0	0	0	0	0	0	0	.000	1	3	0	1.000
Borbon, p	2	2	1	0	0	0	0	0	0	.000	0	0	0	.000
Morgan, 2b	3	7	2	0	0	0	0	0	0	.000	9	5	0	1.000
Totals	3	99	19	25	45	5	3	3	17	.253	81	32	2	.983

CINCINNATI REDS' PITCHING RECORDS

Pitcher	G.	GS.	CG.	IP.	H.	R.	ER.	BB.	SO.	HB.	WP.	W.	L.	Pct.	ERA.
Borbon	2	0	0	4⅓	4	0	0	0	0	0	0	0	0	.000	0.00
Gullett	1	1	0	8	2	1	1	3	4	0	0	1	0	1.000	1.13
Nolan	1	1	0	5⅔	6	1	1	2	1	0	0	0	0	.000	1.59
Zachry	1	1	0	5	6	2	2	3	3	0	0	1	0	1.000	3.60
Eastwick	2	0	0	3	7	5	4	2	2	0	2	1	0	1.000	12.00
Sarmiento	1	0	0	1	2	2	2	1	0	0	0	0	0	.000	18.00
Totals	3	3	0	27	27	11	10	12	9	0	2	3	0	1.000	3.33

No shutouts.   Save—Borbon.

PHILADELPHIA PHILLIES' PITCHING RECORDS

Pitcher	G.	GS.	CG.	IP.	H.	R.	ER.	BB.	SO.	HB.	WP.	W.	L.	Pct.	ERA.
Underwood	1	0	0	⅓	1	0	0	2	0	0	0	0	0	.000	0.00
Lonborg	1	1	0	5⅓	2	3	1	2	2	0	0	0	1	.000	1.69
Kaat	1	1	0	6	2	2	2	2	1	0	0	0	0	.000	3.00
Carlton	1	1	0	7	8	5	4	5	6	0	0	0	1	.000	5.14
Reed	2	0	0	4⅔	6	4	4	2	2	0	0	0	0	.000	7.71
McGraw	2	0	0	2⅓	4	3	3	1	5	0	2	0	0	.000	11.57
Garber	2	0	0	⅔	2	2	1	1	0	0	0	0	1	.000	13.50
Totals	3	3	0	26⅓	25	19	15	15	16	0	2	0	3	.000	5.13

No shutouts or saves.

COMPOSITE SCORE BY INNINGS

Cincinnati	0	0	1	0	0	6	6	3	3	—	19
Philadelphia	1	1	0	1	1	0	2	2	3	—	11

Sacrifice hits—Armbrister, Boone, Kaat, Lonborg.
Sacrifice flies—Perez 2, Foster, Cash, Schmidt.
Stolen bases—Griffey 2, Morgan 2, Bench.
Caught stealing—Geronimo, Maddox.
Double plays—Morgan (unassisted); Rose, Bench and Perez; Concepcion, Morgan and Perez; Schmidt (unassisted); Schmidt and Cash; Bowa, Cash and Allen.
Left on bases—Cincinnati 20—9, 5, 6; Philadelphia 25—5, 10, 10.
Hit by pitcher—None.

Passed balls—None.
Balks—None.
Time of games—First game, 2:39; second game, 2:24; third game, 2:43.
Attendance—First game, 62,640; second game, 62,651; third game, 55,047.
Umpires—Sudol, Dale, Stello, Vargo, Harvey and Tata.
Official scorers—Bob Hertzel, Cincinnati Enquirer; Bob Kenney, Camden Courier-Post.

AMERICAN LEAGUE
Championship Series of 1977

	W.	L.	Pct.
New York (East)	3	2	.600
Kansas City (West)	2	3	.400

There they were, Yankee Manager Billy Martin and his boss, George Steinbrenner, shaking hands and embracing in their mutual joy after the Bronx Bombers had disposed of the Kansas City Royals in five games of the American League Championship Series.

The joy expressed in that setting was pure ecstasy. The Yankees, billed as "the best club money can buy," had to score three runs in the ninth inning to overtake the Royals in the final game, 5-3.

It was the second straight year the Yankees had conquered the Royals for the A.L. pennant.

Pitchers Mike Torrez and Sparky Lyle were the key men in the final game triumph. They held the Royals off the scoreboard on only four hits for the last 6⅔ innings, while the Yankees fought back from a 3-1 deficit.

The evening started in what had become typical Yankee high drama when Martin benched star outfielder Reggie Jackson, a 1-for-14 performer in the first four games.

Kansas City aggressively took a 2-0 lead in the first inning. With one out Hal McRae got an infield single. George Brett followed with a triple to right-center. When he came up from his hard slide, Brett fired a right hand in the direction of the New York third baseman Graig Nettles and the two wrestled to the ground. Both benches emptied. (In game two, McRae had set the fierce tempo in bowling over Yankee second baseman Willie Randolph on a force play in the sixth inning.)

After order was restored, Al Cowens' grounder scored Brett. A run-scoring single by Cowens in the third made the score 3-1. Enter third-game loser Torrez for a 5⅓ inning scoreless stint. Lyle, who hurled 5⅓ innings of scoreless ball to win the fourth game, followed with his second straight victory by setting down the Royals for the final 1⅓ innings.

The Yanks struck for one run in the eighth, with Jackson's pinch-single being a key blow. Kansas City Manager Whitey Herzog, who had already called on three pitchers—excusing starter Paul Splittorff after an impressive seven-inning performance—went to his ace starter and 20-game winner Dennis Leonard in the ninth.

Paul Blair, who started in right field in place of Jackson, opened with a single. Pinch-hitter Roy White drew a walk. Lefthander Larry Gura, who had been routed for six hits and four runs in two innings a day earlier, was summoned by Herzog to face Mickey Rivers.

Rivers, who had gone 2-for-2 against Gura's deliveries in Game 4, slapped a single to right, scoring Blair and sending White to third. Mark Littell then took the mound and surrendered a sacrifice fly to Randolph for the go-ahead run. An insurance run followed on Brett's error.

Kansas City and New York had split their 10-game series during the 1977 season, but it was the Royals who showed no timidity, waltzing right into Yankee Stadium for a stunning 7-2 first game victory.

The Royals flexed their muscles with three home runs and almost pulled off a triple play to end the game.

Lefthander Splittorff stifled the Yankees' bats, before being relieved by Doug Bird after surrendering his first walk of the game to Chambliss, leading off the ninth inning.

McRae's previously mentioned bodyblock of second baseman Randolph was the cause celebre in the second game.

Aroused by what they considered violent tactics by McRae, the Yankees broke a 2-2 tie with three runs in their half of the sixth. And lefty Ron Guidry held Kansas City to three hits in a 6-2 victory.

Thus, the scene shifted to Royals Stadium for Game 3 and Kansas City righthander Dennis Leonard was in complete control, limiting New York to four hits in a 6-2 triumph.

The Yankees pulled away to a 4-0 lead in three innings against Larry Gura in Game 4.

But Yankee starter Ed Figueroa couldn't stand prosperity and departed in the fourth with a 5-3 lead. Reliever Dick Tidrow yielded a run-producing double by Frank White.

Then Lyle entered with runners on first and third and two out in a one-run ball game. He quickly enticed Brett to fly out. For the next five innings, Sparky faced 16 batters, one over the minimum, while permitting only two hits.

Meanwhile, Mickey Rivers, who had 4-for-5, scored an insurance run in the ninth for the 6-4 final score.

GAME OF WEDNESDAY, OCTOBER 5, AT NEW YORK

Kansas City	AB.	R.	H.	RBI.	PO.	A.
Patek, ss	4	1	2	2	6	0
McRae, dh	5	1	1	2	0	0
Brett, 3b	5	0	0	0	2	0
Cowens, rf	4	2	3	1	4	0
Otis, cf	4	0	0	0	2	0
Mayberry, 1b	3	1	1	2	3	0
Zdeb, lf	4	0	0	0	3	0
Porter, c	2	1	1	0	3	0
F. White, 2b	4	1	1	0	4	0
Splittorff, p	0	0	0	0	0	2
Bird, p	0	0	0	0	0	0
Totals	35	7	9	7	27	4

New York	AB.	R.	H.	RBI.	PO.	A.
Rivers, cf	4	1	3	0	4	0
Nettles, 3b	4	0	0	0	0	2
Munson, c	4	1	1	2	4	1
Jackson, rf	4	0	0	0	1	0
Piniella, lf	4	0	1	0	2	0
Chambliss, 1b	3	0	1	0	5	2
Johnson, dh	4	0	2	0	0	0
Randolph, 2b	4	0	1	0	4	1
Dent, ss	3	0	0	0	6	3
R. White, ph	1	0	0	0	0	0
Gullett, p	0	0	0	0	0	0
Tidrow, p	0	0	0	0	1	2
Lyle, p	0	0	0	0	0	0
Totals	35	2	9	2	27	11

Kansas City	2	2	2	0	0	0	0	1	0 – 7
New York	0	0	2	0	0	0	0	0	0 – 2

Kansas City	IP.	H.	R.	ER.	BB.	SO.
Splittorff (Winner)	8*	8	2	2	1	2
Bird	1	1	0	0	0	0

New York	IP.	H.	R.	ER.	BB.	SO.
Gullett (Loser)	2	4	4	4	2	0
Tidrow	6⅔	5	3	3	2	3
Lyle	⅓	0	0	0	0	0

*Pitched to one batter in ninth.

Errors—None. Double play—Kansas City 1. Left on base—Kansas City 5, New York 7. Two-base hits—Patek, Randolph, Rivers. Home runs—McRae, Mayberry, Munson, Cowens. Stolen base—Zdeb. Umpires—Neudecker, Goetz, McKean, Springstead, Bremigan and Deegan. Time—2:40. Attendance—54,930.

GAME OF THURSDAY, OCTOBER 6, AT NEW YORK (N)

Kansas City	AB.	R.	H.	RBI.	PO.	A.	New York	AB.	R.	H.	RBI.	PO.	A.
Patek, ss	3	1	1	1	1	3	Rivers, cf	5	0	0	0	7	0
McRae, dh	2	0	0	0	0	0	Nettles, 3b	4	0	0	0	1	0
Brett, 3b	4	0	1	0	0	3	Munson, c	4	1	3	0	7	2
Cowens, rf	4	0	0	0	0	0	Jackson, rf	4	1	1	0	3	0
Otis, cf	4	0	0	0	3	1	Blair, rf	0	0	0	0	0	0
Mayberry, 1b	3	0	0	0	9	1	Piniella, lf	4	1	1	0	1	0
Zdeb, lf	3	0	0	0	1	0	Johnson, dh	4	2	2	2	0	0
Porter, c	1	1	0	0	3	0	Chambliss, 1b	2	0	0	0	3	1
Wathan, ph-c	1	0	0	0	2	0	Randolph, 2b	4	1	2	1	3	1
White, 2b	3	0	1	0	4	3	Dent, ss	3	0	1	1	2	2
Hassler, p	0	0	0	0	1	0	Guidry, p	0	0	0	0	1	0
Littell, p	0	0	0	0	0	0	Totals	34	6	10	4	27	7
Mingori, p	0	0	0	0	0	0							
Totals	28	2	3	1	24	11							

Kansas City	0	0	1	0	0	1	0	0	0 – 2
New York	0	0	0	0	2	3	0	1	x – 6

Kansas City	IP.	H.	R.	ER.	BB.	SO.
Hassler (Loser)	5⅔	5	3	3	0	3
Littell	2	5	3	1	3·	1
Mingori	⅓	0	0	0	0	1

New York	IP.	H.	R.	ER.	BB.	SO.
Guidry (Winner)	9	3	2	2	3	7

Errors—Dent, Brett. Left on base—Kansas City 3, New York 7. Two-base hits—Patek, Johnson. Home run—Johnson. Stolen base—Jackson. Sacrifice fly—Patek. Balk—Hassler. Umpires—Goetz, McKean, Springstead, Bremigan, Deegan and Neudecker. Time—2:58. Attendance—56,230.

GAME OF FRIDAY, OCTOBER 7, AT KANSAS CITY (N)

New York	AB.	R.	H.	RBI.	PO.	A.	Kansas City	AB.	R.	H.	RBI.	PO.	A.
Rivers, cf	4	0	0	0	2	0	Poquette, rf	3	0	1	0	3	0
R. White, lf	4	1	2	0	2	0	Otis, ph-cf	2	0	1	2	1	0
Munson, c	4	0	0	0	4	1	McRae, lf	4	2	2	0	2	1
Jackson, rf	3	0	0	0	2	0	Zdeb, lf	0	0	0	0	0	0
Chambliss, 1b	4	0	0	0	9	3	Brett, 3b	4	1	2	0	1	1
Nettles, 3b	3	1	1	0	0	4	Cowens, cf-rf	4	0	0	2	2	0
Piniella, dh	3	0	1	1	0	0	Mayberry, 1b	4	0	1	1	12	0
Randolph, 2b	3	0	0	0	1	3	Lahoud, dh	1	2	0	0	0	0
Dent, ss	2	0	0	0	0	2	Wathan, ph-dh	1	0	0	0	0	0
Johnson, ph	1	0	0	0	0	0	Porter, c	4	1	3	0	6	0
Stanley, ss	0	0	0	0	0	0	Patek, ss	2	0	1	1	0	5
Torrez, p	0	0	0	0	2	1	F. White, 2b	4	0	1	0	0	3
Lyle, p	0	0	0	0	0	0	Leonard, p	0	0	0	0	0	0
Totals	31	2	4	1	24	12	Totals	33	6	12	6	27	10

New York	0	0	0	0	0	2	0	0	0 – 2
Kansas City	0	1	1	0	1	2	1	0	x – 6

New York	IP.	H.	R.	ER.	BB.	SO.
Torrez (Loser)	5⅔	8	5	5	2	1
Lyle	2⅓	4	1	1	0	1

Kansas City	IP.	H.	R.	ER.	BB.	SO.
Leonard (Winner)	9	4	2	1	1	4

Errors—R. White, Mayberry. Left on base—New York 3, Kansas City 7. Two-base hits—R. White 2, McRae 2, Piniella, Otis, Mayberry. Stolen bases—F. White, Otis. Sacrifice hits—Patek 2. Umpires—McKean, Springstead, Bremigan, Deegan, Neudecker and Goetz. Time—2:19. Attendance—41,285.

GAME OF SATURDAY, OCTOBER 8, AT KANSAS CITY

New York	AB.	R.	H.	RBI.	PO.	A.
Rivers, cf	5	2	4	1	4	0
Nettles, 3b	5	0	2	1	0	3
Munson, c	4	1	1	2	4	0
Jackson, rf	3	0	0	0	2	0
Blair, rf	1	0	1	0	1	0
Piniella, lf	5	0	2	1	3	0
Johnson, dh	4	0	1	0	0	0
R. White, pr-dh	0	0	0	0	0	0
Chambliss, 1b	4	0	0	0	10	0
Randolph, 2b	4	2	1	0	2	2
Dent, ss	3	1	1	1	1	4
Figueroa, p	0	0	0	0	0	0
Tidrow, p	0	0	0	0	0	0
Lyle, p	0	0	0	0	0	0
Totals	38	6	13	6	27	9

Kansas City	AB.	R.	H.	RBI.	PO.	A.
Poquette, lf	3	0	0	0	0	0
Zdeb, ph-lf	2	0	0	0	0	0
McRae, dh	3	1	2	0	0	0
Brett, 3b	4	0	2	1	1	3
Cowens, rf	3	0	0	0	3	0
Mayberry, 1b	2	0	0	0	5	0
Wathan, 1b	2	0	0	0	6	0
Porter, c	4	0	0	0	3	0
Otis, cf	3	1	0	0	4	0
Patek, ss	4	2	3	1	0	4
F. White, 2b	3	0	1	2	4	4
Gura, p	0	0	0	0	0	0
Pattin, p	0	0	0	0	1	2
Mingori, p	0	0	0	0	0	0
Bird, p	0	0	0	0	0	0
Totals	33	4	8	4	27	13

New York					1	2	1	1	0	0		0	0	1 – 6
Kansas City					0	0	2	2	0	0		0	0	0 – 4

New York	IP.	H.	R.	ER.	BB.	SO.
Figueroa	3⅓	5	4	4	2	3
Tidrow	⅓	1	0	0	1	0
Lyle (Winner)	5⅓	2	0	0	0	1

Kansas City	IP.	H.	R.	ER.	BB.	SO.
Gura (Loser)	2*	6	4	4	1	2
Pattin	6†	6	2	1	0	0
Mingori	⅓	0	0	0	0	0
Bird	⅔	1	0	0	0	0

*Pitched to two batters in third.
†Pitched to one batter in ninth.

Errors—Patek, Mayberry. Double plays—New York 1, Kansas City 1. Left on base—New York 8, Kansas City 6. Two-base hits—Rivers, Dent, Munson, Patek, F. White, Piniella. Three-base hits—Patek, Brett. Sacrifice hit—Dent. Sacrifice flies—F. White, Munson. Wild pitch—Mingori. Umpires—Springstead, Bremigan, Deegan, Neudecker, Goetz and McKean. Time—3:08. Attendance 41,135.

GAME OF SUNDAY, OCTOBER 9, AT KANSAS CITY (N)

New York	AB.	R.	H.	RBI.	PO.	A.
Rivers, cf	5	2	2	1	2	0
Randolph, 2b	3	1	1	1	3	2
Munson, c	5	0	1	1	7	1
Piniella, lf	5	0	2	0	3	1
Johnson, dh	2	1	0	0	0	0
Jackson, ph-dh	2	0	1	1	0	0
Nettles, 3b	4	0	0	0	0	4
Chambliss, 1b	4	0	0	0	8	1
Blair, rf	4	1	1	0	1	0
Dent, ss	3	0	1	0	1	3
R. White, ph	0	1	0	0	0	0
Stanley, ss	0	0	0	0	1	0
Guidry, p	0	0	0	0	1	0
Torrez, p	0	0	0	0	0	0
Lyle, p	0	0	0	0	0	0
Totals	37	5	10	4	27	12

Kansas City	AB.	R.	H.	RBI.	PO.	A.
Patek, ss	5	0	0	0	1	6
McRae, lf	4	2	3	0	0	0
Brett, 3b	3	1	1	1	1	3
Cowens, rf	4	0	2	2	5	0
Otis, cf	3	0	1	0	1	0
Wathan, 1b	2	0	0	0	11	0
LaCock, ph-1b	1	0	0	0	4	0
Rojas, 2b	4	0	1	0	0	0
Porter, c	4	0	1	0	3	0
F. White, 2b	4	0	1	0	1	6
Splittorff, p	0	0	0	0	0	1
Bird, p	0	0	0	0	0	0
Mingori, p	0	0	0	0	0	0
Leonard, p	0	0	0	0	0	0
Gura, p	0	0	0	0	0	0
Littell, p	0	0	0	0	0	0
Totals	34	3	10	3	27	16

New York					0	0	1	0	0	0		0	1	3 – 5
Kansas City					2	0	1	0	0	0		0	0	0 – 3

New York	IP.	H.	R.	ER.	BB.	SO.
Guidry	2⅓	6	3	3	0	1
Torrez	5⅓	3	0	0	3	4
Lyle (Winner)	1⅓	1	0	0	0	1

Kansas City	IP.	H.	R.	ER.	BB.	SO.
Splittorff	7*	6	2	2	2	2
Bird	⅓	2	0	0	0	1
Mingori	⅔	0	0	0	0	0
Leonard (Loser)	0†	1	2	2	1	0
Gura	0‡	1	1	0	0	0
Littell	1	0	0	0	0	0

*Pitched to one batter in eighth.
†Pitched to two batters in ninth.
‡Pitched to one batter in ninth.

Error—Brett. Double play—New York 1. Left on base—New York 9, Kansas City 7. Two-base hits—Piniella, McRae, Johnson. Three-base hit—Brett. Stolen bases—Rivers, Rojas, Otis. Sacrifice fly—Randolph. Umpires—Bremigan, Deegan, Neudecker, Springstead, Goetz and McKean. Time—3:04. Attendance—41,133.

NEW YORK YANKEES' BATTING AND FIELDING AVERAGES

Player—Position	G.	AB.	R.	H.	TB.	2B.	3B.	HR.	RBI.	B.A.	PO.	A.	E.	F.A.
Johnson, dh-ph	5	15	2	6	11	2	0	1	2	.400	0	0	0	.000
Blair, rf	3	5	1	2	2	0	0	0	0	.400	2	0	0	1.000
R. White, ph-lf-pr-dh	4	5	2	2	4	2	0	0	0	.400	2	0	1	.667
Rivers, cf	5	23	5	9	11	2	0	0	2	.391	19	0	0	1.000
Piniella, lf-dh	5	21	1	7	10	3	0	0	2	.333	9	1	0	1.000
Munson, c	5	21	3	6	10	1	0	1	5	.286	24	4	0	1.000
Randolph, 2b	5	18	4	5	6	1	0	0	2	.278	13	9	0	1.000
Dent, ss	5	14	1	3	4	1	0	0	2	.214	10	14	1	.960
Nettles, 3b	5	20	1	3	3	0	0	0	1	.150	2	12	0	1.000
Jackson, rf-ph-dh	5	16	1	2	2	0	0	0	1	.125	10	1	0	1.000
Chambliss, 1b	5	17	0	1	1	0	0	0	0	.059	35	7	0	1.000
Figueroa, p	1	0	0	0	0	0	0	0	0	.000	0	0	0	.000
Guidry, p	2	0	0	0	0	0	0	0	0	.000	2	0	0	1.000
Gullett, p	1	0	0	0	0	0	0	0	0	.000	0	0	0	.000
Lyle, p	4	0	0	0	0	0	0	0	0	.000	0	0	0	.000
Stanley, ss	2	0	0	0	0	0	0	0	0	.000	1	0	0	1.000
Tidrow, p	2	0	0	0	0	0	0	0	0	.000	1	2	0	1.000
Torrez, p	2	0	0	0	0	0	0	0	0	.000	2	1	0	1.000
Totals	5	175	21	46	64	12	0	2	17	.263	132	51	2	.989

KANSAS CITY ROYALS' BATTING AND FIELDING AVERAGES

Player—Position	G.	AB.	R.	H.	TB.	2B.	3B.	HR.	RBI.	B.A.	PO.	A.	E.	F.A.
McRae, dh-lf	5	18	6	8	14	3	0	1	2	.444	2	1	0	1.000
Patek, ss	5	18	4	7	12	3	1	0	5	.389	8	18	1	.963
Porter, c	5	15	3	5	5	0	0	0	0	.333	18	0	0	1.000
Brett, 3b	5	20	2	6	10	0	2	0	2	.300	5	12	2	.895
F. White, 2b	5	18	1	5	6	1	0	0	2	.278	13	16	0	1.000
Cowens, rf-cf	5	19	2	5	8	0	0	1	5	.263	14	0	0	1.000
Rojas, dh	1	4	0	1	1	0	0	0	0	.250	0	0	0	.000
Mayberry, 1b	4	12	1	2	6	1	0	1	3	.167	29	1	2	.938
Poquette, rf-lf	2	6	0	1	1	0	0	0	0	.167	3	0	0	1.000
Otis, cf-ph	5	16	1	2	3	1	0	0	2	.125	11	1	0	1.000
Bird, p	3	0	0	0	0	0	0	0	0	.000	0	0	0	.000
Gura, p	2	0	0	0	0	0	0	0	0	.000	0	0	0	.000
Hassler, p	1	0	0	0	0	0	0	0	0	.000	1	0	0	1.000
Leonard, p	2	0	0	0	0	0	0	0	0	.000	0	0	0	.000
Littell, p	2	0	0	0	0	0	0	0	0	.000	0	0	0	.000
Mingori, p	3	0	0	0	0	0	0	0	0	.000	0	0	0	.000
Pattin, p	1	0	0	0	0	0	0	0	0	.000	1	2	0	1.000
Splittorff, p	2	0	0	0	0	0	0	0	0	.000	0	3	0	1.000
LaCock, ph-1b	1	1	0	0	0	0	0	0	0	.000	4	0	0	1.000
Lahoud, dh	1	1	2	0	0	0	0	0	0	.000	0	0	0	.000
Wathan, ph-c-dh-1b	4	6	0	0	0	0	0	0	0	.000	19	0	0	1.000
Zdeb, lf-ph	4	9	0	0	0	0	0	0	0	.000	4	0	0	1.000
Totals	5	163	22	42	66	9	3	3	21	.258	132	54	5	.974

NEW YORK YANKEES' PITCHING RECORDS

Pitcher	G.	GS.	CG.	IP.	H.	R.	ER.	BB.	SO.	HB.	WP.	W.	L.	Pct.	ERA.
Lyle	4	0	0	9⅓	7	1	1	0	3	0	0	2	0	1.000	0.96
Tidrow	2	0	0	7	6	3	3	3	3	0	0	0	0	.000	3.86
Guidry	2	2	1	11⅓	9	5	5	3	8	0	0	1	0	1.000	3.97
Torrez	2	1	0	11	11	5	5	5	5	0	0	1	0	1.000	4.09
Figueroa	1	1	0	3⅓	5	4	4	2	3	0	0	0	1	.000	10.80
Gullett	1	1	0	2	4	4	4	2	0	0	0	0	1	.000	18.00
Totals	5	5	1	44	42	22	22	15	22	0	0	3	2	.600	4.50

No shutouts or saves

KANSAS CITY ROYALS' PITCHING RECORDS

Pitcher	G.	GS.	CG.	IP.	H.	R.	ER.	BB.	SO.	HB.	WP.	W.	L.	Pct.	ERA.
Bird	3	0	0	2	4	0	0	1	0	0	0	0	0	.000	0.00
Mingori	3	0	0	1⅓	0	0	0	1	0	1	0	0	0	.000	0.00
Pattin	1	0	0	6	6	2	1	0	0	0	0	0	0	.000	1.50

Pitcher	G.	GS.	CG.	IP.	H.	R.	ER.	BB.	SO.	HB.	WP.	W.	L.	Pct.	ERA.
Splittorff	2	2	0	15	14	4	4	3	4	0	0	1	0	1.000	2.40
Leonard	2	1	1	9	5	4	3	2	4	0	0	1	1	.500	3.00
Littell	2	0	0	3	5	3	1	3	1	0	0	0	0	.000	3.00
Hassler	1	1	0	5⅔	5	3	3	0	3	0	0	0	1	.000	4.76
Gura	2	1	0	2	7	5	4	1	2	0	0	0	1	.000	18.00
Totals	5	5	1	44	46	21	16	9	16	0	1	2	3	.400	3.27

No shutouts or saves.

COMPOSITE SCORE BY INNINGS

New York	1	2	4	1	3	3	0	2	5 – 21
Kansas City	4	3	7	2	1	3	1	1	0 – 22

Sacrifice hits—Dent, Patek 2.
Sacrifice flies—Munson, Randolph, Patek, F. White.
Stolen bases—Jackson, Rivers, Otis 2, Rojas, F. White, Zdeb.
Caught stealing—Brett, Cowens, McRae, F. White.
Double plays—Nettles, Randolph and Chambliss 2; Brett and F. White; Pattin and Brett.
Left on bases—New York 7, 7, 3, 8, 9—34; Kansas City 5, 3, 7, 6, 7—28.
Hit by pitcher—None.
Passed balls—None.
Balk—Hassler.
Time of games—First game, 2:40; second game, 2:58; third game, 2:19; fourth game, 3:08; fifth game, 3:04.
Attendance—First game, 54,930; second game, 56,230; third game, 41,285; fourth game, 41,135; fifth game, 41,133.
Umpires—Neudecker, Goetz, McKean, Springstead, Bremigan and Deegan.
Official scorers—Maury Allen, New York Post; Del Black, Kansas City Star.

NATIONAL LEAGUE
Championship Series of 1977

	W.	L.	Pct.
Los Angeles (West)	3	1	.750
Philadelphia (East)	1	3	.250

The Los Angeles Dodgers returned to their second World Series in four seasons after subduing the repeating East Division champions, the Philadelphia Phillies, in four games, one of which pivoted on a controversial call—a decision which, accurate or not, heavily influenced the outcome of an entire season.

In winning the title, the Dodgers became the first club in the nine-year history of the Championship Series to lose the first game at home and then come back to win the series. That initial game featured a pitching matchup of two of the league's outstanding lefthanders, Steve Carlton and Tommy John, each a prominent contender for the Cy Young Award later won by Carlton. Neither fared well, however. John, in large part due to poor defensive play, and Carlton, because of control problems.

John exited in the fifth inning after allowing four runs, all unearned. With two out in the first inning a poor throw by shortstop Bill Russell allowed Mike Schmidt to reach base. Greg Luzinski capitalized on the miscue, driving a 1-2 pitch over the center field wall for a 2-0 Philadelphia lead. In the fourth inning, it was again a Russell mistake, this time a failure to touch second on a forceout, that opened the gates for two more runs. A tally off reliever Elias Sosa an inning later brought the count to 5-1 going into the home seventh.

In that inning, walks to pinch-hitter Jerry Grote and Reggie Smith, sand-wiched around a Davey Lopes single, loaded the bases. After fouling away three full-count deliveries, Ron Cey, one of four Dodgers to hit thirty or more home runs in 1977, belted a game-tying grand slam.

But Gene Garber and Tug McGraw blanked the Dodgers the rest of the way, and when Bake McBride, Larry Bowa and Schmidt singled in the ninth, the Phillies had captured at least a split at Dodger Stadium.

Los Angeles prevailed in game two, 7-1, on the strength of the second Dodger grand slam in as many nights. This time it was Dusty Baker, also a member of the thirty-home run club. The fourth-inning blast broke a 1-1 tie.

Righthander Don Sutton scattered nine hits and did not walk a batter in going the route.

The season had come down to a best-of-three series, and the Phillies had ample reason for their swagger. They had won 60 of 81 games at the Vet during the regular season. Four of the six encounters with their playoff oppo-nent had gone their way. And for a time it did seem that this advantage might tip the scales. Dodger starter Burt Hooton was visibly unnerved by the crowd's incessant hooting which accompanied his every delivery. With the bases loaded, plate umpire Harry Wendelstedt waved Larry Christenson, McBride, and Bowa to first with free passes. What had been a 2-0 deficit had become a 3-2 lead. After eight innings, the Phils had stretched their lead to 5-3.

With two outs in the ninth inning, no one on base, and the dependable Gene Garber having retired on ground balls all eight batters he had faced, Dodger Manager Tommy Lasorda was but one out from falling into a Dodger Blue trance.

But then it happened. In the space of a few short minutes the Phillies' season unraveled. Ironically, it was the Dodgers' bench, considered inferior in pre-series analyses, that did the damage. Aging Vic Davalillo, obtained from the Mexican League in August, beat out a drag bunt. Then Manny Mota, a Davalillo contemporary, sent a two-strike pitch to deep left field. Luzinski, oddly unreplaced by Jerry Martin, a more capable fielder, got his glove on it but could not hang on as he bulled into the wall. Mota had a double, scoring Davalillo, and when the relay escaped second baseman Sizemore, Mota took third.

Lopes followed with a shot off the glove of third baseman Schmidt that Larry Bowa alertly rebounded and threw to first. Bruce Froemming ruled Lopes safe and the game was tied. The Phillies insisted otherwise.

Lopes became the game-winning run when, after moving up a base on an errant Garber pickoff attempt, he scored on a Bill Russell bouncer through the middle.

If the Dodgers were relaxed and assured before the fourth and what proved to be the final game, the Phillies could be excused for being less than that. Lopes had indeed appeared to be out on television replays but not by so great a margin that Froemming could be castigated or reproached with any fairness.

In a game played almost entirely in a steady downpour of rain, Los Angeles took a third straight win and with it the title. Baker's two-run homer in the second inning was more than enough for Tommy John. Stranding nine runners, he bested Carlton, 4-1.

GAME OF TUESDAY, OCTOBER 4, AT LOS ANGELES (N)

Philadelphia	AB.	R.	H.	RBI.	PO.	A.
McBride, cf	5	1	2	0	3	0
Bowa, ss	5	2	1	0	0	5
Schmidt, 3b	5	2	1	1	1	5
Luzinski, lf	3	1	1	2	1	0
Johnson, 1b	4	0	1	2	8	0
Hutton, 1b	1	0	0	0	5	0
Martin, rf	3	0	0	0	1	0
Johnstone, ph-rf	1	0	0	0	0	0
McCarver, c	3	1	1	0	4	0
Boone, c	0	0	0	0	1	0
Sizemore, 2b	3	0	0	0	3	2
Carlton, p	2	0	2	1	0	0
Garber, p	0	0	0	0	0	1
Hebner, ph	1	0	0	0	0	0
McGraw, p	0	0	0	0	0	0
Totals	36	7	9	6	27	13

Los Angeles	AB.	R.	H.	RBI.	PO.	A.
Lopes, 2b	5	1	2	1	3	3
Russell, ss	5	1	0	0	2	3
Smith, rf	4	1	0	0	1	0
Cey, 3b	4	1	2	4	2	4
Garvey, 1b	4	0	3	0	12	0
Baker, lf	3	0	1	0	0	0
Burke, cf	3	0	0	0	1	0
Monday, ph-cf	1	0	0	0	0	0
Yeager, c	4	0	0	0	6	1
John, p	1	0	0	0	0	1
Garman, p	0	0	0	0	0	0
Lacy, ph	1	1	1	0	0	0
Hough, p	0	0	0	0	0	1
Grote, ph	0	0	0	0	0	0
Sosa, p	1	0	0	0	0	0
Totals	36	5	9	5	27	13

Philadelphia	2	0	0		0	2	1		0	0	2 — 7
Los Angeles	0	0	0		0	1	0		4	0	0 — 5

Philadelphia	IP.	H.	R.	ER.	BB.	SO.
Carlton	6⅔	9	5	5	3	3
Garber (Winner)	1⅓	0	0	0	0	2
McGraw (Save)	1	0	0	0	0	0

Los Angeles	IP.	H.	R.	ER.	BB.	SO.
John	4⅔	4	4	0	3	3
Garman	⅓	0	0	0	0	1
Hough	2	2	1	1	0	3
Sosa (Loser)	2	3	2	2	0	1

Errors—Russell 2. Double play—Los Angeles 1. Left on bases—Philadelphia 7, Los Angeles 7. Home runs—Luzinski, Cey. Stolen bases—Luzinski, Garvey. Sacrifice hit—Sizemore. Hit by pitcher—By John (Carlton). Balks—Carlton, Sosa. Umpires—Pryor, Engel, Wendelstedt, Froemming, Rennert and Runge. Time—2:35. Attendance—55,968.

GAME OF WEDNESDAY, OCTOBER 5, AT LOS ANGELES (N)

Philadelphia	AB.	R.	H.	RBI.	PO.	A.
McBride, cf	4	1	2	1	0	1
Bowa, ss	4	0	1	0	0	5
Schmidt, 3b	4	0	0	0	1	1
Luzinski, lf	4	0	1	0	0	0
Hebner, 1b	4	0	2	0	11	0
Johnstone, rf	4	0	1	0	4	0
Boone, c	4	0	1	0	6	1
Sizemore, 2b	4	0	1	0	2	1
Lonborg, p	1	0	0	0	0	2
Hutton, ph	1	0	0	0	0	0
Reed, p	0	0	0	0	0	0
Brown, ph	1	0	0	0	0	0
Brusstar, p	0	0	0	0	0	0
Totals	35	1	9	1	24	11

Los Angeles	AB.	R.	H.	RBI.	PO.	A.
Lopes, 2b	4	0	1	1	2	1
Russell, ss	4	2	2	0	3	2
Smith, rf	4	1	2	1	2	0
Cey, 3b	3	1	1	0	2	1
Garvey, 1b	3	1	0	0	7	1
Baker, lf	4	1	1	4	3	0
Monday, cf	3	1	1	0	3	0
Burke, cf	0	0	0	0	0	0
Yeager, c	3	0	1	0	5	0
Sutton, p	3	0	0	0	0	2
Totals	31	7	9	7	27	7

Philadelphia	0	0	1		0	0	0		0	0	0 — 1
Los Angeles	0	0	1		4	0	1		1	0	x — 7

Philadelphia	IP.	H.	R.	ER.	BB.	SO.
Lonborg (Loser)	4	5	5	5	1	1
Reed	2	2	1	1	1	2
Brusstar	2	2	1	1	0	2

Los Angeles	IP.	H.	R.	ER.	BB.	SO.
Sutton (Winner)	9	9	1	1	0	4

Errors—Sizemore, Lopes. Double plays—Los Angeles 2. Left on bases—Philadelphia 7, Los Angeles 3. Two-base hits—Luzinski, Monday. Three-base hit—Smith. Home runs—McBride, Baker. Stolen base—Cey. Sacrifice hit—Cey. Umpires—Engel, Wendelstedt, Froemming, Rennert, Runge and Pryor. Time—2:14. Attendance—55,973.

GAME OF FRIDAY, OCTOBER 7, AT PHILADELPHIA

Los Angeles	AB.	R.	H.	RBI.	PO.	A.
Lopes, 2b	5	1	1	1	3	3
Russell, ss	5	0	2	1	5	2
Smith, rf	5	0	0	0	2	0
Cey, 3b	4	1	1	0	1	4
Garvey, 1b	4	1	1	0	9	0
Baker, lf	4	1	2	2	0	0
Monday, cf	3	0	1	0	3	0
Grote, c	0	0	0	0	0	0
Yeager, c	2	0	1	1	3	0
Davalillo, ph	1	1	1	0	0	0
Burke, cf	0	0	0	0	1	0
Hooton, p	1	0	1	0	0	1
Rhoden, p	1	0	0	0	0	0
Goodson, ph	1	0	0	0	0	0
Rau, p	0	0	0	0	0	0
Sosa, p	0	0	0	0	0	1
Rautzhan, p	0	0	0	0	0	0
Mota, ph	1	1	1	0	0	0
Garman, p	0	0	0	0	0	0
Totals	37	6	12	5	27	11

Philadelphia	AB.	R.	H.	RBI.	PO.	A.
McBride, rf	4	0	0	1	1	1
Bowa, ss	4	0	0	1	0	5
Schmidt, 3b	4	0	0	0	1	6
Luzinski, lf	3	0	1	0	0	1
Martin, pr	0	0	0	0	0	0
Hebner, 1b	5	2	1	0	14	0
Maddox, cf	4	1	1	1	3	0
Boone, c	4	1	2	0	6	0
Sizemore, 2b	3	1	1	0	2	3
Christenson, p	0	0	0	1	0	0
Brusstar, p	0	0	0	0	0	0
Hutton, ph	1	0	0	0	0	0
Reed, p	0	0	0	0	0	0
McCarver, ph	1	0	0	0	0	0
Garber, p	0	0	0	0	0	1
Totals	33	5	6	4	27	17

Los Angeles	0	2	0	1	0	0	0	0	3 – 6
Philadelphia	0	3	0	0	0	0	0	2	0 – 5

Los Angeles	IP.	H.	R.	ER.	BB.	SO.
Hooton	1⅔	2	3	3	4	1
Rhoden	4⅓	2	0	0	2	0
Rau	1	0	0	0	0	1
Sosa	⅔	2	2	1	0	0
Rautzhan (Winner)	⅓	0	0	0	0	0
Garman (Save)	1	0	0	0	0	0

Philadelphia	IP.	H.	R.	ER.	BB.	SO.
Christenson	3⅓	7	3	3	0	2
Brusstar	⅔	0	0	0	1	0
Reed	2	1	0	0	1	2
Garber (Loser)	3	4	3	2	0	0

Errors—Cey, Sizemore, Garber, Smith. Double play—Philadelphia 1. Left on bases—Los Angeles 6, Philadelphia 9. Two-base hits—Baker, Hooton, Cey, Russell, Hebner, Mota. Sacrifice hit—Garber. Hit by pitcher—By Garman (Luzinski). Passed ball—Boone. Umpires—Wendelstedt, Froemming, Rennert, Runge, Pryor and Engel. Time—2:51. Attendance—63,719.

GAME OF SATURDAY, OCTOBER 8, AT PHILADELPHIA (N)

Los Angeles	AB.	R.	H.	RBI.	PO.	A.
Lopes, 2b	3	0	0	0	1	3
Russell, ss	4	0	1	1	1	5
Smith, rf	3	0	1	0	2	0
Cey, 3b	2	1	0	0	2	5
Garvey, 1b	2	0	0	0	12	0
Baker, lf	3	2	1	2	0	0
Burke, cf	4	0	0	0	1	0
Yeager, c	4	1	1	0	8	0
John, p	4	0	1	0	0	0
Totals	29	4	5	3	27	13

Philadelphia	AB.	R.	H.	RBI.	PO.	A.
McBride, rf	5	0	0	0	2	0
Bowa, ss	4	0	0	0	2	2
Schmidt, 3b	3	0	0	0	1	3
Luzinski, lf	4	1	1	0	3	0
Hebner, 1b	4	0	2	0	7	0
Maddox, cf	3	0	2	1	3	0
McCarver, c	2	0	0	0	3	0
Reed, p	0	0	0	0	0	0
Brown, ph	1	0	0	0	0	0
McGraw, p	0	0	0	0	0	0
Martin, ph	1	0	0	0	0	0
Garber, p	0	0	0	0	0	0
Sizemore, 2b	3	0	1	0	3	2
Carlton, p	2	0	0	0	1	0
Boone, c	2	0	1	0	5	1
Totals	34	1	7	1	27	8

Los Angeles	0	2	0	0	2	0	0	0	0 – 4
Philadelphia	0	0	0	1	0	0	0	0	0 – 1

Los Angeles	IP.	H.	R.	ER.	BB.	SO.
John (Winner)	9	7	1	1	2	8

Philadelphia	IP.	H.	R.	ER.	BB.	SO.
Carlton (Loser)	5*	4	4	4	5	3
Reed	1	0	0	0	0	1
McGraw	2	1	0	0	2	3
Garber	1	0	0	0	0	1

*Pitched to on batter in sixth.

Errors—None. Double plays—Philadelphia 2. Left on bases—Los Angeles 6, Philadelphia 9. Two-base hit—Hebner. Home run—Baker. Stolen base—Smith. Sacrifice hit—Garvey. Hit by pitcher—By John (Maddox). Wild pitch—Carlton. Umpires—Froemming, Rennert, Runge, Pryor, Engel and Wendelstedt. Time—2:39. Attendance—64,924.

LOS ANGELES DODGERS' BATTING AND FIELDING AVERAGES

Player—Position	G.	AB.	R.	H.	TB.	2B.	3B.	HR.	RBI.	B.A.	PO.	A.	E.	F.A.
Davalillo, ph	1	1	1	1	1	0	0	0	0	1.000	0	0	0	.000
Hooton, p	1	1	0	1	2	1	0	0	0	1.000	0	1	0	1.000
Lacy, ph	1	1	1	1	1	0	0	0	0	1.000	0	0	0	.000
Mota, ph	1	1	1	1	1	0	0	0	0	1.000	0	0	0	.000
Baker, lf	4	14	4	5	12	1	0	2	8	.357	3	0	0	1.000
Cey, 3b	4	13	4	4	8	1	0	1	4	.308	7	14	1	.955
Garvey, 1b	4	13	2	4	4	0	0	0	0	.308	40	1	0	1.000
Monday, ph-cf	3	7	1	2	3	1	0	0	0	.286	6	0	0	1.000
Russell, ss	4	18	3	5	6	1	0	0	2	.278	11	12	2	.920
Lopes, 2b	4	17	2	4	4	0	0	0	3	.235	9	10	1	.950
Yeager, c	4	13	1	3	3	0	0	0	2	.231	22	1	0	1.000
John, p	2	5	0	1	1	0	0	0	0	.200	0	1	0	1.000
Smith, rf	4	16	2	3	5	0	1	0	1	.188	7	0	1	.875
Garman, p	2	0	0	0	0	0	0	0	0	.000	0	0	0	.000
Grote, ph-c	2	0	0	0	0	0	0	0	0	.000	0	0	0	.000
Hough, p	1	0	0	0	0	0	0	0	0	.000	0	1	0	1.000
Rau, p	1	0	0	0	0	0	0	0	0	.000	0	0	0	.000
Rautzhan, p	1	0	0	0	0	0	0	0	0	.000	0	0	0	.000
Goodson, ph	1	1	0	0	0	0	0	0	0	.000	0	0	0	.000
Rhoden, p	1	1	0	0	0	0	0	0	0	.000	0	0	0	.000
Sosa, p	2	1	0	0	0	0	0	0	0	.000	0	1	0	1.000
Sutton, p	1	3	0	0	0	0	0	0	0	.000	0	2	0	1.000
Burke, cf	4	7	0	0	0	0	0	0	0	.000	3	0	0	1.000
Totals	4	133	22	35	52	6	1	3	20	.263	108	44	5	.968

PHILADELPHIA PHILLIES' BATTING AND FIELDING AVERAGES

Player—Position	G.	AB.	R.	H.	TB.	2B.	3B.	HR.	RBI.	B.A.	PO.	A.	E.	F.A.
Carlton, p	2	4	0	2	2	0	0	0	0	.500	0	0	0	.000
Maddox, cf	2	7	1	3	3	0	0	0	2	.429	6	0	0	1.000
Boone, c	4	10	1	4	4	0	0	0	0	.400	18	2	0	1.000
Hebner, ph-1b	4	14	2	5	7	2	0	0	0	.357	32	0	0	1.000
Luzinski, lf	4	14	2	4	8	1	0	1	2	.286	4	1	0	1.000
Johnson, 1b	1	4	0	1	1	0	0	0	2	.250	8	0	0	1.000
Sizemore, 2b	4	13	1	3	3	0	0	0	0	.231	10	8	2	.900
McBride, cf-rf	4	18	2	4	7	0	0	1	2	.222	6	2	0	1.000
Johnstone, ph-rf	2	5	0	1	1	0	0	0	0	.200	4	0	0	1.000
McCarver, c-ph	3	6	1	1	1	0	0	0	0	.167	7	0	0	1.000
Bowa, ss	4	17	2	2	2	0	0	0	1	.118	0	17	0	1.000
Schmidt, 3b	4	16	2	1	1	0	0	0	1	.063	4	15	0	1.000
Brusstar, p	2	0	0	0	0	0	0	0	0	.000	0	0	0	.000
Christenson, p	1	0	0	0	0	0	0	0	1	.000	0	0	0	.000
Garber, p	3	0	0	0	0	0	0	0	0	.000	0	2	1	.667
McGraw, p	2	0	0	0	0	0	0	0	0	.000	0	0	0	.000
Reed, p	3	0	0	0	0	0	0	0	0	.000	0	0	0	.000
Lonborg, p	1	1	0	0	0	0	0	0	0	.000	0	2	0	1.000
Brown, ph	2	2	0	0	0	0	0	0	0	.000	0	0	0	.000
Hutton, 1b-ph	3	3	0	0	0	0	0	0	0	.000	5	0	0	1.000
Martin, rf-pr-ph	3	4	0	0	0	0	0	0	0	.000	1	0	0	1.000
Totals	4	138	14	31	40	3	0	2	12	.225	105	49	3	.981

LOS ANGELES DODGERS' PITCHING RECORDS

Pitcher	G.	GS.	CG.	IP.	H.	R.	ER.	BB.	SO.	HB.	WP.	W.	L.	Pct.	ERA.
Rhoden	1	0	0	4⅓	2	0	0	2	0	0	0	0	0	.000	0.00
Garman	2	0	0	1⅓	0	0	0	1	1	0	0	0	0	.000	0.00
Rau	1	0	0	1	0	0	0	0	0	0	0	0	0	.000	0.00
Rautzhan	1	0	0	⅓	0	0	0	0	0	0	0	0	0	.000	0.00
John	2	2	1	13¾	11	5	1	5	11	2	0	1	0	1.000	0.66
Sutton	1	1	0	9	9	1	1	0	4	0	0	1	0	1.000	1.00
Hough	1	0	0	2	2	1	1	0	3	0	0	0	0	.000	4.50
Sosa	2	0	0	2⅔	5	4	3	0	0	0	0	0	1	.000	10.13
Hooton	1	1	0	1⅔	2	3	3	4	1	0	0	0	0	.000	16.20
Totals	4	4	2	36	31	14	9	11	21	3	0	3	1	.750	2.25

No shutouts. Save—Garman.

PHILADELPHIA PHILLIES' PITCHING RECORDS

Pitcher	G.	GS.	CG.	IP.	H.	R.	ER.	BB.	SO.	HB.	WP.	W.	L.	Pct.	ERA.
McGraw	2	0	0	3	1	0	0	2	3	0	0	0	0	.000	0.00
Reed	3	0	0	5	3	1	1	2	5	0	0	0	0	.000	1.80
Garber	3	0	0	5⅓	4	3	2	0	3	0	0	1	1	.500	3.38
Brusstar	2	0	0	2⅔	2	1	1	1	2	0	0	0	0	.000	3.38
Carlton	2	2	0	11⅔	13	9	9	8	6	0	1	0	1	.000	6.94
Christenson	1	1	0	3⅓	7	3	3	0	2	0	0	0	0	.000	8.10
Lonborg	1	1	0	4	5	5	5	1	1	0	0	0	1	.000	11.25
Totals	4	4	0	35	35	22	21	14	22	0	1	1	3	.250	5.40

No shutouts. Save—McGraw.

COMPOSITE SCORE BY INNINGS

Los Angeles	0	4	1	5	3	1	5	0	3 — 22
Philadelphia	2	3	1	1	2	1	0	2	2 — 14

Sacrifice hits—Cey, Garvey, Garber, Sizemore.
Sacrifice flies—None.
Stolen bases—Cey, Garvey, Smith, Luzinski.
Caught stealing—Lopes.
Double plays—Russell, Lopes and Garvey; Garvey and Russell; Russell and Garvey; McBride and Boone; Bowa, Sizemore and Hebner 2.
Left on bases—Los Angeles 7, 3, 6, 6—22; Philadelphia 7, 7, 9, 9—32.
Hit by pitcher—By John 2 (Carlton, Maddox); by Garman (Luzinski).
Passed ball—Boone.
Balks—Sosa, Carlton.
Time of games—First game, 2:35, second game, 2:14; third game, 2:51; fourth game, 2:39.
Attendance—First game, 55,968; second game, 55,973; third game, 63,719; fourth game, 64,924.
Umpires—Pryor, Engel, Wendelstedt, Froemming, Rennert and Runge.
Official scorers—Gordon Verrell, Long Beach Independent Press-Telegram; Paul Giordano, Levittown Courier Times.

AMERICAN LEAGUE
Championship Series of 1978

	W.	L.	Pct.
New York (East)	3	1	.750
Kansas City (West)	1	3	.250

If you listened to the Royals, things had fallen just right for them in this third try at stopping the Yankees in the American League Championship Series. Kansas City would have its ace Dennis Leonard facing New York and virtually untested Jim Beattie since Ron Guidry had been forced to pitch in the Yankees' one-game playoff against the Boston Red Sox. But as is often the case, things just didn't work out the way they were planned, with the Yankees winning the A.L. pennant three games to one.

New York ripped Leonard and three other Royals' pitchers for 16 hits and the 7-1 score could have been worse as the Yanks stranded another 12 runners. While the Yankees were busy circling the base paths, Beattie, with help from Ken Clay, was limiting the Royals to just two hits.

New York went in front 1-0 in the second on a Bucky Dent single after a Roy White double. A double by Reggie Jackson and a triple by Graig Nettles increased the lead to 2-0 in the third. Leonard exited in the fifth after a leadoff single by Lou Piniella and was relieved by Steve Mingori. Jackson walked after a passed ball moved Piniella to second, and Chris Chambliss and Brian Doyle followed with run-scoring singles for a 4-0 Yankee lead.

In the Kansas City sixth, Beattie's control deserted him. After George

Brett doubled to start the inning, Beattie walked Amos Otis and Pete LaCock to load the bases. Enter Clay with one out. He pitched out of trouble allowing one run on a sacrifice fly by Hal McRae and ending the inning on an Al Cowens ground out. Clay, in his relief role, did not allow a hit over the last 3⅔ innings.

Meanwhile, Jackson, who was on base five times, put the game out of reach in the eighth. Royals' reliever Al Hrabosky was summoned with two runners on. The "Mad Hungarian" went through his usual psyching routine but Jackson wasn't impressed. He blasted a three-run homer to right-center, clinching the verdict.

With the Yankees now relaxed entering Game Two, the Royals lowered the boom with a hitting barrage of their own. Kansas City jumped to a 5-0 lead after just two innings, knocking out New York starter Ed Figueroa. Singles by George Brett and Amos Otis and a sacrifice fly by Darrell Porter gave the Royals their run in the first, and four runs in the second came by way of five singles and a Bucky Dent error. The Yankees cut the lead to 5-2 off Royal starter Larry Gura in the seventh, knocking Gura out, but Freddie Patek enlisted some unexpected power in the bottom of the inning, crashing a two-run homer in the three-run inning as the Royals went on to a 10-4 win.

All George Brett did in game three was hit three homers, all off Catfish Hunter, but it was a Thurman Munson blow that decided the contest in favor of New York. Brett's first homer led off the game. But Jackson matched the clout in the New York second. No. 2 for Brett came in the third for a 2-1 Royal lead, but singles by Jackson and Pinella, following a Munson double, gave the Yankees a 3-2 lead in the fourth.

Brett's third homer tied the game leading off the fifth. But the Yankees went ahead again in the sixth on singles by White and Munson and a sacrifice fly by Jackson. In the eighth, Kansas City regained the lead, 5-4, and it was done without the aid of Brett. Porter scored Otis with a single, after Otis had doubled, and Porter scored the go-ahead run on a force out by Cowens. But the bottom of the eighth was the Royals' undoing. With one out, White singled off Royals' starter Paul Splittorff and with the righthanded-hitting Munson coming up, K. C. Manager Whitey Herzog called in reliever Doug Bird.

On the third delivery, Munson rocketed a home run into the left center field bullpen. Rich Gossage stopped the Royals in the ninth.

With a 2-1 lead in the series, the Yankees now would be hard to beat. Guidry would be the pitcher in the crucial fourth game, while the Royals would come back with Leonard. It turned out to be a masterful pitching exhibition by both hurlers.

Brett greeted Guidry with a triple leading off the game and scored on a McRae single. McRae promptly stole second but was left there as Guidry retired the side. It was to be the only run yielded by Guidry in eight-plus innings.

Nettles tied the game for the Yankees with a leadoff homer in the second. Leonard then settled down to retire ten consecutive batters, five on strikeouts, until one man was out in the sixth. It was then he made his final mistake, with White hitting it for a homer and a 2-1 Yankee lead.

Guidry was also sailing along and escaped a two-out, first and third situation in the fourth by fanning Patek. However, when Otis led off the ninth with a double, manager Bob Lemon called on Gossage. He didn't disappoint Lemon. Throwing nothing but bullets, Gossage struck out pinch-hitter Clint Hurdle and retired Porter and pinch-hitter Pete LaCock on fly balls to seal the New York victory.

Gossage capsuled the entire Yankee season after his fireman's effort. "We almost expected it to go to tomorrow," Gossage admitted. "We've done everything the hard way." But certainly the winning way.

GAME OF TUESDAY, OCTOBER 3, AT KANSAS CITY (N)

New York	AB.	R.	H.	RBI.	PO.	A.
Rivers, cf	5	0	2	0	3	0
Blair, pr-cf	1	1	0	0	2	0
Munson, c	5	0	1	0	6	0
Piniella, rf	5	2	2	0	6	0
Jackson, dh	3	2	3	3	0	0
Nettles, 3b	5	1	2	1	1	1
Chambliss, 1b	5	0	2	1	4	0
R. White, lf	4	1	1	0	1	0
Doyle, 2b	5	0	2	1	2	4
Dent, ss	5	0	1	1	0	1
Beattie, p	0	0	0	0	2	0
Clay, p	0	0	0	0	0	0
Totals	43	7	16	7	27	6

Kansas City	AB.	R.	H.	RBI.	PO.	A.
Braun, lf	4	0	0	0	5	0
Brett, 3b	4	1	1	0	2	4
Otis, cf	2	0	0	0	1	0
Porter, c	3	0	0	0	4	1
LaCock, 1b	2	0	0	0	9	0
McRae, dh	2	0	0	1	0	0
Cowens, rf	4	0	1	0	1	0
Patek, ss	3	0	0	0	4	3
Hurdle, ph	0	0	0	0	0	0
F. White, 2b	3	0	0	0	1	3
Poquette, ph	1	0	0	0	0	0
Leonard, p	0	0	0	0	0	0
Mingori, p	0	0	0	0	0	0
Hrabosky, p	0	0	0	0	0	0
Bird, p	0	0	0	0	0	1
Totals	28	1	2	1	27	12

New York	0	1	1	0	2	0	0	3	0 – 7
Kansas City	0	0	0	0	0	1	0	0	0 – 1

New York	IP.	H.	R.	ER.	BB.	SO.
Beattie (Winner)	5⅓	2	1	1	5	3
Clay (Save)	3⅔	0	0	0	3	2

Kansas City	IP.	H.	R.	ER.	BB.	SO.
Leonard (Loser)	4*	9	3	3	0	2
Mingori	3⅔	5	3	3	3	0
Hrabosky	⅓	1	1	1	0	0
Bird	1	1	0	0	0	1

*Pitched to one batter in fifth.

Errors—Otis, Brett. Left on bases—New York 12, Kansas City 9. Two-base hits—R. White, Jackson, Brett. Three-base hit—Nettles. Home run—Jackson. Stolen bases—LaCock, Otis. Sacrifice fly—McRae. Passed ball—Porter. Umpires—DiMuro, Garcia, Luciano, Kunkel, Phillips and Cooney. Time—2:57. Attendance—41,143.

GAME OF WEDNESDAY, OCTOBER 4, AT KANSAS CITY

New York	AB.	R.	H.	RBI.	PO.	A.
Rivers, cf	3	0	2	0	1	0
Thomasson, ph-cf	1	0	0	0	0	0
Munson, c	5	0	0	0	2	1
Piniella, lf	5	0	0	3	0	0
Jackson, rf	4	1	1	0	4	0
Nettles, 3b	4	1	1	0	1	2
Chambliss, 1b	4	1	4	1	10	1
R. White, dh	4	1	1	0	0	0
Stanley, 2b	2	0	1	0	1	2
Johnson, ph	1	0	0	0	0	0
Doyle, 2b	0	0	0	0	0	0
Blair, ph-2b	1	0	0	0	1	0
Dent, ss	4	0	2	3	0	4
Figueroa, p	0	0	0	0	0	0
Tidrow, p	0	0	0	0	0	2
Lyle, p	0	0	0	0	1	0
Totals	38	4	12	4	24	13

Kansas City	AB.	R.	H.	RBI.	PO.	A.
Brett, 3b	5	2	2	0	0	1
McRae, dh	3	0	2	0	0	0
Otis, cf	5	1	3	1	3	0
Porter, c	4	0	2	2	3	0
LaCock, 1b	5	1	2	1	11	1
Hurdle, lf	3	1	2	1	0	0
Wilson, pr-lf	1	0	0	0	1	0
Cowens, rf	4	2	1	0	0	0
Patek, ss	4	2	1	2	2	1
F. White, 2b	4	1	1	2	6	5
Gura, p	0	0	0	0	1	4
Pattin, p	0	0	0	0	0	0
Hrabosky, p	0	0	0	0	0	0
Totals	38	10	16	9	27	12

New York	0	0	0	0	0	0	2	2	0 – 4
Kansas City	1	4	0	0	0	0	3	2	x – 10

New York	IP.	H.	R.	ER.	BB.	SO.
Figueroa (Loser)	1*	5	5	3	0	0
Tidrow	5⅔	8	3	3	2	1
Lyle	1⅓	3	2	2	0	0

Kansas City	IP.	H.	R.	ER.	BB.	SO.
Gura (Winner)	6⅓	8	2	2	2	2
Pattin	⅔†	2	2	2	0	0
Hrabosky	2	2	0	0	0	1

*Pitched to four batters in second.
†Pitched to two batters in seventh.

Errors—Patek, Dent. Double plays—Kansas City 2. Left on bases—New York 9, Kansas City 8. Two-base hit—LaCock. Three-base hit—Hurdle. Home run—Patek. Stolen bases—Otis 2. Sacrifice hit—McRae. Sacrifice fly—Porter. Umpires—Garcia, Luciano, Kunkel, Phillips, Cooney and DiMuro. Time—2:42. A—41,158.

GAME OF FRIDAY, OCTOBER 6, AT NEW YORK

Kansas City	AB.	R.	H.	RBI.	PO.	A.	New York	AB.	R.	H.	RBI.	PO.	A.
Brett, 3b	5	3	3	3	0	1	Rivers, cf	1	0	1	0	2	1
McRae, dh	5	0	0	0	0	0	Blair, ph-cf	3	0	0	0	3	0
Otis, cf	3	1	2	0	2	0	R. White, lf	4	2	2	0	1	0
Porter, c	4	1	2	1	4	0	Thomasson, lf	0	0	0	0	1	0
LaCock, 1b	3	0	2	0	5	0	Munson, c	4	2	3	2	7	1
Hurdle, lf	4	1	2	1	6	1	Jackson, dh	3	2	2	3	0	0
Wilson, pr-lf	0	0	0	0	1	0	Piniella, rf	4	0	2	0	2	0
Cowens, rf	4	0	0	1	4	0	Nettles, 3b	3	0	0	0	1	1
Patek, ss	3	0	0	0	1	2	Chambliss, 1b	3	0	0	0	6	0
F. White, 2b	3	0	0	0	1	2	Stanley, 2b	3	0	0	0	2	4
Braun, ph	1	0	0	0	0	0	Dent, ss	3	0	0	0	2	2
Splittorff, p	0	0	0	0	0	0	Hunter, p	0	0	0	0	0	1
Bird, p	0	0	0	0	0	0	Gossage, p	0	0	0	0	0	1
Hrabosky, p	0	0	0	0	0	0	Totals	31	6	10	5	27	8
Totals	35	5	10	5	24	6							

Kansas City	1	0	1	0	1	0	0	2	0 – 5
New York	0	1	0	2	0	1	0	2	x – 6

Kansas City	IP.	H.	R.	ER.	BB.	SO.
Splittorff	7⅓	9	5	4	0	2
Bird (Loser)	0*	1	1	1	0	0
Hrabosky	⅔	0	0	0	0	1

New York	IP.	H.	R.	ER.	BB.	SO.
Hunter	6	7	3	3	3	5
Gossage (Winner)	3	3	2	2	0	2

*Pitched to one batter in eighth.

Error—Patek. Double plays—Kansas City 2, New York 1. Left on bases—Kansas City 6, New York 2. Two-base hits—LaCock, Porter, Munson, Otis. Three-base hit—LaCock. Home runs—Brett 3, Jackson, Munson. Stolen base—Otis. Sacrifice fly—Jackson. Passed ball—Munson. Umpires—Luciano, Kunkel, Phillips, Cooney, DiMuro and Garcia. Time—2:13. Attendance—55,535.

GAME OF SATURDAY, OCTOBER 7, AT NEW YORK (N)

Kansas City	AB.	R.	H.	RBI.	PO.	A.	New York	AB.	R.	H.	RBI.	PO.	A.
Brett, 3b	4	1	1	0	1	2	Rivers, cf	2	0	0	0	2	0
McRae, dh	4	0	1	1	0	0	Blair, cf	1	0	0	0	2	0
Otis, cf	4	0	1	0	2	0	R. White, lf	4	1	1	1	1	0
Cowens, rf	3	0	0	0	0	0	Thomasson, lf	0	0	0	0	1	0
Hurdle, ph	1	0	0	0	0	0	Munson, c	4	0	1	0	7	2
Porter, c	3	0	1	0	10	0	Jackson, dh	3	0	0	0	0	0
Wathan, 1b	3	0	0	0	7	0	Piniella, rf	3	0	0	0	2	0
LaCock, ph	1	0	0	0	0	0	Nettles, 3b	3	1	2	1	3	3
F. White, 2b	3	0	2	0	1	2	Chambliss, 1b	3	0	0	0	8	0
Patek, ss	3	0	0	0	2	2	Doyle, 2b	2	0	0	0	1	2
Wilson, lf	3	0	1	0	0	0	Dent, ss	3	0	0	0	0	1
Leonard, p	0	0	0	0	1	0	Guidry, p	0	0	0	0	0	0
Totals	32	1	7	1	24	6	Gossage, p	0	0	0	0	0	0
							Totals	28	2	4	2	27	8

Kansas City	1	0	0	0	0	0	0	0	0 – 1
New York	0	1	0	0	1	0	0	0	x – 2

Kansas City	IP.	H.	R.	ER.	BB.	SO.
Leonard (Loser)	8	4	2	2	2	9

New York	IP.	H.	R.	ER.	BB.	SO.
Guidry (Winner)	8*	7	1	1	1	7
Gossage (Save)	1	0	0	0	0	1

*Pitched to one batter in ninth.

Errors—None. Double play—New York 1. Left on bases—Kansas City 5, New York 4. Two-base hit—Otis. Three-base hit—Brett. Home runs—Nettles, R. White. Stolen base—McRae. Wild pitch—Leonard. Umpires—Kunkel, Phillips, Cooney, DiMuro, Garcia and Luciano. Time—2:20. Attendance—56,356.

NEW YORK YANKEES' BATTING AND FIELDING AVERAGES

Player—Position	G.	AB.	R.	H.	TB.	2B.	3B.	HR.	RBI.	B.A.	PO.	A.	E.	F.A.
Jackson, dh-rf	4	13	5	6	13	1	0	2	6	.462	4	0	0	1.000
Rivers, cf	4	11	0	5	5	0	0	0	0	.455	8	1	0	1.000
Chambliss, 1b	4	15	1	6	6	0	0	0	2	.400	28	1	0	1.000
Nettles, 3b	4	15	3	5	10	0	1	1	2	.333	6	7	0	1.000
R. White, lf-dh	4	16	5	5	9	1	0	1	1	.313	3	0	0	1.000
Doyle, 2b	3	7	0	2	2	0	0	0	1	.286	3	6	0	1.000
Munson, c	4	18	2	5	9	1	0	1	2	.278	22	4	0	1.000
Piniella, rf-lf	4	17	2	4	4	0	0	0	0	.235	13	0	0	1.000
Dent, ss	4	15	0	3	3	0	0	0	4	.200	2	8	1	.909
Stanley, 2b	2	5	0	1	1	0	0	0	0	.200	3	3	0	1.000
Beattie, p	1	0	0	0	0	0	0	0	0	.000	2	0	0	1.000
Clay, p	1	0	0	0	0	0	0	0	0	.000	0	0	0	.000
Figueroa, p	1	0	0	0	0	0	0	0	0	.000	0	0	0	.000
Guidry, p	1	0	0	0	0	0	0	0	0	.000	0	1	0	1.000
Hunter, p	1	0	0	0	0	0	0	0	0	.000	0	1	0	1.000
Lyle, p	1	0	0	0	0	0	0	0	0	.000	1	1	0	1.000
Tidrow, p	1	0	0	0	0	0	0	0	0	.000	0	2	0	1.000
Gossage, p	2	0	0	0	0	0	0	0	0	.000	0	1	0	1.000
Johnson, ph	1	1	0	0	0	0	0	0	0	.000	0	0	0	.000
Thomasson, ph-cf-lf	3	1	0	0	0	0	0	0	0	.000	2	0	0	1.000
Blair, pr-cf-ph-2b	4	6	1	0	0	0	0	0	0	.000	8	0	0	1.000
Totals	4	140	19	42	62	3	1	5	18	.300	105	35	1	.993

KANSAS CITY ROYALS' BATTING AND FIELDING AVERAGES

Player—Position	G.	AB.	R.	H.	TB.	2B.	3B.	HR.	RBI.	B.A.	PO.	A.	E.	F.A.
Otis, cf	4	14	2	6	8	2	0	0	1	.429	8	0	1	.889
Brett, 3b	4	18	7	7	19	1	1	3	3	.389	3	8	1	.917
Hurdle, ph-lf	4	8	1	3	5	0	1	0	1	.375	6	1	0	1.000
LaCock, 1b-ph	4	11	1	4	8	2	1	0	1	.364	25	1	0	1.000
Porter, c	4	14	1	5	6	1	0	0	3	.357	21	1	0	1.000
Wilson, pr-lf	3	4	0	1	1	0	0	0	0	.250	0	0	0	.000
F. White, 2b	4	13	1	3	3	0	0	0	2	.231	9	12	0	1.000
McRae, dh	4	14	0	3	3	0	0	0	2	.214	0	0	0	.000
Cowens, rf	4	15	2	2	2	0	0	0	1	.133	5	0	0	1.000
Patek, ss	4	13	2	1	4	0	0	1	2	.077	9	8	2	.895
Gura, p	1	0	0	0	0	0	0	0	0	.000	1	4	0	1.000
Mingori, p	1	0	0	0	0	0	0	0	0	.000	0	0	0	.000
Pattin, p	1	0	0	0	0	0	0	0	0	.000	0	0	0	.000
Splittorff, p	1	0	0	0	0	0	0	0	0	.000	0	1	0	1.000
Bird, p	2	0	0	0	0	0	0	0	0	.000	1	0	0	1.000
Leonard, p	2	0	0	0	0	0	0	0	0	.000	0	0	0	.000
Hrabosky, p	1	1	0	0	0	0	0	0	0	.000	0	0	0	.000
Poquette, ph	1	3	0	0	0	0	0	0	0	.000	7	0	0	1.000
Wathan, ph	1	3	0	0	0	0	0	0	0	.000	7	0	0	1.000
Braun, lf-ph	2	5	0	0	0	0	0	0	0	.000	5	0	0	1.000
Totals	4	133	17	35	59	6	3	4	16	.263	102	36	4	.972

NEW YORK YANKEES' PITCHING RECORDS

Pitcher	G.	GS.	CG.	IP.	H.	R.	ER.	BB.	SO.	HB.	WP.	W.	L.	Pct.	ERA.
Clay	1	0	0	3⅔	0	0	0	3	2	0	0	0	0	.000	0.00
Guidry	1	1	0	8	7	1	1	1	7	0	0	1	0	1.000	1.13
Beattie	1	1	0	5⅓	2	1	1	5	3	0	0	1	0	1.000	1.69
Hunter	1	1	0	6	7	3	3	3	5	0	0	0	0	.000	4.50
Gossage	2	0	0	4	3	2	2	0	3	0	0	1	0	1.000	4.50
Tidrow	1	0	0	5⅔	8	3	3	2	1	0	0	0	0	.000	4.76
Lyle	1	0	0	1⅓	3	2	2	0	0	0	0	0	0	.000	13.50
Figueroa	1	1	0	1	5	5	3	0	0	0	0	0	1	.000	27.00
Totals	4	4	0	35	35	17	15	14	21	0	0	3	1	.750	3.86

Saves—Clay, Gossage. No shutouts.

KANSAS CITY ROYALS' PITCHING RECORDS

Pitcher	G.	GS.	CG.	IP.	H.	R.	ER.	BB.	SO.	HB.	WP.	W.	L.	Pct.	ERA.
Gura	1	1	0	6⅓	8	2	2	2	2	0	0	1	0	1.000	2.84
Hrabosky	3	0	0	3	3	1	1	0	2	0	0	0	0	.000	3.00
Leonard	2	2	1	12	13	5	5	2	11	0	1	0	2	.000	3.75
Splittorff	1	1	0	7⅓	9	5	4	0	2	0	0	0	0	.000	4.91
Mingori	1	0	0	3⅔	5	3	3	3	0	0	0	0	0	.000	7.36
Bird	2	0	0	1	2	1	1	0	1	0	0	0	1	.000	9.00
Pattin	1	0	0	⅔	2	2	2	0	0	0	0	0	0	.000	27.00
Totals	4	4	1	34	42	19	18	7	18	0	1	1	3	.250	4.76

No shutouts or saves.

COMPOSITE SCORE BY INNINGS

New York	0	3	1	2	2	2	2	7	0 – 19
Kansas City	3	4	1	0	1	1	3	4	0 – 17

Sacrifice hit—McRae.
Sacrifice flies—McRae, Porter, Jackson.
Stolen bases—LaCock, Otis 4, McRae.
Caught stealing—Jackson, McRae, Patek, Wilson.
Double plays—Brett, White and LaCock; Patek, White and LaCock; Rivers and Nettles; White, Patek and LaCock; Hurdle and Porter; Nettles and Chambliss.
Left on bases—Kansas City 28—9, 8, 6, 5; New York 27—12, 9, 4, 2.
Hit by pitchers—None.
Passed balls—Porter, Munson.
Balks—None.
Time of games—First game, 2:57; second game, 2:42; third game, 2:13; fourth game, 2:20.
Attendance—First game, 41,143; second game, 41,158; third game, 55,535; fourth game, 56,356.
Umpires—DiMuro, Garcia, Luciano, Kunkel, Phillips and Cooney.
Official scorers—Phil Pepe, New York Daily News; Del Black, Kansas City Star; Ken Leiker, Topeka Capital-Journal.

NATIONAL LEAGUE
Championship Series of 1978

	W.	L.	Pct.
Los Angeles (West)	3	1	.750
Philadelphia (East)	1	3	.250

As he made the long run from center field to the dugout, with Dodgers celebrating around him, Garry Maddox must have been in a daze. Two plays earlier, Maddox had dropped a two-out line drive off the bat of Dusty Baker prolonging Los Angeles' tenth inning. And when Bill Russell followed with a single that scored Ron Cey from second base, the Dodgers had wrapped up their second consecutive National League title and handed the Phillies their third straight loss.

The series began in Philadelphia with Phils' manager Danny Ozark proclaiming a three-game sweep. However, after the Dodgers shelled four Phillies' pitchers for four home runs in the opener, Ozark amended his statement.

In the 9-5 Dodger victory, Steve Garvey's three-run homer followed a Davey Lopes double, a Schmidt error on Russell's grounder and a run-scoring single by Reggie Smith. One inning later, Rick Monday blasted a triple to deep center field and Lopes cracked a two-run homer for a 6-1 Los Angeles lead against battered Phillies' starter Larry Christenson.

In Game Two, the Phillies sent Dick Ruthven to face the Dodgers' Tommy John. Ruthven had been the ace of the staff during the second half of the season after being acquired from the Atlanta Braves, having won 11 of 15 decisions. And after pitching perfect ball against Los Angeles for the first three innings, it looked as though Ruthven and the Phillies might be ready to get back at the Dodgers.

But Los Angeles turned to the long ball once again. Lopes greeted Ruthven with a home run leading off the fourth and that was to be all John ever needed. The Dodger lefty allowed only four singles, induced hard-hitting Philadelphia to bounce into three double plays and watched as his fielders gobbled up the 18 ground balls that came weakly off the Phillies' bats.

Lopes continued to wreak havoc on Phillie pitching, driving in a run in the fifth on a single and another in the seventh with a triple. Steve Yeager knocked in the other Dodger run with a single in the 4-0 win and the teams traveled to Los Angeles with the Dodgers waiting to supply the knockout punch. But Steve Carlton had other thoughts in mind.

Carlton stopped the Dodgers in Game Three, more with his bat than with his arm. He staked the Phils to a 4-0 second-inning lead with a cannon-like three-run homer to center field off Don Sutton. The blast had followed a run-scoring single by Ted Sizemore. When the Dodgers crawled to within 4-3 after three innings, Carlton let his bat do the talking again.

Lopes opened the gates for the Phils' three-run sixth with a two-out error on Tim McCarver's grounder. Sizemore followed with a single and Carlton knocked in McCarver with another single. Sizemore scored when Smith's throw from right field sailed past third base, and Carlton then scored on Jerry Martin's pinch-double. That was to be all the Phillies needed, though Luzinski added a homer in the ninth for good measure and a 9-4 victory, paving the way for Game Four and one of the most exciting games in Championship Series history.

Barring Maddox' error, the game was probably lost by the Phillies in the first inning. Schmidt doubled down the left field line to start the game off Doug Rau and Larry Bowa walked and Maddox singled, loading the bases with none out. But Rau escaped with no runs scored. He struck out the dangerous Luzinski and retired Jose Cardenal on a liner to short and Martin on a foul pop to the catcher.

Los Angeles jumped to a 1-0 lead in the second when Baker scored Ron Cey with a single off Randy Lerch. But the Phillies came right back in the third, taking a 2-1 lead on a two-run homer by Luzinski. Cey evened matters with a homer of his own in the fourth, and Garvey gave the Dodgers the lead again with a homer in the sixth, knocking out Lerch.

Rau had given way to Rick Rhoden in the sixth and Phillie reliever Warren Brusstar, hitting for Phillie reliever Warren Brusstar, tied the game again with a homer in the seventh. And that's the way it stayed until the memorable tenth. Tug McGraw had relieved Ron Reed in the ninth and appeared in command, retiring five straight batters. But with two down in the tenth, McGraw walked Cey on four pitches and Baker followed with the liner that Maddox mishandled, Cey stopping at second. It was now McGraw against Russell. And on the second pitch, Russell singled to center, scoring Cey and giving the Dodgers the game and series.

GAME OF WEDNESDAY, OCTOBER 4, AT PHILADELPHIA (N)

Los Angeles	AB.	R.	H.	RBI.	PO.	A.
Lopes, 2b	5	2	3	2	3	3
Russell, ss	5	1	1	0	1	2
Smith, rf	3	1	1	1	1	0
North, cf	1	0	0	0	0	0
Garvey, 1b	5	3	3	4	6	1
Cey, 3b	5	0	2	1	0	1
Baker, lf	3	0	1	0	1	0
Monday, cf-rf	4	1	1	0	4	0
Yeager, c	4	1	1	1	10	0
Hooton, p	2	0	0	0	1	0
Welch, p	2	0	0	0	0	1
Totals	39	9	13	9	27	8

Philadelphia	AB.	R.	H.	RBI.	PO.	A.
McBride, rf	5	1	1	0	1	0
Bowa, ss	5	1	3	0	0	4
Maddox, cf	5	0	2	2	4	0
Luzinski, lf	4	1	1	0	1	1
Hebner, 1b	4	0	1	1	11	0
Schmidt, 3b	3	0	0	1	2	4
Boone, c	4	0	1	0	6	1
Sizemore, 2b	4	1	2	0	2	3
Christenson, p	1	0	0	0	0	0
Brusstar, p	0	0	0	0	0	0
Gonzalez, ph	1	0	0	0	0	0
Eastwick, p	0	0	0	0	0	0
McCarver, ph	1	0	0	0	0	0
McGraw, p	0	0	0	0	0	0
Martin, ph	1	1	1	1	0	0
Totals	38	5	12	5	27	13

Los Angeles	0	0	4		2	1	1		0	0	1 – 9
Philadelphia	0	1	0		0	3	0		0	0	1 – 5

Los Angeles	IP.	H.	R.	ER.	BB.	SO.
Hooton	4⅔	10	4	4	0	5
Welch (Winner)	4⅓	2	1	1	0	5

Philadelphia	IP.	H.	R.	ER.	BB.	SO.
Christenson (Loser)	4⅓	7	7	6	1	3
Brusstar	⅔	1	0	0	0	0
Eastwick	1	3	1	1	0	1
McGraw	3	2	1	1	3	3

Errors—Lopes, Schmidt. Double plays—Los Angeles 1, Philadelphia 1. Left on bases—Los Angeles 8, Philadelphia 7. Two-base hit—Lopes. Three-base hits—Luzinski, Monday, Garvey. Home runs—Garvey 2, Lopes, Yeager, Martin. Sacrifice fly—Schmidt. Hit by pitcher—By Eastwick (Smith). Umpires—Weyer, Colosi, Olsen, Davidson, W. Williams and McSherry. Time—2:37. Attendance—63,460.

GAME OF THURSDAY, OCTOBER 5, AT PHILADELPHIA

Los Angeles	AB.	R.	H.	RBI.	PO.	A.
Lopes, 2b	4	1	3	3	4	4
Russell, ss	4	0	1	0	1	9
Smith, rf	4	0	1	0	0	0
North, cf	0	0	0	0	0	0
Garvey, 1b	4	0	0	0	16	0
Cey, 3b	4	0	0	0	0	7
Baker, lf	4	1	1	0	0	0
Monday, cf-rf	4	1	1	0	2	0
Yeager, c	3	1	1	1	4	1
John, p	3	0	0	0	0	0
Totals	34	4	8	4	27	21

Philadelphia	AB.	R.	H.	RBI.	PO.	A.
Schmidt, 3b	4	0	1	0	0	4
Bowa, ss	4	0	0	0	1	4
Maddox, cf	4	0	1	0	5	0
Luzinski, lf	3	0	1	0	2	0
Cardenal, 1b	2	0	0	0	10	0
Boone, c	3	0	1	0	5	0
Martin, rf	2	0	0	0	1	0
Sizemore, 2b	3	0	0	0	3	1
Ruthven, p	1	0	0	0	0	0
Brusstar, p	0	0	0	0	0	0
Morrison, ph	1	0	0	0	0	0
Reed, p	0	0	0	0	0	0
Foote, ph	1	0	0	0	0	0
McGraw, p	0	0	0	0	0	0
Totals	28	0	4	0	27	9

Los Angeles	0	0	0		1	2	0		1	0	0 – 4
Philadelphia	0	0	0		0	0	0		0	0	0 – 0

Los Angeles	IP.	H.	R.	ER.	BB.	SO.
John (Winner)	9	4	0	0	2	4

Philadelphia	IP.	H.	R.	ER.	BB.	SO.
Ruthven (Loser)	4⅔	6	3	3	0	3
Brusstar	1⅓	0	0	0	0	0
Reed	2	2	1	1	0	1
McGraw	1	0	0	0	1	0

Errors—None. Double plays—Los Angeles 3. Left on bases—Los Angeles 5, Philadelphia 3. Two-base hits—Smith, Baker. Three-base hit—Lopes. Home run—Lopes. Stolen base—Yeager. Sacrifice hit—John. Umpires—Colosi, Olsen, Davidson, W. Williams, McSherry and Weyer. Time—2:06. Attendance—60,642.

GAME OF FRIDAY, OCTOBER 6, AT LOS ANGELES

Philadelphia	AB.	R.	H.	RBI.	PO.	A.
McBride, rf	3	0	0	0	0	0
Martin, ph-rf	2	0	1	1	1	0
Bowa, ss	5	0	1	0	2	5
Maddox, cf	5	1	1	0	3	0
Luzinski, lf	5	1	3	1	1	0
Hebner, 1b	4	0	0	0	10	0
Schmidt, 3b	4	1	1	0	1	5
McCarver, c	3	2	0	1	8	0
Sizemore, 2b	2	2	2	1	1	2
Carlton, p	4	2	2	4	0	0
Totals	37	9	11	8	27	12

Los Angeles	AB.	R.	H.	RBI.	PO.	A.
Lopes, 2b	4	0	0	0	2	2
North, cf	4	0	0	0	2	0
Smith, rf	4	1	1	0	2	0
Garvey, 1b	4	2	2	2	16	2
Cey, 3b	3	1	1	1	2	3
Baker, lf	3	0	1	0	0	0
Russell, ss	4	0	2	1	0	2
Yeager, c	3	0	0	0	2	0
Lacy, ph	1	0	0	0	0	0
Sutton, p	2	0	0	0	0	1
Rautzhan, p	0	0	0	0	0	1
Mota, ph	1	0	1	0	0	0
Hough, p	0	0	0	0	1	1
Ferguson, ph	1	0	0	0	0	0
Totals	34	4	8	4	27	12

Philadelphia									
Philadelphia	0	4	0	0	0	3	1	0	1 – 9
Los Angeles	0	1	2	0	0	0	0	1	0 – 4

Philadelphia	IP.	H.	R.	ER.	BB.	SO.
Carlton (Winner)	9	8	4	4	2	8

Los Angeles	IP.	H.	R.	ER.	BB.	SO.
Sutton (Loser)	5⅔	7	7	4	2	0
Rautzhan	1⅓	3	1	1	2	0
Hough	2	1	1	1	0	1

Errors—Lopes, Smith, Schmidt. Double plays—Philadelphia 2. Left on bases—Philadelphia 7, Los Angeles 5. Two-base hits—Schmidt, Martin, Russell, Garvey, Mota. Home runs—Carlton, Luzinski, Garvey. Sacrifice hits—Sizemore, Hebner. Umpires—Olsen, Davidson, W. Williams, McSherry, Weyer and Colosi. Time—2:18. Attendance —55,043.

GAME OF SATURDAY, OCTOBER 7, AT LOS ANGELES

Philadelphia	AB.	R.	H.	RBI.	PO.	A.
Schmidt, 3b	4	0	1	0	0	5
Bowa, ss	4	1	2	0	2	3
Maddox, cf	5	0	1	0	4	0
Luzinski, lf	4	1	1	2	1	0
Cardenal, 1b	4	0	1	0	11	0
Martin, rf	4	0	0	0	5	0
Boone, c	4	0	0	0	5	1
Sizemore, 2b	4	0	1	0	1	2
Lerch, p	2	0	0	0	0	1
Brusstar, p	0	0	0	0	0	0
McBride, ph	1	1	1	1	0	0
Reed, p	0	0	0	0	0	0
Hebner, ph	1	0	0	0	0	0
McGraw, p	0	0	0	0	0	0
Totals	37	3	8	3	29	12

Los Angeles	AB.	R.	H.	RBI.	PO.	A.
Lopes, 2b	5	0	1	0	1	1
North, cf	3	0	0	0	7	0
Monday, ph-cf	2	0	0	0	0	0
Smith, rf	5	0	0	0	2	0
Garvey, 1b	5	1	2	1	6	2
Cey, 3b	4	3	2	1	0	2
Baker, lf	5	0	4	1	4	0
Russell, ss	4	0	3	1	2	1
Yeager, c	3	0	1	0	5	1
Lacy, ph	1	0	0	0	0	0
Grote, c	0	0	0	0	2	0
Rau, p	1	0	0	0	1	0
Mota, ph	0	0	0	0	0	0
Rhoden, p	1	0	0	0	0	2
Ferguson, ph	1	0	0	0	0	0
Forster, p	0	0	0	0	0	0
Totals	40	4	13	4	30	9

Philadelphia									
Philadelphia	0	0	2	0	0	0	1	0	0 – 3
Los Angeles	0	1	0	1	0	1	0	0	1 – 4

Two out when winning run scored.

Philadelphia	IP.	H.	R.	ER.	BB.	SO.
Lerch	5⅓	7	3	3	0	0
Brusstar	⅔	1	0	0	1	0
Reed	2	4	0	0	0	1
McGraw (Loser)	1⅔	1	1	0	1	2

Los Angeles	IP.	H.	R.	ER.	BB.	SO.
Rau	5	5	2	2	2	1
Rhoden	4	2	1	1	1	3
Forster (Winner)	1	1	0	0	0	2

Errors—Boone, Maddox. Double play—Philadelphia 1. Left on bases—Philadelphia 7, Los Angeles 10. Two-base hits—Schmidt, Cey, Baker. Three-base hit—Sizemore. Home runs—Luzinski, Cey, Garvey, McBride. Stolen base—Lopes. Sacrifice hit—Mota. Umpires—Davidson, W. Williams, McSherry, Weyer, Colosi and Olsen. Time—2:53. Attendance—55,124.

LOS ANGELES DODGERS' BATTING AND FIELDING AVERAGES

Player—Position	G.	AB.	R.	H.	TB.	2B.	3B.	HR.	RBI.	B.A.	PO.	A.	E.	F.A.
Mota, ph	2	1	0	1	2	1	0	0	0	1.000	0	0	0	.000
Baker, lf	4	15	1	7	9	2	0	0	1	.467	5	0	0	1.000
Russell, ss	4	17	1	7	8	1	0	0	2	.412	4	14	0	1.000
Garvey, 1b	4	18	6	7	22	1	1	4	7	.389	44	5	0	1.000
Lopes, 2b	4	18	3	7	16	1	1	2	5	.389	10	10	2	.909
Cey, 3b	4	16	4	5	9	1	0	1	3	.313	2	13	0	1.000
Yeager, c	4	13	2	3	6	0	0	1	2	.231	21	2	0	1.000
Monday, cf-rf-ph	3	10	2	2	4	0	1	0	0	.200	6	0	0	1.000
Smith, rf	4	16	2	3	4	1	0	0	1	.188	5	0	1	.833
Grote, c	1	0	0	0	0	0	0	0	0	.000	2	0	0	1.000
Hough, p	1	0	0	0	0	0	0	0	0	.000	1	1	0	1.000
Forster, p	1	0	0	0	0	0	0	0	0	.000	0	0	0	.000
Rautzhan, p	1	0	0	0	0	0	0	0	0	.000	0	1	0	1.000
Rau, p	1	1	0	0	0	0	0	0	0	.000	1	0	0	1.000
Rhoden, p	1	1	0	0	0	0	0	0	0	.000	0	2	0	1.000
Hooton, p	1	2	0	0	0	0	0	0	0	.000	1	0	0	1.000
Sutton, p	1	2	0	0	0	0	0	0	0	.000	0	1	0	1.000
Welch, p	1	2	0	0	0	0	0	0	0	.000	0	1	0	1.000
Ferguson, ph	2	2	0	0	0	0	0	0	0	.000	0	0	0	.000
Lacy, ph	2	2	0	0	0	0	0	0	0	.000	0	0	0	.000
John, p	1	3	0	0	0	0	0	0	0	.000	0	0	0	.000
North, cf	4	8	0	0	0	0	0	0	0	.000	9	0	0	1.000
Totals	4	147	21	42	80	8	3	8	21	.286	111	50	3	.982

PHILADELPHIA PHILLIES' BATTING AND FIELDING AVERAGES

Player—Position	G.	AB.	R.	H.	TB.	2B.	3B.	HR.	RBI.	B.A.	PO.	A.	E.	F.A.
Carlton, p	1	4	2	2	5	0	0	1	4	.500	0	0	0	.000
Sizemore, 2b	4	13	3	5	7	0	1	0	1	.385	7	8	0	1.000
Luzinski, lf	4	16	3	6	14	0	1	2	3	.375	5	1	0	1.000
Bowa, ss	4	18	2	6	6	0	0	0	0	.333	5	16	0	1.000
Maddox, cf	4	19	1	5	5	0	0	0	2	.263	16	0	1	.941
McBride, rf-ph	3	9	2	2	5	0	0	1	1	.222	1	0	0	1.000
Martin, ph-rf	4	9	1	2	6	1	0	1	2	.222	7	0	0	1.000
Schmidt, 3b	4	15	1	3	5	2	0	0	1	.200	3	18	2	.913
Boone, c	3	11	0	2	2	0	0	0	0	.182	16	2	1	.947
Cardenal, 1b	2	6	0	1	1	0	0	0	0	.167	21	0	0	1.000
Hebner, 1b-ph	3	9	0	1	1	0	0	0	1	.111	21	0	0	1.000
Christenson, p	1	1	0	0	0	0	0	0	0	.000	0	0	0	.000
Eastwick, p	1	0	0	0	0	0	0	0	0	.000	0	0	0	.000
Reed, p	2	0	0	0	0	0	0	0	0	.000	0	0	0	.000
Brusstar, p	3	0	0	0	0	0	0	0	0	.000	0	0	0	.000
McGraw, p	3	0	0	0	0	0	0	0	0	.000	0	0	0	.000
Foote, ph	1	1	0	0	0	0	0	0	0	.000	0	0	0	.000
Gonzalez, ph	1	1	0	0	0	0	0	0	0	.000	0	0	0	.000
Morrison, ph	1	1	0	0	0	0	0	0	0	.000	0	0	0	.000
Ruthven, p	1	1	0	0	0	0	0	0	0	.000	0	0	0	.000
Lerch, p	1	2	0	0	0	0	0	0	0	.000	0	1	0	1.000
McCarver, ph-c	2	4	2	0	0	0	0	0	1	.000	8	0	0	1.000
Totals	4	140	17	35	57	3	2	5	16	.250	110	46	4	.975

LOS ANGELES DODGERS' PITCHING RECORDS

Pitcher	G.	GS.	CG.	IP.	H.	R.	ER.	BB.	SO.	HB.	WP.	W.	L.	Pct.	ERA.
John	1	1	1	9	4	0	0	2	4	0	0	1	0	1.000	0.00
Forster	1	0	0	1	1	0	0	2	0	0	1	1	0	1.000	0.00
Welch	1	0	0	4⅓	2	1	1	0	5	0	0	1	0	1.000	2.08
Rhoden	1	0	0	4	2	1	1	1	3	0	0	0	0	.000	2.25
Rau	1	1	0	5	5	2	2	2	1	0	0	0	0	.000	3.60
Hough	1	0	0	2	1	1	1	0	1	0	0	0	0	.000	4.50
Sutton	1	1	0	5⅔	7	7	4	2	0	0	0	0	1	.000	6.35
Rautzhan	1	0	0	1⅓	3	1	1	2	0	0	0	0	0	.000	6.75
Hooton	1	1	0	4⅔	10	4	4	0	5	0	0	0	0	.000	7.71
Totals	4	4	1	37	35	17	14	9	21	0	0	3	1	.750	3.41

Shutout—John. No saves.

PHILADELPHIA PHILLIES' PITCHING RECORDS

Pitcher	G.	GS.	CG.	IP.	H.	R.	ER.	BB.	SO.	HB.	WP.	W.	L.	Pct.	ERA.
Brusstar	3	0	0	2⅔	2	0	0	1	0	0	0	0	0	.000	0.00
McGraw	3	0	0	5⅔	3	2	1	5	5	0	0	0	1	.000	1.59
Reed	2	0	0	4	6	1	1	0	2	0	0	0	0	.000	2.25

Pitcher	G.	GS.	CG.	IP.	H.	R.	ER.	BB.	SO.	HB.	WP.	W.	L.	Pct.	ERA.
Carlton	1	1	1	9	8	4	4	2	8	0	0	1	0	1.000	4.00
Lerch	1	1	0	5⅓	7	3	3	0	0	0	0	0	0	.000	5.06
Ruthven	1	1	0	4⅔	6	3	3	0	3	0	0	0	0	.000	5.79
Eastwick	1	0	0	1	3	1	1	0	1	1	0	0	0	.000	9.00
Christenson	1	1	0	4⅓	7	7	6	1	3	0	0	0	1	.000	12.46
Totals	4	4	1	36⅔	42	21	19	9	22	1	0	1	3	.250	4.66

No shutouts or saves.

COMPOSITE SCORE BY INNINGS

Los Angeles	0	2	6	4	3	2	1	1	1	1 – 21
Philadelphia	0	5	2	0	3	3	2	0	2	0 – 17

Sacrifice hits—John, Sizemore, Hebner, Mota.
Sacrifice fly—Schmidt.
Stolen bases—Yeager, Lopes.
Caught stealing—Schmidt, Garvey.
Double plays—Russell and Garvey; Bowa, Sizemore and Hebner; Russell, Lopes and Garvey; Lopes, Russell and Garvey; Cey, Lopes and Garvey; Sizemore, Bowa and Hebner 2; Sizemore, Bowa and Cardenal.
Left on bases—Los Angeles 28—8, 5, 5, 10; Philadelphia 24—7, 3, 7, 7.
Hit by pitcher—By Eastwick (Smith).
Passed balls—None.
Balks—None.
Time of games—First game, 2:37; second game, 2:06; third game, 2:18; fourth game, 2:53.
Attendance—First game, 63,460; second game, 60,642; third game, 55,043; fourth game, 55,124.
Umpires—Weyer, Colosi, Olsen, Davidson, W. Williams and McSherry.
Official scorers—Dick Robinson, Pasadena Star-News; Bob Kenney, Camden Courier-Post.

AMERICAN LEAGUE
Championship Series of 1979

	W.	L.	Pct.
Baltimore (East)	3	1	.750
California (West)	1	3	.250

"I've seen that play a hundred times before," said Baltimore shortstop Mark Belanger. "But by another third baseman."

"I thought of Brooks Robinson," said Brooks Robinson.

Memories. Of diving stops. Of World Series gems. Of Brooks Robinson.

But Brooks was retired and those sparkling plays were now only memories. . . . The California Angels had the bases loaded with one out in the fifth inning, trailing the Baltimore Orioles, 3-0, in the fourth game of the American League Championship Series. The Orioles led the Series two games to one, but the potential tying runs were on the bases.

Shortstop Jim Anderson was at the plate against Scott McGregor with 43,199 Anaheim Stadium fans on their feet, sensing their Angels were going to turn things around.

Anderson swung at the second pitch and hit a vicious one-hopper down the third base line. It looked like at least a double as the ball sped over the bag. Two runs would have scored for sure, maybe three. Doug DeCinces, who had never really escaped the shadow of Brooks Robinson at third base in the eyes of Orioles' rooters, dived to his right and somehow snared the ball. He recovered, straightened up and, while standing on third, threw to first to complete the double play and end the Angels' threat.

McGregor went on to hurl a six-hit shutout and the Orioles won 8-0 for a 3-1 Series triumph and their first visit to the World Series since 1971.

Pat Kelly's seventh-inning homer closed out the scoring and was the second three-run blast off California reliever John Montague. However, it was far less dramatic than the first one.

With two out in the 10th inning of the first game, the score deadlocked, 3-3, and DeCinces and Al Bumbry aboard via a single and intentional walk, respectively, pinch-hitter John Lowenstein strolled to the plate against Montague.

Lowenstein, sidelined for much of the latter part of the season because of a severely sprained ankle, sliced a two-strike pitch to the opposite field, just over the left-field wall to break up the game before 52,787 at Baltimore's Memorial Stadium.

Jim Palmer hurled the first nine innings, yielding seven hits, including a homer and double by Dan Ford, before Don Stanhouse pitched a perfect 10th inning to gain credit for the victory.

The Orioles sent 23-game winner Mike Flanagan to the mound in Game 2 and, after Ford connected off Flanagan in the first inning for his second homer in as many games, the AL Cy Young Award winner was given a 9-1 cushion in the first three innings, only to see it dwindle to one run before Stanhouse slowed the game down to his pace and saved a 9-8 victory.

The Orioles had scored four runs in their half of the first and added four more in the second, highlighted by first baseman Eddie Murray's 400-foot homer, before Kiko Garcia's RBI single in the third made the score 9-1.

After the Angels cuffed Flanagan for single runs in the sixth and seventh, they knocked the lefthander from the mound in the eighth, scoring three more runs, aided by a Murray error.

Stanhouse put gasoline on the fire for Flanagan in the eighth when he yielded a run-scoring single by Don Baylor and a sacrifice fly, reducing Baltimore's lead to 9-6.

In the ninth, Stanhouse permitted a walk, a pinch-double by Willie Davis, an infield out for one run and an RBI single by Carney Lansford, sending Baltimore skipper Earl Weaver to the mound.

"I was going to leave him (Stanhouse) in there until they tied the score," Weaver said later, after watching the Angels load the bases on a single by Ford and an intentional walk to Baylor, before Brian Downing grounded into a forceout to put a halt to the nail-biting.

With no days off for travel, the scene shifted to Anaheim Stadium for Game 3, where high drama once again dominated.

The Orioles were only two outs away from sweeping the series when the Angels struck back for a 4-3 victory.

Dennis Martinez spaced seven hits in the first eight innings prior to permitting a one-out double to Rod Carew in the ninth, bringing Stanhouse to the mound for the third straight game.

A walk to Downing preceded Bobby Grich's liner to center field where Al Bumbry, unable to hear the crack of the bat because of the roar of the crowd, got a late jump on the ball and dropped it for an error as Carew scored to tie the game, 3-3, with Downing stopping at second.

When Larry Harlow followed with a looping double down the left field line, Downing raced home with the winning run.

The ecstasy was short-lived for the Angels, who finally made it to the playoffs after 19 years of trying.

GAME OF WEDNESDAY, OCTOBER 3 AT BALTIMORE (N)

California	AB.	R.	H.	RBI.	PO.	A.
Miller, cf	5	1	1	0	2	1
Lansford, 3b	4	0	0	0	0	3
Ford, rf	4	1	2	2	3	0
Baylor, dh	4	0	0	0	0	0
Carew 1b	4	1	3	0	8	1
Downing, c	4	0	0	0	9	0
Grich, 2b	3	0	1	1	1	3
Harlow, lf	4	0	0	0	4	0
Anderson, ss	3	0	0	1	1	2
Davis, ph	1	0	0	0	0	0
Campaneris, ss	0	0	0	0	0	0
Ryan, p	0	0	0	0	0	0
Montague, p	0	0	0	0	1	1
Totals	36	3	7	3	29	11

Baltimore	AB.	R.	H.	RBI.	PO.	A.
Bumbry, cf	4	1	0	0	3	0
Belanger, ss	4	0	1	1	0	5
Lowenstein, ph	1	1	1	3	0	0
Singleton, rf	3	0	0	0	1	0
Murray, 1b	2	0	0	0	13	1
Kelly, lf	3	1	1	0	3	0
May, dh	4	0	0	0	0	0
DeCinces, 3b	3	2	1	1	2	3
Dauer, 2b	3	0	1	0	3	3
Dempsey, c	3	1	1	1	4	1
Crowley, ph	1	0	0	0	0	0
Palmer, p	0	0	0	0	1	1
Stanhouse, p	0	0	0	0	0	0
Totals	31	6	6	6	30	14

```
California ......................... 1 0 1   0 0 0   0 0 0   0 – 3
Baltimore .......................... 0 0 2   1 0 0   0 0 0   3 – 6
        Two out when winning run scored.
```

California	IP.	H.	R.	ER.	BB.	SO.
Ryan	7	4	3	1	3	8
Montague (Loser)	2⅔	2	3	3	2	1

Baltimore	IP.	H.	R.	ER.	BB.	SO.
Palmer	9	7	3	3	2	3
Stanhouse (Winner)	1	0	0	0	0	0

Error—Grich. Double plays—California 2. Left on bases—California 5, Baltimore 3. Two-base hits—Ford, Dempsey, Carew, Grich. Home runs—Ford, Lowenstein. Stolen base—Kelly. Caught stealing—Carew, Murray. Sacrifice hit—Dauer. Sacrifice fly—DeCinces. Wild pitch—Ryan. Passed ball—Dempsey. Umpires—Barnett, Ford, Evans, Denkinger, Clark and Kosc. Time—3:10. Attendance—52,787.

GAME OF THURSDAY, OCTOBER 4, AT BALTIMORE

California	AB.	R.	H.	RBI.	PO.	A.
Carew, 1b	5	2	1	1	10	0
Lansford, 3b	5	1	3	3	0	1
Ford, rf	5	1	2	1	0	0
Baylor, dh	4	1	2	1	0	0
Downing, c	4	0	1	1	6	0
Grich, 2b	3	0	0	1	1	3
Clark, lf	3	0	0	0	3	0
Harlow, ph	0	0	0	0	0	0
Miller, cf	4	1	0	0	2	0
Anderson, ss	2	0	0	2	3	2
Rettenmund, ph	0	0	0	0	0	0
Thon, pr-ss	0	1	1	0	0	0
Davis, ph	1	1	1	0	0	0
Frost, p	0	0	0	0	0	0
Clear, p	0	0	0	0	0	0
Aase, p	0	0	0	0	0	0
Totals	36	8	10	8	24	7

Baltimore	AB.	R.	H.	RBI.	PO.	A.
Bumbry, cf	4	2	3	0	3	0
Garcia, ss	5	1	2	2	2	9
Singleton, rf	5	1	1	0	0	0
Murray, 1b	4	2	2	4	13	0
Lowenstein, lf	4	1	1	1	0	0
Kelly, dh	3	1	1	1	2	0
DeCinces, 3b	4	0	0	0	3	5
Dauer, 2b	4	0	1	0	2	0
Dempsey, c	0	0	0	0	0	0
Flanagan, p	0	0	0	0	0	0
Stanhouse, p	0	0	0	0	0	0
Totals	34	9	11	8	27	16

```
California ......................... 0 0 0   0 0 1   1 3   2 – 8
Baltimore .......................... 4 1 0   0 0 0   0 0   x – 9
```

California	IP.	H.	R.	ER.	BB.	SO.
Frost (Loser)	1⅓	5	6	5	3	0
Clear	5⅔	4	3	3	2	3
Aase	1	2	0	0	0	2

Baltimore	IP.	H.	R.	ER.	BB.	SO.
Flanagan (Winner)	7*	6	6	4	1	2
Stanhouse	2	4	2	2	2	0

*Pitched to three batters in eighth.

Errors—Ford, Murray. Double play—California 1. Left on bases—California 6, Baltimore 6. Two-base hits—Carew, Davis. Home runs—Ford, Murray. Stolen bases—Bumbry 2. Sacrifice flies—Grich, Downing. Wild pitch—Clear. Umpires—Ford, Evans, Denkinger, Clark, Kosc and Barnett. Time—2:51. Attendance—52,108.

GAME OF FRIDAY, OCTOBER 5, AT CALIFORNIA

Baltimore	AB.	R.	H.	RBI.PO.	A.
Bumbry, cf	5	1	1	0	1	0
Garcia, ss	3	0	0	0	2	2
Crowley, ph	1	0	1	1	0	0
Belanger, pr-ss	1	0	0	0	0	0
Singleton, rf	4	2	2	0	2	1
Murray, 1b	2	0	2	0	8	2
May, dh	3	0	1	1	0	0
DeCinces, 3b	3	0	0	1	0	1
Roenicke, lf	1	0	0	0	2	1
Lowenstein, ph-lf	1	0	0	0	2	0
Dauer, 2b	4	0	1	0	3	4
Skaggs, c	4	0	0	0	3	1
D. Martinez, p	0	0	0	0	2	0
Stanhouse, p	0	0	0	0	0	0
Totals	32	3	8	3	25	12

California	AB.	R.	H.	RBI.PO.	A.
Miller, cf	4	0	1	0	7	1
Lansford, 3b	4	1	1	0	0	3
Ford, rf	4	0	1	1	2	0
Baylor, dh	4	1	1	1	0	0
Carew, 1b	4	1	2	0	7	0
Downing, c	3	1	1	0	8	0
Grich, 2b	4	0	0	0	1	1
Harlow, lf	4	0	1	1	2	0
Anderson, ss	3	0	1	0	0	3
Tanana, p	0	0	0	0	0	0
Aase, p	0	0	0	0	0	1
Totals	34	4	9	3	27	9

Baltimore	0	0	0	1	0	1	1	0	0 – 3
California	1	0	0	1	0	0	0	0	2 – 4

One out when winning run scored.

Baltimore	IP.	H.	R.	ER.	BB.	SO.
D. Martinez	8⅓	8	3	3	0	4
Stanhouse (Loser)	0†	1	1	0	1	0

California	IP.	H.	R.	ER.	BB.	SO.
Tanana	5*	6	2	2	2	3
Aase (Winner)	4	2	1	1	2	4

*Pitched to three batters in sixth.
†Pitched to three batters in ninth.

Errors—Garcia, Murray, Bumbry. Double plays—Baltimore 2, California 2. Left on bases—Baltimore 8, California 6. Two-base hits—Singleton, Carew, Harlow. Three-base hit—Bumbry. Home run—Baylor. Stolen bases—Lansford, Carew. Sacrifice fly—DeCinces. Hit by pitcher—By Tanana (Roenicke). Umpires—Evans, Denkinger, Clark, Kosc, Barnett and Ford. Time—2:59. Attendance—43, 199.

GAME OF SATURDAY, OCTOBER 6, AT CALIFORNIA

Baltimore	AB.	R.	H.	RBI.PO.	A.
Bumbry, cf	3	1	0	0	3	0
Garcia, ss	5	0	1	0	2	5
Belanger, ss	0	0	0	0	0	1
Singleton, rf	4	1	3	2	2	0
Murray, 1b	4	1	1	1	10	0
Lowenstein, lf	1	0	0	0	1	0
Roenicke, ph-lf	4	1	1	1	1	0
Kelly, dh	4	1	2	3	0	0
DeCinces, 3b	4	1	2	0	2	2
Smith, 2b	4	0	0	0	1	2
Dauer, 2b	0	0	0	0	1	0
Dempsey, c	3	2	2	1	4	0
McGregor, p	0	0	0	0	0	0
Totals	36	8	12	8	27	10

California	AB.	R.	H.	RBI.PO.	A.
Carew, 1b	4	0	1	0	9	0
Lansford, 3b	4	0	1	0	4	1
Ford, rf	4	0	0	0	1	0
Baylor, lf	4	0	0	0	4	0
Downing, c	4	0	1	0	4	0
Grich, 2b	3	0	1	0	1	5
Rettenmund, dh	2	0	0	0	0	0
Miller, cf	3	0	2	0	3	0
Anderson, ss	3	0	0	0	1	3
Knapp, p	0	0	0	0	0	0
LaRoche, p	0	0	0	0	0	0
Frost, p	0	0	0	0	0	0
Montague, p	0	0	0	0	0	1
Barlow, p	0	0	0	0	0	0
Totals	31	0	6	0	27	10

Baltimore	0	0	2	1	0	0	5	0	0 – 8
California	0	0	0	0	0	0	0	0	0 – 0

Baltimore	IP.	H.	R.	ER.	BB.	SO.
McGregor (Winner)	9	6	0	0	1	4

California	IP.	H.	R.	ER.	BB.	SO.
Knapp (Loser)	2⅓	5	2	2	1	0
LaRoche	1⅓	2	1	1	1	1
Frost	3	3	4	4	2	1
Montague	1⅓	2	1	1	0	1
Barlow	1	0	0	0	0	0

Error—Garcia. Double plays—Baltimore 3, California 2. Left on bases—Baltimore 6, California 5. Two-base hits—DeCinces, Dempsey, Singleton. Home run—Kelly. Stolen bases—Kelly, Dempsey. Sacrifice fly—Singleton. Wild pitch—Frost. Umpires—Denkinger, Clark, Kosc, Barnett, Ford and Evans. Time—2:56. Attendance—43,199.

BALTIMORE ORIOLES' BATTING AND FIELDING AVERAGES

Player—Position	G.	AB.	R.	H.	TB.	2B.	3B.	HR.	RBI.	B.A.	PO.	A.	E.	F.A.
Crowley, ph	2	2	0	1	1	0	0	0	1	.500	0	0	0	.000
Murray, 1b	4	12	3	5	8	0	0	1	5	.417	44	3	2	.959
Dempsey, c	3	10	3	4	6	2	0	0	2	.400	10	1	0	1.000
Singleton, rf	4	16	4	6	8	2	0	0	2	.375	5	1	0	1.000
Kelly, lf-dh	3	11	3	4	7	0	0	1	4	.364	3	0	0	1.000
DeCinces, 3b	4	13	4	4	5	1	0	0	3	.308	5	8	0	1.000
Garcia, ss	3	11	1	3	3	0	0	0	2	.273	6	16	2	.917
Bumbry, cf	4	16	5	4	6	0	1	0	0	.250	10	0	1	.909
Roenicke, lf-ph	2	5	1	1	1	0	0	0	1	.200	3	1	0	1.000
Belanger, ss-pr	3	5	0	1	1	0	0	0	0	.200	0	6	0	1.000
Dauer, 2b	4	11	0	2	2	0	0	0	0	.182	10	12	0	1.000
Lowenstein, ph-lf	4	6	2	1	4	0	0	1	3	.167	6	0	0	1.000
May, dh	2	7	0	1	1	0	0	0	1	.143	0	0	0	.000
D. Martinez, p	1	0	0	0	0	0	0	0	0	.000	2	0	0	1.000
Palmer, p	1	0	0	0	0	0	0	0	0	.000	1	1	0	1.000
Flanagan, p	1	0	0	0	0	0	0	0	0	.000	0	0	0	.000
McGregor, p	1	0	0	0	0	0	0	0	0	.000	0	0	0	.000
Stanhouse, p	3	0	0	0	0	0	0	0	0	.000	0	0	0	.000
Skaggs, c	1	4	0	0	0	0	0	0	0	.000	3	1	0	1.000
Smith, 2b	1	4	0	0	0	0	0	0	0	.000	1	2	0	1.000
Totals	4	133	26	37	53	5	1	3	25	.278	109	52	5	.970

CALIFORNIA ANGELS' BATTING AND FIELDING AVERAGES

Player—Position	G.	AB.	R.	H.	TB.	2B.	3B.	HR.	RBI.	B.A.	PO.	A.	E.	F.A.
Davis, ph	2	2	1	1	2	1	0	0	0	.500	0	0	0	.000
Carew, 1b	4	17	4	7	10	3	0	0	1	.412	34	1	0	1.000
Ford, rf	4	17	2	5	12	1	0	2	4	.294	6	0	1	.857
Lansford, 3b	4	17	2	5	5	0	0	0	3	.294	4	8	0	1.000
Miller, cf	4	16	2	4	4	0	0	0	0	.250	14	2	0	1.000
Downing, c	4	15	1	3	3	0	0	0	1	.200	27	0	0	1.000
Baylor, dh-lf	4	16	2	3	6	0	0	1	2	.188	4	0	0	1.000
Grich, 2b	4	13	0	2	3	1	0	0	2	.154	4	12	1	.941
Harlow, lf-ph	3	8	0	1	2	1	0	0	1	.125	6	0	0	1.000
Anderson, ss	4	11	0	1	1	0	0	0	0	.091	4	11	0	1.000
Thon, pr-ss	1	0	1	0	0	0	0	0	0	.000	0	0	0	.000
Barlow, p	1	0	0	0	0	0	0	0	0	.000	0	0	0	.000
Campaneris, ss	1	0	0	0	0	0	0	0	0	.000	0	0	0	.000
Clear, p	1	0	0	0	0	0	0	0	0	.000	0	0	0	.000
Knapp, p	1	0	0	0	0	0	0	0	0	.000	0	0	0	.000
LaRoche, p	1	0	0	0	0	0	0	0	0	.000	0	0	0	.000
Ryan, p	1	0	0	0	0	0	0	0	0	.000	0	0	0	.000
Tanana, p	1	0	0	0	0	0	0	0	0	.000	0	0	0	.000
Montague, p	2	0	0	0	0	0	0	0	0	.000	1	2	0	1.000
Aase, p	2	0	0	0	0	0	0	0	0	.000	0	1	0	1.000
Frost, p	2	0	0	0	0	0	0	0	0	.000	0	0	0	.000
Rettenmund, ph-dh	2	2	0	0	0	0	0	0	0	.000	0	0	0	.000
Clark, lf	1	3	0	0	0	0	0	0	0	.000	3	0	0	1.000
Totals	4	137	15	32	48	7	0	3	14	.234	107	37	2	.986

CALIFORNIA ANGELS' PITCHING RECORDS

Pitcher	G.	GS.	CG.	IP.	H.	R.	ER.	BB.	SO.	HB.	WP.	W.	L.	Pct.	ERA.
Barlow	1	0	0	1	0	0	0	0	0	0	0	0	0	.000	0.00
Ryan	1	1	0	7	4	3	1	3	8	0	1	0	0	.000	1.29
Aase	2	0	0	5	4	1	1	2	6	0	0	1	0	1.000	1.80
Tanana	1	1	0	5	6	2	2	2	3	1	0	0	0	.000	3.60
Clear	1	0	0	5⅓	4	3	3	2	2	0	1	0	0	.000	4.76
LaRoche	1	0	0	1⅓	2	1	1	1	1	0	0	0	0	.000	6.75
Knapp	1	1	0	2⅓	5	2	2	1	0	0	0	0	1	.000	7.71
Montague	2	0	0	4	4	4	4	2	2	0	0	0	1	.000	9.00
Frost	2	1	0	4½	8	10	9	5	1	0	1	0	1	.000	18.69
Totals	4	4	0	35⅔	37	26	23	18	24	1	3	1	3	.250	5.80

No shutouts or saves.

BALTIMORE ORIOLES' PITCHING RECORDS

Pitcher	G.	GS.	CG.	IP.	H.	R.	ER.	BB.	SO.	HB.	WP.	W.	L.	Pct.	ERA.
McGregor	1	1	1	9	6	0	0	1	4	0	0	1	0	1.000	0.00
Palmer	1	1	0	9	7	3	3	2	3	0	0	0	0	.000	3.00
D. Martinez	1	1	0	8⅓	8	3	3	0	4	0	0	0	0	.000	3.24
Flanagan	1	1	0	7	6	6	4	1	2	0	0	1	0	1.000	5.14
Stanhouse	3	0	0	3	5	3	2	3	0	0	0	1	1	.500	6.00
Totals	4	4	1	36⅓	32	15	12	7	13	0	0	3	1	.750	2.97

Shutout—McGregor. No saves.

COMPOSITE SCORE BY INNINGS

Baltimore	4	4	5	3	0	1	6	0	0	3 — 26
California	3	0	1	1	0	2	1	3	4	0 — 15

Sacrifice hit—Dauer.

Sacrifice flies—DeCinces 2, Grich, Downing, Singleton.

Stolen bases—Bumbry 2, Kelley 2, Lansford, Carew, Dempsey.

Caught stealing—Carew, Murray.

Double plays—Lansford, Grich and Carew 2; Miller and Carew; Anderson, Grich and Carew 2; Roenicke, Garcia and Dauer; Dauer and Murray; Miller and Downing; Smith, Garcia and Murray; Lansford and Carew; DeCinces and Murray; Garcia, Smith and Murray.

Left on bases—Baltimore 3, 6, 8, 6—23; California 5, 6, 6, 5—22.

Hit by pitcher—By Tanana (Roenicke).

Passed ball—Dempsey.

Balks—None.

Time of games—First game, 3:10; second game, 2:51; third game, 2:59; fourth game, 2:56.

Attendance—First game, 52,787; second game, 52,108; third game, 43,199; fourth game, 43,199.

Umpires—Barnett, Ford, Evans, Denkinger, Clark and Kosc.

Official scorers—Jim Henneman, Baltimore News-American; Tracy Ringolsby, Long Beach Independent Press-Telegram.

NATIONAL LEAGUE
Championship Series of 1979

	W.	L.	Pct.
Pittsburgh (East)	3	0	1.000
Cincinnati (West)	0	3	.000

Can you picture Willie Stargell searching through his locker like a man possessed?

As Willie tells the story, while the Pirates were at Cincinnati for the first two games of their three-game sweep of the National League Championship Series, someone broke into his locker and swiped his final batch of 100 gold cloth stars—those stars he awarded to his teammates for various accomplishments during the season.

"The bag came up missing and still is," lamented Stargell, after he was unanimously selected the Most Valuable Player in the Series for batting .455 with 13 total bases and six RBIs. "It's a dirty trick for someone to pull on us now.

"When I found out they were missing, I ordered 3,000 more. If I have a choice, the entire squad will get a star for this one."

Stargell's contributions were headline material in papers across the country: A three-run, 11th-inning homer that decided a 5-2 win in the opener; a single and double in the Pirates' 10-inning 3-2 triumph in Game 2; a homer and two-run double in the 7-1 clinching victory.

It was sweet revenge for the Pirates' dauntless 38-year-old captain and main inspirational force, even if he couldn't celebrate the conquest of the Reds by awarding stars to his teammates, because the Pirates had been swept by the Reds in the NL playoffs in 1970 and 1975.

After a 45-minute delay by rain at the start of Game 1, the Pirates, losers in eight of 12 games with the Reds in '79, bolted to a 2-0 lead in the third inning. Phil Garner sliced a homer to right field, Omar Moreno tripled on a drive that eluded the diving Dave Collins in right and Tim Foli contributed a sacrifice fly.

But the Reds rebounded with a pair in the fourth on a single by Dave Concepcion and a homer by George Foster off Pittsburgh starting pitcher John Candelaria.

The deadlock persisted until the top half of the 11th. For two innings in relief of starter Tom Seaver, righthander Tom Hume was in command. But Foli and Dave Parker singled before Stargell's first-pitch homer settled the issue and sent flocks of the 55,006 spectators streaming for the exits.

A single by Concepcion and walks to Foster and Johnny Bench gave Reds' diehards one last hope in their half, before Don Robinson fanned Ray Knight to end the threat.

After using five pitchers in the first game, Pittsburgh manager Chuck Tanner came right back with six hurlers for a 3-2 verdict in 10 innings in Game 2.

Controversy surrounded the victory, however.

With the score tied 1-1 in the Pirates' half of the fifth, Garner lashed a liner to right field. The Reds' Collins dived for the ball, but second base umpire Frank Pulli ruled a trap. Television replays showed that Collins had made a clean grab.

Garner advanced on a sacrifice by pitcher Jim Bibby and scored on Foli's double, giving the Pirates a 2-1 lead.

The Reds knotted the score with one out in the ninth on a pinch-double by Hector Cruz and another two-bagger by Collins.

The rally continued when Dave Roberts walked Joe Morgan. Don Robinson was summoned by Tanner and proceeded to strike out Concepcion and retire Foster on a groundout.

Then Moreno and Parker singled around a Foli sacrifice in the 10th to make Robinson the winner and saddle Doug Bair with the loss.

A 30-minute rain delay preceded Game 3 as the scene shifted upriver to Pittsburgh on October 5.

Robinson, who saved Game 1, was extremely impressive as he set down five straight batters in the second game.

While Stargell was providing the slugging feats, the Pirates' pitching staff was limiting the once-feared Cincinnati offense to five runs in three games, climaxed by Bert Blyleven's route-going performance, only his fifth complete game of the year and first since August 15.

Blyleven put to rest frequent reports that he couldn't win the big games by becoming the only starter to go the distance. He scattered eight hits and fanned nine, losing his shutout bid in the sixth inning when Bench tagged him for a home run.

And the Bucs' bats went to work early, getting single runs in the first and second and two runs each in the third and fourth. Stargell and Bill Madlock socked homers in the third.

GAME OF TUESDAY, OCTOBER 2, AT CINCINNATI (N)

Pittsburgh	AB.	R.	H.	RBI.	PO.	A.
Moreno, cf	5	1	1	0	2	0
Foli, ss	4	0	2	1	1	6
Alexander, pr	0	1	0	0	0	0
B. Robinson, lf	0	0	0	0	0	0
Parker, rf	4	1	1	0	2	0
Stargell, 1b	4	1	1	3	17	0
Milner, lf	5	0	0	0	1	0
Stennett, 2b	0	0	0	0	0	1
Madlock, 3b	5	0	2	0	0	4
Ott, c	5	0	1	0	7	2
Garner, 2b-ss	4	1	2	1	3	5
Candelaria, p	3	0	0	0	0	0
Romo, p	0	0	0	0	0	0
Tekulve, p	0	0	0	0	0	1
Easler, ph	1	0	0	0	0	0
Jackson, p	1	0	0	0	0	0
D. Robinson, p	0	0	0	0	0	0
Totals	41	5	10	5	33	19

Cincinnati	AB.	R.	H.	RBI.	PO.	A.
Collins, rf	5	0	2	0	3	0
Morgan, 2b	4	0	0	0	3	4
Concepcion, ss	5	1	2	0	1	6
Foster, lf	3	1	1	2	1	0
Bench, c	3	0	2	0	7	0
Knight, 3b	5	0	0	0	0	1
Driessen, 1b	4	0	0	0	14	0
Cruz, cf	4	0	0	0	3	0
Seaver, p	2	0	0	0	0	0
Auerbach, ph	1	0	0	0	0	0
Hume, p	1	0	0	0	0	2
Tomlin, p	0	0	0	0	1	0
Totals	37	2	7	2	33	13

Pittsburgh	0	0	2	0	0	0	0	0	0	0	3 – 5
Cincinnati	0	0	0	2	0	0	0	0	0	0	0 – 2

Pittsburgh	IP.	H.	R.	ER.	BB.	SO.
Candelaria	7	5	2	2	1	4
Romo	⅓	1	0	0	1	1
Tekulve	1⅔	0	0	0	1	0
Jackson (Winner)	1⅔	1	0	0	1	2
D. Robinson (Save)	⅓	0	0	0	1	1

Cincinnati	IP.	H.	R.	ER.	BB.	SO.
Seaver	8	5	2	2	2	5
Hume (Loser)	2⅓	5	3	3	0	1
Tomlin	⅔	0	0	0	1	1

Errors—None. Double plays—Pittsburgh 2, Cincinnati 1. Left on bases—Pittsburgh 7, Cincinnati 7. Three-base hits—Bench, Moreno. Home runs—Garner, Foster, Stargell. Stolen bases—Madlock 2, Collins. Caught stealing—Bench. Sacrifice fly—Foli. Umpires—Kibler, Montague, Dale, Pulli, Stello and Quick. Time—3:14. Attendance—55,006.

GAME OF WEDNESDAY, OCTOBER 3, AT CINCINNATI

Pittsburgh	AB.	R.	H.	RBI.	PO.	A.
Moreno, cf	5	1	2	0	4	0
Foli, ss	4	1	2	1	2	1
Parker, rf	5	0	2	1	4	0
Stargell, 1b	3	0	2	0	6	1
Milner, lf	2	0	0	0	0	0
B. Robinson, lf	2	0	0	0	3	0
Madlock, 3b	5	0	0	1	1	0
Ott, c	4	0	2	0	9	1
Garner, 2b	4	1	1	0	1	3
Bibby, p	0	0	0	0	0	1
Jackson, p	0	0	0	0	0	0
Romo, p	0	0	0	0	0	0
Tekulve, p	1	0	0	0	0	0
Roberts, p	0	0	0	0	0	0
D. Robinson, p	0	0	0	0	0	0
Totals	35	3	11	3	30	7

Cincinnati	AB.	R.	H.	RBI.	PO.	A.
Collins, rf	5	0	1	1	0	0
Morgan, 2b	3	0	0	0	6	6
Concepcion, ss	5	0	2	0	1	8
Foster, lf	3	0	1	0	3	2
Bench, c	5	0	0	0	5	1
Driessen, 1b	4	1	1	0	12	0
Knight, 3b	5	0	2	0	0	2
Geronimo, cf	3	0	0	0	3	0
Pastore, p	0	0	0	1	0	0
Spilman, ph	1	0	0	0	0	0
Tomlin, p	0	0	0	0	0	0
Hume, p	0	0	0	0	0	0
Cruz, ph	1	1	1	0	0	0
Bair, p	0	0	0	0	0	1
Totals	35	2	8	2	30	20

Pittsburgh	0	0	0	1	1	0	0	0	0	1 – 3
Cincinnati	0	1	0	0	0	0	0	0	1	0 – 2

Pittsburgh	IP.	H.	R.	ER.	BB.	SO.
Bibby	7	4	1	1	4	5
Jackson	⅓	0	0	0	0	0
Romo	0*	2	0	0	0	0
Tekulve	1	2	1	1	1	2
Roberts	0†	0	0	0	1	0
D. Robinson (Winner)	1⅔	0	0	0	0	2

Cincinnati	IP.	H.	R.	ER.	BB.	SO.
Pastore	7	7	2	2	3	1
Tomlin	⅔	1	0	0	0	1
Hume	1⅓	1	0	0	0	1
Bair (Loser)	1	2	1	1	1	0

*Pitched to two batters in eighth.
†Pitched to one batter in ninth.

Errors—None. Double play—Cincinnati 1. Left on bases—Pittsburgh 9, Cincinnati 11. Two-base hits—Concepcion, Foli, Stargell, Cruz, Collins. Stolen bases—Morgan, Knight, Collins, Caught stealing—Concepcion. Sacrifice hits—Bibby 2, Geronimo, Foli. Sacrifice fly—Pastore. Wild pitch—Tekulve. Umpires—Montague, Dale, Pulli, Stello, Quick and Kibler. Time—3:24. Attendance—55,000.

GAME OF FRIDAY, OCTOBER 5, AT PITTSBURGH

Cincinnati	AB.	R.	H.	RBI.	PO.	A.
Collins, rf	4	0	2	0	2	0
Morgan, 2b	4	0	0	0	3	1
Concepcion, ss	4	0	2	0	1	0
Foster, lf	4	0	0	0	2	0
Bench, c	4	1	1	1	5	1
Driessen, 1b	4	0	0	0	6	0
Knight, 3b	4	0	2	0	0	2
Geronimo, cf	4	0	1	0	5	0
LaCoss, p	0	0	0	0	0	1
Norman, p	1	0	0	0	0	0
Leibrandt, p	0	0	0	0	0	0
Auerbach, ph	1	0	0	0	0	0
Soto, p	0	0	0	0	0	0
Spilman, ph	1	0	0	0	0	0
Tomlin, p	0	0	0	0	0	1
Hume, p	0	0	0	0	0	0
Totals	35	1	8	1	24	6

Pittsburgh	AB.	R.	H.	RBI.	PO.	A.
Moreno, cf	2	1	0	0	1	0
Foli, ss	4	0	0	1	0	2
Parker, rf	3	1	1	1	3	0
Stargell, 1b	4	1	2	3	9	1
Milner, lf	2	0	0	0	0	0
B. Robinson, lf	1	0	0	0	0	0
Madlock, 3b	2	1	1	1	0	3
Ott, c	4	0	0	0	9	0
Garner, 2b	4	2	2	0	4	1
Blyleven, p	3	1	1	0	1	1
Totals	29	7	7	6	27	8

Cincinnati	0	0	0	0	0	1	0	0	0 – 1
Pittsburgh	1	1	2	2	0	0	0	1	x – 7

Cincinnati	IP.	H.	R.	ER.	BB.	SO.
LaCoss (Loser)	1⅔	1	2	2	4	0
Norman	2	4	4	4	1	1
Leibrandt	⅓	0	0	0	0	0
Soto	2	0	0	0	0	1
Tomlin	1⅔	2	1	0	1	1
Hume	⅓	0	0	0	0	0

Pittsburgh	IP.	H.	R.	ER.	BB.	SO.
Blyleven (Winner)	9	8	1	1	0	9

Error—Geronimo. Left on bases—Cincinnati 7, Pittsburgh 8. Two-base hits—Knight, Stargell. Three-base hit—Garner. Home runs—Stargell, Madlock, Bench. Stolen bases—Moreno, Parker. Sacrifice hits—Moreno, Blyleven. Sacrifice flies—Parker, Foli. Balk—Leibrandt. Umpires—Dale, Pulli, Stello, Quick, Kibler and Montague. Time—2:45. Attendance—42,240.

PITTSBURGH PIRATES' BATTING AND FIELDING AVERAGES

Player—Position	G.	AB.	R.	H.	TB.	2B.	3B.	HR.	RBI.	B.A.	PO.	A.	E.	F.A.
Stargell, 1b	3	11	2	5	13	2	0	2	6	.455	32	2	0	1.000
Garner, 2b-ss	3	12	4	5	10	0	1	1	1	.417	8	9	0	1.000
Foli, ss	3	12	1	4	5	1	0	0	3	.333	3	9	0	1.000
Parker, rf	3	12	2	4	4	0	0	0	2	.333	9	0	0	1.000
Blyleven, p	1	3	1	1	1	0	0	0	0	.333	1	1	0	1.000
Madlock, 3b	3	12	1	3	6	0	0	1	2	.250	7	7	0	1.000
Moreno, cf	3	12	3	3	5	0	1	0	0	.250	7	0	0	1.000
Ott, c	3	13	0	3	3	0	0	0	0	.231	25	3	0	1.000
Alexander, pr	1	0	1	0	0	0	0	0	0	.000	0	0	0	.000
Bibby, p	1	0	0	0	0	0	0	0	0	.000	0	1	0	1.000
Stennett, 2b	1	0	0	0	0	0	0	0	0	.000	0	0	0	.000
Roberts, p	1	0	0	0	0	0	0	0	0	.000	0	0	0	.000
D. Robinson, p	2	0	0	0	0	0	0	0	0	.000	0	0	0	.000
Romo, p	2	0	0	0	0	0	0	0	0	.000	0	0	0	.000
Easler, ph	1	1	0	0	0	0	0	0	0	.000	0	1	0	1.000
Tekulve, p	2	1	0	0	0	0	0	0	0	.000	0	0	0	.000
Jackson, p	2	1	0	0	0	0	0	0	0	.000	0	0	0	.000
Candelaria, p	1	3	0	0	0	0	0	0	0	.000	3	0	0	1.000
B. Robinson, lf	3	3	0	0	0	0	0	0	0	.000	1	0	0	1.000
Milner, lf	3	9	0	0	0	0	0	0	0	.000	1	0	0	1.000
Totals	3	105	15	28	47	3	2	4	14	.267	90	34	0	1.000

CINCINNATI REDS' BATTING AND FIELDING AVERAGES

Player—Position	G.	AB.	R.	H.	TB.	2B.	3B.	HR.	RBI.	B.A.	PO.	A.	E.	F.A.
Concepcion, ss	3	14	1	6	7	1	0	0	0	.429	3	14	0	1.000
Collins, rf	3	14	0	5	6	1	0	0	1	.357	5	0	0	1.000
Knight, 3b	3	14	0	4	5	1	0	0	0	.286	0	5	0	1.000
Bench, c	3	12	1	3	8	0	1	1	1	.250	17	2	0	1.000
Foster, lf	3	10	1	2	5	0	0	1	2	.200	6	2	0	1.000
Cruz, cf-ph	2	5	1	1	2	1	0	0	0	.200	3	0	0	1.000
Geronimo, cf	2	7	0	1	1	0	0	0	0	.143	8	0	1	.889
Driessen, 1b	3	12	1	1	1	0	0	0	0	.083	32	0	0	1.000
Pastore, p	1	0	0	0	0	0	0	0	1	.000	0	0	0	.000
Bair, p	1	0	0	0	0	0	0	0	0	.000	0	1	0	1.000
LaCoss, p	1	0	0	0	0	0	0	0	0	.000	0	1	0	1.000
Leibrandt, p	1	0	0	0	0	0	0	0	0	.000	0	0	0	.000
Soto, p	1	0	0	0	0	0	0	0	0	.000	0	0	0	.000
Tomlin, p	3	0	0	0	0	0	0	0	0	.000	1	1	0	1.000
Norman, p	1	1	0	0	0	0	0	0	0	.000	0	0	0	.000
Hume, p	3	1	0	0	0	0	0	0	0	.000	0	2	0	1.000
Seaver, p	1	2	0	0	0	0	0	0	0	.000	0	0	0	.000
Auerbach, ph	2	2	0	0	0	0	0	0	0	.000	0	0	0	.000
Spilman, ph	2	2	0	0	0	0	0	0	0	.000	0	0	0	.000
Morgan, 2b	3	11	0	0	0	0	0	0	0	.000	12	11	0	1.000
Totals	3	107	5	23	35	4	1	2	5	.215	87	39	1	.992

PITTSBURGH PIRATES' PITCHING RECORDS

Pitcher	G.	GS.	CG.	IP.	H.	R.	ER.	BB.	SO.	HB.	WP.	W.	L.	Pct.	ERA.
D. Robinson	2	0	0	2	0	0	0	1	3	0	0	1	0	1.000	0.00
Jackson	2	0	0	2	1	0	0	1	2	0	0	1	0	1.000	0.00
Romo	2	0	0	⅓	3	0	0	1	1	0	0	0	0	.000	0.00
Roberts	1	0	0	0	0	0	0	1	0	0	0	0	0	.000	0.00
Blyleven	1	1	1	9	8	1	1	0	9	0	0	1	0	1.000	1.00
Bibby	1	1	0	7	4	1	1	4	5	0	0	0	0	.000	1.29
Candelaria	1	1	0	7	5	2	2	1	4	0	0	0	0	.000	2.57
Tekulve	2	0	0	2⅔	2	1	1	2	2	0	1	0	0	.000	3.38
Totals	3	3	1	30	23	5	5	11	26	0	1	3	0	1.000	1.50

No shutouts. Save—D. Robinson.

CINCINNATI REDS' PITCHING RECORDS

Pitcher	G.	GS.	CG.	IP.	H.	R.	ER.	BB.	SO.	HB.	WP.	W.	L.	Pct.	ERA.
Tomlin	3	0	0	3	3	1	0	2	3	0	0	0	0	.000	0.00
Soto	1	0	0	2	0	0	0	0	1	0	0	0	0	.000	0.00
Leibrandt	1	0	0	⅓	0	0	0	0	0	0	0	0	0	.000	0.00
Seaver	1	1	0	8	5	2	2	2	5	0	0	0	0	.000	2.25
Pastore	1	1	0	7	7	2	2	3	1	0	0	0	0	.000	2.57
Hume	3	0	0	4	6	3	3	0	2	0	0	0	1	.000	6.75
Bair	1	0	0	1	2	1	1	1	0	0	0	0	1	.000	9.00
LaCoss	1	1	0	1⅔	1	2	2	4	0	0	0	0	1	.000	10.80
Norman	1	0	0	2	4	4	4	1	1	0	0	0	0	.000	18.00
Totals	3	3	0	29	28	15	14	13	13	0	0	0	3	.000	4.34

No shutouts or saves.

COMPOSITE SCORE BY INNINGS

Pittsburgh	1	1	4	3	1	0	0	1	0	1	3	– 15
Cincinnati	0	1	0	2	0	1	0	0	1	0	0	– 5

Sacrifice hits—Bibby 2, Geronimo, Foli, Moreno, Blyleven.

Sacrifice flies—Foli 2, Pastore, Parker.

Stolen bases—Madlock 2, Collins 2, Morgan, Knight, Moreno, Parker.

Caught stealing—Bench, Concepcion.

Double plays—Concepcion, Morgan and Driessen 2; Garner, Foli and Stargell; Madlock, Garner and Stargell.

Left on bases—Pittsburgh 7, 9, 8—24; Cincinnati 7, 11, 7—25.

Hit by pitcher—None.

Passed balls—None.

Balk—Leibrandt.

Time of games—First game, 3:14; second game, 3:24; third game, 2:45.

Attendance—First game, 55,006; second game, 55,000; third game, 42,240.

Umpires—Kibler, Montague, Dale, Pulli, Stello and Quick.

Official scorers—Earl Lawson, Cincinnati Post; Dan Donovan, Pittsburgh Press.

AMERICAN LEAGUE
Championship Series of 1980

	W.	L.	Pct.
Kansas City (West)	3	0	1.000
New York (East)	0	3	.000

The Kansas City Royals were driven by the idea of beating the New York Yankees. Yes, beating those same Big Apple brutes who had sent the Royals away unhappy with playoff losses in 1976, '77 and '78.

The idea of beating the Yankees was almost haunting to the Royals, even to a player like THE SPORTING NEWS 1980 American League Fireman of the Year Dan Quisenberry, who wasn't with Kansas City during those second-best seasons.

"I thought to myself, 'Hey, you know all the years the Royals had short relief problems and they blew leads—that's how they lost all those playoff games. You're the guy who is supposed to turn all that around this year. What are you walking all these guys for?' " Quisenberry commented before he set down the Yankees to extinguish an eight-inning threat and preserve a 4-2 victory in Game 3, enabling the Royals to sweep the A.L. Championship Series from the Yanks.

"Our fans think we've already won the World Series by beating the Yankees," said George Brett, whose towering three-run homer into the third tier of seats at Yankee Stadium off ace reliever Rich Gossage erased a 2-1 deficit and provided the winning touch to the third game triumph.

Gossage, unhittable for the final eight weeks of the season, entered the contest after Tommy John yielded a two-out double by Willie Wilson. U.L. Washington greeted Gossage by beating out an infield chopper.

The stage was set. As Gossage put it: "It was power versus power."

In one classic swipe of the bat, Brett slayed the giants.

The Royals didn't begin the series with the glee that climaxed it. In fact, there was doubt in the mind of their starting pitcher Larry Gura after Rick Cerone and Lou Piniella hit back-to-back homers for a 2-0 lead in the second inning of Game 1.

Gura didn't exactly dazzle the Yanks but he did manage to scatter 10 hits and pitch the Royals to a 7-2 verdict and a one-game edge.

Frank White began the Kansas City comeback with a two-out, two-run double in the second and Willie Aikens sent two more runs home with a third-inning single. Brett blasted a homer in the seventh and Wilson doubled in the final two tallies in the eighth.

The Royals put together four straight hits for all their runs in the third inning and shaded the Yanks, 3-2, in Game 2. Darrell Porter and White singled before Wilson cleared the sacks with a triple and Washington completed the outburst with a two-base hit.

The Yankees had an inside-the-park homer by Graig Nettles and a run-scoring double by Willie Randolph for their only runs.

However, the most talked about New York play occurred in the eighth when Randolph was thrown out at the plate attempting to score from first on a two-out double by Bob Watson. Blustery Yankees Owner George Steinbrenner wanted third base coach Mike Ferraro fired. The consensus: when left fielder Wilson overthrew the relay man the runner had to score. Brett, backing up Washington, snared the throw and gunned Randolph out at the plate with a perfect peg.

White, who was voted MVP of the series with his 5-for-11 and several outstanding plays in the field, staked the Royals to a 1-0 lead in Game 3 before the Yanks rallied for two runs in the sixth—one coming off starter Paul Splittorff and the other coming off Quisenberry.

Center stage was set for the Brett-Gossage confrontation.

"We all kept hollering, 'It's going to happen, it's going to happen,' " said White. "We just knew they couldn't keep getting George (0 for his last 7) out like that."

The rest is history.

GAME OF WEDNESDAY, OCTOBER 8, AT KANSAS CITY

New York	AB.	R.	H.	RBI.	PO.	A.	Kansas City	AB.	R.	H.	RBI.	PO.	A.
Randolph, 2b	5	0	2	0	0	5	Wilson, lf	5	0	1	2	2	0
Dent, ss	4	0	2	0	3	3	Washington, ss	4	0	1	0	1	3
Watson, 1b	4	0	2	0	11	2	G. Brett, 3b	3	2	2	1	1	2
Jackson, rf	4	0	0	0	1	0	McRae, dh	3	0	0	0	0	0
Soderholm, dh	4	0	1	0	0	0	Otis, cf	4	2	2	0	5	0
Cerone, c	4	1	1	1	6	1	Wathan, rf	1	1	0	0	4	0
Piniella, lf	3	1	1	1	1	0	Hurdle, rf	0	0	0	0	0	0
Rodriguez, 3b	4	0	1	0	1	2	Aikens, 1b	4	0	1	2	7	0
Brown, cf	4	0	0	0	1	0	LaCock, 1b	0	0	0	0	0	0
Guidry, p	0	0	0	0	0	1	Porter, c	4	1	0	0	5	0
Davis, p	0	0	0	0	0	2	White, 2b	4	1	3	2	2	3
Underwood, p	0	0	0	0	0	1	Gura, p	0	0	0	0	0	1
Totals	36	2	10	2	24	17	Totals	32	7	10	7	27	9

New York	0	2	0	0	0	0	0	0	0 – 2
Kansas City	0	2	2	0	0	0	1	2	x – 7

New York	IP.	H.	R.	ER.	BB.	SO.
Guidry (Loser)	3	5	4	4	4	2
Davis	4	3	1	1	1	3
Underwood	1	2	2	0	0	2
Kansas City	IP.	H.	R.	ER.	BB.	SO.
Gura (Winner)	9	10	2	2	1	4

Game-winning RBI—Aikens.

Error—Watson. Double play—New York 1. Left on bases—New York 9, Kansas City 7. Two-base hits—Randolph, G. Brett, Rodriguez, White, Watson, Otis, Wilson. Home runs—Cerone, Piniella, G. Brett. Stolen bases—Otis, White. Sacrifice hit—Dent. Hit by pitcher—By Davis (McRae). Wild pitch—Guidry. Umpires—Palermo, Brinkman, McCoy, Haller, Kaiser and Maloney. Time—3:00. Attendance—42,598.

GAME OF THURSDAY, OCTOBER 9, AT KANSAS CITY (N)

New York	AB.	R.	H.	RBI.	PO.	A.	Kansas City	AB.	R.	H.	RBI.	PO.	A.
Randolph, 2b	4	0	2	1	1	1	Wilson, lf	3	1	1	2	2	1
Murcer, dh	4	0	0	0	0	0	Washington, ss	3	0	1	1	3	1
Watson, 1b	4	0	1	0	6	2	G. Brett, 3b	4	0	0	0	0	3
Jackson, rf	4	0	2	0	2	0	McRae, dh	3	0	0	0	0	0
Gamble, lf	4	0	0	0	1	0	Otis, cf	4	0	1	0	3	0
Cerone, c	4	0	2	0	4	1	Wathan, rf	3	0	0	0	3	0
Nettles, 3b	4	1	1	1	0	1	Hurdle, rf	0	0	0	0	0	0
Dent, ss	3	0	0	0	3	2	Aikens, 1b	3	0	0	0	7	0
Brown, cf	2	1	0	0	5	0	Porter, c	3	1	1	0	8	1
May, p	0	0	0	0	2	2	White, 2b	3	1	2	0	1	2
							Leonard, p	0	0	0	0	0	0
							Quisenberry, p	0	0	0	0	0	0
Totals	33	2	8	2	24	9	Totals	29	3	6	3	27	8

New York	0	0	0		0	2	0		0	0	0 – 2
Kansas City	0	0	3		0	0	0		0	0	x – 3

New York	IP.	H.	R.	ER.	BB.	SO.
May (Loser)	8	6	3	3	3	4

Kansas City	IP.	H.	R.	ER.	BB.	SO.
Leonard (Winner)	8*	7	2	2	1	8
Quisenberry (Save)	1	1	0	0	0	0

*Pitched to one batter in ninth.

Game-winning RBI—Wilson.

Errors—None. Double play—Kansas City 1. Left on bases—New York 5, Kansas City 5. Two-base hits—Washington, Randolph, Watson. Three-base hit—Wilson. Home run—Nettles. Stolen base—Otis. Umpires—Brinkman, McCoy, Haller, Kaiser, Maloney and Palermo. Time—2:51. Attendance—42,633.

GAME OF FRIDAY, OCTOBER 10, AT NEW YORK (N)

Kansas City	AB.	R.	H.	RBI.	PO.	A.	New York	AB.	R.	H.	RBI.	PO.	A.
Wilson, lf	5	1	2	0	2	0	Randolph, 2b	4	0	1	0	1	3
Washington, ss	4	1	2	0	1	3	Dent, ss	4	0	0	0	3	7
G. Brett, 3b	4	1	1	3	1	2	Watson, 1b	4	0	3	0	4	1
McRae, dh	4	0	2	0	0	0	Jackson, rf	3	1	1	0	2	0
Otis, cf	4	0	1	0	3	0	Soderholm, dh	2	0	0	0	0	0
Aikens, 1b	4	0	3	0	8	1	Gamble, ph-dh	1	1	1	0	0	0
Porter, c	3	0	0	0	4	0	Cerone, c	4	0	1	1	4	2
Hurdle, rf	2	0	0	0	1	0	Piniella, lf	2	0	0	0	4	0
Wathan, ph-rf	2	0	0	0	0	0	Spencer, ph	1	0	0	0	0	0
White, 2b	4	1	1	1	6	5	Lefebvre, lf	0	0	0	0	0	0
Splittorff, p	0	0	0	0	0	1	Rodriguez, 3b	2	0	1	0	1	0
Quisenberry, p	0	0	0	0	1	0	Nettles, ph-3b	2	0	0	0	0	1
							Brown, cf	4	0	0	0	1	0
							John, p	0	0	0	0	0	1
							Gossage, p	0	0	0	0	0	0
							Underwood, p	0	0	0	0	0	1
Totals	36	4	12	4	27	12	Totals	33	2	8	1	27	16

Kansas City	0	0	0		0	1	0		3	0	0 – 4
New York	0	0	0		0	0	2		0	0	0 – 2

Kansas City	IP.	H.	R.	ER.	BB.	SO.
Splittorff	5⅓	5	1	1	2	3
Quisenberry (Winner)	3⅔	3	1	0	2	1

New York	IP.	H.	R.	ER.	BB.	SO.
John	6⅔	8	2	2	1	3
Gossage (Loser)	⅓	3	2	2	0	0
Underwood	2	1	0	0	0	1

Game-winning RBI—G. Brett.

Error—White. Double plays—Kansas City 2, New York 1. Left on bases—Kansas City 6, New York 8. Two-base hits—Watson, Jackson, Wilson. Three-base hit—Watson. Home runs—White, G. Brett. Wild pitch—John. Balk—Splittorff. Umpires—McCoy, Haller, Kaiser, Maloney, Palermo and Brinkman. Time—2:59. Attendance—56,588.

KANSAS CITY ROYALS' BATTING AND FIELDING AVERAGES

Player—Position	G.	AB.	R.	H.	TB.	2B.	3B.	HR.	RBI.	B.A.	PO.	A.	E.	F.A.
White, 2b	3	11	3	6	10	1	0	1	3	.545	9	10	1	.950
Washington, ss	3	11	1	4	5	1	0	0	1	.364	5	7	0	1.000
Aikens, 1b	3	11	0	4	4	0	0	2	2	.364	22	1	0	1.000
Otis, cf.	3	12	2	4	5	1	0	0	0	.333	11	0	0	1.000
Wilson, lf	3	13	2	4	8	2	1	0	4	.308	6	1	0	1.000
G. Brett, 3b	3	11	3	3	10	1	0	2	4	.273	2	7	0	1.000
McRae, dh	3	10	0	2	2	0	0	0	0	.200	0	0	0	.000
Porter, c	3	10	2	1	1	0	0	0	0	.100	17	1	0	1.000
Quisenberry, p	2	0	0	0	0	0	0	0	0	.000	1	0	0	1.000
Gura, p.	1	0	0	0	0	0	0	0	0	.000	0	1	0	1.000
LaCock, 1b	1	0	0	0	0	0	0	0	0	.000	0	0	0	.000
Leonard, p	1	0	0	0	0	0	0	0	0	.000	0	0	0	.000
Splittorff, p	1	0	0	0	0	0	0	0	0	.000	0	1	0	1.000
Hurdle, rf	3	2	0	0	0	0	0	0	0	.000	1	0	0	1.000
Wathan, rf-ph	3	6	1	0	0	0	0	0	0	.000	7	0	0	1.000
Totals	3	97	14	28	45	6	1	3	14	.289	81	29	1	.991

NEW YORK YANKEES' BATTING AND FIELDING AVERAGES

Player—Position	G.	AB.	R.	H.	TB.	2B.	3B.	HR.	RBI.	B.A.	PO.	A.	E.	F.A.
Watson, 1b	3	12	0	6	11	3	1	0	0	.500	28	5	1	.971
Randolph, 2b	3	13	0	5	7	2	0	0	1	.385	2	9	0	1.000
Cerone, c	3	12	1	4	7	0	0	1	2	.333	14	4	0	1.000
Rodriguez, 3b	2	6	0	2	3	1	0	0	0	.333	2	2	0	1.000
Jackson, rf	3	11	1	3	4	1	0	0	0	.273	5	0	0	1.000
Piniella, lf	2	5	1	1	4	0	0	1	1	.200	5	0	0	1.000
Gamble, lf-ph-dh	2	5	1	1	1	0	0	0	0	.200	1	0	0	1.000
Dent, ss	3	11	0	2	2	0	0	0	0	.182	9	12	0	1.000
Nettles, 3b-ph	2	6	1	1	4	0	0	1	1	.167	0	2	0	1.000
Soderholm, dh	2	6	0	1	1	0	0	0	0	.167	0	0	0	.000
Underwood, p	2	0	0	0	0	0	0	0	0	.000	0	2	0	1.000
Davis, p	1	0	0	0	0	0	0	0	0	.000	0	2	0	1.000
Gossage, p	1	0	0	0	0	0	0	0	0	.000	0	0	0	.000
Guidry, p	1	0	0	0	0	0	0	0	0	.000	0	1	0	1.000
John, p	1	0	0	0	0	0	0	0	0	.000	0	1	0	1.000
Lefebvre, lf	1	0	0	0	0	0	0	0	0	.000	0	0	0	.000
May, p	1	0	0	0	0	0	0	0	0	.000	2	2	0	1.000
Spencer, ph	1	1	0	0	0	0	0	0	0	.000	0	0	0	.000
Murcer, dh	1	4	0	0	0	0	0	0	0	.000	0	0	0	.000
Brown, cf	3	10	1	0	0	0	0	0	0	.000	7	0	0	1.000
Totals	3	102	6	26	44	7	1	3	5	.255	75	42	1	.992

KANSAS CITY ROYALS' PITCHING RECORDS

Pitcher	G.	GS.	CG.	IP.	H.	R.	ER.	BB.	SO.	HB.	WP.	W.	L.	Pct.	ERA.
Quisenberry	2	0	0	4⅔	4	1	0	2	1	0	0	1	0	1.000	0.00
Splittorff	1	1	0	5⅓	5	1	1	2	3	0	0	0	0	.000	1.69
Gura	1	1	1	9	10	2	2	1	4	0	0	1	0	1.000	2.00
Leonard	1	1	0	8	7	2	2	1	8	0	0	1	0	1.000	2.25
Totals	3	3	1	27	26	6	5	6	16	0	0	3	0	1.000	1.67

No shutouts. Save—Quisenberry.

NEW YORK YANKEES' PITCHING RECORDS

Pitcher	G.	GS.	CG.	IP.	H.	R.	ER.	BB.	SO.	HB.	WP.	W.	L.	Pct.	ERA.
Underwood	2	0	0	3	3	2	0	3	0	0	0	0	0	.000	0.00
Davis	1	0	0	4	3	1	1	3	1	0	0	0	0	.000	2.25
John	1	1	0	6⅔	8	2	2	1	3	0	1	0	0	.000	2.70
May	1	1	1	8	6	3	3	3	4	0	0	0	1	.000	3.38
Guidry	1	1	0	3	5	4	4	4	2	0	1	0	1	.000	12.00
Gossage	1	0	0	⅓	3	2	2	0	0	0	0	0	1	.000	54.00
Totals	3	3	1	25	28	14	12	9	15	1	2	0	3	.000	4.32

No shutouts or saves.

COMPOSITE SCORE BY INNINGS

Kansas City	0	2	5	0	1	0	4	2	0 —	14
New York	0	2	0	0	2	2	0	0	0 —	6

Game-winning RBIs—Aikens, Wilson, G. Brett.
Sacrifice hit—Dent.
Sacrifice flies—None.
Stolen bases—Otis 2, White.
Caught stealing—McRae 3, Washington, Otis.
Double plays—Randolph, Dent and Watson; White, Washington and Aikens; Dent, Randolph and Watson; Splittorff, White and Aikens; Washington and White.
Left on bases—Kansas City 7, 5, 6—18; New York 9, 5, 8—22.
Hit by pitcher—By Davis (McRae).
Passed balls—None.
Balk—Splittorff.
Time of games—First game, 3:00; second game, 2:51; third game, 2:59.
Attendance—First game, 42,598; second game, 42,633; third game, 56,588.
Umpires—Palermo, Brinkman, McCoy, Haller, Kaiser and Maloney.
Official scorers—Red Foley, New York Daily News; Don Pfannenstiel, Independence (Mo.) Examiner.

NATIONAL LEAGUE
Championship Series of 1980

	W.	L.	Pct.
Philadelphia (East)	3	2	.600
Houston (West)	2	3	.400

The 1980 National League Championship Series had everything anyone could ever hope for. It had controversy. It had rallies. It had high-drama. It had more rallies. It had heartbreak. Most of all, it had two teams that wouldn't give up.

Not until Garry Maddox cradled that final fly ball by Enos Cabell in the 10th inning of the fifth game October 12 did the Philadelphia Phillies finally gain an edge for an 8-7 victory and a three games to two elimination of the West Division champion Houston Astros.

That Maddox would catch the final out and drive in the winning run with a 10th inning double to center field was poetic justice for the Gold Glove-winning center fielder. It was Maddox who dropped a routine fly ball by Bill Russell which set the stage for the Dodgers to beat the Phillies and capture the 1978 Championship Series. Adding fuel to the fire, there were two fly balls in San Diego in August and another on September 28 against Montreal which caused Garry to be benched for the final seven games of the regular season.

"I can't begin to tell you how I feel right now," said Maddox, whose two-base hit plated the doubling Del Unser to ice a see-saw decision and send the Phillies to the World Series for the first time since 1950. "This pennant is one of the most exciting things to ever happen to me. It has been a long time coming for me, my teammates and the fans of Philadelphia."

The Phillies rebounded from a 1-0 deficit in the first game when Greg Luzinski slammed a two-run homer to left field in the seventh inning and Greg Gross plated Maddox with a pinch-single in the eighth for a 3-1 verdict.

The Phils were on the threshold of a second consecutive victory at Veterans Stadium after Steve Carlton and Tug McGraw had collaborated in the opener. However, Bake McBride held up at third base on a single by Lonnie Smith, loading the bases, in a controversial play with the score tied, 3-3, in the ninth inning. Third base coach Lee Elia held up his arms to stop McBride and then motioned feverishly to send McBride when Smith's looper fell safely in right field. Houston reliever Frank LaCorte slammed the door by fanning Manny Trillo and getting Maddox on a foul pop.

The Astros rallied with a four-run outburst in the 10th inning to take a 7-4 decision, sending the series to Houston tied at one game apiece.

Terry Puhl opened the 10th with a single. After a sacrifice by Cabell and an intentional walk to Joe Morgan, Puhl scored on a single by Jose Cruz. Rafael Landestoy, running for Morgan, beat a throw home on a grounder to shortstop Larry Bowa by Cesar Cedeno before Dave Bergman capped the outburst with a two-run triple.

Joe Niekro, Houston's two-time 20-game winner, and injury-plagued Larry Christenson of the Phillies spun zeroes at one another in Game 3. The

Phils fired 10 blanks at Niekro while Christenson was shutting out the Astros for six frames and McGraw for three more.

In the 11th, Morgan crashed a leadoff triple and Cruz and Art Howe were walked intentionally, before Dennis Walling's sacrifice fly scored pinch-runner Landestoy and made a winner of Dave Smith for one inning of work.

The victory was costly to the Astros, however, as outfielder Cedeno suffered a compound dislocation of the right ankle when he stepped awkwardly on first base while trying to beat a double-play relay in the sixth inning.

Game 4 abounded in controversy, was protested by both clubs and ended up in a 5-3, 10-inning triumph by the Phillies to tie the series at two games each.

McBride and Trillo started the confusion in the fourth inning with singles off Vern Ruhle. When Maddox stroked a soft liner back to the mound controversy turned to chaos.

Ruhle fielded the ball and threw to first base for an apparent double play. Philadelphia players streamed from the dugout, insisting that Ruhle had trapped the ball. Houston players maintained the ball had been caught. Slow-motion replays from numerous angles were inconclusive.

During the confusion, Houston first baseman Howe strolled over to second base and claimed a triple play.

Plate umpire Doug Harvey, with nearly two decades of National League experience, reset the play after conferring with fellow umpires and meeting with N.L. President Chub Feeney, who was in a first base box seat.

"Maddox hits the ball and steps in front of me," Harvey began. "There are runners out there wondering if it's a catch or a trap. My first reaction is no catch and I put my hands down to signal fair ball in play. But I see the pitcher throw to first as though he's going for the double play.

"So I ask for help and they tell me the pitcher caught the ball, and that's good enough for me."

Inasmuch as time had been called before Howe tagged second base, Harvey disallowed the putout, returned McBride to second and ordered the game to go on. The rhubarb consumed 20 minutes and prompted an official protest by each club before the Phillies were retired without any scoring.

After the Astros had taken a 2-0 lead with single runs in the fourth and fifth, there was another argument in their half of the sixth when Gary Woods was called out for leaving base too soon while attempting to score on a fly ball by Luis Pujols.

The Phillies took a 3-2 lead in the eighth when Gross, pinch-hitting for Carlton, singled and scored on singles by Smith and Pete Rose. Schmidt's infield single scored Smith and Trillo followed with a sacrifice fly.

After the Astros once again tied the score in the ninth on a run-scoring single by Puhl, Rose singled and raced home bowling over catcher Bruce Bochy, when pinch-hitter Luzinski doubled. Trillo also doubled, driving in Luzinski.

Bochy was in the game only because Alan Ashby suffered a rib separation in the West Division playoff with Los Angeles and Pujols was sidelined with an ankle injury when struck by an eighth-inning foul tip.

The topsy-turvy fifth game saw the Astros' 5-2 lead evaporate into a 7-5 deficit before they staged a rally in the eighth inning to force extra innings.

GAME OF TUESDAY, OCTOBER 7, AT PHILADELPHIA (N)

Houston	AB.	R.	H.	RBI.	PO.	A.
Landestoy, 2b	5	0	0	0	1	2
Cabell, 3b	4	0	1	0	0	2
Cruz, lf	3	1	1	0	5	0
Cedeno, cf	3	0	1	0	1	0
Howe, 1b	4	0	0	0	8	1
Woods, rf	4	0	2	1	1	0
Pujols, c	3	0	0	0	5	1
Bergman, pr	0	0	0	0	0	0
Reynolds, ss	2	0	0	0	2	4
Puhl, ph	1	0	0	0	0	0
Forsch, p	2	0	2	0	1	0
Leonard, ph	1	0	0	0	0	0
Totals	32	1	7	1	24	10

Philadelphia	AB.	R.	H.	RBI.	PO.	A.
Rose, 1b	4	1	2	0	11	1
McBride, rf	4	0	1	0	2	0
Schmidt, 3b	3	0	0	0	0	4
Luzinski, lf	4	1	1	2	0	0
Unser, lf	0	0	0	0	1	0
Trillo, 2b	4	0	0	0	5	8
Maddox, cf	3	1	1	0	3	0
Bowa, ss	2	0	1	0	1	1
Boone, c	3	0	1	0	4	1
Carlton, p	2	0	0	0	0	0
Gross, ph	1	0	1	1	0	0
McGraw, p	0	0	0	0	0	0
Totals	30	3	8	3	27	15

Houston	0	0	1	0	0	0	0	0	0 — 1
Philadelphia	0	0	0	0	0	2	1	0	x — 3

Houston	IP.	H.	R.	ER.	BB.	SO.
Forsch (Loser)	8	8	3	3	1	5

Philadelphia	IP.	H.	R.	ER.	BB.	SO.
Carlton (Winner)	7	7	1	1	3	3
McGraw (Save)	2	0	0	0	1	1

Game-winning RBI—Luzinski.
Error—Bowa. Double play—Philadelphia 1. Left on bases—Houston 9, Philadelphia 5. Home run—Luzinski. Stolen bases—McBride, Maddox. Sacrifice hits—Forsch, Bowa. Umpires—Engel, Tata, Froemming, Harvey, Vargo and Crawford. Time—2:35. Attendance—65,277.

GAME OF WEDNESDAY, OCTOBER 8, AT PHILADELPHIA (N)

Houston	AB.	R.	H.	RBI.	PO.	A.
Puhl, rf	5	1	3	2	3	0
Cabell, 3b	4	0	0	0	0	0
Morgan, 2b	2	1	1	0	4	0
Landestoy, pr-2b	0	1	0	0	0	1
Cruz, lf	4	1	2	2	4	0
Cedeno, cf	5	1	1	1	3	0
Howe, 1b	4	0	0	0	5	1
Bergman, 1b	1	0	1	2	1	1
Ashby, c	5	0	0	0	9	2
Reynolds, ss	3	1	0	0	1	1
Ryan, p	1	1	0	0	0	2
Sambito, p	0	0	0	0	0	0
D. Smith, p	0	0	0	0	0	0
Leonard, ph	1	0	0	0	0	0
LaCorte, p	1	0	0	0	0	0
Andujar, p	0	0	0	0	0	0
Totals	36	7	8	7	30	8

Philadelphia	AB.	R.	H.	RBI.	PO.	A.
Rose, 1b	4	0	2	0	14	2
McBride, rf	5	0	1	0	2	0
Schmidt, 3b	6	1	2	0	0	3
Luzinski, lf	4	1	2	1	3	0
L. Smith, pr-lf	1	1	1	0	0	0
Trillo, 2b	3	0	1	0	2	7
Maddox, cf	5	0	2	2	2	0
Bowa, ss	4	1	2	0	0	4
Boone, c	4	0	1	0	5	0
Ruthven, p	2	0	0	0	2	0
Gross, ph	0	0	0	0	0	0
McGraw, p	0	0	0	0	0	0
Unser, ph	1	0	0	0	0	0
Reed, p	0	0	0	0	0	0
Saucier, p	0	0	0	0	0	0
G. Vukovich, ph	1	0	0	0	0	0
Totals	40	4	14	3	30	16

Houston	0	0	1	0	0	0	1	1	0	4 — 7
Philadelphia	0	0	0	2	0	0	0	1	0	1 — 4

Houston	IP.	H.	R.	ER.	BB.	SO.
Ryan	6⅓	8	2	2	1	6
Sambito	⅓	0	0	0	1	1
D. Smith	1⅓	2	1	1	1	2
LaCorte (Winner)	1*	4	1	0	1	1
Andujar (Save)	1	0	0	0	1	0

Philadelphia	IP.	H.	R.	ER.	BB.	SO.
Ruthven	7	3	2	2	5	4
McGraw	1	2	1	1	0	0
Reed (Loser)	1⅓	2	4	4	1	1
Saucier	⅔	1	0	0	1	0

*Pitched to two batters in tenth.

Game-winning RBI—Cruz.
Errors—Schmidt, McBride, Reynolds. Double play—Philadelphia 1. Left on bases—Houston 8, Philadelphia 14. Two-base hits—Schmidt, Luzinski, Puhl, Morgan. Three-base hit—Bergman. Sacrifice hits—Trillo 2, Ryan, Gross, Cabell. Umpires—Tata, Froemming, Harvey, Vargo, Crawford and Engel. Time—3:34. Attendance—65,476.

GAME OF FRIDAY, OCTOBER 10, AT HOUSTON

Philadelphia	AB.	R.	H.	RBI.	PO.	A.
Rose, 1b	5	0	1	0	13	0
McBride, rf	5	0	1	0	1	0
Schmidt, 3b	5	0	1	0	0	2
Luzinski, lf	5	0	0	0	2	0
Trillo, 2b	5	0	2	0	4	5
Maddox, cf	4	0	2	0	6	0
Bowa, ss	3	0	0	0	2	4
Boone, c	4	0	0	0	3	1
Unser, ph	1	0	0	0	0	0
Moreland, c	0	0	0	0	0	0
Christenson, p	2	0	0	0	0	1
G. Vukovich, ph	1	0	0	0	0	0
Noles, p	0	0	0	0	0	1
McGraw, p	1	0	0	0	0	0
Totals	41	0	7	0	31	14

Houston	AB.	R.	H.	RBI.	PO.	A.
Puhl, rf-cf	4	0	2	0	5	0
Cabell, 3b	4	0	2	0	1	4
Morgan, 2b	4	0	1	0	0	2
Landestoy, pr	0	1	0	0	0	0
Cruz, lf	2	0	1	0	7	0
Cedeño, cf	3	0	0	0	1	0
Bergman, 1b	1	0	0	0	5	0
Howe, c	0	0	0	0	0	0
Walling, 1b-rf	3	0	0	1	5	0
Pujols, c	3	0	0	0	5	0
Reynolds, ss	3	0	0	0	3	5
Niekro, p	3	0	0	0	1	0
Woods, ph	1	0	0	0	0	0
Smith, p	0	0	0	0	0	0
Totals	31	1	6	1	33	11

Philadelphia ... 0 0 0   0 0 0   0 0 0   0 0—0
Houston ... 0 0 0   0 0 0   0 0 0   0 1—1
One out when winning run scored.

Philadelphia	IP.	H.	R.	ER.	BB.	SO.
Christenson	6	3	0	0	4	2
Noles	1⅓	1	0	0	1	0
McGraw (Loser)	3	2	1	1	3	1

Houston	IP.	H.	R.	ER.	BB.	SO.
Niekro	10	6	0	0	1	2
Smith (Winner)	1	1	0	0	1	2

Game-winning RBI—Walling.
Errors—Christenson, Bergman. Double plays—Philadelphia 2. Left on bases—Philadelphia 11, Houston 10. Two-base hits—Puhl, Trillo, Maddox. Three-base hits—Cruz, Morgan. Stolen bases—Schmidt, Maddox. Sacrifice hits—Reynolds, Cabell. Sacrifice fly—Walling. Hit by pitch—By Niekro (Maddox). Passed ball—Pujols. Umpires—Froemming, Harvey, Vargo, Crawford, Engel and Tata. Time—3:22. Attendance—44,443.

GAME OF SATURDAY, OCTOBER 11, AT HOUSTON

Philadelphia	AB.	R.	H.	RBI.	PO.	A.
L. Smith, lf	4	1	2	0	2	1
Unser, lf-rf	1	0	0	0	1	0
Rose, 1b	4	2	2	1	6	2
Schmidt, 3b	5	0	2	1	3	5
McBride, rf	4	0	2	0	3	2
Luzinski, ph	1	1	1	1	0	0
McGraw, p	0	0	0	0	0	0
Trillo, 2b	4	0	2	2	3	0
Maddox, cf	4	0	0	0	6	0
Bowa, ss	5	0	1	0	0	0
Boone, c	4	0	0	0	4	1
Carlton, p	2	0	0	0	0	1
Noles, p	0	0	0	0	1	1
Saucier, p	0	0	0	0	0	0
Reed, p	0	0	0	0	1	0
Gross, ph	1	1	1	0	0	0
Brusstar, p	1	0	0	0	0	0
G. Vukovich, lf	0	0	0	0	0	0
Totals	40	5	13	5	30	13

Houston	AB.	R.	H.	RBI.	PO.	A.
Puhl, cf	3	0	1	1	2	0
Cabell, 3b	4	1	1	0	0	2
Morgan, 2b	3	0	0	0	1	4
Woods, rf	2	0	0	0	0	0
Walling, ph	1	0	0	0	0	0
Leonard, rf	1	0	0	0	2	1
Howe, 1b	3	0	1	1	12	1
Cruz, lf	3	0	0	0	2	0
Pujols, c	3	1	1	0	3	0
Bochy, c	1	0	0	0	5	1
Landestoy, ss	3	1	1	1	2	4
Ruhle, p	3	0	0	0	1	1
D. Smith, p	0	0	0	0	0	0
Sambito, p	0	0	0	0	0	0
Totals	30	3	5	3	30	14

Philadelphia ... 0 0 0   0 0 0   0 3 0   2—5
Houston ... 0 0 0   1 1 0   0 0 1   0—3

Philadelphia	IP.	H.	R.	ER.	BB.	SO.
Carlton	5⅓	4	2	2	5	3
Noles	1⅓	0	0	0	2	0
Saucier	0*	0	0	0	1	0
Reed	⅓	0	0	0	0	0
Brusstar (Winner)	2	1	1	1	1	0
McGraw (Save)	1	0	0	0	0	1

Houston	IP.	H.	R.	ER.	BB.	SO.
Ruhle	7†	8	3	3	1	3
D. Smith	0‡	1	0	0	0	0
Sambito (Loser)	3	4	2	2	1	5

*Pitched to one batter in seventh.
†Pitched to three batters in eighth.
‡Pitched to one batter in eighth.

Game-winning RBI—Luzinski.
Error—Landestoy. Double plays—Philadelphia 3, Houston 2. Left on bases—Philadelphia 8, Houston 8. Two-base hits—Howe, Cabell, Luzinski, Trillo. Three-base hit—Pujols. Stolen bases—McBride, L. Smith, Landestoy, Woods, Puhl, Bowa. Sacrifice hit—Howe, Trillo. Sacrifice flies—Howe, Trillo. Umpires—Harvey, Vargo, Crawford, Engel, Tata and Froemming. Time—3:55. Attendance—44,952.

GAME OF SUNDAY, OCTOBER 12, AT HOUSTON (N)

Philadelphia	AB.	R.	H.	RBI.	PO.	A.	Houston	AB.	R.	H.	RBI.	PO.	A.
Rose, 1b	3	0	1	1	9	2	Puhl, cf	6	3	4	0	3	0
McBride, rf	3	0	0	0	3	1	Cabell, 3b	5	0	1	0	0	1
Moreland, ph	1	0	1	1	0	0	Morgan, 2b	4	0	0	0	4	2
Aviles, pr	0	1	0	0	0	0	Landestoy, 2b	1	0	1	1	2	1
McGraw, p	0	0	0	0	0	0	Cruz, lf	3	1	2	1	1	0
G. Vukovich, ph	1	0	0	0	0	0	Walling, rf	5	2	1	1	0	0
Ruthven, p	0	0	0	0	0	3	LaCorte, p	0	0	0	0	0	0
Schmidt, 3b	5	0	0	0	0	0	Howe, 1b	4	0	2	1	4	0
Luzinski, lf	3	0	1	0	0	0	Bergman, pr-1b	1	0	0	0	2	1
Smith, pr	0	0	0	0	0	0	Pujols, c	1	0	0	0	8	1
Christenson, p	0	0	0	0	0	0	Ashby, ph-c	3	0	1	1	2	0
Reed, p	0	0	0	0	0	0	Reynolds, ss	5	1	2	0	2	2
Unser, ph-rf	2	2	2	1	0	0	Ryan, p	3	0	0	0	1	1
Trillo, 2b	5	1	3	2	4	5	Sambito, p	0	0	0	0	0	0
Maddox, cf	4	1	1	1	6	0	Forsch, p	0	0	0	0	0	0
Bowa, ss	5	1	2	0	1	2	Woods, ph-rf	1	0	0	0	0	0
Boone, c	3	1	2	2	6	0	Heep, ph	1	0	0	0	0	0
Bystrom, p	2	0	0	0	0	0							
Brusstar, p	0	0	0	0	0	0							
Gross, lf	2	1	1	0	1	0							
Totals	39	8	13	8	30	13	Totals	43	7	14	6	30	9

Philadelphia	0	2	0	0	0	0	0	5	0	1—8
Houston	1	0	0	0	0	1	3	2	0	0—7

Philadelphia	IP.	H.	R.	ER.	BB.	SO.
Bystrom	5⅓	7	2	1	2	1
Brusstar	⅔	0	0	0	0	0
Christenson	⅔	2	3	3	1	0
Reed	⅓	1	0	0	0	0
McGraw	1	4	2	2	0	2
Ruthven (Winner)	2	0	0	0	0	0
Houston	IP.	H.	R.	ER.	BB.	SO.
Ryan	7*	8	6	6	2	8
Sambito	⅓	0	0	0	0	0
Forsch	⅔	2	1	1	0	1
LaCorte (Loser)	2	3	1	1	1	1

*Pitched to four batters in eighth.

Game-winning RBI—Maddox.
Errors—Trillo, Luzinski. Double plays—Houston 2. Left on bases—Philadelphia 5, Houston 10. Two-base hits—Cruz, Reynolds, Unser, Maddox. Three-base hits—Howe, Trillo. Stolen base—Puhl. Sacrifice hits—Cabell, Boone. Wild pitch—Christenson. Umpires—Vargo, Crawford, Engel, Tata, Froemming and Harvey. Time—3:38. Attendance—44,802.

PHILADELPHIA PHILLIES' BATTING AND FIELDING AVERAGES

Player-Position	G.	AB.	R.	H.	TB.	2B.	3B.	HR.	RBI.	B.A.	PO.	A.	E.	F.A.
Gross, ph-lf	4	4	2	3	3	0	0	0	1	.750	1	0	0	1.000
L. Smith, pr-lf	3	5	2	3	3	0	0	0	0	.600	2	1	0	1.000
Rose, 1b	5	20	3	8	8	0	0	0	2	.400	53	7	0	1.000
Unser, lf-ph-rf	5	5	2	2	3	1	0	0	1	.400	2	0	0	1.000
Trillo, 2b	5	21	1	8	12	2	1	0	4	.381	18	25	1	.977
Bowa, ss	5	19	2	6	6	0	0	0	0	.316	4	11	1	.938
Maddox, cf	5	20	2	6	8	2	0	0	3	.300	23	0	0	1.000
Luzinski, lf-ph	5	17	3	5	10	2	0	1	4	.294	5	0	1	.833
McBride, rf	5	21	0	5	5	0	0	0	0	.238	11	3	1	.933
Boone, c	5	18	1	4	4	0	0	0	2	.222	22	3	0	1.000
Schmidt, 3b	5	24	1	5	6	1	0	0	1	.208	3	17	1	.952
Reed, p	3	0	0	0	0	0	0	0	0	.000	1	0	0	1.000
Noles, p	2	0	0	0	0	0	0	0	0	.000	1	2	0	1.000
Saucier, p	2	0	0	0	0	0	0	0	0	.000	0	0	0	.000

Player—Position	G.	AB.	R.	H.	TB.	2B.	3B.	HR.	RBI.	B.A.	PO.	A.	E.	F.A.
Aviles, pr	1	0	1	0	0	0	0	0	0	.000	0	0	0	.000
McGraw, p	5	1	0	0	0	0	0	0	0	.000	0	0	0	.000
Brusstar, p	2	1	0	0	0	0	0	0	0	.000	0	0	0	.000
Moreland, c-ph	2	1	0	0	0	0	0	0	1	.000	0	0	0	.000
Christenson, p	2	2	0	0	0	0	0	0	0	.000	0	1	1	.500
Ruthven, p.	2	2	0	0	0	0	0	0	0	.000	0	2	0	1.000
Bystrom, p	1	2	0	0	0	0	0	0	0	.000	0	0	0	.000
G. Vukovich, ph-lf	4	3	0	0	0	0	0	0	0	.000	0	0	0	.000
Carlton, p	2	4	0	0	0	0	0	0	0	.000	0	1	0	1.000
Totals	5	190	20	55	68	8	1	1	19	.290	148	71	6	.973

HOUSTON ASTROS' BATTING AND FIELDING AVERAGES

Player—Position	G.	AB.	R.	H.	TB.	2B.	3B.	HR.	RBI.	B.A.	PO.	A.	E.	F.A.
Forsch, p	2	2	0	2	2	0	0	0	0	.000	1	0	0	1.000
Puhl, ph-rf-cf	5	19	4	10	12	2	0	0	3	.526	13	0	0	1.000
Cruz, lf	5	15	3	6	9	1	1	0	4	.400	19	0	0	1.000
Bergman, pr-1b	4	3	0	1	3	0	1	0	2	.333	8	2	1	.909
Woods, rf-ph	4	8	0	2	2	0	0	0	1	.250	1	0	0	1.000
Cabell, 3b	5	21	1	5	6	1	0	0	0	.238	1	9	0	1.000
Landestoy, 2b-pr-ss	5	9	3	2	2	0	0	0	2	.222	5	8	1	.929
Howe, 1b-ph	5	15	0	3	6	1	1	0	2	.200	29	3	0	1.000
Cedeno, cf	3	11	1	2	2	0	0	0	0	.182	5	0	0	1.000
Morgan, 2b	4	13	1	2	5	1	1	0	0	.154	9	8	0	1.000
Reynolds, ss	4	13	2	2	3	1	0	0	0	.154	8	12	1	.952
Ashby, c-ph	2	8	0	1	1	0	0	0	1	.125	11	2	0	1.000
Walling, 1b-rf-ph	3	9	2	1	1	0	0	0	2	.111	6	0	0	1.000
Pujols, c	4	10	1	1	3	0	1	0	0	.100	21	2	0	1.000
Sambito, p	3	0	0	0	0	0	0	0	0	.000	0	0	0	.000
D. Smith, p	3	0	0	0	0	0	0	0	0	.000	0	0	0	.000
Andujar, p	1	0	0	0	0	0	0	0	0	.000	0	0	0	.000
LaCorte, p	2	1	0	0	0	0	0	0	0	.000	0	0	0	.000
Bochy, c	1	1	0	0	0	0	0	0	0	.000	5	1	0	1.000
Heep, ph	1	1	0	0	0	0	0	0	0	.000	0	0	0	.000
Leonard, ph-rf	3	3	0	0	0	0	0	0	0	.000	2	1	0	1.000
Niekro, p	1	3	0	0	0	0	0	0	0	.000	1	1	0	1.000
Ruhle, p	1	3	0	0	0	0	0	0	0	.000	1	1	0	1.000
Ryan, p	2	4	1	0	0	0	0	0	0	.000	1	3	0	1.000
Totals	5	172	19	40	57	7	5	0	18	.233	147	52	3	.985

PHILADELPHIA PHILLIES' PITCHING RECORDS

Pitcher	G.	GS.	CG.	IP.	H.	R.	ER.	BB.	SO.	HB.	WP.	W.	L.	Pct.	ERA.
Noles	2	0	0	2⅔	1	0	0	3	0	0	0	0	0	.000	0.00
Saucier	2	0	0	⅔	1	0	0	2	0	0	0	0	0	.000	0.00
Bystrom	1	1	0	5⅓	7	2	1	2	1	0	0	0	0	.000	1.69
Ruthven	2	1	0	9	3	2	2	5	4	0	0	1	0	1.000	2.00
Carlton	2	2	0	12⅓	11	3	3	8	6	0	0	1	0	1.000	2.19
Brusstar	2	0	0	2⅔	1	1	1	1	0	0	0	1	0	1.000	3.38
Christenson	2	1	0	6⅔	5	3	3	5	2	0	1	0	0	.000	4.05
McGraw	5	0	0	8	8	4	4	4	5	0	0	0	1	.000	4.50
Reed	3	0	0	2	3	4	4	1	1	0	0	0	1	.000	18.00
Totals	5	5	0	49⅓	40	19	18	31	19	0	1	3	2	.600	3.28

No shutouts. Saves—McGraw 2.

HOUSTON ASTROS' PITCHING RECORDS

Pitcher	G.	GS.	CG.	IP.	H.	R.	ER.	BB.	SO.	HB.	WP.	W.	L.	Pct.	ERA.
Niekro	1	1	0	10	6	0	0	1	2	1	0	0	0	.000	0.00
Andujar	1	0	0	1	0	0	0	1	0	0	0	0	0	.000	0.00
LaCorte	2	0	0	3	7	2	1	2	2	0	0	1	1	.500	3.00
Ruhle	1	1	0	7	8	3	3	1	3	0	0	0	0	.000	3.86
D. Smith	3	0	0	2⅓	4	1	1	2	4	0	0	1	0	1.000	3.86
Forsch	2	1	1	8⅔	10	4	4	1	6	0	0	0	1	.000	4.15
Sambito	3	0	0	3⅔	4	2	2	2	6	0	0	0	1	.000	4.91
Ryan	2	2	0	13⅓	16	8	8	3	14	0	0	0	0	.000	5.40
Totals	5	5	1	49	55	20	19	13	37	1	0	2	3	.400	3.49

Shutout—Niekro-D. Smith (combined). Save—Andujar.

COMPOSITE SCORE BY INNINGS

Philadelphia	0	2	0		2	0	2		1	9	0	4	0 – 20
Houston	1	0	2		1	1	1		4	3	1	4	1 – 19

Game-winning RBIs—Luzinski 2, Cruz, Walling, Maddox.

Sacrifice hits—Cabell 3, Trillo 2, Forsch, Bowa, Ryan, Gross, Reynolds, Sambito, Boone.

Sacrifice flies—Walling, Howe, Trillo.

Stolen bases—Maddox 2, McBride 2, Puhl 2, Schmidt, L. Smith, Landestoy, Woods, Bowa.

Caught stealing—Rose 2, Maddox, Cabell.

Double plays—Bowa, Trillo and Rose 3; Trillo, Bowa and Rose; Ruhle and Howe; Leonard, Bochy and Morgan; L. Smith and Schmidt; McBride, Boone, Noles and Schmidt; McBride and Rose; Reynolds, Morgan and Howe; Cabell, Morgan and Howe.

Left on bases—Philadelphia 5, 14, 11, 8, 5—43; Houston—9, 8, 10, 8, 10—45.

Hit by pitcher—By Niekro (Maddox).

Passed ball—Pujols.

Balks—None.

Time of games—First game, 2:35; second game, 3:34; third game, 3:22; fourth game, 3:55; fifth game, 3:38.

Attendance—First game, 65,277; second game, 65.476; third game, 44,443; fourth game, 44,952; fifth game, 44,802.

Umpires—Engel, Tata, Froemming, Harvey, Vargo and Crawford.

Official scorers—John Black, Rosenberg (Tex.) Herald-Coaster; Paul Giordano, Bucks County (Pa.) Courier; Ivy McLemore, Houston Post.

PETE ROSE bowls over catcher Bruce Bochy for deciding run in fourth game of N.L. Championship Series.

CHAMPIONSHIP SERIES STANDINGS
Series Won and Lost

American League—East Division

	W.	L.	Pct.
Boston	1	0	1.000
New York	3	1	.750
Baltimore	4	2	.667
Detroit	0	1	.000
	8	4	.667

American League—West Division

	W.	L.	Pct.
Oakland	3	2	.600
Kansas City	1	3	.250
Minnesota	0	2	.000
California	0	1	.000
	4	8	.333

National League—East Division

	W.	L.	Pct.
New York	2	0	1.000
Pittsburgh	2	4	.333
Philadelphia	1	3	.250
	5	7	.417

National League—West Division

	W.	L.	Pct.
Los Angeles	3	0	1.000
Cincinnati	4	2	.667
Atlanta	0	1	.000
San Francisco	0	1	.000
Houston	0	1	.000
	7	5	.583

Games Won and Lost

American League—East Division

	W.	L.	Pct.
Boston	3	0	1.000
Baltimore	15	7	.682
New York	9	8	.529
Detroit	2	3	.400
	29	18	.617

American League—West Division

	W.	L.	Pct.
Kansas City	8	9	.471
Oakland	9	11	.450
California	1	3	.250
Minnesota	0	6	.000
	18	29	.383

National League—East Division

	W.	L.	Pct.
New York	6	2	.750
Pittsburgh	9	13	.409
Philadelphia	5	11	.313
	20	26	.435

National League—West Division

	W.	L.	Pct.
Los Angeles	9	3	.750
Cincinnati	14	8	.636
Houston	2	3	.400
San Francisco	1	3	.250
Atlanta	0	3	.000
	26	20	.565

Series Played, Games Played, Games Played at Home, Games Played Abroad

AMERICAN LEAGUE

East Division

	Ser.	G.	Ho.	Abr.
Baltimore	6	22	11	11
New York	4	17	8	9
Detroit	1	5	3	2
Boston	1	3	2	1
	11	47	24	23

West Division

	Ser.	G.	Ho.	Abr.
Oakland	5	20	9	11
Kansas City	4	17	9	8
Minnesota	2	6	3	3
California	1	4	2	2
	11	47	23	24

NATIONAL LEAGUE

East Division

	Ser.	G.	Ho.	Abr.
Pittsburgh	6	22	10	12
Philadelphia	4	16	8	8
New York	2	8	4	4
	12	46	22	24

West Division

	Ser.	G.	Ho.	Abr.
Cincinnati	6	22	11	11
Los Angeles	3	12	6	6
Houston	1	5	3	2
San Francisco	1	4	2	2
Atlanta	1	3	2	1
	12	46	24	22

GAMES PLAYED IN EACH CITY

AMERICAN LEAGUE (47)		NATIONAL LEAGUE (46)	
Baltimore	11	Cincinnati	11
Oakland	9	Pittsburgh	10
Kansas City	9	Philadelphia	8
New York	8	Los Angeles	6
Detroit	3	New York	4
Minnesota (Bloomington)	3	Houston	3
Boston	2	Atlanta	2
California	2	San Francisco	2

CHAMPIONSHIP SERIES SHUTOUT GAMES

AMERICAN LEAGUE (8)

October 5, 1969—McNally, Baltimore 1, Minnesota 0; 3 hits (11 innings).
October 8, 1972—Odom, Oakland 5, Detroit 0; 3 hits.
October 10, 1972—Coleman, Detroit 3, Oakland 0; 7 hits.
October 6, 1973—Palmer, Baltimore 6, Oakland 0; 5 hits.
October 11, 1973—Hunter, Oakland 3, Baltimore 0; 5 hits.
October 6, 1974—Holtzman, Oakland 5, Baltimore 0; 5 hits.
October 8, 1974—Blue, Oakland 1, Baltimore 0; 2 hits.
October 6, 1979—McGregor, Baltimore 8, California 0; 6 hits.

NATIONAL LEAGUE (6)

October 3, 1970—Nolan and Carroll, Cincinnati 3, Pittsburgh 0; 8 hits (10 innings).
October 7, 1973—Matlack, New York 5, Cincinnati 0; 2 hits.
October 5, 1974—Sutton, Los Angeles 3, Pittsburgh 0; 4 hits.
October 8, 1974—Kison and Hernandez, Pittsburgh 7, Los Angeles 0; 4 hits.
October 4, 1978—John, Los Angeles 4, Philadelphia 0; 4 hits.
October 10, 1980—Niekro and D. Smith, Houston 1, Philadelphia 0; 7 hits (11 innings).

CHAMPIONSHIP SERIES EXTRA-INNING GAMES (16)

October 4, 1969—at Baltimore, 12 innings, Baltimore AL East 4, Minnesota AL West 3.
October 5, 1969—at Baltimore, 11 innings, Baltimore AL East 1, Minnesota AL West 0.
October 3, 1970—at Pittsburgh, 10 innings, Cincinnati NL West 3, Pittsburgh NL East 0.
October 7, 1972—at Oakland, 11 innings, Oakland AL West 3, Detroit AL East 2.
October 11, 1972—at Detroit, 10 innings, Detroit AL East 4, Oakland AL West 3.
October 9, 1973—at Oakland, 11 innings, Oakland AL West 2, Baltimore AL East 1.
October 9, 1973—at New York, 12 innings, Cincinnati NL West 2, New York NL East 1.
October 7, 1975—at Pittsburgh, 10 innings, Cincinnati NL West 5, Pittsburgh NL East 3.
October 7, 1978—at Los Angeles, 10 innings, Los Angeles NL West 4, Philadelphia NL East 3.
October 2, 1979—at Cincinnati, 11 innings, Pittsburgh NL East 5, Cincinnati NL West 2.
October 3, 1979—at Cincinnati, 10 innings, Pittsburgh NL East 3, Cincinnati NL West 2.
October 3, 1979—at Baltimore, 10 innings, Baltimore AL East 6, California AL West 3.
October 8, 1980—at Philadelphia, 10 innings, Houston NL West 7, Philadelphia NL East 4.
October 10, 1980—at Houston, 11 innings, Houston NL West 1, Philadelphia NL East 0.
October 11, 1980—at Houston, 10 innings, Philadelphia NL East 5, Houston NL West 3.
October 12, 1980—at Houston, 10 innings, Philadelphia NL East 8, Houston NL West 7.

WINNING, LOSING CLUBS

AMERICAN LEAGUE WINNING CLUBS

Baltimore (East)	4	1969-70-71-79.
Oakland (West)	3	1972-73-74.
New York (East)	3	1976-77-78.
Boston (East)	1	1975.
Kansas City (West)	1	1980.

East Division Has Won 8, Lost 4

AMERICAN LEAGUE LOSING CLUBS

Kansas City (West)	3	1976-77-78.
Baltimore (East)	2	1973-74.
Minnesota (West)	2	1969-70.
Oakland (West)	2	1971-75.
Detroit (East)	1	1972.
California (West)	1	1979.
New York (East)	1	1980.

NATIONAL LEAGUE WINNING CLUBS

Cincinnati (West) .... 4—1970-72-75-76.
Los Angeles (West) .... 3—1974-77-78.
New York (East) .... 2—1969-73.
Pittsburgh (East) .... 2—1971-79.
Philadelphia (East) .... 1—1980.

West Division Has Won 7, Lost 5

NATIONAL LEAGUE LOSING CLUBS

Pittsburgh (East) .... 4—1970-72-74-75.
Philadelphia (East) .... 3—1976-77-78.
Cincinnati (West) .... 2—1973-79.
Atlanta (West) .... 1—1969.
San Francisco (West) .... 1—1971.
Houston (West)........................ 1—1980.

SERIES WON

3-game Series—3—Baltimore AL, 1969, 1970, 1971.
      3—Cincinnati NL, 1970, 1975, 1976.
      1—Boston AL, 1975.
      1—New York NL, 1969.
      1—Pittsburgh NL, 1979.
      1—Kansas City AL, 1980.

4-game Series—3—Los Angeles NL, 1974, 1977, 1978.
      1—Oakland AL, 1974.
      1—Pittsburgh NL, 1971.
      1—New York AL, 1978.
      1—Baltimore AL, 1979.

5-game Series—2—New York AL, 1976, 1977.
      2—Oakland AL, 1972, 1973.
      1—Cincinnati NL, 1972.
      1—New York NL, 1973.
      1—Philadelphia NL, 1980.

SERIES LOST

3-game Series—2—Minnesota AL, 1969, 1970.
      2—Oakland AL, 1971, 1975.
      2—Pittsburgh NL, 1970, 1975.
      1—Atlanta NL, 1969.
      1—Philadelphia NL, 1976.
      1—Cincinnati NL, 1979.
      1—New York AL, 1980.

4-game Series—2—Philadelphia NL, 1977, 1978.
      1—Baltimore AL, 1974.
      1—Pittsburgh NL, 1974.
      1—San Francisco NL, 1971.
      1—Kansas City AL, 1978.
      1—California AL, 1979.

5-game Series—2—Kansas City AL, 1976, 1977.
      1—Baltimore AL, 1973.
      1—Cincinnati NL, 1973.
      1—Detroit AL, 1972.
      1—Pittsburgh NL, 1972.
      1—Houston NL, 1980.

.400 Hitters Playing in All Games, Each Series
(9 or more at-bats)
AMERICAN LEAGUE (24)

Player and Club	Year	G.	AB.	R.	H.	2B.	3B.	HR.	TB.	B.A.
Robinson, Brooks C., Baltimore	1970	3	12	3	7	2	0	0	9	.583
White, Frank, Kansas City	1980	3	11	3	6	1	0	1	10	.545
Chambliss, C. Christopher, New York	1976	5	21	5	11	1	1	2	20	.524
Robinson, Brooks C., Baltimore	1969	3	14	1	7	1	0	0	8	.500
Oliva, Antonio, Minnesota	1970	3	12	2	6	2	0	1	11	.500
Bando, Salvatore L., Oakland	1975	3	12	1	6	2	0	0	8	.500
Watson, Robert J., New York	1980	3	12	0	6	3	1	0	11	.500
Jackson, Reginald M., New York	1978	4	13	5	6	1	0	2	13	.462
Yastrzemski, Carl M., Boston	1975	3	11	4	5	1	0	1	9	.455
Rivers, John M., New York	1978	4	11	0	5	0	0	0	5	.455
Burleson, Richard P., Boston	1975	3	9	2	4	2	0	0	6	.444
Brett, George H., Kansas City	1976	5	18	4	8	1	1	1	14	.444
McRae, Harold A., Kansas City	1977	5	18	6	8	3	0	1	14	.444
Munson, Thurman L., New York	1976	5	23	3	10	2	0	0	12	.435
Powell, John W., Baltimore	1970	3	14	2	6	2	0	1	11	.429
Otis, Amos J., Kansas City	1978	4	14	2	6	2	0	0	8	.429
Fisk, Carlton E., Boston	1975	3	12	4	5	1	0	0	6	.417
Jackson, Reginald M., Oakland	1975	3	12	1	5	0	0	1	8	.417
Murray, Eddie C., Baltimore	1979	4	12	3	5	0	0	1	8	.417
Carew, Rodney C., California	1979	4	17	4	7	3	0	0	10	.412
Blair, Paul L., Baltimore	1969	3	15	1	6	2	0	1	11	.400
Johnson, Clifford, New York	1977	5	15	2	6	2	0	1	11	.400
Chambliss, C. Christopher, New York	1978	4	15	1	6	0	0	0	6	.400
Cooper, Cecil C., Boston	1975	3	10	0	4	2	0	0	6	.400

.400 Hitters Playing in All Games, Each Series
(9 or more at-bats)
NATIONAL LEAGUE (24)

Player and Club	Year	G.	AB.	R.	H.	2B.	3B.	HR.	TB.	B.A.
Johnstone, John W., Philadelphia	1976	3	9	1	7	1	1	0	10	.778
Shamsky, Arthur L., New York	1969	3	13	3	7	0	0	0	7	.538
Puhl, Terry S., Houston	1980	5	19	4	10	2	0	0	12	.526
Stargell, Wilver D., Pittsburgh	1970	3	12	0	6	1	0	0	7	.500
Zisk, Richard W., Pittsburgh	1975	3	10	0	5	1	0	0	6	.500
Baker, Johnnie B., Los Angeles	1978	4	15	1	7	2	0	0	9	.467
Cepeda, Orlando M., Atlanta	1969	3	11	2	5	2	0	1	10	.455
Concepcion, David I., Cincinnati	1975	3	11	2	5	0	0	1	8	.455
Stargell, Wilver D., Pittsburgh	1979	3	11	2	5	2	0	2	13	.455
Rose, Peter E., Cincinnati	1972	5	20	1	9	4	0	0	13	.450
Robertson, Robert E., Pittsburgh	1971	4	16	5	7	1	0	4	20	.438
Jones, Cleon J., New York	1969	3	14	4	6	2	0	1	11	.429
McCovey, Willie L., San Francisco	1971	4	14	2	6	0	0	2	12	.429
Rose, Peter E., Cincinnati	1976	3	14	3	6	2	1	0	10	.429
Concepcion, David I., Cincinnati	1979	3	14	1	6	1	0	0	7	.429
Cash, David, Pittsburgh	1971	4	19	5	8	2	0	0	10	.421
Tolan, Robert, Cincinnati	1970	3	12	3	5	0	0	1	8	.417
Perez, Atanasio R., Cincinnati	1975	3	12	3	5	0	0	1	8	.417
Garner, Philip M., Pittsburgh	1979	3	12	4	5	0	1	1	10	.417
Russell, William E., Los Angeles	1978	4	17	1	7	1	0	0	8	.412
Rose, Peter E., Philadelphia	1980	5	20	3	8	0	0	0	8	.400
Stargell, Wilver D., Pittsburgh	1974	4	15	3	6	0	0	2	12	.400
Cruz, Jose D., Houston	1980	5	15	3	6	1	1	0	9	.400
Boone, Robert R., Philadelphia	1977	4	10	1	4	0	0	0	4	.400

LEADING BATSMEN, CHAMPIONSHIP SERIES

PLAYING IN ALL GAMES, EACH SERIES (4 or more hits)

AMERICAN LEAGUE

Year	Player and Club	G.	AB.	R.	H.	2B.	3B.	HR.	TB.	B.A.
1969—Brooks C. Robinson, Baltimore		3	14	1	7	1	0	0	8	.500
1970—Brooks C. Robinson, Baltimore		3	12	3	7	2	0	0	9	.583
1971—Brooks C. Robinson, Baltimore		3	11	2	4	1	0	1	8	.364
Salvatore L. Bando, Oakland		3	11	3	4	2	0	1	9	.364
1972—Mateo R. Alou, Oakland		5	21	2	8	4	0	0	12	.381
1973—Dagoberto B. Campaneris, Oakland		5	21	3	7	1	0	2	14	.333
1974—Raymond E. Fosse, Oakland		4	12	1	4	1	0	1	8	.333
1975—Salvatore L. Bando, Oakland		3	12	1	6	2	0	0	8	.500
1976—C. Christopher Chambliss, New York		5	21	5	11	1	1	2	20	.524
1977—Harold A. McRae, Kansas City		5	18	6	8	3	0	1	14	.444
1978—Reginald M. Jackson, New York		4	13	5	6	1	0	2	13	.462
1979—Murray, Eddie C. Baltimore		4	12	3	5	0	0	1	8	.417
1980—White, Frank, Kansas City		3	11	3	6	1	0	1	10	.545

NATIONAL LEAGUE

Year	Player and Club	G.	AB.	R.	H.	2B.	3B.	HR.	TB.	B.A.
1969—Arthur L. Shamsky, New York		3	13	3	7	0	0	0	7	.538
1970—Wilver D. Stargell, Pittsburgh		3	12	0	6	1	0	0	7	.500
1971—Robert E. Robertson, Pittsburgh		4	16	5	7	1	0	4	20	.438
1972—Peter E. Rose, Cincinnati		5	20	1	9	4	0	0	13	.450
1973—Peter E. Rose, Cincinnati		5	21	3	8	1	0	2	15	.381
1974—Wilver D. Stargell, Pittsburgh		4	15	3	6	0	0	2	12	.400
1975—Richard W. Zisk, Pittsburgh		3	10	0	5	1	0	0	6	.500
1976—John W. Johnstone, Philadelphia		3	9	1	7	1	1	0	10	.778
1977—Robert R. Boone, Philadelphia		4	10	1	4	0	0	0	4	.400
1978—Johnnie B. Baker, Los Angeles		4	15	1	7	2	0	0	9	.467
1979—Stargell, Wilver D., Pittsburgh		3	11	2	5	2	0	2	13	.455
1980—Puhl, Terry S., Houston		5	19	4	10	2	0	0	12	.526

CLUB BATTING

AMERICAN LEAGUE

Year–Club	G.	AB.	R.	H.	TB.	2B.	3B.	HR.	SH.	SF.	SB.	BB.	SO.	RBI.	B.A.
1969—Baltimore, East	3	123	16	36	58	8	1	4	2	0	0	13	14	15	.293
Minnesota, West	3	110	5	17	25	3	1	1	0	1	2	12	27	5	.155
1970—Baltimore, East	3	109	27	36	61	7	0	6	1	2	1	12	19	24	.330
Minnesota, West	3	101	10	24	39	4	1	3	1	0	0	9	22	10	.238
1971—Baltimore, East	3	95	15	26	47	7	1	4	0	1	0	13	14	14	.274
Oakland, West	3	96	7	22	41	8	1	3	2	0	0	5	16	7	.229
1972—Detroit, East	5	162	10	32	52	6	1	4	3	0	0	13	25	10	.198
Oakland, West	5	170	13	38	49	8	0	1	4	1	7	12	35	10	.224
1973—Baltimore, East	5	171	15	36	52	7	0	3	0	0	1	16	25	15	.211
Oakland, West	5	160	15	32	54	5	1	5	4	1	3	17	39	15	.200
1974—Baltimore, East	4	124	7	22	32	1	0	3	2	0	0	5	20	7	.177
Oakland, West	4	120	11	22	37	4	1	3	2	1	3	22	16	11	.183
1975—Boston, East	3	98	18	31	45	8	0	2	5	1	3	3	12	14	.316
Oakland, West	3	98	7	19	28	6	0	1	0	0	0	9	14	7	.194
1976—New York, East	5	174	23	55	84	13	2	4	2	1	4	16	15	21	.316
Kansas City, West	5	162	24	40	60	6	4	2	0	4	5	11	18	24	.247
1977—New York, East	5	175	21	46	64	12	0	2	1	2	2	9	16	17	.263
Kansas City, West	5	163	22	42	66	9	3	3	2	2	5	15	22	21	.258
1978—New York, East	4	140	19	42	62	3	1	5	0	1	0	7	18	18	.300
Kansas City, West	4	133	17	35	59	6	3	4	1	2	6	14	21	16	.263
1979—Baltimore, East	4	133	26	37	53	5	1	3	1	3	5	18	24	25	.278
California, West	4	137	15	32	48	7	0	3	0	2	2	7	13	14	.234
1980—New York, East	3	102	6	26	44	7	1	3	1	0	0	6	16	5	.255
Kansas City, West	3	97	14	28	45	6	1	3	0	0	3	9	15	14	.289

CLUB BATTING

NATIONAL LEAGUE

Year–Club	G.	AB.	R.	H.	TB.	2B.	3B.	HR.	SH.	SF.	SB.	BB.	SO.	RBI.	B.A.
1969—New York, East	3	113	27	37	65	8	1	6	1	0	5	10	25	24	.327
Atlanta, West	3	106	15	27	51	9	0	5	0	1	1	11	20	15	.255
1970—Pittsburgh, East	3	102	3	23	29	6	0	0	2	0	0	12	19	3	.225
Cincinnati, West	3	100	9	22	36	3	1	3	0	0	1	8	12	8	.220
1971—Pittsburgh, East	4	144	24	39	67	4	0	8	1	0	2	5	33	23	.271
San Francisco, West	4	132	25	31	51	5	0	5	4	0	2	16	28	14	.235
1972—Pittsburgh, East	5	158	15	30	47	6	1	3	2	0	0	9	27	14	.190
Cincinnati, West	5	166	19	42	67	9	2	4	3	1	4	10	28	16	.253

NATIONAL LEAGUE

Year–Club	G.	AB.	R.	H.	TB.	2B.	3B.	HR.	SH.	SF.	SB.	BB.	SO.	RBI.	B.A.
1973–New York, East	5	168	23	37	51	5	0	3	3	1	0	19	28	22	.220
Cincinnati, West	5	167	8	31	52	6	0	5	3	1	0	13	42	8	.186
1974–Pittsburgh, East	4	129	10	25	35	1	0	3	2	0	1	8	17	10	.194
Los Angeles, West	4	138	20	37	56	8	1	3	1	0	5	30	16	19	.268
1975–Pittsburgh, East	3	101	7	20	26	3	0	1	0	0	0	10	18	7	.198
Cincinnati, West	3	102	19	29	45	4	0	4	0	3	11	9	28	18	.284
1976–Philadelphia, East	3	100	11	27	40	8	1	1	3	2	0	12	9	11	.270
Cincinnati, West	3	99	19	25	45	5	3	3	1	3	5	15	16	17	.253
1977–Philadelphia, East	4	138	14	31	40	3	0	2	2	0	1	11	21	12	.225
Los Angeles, West	4	133	22	35	52	6	1	3	2	0	3	14	22	20	.263
1978–Philadelphia, East	4	140	17	35	57	3	2	5	2	1	0	9	21	16	.250
Los Angeles, West	4	147	21	42	8	8	3	8	2	0	2	9	22	21	.286
1979–Pittsburgh, East	3	105	15	28	47	3	2	4	5	3	4	13	13	14	.267
Cincinnati, West	3	107	5	23	35	4	1	2	1	1	4	11	26	5	.215
1980–Philadelphia, East	5	189	20	55	68	8	1	1	5	1	7	13	37	19	.291
Houston, West	5	172	19	40	57	7	5	0	7	2	4	31	19	18	.233

CLUB FIELDING, LEFT ON BASES, PLAYERS, PITCHERS USED

AMERICAN LEAGUE

Year–Team, Division	G.	PO.	A.	E.	DP.	PB.	F.A.	LOB.	Pl.	Pi.
1969–Baltimore, East	3	96	31	1	2	0	.992	28	20	7
Minnesota, West	3	94	34	5	3	0	.962	22	22	9
1970–Baltimore, East	3	81	29	0	3	0	1.000	20	14	4
Minnesota, West	3	78	28	6	5	0	.946	20	24	9
1971–Baltimore, East	3	81	31	1	3	0	.991	19	15	4
Oakland, West	3	75	15	0	4	0	1.000	15	20	7
1972–Detroit, East	5	139	48	7	4	0	.964	30	24	8
Oakland, West	5	138	59	3	5	1	.985	38	25	8
1973–Baltimore, East	5	135	51	2	2	1	.989	36	23	7
Oakland, West	5	138	47	4	4	0	.979	34	22	6
1974–Baltimore, East	4	105	50	4	4	0	.975	16	22	7
Oakland, West	4	108	43	2	4	1	.987	30	20	5
1975–Boston, East	3	81	33	4	3	0	.966	14	14	5
Oakland, West	3	75	40	6	4	0	.950	19	22	7
1976–New York, East	5	132	60	6	3	1	.970	41	22	6
Kansas City, West	5	129	51	4	5	0	.978	22	24	9
1977–New York, East	5	132	51	2	2	0	.989	34	18	6
Kansas City, West	5	132	54	5	2	0	.974	28	22	8
1978–New York, East	4	105	35	1	2	1	.993	27	21	8
Kansas City, West	4	102	36	4	4	1	.972	28	20	7
1979–Baltimore, East	4	109	52	5	5	1	.970	23	20	5
California, West	4	107	37	2	7	0	.986	22	23	9
1980–New York, East	3	75	42	1	2	0	.991	22	20	6
Kansas City, West	3	81	29	1	3	0	.991	18	15	4

NATIONAL LEAGUE

Year–Team, Division	G.	PO.	A.	E.	DP.	PB.	F.A.	LOB.	Pl.	Pi.
1969–New York, East	3	81	23	2	2	1	.981	19	17	6
Atlanta, West	3	78	37	6	4	1	.950	23	23	9
1970–Pittsburgh, East	3	81	37	2	3	0	.983	29	18	5
Cincinnati, West	3	84	39	1	1	0	.992	18	20	7
1971–Pittsburgh, East	4	105	32	3	3	1	.979	26	21	7
San Francisco, West	4	102	37	4	1	1	.972	33	22	9
1972–Pittsburgh, East	5	131	38	4	3	0	.977	24	23	10
Cincinnati, West	5	132	53	4	3	1	.979	30	21	8
1973–New York, East	5	142	44	4	3	0	.979	30	17	6
Cincinnati, West	5	138	59	2	3	0	.990	35	24	9
1974–Pittsburgh, East	4	105	37	4	2	1	.973	24	22	8
Los Angeles, West	4	108	46	7	8	1	.957	44	22	7
1975–Pittsburgh, East	3	78	20	2	3	2	.980	21	24	10
Cincinnati, West	3	84	31	1	2	0	.991	17	18	7
1976–Philadelphia, East	3	79	34	2	3	0	.983	25	22	7
Cincinnati, West	3	81	32	2	3	0	.983	20	18	6
1977–Philadelphia, East	4	105	49	3	3	1	.981	32	21	7
Los Angeles, West	4	108	44	5	3	0	.968	22	23	9
1978–Philadelphia, East	4	110	46	4	4	0	.975	24	22	8
Los Angeles, West	4	111	50	3	4	0	.982	28	22	9
1979–Pittsburgh, East	3	90	34	0	2	0	1.000	24	20	8
Cincinnati, West	3	87	39	1	2	0	.992	25	20	9
1980–Philadelphia, East	5	148	71	6	7	0	.973	43	23	9
Houston, West	5	147	52	3	4	1	.985	45	24	7

CHAMPIONSHIP SERIES HOME RUNS

AMERICAN LEAGUE (75)

1969—4—Baltimore (East), Frank Robinson (1), Mark H. Belanger (1), John W. Powell (1), Paul L. Blair (1).
 1—Minnesota (West), Antonio Oliva (1).
1970—6—Baltimore (East), David A. Johnson (2), Miguel Cuellar (1), Donald A. Buford (1), John W. Powell (1), Frank Robinson (1).
 3—Minnesota (West), Harmon C. Killebrew (2), Antonio Oliva (1).
1971—4—Baltimore (East), John W. Powell (2), Brooks C. Robinson (1), Elrod J. Hendricks (1).
 3—Oakland (West), Reginald M. Jackson (2), Salvatore L. Bando (1).
1972—4—Detroit (East), Norman D. Cash (1), Albert W. Kaline (1), William A. Freehan (1), Richard J. McAuliffe (1).
 1—Oakland (West), Michael P. Epstein (1).
1973—5—Oakland (West), Salvatore L. Bando (2), Dagoberto B. Campaneris (2), Joseph O. Rudi (1).
 3—Baltimore (East), Earl C. Williams (1), Andrew A. Etchebarren (1), Robert A. Grich (1).
1974—3—Baltimore (East), Paul L. Blair (1), Brooks C. Robinson (1), Robert A. Grich (1).
 3—Oakland (West), Salvatore L. Bando (2), Raymond E. Fosse (1).
1975—2—Boston (East), Carl M. Yastrzemski (1), Americo P. Petrocelli (1).
 1—Oakland (West), Reginald M. Jackson (1).
1976—4—New York (East), Graig Nettles (2), C. Christopher Chambliss (2).
 2—Kansas City (West), John C. Mayberry (1), George H. Brett (1).
1977—3—Kansas City (West), Harold A. McRae (1), John C. Mayberry (1), Alfred E. Cowens (1).
 2—New York (East), Thurman L. Munson (1), Clifford Johnson (1).
1978—5—New York (East), Reginald M. Jackson (2), Thurman L. Munson (1), Graig Nettles (1), Roy H. White (1).
 4—Kansas City (West), George H. Brett (3), Freddie J. Patek (1).
1979—3—Baltimore (East), John L. Lowenstein (1), Eddie C. Murray (1), H. Patrick Kelly (1).
 3—California (West), Darnell G. Ford (2), Donald E. Baylor (1).
1980—3—New York (East), Richard A. Cerone (1), Louis V. Piniella (1), Graig Nettles (1).
 3—Kansas City (West), George H. Brett (2), Frank White (1).

NATIONAL LEAGUE (82)

1969—6—New York (East), Tommie L. Agee (2), Kenneth G. Boswell (2), Cleon J. Jones (1), R. Wayne Garrett (1).
 5—Atlanta (West), Henry L. Aaron (3), A. Antonio Gonzalez (1), Orlando M. Cepeda (1).
1970—3—Cincinnati (West), Robert Tolan (1), Atanasio R. Perez (1), Johnny L. Bench (1).
 0—Pittsburgh (East).
1971—8—Pittsburgh (East), Robert E. Robertson (4), Richard J. Hebner (2), Eugene A. Clines (1), Albert Oliver (1).
 5—San Francisco (West), Willie L. McCovey (2), Rigoberto Fuentes (1), Willie H. Mays (1), Chris E. Speier (1).
1972—4—Cincinnati (West), Joe L. Morgan (2), Cesar F. Geronimo (1), Johnny L. Bench (1).
 3—Pittsburgh (East), Albert Oliver (1), Manuel D. Sanguillen (1), Roberto W. Clemente (1).
1973—5—Cincinnati (West), Peter E. Rose (2), Johnny L. Bench (1), Denis J. Menke (1), Atanasio R. Perez (1).
 3—New York (East), Daniel J. Staub (3).

1974—3—Los Angeles (West), Steven P. Garvey (2), Ronald C. Cey (1).
      3—Pittsburgh (East), Wilver D. Stargell (2), Richard J. Hebner (1).
1975—4—Cincinnati (West), Donald E. Gullett (1), Atanasio R. Perez (1), David I.
        Concepcion (1), Peter E. Rose (1).
      1—Pittsburgh (East), Albert Oliver (1).
1976—3—Cincinnati (West), George A. Foster (2), Johnny L. Bench (1).
      1—Philadelphia (East), Gregory M. Luzinski (1).
1977—3—Los Angeles (West), Johnnie B. Baker (2), Ronald C. Cey (1).
      2—Philadelphia (East), Gregory M. Luzinski (1), Arnold R. McBride (1).
1978—8—Los Angeles (West), Steven P. Garvey (4), David E. Lopes (2), Stephen W.
        Yeager (1), Ronald C. Cey (1).
      5—Philadelphia (East), Gregory M. Luzinski (2), Jerry L. Martin (1), Steven
        N. Carlton (1), Arnold R. McBride (1).
1979—4—Pittsburgh (East), Wilver D. Stargell (2), Philip M. Garner (1), Bill Mad-
        lock (1).
      2—Cincinnati, (West), George A. Foster (1), Johnny L. Bench (1).
1980—1—Philadelphia (East), Gregory M. Luzinski (1).
      0—Houston (West).

GEORGE BRETT exalts after his three-run homer off Rich Gossage gave Royals A.L. pennant.

CHAMPIONSHIP SERIES PLAYERS, 1969 THROUGH 1980
(Players Appearing in One or More Games)

– A –

Aaron, Henry L.–Atlanta NL 1969.

Aaron, Tommie L.–Atlanta NL 1969.

Aase, Donald W.–California AL 1979.

Abbott, W. Glenn–Oakland AL 1975.

Agee, Tommie L.–New York NL 1969.

Aikens, Willie M.–Kansas City AL 1980.

Alexander, Doyle L.–Baltimore AL 1973.

Alexander, Matthew–Pittsburgh NL 1979.

Allen, Richard A.–Philadelphia NL 1976.

Alley, L. Eugene–Pittsburgh NL 1970-71-72.

Allison, W. Robert–Minnesota AL 1969-70.

Alomar, Santos–New York AL 1976.

Alou, Felipe R.–Atlanta NL 1969.

Alou, Jesus M.–Oakland AL 1973-74.

Alou, Mateo R.–Pittsburgh NL 1970; Oakland AL 1972.

Alyea, Garrabrant R.–Minnesota AL 1970.

Anderson, James L.–California AL 1979.

Andrews, Michael J.–Oakland AL 1973.

Andujar, Joaquin–Houston NL 1980.

Armbrister, Edison R.–Cincinnati NL 1973-75-76.

Ashby, Alan D.–Houston NL 1980.

Aspromonte, Robert T.–Atlanta NL 1969.

Auerbach, Frederick S.–Los Angeles NL 1974; Cincinnati NL 1979.

Aviles, Ramon A.A.–Philadelphia NL 1980.

– B –

Bair, C. Douglas–Cincinnati NL 1979.

Baker, Frank W.–Baltimore AL 1973-74.

Baker, Johnnie B.–Los Angeles NL 1977-78.

Bando, Salvatore L.–Oakland AL 1971-72-73-74-75.

Barlow, Michael R.–California AL 1979.

Barr, James L.–San Francisco NL 1971.

Baylor, Donald E.–Baltimore AL 1973-74; California AL 1979.

Beattie, James L.–New York AL 1978.

Belanger, Mark H.–Baltimore AL 1969-70-71-73-74-79.

Bench, Johnny L.–Cincinnati NL 1970-72-73-75-76-79.

Beniquez, Juan J.–Boston AL 1975.

Bergman, David B.–Houston NL 1980.

Bibby, James B.–Pittsburgh NL 1979.

Billingham, John E.–Cincinnati NL 1972-73.

Bird, J. Douglas–Kansas City AL 1976-77-78.

Blair, Paul L.–Baltimore AL 1969-70-71-73-74; New York AL 1977-78.

Blass, Stephen R.–Pittsburgh NL 1971-72.

Blefary, Curtis L.–Oakland AL 1971.

Blue, Vida R.–Oakland AL 1971-72-73-74-75.

Blyleven, Rikalbert–Minnesota AL 1970; Pittsburgh NL 1979.

Bochy, Bruce D.–Houston NL 1980.

Bonds, Bobby L.–San Francisco NL 1971.

Boone, Robert R.–Philadelphia NL 1976-77-78-80.

Borbon, Pedro R.–Cincinnati NL 1972-73-75-76.

Bosman, Richard A.–Oakland AL 1975.

Boswell, David W.–Minnesota AL 1969.

Boswell, Kenneth G.–New York NL 1969-73.

Bourque, Patrick D.–Oakland AL 1973.

Bowa, Lawrence R.–Philadelphia NL 1976-77-78-80.

Boyer, Cletis L.–Atlanta NL 1969.

Braun, Stephen R.–Kansas City AL 1978.

Bravo, Angel A.–Cincinnati NL 1970.

Brett, George H.–Kansas City AL 1976-77-78-80.

Brett, Kenneth A.–Pittsburgh NL 1974-75.

Briles, Nelson K.–Pittsburgh NL 1972.

Brinkman, Edwin A.–Detroit AL 1972.

Britton, James A.–Atlanta NL 1969.

Brown, Isaac–Detroit AL 1972.

Brown, Larry L.–Baltimore AL 1973.

Brown, Ollie L.–Philadelphia NL 1976-77.

Brown, R.L. Bobby–New York AL 1980.

Brown, W. Gates—Detroit AL 1972.

Brusstar, Warren S.—Philadelphia NL 1977-78-80.

Bryant, Ronald R.—San Francisco NL 1971.

Buckner, William J.—Los Angeles NL 1974.

Buford, Donald A.—Baltimore AL 1969-70-71.

Bumbry, Alonza B.—Baltimore AL 1973-74-79.

Burke, Glenn L.—Los Angeles NL 1977.

Burleson, Richard P.—Boston AL 1975.

Bystrom, Martin E.—Philadelphia NL 1980.

— C —

Cabell, Enos M.—Baltimore AL 1974; Houston NL 1980.

Campaneris, Dagoberto B.—Oakland AL 1971-72-73-74-75; California AL 1979.

Candelaria, John R.—Pittsburgh NL 1975-79.

Carbo, Bernardo—Cincinnati NL 1970.

Cardenal, Jose D.—Philadelphia NL 1978.

Cardenas, Leonardo A.—Minnesota AL 1969-70.

Carew, Rodney C.—Minnesota AL 1969-70; California AL 1979.

Carlton, Steven N.—Philadelphia NL 1976-77-78-80.

Carrithers, Donald G.—San Francisco NL 1971.

Carroll, Clay P.—Cincinnati NL 1970-72-73-75.

Carty, Ricardo A. J.—Atlanta NL 1969.

Cash, David—Pittsburgh NL 1970-71-72; Philadelphia NL 1976.

Cash, Norman D.—Detroit AL 1972.

Cedeno, Cesar—Houston NL 1980.

Cepeda, Orlando M.—Atlanta NL 1969.

Cerone, Richard A.—New York AL 1980.

Cey, Ronald C.—Los Angeles NL 1974-77-78.

Chambliss, C. Christopher—New York AL 1976-77-78.

Chance, W. Dean—Minnesota AL 1969.

Chaney, Darrel L.—Cincinnati NL 1972-73.

Christenson, Larry R.—Philadelphia NL 1977-78-80.

Clark, Robert C.—California AL 1979.

Clay, Kenneth E.—New York AL 1978.

Clear, Mark A.—California AL 1979.

Clemente, Roberto W.—Pittsburgh NL 1970-71-72.

Cleveland, Reginald L.—Boston AL 1975.

Cline, Tyrone A.—Cincinnati NL 1970.

Clines, Eugene A.—Pittsburgh NL 1971-72-74.

Cloninger, Tony L.—Cincinnati NL 1970.

Coggins, Richard A.—Baltimore AL 1973-74.

Coleman, Joseph H.—Detroit AL 1972.

Collins, David S.—Cincinnati NL 1979.

Concepcion, David I.—Cincinnati NL 1970-72-75-76-79.

Conigliaro, William M.—Oakland AL 1973.

Cooper, Cecil C.—Boston AL 1975.

Cowens, Alfred E.—Kansas City AL 1976-77-78.

Crawford, Willie M.—Los Angeles NL 1974.

Crosby, Edward C.—Cincinnati NL 1973.

Crowley, Terrence M.—Baltimore AL 1973-79; Cincinnati NL 1975.

Cruz, Hector—Cincinnati NL 1979.

Cruz, Jose—Houston NL 1980.

Cuellar, Miguel—Baltimore AL 1969-70-71-73-74.

Cullen Timothy L.—Oakland AL 1972.

Cumberland, John S.—San Francisco NL 1971.

— D —

Dauer, Richard F.—Baltimore AL 1979.

Davalillo, Victor J.—Pittsburgh NL 1971-72; Oakland AL 1973; Los Angeles NL 1977.

Davis, H. Thomas—Oakland AL 1971; Baltimore AL 1973-74.

Davis, Ronald G.—New York AL 1980.

Davis, William H.—California AL 1979.

DeCinces, Douglas V.—Baltimore AL 1979.

Demery, Lawrence C.—Pittsburgh NL 1974-75.

Dempsey, J. Rikard—Baltimore AL 1979.

Dent, Russell E.—New York AL 1977-78-80.

Didier, Robert D.—Atlanta NL 1969.

Dietz, Richard A.—San Francisco NL 1971.

Downing, Alphonso E.—Los Angeles NL 1974.

Downing, Brian J.—California AL 1979.

Doyle, Brian R.—New York AL 1978.

Doyle, Paul S.—Atlanta NL 1969.

Doyle, R. Dennis—Boston AL 1975.

Drago, Richard A.—Boston AL 1975.

Driessen, Daniel D.—Cincinnati NL 1973-76-79.

Duffy, Frank T.—San Francisco NL 1971.

Duncan, David E.—Oakland AL 1971-72.

Dyer, Don R.—Pittsburgh NL 1975.

— E —

Easler, Michael A.—Pittsburgh NL 1979.

Eastwick, Rawlins J.—Cincinnati NL 1975-76; Philadelphia NL 1978.

Ellis, Dock P.—Pittsburgh NL 1970-71-72-75; New York AL 1976.

Epstein, Michael P.—Oakland AL 1971-72.

Etchebarren, Andrew A.—Baltimore AL 1969-70-71-73-74.

Evans, Dwight W.—Boston AL 1975.

— F —

Ferguson, Joseph V.—Los Angeles NL 1974-78.

Figueroa, Eduardo—New York AL 1976-77-78.

Fingers, Roland G.—Oakland AL 1971-72-73-74-75.

Fisk, Carlton E.—Boston AL 1975.

Flanagan, Michael K.—Baltimore AL 1979.

Flynn, R. Douglas—Cincinnati NL 1976.

Foli, Timothy J.—Pittsburgh NL 1979.

Foote, Barry C.—Philadelphia NL 1978.

Ford, Darnell G.—California AL 1979.

Forsch, Kenneth R.—Houston NL 1980.

Forster, Terry J.—Los Angeles NL 1978.

Fosse, Raymond E.—Oakland AL 1973-74-75.

Foster, George A.—Cincinnati NL 1972-75-76-79.

Freehan, William A.—Detroit AL 1972.

Frost, C. David—California AL 1979.

Fryman, Woodrow T.—Detroit AL 1972.

Fuentes, Rigoberto—San Francisco NL 1971.

— G —

Gagliano, Philip J.—Cincinnati NL 1973.

Gallagher, Alan M.—San Francisco NL 1971.

Gamble, Oscar C.—New York AL 1976-80.

Garber, H. Eugene—Philadelphia NL 1976-77.

Garcia, Alfonso R.—Baltimore AL 1979.

Garland, M. Wayne—Baltimore AL 1974.

Garman, Michael D.—Los Angeles NL 1977.

Garner, Philip M.—Oakland AL 1975; Pittsburgh NL 1979.

Garrett, R. Wayne—New York NL 1969-73.

Garrido, Gil G.—Atlanta NL 1969.

Garvey, Steven P.—Los Angeles NL 1974-77-78.

Gaspar, Rodney E.—New York NL 1969.

Gentry, Gary E.—New York NL 1969.

Geronimo, Cesar F.—Cincinnati NL 1972-73-75-76-79.

Gibbon, Joseph C.—Pittsburgh NL 1970.

Giusti, J. David—Pittsburgh NL 1970-71-72-74-75.

Gonzalez, A. Antonio—Atlanta NL 1969.

Gonzalez, Julio C.—Philadelphia NL 1978.

Goodson, J. Edward—Los Angeles NL 1977.

Gossage, Richard M.—New York AL 1978-80.

Granger, Wayne A.—Cincinnati NL 1970.

Grant, James T.—Oakland AL 1971.

Green, Richard L.—Oakland AL 1971-72-73-74.

Grich, Robert A.—Baltimore AL 1973-74; California AL 1979.

Griffey, G. Kenneth—Cincinnati NL 1973-75-76.

Grimsley, Ross A.—Cincinnati NL 1972-73; Baltimore AL 1974.

Gross, Gregory E.—Philadelphia NL 1980.

Grote, Gerald W.—New York NL 1969-73; Los Angeles NL 1977-78.

Grzenda, Joseph C.—Minnesota AL 1969.

Guidry, Ronald A.—New York AL 1976-77-78-80.

Gullett, Donald E.—Cincinnati NL 1970-72-73-75-76; New York AL 1977.

Gura, Lawrence C.—Kansas City AL 1976-77-78-80.

— H —

Hague, Joe C.—Cincinnati NL 1972.

Hahn, Donald A.—New York NL 1973.

Hall, Richard W.—Baltimore AL 1969-70.

Hall, Thomas E.—Minnesota AL 1969-70; Cincinnati NL 1972-73; Kansas City AL 1976.

Haller, Thomas F.—Detroit AL 1972.

Hamilton, David E.—Oakland AL 1972.

Hamilton, Steve A.—San Francisco NL 1971.

Harlow, Larry D.—California AL 1979.

Harmon, Terry W.—Philadelphia NL 1976.

Harper, Tommy—Oakland AL 1975.

Harrelson, Derrel M.—New York NL 1969-73.

Hart, James R.—San Francisco NL 1971.

Hassler, Andrew E.—Kansas City AL 1976-77.

Hebner, Richard J.—Pittsburgh NL 1970-71-72-74-75; Philadelphia NL 1977-78.

Heep, Daniel W.—Houston NL 1980.

Hegan, J. Michael—Oakland AL 1971-72.

Helms, Tommy V.—Cincinnati NL 1970.

Henderson, Kenneth J.—San Francisco NL 1971.

Hendrick, George A.—Oakland AL 1972.

Hendricks, Elrod J.—Baltimore AL 1969-70-71-74; New York AL 1976.

Hernandez, Jacinto—Pittsburgh NL 1971.

Hernandez, Ramon G.—Pittsburgh NL 1972-74-75.

Hiller, John F.—Detroit AL 1972.

Holt, James W.—Minnesota AL 1970; Oakland AL 1974-75.

Holtzman, Kenneth D.—Oakland AL 1972-73-74-75.

Hood, Donald H.—Baltimore AL 1973.

Hooton, Burt C.—Los Angeles NL 1977-78.

Hopkins, Donald—Oakland AL 1975.

Horlen, Joel E.—Oakland AL 1972.

Horton, William W.—Detroit AL 1972.

Hough, Charles O.—Los Angeles NL 1974-77-78.

Howe, Arthur H.—Pittsburgh NL 1974; Houston NL 1980.

Hrabosky, Alan T.—Kansas City AL 1978.

Hume, Thomas H.—Cincinnati NL 1979.

Hunter, James A.—Oakland AL 1971-72-73-74; New York AL 1976-78.

Hurdle, Clinton M.—Kansas City AL 1978-80.

Hutton, Thomas G.—Philadelphia NL 1976-77.

— J —

Jackson, Grant D.—Baltimore AL 1973-74; New York AL 1976; Pittsburgh NL 1979.

Jackson, Reginald M.—Oakland AL 1971-72-73-74-75; New York AL 1977-78-80.

Jackson, R. Sonny—Atlanta NL 1969.

Jarvis, R. Patrick—Atlanta NL 1969.

Jeter, Johnny—Pittsburgh NL 1970.

John, Thomas E.—Los Angeles NL 1977-78; New York AL 1980.

Johnson, Clifford—New York AL 1977-78.

Johnson, David A.—Baltimore AL 1969-70-71; Philadelphia NL 1977.

Johnson, Deron R.—Oakland AL 1973.

Johnson, Jerry M.—San Francisco NL 1971.

Johnson, Robert D.—Pittsburgh NL 1971-72.

Johnstone, John W.—Philadelphia NL 1976-77.

Jones, Cleon J.—New York NL 1969-73.

Joshua, Von E.—Los Angeles NL 1974.

— K —

Kaat, James L.—Minnesota AL 1970; Philadelphia NL 1976.

Kaline, Albert W.—Detroit AL 1972.

Kelly, Patrick H.—Baltimore AL 1979.

Killebrew, Harmon C.—Minnesota AL 1969-70.

King, Harold—Cincinnati NL 1973.

Kingman, David A.—San Francisco NL 1971.

Kirkpatrick, Edgar L.—Pittsburgh NL 1974-75.

Kison, Bruce E.—Pittsburgh NL 1971-72-74-75.

Knapp, Christian R.—California AL 1979.

Knight, C. Ray—Cincinnati NL 1979.

Knowles, Darold D.—Oakland AL 1971.

Knox, John C.—Detroit AL 1972.

Koosman, Jerry M.—New York NL 1969-73.

Kosco, Andrew J.—Cincinnati NL 1973.

Kranepool, Edward E.—New York NL 1969-73.

Kubiak, Theodore R.—Oakland AL 1972-73.

— L —

LaCock, Ralph P.—Kansas City AL 1977-78-80.

LaCorte, Frank J.—Houston NL 1980.

LaCoss, Michael J.—Cincinnati NL 1979.

Lacy, Leondaus—Los Angeles NL 1974-77-78.

LaGrow, Lerrin H.—Detroit AL 1972.

Lahoud, Joseph M.—Kansas City AL 1977.

Landestoy, Rafael S.C.—Houston NL 1980.

Lanier, Harold C.—San Francisco NL 1971.

Lansford, Carney R.—California AL 1979.

LaRoche, David E.—California AL 1979.

Lefebvre, Joseph H.—New York AL 1980.

Leibrandt, Charles L.—Cincinnati NL 1979.

Leonard, Dennis P.—Kansas City AL 1976-77-78-80.

Leonard, Jeffrey N.—Houston NL 1980.

Lerch, Randy L.—Philadelphia NL 1978.

Lewis, Allan S.—Oakland AL 1973.

Lindblad, Paul A.—Oakland AL 1975.

Littell, Mark A.—Kansas City AL 1976-77.

Locker, Robert A.—Oakland AL 1971-72.

Lolich, Michael S.—Detroit AL 1972.

Lonborg, James R.—Philadelphia NL 1976-77.

Lopes, David E.—Los Angeles NL 1974-77-78.

Lopez, Marcelino P.—Baltimore AL 1969.

Lowenstein, John L.—Baltimore AL 1979.

Lum, Michael K.—Atlanta NL 1969; Cincinnati NL 1976.

Luzinski, Gregory M.—Philadelphia NL 1976-77-78-80.

Lyle, Albert W.—New York AL 1976-77-78.

Lynn, Fredric M.—Boston AL 1975.

— M —

Maddox, Elliott—New York AL 1976.

Maddox, Garry L.—Philadelphia NL 1976-77-78-80.

Madlock, Bill—Pittsburgh NL 1979.

Mangual, Angel L.—Oakland AL 1971-72-73-74.

Manuel, Charles F.—Minnesota AL 1969-70.

Marichal, Juan A.—San Francisco NL 1971.

Marquez, Gonzalo—Oakland AL 1972.

Marshall, Michael G.—Los Angeles NL 1974.

Martin, Jerry L.—Philadelphia NL 1976-77-78.

Martin, Joseph C.—New York NL 1969.

Martinez, J. Buck—Kansas City AL 1976.

Martinez, J. Dennis—Baltimore AL 1979.

Martinez, Teodoro N.—Oakland AL 1975.

Mason, James P.—New York AL 1976.

Matlack, Jonathan T.—New York NL 1973.

Maxvill, C. Dallan—Oakland AL 1972-74.

May, Carlos—New York AL 1976.

May, David L.—Baltimore AL 1969.

May, Lee A.—Cincinnati NL 1970; Baltimore AL 1979.

May, Milton S.—Pittsburgh NL 1971-72.

May, Rudolph—New York AL 1980.

Mayberry, John C.—Kansas City AL 1976-77.

Mays, Willie H.—San Francisco NL 1971; New York NL 1973.

Mazeroski, Williams S.—Pittsburgh NL 1970-71-72.

McAuliffe, Richard J.—Detroit AL 1972.

McBride, Arnold R.—Philadelphia NL 1977-78-80.

McCarver, J. Timothy—Philadelphia NL 1976-77-78.

McCovey, Willie L.—San Francisco NL 1971.

McEnaney, William H.—Cincinnati NL 1975.

McGlothlin, James M.—Cincinnati NL 1972.

McGraw, Frank E.—New York NL 1969-73; Philadelphia NL 1976-77-78-80.

McGregor, Scott H.—Baltimore AL 1979.

McMahon, Donald J.—San Francisco NL 1971.

McMullen, Kenneth L.—Los Angeles NL 1974.

McNally, David A.—Baltimore AL 1969-70-71-73-74.

McRae, Harold A.—Cincinnati NL 1970-72; Kansas City AL 1976-77-78-80.

Mendoza, Mario—Pittsburgh NL 1974.

Menke, Denis J.—Cincinnati NL 1972-73.

Merritt, James J.—Cincinnati NL 1970.

Messersmith, John A.—Los Angeles NL 1974.

Millan, Felix B. M.—Atlanta NL 1969; New York NL 1973.

Miller, Richard A.—California AL 1979.

Miller, Robert L.—Minnesota AL 1969; Pittsburgh NL 1971-72.

Milner, John D.—New York NL 1973; Pittsburgh NL 1979.

Mincher, Donald R.—Oakland AL 1972.

Mingori, Stephen B.—Kansas City AL 1976-77-78.

Mitterwald, George E.—Minnesota AL 1969-70.

Monday, Robert J.—Oakland AL 1971; Los Angeles NL 1977-78.

Montague, John E.—California AL 1979.

Moose, Robert R.—Pittsburgh NL 1970-71-72.

Moreland, B. Keith—Philadelphia NL 1980.

Moreno, Omar R.—Pittsburgh NL 1979.

Moret, Rogelio—Boston AL 1975.

Morgan, Joe L.—Cincinnati NL 1972-73-75-76-79; Houston NL 1980.

Morrison, James F.—Philadelphia NL 1978.

Mota, Manuel R.—Los Angeles NL 1974-77-78.

Motton, Curtell H.—Baltimore AL 1969-71-74.

Munson, Thurman, L.—New York AL 1976-77-78.

Murcer, Bobby R.—New York AL 1980.

Murray, Eddie C.—Baltimore AL 1979.

— N —

Neibauer, Gary W.—Atlanta NL 1969.

Nelson, David E.—Kansas City AL 1976.

Nelson, Roger E.—Cincinnati NL 1973.

Nettles, Graig—Minnesota AL 1969; New York AL 1976-77-78-80.

Niekro, Joseph F.—Detroit AL 1972; Houston NL 1980.

Niekro, Philip H.—Atlanta NL 1969.

Nolan, Gary L.—Cincinnati NL 1970-72-75-76.

Noles, Dickie R.—Philadelphia NL 1980.

Norman, Fredie H.—Cincinnati NL 1973-75-79.

North, William A.—Oakland AL 1974-75; Los Angeles NL 1978.

Northrup, James T.—Detroit AL 1972.

— O —

Oates, Johnny L.—Philadelphia NL 1976.

Odom, Johnny L.—Oakland AL 1972-73-74.

Oliva, Antonio—Minnesota AL 1969-70.

Oliver, Albert—Pittsburgh NL 1970-71-72-74-75.

Otis, Amos J.—Kansas City AL 1976-77-78-80.

Ott, N. Edward—Pittsburgh NL 1979.

— P —

Paciorek, Thomas M.—Los Angeles NL 1974.

Pagan, Jose A.—Pittsburgh NL 1970-71.

Palmer, James A.—Baltimore AL 1969-70-71-73-74-79.

Pappas, Milton S.—Atlanta NL 1969.

Parker, David G.—Pittsburgh NL 1974-75-79.

Parker, Harry W.—New York NL 1973.

Pastore, Frank E.—Cincinnati, NL 1979.

Patek, Freddie J.—Pittsburgh NL 1970; Kansas City AL 1976-77-78.

Pattin, Martin W.—Kansas City AL 1976-77-78.

Perez, Atanasio R.—Cincinnati NL 1970-72-73-75-76.

Perranoski, Ronald P.—Minnesota AL 1969-70.

Perry, Gaylord J.—San Francisco NL 1971.

Perry, James E.—Minnesota AL 1969-70.

Petrocelli, Americo P.—Boston AL 1975.

Pina, Horacio—Oakland AL 1973.

Piniella, Louis V.—New York AL 1976-77-78-80.

Pizarro, Juan—Pittsburgh NL 1974.

Popovich, Paul E.—Pittsburgh NL 1974.

Poquette, Thomas A.—Kansas City AL 1976-77-78.

Porter, Darrell R.—Kansas City AL 1977-78-80.

Powell, John W.—Baltimore AL 1969-70-71-73-74.

Puhl, Terry S.—Houston NL 1980.

Pujols, Luis B.—Houston NL 1980.

— Q —

Quilici, Frank R.—Minnesota AL 1970.

Quirk, James P.—Kansas City AL 1976.

Quisenberry, Daniel R.—Kansas City AL 1980.

— R —

Randolph, William L.—Pittsburgh NL 1975; New York AL 1976-77-80.

Ratliff, Paul H.—Minnesota AL 1970.

Rau, Douglas J.—Los Angeles NL 1974-77-78.

Rautzhan, Clarence G.—Los Angeles NL 1977-78.

Reed, Ronald L.—Atlanta NL 1969; Philadelphia NL 1976-77-78-80.

Reese, Richard B.—Minnesota AL 1969-70.

Renick, W. Richard—Minnesota AL 1969-70.

Rettenmund, Mervin W.—Baltimore AL 1969-70-71-73; Cincinnati NL 1975; California AL 1979.

Reuss, Jerry—Pittsburgh NL 1974-75.

Reynolds, G. Craig—Pittsburgh NL 1975; Houston NL 1980.

Reynolds, Robert A.—Baltimore AL 1973-74.

Rhoden, Richard A.—Los Angeles NL 1977-78.

Richert, Peter G.—Baltimore AL 1969.

Rivers, John M.—New York AL 1976-77-78.

Roberts, David A.—Pittsburgh NL 1979.

Robertson, Robert E.—Pittsburgh NL 1970-71-72-74-75.

Robinson, Brooks C.—Baltimore AL 1969-70-71-73-74.

Robinson, Don A.—Pittsburgh NL 1979.

Robinson, Frank—Baltimore AL 1969-70-71.

Robinson, William H.—Pittsburgh NL 1975-79.

Rodriguez, Aurelio—Detroit AL 1972; New York AL 1980.

Roenicke, Gary S.—Baltimore AL 1979.

Rojas, Octavio—Kansas City AL 1976-77.

Romo, Enrique—Pittsburgh NL 1979.

Rooker, James P.—Pittsburgh NL 1974-75.

Rosario, Angel—San Francisco NL 1971.

Rose, Peter E.—Cincinnati NL 1970-72-73-75-76; Philadelphia NL 1980.

Roseboro, John—Minnesota AL 1969.

Rudi, Joseph O.—Oakland AL 1971-72-73-74-75.

Ruhle, Vernon G.—Houston NL 1980.

Russell, William E.—Los Angeles NL 1974-77-78.

Ruthven, Richard D.—Philadelphia NL 1978-80.

Ryan, L. Nolan—New York NL 1969; California AL 1979; Houston NL 1980.

– S –

Salmon, Ruthford E.—Baltimore AL 1969.

Sambito, Joseph C.—Houston NL 1980.

Sanguillen, Manuel de J.—Pittsburgh NL 1970-71-72-74-75.

Sarmiento, Manuel E.—Cincinnati NL 1976.

Saucier, Kevin A.—Philadelphia NL 1980.

Scherman, Frederick J.—Detroit AL 1972.

Schmidt, Michael J.—Philadelphia NL 1976-77-78-80.

Seaver, G. Thomas—New York NL 1969-73; Cincinnati NL 1979.

Seelbach, Charles F.—Detroit AL 1972.

Segui, Diego P.—Oakland AL 1971.

Shamsky, Arthur L.—New York NL 1969.

Sims, Duane B.—Detroit AL 1972.

Singleton, Kenneth W.—Baltimore AL 1979.

Sizemore, Ted C.—Philadelphia NL 1977-78.

Skaggs, David L.—Baltimore AL 1979.

Smith, Billy E.—Baltimore AL 1979.

Smith, C. Reginald—Los Angeles NL 1977-78.

Smith, David S.—Houston NL 1980.

Smith, Lonnie—Philadelphia NL 1980.

Soderholm, Eric T.—New York AL 1980.

Solomon, Eddie—Los Angeles NL 1974.

Sosa, Elias—Los Angeles NL 1977.

Soto, Mario M.—Cincinnati NL 1979.

Speier, Chris E.—San Francisco NL 1971.

Spencer, James L.—New York AL 1980.

Spilman, Harry W.—Cincinnati NL 1979.

Splittorff, Paul W.—Kansas City AL 1976-77-78-80.

Stahl, Larry F.—Cincinnati NL 1973.

Stanhouse, Donald J.—Baltimore AL 1979.

Stanley, Frederick B.—New York AL 1976-77-78.

Stanley, Mitchell J.—Detroit AL 1972.

Stargell, Wilver D.—Pittsburgh NL 1970-71-72-74-75-79.

Staub, Daniel J.—New York NL 1973.

Stennett, Renaldo A.—Pittsburgh NL 1972-74-75-79.

Stewart, James F.—Cincinnati NL 1970.

Stinson, G. Robert—Kansas City AL 1976.

Stone, George H.—Atlanta NL 1969; New York NL 1973.

Sutton, Donald H.—Los Angeles NL 1974-77-78.

– T –

Tanana, Frank D.—California AL 1979.

Taveras, Franklin—Pittsburgh NL 1974-75.

Taylor, Antonio—Detroit AL 1972.
Taylor, Ronald W.—New York NL 1969.
Tekulve, Kenton C.—Pittsburgh NL 1975-79.
Tenace, F. Gene—Oakland AL 1971-72-73-74-75.
Thomasson, Gary L.—New York AL 1978.
Thompson, Danny L.—Minnesota AL 1970.
Thon, Richard W.—California AL 1979.
Tiant, Luis C.—Minnesota AL 1970; Boston AL 1975.
Tidrow, Richard W.—New York AL 1976-77-78.
Tillman, J. Robert—Atlanta NL 1969.
Todd, James R.—Oakland AL 1975.
Tolan, Robert—Cincinnati NL 1970-72; Philadelphia NL 1976.
Tomlin, David A.—Cincinnati NL 1973-79.
Torrez, Michael A.—New York AL 1977.
Tovar, Cesar L.—Minnesota AL 1969-70; Oakland AL 1975.
Trillo, J. Manuel—Oakland AL 1974; Philadelphia NL 1980.

— U —

Uhlaender, Theodore O.—Minnesota AL 1969; Cincinnati NL 1972.
Underwood, Thomas G.—Philadelphia NL 1976; New York AL 1980.
Unser, Delbert B.—Philadelphia NL 1980.
Upshaw, Cecil L.—Atlanta NL 1969.

— V —

Velez, Otoniel—New York AL 1976.
Vukovich, George S.—Philadelphia NL 1980.

— W —

Walker, J. Luke—Pittsburgh NL 1970-72.
Walling, Dennis M.—Houston NL 1980.
Washington, Claudell—Oakland AL 1974-75.
Washington, Herbert L.—Oakland AL 1974.
Washington, U. L.—Kansas City AL 1980.
Wathan, John D.—Kansas City AL 1976-77-78-80.
Watson, Robert J.—New York AL 1980.
Watt, Eddie D.—Baltimore AL 1969-71-73.
Weis, Albert J.—New York NL 1969.
Welch, Robert L.—Los Angeles NL 1978.
White, Frank—Kansas City AL 1976-77-78-80.
White, Roy H.—New York AL 1976-77-78.
Wilcox, Milton E.—Cincinnati NL 1970.
Williams, Billy L.—Oakland AL 1975.
Williams, Earl C.—Baltimore AL 1973-74.
Williams, Stanley W.—Minnesota AL 1970.
Wilson, Willie J.—Kansas City AL 1978-80.
Wise, Richard C.—Boston AL 1975.
Wohlford, James E.—Kansas City AL 1976.
Woods, Gary L.—Houston NL 1980.
Woodson, Richard L.—Minnesota AL 1969-70.
Woodward, William F.—Cincinnati NL 1970.
Worthington, Allan F.—Minnesota AL 1969.
Wynn, James S.—Los Angeles NL 1974.

— Y —

Yastrzemski, Carl M.—Boston AL 1975.
Yeager, Stephen W.—Los Angeles NL 1974-77-78.

— Z —

Zachary, W. Chris—Detroit AL 1972.
Zachry, Patrick P.—Cincinnati NL 1976.
Zdeb, Joseph E.—Kansas City AL 1977.
Zepp, William C.—Minnesota AL 1970.
Zisk, Richard W.—Pittsburgh NL 1974-75.

CHAMPIONSHIP SERIES MANAGERS (24)

Alston, Walter E.—Los Angeles NL 1974.
Anderson, George L.—Cincinnati NL 1970-72-73-75-76.
Berra, Lawrence P.—New York NL 1973.
Dark, Alvin R.—Oakland AL 1974-75.
Fox, Charles F.—San Francisco NL 1971.
Fregosi, James L.—California AL 1979.
Frey, James G.—Kansas City AL 1980.
Green, G. Dallas—Philadelphia NL 1980.
Harris, C. Luman—Atlanta NL 1969.

Herzog, Dorrell N. E.—Kansas City AL 1976-77-78.

Hodges, Gilbert R.—New York NL 1969.

Howser, Richard D.—New York AL 1980.

Johnson, Darrell D.—Boston AL 1975.

Lasorda, Thomas C.—Los Angeles NL 1977-78.

Lemon, Robert G.—New York AL 1978.

Martin, Alfred M.—Minnesota AL 1969; Detroit AL 1972; New York AL 1976-77.

McNamara, John F.—Cincinnati NL 1979.

Murtaugh, Daniel E.—Pittsburgh NL 1970-71-74-75.

Ozark, Daniel L.—Philadelphia NL 1976-77-78.

Rigney, William J.—Minnesota AL 1970.

Tanner, Charles W.—Pittsburgh NL 1979.

Virdon, William C.—Pittsburgh NL 1972; Houston NL 1980.

Weaver, Earl S.—Baltimore AL 1969-70-71-73-74-79.

Williams, Richard H.—Oakland AL 1971-72-73.

REGGIE JACKSON—author of most Championship Series records.

INDIVIDUAL SERIES SERVICE

Most Series Played

A. L.—8— Jackson, Reginald M., Oakland, 1971, 1972, 1973, 1974, 1975; New York, 1977, 1978, 1980.

N. L.—7— Hebner, Richard J., Pittsburgh, 1970, 1971, 1972, 1974, 1975; Philadelphia, 1977, 1978.

Most Series Played, One Club

N. L.—6— Johnny L. Bench, Cincinnati, 1970, 1972, 1973, 1975, 1976, 1979.
Wilver D. Stargell, Pittsburgh, 1970, 1971, 1972, 1974, 1975, 1979.

A. L.—6— Mark H. Belanger, Baltimore, 1969, 1970, 1971, 1973, 1974, 1979.
James A. Palmer, Baltimore, 1969, 1970, 1971, 1973, 1974, 1979.

Most Clubs, Total Series

Both Leagues—3— Davalillo, Victor J., Pittsburgh NL, 1971, 1972; Oakland AL, 1973; Los Angeles NL, 1977.

Hall, Thomas E., Minnesota AL, 1969, 1970; Cincinnati NL 1972, 1973; Kansas City AL, 1976.

Rettenmund, Mervin W., Baltimore AL, 1969, 1970, 1971, 1973; Cincinnati NL, 1975; California AL, 1979.

Jackson, Grant D., Baltimore AL, 1973, 1974; New York AL, 1976; Pittsburgh NL, 1979.

Ryan, L. Nolan, New York NL, 1969; California AL, 1979; Houston NL, 1980.

A. L.-N. L.—2-Held by many players.

Most Consecutive Series Played

A. L.—5— Salvatore L. Bando, Vida R. Blue, Dagoberto B. Campaneris, Roland G. Fingers, Reginald M. Jackson, Joseph O. Rudi, F. Gene Tenace, Oakland, 1971 through 1975.

N. L.—3— Held by many players.

Most Series Playing in All Games

A. L.—8— Reginald M. Jackson, Oakland, 1971, 1972, 1973, 1974, 1975; New York, 1977, 1978, 1980; 32 games.

N. L.—6— Johnny L. Bench, Cincinnati, 1970, 1972, 1973, 1975, 1976, 1979; 22 games.

Wilver D. Stargell, Pittsburgh, 1970, 1971, 1972, 1974, 1975, 1979; 22 games.

Peter E. Rose, Cincinnati, 1970, 1972, 1973, 1975, 1976; Philadelphia, 1980; 24 games.

Most Games, Total Series

A. L.—32— Jackson, Reginald M., Oakland, 1971, 1972, 1973, 1974, 1975; New York, 1977, 1978, 1980; 8 Series, 32 consecutive games.

N. L.—25— Hebner, Richard J., Pittsburgh, 1970, 1971, 1972, 1974, 1975; Philadelphia, 1977, 1978; 7 Series, 22 consecutive games.

Most Games, Total Series, One Club

N. L.—22— Johnny L. Bench, Cincinnati, 1970, 1972, 1973, 1975, 1976, 1979; 6 Series.

Wilver D. Stargell, Pittsburgh, 1970, 1971, 1972, 1974, 1975, 1979; 6 Series.

A. L.—21— Mark H. Belanger, Baltimore, 1969, 1970, 1971, 1973, 1974, 1979; 6 Series.

Most Times on Winning Club, Playing One or More Games Each Series

N. L.—5— Peter E. Rose, Cincinnati, 1970, 1972, 1975, 1976; Philadelphia, 1980.

A. L.—5— Paul L. Blair, Baltimore, 1969, 1970, 1971; New York, 1977, 1978.
James A. Hunter, Oakland, 1972, 1973, 1974; New York, 1976, 1978.

Most Times, Playing on Winning Club—Continued

Reginald M. Jackson, Oakland, 1972, 1973, 1974; New York, 1977, 1978.
Both Leagues—5—Donald E. Gullett, Cincinnati NL, 1970, 1972, 1975, 1976; New York AL, 1977.

Most Times on Losing Club, Playing One or More Games Each Series

N. L.—6—Hebner, Richard J., Pittsburgh, 1970, 1972, 1974, 1975; Philadelphia, 1977, 1978.
A. L.—3—Held by many players.

Most Positions Played, Total Series

N. L.—4—Rose, Peter E., Cincinnati, 1970, 1972, 1973, 1975, 1976; Philadelphia, 1980; 24 games, right field, left field, third base, first base.
A. L.—3—Tovar, Cesar L., Minnesota, 1969, 1970; Oakland, 1975; 8 games, center field, second base, left field.
    Rettenmund, Mervin W., Baltimore, 1969, 1970, 1971, 1973; California, 1979; 10 games, left field, center field, right field.
    Tenace, F. Gene, Oakland, 1971, 1972, 1973, 1974, 1975; 18 games, catcher, second base, first base.
    Blair, Paul L., Baltimore, 1969, 1970, 1971, 1973, 1974; New York, 1977, 1978; 25 games, center field, right field, second base.

Most Positions Played, Series

A. L.—3—Tovar, Cesar L., Minnesota, 1970, center field, second base, left field; 3-game Series, 3 games.
N. L.—2—Held by many players.

Oldest Championship Series Player (Non-Pitcher)

N. L.—Mays, Willie H., New York; 42 years, 5 months, 4 days on October 10, 1973.
A. L.—Davis, William H., California; 39 years, 5 months, 19 days on October 4, 1979.

Oldest Championship Series Pitcher

N. L.—McMahon, Donald J., San Francisco; 41 years, 9 months, 2 days on October 6, 1971.
A. L.—Worthington, Allan F., Minnesota; 40 years, 8 months, 1 day on October 6, 1969.

Youngest Championship Series Player (Non-Pitcher)

A. L.—Washington, Claudell, Oakland; 20 years, 1 month, 5 days on October 5, 1974.
N. L.—Speier, Chris E., San Francisco; 21 years, 3 months, 4 days on October 2, 1971.

Youngest Championship Series Pitcher

A. L.—Blyleven, Rikalbert, Minnesota; 19 years, 5 months, 29 days on October 5, 1970.
N. L.—Gullett, Donald E., Cincinnati; 19 years, 8 months, 28 days on October 4, 1970.

Most Years Between First and Second Series

N. L.—11—Ryan, L. Nolan, New York NL, 1969; Houston NL, 1980 (played in AL Series in 1979).
     7—Lum, Michael K., Atlanta, 1969; Cincinnati, 1976.
        Reed, Ronald L., Atlanta, 1969; Philadelphia, 1976.
Both Leagues—10—Ryan, L. Nolan, New York NL, 1969; California AL, 1979.
A. L.— 8—Rodriguez, Aurelio, Detroit, 1972; New York, 1980.

Most Years Between First and Last Series

N. L.—11—McGraw, Frank E., New York, 1969; Philadelphia, 1980.
        Ryan, L. Nolan, New York, 1969; Houston, 1980.

Reed, Ronald L., Atlanta, 1969; Philadelphia, 1980.
A. L. — 11— Nettles, Graig, Minnesota, 1969; New York, 1980.

INDIVIDUAL BATTING

Highest Batting Average, Total Series (10 or More Games and 30 or More At-Bats)

A. L. — .386 — Rivers, John M., New York, 1976, 1977, 1978; 3 Series, 14 games, 57 at-bats, 22 hits.

N. L. — .382 — Rose, Peter E., Cincinnati, 1970, 1972, 1973, 1975, 1976; Philadelphia, 1980; 6 Series, 24 games, 102 at-bats, 39 hits.

Highest Batting Average, Series (Playing All Games)

3-game Series — N. L. — .778 — Johnstone, John W., Philadelphia, 1976.
                A. L. — .583 — Robinson, Brooks C., Baltimore, 1970.
4-game Series — N. L. — .467 — Baker, Johnnie B., Los Angeles, 1978.
                A. L. — .462 — Jackson, Reginald M., New York, 1978.
5-game Series — A. L. — .524 — Chambliss, C. Christopher, New York, 1976.
                N. L. — .526 — Puhl, Terry S., Houston, 1980.

Highest Slugging Average, Total Series (10 or More Games and 30 or More At-Bats)

N. L. — .816 — Garvey, Steven P., Los Angeles, 1974, 1977, 1978; 3 Series, 12 games, 49 at-bats, 18 hits, 2 doubles, 1 triple, 6 home runs, 40 total bases.

A. L. — .791 — Brett, George H., Kansas City, 1976, 1977, 1978, 1980; 4 Series, 17 games, 67 at-bats, 24 hits, 3 doubles, 4 triples, 6 home runs, 53 total bases.

Highest Slugging Average, Series (10 or More At-Bats)

3-game Series — N. L. — 1.182 — Stargell, Wilver D., Pittsburgh, 1979.
                A. L. — .917 — Oliva, Antonio, Minnesota, 1970.
                            Jackson, Reginald M., Oakland, 1971.
                            Watson, Robert J., New York, 1980.
4-game Series — N. L. — 1.250 — Robertson, Robert E., Pittsburgh, 1971.
                A. L. — 1.056 — Brett, George H., Kansas City, 1978.
5-game Series — A. L. — .952 — Chambliss, C. Christopher, New York, 1976.
                N. L. — .800 — Staub, Daniel J., New York, 1973.

Most At-Bats, Total Series

A. L. — 115 — Jackson, Reginald M., Oakland, 1971, 1972, 1973, 1974, 1975; New York, 1977, 1978, 1980; 8 Series, 32 games.

N. L. — 102 — Rose, Peter E., Cincinnati, 1970, 1972, 1973, 1975, 1976; Philadelphia, 1980; 6 series, 24 games.

Most At-Bats, Series

3-game Series — A. L. — 15 — Belanger, Mark H., Baltimore, 1969.
                            Blair, Paul L., Baltimore, 1969.
                N. L. — 14 — Held by many players.
4-game Series — N. L. — 19 — Cash, David, Pittsburgh, 1971.
                            Maddox, Garry L., Philadelphia, 1978.
                A. L. — 18 — Brett, George H., Kansas City, 1978.
                            Munson, Thurman L., New York, 1978.
5-game Series — N. L. — 24 — Schmidt, Michael J., Philadelphia, 1980.
                A. L. — 23 — Munson, Thurman L., New York, 1976.
                            Rivers, John M., New York, 1976, 1977.

Most Consecutive Hitless Times at Bat, Total Series

Both Leagues — 31 — North, William A., Oakland AL, 1974 (last 13 times at bat), 1975 (all 10 times at bat); Los Angeles NL, 1978 (all 8 times at bat).

Most Consecutive Hitless Times at Bat, Total Series—Continued

N. L.—30—Geronimo, Cesar F., Cincinnati, 1973 (last 13 times at bat), 1975 (all 10 times at bat), 1976 (first 7 times at bat).

A. L.—24—Campaneris, Dagoberto B., Oakland, 1974 (last 13 times at bat), 1975 (all 11 times at bat); California, 1979 (0 times at bat).

Most At-Bats, Total Series, No Hits

N. L.—11—Didier, Robert D., Atlanta, 1969.
Kirkpatrick, Edgar L., Pittsburgh, 1974 (9), 1975 (2).

A. L.—10—Allison, W. Robert, Minnesota, 1969 (8), 1970 (2).
Brown, R. L. Bobby, New York, 1980 (10).

Most At-Bats, Game, Nine Innings

A. L.—6—Blair, Paul L., Baltimore, October 6, 1969.
N. L.—5—Held by many players.

Most At-Bats, Extra-Inning Game

A. L.—6—Buford, Donald A., Baltimore, October 4, 1969; 12 innings.
N. L.—6—Perez, Atanasio R., Cincinnati, October 9, 1973; 12 innings.
Schmidt, Michael J., Philadelphia, October 8, 1980; 10 innings.
Puhl, Terry S., Houston, October 12, 1980; 10 innings.

Most At-Bats, Game, Nine Innings, No Hits

A. L.-N. L.—5—Held by many players.

Most At-Bats, Extra-Inning Game, No Hits

A. L.—6—Buford, Donald A., Baltimore, October 4, 1969; 12 innings.
N. L.—5—Held by many players.

Most At-Bats, Inning

N. L.—2—Garrett, R. Wayne, New York, October 7, 1973; ninth inning.
A. L.—2—Robinson, Frank, Baltimore, October 3, 1970; fourth inning.
McNally, David A., Baltimore, October 4, 1970; ninth inning.
Rettenmund, Mervin W., Baltimore, October 6, 1973; first inning.

Most Times Faced Pitcher, Inning

N. L.—2—Garrett, R. Wayne, New York, October 7, 1973; ninth inning.
A. L.—2—Robinson, Frank, Baltimore, October 3, 1970; fourth inning.
McNally, David A., Baltimore, October 4, 1970; ninth inning.
Rettenmund, Mervin W., Baltimore, October 6, 1973; first inning.

Most Runs, Total Series

A. L.—16—Brett, George H., Kansas City, 1976, 1977, 1978, 1980; 4 Series, 17 games.
N. L.—14—Rose, Peter E., Cincinnati, 1970, 1972, 1973, 1975, 1976; Philadelphia, 1980; 6 Series, 24 games.

Most Runs, Series

3-game Series—A. L.—5—Belanger, Mark H., Baltimore, 1970.
N. L.—4—Held by many players.
4-game Series—A. L.—7—Brett, George H., Kansas City, 1978.
N. L.—6—Garvey, Steven P., Los Angeles, 1978.
5-game Series—A. L.—6—McRae, Harold A., Kansas City, 1977.
N. L.—5—Morgan, Joe L., Cincinnati, 1972.
Millan, Felix B. M., New York, 1973.

Most Runs, Game

N. L.—4—Robertson, Robert E., Pittsburgh, October 3, 1971.
Garvey, Steven P., Los Angeles, October 9, 1974.

A. L.—3—Buford, Donald A., Baltimore, October 6, 1969.
Belanger, Mark H., Baltimore, October 4, 1970.
Rivers, John M., New York, October 14, 1976.
Brett, George H., Kansas City, October 6, 1978.

Most Runs, Inning

A. L.-N. L.—1—Held by many players.

Most Hits, Total Series

N. L.—39—Rose, Peter E., Cincinnati, 1970, 1972, 1973, 1975, 1976; Philadelphia, 1980; 6 Series, 24 games.
A. L.—30—Jackson, Reginald M., Oakland, 1971, 1972, 1973, 1974, 1975; New York, 1977, 1978, 1980; 8 Series, 32 games.

Most Hits, Series

3-game Series—A. L.— 7—Robinson, Brooks C., Baltimore, 1969, 1970.
N. L.— 7—Shamsky, Arthur L., New York, 1969.
Johnstone, John W., Philadelphia, 1976.
4-game Series—N. L.— 8—Cash, David, Pittsburgh, 1971.
A. L.— 7—Brett, George H., Kansas City, 1978.
Carew, Rodney C., California, 1979.
5-game Series—A. L.—11—Chambliss, C. Christopher, New York, 1976.
N. L.—10—Puhl, Terry S., Houston, 1980.

Most Hits, Two Consecutive Series

N. L.—17—Rose, Peter E., Cincinnati, 1972 (9), 1973 (8).
A. L.—14—Robinson, Brooks C., Baltimore, 1969 (7), 1970 (7).
Rivers, John M., New York, 1977 (9), 1978 (5).

Most Series, One or More Hits

A. L.—8—Jackson, Reginald M., Oakland, 1971, 1972, 1973, 1974, 1975; New York, 1977, 1978, 1980.
N. L.—7—Hebner, Richard J., Pittsburgh, 1970, 1971, 1972, 1974, 1975; Philadelphia, 1977, 1978.

Most Consecutive Hits, Total Series

N. L.—6—Garvey, Steven P., Los Angeles, October 9, 1974 (4), October 4, 1977 (2).
A. L.—5—Bando, Salvatore L., Oakland, October 5 (4), October 7 (1), 1975.
Rivers, John M., New York, October 13 (1), October 14 (4), 1976.
Chambliss, C. Christopher, New York, October 3 (1), October 4 (4), 1978.

Most Consecutive Hits, One Series

A. L.—5—Bando, Salvatore L., Oakland, October 5 (4), October 7 (1), 1975.
Rivers, John M., New York, October 13 (1), October 14 (4), 1976.
Chambliss, C. Christopher, New York, October 3 (1), October 4 (4), 1978.
N. L.—4—Hebner, Richard J., Pittsburgh, October 5 (2), October 6 (2), 1971.
Cey, Ronald C., Los Angeles, October 6, 1974.
Garvey, Steven P., Los Angeles, October 9, 1974.
Baker, Johnnie B., Los Angeles, October 7, 1978; 10 innings.

Most Hits, Game

A. L.—5—Blair, Paul L., Baltimore, October 6, 1969.
N. L.—4—Robertson, Robert E., Pittsburgh, October 3, 1971.
Cey, Ronald C., Los Angeles, October 6, 1974.
Garvey, Steven P., Los Angeles, October 9, 1974.
Baker, Johnnie B., Los Angeles, October 7, 1978; 10 innings.
Puhl, Terry S., Houston, October 12, 1980.

Most Times Reached First Base Safely, Nine-Inning Game (Batting 1.000)

A. L.—5— Jackson, Reginald M., New York, October 3, 1978; 2 bases on balls, 1 single, 1 double, 1 home run.

N. L.—5— Millan, Felix B. M., Atlanta, October 5, 1969; 3 bases on balls, 2 singles.

Getting All Club's Hits, Game (Most)

N. L.—2— Clemente, Roberto W., Pittsburgh, October 10, 1972.
　　　　　Kosco, Andrew J., Cincinnati, October 7, 1973.
A. L.—1— Jackson, Reginald M., Oakland, October 9, 1974.

Most Consecutive Games, One or More Hits, Total Series

N. L.—14— Rose, Peter E., Cincinnati, 1973 (last 3), 1975 (3), 1976 (3); Philadelphia, 1980 (5).
A. L.— 9— Robinson, Brooks C., Baltimore, 1969 (3), 1970 (3), 1971 (3).
　　　　　 Patek, Freddie J., Kansas City, 1976 (5), 1977 (first 4).
　　　　　 Brett, George H., Kansas City, 1977 (last 4), 1978 (4), 1980 (first 1).

Most Hits, Two Consecutive Games, One Series

A. L.—6— Robinson, Brooks C., Baltimore, October 4 (4), October 5 (2), 1969, first game 12 innings, second game 11 innings.
　　　　　Bando, Salvatore L., Oakland, October 5 (4), October 7 (2), 1975.
　　　　　Rivers, John M., New York, October 8 (4), October 9 (2), 1977.
　　　　　Chambliss, C. Christopher, New York, October 3 (2), October 4 (4), 1978.
N. L.—6— Shamsky, Arthur L., New York, October 4 (3), October 5 (3), 1969.
　　　　　Robertson, Robert E., Pittsburgh, October 2 (2), October 3 (4), 1971.
　　　　　Johnstone, John W., Philadelphia, October 10 (3), October 12 (3), 1976.
　　　　　Lopes, David E., Los Angeles, October 4 (3), October 5 (3), 1978.

Most Hits, Inning

A. L.-N. L.—1—Held by many players.

Most One-Base Hits, Total Series.

N. L.—28— Rose, Peter E., Cincinnati, 1970, 1972, 1973, 1975, 1976; Philadelphia, 1980; 6 Series, 24 games.
A. L.—20— Jackson, Reginald M., Oakland, 1971, 1972, 1973, 1974, 1975; New York, 1977, 1978, 1980; 8 Series, 32 games.

Most One-Base Hits, Series

3-game Series—N. L.— 7— Shamsky, Arthur L., New York, 1969.
　　　　　　　　A. L.— 6— Robinson, Brooks C., Baltimore, 1969.
4-game Series—N. L.— 7— Russell, William E., Los Angeles, 1974.
　　　　　　　　A. L.— 6— Chambliss, C. Christopher, New York, 1978.
5-game Series—A. L.— 8— Munson, Thurman L., New York, 1976.
　　　　　　　　N. L.— 8— Rose, Peter E., Philadelphia, 1980.
　　　　　　　　　　　　　 Puhl, Terry S., Houston, 1980.

Most One-Base Hits, Game

A. L.—4— Robinson, Brooks C., Baltimore, October 4, 1969; 12 innings.
　　　　　Chambliss, C. Christopher, New York, October 4, 1978.
N. L.—4— Puhl, Terry S., Houston, October 12, 1980; 10 innings.
N. L.—Nine-inning record—3—Held by many players.

Most One-Base Hits, Inning

A. L.-N. L.—1—Held by many players.

Most Two-Base Hits, Total Series

N. L.—7— Rose, Peter E., Cincinnati, 1970, 1972, 1973, 1975, 1976; Philadelphia, 1980; 6 Series, 24 games.
　　　　　Hebner, Richard J., Pittsburgh, 1970, 1971, 1972, 1974, 1975; Philadelphia, 1977, 1978; 7 Series, 25 games.

A. L.—6— Robinson, Brooks C., Baltimore, 1969, 1970, 1971, 1973, 1974; 5 Series, 18 games.
White, Roy H., New York, 1976, 1977, 1978; 3 Series, 13 games.

Most Two-Base Hits, Series

3-game Series—N. L.— 3— Morgan, Joe L., Cincinnati, 1975.
A. L.— 3— Watson, Robert J., New York, 1980.
4-game Series—N. L.— 3— Cey, Ronald C., Los Angeles, 1974.
A. L.— 3— Carew, Rodney C., California, 1979.
5-game Series—A. L.— 4— Alou, Mateo R., Oakland, 1972.
N. L.— 4— Rose, Peter E., Cincinnati, 1972.

Most Two-Base Hits, Game

A. L.-N. L.—2—Held by many players.

Most Two-Base Hits, Inning

A. L.-N. L.—1—Held by many players.

Most Three-Base Hits, Total Series

A. L.—4— Brett, George H., Kansas City, 1976, 1977, 1978, 1980; 4 Series, 17 games.
N. L.—2— Lopes, David E., Los Angeles, 1974, 1977, 1978; 3 Series, 12 games.
Bench, Johnny L., Cincinnati, 1970, 1972, 1973, 1975, 1976, 1979; 6 Series, 22 games.

Most Three-Base Hits, Series

A. L.—2— Brett, George H., Kansas City, 1977; 5-game Series.
N. L.— 1— Held by many players.

Most Three-Base Hits, Game

A. L.-N. L.—1—Held by many players.

Most Three-Base Hits, Game, Batting in Three Runs

A. L.-N. L—Never accomplished.

Most Home Runs, Total Series

N. L.—6— Garvey, Steven P., Los Angeles, 1974, 1977, 1978; 3 Series, 12 games.
A. L.—6— Brett, George H., Kansas City, 1976, 1977, 1978, 1980; 4 Series, 17 games.

Three or More Home Runs, Total Series

National League			American League		
Player	Series	HR.	Player	Series	HR.
Garvey, Steven P.	3	6	Brett, George H.	4	6
Bench, Johnny L.	6	5	Bando, Salvatore L.	5	5
Luzinski, Gregory M.	4	5	Jackson, Reginald M.	8	5
Robertson, Robert E.	5	4	Powell, John W.	5	4
Stargell, Wilver D.	6	4	Nettles, Graig	5	4
Aaron, Henry L.	1	3			
Staub, Daniel J.	1	3			
Cey, Ronald C.	3	3			
Foster, George A.	4	3			
Oliver, Albert	5	3			
Perez, Atanasio R.	5	3			
Rose, Peter E.	6	3			
Hebner, Richard J.	7	3			

Most Home Runs, Series

3-game Series—N. L.— 3— Aaron, Henry L., Atlanta, 1969.
A. L.— 2— Johnson, David A., Baltimore, 1970
Killebrew, Harmon C., Minnesota, 1970.

Most Home Runs, Series—Continued

                        Powell, John W., Baltimore, 1971.
                        Jackson, Reginald M., Oakland, 1971.
                        Brett, George H., Kansas City, 1980.
4-game Series—N. L.— 4— Robertson, Robert E., Pittsburgh, 1971.
                        Garvey, Steven P., Los Angeles, 1978.
         A. L.— 3— Brett, George H., Kansas City, 1978.
5-game Series—N. L.— 3— Staub, Daniel J., New York, 1973.
         A. L.— 2— Campaneris, Dagoberto B., Oakland, 1973.
                        Bando, Salvatore L., Oakland, 1973.
                        Chambliss, C. Christopher, New York, 1976.
                        Nettles, Graig, New York, 1976.

Most Series, One or More Home Runs

N. L.— 5— Bench, Johnny L., Cincinnati, 1970 (1), 1972 (1), 1973 (1), 1976 (1), 1979
          (1).
A. L.— 3— Bando, Salvatore L., Oakland, 1971 (1), 1973 (2), 1974 (2).
          Powell, John W., Baltimore, 1969 (1), 1970 (1), 1971 (2).
          Jackson, Reginald M., Oakland, 1971 (1), 1975 (1); New York, 1978 (2).
          Brett, George H., Kansas City, 1976 (1), 1978 (3), 1980 (2).
          Nettles, Graig, New York, 1976 (2), 1978 (1), 1980 (1).

Most Series, Two or More Home Runs

N. L.— 2— Garvey, Steven P., Los Angeles, 1974 (2), 1978 (4).
          Stargell, Wilver D., Pittsburgh, 1974 (2), 1979 (2).
A. L.— 2— Bando, Salvatore L., Oakland, 1973 (2), 1974 (2).
          Jackson, Reginald M., Oakland, 1971 (2); New York, 1978 (2).
          Brett, George H., Kansas City, 1978 (3), 1980 (2).

Most Home Runs, Game

N. L.— 3— Robertson, Robert E., Pittsburgh, October 3, 1971.
       2— Staub, Daniel J., New York, October 8, 1973.
          Garvey, Steven P., Los Angeles, October 9, 1974.
          Garvey, Steven P., Los Angeles, October 4, 1978.
A. L.— 3— Brett, George H., Kansas City, October 6, 1978.
       2— Powell, John W., Baltimore, October 4, 1971.
          Jackson, Reginald M., Oakland, October 5, 1971.
          Bando, Salvatore L., Oakland, October 7, 1973.
          Nettles, Graig, New York, October 13, 1976.

Most Home Runs with Bases Filled, Game

A. L.— 1— Cuellar, Miguel, Baltimore, October 3, 1970; fourth inning.
N. L.— 1— Cey, Ronald C., Los Angeles, October 4, 1977; seventh inning.
          Baker, Johnnie B., Los Angeles, October 5, 1977; fourth inning.

Inside-the-Park Home Runs

Nettles, Graig, New York, October 9, fifth inning, 0 on base.

Most Home Runs, Pinch-Hitter, Game

N. L.— 1— Martin, Jerry L., Philadephia, October 4, 1978; ninth inning.
          McBride, Arnold R., Philadelphia, October.7, 1978; seventh inning.
A. L.— 1— Lowenstein, John L., Baltimore, October 3, 1979; tenth inning.

Hitting Home Run, Leadoff Batter, Start of Game

A. L.— Campaneris, Dagoberto B., Oakland, October 7, 1973; at Baltimore.
       Brett, George H., Kansas City, October 6, 1978; at New York.
N. L.— Never accomplished.

Home Runs Winning 1-0 Games

A. L.— Bando, Salvatore L., Oakland, October 8, 1974; fourth inning.
N. L.— Never accomplished.

Most Home Runs, Game, by Pitcher

   A. L.— 1— Cuellar, Miguel, Baltimore, October 3, 1970; 3 on base.

   N. L.— 1— Gullett, Donald E., Cincinnati, October 4, 1975; 1 on base.

          Carlton, Steven N., Philadelphia, October 6, 1978; 2 on base.

Most Home Runs, Game, by Rookie

   N. L.— 1— Garrett, R. Wayne, New York, October 6, 1969.

          Clines, Eugene A., Pittsburgh, October 3, 1971.

          Speier, Chris E., San Francisco, October 6, 1971.

   A. L.— Never accomplished.

Most Consecutive Games, Series, Hitting One or More Home Runs

   N. L.— 3— Aaron, Henry L., Atlanta, October 4, 5, 6, 1969.

   A. L.— 2— Killebrew, Harmon C., Minnesota, October 3, 4, 1970.

          Johnson, David A., Baltimore, October 4, 5, 1970.

          Campaneris, Dagoberto B., Oakland, October 7, 9, 1973; second game
            11 innings.

          Bando, Salvatore L., Oakland, October 6, 8, 1974.

          Ford, Darnell G., California, October 3, 4, 1979.

Most Home Runs, Two Consecutive Games, One Series, Hitting Homer in Each Game

   N. L.— 4— Robertson, Robert E., Pittsburgh, October 3 (3), 5 (1), 1971.

   A. L.— 2— Killebrew, Harmon C., Minnesota, October 3, 4, 1970.

          Johnson, David A., Baltimore, October 4, 5, 1970.

          Campaneris, Dagoberto B., Oakland, October 7, 9, 1973; second game
            11 innings.

          Bando, Salvatore L., Oakland, October 6, 8, 1974.

          Ford, Darnell G., California, October 3, 4, 1979.

Hitting Home Run in First Championship Series At-Bat

   A. L.— Robinson, Frank, Baltimore, October 4, 1969; fourth inning (walked in
         first inning).

          Cash, Norman D., Detroit, October 7, 1972; second inning.

          Ford, Darnell G., California, October 3, 1979; first inning.

          Lowenstein, John L., Baltimore, October 3, 1979; tenth inning (pinch-hit).

          Cerone, Richard A., New York, October 8, 1980; first inning.

   N. L.— Morgan, Joe L., Cincinnati, October 7, 1972; first inning.

Most Home Runs, Inning

   A. L.-N. L.— 1— Held by many players.

Most Home Runs, Two Consecutive Innings

   N. L.— 2— Staub, Daniel J., New York, October 8, 1973, first and second innings.

   A. L.— Never accomplished.

Most Long Hits, Total Series

   A. L.— 13— Brett, George H., Kansas City, 1976, 1977, 1978, 1980; 4 Series, 17
         games.

   N. L.— 11— Rose, Peter E., Cincinnati, 1970, 1972, 1973, 1975, 1976; Philadelphia,
         1980; 6 Series, 24 games.

          Bench, Johnny L., Cincinnati, 1970, 1972, 1973, 1975, 1976, 1979; 6
         Series, 22 games.

          Luzinski, Gregory M., Philadelphia, 1976, 1977, 1978, 1980; 4 Series,
         16 games.

Most Long Hits, Series

   3-game Series—N. L.— 5— Aaron, Henry L., Atlanta, 1969.

                A. L.— 4— Watson, Robert J., New York, 1980.

   4-game Series—N. L.— 6— Garvey, Steven P., Los Angeles, 1978.

                A. L.— 5— Brett, George H., Kansas City, 1978.

Most Long Hits, Series—Continued

    5-game Series—N. L.—4—Rose, Peter E., Cincinnati, 1972.
                          Oliver, Albert, Pittsburgh, 1972.
                A. L.—4—Held by many players.

Most Long Hits, Game

    N. L.—4—Robertson, Robert E., Pittsburgh, October 3, 1971; 3 home runs, 1
        double.
    A. L.—3—Blair, Paul L., Baltimore, October 6, 1969; 2 doubles, 1 home run.
        Brett, George H., Kansas City, October 6, 1978; 3 home runs.

Most Long Hits, Two Consecutive Games, Series

    N. L.—5—Robertson, Robert E., Pittsburgh, October 3 (4), 3 home runs, 1 double;
        October 5 (1), 1 home run, 1971.
    A. L.—4—Brett, George H., Kansas City, October 6 (3), 3 home runs; October 7
        (1), 1 triple, 1978.

Most Long Hits, Inning

    A. L.-N. L.—1—Held by many players.

Most Total Bases, Total Series

    N. L.—57—Rose, Peter E., Cincinnati, 1970, 1972, 1973, 1975, 1976; Philadelphia,
        1980; 6 Series, 24 games.
    A. L.—53—Brett, George H., Kansas City, 1976, 1977, 1978, 1980; 4 Series, 17
        games.

Most Total Bases, Series

    3-game Series—N. L.—16—Aaron, Henry L., Atlanta, 1969.
                  A. L.—11—Held by many players.
    4-game Series—N. L.—22—Garvey, Steven P., Los Angeles, 1978.
                  A. L.—19—Brett, George H., Kansas City, 1978.
    5-game Series—A. L.—20—Chambliss, C. Christopher, New York, 1976.
                  N. L.—15—Rose, Peter E., Cincinnati, 1973.

Most Total Bases, Game

    N. L.—14—Robertson, Robert E., Pittsburgh, October 3, 1971; 3 home runs, 1
        double.
    A. L.—12—Brett, George H., Kansas City, October 6, 1978; 3 home runs.

Most Total Bases, Inning

    A. L.-N. L.—4—Held by many players.

Most Runs Batted In, Total Series

    A. L.—15—Jackson, Reginald M., Oakland, 1971, 1972, 1973, 1974, 1975; New
        York, 1977, 1978, 1980; 8 Series, 32 games.
    N. L.—13—Perez, Atanasio R., Cincinnati, 1970, 1972, 1973, 1975, 1976; 5 Series,
        19 games.

Most Runs Batted In, Series

    3-game Series—N. L.—7—Aaron, Henry L., Atlanta, 1969.
                  A. L.—6—Blair, Paul L., Baltimore, 1969.
                        Powell, John W., Baltimore, 1970.
    4-game Series—N. L.—8—Baker, Johnnie B., Los Angeles, 1977.
                  A. L.—6—Jackson, Reginald M., New York, 1978.
    5-game Series—A. L.—8—Chambliss, C. Christopher, New York, 1976.
                  N. L.—5—Staub, Daniel J., New York, 1973.

Most Runs Batted In, Game

    A. L.—5—Blair, Paul L., Baltimore, October 6, 1969.
    N. L.—5—Robertson, Robert E., Pittsburgh, October 3, 1971

Most Runs Batted In, Inning

A. L.—4—Cuellar, Miguel, Baltimore, October 3, 1970; bases-loaded home run in
            fourth inning.
N. L.—4—Cey, Ronald C., Los Angeles, October 4, 1977; bases-loaded home run in
            seventh inning.
            Baker, Johnnie B., Los Angeles, October 5, 1977; bases-loaded home
            run in fourth inning.

Most Consecutive Games, One or More Runs Batted In, Total Series

A. L.—4—Patek, Freddie J., Kansas City, 1977 (first 4); 5 runs batted in.
N. L.—4—Perez, Atanasio R., Cincinnati, 1973 (last 2), 1975 (first 2); 6 runs batted
            in.
            Lopes, David E., Los Angeles, 1974 (last 1), 1977 (first 3); 4 runs batted
            in.
            Luzinski, Gregory M., Philadelphia, 1976 (3), 1977 (first 1); 5 runs
            batted in.
            Maddox, Garry L., Philadelphia, 1976 (last 1), 1977 (2), 1978 (first 1); 5
            runs batted in.
            Foster, George A., Cincinnati, 1976 (3), 1979 (first 1); 6 runs batted in.
            Luzinski, Gregory M., Philadelphia, 1978 (last 2), 1980 (first 2); 6 runs
            batted in.

Batting in All Club's Runs, Game (Most)

A. L.—3—Campaneris, Dagoberto B., Oakland, October 5, 1974.
N. L.—2—Foster, George A., Cincinnati, October 2, 1979; 11 innings.

Most Game-Winning RBIs, Total Series (Since 1980)

N. L.—2—Luzinski, Gregory M., Philadelphia, 1980.
A. L.—1—Held by many players.

Most Game-Winning RBIs, Series (Since 1980)

N. L.—2—Luzinski, Gregory M., Philadelphia, 1980.
A. L.—1—Held by many players.

Most Bases on Balls, Total Series

N. L.—21—Morgan, Joe L., Cincinnati, 1972, 1973, 1975, 1976, 1979; Houston,
            1980; 6 Series, 23 games.
A. L.—13—Tenace, F. Gene, Oakland, 1971, 1972, 1973, 1974, 1975; 5 Series, 18
            games.

Most Bases on Balls, Series

3-game Series—A. L.—6—Killebrew, Harmon C., Minnesota, 1969.
               N. L.—6—Morgan, Joe L., Cincinnati, 1976.
4-game Series—N. L.—9—Wynn, James S., Los Angeles, 1974.
               A. L.—5—Jackson, Reginald M., Oakland, 1974.
                        Murray, Eddie C., Baltimore, 1979.
5-game Series—N. L.—8—Cruz, Jose, Houston, 1980.
               A. L.—5—White, Roy H., New York, 1976.

Most Consecutive Bases on Balls, One Series

A. L.—4—Killebrew, Harmon C., Minnesota, October 4 (3), October 5 (1), 1969.
N. L.—3—Foster, George A., Cincinnati, October 2 (1), October 3 (2), 1979.

Most Bases on Balls, Game

A. L.-N. L.—3—Held by many players.

Most Bases on Balls With Bases Filled, Game

A. L.—1—Cash, Norman D., Detroit, October 11, 1972; tenth inning.
            Tenace, F. Gene, Oakland, October 9, 1974; fifth inning.
N. L.—1—Lopes, David E., Los Angeles, October 5, 1974; second inning.
            Dyer, Don R., Pittsburgh, October 7, 1975; ninth inning.

Most Bases on Balls With Bases Filled, Game—Continued

> Christenson, Larry R., Philadelphia, October 7, 1977; second inning.
> McBride, Arnold R., Philadelphia, October 7, 1977; second inning.
> Bowa, Lawrence R., Philadelphia, October 7, 1977; second inning.
> Rose, Peter E., Philadelphia, October 12, 1980; eighth inning.

Most Bases on Balls, Two Consecutive Games

> A. L.—5— Killebrew, Harmon C., Minnesota, October 4 (3), October 5 (2), 1969; first game 12 innings, second game 11 innings.
> N. L.—5—Wynn, James S., Los Angeles, October 5 (2), October 6 (3), 1974.

Most Bases on Balls, Inning

> A. L.-N. L.—1—Held by many players.

Most Strikeouts, Total Series

> A. L.— 27—Jackson, Reginald M., Oakland, 1971, 1972, 1973, 1974, 1975; New York, 1977, 1978, 1980; 8 Series, 32 games.
> N. L.— 24— Geronimo, Cesar F., Cincinnati, 1972, 1973, 1975, 1976, 1979; 5 Series, 17 games.

Most Strikeouts, Series

> 3-game Series—A. L.— 7— Cardenas, Leonardo A., Minnesota, 1969.
>   N. L.— 7— Geronimo, Cesar F., Cincinnati, 1975.
> 4-game Series—N. L.— 6— Clemente, Roberto W., Pittsburgh, 1971.
>   Stargell, Wilver D., Pittsburgh, 1971.
>   A. L.— 5— Otis, Amos J., Kansas City, 1978.
> 5-game Series—N. L.— 7— Perez, Atanasio R., Cincinnati, 1972.
>   Geronimo, Cesar F., Cincinnati, 1973.
>   A. L.— 6— Jackson, Reginald M., Oakland, 1972.
>   Jackson, Reginald M., Oakland, 1973.
>   Bando, Salvatore L., Oakland, 1973.
>   Johnson, Deron R., Oakland, 1973.

Most Consecutive Strikeouts, One Series (Consecutive at-bats)

> N. L.— 7— Geronimo, Cesar F., Cincinnati, October 4 (1), October 5 (3), October 7 (3), 1975, third game 10 innings, one base on balls during streak.
> A. L.— 4— Cardenas, Leonardo A., Minnesota, October 4 (2), October 5 (2), 1969; first game 12 innings, second game 11 innings.
>   Boswell, David W., Minnesota, October 5, 1969; 11 innings.
>   Bando, Salvatore L., Oakland, October 9 (2), October 10 (2), 1973; first game 11 innings, one base on balls during streak.

Most Consecutive Strikeouts, One Series (Consecutive plate appearances)

> N. L.— 5— Geronimo, Cesar F., Cincinnati, October 6 (1), October 7 (3), October 9 (1), 1973; third game 12 innings.
> A. L.— 4— Cardenas, Leonardo A., Minnesota, October 4 (2), October 5 (2), 1969; first game 12 innings, second game 11 innings.
>   Boswell, David W., Minnesota, October 5, 1969; 11 innings.

Most Strikeouts, Game

> A. L.— 4— Boswell, David W., Minnesota, October 5, 1969; consecutive, 11 innings.
> Nine-inning record—A. L.-N. L.—3—Held by many players.

Most Strikeouts, Inning

> A. L.-N. L.—1—Held by many players.

Most Sacrifice Hits, Total Series

> A. L.— 3— Green, Richard L., Oakland, 1971, 1972, 1973, 1974; 4 Series, 17 games.
> N. L.— 3— Cabell, Enos M., Houston, 1980; 1 Series, 5 games.

Most Sacrifice Hits, Series

3-game Series—N. L.— 2— Ellis, Dock P., Pittsburgh, 1970.
Bibby, James B., Pittsburgh, 1979.
A. L.— 1— Held by many players.
4-game Series—N. L.— 2— Perry, Gaylord J. San Francisco, 1971.
A. L.— 2— Belanger, Mark H., Baltimore, 1974.
5-game Series—N. L.— 3— Cabell, Enos M., Houston, 1980.
A. L.— 2— Bando, Salvatore L., Oakland, 1972.
Patek, Freddie J., Kansas City, 1977.

Most Sacrifice Hits, Game

A. L.— 2— Patek, Freddie J., Kansas City, October 7, 1977.
N. L.— 2— Ellis, Dock P., Pittsburgh, October 3, 1970; 10 innings.
Perry, Gaylord J., San Francisco, October 2, 1971.
Bibby, James B., Pittsburgh, October 3, 1979.
Trillo, J. Manuel, Philadelphia, October 8, 1980; 10 innings.

Most Sacrifice Flies, Total Series

A. L.— 2— McRae, Harold A., Kansas City, 1976, 1977, 1978, 1980; 4 Series, 17 games.
DeCinces, Douglas V., Baltimore, 1979; 1 Series, 4 games.
N. L.— 2— Perez, Atanasio R., Cincinnati, 1970, 1972, 1973, 1975, 1976; 5 Series, 19 games.
Schmidt, Michael J., Philadelphia, 1976, 1977, 1978, 1980; 4 Series, 16 games.
Foli, Timothy J., Pittsburgh, 1979; 1 Series, 3 games.

Most Sacrifice Flies, Series

N. L.— 2— Perez, Atanasio R., Cincinnati, 1976; 3-game Series.
Foli, Timothy J., Pittsburgh, 1979; 3-game Series.
A. L.— 2— DeCinces, Douglas V., Baltimore, 1979; 4-game Series.

Most Sacrifice Flies, Game

A. L.-N. L.—1—Held by many players.

Most Hit by Pitch, Total Series

N. L.— 3— Hebner, Richard J., Pittsburgh, 1971 (1), 1972 (1), 1974 (1).
A. L.— 2— McRae, Harold A., Kansas City, 1976 (1), 1980 (1).

Most Hit by Pitch, Series

A. L.-N. L.—1—Held by many players.

Most Hit by Pitch, Game

A. L.-N. L.—1—Held by many players.

Most Times Awarded First Base on Catcher's Interference, Game

N. L.— 1— Hebner, Richard J., Pittsburgh, October 8, 1974, fifth inning.
A. L.—Never accomplished.

Most Grounded Into Double Play, Total Series

N. L.— 3— Jones, Cleon J., New York, 1969, 1973; 2 Series, 8 games.
Cedeno, Cesar, Houston, 1980; 1 Series, 3 games.
A. L.— 3— Taylor, Antonio, Detroit, 1972; 1 Series, 4 games.
Powell, John W., Baltimore, 1969, 1970, 1971, 1973, 1974; 5 Series, 12 games.
Randolph, William L., New York, 1976, 1977, 1980; 3 Series, 13 games.

Most Grounded Into Double Play, Series

A. L.— 3— Taylor, Antonio, Detroit, 1972; 15 at-bats in 4 games of 5-game Series.
N. L.— 3— Cedeno, Cesar, Houston, 1980; 11 at-bats in 3 games of 5-game Series.

Most Grounded Into Double Play, Game

    A. L.—3—Taylor, Antonio, Detroit, October 10, 1972.
    N. L.—2—Jones, Cleon J., New York, October 4, 1969.

INDIVIDUAL PINCH-HITTING

Most Series Appeared as Pinch-Hitter

    Both Leagues—4—Davalillo, Victor J., Pittsburgh NL, 1971, 1972; Oakland AL,
        1973; Los Angeles NL, 1977; 5 games.
    A. L.—3—Motton, Curtell H., Baltimore, 1969, 1971, 1974; 4 games.
        Holt, James W., Minnesota, 1970; Oakland, 1974, 1975; 4 games.
    N. L.—3—Armbrister, Edison R., Cincinnati, 1973, 1975, 1976; 5 games.
        Davalillo, Victor J., Pittsburgh, 1971, 1972; Los Angeles, 1977; 4 games.
        Hebner, Richard J., Pittsburgh, 1971; Philadelphia, 1977, 1978; 3
        games.
        Mota, Manuel R., Los Angeles, 1974, 1977, 1978; 6 games.
        McCarver, J. Timothy, Philadelphia, 1976, 1977, 1978; 3 games.

Most Games, Pinch-Hitter, Total Series

    N. L.—6—Mota, Manuel R., Los Angeles, 1974 (3), 1977 (1), 1978 (2); 6 plate ap-
        pearances, 5 at-bats.
    A. L.—4—Held by many players.

Most Games, Pinch-Hitter, Series

    A. L.—4—Hendrick, George A., Oakland, 1972.
    N. L.—4—Stahl, Larry F., Cincinnati, 1973.

Most At-Bats, Pinch-Hitter, Total Series

    N. L.—5—Mota, Manuel R., Los Angeles, 1974 (3), 1977 (1), 1978 (1).
    A. L.—4—Hendrick, George A., Oakland, 1972.
        Mangual, Angel L., Oakland, 1972 (3), 1973 (1).
        Alou, Jesus M., Oakland, 1973 (3), 1974 (1).
        Motton, Curtell H., Baltimore, 1969 (2), 1971 (1), 1974 (1).
        Crowley, Terrence M., Baltimore, 1973 (2), 1979 (2).

Most At-Bats, Pinch-Hitter, Series

    A. L.—4—Hendrick, George A., Oakland, 1972.
    N. L.—4—Stahl, Larry F., Cincinnati, 1973.

Most Plate Appearances, Pinch-Hitter, Total Series

    N. L.—6—Mota, Manuel R., Los Angeles, 1974 (3), 1977 (1), 1978 (2).
    A. L.—4—Held by many players.

Most Runs, Pinch-Hitter, Total Series

    N. L.—2—Cline, Tyrone A., Cincinnati, 1970; 1 Series, 2 games.
    A. L.—1—Held by many players.

Most Runs, Pinch-Hitter, Series

    N. L.—2—Cline, Tyrone A., Cincinnati, 1970; 2 games.
    A. L.—1—Held by many players.

Most Hits, Pinch-Hitter, Total Series

    N. L.—3—Popovich, Paul E., Pittsburgh, 1974; 1 Series, 3 games.
        Mota, Manuel R., Los Angeles, 1974, 1977, 1978; 3 Series, 6 games.
    A. L.—2—Marquez, Gonzalo, Oakland, 1972; 1 Series, 3 games.
        Motton, Curtell H., Baltimore, 1969, 1971, 1974; 3 Series, 4 games.
        Alou, Jesus M., Oakland, 1973, 1974; 2 Series, 4 games.

Most Hits, Pinch-Hitter, Series

N. L.—3— Popovich, Paul E., Pittsburgh, 1974; 3 games.
A. L.—2— Marquez, Gonzalo, Oakland, 1972; 3 games.

Most Consecutive Hits, Pinch-Hitter

N. L.—3— Popovich, Paul E., Pittsburgh, October 5, 6, 9, 1974.
A. L.—2— Motton, Curtell H., Baltimore, October 5, 1969; October 3, 1971.

Most One-Base Hits, Pinch-Hitter, Total Series

N. L.—3— Popovich, Paul E., Pittsburgh, 1974; 1 Series, 3 games.
A. L.—2— Marquez, Gonzalo, Oakland, 1972; 1 Series, 3 games.
      Alou, Jesus M., Oakland, 1973, 1974; 2 Series, 4 games.

Most One-Base Hits, Pinch-Hitter, Series

N. L.—3— Popovich, Paul E., Pittsburgh, 1974; 3 games.
A. L.—2— Marquez, Gonzalo, Oakland, 1972; 3 games.

Most Two-Base Hits, Pinch-Hitter, Total Series

N. L.—2— Mota, Manuel R., Los Angeles, 1974, 1977, 1978; 3 Series, 6 games.
A. L.—1— Held by many players.

Most Three-Base Hits, Pinch-Hitter, Total Series

N. L.—1— Cline, Tyrone A., Cincinnati, 1970; 1 Series, 2 games.
A. L.—Never accomplished.

Home Runs by Pinch-Hitters

N. L.—Martin, Jerry L., Philadelphia, October 4, 1978; ninth inning.
      McBride, Arnold R., Philadelphia, October 7, 1978; seventh inning.
A. L.—Lowenstein, John L., Baltimore, October 3, 1979; tenth inning.

Most Total Bases, Pinch-Hitter, Total Series

N. L.—6— Martin, Jerry L., Philadelphia, 1977, 1978; 2 Series, 3 games.
A. L.—4— Lowenstein, John L., Baltimore, 1979; 1 Series, 2 games.

Most Total Bases, Pinch-Hitter, Series

N. L.—6— Martin, Jerry L., Philadelphia, 1978; 2 games.
A. L.—4— Lowenstein, John L., Baltimore, 1979; 2 games.

Most Total Bases, Pinch-Hitter, Game

N. L.—4— Martin, Jerry L., Philadelphia, October 4, 1978; home run in ninth inning.
      McBride, Arnold R., Philadelphia, October 7, 1978; home run in seventh inning.
A. L.—4— Lowenstein, John L., Baltimore, October 3, 1979; home run in tenth inning.

Most Runs Batted In, Pinch-Hitter, Total Series

A. L.—3— Lowenstein, John L., Baltimore, 1979; 1 Series, 2 games.
N. L.—2— Martin, Joseph C., New York, 1969; 1 Series, 2 games.
      Martin, Jerry L., Philadelphia, 1977, 1978; 2 Series, 3 games.

Most Runs Batted In, Pinch-Hitter, Series

A. L.—3— Lowenstein, John L., Baltimore, 1979; 2 games.
N. L.—2— Martin, Joseph C., New York, 1969; 2 games.
      Martin, Jerry L., Philadelphia, 1978; 2 games.

Most Runs Batted In, Pinch-Hitter, Game

A. L.—3— Lowenstein, John L., Baltimore, 1979; tenth inning.
N. L.—2— Martin, Joseph C., New York, October 4, 1969; eighth inning.

Most Bases on Balls, Pinch-Hitter, Total Series

Both Leagues—2—Rettenmund, Mervin W., Baltimore AL, 1969; Cincinnati NL, 1975; California AL, 1979; 3 Series, 4 games.

N. L.—2—Hague, Joe C., Cincinnati, 1972; 1 Series, 3 games.

A. L.—1—Held by many players.

Bases on Balls with Bases Filled by Pinch-Hitters, Game

N. L.—Dyer, Don R., Pittsburgh, October 7, 1975; ninth inning.

A. L.—Never accomplished.

Most Strikeouts, Pinch-Hitter, Total Series

N. L.—2—Armbrister, Edison R., Cincinnati, 1973, 1975, 1976; 3 Series, 5 games.
Monday, Robert J., Los Angeles, 1977, 1978; 2 Series, 2 games.
Leonard, Jeffrey N., Houston, 1980; 1 Series, 2 games.
Woods, Gary L., Houston, 1980; 1 Series, 2 games.

A. L.—1—Held by many players.

Most Strikeouts, Pinch-Hitter, Series

N. L.—2—Armbrister, Edison R., Cincinnati, 1973; 2 games.
Leonard, Jeffrey N., Houston, 1980; 2 games.
Woods, Gary L., Houston, 1980; 2 games.

A. L.—1—Held by many players.

Sacrifice Hits by Pinch-Hitters, Game

A. L.—Andrews, Michael J., Oakland, October 9, 1973; eighth inning.

N. L.—Armbrister, Edison R., Cincinnati, October 12, 1976; ninth inning.
Mota, Manuel R., Los Angeles, October 7, 1978; fifth inning.
Gross, Gregory E., Philadelphia, October 8, 1980; seventh inning.

Sacrifice Flies by Pinch-Hitters, Game

N. L.—Armbrister, Edison R., Cincinnati, October 7, 1975; tenth inning.

A. L.—Never accomplished.

Hit by Pitches by Pinch-Hitters, Game

A. L.-N. L.—Never accomplished.

Grounding into Double Play by Pinch-Hitters, Game

A. L.—Renick, W. Richard, Minnesota, October 6, 1969; sixth inning.
Roenicke, Gary S., Baltimore, October 6, 1979; third inning.

N. L.—Hart, James R., San Francisco, October 3, 1971; eighth inning.
Mota, Manuel R., Los Angeles, October 9, 1974; eighth inning.
Ferguson, Joseph V., Los Angeles, October 6, 1978; ninth inning.

INDIVIDUAL BASE RUNNING

Most Stolen Bases, Total Series

N. L.—8—Morgan, Joe L., Cincinnati, 1972, 1973, 1975, 1976, 1979; Houston, 1980; 6 Series, 23 games.

A. L.—8—Otis, Amos J., Kansas City, 1976, 1977, 1978, 1980; 4 Series, 13 games.

Most Stolen Bases, Series

3-game Series—N. L.—4—Morgan, Joe L., Cincinnati, 1975.
A. L.—2—Beniquez, Juan J., Boston, 1975.
Otis, Amos J., Kansas City, 1980.

4-game Series—A. L.—4—Otis, Amos J., Kansas City, 1978.
N. L.—3—Lopes, David E., Los Angeles, 1974.

5-game Series—A. L.— 3— Campaneris, Dagoberto B., Oakland, 1973.
N. L.— 2— Bench, Johnny L., Cincinnati, 1972.
Maddox, Garry L., Philadelphia, 1980.
McBride, Arnold R., Philadelphia, 1980.
Puhl, Terry S., Houston, 1980.

Most Stolen Bases, Game

N. L.— 3— Morgan, Joe L., Cincinnati, October 4, 1975.
Griffey, G. Kenneth, Cincinnati, October 5, 1975.
A. L.— 2— Held by many players.

Most Times Stealing Home, Game

A. L.— 1— Jackson, Reginald M., Oakland, October 12, 1972; second inning (front end of double steal).
N. L.—Never accomplished.

Most Stolen Bases, Inning

N. L.— 2— Morgan, Joe L., Cincinnati, October 4, 1975; third inning.
Griffey, G. Kenneth, Cincinnati, October 5, 1975; sixth inning.
A. L.— 2— Campaneris, Dagoberto B., Oakland, October 8, 1972; first inning.
Jackson, Reginald M., Oakland, October 12, 1972; second inning.
Beniquez, Juan J., Boston, October 4, 1975; seventh inning.

Most Caught Stealing, Total Series

A. L.— 6— McRae, Harold A., Kansas City, 1976, 1977, 1978, 1980; 1 stolen base.
N. L.— 2— Tolan, Robert, Cincinnati, 1970, 1972; Philadelphia, 1976; 3 Series, 11 games, 1 stolen base.

Most Caught Stealing, Series

3-game Series—A. L.— 3— McRae, Harold A., Kansas City, 1980; 0 stolen bases.
N. L.— 1— Held by many players.
4-game Series—A. L.— 2— Blair, Paul L., Baltimore, 1974; 0 stolen bases.
Washington, Herbert L., Oakland, 1974; 0 stolen bases.
N. L.— 1— Held by many players.
5-game Series—A. L.— 3— Patek, Freddie J., Kansas City, 1976; 0 stolen bases.
N. L.— 2— Rose, Peter E., Philadelphia, 1980; 0 stolen bases.

Most Caught Stealing, Game

A. L.— 2— Robinson, Brooks C., Baltimore, October 4, 1969; 12 innings.
Nine-inning record—A. L.-N. L.—1—Held by many players.

Most Caught Stealing, Inning

A. L.-N. L.—1—Held by many players.

INDIVIDUAL PINCH-RUNNING

Most Games, Pinch-Runner, Total Series

A. L.— 3— Odom, Johnny L., Oakland, 1972, 1974; 2 Series, 0 runs.
N. L.— 3— Concepcion, David I., Cincinnati, 1970, 1972; 2 Series, 0 runs.

Most Games, Pinch-Runner, Series

A. L.— 2— Lewis, Allan S., Oakland, 1973.
Odom, Johnny L., Oakland, 1974.
Washington, Herbert L., Oakland, 1974.
Wilson, Willie J., Kansas City, 1978.
N. L.— 2— Gaspar, Rodney E., New York, 1969.
Jeter, Johnny, Pittsburgh, 1970.
Concepcion, David I., Cincinnati, 1972.
Landestoy, Rafael S.C., Houston, 1980.
Smith, Lonnie, Philadelphia, 1980.

Most Runs, Pinch-Runner, Total Series

    N. L.—2—Clines, Eugene A., Pittsburgh, 1972, 1974; 2 Series, 2 games.
            Landestoy, Rafael S.C., Houston, 1980; 1 Series, 2 games.
    A. L.—1—Held by many players.

Most Runs, Pinch-Runner, Series

    N. L.—2—Landestoy, Rafael S.C., Houston, 1980; 2 games.
    A. L.—1—Held by many players.

Most Stolen Bases, Pinch-Runner, Game

    A. L.-N. L.—Never accomplished.

Most Caught Stealing, Pinch-Runner, Total Series

    A. L.—2—Washington, Herbert L., Oakland, 1974; 1 Series, 2 games.
    N. L.—Never accomplished.

Most Caught Stealing, Pinch-Runner, Series

    A. L.—2—Washington, Herbert L., Oakland, 1974; 2 games.
    N. L.—Never accomplished.

Most Caught Stealing, Pinch-Runner, Game

    A. L.—1—Washington, Herbert L., Oakland, October 6, 8, 1974.
            Alomar, Santos, New York, October 14, 1976.
    N. L.—Never accomplished.

CLUB BATTING

Highest Batting Average, Series, One Club

    3-game Series—A. L.—.330—Baltimore vs. Minnesota, 1970.
                N. L.—.327—New York vs. Atlanta, 1969.
    4-game Series—A. L.—.300—New York vs. Kansas City, 1978.
                N. L.—.286—Los Angeles vs. Philadelphia, 1978.
    5-game Series—A. L.—.316—New York vs. Kansas City, 1976.
                N. L.—.291—Philadelphia vs. Houston, 1980.

Highest Batting Average, Series, Both Clubs

    3-game Series—N. L.—.292—New York .327, Atlanta .255, 1969.
                A. L.—.286—Baltimore .330, Minnesota .238, 1970.
    4-game Series—A. L.—.282—New York .300, Kansas City .263, 1978.
                N. L.—.268—Los Angeles .286, Philadelphia .250, 1978.
    5-game Series—A. L.—.283—New York .316, Kansas City .247, 1976.
                N. L.—.263—Philadelphia .291, Houston .233, 1980.

Highest Batting Average, Series, Championship Series Loser

    3-game Series—N. L.—.270—Philadelphia vs. Cincinnati, 1976.
                A. L.—.255—New York vs. Kansas City, 1980.
    4-game Series—N. L.—.250—Philadelphia vs. Los Angeles, 1978.
                A. L.—.263—Kansas City vs. New York, 1978.
    5-game Series—A. L.—.258—Kansas City vs. New York, 1977.
                N. L.—.233—Houston vs. Philadelphia, 1980.

Lowest Batting Average, Series, One Club

    3-game Series—A. L.—.155—Minnesota vs. Baltimore, 1969.
                N. L.—.198—Pittsburgh vs. Cincinnati, 1975.
    4-game Series—A. L.—.177—Baltimore vs. Oakland, 1974.
                N. L.—.194—Pittsburgh vs. Los Angeles, 1974.
    5-game Series—N. L.—.186—Cincinnati vs. New York, 1973.
                A. L.—.198—Detroit vs. Oakland, 1972.

Lowest Batting Average, Series, Both Clubs

3-game Series—N. L.—.223—Pittsburgh .225, Cincinnati .220, 1970.
            A. L.—.227—Baltimore .293, Minnesota .155, 1969.
4-game Series—A. L.—.180—Oakland .183, Baltimore .177, 1974.
            N. L.—.232—Los Angeles .268, Pittsburgh .194, 1974.
5-game Series—A. L.—.205—Baltimore .211, Oakland .200, 1973.
            N. L.—.203—New York .220, Cincinnati .186, 1973.

Lowest Batting Average, Series, Championship Series Winner

3-game Series—N. L.—.220—Cincinnati vs. Pittsburgh, 1970.
            A. L.—.274—Baltimore vs. Oakland, 1971.
4-game Series—A. L.—.183—Oakland vs. Baltimore, 1974.
            N. L.—.263—Los Angeles vs. Philadelphia, 1977.
5-game Series—A. L.—.200—Oakland vs. Baltimore, 1973.
            N. L.—.220—New York vs. Cincinnati, 1973.

Highest Slugging Average, Series, One Club

3-game Series—N. L.—.575 —New York vs. Atlanta, 1969.
            A. L.—.560 —Baltimore vs. Minnesota, 1970.
4-game Series—N. L.—.544 —Los Angeles vs. Philadelphia, 1978.
            A. L.—.4436—Kansas City vs. New York, 1978.
                  .4428—New York vs. Kansas City, 1978.
5-game Series—A. L.—.483 —New York vs. Kansas City, 1976.
            N. L.—.404 —Cincinnati vs. Pittsburgh, 1972.

Highest Slugging Average, Series, Both Clubs

3-game Series—N. L.—.530—New York .575, Atlanta .481, 1969.
            A. L.—.476—Baltimore .560, Minnesota .386, 1970.
4-game Series—N. L.—.477—Los Angeles .544, Philadelphia .407, 1978.
            A. L.—.443—Kansas City .4436, New York .4428, 1978.
5-game Series—A. L.—.429—New York .483, Kansas City .370, 1976.
            N. L.—.352—Cincinnati .404, Pittsburgh .297, 1972.

Lowest Slugging Average, Series, One Club

3-game Series—A. L.—.227—Minnesota vs. Baltimore, 1969.
            N. L.—.257—Pittsburgh vs. Cincinnati, 1975.
4-game Series—A. L.—.258—Baltimore vs. Oakland, 1974.
            N. L.—.271—Pittsburgh vs. Los Angeles, 1974.
5-game Series—A. L.—.288—Oakland vs. Detroit, 1972.
            N. L.—.297—Pittsburgh vs. Cincinnati, 1972.

Lowest Slugging Average, Series, Both Clubs

3-game Series—N. L.—.322—Cincinnati .360, Pittsburgh .284, 1970.
            A. L.—.356—Baltimore .472, Minnesota .227, 1969.
4-game Series—A. L.—.283—Oakland .308, Baltimore .258, 1974.
            N. L.—.339—Los Angeles .391, Philadelphia .290, 1977.
5-game Series—A. L.—.304—Detroit .321, Oakland .288, 1972.
            N. L.—.307—Cincinnati .311, New York .304, 1973.

Most At-Bats, Total Series, One Club

A. L.— 755— Baltimore, 6 Series, 22 games.
N. L.— 741— Cincinnati; 6 Series, 22 games.

Most At-Bats, Series, One Club

3-game Series—A. L.— 123— Baltimore vs. Minnesota, 1969.
            N. L.— 113— New York vs. Atlanta, 1969.
4-game Series—N. L.— 147— Los Angeles vs. Philadelphia, 1978.
            A. L.— 140— New York vs. Kansas City, 1978.
5-game Series—N. L.— 189— Philadelphia vs. Houston, 1980.
            A. L.— 175— New York vs. Kansas City, 1977.

Most At-Bats, Series, Both Clubs
3-game Series—A. L.— 233— Baltimore 123, Minnesota 110, 1969.
N. L.— 219— New York 113, Atlanta 106, 1969.
4-game Series—N. L.— 287— Los Angeles 147, Philadelphia 140, 1978.
A. L.— 273— New York 140, Kansas City 133, 1978.
5-game Series—A. L.— 361— Philadelphia 189, Houston 172, 1980.
N. L.— 335— New York 168, Cincinnati 167, 1973.

Fewest At-Bats, Series, One Club
3-game Series—A. L.— 95— Baltimore vs. Oakland, 1971.
N. L.— 99— Cincinnati vs. Philadelphia, 1976.
4-game Series—A. L.— 120— Oakland vs. Baltimore, 1974.
N. L.— 129— Pittsburgh vs. Los Angeles, 1974.
5-game Series—N. L.— 158— Pittsburgh vs. Cincinnati, 1972.
A. L.— 160— Oakland vs. Baltimore, 1973.

Fewest At-Bats, Series, Both Clubs
3-game Series—A. L.— 191— Oakland 96, Baltimore 95, 1971.
N. L.— 199— Philadelphia 100, Cincinnati 99, 1976.
4-game Series—A. L.— 244— Baltimore 124, Oakland 120, 1974.
N. L.— 267— Los Angeles 138, Pittsburgh 129, 1974.
5-game Series—N. L.— 324— Cincinnati 166, Pittsburgh 158, 1972.
A. L.— 331— Baltimore 171, Oakland 160, 1973.

Most At-Bats, Game, One Club
A. L.— 44— Baltimore vs. Minnesota, October 6, 1969.
N. L.— 43— Houston vs. Philadelphia, October 12, 1980; 10 innings.
N. L.—Nine-inning record—42—New York vs. Atlanta, October 5, 1969.

Most At-Bats, Game, Nine Innings, Both Clubs
A. L.— 80— Baltimore 44, Minnesota 36, October 6, 1969.
N. L.— 77— New York 42, Atlanta 35, October 5, 1969.
Los Angeles 39, Philadelphia 38, October 4, 1978.

Most At-Bats, Extra-Inning Game, Both Clubs
N. L.— 82— Houston 43, Philadelphia 39, October 12, 1980; 10 innings.
A. L.— 81— Baltimore 43, Minnesota 38, October 4, 1969; 12 innings.

Fewest Official At-Bats, Game, One Club
N. L.— 27— Cincinnati vs. New York, October 7, 1973.
Pittsburgh vs. Los Angeles, October 9, 1974.
A. L.— 28— Detroit vs. Oakland, October 10, 1972; batted 8 innings.
Oakland vs. Baltimore, October 9, 1974.
Kansas City vs. New York, October 12, 1976.
Kansas City vs. New York, October 6, 1977.
Kansas City vs. New York, October 3, 1978.
New York vs. Kansas City, October 7, 1978; batted 8 innings.

Fewest Official At-Bats, Game, Both Clubs
A. L.— 57— Baltimore 29, Oakland 28, October 9, 1974.
N. L.— 58— Cincinnati 30, New York 28, October 6, 1973.
New York 31, Cincinnati 27, October 7, 1973.

Most At-Bats, Inning, One Club
A. L.— 9— Baltimore vs. Minnesota, October 3, 1970; fourth inning.
Baltimore vs. Minnesota, October 4, 1970; ninth inning.
Kansas City vs. New York, October 4, 1978; second inning.
N. L.— 8— San Francisco vs. Pittsburgh, October 6, 1971; second inning.
New York vs. Cincinnati, October 7, 1973; ninth inning.
Philadelphia vs. Los Angeles, October 4, 1978; fifth inning.

Most At-Bats, Inning, Both Clubs

A. L.— 15— Baltimore 9, Minnesota 6, October 3, 1970; fourth inning.
N. L.— 15— Philadelphia 8, Houston 7, October 12, 1980; eighth inning.

Most Men Facing Pitcher, Inning, One Club

N. L.— 10— New York vs. Cincinnati, October 7, 1973; ninth inning.
A. L.— 10— Baltimore vs. Minnesota, October 3, 1970; fourth inning.
       Baltimore vs. Minnesota, October 4, 1970; ninth inning.
       Baltimore vs. Oakland, October 6, 1973; first inning.

Most Men Facing Pitcher, Inning, Both Clubs

A. L.— 16— Baltimore 10, Minnesota 6, October 3, 1970; fourth inning.
N. L.— 16— Philadelphia 9, Houston 7, October 12, 1980; eighth inning.

Most Runs, Total Series, One Club

A. L.— 106— Baltimore; 6 Series, 22 games.
N. L.— 79— Cincinnati; 6 Series, 22 games.

Most Runs, Series, One Club

3-game Series—A. L.— 27— Baltimore vs. Minnesota, 1970.
              N. L.— 27— New York vs. Atlanta, 1969.
4-game Series—A. L.— 26— Baltimore vs. California, 1979.
              N. L.— 24— Pittsburgh vs. San Francisco, 1971.
5-game Series—A. L.— 24— Kansas City vs. New York, 1976.
              N. L.— 23— New York vs. Cincinnati, 1973.

Most Runs, Series, Both Clubs

3-game Series—N. L.— 42— New York 27, Atlanta 15, 1969.
              A. L.— 37— Baltimore 27, Minnesota 10, 1970.
4-game Series—A. L.— 41— Baltimore 26, California 15, 1979.
              N. L.— 39— Pittsburgh 24, San Francisco 15, 1971.
5-game Series—A. L.— 47— Kansas City 24, New York 23, 1976.
              N. L.— 39— Philadelphia 20, Houston 19, 1980.

Most Runs, Series, Championship Series Loser

3-game Series—N. L.— 15— Atlanta vs. New York, 1969.
              A. L.— 10— Minnesota vs. Baltimore, 1970.
4-game Series—N. L.— 17— Philadelphia vs. Los Angeles, 1978.
              A. L.— 17— Kansas City vs. New York, 1978.
5-game Series—A. L.— 24— Kansas City vs. New York, 1976.
              N. L.— 19— Houston vs. Philadelphia, 1980.

Fewest Runs, Series, One Club

3-game Series—N. L.— 3— Pittsburgh vs. Cincinnati, 1970.
              A. L.— 5— Minnesota vs. Baltimore, 1969.
4-game Series—A. L.— 7— Baltimore vs. Oakland, 1974.
              N. L.— 10— Pittsburgh vs. Los Angeles, 1974.
5-game Series—N. L.— 8— Cincinnati vs. New York, 1973.
              A. L.— 10— Detroit vs. Oakland, 1972.

Fewest Runs, Series, Both Clubs

3-game Series—N. L.— 12— Cincinnati 9, Pittsburgh 3, 1970.
              A. L.— 20— Kansas City 14, New York 6, 1980.
4-game Series—A. L.— 18— Oakland 11, Baltimore 7, 1974.
              N. L.— 30— Los Angeles 20, Pittsburgh 10, 1974.
5-game Series—A. L.— 23— Oakland 13, Detroit 10, 1972.
              N. L.— 31— New York 23, Cincinnati 8, 1973.

Most Runs, Game, One Club

N. L.— 12— Los Angeles vs. Pittsburgh, October 9, 1974.
A. L.— 11— Baltimore vs. Minnesota, October 6, 1969.
       Baltimore vs. Minnesota, October 4, 1970.

Largest Score, Shutout Game

  A. L.—Baltimore 8, California 0, October 6, 1979.
  N. L.—Pittsburgh 7, Los Angeles 0, October 8, 1974.

Most Earned Runs, Game, One Club

  N. L.—12— Los Angeles vs. Pittsburgh, October 9, 1974.
  A. L.—10— Baltimore vs. Minnesota, October 4, 1970.

Most Runs, Game, Both Clubs

  N. L.—17— New York 11, Atlanta 6, October 5, 1969.
  A. L.—17— Baltimore 9, California 8, October 4, 1979.

Most Players, One or More Runs, Game, One Club

  A. L.—9— Baltimore vs. Minnesota, October 3, 1970.
  N. L.—8— New York vs. Atlanta, October 5, 1969.

Most Players, One or More Runs, Game, Both Clubs

  A. L.—14— Baltimore 9, Minnesota 5, October 3, 1970.
           Baltimore 7, California 7, October 4, 1979.
  N. L.—13— New York 8, Atlanta 5, October 5, 1969.

Most Innings Scored, Game, One Club

  N. L.—6— New York vs. Atlanta, October 5, 1969.
          Los Angeles vs. Pittsburgh, October 9, 1974.
  A. L.—5— Baltimore vs. Minnesota, October 6, 1969.
          Kansas City vs. New York, October 7, 1977.
          New York vs. Kansas City, October 8, 1977.
          California vs. Baltimore, October 4, 1979.

Most Innings Scored, Game, Both Clubs

  A. L.—8— New York 4, Kansas City 4, October 6, 1978.
          Calforinia 5, Baltimore 3, October 4, 1979.
  N. L.—8— New York 6, Atlanta 2, October 5, 1969.
          Pittsburgh 5, San Francisco 3, October 3, 1971.
          Los Angeles 5, Philadelphia 3, October 4, 1978.

Most Runs, Inning, One Club

  A. L.—7— Baltimore vs. Minnesota, October 3, 1970; fourth inning.
          Baltimore vs. Minnesota, October 4, 1970; ninth inning.
  N. L.—5— New York vs. Atlanta, October 4, 1969; eighth inning.
          Atlanta vs. New York, October 5, 1969; fifth inning.
          New York vs. Cincinnati, October 8, 1973; second inning.
          Pittsburgh vs. Los Angeles, October 8, 1974; first inning.
          Philadelphia vs. Houston, October 12, 1980; eighth inning.

Most Runs, Inning, Both Clubs

  A. L.—8— Baltimore 7, Minnesota 1, October 3, 1970; fourth inning.
  N. L.—7— San Francisco 4, Pittsburgh 3, October 6, 1971; second inning.
          Philadelphia 5, Houston 2, October 12, 1980; eighth inning.

Most Runs, First Inning, One Club

  N. L.—5— Pittsburgh vs. Los Angeles, October 8, 1974.
  A. L.—4— Baltimore vs. Oakland, October 6, 1973.
          Baltimore vs. California, October 4, 1979.

Most Runs, Second Inning, One Club

  N. L.—5— New York vs. Cincinnati, October 8, 1973.
  A. L.—4— Kansas City vs. New York, October 4, 1978.
          Baltimore vs. California, October 4, 1979.

Most Runs, Third Inning, One Club

N. L.— 4— Los Angeles vs. Philadelphia, October 4, 1978.
A. L.— 3— Baltimore vs. Minnesota, October 5, 1970.
Kansas City vs. New York, October 9, 1980.

Most Runs, Fourth Inning, One Club

A. L.— 7— Baltimore vs. Minnesota, October 3, 1970.
N. L.— 4— Los Angeles vs. Philadelphia, October 5, 1977.

Most Runs, Fifth Inning, One Club

N. L.— 5— Atlanta vs. New York, October 5, 1969.
A. L.— 4— Oakland vs. Detroit, October 8, 1972.
Baltimore vs. Oakland, October 5, 1974.

Most Runs, Sixth Inning, One Club

N. L.— 4— Pittsburgh vs. San Francisco, October 6, 1971.
Cincinnati vs. Philadelphia, October 10, 1976.
A. L.— 3— New York vs. Kansas City, October 12, 1976.
New York vs. Kansas City, October 6, 1977.

Most Runs, Seventh Inning, One Club

A. L.— 5— Boston vs. Oakland, October 4, 1975.
Baltimore vs. California, October 6, 1979.
N. L.— 4— Pittsburgh vs. San Francisco, October 3, 1971.
Cincinnati vs. Philadelphia, October 12, 1976.
Los Angeles vs. Philadelphia, October 4, 1977.

Most Runs, Eighth Inning, One Club

N. L.— 5— New York vs. Atlanta, October 4, 1969.
Philadelphia vs. Houston, October 12, 1980.
A. L.— 3— Oakland vs. Baltimore, October 6, 1974.
Kansas City vs. New York, October 10, 1976.
Kansas City vs. New York, October 14, 1976.
New York vs. Kansas City, October 3, 1978.
California vs. Baltimore, October 4, 1979.

Most Runs, Ninth Inning, One Club

A. L.— 7— Baltimore vs. Minnesota, October 4, 1970.
N. L.— 4— New York vs. Cincinnati, October 7, 1973.

Most Runs, Tenth Inning, One Club

N. L.— 4— Houston vs. Philadelphia, October 8, 1980.
A. L.— 3— Detroit vs. Oakland, October 11, 1972.
Baltimore vs. California, October 3, 1979.

Most Runs, Eleventh Inning, One Club

N. L.— 3— Pittsburgh vs. Cincinnati, October 2, 1979.
A. L.— 2— Oakland vs. Detroit, October 7, 1972.

Most Runs, Twelfth Inning, One Club

A. L.— 1— Baltimore vs. Minnesota, October 4, 1969.
N. L.— 1— Cincinnati vs. New York, October 9, 1973.

Most Runs, Extra Inning, One Club

N. L.— 4— Houston vs. Philadelphia, October 8, 1980; tenth inning.
A. L.— 3— Detroit vs. Oakland, October 11, 1972; tenth inning.
Baltimore vs. California, October 3, 1979; tenth inning.

Most Runs, Extra Inning, Both Clubs

A. L.— 5— Detroit 3, Oakland 2, October 11, 1972; tenth inning.
N. L.— 5— Houston 4, Philadelphia 1, October 8, 1980; tenth inning.

Most Hits, Total Series, One Club

A. L.— 193— Baltimore; 6 Series, 22 games.
N. L.— 172— Cincinnati; 6 Series, 22 games.

Most Hits, Series, One Club

3-game Series—N. L.—37— New York vs. Atlanta, 1969.
              A. L.—36— Baltimore vs. Minnesota, 1969, 1970.
4-game Series—N. L.—42— Los Angeles vs. Philadelphia, 1978.
              A. L.—42— New York vs. Kansas City, 1978.
5-game Series—A. L.—55— New York vs. Kansas City, 1976.
              N. L.—55— Philadelphia vs. Houston, 1980.

Most Hits, Series, Both Clubs

3-game Series—N. L.—64— New York 37, Atlanta 27, 1969.
              A. L.—60— Baltimore 36, Minnesota 24, 1970.
4-game Series—N. L.—77— Los Angeles 42, Philadelphia 35, 1978.
              A. L.—77— New York 42, Kansas City 35, 1978.
5-game Series—A. L.—95— New York 55, Kansas City 40, 1976.
              N. L.—95— Philadelphia 55, Houston 40, 1980.

Fewest Hits, Series, One Club

3-game Series—A. L.—17— Minnesota vs. Baltimore, 1969.
              N. L.—20— Pittsburgh vs. Cincinnati, 1975.
4-game Series—A. L.—22— Baltimore vs. Oakland, 1974.
                      Oakland vs. Baltimore, 1974.
              N. L.—25— Pittsburgh vs. Los Angeles, 1974.
5-game Series—N. L.—30— Pittsburgh vs. Cincinnati, 1972.
              A. L.—32— Detroit vs. Oakland, 1972.
                      Oakland vs. Baltimore, 1973.

Fewest Hits, Series, Both Clubs

3-game Series—N. L.—45— Pittsburgh 23, Cincinnati 22, 1970.
              A. L.—48— Baltimore 26, Oakland 22, 1971.
4-game Series—A. L.—44— Baltimore 22, Oakland 22, 1974.
              N. L.—62— Los Angeles 37, Pittsburgh 25, 1974.
5-game Series—A. L.—68— Baltimore 36, Oakland 32, 1973.
              N. L.—68— New York 37, Cincinnati 31, 1973.

Most Hits, Game, One Club

A. L.—18— Baltimore vs. Minnesota, October 6, 1969.
N. L.—15— Pittsburgh vs. San Francisco, October 3, 1971.

Most Hits, Game, Both Clubs

A. L.—28— Baltimore 18, Minnesota 10, October 6, 1969.
             Kansas City 16, New York 12, October 4, 1978.
N. L.—27— Houston 14, Philadelphia 13, October 12, 1980; 10 innings.
N. L.—Nine-inning record—25—Los Angeles 13, Philadelphia 12, October 4, 1978.

Fewest Hits, Game, One Club

A. L.—1— Oakland vs. Baltimore, October 9, 1974.
N. L.—2— Pittsburgh vs. Cincinnati, October 10, 1972.
          Cincinnati vs. New York, October 7, 1973.

Fewest Hits, Game, Both Clubs

A. L.—6— Oakand 4, Baltimore 2, October 8, 1974.
          Baltimore 5, Oakland 1, October 9, 1974.
N. L.—9— San Francisco 5, Pittsburgh 4, October 5, 1971.
          Cincinnati 6, New York 3, October 6, 1973.
          New York 7, Cincinnati 2, October 7, 1973.

Most Players, One or More Hits, Game, One Club

N. L.— 10— Los Angeles vs. Philadelphia, October 7, 1977.
A. L.— 9— Baltimore vs. Minnesota, October 3, 1970.
                New York vs. Kansas City, October 13, 1976.
                New York vs. Kansas City, October 3, 1978.
                Kansas City vs. New York, October 4, 1978.

Most Players, One or More Hits, Game, Both Clubs

A. L.— 16— Kansas City 9, New York 7, October 4, 1978.
N. L.— 16— Los Angeles 8, Philadelphia 8, October 4, 1978.
                Houston 8, Philadelphia 8, October 12, 1980; 10 innings.

Most Hits, Inning, One Club

A. L.— 7— Baltimore vs. Minnesota, October 3, 1970; fourth inning.
N. L.— 5— San Francisco vs. Pittsburgh, October 6, 1971; second inning.
                Cincinnati vs. Pittsburgh, October 8, 1972; first inning.
                New York vs. Cincinnati, October 7, 1973; ninth inning.
                Los Angeles vs. Pittsburgh, October 6, 1974; eighth inning.
                Philadelphia vs. Los Angeles, October 4, 1978; fifth inning.
                Philadelphia vs. Houston, October 12, 1980; eighth inning.

Most Hits, Inning, Both Clubs

A. L.— 9— Baltimore 7, Minnesota 2, October 3, 1970; fourth inning.
N. L.— 9— Philadelphia 5, Houston 4, October 12, 1980; eighth inning.

Most Consecutive Hits, Inning, One Club (Consecutive at-bats)

A. L.— 7— Baltimore vs. Minnesota, October 3, 1970; fourth inning; sacrifice fly
                during streak.
N. L.— 5— Cincinnati vs. Pittsburgh, October 8, 1972; first inning.
                New York vs. Cincinnati, October 7, 1973; ninth inning; two walks
                during streak.
                Los Angeles vs. Pittsburgh, October 6, 1974; eighth inning.

Most Consecutive Hits, Inning, One Club (Consecutive plate appearances)

N. L.— 5— Cincinnati vs. Pittsburgh, October 8, 1972; first inning.
                Los Angeles vs. Pittsburgh, October 6, 1974; eighth inning.
A. L.— 4— Baltimore vs. Minnesota, October 3, 1970; fourth inning.
                Boston vs. Oakland, October 5, 1975; fourth inning.
                New York vs. Kansas City, October 10, 1976; third inning.
                Kansas City vs. New York, October 9, 1980; third inning.

Most One-Base Hits, Total Series, One Club

A. L.— 132— Baltimore; 6 Series, 22 games.
N. L.— 120— Pittsburgh; 6 Series, 22 games.

Most One-Base Hits, Series, One Club

3-game Series—A. L.— 23— Baltimore vs. Minnesota, 1969, 1970.
                  N. L.— 22— New York vs. Atlanta, 1969.
4-game Series—A. L.— 33— New York vs. Kansas City, 1978.
                  N. L.— 27— Pittsburgh vs. San Francisco, 1971.
5-game Series—N. L.— 45— Philadelphia vs. Houston, 1980.
                  A. L.— 36— New York vs. Kansas City, 1976.

Most One-Base Hits, Series, Both Clubs

3-game Series—A. L.— 39— Baltimore 23, Minnesota 16, 1970.
                  N. L.— 37— Cincinnati 21, Pittsburgh 16, 1975.
4-game Series—A. L.— 55— New York 33, Kansas City 22, 1978.
                  N. L.— 51— Philadelphia 26, Los Angeles 25, 1977.
5-game Series—A. L.— 64— New York 36, Kansas City 28, 1976.
                  N. L.— 73— Philadelphia 45, Houston 28, 1980.

Fewest One-Base Hits, Series, One Club

3-game Series—A. L.— 10— Oakand vs. Baltimore, 1971.
N. L.— 13— Atlanta vs. New York, 1969.
4-game Series—A. L.— 14— Oakland vs. Baltimore, 1974.
N. L.— 21— San Francisco vs. Pittsburgh, 1971.
Pittsburgh vs. Los Angeles, 1974.
5-game Series—N. L.— 20— Pittsburgh vs. Cincinnati, 1972.
Cincinnati vs. New York, 1973.
A. L.— 21— Detroit vs. Oakland, 1972.
Oakland vs. Baltimore, 1973.

Fewest One-Base Hits, Series, Both Clubs

3-game Series—A. L.— 24— Baltimore 14, Oakland 10, 1971.
N. L.— 31— Philadelphia 17, Cincinnati 14, 1976.
4-game Series—A. L.— 32— Baltimore 18, Oakland 14, 1974.
N. L.— 46— Los Angeles 25, Pittsburgh 21, 1974.
5-game Series—A. L.— 47— Baltimore 26, Oakland 21, 1973.
N. L.— 47— Cincinnati 27, Pittsburgh 20, 1972.

Most One-Base Hits, Game, One Club

A. L.— 13— Kansas City vs. New York, October 4, 1978.
N. L.— 12— Philadelphia vs. Houston, October 8, 1980; 10 innings.
N. L.—Nine-inning record—10— New York vs. Cincinnati, October 10, 1973.
Cincinnati vs. Pittsburgh, October 5, 1975.
Philadelphia vs. Los Angeles, October 4, 1978.

Most One-Base Hits, Game, Both Clubs

A. L.— 25— Kansas City 13, New York 12, October 4, 1978.
N. L.— 17— Los Angeles 9, Pittsburgh 8, October 6, 1974.
Philadelphia 12, Houston 5, October 8, 1980; 10 innings.

Fewest One-Base Hits, Game, One Club

A. L.— 0— Oakland vs. Baltimore, October 9, 1974.
N. L.— 1— Pittsburgh vs. Cincinnati, October 10, 1972.

Fewest One-Base Hits, Game, Both Clubs

N. L.— 4— New York 2, Cincinnati 2, October 6, 1973.
A. L.— 5— Oakland 3, Baltimore 2, October 9, 1973; 11 innings.
Oakland 3, Baltimore 2, October 8, 1974.
Baltimore 5, Oakland 0, October 9, 1974.

Most One-Base Hits, Inning, One Club

A. L.— 5— Kansas City vs. New York, October 4, 1978; second inning.
N. L.— 5— New York vs. Cincinnati, October 7, 1973; ninth inning.
Philadelphia vs. Los Angeles, October 4, 1978; fifth inning.

Most One-Base Hits, Inning, Both Clubs

N. L.— 8— Philadelphia 4, Houston 4, October 12, 1980; eighth inning.
A. L.— 7— Kansas City 5, New York 2, October 4, 1978; second inning.
New York 4, Kansas City 3, October 4, 1978; eighth inning.

Most Two-Base Hits, Total Series, One Club

A. L.— 35— Baltimore; 6 Series, 22 games.
New York; 4 Series, 17 games.
N. L.— 31— Cincinnati; 6 Series, 22 games.

Most Two-Base Hits, Series, One Club

3-game Series—N. L.— 9— Atlanta vs. New York, 1969.
A. L.— 8— Baltimore vs. Minnesota, 1969.
Oakland vs. Baltimore, 1971.
Boston vs. Oakland, 1975.

4-game Series—N. L.— 8— Los Angeles vs. Pittsburgh, 1974.
    Los Angeles vs. Philadelphia, 1978.
    A. L.— 7— California vs. Baltimore, 1979.
5-game Series—A. L.— 13— New York vs. Kansas City, 1976.
    N. L.— 9— Cincinnati vs. Pittsburgh, 1972.

Most Two-Base Hits, Series, Both Clubs

3-game Series—N. L.— 17— Atlanta 9, New York 8, 1969.
    A. L.— 15— Oakland 8, Baltimore 7, 1971.
4-game Series—A. L.— 12— California 7, Baltimore 5, 1979.
    N. L.— 11— Los Angeles 8, Philadelphia 3, 1978.
5-game Series—A. L.— 21— New York 12, Kansas City 9, 1977.
    N. L.— 15— Cincinnati 9, Pittsburgh 6, 1972.
    Philadelphia 8, Houston 7, 1980.

Fewest Two-Base Hits, Series, One Club

3-game Series—A. L.— 3— Minnesota vs. Baltimore, 1969.
    N. L.— 3— Cincinnati vs. Pittsburgh, 1970.
    Pittsburgh vs. Cincinnati, 1975, 1979.
4-game Series—A. L.— 1— Baltimore vs. Oakland, 1974.
    N. L.— 1— Pittsburgh vs. Los Angeles, 1974.
5-game Series—A. L.— 5— Oakland vs. Baltimore, 1973.
    N. L.— 5— New York vs. Cincinnati, 1973.

Fewest Two-Base Hits, Series, Both Clubs

3-game Series—N. L.— 7— Cincinnati 4, Pittsburgh 3, 1975, 1979.
    A. L.— 11— Baltimore 8, Minnesota 3, 1969.
    Baltimore 7, Minnesota 4, 1970.
4-game Series—A. L.— 5— Oakland 4, Baltimore 1, 1974.
    N. L.— 9— San Francisco 5, Pittsburgh 4, 1971.
    Los Angeles 8, Pittsburgh 1, 1974.
    Los Angeles 6, Philadelphia 3, 1977.
5-game Series—N. L.— 11— Cincinnati 6, New York 5, 1973.
    A. L.— 12— Baltimore 7, Oakland 5, 1973.

Most Two-Base Hits, Game, One Club

A. L.— 6— Baltimore vs. Minnesota, October 6, 1969.
N. L.— 6— Philadelphia vs. Cincinnati, October 12, 1976.

Most Two-Base Hits, Game, Both Clubs

A. L.— 9— Oakland 5, Baltimore 4, October 3, 1971.
N. L.— 7— Cincinnati 5, Philadelphia 2, October 9, 1976.

Most Two-Base Hits, Inning, One Club

A. L.— 3— Oakland vs. Baltimore, October 10, 1973; second inning.
    Boston vs. Oakland, October 4, 1975; seventh inning.
N. L.— 3— Atlanta vs. New York, October 4, 1969; third inning, consecutive.
    Cincinnati vs. Pittsburgh, October 8, 1972; first inning, consecutive.
    Cincinnati vs. Philadelphia, October 9, 1976; eighth inning.

Most Three-Base Hits, Total Series, One Club

A. L.— 11— Kansas City; 4 Series, 17 games.
N. L.— 7— Cincinnati; 6 Series, 22 games.

Most Three-Base Hits, Series, One Club

3-game Series—N. L.— 3— Cincinnati vs. Philadelphia, 1976.
    A. L.— 1— Held by many clubs.
4-game Series—A. L.— 3— Kansas City vs. New York, 1978.
    N. L.— 3— Los Angeles vs. Philadelphia, 1978.
5-game Series—N. L.— 5— Houston vs. Philadelphia, 1980.
    A. L.— 4— Kansas City vs. New York, 1976.

Most Three-Base Hits, Series, Both Clubs

3-game Series—N. L.—4— Cincinnati 3, Philadelphia 1, 1976.
        A. L.— 2— Baltimore 1, Minnesota 1, 1969.
                Baltimore 1, Oakland 1, 1971.
                Kansas City 1, New York 1, 1980.
4-game Series—N. L.—5— Los Angeles 3, Philadelphia 2, 1978.
        A. L.— 4— Kansas City 3, New York 1, 1978.
5-game Series—A. L.— 6— Kansas City 4, New York 2, 1976.
        N. L.— 6— Houston 5, Philadelphia 1, 1980.

Fewest Three-Base Hits, Series, One Club

A. L.-N. L.—0—Held by many clubs in Series of all lengths.

Fewest Three-Base Hits, Series, Both Clubs

3-game Series—N. L.— 0— Cincinnati 0, Pittsburgh 0, 1975.
        A. L.— 0— Boston 0, Oakland 0, 1975.
4-game Series—N. L.— 0— Pittsburgh 0, San Francisco 0, 1971.
        A. L.— 1— Oakland 1, Baltimore 0, 1974.
                Baltimore 1, California 0, 1979.
5-game Series—N. L.— 0— Cincinnati 0, New York 0, 1973.
        A. L.— 1— Detroit 1, Oakland 0, 1972.
                Oakland 1, Baltimore 0, 1973.

Most Three-Base Hits, Game, One Club

A. L.—2— Kansas City vs. New York, October 13, 1976.
        Kansas City vs. New York, October 8, 1977.
N. L.—2— Cincinnati vs. Philadelphia, October 9, 1976.
        Los Angeles vs. Philadelphia, October 4, 1978.
        Houston vs. Philadelphia, October 10, 1980; 11 innings.

Most Three-Base Hits, Game, Both Clubs

N. L.—3— Los Angeles 2, Philadelphia 1, October 4, 1978.
A. L.—2— Baltimore 1, Minnesota 1, October 6, 1969.
        Kansas City 1, New York 1, October 9, 1976.
        Kansas City 2, New York 0, October 13, 1976.
        Kansas City 2, New York 0, October 8, 1977.

Most Three-Base Hits, Inning, One Club

A. L.—2— Kansas City vs. New York, October 8, 1977; third inning.
N. L.—1— Held by many clubs.

Most Home Runs, Total Series, One Club

A. L.—23— Baltimore; 6 Series, 22 games.
N. L.—21— Cincinnati; 6 Series, 22 games.

Most Home Runs, Series, One Club

3-game Series—N. L.— 6— New York vs. Atlanta, 1969.
        A. L.— 6— Baltimore vs. Minnesota, 1970.
4-game Series—N. L.— 8— Pittsburgh vs. San Francisco, 1971.
                Los Angeles vs. Philadelphia, 1978.
        A. L.— 5— New York vs. Kansas City, 1978.
5-game Series—A. L.— 5— Oakland vs. Baltimore, 1973.
        N. L.— 5— Cincinnati vs. New York, 1973.

Most Home Runs, Series, Both Clubs

3-game Series—N. L.—11—New York 6, Atlanta 5, 1969.
        A. L.— 9—Baltimore 6, Minnesota 3, 1970.
4-game Series—N. L.—13—Pittsburgh 8, San Francisco 5, 1971.
                Los Angeles 8, Philadelphia 5, 1978.
        A. L.— 9— New York 5, Kansas City 4, 1978.

5-game Series—A. L.— 8—Oakland 5, Baltimore 3, 1973.
                N. L.— 8—Cincinnati 5, New York 3, 1973.

Fewest Home Runs, Series, One Club

3-game Series—N. L.— 0— Pittsburgh vs. Cincinnati, 1970.
                A. L.— 1— Minnesota vs. Baltimore, 1969.
                         Oakland vs. Boston, 1975.
4-game Series—N. L.— 2— Philadelphia vs. Los Angeles, 1977.
                A. L.— 3— Oakland vs. Baltimore, 1974.
                         Baltimore vs. Oakland, 1974.
                         Baltimore vs. California, 1979.
                         California vs. Baltimore, 1979.
5-game Series—N. L.— 0— Houston vs. Philadelphia, 1980.
                A. L.— 1— Oakland vs. Detroit, 1972.

Fewest Home Runs, Series, Both Clubs

3-game Series—A. L.— 3— Boston 2, Oakland 1, 1975.
                N. L.— 3— Cincinnati 3, Pittsburgh 0, 1970.
4-game Series—N. L.— 5— Los Angeles 3, Philadelphia 2, 1977.
                A. L.— 6— Oakland 3, Baltimore 3, 1974.
                         Baltimore 3, California 3, 1979.
5-game Series—N. L.— 1— Philadelphia 1, Houston 0.
                A. L.— 5— Detroit 4, Oakland 1, 1972.
                         Kansas City 3, New York 2, 1977.

Most Consecutive Games, Total Series, One or More Home Runs

A. L.— 5— New York, last three games vs. Kansas City, 1976 (4 home runs), first
          two games vs. Kansas City, 1977 (2 home runs).
N. L.— 5— Los Angeles, last game vs. Philadelphia, 1977 (1 home run), all four
          games vs. Philadelphia, 1978 (8 home runs).

Most Consecutive Games, Series, One or More Home Runs

N. L.— 4— Los Angeles vs. Philadelphia, October 4, 5, 6, 7, 1978; 8 home runs.
A. L.— 3— Baltimore vs. Minnesota, October 3, 4, 5, 1970; 6 home runs.
          New York vs. Kansas City, October 12, 13, 14, 1976; 4 home runs.

Most Home Runs With Bases Filled, Total Series, One Club

N. L.— 2— Los Angeles; 3 Series, 12 games.
A. L.— 1— Baltimore; 5 Series, 18 games.

Most Home Runs With Bases Filled, Series, One Club

N. L.— 2— Los Angeles vs. Philadelphia, 1977.
A. L.— 1— Baltimore vs. Minnesota, 1970.

Most Home Runs, Game, One Club

A. L.— 4— Baltimore vs. Oakland, October 4, 1971.
          Oakland vs. Baltimore, October 7, 1973.
N. L.— 4— Pittsburgh vs. San Francisco, October 3, 1971.
          Los Angeles vs. Philadelphia, October 4, 1978.

Most Home Runs, Game, Both Clubs

A. L.— 5— Kansas City 3, New York 2, October 6, 1978.
N. L.— 5— New York 3, Atlanta 2, October 6, 1969.
          Pittsburgh 4, San Francisco 1, October 3, 1971.
          Los Angeles 4, Philadelphia 1, October 4, 1978.

Most Home Runs, Inning, One Club

A. L.— 3— Baltimore vs. Minnesota, October 3, 1970; fourth inning (first 2 consec-
          utive).
N. L.— 2— Cincinnati vs. Pittsburgh, October 5, 1970; first inning (consecutive).
          San Francisco vs. Pittsburgh, October 2, 1971; fifth inning.

Most Home Runs, Inning, One Club—Continued

San Francisco vs. Pittsburgh, October 6, 1971; second inning.
Pittsburgh vs. Los Angeles, October 8, 1974; first inning.
Cincinnati vs. Philadelphia, October 12, 1976; ninth inning (consecutive).
Pittsburgh vs. Cincinnati, October 5, 1979; third inning.

Most Home Runs, Inning, Both Clubs

A. L.—3— Baltimore 3, Minnesota 0, October 3, 1970, fourth inning.
N. L.—3— San Francisco 2, Pittsburgh 1, October 6, 1971, second inning.

Most Consecutive Home Runs, Inning, One Club

A. L.—2— Baltimore (Cuellar and Buford) vs. Minnesota, October 3, 1970; fourth inning.
Minnesota (Killebrew and Oliva) vs. Baltimore, October 4, 1970; fourth inning.
Oakland (Rudi and Bando) vs. Baltimore, October 7, 1973; sixth inning.
New York (Cerone and Piniella) vs. Kansas City, October 8, 1980; second inning.
N. L.—2— Cincinnati (Perez and Bench) vs. Pittsburgh, October 5, 1970; first inning.
Cincinnati (Foster and Bench) vs. Philadelphia, October 12, 1976; ninth inning.

Most Long Hits, Total Series, One Club

A. L.—61— Baltimore; 6 Series, 22 games.
N. L.—59— Cincinnati; 6 Series, 22 games.

Most Long Hits, Series, One Club

3-game Series—N. L.—15—New York vs. Atlanta, 1969.
                A. L.—13—Baltimore vs. Minnesota, 1969, 1970.
4-game Series—N. L.—19—Los Angeles vs. Philadelphia, 1978.
                A. L.—13—Kansas City vs. New York, 1978.
5-game Series—A. L.—19—New York vs. Kansas City, 1976.
                N. L.—15—Cincinnati vs. Pittsburgh, 1972.

Most Long Hits, Series, Both Clubs

3-game Series—N. L.—29—New York 15, Atlanta 14, 1969.
                A. L.—24—Baltimore 12, Oakland 12, 1971.
4-game Series—N. L.—29—Los Angeles 19, Philadelphia 10, 1978.
                A. L.—22—Kansas City 13, New York 9, 1978.
5-game Series—A. L.—31—New York 19, Kansas City 12, 1976.
                N. L.—25—Cincinnati 15, Pittsburgh 10, 1972.

Fewest Long Hits, Series, One Club

3-game Series—N. L.—4— Pittsburgh vs. Cincinnati, 1975.
                A. L.—5— Minnesota vs. Baltimore, 1969.
4-game Series—N. L.—4— Pittsburgh vs. Los Angeles, 1974.
                A. L.—4— Baltimore vs. Oakland, 1974.
5-game Series—N. L.—8— New York vs. Cincinnati, 1973.
                A. L.—9— Oakland vs. Detroit, 1972.

Fewest Long Hits, Series, Both Clubs

3-game Series—N. L.—12—Cincinnati 8, Pittsburgh 4, 1975.
                A. L.—17—Boston 10, Oakland 7, 1975.
4-game Series—A. L.—12—Oakland 8, Baltimore 4, 1974.
                N. L.—15—Los Angeles 10, Philadelphia 5, 1977.
5-game Series—N. L.—19—Cincinnati 11, New York 8, 1973.
                A. L.—20—Detroit 11, Oakland 9, 1972.

Most Long Hits, Game, One Club

    A. L.— 8— Baltimore vs. Minnesota, October 6, 1969; 6 doubles, 1 triple, 1 home run.

    N. L.— 8— Cincinnati vs. Philadelphia, October 9, 1976; 5 doubles, 2 triples, 1 home run.

Most Long Hits, Game, Both Clubs

    A. L.— 12— Oakland 6 (5 doubles, 1 home run), Boston 6 (4 doubles, 2 home runs), October 5, 1975.

    N. L.— 11— New York 7 (4 doubles, 3 home runs), Atlanta 4 (2 doubles, 2 home runs), October 6, 1969.

Most Extra Bases on Long Hits, Total Series, One Club

    A. L.— 110— Baltimore; 6 Series, 22 games (35 on doubles, 6 on triples, 69 on home runs).

    N. L.— 108— Cincinnati; 6 Series, 22 games (31 on doubles, 14 on triples, 63 on home runs).

Most Extra Bases on Long Hits, Series, One Club

    3-game Series—N. L.— 28— New York vs. Atlanta, 1969.
                    A. L.— 25— Baltimore vs. Minnesota, 1970.
    4-game Series—N. L.— 38— Los Angeles vs. Philadelphia, 1978.
                    A. L.— 24— Kansas City vs. New York, 1978.
    5-game Series—A. L.— 29— New York vs. Kansas City, 1976.
                    N. L.— 25— Cincinnati vs. Pittsburgh, 1972.

Most Extra Bases on Long Hits, Series, Both Clubs

    3-game Series—N. L.— 52— New York 28, Atlanta 24, 1969.
                    A. L.— 40— Baltimore 25, Minnesota 15, 1970.
                        Baltimore 21, Oakland 19, 1971.
    4-game Series—N. L.— 60— Los Angeles 38, Philadelphia 22, 1978.
                    A. L.— 44— Kansas City 24, New York 20, 1978.
    5-game Series—A. L.— 49— New York 29, Kansas City 20, 1976.
                    N. L.— 42— Cincinnati 25, Pittsburgh 17, 1972.

Fewest Extra Bases on Long Hits, Series, One Club

    3-game Series—N. L.— 6— Pittsburgh vs. Cincinnati, 1970, 1975.
                    A. L.— 8— Minnesota vs. Baltimore, 1969.
    4-game Series—N. L.— 9— Philadelphia vs. Los Angeles, 1977.
                    A. L.— 10— Baltimore vs. Oakland, 1974.
    5-game Series—A. L.— 11— Oakland vs. Detroit, 1972.
                    N. L.— 13— Philadelphia vs. Houston, 1980.

Fewest Extra Bases on Long Hits, Series, Both Clubs

    3-game Series—N. L.— 20— Cincinnati 14, Pittsburgh 6, 1970.
                    A. L.— 23— Boston 14, Oakland 9, 1975.
    4-game Series—A. L.— 25— Oakland 15, Baltimore 10, 1974.
                    N. L.— 26— Los Angeles 17, Philadelphia 9, 1977.
    5-game Series—N. L.— 30— Houston 17, Philadelphia 13, 1980.
                    A. L.— 31— Detroit 20, Oakland 11, 1972.

Most Total Bases, Total Series, One Club

    A. L.— 303— Baltimore; 6 Series, 22 games.
    N. L.— 280— Cincinnati; 6 Series, 22 games.

Most Total Bases, Series, One Club

    3-game Series—N. L.— 65— New York vs. Atlanta, 1969.
                    A. L.— 61— Baltimore vs. Minnesota, 1970.
    4-game Series—N. L.— 80— Los Angeles vs. Philadelphia, 1978.
                    A. L.— 62— New York vs. Kansas City, 1978.
    5-game Series—A. L.— 84— New York vs. Kansas City, 1976.
                    N. L.— 68— Philadelphia vs. Houston, 1980.

Most Total Bases, Series, Both Clubs

3-game Series—N. L.— 116—New York 65, Atlanta 51, 1969.
          A. L.—100—Baltimore 61, Minnesota 39, 1970.
4-game Series—N. L.—137—Los Angeles 80, Philadelphia 57, 1978.
          A. L.—121—New York 62, Kansas City 59, 1978.
5-game Series—A. L.—144—New York 84, Kansas City 60, 1976.
          N. L.—125—Philadelphia 68, Houston 57, 1980.

Fewest Total Bases, Series, One Club

3-game Series—A. L.—25—Minnesota vs. Baltimore, 1969.
          N. L.—26—Pittsburgh vs. Cincinnati, 1975.
4-game Series—A. L.—32—Baltimore vs. Oakland, 1974.
          N. L.—35—Pittsburgh vs. Los Angeles, 1974.
5-game Series—N. L.—47—Pittsburgh vs. Cincinnati, 1972.
          A. L.—49—Oakland vs. Detroit, 1972.

Fewest Total Bases, Series, Both Clubs

3-game Series—N. L.— 65—Cincinnati 36, Pittsburgh 29, 1970.
          A. L.— 73—Boston 45, Oakland 28, 1975.
4-game Series—A. L.— 69—Oakland 37, Baltimore 32, 1974.
          N. L.— 91—Los Angeles 56, Pittsburgh 35, 1974.
5-game Series—A. L.— 101—Detroit 52, Oakland 49, 1972.
          N. L.—103—Cincinnati 52, New York 51, 1973.

Most Total Bases, Game, One Club

N. L.—30—Los Angeles vs. Philadelphia, October 4, 1978.
A. L.—29—Baltimore vs. Minnesota, October 6, 1969.

Most Total Bases, Game, Both Clubs

N. L.—47—Los Angeles 30, Philadelphia 17, October 4, 1978.
A. L.—43—Baltimore 29, Minnesota 14, October 6, 1969.

Fewest Total Bases, Game, One Club

N. L.—2—Cincinnati vs. New York, October 7, 1973.
A. L.—2—Baltimore vs. Oakland, October 8, 1974.
          Oakland vs. Baltimore, October 9, 1974.

Fewest Total Bases, Game, Both Clubs

A. L.— 7—Baltimore 5, Oakland 2, October 9, 1974.
N. L.—12—New York 10, Cincinnati 2, October 7, 1973.

Most Total Bases, Inning, One Club

A. L.—16—Baltimore vs. Minnesota, October 3, 1970; fourth inning.
N. L.—11—San Francisco vs. Pittsburgh, October 6, 1971; second inning.

Most Total Bases, Inning, Both Clubs

A. L.—18—Baltimore 16, Minnesota 2, October 3, 1970; fourth inning.
N. L.—17—San Francisco 11, Pittsburgh 6, October 6, 1971; second inning.

Most Runs Batted In, Total Series, One Club

A. L.—100—Baltimore; 6 Series, 22 games.
N. L.— 72—Cincinnati; 6 Series, 22 games.

Most Runs Batted In, Series, One Club

3-game Series—A. L.—24—Baltimore vs. Minnesota, 1970.
          N. L.—24—New York vs. Atlanta, 1969.
4-game Series—A. L.—25—Baltimore vs. California, 1979.
          N. L.—23—Pittsburgh vs. San Francisco, 1971.
5-game Series—A. L.—24—Kansas City vs. New York, 1976.
          N. L.—22—New York vs. Cincinnati, 1973.

Most Runs Batted In, Series, Both Clubs

    3-game Series—N. L.—39—New York 24, Atlanta 15, 1969.
                   A. L.—34—Baltimore 24, Minnesota 10, 1970.
    4-game Series—A. L.—39—Baltimore 25, California 14, 1979.
                   N. L.—37—Pittsburgh 23, San Francisco 14, 1971.
                          Los Angeles 21, Philadelphia 16, 1978.
    5-game Series—A. L.—45—Kansas City 24, New York 21, 1976.
                   N. L.—37—Philadelphia 19, Houston 18, 1980.

Fewest Runs Batted In, Series, One Club

    3-game Series—N. L.— 3—Pittsburgh vs. Cincinnati, 1970.
                   A. L.— 5—Minnesota vs. Baltimore, 1969.
                          New York vs. Kansas City, 1980.
    4-game Series—A. L.— 7—Baltimore vs.Oakland, 1974.
                   N. L.—10—Pittsburgh vs. Los Angeles, 1974.
    5-game Series—N. L.— 8—Cincinnati vs. New York, 1973.
                   A. L.—10—Oakland vs. Detroit, 1972.
                          Detroit vs. Oakland, 1972.

Fewest Runs Batted In, Series, Both Clubs

    3-game Series—N. L.—11—Cincinnati 8, Pittsburgh 3, 1970.
                   A. L.—19—Kansas City 14, New York 5, 1980.
    4-game Series—A. L.—18—Oakland 11, Baltimore 7, 1974.
                   N. L.—29—Los Angeles 19, Pittsburgh 10, 1974.
    5-game Series—A. L.—20—Oakland 10, Detroit 10, 1972.
                   N. L.—30—Cincinnati 16, Pittsburgh 14, 1972.
                          New York 22, Cincinnati 8, 1973.

Most Runs Batted In, Game, One Club

    N. L.—11—New York vs. Atlanta, October 5, 1969.
           Los Angeles vs. Pittsburgh, October 9, 1974.
    A. L.—10—Baltimore vs. Minnesota, October 6, 1969.
           Baltimore vs. Minnesota, October 4, 1970.

Most Runs Batted In, Game, Both Clubs

    N. L.—17—New York 11, Atlanta 6, October 5, 1969.
    A. L.—16—Baltimore 8, California 8, October 4, 1979.

Most Runs Batted In, Inning, One Club

    A. L.—7—Baltimore vs. Minnesota, October 3, 1970; fourth inning.
    N. L.—5—Atlanta vs. New York, October 5, 1969; fifth inning.
           New York vs. Cincinnati, October 8, 1973; second inning.
           Pittsburgh vs. Los Angeles, October 8, 1974; first inning.
           Philadelphia vs. Houston, October 12, 1980; eighth inning.

Most Runs Batted In, Inning, Both Clubs

    A. L.—8—Baltimore 7, Minnesota 1, October 3, 1970; fourth inning.
    N. L.—7—San Francisco 4, Pittsburgh 3, October 6, 1971; second inning.
           Philadelphia 5, Houston 2, October 12, 1980; eighth inning.

Fewest Runs Batted In, Game, Both Clubs

    A. L.—1—Baltimore 1, Minnesota 0, October 5, 1969; 11 innings.
           Oakland 1, Baltimore 0, October 8, 1974.
    N. L.—1—Houston 1, Philadelphia 0, October 10, 1980; 11 innings.

Most Bases on Balls, Total Series, One Club

    A. L.—77—Baltimore; 6 Series, 22 games.
    N. L.—66—Cincinnati; 6 Series, 22 games.

Most Bases on Balls, Series, One Club

   3-game Series—N. L.—15—Cincinnati vs. Philadelphia, 1976.
                A. L.—13—Baltimore vs. Minnesota, 1969.
                       Baltimore vs. Oakland, 1971.
   4-game Series—N. L.—30—Los Angeles vs. Pittsburgh, 1974.
                A. L.—22—Oakland vs. Baltimore, 1974.
   5-game Series—N. L.—31—Houston vs. Philadelphia, 1980.
                A. L.—17—Oakland vs. Baltimore, 1973.

Most Bases on Balls, Series, Both Clubs

   3-game Series—N. L.—27—Cincinnati 15, Philadelphia 12, 1976.
                A. L.—25—Baltimore 13, Minnesota 12, 1969.
   4-game Series—N. L.—38—Los Angeles 30, Pittsburgh 8, 1974.
                A. L.—27—Oakland 22, Baltimore 5, 1974.
   5-game Series—N. L.—44—Houston 31, Philadelphia 13, 1980.
                A. L.—33—Oakland 17, Baltimore 16, 1973.

Fewest Bases on Balls, Series, One Club

   3-game Series—A. L.— 3—Boston vs. Oakland, 1975.
                N. L.— 8—Cincinnati vs. Pittsburgh, 1970.
   4-game Series—A. L.— 5—Baltimore vs. Oakland, 1974.
                N. L.— 5—Pittsburgh vs. San Francisco, 1971.
   5-game Series—A. L.— 9—New York vs. Kansas City, 1977.
                N. L.— 9—Pittsburgh vs. Cincinnati, 1972.

Fewest Bases on Balls, Series, Both Clubs

   3-game Series—A. L.— 12—Oakland 9, Boston 3, 1975.
                N. L.— 19—Pittsburgh 10, Cincinnati 9, 1975.
   4-game Series—N. L.— 18—Los Angeles 9, Philadelphia 9, 1978.
                A. L.— 21—Kansas City 14, New York 7, 1978.
   5-game Series—N. L.— 19—Cincinnati 10, Pittsburgh 9, 1972.
                A. L.— 24—Kansas City 15, New York 9, 1977.

Most Bases on Balls, Game, One Club

   A. L.—11—Oakland vs. Baltimore, October 9, 1974.
   N. L.—11—Los Angeles vs. Pittsburgh, October 9, 1974.

Most Bases on Balls, Game, Both Clubs

   A. L.—14—Oakland 11, Baltimore 3, October 9, 1974.
   N. L.—12—Los Angeles 11, Pittsburgh 1, October 9, 1974.
              Houston 7, Philadelphia 5, October 8, 1980; 10 innings.

Fewest Bases on Balls, Game, One Club

   A. L.-N. L.—0—Held by many clubs.

Fewest Bases on Balls, Game, Both Clubs

   A. L.— 1—Oakland 1, Baltimore 0, October 8, 1974.
            New York 1, Kansas City 0, October 9, 1976.
   N. L.— 2—Cincinnati 2, Pittsburgh 0, October 10, 1972.

Most Bases on Balls, Inning, One Club

   A. L.—4—Oakland vs. Baltimore, October 9, 1974; fifth inning, consecutive.
   N. L.—4—Philadelphia vs. Los Angeles, October 7, 1977; second inning, consecutive.

Most Bases on Balls, Inning, Both Clubs

   N. L.—5—Philadelphia 3, Cincinnati 2, October 9, 1976; first inning.
   A. L.—4—Made in many innings.

Most Strikeouts, Total Series, One Club

   N. L.—152— Cincinnati; 6 Series, 22 games.
   A. L.—124— Baltimore; 6 Series, 22 games.

Most Strikeouts, Series, One Club

3-game Series—N. L.—28—Cincinnati vs. Pittsburgh, 1975.
      A. L.—27—Minnesota vs. Baltimore, 1969.
4-game Series—N. L.—33—Pittsburgh vs. San Francisco, 1971.
      A. L.—24—Baltimore vs. California, 1979.
5-game Series—N. L.—42—Cincinnati vs. New York, 1973.
      A. L.—39—Oakland vs. Baltimore, 1973.

Most Strikeouts, Series, Both Clubs

3-game Series—N. L.—46—Cincinnati 28, Pittsburgh 18, 1975.
      A. L.—41—Minnesota 27, Baltimore 14, 1969.
         Minnesota 22, Baltimore 19, 1970.
4-game Series—N. L.—61—Pittsburgh 33, San Francisco 28, 1971.
      A. L.—39—Kansas City 21, New York 18, 1978.
5-game Series—N. L.—70—Cincinnati 42, New York 28, 1973.
      A. L.—64—Oakland 39, Baltimore 25, 1973.

Fewest Strikeouts, Series, One Club

3-game Series—N. L.— 9—Philadelphia vs. Cincinnati, 1976.
      A. L.—12—Boston vs. Oakland, 1975.
4-game Series—A. L.—13—California vs. Baltimore, 1979.
      N. L.—16—Los Angeles vs. Pittsburgh, 1974.
5-game Series—A. L.—15—New York vs. Kansas City, 1976.
      N. L.—19—Houston vs. Philadelphia, 1980.

Fewest Strikeouts, Series, Both Clubs

3-game Series—N. L.—25—Cincinnati 16, Philadelphia 9, 1976.
      A. L.—26—Oakland 14, Boston 12, 1975.
4-game Series—N. L.—33—Pittsburgh 17, Los Angeles 16, 1974.
      A. L.—36—Baltimore 20, Oakland 16, 1974.
5-game Series—A. L.—33—Kansas City 18, New York 15, 1976.
      N. L.—55—Cincinnati 28, Pittsburgh 27, 1972.

Most Strikeouts, Game, Nine Innings, One Club

A. L.—14—Oakland vs. Detroit, October 10, 1972.
N. L.—13—Pittsburgh vs. San Francisco, October 3, 1971.
    Cincinnati vs. New York, October 6, 1973.

Most Strikeouts, Extra-Inning Game, One Club

N. L.—15—Cincinnati vs. Pittsburgh, October 7, 1975; 10 innings.
A. L.—Less than nine-inning record.

Most Strikeouts, Game, Nine Innings, Both Clubs

N. L.—20—New York 12, Atlanta 8, October 5, 1969.
A. L.—19—Minnesota 12, Baltimore 7, October 5, 1970.
    Oakland 12, Baltimore 7, October 6, 1973.

Most Strikeouts, Extra-Inning Game, Both Clubs

N. L.—23—Cincinnati 15, Pittsburgh 8, October 7, 1975; 10 innings.
A. L.—Less than nine-inning record.

Fewest Strikeouts, Game, One Club

N. L.—0— Pittsburgh vs. Los Angeles, October 6, 1974.
A. L.—1— Baltimore vs. Oakland, October 11, 1973.
    New York vs. Kansas City, October 13, 1976.
    Kansas City vs. New York, October 4, 1978.

Fewest Strikeouts, Game, Both Clubs

A. L.—3— Oakland 2, Baltimore 1, October 11, 1973.
    Kansas City 2, New York 1, October 13, 1976.
N. L.—4— Philadelphia 2, Cincinnati 2, October 12, 1976.

Most Consecutive Strikeouts, Game, One Club

A. L.—4—Oakland vs. Detroit, October 10, 1972; 1 in fourth inning, 3 in fifth
        inning.
        Baltimore vs. California, October 3, 1979; 3 in first inning, 1 in second
        inning.
N. L.—4—Pittsburgh vs. Cincinnati, October 5, 1970; 2 in sixth inning, 2 in sev-
        enth inning.
        Cincinnati vs. Pittsburgh, October 7, 1975; 3 in first inning, 1 in second
        inning.

Most Strikeouts, Inning, One Club

A. L.-N. L.—3—Held by many clubs.

Most Strikeouts, Inning, Both Clubs

A. L.—5—Oakland 3, Baltimore 2, October 6, 1973; first inning.
        Boston 3, Oakland 2, October 4, 1975; second inning.
N. L.—5—New York 3, Atlanta 2, October 5, 1969; third inning.
        New York 3, Atlanta 2, October 6, 1969; third inning.
        Philadelphia 3, Los Angeles 2, October 4, 1977; seventh inning.

Most Sacrifice Hits, Total Series, One Club

A. L.—12—Oakland; 5 Series, 20 games.
N. L.—12—Pittsburgh; 6 Series, 22 games.
        Philadelphia; 4 Series, 16 games.

Most Sacrifice Hits, Series, One Club

3-game Series—A. L.—5—Boston vs. Oakland, 1975.
              N. L.—5—Pittsburgh vs. Cincinnati, 1979.
4-game Series—N. L.—4—San Francisco vs. Pittsburgh, 1971.
              A. L.—2—Baltimore vs. Oakland, 1974.
                      Oakland vs. Baltimore, 1974.
5-game Series—N. L.—7—Houston vs. Philadelphia, 1980.
              A. L.—4—Oakland vs. Detroit, 1972.
                      Oakland vs. Baltimore, 1973.

Most Sacrifice Hits, Series, Both Clubs

3-game Series—A. L.— 5—Boston 5, Oakland 0, 1975.
              N. L.— 6—Pittsburgh 5, Cincinnati 1, 1979.
4-game Series—N. L.— 5—San Francisco 4, Pittsburgh 1, 1971.
              A. L.— 4—Baltimore 2, Oakland 2, 1974.
5-game Series—N. L.— 12—Houston 7, Philadelphia 5, 1980.
              A. L.— 7—Oakland 4, Detroit 3, 1972.

Fewest Sacrifice Hits, Series, One Club

3-game Series—A. L.—N. L.—0—Held by many clubs.
4-game Series—A. L.—0—New York vs. Kansas City, 1978.
                      California vs. Baltimore, 1979.
              N. L.—1—Pittsburgh vs. San Francisco, 1971.
                      Los Angeles vs. Pittsburgh, 1974.
5-game Series—A. L.—0—Baltimore vs. Oakland, 1973.
                      Kansas City vs. New York, 1976.
              N. L.—2—Pittsburgh vs. Cincinnati, 1972.

Fewest Sacrifice Hits, Series, Both Clubs

3-game Series—N. L.—0—Cincinnati 0, Pittsburgh 0, 1975.
              A. L.—1—New York 1, Kansas City 0, 1980.
4-game Series—A. L.—1—Kansas City 1, New York 0, 1978.
                      Baltimore 1, California 0, 1979.
              N. L.—3—Pittsburgh 2, Los Angeles 1, 1974.
5-game Series—A. L.—2—New York 2, Kansas City 0, 1976.
              N. L.—5—Cincinnati 3, Pittsburgh 2, 1972.

Most Sacrifice Hits, Game, One Club

    N. L.—3— Pittsburgh vs. Cincinnati, October 3, 1979; 10 innings.
              Philadelphia vs. Houston, October 8, 1980; 10 innings.
    Nine-Inning Record—A. L.-N. L.—2—Held by many clubs.

Most Sacrifice Hits, Game, Both Clubs

    N. L.—4— Pittsburgh 3, Cincinnati 1, October 3, 1979; 10 innings.
          3— San Francisco 2, Pittsburgh 1, October 2, 1971.
              Cincinnati 2, Pittsburgh 1, October 11, 1972.
    A. L.—2— Made in many games.

Most Sacrifice Hits, Inning, One Club

    N. L.—2— Philadelphia vs. Cincinnati, October 10, 1976; fourth inning.
    A. L.—1— Held by many clubs.

Most Sacrifice Flies, Total Series, One Club

    N. L.—9— Cincinnati; 6 Series, 22 games.
    A. L.—8— Kansas City; 3 Series, 14 games.

Most Sacrifice Flies, Series, One Club

    3-game Series—N. L.—3— Cincinnati vs. Pittsburgh, 1975.
                     Cincinnati vs. Philadelphia, 1976.
                     Pittsburgh vs. Cincinnati, 1979.
             A. L.—2— Baltimore vs. Minnesota, 1970.
    4-game Series—A. L.—3— Baltimore vs. California, 1979.
             N. L.—1— Philadelphia vs. Los Angeles, 1978.
    5-game Series—A. L.—4— Kansas City vs. New York, 1976.
             N. L.—2— Houston vs. Philadelphia, 1980.

Most Sacrifice Flies, Series, Both Clubs

    3-game Series—N. L.—5— Cincinnati 3, Philadelphia 2, 1976.
             A. L.—2— Baltimore 2, Minnesota 0, 1970.
    4-game Series—A. L.—5— Baltimore 3, California 2, 1979.
             N. L.—1— Philadelphia 1, Los Angeles 0, 1978.
    5-game Series—A. L.—5— Kansas City 4, New York 1, 1976.
             N. L.—3— Houston 2, Philadelphia 1, 1980.

Most Sacrifice Flies, Game, One Club

    A. L.—2— Kansas City vs. New York, October 13, 1976.
              California vs. Baltimore, October 4, 1979.
    N. L.—2— Pittsburgh vs. Cincinnati, October 5, 1979.

Most Sacrifice Flies, Game, Both Clubs

    A. L.—2— Kansas City 2, New York 0, October 13, 1976.
              Kansas City 1, New York 1, October 8, 1977.
              California 2, Baltimore 0, October 4, 1979.
    N. L.—2— Cincinnati 1, Philadelphia 1, October 9, 1976.
              Cincinnati 1, Philadelphia 1, October 12, 1976.
              Pittsburgh 2, Cincinnati 0, October 5, 1979.
              Houston 1, Philadelphia 1, October 11, 1980; 10 innings.

Most Sacrifice Flies, Inning, One Club

    A. L.-N. L.—1—Held by many clubs.

Most Hit by Pitch, Total Series, One Club

    N. L.—7— Pittsburgh; 6 Series, 22 games.
    A. L.—6— Oakland; 5 Series, 20 games.

Most Hit by Pitch, Series, One Club

    3-game Series—A. L.— 1— Baltimore vs. Minnesota, 1970.
                     Kansas City vs. New York, 1980.

Most Hit by Pitch, Series, One Club—Continued

 N. L.— 1— Atlanta vs. New York, 1969.
  Pittsburgh vs. Cincinnati, 1975.
4-game Series—N. L.— 3— Philadelphia vs. Los Angeles, 1977.
 A. L.— 1— Oakland vs. Baltimore, 1974.
  Baltimore vs. California, 1979.
5-game Series—A. L.— 3— Oakland vs. Detroit, 1972.
 N. L.— 2— Pittsburgh vs. Cincinnati, 1972.

Most Hit by Pitch, Series, Both Clubs

3-game Series—A. L.— 1— Baltimore 1, Minnesota 0, 1970.
  Kansas City 1, New York 0, 1980.
 N. L.— 1— Atlanta 1, New York 0, 1969.
  Pittsburgh 1, Cincinnati 0, 1975.
4-game Series—N. L.— 3— Pittsburgh 2, San Francisco 1, 1971.
  Philadelphia 3, Los Angeles 0, 1977.
 A. L.— 1— Oakland 1, Baltimore 0, 1974.
  Baltimore 1, California 0, 1979.
5-game Series—A. L.— 4— Baltimore 2, Oakland 2, 1973.
 N. L.— 2— Pittsburgh 2, Cincinnati 0, 1972.

Fewest Hit by Pitch, Series, One Club

A. L.-N. L.—0—Held by many clubs in Series of all lengths.

Fewest Hit by Pitch, Series, Both Clubs

3-game Series—N. L.— 0— Cincinnati 0, Pittsburgh 0, 1970, 1979.
  Cincinnati 0, Philadelphia 0, 1976.
 A. L.— 0— Baltimore 0, Minnesota 0, 1969.
  Baltimore 0, Oakland 0, 1971.
  Boston 0, Oakland 0, 1975.
4-game Series—A. L.— 0— Kansas City 0, New York 0, 1978.
 N. L.— 1— Los Angeles 1, Philadelphia 0, 1978.
5-game Series—A. L.— 0— New York 0, Kansas City 0, 1977.
 N. L.— 1— Cincinnati 1, New York 0, 1973.
  Philadelphia 1, Houston 1, 1980.

Most Hit by Pitch Game, One Club

A. L.— 2— Oakland vs. Detroit, October 12, 1972.
N. L.— 1— Held by many clubs.

Most Hit by Pitch, Game, Both Clubs

N. L.— 2— San Francisco 1, Pittsburgh 1, October 3, 1971.
A. L.— 2— Oakland 2, Detroit 0, October 12, 1972.
  Oakland 1, Baltimore 1, October 11, 1973.

Most Hit by Pitch, Inning, One Club

A. L.-N. L.—1—Held by many clubs.

CLUB PINCH-HITTING

Most Times Pinch-Hitter Used, Series, One Club

3-game Series—A. L.— 10— Minnesota vs. Baltimore, 1970.
 N. L.— 9— Pittsburgh vs. Cincinnati, 1975.
4-game Series—N. L.— 8— Los Angeles vs. Pittsburgh, 1974.
  Philadelphia vs. Los Angeles, 1977, 1978.
 A. L.— 5— Kansas City vs. New York, 1978.
  Baltimore vs. California, 1979.
5-game Series—N. L.—15— Cincinnati vs. New York, 1973.
 A. L.—14— Oakland vs. Detroit, 1972.

Most Times Pinch-Hitter Used, Series, Both Clubs

3-game Series—N. L.—14—Pittsburgh 9, Cincinnati 5, 1975.
            A. L.—10—Minnesota 10, Baltimore 0, 1970.
4-game Series—N. L.—15—Philadelphia 8, Los Angeles 7, 1978.
            A. L.— 9—Kansas City 5, New York 4, 1978.
                    Baltimore 5, California 4, 1979.
5-game Series—A. L.—22—Oakland 14, Detroit 8, 1972.
            N. L.—20—Philadelphia 11, Houston 9, 1980.

Fewest Times Pinch-Hitter Used, Series, One Club

3-game Series—A. L.— 0— Baltimore vs. Minnesota, 1970.
                    Boston vs. Oakland, 1975.
            N. L.— 1— Pittsburgh vs. Cincinnati, 1979.
4-game Series—A. L.— 3— Oakland vs. Baltimore, 1974.
                    Baltimore vs. Oakland, 1974.
            N. L.—5— San Francisco vs. Pittsburgh, 1971.
5-game Series—N. L.— 1— New York vs. Cincinnati, 1973.
            A. L.— 3— Baltimore vs. Oakland, 1973.

Fewest Times Pinch-Hitter Used, Series, Both Clubs

3-game Series—A. L.— 4— New York 3, Kansas City 1, 1980.
            N. L.— 6—Cincinnati 4, Pittsburgh 2, 1970.
                    Cincinnati 5, Pittsburgh 1, 1979.
4-game Series—A. L.— 6—Oakland 3, Baltimore 3, 1974.
            N. L.—11—Pittsburgh 6, San Francisco 5, 1971.
5-game Series—A. L.— 9— Kansas City 5, New York 4, 1977.
            N. L.—13—Cincinnati 7, Pittsburgh 6, 1972.

Most At-Bats, Pinch-Hitters, Total Series, One Club

N. L.—31—Philadelphia, 1976, 1977, 1978, 1980; 4 Series, 16 games.
A. L.—30—Oakland, 1971, 1972, 1973, 1974, 1975; 5 Series, 20 games.

Most At-Bats, Pinch-Hitters, Series, One Club

3-game Series—A. L.— 9—Minnesota vs. Baltimore, 1970.
            N. L.— 7—Pittsburgh vs. Cincinnati, 1975.
4-game Series—N. L.— 8—Philadelphia vs. Los Angeles, 1977, 1978.
            A. L.— 4— New York vs. Kansas City, 1978.
                    Kansas City vs. New York, 1978.
                    Baltimore vs. California, 1979.
5-game Series—N. L.—14—Cincinnati vs. New York, 1973.
            A. L.—13—Oakland vs. Detroit, 1972.

Most At-Bats, Pinch-Hitters, Series, Both Cubs

3-game Series—A. L.— 9—Minnesota 9, Baltimore 0, 1970.
            N. L.— 8—Atlanta 6, New York 2, 1969.
                    Pittsburgh 7, Cincinnati 1, 1975.
4-game Series—N. L.—14—Philadelphia 8, Los Angeles 6, 1978.
            A. L.— 8—New York 4, Kansas City 4, 1978.
5-game Series—A. L.—20—Oakland 13, Detroit 7, 1972.
            N. L.—18—Philadelphia 10, Houston 8, 1980.

Most Plate Appearances, Pinch-Hitters, Total Series, Club

A. L.—36—Oakland, 1971, 1972, 1973, 1974, 1975; 5 Series, 20 games.
N. L.—36—Cincinnati, 1970, 1972, 1973, 1975, 1976, 1979; 6 Series, 22 games.

Most Plate Appearances, Pinch-Hitters, Series, One Club

3-game Series—A. L.— 10—Minnesota vs. Baltimore, 1970.
            N. L.— 9—Pittsburgh vs. Cincinnati, 1975.
4-game Series—N. L.— 8—Los Angeles vs. Pittsburgh, 1974.
                    Philadelphia vs. Los Angeles, 1977, 1978.

Most Plate Appearances, Pinch-Hitters, Series, One Club—Continued

    A. L.— 5—Kansas City vs. New York, 1978.
           Baltimore vs. California, 1979.
  5-game Series—N. L.—15—Cincinnati vs. New York, 1973.
        A. L.—14—Oakland vs. Detroit, 1972.

Most Plate Appearances, Pinch-Hitters, Series, Both Clubs

  3-game Series—N. L.—12—Pittsburgh 9, Cincinnati 3, 1975.
        A. L.—10—Minnesota 10, Baltimore 0, 1970.
  4-game Series—N. L.—15—Philadelphia 8, Los Angeles 7, 1978.
        A. L.— 9—Kansas City 5, New York 4, 1978.
           Baltimore 5, California 4, 1979.
  5-game Series—A. L.—22—Oakland 14, Detroit 8, 1972.
        N. L.—20—Philadelphia 11, Houston 9, 1980.

Most Pinch-Hitters, Game, One Club

  A. L.—6—Oakland vs. Detroit, October 10, 1972.
  N. L.—5—Los Angeles vs. Pittsburgh, October 8, 1974.

Most Pinch-Hitters, Game, Both Clubs

  A. L.—7—Oakland 6, Detroit 1, October 10, 1972.
  N. L.—6—Pittsburgh 3, Cincinnati 3, October 5, 1975.
        Los Angeles 4, Philadelphia 2, October 7, 1978; 10 innings.
        Philadelphia 3, Houston 3, October 12, 1980; 10 innings.

Most Plate Appearances, Pinch-Hitters, Game, One Club

  A. L.—6—Oakland vs. Detroit, October 10, 1972.
  N. L.—5—Los Angeles vs. Pittsburgh, October 8, 1974.

Most Plate Appearances, Pinch-Hitters, Game, Both Clubs

  A. L.—7—Oakland 6, Detroit 1, October 10, 1972.
  N. L.—6—Los Angeles 4, Philadelphia 2, October 7, 1978; 10 innings.
        Philadelphia 3, Houston 3, October 12, 1980; 10 innings.
  N. L.—Nine-inning record-5-Held by many clubs.

Most At-Bats, Pinch-Hitters, Game, One Club

  A. L.—6—Oakland vs. Detroit, October 10, 1972.
  N. L.—4—Cincinnati vs. New York, October 9, 1973; 12 innings.
        Los Angeles vs. Pittsburgh, October 8, 1974.

Most At-Bats, Pinch-Hitters, Game, Both Clubs

  A. L.—7—Oakland 6, Detroit 1, October 10, 1972.
  N. L.—6—Philadelphia 3, Houston 3, October 12, 1980; 10 innings.
  Nine-inning record—5—Los Angeles 3, Philadelphia 2, October 7, 1977.

Most Pinch-Hitters, Inning, One Club

  A. L.—3—Oakland vs. Detroit, October 10, 1972; seventh inning.
        Oakland vs. Baltimore, October 10, 1973; eighth inning.
  N. L.—3—Cincinnati vs. Pittsburgh, October 5, 1975; sixth inning.
        Philadelphia vs. Cincinnati, October 9, 1976; ninth inning.

Most Runs, Pinch-Hitters, Series, One Club

  N. L.—3—Los Angeles vs. Philadelphia, 1977; 4-game Series.
        Philadelphia vs. Houston, October 11, 1980; 10 innings.
  A. L.—2—Oakland vs. Detroit, 1972; 5-game Series.

Most Runs, Pinch-Hitters, Series, Both Clubs

  A. L.—3—Oakland 2, Detroit 1, 1972; 5-game Series.
  N. L.—3—Los Angeles 3, Philadelphia 0, 1977; 4-game Series.

Most Runs, Pinch-Hitters, Game, One Club

  N. L.—2—Los Angeles vs. Philadelphia, October 7, 1977.

Philadelphia vs. Houston, October 11, 1980; 10 innings.

A. L.— 1— Held by many clubs.

Most Runs, Pinch-Hitters, Inning, One Club

N. L.— 2— Los Angeles vs. Philadelphia, October 7, 1977; ninth inning.

A. L.— 1— Held by many clubs.

Most Hits, Pinch-Hitters, Series, One Club

N. L.— 4— Pittsburgh vs. Los Angeles, 1974; 4-game Series.
Los Angeles vs. Pittsburgh, 1974; 4-game Series.
Philadelphia vs. Houston, 1980; 5-game Series.

A. L.— 3— Oakland vs. Detroit, 1972; 5-game Series.

Most Hits, Pinch-Hitters, Series, Both Clubs

N. L.— 8— Pittsburgh 4, Los Angeles 4, 1974; 4-game Series.

A. L.— 4— Oakland 3, Detroit 1, 1972; 5-game Series.

Most Hits, Pinch-Hitters, Game, One Club

A. L.— 2— Oakland vs. Baltimore, October 5, 1974.

N. L.— 2— Held by many clubs.

Most Hits, Pinch-Hitters, Game, Both Clubs

N. L.— 4— Los Angeles 2, Pittsburgh 2, October 6, 1974.

A. L.— 2— Oakland 2, Baltimore 0, October 5, 1974.

Most Consecutive Hits, Pinch-Hitters, Game, One Club

A. L.— 2— Oakland vs. Baltimore, October 5, 1974; J. Alou singled and C. Washington doubled in ninth inning.

N. L.— 2— Pittsburgh vs. Los Angeles, October 6, 1974; Popovich and Zisk singled in seventh inning.
Los Angeles vs. Pittsburgh, October 6, 1974; Crawford and Mota singled in eighth inning.
Los Angeles vs. Philadelphia, October 7, 1977; Davalillo singled and Mota doubled in ninth inning.

Most Hits, Pinch-Hitters, Inning, One Club

A. L.— 2— Oakland vs. Baltimore, October 5, 1974; ninth inning

N. L.— 2— Pittsburgh vs. Los Angeles, October 6, 1974; seventh inning.
Los Angeles vs. Pittsburgh, October 6, 1974; eighth inning.
Los Angeles vs. Philadelphia, October 7, 1977; ninth inning.

Most One-Base Hits, Pinch-Hitters, Series, One Club

N. L.— 4— Pittsburgh vs. Los Angeles, 1974; 4-game Series.

A. L.— 3— Oakland vs. Detroit, 1972; 5-game Series.

Most One-Base Hits, Pinch-Hitters, Series, Both Clubs

N. L.— 7— Pittsburgh 4, Los Angeles 3, 1974; 4-game Series.

A. L.— 4— Oakland 3, Detroit 1, 1972; 5-game Series.

Most Two-Base Hits, Pinch-Hitters, Series, One Club

A. L.-N. L.—1—Held by many clubs.

Most Two-Base Hits, Pinch-Hitters, Series, Both Clubs

N. L.— 2— Los Angeles 1, Philadelphia 1, 1978; 4-game Series.

A. L.— 1— Made in many Series.

Most Three-Base Hits, Pinch-Hitters, Series, One Club

N. L.— 1— Cincinnati vs. Pittsburgh, 1970; 3-game Series.

A. L.—Never accomplished.

Most Home Runs, Pinch-Hitters, Series, One Club

N. L.— 2— Philadelphia vs. Los Angeles, 1978; 4-game Series.

A. L.— 1— Baltimore vs. California, 1979; 4-game Series.

Most Total Bases, Pinch-Hitters, Series, One Club

N. L.— 10— Philadelphia vs. Los Angeles, 1978; 4-game Series.
A. L.— 5— Baltimore vs. California, 1979; 4-game Series.

Most Total Bases, Pinch-Hitters, Series, Both Clubs

N. L.— 12— Philadelphia 10, Los Angeles 2, 1978; 4-game Series.
A. L.— 7— Baltimore 5, California 2, 1979; 4-game Series.

Most Runs Batted In, Pinch-Hitters, Series, One Club

A. L.— 4— Baltimore vs. California, 1979; 4-game Series.
N. L.— 4— Philadelphia vs. Houston, 1980; 5-game Series.

Most Runs Batted In, Pinch-Hitters, Series, Both Clubs

N. L.— 5— Philadelphia 4, Houston 1, 1980; 5-game Series.
A. L.— 4— Baltimore 4, California 0, 1979; 4-game Series.

Most Runs Batted In, Pinch-Hitters, Game, One Club

A. L.— 3— Baltimore vs. California, October 3, 1979; 10 innings.
N. L.— 2— New York vs. Atlanta, October 4, 1969.
    Los Angeles vs. Pittsburgh, October 6, 1974.

Most Runs Batted In, Pinch-Hitters, Game, Both Clubs

A. L.— 3— Baltimore vs. California, October 3, 1979; 10 innings.
        2— Kansas City 2, New York 0, October 7, 1977.
N. L.— 2— New York 2, Atlanta 0, October 4, 1969.
    Los Angeles 2, Pittsburgh 0, October 6, 1974.
    Cincinnati 1, Pittsburgh 1, October 7, 1975; 10 innings.
    Houston 1, Philadelphia 1, October 12, 1980; 10 innings.

Most Runs Batted In, Pinch-Hitters, Inning, One Club

A. L.— 3— Baltimore vs. California, October 3, 1979; tenth inning.
N. L.— 2— New York vs. Atlanta, October 4, 1969; eighth inning.
    Los Angeles vs. Pittsburgh, October 6, 1974; eighth inning.

Most Bases on Balls, Pinch-Hitters, Series, One Club

A. L.— 2— Oakland vs. Boston, 1975; 3-game Series.
    California vs. Baltimore, 1979; 4-game Series.
N. L.— 2— Cincinnati vs. Pittsburgh, 1972; 5-game Series.
    Pittsburgh vs. Cincinnati, 1975; 3-game Series.

Most Bases on Balls, Pinch-Hitters, Series, Both Clubs

N. L.— 3— Cincinnati 2, Pittsburgh 1, 1972; 5-game Series.
    Pittsburgh 2, Cincinnati 1, 1975; 3-game Series.
A. L.— 3— California 2, Baltimore 1, 1979; 4-game Series.

Most Bases on Balls, Pinch-Hitters, Game, One Club

N. L.— 2— Pittsburgh vs. Cincinnati, October 7, 1975; 10 innings.
A. L.— 2— California vs. Baltimore, October 4, 1979.

Most Bases on Balls, Pinch-Hitters, Game, Both Clubs

N. L.— 3— Pittsburgh 2, Cincinnati 1, October 7, 1975; 10 innings.
A. L.— 2— Detroit 1, Oakland 1, October 11, 1972; 10 innings.
    California 2, Baltimore 0, October 4, 1979.

Most Bases on Balls, Pinch-Hitters, Inning, One Club

N. L.— 2— Pittsburgh vs. Cincinnati, October 7, 1975; ninth inning.
A. L.— 1— Held by many clubs.

Most Strikeouts, Pinch-Hitters, Series, One Club

N. L.— 7— Cincinnati vs. New York, 1973; 5-game Series.
A. L.— 4— Minnesota vs. Baltimore, 1970; 3-game Series.
    Oakland vs. Detroit, 1972; 5-game Series.

Most Strikeouts, Pinch-Hitters, Series, Both Clubs

   N. L.— 7— Cincinnati 7, New York 0, 1973; 5-game Series.
   A. L.— 4— Minnesota 4, Baltimore 0, 1970; 3-game Series.
         Oakland 4, Detroit 0, 1972; 5-game Series.

Most Strikeouts, Pinch-Hitters, Game, One Club

   A. L.— 4— Oakland vs. Detroit, October 10, 1972.
   N. L.— 3— Cincinnati vs. New York, October 7, 1973.

Most Strikeouts, Pinch-Hitters, Inning, One Club

   A. L.— 2— Oakland vs. Baltimore, October 5, 1971; ninth inning, consecutive.
   N. L.— 2— Cincinnati vs. New York, October 7, 1973; eighth inning, consecutive.

Most Sacrifice Hits, Pinch-Hitters, Game, One Club

   A. L.— 1— Oakland vs. Baltimore, October 9, 1973; 11 innings.
   N. L.— 1— Cincinnati vs. Philadelphia, October 12, 1976.
         Los Angeles vs. Philadelphia, October 7, 1978; 10 innings.
         Philadelphia vs. Houston, October 8, 1980; 10 innings.

Most Sacrifice Flies, Pinch-Hitters, Game, One Club

   N. L.— 1— Cincinnati vs. Pittsburgh, October 7, 1975; 10 innings.
   A. L.—Never accomplished.

Most Hit by Pitch, Pinch-Hitters, Game, One Club

   A. L.-N. L.—Never accomplished.

Most Grounded into Double Plays, Pinch-Hitters, Game, One Club

   A. L.— 1— Minnesota vs. Baltimore, October 6, 1969.
         Baltimore vs. California, October 6, 1979.
   N. L.— 1— San Francisco vs. Pittsburgh, October 3, 1971.
         Los Angeles vs. Pittsburgh, October 9, 1974.
         Los Angeles vs. Philadelphia, October 6, 1978.

CLUB BASE RUNNING

Most Stolen Bases, Total Series, One Club

   N. L.— 25— Cincinnati; 6 Series, 22 games.
   A. L.— 19— Kansas City; 4 Series, 17 games.

Most Stolen Bases, Series, One Club

   3-game Series—N. L.— 11— Cincinnati vs. Pittsburgh, 1975.
            A. L.— 3— Boston vs. Oakland, 1975.
                   Kansas City vs. New York, 1980.
   4-game Series—A. L.— 6— Kansas City vs. New York, 1978.
            N. L.— 5— Los Angeles vs. Pittsburgh, 1974.
   5-game Series—A. L.— 7— Oakland vs. Detroit, 1972.
            N. L.— 7— Philadelphia vs. Houston, 1980.

Most Stolen Bases, Series, Both Clubs

   3-game Series—N. L.— 11— Cincinnati 11, Pittsburgh 0, 1975.
            A. L.— 3— Boston 3, Oakland 0, 1975.
                   Kansas City 3, New York 0, 1980.
   4-game Series—A. L.— 7— Baltimore 5, California 2, 1979.
            N. L.— 6— Los Angeles 5, Pittsburgh 1, 1974.
   5-game Series—A. L.— 9— Kansas City 5, New York 4, 1976.
            N. L.— 11— Philadelphia 7, Houston 4, 1980.

Fewest Stolen Bases, Series, One Club

   A. L.-N. L.— 0—Held by many clubs in Series of all lengths.

Fewest Stolen Bases, Series, Both Clubs

3-game Series—A. L.— 0— Baltimore 0, Oakland 0, 1971.
          N. L.— 1— Cincinnati 1, Pittsburgh 0, 1970.
4-game Series—N. L.— 2— Los Angeles 2, Philadelphia 0, 1978.
          A. L.— 3— Oakland 3, Baltimore 0, 1974.
5-game Series—N. L.— 0— Cincinnati 0, New York 0, 1973.
          A. L.— 4— Oakland 3, Baltimore 1, 1973.

Most Stolen Bases, Game, One Club

N. L.— 7— Cincinnati vs. Pittsburgh, October 5, 1975.
A. L.— 3— Oakland vs. Detroit, October 12, 1972.
          Kansas City vs. New York, October 10, 1976.

Most Stolen Bases, Game, Both Clubs

N. L.— 7— Cincinnati 7, Pittsburgh 0, October 5, 1975.
A. L.— 3— Made in many games.

Longest Game, No Stolen Bases, One Club

A. L.— 12 innings— Baltimore vs. Minnesota, October 4, 1969.
N. L.— 12 innings— New York vs. Cincinnati, October 9, 1973.
          Cincinnati vs. New York, October 9, 1973.

Longest Game, No Stolen Bases, Both Clubs

N. L.— 12 innings— New York 0, Cincinnati 0, October 9, 1973.
A. L.— 11 innings— Detroit 0, Oakland 0, October 7, 1972.
          Baltimore 0, Oakland 0, October 9, 1973.

Most Stolen Bases, Inning, One Club

A. L.— 3— Oakland vs. Detroit, October 12, 1972; second inning.
N. L.— 2— New York vs. Atlanta, October 5, 1969; first inning.
          Cincinnati vs. Pittsburgh, October 4, 1975; third inning.
          Cincinnati vs. Pittsburgh, October 5, 1975; first inning, fourth inning,
          sixth inning.

Most Caught Stealing, Series, One Club

3-game Series—A. L.— 5— Kansas City vs. New York, 1980.
          N. L.— 2— Pittsburgh vs. Cincinnati, 1970.
          Cincinnati vs. Pittsburgh, 1979.
4-game Series—A. L.— 3— Oakland vs. Baltimore, 1974.
          Baltimore vs. Oakland, 1974.
          Kansas City vs. New York, 1978.
          N. L.— 1— Held by many clubs.
5-game Series—A. L.— 5— Kansas City vs. New York, 1976.
          N. L.— 3— Philadelphia vs. Houston, 1980.

Most Caught Stealing, Series, Both Clubs

3-game Series—A. L.— 5— Kansas City 5, New York 0, 1980.
          N. L.— 3— Pittsburgh 2, Cincinnati 1, 1970.
4-game Series—A. L.— 6— Oakland 3, Baltimore 3, 1974.
          N. L.— 2— Los Angeles 1, Philadelphia 1, 1978.
5-game Series—A. L.— 8— Kansas City 5, New York 3, 1976.
          N. L.— 4— Philadelphia 3, Houston 1, 1980.

Fewest Caught Stealing, Series, One Club

3-game Series—A. L.— N. L.— 0—Held by many clubs.
4-game Series—N. L.— 0— Held by many clubs.
          A. L.— 1— New York vs. Kansas City, 1978.
          Baltimore vs. California, 1979.
          California vs. Baltimore, 1979.
5-game Series—A. L.— 0— New York vs. Kansas City, 1977.
          N. L.— 0— New York vs. Cincinnati, 1973.

Fewest Caught Stealing, Series, Both Clubs

3-game Series—N. L.— 0— Cincinnati 0, Pittsburgh 0, 1975.
A. L.— 0— Baltimore 0, Minnesota 0, 1970.
Boston 0, Oakland 0, 1975.
4-game Series—N. L.— 0— Los Angeles 0, Pittsburgh 0, 1974.
A. L.— 4— Kansas City 3, New York 1, 1978.
5-game Series—N. L.— 1— Cincinnati 1, New York 0, 1973.
A. L.— 4— Detroit 2, Oakland 2, 1972.
Kansas City 4, New York 0, 1977.

Most Caught Stealing, Game, One Club

A. L.— 2— Held by many clubs.
N. L.— 1— Held by many clubs.

Most Caught Stealing, Game, Both Clubs

A. L.— 3— Baltimore 2, Oakland 1, October 10, 1973.
Kansas City 2, New York 1, October 12, 1976.
N. L.— 2— Pittsburgh 1, Cincinnati 1, October 5, 1970.
Los Angeles 1, Philadelphia 1, October 7, 1978; 10 innings.

Most Caught Stealing, Inning, One Club

A. L.-N. L.— 1— Held by many clubs.

Most Left on Bases, Total Series, One Club

N. L.— 148— Pittsburgh; 6 Series, 22 games.
A. L.— 142— Baltimore; 6 Series, 22 games.

Most Left on Bases, Series, One Club

3-game Series—N. L.— 29— Pittsburgh vs. Cincinnati, 1970.
A. L.— 28— Baltimore vs. Minnesota, 1969.
4-game Series—N. L.— 44— Los Angeles vs. Pittsburgh, 1974.
A. L.— 30— Oakland vs. Baltimore, 1974.
5-game Series—N. L.— 45— Houston vs. Philadelphia, 1980.
A. L.— 41— New York vs. Kansas City, 1976.

Most Left on Bases, Series, Both Clubs

3-game Series—A. L.— 50— Baltimore 28, Minnesota 22, 1969.
N. L.— 49— Cincinnati 25, Pittsburgh 24, 1979.
4-game Series—N. L.— 68— Los Angeles 44, Pittsburgh 24, 1974.
A. L.— 55— Kansas City 28, New York 27, 1978.
5-game Series—N. L.— 88— Houston 45, Philadelphia 43, 1980.
A. L.— 70— Baltimore 36, Oakland 34, 1973.

Fewest Left on Bases, Series, One Club

3-game Series—A. L.— 14— Boston vs. Oakland, 1975.
N. L.— 17— Cincinnati vs. Pittsburgh, 1975.
4-game Series—A. L.— 16— Baltimore vs. Oakland, 1974.
N. L.— 22— Los Angeles vs. Philadelphia, 1977.
5-game Series—A. L.— 22— Kansas City vs. New York, 1976.
N. L.— 24— Pittsburgh vs. Cincinnati, 1972.

Fewest Left on Bases, Series, Both Clubs

3-game Series—A. L.— 33— Oakland 19, Boston 14, 1975.
N. L.— 38— Pittsburgh 21, Cincinnati 17, 1975.
4-game Series—A. L.— 45— Baltimore 23, California 22, 1979.
N. L.— 52— Los Angeles 28, Philadelphia 24, 1978.
5-game Series—N. L.— 54— Cincinnati 30, Pittsburgh 24, 1972.
A. L.— 62— New York 34, Kansas City 28, 1977.

Most Left on Bases, Game, One Club

N. L.— 14— Philadelphia vs. Houston, October 8, 1980; 10 innings.

Most Left on Bases, Game, One Club—Continued

N. L.—Nine-inning record—13—Los Angeles vs. Pittsburgh, October 5, 1974.
A. L.—13—Baltimore vs. Oakland, October 5, 1971.

Most Left on Bases, Two Consecutive Games, One Club

N. L.—25—Los Angeles vs. Pittsburgh, October 5 (13), October 6 (12), 1974.
A. L.—21—Baltimore vs. Oakland, October 6 (12), October 7 (9), 1973.
            New York vs. Kansas City, October 3 (12), October 4 (9), 1978.

Most Left on Bases, Shutout Defeat, One Club

A. L.—10—Oakland vs. Detroit, October 10, 1972 (lost 3-0).
N. L.—11—Philadelphia vs. Houston, October 10, 1980 (lost 1-0 in 11 innings).
Nine-inning record—10—Los Angeles vs. Pittsburgh, October 8, 1974 (lost 7-0).

Most Left on Bases, Game, Both Clubs

N. L.—22—Philadelphia 14, Houston 8, October 8, 1980; 10 innings.
N. L.—Nine-inning record—20—Cincinnati 10, New York 10, October 10, 1973.
            Los Angeles 13, Pittsburgh 7, October 5, 1974.
            Los Angeles 12, Pittsburgh 8, October 6, 1974.
A. L.—21—Baltimore 12, Oakland 9, October 6, 1973.
            New York 12, Kansas City 9, October 3, 1978.

Fewest Left on Bases, Game, One Club

N. L.—1—Pittsburgh vs. Cincinnati, October 7, 1972.
            Pittsburgh vs. Los Angeles, October 9, 1974.
A. L.—2—Detroit vs. Oakland, October 8, 1972.
            Kansas City vs. New York, October 9, 1976.
            New York vs. Kansas City, October 6, 1978.

Fewest Left on Bases, Game, Both Clubs

A. L.—6—Oakland 4, Detroit 2, October 8, 1972.
N. L.—8—Cincinnati 6, Pittsburgh 2, October 10, 1972.
            Los Angeles 5, Philadelphia 3, October 5, 1978.

CLUB PINCH-RUNNING

Most Pinch-Runners Used, Total Series, One Club

A. L.—12—Oakland, 1971, 1972, 1973, 1974, 1975; 5 Series, 20 games.
N. L.— 7—Pittsburgh, 1970, 1971, 1972, 1974, 1975, 1979; 6 Series, 22 games.

Most Pinch-Runners Used, Series, One Club

A. L.—5—Oakland vs. Baltimore, 1974; 4-game Series.
N. L.—3—New York vs. Atlanta, 1969; 3-game Series.
            Cincinnati vs. Pittsburgh, 1972; 5-game Series.
            Houston vs. Philadelphia, 1980; 5-game Series.
            Philadelphia vs. Houston, 1980; 5-game Series.

Most Pinch-Runners Used, Series, Both Clubs

A. L.—8—Oakland 5, Baltimore 3, 1974; 4-game Series.
N. L.—6—Houston 3, Philadelphia 3, 1980; 5-game Series.

Fewest Pinch-Runners Used, Series, One Club

A. L.-N. L.—0—Held by many clubs.

Fewest Pinch-Runners Used, Series, Both Clubs

A. L.—0—Baltimore 0, Minnesota 0, 1969; 3-game Series.
            Kansas City 0, New York 0, 1980; 3-game Series.
N. L.—0—Philadelphia 0, Los Angeles 0, 1978; 4-game Series.

Most Pinch-Runners Used, Game, One Club

N. L.— 2— Cincinnati vs. Pittsburgh, October 11, 1972.
        Philadelphia vs. Houston, October 12, 1980; 10 innings.
A. L..— 2— Oakland vs. Detroit, October 7, 1972; 11 innings.
        Detroit vs. Oakland, October 12, 1972.
        Oakland vs. Baltimore, October 6, 1974.
        Baltimore vs. Oakland, October 9, 1974.
        Oakland vs. Boston, October 4, 1975.

Most Pinch-Runners Used, Game, Both Clubs

A. L.— 3— Oakland 2, Baltimore 1, October 6, 1974.
        Baltimore 2, Oakland 1, October 9, 1974.
N. L.— 3— Philadelphia 2, Houston 1, October 12, 1980; 10 innings.

Most Pinch-Runners Used, Inning, One Club

A. L.— 2— Oakland vs. Detroit, October 7, 1972; eleventh inning.
        Baltimore vs. Oakland, October 9, 1974; ninth inning.
N. L.— 1— Held by many clubs.

INDIVIDUAL FIELDING

FIRST BASEMEN'S FIELDING RECORDS

Most Series Played

A. L.— 5— Powell, John W., Baltimore, 1969, 1970, 1971, 1973, 1974; 12 games.
N. L.— 5— Perez, Atanasio R., Cincinnati, 1970, 1972, 1973, 1975, 1976; 17 games.
        Robertson, Robert E., Pittsburgh, 1970, 1971, 1972, 1974, 1975; 11 games.

Most Games Played, Total Series

N. L.— 17— Perez, Atanasio R. Cincinnati, 1970, 1972, 1973, 1975, 1976; 5 Series.
A. L.— 14— Chambliss, C. Christopher, New York, 1976, 1977, 1978; 3 Series.

Highest Fielding Average, Series, With Most Chances Accepted

3-game Series—A. L.— 1.000— Powell, John W., Baltimore, 1969; 34 chances accepted.
              N. L.— 1.000— Stargell, Wilver D., Pittsburgh, 1979; 34 chances accepted.
4-game Series—N. L.— 1.000— Garvey, Steven P., Los Angeles, 1978; 49 chances accepted.
              A. L.— 1.000— Tenace, F. Gene, Oakland, 1974; 37 chances accepted.
5-game Series—N. L.— 1.000— Rose, Peter E., Philadelphia, 1980; 60 chances accepted.
              A. L.— 1.000— Epstein, Michael P., Oakland, 1972; 57 chances accepted.

Most Consecutive Errorless Games, Total Series

N. L.— 16— Perez, Atanasio R., Cincinnati, October 3, 1970 through October 10, 1976.
A. L.— 12— Powell, John W., Baltimore, October 4, 1969 through October 9, 1974.
        Chambliss, C. Christopher, New York, October 12, 1976 through October 7, 1978.

Most Putouts, Total Series

N. L.— 147— Perez, Atanasio R., Cincinnati, 1970, 1972, 1973, 1975, 1976; 5 Series, 17 games.
A. L.— 115— Powell, John W., Baltimore, 1969, 1970, 1971, 1973, 1974; 5 Series, 12 games.

Most Putouts, Series

3-game Series—A. L.— 34—Powell, John W., Baltimore, 1969.
N. L.— 32—Driessen, Daniel, Cincinnati, 1979.
Stargell, Wilver D., Pittsburgh, 1979.
4-game Series—N. L.— 44—Garvey, Steven P., Los Angeles, 1978.
A. L.— 44—Murray, Eddie C., Baltimore, 1979.
5-game Series—A. L.— 55—Epstein, Michael P., Oakland, 1972.
N. L.— 53—Rose, Peter E., Philadelphia, 1980.

Most Putouts, Game

N. L.— 17—Stargell, Wilver D., Pittsburgh, October 2, 1979; 11 innings.
16—Garvey, Steven P., Los Angeles, October 5, 1978.
Garvey, Steven P., Los Angeles, October 6, 1978.
A. L.— 15—Chambliss, C. Christopher, New York, October 14, 1976.

Most Putouts, Inning

A. L.-N.L.—3—Held by many first basemen.

Fewest Putouts, Game, Nine Innings

N. L.— 1—Robertson, Robert E., Pittsburgh, October 2, 1971.
A. L.— 2—Cash, Norman, D., Detroit, October 8, 1972.
Cooper, Cecil C., Boston, October 4, 1975.

Most Assists, Total Series

N. L.— 14—Perez, Atanasio R., Cincinnati, 1970, 1972, 1973, 1975, 1976; 5 Series,
17 games.
A. L.— 11—Chambliss, C. Christopher, New York, 1976, 1977, 1978; 3 Series, 14
games.

Most Assists, Series

3-game Series—A. L.— 5— Reese, Richard B., Minnesota, 1969.
Watson, Robert J., New York, 1980.
N. L.— 5— Perez, Atanasio R., Cincinnati, 1975.
4-game Series—N. L.— 5— Garvey, Steven P., Los Angeles, 1978.
A. L.— 3— Murray, Eddie C., Baltimore, 1979.
5-game Series—A. L.— 7— Chambliss, C. Christopher, New York, 1977.
N. L.— 7— Rose, Peter E., Philadelphia, 1980.

Most Assists, Game

N. L.— 3— Perez, Atanasio R., Cincinnati, October 4, 1975.
A. L.— 3— Reese, Richard B., Minnesota, October 5, 1969; 11 innings.
Chambliss, C. Christopher, New York, October 7, 1977.

Most Assists, Inning

A. L.— 2— Chambliss, C. Christopher, New York, October 5, 1977; sixth inning.
Chambliss, C. Christopher, New York, October 7, 1977; second inning.
N. L.— 2— Milner, John D., New York, October 7, 1973; second inning.
Garvey, Steven P., Los Angeles, October 7, 1978; fifth inning.
Rose, Peter E., Philadelphia, October 11, 1980; seventh inning.

Most Chances Accepted, Total Series

N. L.— 161— Perez, Atanasio R., Cincinnati, 1970, 1972, 1973, 1975, 1976; 5 Series,
17 games.
A. L.— 124— Chambliss, C. Christopher, New York, 1976, 1977, 1978; 3 Series, 14
games.

Most Chances Accepted, Series

3-game Series—A. L.— 34—Powell, John W., Baltimore, 1969.
N. L.— 34—Stargell, Wilver D., Pittsburgh, 1979.
4-game Series—N. L.— 49—Garvey, Steven P., Los Angeles, 1978.
A. L.— 47—Murray, Eddie C., Baltimore, 1979.

5-game Series—N. L.— 60— Rose, Peter E., Philadelphia, 1980.
A. L.— 57— Epstein, Michael P., Oakland, 1972.

Most Chances Accepted, Game

N. L.— 18— Garvey, Steven P., Los Angeles, October 6, 1978; 16 putouts, 2 assists, 0 errors.
A. L.— 15— Epstein, Michael P., Oakland, October 8, 1972; 13 putouts, 2 assists, 0 errors.
Chambliss, C. Christopher, New York, October 14, 1976; 15 putouts, 0 assists, 0 errors.

Most Chances Accepted, Inning

A. L.-N. L.—3—Held by many first basemen.

Fewest Chances Offered, Game, Nine Innings

N. L.— 2— Robertson, Robert E., Pittsburgh, October 2, 1971; 1 putout, 1 assist, 0 errors.
A. L.— 3— Cooper, Cecil C., Boston, October 4, 1975; 2 putouts, 0 assists, 1 error.

Most Errors, Total Series

A. L.— 2— Mayberry, John C., Kansas City, 1976, 1977; 2 Series, 9 games.
Murray, Eddie C., Baltimore, 1979; 1 Series, 4 games.
N. L.— 2— Cepeda, Orlando M., Atlanta, 1969; 1 Series, 3 games.

Most Errors, Series

3-game Series—N. L.— 2— Cepeda, Orlando M., Atlanta, 1969.
A. L.— 1— Cooper, Cecil C., Boston, 1975.
4-game Series—A. L.— 2— Murray, Eddie C., Baltimore, 1979.
N. L.— 1— McCovey, Willie L., San Francisco, 1971.
Garvey, Steven P., Los Angeles, 1974.
5-game Series—A. L.— 2— Mayberry, John C., Kansas City, 1977.
N. L.—Never accomplished.

Most Errors, Game

A. L.-N. L.—1—Held by many first basemen.

Most Double Plays, Total Series

N. L.— 13— Garvey, Steven P., Los Angeles, 1974, 1977, 1978; 3 Series, 12 games.
A. L.— 9— Powell, John W., Baltimore, 1969, 1970, 1971, 1973, 1974; 5 Series, 12 games.

Most Double Plays, Series

3-game Series—A. L.— 3— Held by many first basemen.
N. L.— 2— Held by many first basemen.
4-game Series—N. L.— 6— Garvey, Steven P., Los Angeles, 1974.
A. L.— 6— Carew, Rodney C., California, 1979.
5-game Series—A. L.— 5— Epstein, Michael P., Oakland, 1972.
N. L.— 5— Rose, Peter E., Philadelphia, 1980.

Most Double Plays Started, Series

3-game Series—A. L.— 1— Reese, Richard B., Minnesota, 1970.
Tenace, F. Gene, Oakland, 1975.
N. L.—Never accomplished.
4-game Series—N. L.— 1— Garvey, Steven P., Los Angeles, 1977.
A. L.—Never accomplished.
5-game Series—N. L.— 1— Milner, John D., New York, 1973.
A. L.— 1— Williams, Earl C., Baltimore, 1973.
Chambliss, C. Christopher, New York, 1976.

Most Double Plays, Game

N. L.— 3— Garvey, Steven P., Los Angeles, October 5, 1978.

Most Double Plays, Game—Continued

A. L.—3— Reese, Richard B., Minnesota, October 3, 1970.
Epstein, Michael P., Oakland, October 10, 1972.
Tenace, F. Gene, Oakland, October 5, 1975.
Murray, Eddie C., Baltimore, October 6, 1979.

Most Double Plays Started, Game

A. L.-N. L.—1—Held by many first basemen.

Most Unassisted Double Plays, Game

A. L.-N. L.—1—Never accomplished.

SECOND BASEMEN'S FIELDING RECORDS

Most Series Played

N. L.— 6— Morgan, Joe L., Cincinnati, 1972, 1973, 1975, 1976, 1979; Houston, 1980; 23 games.
A. L.— 4— Green, Richard L., Oakland, 1971, 1972, 1973, 1974; 17 games.
White, Frank, Kansas City, 1976, 1977, 1978, 1980; 16 games.

Most Games Played, Total Series

N. L.— 19— Morgan, Joe L., Cincinnati, 1972, 1973, 1975, 1976, 1979; 5 Series.
A. L.— 17— Green, Richard L., Oakland, 1971, 1972, 1973, 1974; 4 Series.

Highest Fielding Average, Series, With Most Chances Accepted

3-game Series—N. L.—1.000— Helms, Tommy V., Cincinnati, 1970; 23 chances accepted.
Morgan, Joe L., Cincinnati, 1979; 23 chances accepted.
A. L.—1.000— Johnson, David A., Baltimore, 1969; 16 chances accepted.
4-game Series—A. L.—1.000— Dauer, Richard F., Baltimore, 1979; 22 chance accepted.
N. L.—1.000— Sizemore, Ted C., Philadelphia, 1978; 15 chances accepted.
5-game Series—N. L.—1.000— Morgan, Joe L., Cincinnati, 1973; 39 chances accepted.
A. L.—1.000— White, Frank, Kansas City, 1977; 29 chances accepted.

Most Consecutive Errorless Games, Total Series

N. L.— 23— Morgan, Joe L., Cincinnati, Houston, October 7, 1972 through October 12, 1980.
A. L.— 15— White, Frank, Kansas City, October 9, 1976 through October 10, 1980.

Most Putouts, Total Series

N. L.—55— Morgan, Joe L., Cincinnati, 1972, 1973, 1975, 1976, 1979; Houston, 1980; 6 Series, 23 games.
A. L.— 37— White, Frank, Kansas City, 1976, 1977, 1978, 1980; 4 Series, 16 games.

Most Putouts, Series

3-game Series—N. L.—12—Morgan, Joe L., Cincinnati, 1979.
A. L.—11—Johnson, David A., Baltimore, 1970.
4-game Series—A. L.—13—Grich, Robert A., Baltimore, 1974.
N. L.—11—Cash, David, Pittsburgh, 1971.
5-game Series—A. L.—16—Grich, Robert A., Baltimore, 1973.
N. L.—18—Trillo, J. Manuel, Philadelphia, 1980.

Most Putouts, Game

A. L.— 7— Grich, Robert A., Baltimore, October 6, 1974.
N. L.— 6— Cash, David, Philadelphia, October 12, 1976.
　　　　　 Morgan, Joe L., Cincinnati, October 3, 1979; 10 innings.

Most Putouts, Inning

N. L.— 3— Morgan, Joe L., Cincinnati, October 10, 1976; eighth inning.
A. L.— 3— Grich, Robert A., Baltimore, October 11, 1973; third inning.
　　　　　 Green, Richard L., Oakland, October 8, 1974; seventh inning.

Most Assists, Total Series

N. L.— 78— Morgan, Joe L., Cincinnati, 1972, 1973, 1975, 1976, 1979; Houston, 1980; 6 Series, 23 games.
A. L.— 49— White, Frank, Kansas City, 1976, 1977, 1978, 1980; 4 Series, 16 games.

Most Assists, Series

3-game Series—N. L.— 12— Helms, Tommy V., Cincinnati, 1970.
　　　　　　　　　　A. L.— 11— Johnson, David A., 1969.
4-game Series—N. L.— 18— Lopes, David E., Los Angeles, 1974.
　　　　　　　　　　A. L.— 12— Grich, Robert A., Baltimore, 1974.
　　　　　　　　　　　　　　　 White, Frank, Kansas City, 1978.
　　　　　　　　　　　　　　　 Grich, Robert A., California, 1979.
　　　　　　　　　　　　　　　 Dauer, Richard F., Baltimore, 1979.
5-game Series—N. L.— 27— Morgan, Joe L., Cincinnati, 1973.
　　　　　　　　　　A. L.— 16— White, Frank, Kansas City, 1977.

Most Assists, Game

N. L.— 8— Trillo, J. Manuel, Philadelphia, October 7, 1980.
A. L..— 6— Johnson, David A., Baltimore, October 6, 1969.
　　　　　 Doyle, R. Dennis, Boston, October 7, 1975.
　　　　　 White, Frank, Kansas City, October 9, 1977.

Most Assists, Inning

A. L.-N. L.—2—Held by many second basemen.

Most Chances Accepted, Total Series

N. L.— 133— Morgan, Joe L., Cincinnati, 1972, 1973, 1975, 1976, 1979; Houston, 1980; 6 Series, 23 games.
A. L.— 86— White, Frank, Kansas City, 1976, 1977, 1978, 1980; 4 Series, 16 games.

Most Chances Accepted, Series

3-game Series—N. L.— 23— Helms, Tommy V., Cincinnati, 1970.
　　　　　　　　　　　　　　　 Morgan, Joe L., Cincinnati, 1979.
　　　　　　　　　　A. L.— 19— White, Frank, Kansas City, 1980.
4-game Series—N. L.— 27— Lopes, David E., Los Angeles, 1974.
　　　　　　　　　　A. L.— 25— Grich, Robert A., Baltimore, 1974.
5-game Series—N. L.— 43— Trillo, J. Manuel, Philadelphia, 1980.
　　　　　　　　　　A. L.— 29— White, Frank, Kansas City, 1977.

Most Chances Accepted, Game

N. L.— 13— Trillo, J. Manuel, Philadelphia, October 7, 1980; 5 putouts, 8 assists, 0 errors.
A. L.— 12— Grich, Robert A., Baltimore, October 6, 1974; 7 putouts, 5 assists, 1 error.

Most Chances Accepted, Inning

A. L.-N. L.—3—Held by many second basemen.

Fewest Chances Offered, Game

A. L.— 0— Thompson, Danny L., Minnesota, October 4, 1970.

Fewest Chances Offered, Game—Continued

    N. L.—1— Cash, David, Pittsburgh, October 9, 1972.
           Millan, Felix B. M., New York, October 7, 1973.

Most Errors, Total Series

    A. L.—4— Green, Richard L., Oakland, 1971, 1972, 1973, 1974; 4 Series, 17 games.
    N. L.—4— Lopes, David E., Los Angeles, 1974, 1977, 1978; 3 Series, 12 games.

Most Errors, Series

    3-game Series—A. L.— N. L.—1—Held by many second basemen.
    4-game Series—A. L.—2— Green, Richard L., Oakland, 1974.
               N. L.—2— Sizemore, Ted C., Philadelphia, 1977.
                      Lopes, David E., Los Angeles, 1978.
    5-game Series—A. L.—2— Green, Richard L., Oakland, 1973.
               N. L.—1— Cash, David, Pittsburgh, 1972.

Most Errors, Game

    A. L.—2— Green, Richard L., Oakland, October 9, 1973; 11 innings.
           Green, Richard L., Oakland, October 8, 1974.
    N. L.—1— Held by many second basemen.

Most Errors, Inning

    A. L.-N. L.—1—Held by many second basemen.

Most Double Plays, Total Series

    A. L.—11— Green, Richard L., Oakland, 1971, 1972, 1973, 1974; 4 Series, 17 games.
    N. L.—14— Morgan, Joe L., Cincinnati, 1972, 1973, 1975, 1976, 1979; Houston, 1980; 6 Series, 23 games.

Most Double Plays, Series

    3-game Series—N. L.—3— Cash, David, Pittsburgh, 1970.
               A. L.—3— Johnson, David A., Baltimore, 1970, 1971.
                     Green, Richard L., Oakland, 1971.
                     White, Frank, Kansas City, 1980.
    4-game Series—N. L.—4— Lopes, David E., Los Angeles, 1974.
                     Sizemore, Ted C., Philadelphia, 1978.
               A. L.—4— Grich, Robert A., California, 1979.
    5-game Series—A. L.—4— Green, Richard L., Oakland, 1973.
               N. L.—4— Trillo, J. Manuel, Philadelphia, 1980.

Most Double Plays Started, Series

    3-game Series—A. L.—2— Johnson, David A., Baltimore, 1970.
               N. L.—2— Stennett, Renaldo A., Pittsburgh, 1975.
    4-game Series—N. L.—3— Sizemore, Ted C., Philadelphia, 1978.
               A. L.—1— Held by many second basemen.
    5-game Series—N. L.—2— Morgan, Joe L., Cincinnati, 1972.
               A. L.—1— Held by many second basemen.

Most Double Plays, Game

    N. L.—3— Lopes, David E., Los Angeles, October 5, 1978.
    A. L.—2— Held by many second basemen.

Most Double Plays Started, Game

    N. L.—2— Stennett, Renaldo A., Pittsburgh, October 5, 1975.
           Sizemore, Ted C., Philadelphia, October 6, 1978.
    A. L.—1— Held by many second basemen.

Most Unassisted Double Plays, Game

    N. L.—1— Morgan, Joe L., October 10, 1976.
    A. L.—Never accomplished.

THIRD BASEMEN'S FIELDING RECORDS

Most Series Played

N. L.—5— Hebner, Richard J., Pittsburgh, 1970, 1971, 1972, 1974, 1975; 18 games.
A. L.—5— Robinson, Brooks C., Baltimore, 1969, 1970, 1971, 1973, 1974; 18 games.
Bando, Salvatore L., Oakland, 1971, 1972, 1973, 1974, 1975; 20 games.

Most Games Played, Total Series

A. L.— 20— Bando, Salvatore L., Oakland, 1971, 1972, 1973, 1974, 1975; 5 Series.
N. L.— 18— Hebner, Richard J., Pittsburgh, 1970, 1971, 1972, 1974, 1975; 5 Series.

Highest Fielding Average, Series, With Most Chances Accepted

3-game Series— A. L.— 1.000— Robinson, Brooks C., Baltimore, 1969; 16 chances accepted.
N. L.— 1.000— Madlock, Bill, Pittsburgh, 1979; 8 chances accepted.
4-game Series—N. L.— 1.000— Schmidt, Michael J., Philadelphia, 1977; 19 chances accepted.
A. L.— 1.000— Robinson, Brooks C., Baltimore, 1974; 17 chances accepted.
5-game Series— A. L.— 1.000— Bando, Salvatore L., Oakland, 1972; 22 chances accepted.
N. L.— 1.000— Hebner, Richard J., Pittsburgh, 1972; 16 chances accepted.

Most Consecutive Errorless Games, Total Series

A. L.— 17— Bando, Salvatore L., Oakland, October 3, 1971 through October 9, 1974.
N. L.— 13— Hebner, Richard J., Pittsburgh, October 6, 1971 through October 7, 1975.

Most Putouts, Total Series

A. L.— 25— Bando, Salvatore L., Oakland, 1971, 1972, 1973, 1974, 1975; 5 Series, 20 games.
N. L.— 14— Hebner, Richard J., Pittsburgh, 1970, 1971, 1972, 1974, 1975; 5 Series, 18 games.
Schmidt, Michael J., Philadelphia, 1976, 1977, 1978, 1980; 4 Series, 16 games.

Most Putouts, Series

3-game Series— A. L.— 6— Robinson, Brooks C., Baltimore, 1969.
Killebrew, Harmon C., Minnesota, 1969.
Bando, Salvatore L., Oakland, 1971.
N. L.— 5— Perez, Atanasio R., Cincinnati, 1970.
4-game Series—N. L.— 7— Cey, Ronald C., Los Angeles, 1977.
A. L.— 6— Nettles, Graig, New York, 1978.
5-game Series— A. L.— 7— Bando, Salvatore L., Oakland, 1973.
N. L.— 5— Hebner, Richard J., Pittsburgh, 1972.

Most Putouts, Game

A. L.— 4— Lansford, Carney R., California, October 6, 1979.
N. L.— 3— Perez, Atanasio R., Cincinnati, October 5, 1970.
Hebner, Richard J., Pittsburgh, October 10, 1972.
Schmidt, Michael J., Philadelphia, October 11, 1980; 10 innings.

Most Putouts, Inning

A. L.-N. L.— 2— Held by many third basemen.

Most Assists, Total Series

N. L.— 59— Schmidt, Michael J., Philadelphia, 1976, 1977, 1978, 1980; 4 Series, 16 games.

Most Assists, Total Series—Continued

A. L.— 49— Robinson, Brooks C., Baltimore, 1969, 1970, 1971, 1973, 1974; 5 Series, 18 games.

Most Assists, Series

3-game Series—A. L.— 11— Bando, Salvatore L., Oakland, 1975.
N. L.— 9— Schmidt, Michael J., Philadelphia, 1976.
4-game Series—N. L.— 18— Schmidt, Michael J., Philadelphia, 1978.
A. L.— 13— Robinson, Brooks C., Baltimore, 1974.
5-game Series—N. L.— 17— Schmidt, Michael J., Philadelphia, 1980.
A. L.— 16— Bando, Salvatore L., Oakland, 1972.

Most Assists, Game, Nine Innings

N. L.— 7— Cey, Ronald C., Los Angeles, October 5, 1978.
A. L.— 6— Bando, Salvatore L., Oakland, October 8, 1972.

Most Assists, Extra-Inning Game

A. L.— 7— Rodriguez, Aurelio, Detroit, October 11, 1972; 10 innings.
N. L.—Less than nine-inning record.

Most Assists, Inning

N. L.— 3— Cey, Ronald C., Los Angeles, October 4, 1977; fourth inning.
A. L.— 2— Held by many third basemen.

Most Chances Accepted, Total Series

N. L.— 73— Schmidt, Michael J., Philadelphia, 1976, 1977, 1978, 1980; 4 Series, 16 games.
A. L.— 72— Bando, Salvatore L., Oakland, 1971, 1972, 1973, 1974, 1975; 5 Series, 20 games.

Most Chances Accepted, Series

3-game Series—A. L.— 16— Robinson, Brooks C., Baltimore, 1969.
N. L.— 13— Schmidt, Michael J., Philadelphia, 1976.
4-game Series—N. L.— 21— Cey, Ronald C., Los Angeles, 1977.
Schmidt, Michael J., Philadelphia, 1978.
A. L.— 17— Robinson, Brooks C., Baltimore, 1974.
5-game Series—A. L.— 22— Bando, Salvatore L., Oakland, 1972.
N. L.— 20— Schmidt, Michael J., Philadelphia, 1980.

Most Chances Accepted, Game

N. L.— 8— Hebner, Richard J., Pittsburgh, October 10, 1972; 3 putouts, 5 assists, 0 errors.
Schmidt, Michael J., Philadelphia, October 11, 1980; 10 innings; 3 putouts, 5 assists, 0 errors.
A. L.— 7— Bando, Salvatore L., Oakland, October 8, 1972; 1 putout, 6 assists, 0 errors.
Rodriguez, Aurelio, Detroit, October 11, 1972; 10 innings; 0 putouts, 7 assists, 1 error.
Nettles, Graig, New York, October 10, 1976; 2 putouts, 5 assists, 0 errors.

Most Chances Accepted, Inning

A. L.-N. L.—3—Held by many third basemen.

Fewest Chances Offered, Game

A. L.— 0— Robinson, Brooks C., Baltimore, October 5, 1970.
Rodriguez, Aurelio, Detroit, October 10, 1972.
N. L.— 0— Held by many players.

Most Errors, Total Series

A. L.— 6— Brett, George H., Kansas City, 1976, 1977, 1978, 1980; 4 Series, 17 games.

N. L.— 4— Schmidt, Michael J., Philadelphia, 1976, 1977, 1978, 1980; 4 Series, 16
      games.

Most Errors, Series

3-game Series—A. L.— N. L.— 1—Held by many third basemen.
4-game Series—N. L.— 2— Cey, Ronald C., Los Angeles, 1974.
                Schmidt, Michael J., Philadelphia, 1978.
          A. L.— 1— Brett, George H., Kansas City, 1978.
5-game Series—A. L.— 3— Brett, George H., Kansas City, 1976.
          N. L.— 1— Held by many third basemen.

Most Errors, Game

A. L.— 2— Brett, George H., Kansas City, October 9, 1976.
N. L.— 2— Cey, Ronald C., Los Angeles, October 5, 1974.

Most Errors, Inning

A. L.— 2— Brett, George H., Kansas City, October 9, 1976; first inning.
N. L.— 1— Held by many third basemen.

Most Double Plays, Total Series

A. L.— 5— Bando, Salvatore L., Oakland, 1971, 1972, 1973, 1974, 1975; 5 Series, 20
      games.
N. L.— 4— Schmidt, Michael J., Philadelphia, 1976, 1977, 1978, 1980; 4 Series, 16
      games.

Most Double Plays, Series

3-game Series—A. L.— 2— Bando, Salvatore L., Oakland, 1971.
          N. L.— 2— Schmidt, Michael J., Philadelphia, 1976.
4-game Series—A. L.— 3— Lansford, Carney R. California, 1979.
          N. L.— 1— Cey, Ronald C., Los Angeles, 1974, 1978.
                Hebner, Richard J., Pittsburgh, 1974.
5-game Series—A. L.— 2— Held by many third basemen.
          N. L.— 2— Schmidt, Michael J., Philadelphia, 1980.

Most Double Plays Started, Series

3-game Series—A. L.— 2— Bando, Salvatore L., Oakland, 1971.
          N. L.— 2— Schmidt, Michael J., Philadelphia, 1976.
4-game Series—A. L.— 3— Lansford, Carney R., California, 1979.
          N. L.— 1— Cey, Ronald C., Los Angeles, 1974, 1978.
                Hebner, Richard J., Pittsburgh, 1974.
5-game Series—A. L.— 2— Rodriguez, Aurelio, Detroit, 1972.
                Nettles, Graig, New York, 1977.
          N. L.— 1— Hebner, Richard J., Pittsburgh, 1972.
                Cabell, Enos M., Houston, 1980.

Most Double Plays, Game

N. L.— 2— Schmidt, Michael J., Philadelphia, October 9, 1976.
      Schmidt, Michael J., Philadelphia, October 11, 1980; 10 innings.
A. L.— 1— Held by many third basemen.

Most Double Plays Started, Game

N. L.— 2— Schmidt, Michael J., Philadelphia, October 9, 1976.
A. L.— 1— Held by many third basemen.

Most Unassisted Double Plays, Game

N. L.— 1— Schmidt, Michael J., Philadelphia, October 9, 1976.
A. L.—Never accomplished.

SHORTSTOPS' FIELDING RECORDS

Most Series Played

    A. L.— 6— Belanger, Mark H., Baltimore, 1969, 1970, 1971, 1973, 1974, 1979; 21 games.

              Campaneris, Dagoberto B., Oakland, 1971, 1972, 1973, 1974, 1975, California, 1979; 18 games.

    N. L.— 5— Concepcion, David I., Cincinnati, 1970, 1972, 1975, 1976, 1979; 13 games.

Most Games Played, Total Series

    A. L.— 21— Belanger, Mark H., Baltimore, 1969, 1970, 1971, 1973, 1974, 1979; 6 Series.

    N. L.— 16— Bowa, Lawrence R., Philadelphia, 1976, 1977, 1978, 1980; 4 Series.

Highest Fielding Average, Series, With Most Chances Accepted

    3-game Series—A. L.— 1.000— Dent, Russell E., New York, 1980; 21 chances accepted.

                  N. L.— 1.000— Concepcion, David I., Cincinnati, 1979; 17 chances accepted.

    4-game Series—N. L.— 1.000— Russell, William E., Los Angeles, 1974; 29 chances accepted.

                  A. L.— 1.000— Campaneris, Dagoberto B., Oakland, 1974; 20 chances accepted.

    5-game Series—A. L.— 1.000— Patek, Freddie J., Kansas City, 1976; 31 chances accepted.

                  N. L.— 1.000— Harrelson, Derrel M., New York, 1973; 26 chances accepted.

Most Consecutive Errorless Games, Total Series

    A. L.— 17— Belanger, Mark H., Baltimore, October 4, 1969 through October 8, 1974.

    N. L.— 11— Bowa, Lawrence R., Philadelphia, October 9, 1976 through October 7, 1980.

Most Putouts, Total Series

    A. L.— 31— Belanger, Mark H., Baltimore, 1969, 1970, 1971, 1973, 1974, 1979; 6 Series, 21 games.

    N. L.— 28— Russell, William E., Los Angeles, 1974, 1977, 1978; 3 Series, 12 games.

Most Putouts, Series

    3-game Series—A. L.— 13— Cardenas, Leonardo A., Minnesota, 1969.

                  N. L.— 6— Held by many shortstops.

    4-game Series—N. L.— 13— Russell, William E., Los Angeles, 1974.

                  A. L.— 9— Patek, Freddie J., Kansas City, 1978.

    5-game Series—A. L.— 13— Patek, Freddie J., Kansas City, 1976.

                  N. L.— 12— Harrelson, Derrel M., New York, 1973.

Most Putouts, Game

    N. L.— 6— Russell, William E., Los Angeles, October 8, 1974.

    A. L.— 6— Belanger, Mark H., Baltimore, October 5, 1974.

            Dent, Russell E., New York, October 5, 1977.

            Patek, Freddie J., Kansas City, October 5, 1977.

Most Putouts, Inning

    A. L.— 3— Belanger, Mark H., Baltimore, October 5, 1974; third inning.

            Patek, Freddie J., Kansas City, October 5, 1977; second inning.

    N. L.— 2— Held by many shortstops.

Most Assists, Total Series

    A. L.— 69— Belanger, Mark H., Baltimore, 1969, 1970, 1971, 1973, 1974, 1979; 6 Series, 21 games.

N. L.—55— Bowa, Lawrence R., Philadelphia, 1976, 1977, 1978, 1980; 4 Series, 16
     games.

Most Assists, Series

    3-game Series—A. L.— 14— Belanger, Mark H., Baltimore, 1970.
                   N. L.— 14— Concepcion, David I., Cincinnati, 1979.
    4-game Series—A. L.— 17— Campaneris, Dagoberto B., Oakland, 1974.
                   N. L.— 17— Bowa, Lawrence R., Philadelphia, 1977.
    5-game Series—A. L.— 18— Patek, Freddie J., Kansas City, 1976, 1977.
                   N. L.— 16— Chaney, Darrel L., Cincinnati, 1972.

Most Assists, Game

    N. L.—9— Russell, William E., Los Angeles, October 5, 1978.
    A. L.—9— Garcia, Alfonso R., Baltimore, October 4, 1979.

Most Assists, Inning

    A. L.—3— Belanger, Mark H., Baltimore, October 7, 1973; seventh inning.
    N. L.—3— Concepcion, David I., Cincinnati, October 3, 1979; fourth inning.

Most Chances Accepted, Total Series

    A. L.— 100— Belanger, Mark H., Baltimore, 1969, 1970, 1971, 1973, 1974, 1979; 6
               Series, 21 games.
    N. L.— 70— Russell, William E., Los Angeles, 1974, 1977, 1978; 3 Series, 12
               games.

Most Chances Accepted, Series

    3-game Series—A. L.— 25— Cardenas, Leonardo A., Minnesota, 1969.
                   N. L.— 17— Concepcion, David I., Cincinnati, 1979.
    4-game Series—N. L.— 29— Russell, William E., Los Angeles, 1974.
                   A. L.— 22— Garcia, Alfonso R., Baltimore, 1979.
    5-game Series—A. L.— 31— Patek, Freddie J., Kansas City, 1976.
                   N. L.— 26— Harrelson, Derrel M., New York, 1973.

Most Chances Accepted, Game

    N. L.— 13— Russell, William E., Los Angeles, October 8, 1974; 6 putouts, 7 assists,
              0 errors.
    A. L.— 11— Cardenas, Leonardo A., Minnesota, October 5, 1969; 11 innings; 6
              putouts, 5 assists, 1 error.
              Garcia, Alfonso R., Baltimore, October 4, 1979; 2 putouts, 9 assists, 0
              errors.

Most Chances Accepted, Inning

    A. L.-N. L.—3—Held by many shortstops.

Fewest Chances Offered, Game

    A. L.— 0— Campaneris, Dagoberto B., Oakland, October 3, 1971.
    N. L.— 0— Garrido, Gil G., Atlanta, October 5, 1969.
              Bowa, Lawrence R., Philadelphia, October 11, 1980; 10 innings.

Most Errors, Total Series

    N. L.—3— Chaney, Darrel L., Cincinnati, 1972, 1973; 2 Series, 10 games.
    A. L.—3— Cardenas, Leonardo A., Minnesota, 1969, 1970; 2 Series; 6 games.
              McAuliffe, Richard J., Detroit, 1972; 1 Series, 4 games.
              Patek, Freddie J., Kansas City, 1976, 1977, 1978; 3 Series, 14 games.

Most Errors, Series

    3-game Series—A. L.— 2— Cardenas, Leonardo A., Minnesota, 1970.
                   N. L.— 1— Held by many shortstops.
    4-game Series—A. L.— 2— Patek, Freddie J., Kansas City, 1978.
                           Garcia, Alfonso R., Baltimore, 1979.
                   N. L.— 2— Russell, William E., Los Angeles, 1977.
    5-game Series—A. L.— 3— McAuliffe, Richard J., Detroit, 1972.
                   N. L.— 3— Chaney, Darrel L., Cincinnati, 1972.

Most Errors, Game

    A. L.— 2— Cardenas, Leonardo A., Minnesota, October 4, 1970.
    N. L.— 2— Alley, L. Eugene, Pittsburgh, October 10, 1972.
                 Russell, William E., Los Angeles, October 4, 1977.

Most Errors, Inning

    N. L.— 2— Alley, L. Eugene, Pittsburgh, October 10, 1972; fourth inning.
    A. L.— 1— Held by many shortstops.

Most Double Plays, Total Series

    N. L.— 12— Russell, William E., Los Angeles, 1974, 1977, 1978; 3 Series, 12 games.
    A. L.— 10— Belanger, Mark H., Baltimore, 1969, 1970, 1971, 1973, 1974, 1979; 6
              Series, 21 games.

Most Double Plays, Series

    3-game Series—N. L.— 3— Garrido, Gil C., Atlanta, 1969.
                         Alley, L. Eugene, Pittsburgh, 1970.
              A. L.— 3— Held by many shortstops.
    4-game Series—N. L.— 6— Russell, William E., Los Angeles, 1974.
              A. L.— 3— Garcia, Alfonso R., Baltimore, 1979.
    5-game Series—A. L.— 3— Patek, Freddie J., Kansas City, 1976.
              N. L.— 3— Bowa, Lawrence R., Philadelphia, 1980.

Most Double Plays Started, Series

    3-game Series—N. L.— 3— Alley, L. Eugene, Pittsburgh, 1970.
              A. L.— 2— Belanger, Mark H., Baltimore, 1971.
                         Campaneris, Dagoberto B., Oakland, 1975.
    4-game Series—N. L.— 3— Russell, William E., Los Angeles, 1974.
              A. L.— 2— Belanger, Mark H., Baltimore, 1974.
                         Anderson, James L., California, 1979.
    5-game Series—N. L.— 3— Bowa, Lawrence R., Philadelphia, 1980.
              A. L.— 2— Maxvill, C. Dallan, Oakland, 1972.
                       Patek, Freddie J., Kansas City, 1976.

Most Double Plays, Game

    A. L.— 3— Campaneris, Dagoberto B., Oakland, October 5, 1975.
    N. L.— 3— Russell, William E., Los Angeles, October 8, 1974.

Most Double Plays Started, Game

    A. L.— 2— Maxvill, C. Dallan, Oakland, October 10, 1972.
              Campaneris, Dagoberto B., Oakland, October 5, 1975.
               Patek, Freddie J., Kansas City, October 10, 1976.
    N. L.— 2— Alley, L. Eugene, Pittsburgh, October 4, 1970.
              Russell, William E., Los Angeles, October 8, 1974.
              Bowa, Lawrence R., Philadelphia, October 8, 1977.
              Bowa, Lawrence R., Philadelphia, October 10, 1980; 11 innings.

Most Unassisted Double Plays, Game

    N. L.— 1— Russell, William E., Los Angeles, October 8, 1974.
    A. L.—Never accomplished.

OUTFIELDERS' FIELDING RECORDS

Most Series Played

    A. L.— 8—Jackson, Reginald M., Oakland, 1971, 1972, 1973, 1974, 1975; New
              York, 1977, 1978, 1980; 25 games.
    N. L.— 5—Geronimo, Cesar F., Cincinnati, 1972, 1973, 1975, 1976, 1979; 17 games.

Most Games Played, Total Series

A. L.—25—Jackson, Reginald M., Oakland, 1971, 1972, 1973, 1974, 1975; New York, 1977, 1978, 1980; 8 Series.

N. L.—17—Geronimo, Cesar F., Cincinnati, 1972, 1973, 1975, 1976, 1979; 5 Series.

Highest Fielding Average, Series, With Most Chances Accepted

3-game Series—N. L.—1.000—Parker, David G., Pittsburgh, 1975; 14 chances accepted.

A. L.—1.000—Oliva, Antonio, Minnesota, 1970; 12 chances accepted.

4-game Series—A. L.—1.000—Miller, Richard A., California, 1979; 16 chances accepted.

N. L.—1.000—Stargell, Wilver D., Pittsburgh, 1974, 13 chances accepted.

5-game Series—N.L.—1.000—Maddox, Garry L., Philadelphia, 1980; 23 chances accepted.

A. L.—1.000—Jackson, Reginald M., Oakland, 1973; 19 chances accepted.

Rivers, John M., New York, 1977; 19 chances accepted.

Most Consecutive Errorless Games, Total Series

A. L.—24—Blair, Paul L., Oakland, New York, October 4, 1969 through October 7, 1978; 41 chances accepted.

N. L.—16—Oliver, Albert, Pittsburgh, October 2, 1971 through October 7, 1975; 37 chances accepted.

Geronimo, Cesar F., Cincinnati; October 7, 1972 through October 3, 1979; 50 chances accepted.

Most Putouts, Total Series

A. L.—66—Jackson, Reginald M., Oakland, 1971, 1972, 1973, 1974, 1975; New York, 1977, 1978, 1980; 8 Series, 25 games.

N. L.—54—Maddox, Garry L., Philadelphia, 1976, 1977, 1978, 1980; 4 Series, 14 games.

Most Putouts, Series

3-game Series—N. L.—13—Geronimo, Cesar F., Cincinnati, 1975.
Parker, David G., Pittsburgh, 1975.

A. L.—12—Lynn, Fredric M., Boston, 1975.

4-game Series—N. L.—16—Maddox, Garry L., Philadelphia, 1978.

A. L.—14—North, William A., Oakland, 1974.
Miller, Richard A., California, 1979.

5-game Series—N. L.—23—Maddox, Garry L., Philadelphia, 1980.

A. L.—19—Jackson, Reginald M., Oakland, 1973.
Rivers, John M., New York, 1977.

Most Putouts, Game, Center Field

N. L.—8—Oliver, Albert, Pittsburgh, October 7, 1972.
Hahn, Donald A., New York, October 8, 1973.

A. L.—7—Lynn, Fredric M., Boston, October 4, 1975.
Rivers, John M., New York, October 6, 1977.
Miller, Richard A., California, October 5, 1979.

Most Putouts, Game, Left Field

A. L.—7—White, Roy H., New York, October 13, 1976.

N. L.—7—Stennett, Renaldo A., Pittsburgh, October 7, 1972.
Cruz, Jose, Houston, October 10, 1980; 11 innings.

Most Putouts, Game, Right Field

A. L.—7—Jackson, Reginald M., Oakland, October 10, 1973.
Washington, Claudell, Oakland, October 9, 1974.

N. L.—5—Held by many right fielders.

Most Consecutive Putouts, Game

    A. L.— 3— Hurdle, Clinton M., Kansas City, October 6, 1978; 3 in seventh inning; left field.

    N. L.— 3— Tolan, Robert, Cincinnati, October 7, 1972; 2 in third inning, 1 in fourth inning; center field.

          Geronimo, Cesar F., Cincinnati, October 7, 1975; 1 in third inning, 2 in fourth inning; center field.

Most Putouts, Inning, Outfielder

    A. L.— 3— Jackson, Reginald M., New York, October 7, 1977; right field, fourth inning.

          Hurdle, Clinton M., Kansas City, October 6, 1978; left field, seventh inning, consecutive.

    N. L.— 2— Held by many outfielders.

Most Assists, Total Series

    A. L.— 3— Oliva, Antonio, Minnesota, 1969, 1970; 2 Series, 6 games.

          Jackson, Reginald M., Oakland, 1971, 1972, 1973, 1974, 1975; New York, 1977, 1978, 1980; 8 Series, 25 games.

    N. L.— 5— McBride, Arnold R., Philadelphia, 1977, 1978, 1980; 3 Series, 11 games.

Fewest Assists, Total Series (Most Games)

    A. L.— 0— Blair, Paul L., Baltimore, 1969, 1970, 1971, 1973, 1974; New York, 1977, 1978; 7 Series, 24 games.

    N. L.— 0— Maddox, Garry L., Philadelphia, 1976, 1977, 1978, 1980; 4 series, 14 games.

          Stargell, Wilver D., Pittsburgh, 1970, 1971, 1972, 1974, 4 Series, 12 games.

Most Assists, Series

    3-game Series— A. L.— 2— Oliva, Antonio, Minnesota, 1970.

                    Yastrzemski, Carl M., Boston, 1975.

          N. L.— 2— Foster, George A., Cincinnati. 1979.

    4-game Series— N. L.— 2— McBride, Arnold R., Philadelphia, 1977.

          A. L.— 2— Miller, Richard, A., California, 1979.

    5-game Series— N. L.— 3— McBride, Arnold R., Philadelphia, 1980.

          A. L.— 1— Held by many outfielders.

Most Assists, Game

    A. L.— 2— Oliva, Antonio, Minnesota, October 4, 1970.

    N. L.— 2— Foster, George A., Cincinnati, October 3, 1979; 10 innings.

          McBride, Arnold R., Philadelphia, October 11, 1980; 10 innings.

Most Chances Accepted, Total Series

    A. L.— 69— Jackson, Reginald M., Oakland, 1971, 1972, 1973, 1974, 1975; New York, 1977, 1978, 1980; 8 Series, 25 games.

    N. L.— 55— Geronimo, Cesar F., Cincinnati, 1972, 1973, 1975, 1976, 1979; 5 Series, 17 games.

Most Chances Accepted, Series

    3-game Series— N. L.— 14— Parker, David G., Pittsburgh, 1975.

          A. L.— 13— Lynn, Fredric M., Boston, 1975.

    4-game Series— N. L.— 16— Maddox, Garry L., Philadelphia, 1978.

          A. L.— 16— Miller, Richard A., California, 1979.

    5-game Series— N. L.— 23— Maddox, Garry L., Philadelphia, 1980.

          A. L.— 19— Jackson, Reginald M., Oakland, 1973.

          Rivers, John M., New York, 1977.

Most Chances Accepted, Game, Center Field

    N. L.— 8— Oliver, Albert, Pittsburgh, October 7, 1972; 8 putouts, 0 assists, 0 errors.

Hahn, Donald A., New York, October 8, 1973; 8 putouts, 0 assists, 0 errors.
A. L.— 8— Miller, Richard A., California, October 5, 1979; 7 putouts, 1 assist, 0 errors.

Most Chances Accepted, Game, Left Field

A. L.— 7— White, Roy H., New York, October 13, 1976; 7 putouts, 0 assists, 0 errors.
Hurdle, Clinton M., Kansas City, October 6, 1978; 6 putouts, 1 assist, 0 errors.
N. L.— 7— Stennett, Renaldo A., Pittsburgh, October 7, 1972; 7 putouts, 0 assists, 0 errors.
Cruz, Jose, Houston, October 10, 1980; 7 putouts, 0 assists, 0 errors.

Most Chances Accepted, Game, Right Field

A. L.— 7— Jackson, Reginald M., Oakland, October 10, 1973; 7 putouts, 0 assists, 0 errors.
Washington, Claudell, Oakland, October 9, 1974; 7 putouts, 0 assists, 0 errors.
N. L.— 5— Held by many right fielders.

Longest Game, No Chances Offered, Outfielder

N. L.—12 innings— Hahn, Donald A., New York, October 9, 1973.
A. L.—11 innings— Alou, Mateo R., Oakland, October 7, 1972.

Most Chances Accepted, Inning

N. L.— 3— Parker, David G., Pittsburgh, October 5, 1975; sixth inning.
A. L.— 3— Oliva, Antonio, Minnesota, October 4, 1970; fourth inning.
Jackson, Reginald M., New York, October 7, 1977; fourth inning.
Hurdle, Clinton M., Kansas City, October 6, 1978; seventh inning.
Miller, Richard A., California, October 5, 1979; sixth inning.

Most Errors, Total Series

N. L.— 2— Smith, C. Reginald, Los Angeles, 1977, 1978; 2 Series, 8 games.
A. L.— 2— Oliva, Antonio, Minnesota, 1969, 1970; 2 Series, 6 games.
Washington, Claudell, Oakland, 1974, 1975; 2 Series, 5 games.
Gamble, Oscar C., New York, 1976, 1980; 2 Series, 4 games.
Bumbry, Alonza B., Baltimore, 1973, 1979; 2 Series, 6 games.

Most Errors, Series

A. L.— 2— Oliva, Antonio, Minnesota, 1969; 3-game Series.
Washington, Claudell, Oakland, 1975; 3-game Series.
Gamble, Oscar C., New York, 1976; 5-game Series.
N. L.— 1— Held by many outfielders.

Most Errors, Game

A. L.— 2— Oliva, Antonio, Minnesota, October 6, 1969.
N. L.— 1— Held by many outfielders.

Most Errors, Inning

A. L.-N. L.—1—Held by many outfielders.

Most Double Plays, Total Series

N. L.— 3— McBride, Arnold R., Philadelphia, 1977, 1978, 1980; 3 Series, 11 games.
A. L.— 2— Miller, Richard A., California, 1979; 1 Series, 4 games.

Most Double Plays, Game

N. L.— 2— McBride, Arnold R., Philadelphia, October 11, 1980; 10 innings.
A. L.—N. L.—Nine-inning record—1—Held by many outfielders.

Most Double Plays Started, Game

N. L.— 2— McBride, Arnold R., Philadelphia, October 11, 1980; 10 innings.
A. L.—N. L.—Nine-inning record—1—Held by many outfielders.

Most Unassisted Double Plays, Game

    A. L.-N. L.—Never accomplished.

CATCHERS' FIELDING RECORDS

Most Series Played

    N. L.— 6— Bench, Johnny L., Cincinnati, 1970, 1972, 1973, 1975, 1976, 1979; 22 games.

    A. L.— 5— Etchebarren, Andrew A., Baltimore, 1969, 1970, 1971, 1973, 1974; 12 games.

Most Games Caught, Total Series

    N. L.— 22— Bench, Johnny L., Cincinnati, 1970, 1972, 1973, 1975, 1976, 1979; 6 Series.

    A. L.— 14— Munson, Thurman L., New York, 1976, 1977, 1978; 3 Series.

Highest Fielding Average, Series, With Most Chances Accepted

    3-game Series—N. L.— 1.000—Ott, N. Edward, Pittsburgh, 1979; 28 chances accepted.

        A. L.— 1.000—Etchebarren, Andrew A., Baltimore, 1970; 19 chances accepted.

    4-game Series—N. L.— 1.000—Dietz, Richard A., San Francisco, 1971; 36 chances accepted.

        A. L.— 1.000—Downing, Brian J., California, 1979; 27 chances accepted.

    5-game Series—N. L.— 1.000—Bench, Johnny L., Cincinnati, 1973; 33 chances accepted.

        A. L.— 1.000—Etchebarren, Andrew A., Baltimore, 1973; 32 chances accepted.

Most Consecutive Errorless Games, Total Series

    N. L.— 17— Bench, Johnny L., Cincinnati, October 9, 1972 through October 5, 1979.

    A. L.— 12— Etchebarren, Andrew A., Baltimore, October 4, 1969 through October 8, 1974.

        Munson, Thurman L., New York, October 12, 1976 through October 7, 1978.

Most Putouts, Total Series

    N. L.— 125— Bench, Johnny L., Cincinnati, 1970, 1972, 1973, 1975, 1976, 1979; 6 Series, 22 games.

    A. L.— 78— Etchebarren, Andrew A., Baltimore, 1969, 1970, 1971, 1973, 1974; 5 Series, 12 games.

Most Putouts, Series

    3-game Series—N. L.— 29—Sanguillen, Manuel D., Pittsburgh, 1975.

        A. L.— 19— Etchebarren, Andrew A., Baltimore, 1970.

    4-game Series—N. L.— 34— Dietz, Richard A., San Francisco, 1971.

        A. L.— 27— Downing, Brian J., California, 1979.

    5-game Series—N. L.— 42— Grote, Gerald W., New York, 1973.

        A. L.— 30— Etchebarren, Andrew A., Baltimore, 1973.

Most Putouts, Game, Nine Innings

    A. L.— 14— Freehan, William A., Detroit, October 10, 1972.

    N. L.— 14— Dietz, Richard A., San Francisco, October 3, 1971.

Most Putouts, Extra-Inning Game

    N. L.— 15— Sanguillen, Manuel D., Pittsburgh, October 7, 1975; 10 innings.

    A. L.—Less than nine-inning record.

Fewest Putouts, Game

    A. L.— 1— Fosse, Raymond E., Oakland, October 11, 1973.
             Martinez, J. Buck, Kansas City, October 13, 1976.
    N. L.— 2— Sanguillen, Manuel D., Pittsburgh, October 3, 1970; 10 innings.
             Sanguillen, Manuel D., Pittsburgh, October 7, 1972.
             Yeager, Stephen W., Los Angeles, October 6, 1978.

Most Putouts, Inning

    A. L.-N. L.—3—Held by many catchers.

Most Assists, Total Series

    N. L.— 18— Bench, Johnny L., Cincinnati, 1970, 1972, 1973, 1975, 1976, 1979; 6
             Series, 22 games.
    A. L.— 14— Munson, Thurman L., New York, 1976, 1977, 1978; 3 Series, 14 games.

Most Assists, Series

    3-game Series—A. L.— 4— Mitterwald, George E., Minnesota, 1969.
                     Cerone, Richard A., New York, 1980.
             N. L.— 4— Bench, Johnny L., Cincinnati, 1975, 1976.
    4-game Series—A. L.— 4— Munson, Thurman L., New York, 1978.
             N. L.— 2— Held by many catchers.
    5-game Series—A. L.— 6— Munson, Thurman L., New York, 1976.
             N. L.— 3— Bench, Johnny L., Cincinnati, 1972.
                     Boone, Robert R., Philadelphia, 1980.

Most Assists, Game

    N. L.— 3— Bench, Johnny L., Cincinnati, October 3, 1970; 10 innings.
             Bench, Johnny L., Cincinnati, October 5, 1975.
    A. L.— 2— Held by many catchers.

Most Assists, Inning

    N. L.— 2— Bench, Johnny L., Cincinnati, October 7, 1973; eighth inning.
    A. L.— 1— Held by many catchers.

Most Chances Accepted, Total Series

    N. L.— 143— Bench, Johnny L., Cincinnati, 1970, 1972, 1973, 1975, 1976, 1979; 6
             Series, 22 games.
    A. L.— 81— Etchebarren, Andrew A., Baltimore, 1969, 1970, 1971, 1973, 1974; 5
             Series, 12 games.

Most Chances Accepted, Series

    3-game Series—N. L.— 30— Sanguillen, Manuel D., Pittsburgh, 1975.
                  A. L.— 19— Etchebarren, Andrew A., Baltimore, 1970.
    4-game Series—N. L.— 36— Dietz, Richard A., San Francisco, 1971.
                  A. L.— 27— Downing, Brian J., California, 1979.
    5-game Series—N. L.— 43— Grote, Gerald W., New York, 1973.
                  A. L.— 32— Etchebarren, Andrew A., Baltimore, 1973.

Most Chances Accepted, Game

    A. L.— 15— Freehan, William A., Detroit, October 10, 1972; 14 putouts, 1 assist, 0
             errors.
    N. L.— 15— Dietz, Richard A., San Francisco, October 3, 1971; 14 putouts, 1 assist,
             0 errors.
             Sanguillen, Manuel D., Pittsburgh, October 7, 1975; 10 innings; 15
             putouts, 0 assists, 1 error.

Most Chances Accepted, Inning

    A. L.-N. L.—3—Held by many catchers.

Fewest Chances Offered, Game

    A. L.-N. L.—2—Held by many catchers.

Most Errors, Total Series

    N. L.—5—Sanguillen, Manuel D., Pittsburgh, 1970, 1971, 1972, 1974, 1975; 5 Series, 19 games.

    A. L.—2—Munson, Thurman L., New York, 1976, 1977, 1978; 3 Series, 14 games.

Most Errors, Series

    3-game Series—A. L.— 1— Ratliff, Paul H., Minnesota, 1970.

                   N. L.— 1— Sanguillen, Manuel D., Pittsburgh, 1970, 1975.

    4-game Series—N. L.— 2— Sanguillen, Manuel D., Pittsburgh, 1974.

                 A. L.—Never accomplished.

    5-game Series—A. L.— 2— Munson, Thurman L., New York, 1976.

                 N. L.— 1— Bench, Johnny L., Cincinnati, 1972.

                          Sanguillen, Manuel D., Pittsburgh, 1972.

                          Grote, Gerald W., New York, 1973.

Most Errors, Game

    A. L.—2—Munson, Thurman L., New York, October 10, 1976.

    N. L.—2—Sanguillen, Manuel D., Pittsburgh, October 6, 1974.

Most Errors, Inning

    A. L.-N. L.—1—Held by many catchers.

Most Passed Balls, Total Series

    N. L.—4—Sanguillen, Manuel D., Pittsburgh, 1970, 1971, 1972, 1974, 1975; 5 Series, 19 games.

    A. L.—2—Munson, Thurman L., New York, 1976, 1977, 1978; 3 Series, 14 games.

Most Passed Balls, Series

    N. L.—2—Sanguillen, Manuel D., Pittsburgh, 1975; 3-game Series.

    A. L.— 1— Held by many catchers.

Most Passed Balls, Game

    N. L.—2—Sanguillen, Manuel D., Pittsburgh, October 4, 1975.

    A. L.— 1— Held by many catchers.

Most Passed Balls, Inning

    A L.-N. L.—1—Held by many catchers.

Most Double Plays Total Series

    A. L.—4— Fosse, Raymond E., Oakland, 1973, 1974, 1975; 3 Series, 10 games.

    N. L.—3— Sanguillen, Manuel D., Pittsburgh, 1970, 1971, 1972, 1974, 1975; 5 Series, 19 games.

Most Double Plays, Series

    3-game Series—A. L.— 2— Mitterwald, George E., Minnesota, 1970.

    4-game Series—A. L.— 1— Fosse, Raymond E., Oakland, 1974.

                     Porter, Darrell R., Kansas City, 1978.

                     Downing, Brian J., California, 1979.

    5-game Series—A. L.— 2— Fosse, Raymond E., Oakland, 1973.

                 N. L.—1—Held by many catchers in Series of all lengths.

Most Double Plays Started, Series

    3-game Series—N. L.— 1— Didier, Robert D., Atlanta, 1969.

                 A. L.—Never accomplished.

    4-game Series—N. L.— 1— Dietz, Richard A., San Francisco, 1971.

                 A. L.— 1— Fosse, Raymond E., Oakland, 1974.

    5-game Series—A. L.— 2— Fosse, Raymond E., Oakland, 1973.

                 N. L.— 1— May, Milton S., Pittsburgh, 1972.

Most Double Plays, Game

    A. L.-N. L.—1—Held by many catchers.

Most Double Plays Started, Game

    A. L.-N. L.—1—Held by many catchers.

Most Unassisted Double Plays, Game

    A. L.-N. L.—Never accomplished.

Most Players Caught Stealing, Total Series

    A. L.— 12— Munson, Thurman L., New York, 1976, 1977, 1978; 3 Series, 14 games.
    N. L.— 3— Bench, Johnny L., Cincinnati, 1970, 1972, 1973, 1975, 1976, 1979; 6 Series, 22 games.
                Boone, Robert R., Philadelphia, 1976, 1977, 1978, 1980; 4 Series, 14 games.

Most Players Caught Stealing, Series

    3-game Series—A. L.— 4— Mitterwald, George E., Minnesota, 1969.
               N. L.— 1— Held by many catchers.
    4-game Series—A. L.— 3— Fosse, Raymond E., Oakland, 1974.
                           Munson, Thurman L., New York, 1978.
               N. L.— 1— Held by many catchers.
    5-game Series—A. L.— 5— Munson, Thurman L., New York, 1976.
               N. L.— 1— Held by many catchers.

Most Players Caught Stealing, Inning

    A. L.-N. L.—1—Held by many catchers.

Most Players Caught Stealing, Game

    A. L.— 2— Held by many catchers.
    N. L.— 1— Held by many catchers.

PITCHERS' FIELDING RECORDS

Most Series Pitched

    Both Leagues—6—Gullett, Donald E., Cincinnati NL, 1970, 1972, 1973, 1975, 1976; New York AL, 1977; 10 games.
    A. L.— 6— Hunter, James A., Oakland, 1971, 1972, 1973, 1974; New York, 1976, 1978; 10 games.
              Palmer, James A., Baltimore, 1969, 1970, 1971, 1973, 1974, 1979; 8 games.
    N. L.— 6— McGraw, Frank E., New York, 1969, 1973; Philadelphia, 1976, 1977, 1978, 1980; 15 games.

Most Games Pitched, Total Series

    N. L.— 15— McGraw, Frank E., New York, 1969, 1973; Philadelphia, 1976, 1977, 1978, 1980; 6 Series.
    A. L.— 11— Fingers, Roland G., Oakland, 1971, 1972, 1973, 1974, 1975; 5 Series.

Most Games Pitched, Series

    3-game Series—N. L.— 3— Upshaw, Cecil L., Atlanta, 1969; $6\frac{1}{3}$ innings.
                           Tomlin, David A., Cincinnati, 1979; 3 innings.
                           Hume, Thomas H., Cincinnati, 1979; 4 innings.
               A. L.— 3— Perranoski, Ronald P., Minnesota, 1969; $4\frac{2}{3}$ innings.
                           Todd, James R., Oakland, 1975; 1 inning.
    4-game Series—N. L.— 4— Giusti, J. David, Pittsburgh, 1971; $5\frac{1}{3}$ innings.
               A. L.— 3— Hrabosky, Alan T., Kansas City, 1978; 3 innings.
                           Stanhouse, Donald J., Baltimore, 1979; 3 innings.
    5-game Series—N. L.— 5— McGraw, Frank E., Philadelphia, 1980; 8 innings.
               A. L.— 4— Blue, Vida R., Oakland, 1972; $5\frac{1}{3}$ innings.
                         Lyle, Albert W., New York, 1977; $9\frac{1}{3}$ innings.

Highest Fielding Average, Series, With Most Chances Accepted

3-game Series—N. L.—1.000—Gullett, Donald E., Cincinnati, 1975; 5 chances accepted.

    A. L.—1.000—Boswell, David W., Minnesota, 1969; 5 chances accepted.

                Lindblad, Paul A., Oakland, 1975; 5 chances accepted.

                Wise, Richard C., Boston, 1975; 5 chances accepted.

4-game Series—N. L.—1.000—Marichal, Juan A., San Francisco, 1971; 6 chances accepted.

    A. L.—1.000—Cuellar, Miguel, Baltimore, 1974; 5 chances accepted.

                Hunter, James A., Oakland, 1974; 5 chances accepted.

                Gura, Lawrence C., Kansas City, 1978; 5 chances accepted.

5-game Series—N. L.—1.000—Blass, Stephen R., Pittsburgh, 1972; 4 chances accepted.

                Ryan, L. Nolan, Houston, 1980; 4 chances accepted.

    A. L.—1.000—Lolich, Michael S., Detroit, 1972; 4 chances accepted.

Most Consecutive Errorless Games, Total Series

N. L.—13—Giusti, J. David, Pittsburgh, October 4, 1970 through October 7, 1975.
    McGraw, Frank E., New York, Philadelphia, October 10, 1973 through October 12, 1980.

A. L.—11—Fingers, Roland G., Oakland, October 3, 1971 through October 5, 1975.

Most Putouts, Total Series

N. L.—5—Gullett, Donald E., Cincinnati, 1970, 1972, 1973, 1975, 1976; 5 Series, 9 games.

A. L.—4—Hunter, James A., Oakland, 1971, 1972, 1973, 1974; New York, 1976, 1978; 6 Series, 10 games.
    Palmer James A., Baltimore, 1969, 1970, 1971, 1973, 1974, 1979; 6 Series, 8 games.

Most Putouts, Series

3-game Series—N. L.—4—Gullett, Donald E., Cincinnati, 1975.
    A. L.—2—Wise, Richard, C., Boston, 1975.
4-game Series—A. L.—3—Hunter, James A., Oakland, 1974.
    N. L.—2—Marichal, Juan A., San Francisco, 1971.
        Sutton, Donald H., Los Angeles, 1974.
5-game Series—N. L.—2—McGraw, Frank E., New York, 1973.
        Ruthven, Richard D., Philadelphia, 1980.
    A. L.—2—Odom, Johnny L., Oakland, 1972.
        Torrez, Michael A., New York, 1977.
        Guidry, Ronald A., New York, 1977.
        May, Rudolph, New York, 1980.

Most Putouts, Game

N. L.—4—Gullett, Donald E., Cincinnati, October 4, 1975.
A. L.—2—Held by many pitchers.

Most Putouts, Inning

A. L.—2—Torrez, Michael A., New York, October 7, 1977; second inning.
N. L.—2—Gullett, Donald E., Cincinnati, October 4, 1975; third inning.

Most Assists, Total Series

    A. L.— 12— Cuellar, Miguel, Baltimore, 1969, 1970, 1971, 1973, 1974; 5 Series, 6
          games.
    N. L.— 6— Sutton, Donald H., Los Angeles, 1974, 1977, 1978; 3 Series, 4 games.

Most Assists, Series

    3-game Series—A. L.— 4— Boswell, David W., Minnesota, 1969.
                      Lindblad, Paul A., Oakland, 1975.
              N. L.— 3— Niekro, Philip H., Atlanta, 1969.
                      Ellis, Dock P., Pittsburgh, 1970.
                      Zachry, Patrick P., Cincinnati, 1976.
    4-game Series—A. L.— 5— Cuellar, Miguel, Baltimore, 1974.
              N. L.— 4— Marichal, Juan A., San Francisco, 1971.
    5-game Series—N. L.— 3— Blass, Stephen R., Pittsburgh, 1972.
                      Seaver, G. Thomas, New York, 1973.
                      Ryan, L. Nolan, Houston, 1980.
              A. L.— 3— Held by many pitchers.

Most Assists, Game

    N. L.— 4— Marichal, Juan A., San Francisco, October 5, 1971.
    A. L.— 4— Boswell, David W., Minnesota, October 5, 1969; 11 innings.
              Lindblad, Paul A., Oakland, October 7, 1975.
              Gura, Lawrence C., Kansas City, October 4, 1978.

Most Assists, Inning

    N. L.— 3— Zachry, Patrick P., Cincinnati, October 10, 1976; fourth inning.
    A. L.— 2— Held by many pitchers.

Most Chances Accepted, Total Series

    A. L.— 13— Cuellar, Miguel, Baltimore, 1969, 1970, 1971, 1973, 1974; 5 Series, 6
          games.
    N. L.— 8— Sutton, Donald H., Los Angeles, 1974, 1977, 1978; 3 Series, 4 games.

Most Chances Accepted, Series

    3-game Series—N. L.— 5— Gullett, Donald E., Cincinnati, 1975.
              A. L.— 5— Boswell, David W., Minnesota, 1969.
                      Wise, Richard C., Boston, 1975.
                      Lindblad, Paul A., Oakland, 1975.
    4-game Series—N. L.— 6— Marichal, Juan A., San Francisco, 1971.
              A. L.— 5— Hunter, James A., Oakland, 1974.
                      Cuellar, Miguel, Baltimore, 1974.
                      Gura, Lawrence C., Kansas City, 1978.
    5-game Series—N. L.— 4— Blass, Stephen R., Pittsburgh, 1972.
                      Ryan, L. Nolan, Houston, 1980.
              A. L.— 4— Lolich, Michael S., Detroit, 1972.

Most Chances Accepted, Game

    N. L.— 6— Marichal, Juan A., San Francisco, October 5, 1971.
    A. L.— 5— Boswell, David W., Minnesota, October 5, 1969; 11 innings.
              Wise, Richard C., Boston, October 7, 1975.
              Lindblad, Paul A., Oakland, October 7, 1975.
              Gura, Lawrence C., Kansas City, October 4, 1978.

Most Chances Accepted, Inning

    N. L.— 3— Zachry, Patrick P., Cincinnati, October 10, 1976; fourth inning.
    A. L.— 2— Held by many pitchers.

Most Errors, Total Series

    A. L.— 1— Bird, J. Douglas, Kansas City, 1976.
    N. L.— 1— Held by many pitchers.

Most Errors, Series

    A. L.—1— Bird, J. Douglas, Kansas City, 1976.
    N. L.—1— Held by many pitchers.

Most Errors, Game

    A. L.—1— Bird, J. Douglas, Kansas City, October 13, 1976.
    N. L.—1— Held by many pitchers.

Most Double Plays, Total Series

    A. L.-N. L.—1—Held by many pitchers.

Most Double Plays Started, Total Series

    A. L.-N. L.—1—Held by many pitchers.

Most Unassisted Double Plays, Game

    A. L.-N. L.—Never accomplished.

CLUB FIELDING

Highest Fielding Average, Series, One Club

    3-game Series—A. L.— 1.000— Baltimore vs. Minnesota, 1970.
                          Oakland vs. Baltimore, 1971.
              N. L.— 1.000— Pittsburgh vs. Cincinnati, 1979.
    4-game Series—A. L.— .993— New York vs. Kansas City, 1978.
              N. L.— .982— Los Angeles vs. Philadelphia, 1978.
    5-game Series—N. L.— .990— Cincinnati vs. New York, 1973.
              A. L.— .989— Baltimore vs. Oakland, 1973.
                          New York vs. Kansas City, 1977.

Highest Fielding Average, Series, Both Clubs

    3-game Series—N. L.—.996—Pittsburgh 1.000, Cincinnati .992, 1979.
              A. L.—.995—Oakland 1.000, Baltimore .991, 1971.
    4-game Series—A. L.—.982—New York .993, Kansas City, 1978.
              N. L.—.978—Los Angeles .982, Philadelphia .975, 1978.
    5-game Series—N. L.—.985—Cincinnati .990, New York .979, 1973.
              A. L.—.984—Baltimore .989, Oakland .979, 1973.

Lowest Fielding Average, Series, One Club

    3-game Series—A. L.—.946—Minnesota vs. Baltimore, 1970.
              N. L.—.950—Atlanta vs. New York, 1969.
    4-game Series—N. L.—.957—Los Angeles vs. Pittsburgh, 1974.
              A. L.—.970—Baltimore vs. California, 1979.
    5-game Series—A. L.—.964—Detroit vs. Oakland, 1972.
              N. L.—.973—Philadelphia vs. Houston, 1980.

Lowest Fielding Average, Series, Both Clubs

    3-game Series—A. L.—.958—Boston .966, Oakland .950, 1975.
              N. L.—.965—New York .981, Atlanta .950, 1969.
    4-game Series—N. L.—.964—Pittsburgh .973, Los Angeles .957, 1974.
              A. L.—.978—California .986, Baltimore .970, 1979.
    5-game Series—A. L.—.974—Kansas City .978, New York .970, 1976.
              N. L.—.978—Cincinnati .979, Pittsburgh .977, 1972.

Most Putouts, Total Series

    A. L.— 607— Baltimore; 6 Series, 22 games.
    N. L.— 606— Cincinnati; 6 Series, 22 games.

Most Putouts, Series, One Club

    3-game Series—A. L.— 96— Baltimore vs. Minnesota, 1969.
              N. L.— 90— Pittsburgh vs. Cincinnati, 1979.

4-game Series—N. L.— 111— Los Angeles vs. Philadelphia, 1978.
            A. L.— 109— Baltimore vs. California, 1979.
5-game Series—N. L.— 148— Philadelphia vs. Houston, 1980.
            A. L.— 139— Detroit vs. Oakland, 1972.

Most Putouts, Series, Both Clubs

3-game Series—A. L.— 190— Baltimore 96, Minnesota 94, 1969.
            N. L.— 177— Pittsburgh 90, Cincinnati 87, 1979.
4-game Series—N. L.— 221— Los Angeles 111, Philadelphia 110, 1978.
            A. L.— 216— Baltimore 109, California 107, 1979.
5-game Series—N. L.— 295— Philadelphia 148, Houston 147, 1980.
            A. L.— 277— Detroit 139, Oakland 138, 1972.

Fewest Putouts, Series, One Club

3-game Series—A. L.— 75— Oakland vs. Baltimore, 1971.
                         Oakland vs. Boston, 1975.
                         New York vs. Kansas City, 1980.
            N. L.— 78— Atlanta vs. New York, 1969.
                         Pittsburgh vs. Cincinnati, 1975.
4-game Series—A. L.— 102— Kansas City vs. New York, 1978.
            N. L.— 102— San Francisco vs. Pittsburgh, 1971.
5-game Series—A. L.— 129— Kansas City vs. New York, 1976.
            N. L.— 131— Pittsburgh vs. Cincinnati, 1972.

Fewest Putouts, Series, Both Clubs

3-game Series—A. L.— 156— Baltimore 81, Oakland 75, 1971.
                         Boston 81, Oakland 75, 1975.
                         Kansas City 81, New York 75, 1980.
            N. L.— 159— New York 81, Atlanta 78, 1969.
4-game Series—A. L.— 207— New York 105, Kansas City 102, 1978.
            N. L.— 207— Pittsburgh 105, San Francisco 102, 1971.
5-game Series—A. L.— 261— New York 132, Kansas City 129, 1976.
            N. L.— 263— Cincinnati 132, Pittsburgh 131, 1972.

Most Players, One or More Putouts, Game, One Club

N. L.— 11— Houston vs. Philadelphia, October 12, 1980; 10 innings.
A. L.—N. L.—Nine-inning record—10—Held by many clubs.

Most Players, One or More Putouts, Game, Both Clubs

N. L.— 20— Cincinnati 10, Pittsburgh 10, October 8, 1972.
A. L.— 18— Boston 10, Oakland 8, October 7, 1975.

Most Putouts, Catchers, Inning, Both Clubs

A. L.— 5— Baltimore 3, Oakland 2, October 6, 1973; first inning.
            Oakland 3, Boston 2, October 4, 1975; second inning.
N. L.— 5— Atlanta 3, New York 2, October 5, 1969; third inning.
            Atlanta 3, New York 2, October 6, 1969; third inning.
            Los Angeles 3, Philadelphia 2, October 4, 1977; seventh inning.

Most Putouts, Outfield, Game, One Club

N. L.— 18— Pittsburgh vs. Cincinnati, October 7, 1972.
A. L.— 14— Boston vs. Oakland, October 4, 1975.
            New York vs. Kansas City, October 13, 1976.

Most Putouts, Outfield, Game, Both Clubs

A. L.— 26— New York 14, Kansas City 12, October 13, 1976.
N. L.— 25— Pittsburgh 18, Cincinnati 7, October 7, 1972.

Fewest Putouts, Outfield, Game, Nine Innings, One Club

N. L.— 1— Atlanta vs. New York, October 4, 1969.
            Cincinnati vs. Pittsburgh, October 5, 1970.

Fewest Putouts, Outfield, Game, Nine Innings, One Club—Continued

    A. L.—2— Oakland vs. Boston, October 5, 1975; fielded 8 innings.
          3— Baltimore vs. Minnesota, October 3, 1970.
             Baltimore vs. Oakland, October 10, 1973.
             Kansas City vs. New York, October 12, 1976; fielded 8 innings.
             New York vs. Kansas City, October 8, 1980; fielded 8 innings.

Fewest Putouts, Outfield, Extra-Inning Game, One Club

    N. L.—3— Cincinnati vs. Pittsburgh, October 3, 1970; 10 innings.
    A. L.—4— Baltimore vs. Oakland, October 9, 1973; fielded 10 innings of 11-inning
          game.

Fewest Putouts, Outfield, Game, Nine Innings, Both Clubs

    N. L.—5— Pittsburgh 4, Cincinnati 1, October 5, 1970.
    A. L.—7— Minnesota 4, Baltimore 3, October 3, 1970.

Fewest Putouts, Outfield, Extra-Inning Game, Both Clubs

    N. L.—12— Cincinnati 7, Pittsburgh 5, October 2, 1979; 11 innings.
    A. L.—14— Minnesota 9, Baltimore 5, October 4, 1969; 12 innings.
             Baltimore 8, Minnesota 6, October 5, 1969; 11 innings.
             Oakland 10, Baltimore 4, October 9, 1973; 11 innings.

Most Putouts, Outfield, Inning, One Club

    A. L.-N. L.—3—Held by many clubs.

Most Putouts, Outfield, Inning, Both Clubs

    A. L.—6— Baltimore 3, Oakland 3, October 11, 1973; seventh inning.
    N. L.—5— New York 3, Atlanta 2, October 5, 1969; seventh inning.
             Pittsburgh 3, Cincinnati 2, October 7, 1972; third inning.
             Los Angeles 3, Philadelphia 2, October 7, 1978; third inning.

Most Assists, Total Series

    N. L.— 253— Cincinnati; 6 Series, 22 games.
    A. L.— 244— Baltimore; 6 Series, 22 games.

Most Assists, Series, One Club

    3-game Series—A. L.— 41—New York vs. Kansas City, 1980.
               N. L.—39—Cincinnati vs. Pittsburgh, 1970, 1979.
    4-game Series—A. L.— 52—Baltimore vs. California, 1979.
               N. L.—50—Los Angeles vs. Philadelphia, 1978.
    5-game Series—N. L.—71—Philadelphia vs. Houston, 1980.
               A. L.—60—New York vs. Kansas City, 1976.

Most Assists, Series, Both Clubs

    3-game Series—N. L.— 76—Cincinnati 39, Pittsburgh 37, 1970.
               A. L.— 73—Oakland 40, Boston 33, 1975.
    4-game Series—N. L.— 96—Los Angeles 50, Philadelphia 46, 1978.
               A. L.— 93— Baltimore 50, Oakland 43, 1974.
    5-game Series—A. L.— 111—New York 60, Kansas City 51, 1976.
               N. L.—123—Philadelphia 71, Houston 52, 1980.

Fewest Assists, Series, One Club

    3-game Series—A. L.— 15—Oakland vs. Baltimore, 1971.
               N. L.—20—Pittsburgh vs. Cincinnati, 1975.
    4-game Series—N. L.—32—Pittsburgh vs. San Francisco, 1971.
               A. L.—35—New York vs. Kansas City, 1978.
    5-game Series—N. L.—38—Pittsburgh vs. Cincinnati, 1972.
               A. L.—47—Oakland vs. Baltimore, 1973.

Fewest Assists, Series, Both Clubs

    3-game Series—A. L.— 46—Baltimore 31, Oakland 15, 1971.
               N. L.—51—Cincinnati 31, Pittsburgh 20, 1975.

4-game Series—N. L.—69—San Francisco 37, Pittsburgh 32, 1971.
A. L.—71—Kansas City 36, New York 35, 1978.
5-game Series—N. L.—91—Cincinnati 53, Pittsburgh 38, 1972.
A. L.—98—Baltimore 51, Oakland 47, 1973.

Most Assists, Game, One Club

N. L.—21—Los Angeles vs. Philadelphia, October 5, 1978.
A. L.—18—Boston vs. Oakland, October 7, 1975.

Most Assists, Game, Both Clubs

A. L.—33—Boston 18, Oakland 15, October 7, 1975.
N. L.—32—Pittsburgh 19, Cincinnati 13, October 2, 1979; 11 innings.
30—Los Angeles 21, Philadelphia 9, October 5, 1978.

Most Players, One or More Assists, Game, One Club

N. L.—8—Cincinnati vs. New York, October 10, 1973.
A. L.—8—New York vs. Kansas City, October 8, 1980.

Most Players, One or More Assists, Game, Both Clubs

N. L.—14—Philadelphia 7, Houston 7, October 11, 1980; 10 innings.
N. L.—Nine-inning record—13—New York 7, Atlanta 6, October 4, 1969.
Pittsburgh 7, Cincinnati 6, October 9, 1972.
Cincinnati 8, New York 5, October 10, 1973.
A. L.—13—Oakland 7, Boston 6, October 7, 1975.

Fewest Assists, Game, One Club

A. L.—2—Boston vs. Oakland, October 4, 1975.
N. L.—2—Pittsburgh vs. Cincinnati, October 7, 1972.
Pittsburgh vs. Cincinnati, October 7, 1975, 10 innings.

Fewest Assists, Game, Both Clubs

N. L.—10—Cincinnati 8, Pittsburgh 2, October 7, 1975; 10 innings.
A. L.—11—Oakland 6, Baltimore 5, October 6, 1973.

Most Assists, Outfield, Game, One Club

N. L.—3—Philadelphia vs. Houston, October 11, 1980; 10 innings.
N. L.—Nine-inning record—2—Pittsburgh vs. Cincinnati, October 9, 1972.
Cincinnati vs. New York, October 10, 1973.
Philadelphia vs. Los Angeles, October 7, 1977.
A. L.—2—Minnesota vs. Baltimore, October 4, 1970.
Boston vs. Oakland, October 5, 1975.
Baltimore vs. California, October 5, 1979.

Most Assists, Outfield, Game, Both Clubs

N. L.—4—Philadelphia 3, Houston 1, October 11, 1980; 10 innings.
N. L.—Nine-inning record—3—Pittsburgh 2, Cincinnati 1, October 9, 1972.
A. L.—3—Minnesota 2, Baltimore 1, October 4, 1970.
Boston 2, Oakland 1, October 5, 1975.
Baltimore 2, California 1, October 5, 1979.

Most Assists, Outfield, Inning, One Club

N. L.—2—Cincinnati vs. New York, October 10, 1973; fifth inning.
A. L.—1—Held by many clubs.

Fewest Chances Offered, Outfield, Game, Nine Innings, One Club

N. L.—1—Cincinnati vs. Pittsburgh, October 5, 1970.
A. L.—2—Kansas City vs. New York, October 7, 1978.

Fewest Chances Offered, Outfield, Extra-Inning Game, One Club

N. L.—3—Cincinnati vs. Pittsburgh, October 3, 1970; 10 innings.
A. L.—4—Baltimore vs. Oakland, October 9, 1973; fielded 10 innings of 11-inning game.

Fewest Chances Offered, Outfield, Game, Nine Innings, Both Clubs

N. L.— 5— Pittsburgh 4, Cincinnati 1, October 5, 1970.
A. L.— 7— Minnesota 4, Baltimore 3, October 3, 1970.

Fewest Chances Offered, Outfield, Extra-Inning Game, Both Clubs

N. L.— 12— Cincinnati 7, Pittsburgh 5, October 2, 1979; 11 innings.
A. L.— 14— Baltimore 8, Minnesota 6, October 5, 1969; 11 innings.
       Oakland 10, Baltimore 4, October 9, 1973; 11 innings.

Most Errors, Outfield, Game, One Club

A. L.— 2— Minnesota vs. Baltimore, October 6, 1969.
       Oakland vs. Boston, October 4, 1975.
N. L.— 1— Held by many clubs.

Most Errors, Outfield, Game, Both Clubs

A. L.— 3— Oakland 2, Boston 1, October 4, 1975.
N. L.— 1— Made in many games.

Most Errors, Total Series

A. L.— 15— Oakland; 5 Series, 20 games.
N. L.— 15— Pittsburgh; 6 Series, 22 games.
       Los Angeles; 3 Series, 12 games.
       Philadelphia; 4 Series, 16 games.

Most Errors, Series, One Club

3-game Series—N. L.— 6— Atlanta vs. New York, 1969.
          A. L.— 6— Minnesota vs. Baltimore, 1970.
                  Oakland vs. Boston, 1975.
4-game Series—N. L.— 7— Los Angeles vs. Pittsburgh, 1974.
          A. L.— 5— Baltimore vs. California, 1979.
5-game Series—A. L.— 7— Detroit vs. Oakland, 1972.
          N. L.— 6— Philadelpia vs. Houston, 1980.

Most Errors, Series, Both Clubs

3-game Series—A. L.— 10— Oakland 6, Boston 4, 1975.
          N. L.— 8— Atlanta 6, New York 2, 1969.
4-game Series—N. L.— 11— Los Angeles 7, Pittsburgh 4, 1974.
          A. L.— 7— Baltimore 5, California 2, 1979.
5-game Series—A. L.— 10— Detroit 7, Oakland 3, 1972.
                 New York 6, Kansas City 4, 1976.
          N. L.— 9— Philadelphia 6, Houston 3, 1980.

Fewest Errors, Series, One Club

3-game Series—A. L.— 0— Baltimore vs. Minnesota, 1970.
                 Oakland vs. Baltimore, 1971.
          N. L.— 0— Pittsburgh vs. Cincinnati, 1979.
4-game Series—A. L.— 1— New York vs. Kansas City, 1978.
          N. L.— 3— Pittsburgh vs. San Francisco, 1971.
                 Philadelphia vs. Los Angeles, 1977.
                 Los Angeles vs. Philadelphia, 1978.
5-game Series—N. L.— 2— Cincinnati vs. New York, 1973.
          A. L.— 2— Baltimore vs. Oakland, 1973.
                 New York vs. Kansas City, 1977.

Fewest Errors, Series, Both Clubs

3-game Series—A. L.— 1— Baltimore 1, Oakland 0, 1971.
          N. L.— 1— Cincinnati 1, Pittsburgh 0, 1979.
4-game Series—A. L.— 5— Kansas City 4, New York 1, 1978.
          N. L.— 7— San Francisco 4, Pittsburgh 3, 1971.
                 Philadelphia 4, Los Angeles 3, 1978.
5-game Series—A. L.— 6— Oakland 4, Baltimore 2, 1973.
          N. L.— 6— New York 4, Cincinnati 2, 1973.

Most Errorless Games, Total Series

N. L.— 14— Pittsburgh; 6 Series, 22 games.
A. L.— 13— Oakland; 5 Series, 20 games.
Baltimore; 6 Series, 22 games.

Most Errors, Game, One Club

A. L.— 5— New York vs. Kansas City, October 10, 1976.
N. L.— 5— Los Angeles vs. Pittsburgh, October 8, 1974.

Most Errors, Game, Both Clubs

A. L.— 7— Oakland 4, Boston 3, October 4, 1975.
N. L.— 5— Los Angeles 5, Pittsburgh 0, October 8, 1974.

Most Errors, Infield, Game, One Club

A. L.— 3— Oakland vs. Baltimore, October 9, 1973; 11 innings.
Nine-inning record— 2— Held by many clubs.
N. L.— 2— Held by many clubs.

Most Errors, Infield, Game, Both Clubs

A. L.— 4— Boston 2, Oakland 2, October 4, 1975.
N. L.— 3— Atlanta 2, New York 1, October 5, 1969.
Pittsburgh 2, Cincinnati 1, October 10, 1972.

Longest Errorless Game, One Club

N. L.— 12 innings— Cincinnati vs. New York, October 9, 1973; fielded 12 complete
innings.
A. L.— 11 innings— Baltimore vs. Minnesota, October 5, 1969; fielded 11 complete
innings.
Baltimore vs. Oakland, October 9, 1973; fielded 10 complete
innings of 11-inning game.

Longest Errorless Game, Both Clubs

N. L.— 11 innings— Pittsburgh vs. Cincinnati, October 2, 1979; both clubs fielded
11 complete innings.
A. L.— 9 innings— Made in many games.

Most Errors, Inning, One Club

A. L.— 3— Oakland vs. Boston, October 4, 1975; first inning.
N. L.— 2— Held by many clubs.

Most Passed Balls, Total Series

N. L.— 4— Pittsburgh; 5 Series, 19 games.
A. L.— 2— Oakland; 5 Series, 20 games.
New York; 3 Series, 14 games.
Baltimore; 6 Series, 22 games.

Most Passed Balls, Series, One Club

N. L.— 2— Pittsburgh vs. Cincinnati, 1975; 3-game Series.
A. L.— 1— Held by many clubs.

Most Passed Balls, Series, Both Clubs

A. L.— 2— Kansas City 1, New York 1, 1978.
N. L.— 2— Made in many Series.

Most Passed Balls, Game, One Club

N. L.— 2— Pittsburgh vs. Cincinnati, October 4, 1975.
A. L.— 1— Held by many clubs.

Most Passed Balls, Inning, One Club

A. L.-N. L.— 1— Held by many clubs.

Most Double Plays, Total Series

A. L.— 21— Oakland; 5 Series, 20 games.
N. L.— 17— Philadelphia; 4 Series, 16 games.

Most Double Plays, Series, One Club

3-game Series—A. L.— 5— Minnesota vs. Baltimore, 1970.
              N. L.— 4— Atlanta vs. New York, 1969.
4-game Series—N. L.— 8— Los Angeles vs. Pittsburgh, 1974.
              A. L.— 7— California vs. Baltimore, 1979.
5-game Series—N. L.— 7— Philadelphia vs. Houston, 1980.
              A. L.— 5— Oakland vs. Detroit, 1972.
                      Kansas City vs. New York, 1976.

Most Double Plays, Series, Both Clubs

3-game Series—A. L.— 8— Minnesota 5, Baltimore 3, 1970.
              N. L.— 6— Atlanta 4, New York 2, 1969.
                      Cincinnati 3, Philadelphia 3, 1976.
4-game Series—A. L.— 12— California 7, Baltimore 5, 1979.
              N. L.— 10— Los Angeles 8, Pittsburgh 2, 1974.
5-game Series—N. L.— 11— Philadelphia 7, Houston 4, 1980.
              A. L.— 9— Oakland 5, Detroit 4, 1972.

Fewest Double Plays, Series, One Club

3-game Series—N. L.— 1— Cincinnati vs. Pittsburgh, 1970.
              A. L.— 2— Baltimore vs. Minnesota, 1969.
                      New York vs. Kansas City, 1980.
4-game Series—N. L.— 1— San Francisco vs. Pittsbugh, 1971.
              A. L.— 2— New York vs. Kansas City, 1978.
5-game Series—A. L.— 2— Held by many clubs.
              N. L.— 3— Held by many clubs.

Fewest Double Plays, Series, Both Clubs

3-game Series—N. L.— 4— Pittsburgh 3, Cincinnati 1, 1970.
                      Pittsburgh 2, Cincinnati 2, 1979.
              A. L.— 5— Minnesota 3, Baltimore 2, 1969.
                      Kansas City 3, New York 2, 1980.
4-game Series—N. L.— 4— Pittsburgh 3, San Francisco 1, 1971.
              A. L.— 6— Kansas City 4, New York 2, 1978.
5-game Series—A. L.— 4— Kansas City 2, New York 2, 1977.
              N. L.— 6— Cincinnati 3, Pittsburgh 3, 1972.
                      Cincinnati 3, New York 3, 1973.

Most Double Plays, Game, One Club

A. L.— 4— Oakland vs. Boston, October 5, 1975.
N. L.— 3— Los Angeles vs. Pittsburgh, October 8, 1974.
           Pittsburgh vs. Cincinnati, October 5, 1975.
           Los Angeles vs. Philadelphia, October 5, 1978.
           Philadelphia vs. Houston, October 11, 1980; 10 innings.

Most Double Plays, Game, Both Clubs

A. L.— 6— Oakland 4, Boston 2, October 5, 1975.
N. L.— 5— Pittsburgh 3, Cincinnati 2, October 5, 1975.
           Philadelphia 3, Houston 2, October 11, 1980; 10 innings.

Most Triple Plays, Series, One Club

A. L.-N. L.— Never accomplished.

INDIVIDUAL PITCHING

Most Series Pitched

A. L.— 6— Hunter, James, A., Oakland, 1971, 1972, 1973, 1974; New York, 1976, 1978; 10 games.

Palmer, James A., Baltimore, 1969, 1970, 1971, 1973, 1974, 1979; 8 games.

Both Leagues—6—Gullett, Donald E., Cincinnati NL, 1970, 1972, 1973, 1975, 1976, 9 games; New York AL, 1977; 1 game.

N. L.— 6— McGraw, Frank E., New York, 1969, 1973; Philadelphia, 1976, 1977, 1978, 1980; 15 games.

Most Games Pitched, Total Series

N. L.— 15— McGraw, Frank E., New York, 1969, 1973; Philadelphia, 1976, 1977, 1978, 1980; 6 Series.

A. L.— 11— Fingers, Roland G., Oakland, 1971, 1972, 1973, 1974, 1975; 5 Series.

Most Games Pitched, Series

3-game Series— N. L.— 3— Upshaw, Cecil L., Atlanta, 1969; 6⅓ innings.

Tomlin, David A., Cincinnati, 1979; 3 innings.

Hume, Thomas H., Cincinnati, 1979; 4 innings.

A. L.— 3— Perranoski, Ronald P., Minnesota, 1969; 4⅔ innings.

Todd, James, R., Oakland, 1975; 1 inning.

4-game Series— N. L.— 4— Giusti, J. David, Pittsburgh, 1971; 5⅓ innings.

A. L.— 3— Hrabosky, Alan T., Kansas City, 1978; 3 innings.

Stanhouse, Donald J., Baltimore, 1979; 3 innings.

5-game Series— N. L.— 5— McGraw, Frank E., Philadelphia, 1980; 8 innings.

A. L.— 4— Blue, Vida R., Oakland, 1972; 5⅓ innings.

Lyle, Albert W., New York, 1977; 9 innings.

Most Consecutive Games Pitched, Series

N. L.— 5— McGraw, Frank E., Philadelphia, October 7, 8, 10, 11, 12, 1980.

A. L.— 3— Perranoski, Ronald P., Minnesota, October 4, 5, 6, 1969.

Blue, Vida R., Oakland, October 10, 11, 12, 1972.

Todd, James R., Oakland, October 4, 5, 7, 1975.

Lyle, Albert W., New York, October 7, 8, 9, 1977.

Hrabosky, Alan T., Kansas City, October 3, 4, 6, 1978.

Stanhouse, Donald J., Baltimore, October 3, 4, 5, 1979.

Most Games Started, Total Series

A. L.— 10— Hunter, James A., Oakland, 1971, 1972, 1973, 1974; New York, 1976, 1978; 6 Series.

N. L.— 6— Carlton, Steven N., Philadelphia, 1976, 1977, 1978, 1980; 4 Series.

Most Opening Games Started, Total Series

Both Leagues—4—Gullett, Donald E., Cincinnati NL, 1972, 1975, 1976; New York AL, 1977; won 2, lost 2.

N. L.— 3— Gullett, Donald E., Cincinnati, 1972, 1975, 1976; won 2, lost 1.

Carlton, Steven N., Philadelphia, 1976, 1977, 1980; won 1, lost 1, no decision 1.

A. L.— 3— Cuellar, Miguel, Baltimore, 1969, 1970, 1974; won 1 lost 0, no decision 2.

Hunter, James A., Oakland, 1972, 1974; New York, 1976; won 1, lost 1, no decision 1.

Most Games Started, Series

3-game Series—A. L.— 2— Holtzman, Kenneth D., Oakland, 1975.

N. L.— 1— Held by many pitchers.

4-game Series—A. L.— N. L.— 2—Held by many pitchers.

5-game Series—A. L.— N. L.— 2—Held by many pitchers.

Most Games Finished, Total Series

N. L.— 9— Giusti, J. David, Pittsburgh, 1970, 1971, 1972, 1974, 1975; 5 Series, 13 games.

McGraw, Frank E., New York, Philadelphia, 1969, 1973, 1976, 1977, 1978, 1980; 6 Series, 15 games.

A. L.— 8— Fingers, Roland G., Oakland, 1971, 1972, 1973, 1974, 1975; 5 Series, 11 games.

Most Games Finished, Series

3-game Series—A. L.— 3— Perranoski, Ronald P., Minnesota, 1969.

N. L.— 2— Held by many pitchers.

4-game Series—N. L.— 4— Giusti, J. David, Pittsburgh, 1971.

A. L.— 3— Stanhouse, Donald J., Baltimore, 1979.

5-game Series—A. L.— 4— Lyle, Albert W., New York, 1977.

N. L.— 4— Borbon, Pedro R., Cincinnati, 1973.

Most Complete Games Pitched, Total Series

A. L.— 5— Palmer, James A., Baltimore, 1969, 1970, 1971, 1973, 1974.

N. L.— 2— Sutton, Donald H., Los Angeles, 1974, 1977.

John, Thomas E., Los Angeles, 1977, 1978.

Most Consecutive Complete Games Pitched, Total Series

A. L.— 4— Palmer, James A., Baltimore, 1969 (1), 1970 (1), 1971 (1), 1973 (1); won 4, lost 0.

N. L.— 2— John, Thomas E., Los Angeles, 1977 (1), 1978 (1); won 2, lost 0.

Most Complete Games, Series

A. L.–N. L.–1–Held by many pitchers in Series of all lengths.

Most Games, Total Series, Relief Pitcher

N. L.— 15— McGraw, Frank E., New York, Philadelphia, 1969, 1973, 1976, 1977, 1978, 1980; 27 innings.

A. L.— 11— Fingers, Roland G., Oakland, 1971, 1972, 1973, 1974, 1975; 19⅓ innings.

Most Series, One or More Games as Relief Pitcher

N. L.— 6— McGraw, Frank E., New York, Philadelphia, 1969, 1973, 1976, 1977, 1978, 1980; 15 games as relief pitcher.

A. L.— 5— Fingers, Roland G., Oakland, 1971, 1972, 1973, 1974, 1975, 11 games as relief pitcher.

Most Games, Series, Relief Pitcher

3-game Series—N. L.— 3— Upshaw, Cecil L., Atlana, 1969; 6⅓ innings.

Tomlin, David A., Cincinnati, 1979; 3 innings.

Hume, Thomas H., Cincinnati, 1979; 4 innings.

A. L.— 3— Perranoski, Ronald P., Minnesota, 1969; 4⅔ innings.

Todd, James R., Oakland, 1975; 1 inning.

4-game Series—N. L.— 4— Giusti, J. David, Pittsburgh, 1971; 5⅓ innings.

A. L.— 3— Hrabosky, Alan T., Kansas City, 1978; 3 innings.

Stanhouse, Donald J., Baltimore, 1979; 3 innings.

5-game Series—N. L.— 5— McGraw, Frank E., Philadelphia, 1980; 8 innings.

A. L.— 4— Blue, Vida R., Oakland, 1972; 5⅓ innings.

Lyle, Albert W., New York, 1977; 9⅓ innings.

Most Games Won, Total Series

A. L.— 4— Palmer, James A., Baltimore, 1969, 1970, 1971, 1973, 1974, 1979; won 4, lost 1, 6 Series, 8 games.

Hunter, James A., Oakland, 1971, 1972, 1973, 1974; New York 1976, 1978; won 4, lost 3, 6 Series, 10 games.

N. L.— 3— Kison, Bruce E., Pittsburgh, 1971, 1972, 1974, 1975; won 3, lost 0, 4 Series, 5 games.

Sutton, Donald H., Los Angeles, 1974, 1977, 1978; won 3, lost 1, 3 Series, 4 games.

Pitchers Winning 2 or More Games, Total Series
Both Leagues

Pitcher and Club	Years	W.	L.
Jackson, Grant D., Balt.-N.Y. AL, Pitts. NL	1973-74-76-79	2	0
Ellis, Dock P., Pitts. NL, New York AL	1970-71-72-75-76	2	2
Gullett, Donald E., Cin. NL, N.Y. AL	1970-72-73-75-76-77	2	3

American League

Pitcher and Club	Years	W.	L.
Palmer, James A., Baltimore	1969-70-71-73-74-79	4	1
Hunter, James A., Oakland, New York	1971-72-73-74-76-78	4	3
McNally, David A., Baltimore	1969-70-71-73-74	3	2
Odom, Johnny L., Oakland	1972-73-74	2	0
Hall, Richard W., Baltimore	1969-70	2	0
Lyle, Albert W., New York	1976-77-78	2	0
Splittorff, Paul W., Kansas City	1976-77-78-80	2	0
Guidry, Ronald A., New York	1977-78-80	2	1
Cuellar, Miguel, Baltimore	1969-70-71-73-74	2	2
Gura, Lawrence C., Kansas City	1976-77-78-80	2	2
Holtzman, Kenneth D., Oakland	1972-73-74-75	2	3
Leonard, Dennis P., Kansas City	1976-77-78-80	2	3

National League

Pitcher and Club	Years	W.	L.
Kison, Bruce E., Pittsburgh	1971-72-74-75	3	0
Sutton, Donald H., Los Angeles	1974-77-78	3	1
Eastwick, Rawlins J., Cincinnati, Phila.	1975-76-78	2	0
John, Thomas E., Los Angeles	1977-78	2	0
Seaver, G. Thomas, New York-Cin.	1969-73-79	2	1
Carroll, Clay P., Cincinnati	1970-72-73-75	2	1
Gullett, Donald E., Cincinnati	1970-72-73-75-76	2	2
Carlton, Steven N., Philadelphia	1976-77-78-80	2	3

Most Games Won, Total Series, No Defeats

N. L.— 3— Kison, Bruce W., Pittsburgh, 1971, 1972, 1974.
A. L.— 2— Hall, Richard W., Baltimore, 1969, 1970.
     Odom, Johnny L., Oakland, 1972 (2).
     Splittorff, Paul W., Kansas City, 1976, 1977.
     Lyle, Albert W., New York, 1977 (2).

Most Games Won, Series

3-game Series—A. L.— N. L.—1—Held by many pitchers.
4-game Series—N. L.— 2— Sutton, Donald H., Los Angeles, 1974 (one complete).
     A. L.— 1— Held by many pitchers.
5-game Series—A. L.— 2— Odom, Johnny L., Oakland, 1972 (one complete).
     Hunter, James A., Oakland, 1973 (one complete).
     Lyle, Albert W., New York, 1977 (no complete).
     N. L.— 1— Held by many pitchers.

Most Consecutive Games Won, Total Series

A. L.— 4— Palmer, James A., Baltimore, October 6, 1969; October 5, 1970; October 5, 1971; October 6, 1973; all complete.
N. L.— 3— Kison, Bruce E., Pittsburgh, October 6, 1971; October 9, 1972; October 8, 1974; all incomplete.
     Sutton, Donald H., Los Angeles, October 5, 9, 1974; October 5, 1977; two complete, one incomplete.

Most Consecutive Complete Games Won, Total Series

    A. L.—4— Palmer, James A., Baltimore, October 6, 1969; October 5, 1970; October 5, 1971; October 6, 1973.

    N. L.—2— John, Thomas E., Los Angeles, October 8, 1977; October 5, 1978.

Most Games Won, Series, As Relief Pitcher

    A. L.—2— Lyle, Albert W., New York, 1977; 5-game Series.

    N. L.—1— Held by many pitchers.

Most Opening Games Won, Total Series

    N. L.—2— Gullett, Donald E., Cincinnati, 1975, 1976.

    A. L.—2— Hall, Richard W., Baltimore, 1969, 1970.

Most Games Lost, Total Series

    N. L.—3— Reuss, Jerry, Pittsburgh, 1974, 1975; won 0, 2 Series, 3 games.

    A. L.—3— Holtzman, Kenneth D., Oakland, 1972, 1973, 1974, 1975; won 2, 4 Series, 5 games.

        Hunter, James A., Oakland, 1971, 1972, 1973, 1974; New York, 1976, 1978; won 4, 6 Series, 10 games.

        Leonard, Dennis P., Kansas City, 1976, 1977, 1978; won 1, 3 Series, 6 games.

Both Leagues—3—Gullett, Donald E., Cincinnati NL, 1970, 1972, 1973, 1975, 1976; New York AL, 1977; won 2, 6 Series, 10 games.

Most Games Lost, Total Series, No Victories

    N. L.—3— Reuss, Jerry, Pittsburgh, 1974 (2), 1975.

    A. L.—2— Fryman, Woodrow T., Detroit, 1972 (2).

        Hassler, Andrew E., Kansas City, 1976, 1977.

        Figueroa, Eduardo, New York, 1976, 1978.

Most Consecutive Games Lost, Total Series

    N. L.—3— Reuss, Jerry, Pittsburgh, 1974 (2), 1975.

    A. L.—3— Leonard, Dennis P., Kansas City, 1977, 1978 (2).

Most Games Lost, Series

    3-game Series—A. L.— 2— Holtzman, Kenneth D., Oakland, 1975.

                     N. L.—1— Held by many pitchers.

    4-game Series—A. L.— 2— Leonard, Dennis P., Kansas City, 1978.

                     N. L.—2— Reuss, Jerry, Pittsburgh, 1974.

    5-game Series—A. L.— 2— Fryman, Woodrow T., Detroit, 1972.

                     N. L.—1— Held by many pitchers.

Most Saves, Total Series

    N. L.—5— McGraw, Frank E., New York, 1969, 1973; Philadelphia, 1977, 1980 (2).

    A. L.—2— Fingers, Roland G., Oakland, 1973, 1974.

        Drago, Richard A., Boston, 1975 (2).

Most Saves, Series

    3-game Series—A. L.— 2— Drago, Richard A., Boston, 1975.

                     N. L.—2— Gullett, Donald E., Cincinnati, 1970.

    4-game Series—N. L.— 3— Giusti, J. David, Pittsburgh, 1971.

                     A. L.—1— Held by many pitchers.

    5-game Series—N. L.— 2— McGraw, Frank E., Philadelphia, 1980.

                     A. L.—1— Held by many pitchers.

Most Innings Pitched, Total Series

    A. L.—69⅓— Hunter, James A., Oakland, 1971, 1972, 1973, 1974; New York, 1976, 1978; 6 Series, 10 games.

    N. L.— 40 — Carlton, Steven N., Philadelphia, 1976, 1977, 1978, 1980; 4 Series, 6 games.

Most Innings Pitched, Series

3-game Series—A. L.— 11 — McNally, David A., Baltimore, 1969.
         Holtzman, Kenneth D., Oakland, 1975.
     N. L.— 9⅔—Ellis, Dock P., Pittsburgh, 1970.
4-game Series—N. L.—17 —Sutton, Donald H., Los Angeles, 1974.
     A. L.—12⅔—Cuellar, Miguel, Baltimore, 1974.
5-game Series—A. L.— 19 —Lolich, Michael S., Detroit, 1972.
     N. L.—16⅔—Seaver, G. Thomas, New York, 1973.

Most Innings Pitched, Game

A. L.—11—McNally, David A., Baltimore, October 5, 1969, complete game, won
   1-0.
   Holtzman, Kenneth D., Oakland, October 9, 1973, complete game,
   won 2-1.
N. L.—10—Niekro, Joseph F., Houston, October 10, 1980, incomplete game, no
   decision.

Most Shutouts, Series

A. L.-N. L.—1—Held by many pitchers.

Most Consecutive Scoreless Innings, Total Series

A. L.— 19⅓— Holtzman, Kenneth D., Oakland, October 9, 1973 (9⅔ innings);
   October 6, 1974 (9 innings); October 4, 1975 (⅔ innings).
N. L.— 15⅔— Sutton, Donald H., Los Angeles, October 5, 1974 (9 innings); Octo-
   ber 9, 1974 (6⅔ innings).

Most Consecutive Scoreless Innings, Series

N. L.— 15⅔— Sutton, Donald H., Los Angeles, October 5, 9, 1974.
A. L.— 11 — McNally, David A., Baltimore, October 5, 1969.

Most Consecutive Hitless Innings, Total Series

A. L.— 11 — McNally, David A., Baltimore, October 5 (8 innings), 1969; October
   4 (3 innings), 1970.
N. L.— 6⅔— Billingham, John E., Cincinnati, October 6 (6⅓ innings), October
   10 (⅓ inning), 1973.

Most Consecutive Hitless Innings, Game

A. L.— 8 — McNally, David A., Baltimore, October 5, 1969; 11-inning game.
N. L.— 6⅓— Billingham, John E., Cincinnati, October 6, 1973.

Most Runs Allowed, Total Series

A. L.—25—Hunter, James A., Oakland, 1971, 1972, 1973, 1974; New York, 1976,
   1978; 6 Series, 10 games.
N. L.—21—Carlton, Steven N., Philadelphia, 1976, 1977, 1978, 1980; 4 Series, 6
   games.

Most Earned Runs Allowed, Total Series

A. L.—25—Hunter, James A., Oakland, 1971, 1972, 1973, 1974; New York, 1976,
   1978; 6 Series, 10 games.
N. L.—20—Carlton, Steven N., Philadelphia, 1976, 1977, 1978, 1980; 4 Series, 6
   games.

Most Runs Allowed, Series

3-game Series—A. L.— 9—Perry, James E., Minnesota, 1970.
     N. L.— 9—Niekro, Philip H., Atlanta, 1969.
4-game Series—N. L.—11—Perry, Gaylord J., San Francisco, 1971.
     A. L.— 10—Frost, C. David, California, 1979.
5-game Series—N. L.— 8—Gullett, Donald E., Cincinnati, 1972.
       Ryan, L. Nolan, Houston, 1980.
     A. L.— 8—Blue, Vida R., Oakland, 1973.
       Figueroa, Eduardo, New York, 1976.

Most Earned Runs Allowed, Series

3-game Series—A. L.— 8—Perry, James E., Minnesota, 1970.
              N. L.— 6—Koosman, Jerry M., New York, 1969.
                       Jarvis, R. Patrick, Atlanta, 1969.
4-game Series—N. L.—10—Perry, Gaylord J., San Francisco, 1971.
              A. L.— 9—Frost, C. David, California, 1979.
5-game Series—N. L.— 8—Gullett, Donald E., Cincinnati, 1972.
                       Ryan, L. Nolan, Houston, 1980.
              A. L.— 8—Blue, Vida R., Oakland, 1973.
                       Figueroa, Eduardo, New York, 1976.

Most Runs Allowed, Game

N. L.—9—Niekro, Philip H., Atlanta, October 4, 1969.
A. L.—8—Perry, James E., Minnesota, October 3, 1970.

Most Earned Runs Allowed, Game

A. L.—7—Perry, James E., Minnesota, October 3, 1970.
N. L.—7—Perry, Gaylord J., San Francisco, October 6, 1971.

Most Runs Allowed, Inning

A. L.—6—Perry, James E., Minnesota, October 3, 1970; fourth inning.
N. L.—5—Niekro, Philip H., Atlanta, October 4, 1969; eighth inning.
           Koosman, Jerry M., New York, October 5, 1969; fifth inning.
           Rau, Douglas J., Los Angeles, October 8, 1974, first inning.

Most Earned Runs Allowed, Inning

A. L.—6—Perry, James E., Minnesota, October 3, 1970; fourth inning.
N. L.—5—Koosman, Jerry M., New York, October 5, 1969; fifth inning.

Most Hits Allowed, Total Series

A. L.—57—Hunter, James A., Oakland, 1971, 1972, 1973, 1974; New York, 1976, 1978; 6 Series, 10 games.
N. L.—40—Carlton, Steven N., Philadelphia, 1976, 1977, 1978, 1980; 4 Series, 6 games.

Most Hits Allowed, Series

3-game Series—A. L.— 12—Holtzman, Kenneth D., Oakland, 1975.
              N. L.—10—Jarvis, R. Patrick, Atlanta, 1969.
4-game Series—N. L.— 19—Perry, Gaylord J., San Francisco, 1971.
              A. L.— 13—Leonard, Dennis P., Kansas City, 1978.
5-game Series—A. L.— 18—Gura, Lawrence C., Kansas City, 1976.
              N. L.— 16—Ryan, L. Nolan, Houston, 1980.

Most Hits Allowed, Game

A. L.— 12—Gura, Lawrence C., Kansas City, October 9, 1976.
N. L.—10—Jarvis, R. Patrick, Atlanta, October 6, 1969.
            Perry, Gaylord J., San Francisco, October 6, 1971.
            Hooton, Burt C., Los Angeles, October 4, 1978.

Fewest Hits Allowed Game, Nine Innings

A. L.—2—Blue, Vida R., Oakland, October 8, 1974.
N. L.—2—Grimsley, Ross A., Cincinnati, October 10, 1972.
           Matlack, Jonathan T., New York, October 7, 1973.

Most Hits Allowed, Inning

A. L.—6—Perry, James E., Minnesota, October 3, 1970; fourth inning.
N. L.—5—Blass, Stephen R., Pittsburgh, October 6, 1971; second inning.
           Moose, Robert R., Pittsburgh, October 8, 1972; first inning.
           Hooton, Burt C., Los Angeles, October 4, 1978; fifth inning.

Most Consecutive Hits Allowed, Inning (Consecutive At-Bats)

A. L.— 6— Perry, James E., Minnesota, October 3, 1970; fourth inning (sacrifice fly during streak).

N. L.— 5— Moose, Robert R., Pittsburgh, October 8, 1972; first inning.

Most Consecutive Hits Allowed, Inning (Consecutive Plate Appearances)

N. L.— 5— Moose, Robert R., Pittsburgh, October 8, 1972; first inning.

A. L.— 4— Perry, James E., Minnesota, October 3, 1970; fourth inning.
    Blue, Vida R., Oakland, October 5, 1975; fourth inning.
    May, Rudolph, New York, October 9, 1980; third inning.

Most Two-Base Hits Allowed, Game

N. L.— 4— Seaver, G. Thomas, New York, October 4, 1969.

A. L.— 4— McNally, David A., Baltimore, October 3, 1971.
    Blue, Vida R., Oakland, October 3, 1971.

Most Three-Base Hits Allowed, Game

A. L.— 2— Figueroa, Eduardo, New York, October 8, 1977.

N. L.— 2— Carlton, Steven N., Philadelphia, October 9, 1976.
    Christenson, Larry R., Philadelphia, October 4, 1978.

Most Home Runs Allowed, Total Series

A. L.— 12— Hunter, James A., Oakland, 1971 (4), 1972 (2), 1974 (3), New York, 1978 (3).

N. L.— 6— Blass, Stephen R., Pittsburgh, 1971 (4), 1972 (2).

Most Home Runs Allowed, Series

3-game Series—A. L.— 4— Hunter, James A., Oakland, 1971.
              N. L.— 3— Jarvis, R. Patrick, Atlanta, 1969.
4-game Series—N. L.— 4— Blass, Stephen R., Pittsburgh, 1971.
              A. L.— 3— Hunter, James A., Oakland, 1974; New York, 1978.
5-game Series—A. L.— 4— McNally, David A., Baltimore, 1973.
              N. L.— 2— Blass, Stephen R., Pittsburgh, 1972.
                       Seaver, G. Thomas, New York, 1973.

Most Home Runs Allowed, Game

A. L.— 4— Hunter, James A., Oakland, October 4, 1971.
    McNally, David A., Baltimore, October 7, 1973.

N. L.— 3— Jarvis, R. Patrick, Atlanta, October 6, 1969.

Most Home Runs With Bases Loaded Allowed, Game

A. L.— 1— Perry, James E., Minnesota, October 3, 1970; fourth inning.

N. L.— 1— Carlton, Steven N., Philadelphia, October 4, 1977; seventh inning.
    Lonborg, James R., Philadelphia, October 5, 1977; fourth inning.

Most Home Runs Allowed, Inning

A. L.— 2— Perry, James E., Minnesota, October 3, 1970; fourth inning.
    McNally, David A., Baltimore, October 4, 1970; fourth inning.
    McNally, David A., Baltimore, October 7, 1973; sixth inning.
    Hunter, James A., Oakland, October 5, 1974; fifth inning.
    Gura, Lawrence C., Kansas City, October 8, 1980; second inning.

N. L.— 2— Moose, Robert R., Pittsburgh, October 5, 1970; first inning.
    Blass, Stephen R., Pittsburgh, October 2, 1971; fifth inning.
    Blass, Stephen R., Pittsburgh, October 6, 1971; second inning.
    Rau, Douglas J., Los Angeles, October 8, 1974; first inning.
    Reed, Ronald L., Philadelphia, October 12, 1976; ninth inning.
    Norman, Fredie H., Cincinnati, October 5, 1979; third inning.

Most Consecutive Home Runs Allowed, Inning

N. L.— 2— Moose, Robert R., Pittsburgh, October 5, 1970; first inning.
    Reed, Ronald L., Philadelphia, October 12, 1976; ninth inning.

Most Consecutive Home Runs Allowed, Inning—Continued

A. L.— 2— Perry, James E., Minnesota, October 3, 1970; fourth inning.
McNally, David A., Baltimore, October 4, 1970; fourth inning.
McNally, David A., Baltimore, October 7, 1973; sixth inning.
Gura, Lawrence C., Kansas City, October 8, 1980; second inning.

Most Total Bases Allowed, Game

N. L.— 22— Jarvis, R. Patrick, Atlanta, October 6, 1969.
A. L.— 20— Hunter, James A., New York, October 6, 1978.

Most Bases on Balls, Total Series

N. L.— 23— Carlton, Steven N., Philadelphia, 1976, 1977, 1978, 1980; 4 Series, 6
games.
A. L.— 19— Cuellar, Miguel, Baltimore, 1969, 1970, 1971, 1973, 1974; 5 Series, 6
games.
Palmer, James A., Baltimore, 1969, 1970, 1971, 1973, 1974, 1979; 6
Series, 8 games.

Most Bases on Balls, Series

3-game Series—A. L.— 7—Boswell, David W., Minnesota, 1969.
N. L.— 5—Norman, Fredie H., Cincinnati, 1975.
Carlton, Steven N., Philadelphia, 1976.
4-game Series—A. L.— 13—Cuellar, Miguel, Baltimore, 1974.
N. L.— 8—Reuss, Jerry, Pittsburgh, 1974.
Carlton, Steven N., Philadelphia, 1977.
5-game Series—A. L.— 8—Palmer, James A., Baltimore, 1973.
N. L.— 8—Carlton, Steven N., Philadelphia, 1980.

Most Bases on Balls, Game

A. L.— 9— Cuellar, Miguel, Baltimore, October 9, 1974.
N. L.— 6— Kison, Bruce E., Pittsburgh, October 8, 1974.

Most Bases on Balls, Inning

A. L.— 4— Cuellar, Miguel, Baltimore, October 9, 1974; fifth inning, consecutive.
N. L.— 4— Hooton, Burt E., Los Angeles, October 7, 1977; second inning, consecutive.

Most Consecutive Bases on Balls, Inning

A. L.— 4— Cuellar, Miguel, Baltimore, October 9, 1974; fifth inning.
N. L.— 4— Hooton, Burt E., Los Angeles, October 7, 1977; second inning.

Most Strikeouts, Total Series

A. L.— 46— Palmer, James A., Baltimore, 1969, 1970, 1971, 1973, 1974, 1979; 8
Series, 6 games.
N. L.— 26— Carlton, Steven N., Philadelphia, 1976, 1977, 1978, 1980; 4 Series, 6
games.

Most Strikeouts, Series

3-game Series—N. L.—14—Candelaria, John R., Pittsburgh 1975.
A. L.—12—Palmer, James A., Baltimore, 1970.
4-game Series—N. L.—13—Sutton, Donald H., Los Angeles, 1974.
A. L.—11—Leonard, Dennis P., Kansas City, 1978.
5-game Series—N. L.—17—Seaver, G. Thomas, New York, 1973.
A. L.—15—Palmer, James A., Baltimore, 1973.

Most Strikeouts, Game

A. L.— 14— Coleman, Joseph H., Detroit, October 10, 1972.
N. L.— 14— Candelaria, John R., Pittsburgh, October 7, 1975 (pitched first 7⅔
innings of 10-inning game).

Ten or More Strikeouts by Pitchers in Championship Series Game

AMERICAN LEAGUE

Date	Pitcher and Club	SO.	Score
Oct. 5, 1969	McNally, Baltimore vs. Minnesota (11 inn.)	11	1-0
Oct. 5, 1970	Palmer, Baltimore vs. Minnesota	12	6-1
Oct. 10, 1972	Coleman, Detroit vs. Oakland	14	3-0
Oct. 6, 1973	Palmer, Baltimore, vs. Oakland	12	6-0
Oct. 9, 1973	Cuellar, Baltimore vs. Oakland (10 inn.)	11	1-2

NATIONAL LEAGUE

Date	Pitcher and Club	SO.	Score
Oct. 6, 1973	Seaver, New York vs. Cincinnati (8⅓ inn.)	13	1-2
Oct. 7, 1975	Candelaria, Pitts. vs. Cincinnati (7⅔ inn.)	14	3-5

Most Strikeouts, Game, Relief Pitcher

N. L.—7— Ryan, L. Nolan, New York, October 6, 1969; pitched 7 innings.
A. L.—4— Odom, Johnny L., Oakland, October 6, 1973; pitched 5 innings.
       Torrez, Michael A., New York, October 9, 1977; pitched 5⅓ innings.
       Aase, Donald W., California, October 5, 1979; pitched 4 innings.

Most Consecutive Strikeouts, Game

A. L.—4— Coleman, Joseph H., Detroit, October 10, 1972; 1 in fourth inning, 3 in fifth inning.
       Ryan, L. Nolan, California, October 3, 1979; 3 in first inning, 1 in second inning.
N. L.—4— Wilcox, Milton E., Cincinnati, October 5, 1970; 2 in sixth inning, 2 in seventh inning.
       Candelaria, John R., Pittsburgh, October 7, 1975; 3 in first inning, 1 in second inning.

Most Consecutive Strikeouts, Start of Game

N. L.—4— Candelaria, John R., Pittsburgh, October 7, 1975.
A. L.—4— Ryan, L. Nolan, California, October 3, 1979.

Most Strikeouts, Inning

A. L.-N. L.—3—Held by many pitchers.

Most Hit Batsmen, Total Series

A. L.—2— Fryman, Woodrow T., Detroit, 1972 (2).
N. L.—2— Seaver, G. Thomas, New York, 1969, 1973.
       John, Thomas E., Los Angeles, 1977 (2).
Both Leagues—2—Ellis, Dock P., Pittsburgh NL, 1971, New York AL, 1976.

Most Hit Batsmen, Series

A. L.—2— Fryman, Woodrow T., Detroit, 1972; 5-game Series.
N. L.—2— John, Thomas E., Los Angeles, 1977; 4-game Series.

Most Hit Batsmen, Game

A. L.—2— Fryman, Woodrow T., Detroit, October 12, 1972.
N. L.—1— Held by many pitchers.

Most Hit Batsmen, Inning

A. L.-N. L.—1—Held by many pitchers.

Most Wild Pitches, Total Series

N. L.—3— McGraw, Frank E., New York, 1973; Philadelphia, 1976 (2).
A. L.—2— Palmer, James A., Baltimore, 1969, 1971.
       Zachary, W. Chris, Detroit, 1972 (2).
       McNally, David A., Baltimore, 1973, 1974.

Most Wild Pitches, Series

A. L.—2— Zachary, W. Chris, Detroit, 1972; 5-game Series.

Most Wild Pitches, Series—Continued

   N. L.— 2— Marichal, Juan A., San Francisco, 1971; 4-game Series.
                 McGraw, Frank E., Philadelphia, 1976; 3-game Series.
                  Eastwick, Rawlins J., Cincinnati, 1976; 3-game Series.

Most Wild Pitches, Game

   A. L.— 2— Zachary, W. Chris, Detroit, October 8, 1972.
   N. L.— 2— Marichal, Juan A., San Francisco, October 5, 1971.

Most Wild Pitches, Inning

   A. L.— 2— Zachary, W. Chris, Detroit, October 8, 1972; fifth inning.
   N. L.— 1— Held by many pitchers.

Most Balks, Game

   A. L.— 1— Fryman, Woodrow T., Detroit, October 12, 1972; third inning.
                Hassler, Andrew E., Kansas City, October 6, 1977; fifth inning.
                Splittorff, Paul W., Kansas City, October 10, 1980; third inning.
   N. L.— 1— Brett, Kenneth A., Pittsburgh, October 5, 1975; sixth inning.
                Hernandez, Ramon G., Pittsburgh, October 7, 1975; tenth inning.
                Carlton, Steven N., Philadelphia, October 4, 1977; fifth inning.
                Sosa, Elias, Los Angeles, October 4, 1977; ninth inning.
                Leibrandt, Charles L., October 5, 1979; fourth inning.

CLUB PITCHING

Most Pitchers, Series, One Club

   3-game Series—N. L.— 10— Pittsburgh vs. Cincinnati, 1975.
                A. L.— 9— Minnesota vs. Baltimore, 1969, 1970.
   4-game Series—N. L.— 9— San Francisco vs. Pittsburgh, 1971.
                                Los Angeles vs. Philadelphia, 1977, 1978.
                A. L.— 9— California vs. Baltimore, 1979.
   5-game Series—N. L.— 10— Pittsburgh vs. Cincinnati, 1972.
                A. L.— 9— Kansas City vs. New York, 1976.

Most Pitchers, Series, Both Clubs

   3-game Series—N. L.— 17— Pittsburgh 10, Cincinnati 7, 1975.
                                Cincinnati 9, Pittsburgh 8, 1979.
                A. L.— 16— Minnesota 9, Baltimore 7, 1969.
   4-game Series—N. L.— 17— Los Angeles 9, Philadelphia 8, 1978.
                A. L.— 15— New York 8, Kansas City 7, 1978.
   5-game Series—N. L.— 18— Pittsburgh 10, Cincinnati 8, 1972.
                A. L.— 16— Oakland 8, Detroit 8, 1972.

Fewest Pitchers, Series, One Club

   3-game Series—A. L.— 4— Baltimore vs. Minnesota, 1970.
                            Baltimore vs. Oakland, 1971.
                            Kansas City vs. New York, 1980.
                N. L.— 5— Pittsburgh vs. Cincinnati, 1970.
   4-game Series—A. L.— 5— Oakland vs. Baltimore, 1974.
                            Baltimore vs. California, 1979.
                N. L.— 7— Pittsburgh vs. San Francisco, 1971.
                            Los Angeles vs. Pittsburgh, 1974.
                            Philadelphia vs. Los Angeles, 1977.
   5-game Series—N. L.— 6— New York vs. Cincinnati, 1973.
                A. L.— 6— Oakland vs. Baltimore, 1973.
                            New York vs. Kansas City, 1976, 1977.

Fewest Pitchers, Series, Both Clubs

3-game Series—A. L.— 10— New York 6, Kansas City 4, 1980.
       N. L.— 12— Cincinnati 7, Pittsburgh 5, 1970.
4-game Series—A. L.— 12— Baltimore 7, Oakland 5, 1974.
       N. L.— 15— Pittsburgh 8, Los Angeles 7, 1974.
5-game Series—A. L.— 13— Baltimore 7, Oakland 6, 1973.
       N. L.— 15— Cincinnati 9, New York 6 , 1973.

Most Appearances by Pitchers, Series, One Club

3-game Series—A. L.— 14— Minnesota vs. Baltimore, 1970.
       N. L.— 13— Cincinnati vs. Pittsburgh, 1979.
4-game Series—N. L.— 14— Philadelphia vs. Los Angeles, 1977.
       A. L.— 12— California vs. Baltimore, 1979.
5-game Series—N. L.— 21— Philadelphia vs. Houston, 1980.
       A. L.— 18— Kansas City vs. New York, 1976.

Most Appearances by Pitchers, Series, Both Clubs

3-game Series—N. L.— 25— Cincinnati 13, Pittsburgh 12, 1979.
       A. L.— 18— Minnesota 11, Baltimore 7, 1969.
          Minnesota 14, Baltimore 4, 1970.
4-game Series—N. L.— 26— Philadelphia 14, Los Angeles 12, 1977.
       A. L.— 20— Kansas City 11, New York 9, 1978.
5-game Series—N. L.— 36— Philadelphia 21, Houston 15, 1980.
       A. L.— 29— Oakland 16, Detroit 13, 1972.
          Kansas City 18, New York 11, 1976.

Most Pitchers, Game, One Club

A. L.— 7— Minnesota vs. Baltimore, October 6, 1969.
N. L.— 6— Atlanta vs. New York, October 5, 1969.
      San Francisco vs. Pittsburgh, October 3, 1971.
      Los Angeles vs. Philadelphia, October 7, 1977.
      Pittsburgh vs. Cincinnati, October 3, 1979; 10 innings.
      Cincinnati vs. Pittsburgh, October 5, 1979.
      Philadelphia vs. Houston October 11, 1980; 10 innings.
      Philadelphia vs. Houston, October 12, 1980; 10 innings.

Most Pitchers, Game, Winning Club

N. L.— 6— Los Angeles vs. Philadelphia, October 7, 1977.
      Pittsburgh vs. Cincinnati, October 3, 1979; 10 innings.
      Philadelphia vs. Houston, October 11, 1980; 10 innings.
      Philadelphia vs. Houston, October 12, 1980; 10 innings.
A. L.— 5— Baltimore vs. Minnesota, October 4, 1969; 12 innings.

Most Pitchers, Game, Losing Club

A. L.— 7— Minnesota vs. Baltimore, October 6, 1969.
N. L.— 6— Atlanta vs. New York, October 5, 1969.
      San Francisco vs. Pittsburgh, October 3, 1971.
      Cincinnati vs. Pittsburgh, October 5, 1979.

Most Pitchers, Game, Both Clubs

N. L.— 10— Los Angeles 6, Philadelphia 4, October 7, 1977.
       Pittsburgh 6, Cincinnati 4, October 3, 1979; 10 innings.
       Philadelphia 6, Houston 4, October 12, 1980; 10 innings.
A. L.— 9— Oakland 6, Detroit 3, October 11, 1972; 10 innings.
      Kansas City 6, New York 3, October 9, 1977.

Most Pitchers, Inning, One Club

A. L.— 5— Kansas City vs. New York, October 12, 1976; sixth inning.
N. L.— 3— Made in many games.

Most Complete Games, Series, One Club

3-game Series—A. L.— 2— Baltimore vs. Minnesota, 1969, 1970.
                          Baltimore vs. Oakland, 1971.
              N. L.— 1— Cincinnati vs. Pittsburgh, 1975.
                          Pittsburgh vs. Cincinnati, 1979.
4-game Series—A. L.— 2— Oakland vs. Baltimore, 1974.
              N. L.— 2— San Francisco vs. Pittsburgh, 1971.
                          Los Angeles vs. Philadelphia, 1977.
5-game Series—N. L.— 3— New York vs. Cincinnati, 1973.
              A. L.— 2— Oakland vs. Baltimore, 1973.
                          Baltimore vs. Oakland, 1973.

Most Complete Games, Series, Both Clubs

3-game Series—A. L.— 3— Baltimore 2, Oakland 1, 1971.
              N. L.— 1— Cincinnati 1, Pittsburgh 0, 1975.
                          Pittsburgh 1, Cincinnati 0, 1979.
4-game Series—A. L.— 3— Oakland 2, Baltimore 1, 1974.
              N. L.— 2— San Francisco 2, Pittsburgh 0, 1971.
                          Los Angeles 2, Philadelphia 0, 1977.
                          Los Angeles 1, Philadelphia 1, 1978.
5-game Series—A. L.— 4— Baltimore 2, Oakland 2, 1973.
              N. L.— 3— New York 3, Cincinnati 0, 1973.

Most Saves, Series, One Club

3-game Series—N. L.— 3— Cincinnati vs. Pittsburgh, 1970.
              A. L.— 2— Boston vs. Oakland, 1975.
4-game Series—N. L.— 3— Pittsburgh vs. San Francisco, 1971.
              A. L.— 2— New York vs. Kansas City, 1978.
5-game Series—N. L.— 2— Pittsburgh vs. Cincinnati, 1972.
                          Philadelphia vs. Houston, 1980.
              A. L.— 1— Held by many clubs.

Most Saves, Series, Both Clubs

3-game Series—N. L.— 3— Cincinnati 3, Pittsburgh 0, 1970.
              A. L.— 2— Boston 2, Oakland 0, 1975.
4-game Series—N. L.— 3— Pittsburgh 3, San Francisco 0, 1971.
              A. L.— 2— New York 2, Kansas City 0, 1978.
5-game Series—N. L.— 5— Houston 3, Philadelphia 2, 1980.
              A. L.— 2— Kansas City 1, New York 1, 1976.

Fewest Saves, Series, One Club and Both Clubs

A. L.-N. L.—0—Held by many clubs in Series of all lengths.

Most Runs Allowed, Total Series, One Club

N. L.— 87— Pittsburgh; 6 Series, 22 games.
A. L.— 77— New York; 4 Series, 17 games.

Most Shutouts Won, Total Series

A. L.— 4— Oakland, 1972, 1973, 1974 (2).
N. L.— 2— Los Angeles, 1974, 1978.

Most Shutouts Lost, Total Series

A. L.— 3— Baltimore, 1973, 1974 (2).
N. L.— 2— Pittsburgh, 1970, 1974.
              Philadelphia, 1978, 1980.

Most Shutouts Won, Series, One Club

A. L.— 2— Oakland vs. Baltimore, 1974; 4-game Series.
N. L.— 1— Held by many clubs.

Most Consecutive Shutouts Won, Series, One Club

   A. L.– 2– Oakland vs. Baltimore, October 6, 8, 1974.
   N. L.– 1– Held by many clubs.

Most Shutouts, Series, Both Clubs

   N. L.– 2– Los Angeles 1, Pittsburgh 1, 1974; 4-game Series.
   A. L.– 2– Oakland 1, Detroit 1, 1972; 5-game Series.
            Oakland 1, Baltimore 1, 1973; 5-game Series.
            Oakland 2, Baltimore 0, 1974; 4-game Series.

Most Consecutive Games, Total Series, Without Being Shut Out

   A. L.– 17– Kansas City, October 9, 1976 through October 10, 1980.
            New York, October 9, 1976 through October 10, 1980.
   N. L.– 12– Cincinnati, October 8, 1973 through October 5, 1979.

Most Consecutive Innings Shut Out Opponent, Total Series

   A. L.– 31 – Oakland vs. Baltimore, October 5 (last one-third of fifth inning) to
            October 9, 1974 (first two-thirds of ninth inning).
   N. L.– 18⅓– Houston vs. Philadelphia, October 8 (last one-third of tenth inning)
            to October 11 (through seven innings).

Most Consecutive Innings Shut Out Opponent, Series

   A. L.– 31 – Oakland vs. Baltimore, October 5 (last one-third of fifth inning) to
            October 9, 1974 (first two-thirds of ninth inning).
   N. L.– 18⅓– Houston vs. Philadelphia, October 8 (last one-third of tenth inning)
            to October 11 (through seven innings).

Largest Score, Shutout Game

   A. L.– 8 - 0– Baltimore 8, California 0, October 6, 1979.
   N. L.– 7 - 0– Pittsburgh 7, Los Angeles 0, October 8, 1974.

Longest Shutout Game

   A. L.– 11 innings– Baltimore 1, Minnesota 0, October 5, 1969.
   N. L.– 11 innings– Houston 1, Philadelphia 0, October 10, 1980.

Championship Series 1-0 Games

   A. L.– Baltimore 1, Minnesota 0, October 5, 1969; 11 innings.
         Oakland 1, Baltimore 0, October 8, 1974.
   N. L.– Houston 1, Philadelphia 0, October 10, 1980; 11 innings.

Most Wild Pitches, Series, One Club

   N. L.– 3– San Francisco vs. Pittsburgh, 1971; 4-game Series.
   A. L.– 3– California vs. Baltimore, 1979; 4-game Series.

Most Wild Pitches, Series, Both Clubs

   A. L.– 4– Detroit 2, Oakland 2, 1972; 5-game Series.
   N. L.– 4– San Francisco 3, Pittsburgh 1, 1971; 4-game Series.
            Cincinnati 2, Pittsburgh 2, 1972; 5-game Series.
            Cincinnati 2, Philadelphia 2, 1976; 3-game Series.

Most Balks, Series, One Club

   N. L.– 2– Pittsburgh vs. Cincinnati, 1975; 3-game Series.
   A. L.– 1– Detroit vs.Oakland, 1972; 5-game Series.
            Kansas City vs. New York, 1977; 5-game Series.
            Kansas City vs. New York, 1980; 3-game Series.

Most Balks, Series, Both Clubs

   N. L.– 2– Pittsburgh 2, Cincinnati 0, 1975; 3-game Series.
            Philadelphia 1, Los Angeles 1, 1977; 4-game Series.
   A. L.– 1– Detroit 1, Oakland 0, 1972; 5-game Series.
            Kansas City 1, New York 0, 1977; 5-game Series.
            Kansas City 1, New York 0, 1980; 3-game Series.

Fewest Balks, Series, One Club and Both Clubs
  A. L.-N. L.—0—Held by many clubs in Series of all lengths.

GENERAL CLUB RECORDS

Most Series Played
  A. L.—6— Baltimore, 1969, 1970, 1971, 1973, 1974, 1979; won 4, lost 2.
  N. L.—6— Pittsburgh, 1970, 1971, 1972, 1974, 1975, 1979; won 2, lost 4.
        Cincinnati, 1970, 1972, 1973, 1975 1976, 1979; won 4, lost 2.

Most Series Won
  N. L.—4— Cincinnati, 1970, 1972, 1975, 1976; lost 2.
  A. L.—4— Baltimore, 1969, 1970, 1971, 1979; lost 2.

Most Consecutive Years Winning Series
  A. L.—3— Baltimore, 1969, 1970, 1971.
        Oakland, 1972, 1973, 1974.
        New York, 1976, 1977, 1978.
  N. L.—2— Cincinnati, 1975, 1976.
        Los Angeles, 1977, 1978.

Most Series Lost
  N. L.—4— Pittsburgh, 1970, 1972, 1974, 1975; won 2.
  A. L.—3— Kansas City, 1976, 1977, 1978; won 1.

Most Consecutive Years Losing Series
  A. L.—3— Kansas City, 1976, 1977, 1978.
  N. L.—3— Philadelphia, 1976, 1977, 1978.

Most Times Winning Series in Three Consecutive Games
  A. L.—3— Baltimore, 1969, 1970, 1971.
  N. L.—3— Cincinnati, 1970, 1975, 1976.

Winning Series After Winning First Game
  A. L.—Accomplished 9 times.
  N. L.—Accomplished 8 times.

Winning Series After Losing First Game
  N. L.—Accomplished 4 times.
  A. L.—Accomplished 3 times.

Winning Series After Winning One Game and Losing Two
  N. L.—Cincinnati vs. Pittsburgh, 1972.
        Philadelphia vs. Houston, 1980.
  A. L.—New York vs. Kansas City, 1977.

Winning Series After Losing First Two Games
  A. L.-N. L.—Never accomplished.

Most Games Played, Total Series
  A. L.—22— Baltimore, 6 Series; won 15, lost 7.
  N. L.—22— Pittsburgh, 6 Series; won 9, lost 13.
        Cincinnati, 6 Series; won 14, lost 8.

Most Games Won, Total Series
  A. L.—15— Baltimore, 6 Series; won 15, lost 7.
  N. L.—14— Cincinnati, 6 Series; won 14, lost 8.

Most Games Lost, Total Series
  N. L.—13— Pittsburgh, 6 Series; won 9, lost 13.
  A. L.—11— Oakland, 5 Series; won 9, lost 11.

Most Extra-Inning Games, Total Series

   N. L.— 5— Cincinnati, 6 Series, 22 games; won 3 lost 2.
            Philadelphia, 4 Series, 16 games; won 2, lost 3.
   A. L.— 4— Baltimore, 6 Series, 22 games; won 3, lost 1.

Most Extra-Inning Games Won, Total Series

   N. L.— 3— Cincinnati, 6 Series, 22 games; won 3, lost 1.
   A. L.— 3— Baltimore, 6 Series, 22 games; won 3, lost 1.

Most Extra-Inning Games Lost, Total Series

   N. L.— 3— Philadelphia, 4 Series, 16 games; won 2, lost 3.
   A. L.— 2— Minnesota, 2 Series, 6 games; won 0, lost 2.

Most Extra-Inning Games, Series

   3-game Series—A. L.— 2— Baltimore vs. Minnesota, 1969.
                N. L.— 2— Cincinnati vs. Pittsburgh, 1979.
   4-game Series—N. L.— 1— Los Angeles vs. Philadelphia, 1978.
                A. L.— 1— Baltimore vs. California, 1979.
   5-game Series—N. L.— 4— Philadelphia vs. Houston, 1980.
                A. L.— 2— Detroit vs. Oakland, 1972.

Most Games Decided by One Run, Total Series

   A. L.— 8— Baltimore, 6 Series; won 4, lost 4.
   N. L.— 7— Cincinnati, 6 Series; won 5, lost 2.

Most Games Won by One Run, Total Series

   A. L.— 5— Oakland, 5 Series; won 5, lost 2.
   N. L.— 5— Cincinnati, 6 Series; won 5, lost 2.

Most Games Lost by One Run, Total Series

   A. L.— 4— Baltimore; 6 Series, won 4, lost 4.
   N. L.— 4— Philadelphia; 4 Series, won 1, lost 4.

Most Games Won by One Run, Series, One Club

   3-game Series—A. L.— 2— Baltimore vs. Minnesota, 1969.
                N. L.— 1— Occurred often.
   4-game Series—A. L.— 2— Oakland vs. Baltimore, 1974.
                     New York vs. Kansas City, 1978.
                N. L.— 1— Occurred often.
   5-game Series—A. L.— 2— Oakland vs. Detroit, 1972.
                N. L.— 2— Cincinnati vs. New York, 1973.

Most Games Decided by One Run, Series, Both Clubs

   3-game Series—A. L.— 2— Baltimore (won 2) vs. Minnesota, 1969.
                N. L.— 1— Occurred often.
   4-game Series—A. L.— 2— Oakland (won 2) vs. Baltimore, 1974.
                     New York (won 2) vs. Kansas City, 1978.
                     Baltimore (won 1) vs. California (won 1), 1979.
                N. L.— 2— San Francisco (won 1) vs. Pittsburgh (won 1), 1971.
   5-game Series—A. L.— 3— Oakland (won 2) vs. Detroit (won 1), 1972.
                N. L.— 2— Pittsburgh (won 1) vs. Cincinnati (won 1), 1972.
                     Cincinnati (won 2) vs. New York, 1973.
                     Philadelphia (won 1) vs. Houston (won 1), 1980.

Most Consecutive Series Won, Division

   N. L.— 5— West Division, 1974, 1975, 1976, 1977, 1978.
   A. L.— 5— East Division, 1975, 1976, 1977, 1978, 1979.

Most Consecutive Games Won, League, Total Series

   A. L.— 10— Baltimore, 1969 (3), 1970 (3), 1971 (3), 1973 (first 1).
   N. L.— 6— Cincinnati, 1975 (3), 1976 (3).

Most Consecutive Games Lost, League, Total Series

  A. L.— 6— Minnesota, 1969 (3), 1970 (3).
  N. L.— 5— Philadelphia, 1977 (last 3), 1978 (first 2).

Most Consecutive Games Won, Division

  A. L.— 9— East Division, 1969 (3), 1970 (3), 1971 (3).
  N. L.— 7— West Division, 1974 (last 1), 1975 (3), 1976 (3).

Earliest Date for Championship Series Game

  N. L.—October 2, 1971, at San Francisco; San Francisco 5, Pittsburgh 4.
      October 2, 1979, at Cincinnati; Pittsburgh 5, Cincinnati 2; 11 innings.
  A. L.—October 3, 1970, at Minnesota; Baltimore 10, Minnesota 6.
      October 3, 1971, at Baltimore; Baltimore 5, Oakland 3.
      October 3, 1978, at Kansas City; New York 7, Kansas City 1.
      October 3, 1979, at Baltimore; Baltimore 6, California 3; 10 innings.

Earliest Date for Championship Series Final Game

  N. L.—October 5, 1970, at Cincinnati; Cincinnati 3, Pittsburgh 2; 3-game Series.
      October 5, 1979, at Pittsburgh; Pittsburgh 7, Cincinnati 1; 3-game Series.
  A. L.—October 5, 1970, at Baltimore; Baltimore 6, Minnesota 1; 3-game Series.
      October 5, 1971, at Oakland; Baltimore 5, Oakland 3; 3-game Series.

Latest Date for Championship Series Start

  N. L.—October 9, 1976, at Philadelphia; Cincinnati 6, Philadelphia 3; 3-game
      Series ended at Cincinnati on October 12, 1976.
  A. L.—October 9, 1976, at Kansas City; New York 4, Kansas City 1; 5-game Series
      ended at New York on October 14, 1976.

Latest Date for Championship Series Finish

  A. L.—October 14, 1976-Series started October 9, 1976 at Kansas City; 5-game
      Series ended at New York.
  N. L.—October 12, 1976-Series started October 9, 1976 at Philadelphia; 3-game
      Series ended at Cincinnati.
      October 12, 1980—Series started October 7, 1980 at Philadelphia; 5-game
      Series ended at Houston.

Longest Game

  A. L.—12 innings— Baltimore 4, Minnesota 3, at Baltimore, October 4, 1969.
  N. L.—12 innings— Cincinnati 2, New York 1, at New York, October 9, 1973.

Longest Game by Time, Nine Innings

  N. L.—3 hours, 23 minutes-Pittsburgh 9, San Francisco 4, at San Francisco,
      October 3, 1971.
  A. L.—3 hours, 13 minutes-New York 7, Kansas City 6, at New York, October 14,
      1976.

Longest Game by Time, Extra Innings

  N. L.—3 hours, 55 minutes-Philadelphia 5, Houston 3, at Houston, October 11,
      1980, 10 innings.
  A. L.—3 hours, 29 minutes-Baltimore 4, Minnesota 3, at Baltimore, October 4,
      1969, 12 innings.

Shortest Game by Time

  A. L.—1 hour, 57 minutes-Oakland 1, Baltimore 0, at Baltimore, October 8, 1974.
  N. L.—1 hour, 57 minutes-Pittsburgh 5, Cincinnati 1, at Pittsburgh, October 7,
      1972.

MOST PLAYERS USED AT POSITIONS

Most Players, Series, One Club

3-game Series—A. L.— 24— Minnesota vs. Baltimore, 1970.
N. L.— 24— Pittsburgh vs. Cincinnati, 1975.
4-game Series—N. L.— 23— Los Angeles vs. Philadelphia, 1977.
A. L.— 23— California vs. Baltimore, 1979.
5-game Series—A. L.— 25— Oakland vs. Detroit, 1972.
N. L.— 24— Cincinnati vs. New York, 1973.
Houston vs. Philadelphia, 1980.

Most Players, Series, Both Clubs

3-game Series—A. L.— 42— Minnesota 22, Baltimore 20, 1969.
N. L.— 42— Pittsburgh 24, Cincinnati 18, 1975.
4-game Series—N. L.— 44— Los Angeles 22, Pittsburgh 22, 1974.
Los Angeles 23, Philadelphia 21, 1977.
Los Angeles 22, Philadelphia 22, 1978.
A. L.— 43— California 23, Baltimore 20, 1979.
5-game Series—A. L.— 49— Oakland 25, Detroit 24, 1972.
N. L.— 47— Houston 24, Philadelphia 23, 1980.

Fewest Players, Series, One Club

3-game Series—A. L.— 14— Baltimore vs. Minnesota, 1970.
Boston vs. Oakland, 1975.
N. L.— 17— New York vs. Atlanta, 1969.
4-game Series—A. L.— 20— Oakland vs. Baltimore, 1974.
Kansas City vs. New York, 1978.
Baltimore vs. California, 1979.
N. L.— 21— Pittsburgh vs. San Francisco, 1971.
5-game Series—N. L.— 17— New York vs. Cincinnati, 1973.
A. L.— 18— New York vs. Kansas City, 1977.

Fewest Players, Series, Both Clubs

3-game Series—A. L.— 35— Oakland 20, Baltimore 15, 1971.
New York 20, Kansas City 15, 1980.
N. L.— 38— Cincinnati 20, Pittsburgh 18, 1970.
4-game Series—A. L.— 41— New York 21, Kansas City 20, 1978.
N. L.— 43— San Francisco 22, Pittsburgh 21, 1971.
5-game Series—A. L.— 40— Kansas City 22, New York 18, 1977.
N. L.— 41— Cincinnati 24, New York 17, 1973.

Most Times, One Club Using Only Nine Players in Game, Series

3-game Series—A. L.— 2— Baltimore vs. Minnesota, 1970.
N. L.— 1— Cincinnati vs. Pittsburgh, 1975.
4-game Series—N. L.— 1— Los Angeles vs. Pittsburgh, 1974.
Los Angeles vs. Philadelphia, 1977.
A. L.— 0— Never accomplished.
5-game Series—N. L.— 3— New York vs. Cincinnati, 1973.
A. L.— 0— Never accomplished.

Most Players, Game, One Club

A. L.— 20— Oakland vs. Detroit, October 10, 1972.
Oakland vs. Detroit, October 11, 1972; 10 innings.
N. L.— 20— Philadelphia vs. Houston, October 12, 1980; 10 innings.
N. L.—Nine-inning record—19— Los Angeles vs. Philadelphia, October 7, 1977.

Most Players, Nine-Inning Game, Both Clubs

N. L.— 34— Los Angeles, 19, Philadelphia 15, October 7, 1977.
A. L.— 33— New York 18, Kansas City 15, October 13, 1976.

Most Players, Extra-Inning Game, Both Clubs

   A. L.—34— Oakland 20, Detroit 14, October 11, 1972; 10 innings.

   N. L.—37—Philadelphia 20, Houston 17, October 12, 1980; 10 innings.

FIRST BASEMEN

Most First Basemen, Series, One Club

   3-game Series—A. L.— 3— Oakland vs. Boston, 1975.
                N. L.— 2— Held by many clubs.
   4-game Series—N. L.— 3— Philadelphia vs. Los Angeles, 1977.
                A. L.— 2— Held by many clubs.
   5-game Series—A. L.— 3— Oakland vs. Baltimore, 1973.
                           Kansas City vs. New York, 1977.
                N. L.— 3— Houston vs. Philadelphia, 1980.

Most First Basemen, Series, Both Clubs

   3-game Series—A. L.— 4— Oakland 3, Boston 1, 1975.
                N. L.— 4— Cincinnati 2, Pittsburgh 2, 1970.
   4-game Series—A. L.— 4— Baltimore 2, Oakland 2, 1974.
                N. L.— 4— Philadelphia 3, Los Angeles 1, 1977.
   5-game Series—A. L.— 5— Oakland 3, Baltimore 2, 1973.
                N. L.— 4— Houston 3, Philadelphia 1, 1980.

Most First Basemen, Game, One Club

   A. L.-N. L.—2—Made in many games.

Most First Basemen, Game, Both Clubs

   A. L.-N. L.—3—Made in many games.

SECOND BASEMEN

Most Second Basemen, Series, One Club

   3-game Series—A. L.— 3— Minnesota vs. Baltimore, 1970.
                           Oakland vs. Boston, 1975.
                N. L.— 2— Held by many clubs.
   4-game Series—A. L.— 3— New York vs. Kansas City, 1978.
                N. L.— 1— Held by many clubs.
   5-game Series—A. L.— 4— Oakland vs. Detroit, 1972.
                N. L.— 2— Pittsburgh vs. Cincinnati, 1972.
                           Houston vs. Philadelphia, 1980.

Most Second Basemen, Series, Both Clubs

   3-game Series—A. L.— 4— Minnesota 3, Baltimore 1, 1970.
                           Oakland 3, Boston 1, 1975.
                N. L.— 3— Made in many Series.
   4-game Series—A. L.— 4— New York 3, Kansas City 1, 1978.
                N. L.— 2— Made in many Series.
   5-game Series—A. L.— 6— Oakland 4, Detroit 2, 1972.
                N. L.— 3— Pittsburgh 2, Cincinnati 1, 1972.
                           Houston 2, Philadelphia 1, 1980.

Most Second Basemen, Game, One Club

   A. L.—3— Minnesota vs. Baltimore, October 3, 1970.
            Oakland vs. Detroit, October 7, 1972; 11 innings.
            Oakland vs. Detroit, October 10, 1972.
            Oakland vs. Boston, October 7, 1975.
            New York vs. Kansas City, October 4, 1978.
   N. L.—2— Made in many games.

Most Second Basemen, Game, Both Clubs

A. L.— 4— Minnesota 3, Baltimore 1, October 3, 1970.
Oakland 3, Detroit 1, October 7, 1972; 11 innings.
Oakland 3, Detroit 1, October 10, 1972.
Oakland 3, Boston 1, October 7, 1975.
New York 3, Kansas City 1, October 4, 1978.
N. L.— 3— Made in many games.

THIRD BASEMEN

Most Third Basemen, Series, One Club

3-game Series—A. L.— 2— Minnesota vs. Baltimore, 1970.
New York vs. Kansas City, 1980.
N. L.— 2— Cincinnati vs. Pittsburgh, 1970.
Pittsburgh vs. Cincinnati, 1970.
4-game Series—N. L.— 3— San Francisco vs. Pittsburgh, 1971.
A.L.— 1— Held by all clubs.
5-game Series—A. L.— 2— Baltimore vs. Oakland, 1973.
N. L.— 2— Cincinnati vs. New York, 1973.

Most Third Basemen, Series, Both Clubs

3-game Series—N. L.— 4— Cincinnati 2, Pittsburgh 2, 1970.
A. L.— 3— Minnesota 2, Baltimore 1, 1970.
New York 2, Kansas City 1, 1980.
4-game Series—N. L.— 5— San Francisco 3, Pittsburgh 2, 1971.
A. L.— 2— Made in all Series.
5-game Series—A. L.— 3— Baltimore 2, Oakland 1, 1973.
N. L.— 3— Cincinnati 2, New York 1, 1973.

Most Third Basemen, Game, One Club

A. L.— 2— Baltimore vs. Oakland, October 7, 1973.
New York vs. Kansas City, October 10, 1980.
N. L.— 2— Held by many clubs.

Most Third Basemen, Game, Both Clubs

A. L.— 3— Baltimore 2, Oakland 1, October 7, 1973.
New York 2, Kansas City 1, October 10, 1980.
N. L.— 3— Made in many games.

SHORTSTOPS

Most Shortstops, Series, One Club

3-game Series—N. L.— 3— Pittsburgh vs. Cincinnati, 1975.
A. L.— 1— Held by many clubs.
4-game Series—N. L.— 3— Pittsburgh vs. Los Angeles, 1974.
A. L.— 3— California vs. Baltimore, 1979.
5-game Series—A. L.— 4— Oakland vs. Detroit, 1972.
N. L.— 3— Cincinnati vs. New York, 1973.

Most Shortstops, Series, Both Clubs

3-game Series—N. L.— 4— Cincinnati 2, Pittsburgh 2, 1970.
Pittsburgh 3, Cincinnati 1, 1975.
A. L.— 2— Made in all Series.
4-game Series—A. L.— 5— California 3, Baltimore 2, 1979.
N. L.— 4— Pittsburgh 3, Los Angeles 1, 1974.
5-game Series—A. L.— 6— Oakland 4, Detroit 2, 1972.
N. L.— 4— Cincinnati 3, New York 1, 1973.

Most Shortstops, Game, One Club

N. L.— 3— Cincinnati vs. New York, October 9, 1973; 12 innings.
Pittsburgh vs. Los Angeles, October 6, 1974.
Pittsburgh vs. Cincinnati, October 7, 1975; 10 innings.
A. L.— 3— Oakland vs. Detroit, October 11, 1972; 10 innings.
Nine-inning record— 2— Held by many clubs.

Most Shortstops, Game, Both Clubs

A. L.— 4— Oakland 3, Detroit 1, October 11, 1972; 10 innings.
Nine-inning record— 3— Made in many games.
N. L.— 4— Cincinnati 3, New York 1, October 9, 1973; 12 innings.
Pittsburgh 3, Los Angeles 1, October 6, 1974.
Pittsburgh 3, Cincinnati 1, October 7, 1975; 10 innings.

LEFT FIELDERS

Most Left Fielders, Series, One Club

3-game Series—N. L.— 4— Cincinnati vs. Pittsburgh, 1970.
          A. L.— 3— New York vs. Kansas City, 1980.
4-game Series—A. L.— 3— Kansas City vs. New York, 1978.
          New York vs. Kansas City, 1978.
          Baltimore vs. California, 1979.
          California vs. Baltimore, 1979.
    N. L.— 2— Los Angeles vs. Pittsburgh, 1974.
          Pittsburgh vs. Los Angeles, 1974.
5-game Series—A. L.— 3— Detroit vs. Oakland, 1972.
          Kansas City vs. New York, 1977.
    N. L.— 5— Philadelphia vs. Houston, 1980.

Most Left Fielders, Series, Both Clubs

3-game Series—N. L.— 6— Cincinnati 4, Pittsburgh 2, 1970.
          A. L.— 4— Baltimore 2, Minnesota 2, 1970.
          Baltimore 2, Oakland 2, 1971.
          New York 3, Kansas City 1, 1980.
4-game Series—A. L.— 6— Kansas City 3, New York 3, 1978.
          Baltimore 3, California 3, 1979.
    N. L.— 4— Los Angeles 2, Pittsburgh 2, 1974.
5-game Series—A. L.— 5— Kansas City 3, New York 2, 1977.
    N. L.— 6— Philadelphia 5, Houston 1, 1980.

Most Left Fielders, Game, One Club

N. L.— 3— Philadelphia vs. Cincinnati, October 12, 1976.
Philadelphia vs. Houston, October 11, 1980; 10 innings.
A. L.— 2— Held by many clubs.

Most Left Fielders, Game, Both Clubs

A. L.— 4— Kansas City 2, New York 2, October 6, 1978.
N. L.— 4— Cincinnati 2, Pittsburgh 2, October 3, 1970; 10 innings.
Philadelphia 3, Cincinnati 1, October 12, 1976.
Philadelphia 3, Houston 1, October 11, 1980; 10 innings.

CENTER FIELDERS

Most Center Fielders, Series, One Club

3-game Series—A. L.— 2— Held by many clubs.
          N. L.— 2— Cincinnati vs. Pittsburgh, 1979.
4-game Series—A. L.— 3— New York vs. Kansas City, 1978.
          N. L.— 2— Held by many clubs.
5-game Series—A. L.— 3— Oakland vs. Baltimore, 1973.

N. L.—2—Cincinnati vs. New York, 1973.
New York vs. Cincinnati, 1973.
Houston vs. Philadelphia, 1980.

Most Center Fielders, Series, Both Clubs

3-game Series—A. L.— 4— Baltimore 2, Oakland 2. 1971.
N. L.— 3— Cincinnati 2, Pittsburgh, 1979.
4-game Series—A. L.— 4— New York 3, Kansas City 1, 1978.
N. L.— 4— Los Angeles 2, Philadelphia 2, 1977.
5-game Series—A. L.— 5— Oakland 3, Baltimore 2, 1973.
N. L.— 4— Cincinnati 2, New York 2, 1973.

Most Center Fielders, Game, One Club

A. L.-N. L.—2—Held by many clubs.

Most Center Fielders, Game, Both Clubs

A. L.-N. L.—3—Made in many games.

RIGHT FIELDERS

Most Right Fielders, Series, One Club

3-game Series— N. L.— 2— New York vs. Atlanta, 1969.
Philadelphia vs. Cincinnati, 1976.
A. L.— 2— Kansas City vs. New York, 1980.
4-game Series— N. L.— 3— Held by many clubs.
A. L.— 2— Held by many clubs.
5-game Series— N. L.— 4— Houston vs. Philadelphia, 1980.
A. L.— 3— Baltimore vs. Oakland, 1973.
Kansas City vs. New York, 1976.

Most Right Fielders, Series, Both Clubs

3-game Series— N. L.— 3— New York 2, Atlanta 1, 1969.
Philadelphia 2, Cincinnati 1, 1976.
A. L.— 3— Kansas City 2, New York 1, 1980.
4-game Series— N. L.— 6— Los Angeles 3, Pittsburgh 3, 1974.
A. L.— 4— Baltimore 2, Oakland 2, 1974.
5-game Series— N. L.— 6— Houston 4, Philadelphia 2, 1980.
A. L.— 5— Kansas City 3, New York 2, 1976.

Most Right Fielders, Game, One Club

A. L.-N. L.—2—Made in many games.

Most Right Fielders, Game, Both Clubs

A. L.— 4— Kansas City 2, New York 2, October 13, 1976.
N. L.— 4— Pittsburgh 2, Los Angeles 2, October 8, 1974.
Houston 2, Philadelphia 2, October 11, 1980; 10 innings.

CATCHERS

Most Catchers, Series, One Club

3-game Series—N. L.— 3— Philadelphia vs. Cincinnati, 1976.
A. L.— 2— Held by many clubs.
4-game Series—A. L.— 2— Baltimore vs. Oakland, 1974.
Baltimore vs. California, 1979.
N. L.— 2— Los Angeles vs. Pittsburgh, 1974.
Los Angeles vs. Philadelphia, 1977, 1978.
Philadelphia vs. Los Angeles, 1977, 1978.
5-game Series—A. L.— 3— Kansas City vs. New York, 1976.
N. L.— 3— Houston vs. Philadelphia, 1980.

Most Catchers, Series, Both Clubs

  3-game Series—N. L.—4— Philadelphia 3, Cincinnati 1, 1976.
                A. L.—4— Baltimore 2, Minnesota 2, 1969, 1970.
                        Baltimore 2, Oakland 2, 1971.
  4-game Series—N. L.—4— Los Angeles 2, Philadelphia 2, 1977, 1978.
                A. L.—3— Baltimore 2, Oakland 1, 1974.
                        Baltimore 2, California 1, 1979.
  5-game Series—N. L.—5— Houston 3, Philadelphia 2, 1980.
                A. L.—4— Made in many Series.

Most Catchers, Game, One Club

  A. L.-N. L.—2—Held by many clubs.

Most Catchers, Game, Both Clubs

  A. L.—4— Baltimore 2, Minnesota 2, October 4, 1969; 12 innings.
  Nine-inning record—A. L.-N. L.—3—Made in many games.

PITCHERS

See CLUB PITCHING RECORDS on page 462.

RECORDS OF CHAMPIONSHIP SERIES MANAGERS
AMERICAN LEAGUE (11)

		Series		Games	
	Series	Won	Lost	Won	Lost
Dark, Alvin R., Oakland (West)	2	1	1	3	4
Fregosi, James L., California (West)	1	0	1	1	3
Frey, James G., Kansas City (West)	1	1	0	3	0
Herzog, Dorrell N. E., Kansas City (West)	3	0	3	5	9
Howser, Richard D., New York (East)	1	0	1	0	3
Johnson, Darrell D., Boston (East)	1	1	0	3	0
Lemon, Robert G., New York (East)	1	1	0	3	1
Martin, Alfred M., Minnesota (West), Detroit (East), New York (East)	4	2	2	8	10
Rigney, William J., Minnesota (West)	1	0	1	0	3
Weaver, Earl S., Baltimore (East)	6	4	2	15	7
Williams, Richard H., Oakland (West)	3	2	1	6	7

NATIONAL LEAGUE (13)

		Series		Games	
	Series	Won	Lost	Won	Lost
Alston, Walter E., Los Angeles (West)	1	1	0	3	1
Anderson, George L., Cincinnati (West)	5	4	1	14	5
Berra, Lawrence P., New York (East)	1	1	0	3	2
Fox, Charles F., San Francisco (West)	1	0	1	1	3
Green, G. Dallas, Philadelphia (East)	1	1	0	3	2
Harris, C. Luman, Atlanta (East)	1	0	1	0	3
Hodges, Gilbert R., New York (East)	1	1	0	3	0
Lasorda, Thomas C., Los Angeles (West)	2	2	0	6	2
McNamara, John F., Cincinnati (West)	1	0	1	0	3
Murtaugh, Daniel E., Pittsburgh (East)	4	1	3	4	10
Ozark, Daniel L., Philadelphia (East)	3	0	3	2	9
Tanner, Charles W., Pittsburgh (East)	1	1	0	3	0
Virdon, William C., Pitts. (East), Hous. (West)	2	0	2	4	6

Most Series, Manager

A. L.— 6— Weaver, Earl S., Baltimore, 1969, 1970, 1971, 1973, 1974, 1979; won 4, lost 2.

N. L.— 5— Anderson, George L., Cincinnati, 1970, 1972, 1973, 1975, 1976; won 4, lost 1.

Most Championship Series Winners Managed

N. L.— 4— Anderson, George L., Cincinnati, 1970, 1972, 1975, 1976.

A. L.— 4— Weaver, Earl S., Baltimore, 1969, 1970, 1971, 1979.

Most Championship Series Losers Managed

A. L.— 3— Herzog, Dorrell N. E., Kansas City, 1976, 1977, 1978.

N. L.— 3— Murtaugh, Daniel E., Pittsburgh, 1970, 1974, 1975.

          Ozark, Daniel L., Philadelphia, 1976, 1977, 1978.

Most Different Clubs Managed, League

A. L.— 3— Martin, Alfred M., Minnesota 1970, Detroit 1972, New York 1976, 1977.

N. L.— 2— Virdon, William C., Pittsburgh 1972, Houston 1980.

CHAMPIONSHIP SERIES UMPIRES
AMERICAN LEAGUE (41)

Anthony, G. Merlyn 1973
Barnett, Lawrence R. 1972, 1976, 1979
Berry, Charles 1970
Bremigan, Nicholas G. 1977
Brinkman, Joseph N. 1976, 1980
Chylak, Nestor 1969, 1972, 1973
Clark, Alan M. 1979
Cooney, Terrance J. 1978
Deegan, William E. 1970, 1974, 1977
Denkinger, Donald A. 1972, 1975, 1979
DiMuro, Louis J...................................1971, 1975, 1978
Evans, James B. 1975, 1979
Flaherty, John F. 1969, 1972
Ford, R. Dale 1979
Frantz, Arthur F. 1972, 1976
Garcia, Richard R. 1978
Goetz, Russell 1970, 1974, 1977
Haller, William E.................................1970, 1973, 1976, 1980
Honochick, G. James 1970
Kaiser, Kenneth 1980
Kosc, Gregory J...................................1979
Kunkel, William G...............................1971, 1975, 1978
Luciano, Ronald M..............................1971, 1975, 1978
Maloney, George P. 1973, 1976, 1980
McCoy, Larry S. 1973, 1976, 1980
McKean, James G. 1977
Morgenweck, Henry C.........................1975
Napp, Larry A. 1971, 1974
Neudecker, Jerome A. 1970, 1974, 1977
Odom, James C.....................................1970, 1973
O'Donnell, James M.............................1971
Palermo, Stephen M............................1980
Phillips, David R. 1974, 1978
Rice, John L..1969, 1972
Runge, Edward P. 1969
Satchell, Derold L. 1970
Soar, A. Henry......................................1971
Springstead, Martin J. 1970, 1974, 1977

CHAMPIONSHIP SERIES UMPIRES

AMERICAN LEAGUE (41)—Continued

Stevens, John W. 1970
Stewart, Robert W. 1969
Umont, Frank...1969

NOTE—Six umpires used per game except on October 3, 1970 (major league umpires on strike), when four substitute umpires used.

NATIONAL LEAGUE (35)

Barlick, Albert J. 1969
Blandford, Fred....................................1970
Burkhart, William K. 1972
Colosi, Nicholas 1970, 1974, 1978
Crawford, Henry C. 1971, 1974, 1980
Dale, Jerry P..1973, 1976, 1979
Davidson, David L..................................1971, 1974, 1978
Donatelli, August J. 1969, 1972
Engel, Robert A.....................................1970, 1973, 1977, 1980
Froemming, Bruce N.............................1973, 1977, 1980
Gorman, Thomas D...............................1971, 1975
Grimsley, John W. 1970
Grygiel, George R. 1970
Harvey, H. Douglas 1970, 1972, 1976, 1980
Kibler, John W. 1972, 1975, 1979
Landes, Stanley 1970
McSherry, John P. 1974, 1978
Montague, Edward M. 1979
Morgenweck, Henry C...........................1970
Olsen, Andrew H.....................................1971, 1975, 1978
Pelekoudas, Chris G..............................1969, 1973
Pryor, J. Paul..1970, 1974, 1977
Pulli, Frank V. 1975, 1979
Quick, James E.......................................1979
Rennert, Laurence H.............................1977
Runge, Paul E. 1977
Steiner, Melvin J. 1969
Stello, Richard J.....................................1971, 1976, 1979
Sudol, Edward L. 1969, 1973, 1976
Tata, Terry A. 1976, 1980
Vargo, Edward P.....................................1969, 1973, 1976, 1980
Wendelstedt, Harry H. 1970, 1972, 1977
Weyer, Lee H. 1971, 1974, 1978
Williams, Arthur....................................1975
Williams, William G. 1972, 1975, 1978

NOTE—Six umpires used per game except on October 3, 1970 (major league umpires on strike), when four substitute umpires used.

Most Games Umpired

N. L.—16— Engel, Robert A.; 4 Series.
               Vargo, Edward P.; 4 Series.
A. L.—15— Haller, William E.; 4 Series.

ATTENDANCE

CHAMPIONSHIP SERIES ATTENDANCE

AMERICAN LEAGUE

Year	G.	Game 1	Game 2	Game 3	Game 4	Game 5	Total
1969	3	39,324	41,704	32,735	....	....	113,763
1970	3	26,847	27,470	27,608	....	....	81,945
1971	3	42,621	35,003	33,176	....	....	110,800
1972	5	29,536	31,088	41,156	37,615	50,276	189,671
1973	5	41,279	48,425	34,367	27,497	24,265	175,833
1974	4	41,609	42,810	32,060	28,136	....	144,615
1975	3	35,578	35,578	49,358	....	....	120,514
1976	5	41,077	41,091	56,808	56,355	56,821	252,152
1977	5	54,930	56,230	41,285	41,135	41,133	234,713
1978	4	41,143	41,158	55,535	56,356	....	194,192
1979	4	52,787	52,108	43,199	43,199	....	191,293
1980	3	42,598	42,633	56,588	......	......	141,819

NATIONAL LEAGUE

Year	G.	Game 1	Game 2	Game 3	Game 4	Game 5	Total
1969	3	50,122	50,270	53,195	....	....	153,587
1970	3	33,088	39,317	40,538	....	....	112,943
1971	4	40,977	42,562	38,322	35,482	....	157,348
1972	5	50,476	50,584	52,420	39,447	41,887	234,814
1973	5	53,431	54,041	53,967	50,786	50,323	262,548
1974	4	40,638	49,247	55,953	54,424	....	200,262
1975	3	54,633	54,752	46,355	....	....	155,740
1976	3	62,640	62,651	55,047	....	....	180,338
1977	4	55,968	55,973	63,719	64,924	....	240,584
1978	4	63,460	60,642	55,043	55,124	....	234,269
1979	3	55,006	55,000	42,240	....	....	152,246
1980	5	65,277	65,476	44,443	44,952	44,802	264,950

ATTENDANCE RECORDS
SINGLE GAME

AMERICAN LEAGUE

Club	Largest Attendance	Smallest Attendance
Baltimore	52,787 (Oct. 3, 1979)	27,608 (Oct. 5, 1970)
Boston	35,578 (Oct. 4, 1975)	35,578 (Oct. 4, 1975)
	(Oct. 5, 1975)	(Oct. 5, 1975)
California	43,199 (Oct. 5, 1979)	43,199 (Oct. 5, 1979)
	(Oct. 6, 1979)	(Oct. 6, 1979)
Detroit	50,276 (Oct. 12, 1972)	37,615 (Oct. 11, 1972)
Kansas City	42,633 (Oct. 9, 1980)	41,077 (Oct. 9, 1976)
Minnesota	32,735 (Oct. 6, 1969)	26,847 (Oct. 3, 1970)
New York	56,821 (Oct. 14, 1976)	54,930 (Oct. 5, 1977)
Oakland	49,358 (Oct. 7, 1975)	24,265 (Oct. 11, 1973)

NATIONAL LEAGUE

Club	Largest Attendance	Smallest Attendance
Atlanta	50,270 (Oct. 5, 1969)	50,122 (Oct. 4, 1969)
Cincinnati	55,047 (Oct. 12, 1976)	39,447 (Oct. 10, 1972)
Houston	44,952 (Oct. 11, 1980)	44,443 (Oct. 10, 1980)
Los Angeles	55,973 (Oct. 5, 1977)	54,424 (Oct. 9, 1974)
New York	53,967 (Oct. 8, 1973)	50,323 (Oct. 10, 1973)
Philadelphia	65,476 (Oct. 8, 1980)	60,642 (Oct. 5, 1978)
Pittsburgh	50,584 (Oct. 8, 1972)	33,088 (Oct. 3, 1970)
San Francisco	42,562 (Oct. 3, 1971)	40,977 (Oct. 2, 1971)

Largest Attendance, Game

    N. L.— 64,924— At Philadelphia, October 8, 1977; Los Angeles 4, Philadelphia 1; fourth game.

    A. L.— 56,821— At New York, October 14, 1976; New York 7, Kansas City 6; fifth game.

Smallest Attendance, Game

    A. L.— 24,265— At Oakland, October 11, 1973; Oakland 3, Baltimore 0; fifth game.

    N. L.— 33,088— At Pittsburgh, October 3, 1970; Cincinnati 3, Pittsburgh 0; first game.

Largest Attendance, Series

    3-game Series—N. L.—180,338—Cincinnati vs. Philadelphia, 1976.

                A. L.—141,819—Kansas City vs. New York, 1978.

    4-game Series—N. L.—240,584—Philadelphia vs. Los Angeles, 1977.

                A. L.—194,192—New York vs. Kansas City, 1978.

    5-game Series—N. L.—264,950—Philadelphia vs. Houston, 1980.

                A. L.—252,152—New York vs. Kansas City, 1976.

Smallest Attendance, Series

    3-game Series—A. L.— 81,945—Baltimore vs. Minnesota, 1970.

                N. L.—112,943—Pittsburgh vs. Cincinnati, 1970.

    4-game Series—A. L.—144,615—Baltimore vs. Oakland, 1974.

                N. L.—157,348—San Francisco vs. Pittsburgh, 1971.

    5-game Series—A. L.—175,833—Baltimore vs. Oakland, 1973.

                N. L.—234,814—Pittsburgh vs. Cincinnati, 1972.

Index to Championship Series Records

CLUB PINCH-RUNNING

INDIVIDUAL FIELDING

CLUB FIELDING

INDIVIDUAL PITCHING

CLUB PITCHING

GENERAL SERIES RECORDS